Preface

This is a book you need if you are a student of the Bible. No matter how well you may know your Bible, it offers many new and progressive avenues of thought and inspiration. And it is a book you need if you are not already a student; it provides challenges that can make you want to be one.

This is many things in one: a study book, a history, a reference book, and an enlightening experience. It ties the sixty-six books of the Bible into one complete whole so that you see the continuity of history, God's unbreakable and inviolable covenant, and the development of the divine plan and purpose for man's salvation through His Messiah.

The subject matter is presented in a manner that can make you more aware than ever before of every portion of your Bible. At the same time it fosters spiritualization of thought, encouraging you to carry its history forward into the present in order to appropriate its spiritual value and find parallels in your own life.

This book also offers many tools: clear and concise text, and *visualization* by chart whereby Scriptural subjects have been stripped to their essence for fresh inspiration. It abounds in *correlation*, cross-reference study in action; ideas presented in various sections of the Bible can either be traced through to their fuller unfolding record or united with their actual Biblical fulfillment. A chapter on *appropriation* gives concrete examples of how to translate events and terms into practical application.

The approach is unique and individual: it seeks at every point to carry you not only forward in your Bible reading and study but upward and outward to a richer appreciation and comprehension of your Bible's treasures.

The author has taught a nondenominational Bible course to adult groups throughout the United States for more than thirty-five years, and this volume is the outgrowth of those years of teaching and research. This is not merely a book *about* the Bible, it is a study of the Bible *itself.* The King James Version has been used as its basis; quotations have been liberal and deliberate to challenge the reader to hear the Word behind the words.

Acknowledgement with much gratitude and appreciation is made to: my editors, Ruth Chapman, who also designed the book, and H. L. Kirk; my secretary, Sylvia B. Miller; James D. Norris, who so ably realized in type the author's chart patterns; and to those friends who, knowing about the work, gave encouragement as it progressed.

B.M.S.

A Note on Dates

Early Biblical history is shrouded in the sometimes confusing mist of the distant past and it is therefore not possible to give exact dates. What scholars cited with assurance a generation ago as the precise timing of an event has frequently required revision in the light of archaeological discovery and other investigation. Uncertainty as to precisely when an event took place or when a minor prophet was born or died is however perhaps of less immediate consequence than the fact that a certain event did transpire or that the prophet lived, spoke, or wrote.

The author has used a generally accepted range of dates; where there is wide disagreement in sound scholarship about matters of placement in time, that fact has been noted. Biblical dates will undoubtedly continue to be subject to revision as new discoveries come to verify the kernel of truth underlying the record as it has come down to us.

Abbreviations

BOOKS OF THE OLD TESTAMENT

Gen., *Genesis*	II Chron., *II Chronicles*	Dan., *Daniel*
Ex., *Exodus*	Ezra, *Ezra*	Hos., *Hosea*
Lev., *Leviticus*	Neh., *Nehemiah*	Joel, *Joel*
Num., *Numbers*	Es., *Esther*	Amos, *Amos*
Deut., *Deuteronomy*	Job, *Job*	Ob., *Obadiah*
Josh., *Joshua*	Ps., *Psalms*	Jon., *Jonah*
Ju., *Judges*	Pr., *Proverbs*	Mic., *Micah*
Ru., *Ruth*	Ec., *Ecclesiastes*	Na., *Nahum*
I Sam., *I Samuel*	Song., *Song of Solomon*	Hab., *Habakkuk*
II Sam., *II Samuel*	Is., *Isaiah*	Zeph., *Zephaniah*
I Ki., *I Kings*	Jer., *Jeremiah*	Hag., *Haggai*
II Ki., *II Kings*	La., *Lamentations*	Zech., *Zechariah*
I Chron., *I Chronicles*	Ezek., *Ezekiel*	Mal., *Malachi*

BOOKS OF THE NEW TESTAMENT

Mt., *Matthew*	Eph., *Ephesians*	Heb., *Hebrews*
Mk., *Mark*	Phil., *Philippians*	Ja., *James*
Lu., *Luke*	Col., *Colossians*	I Pet., *I Peter*
Jn., *John*	I Th., *I Thessalonians*	II Pet., *II Peter*
Acts, *Acts*	II Th., *II Thessalonians*	I Jn., *I John*
Rom., *Romans*	I Tim., *I Timothy*	II Jn., *II John*
I Cor., *I Corinthians*	II Tim., *II Timothy*	III Jn., *III John*
II Cor., *II Corinthians*	Tit., *Titus*	Jude, *Jude*
Gal., *Galatians*	Philem., *Philemon*	Rev., *Revelation*

AV = Authorized Version (King James)	LXX = Septuagint	RV = Revised Version
ASV = American Standard Version	Macc. = Maccabees	RV (marg.) = margin of RV

Getting
Better
Acquainted
with
Your Bible

BERENICE MYERS SHOTWELL

Shadwold Press   Kennebunkport   Maine

This book is lovingly dedicated
to
all students of the Bible
who are earnestly endeavoring to hear the Word
that shines through the words

ISBN 0-960302b-0-3 H

ISBN 0-960302b-1-1 S

Contents

Preface   iii

PART I   THE BIBLE: ITS DESIGN AND SCOPE

1   *The Bible and Its Preservation*   3
   Scope of Old and New Testament Literature   12
   Divisions and Books of the Old Testament   13
   New Testament Literature   20
   Divisions and Books of the New Testament   21

PART II   OLD TESTAMENT

2   *Life and Customs of Bible Times*   27
   Nomadic Life 29, Agricultural Life 34, Hebrew Society 36,
   Dress 42, Meals 43, Hospitality 44, Blood Revenge 45,
   Covenants 46, Worship 47, Festivals 58, Fasts 61,
   Language 63, Glossary 63

3   *Old Testament History*   65
   Outline of Old Testament History   73
   Intertestamental Period   92
   The Plumbline   94

4   *Great Old Testament Characters*   95
   Adam 96, Noah 98, Abraham 100, Jacob 102, Joseph 104,
   Moses 106, Joshua 108, Samuel 110, David 112, Solomon
   116, Elijah 118, Elisha 120, Asa 122, Jehoshaphat 123,
   Isaiah 124, Hezekiah 126, Josiah 127, Jeremiah 128,
   Ezekiel 130, Daniel 132, Zerubbabel 134, Ezra 136,
   Nehemiah 138

   Genealogy from Adam to David   114

5 *Correlation—Old Testament Subjects*   141
   Names of God   142
   Creation: First Account   143
   Creation: Second Account   145
   The Record of the Fall of Man—The Fulfillment
      of the Promise of the Redeemer   147
   The Covenant between God and Men   148
   The Ten Plagues   149
   The Twelve Sons of Jacob   150
   Jacob's Prophecies to His Twelve Sons   152
   Moses' Blessings to the Twelve Tribes   154
   A New Name   156
   The Law: Three Stages   157
   The Remnant   158
   The Tabernacle   159
   Ark of the Covenant   161
   The Temple   162
   Satan   165
   Principal Biblical Terms for Satan   166
   Old Testament Miracles   167
   Jerusalem   174
   Silences of Biblical History   175

6 *A Study of Job*   179

7 *A Condensation of the Psalms*   204

PART III   NEW TESTAMENT

8 *Life and Ministry of Jesus*   213
   Jesus' Early Years   223
     Genealogies of Jesus Christ   224
   Public Ministry   239
   Judaean Ministry   240
   Galilean Ministry   245
   Peraean Ministry   284
   The Week Preceding Resurrection (Passion Week)   299
   The Forty Days from Resurrection to Ascension   328
   Jesus' Miracles   335
   Jesus' Parables   336
   Jesus' Discourses   336
   Principal Messianic Prophecies of
     Old Testament Fulfilled in New Testament   337
   A Harmony of the Four Gospels   338

9 *Correlation—Jesus*   344
   Jesus' Foreknowledge of Events   345
   Questions Asked by Jesus   349
   Swelling Tide of Hatred   352
   Types of Womanhood   356
   Changing Concepts of Womanhood   357
   Healing Work of Jesus   358

Jesus' Four Raisings from the Dead   370
Jesus' Training of His Twelve Apostles   372

10 *The Work of the Twelve Apostles*   374
Apostolic Church, 30-63 A.D.   383
Apostolic Healing   384
Raisings from the Dead by the Apostles   386

11 *Life and Ministry of Paul*   387
Early Life   388
First Missionary Journey   393
Second Missionary Journey   397
Third Missionary Journey   406
Voyage to Rome and Imprisonments   429
Parallels in the Lives of Paul and Jesus   441

12 *Paul's Doctrinal Teachings*   445

13 *Correlation—Christian and Church*   453
"Put Off . . . the Old Man"   454
"Put on the New Man"   456
The Spiritual Nature of the Perfect Man   458
The True Church   459
Edifying (Building Up) of the Church   460
Redemptive Healing Mission of the
    Christian Church   462
The Israel of God   464
Mysteries   465
Apostolic Church, 61-96 A.D.   468

14 *The Epistle to the Hebrews*   470

15 *The First Epistle of John*   482
"Love Not the World"   486

16 *The Revelation of St. John the Divine*   488
Over-all View of the Book of Revelation   492
An Outline of the Book of Revelation   495
Panorama of the Apocalypse   506
Old Testament Terms in the Apocalypse   508
Paradise of God in Contrast to Eden   522
Glimpses of the Fourth Dimension   524
Summation   526

PART IV   APPROPRIATION

17 *Appropriation of Scriptural Lessons*   529
A Season and a Time   530
Steps in Israel's Spiritual Journey   533
The Godhead   534
Significance of Certain Numbers in Scripture   536
"Out of Egypt Have I Called My Son"   540
A Lesson from Old Testament History   542

Ten Ascending Steps in the Life of Jesus
and of the Christian   544
Some Lessons from Jesus' Early Life   546
An Example of Enduring Trust   547
Place and Time as Dimensions of Thought   548
Spiritual Growth of the Christian   549
Example of Deliverance through Prayer   550
The Span from Genesis to Revelation   551

Notes   552

INDEX   555

Illustrations

Caves of the Dead Sea Scrolls   7
Wycliffe's Bible   8
Tyndale's Version   8
Facsimile page, Gutenberg Bible   9
King James Bible   9
Bedouin shepherd near Bethlehem   30
Oasis near Jericho   31
Two Bedouin tribesmen   32
Solomon's stables at Megiddo   32
Ancient cistern in the Negeb   33
Stone water pots   34
Nomad's tent near an oasis   35
Threshing floor   36
Storage jar of Jeremiah's time   36
Cuneiform tablet from the twelfth century B.C.   37
First-century earthenware bottle from Petra   43
Four-horned limestone altar of Solomon's day   49
Altar of burnt offering   50
Altar of incense   51
High priest's breastplate   52
Seven-branch golden candlestick   53
Ancient trumpets   54
Excavation of the Flood level at Ur   66
Pottery figurines of Flood level at Ur   67
World's oldest wall, Jericho   68
Excavation at Sarepta (Zarephath)   69
Pools of Solomon   70,   71
Sennacherib's prism   71
Cyrus' cylinder   72
Airview of the ruin-mounds of Shushan   140
Israel's camp in the Wilderness   159
Tabernacle uncovered   159
The Tabernacle   160

Laver of brass   161
Ark of the Covenant   161
Ground plan of Solomon's Temple   162
Bronze altar of the Temple, restored   163
Plan of Herod's Temple and courts   164
Copper coins of Herod the Great   215
Sectarian Manual of Discipline   218
Excavation of Khirbet Qumran   219
Masada, summer palace of Herod the Great   221
Hills around Bethlehem   222
Street of arches in Old Jerusalem   230
A tranquil scene of the Jordan   233
The Judaean Wilderness   235
A curve of the Galilean shore line   237
Dead Sea by moonlight   243
A fisherman casting his net   245
One of the four sources of the Jordan   247
Site of Pool of Bethesda   251
Horns of Hattin   257
Washing of hands   273
Tower of David   279
View across the Kidron to the Mount of Olives   284
Ancient olive trees in the Garden of Gethsemane   316-319
Sanhedrin in session   321
Aerial view of the Old City of Jerusalem   325
"The street called Straight"   390
Temple of Zeus at Salamis on Cyprus   393
The Cilician Gates near Tarsus   398
Ruins of Philippi   399
Roman scourges   400
Rocky plateau of the Acropolis, Athens   401
The Areopagus, or Mars' Hill   403
Drawing of the statue of Diana of the Ephesians   407
Theater at Pergamum   408
Temple of Diana at Sardis   409
Reconstruction of Temple of Diana, Ephesus   413
Great theater at Ephesus   414
Ruins at Miletus   423
Roman pillars at Caesarea   426
Merchant ship from a Greek vase painting   428
St. Paul's Islands near Malta (Melita)   431
Isle of Patmos   489

Maps

The World of the Patriarchs   28
The Exodus and Wilderness Wandering   76
Palestine as Divided among the Tribes   78
The United Kingdom under David and Solomon   80
The Divided Kingdom: Judah and Israel   82
Probable Settlement of Noah's Descendants   114
Palestine in the Time of Jesus   238
Ancient Jerusalem   325
Paul's First Missionary Journey   392
Paul's Second Missionary Journey   397
Paul's Third Missionary Journey   406
Paul's Voyage to Rome   429

Part I

THE BIBLE:
ITS DESIGN
AND SCOPE

1

The Bible and Its Preservation

The universal truths and the beauties and consolations of the Bible are the world's heritage, a religious literature unsurpassed in loveliness and sublimity. These are available to all men, but fully to hear the Word of God one must look perceptively beyond the written words. In the Bible the history of the Messianic people and the golden thread of spiritual truth and revelation are closely interwoven—the one transfigured in character by the other, as when a strong light held behind translucent paper illumines the paper with light.

The Bible truths provide a practical guide and impetus for every good thought and action—from the smallest detail of daily living to the fullness of a consecrated life. At every level a study of the Bible is rewarding, but to benefit from its greatest richness everyone must approach it for himself in the attitude of "What is this saying to *me*?"

The Bible is sacred literature, telling over and over again of God's presence, always availing and always available. The Bible is an ancient Oriental literature. The language and customs of the ancient Israelites are in many ways unlike those of the twentieth-century Western man. The Old Testament is a rich historical and spiritual storehouse which grew out of the life of this Oriental people, the life of a small nation continually tried in its loyalty to its God.

To the English-speaking world *Bible* designates primarily the Christian Scriptures—the Old and New Testaments—consisting of thirty-nine books in the Old and twenty-seven in the New. "Bible" is derived from the Greek word *biblos* (book, the pith of the Egyptian papyrus plant used in ancient times to make writing material); "testament" (Latin *testamentum*) means "covenant" or "will." The Old and New Testaments are thus translated literally "Old Covenant" and "New Covenant." The Old Testament was written originally in Hebrew, the language of the Israelites, with a few portions in Aramaic; the New was written in Greek, the language of the Graeco-Roman world of the first century A.D.

Preservation of Text

The sixty-six books we now have in our Bible passed through centuries of scrutiny and selection. Other writings were eventually discarded because they were not considered inspired sources of doctrine or reliable history. Rabbinical scholars exercised great care and discrimination to safeguard the authenticity of Old Testament books, and the early Christian Church Fathers were equally scrupulous to ascertain the genuineness of New Testament writings.

The word canon is derived from the Greek *kanohn,* "a straight rod," "a rule," "a standard," "a catalogue," and the term is applied Biblically to the collection of sacred books considered divinely inspired and authoritative.

Development of Old Testament Canon

The sacred literature of the Old Testament, which preserved the divine revelations of God to the chosen race of Israel and memorialized its history, varies in character from the historical, the prophetic, the legal and priestly to the poetic and devotional. Its composition covered a long period of time, not a single age, and its production took place under a wide variety of circumstances. The Law, the Prophets, and the Writings constitute the three divisions of Hebrew Scripture.

The first stage of its transmission was oral—from father to son and from generation to generation. The ordinances which Moses gave to his nation were at first circulated by word of mouth. They included not only the Ten Commandments but also civic and social legislation relating to the community life of Israel. These legislations were developed and elaborated by the priests as they taught the Law to the people; this method of oral law (*torah*) survived long in Israel, adapting itself to Israel's changing economic and social conditions, later to crystallize into written law codes during various periods of the national history.

Along with the Law was transmitted orally through the centuries the folklore of the Hebrew race, songs of the exploits of its military leaders and heroes, and the stories of the religious experiences unique to the Israelites as the covenant people. In time these were collected and written into separate histories, possibly by scholars of the schools of the prophets originally founded by Samuel.

All these writings existed in fragmentary form up to the Exile (586 B.C.). During the Captivity concerted efforts were made to preserve and assemble existing records. Priestly scribes then edited and wove these segments into a unified whole.

The Law

The five books of the Law (Torah, Pentateuch—Genesis, Exodus, Leviticus, Numbers, Deuteronomy—reached their final form shortly after the Exile and became canon in the time of Ezra and Nehemiah (*ca.* 445 B.C.). Although these are attributed to Moses, modern Biblical criticism finds evidence that the Pentateuch is a compilation from five principal sources: the Jehovistic and Elohistic Documents, the Deuteronomic, Holiness, and Priestly Codes (J,E,D,H,P). These sources include the oral and written Mosaic history and law as well as additional history and advancing law codes based on changing social conditions in Israel. In its composite form the Pentateuch is a masterpiece of interwoven records illumined by the revelation of God's purposeful design.

The **Jehovistic Document** (J), *ca.* 850 B.C., so named because the Deity is called Jehovah (Yahweh), was written from the viewpoint of the southern kingdom of Judah. It traced the beginnings of the patriarchal and national history of Israel from Adam to the conquest of Canaan.

The **Elohistic Document** (E), *ca.* 750 B.C., in which the Deity is called Elohim, was written from the viewpoint of the northern kingdom of Israel and reflects the powerful religious influence of Elijah. This document parallels the history of J from Abram to Joshua. (A composite record [JE] appeared *ca.* 650 B.C.)

The **Deuteronomic Code** (D), "the book of the law," dating *ca.* 621 B.C., was discovered in the Temple in Jerusalem during the reign of King Josiah (II Ki. 22:8). It was probably written in the century preceding its discovery and gave a restatement and amplified codification of earlier Mosaic legislation. Chapters 12-26 and 28 of our book of Deuteronomy contain this code.

The **Holiness Code** (H), *ca.* 560 B.C., was a body of laws now incorporated in Leviticus, chapters 17-26. Its author was one in spirit with Ezekiel, and its great emphasis is on holiness—the holiness of God, of worship, and of God's people.

The **Priestly Code** (P), *ca.* 500-450 B.C., was prepared by a priestly writer or writers during the early post-exilic period when the religious institutions of the highly organized priestly system of the Second Temple were set up. This code, expressing a lofty conception of the majesty of God and the highest development of ritual religion, forms the framework of the first five books of the Bible. Its ritual portions are to be found in Exodus, Leviticus, and Numbers.

The Prophets

The prophetic literature of the Old Testament was the result of the vigorous reformative efforts of Israel's major and minor prophets. The early seers had left no record of their utterances; with the advance of the nation's culture, however, reading and writing became more general, and from the middle of the eighth to the fifth century B.C. these great moral teachers, contemporaries of kings and statesmen, not only fought the social evils of their era and taught the will and revelations of God to their people but wrote down their messages for future generations.

By 150 B.C., in addition to the record of Israel's early history and law codes, the Hebrew Scripture included a second group of canonical books, historical and prophetic, called the Prophets. These included Joshua, Judges, I and II Samuel, I and II Kings, Isaiah, Jeremiah, Ezekiel, and twelve Minor Prophets: Hosea, Joel, Amos, Obadiah, Jonah, Micah, Nahum, Habakkuk, Zephaniah, Haggai, Zechariah, Malachi. Modern study prefers to group the book of Joshua with the first five books of the Law under the title Hexateuch ("six books") because its literary style and theological viewpoint bear the imprint of the Priestly Code.

The Writings (Hagiographa)

In the next several centuries following the return of Judah to Palestine the books of exile and restoration history appeared. The sayings and practical precepts of Israel's wise men, who sought to solve the great problems of life (the Wisdom Literature: Job, Proverbs, Ecclesiastes), had been collected, as had the lyrics of poet and psalmist long used in Hebrew worship. This third great group of poetic, prophetic, and historic books, consisting of Job, Psalms, Proverbs (three devotional books used in synagogue worship), Song of Solomon, Ruth, Lamentations, Ecclesiastes, Esther (the "Five Rolls" read yearly at special Jewish festivals), Daniel, Ezra, Nehemiah, I and II Chronicles, ranked as Scripture before the close of the first century B.C. Their canonicity was accepted when the Old Testament canon of thirty-nine books was officially set by a synod of rabbis at the Council of Jamnia, near Joppa, in 90 A.D.

Apocrypha

Beside these Old Testament canonical books there was in existence a body of religious literature never used in the Palestinian synagogues. These books—of uncertain origin or written by anonymous authors using the names of great historic figures and claiming a "hidden" wisdom—gradually came to be rejected as spurious or lacking divine inspiration. As generally understood by Protestant Christians, *Apocrypha* denotes the fourteen books which appeared in the Greek Septuagint (LXX) in addition to the Old Testament books. These were translated into Old Latin and carried over mainly in this form into the Latin Vulgate by Jerome.

I and II Esdras
Tobit
Judith
Additions to book of Esther
Wisdom of Solomon
Ecclesiasticus, or the Wisdom of Jesus the Son of Sirach
Baruch (including Epistle of Jeremy, Baruch chap. 6)
Song of the Three Holy Children ⎫ Added to
History of Susanna   ⎬ book of
History of Bel and the Dragon   ⎭ Daniel
The Prayer of Manasses
I and II Maccabees

The question whether these books should be included in the canon was re-examined during the Renaissance and Reformation in the fifteenth and sixteenth centuries; because these books had never been part of Hebrew Scripture, they were not accepted by Protestant Christians as canonical. Wycliffe's Bible (1382) did include them, between the Old and New Testaments, as did the Coverdale Bible (1535) and the King James Bible (1611), although they were omitted from the latter version as early as 1629. At the Council of Trent (Italy) in 1546 these books (with the exception of I and II Esdras and the Prayer of Manasses) were officially accepted by the Roman Catholic Church as part of its Old Testament canon.

Development of New Testament Canon

Although marked lines cannot be drawn in the process of the development of New Testament canon, three stages may be seen clearly: (1) the appearance of the apostolic epistles and gospel records, circulated among the churches in fragmentary form, the substance of which were known and quoted by the Apostolic Fathers; (2) a growing acceptance of their authenticity in the second and third centuries; (3) their formal canonization in 397 A.D.

The New Testament text has come down to us in Greek in the vernacular *koine* used in the first-century Graeco-Roman world. The original manuscripts no longer exist, but many Greek manuscripts dating from the second century to the fifteenth (when printing was invented by Gutenberg in Mainz, Germany, in 1450) have since come to light to authenticate the New Testament text. Like the Old Testament, it was preserved in manuscript form and copied by hand by layman and scribe on perishable papyrus.

The canon of the New Testament developed slowly. The gospel of Jesus was at first testified to by word of mouth by apostles and Christian converts and only gradually preserved in writing to meet the need of a growing Church. Not till the close of the first century A.D. did the Church have a Scripture of its own, and even then this was not a cohesive whole. Rather, it consisted of scattered gospel records and epistles possessed by widely separated churches and honored because these told of the life and words of Jesus or of the teachings of the apostles, but by the close of the century or early in the second the Synoptic Gospels were already grouped together, as were some of Paul's Epistles.

Certain early-church ecclesiastics were influential in the selection of the New Testament books. *Marcion,* a Christian Gnostic of Rome, accepted Luke's Gospel and ten of Paul's Epistles in 140 A.D. *Justin Martyr,* a Palestinian church father, referred in 150 A.D. to the three Synoptic Gospels of Matthew, Mark, and Luke. *Tertullian,* 150-222 A.D., an early Latin church father, a native of Carthage, accepted the four Gospels and most of the New Testament books, while *Clement of Alexandria* (Egypt), 165-220 A.D., also a Christian church father, mentioned all the New Testament books except James, II Peter, and III John. *Irenaeus,* bishop of Lyons in Gaul in 180 A.D., was a pupil of Polycarp, who had been a disciple of John. Irenaeus accepted as canonical most of the New Testament books, and henceforth Paul's Epistles became doctrine for the Church. The eminent Alexandrian theologian *Origen,* 185-254 A.D., catalogued most of the New Testament books as genuine. One of the lists made by *Eusebius,* 260-340 A.D., bishop of Caesarea in Palestine, agrees with present canon. *Jerome,* 340-420 A.D., the Latin church father and scholar who produced the Latin Vulgate, accepted all the present New Testament books as authoritative, distinguishing canonical from apocryphal writings. *Augustine,* Numidian bishop of Hippo (Africa), 354-430 A.D., whose influence was great in the Church, also accepted all the New Testament books as genuine.

The present canon of the New Testament closed when its twenty-seven books were accepted as authoritative Scripture at the Council of Carthage in 397 A.D.

Principal Versions

The preservation of the texts of both Old and New Testaments was a miracle in itself as none of the original manuscripts exist. Writings were painstakingly copied by hand from generation to generation on long scrolls of animal skins carefully sewn together or on papyrus rolls. As the years passed the books of the Law, the Prophets, and the Writings wore out and were recopied. The worn scrolls were usually buried, so that until recently available copies were not much more than a thousand years old. (With the discovery in 1947 of the Dead Sea Scrolls in the cliffs above the Dead Sea a number of much older manuscripts, written almost two thousand years ago, have come to light.) Often errors crept into the text with the copying. Texts suffered alterations by editorial revisions and additions of the copyists. Changes also occurred as the Old and New Testaments were translated from one language to another and new versions appeared. The ancient versions which were preserved have been of great value to scholars in determining the original text.

The Old Testament, written in Hebrew with a few portions in Aramaic, was preserved in the second century A.D. in the **Massora,** an authoritative Hebrew text prepared by Jewish scholars. It followed soon after the canonization of the Old Testament books. All Hebrew manuscripts after the second century were based on the Massora, which stabilized the text by introduction of a system of vowel sounds and by accent marks for punctuation.

The *Targums,* Aramaic oral translations or paraphrases of the Old Testament Hebrew text, were put into writing by the fifth century A.D.

The **Septuagint,** known also as the LXX, was a celebrated Greek version of Hebrew Scripture, translated between 250 and 50 B.C. for the Jews of Alexandria and used by Jews of the Diaspora in the Mediterranean world. It was the version widely used in the early Christian Church. This oldest complete version included the Apocrypha.

The **Peshitta** was the Syriac version of the Old and New Testaments. The Old Testament was in close agreement with the Massoretic Hebrew text; its New Testament conformed to the Greek. Portions of the Peshitta were in circulation by the end of the second century A.D. among Syriac Christians. It underwent revision, and since the fifth century has been the national version of the Syrian Church.

The Sahadic and Bohairic versions circulated by Christians of Egypt were in Coptic. By 200 A.D. the Old Testament was translated from the LXX into the two dialects of Upper and Lower Egypt respectively; by 250 the New Testament also existed in both dialects.

An Armenian version preserved the Old Testament text from the Greek LXX and the New Testament from a Syriac text. This translation circulated in the Christian communities of eastern Asia around 400 A.D.

The first of the Old Latin versions appeared among Latin-speaking Jews of Carthage early in the third century A.D. In 385 A.D. Jerome translated the

In these caves of the Judaean hills the first Dead Sea Scrolls were found in 1947. American Bible Society.

New Testament from Old Latin into Latin with the aid of Greek manuscripts, and from 390 through 404 translated the Old Testament from the Hebrew text. This translation of Old and New Testaments was called the **Vulgate**, and became the Bible of the Western world for the next thousand years. In 1593 A.D. it became the official Latin version of the Roman Catholic Church.

History of the English Bible

Wycliffe's Bible

Before the time of Wycliffe the only Bible England possessed was the Latin Bible, although earlier attempts had been made to translate portions into Anglo-Saxon. John Wycliffe, the English religious reformer, made the first complete English translation in 1382 (Old Testament partly the work of Nicholas de Hereford). It was an exact translation in manuscript form of the Latin Vulgate into early English, to make Scripture available to the common people who could not read Latin. It had a wide circulation, but it aroused great resistance on the part of the Church and such translations were forbidden by threat of excommunication. A second improved Wycliffe version, attributed to his friend John Purvey, appeared soon after Wycliffe's death and attained wide popularity; about 140 copies have survived. An Oxford scholar of repute, Wycliffe escaped persecution, but after his death his bones were exhumed, burned, and thrown into the river Swift "to the damnation and destruction of his memory." Both his friends de Hereford and Purvey were forced to recant under torture. Parliament passed a bill making circulation of the English-language Bible a crime, and by 1401 English Bibles were ordered burned.

Tyndale's Bible

William Tyndale, an Oxford student, went to Cambridge to study Greek under the Dutch scholar Erasmus. Inspired by the revival of Greek learning and spurred by the new invention of printing, Tyndale

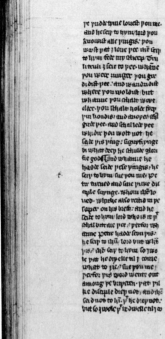

Above: Wycliffe's Bible, 1382 A.D. This first complete English translation was handwritten and illuminated. Below: Tyndale's Version, 1535 A.D., was the first printed English Bible. Both photographs, American Bible Society.

determined he would give a reliable English version of the Scriptures to the people in the language they could understand. Forced to flee from England he made his translation of the New Testament at Hamburg, then at Cologne. It was printed at Worms in 1525-1526 and copies were shipped to England, where it was eagerly received by the people. By 1530 15,000 copies had flooded England, but opposition by clergy and king caused them to be sought out and burned. From 1530 to 1534 Tyndale translated the Pentateuch and the book of Jonah and revised his New Testament. Betrayed by enemies, he was imprisoned near Brussels for more than a year and martyred in 1536—strangled and burned at the stake—for the work he had done. Tyndale's translation was not from the Latin Vulgate, as Wycliffe's had been, but from early Greek and Hebrew texts. The excellence of this translation and the simplicity and directness of its style made it the basis of many later translations. As Luther's translation had molded the vernacular of the German people, Tyndale's beautiful and vigorous diction shaped the English language of the Elizabethan period (1570-1610).

Coverdale's Bible

In 1534 the mood of England began to change. A petition was made to King Henry VIII to permit the translation of the Bible into English by scholars whom he would appoint, and in 1535 Miles Coverdale's translation from the Latin Vulgate and German versions (including Luther's), together with Tyndale's Pentateuch and Tyndale's 1534 New Testament revision, gave England its first complete printed English Bible. Two new editions were published in 1537 by license of the king, and from this time the English Bible circulated freely.

Matthew's Bible

This was a composite edition produced in 1537 by Thomas Matthew (whose real name is believed to have been John Rogers), a close associate of Tyndale. It included Tyndale's Pentateuch, the Joshua to II Chronicles left in manuscript form by Tyndale, and his revision of the New Testament, as well as Coverdale's translation from Ezra to Malachi.

Through the remainder of the sixteenth century a number of Bibles appeared. The *Great Bible* (1539), so named because of its size, was a revision of Matthew's Bible and was appointed for use in every parish church. The *Geneva Bible* (1560) was a revision of the Great Bible and the first English text to number chapters and verses; it attained a great popularity. The *Bishop's Bible* (1568) was an inferior edition published by a group of noted bishops and other clergymen to replace the Geneva Bible. Seeing the desirability of having a translation for English Roman Catholics,

Above: Facsimile page from Gutenberg Bible (Latin), 1450-1455 A.D. Below: King James Bible, 1611. Both photographs, American Bible Society.

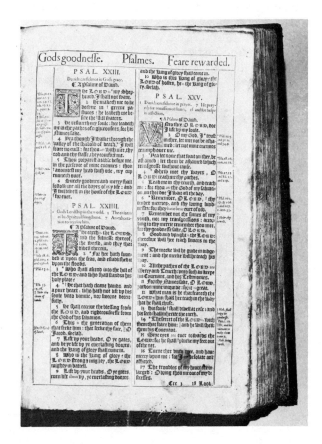

Catholic scholars of the English college of Douai, Flanders, produced a New Testament which was published in 1582 at Rheims, France, and an Old Testament in 1609 at Douai, hereafter known as the *Rheims and Douai Bible.*

The Authorized Version (AV) or King James Bible, 1611   Because of imperfections and disagreements of existing translations, a new version was undertaken by England's best scholars, an idea enthusiastically supported by King James I. Forty-seven Biblical scholars were commissioned to produce a version acceptable to Puritan and Anglican Protestants. Other scholars throughout the land were invited to give assistance in cases of special difficulty. It was not a new translation but one that deliberately drew on the best of every preceding English version as well as foreign translations. The result was that from its inception it held first place among all versions by reason of its beauty of language and intrinsic merit. It was destined to leave an indelible imprint on English religion and to become a standard for English literature.

Revised Version (RV or ERV)   For two hundred fifty years the King James Version stood alone. Then began a whole new era of textual criticism. Progress had been made in Hebrew and Greek learning and scholars now had ready access to a newly discovered and more reliable Greek text than that on which the Authorized Version was based.

In 1870, at the instigation of the Convocation of Canterbury of the Church of England, Hebrew and Greek scholars, in two companies of twenty-seven each, undertook a revision. One company, working forty days a year for ten years, translated the New Testament, which was published in 1881; the other company worked on the Old Testament a total of 792 days during fourteen years, and in 1885 the entire Bible was published. The English language had undergone many changes since the Elizabethan period and numerous words had taken on different meanings. Thus into the Revised were incorporated the advancing results of scholarship.

In close relation to the English Revised Version was the *American Revised Version* (ARV), published in 1901. Since the turn of the twentieth century various Bibles have appeared, many of them in modern English: *The Twentieth Century New Testament,* 1902; Weymouth's *The New Testament in Modern Speech,* 1903; Ferrar Fenton's *The Holy Bible in Modern English,* 1903; Moffatt's *A New Translation of the Bible,* 1922; Smith-Goodspeed's *The Bible, An American Translation,* 1931; Ogden's *The Bible in Basic English,* 1949; Charles K. Williams' *The New Testament, A New Translation in Plain English,* 1952; *Revised Standard Version of the Holy Bible* (RSV), 1952; J. B. Phillips' *New Testament in Modern Speech,* 1958; *The Jerusalem Bible,* 1966; *The New English Bible,* 1961-1970; *The New American Bible,* 1970, a new translation for Roman Catholics; *The Anchor Bible* (thirty-eight-volume translation and commentary), publication begun in 1964.

Design and Scope of the Bible

The sixty-six books of Christian Scripture are knit together by the central theme of God's purpose of redemption for the family of mankind through His Son Jesus Christ. Prophet, priest, historian, statesman, king, reformer, poet, psalmist, seer, apostle alike contributed to the wealth of this material. The Bible is the record of God's love for man seen in a threefold aspect—God's self-revelation, the Messianic idea, and the history of redemption.

1. Its pages begin with the doctrine of God as Creator of the universe and man, and reveal progressively the fullness of God's nature, will, and kingdom. It is the voice of God saying, "I am the first, and I am the last; and beside me there is no God" (Is. 44:6).

2. God's redemptive plan for a mankind in need of salvation is developed in the Messianic idea. This idea is first seen in the promise of a Redeemer in the "seed" of the woman: "I [God] will put enmity between thee [the serpent] and the woman, and between thy seed and her seed; it shall bruise thy head, and thou shalt bruise his heel" (Gen. 3:15). The Messianic line began with Seth, Adam's third son, and became definitive in the covenant with Abraham and his descendants, with Israel, and with the royal line of David, to be made fully manifest in Jesus, son of Mary. All of the Old Testament leads forward to the advent of the Messiah, "the anointed"; after his coming everything is a working out from his life, his teachings, and his Church.

3. The history of redemption is one of the principal themes of the Biblical system. The Bible records the redemption of the Children of Israel through God's covenant, as developed in the Law and the Prophets; and the redemption of all men through Jesus Christ, his gospel, and his Church; and closes with the visions of the Apocalypse which prophesy the

final triumph of the kingdom of God and His Christ.

Three major elements within Scripture itself bear witness to its divine inspiration. The first is **monotheism**. In the almost completely polytheistic world of the Israelite the concept of only one God, invisible Spirit, was a startling idea that was to permeate human consciousness as enlightened thought advanced in the knowledge of this One God. The second element is **unity**. Although the books of the Bible were written during a period of approximately fifteen centuries and by many authors, they maintain the unity of its grand theme of redemption. The third element that gives proof of divine influence is **prophecy**. The Old Testament contains Messianic promises and prophecies fulfilled centuries later in a way no prophet of himself could have foreseen. David, a thousand years before the Messiah, made prophecies which were fulfilled in Jesus; Isaiah prophesied of the Messiah more than seven hundred years before Jesus' Advent; so did Jeremiah, Daniel, and many of the Minor Prophets.

The threefold aspect and progression of the divine plan:

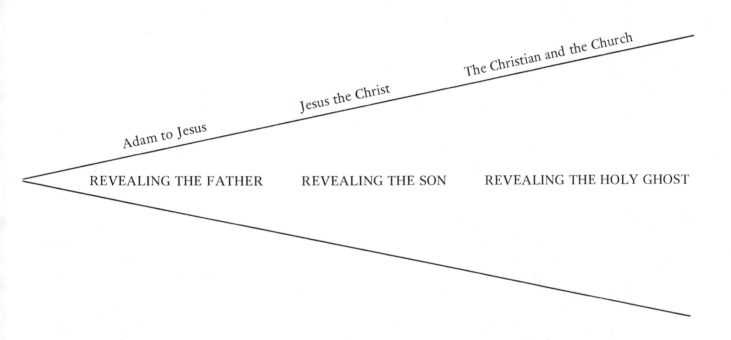

REVEALING THE FATHER   REVEALING THE SON   REVEALING THE HOLY GHOST

SCOPE OF OLD AND NEW TESTAMENT LITERATURE

Although the Bible as we think of it today has come to us in one volume, it is really a library of sixty-six books. There are five divisions in the Old Testament and five in the New. The Old Testament records the history and spiritual development of the Children of Israel in their preparation for the reception of the Messiah; the New Testament records the outgrowth of Jesus' life and gospel, and the establishment of his kingdom. The whole is an expanding revelation.

NEW TESTAMENT

OLD TESTAMENT

Consummation of Kingdom

Christ's Advent

Promulgation of the Gospel

Preparation for Coming of the Messiah

EPISTLES
(21)

PROPHECY
(1)

General

PROPHECY
(17)

GOSPELS
(4)

HISTORY
(1)

Pauline

Revelation

Minor
Prophets

Major
Prophets

James
I Peter
II Peter
I John
II John
III John
Jude

POETRY
(5)

Matthew
Mark
Luke
John

The Acts
of the
Apostles

Romans
I Corinthians
II Corinthians
Galatians
Ephesians
Philippians
Colossians
I Thessalonians
II Thessalonians
I Timothy
II Timothy
Titus
Philemon

Hebrews

Hosea
Joel
Amos
Obadiah
Jonah
Micah
Nahum
Habakkuk
Zephaniah
Haggai
Zechariah
Malachi

Isaiah
Jeremiah
Lamentations
Ezekiel
Daniel

HISTORY
(12)

Job
Psalms
Proverbs
Ecclesiastes
Song of
Solomon

LAW
(5)

Joshua
Judges
Ruth
I Samuel
II Samuel
I Kings
II Kings
I Chron.
II Chron.
Ezra
Nehemiah
Esther

Genesis
Exodus
Leviticus
Numbers
Deuteronomy

DIVISIONS AND BOOKS OF THE OLD TESTAMENT

Five Divisions: LAW, HISTORY,
POETRY, MAJOR PROPHETS, MINOR PROPHETS

Pre-Mosaic Period	Israel in Egypt	Exodus	Wilderness Wandering
Adam to Joseph	1880-1450 B.C.*	1450 B.C.	1450-1410 B.C.

THE FIVE BOOKS OF THE LAW (PENTATEUCH)

GENESIS	EXODUS	LEVITICUS	NUMBERS	DEUTERONOMY
Genesis sets forth the basic structure of the whole Bible and sounds its keynote of salvation: —God and His creation —A second account of creation; the beginning of the moral history of mankind —The divine plan of redemption (3:15) History from Adam through patriarchs Abraham, Isaac, Jacob, Joseph—God's covenant with Abraham and his seed	Israel's bondage in Egypt Call and commission of Moses Exodus of Israel from Egypt At Mount Sinai God's covenant is made with Israel—Moses is given the Decalogue, also civil and ceremonial laws to govern Israel as a nation The erection of the Tabernacle Israel ("my first-born") is chosen to the worship of the One God	Development in detail of Mosaic legislation —specific precepts of worship to be followed by the priests, Levites, and the people Sacrificial and priestly types of religious worship by which Israel is to establish her communion with God These Levitical laws are to govern the nation throughout its history and to consecrate Israel to God The keynote of the book is the word *holy*	The first numbering of the Children of Israel at Sinai Their journey to Kadesh-barnea — twelve spies search out the land of Canaan for forty days — Israel fears to go forward Forty years of wandering in the wilderness Valuable training of the nation in observance of its civil and religious institutions Second numbering of the people in plains of Moab	The addresses of Moses and the restating of the Law to a new generation of Israel about to enter the land of Canaan Moses reviews the vital lessons of the past forty years and magnifies God's unceasing goodness to Israel Moses urges upon Israel proper measures of protection for the future: gratitude for God's mercy, obedience to the Law, separateness, and abstinence from idolatry

Israel's preparation for its Messianic mission:

Here appears the first promise of the Redeemer, and with the turning of men to God (4:26) begins their preparation for the reception of God's revelation of Himself.	Worship of the One God (monotheism) is a developing step in the great work of redemption—a redemption not for the Israelites alone, but for all men.	Israel (chosen of God to bring forth the Messiah) is to be a holy people set apart to the service of God —"Holiness is separateness. . . ."	Israel is found wanting in faith and courage. The forty years of wandering constitute a period of needed discipline to learn reliance upon God.	Renewed emphasis is placed upon obedience to the Law—a matter of life and death—for Israel must be prepared to maintain its part of the covenant with God.

*Exodus 12:40 reads: "Now the sojourning of the children of Israel, who dwelt in Egypt, was four hundred and thirty years." The LXX adds "and in the land of Canaan" after "Egypt," thus beginning the 430-year period from Abraham's entrance into Canaan and reducing Israel's sojourn in Egypt to 215 years.

DIVISIONS AND BOOKS OF THE OLD TESTAMENT (Continued)

Conquest of Canaan	Period of Judges	Reign of Saul	Reign of David
1410-1370 B.C.	*ca.* 1370-1028 B.C.	1028-1013 B.C.	1013-973 B.C.
Under Joshua and elders	Fifteen judges	Israel's first king	7½ years over Judah 33 years over the United Kingdom

THE TWELVE BOOKS OF HISTORY

JOSHUA	JUDGES	RUTH	I SAMUEL	II SAMUEL
The entrance of the Children of Israel into Canaan, the promised land, under Joshua, successor to Moses	History of the Israelites under fourteen judges, from Othniel to Eli	This book is believed to be connected historically with the period of the Judges, although written at a later date	Closing period of Judges and transition to Hebrew monarchy	David becomes king of Judah, reigns seven and a half years with his capital at Hebron
The conquest of Canaan takes place under Joshua's leadership and in accord with God's directing —Israel must earn its heritage	Israel's repeated desertion of its religious principles brings about oppression after oppression by its enemies—Israel "went a whoring after other gods ... they turned quickly out of the way which their fathers walked in...."	Ruth, a young Moabitish widow, forsakes her homeland to follow her mother-in-law Naomi to Judah—she chooses to worship the God of Israel	Samuel, fifteenth judge, is dedicated when still a child to the service of God—he is established as a prophet—founds first groups for religious instruction	David becomes king of all Israel (United Kingdom), reigns thirty-three years with his capital at Jerusalem
Division of the land among the twelve tribes with exception of tribe of Levi	When Israel "cried unto the Lord," judges were raised up one by one to deliver a repentant people	Ruth becomes the wife of Boaz of Bethlehem, and through her son Obed becomes an ancestress of David—her name appears in the genealogy of Jesus	Israel demands a king —Saul becomes its first king—Saul's presumption and disobedience cause his rejection	David centralizes religious worship in Jerusalem (Zion)
Joshua's final counsels—calls to remembrance God's mercies —exhorts Israel to "cleave unto the Lord"			Samuel anoints the shepherd David to be king—David's rise and Saul's fall	David's sin with Bathsheba—his deep repentance
				God's covenant with David and his house "thy throne shall be established for ever"

Preparation for mission:

Israel warned utterly to eschew all idolatry and all contact with the idolatrous Canaanites, else they shall be "scourges in your sides, and thorns in your eyes, until ye perish from off this good land."	Israel, failing to cleave to the One God and to obey His commandments, corrupts itself among the pagan people of Canaan, is disciplined repeatedly for apostasy, and yet is shown God's mercy again and again.	Amid the conflicts and distresses of the long period of the Judges, the enduring values of family life, love, fidelity, and true worship of God are clearly seen, with their recompense and full reward.	Israel's determination to have "a king to judge us like all the nations" disavows and rejects God's divine sovereignty. This choice is to bring centuries of corrupt worldly government, unrest, and suffering.	David, loving God and acknowledging God's sovereignty over Israel, shows true kingship, a kingship that is blessed of God by His covenant. Israel thus gains national unity and a higher conception of righteousness

Reign of Solomon	Divided Kingdom	Captivities	Restoration of Judah
973-933/32 B.C.	933/32 B.C.	722 B.C.—Israel into Assyria	536 B.C.—return under Zerubbabel
	Kingdom of Judah Kingdom of Israel	586 B.C.—Judah into Babylon	458 B.C.—return under Ezra

I and II KINGS	I and II CHRONICLES	EZRA	NEHEMIAH	ESTHER
History from death of David to Judah's captivity	History from death of Saul to the captivity of Judah	Close of the Exile of Judah and beginning of the Restoration	A continuation of book of Ezra	Events recorded are believed to have transpired between first and second expeditions of Jews to Jerusalem
Reign of Solomon— the building and dedication of the Temple	The chronicler, writing from the viewpoint of the restoration of Judah, chooses events which teach religious lessons— supplements history of I and II Kings— deals wholly with Kingdom of Judah and the Davidic line	First return: a remnant of the people of Judah (Jews) returns to its own land led by Zerubbabel (of the Messianic line)	Nehemiah's first journey to Jerusalem from Persia (445 B.C.) —rebuilds the wall— acts as governor for twelve years—corrects social and religious abuses	Concerns crisis in history of those Jews who choose to remain in the Persian Empire
Division of the kingdom—contemporary history of the two kingdoms Israel and Judah		The Temple is rebuilt (Second Temple) with the encouragement of the prophets	Ezra instructs people in the Law—renewal of the covenant— purification of Temple worship	Esther, a Jewess, becomes queen—Haman, the king's favorite, conspires against the Jews throughout the Empire—Esther courageously intervenes to save her people from extermination
Apostate Israel rapidly sinks into corruption—idolatrous Judah experiences periods of reformation	Genealogies place special emphasis upon Judah, Levi, and the house of David	Second return: another Jewish remnant returns to Judah led by Ezra, scribe and priest	Nehemiah's second journey to Jerusalem —he institutes radical reforms—Nehemiah and Ezra zealously consolidate the Jewish religious system	Feast of Purim instituted to commemorate this deliverance
Israel carried captive to Assyria—Jerusalem falls, Judah carried captive to Babylon	Religious importance of Jerusalem and of Levitical order are accented	Ezra inaugurates a religious reformation in Judah and enforces the law of Moses		
With building of Temple Israel rededicates itself to God, but materialism soon leads away from pure worship. Unity is disrupted by discontent and the kingdom is divided. Accumulation of sins brings enslavement.	Judah, having learned in captivity a purer monotheism, now returns to former inheritance in Palestine in order to proceed to fulfill the high purpose for which God has chosen it: to bring forth the Messiah.	A record of action! In two instances a faithful willing remnant of Judah rises up and prayerfully journeys to Jerusalem, in each case thankful for God's mercy in the renewed opportunity to prove itself worthy.	Judah's one high purpose must be the rebuilding of holy Jerusalem and the establishment of a pure monotheism. Persistent watchfulness and stern discipline are required to maintain Israel's ancient covenant with God.	God's people, wherever they may be and under whatever circumstances, are always under His providence. The enemies of God's people, hateful in intent, are turned back from their wicked purposes and punished.

15

These poetical writings were collected and edited in their final form during the post-exilic age, prior to the second century B.C.

THE FIVE BOOKS OF POETRY

JOB	PSALMS	PROVERBS	ECCLESIASTES	SONG OF SOLOMON
A dramatic poem—its subject, Why do those who are righteous suffer affliction? Job, a devout patriarch, is visited with afflictions, against which he rebels as undeserved—his three friends debate with him, ascribing his suffering to sin, but Job maintains his righteousness — through magnifying God's greatness and wisdom Job ceases to contend with the Almighty—human reason is subordinated—he is humbled and restored	A collection of lyric poetry which mirrors the spiritual riches of Israel's religious experience—these songs of praise, prayer, penitence, and thanksgiving echo the deep longings and aspirations of the heart in its search for God—in sublime language God is exalted as sovereign Creator and His works are magnified Some of these devotional hymns prophesy the nature and redeeming work of God's Messiah	Proverbs treats of the excellent and eternal wisdom of God, with Him "from the beginning, or ever the earth was," and sets forth practical moral and spiritual maxims for guidance in daily conduct "The fear of the Lord is the beginning of wisdom: and the knowledge of the holy is understanding" keynotes the book—wisdom is exalted as an essential of life, attainment of which leads to godliness, preservation, stability, and well-being	Its subject: the search for the value and purpose of human life Weighing thoroughly the transitory values of worldly wisdom, pleasure, labor, riches, power, and life itself, the Preacher deduces that "all is vanity" He infers that human life has value only as man remembers his Creator, and he concludes: "Fear God, and keep his commandments: for this is the whole duty of man. For God shall bring every work into judgment. . . ."	Also known as Canticles (from Vulgate)—a love poem or collection of love poems of singular beauty Biblical scholars hold varying opinions concerning the kind of love of which it speaks—it has been interpreted in three ways: literally, typically, and allegorically The Jews held that it alluded to the love between God and His chosen people, while early Christians applied its allegorical meaning to Christ and his Church

The Period of the Prophets

The period of the writing prophets, major and minor, is without parallel in religious annals. The prophets made a lasting impress upon their nation, politically, socially, and religiously. Their message was twofold: for their day and situation, for all time and world salvation. They developed for the Hebrew mind a vastly higher and more spiritual conception of the nature of God—of His justice, righteousness, mercy, and unfailing love to His covenant people—than had ever been known before. Coming in a period of declension and apostasy, the prophets held aloft a spiritual standard for Israel, severely condemning the gross iniquity and flagrant disobedience of their people. Foreseeing the burden of captivity, they comforted them with promises of a restored remnant and future glory. Woven throughout their prophecies are the hopes and expectations of Israel for a Messianic King, salvation for the Gentiles (the nations), the Day of the Lord, and the establishing of God's kingdom on earth.

The books of the prophets do not extend history in point of time, but are contemporary with the latter Old Testament books of history, i.e. from Second Kings through Esther.

Isaiah	Jeremiah	Ezekiel	Daniel
Pre-exilic	Pre-exilic	Exilic	Exilic
740-701 B.C.	626-585 B.C.	592-570 B.C.	606-536 B.C.
To Judah	To Judah	To Judah	To Judah

THE FIVE BOOKS OF THE MAJOR PROPHETS

ISAIAH	JEREMIAH	LAMENTATIONS	EZEKIEL	DANIEL
Isaiah prophesies during critical period when Assyria is invading Palestine His stern denunciations of Judah's moral and religious declension—his prophecies against heathen nations—sublime prophecies of the coming Messiah and his work Prophecies of restoration, redemption, and future glory of Israel —the Messianic salvation is to include the Gentiles (Chs. 40-55 attributed to Second Isaiah, 540 B.C.; chs. 56-66 to Third Isaiah, 450 B.C.)	Jeremiah prophesies prior to the fall of Assyria and during rise of Babylonian Empire Warnings and admonitions to a backsliding and rebellious Judah Prophecies: concerning the fall of Jerusalem; seventy years' captivity in Babylon, and the restoration; concerning the Messiah, the Branch; and his kingship over all the earth King and people persecute Jeremiah—his unceasing labors to reform and save Judah	Written anonymously but attributed by tradition to Jeremiah—a lamentation over fall and desolation of Jerusalem and the ravaging of the city by the Babylonians The sins of the nation are the totality of the sins of its people, and its judgment has come He weeps for the suffering, humiliation, and reproach of Judah—grieves for beloved Jerusalem now violently stripped of its sanctuary, its beauty, and its joy	Ezekiel, captive in Babylon, labors among his people in exile His messages are inspired visions, apocalyptic in form He foretells the certain and direful fall of Jerusalem, the result of Judah's sins After the fall of Jerusalem he comforts and sustains Judah with predictions of restoration and of future glory—faithful to his high office as watchman, he zealously holds before his people the high destiny of a united Israel	This book is in two parts: Personal history of Daniel in captivity—he and his companions, uncompromisingly loyal to the worship of the One God and subjected to severe trials of their faith, are miraculously protected Daniel's apocalyptic visions of world powers ("the times of the Gentiles") extending to the establishment of the Messianic Kingdom—his prophecies of the great tribulation and "the time of the end"

The Developing Conception of God and of Man's Obligation to Him:

To Isaiah God is "the Holy One of Israel," its "Maker," and Zion is the place of His habitation. He defines Israel's true mission. Through Israel is to come Messiah, and through Messiah is to come redemption for all nations.	Israel must throughly amend its sinful ways and to this end it suffers chastisement. Jeremiah foresees the new covenant when God's law shall be written in the heart and shall bring individual responsibility.	Jeremiah takes the first step in the repentance of his people when in "godly sorrow" he weeps over their sins and mourns over Jerusalem. Out of affliction must come genuine contrition and true reformation.	Ezekiel defines the individual's responsibility to God. Man must stand wholly upon the merit of righteousness. "The soul that sinneth, it shall die." "In his righteousness that he hath done he shall live."	Holding to a pure monotheism, these representative captives endure fiery trials. Their God is acknowledged by the heathen as supreme, as "the living God," whose kingdom shall be unto the end.

Hosea	Joel	Amos	Obadiah	Jonah	Micah
Pre-exilic 750-735 B.C.	Post-exilic ? *ca.* 500 B.C. ?	Pre-exilic *ca.* 760 B.C.	Exilic 586 B.C. (?)	Pre-exilic 780 B.C. (?)	Pre-exilic 738-700 B.C.
To Israel		To Israel		To Israel	To Israel and Judah

THE TWELVE BOOKS OF THE MINOR PROPHETS (termed Minor because of smaller literary output)

HOSEA	JOEL	AMOS	OBADIAH	JONAH	MICAH
The tragedy of Hosea's marriage to an unfaithful wife is made a parable to teach adulterous Israel, seeking other lovers As Hosea's love remains constant for his adulterous wife, so God's love remains unchanged for apostate Israel Reconciliation to God is promised to Israel after the expiation of its sins	Judah has fallen away from its communion with God (daily sacrifice has ceased [1:9])—Joel sees a national calamity, a devastating plague of locusts, as an instance of divine judgment and as a foreshadowing of the terrible Day of the Lord—he calls Judah to repentance He comforts Judah with the promise of God's temporal and spiritual blessings	Amos of Judah prophesies in Israel—vainly he rebukes the rich for oppressing the poor, and calls for social justice Foretells the captivity of Israel for incorrigible wickedness Punishment shall not be turned away from the nations which continually transgress God has set His "plumbline" of justice in the midst of them	The occasion of Obadiah's prophecy is the cruelty of the Edomites, descendants of Esau, against the house of Jacob at a time of Judah's helplessness He prophecies total destruction of Edom because of its participation in and exultation over Judah's downfall Edom's strong confederacy shall be of no avail—Edom shall suffer a like cruelty—God will deliver Judah	Jonah is sent to Nineveh, capital of Assyria, to proclaim God's judgment against it Fearing God will spare this wicked city, Jonah disobediently flees by ship —thrown into the sea, is swallowed by a great fish—by prayer is miraculously delivered—he then preaches to Nineveh and its people repent Through the object lesson of a gourd, God teaches him the worth of human life	Micah's twofold message: 1. Pronounces judgment upon Samaria and Judah— denounces rulers who oppress and pervert justice 2. Prophesies restoration and hope in the Messiah: "This man shall be the peace, when the Assyrian shall come into our land"—God's unceasing kindness requires more than burnt offerings— God delights in mercy

The Developing Conception of God and of Man's Obligation to Him:

God is still mercifully maintaining His tender loving relationship with faithless Israel and His love will redeem: "I will even betroth thee unto me in faithfulness: and thou shalt know the Lord."	Sin brings upon itself a devastating divine judgment, yet God is gracious and merciful, ready to deliver those who call upon His name. "Turn ye even to me with all your heart, and with fasting.... And rend your heart, and not your garments...."	The One God is a God of holiness and of righteousness whose justice is impartially exercised upon all nations. "Let judgment run down as waters, and righteousness as a mighty stream."	The covenant people are assured continuance and deliverance in the midst of trial and suffering. "Upon mount Zion shall be deliverance, and there shall be holiness; and the house of Jacob shall possess their possessions."	Israel's narrow conception of God—as the God of the Hebrews only—gives place in a degree to a broader conception of His universal love. The repentant of every nation are seen as the object of divine mercy and benevolence.	The moral essence of prophetic religion: "He hath shewed thee, O man, what is good and what doth the Lord require of thee, but to do justly, and to love mercy, and to walk humbly with thy God?"

Nahum	Habakkuk	Zephaniah	Haggai	Zechariah	Malachi
Pre-exilic 615 B.C. To Judah	Pre-exilic 600 B.C. To Judah	Pre-exilic 627 B.C. To Judah	Post-exilic 520-518 B.C. To restored Judah	Post-exilic 520-518 B.C. To restored Judah	Post-exilic *ca.* 432 B.C. To restored Judah

NAHUM	HABAKKUK	ZEPHANIAH	HAGGAI	ZECHARIAH	MALACHI
Nahum prophesies the fall of Nineveh —he gives a vivid picture of the wickedness, drunkenness, whoredom, and idolatry of this Gentile city—for his burden of sin and apostasy the city incurs God's severe judgment "The Lord is slow to anger, and great in power, and will not at all acquit the wicked. . . . Behold, I am against thee, saith the Lord of hosts. . . ."	Habakkuk is shown of God that the Chaldeans will be used to refine Judah—observing that the iniquity of Chaldea far exceeds that of Judah, he is sorely perplexed From his watchtower he sees, through prayer and faith, a vision of the ultimate triumph of God's purposes — beholding God's omnipotence, he dedicates himself in trust and joy	As the crisis of Judah's captivity approaches, Zephaniah, a contemporary of Jeremiah, thunders the terrible judgments of God, first upon Judah and Jerusalem, then upon heathen nations—he vividly portrays the awful Day of the Lord He prophesies of a pure remnant whose reproach for sin has been removed and who will not see evil any more—God rejoices over it	In four short discourses Haggai rebukes the remnant, now returned to Jerusalem, for neglecting the rebuilding of the Temple — rouses them to build, prophesying the greater glory of this second Temple—and shows the disastrous results of their delay upon the nation's interests Pronounces God's blessing upon Zerubbabel's work	Zechariah encourages the remnant to rebuild the Temple. Through a series of visions he portrays Zerubbabel's Temple as a type of Christ's Church, and restored Jerusalem as a type of spiritual Zion Far-seeing in his vision, he foretells both advents of the Messiah King, first in rejection, second in power	Malachi upholds the civil, social, and religious reforms of Nehemiah and stresses a strict observance of the Mosaic Law He, like Zechariah, foresees both advents of the Messiah Old Testament history closes with Malachi's inspired prediction of "the Sun of righteousness [which shall] arise with healing in his wings. . . ."
The unrepentant, who heed not God's redemptive mercies but go their way unchecked, have passed the point of correction. Their sin is ripe for destruction. "There is no healing of thy bruise. . . ."	"The just shall live by his faith." As God in His goodness has delivered His people in times past, so He will always deliver them. Though the vision tarry, Israel must wait in faith and rejoicing.	God is seen as the God of the universe. None shall escape His judgments. Yet His love rests upon men. He will "turn to the people a pure language, that they may all call upon the name of the Lord, to serve him with one consent."	The first responsibility of the restored remnant is to rebuild God's temple inwardly and outwardly. Recipients of His blessing must not permit selfish personal considerations to be of first importance.	"Be ye not as your fathers. . . ." Israel is to build from the basis of higher ideals and more spiritual types. "Behold the man whose name is The BRANCH. . . . Even he shall build the temple of the Lord. . . ."	Last of O.T. prophecy. Israel's centuries of preparation are moving toward their climax and fulfillment. Now Israel stands waiting for the Messiah —for the promised "messenger of the covenant."

New Testament Literature

"All experience comes to be but more and more the pressure of Christ's life upon ours."–Phillips Brooks

The Old Testament does not become obsolete in the light of the New, but one finds in the New the fulfillment of the Old. In the former God's revelation came through His servants and prophets; in the latter it came through His Son. Under the Old Covenant there were many mediators, under the New Covenant only one.

The New Testament is especially important to Christians, recording as it does the life of our Lord. It strikes a responsive chord in the soul because it attests the immortality of man and marks the way of hope and full salvation. It was written by those whose lives had been transformed by this Life and whose faith rested on a living Lord. The Church itself produced the New Testament within the first century A.D. for its Christian community. Those who come to it in faith find in its pages that same transforming Spirit and power. Dr. James Moffatt, whose translation of the Bible into modern English is one of the most meaningful, describes the New Testament as "the literature of a Life which disturbs whatever is lifeless."

The New Testament was written in Hellenistic Greek (*koine*). Its twenty-seven books fall naturally under five general headings: Gospels, History, Pauline Epistles, General Epistles, and Revelation.

1. The Four Gospels are the records of Jesus' life as the Son of man and as the Son of God. The first three—Matthew, Mark, and Luke—deal chiefly with Jesus' ministry in Galilee, often giving the same events, in the same order and in the same words. Therefore they are termed the Synoptic Gospels. The Abingdon Bible Commentary says that these three begin on the plane of human history, the fourth on the heights of divine reality. John's Gospel differs markedly in emphasis from the Synoptics; it does not duplicate but supplements their biographies, giving Jesus' ministry in Judaea and his important visits to Jerusalem and choosing sayings and incidents which present the divine aspect of the Master's character and the profound theology of his teachings. John alone gives the great discourses in which Christ revealed himself as "the bread of life," "the light of the world," "the good shepherd," "the way, the truth, and the life," "the true vine."

2. The book of Acts records the history of the spread of Christ's gospel and the growth of the Apostolic Church. Numerous churches were founded and firmly grounded as the "good news" of salvation through faith in Jesus Christ was preached to the Jews of Palestine under the faithful supervision of the Twelve, and as it was carried to the Gentiles of Asia Minor, Greece, and Rome through the great missionary labors of Paul.

3 and 4. Hand in hand with the organization of the visible Church came the formation of Christian doctrine as its members were instructed in the rudiments of the gospel. This doctrine is preserved in the unique body of literature of the Pauline and General Epistles. The Pauline Epistles (fourteen in number, if Hebrews is included) were written primarily to individual churches. In them Paul formulated and expounded the fundamental doctrines of redemption, reconciliation, justification by faith, grace, and salvation. They guided and guarded the Christian and the Church amid persecution and heresy, and laid the foundation of Christian conduct and fellowship. The seven General Epistles, so-called because written to churches in general, gave comfort in trial, warning against heretical teachings, and admonitions concerning Christian duty and practice.

5. Revelation is a book of prophecy, a Christian apocalypse, written to encourage a persecuted Church to endure. It portrays the glory and power of Christ at his Second Advent and depicts the mighty conquest of good over evil, culminating in the final supremacy of God's kingdom.

DIVISIONS AND BOOKS OF THE NEW TESTAMENT

Five Divisions: GOSPELS, HISTORY, PAULINE EPISTLES, GENERAL EPISTLES, PROPHECY

Written before 70 A.D. (61/62?)	Written before 70 A.D. (57?)	Written before 70 A.D. (61-63?)	Written *ca.* 80-90 A.D.	Written *ca.* 63 A.D.
THE FOUR GOSPELS				**HISTORY**
MATTHEW	**MARK**	**LUKE**	**JOHN**	**THE ACTS OF THE APOSTLES**
A life of Jesus Christ written for Israel, primarily for those who had a knowledge of the Old Testament covenant and of the Messianic prophecies	A life of Jesus Christ written for Gentiles, primarily for Romans unfamiliar with Hebrew Scripture, customs, and religious expectations	A life of Jesus Christ written for Gentiles of the Greek-speaking world—the most complete and orderly history of the Four Gospels	A life of Jesus Christ written for the Church—it supplements history of the Synoptic Gospels and interprets the deep spiritual meanings of his mission	A history of early Christianity from founding of the Church at Pentecost through Paul's first imprisonment at Rome (30-63 A.D.)—written by Luke—marks the dispensation of grace in the descent of the Holy Ghost upon men
This Gospel presents Jesus as the Messiah of Israel, the fulfillment of the Abrahamic covenant and the fulfillment of the Davidic covenant of kingship	Presents Jesus as Son and Servant in his ministry of power, vividly portraying his mighty deeds—it early served as source material for Matthew and Luke	Presents Jesus as the Son of man in his humanity and divinity, emphasizing his compassionate ministry and his universal mission of salvation	John presents Jesus as the Son of God, "the only begotten of the Father," laying stress on the divinity of his words and works	It alone records the work of the twelve apostles and the missionary labors of Paul as Christianity spread from Jerusalem to Rome
KEYNOTE: "The kingdom of heaven is at hand." Mt. 4:17; 10:7	*KEYNOTE:* "The Son of man came not to be ministered unto, but to minister...." Mk. 10:45	*KEYNOTE:* "The Son of man is come to seek and to save that which was lost." Lu. 19:10	*KEYNOTE:* "In him was life; and the life was the light of men." Jn. 1:4	As the Son and his "acts" fill the Gospels, glorifying the Father, so the Holy Spirit fills the "acts" of the apostles, glorifying both the Father and the Son
"In Matt. God says to us, 'Behold thy King' (Zech. ix. 9)."*	"In Mark He says, 'Behold My Servant' (Isa. xl. 1)."*	"In Luke He says, 'Behold the Man' (Zech. vi. 12)."*	"In John He says, 'Behold your God' (Isa. xl. 9)."*	

*E. W. Bullinger, *Number in Scripture*, p. 159.

| Written at Corinth 58 A.D. | Written at Ephesus 57 A.D.
 Written in Macedonia 57 A.D. | Written at Corinth 57 A.D. | Written at Rome 62/63 A.D. | Written at Rome 62/63 A.D. |

THE THIRTEEN EPISTLES OF PAUL AND THE EPISTLE TO THE HEBREWS

ROMANS	I and II CORINTHIANS	GALATIANS	EPHESIANS	PHILIPPIANS
Foremost of all Paul's writings—his subject is "the gospel of God" and the power of that gospel to save both Jew and Gentile A clear exposition of basic Christian doctrines: redemption and salvation through Christ Jesus to a whole world under sin; justification by faith, not by the Law; the Christian's position under grace God's promises to both Israel and the Gentiles are shown to be in agreement	The Corinthian church, founded by Paul, was composed of Jewish and Gentile converts—in his absence there arose immoralities, divisions, and factions—false teachers attempted to Judaize the church—Paul's apostolic authority was repudiated He vehemently justifies his apostleship—the church sorrows to repentance—with tender concern he exhorts to Christian conduct, discipline, and love—acts to correct church problems	The churches of Galatia, founded by Paul, were being drawn away from the pure gospel by Jewish zealots who pressed Judaic practices upon Gentile converts He defends the gospel he teaches as the true gospel—asserts his apostleship as of Christ He sets forth the doctrines of justification by faith and of adoption or spiritual sonship, and contrasts the weakness and bondage of the law with the power and liberty of the gospel	The theme is the Church in its glory and fullness Paul reveals the deep "mystery" of Christ's Church whereby those united in godly love constitute the "members of his body" over which Christ is head Its members are exhorted to walk worthy of their spiritual calling to the end that the Church may be edified, to put off "the old man" and to put on "the new man," to prove faithful and strong in Christian warfare	In this tender, affectionate letter Paul assures the church in Philippi that his present afflictions, instead of retarding his mission, are furthering the gospel of Christ—with unrestrained love he rejoices in the spiritual victory, dominion, and peace which he has attained in Christ He presses upon Christians the necessity of working out their own salvation, holding before them anew Christ Jesus' perfection

The Christian's walk toward the goal of perfection:

Paul urges all men to be Christlike, to "walk not after the flesh, but after the Spirit," for the power and grace of "the law of the Spirit of life in Christ Jesus" makes them free from "the law of sin and death."	The apostle's love for Christ finds expression in a patient, solicitous ministry of reconciliation, correcting errors that lead away from the gospel of Christ. He charges all to be "as the ministers of God."	Paul reminds the followers of Christ that, having received the gift of grace by faith, they are already justified and should henceforth show forth not the lustful works of the flesh but the pure fruits of the Spirit.	Paul earnestly beseeches every Christian, a member by God's grace, to grow "unto the measure of the stature of the fulness of Christ," and thus to show forth the glory and unity of Christ's Church on earth.	By the example of Paul, this faithful apostle, still striving in humility to attain perfection and the power of Christ's resurrection, Christians are persuaded to be "thus minded" and to surrender all for Christ.

Written at Rome 62/63 A.D.	Written at Corinth 52/53 A.D.	Written in Macedonia 66/67 A.D. Written at Rome 67/68 A.D.	Written in Macedonia 66/67 A.D. Written at Rome 62/63 A.D.	Written from Italy 65-68 A.D.

COLOSSIANS	I and II THESSALONIANS	I and II TIMOTHY	TITUS and PHILEMON	HEBREWS
Paul writes to guard the church against false philosophies and mysticism which are perverting the true gospel Christ's pre-eminence in the universe and in the Church is set forth, "for it pleased the Father that in him should all fulness dwell" Men need no other gospel than that of Christ Jesus, for in Christ alone is redemption and reconciliation "Set your affection on things above, not on things on the earth."	Shortly after the founding of the Gentile church of Thessalonica these two Epistles were written to confirm the faith of its new converts and to instruct and comfort them regarding the resurrection of the dead, the Second Coming of Christ and the Day of the Lord (the Day of Christ) Paul exhorts them to patience regarding Christ's coming, explaining that "that man of sin . . . the son of perdition [antichrist]" must first be revealed	Paul lovingly instructs Timothy, a co-worker in the faith, "how thou oughtest to behave thyself in the house of God" as a good minister of Jesus Christ, and thus by the example of godliness profit the churches—gives careful directives for the safeguarding of the churches against heresies—deals with the qualifications of ministers, with church organization and discipline Paul's solemn charge to Timothy to uphold sound doctrine	Having placed Titus, a co-worker in the gospel, in charge of the church in Crete, Paul sets forth for him the qualifications of those occupying office within the church, that they may be found faithful and blameless ——— Philemon is a personal letter from Paul concerning Onesimus, Philemon's runaway slave, whom Paul has converted—Paul tactfully requests Philemon's loving reception and forgiveness of Onesimus	This epistle addressed to Hebrew Christians was written anonymously—Pauline in spirit, it is attributed by many scholars to Paul It sets forth the pre-eminence of Christ, our "great high priest" and "mediator of the new covenant," and his atoning work as contrasted with the Levitical priesthood and ceremonialism of Mosaic Law—Christ's one perfect sacrifice gives man access to God "by a new and living way"

Paul's prayer is that every man come to perfection. Having himself experienced the working of the "indwelling Christ," he comforts Christians with "this mystery . . . which is Christ in you, the hope of glory."	Christians are reminded that they "are all the children of light, and the children of the day," and are urged to the unwearied practice of Christian virtues, patient waiting, watchfulness, and well-doing.	Paul charges the Christian through Timothy to be "a good soldier of Jesus Christ," and to "study to shew thyself approved unto God, a workman that needeth not to be ashamed, rightly dividing the word of truth."	Paul charges the Christian through Titus to follow sound doctrine and to maintain good works "in this present world." ——— Paul pleads for the practice of Christian brotherhood, forgiveness and love.	Christians are encouraged to hold fast the faith unto the fullness of Christ's coming. "Having an high priest over the house of God; Let us draw near with a true heart in full assurance of faith. . . ."

DIVISIONS AND BOOKS OF THE NEW TESTAMENT *(Continued)*

Written *ca.* 61 A.D.	Written *ca.* 62 A.D. Written *ca.* 66 A.D.	Written *ca.* 90 A.D.	Written *ca.* 66 A.D.	Written *ca.* 96 A.D.

THE GENERAL EPISTLES

PROPHECY

JAMES	I and II PETER	I, II, and III JOHN	JUDE	REVELATION
The author has been identified as "the Lord's brother" and a pillar of the church in Jerusalem—the Epistle is addressed to Jewish Christians throughout the Roman Empire It emphasizes simple fundamental Christian ethics and practical application of Jesus' Sermon on the Mount, a fulfilling of "the royal law" of love with regard to trial, temptation, faith, righteous works, respect of persons, government of the tongue, effectual prayer	Peter, cherishing his association with the Master, gives witness to the sufferings and glory of Christ—calls the Christians of Asia Minor to witness and to suffer for Christ Peter, like Paul, is aware of his coming martyrdom—he desires his own firsthand knowledge of Jesus Christ to become known to all Christians in order to safeguard them from "damnable heresies"—he nourishes faith in Christ's Second Coming	First John is a pastoral letter solicitous of "my little children" in the world—its keynote is "love," and its message the sacred obligations of love—a warning against the spirit of antichrist "already . . . in the world" Second John is a brief exhortation to abide in Christian love and doctrine Third John is a brief personal letter commending Gaius' Christian hospitality to itinerant ministers	Jude pours into a brief letter a powerful message of warning that Christians safeguard themselves against false and ungodly teachers who are corrupting the pure gospel delivered them by the apostles—he calls such wicked teachers "filthy dreamers," "clouds . . . without water, . . . trees whose fruit withereth, without fruit, twice dead. . . ." He foresees a terrible punishment of the ungodly, but a saving of those who are constant in faith	The Revelation of Jesus Christ recorded by John—message of encouragement in time of severe persecution of Christians within Roman Empire—given to the seven churches of Asia but embracing the church universal Written in apocalyptic language, it is couched in a series of visions which portray the struggle between good and evil, culminating in the final overthrow of evil and the triumph of God's kingdom—depicts the coming of Christ in glory

The Christian's walk toward the goal of perfection:

James exhorts to active evidence of Christian profession, "Be ye doers of the word, and not hearers only"; to long patience; and to the bridling and taming of the tongue, an "unruly" little member.	Peter sounds a deep note of encouragement and comfort to the Christian facing suffering or persecution. "If ye be reproached for the name of Christ, happy are ye; for the spirit of glory and of God resteth upon you. . . ."	With simplicity and clarity John defines love: the love of the Father for His children, their love for the Father, and brotherly love one for another. "Beloved, let us love one another: for love is of God. . . ."	Jude counsels the Christian to eschew false teachings, to contend earnestly for the faith and to be constant in it, "building up yourselves on your most holy faith. . . . Keep yourselves in the love of God."	John beholds and foretells the full salvation of the righteous, the perfect union of God and man, and the fulfillment of the covenant. God and His Christ are seen to be supreme "as in heaven, so in earth."

Part II

OLD
TESTAMENT

2

Life and Customs of Bible Times

The unfolding drama of Biblical history is set against the life of the Middle East—a life essentially Oriental and one that sometimes seems completely foreign to today's complex society. The customs of the Hebrew people sprang from the driving forces that molded their destiny, much as the aspirations of the Pilgrims for religious freedom resulted in a new culture in North America. A knowledge of Hebrew customs is essential to a richer understanding of the Bible because they are interwoven as warp and woof of daily living into the Biblical record and form the colorful fabric of its background. Although these ways of life relate mainly to the Hebrews, many were common property with the other peoples of the ancient Middle East—Babylonians, Assyrians, Egyptians. We know through archeological finds that these more powerful nations possessed highly developed civilizations and forms of religious worship, but it is the Hebrew culture that has left its lasting imprint on Western thought in the Judaeo-Christian heritage and is therefore the one that claims our chief attention.

Israel's historians, prophets, priests, poets, and scribes wrote to their small nation to remind it of its destiny. These men were seers with a vision of the one God, and they manifested the special genius of the Hebrew mind in translating history, everyday occurrences, and material objects into spiritual lessons and spiritual counterparts. The expressive metaphors, symbols, and figures that abound in their writings were frequently drawn from the social and religious life of their periods. Because this is true, everything we can learn today about how the ancient Israelites lived and thought contributes to our appreciation of the written text of the Bible. We can better understand, too, why the Messiah came forth from this distinctive culture. Jesus' reference to many of these customs, and his retention of religious forms so familiar to his people—as well as his fulfillment of their types—served to intensify the meaning of his ministry, sacrifice, and victory.

The modern reader of the Bible often studies the social and religious customs of the Hebrews chiefly for the light they throw on the historical past, but if he restricts himself to this level one can lose sight of their inspirational value. If he will not relegate these customs to a bygone age, he can see something of their deeper meanings for today, making the transition from literal to spiritual, and will be able to apply these to his own Christian experience and progress. His own life might be likened to that of the Israelite, in which he is no longer a nomad in a wilderness world but a dweller in the promised kingdom, his real home not a temporal abode of the flesh but an imperishable habitation of the spirit, his worship advanced beyond the ceremonial to inner self-surrender and dedication.

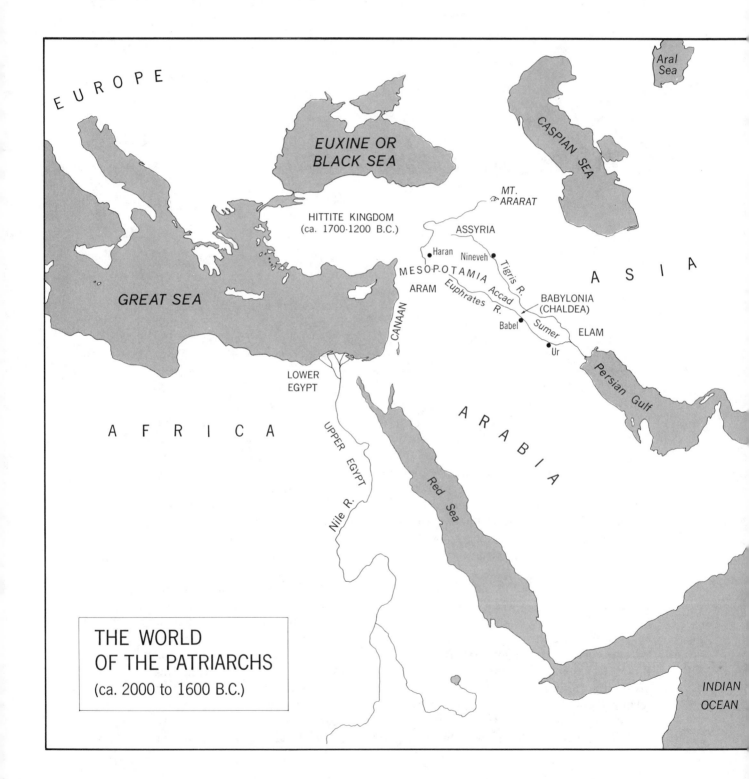

THE WORLD
OF THE PATRIARCHS
(ca. 2000 to 1600 B.C.)

Nomadic Life

The Semites, of whom the Hebrews were a small branch, were, according to the Biblical record, descendants of Shem, the eldest son of Noah. The original home of these pastoral nomads was the desert reaches and fertile oases of the Arabian peninsula, the extensive region that stretched from the Persian Gulf on the east to the Red Sea on the west and from the Armenian mountains on the north to the Indian Ocean on the south.

Driven by the necessity for survival, hordes of Semites poured out of the desert periodically from about 3500 to 1500 B.C., carrying with them their desert ideals and nomadic ways. An early migration wave went into Africa to fuse with the inhabitants of the upper Nile valley; another later invaded the lower Nile valley to rule as the Hyksos or Shepherd Kings of Egypt's XVth and XVIth dynasties (ca. 1720 to 1550 B.C.). Another wave pushed to the north to settle in the seacoast plains above Palestine to found the maritime nation of Phoenicia. But of particular interest to us are the Semites who swept into the Tigris-Euphrates valley to the northeast. Many of these settled in Upper Mesopotamia, the northwestern portion of this valley, to form an element of the later Assyrian Empire (ca. 1110-606 B.C.), while others settled in Lower Mesopotamia (Accad and Sumer), the rich alluvial plain in the southeastern portion of this valley, there to mingle with the Sumerians. With the rise to power of the city-state of Babylon they became known as the Babylonians.

Babylonia became a great civilization, making remarkable advances in the sciences of astronomy, numbers, and architecture, all of these closely allied to a highly sophisticated polytheistic religion. From its culture sprang cuneiform writing and one of the oldest codes of law known to history—the Code of Hammurabi. From Babylonia new migrations swept west across the Fertile Crescent above the Arabian desert (ca. 2500 B.C.) to locate in Syria (Aram) and Canaan; the Canaanitish colonies thus founded reproduced Babylonian culture and worship in their city-states. The Semitic tribes that continued to live a nomadic life in the deserts of Arabia, Syria, and Africa are known as Arabs (Bedouins).

Abram (Abraham), termed the father of the Hebrew race, and his nephew Lot, direct descendants of Shem, followed the arc of the Fertile Crescent as they migrated from the ancient city of Ur in southern Babylonia to Haran in upper Mesopotamia and thence to Canaan (ca. 2095 B.C.). From Abram sprang the Israelites, Ishmaelites, Edomites, and Midianites; from Lot came the Ammonites and Moabites. The early Hebrews were proportionately much less significant to any of the powerful nations in the Old Testament period than they are to the religiously aware people of the Western world today. Yet this relatively insignificant segment of the Semitic family provided the soil in which a monotheistic religion would develop, flourish, and flower in the Advent of the Christ.

The call of Abram by the Almighty took him out of Babylonian polytheism and set his feet in the path of monotheism; worship of one God was fostered by his son Isaac, his grandson Jacob, and their descendants. The distinctive religion that began with Abraham was given form nearly seven hundred years later by the great lawgiver Moses when Israel became the covenant nation and received the Sinaitic law. Henceforth the Israelites regarded themselves "a chosen people," set apart from other nations to the service of God. The covenant provisions of Sinai set the pattern of the nation's religious beliefs and shaped the laws of its singular society. To preserve the purity of monotheistic worship from sensual heathen rites and to prevent a pernicious mixture with paganism they were forbidden by Mosaic law to serve heathen gods, have social intercourse with idolatrous neighbors, or marry their neighbors' sons and daughters. Israel's leaders and prophets labored throughout the centuries of Old Testament history to keep Israel a separate people, faithful to God's covenant.

Hebrew life in the Patriarchal Age (from Abraham to Moses) was nomadic and the mores of the people grew out of an austere nomadic life. The mode of existence of Abraham, Lot, Isaac, Jacob, and his descendants in Canaan was largely dictated by the ruggedness of their environment—"a desert land . . . the waste howling wilderness" (Deut. 32:10).

Canaan, the early name for Palestine, was the small territory between the Mediterranean and the Jordan River and from Syria to the border of Egypt. This narrow strip (some 150 miles long and ranging from 20 to 60 miles wide) was dominated by the Central Range of mountains running north and south close to the deep valley of the Jordan on the east, while to the west lay the productive coastal plains.

In the northern portion of the land were rich highlands, well watered by springs; in the central portion, bordered on the north by the fertile Plain of Esdraelon and intersected by the spur of the Carmel range, were high mountain peaks, rolling hills, and deep valleys. Its southern portion was a barren mountainous plateau broken by numerous gorges and valleys that dropped precipitously on one side into the Jordan-Dead Sea rift and on the other sloped gently toward the seacoast into the fruitful lowlands or Shephelah. Much of southern Canaan was wilderness terrain, particularly the desert strip along the Dead Sea. Today we are inclined to think of a desert as a wasteland of sand, but the wildernesses of the Judaean highlands, although semi-arid and treeless and watered by scanty springs, furnished rich herbage for animal subsistence, especially after periods of seasonal rainfall. (*Wilderness* is often translated *desert* in AV and is frequently a synonym for it.)

As shepherds, the patriarchal families roved central and lower Canaan, including the parched Negeb desert to the south, finding it well suited to pastoral life (Ho. 9:10). They also may have roamed the rich plateaus east of the Jordan, territory that later became a part of Palestine. They lived in tents, moving from place to place as pasturage was exhausted. Their habits were tribal, their laws the harsh justice of the desert, their ritual worship colored by that of their Semitic ancestors (see Worship, p. 47). Many of their nomadic customs are still practiced among Bedouin tribes in the twentieth century.

Cattle Breeding

The chief occupation of the Hebrew nomads was the care and breeding of their livestock: sheep, goats, oxen, bullocks, heifers, donkeys, and camels. They measured their wealth by their flocks and herds—from the poor man with his one ewe lamb (II Sam. 12:2,3) to the tribal chieftains with their vast numbers of sheep and goats. Abraham, Isaac, and Jacob were typical tribal chieftains (Gen. 12:16; 26:14; 30:43;

A Bedouin shepherd leads his flock through the hills near Bethlehem. The garb of these modern inhabitants is much like that of their ancestors as are many of their customs.

32:3-15). Job's wealth included thousands of animals (Job 1:3), as well as land and other possessions.

Goats thrived on the rough pasturage of the rocky hills, while sheep preferred the soft green grasses of the lower levels. Goats supplied milk and meat, and their skins and hair were used as material for tents and clothing. Sheep also provided meat and oil for food, as well as skins and wool for clothing. Both were used as sacrificial offerings (see Sacrifice, p. 55).

Every man and boy was more or less a shepherd. The shepherd walked ahead to lead his flock to pasturage and water. He protected them day and night against the attacks of wild beasts, tended their wounds, sought the strays, and carried the young on his shoulders. At evening he counted them as they passed under his rod into the sheepfold.

Hebrew writers and prophets drew some of their most telling metaphors from this pastoral occupation, so common to Israel. As a shepherd was to his flock, so was God to His people, guiding, nourishing, and guarding them with His love: "He shall gather the lambs with his arm, and carry them in his bosom" (Is. 40:11). "I [will] seek out my sheep, and will deliver them out of all places where they have been scattered in the cloudy and dark day" (Ezek. 34:12; compare Jer. 31:10). "The Lord is my shepherd; I shall not want," sang the Psalmist David (Ps. 23). Israel's expected Messiah was portrayed as a shepherd feeding his flock (Ezek. 34:23).

Jesus Christ was the Good Shepherd, calling men to enter the kingdom of heaven and patiently showing them the way. He fed their souls, ministered to their needs, and rejoiced in their salvation (Jn. 10:1-18; Heb. 13:20; I Pet. 2:25).

Oxen were beasts of burden and a source of food in Abraham's day. In Canaan, after the Wandering, they became draft animals for plowing and threshing (Deut. 25:4; I Ki. 19:19). Like sheep and goats, they were designated "clean" animals by Levitical law (Lev. 11:3) and were used in great numbers as sacrificial offerings (22,000 oxen were sacrificed as a peace offering at the dedication of Solomon's Temple [I Ki. 8:63]). The domesticated donkey (ass) was also a valuable burden-bearer because of its tractable nature and its surefootedness over mountain terrain. The ass was a symbol of patience, peace, and humility; a white ass the symbol of royalty. On the day of his triumphal entry into Jerusalem Jesus rode from Bethphage on a donkey colt (Jn. 12:14,15).

Camels were highly valued for desert traveling. They were bred by the Hebrews for sale to merchants and traders who traveled the great caravan routes between Egypt, Arabia, and Mesopotamia; fittingly have they been termed "ships of the desert." The

The vegetation of this oasis near Jericho contrasts sharply with the stark nearby mountains and the wastes of the Judaean desert. Israel Government Tourist Office.

one-humped camel was most common in Biblical lands. Provided by nature with a heavy coat of hair that insulated it against external temperatures, with the ability to retain the water content in its blood plasma even when the water in the tissues had been greatly depleted, with a hump that stored fat and thick padded soles that could resist the burning sands of the desert, this species was particularly well adapted to desert travel. It could carry loads weighing from 500 to 700 pounds and travel tirelessly as long as 18 hours at a stretch. It supplied milk, hair, and leather for the Hebrew economy, but its meat was forbidden as food (Lev. 11:4). (See Gen. 12:16; Job 1:3.)

Horses

Hebrew nomads do not appear to have possessed horses. The first mention in Scripture of such animals is of those owned by the Egyptians in the time of Joseph (Gen. 47:17; 49:17; 50:9), used to draw the

Two Bedouin tribesmen pose for the author near Jericho.

chariots of the Pharaohs and as mounts for their warriors (Ex. 14:9). Not until the reigns of David and Solomon (1013-932 B.C.) were horses introduced into Palestine in any great number (II Sam. 8:4). Since the mountain regions of Palestine did not readily lend themselves to the use of horses for travel, these animals were employed mainly for war. Solomon imported thousands from the Egyptians and also carried on an extensive trade in horses with the Hittites of Asia Minor (II Chron. 1:16,17). Twentieth-century archeological excavation at Solomon's chariot city of Megiddo unearthed stables for hundreds of horses, confirming the Biblical record (II Chron. 1:14). Deuteronomic law forbade Israelitish kings to amass horses for war (Deut. 17:16; compare Ps. 20:7; 33:17; Is. 31:1). Throughout Palestinian history, in fact, the usual beasts of burden were the donkey and the ox, not the horse.

Solomon's stables at Megiddo provided space for 450 horses or more. Two stone feed troughs (mangers) stand in the center. Courtesy of the Oriental Institute, University of Chicago.

A white horse was symbolic of conquest and of victory, and in the book of Revelation Christ as "King of kings" rides the white horse of victory and leads the armies of heaven (Rev. 17:14; 19:11-16).

Tents

During the centuries the Hebrews were nomads they were tent-dwellers; their portable lodgings were particularly suited to their mode of life. Made of black cloth of woven goat's hair sewn together in strips, tents were easy to set up, take down, and transport by donkey or camel. The women wove the cloth and pitched the tents.

A tribal encampment sometimes included hundreds of tents. The average tent in Biblical times was probably much like that of the modern Bedouin. It had nine poles, six to seven feet high, in three rows;

Ancient cistern in the Negeb, lined with rough-hewn stone blocks, with terraced fields in the background. Reprinted by permission of Farrar, Straus & Geroux, Inc. from *Rivers in the Desert* by Nelson Glueck, copyright 1959 by Nelson Glueck.

over these the water-resistant cloth was stretched taut by cords pegged into the ground. The center row of poles stood somewhat higher to provide a slanting roof, and the door and side curtains were rolled up during the day to catch the breeze. An inner curtain hung along the center poles, dividing the tent home into two sections. The front part was open to all members of the household and to guests; the back part was reserved for the women and children and used for cooking and storage. The floor was of earth, either bare or covered with a simple woven matting. A wealthy man often had a tent for himself, one for each of his wives with her children and female slaves, and others for his animals. (See Gen. 13:5; 25:27; 31:33; Num. 1:52.)

The Hebrews dwelt in tents during the Wilderness Wandering; even their place of worship, the Tabernacle, was a tent, and after their entrance into Canaan it continued to serve as their principal sanctuary until Solomon erected the Temple in Jerusalem (Ex. 26; II Sam. 7:6; II Chron. 1:3,4).

More solid dwellings of sunbaked brick or of stone supplanted the perishable tents when the Israelites settled in the cities and villages of the Promised Land. Their former manner of life was not

forgotten, however, for annually during the Feast of Tabernacles the people erected boothlike structures on the flat roofs of their houses to commemorate the Wilderness Wandering (see Feast of Tabernacles, p. 61).

By New Testament times tentmaking had become an honorable profession in which men participated; the one famous tentmaker of whom we know was Paul the Apostle (Acts 18:3).

Springs
Wells
Cisterns

Water was precious in semi-arid Palestine, where no rain fell for six months of the year. The country lacked small rivers and the one great river, the Jordan, lay too far below sea level to irrigate more than its own valley. Numerous springs or fountains rose in the chalky limestone hills but many of these, particularly in southern Palestine, were short-lived and flowed abundantly only after the two rainfall seasons of autumn and spring, drying up in the summer.

As a result of these seasonal conditions the people were dependent on wells and cisterns for a continuous supply of water (Gen. 29:2,3). Wells were difficult to dig and to maintain free from shifting sands and from the devastations of marauders. Isaac redug the wells first put down in the days of Abraham, wells that Isaac's jealous Philistine neighbors had choked with sand and stones (Gen. 26:18). The wells were often located at some distance from the villages, and to the women fell the burdensome task of drawing water and carrying it home upon their shoulders in earthen vessels (Gen. 24:11; Ex. 2:16). During the periods of heavy rainfall water was stored in cisterns or reservoirs, pits usually hewn out of limestone, to provide for subsequent months of drought (Pr. 5:15). These, like the wells, were covered with a large flat stone. The water of wells, fountains, and springs was considered

Stone water pots. *Popular and Critical Bible Encyclopaedia.*

"living water," far more desirable and satisfying than the stale, lifeless water of the cisterns (Jer. 2:13).

In many Scriptural passages the words *water, wells,* and *fountains* are used figuratively: of God as the source of salvation and blessing (Ps. 36:9; 107:35; Is. 12:3; Jer. 17:13); of understanding and wisdom (Pr. 16:22; 18:4); of a righteous man (Pr. 10:11; Is. 58:11); of Christ's gospel (Zech. 13:1; Jn. 7:38); of spiritual refreshment (Mt. 10:42; Rev. 7:17); of false teachers (II Pet. 2:17); of heaven's "pure river of water of life" (Rev. 22:1). One of Jesus' most telling metaphors is found in his use of *water* and *well:* "Whosoever drinketh of the water that I shall give him shall never thirst; but the water that I shall give him shall be in him a well of water springing up into everlasting life" (Jn. 4:14).

Agricultural Life

When Israel settled in Canaan under the leadership of Joshua (*ca.* 1410 B.C.), its people ceased to be nomads. (Dr. Nelson Glueck asserts in his *Rivers in the Desert* that, as a result of his study of the potsherds of Edom and Moab, the entrance into Canaan should not be dated earlier than 1300 B.C.) The change to a permanent mode of life added many new customs. The Israelites lived in villages and towns, and adopted the advanced agricultural practices of the Canaanites who had occupied the land for a thousand years. They adapted to their own religious use the Canaanitish harvest festivals and took over ancient Canaanitish sanctuaries for their God Jehovah.

Palestine not only supplied an environment fitted to pastoral life, it also possessed one suitable for agriculture. Its plains and terraced hills were rich and fertile, and where there was water they provided arable land. The chief farming areas lay in the Maritime Plain (the Plain of Sharon to the north and the Plain of Philistia to the south, inhabited by the Philistines), the Plain of Esdraelon, the plains of Galilee, the plains of Shechem and Dothan, the Jordan Plains, the valley of Jericho, the Shephelah of Judaea, and the tablelands east of the Jordan.

When the Israelites, under the leadership of Joshua, began to subdue the Canaanites and finally succeeded in conquering them during the period of the Judges, they dispossessed them of their well-cultivated fields. Settling down, the Israelites turned to farming as their principal means of livelihood and, following

Similar nomads' tents have been pitched near oases for centuries. The Bettmann Archive, Inc.

the successfully tested methods of the Canaanites, became proficient agriculturists in the growing of grain and the cultivation of vineyards and olive orchards (Josh. 24:13). Each husbandman received an allotment of ground—as much as one yoke of oxen could plow in a day (I Sam. 14:14) or as much as a designated amount of seed would sow (Lev. 27:16). Some Israelites, however, chose to continue pastoral pursuits, grazing their flocks and herds in the stony plateaus and hills adjacent to the villages, as such uncultivable land remained common property.

Palestine's intermittent and heavy seasonal rains fell from October through April—the "former rain" of autumn (October-November) and the "latter rain" of spring (March-April). Plowing began as soon as the sun-baked soil was softened by the first showers, and the planting season extended from the middle of October to mid-December. Deuteronomy 11:14 reads: "I will give you the rain of your land in his due season, the first rain and the latter rain, that thou mayest gather in thy corn, and thy wine, and thine oil." Cereal grains such as wheat, barley, millet, and rye were the chief food crops; flax was grown for the

weaving of linen. The harvest season fell between the middle of April and the middle of June. Reaping was done by sickle, and the sheaves were carried to the threshing floors on the backs of men and of donkeys or in carts.

The firstfruits of the land were dedicated to God, the land being regarded as His possession (Lev. 25:23) and its fruitage the manifestation of His blessings to His people (Lev. 26:3-5). This immemorial concept that the land belonged to a deity was incorporated in the Mosaic legislation enacted for the care and use of the land: for its rest each seventh year (Ex. 23:10,11; Lev. 25:3-5), for sowing a field with but only one kind of seed (Lev. 19:19; Deut. 22:9), for tithing (see p. 57), for thank offerings of the people (see p. 55), for agricultural festivals celebrating harvesting (see Feasts, p. 59).

It was natural that this common daily preoccupation with the growing things of the earth should furnish Israel's writers and seers many beautiful metaphors and spiritual lessons. Israel is termed "the choicest vine," "the vineyard of the Lord" (Is. 5:2,7); the suffering Messiah "a tender plant," "a root out of

A threshing floor. *Peloubet's Bible Dictionary.*

a dry ground" (Is. 53:2). The Psalmist promised that "they that sow in tears shall reap in joy" (Ps. 126:5). Hosea admonished "Sow to yourselves in righteousness, reap in mercy; break up your fallow ground" (Ho. 10:12).

Jesus likewise drew many of his vivid parables and metaphors from the familiar lessons of nature and life on the land, among them the parables of the sower and the seed (Mk. 4:1-20), the tares and the wheat (Mt. 13:24-43), the mustard seed (Mk. 4:30-32). In agricultural terms Paul admonished the early Church against sin: "He that soweth to his flesh shall of the flesh reap corruption; but he that soweth to the Spirit shall of the Spirit reap life everlasting" (Gal. 6:7,8). In the Apocalypse John sees Christ reaping with his sickle the harvest of the earth (Rev. 14:15-19).

Threshing Floors

The threshing floor, usually situated on a hill not far from the village, was a circular piece of hard level ground where the ripened grain was separated from its stalks. The harvested sheaves laid upon this floor were either beaten with a hand flail—a wooden handle from which a short stout stick hung loosely—or trampled under the hooves of unmuzzled oxen as they paced round and round (Deut. 25:4). The winnowing or separating of the chaff from the grain took place toward evening, when the breeze was strongest. The winnower tossed the grain up into the wind by means of a fan or pronged fork so that the chaff was blown away. After a thorough sifting of the kernels in one or more sieves, the grain was carefully stored in dry pits or in specially built granaries.

Joseph mourned the death of his father at the threshing floor of Atad (Gen. 50:10). Gideon was threshing when he was called to lead his people against the Midianites (Ju. 6:11). Boaz, a wealthy Bethlehemite, was winnowing barley when Ruth the Moabitess, daughter-in-law of Naomi, sought his protection as a kinsman (Ru. 3:2). David purchased the threshing floor of Araunah (Ornan) to build an altar to God, and later his son Solomon built the Temple on the site of that threshing floor (II Sam. 24:21; I Chron. 21:18-22:11).

The prophets likened the whole earth to God's great threshing floor, subject to sifting by His judgment. Isaiah prophesied "a new sharp threshing instrument having teeth" which would thresh the mountains as chaff (Is. 41:15). Jeremiah wrote of Babylon as a threshing floor whose time of harvest was imminent (Jer. 51:33). Daniel predicted the four heathen kingdoms of Nebuchadnezzar's dream would become "like the chaff of the summer threshing-floors" (Dan. 2:35). Amos spoke of Israel as being sifted "like as corn is sifted in a sieve" (Amos 9:9). John the Baptist referred to the Messiah as coming with the winnowing fan of judgment in hand to garner into the kingdom of heaven the righteous of the earth (Mt. 3:11,12). (See also I Cor. 9:10.)

Hebrew Society

Scriptural history presents family life as patriarchal; the wife became a member of the husband's tribe and progeny was traced through the father. The foundational unit of Hebrew society was the *family*, frequently designated *house* or *household*. This unit was often a large one; it included the father, his wives, his concubines, the children of his wives and concubines, the offspring of his sons and daughters, the hired servants, and slaves (Gen. 7:7; 17:23; Job 1:3). The household was ruled by the father, whose word

A storage jar of Jeremiah's time was found in the ruins of Bethshemesh (modern Ain-Shems). (From Grant, Ain Shems Excavations). Courtesy of the American Schools of Oriental Research.

Cuneiform tablet from the twelfth century B.C., found at Tel Ta'annek (Biblical Taanach), a Canaanite town five miles southeast of Megiddo. Cuneiform writing consisted of ideographic characters impressed by a sharp stylus into wet clay tablets that were later baked. Courtesy of the American Schools of Oriental Research.

was law. He owned his wife and children and exacted their unquestioning obedience. In his hands lay the power of life and death over his children (Ju. 11:30-39), the right to sell his daughters into slavery (Ex. 21:7) and to arrange the marriages of both sons and daughters (Gen. 24:4; 28:2). He guarded the security of the family, managed its business affairs, acted as its head in all religious matters and—in early Hebrew society—as its priest at sacrificial offerings. On him rested the responsibility of educating his sons and instructing his household in the traditions of family and tribe.

As the single family expanded into a group of many families, they became a **clan** united by the ties of kinship on the father's side and by blood brotherhood. A number of clans formed a **tribe**. The tribe was headed by one patriarch, or father, who exercised absolute authority. It was an important social entity, the whole functioning under primitive tribal laws for its own protection. A prime example of this development from family to tribe is seen in Hebrew history—from Abraham to the twelve tribes of Israel fathered by the sons of Jacob (Gen. 46:27; see p. 102). (See also Josh. 7:14; Ps. 122:3,4; Rev. 7:4-8.)

In the patriarchal period the single family unit was almost wholly merged in the larger household interest which in turn was overshadowed by the communal life of the clan and tribe. But after the tribes of Israel settled in Canaan, life was no longer economically dependent on tribal cohesiveness and the individual family gained the place of first importance.

Marriage

Marriage was instituted from earliest times among primitive races to safeguard the sanctity of human relationships and home and to further the welfare and influence of the family; it was the basis of Hebrew society. **Polygamy**, the practice of having more than one wife, was common in nomadic times. There were contributing causes: the necessity for numerous progeny, the barrenness of a wife, the preservation of the clan and tribe from the exigencies of desert life and from decimation by tribal feuds. Hebrews often took

to wife women captured as spoils of war (Deut. 21:10-14). The first mention in Scripture of polygamy is in connection with Lamech in the line of Cain, who had two wives (Gen. 4:19). A wealthy man might possess as many wives as he could afford, a restriction that acted as a curb on polygamy, while a poor man possessed only one. Both David and Solomon had many wives (II Sam. 3:2-5; 5:13; I Ki. 11:1,3). **Concubinage**, the cohabitation of a master with his female slaves or with the handmaids of his wife or wives, was also prevalent and countenanced for the same reasons as polygamy (Gen. 25:6).

Monogamy, the union of one man with one woman, was the ideal state of marriage, although no disgrace was attached to polygamy or to concubinage. Scripture presents monogamy, wherein woman is "an help meet" for man, as a prime ordinance of God (Gen. 2:18,24). The Code of Hammurabi of Babylon, which incorporated Sumerian laws in force long before Hammurabi's own reign and nearly a thousand years before the time of Moses, adhered to monogamy as a fundamental principle.

(The Code of Hammurabi was engraved on a six-foot black diorite pillar set up by Hammurabi, sixth king of the First Dynasty of Babylon [ca. 1728-1686 B.C.]. This stele, today a treasure of the Louvre in Paris, was discovered at Susa, the ancient capital of Elam, by archeologist M. J. de Morgan, in 1901-1902. It contained 51 columns of Babylonian cuneiform characters, seven of which had been erased but whose contents scholars have been able to supply from fragments of other copies of the Code. It records 282 highly systematized laws that regulated the social and commercial life of Babylonia. Certain similarities of style and legislation are apparent between this Code and Mosaic Law.)

The concept of monogamous marriage was in consonance with Israel's monotheistic religion. Mosaic Law disapproved of polygamy and concubinage, restricting but not expressly forbidding them (Deut. 21:15-17). After the Exile, as a purer monotheism emerged, these practices among the Jews gradually faded out and by New Testament times monogamy had become the accepted standard.

Levitical law gave the first specific regulations relating to chastity and marriage among the Israelites

(Lev. 18; 20:11-21). These forbade marriage with near relatives and prohibited the incestuous pollution practiced by the Egyptians and the Canaanites. Mixed marriages, between Israelites and non-Israelites—particularly with the Canaanites—were forbidden, lest the chosen people be tempted to the sin of idolatry and a consequent adulteration of monotheism (Deut. 7:1-3; Josh. 23:11-13). Even so, mixed marriage continued a widespread practice. When Ezra returned from Babylon (458 B.C.) he found so many Israelites with alien wives that he legislated that Israelites "put away" their strange wives (see Ezra 10:2,3). (See also Neh. 13:23-25.)

Under Levitical law a priest was forbidden to marry a harlot, a divorcee, or a woman who had been violated; he was, however, permitted to marry a widow (Lev. 21:7). A high priest could not even marry a widow, but only a virgin of Israel (see also Lev. 21:13,14).

Deuteronomic law laid on a brother-in-law of a childless widow or on the next of kin the duty of marrying the widow to perpetuate the brother's family name (Deut. 25:5-10; compare Gen. 38:8). This was called a **Levirate** marriage. Such a duty was not binding and could be voided by a formal act of agreement in the presence of both parties and of witnesses. A clear example of this practice is seen in the marriage of Boaz the Bethlehemite to Ruth the Moabitesss, widow of his kinsman Mahlon. When Boaz ascertained that her nearest of kin chose not to redeem his right, Boaz purchased all that belonged to Naomi's husband Elimelech and their two sons Chilion and Mahlon, and made Ruth his wife (Ru. 3:12,13; 4:5-10).

Jesus' teachings upheld in principle the Edenic institution of monogamous marriage as a divine decree for the human race (Gen. 2:24; Mt. 19:4-6). His presence sanctioned and blessed the marriage in Cana (Jn. 2:1-11). Only in one instance did Jesus touch on the subject of celibacy, saying of this state "He that is able to receive it, let him receive it" (Mt. 19:12). And in his discourse to the Pharisees regarding resurrection he pointed to the higher life wherein there is no marriage: "They which shall be accounted worthy to obtain that world, and the resurrection from the dead, neither marry, nor are given in marriage: Neither can they die any more: for they are equal unto the angels; and are the children of God, being the children of the resurrection" (Lu. 20:34-36).

Paul upheld marriage as honorable. The apostle saw its necessity for mankind as a moral safeguard against fornication. He advised marriage as a general rule, to be mutually observed in love, but he commended celibacy, which left a person freer of the cares of the world so that he might "attend upon the Lord without distraction" (I Cor. 7).

Betrothal

Parents frequently promised their children in marriage in infancy and the marriage of the young people usually took place in the years of adolescence, for physical maturity came early to the peoples of the East. The choice of a wife for a son or a husband for a daughter was a matter of grave consideration, affecting the interests not only of the family but of the whole clan and tribe. A daughter might be returned to her home discredited if she were unpleasing to her husband or mother-in-law; this could become a source of tribal dissension. The attempt was made to keep the marriage within the tribe in order to safeguard tribal power and wealth. Abraham chose a wife for Isaac from among his kindred (Gen. 24); Isaac sent Jacob to take a wife from among his mother's family (Gen. 28); Hagar chose an Egyptian wife for Ishmael from among her people (Gen. 21:21).

At the time of the formal betrothal the bridegroom or his father gave a dowry of thirty to fifty shekels to the father of the bride. This *mohar* was accompanied by gifts to the bride and her family (Gen. 34:12; Ex. 22:16,17; Deut. 22:28,29; Ru. 4:5,10). Sometimes the dowry took the form of service as in the betrothal of Jacob and Rachel (Gen. 29:18). Gifts made to the bride by father or bridegroom remained her private property (Gen. 24:22,53; 29:24,29; Josh. 15:18-19); often she brought considerable wealth to the marriage, as in the case of daughters who had inherited property (Num. 27:1-8; 36:1-12) and in the case of Abigail (I Sam. 25:39-42). The betrothal contract was considered legally binding at the time of the dowry payment.

During the period of betrothal, which in the Patriarchal Age might last only a few days or in later times as long as twelve months for a virgin or one month for a widow, the bride-to-be remained in the home of her parents or of a friend. Inasmuch as betrothal was considered virtual marriage, any act of unfaithfulness by the bride during this interval was regarded as adultery, punishable by death, in which case the husband-to-be could break the contract by a bill of divorcement (Deut. 22:23,24; 24:1; Mt. 1:18,19). A betrothed or newly married man was exempted from military service for a year (Deut. 20:7; 24:5).

The Hebrew prophets Isaiah, Jeremiah, Hosea, and Malachi employed the metaphors of betrothal and marriage to depict the inviolable covenant between God and His people Israel—"thy Maker is thine husband" (Is. 54:5; compare Jer. 3:14); "I will betroth thee unto me in righteousness . . . in judgment . . . in lovingkindness . . . in mercies . . . in faithfulness. . . ." (Ho. 2:19,20). Paul described the Church as a chaste virgin "espoused" to Christ (II Cor. 11:2).

Wedding

In patriarchal days and for many centuries thereafter the wedding ceremony appears to have been the simple act of the father's leading the bride, veiled and jeweled, into the bridegroom's tent (Gen. 24:67). The marriage was celebrated by a feast that lasted seven days or longer, to which the friends of the family were invited, as in the marriages of Jacob and Samson (Gen. 29:21-23,28; Ju. 14:10-12).

In later times and certainly by Jesus' day, guests were invited to the feast by personal messengers; they were expected to come dressed in wedding garments, borrowing them if they had none of their own. To refuse such an invitation was an insult to the host—reflected in Jesus' parable of the wedding supper, in which the guests bidden to the wedding of the king's son made light of his invitation (Mt. 22:2-14). This custom of personal invitation to a banquet is also seen in Revelation 19:9: "Blessed are they which are called unto the marriage supper of the Lamb." The **bride** was dressed in an elaborate wedding garment and veiled from head to foot. The **bridegroom**, too, was clothed in a festive robe (Is. 6:10). The central feature of the marriage ceremony was the wedding procession, a colorful event marked by singing, music, and the carrying of lighted torches. It took place late in the evening when the bridegroom, in the company of his friends or "children of the bridechamber," led his bride and her attendants to his house or the house of his parents. Then followed a joyful marriage supper and a week of festivities, a custom that still prevails among the peoples of Arabia and Armenia.

The appellation *bridegroom* was applied to Jesus Christ by John the Baptist in describing his pre-eminence (Jn. 3:29), and was also used by Jesus of himself to illustrate his enduring union with his faithful followers (Mt. 9:15; 25:1-12). *Bride* is used figuratively in the book of Revelation to denote the perfection and beauty of Christ's Church and of the New Jerusalem (Rev. 21:2,9).

Status of Wife

The wife was the property of her husband; he was her master and owner and she was regarded as a chattel. Theoretically, in a polygamous marriage wives had equal status, but in practice there was bitter rivalry among them for the husband's favor, and the standing of each wife was determined largely by the husband's affection and by her ability to bear him children. Such rivalry is apparent in the marriages of Jacob to the sisters Leah and Rachel (Gen. 29:30,31) and in those of Elkanah to Hannah and Peninnah (I Sam. 1:2-7). A concubine, although she lived in her master's house and mothered his children, did not have the legal standing of a wife (Gen. 21:9,10).

Despite the fact that marriage was a commercial contract, the love of young people for each other often played a part in the choice, and the joys of conjugal love and happy family life were abundantly evident in Hebrew society. To the women fell the cares of motherhood and the heavy duties of the household. One cannot find a more exquisite portrayal of a virtuous wife and mother than that in Proverbs 31:10-31, which eulogizes "She looketh well to the ways of her household, and eateth not the bread of idleness. Her children arise up, and call her blessed; her husband also, and he praiseth her."

Hebrew women were given recognition and freedom beyond that accorded women of other Oriental nations, and Mosaic legislation protected their human dignity. Some women of strong character manifested independence of spirit and rose to positions of authority and importance. Sarah gave wise counsel to Abraham, Rebekah acted independently of her husband to assure her son Jacob the birthright, Deborah became a judge in Israel, Abigail graciously proferred David the hospitality her husband had refused, Huldah became a prophetess.

Christianity accorded women a much higher recognition of their intrinsic worth, and they actively participated in the work of the early Christian Church (see p. 357).

Divorce

Divorce was prevalent among the Hebrews and other peoples of the East. Because a wife was the property of her husband, he had the traditional right of putting her away if she did not please him (Gen. 21:14). Mosaic law acknowledged this right but tended to restrain it, offering some measure of protection to a wife from the sudden loss of her home and children. The husband could send his wife back to her family if, because of some uncleanness, she had lost favor with him. Specifically, a man could divorce his wife if she were not a virgin (Lev. 21:7,14) or if she had committed adultery (Ex. 20:14), but he was denied the right of divorce in two cases where he himself was at fault (Deut. 22:13-19,29). He could not, however, act capriciously; he was required to take legal steps in the presence of witnesses and to give his wife a written bill of divorce (Deut. 24:1; Is. 50:1; Mal. 2:11-16). A divorced woman could remarry, but in the case of a second divorce or the second husband's death she could not remarry her first husband (Deut. 24:1-4).

In Jesus' day the rabbinical schools of Shammai and Hillel (see p. 296) held greatly divergent opinions as to the permissible grounds for divorce as given in Deuteronomy 24:1, the former confining its interpretation of this passage to adultery or unchaste conduct, the latter extending it to include trifling acts that displeased a husband. Although Jesus acknowledged that Mosaic Law permitted divorce, he condemned this social evil as not in accord with the divine will (Mk. 10:2-12).

Paul taught the Christian that the mutual bond of wedlock was one not to be lightly dissolved. In marriages where one partner was a Christian and the other not, it was Paul's judgment that, if the nonbeliever was willing, they should remain together, for the unconverted one as well as the children would be brought within the pale of Christian influence (I Cor. 7:10-16).

Children

Children played a vital part in the welfare and happiness of the household. They were regarded as treasured gifts, tokens of God's favor, "an heritage of the Lord" (Ps. 127:3-5). Male children were especially esteemed; a father who had many sons was a rich and honored man. Levitical law specified that a male child should be circumcised on the eighth day after birth, at which time he received his name (Lev. 12:3; Lu. 1:59; 2:21).

During their early years Hebrew children were raised by the mother and from her received their first religious instruction. The daughter remained under her mother's care until marriage. It became the father's duty to take over the religious education when a son reached the age of five—to teach him the history of the nation and the exploits of its great leaders, the sacred Law, and other portions of Scripture. This responsibility ceased on the boy's thirteenth birthday, at which time he reached his religious majority and became a "son of the Law," obligated to practice its moral and ritual requirements. This paternal training is clearly portrayed in Proverbs: "My son, hear the instruction of a father. . . ." "My son, despise not the chastening of the Lord. . . ." "My son, attend unto my wisdom. . . ." After synagogues were instituted, children from the age of six attended them for instruction in the Law and the Prophets (see p. 230). By New Testament times elementary schools other than those of the synagogue had been introduced into Palestine, and Talmudic schools (secondary schools or colleges) for the advanced study of Judaism were numerous.

Children were required to render unqualified obedience to their parents—an imperative stated in the Fifth Commandment of the Decalogue (Ex. 20:12). Paul called such obedience "the first commandment with promise" (Eph. 6:1-3). The authority of the father over his children was not restricted to any given age; it certainly extended to the time of marriage, as seen in the father's control of the marriage arrangements for his offspring. Abraham through his servant chose Rebekah for his son Isaac (Gen. 24). Jesus rendered filial obedience to Joseph and Mary beyond the age of twelve (Lu. 2:51). Children held their parents in great honor and reverence; any case of insubordination or disrespect was a serious breach of the Fifth Commandment, and a rebellious or wicked son was subject to capital punishment if his parents concurred in placing a complaint before the town elders (Ex. 21:15,17; Deut. 21:18-21).

The Hebrew prophets lamented the disobedience of Israel against God, their loving Father, seeing it as the crime of rebellious children, and they struggled to wake Israel to her filial obligation (Is. 30:9; 63:8-10; Ezek. 2:3-5; Mal. 1:6). Jesus' obedience was perfect: "I do always those things that please [the Father]" (Jn. 8:29; compare 5:19). Jesus loved little children; he taught that their purity, simplicity, and receptivity were essential qualities for entrance into the kingdom (Mk. 10:14-16). Paul specifically designates as the children of God those "led by the Spirit of God" (Rom. 8:14).

First-born

The first-born son of the Hebrew family was held in special esteem. To him fell the **birthright**—the right to succeed his father as head of the family, clan, or tribe, and the right to inherit a double portion of his father's estate. Abraham gave all he possessed to his son Isaac (Gen. 25:5). To the birthright was usually added the father's blessing, a confirmation that had the force of a modern will (Gen. 27:4). The first-born was reckoned as the son who in point of time was born first in the household, whether the mother was a wife or a concubine (Deut. 21:15-17). The law of primogeniture was not always adhered to, however, as in the case of Ishmael, first-born of Hagar, who was dispossessed at Sarah's word (Gen. 21:10); of Esau, who by his own consent sold his birthright to his younger brother Jacob, and later the father's blessing was conferred upon the second-born (Gen. 25:33; 27:1-41); of Jacob, who blessed Ephraim above Manasseh (Gen. 48:8-20); of David, who chose Solomon instead of his eldest living son Adonijah to succeed to the throne (I Ki. 1:29,30).

If there was no male issue, the father's estate was inherited by the daughters, with the provision that they marry within their own tribe, a precedent set in the case of the daughters of Zelophehad (Num. 27:1-8; 36:1-12).

From the beginning of the nation's religious history the male first-born of the Israelites were considered sacred to Jehovah. Just before the Exodus they were consecrated to the service of God to commemorate their preservation from the tenth plague, which took the lives of Egypt's first-born (Ex. 13:2). When the Mosaic system was instituted at Sinai, the tribe of Levi was substituted for the first-born consecrated in Egypt and was given priestly pre-eminence. Twenty-two thousand Levites replaced the first-born of the other tribes, the 273 remaining males were redeemed at a price of five silver shekels (one shekel = approximately 64 cents), a payment which went to the support of the priests (Num. 3:11,12,40-51). Through succeeding generations every first-born Jewish male child at the age of one month was "presented before the Lord" and redeemed at the same price (Num. 18:15,16), although if a Levite he was exempted. The child Jesus was redeemed by his parents according to this law of Moses (Lu. 2:22,23).

In the Old Testament Israel is called God's son, "my firstborn" (Ex. 4:22). The term *first-born* is applied to Christ—among many brethren (Rom. 8:29), of every creature (Col. 1:15), the "first begotten" of the dead (Rev. 1:5). Those whose names are written in heaven are called "the church of the firstborn" (Heb. 12:23).

Barrenness

A marriage without children was a bitter sorrow to both husband and wife and was accounted a reproach from God. The wife not only grieved because she had no children but also feared for her position as a wife. She was subject to the ridicule and scorn of the other women of the household and the neighborhood. Both Sarai (wife of Abram) and Hannah (wife of Elkanah) suffered this humiliation (Gen. 16:4; 21:9; I Sam. 1:7). The disgrace felt by a barren wife sometimes caused her to give a handmaid to her husband as a secondary wife that she might, through her, lay claim to children and so retain her husband's favor. Sarai, when she saw she was barren, gave Abram her Egyptian slave Hagar (Gen. 16:1-3) and Rachel sought a child of Jacob through her handmaid Bilhah (Gen. 30:1,3). The children of polygamy or concubinage were regarded as legitimate and were welcome members of the household.

Slavery

Slavery was an institution recognized and practiced in all ancient civilizations. In Scripture the **slaves** of the Hebrews are called manservants, maidservants, handmaids, bondservants, or servants. Most of these were non-Hebrew: spoils of war, purchased slaves (often from the slave-traders of Phoenicia), or those born of slave parents. As chattels, they constituted part of the family wealth. The standard price of a slave from five to twenty years of age was 30 silver shekels (Ex. 21:32)—Joseph's brethren sold him for 20 pieces of silver (Gen. 37:28).

To the slaves fell the menial domestic duties and the hard labor of the fields, for the father and sons of a well-to-do Hebrew household held themselves superior to such work. Both male and female slaves served as personal attendants—the men often rising to trusted positions, as did Abraham's stewards (Gen. 15:2; 24:2-4; compare Pr. 17:2), the women becoming secondary wives and concubines. Non-Hebrew slaves could be held in perpetuity; their wives and children were also the property of the master and at his death were bequeathed to his heirs (Lev. 25:44-46).

In Hebrew society, slavery was practiced on a more humane basis than among neighboring nations. The slaves of the Hebrews were accorded many religious rights and privileges: as members of the family group they came under the Abrahamic and Sinaitic covenants, male slaves being circumcised (Gen. 17:13; Deut. 29:10-13); were granted the Sabbath rest (Ex. 20:10); permitted participation in national festivals (Ex. 12:43,44; Deut. 12:11,12,18; 16:10-14); and given instruction in the Law (Deut. 31:10-13; Josh. 8:33-35).

Under Mosaic Law a measure of civil protection and justice was afforded slaves against inhumane treatment by masters; where serious injury was incurred through cruelty, they were given their freedom (Ex. 21:26,27). An escaped slave was not to be returned to his foreign master (Deut. 23:15,16). The penalty of death was imposed for the murder of a slave as well as for that of a freeman (Ex. 21:12; Lev. 24:17), and punishment was meted out where flogging had resulted in immediate death (Ex. 21:20,21).

Hebrew law expressly forbade "man-stealing," specifically the kidnaping of one Hebrew by another for sale as a slave (Ex. 21:16; Deut. 24:7). Hebrews could, however, find themselves reduced to slavery through poverty, debt, or theft. Daughters could be sold at will by the father (Ex. 21:7); a widow's children could be taken in payment of a father's debt (II Ki. 4:1); a man could be sold when he was unable to make restitution for a theft (Ex. 22:3); a man could sell himself voluntarily, as could a woman. Such a slave was not to be treated "with rigour" but as a hired servant. This servitude was not a lasting state, for no Hebrew could remain permanently a slave to another Hebrew since he was regarded as freeborn and primarily a servant of God (Lev. 25:39-43).

A man might be released from his bondage in three ways: by remission of all the claims against him;

by the occurrence of the Year of Jubilee (see p. 59); by the expiration of a six-year period (Ex. 21:2-4; Lev. 25:40; Deut. 15:12; compare Jer. 34:8-17). The Law enjoined that upon his release he be given liberal supplies with which to start a new life (Deut. 15:13,14). The servitude of a female slave was permanent, however, because her position was usually that of a wife or a concubine. If she did not please her master as a wife she could be redeemed by her family: he was not at liberty to sell her to an alien. If he bought her for his son, he was to treat her as a daughter. If he himself took another wife, he must still retain the slave as a wife and treat her justly; if not, her freedom was to be granted without repayment of the purchase money (Ex. 21:7-11). If slaves loved the master and desired to stay with him, the ear of the slave was pierced with an awl and he or she remained a servant forever or until the Year of Jubilee (Ex. 21:5,6; Deut. 15:16,17).

If a Hebrew became the slave of a "stranger," a non-Israelite, he could redeem himself or be redeemed by his kinsmen, or be set free in the Year of Jubilee (Lev. 25:47-55).

A **hired servant** or a **hireling** was one who voluntarily labored for a wage for a stipulated period of time (Is. 21:16). The Law forbade his oppression (Deut. 24:14,15).

Righteous men of Scripture were termed "servants of the Lord," among them Abraham, Jacob, Moses, David, and the prophets. Israel was called "my servant." The Messiah himself came in "the form of a servant" (Phil. 2:7). Paul called himself "a servant of Christ," as did Peter, James, Jude, and John.

In the Graeco-Roman world of New Testament times slavery with all its attendant evils was still rampant. Jesus did not attack the practice of human slavery, his great concern being to free men from the greater bondage of suffering and sin (Lu. 13:16; Jn. 8:32,34-46); but the spiritual principles of love and brotherhood he taught and exemplified became an irresistible moral force that began at once to dissolve the foundations of this social evil.

Neither did Paul, as he journeyed through the Roman Empire, make a militant assault on the institution of slavery; he counseled obedience and faithfulness on the part of the slave, justice and kindness on the part of the master (Eph. 6:5-9; Col. 3:22-4:1; Philemon). At the same time Paul declared the spiritual freedom found in Christ: "He that is called in the Lord, being a servant [slave], is the Lord's freeman: likewise also he that is called, being free, is Christ's servant" (I Cor. 7:22). In this connection he proclaimed: "There is neither Jew nor Greek, there is neither bond nor free, there is neither male nor female: for ye are all one in Christ Jesus" (Gal. 3:28).

Dress

The simplest article of clothing of all primitive civilizations was the **loincloth** made from animal skins or cloth; it was a garment in use by the Hebrews. This was the leather girdle of Elijah and John the Baptist (II Ki. 1:8; Mt. 3:4) and the linen girdle of Jeremiah (Jer. 13:1). Gradually the loincloth was replaced by a close-fitting sleeveless garment—a shirt or **tunic** (AV coat) of wool, linen, or cotton—reaching to the knees. This was the workaday garment worn by all classes, men and women alike—the sheet or shirt of Judges 14:12, the coat of Luke 6:29. The seamless coat of Jesus stripped from him by the Romans at crucifixion was this same inner garment (Jn. 19:23).

The well-to-do adopted a **second tunic** that had wide sleeves and reached to the ankles. This was the "coat of many colours" Jacob gave to his favorite son Joseph (Gen. 37:3) and the garment of Tamar, the daughter of King David (II Sam. 13:18).

Wound around the tunic at the waist was a sash or **girdle** of cloth or leather, varying in size from a single rope to a strip about five inches in width so folded as to provide pockets for miscellaneous articles of money and food, or as a sword belt for a weapon. When a man undertook arduous labor or a journey, he often fastened his girdle securely about his loins, pulling up the tunic until it hung loosely over the girdle. Thus the expression "gird up the loins" came to symbolize vigorous or decisive action. The Israelites ate the first Passover with their loins girded for the exodus from Egypt (Ex. 12:11). Job was commanded "Gird up now thy loins like a man" when God challenged him to answer Him (Job 38:3). Peter urged the Christian "Gird up the loins of your mind" (I Pet. 1:13).

The ordinary outer garment was the **mantle** or **cloak** (Heb. *simlah*)—a long rectangular piece of cloth similar to a blanket, sometimes plain, sometimes striped, seamed at the shoulders but open down the front and sides, hand-woven of wool, goat's hair or camel's hair. So necessary was this article of clothing as a protection against inclement weather and as a covering for warmth at night that, if its owner gave it as a pledge, Mosaic Law required its return before the setting of the sun (Ex. 22:26,27). In many English versions of the Bible the world *simlah* is translated variously as raiment, clothes, garment, apparel. This was the "garment" with which Noah's sons covered their father's nakedness (Gen. 9:23), the "clothes" Jacob rent when he mourned the loss of Joseph (Gen. 37:34), the "raiment" Joseph gave his brethren (Gen. 45:22), the "raiment" of Ruth (Ru. 3:3), and the "apparel" David changed after the death of his child (II Sam. 12:20). The Psalmist spoke of God as "clothed with honour and majesty . . . with light as with a garment" (Ps. 104:1,2).

The mantles of men of high rank are referred to as robes, differing from the *simlah* mainly in quality and decoration. Linen robes, valued for their coolness and cleanliness, were worn by royalty and by the priests (for the distinctive garments of the Aaronic priesthood, see pp. 53-54). Women's robes were similar to men's except in ornamentation.

By New Testament times another type of mantle had come into use, a rectangular woolen or linen cloth with tasseled corners, similar to the Greek *himation* and the Roman *pallium.* This was wrapped around the body and draped over the left shoulder.

These garments varied according to desert or town life as well as in their simplicity of design, texture, and quality, depending on the individual's economic status and occupation. The poor often possessed only one set of raiment. Today the Syrian peasant and the Bedouin still wear flowing robes like those of the ancient Hebrews, finding them highly suitable and adaptable to the rapid changes and extremes of Middle East temperatures.

People of all classes wore **sandals**, plain soles of leather or wood bound onto the feet by thongs or shoelatchets. Within their homes and in places of worship they removed their sandals (Ex. 3:4,5). The priests went barefoot in the performance of their temple duties. To appear in public without shoes was a sign of mourning or an indication of great poverty. When Absalom usurped the kingdom, his father David fled from Jerusalem weeping and barefooted (II Sam. 15:30). The prophet Isaiah, as a warning to Israel not to rely on Egypt and as a sign of the coming captivity of Egypt and Ethiopia, walked barefoot for three years (Is. 20:2-4).

The **headdress** of the Hebrew nomad was like that of the modern Bedouin, a square or rectangular piece of cloth folded triangularly to protect the head, neck, and shoulders from the burning rays of the sun. In later times the Israelites wore more elaborate headdresses of cloth wound round and round to form a turban. This particular headdress (RV turban) is termed in AV a "hood" (Is. 3:23), a "royal diadem" (Is. 62:3), a "mitre" (Zech. 3:5). The priestly turbans were called "bonnets" and were made of fine linen (Lev. 8:13); the high priest's headdress with its frontal plate of gold was also called a "mitre" (Lev. 8:9).

The women wore **veils**. These varied in length, falling to the waist or ankle, and could be drawn over the face or wrapped around the body to provide concealment in the presence of men or strangers. A bride wore a veil in the presence of her betrothed. Rebekah veiled herself at her first meeting with Isaac (Gen. 24:65). Ruth used her veil to carry barley into the city (Ru. 3:15). Moses wore a veil over his face when he gave the people the Decalogue the second time (Ex. 34:33-35). Paul spoke figuratively of the veil upon the hearts of the Jews who could not see that the glory of Christ's grace superseded the glory of Mosaic Law (II Cor. 3:7-16).

Meals

From earliest Biblical times food was prepared by the women. The early breakfast and late morning meal were light, the principal meal being eaten after sunset. The food was served in one earthenware bowl placed on a woven mat on the tent floor. The Hebrew family ate together, either sitting or squatting around this simple table surface, as do the Bedouins and Egyptian fellahin today. Each dipped his hand into the one main dish or scooped its contents with a sop of bread.

A first-century earthenware bottle from Petra, capital of Nabataea (formerly Edom and Moab); 5½ x 1¾ inches. The Metropolitan Museum of Art, gift of William H. Shehadi, 1953.

The fare was chiefly vegetarian. It might consist of parched grains; lentils and beans (often stewed as pottage, Gen. 25:29,34); coarse bread of barley, wheat, or spelt (AV rye); fruits such as grapes and raisins, olives, dates and fresh or pressed figs; nuts, honey, milk and its products. The meat of flocks and herds, particularly of sheep and goats and of certain game, was relished, but meat was enjoyed by the poor only at family feasts and in the entertainment of a guest. When the Israelites settled in Canaan they added to their diet fish, cucumbers, melons, leeks, onions, garlic—foods to which they had been introduced in Egypt (Num. 11:5). The simplicity of the meal served to David and his band of men—grain, pulse [beans, lentils, peas], honey, butter, sheep, cheese (II Sam. 17:28,29)—contrasted strongly with the sumptuous fare of Solomon's table—fine flour, meal, fat oxen, sheep, fattened fowl, and several kinds of game deer (I Ki. 4:22,23).

Mosaic Law carefully prescribed the "clean" meat—animal, fish, fowl—permitted for food, and the prohibited "unclean" meat (Lev. 11). Some of these restrictions were imposed on religious grounds, others for hygienic and sanitary reasons. Clean animals, domesticated and wild, were those that both chewed the cud and had cloven hoofs (ruminating animals digested food better and thus produced healthier meats). Fish that had fins and scales and fowl that did not subsist on carrion were also considered clean. Unclean animals were the camel, rabbit, and hare (which chewed the cud but did not have cloven hoofs), swine (which had cloven hoofs but did not chew the cud), rodents, and reptiles. Also unclean were fish such as shellfish and eels (which resembled serpents, credited with demon spirits), birds of prey and carrion-eating fowl, winged insects (with the exception of four kinds of locusts).

When the Israelites built permanent homes in Canaan their eating habits changed and they advanced to the use of seats or stools and low wooden tables. Gradually the Syrian custom of reclining on low couches at mealtime gained favor among men of the wealthy classes (Amos 6:4; Es. 1:6, RV), and by the third century B.C. this custom was widespread. The guests were seated according to rank, the most honored being given the "highest" place (Lu. 14:8-10). In New Testament times the Greek and Roman way of reclining two or three to a couch, each man resting on his left elbow, was in vogue. The description of John as "leaning on Jesus' bosom" points to this custom (Jn. 13:23), as does the account of a penitent woman who was able to reach and wash the feet of Jesus while he was dining (Lu. 7:37,38).

An invitation to special feasts was extended in advance by the host; on the appointed day when all was in readiness a reminder was sent. The guest arrived in festive garments, for to come dressed in less than his best was an affront to the host. These courtesies are reflected in the parables of the Great Supper and the Marriage of the King's Son (Lu. 14:16-24; Mt. 22:2-13). Other courtesies were observed by the host: the washing of the guest's feet on his arrival, the bestowal of a kiss, the anointing of his head with fragrant oil—all referred to in the narrative of the supper Jesus attended in the house of Simon the Pharisee (Lu. 7:44-46). Jesus himself washed the feet of his apostles at the Last Supper (Jn. 13:4,5).

Hospitality

Hospitality comes from a Greek word meaning "love of strangers." Hospitality was a virtue highly esteemed among all nomadic peoples, being extremely important as a counterbalance to the harshness of desert travel. Proffering this kindness brought blessing; withholding it brought rebuke. The traveler regarded it as his right and the host considered it his duty. Hospitality provided the stranger with shelter, water, food, and protection both for himself and for his animals (Gen. 24:31-33). The laws relating to hospitality were scrupulously observed, for a man never knew when he might find his own life dependent on this courtesy.

The traveler was treated as an honored guest and all the master of the house possessed was placed at his service. The host did not delegate these responsibilities to his servants but waited on his guest himself. The account of Abraham's hospitality to three strangers furnishes an exact picture of that still practiced among today's Bedouins (Gen. 18:1-8). Abraham ran to meet them as they approached his tent; bowing himself to the ground he extended a welcome. He offered water for their feet and rest in the shade of a tree. With his own hands he laid food before his guests and stood while they ate. Lot's observance of the duty of hospitality illustrates the lengths to which a host might go (Gen. 19:1-8; compare Ju. 19:15-21).

Three days was the proper length of stay but the visitor could, by claiming the hospitality of others, remain in the tribal encampment indefinitely. Under the law of hospitality even an enemy or one seeking blood revenge was received as a guest once he entered a tent or so much as touched a tent cord (see Blood Revenge, p. 45). After sharing a meal, he and his host were mutually bound to protect each other during his stay (see Bread and Salt Covenants, p. 46). An avenger could claim the right of exemption from pursuit for at least a day and a half after his departure.

Hospitality to the stranger persisted after Israel entered village and city life. Sometimes a room was set apart in a home as a guest chamber—the Shunammite woman, for instance, made "a little chamber . . . on the wall" for the prophet Elisha (II Ki. 4:10). The number of a man's guests and his liberality in their entertainment added to his merit and prestige. Kings and men of wealth seated many at their tables. Job's hospitality to travelers gave witness to his virtue (Job 31:32). The lavish provision for Solomon's table indicated that daily he entertained many (I Ki. 4:22,23). Jezebel fed four hundred fifty prophets of Baal and four hundred prophets of Asherah at her table (I Ki. 18:19). Nehemiah seated more than a hundred fifty daily at his board (Neh. 5:17). A poor man extended the little he had, often at great personal sacrifice (Ju. 19:20).

In the more advanced society of New Testament times this custom was not so much a necessity to life as a social kindness. It was accounted to a man as righteousness. Jesus and the Twelve relied on hospitality as they journeyed from village to village (Mt. 10:11-14), as did the Seventy (Lu. 10:5-8). Jesus extended hospitality by feeding the five thousand and the four thousand (Mt. 14:14-21; 15:32-38); the Twelve were his guests at the Last Supper (Mt. 26:17-20); and after Resurrection he invited seven of his apostles to partake of a morning meal by the Sea of Galilee (Jn. 21:9,12). His teachings and his own example infused into the spirit of hospitality a deeper sense of mercy, compassion, and brotherhood, as seen in his parable of the good Samaritan (Lu. 10:30-37) and in his admonition to the Pharisees that they feast the poor and unfortunate (Lu. 14:12-14). He made it a divine demand when he taught his followers that to practice kindness and good deeds wherever there is human want or distress is to do it as though to the Son of God: "Inasmuch as ye have done it unto one of the least of these my brethren, ye have done it unto me" (Mt. 25:40).

The spread of apostolic Christianity throughout the Roman world owed much to the custom of hospitality. With full assurance Paul and other Christian missionaries relied on it wherever they went. Hospitality became a Christian virtue that strongly fostered unity among the brethren.

Blood Revenge

The practice of blood revenge was both an ancient custom and a primitive law of the desert, the outgrowth of the necessity to safeguard a man's life and person. This law is mentioned early in Genesis: "Whoso sheddeth man's blood, by man shall his blood be shed" (Gen. 9:6; compare Gen. 4:8-15,23,24). It had its roots deep in the ties of blood kinship. Any grave injustice to a member of the tribe or the killing of one of its members was considered a tribal injury that demanded restitution by the entire tribe. But in actual practice it devolved primarily on the nearest of kin to avenge the wrong, as when two of the sons of Jacob avenged the defilement of their sister Dinah (Gen. 34:25-27) and as when Solomon ordered the death of Joab for his murders of Absalom and Amasa of the house of his father David (II Sam. 18:14; 20:9,10; I Ki. 2:1,5,6,31). This stern law of retaliation served as a restraint against acts of violence among families and tribes.

With Israel's ethical development the practice of blood revenge was tempered with a measure of mercy. Mosaic Law still demanded "life for life, eye for eye, tooth for tooth, hand for hand, foot for foot, burning for burning, wound for wound, stripe for stripe" (Ex. 21:23-25; Lev. 24:17-22), but modified it with provisions of justice (Deut. 19:15-21). Careful distinction was made between murder and accidental killing, and six Levitical cities of refuge were appointed in Palestine where any man who had caused the death of another could find refuge until a fair trial could be held to determine whether the deed had been done wittingly or unintentionally (Num. 35:6,9-32; Deut. 19:1-13; Josh. 20). Three of these cities lay west of the Jordan—Kedesh, Shechem, and Hebron. Three lay east of the Jordan—Golan, Ramoth, and Bezer. They were so chosen that a man could reach one within a day's journey, a distance of about thirty miles.

A deliberate murderer was turned over to "the avenger" (Num. 35:19), but the one who had committed the crime without premeditation could find sanctuary in his city of refuge. If he ventured beyond its borders the avenger could justifiably take his life. Only after the death of the high priest was he at liberty to return to his home. These Mosaic provisions removed the law of retaliation from the sphere of private revenge and feuding and brought the administration of justice under civil magistrates.

Jesus' teachings completely abrogated this ancient law of personal vengeance by the higher law of love. "Thou shalt love thy neighbour as thyself" (Mt. 22:39). "Resist not evil: but whosoever shall smite thee on thy right cheek, turn to him the other also. . . ." (Mt. 5:39). "Love your enemies, bless them that curse you, do good to them that hate you, and pray for them which despitefully use you, and persecute you; That ye may be the children of your Father which is in heaven. . . ." (Mt. 5:44,45). The Church extended the spirit and application of this teaching. Paul wrote "Recompense to no man evil for evil" (Rom. 12:17) and urged men to leave prayerfully to God the execution of justice (Rom. 12:19; compare Rev. 19:2).

binding character (Gen. 31:44-54). Blood was used to seal the national covenant between God and Israel (Ex. 24:6,8): "Moses took half of the blood, and put it in basins; and half of the blood he sprinkled on the altar. . . . And Moses took the blood, and sprinkled it on the people, and said, Behold the blood of the covenant, which the Lord hath made with you. . . ." The blood covenant idea was implicit in the Mosaic sacrificial system of worship.

Ultimate refinement of the blood covenant came with the action of Jesus during the Last Supper when he took the cup and said, "This is my blood of the new testament [new covenant], which is shed for many for the remission of sins" (Mt. 26:28).

Covenants

The general meaning of the word *covenant* (Heb. *berith*) was that of an agreement or contract between two parties. It was considered a solemn pledge whereby men bound themselves to a mutual obligation. Covenants existed not only between individuals but among clans, tribes, kings, and nations. In its definitive religious use *the covenant* designates the compact of God with men, or of men with God.

It was customary to seal a covenant in one of three principal ways: by blood, bread, or salt. There were also several less important ways of concluding covenants: by lifting up the hand (Gen. 14:22), by giving a gift (Gen. 21:28-31), by placing the hand under the thigh (Gen. 24:2-9; 47:29), by setting up a pillar of stones (Gen. 28:22; Josh. 24:26), by the act of taking off and giving of a shoe (Ru. 4:7), by a handshake (II Ki. 10:15; Ezra 10:19).

Blood Covenant

Reaching far back into early Semitic culture, the oldest known form of ratification of an oath between men was the shedding of blood to establish blood kinship. Men entered into this blood covenant either by drinking a drop of each other's blood or by dividing a sacrificial animal in halves and walking between the two parts (Gen. 15:9-18; Jer. 34:18,19). Blood typified life (Gen. 9:4), thus a contract ratified by the shedding of blood—men's own or that of their animals—made the agreement inviolable. The making or confirming of an oath often took place at a shrine or before an altar or pillar stone to invoke the witness of the deity, and this was followed by a sacrificial meal. Such a ceremony gave the compact a sacred

Bread and Salt Covenants

Bread and salt covenants conveyed the same basic idea of kinship as did the blood covenant. Both bread and salt were essential to man's sustenance and thus were considered life-giving substances. When a man ate of another's bread or salt, it typified a pledge of friendship and loyalty, for he shared in the hospitality of the house, as when Abimelech covenanted with Isaac for peace (Gen. 26:28-31) and Laban with Jacob (Gen. 31:44-55).

Bread denoted not only baked foodstuffs but in a general sense the various foods of the table. Christ Jesus gave this term a spiritual meaning when he prayed, "Give us this day our daily bread [Cruden, All things necessary for this life]" (Mt. 6:11). He revealed himself as "the bread of life" sent from heaven, of which if a man partook he would live forever (Jn. 6:35,51).

Salt was used as a seasoning, as a preservative in food (Job 6:6), and also as an antiseptic and a purifier (II Ki. 2:20-22). Every newborn infant was washed and rubbed with salt (Ezek. 16:4). The Hebrews' supply of salt was abundant, readily obtainable from the waters of the Dead Sea by evaporation or from the cliffs of rock salt on its southern border. Salt, as an emblem of purity, accompanied every meat and meal offering, giving each a covenant meaning (Lev. 2:13; Num. 18:19; Ezek. 43:24). It was an essential ingredient of the incense offerings of the sanctuary. A salt covenant implied an agreement free of hypocrisy or duplicity. Jesus referred to salt in its symbolic sense as an essential and vital ingredient of Christian character: "Ye are the salt of the earth: but if the salt have lost his savour, wherewith shall it be salted?" (Mt. 5:13). "Have salt in yourselves, and have peace one with another" (Mk. 9:50). One's speech should be seasoned with the salt of grace (Col. 4:6).

God's Covenant

The word *covenant* has a rich Scriptural significance, as it is through the covenant idea that God made known His relation to men. "The covenant of God with His people is an expression of His love for them. It may be called the divine constitution or ordinance, which is designed to govern human relations with Himself."[1] This divine promise is everlasting and inviolate. The essential requirement on the part of men is that of obedience; Israel was blessed in proportion to its obedience.

In the **Adamic Covenant** God promised a Savior who would redeem mankind from sin (Gen. 3:15).

In the **Noahic Covenant** of grace He promised the continuance of the order of natural law on earth for the benefit and sustenance of men, and Noah ratified it with a blood covenant of sacrificial offerings (Gen. 8:20-9:17).

In the **Abrahamic Covenant**, the greatest in historical importance, the sacred covenant became definitive. In it God promised Abraham a land and a seed, that seed to be a blessing to all nations: "Get thee out of thy country . . . unto a land that I will shew thee: And I will make of thee a great nation . . . and in thee shall all families of the earth be blessed" (Gen. 12:1-3). It was renewed with Abraham after he came up from Egypt to Canaan (Gen. 13:14-17) and later confirmed by the solemn ceremony of the blood covenant (Gen. 15:2-21). At a still later ratification the promise was amplified: "I will establish my covenant between me and thee and thy seed after thee . . . for an everlasting covenant, to be a God unto thee, and to thy seed after thee." At this time circumcision was instituted as a sign of the covenant (Gen. 17:2-14). This promise was renewed to Abraham's son Isaac and to Isaac's son Jacob (Gen. 26:2-5; 28:13-15).

In the **Sinaitic** or **Mosaic Covenant** God renewed His promise to the nation of Israel as a whole. This renewal was accompanied by a theocratic constitution for the nation that was to govern the social and religious life of Israel (Ex. 20-23). When the people swore obedience, Moses sealed the covenant by sprinkling blood of burnt sacrifices first on the altar and then on the people (Ex. 24:5-8). It was renewed with the new generation of Israel in the plains of Moab prior to their entrance into Canaan, and infused with a new vigor by Moses' rehearsal of God's many mercies to the nation and by his warnings of penalties for disobedience (Deut. 29; 30).

In the **Davidic Covenant** God promised David an everlasting seed and an everlasting kingdom: "Thine house and thy kingdom shall be established for ever before thee: thy throne shall be established for ever" (II Sam. 7:8-16). In due time this oath was renewed with David's son Solomon (I Ki. 9:1-7).

The covenant relation between God and Israel was also renewed from time to time on the part of men. Joshua and Israel promised to serve God only (Josh. 24:1-27); Jehoiada and the people of Judah covenanted to be God's people (II Ki. 11:17); King Hezekiah and Judah in solemn ceremony agreed to purify their worship (II Chron. 29:10-36); King Josiah and Judah swore obedience to the Book of the Law (II Ki. 23:2,3); Nehemiah, Ezra, and the returned remnant of Judah pledged themselves to obey Mosaic Law (Neh. 9:2,3,38; 10:1-39).

Because Israel willfully violated her sacred obligation by persistent idolatry, the prophets foretold the **New Covenant** which God would make with spiritual Israel, wherein His law would be written on the heart (Jer. 31:31-34) and mediated by His Messiah (Is. 42:6; Mal. 3:1). (See also The Covenant between God and Men, p. 148.)

God's covenant reached its fulfillment in Jesus Christ, the Immanuel, "God with us." He was the Savior promised through the seed of the woman (Gal. 4:4) and the house of David (Acts 13:23), the blessing promised to Abraham (Gal. 3:16), the fulfillment of the Law through love (Mt. 5:17; 22:37-39), and the establisher of God's spiritual kingdom on earth (Eph. 1:10,11; Rev. 11:15). He was the mediator of the New Covenant, the perfect example of obedience (Mk. 14:36; Heb. 9:15-28; 10:9-17).

Worship

Several Hebrew and Greek words are translated simply *worship* in the Authorized Version. The Hebrew words include those that mean literally "to prostrate," "to fall down," "to bow down," "to reverence"; those in Greek include the meanings "to make obeisance to," "to adore," "to serve," "to praise."

From remote times man has been impelled by an innate religious instinct to the worship of a power outside himself. This instinct appears first to have been expressed in an animistic belief that all natural objects—or nature in general—had conscious life or vitality. Environed in a mysterious universe, wholly at the mercy of its unpredictable moods, men were led to the worship of nature gods of sky, earth, and water. Men's fear and wonder at nature's phenomena in time tended rapidly to multiply lesser deities and to adore natural objects such as the sun, moon, stars, trees, rivers, springs, stones, animals, birds, and the like. The pictographic writings of Sumer indicate a development in Sumerian worship from the sky-god Anu and "the Queen of Heaven" Innini to a pantheon of gods numbering in the thousands. The principal divinities, worshiped at numerous temple towers that dotted the land of Babylonia, were the sun-god Marduk (Bel [Baal] of Is. 46:1 and Merodach of Jer. 50:2), the moon-god Sin, the sea-god Ea, and Ishtar, the goddess of love. In the pantheon of Egypt's deities were the sun-god Ra (Amon, Aton), the Nile-river god Osiris, the fertility goddess Isis, and such lesser gods as the bull, hawk, crocodile, beetle, ibis, and cat.

Men also worshiped the unseen forces of nature: the rising and setting of the sun, the ebbing and flowing of tides, the succession of the seasons, birth and death, thunder, lightning, and rain. All these became personified gods. The malignant forces men could neither comprehend nor control, often called evil spirits, they propitiated with sacrificial offerings—even their own children; the beneficent or life-giving forces they conciliated with gifts.

It is difficult to determine how many of these polytheistic beliefs were accepted and practiced by the Semitic nomads, but they formed the religious background from which the Hebrews emerged. Remnants of these beliefs are found in Genesis: in the concept of God as attached to certain localities, as seen in the narrative of Jacob's experience at Beth-el (Gen. 28:16,17); in Rachel's possession of numerous household gods stolen from her father Laban (Gen. 31:19; 35:2,4); in animal sacrifice in general; in child sacrifice, as in the near-offering of Isaac (Gen. 22) and in the offering of Jephthah's daughter (Ju. 11:30-39).

The life of the Semitic nomads removed them from the corrupt and often lewd practices of the polytheistic temple worship of Babylonian civilization. Their simple, austere manner of living in the awesome stretches of the desert made them men of courage, discipline, and idealism, receptive to lofty conceptions. To the nomad Abram first came the divine call to emerge from polytheism; to him God first revealed Himself as the Almighty God, commanding "Walk before me, and be thou perfect" (Gen. 17:1). Through the revelation of the divine Spirit Hebrew monotheism was born, not through the evolution of current ethnic religions.

The God of Abraham, Isaac, and Jacob further revealed Himself to Moses at Horeb as the I AM THAT I AM—Jehovah, the supreme self-existent One, who by His will called out Israel and separated it from heathen nations (Ex. 3:14). When His law was imparted at Sinai (Horeb), its first two commandments explicitly forbade idolatry: "Thou shalt have no other gods

before me. Thou shalt not make unto thee any graven image, or any likeness of any thing that is in heaven above, or that is in the earth beneath, or that is in the water under the earth: Thou shalt not bow down thyself to them, nor serve them" (Ex. 20:3-5).

Though Israel rejected the visible for the invisible, the many gods for the One, the realization that there was no other god came only gradually; the release of the anthropomorphic concept of Him was also slow and a matter of spiritual growth, as the Old Testament attests (see Names of God, p. 142, and Second Account of Creation, p. 145).

> In the matter of religious practise: (1) Some practises, as idolatry, polytheism, human sacrifice, sensual ceremonies, were utterly condemned from the beginning of the worship of J" [Jehovah]. That they survived, or intruded themselves at later periods, in no wise proves that they were not felt to be condemned by the inward nature of J" worship. It began to make and mark its distinctiveness at the very start, or it could never have done so later. (2) Some practises, as circumcision, sacrifice, feasts, purification, perhaps the Sabbath, which were already in use, or were taken over in Canaan, were gradually changed in form and meaning. Hence we may well expect to find, as we do, that the use and value of these are found to alter from one stage to another, as the growing revelation of God flung its light upon them. (3) Other practises, as the observation of sacred places, stones, trees, animals, etc., continued for a while without explicit condemnation, but were found to be inconsistent with the worship of J", when His self-revelation had become more familiar to the general thought of the people.[2]

The moral and spiritual teachings of the prophets, who labored faithfully to combat the sin of Israel in going after other gods, lifted the standard of religious worship. Though the nation underwent the chastisement of captivity for its idolatry, it emerged with a purer monotheism, a preparatory step for the reception of its Messiah.

Jesus laid his whole emphasis on a spiritual worship, a love of the one omnipotent Father of all. He refined worship in this context in the ultimate way: "God is a Spirit [Moffatt, God is Spirit]; and they that worship him must worship him in spirit and in truth" (Jn. 4:24). The practice of idolatry dominated the Gentile world into which Paul carried the gospel of Christ. It was this gospel which in time was to wean the Gentiles from their pantheistic and polytheistic beliefs to the worship of God as Spirit.

Altars

From earliest times the altar was an essential feature of worship, varying in structure, design, and materials according to different cultures. The primitive altar of the Semites consisted of a single stone, a mound of earth, or a rounded heap of unhewn stones. The stone might be a table altar upon which the sacrificial animal was laid, a natural flat rock with a groove or depression where the blood could run off (Ju. 6:20; I Sam. 14:32-35). Here the lifeblood, the essence, of the sacrifice was dedicated to the deity and regarded as coming into contact with him. The altar marked the temporary abode or nearby presence of the deity; it was simultaneously the place of a man's propitiatory offering and self-surrender and that of his deity's acceptance—the point of reconciliation and union between them.

Archeological excavations have furnished numerous examples of primitive Canaanite altars: among them (from Gezer) a four-sided limestone block with horns, about fifteen inches high and ten inches square; from Megiddo have come several small specimens of horned incense altars, also of limestone, as well as a huge sacrifice altar of unhewn stones measuring twenty-six feet in diameter and four and a half feet high.

The first mention in Scripture of a man-made altar is of that built on a mountain top by Noah to tender his thanksgiving for the preservation of his family from the Flood; the "sweet savour" of his sacrifice rose up before God (Gen. 8:20,21). The patriarchs Abraham, Isaac, and Jacob built memorial altars to mark the particular sites at which God had spoken with them or given them visible manifestation of His presence—a theophany (Gen. 12:7; 26:24,25; 28:16-18). Cairn altars, heaps of stones, also marked spots on which the Hebrews ratified covenants with each other in the sight of God.

When the Mosaic system of worship was developed (see p. 51), the Law specified that altars should be simple structures made of earth or unhewn stones, without steps; any Israelite might build his own and make animal sacrifices and grain offerings upon it (Ex. 20:24-26; Deut. 27:5-7). Family altars and those at local sanctuaries were in use until the reign of King Josiah (638-608 B.C.).

The Tabernacle erected by command of Moses contained three altars: the brazen altar, which stood in the Court of the Congregation; the golden altar, which stood in the Holy Place; and the table of shewbread, also in the Holy Place (see p. 160). The brazen altar (altar of burnt offering) was a hollow structure five cubits square and three cubits high (one cubit equals approximately eighteen inches) made of acacia (shittim) wood overlaid with brass. (The word brass in AV and ASV should be more correctly rendered bronze, since it is a metal alloy of copper and tin.) Each of the four corners of the altar had a hornlike projection overlaid with bronze as well as a bronze ring into which poles were inserted for its transportation. Below

was a grate of bronze on which a fire burned perpetually (Ex. 27:1-8; Lev. 6:13). This altar was used by the priests for the daily morning and evening sacrifice, for those brought by the people, and for the special sacrifices required on feast days (see Sacrifice, p. 55).

The **golden altar** (altar of incense) was also made of acacia wood, but overlaid with gold. It too was a square, one cubit long, one cubit wide, two and a half cubits high, with golden horns and golden rings for carrying. On this altar the priests offered incense morning and evening (Ex. 30:1-10; Lu. 1:8-10; compare Rev. 8:3).

The **table of shewbread** was a small rectangular altar overlaid with gold, two cubits long, one cubit wide, and a cubit and a half high (Ex. 25:23-30). Each Sabbath twelve fresh loaves of unleavened bread sprinkled with frankincense (the number represented the twelve tribes of Israel) were placed in two piles upon it, and the old loaves were eaten by the priests. These loaves were prepared by the Levites, each loaf containing about four-fifths of a peck of fine flour (Lev. 24:5-9). This bread, constantly in the presence and sight of God, was called the "Presence-bread" (RV [marg.] Ex. 25:30), "the continual bread" (Num. 4:7). "This was called the Shewbread, or Bread of the

A four-horned limestone altar of King Solomon's time, found at Megiddo, one of his fortress cities. Courtesy of the Oriental Institute, University of Chicago.

Altar of Burnt Offering (Brazen Altar). *Popular and Critical Bible Encyclopaedia.*

Presence, which symbolized the communion of God's people with Him in the things provided by Him and used in His service."[3]

In Solomon's Temple the brazen altar was immense, twenty cubits square by ten cubits high, to accommodate the numerous sacrifices during Solomon's reign (II Chron. 4:1; 7:4,5). In course of time the sacrificial worship of the people was restricted to this altar in Jerusalem (Deut. 12:5-14,26,27). The golden altar was of cedar covered with gold (I Ki. 6:20), and there were ten tables of shewbread (II Chron. 4:8).

Mention is made in the Old Testament of several other altars: that of King Ahaz, patterned after a model he had seen in Damascus, which displaced Solomon's brazen altar (II Ki. 16:10-15); that of the prophet Ezekiel, a square of twelve cubits, four cubits high, built on four platforms of diminishing size (Ezek. 43:13-17); and that of the Second Temple, erected after Judah's return from exile (Ezra 3:2,3)—an altar used until its desecration in 168 B.C. by Antiochus Epiphanes, who placed upon it an altar to Olympian Zeus (I Macc. 1:57). Judas Maccabaeus replaced this defiled structure in 165 B.C. (I Macc. 4:44-47). The huge altar of burnt offering of Herod's Temple resembled the pattern of Ezekiel's altar and, according to historian Josephus, measured fifty cubits square by fifteen cubits high (dimensions differ in the Mishnah). It was constructed of unhewn stones and approached by a gradual incline also made of unhewn stones. That Herod's Temple contained an altar of incense is confirmed by Luke's record of Zacharias' vision as he stood near it (Lu. 1:11).

Jesus taught a further refinement of worship: no sacrifice at the altar has any merit without the moral and ethical behavior that buttresses it; one's gift to God should not be offered until all grievances with one's fellow men have been corrected (Mt. 5:23,24): "If thou bring thy gift to the altar, and there rememberest that thy brother hath ought against thee; Leave there thy gift before the altar, and go thy way; first be reconciled to thy brother, and then come and offer thy gift."

In Revelation there is seen in heaven only the golden altar, the spiritual counterpart of the altar of incense of the Temple (Rev. 8:3).

High Places

A high place was a local shrine or rustic temple on a hilltop or elevation, with an altar as its central object. This natural setting afforded the worshiper a feeling of exaltation and communion with his god. In time the term *high place* was applied to any sanctuary, whatever its location.

The custom of worshiping on heights was almost universal in the early world. The Babylonians had their mounds and *ziggurats* or artificial elevations (the ruins of an immense *ziggurat* unearthed on the outskirts of Babylon is believed by archeologists to have been the legendary Tower of Babel). The high places of the Canaanites were found throughout their land. The Hebrews likewise regarded hilltops and mountain slopes as natural places of worship. When Abram entered Canaan he built an altar on a mountain east of Beth-el (Gen. 12:8); when he offered Isaac he went to Mount Moriah (Gen. 22:2,9). On the sacred mount of Sinai Moses received his revelations of Jehovah (Ex. 3:1,14; 34:1,2).

On its entrance into Canaan Israel found a civilization over a thousand years old, whose people lived in walled cities and villages and whose idol worship at their sanctuaries was highly developed. Chief among their gods was Baal, the male deity to whom the peasant farmer looked for fertility and productivity of his land and crops. Every town and village had its local Baal, and these many Baals constituted the "Baalim" of Canaanitish worship. Other gods Israel found in the land were Chemosh of the Moabites and Molech of the Ammonites, as well as the bull cult common to all Semitic peoples (Ju. 10:6; I Ki. 11:5,7,8); each of these had specific high places. Moses had explicitly commanded the destruction of heathen high places: "Ye shall drive out all the inhabitants of the land from before you, and destroy all their pictures, and destroy all their molten images, and quite pluck down all their high places" (Num. 33:52).

Conquering the Canaanites, the Israelites inherited the heathen shrines and came into contact with their gross rites and practices. They adapted some of these places, among them Beth-el, Shiloh (where the Ark of the Covenant rested), Ramah, and Gibeon, to the worship of Jehovah (Ju. 21:19; I Sam. 7:17; I Ki. 3:2-4). Here, as at other lesser sanctuaries, they sacrificed, tithed, and observed harvest festivals.

The **groves** so often mentioned in relation to cultic sanctuaries were wooden image poles or artificial trees erected to Ashtoreth (Gr. Astarte), a Phoenician fertility goddess, the consort of Baal. In every instance in which the word *grove* is used in the Authorized Version (with the exception of Genesis

21:33, where it refers to a tamarisk tree) it is correctly translated in the Revised Version as *Asherah* (plural *Asherim*). These Asherim stood beside the stone pillars and altars of Baal, or near green trees, and were worshiped in licentious rituals (Ju. 6:25,26; II Ki. 21:3).

The Israelites failed to obey the Mosaic command to destroy the high places and groves (Ex. 34:12-16; Deut. 16:21). Instead they often worshiped side by side with the Canaanites and married their sons and daughters (Ju. 3:5-7). These sins fostered an admixture of Mosaic religious beliefs and rites with the cultic worship of Baal and Ashtoreth, and such syncretism tended to undermine Israel's monotheism throughout its national career.

Even after Solomon built the Temple on Mount Zion in Jerusalem and decreed it the one high place where all Israel's sacrifices were to be made (I Ki. 11:36; compare Deut. 16:16), the other altars in the land were not abolished. In fact, following the division of Solomon's kingdom, Jeroboam I, first king of the northern kingdom of Israel, deliberately set up idolatrous shrines for his people's use (I Ki. 12:28-31).

The high places of Judah and Israel continued to flourish, particularly in the kingdom of Israel. King Ahab and Queen Jezebel of Israel encouraged Baal worship, feeding at their table the prophets of Baal and the prophets of the groves (I Ki. 18:18,19), while King Manasseh of Judah dared to set up an Asherah in the Temple itself (II Ki. 21:7). The early prophets sternly condemned the idolatry and immorality of these shrines and warned backsliding Israel and Judah of divine judgment. Amos, Hosea, Isaiah, Jeremiah, and Ezekiel thundered their rebuke (Amos 2:4-8; Hos. 4:1, 12-14; Is. 27:9). Jeremiah epitomized the sin of Israelitish worship at high places: "[Israel] is gone up upon every high mountain and under every green tree, and there hath played the harlot" (Jer. 3:6). Ezekiel bluntly warned: "I [God], even I, will bring a sword upon you, and I will destroy your high places. . . . that your altars may be laid waste and made desolate, and your idols may be broken and cease, and your images may be cut down, and your works may be abolished" (Ezek. 6:3,6). The kings Asa, Jehoshaphat, and Hezekiah took partial measures to destroy the high places of Judah; but not until 621 B.C., when the Deuteronomic Code was found in the Temple, did King Josiah, the last of the four godly kings, take drastic and effective measures to wipe them out (II Ki. 23:1-20).

Historically for the Israelite the true high place came to be Mount Zion in Jerusalem, the resting place of the Ark of the Covenant (see p. 161). Zion attained a wealth of meaning in its figurative sense, typifying the heavenly sanctuary and the highest spiritual exaltation: "Out of Zion, the perfection of beauty,

Altar of Incense (Golden Altar). *Popular and Critical Bible Encyclopaedia.*

God hath shined" (Ps. 50:2; compare Ps. 48:2; Joel 3:16,17). Zion is called "my holy hill" (Ps. 2:6), "the mountain of his holiness" (Ps. 48:1), "the place of the name of the Lord of hosts" (Is. 18:7), and is the mount on which the Lamb stands with the redeemed of the earth (Rev. 14:1; compare Heb. 12:22).

Mosaic System

This religious system was instituted by Moses at the beginning of Israel's national history (*ca.* 1450 B.C.) when at Sinai God gave Israel a theocratic constitution in the Ten Commandments, the judgments, and the ordinances. These three component parts formed the Mosaic Covenant. First and foremost was the Decalogue, "the words of the covenant" that united God and Israel (Ex. 34:28). This was proclaimed by God Himself out of fiery flames from the top of the mount (Ex. 20:1-21) and engraved on tables of stone. It embodied the basic precepts of man's duty to God and man's duty to man, and was the core of all subsequent legislation. The judgments and ordinances were given orally to the people by Moses, the judgments to regulate their social life (Ex. 21:1-24:11) and the ordinances to govern their religious life, establishing a tabernacle, a priesthood, and a sacrificial worship to guard and perpetuate the divine covenant (Ex. 24:12-31:18). These three divisions comprised "the law" as used in its general sense in the New Testament (Mt. 5:17,18).

Up to this time the Hebrews had been governed principally by the tribal laws of the desert and by social customs which had assumed the force of law; this was true even during their long sojourn in Egypt. Also in their traditional background was the influence of Babylonian law and justice (see Code of Hammurabi, p. 37), undoubtedly known to them to a degree, for Abram had come from Ur into Canaan and Canaan itself was generally Babylonian in culture. It was natural that some of this ancient civil law should be incorporated in the Mosaic system; but here it received a new moral impetus, being identified in every aspect with the worship of Jehovah.

The Law was first developed orally by Moses and by judges, to whom he delegated authority for the administration of justice (Ex. 18:25,26; Deut. 16:18), as well as by priests and Levites as they taught the Law to the people (Deut. 17:8-11; 19:15-18). This method of oral law (*torah*) survived long in Israel, adapting itself to the nation's changing economic and social conditions. The decisions of the courts and the royal word of kings contributed to changes in the administration of justice; and the teachings of the prophets, emphasizing the moral requirements of Israel's religion, exercised a great influence on the codifiers of Israel's law.

Through the centuries this legislation crystallized into various law codes which were incorporated in the final redaction of the Pentateuch or Torah (*ca.* 500-450 B.C.): the Book of the Covenant (Ex. 20: 22-23:33), Deuteronomic Code (Deut. 12-26), Holiness Code (Lev. 17-26), and Priestly Code (portions of Exodus, Leviticus, and Numbers). (See Preservation of Text, p. 4.) These codes detailed the elaborate ceremonial, civil, and criminal legislation of the Mosaic system: ceremonial laws relating to the sanctuary, priesthood, cleanness and uncleanness, sacrifices,

High priest's breastplate. This nine-inch folded linen square was trimmed with twelve jewels representing the twelve tribes of Israel. *Popular and Critical Bible Encyclopaedia.*

sacred dues, sacred days; constitutional laws relating to the government and the army; criminal laws defining crimes against God, morality, persons, and property; humane laws protecting animals and the poor. Legislation also extended to personal and family rights of parents and children, to marital relations, and to rights of master and slave; to property rights; and to obligations to God.

It was the duty of the priests and Levites to teach the Law to the nation and the obligation of every Hebrew father to instruct his sons in its precepts. Passages from the Law were written on the doorposts of Hebrew homes and inscribed on phylacteries worn by the pious on arm or wrist (Deut. 6:6-9). Later the Law was taught and expounded in the synagogues.

During the intertestamental period, along with the written Torah appeared an oral Torah, minute and numerous interpretations of Mosaic legislations by the scribes and Pharisees (see p. 216). This resulted in a stringent Judaism which governed every facet of Jewish daily life by New Testament times. (Strictly speaking, Judaism refers to the rites and doctrines of the Jews expressed in the written and oral Torah.) Judaism laid on the people the most rigid observance of the letter of the written Law and of the oral traditions they had inherited, so that worship became a heavy burden to the conscientious worshiper. From this burden the Jew was set free by the law of love and grace found in the teachings of Jesus Christ (Jn. 1:17). Jesus did not set aside the Mosaic Law but taught its true practice: "Whatsoever they [scribes and Pharisees] bid you observe, that observe and do; but do not ye after their works: for they say, and do not" (Mt. 23:3). He summed up the essence of the Law in two commandments: "Thou shalt love the Lord thy God with all thy heart, and with all thy soul, and with all thy mind. . . . Thou shalt love thy neighbour as thyself. On these two commandments hang all the law and the prophets" (Mt. 22:37-40).

Aaronic Priesthood

The Aaronic priesthood, drawn from the tribe of Levi, was an essential element of the Mosaic system. This tribe was first set apart to the service of God at Mount Sinai. The Levites rallied to Moses' side when he found the Israelites worshiping the golden calf and aided him in carrying out the punishment of the obstinately idolatrous (Ex. 32:26-29). Because of their loyalty, this tribe was chosen to replace all the first-born of Israel who had been sanctified to Jehovah on the day of exodus from Egypt (Num. 3:11-51; see First-born, p. 40).

Moses appointed a hereditary priesthood in the

family of his brother Aaron, and Aaron and all his sons became priests (Ex. 30:30). An elaborate ceremonial was prescribed for their consecration and that of their successors: ablutions, investiture to their office with priestly garments, anointing of the head with holy oil, and the offering of special sacrifices (Ex. 29). Through succeeding generations the duties of the priests varied with the development of the Mosaic system of worship and the priestly institution reached its most highly organized form with the dedication of the Second Temple (515 B.C.).

The first **high priest** was Aaron; the succession of the high priesthood descended through his third son Eleazar and in turn through Eleazar's son Phineas (Ex. 29:9; Lev. 8; Num. 20:28; 25:10-13). This line did not remain intact, however, for in the days of Samuel, Eli had attained the rank of high priest at the sanctuary in Shiloh although he was descended from Ithamar, the youngest son of Aaron, not from Eleazar. After the death of Eli (I Sam. 3:11-18; 4:15-18), Abiathar of Eli's house shared the high priesthood with Zadok of the line of Eleazar in the reign of David (I Sam. 23:6; I Ki. 1:39). But because Abiathar supported Adonijah's attempted usurpation of his father's throne while Zadok remained loyal to David (I Ki. 1:5,7,8), King Solomon banished Abiathar and gave the high priesthood to the house of Zadok (I Ki. 2:26,27). During the Maccabean period (167-63 B.C.) the office of high priest ceased to be hereditary; it became a political prize.

In the performance of his ceremonial duties the high priest wore the special vestments of his office in addition to the usual garments of a priest (Ex. 28). His outer tunic, "the robe of the ephod," consisted of one woven piece of blue linen, sleeveless and edged at the hem with tassels and bells. The *ephod* worn over this robe was a short, richly embroidered, two-piece linen garment joined at the shoulders by onyx and fastened at the waist with an elaborate girdle. Over the ephod was worn the "breastplate of judgment," a folded square of fine twined linen on which were set twelve precious stones in four rows, each stone bearing the name of one of the twelve tribes of Israel. On his official headdress or linen mitre was a headband of gold engraved with the signet HOLINESS TO THE LORD.

The high priest was dedicated wholly to God's service and revered as the spiritual head of the nation (Lev. 10:6-11; Num. 4:16). According to Levitical law, to preserve his personal holiness and the dignity of his office he was forbidden the outward signs of mourning for the dead, even for his father and mother, which would have defiled him. He was to live within the sacred precincts of the sanctuary, and he could marry only a virgin from among his own people (Lev. 21:10-15).

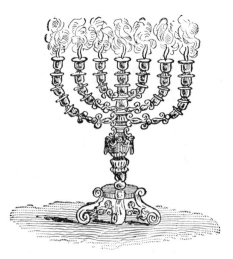

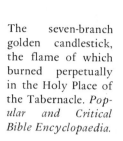

The seven-branch golden candlestick, the flame of which burned perpetually in the Holy Place of the Tabernacle. *Popular and Critical Bible Encyclopaedia.*

As the nation's representative, the high priest consecrated himself each morning and evening by a meal offering on the brazen altar (Lev. 6:19-23). Each morning and evening he also offered incense on the golden altar, the smoke and fragrance symbolic of ascending prayer, and each evening he lit the seven-branch golden candlestick in the Holy Place (Ex. 30:7,8; Lev. 24:1-4).

When there was need for divine guidance in public or national emergencies, the high priest placed two objects or oracles—the Urim and Thummim ("the Lights and the Perfections," Ex. 28:30, RV marg.)—within an inner pouch of the breastplate of judgment so that they rested over his heart, and then went into the Holy Place of the Tabernacle to stand before the veil of the inner sanctuary. Little is known of these two sacred objects, but it is thought they were small carved or marked stones by means of which he cast lots as he sought to divine the will of God (Lev. 8:8; I Sam. 14:41,42; 28:6). This method of seeking divine direction appears to have been discontinued by the time of the prophets, when the will of God was made known to Israel through its spiritually minded seers (but see Ezra 2:63; Neh. 7:65).

One of the holiest duties of the high priest was the yearly atonement for the people. He alone could enter the Holy of Holies, the innermost sanctuary, and this he could do only once a year, on the Day of Atonement, to make solemn expiation for his own sins, for the sins of the priests, and for those of the people (see Day of Atonement, p. 62).

The office of the Aaronic high priesthood typified and foreshadowed the priestly office of Jesus Christ and his atoning work, a point elucidated in particular in the Epistle to the Hebrews (7:26). Jesus Christ came after the higher order of Melchizedek (Heb. 7:17), being divinely anointed not with material oil but "with the oil of gladness above [his] fellows"; "by his own blood" he won redemption for men and entered "into heaven itself, now to appear in the presence of God for us" (Heb. 1:9; 9:12,24).

The **priests** were the lineal male descendants of

Aaron other than the high-priestly line (Ex. 40:12-15), standing in rank and power below the high priest and above the Levites (see p. 54). In the historical record, however, the terms *priest* and *Levite* were often used synonymously until after the Exile. Their sacrificial and ceremonial duties were designed to keep the Israelites ever aware that they were a holy and separate people. In the performance of their office they wore special garments consisting of linen breeches or trousers, embroidered robes, sashes, and turbans (Ex. 28:42; 29:8,9; Lev. 8:13).

A priest was forbidden to mourn the dead, except those of his own family, or to marry a harlot or a divorced woman, that he might be "holy unto his God." While serving in his priestly capacity he must be without blemish; he could not eat of holy things while ceremonially unclean (Lev. 21:1-9, 16-24; 22:1-9).

It was a priestly duty to keep the fire burning day and night on the brazen altar in the outer court of the Tabernacle. Daily on this altar priests made a morning and an evening sacrifice of a lamb on behalf of the people, accompanying it with meal and drink offerings (Ex. 29:38-42; Num. 28:1-8). On the Sabbath the offering was doubled (Num. 28:9,10). At the close of the daily services they pronounced the priestly blessing as prescribed, which assured the people of God's presence and care: "The Lord bless thee, and keep thee: The Lord make his face shine upon thee, and be gracious unto thee: The Lord lift up his countenance upon thee, and give thee peace" (Num. 6:22-27).

The priests daily supplied the high priest with pure olive oil for the golden candlestick (Ex. 27:20, 21), and each Sabbath set out fresh loaves of shewbread and ate the old (Lev. 24:5-9). In later times they also offered incense on the golden altar each morning and evening at the hour of prayer (Lu. 1:8-10). They officiated at the sacrificial offerings brought by the people (Lev. 1-7; see Sacrifice, p. 55) and at special sacrificial ceremonies on feast days (see Feasts, p. 59). They acted as judges in questions concerning that which was ceremonially unclean or profane and administered the rites of purification (Lev. 11-15).

Ancient trumpets. *Peloubet's Bible Dictionary.*

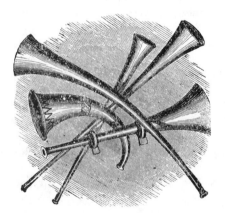

Priests blew the sacred silver trumpets, a privilege reserved to them alone, to assemble the congregation of Israel for journeys during the Wilderness Wandering and for war (Num. 10:1-9). They also sounded the trumpets for the New Moon festivals, for the Feast of Trumpets (Num. 29:1), for set festivals and fasts (Num. 10:10), for the inauguration of the Jubilee year (Lev. 25:9), and for other special occasions such as the crowning of a king (I Ki. 1:39).

Last, one of the principal activities of the priests as well as of the Levites was to teach the people the Mosaic statutes, a service that remained almost wholly their prerogative until after the Exile, when the interpretation of the Law was taken over by the scribes or *sopherim* (Lev. 10:11; Deut. 24:8; 33:10; compare Ezek. 44:23). The priests were supported by redemption money, tithes, firstfruits, and various offerings of the people.

In the religion Jesus Christ founded there was no ecclesiastical organization such as the Aaronic priesthood, for through his redeeming work all true Christians become "an holy priesthood, to offer up spiritual sacrifices, acceptable to God by Jesus Christ"— through his sacrifice he "hath made us kings and priests unto God and his Father" (I Pet. 2:5; Rev. 1:6).

Levites

The Levites as a class were comprised of the non-Aaronic descendants of Levi through his three sons Kohath, Gershon, and Merari. They were the servants of the priests, entering upon their duties at the age of thirty and continuing to the age of fifty (Num. 4:3); the age requirement was later lowered by Moses to twenty-five (Num. 8:24), and to twenty by Hezekiah (II Chron. 31:17; compare Ezra 3:8). The Levites were entrusted with the transportation and care of the Tabernacle, its furniture, and its holy vessels during the Wilderness Wandering (Num. 3:5-9,17-39; 4:1-33). As aides of the priests, they assisted in the lesser tasks of ritual worship (I Chron. 23:27-32), and like the priests were teachers of the Law.

The tribe of Levi received no territory in Canaan, so in lieu of this they were allotted forty-eight cities, known as *Levitical cities,* according to the promise of Moses (Num. 35:1-8). Thirteen of these lay within the territories of the tribes of Judah, Benjamin, and Simeon and were allotted to the Aaronic priesthood; the remaining thirty-five were located in the territories of the other tribes (Josh. 21; I Chron. 6:54-81). All were centers of religious education for the people. The sites chosen for these priestly cities proved wise, for centuries later when the United Kingdom was divided after the death of Solomon the core of the priesthood was preserved in all its strength to the southern Kingdom of Judah. Six of these Levitical cities were particularly designated cities of refuge, sanctuaries to which a man might flee for safety if he had taken a life without premeditation (see p. 45).

The Levites were maintained by the tithes of the people. Their religious duties were enlarged by King David to include those of judges, musicians, singers, porters, treasurers, and officers of the king. David made provision for the organization of the Temple service, dividing the Levites and priests into twenty-four courses or orders; the men of each course came up to the Temple to serve in rotation twice a year for a week at a time (I Chron. 23-26). In the service of the Second Temple the Levites were reduced to a subsidiary order.

Sacrifice

Animal sacrifice was an almost universal custom among primitive peoples and constituted an essential element of worship. It was a highly developed ritual of the great civilizations of Babylonia and Egypt and was a long-established practice among the Semites.

The principal thought underlying the sacrifice of animals and fowls appears to have been the substitution of the life of some innocent creature—a lamb, kid, bullock, turtledove—for the offerer's own life. It was considered a conciliatory gift and by this vicarious means the worshiper hoped to obtain a degree of immunity from the deity's anger and caprice. The most common sacrifice of the early Semitic worshiper was the "peace offering," in which the blood of the victim was poured either on the altar or on the ground and its fat offered to be burned as a "sweet savour"; he and his family ate what remained as a communal feast. A rarer form of animal sacrifice was the "burnt offering," in which the whole animal was offered to the deity and its "sweet savour" rose to heaven.

Offerings, oblations other than living things, were drawn from the fruits of the ground—cereals, vegetables, oil, fruits, salt, wine, incense—and were also propitiatory. Whatever the nature of the sacrifice or offering, it was a personal possession, a thing of value to the individual—the firstling of his flock or the firstfruit of his land—tendered in fear, homage, or thanksgiving.

Up to the time of the Exile in 586 B.C. (before Mosaic Law crystallized into the Levitical law of the Pentateuch) sacrifices were made by the head of the family, the priests receiving only a portion of the animal as their share (I Sam. 1:4; 2:13-16).

The first Biblical record of sacrifice concerns the lamb sacrifice of Abel and the fruit offering of Cain (Gen. 4:3,4). Noah's sacrifice was the incense of a burnt offering of animal and fowl (Gen. 8:20,21). Child-sacrifice was rare among the Hebrews, and in the case of Abraham's intended offering of his son Isaac, a ram was providentially substituted (Gen. 22:13). At the institution of the Passover a lamb was slain by the head of each Israelite household to preserve the life of its first-born (Ex. 12:3-13).

With the inception of the moral law of Sinai came a greater consciousness of sin and guilt for sin, and thus arose a national need for expiation and purification. Sacrificial worship and a priesthood were made an integral part of the Mosaic system to afford the Israelite a means of atoning for his sins and attaining holiness in the sight of God.

The English word *atonement* translates the Hebrew *kaphar,* meaning "to cover," "to cancel," "to expiate." All killing of animals was sacrificial in intent, making use of the blood covenant (Lev. 17:1-9). Every blood sacrifice prefigured in type "the Lamb slain from the foundation of the world" (Rev. 13:8). The eating of blood was prohibited: "The life of the flesh is in the blood: and I have given it to you upon the altar to make an atonement for your souls" (Lev. 17:11-14; compare 7:26,27). The fat, considered as sacred as blood, was never eaten but always burned on the altar—"all the fat is the Lord's" (Lev. 3:16; 7:23-25). Sacrificial animals were drawn from the flocks and herds and were required to be without blemish, never having borne a yoke or been sheared (Lev. 22:18-24; Num. 19:2). Provision was made for the poor, allowing them to substitute turtledoves or pigeons, or even meal offerings, for the more expensive animals. The people's sacrifices were made through the priests in the outer court of the sanctuary according to prescribed ritual for both offerer and priest.

Sacrifices were burned on the altar, either in whole or in part. Any offering burned on the altar was a holy offering, being purified by fire, and any person who touched or partook of that offering was himself made pure.

Fire was long associated with the deity by the peoples of antiquity. "Fire is a frequent emblem of God in the Scriptures on account of its illuminating, purifying, and destructive properties, and appears as the accompaniment and indication of His presence...."[4] A sacred fire had sealed the Abrahamic covenant (Gen. 15:17), marked the presence of God at the burning bush (Ex. 3:2-4), guided and protected the Israelites by a pillar of fire (Ex. 13:21; 14:19, 20), been manifest on Mount Sinai at the giving of the Ten Commandments (Ex. 19:18), accompanied the translation of Elijah (II Ki. 2:11), and was the sign to Elisha of preservation from the Syrian army (II Ki. 6:17).

In some instances sacred fire signified divine

approval in the acceptance of offerings: the "fire of the Lord" consumed the sacrifices of Aaron (Lev. 9:24), of Gideon (Ju. 6:21), of David (I Chron. 21:26), of Solomon (II Chron. 7:1), of Elijah (I Ki. 18:38). As an instrument of God's power, fire was also a symbol of divine judgment, terrible and consuming. Fire from heaven destroyed Sodom and Gomorrah for their wickedness (Gen. 19:24), consumed Nadab and Abihu for their desecration of the altar (Lev. 10:1,2), and so on. God's angels are likened to "a flaming fire" (Ps. 104:4). The baptism of the Holy Ghost comes with fire (Mt. 3:11)—"cloven tongues like as of fire" marked the descent of the Holy Ghost at Pentecost (Acts 2:3). Paul warned that fire would "try every man's work of what sort it is" (I Cor. 3:13-15), and that Christ at his Second Coming would be revealed in "flaming fire" (II Th. 1:7,8). Repeatedly in the book of Revelation fire is used as a descriptive symbol of divine power and judgment.

With the systematizing of sacrificial worship as found in the book of Leviticus the voluntary or freewill offerings of the people fell into five groups (Lev. 1-7). Each type of sacrifice was designed to make a man holy and had its order and purpose in reconciling the worshiper with God.

1. **Whole Burnt Offering** (Lev. 1). This was an animal sacrifice from the herd or flock, a male "without blemish" or, in the case of the poor, a fowl. The offerer, by placing his hand on the head of the animal, identified himself with it, making it a vicarious offering of himself. In the court of the congregation he killed, flayed, and cut the offering into pieces. The priests sprinkled the blood around the altar and laid all the parts on the altar, where they burned all night till consumed—"an offering made by fire, of a sweet savour unto the Lord." The next morning the priests carried the ashes outside the camp (Lev. 6:8-11). The skin of the animal became the property of the officiating priest (Lev. 7:8). *This offering signified the offerer's complete self-dedication, self-surrender, and atonement* (see Rom. 12:1).

A burnt offering of a lamb was made each morning and evening for the community as a whole by the priests—the "continual burnt offering" (Ex. 29:38-42).

2. **Meal Offering** (Lev. 2; designated *meat offering* in AV). This was a vegetable offering of fine flour mixed with oil, seasoned with salt, and accompanied by incense (see Salt, p. 46). It could be presented raw or baked; if baked it contained no leaven or honey; these caused fermentation of the natural substances and thus corrupted them. A handful was burned on the altar as "a sweet savour" and the remainder became the property of the priests, to be eaten by them (compare Lev. 6:14-18; 7:9,10). If of firstfruits, this offering consisted of parched corn from green ears. *This offering signified thankfulness for the bounty of God in the plentifulness of earth's increase, and sought His favor.*

A meal offering also accompanied the daily burnt offering made by the priests for the congregation (Ex. 29:40,41).

One of the high priest's duties was to make this consecration offering daily, morning and evening, on his own behalf. He did not eat of his sacrifice; it was wholly burned (Lev. 6:20-23).

3. **Peace Offering** (Lev. 3). This was an animal sacrifice of the herd or flock, a male or female without blemish—an offering which served as a sacred feast in which God, His priests, and His people jointly partook. Its blood was sprinkled on the altar. Only the internal fat (and, in the case of sheep, the fat of the tail) was offered to be burned as "a sweet savour." The choice parts were waved or heaved before God and then eaten by the priests as their share of the sacrifice (Lev. 7:28-34).

This blood sacrifice was accompanied by a meal offering of four varieties of cake, one of which contained leaven. One cake was also waved and then became the possession of the priests (Lev. 7:11-14). The remaining flesh and cakes were eaten by the offerer and his family in a sacrificial meal (Lev. 7:15-21). Peace offerings were of three kinds: thank, votive, and voluntary offerings. *These were expressive of fellowship, communion, and harmony between God and the offerer.*

4. **Sin Offering** (Lev. 4:1-5:13). This was an animal sacrifice, the victim varying according to the status of the offerer: for the high priest a bullock, for the congregation (represented by the elders) a bullock or a male goat (Num. 15:24), for a ruler a male goat, for one of the people a female goat, a ewe lamb, a pigeon, or a meal offering.

When the sin offering was made for the high priest or for the congregation, the blood was sprinkled seven times before the veil of the sanctuary; some was smeared on the horns of the altar of incense; the remainder was poured out at the base of the altar of burnt offering. In the case of a ruler or a lay member, some of the blood was smeared on the horns of the altar of incense, the remainder poured at the foot of the altar of burnt offering. The fat was burned in atonement and the remaining flesh boiled and eaten by the priests (Lev. 6:29); however, in the case of the offering of the high priest and of the congregation the fat was burned on the altar and the carcass taken outside the camp to be burned (compare Heb.

13:10-14). The high priest did not eat of his own sacrifice (Lev. 6:30).

This sacrifice was made for a sin done in ignorance (RV unwittingly) against the laws and ordinances of God and subsequently brought to the offender's knowledge. It was designed to atone for three specific sins: failing to bear testimony, touching an unclean thing, and making rash oaths. *It signified expiation and atonement.*

Mosaic Law explicitly stated that no atonement was possible for the man who sinned willfully or presumptuously (Num. 15:30; compare Heb. 10:26-29). There were, however, certain permissible exceptions (see next paragraph).

5. **Trespass or Guilt Offering** (Lev. 5:14-6:7). This was a ram sacrifice offered by one who had unwittingly committed sacrilege by defrauding the sanctuary either by consuming what belonged to the priests (Lev. 2:3) or by withholding his full due of tithes, firstfruits, and the like. This guilt offering was to be accompanied by full restitution of what was due plus one-fifth. After the blood and fat of the victim had been offered, what remained was eaten by the priests (Lev. 7:1-7). The trespass offering was also permitted one who had deliberately defrauded his neighbor through lying or deceit but had made full amends plus one-fifth. *It signified penitence, expiation, and atonement.*

Sacrifice also played a part in the purification ritual for uncleanness: the purification of women from childbirth (Lev. 12), cleansing of lepers (Lev. 14), cleansing from bodily discharges (Lev. 15).

Special sacrifices attended the consecration of the priesthood (Ex. 29; Lev. 8; 9).

Extraordinary sacrifices were specified for the Day of Atonement, the Sabbath, the three national festivals (Passover, Feast of Weeks, Feast of Tabernacles), as well as for lesser feasts (see pp. 58-62).

In time this intensive ceremonialism tended to divert Hebrew thought from the real spirit and purpose of sacrifice so that outward symbols took the place of inward purification. The Hebrew prophets (800-400 B.C.), seeing the inadequacy of this system, taught the ethical nature of worship. They did not condemn the sacrificial system as such but spoke out against its hollow ritual, decrying the lack of righteousness, mercy, and justice (Is. 1:11-17; Jer. 6:19,20; Amos 5:22,24; Mic. 6:6-8). Their teachings poured into Israel's devotions a fresh spiritual stimulus which directed the Hebrew mind anew to the exercise of the moral principles of the Law. Hosea epitomized their message: "I desired mercy, and not sacrifice; and the knowledge of God more than burnt offerings" (Ho.

6:6). The Psalmist declared: "The sacrifices of God are a broken spirit: a broken and a contrite heart, O God, thou wilt not despise"; and "Let my prayer be set forth before thee as incense; and the lifting up of my hands as the evening sacrifice" (Ps. 51:17; 141:2).

The types of worship instituted by the Mosaic system were fulfilled in Jesus Christ as God's Messiah. As "the Lamb of God" he literally and figuratively fulfilled the symbolism of blood sacrifice by laying down his life for the sins of men. He himself regarded the giving up of his human life as the great propitiation for sin: "This is my blood of the new testament, which is shed for many for the remission of sins" (Mt. 26:28). New Testament writers saw his sacrifice as a basic and vital fact of Christianity. They related it to that of the paschal lamb (I Cor. 5:7), to the national sin offering of the Day of Atonement (Heb. 9:12), and to the mediation and sealing of the New Covenant with spiritual Israel (Heb. 9:14,15). Peter wrote: "Ye were not redeemed with corruptible things ... But with the precious blood of Christ" (I Pet. 1:18,19; compare Rom. 3:25; I Jn. 1:7). Jesus' supreme sacrifice, "once for all," abrogated the old sacrificial system. His selfless love gave men the true and "living way" of atonement, whereby through faith and life in him they might be reconciled to God (Rom. 5:11; Heb. 9:26; 10:10).

Jesus taught that love itself—love for God and love for one's neighbor—alone keeps the Commandments and is superior to all other sacrifices (Mk. 12:33). Paul urged the believer to present all the faculties of his being as "a living sacrifice, holy, acceptable unto God," man's reasonable service (Rom. 12:1).

Tithing

Tithes were long paid as a tax or tribute to a conqueror or ruler (Gen. 47:24; I Sam. 8:15,17). Scripture records that Abram tithed his spoils of war to Melchizedek, king of Salem (Gen. 14:20; Heb. 7:1-10), and Jacob vowed a tithe to God after his vision at Beth-el (Gen. 28:22).

Tithing to the sanctuary stemmed from an early religious belief of the peoples of the East that the land and all it yielded belonged to a supreme deity who was to be thanked for bountiful crops or to be propitiated in the hope of future blessings. The word *tithe* denotes one-tenth. Mosaic Law required that a tenth of a man's produce of the land and of his flocks and herds be given to God each year as His rightful due, a thank offering for His goodness. Since the tribe of Levi was apportioned no territory in Canaan, this method of tithing furnished the priests and Levites their subsistence in payment for their service to the sanctuary and for their religious instruction of the people (Num. 18:8-24; compare Deut. 18:1-8). The Levites in turn tithed to the priests (Num. 18:25-30). The tithe of the land was of its firstfruits (Deut. 26:2-4,10), and that of flocks and herds was every tenth animal, good or bad, which passed under the owner's rod as he numbered his cattle (Lev. 27:32,33).

Legislation relating to tithing was modified from time to time to meet changing social and economic conditions. Deuteronomic law dictated that the tithe be presented at the central sanctuary, there to provide a feast for the offerer's household and for the Levite (Deut. 12:17-19). Where the journey was too long to transport the offering, it could be converted into money to be spent at the sanctuary or given to the Levites (Deut. 14:22-27). Levitical legislation added one-fifth to the tithe value when agricultural produce was exchanged for money, but the animal tithe could not be commuted (Lev. 27:30-33). Every third year the tithe was stored in local villages to be shared with the stranger, the fatherless, the widow, and the Levite (Deut. 14:28,29).

During religious lapses the practice of tithing to the Levites was slighted. King Hezekiah in his reforms enforced this duty by royal mandate (II Chron. 31:5-7); the prophet Malachi after the Exile sternly reproved the people for withholding their tithes, for by so doing they were defrauding God (Mal. 3:8,9); Nehemiah made tithing an important part of law-keeping (Neh. 10:35-38). The well-known passage of Malachi (3:10), "Bring ye all the tithes into the storehouse. . . ," describes the benediction God pours out on those who tithe in gratitude and trust.

In the first century A.D. the Pharisees tithed with great literalness, giving a tenth even of their garden herbs. Jesus did not condemn their meticulous attention to detail on this point, but he did rebuke their neglect of the more important moral and spiritual dues of righteous judgment, mercy, and faith (Mt. 23:23).

Festivals

Festivals or feasts occupied a natural and important place in the social and religious life of the Hebrews after their entrance into Canaan. With the exception of the Day of Atonement, these were days and seasons of rejoicing before God. The religious festivals can be grouped under three headings: (1) festivals connected with the Sabbath; (2) the three great national festivals; (3) lesser historical feasts.

Sabbath

The festivals connected with the institution of the Sabbath were reckoned on the basis of the sacred number seven, for on the seventh day God rested from His creative work—each seventh day was sacred, as was each seventh month and each seventh year. Principal among these feasts was the weekly Sabbath. The word *sabbath* is derived from the Hebrew *shabbath*, "to break off," "to repose," "to desist." Its origin as a day of rest is uncertain, but it perhaps arose from ancient Babylonian and Canaanitish observances based in some form on the ever-recurring cycles of the moon. Whatever its origin, a periodic day of rest was probably customary in the lives of the nomadic Hebrews.

The first specific mention of the Sabbath occurs in the time of Moses, when the Fourth Commandment of the Decalogue consecrated the seventh day of the week as a holy day commemorating the completion of God's creation (Ex. 20:8-11; compare Gen. 2:2,3). "The children of Israel shall keep the sabbath . . . for a perpetual covenant. It is a sign between me and the children of Israel for ever" (Ex. 31:16,17). The Sabbath began at sundown on the sixth day and terminated at sundown on the seventh; it was a day of cessation from all servile and gainful labor, thus one of rest and refreshment for man and beast. No fire was kindled in the home. Principally this day was one of worship and meditation. A public convocation was held originally in Tabernacle and, later, Temple. For those who could not attend, it was observed faithfully in the home (Lev. 23:3) but its manner of observance is not prescribed.

On this day the priests doubled the burnt offering of the morning and evening sacrifice, and replaced the consecration offering of the shewbread with fresh loaves (Lev. 24:5-8; Num. 28:9,10). Under Mosaic Law the observance of the Sabbath was mandatory (Ex. 35:2,3; Num. 15:32-36).

Sabbath-keeping became a distinguishing mark between the Hebrews and their neighbors, although little is recorded about the Sabbath from the time of Moses to the Exile other than the prophets' exhortations to keep the Sabbath holy (Is. 56:2-7; Jer. 17:22-27) and their rebukes of its repeated desecration: "The house of Israel rebelled against me in the wilderness . . . and my sabbaths they greatly polluted. . . ." (Ezek. 20:13). The Sabbath proved a strong cohesive bond among the Jewish captives in Babylon.

With the development of the synagogue in the intertestamental period, the Sabbath became not only a day of rest and worship but also one devoted to the study of Scripture (see Synagogue, p. 216). With the rise of Judaism in the same period, observance of the Sabbath became a paramount religious duty. So many restrictions were added under scribal and Pharisaic interpretations of the Law that Sabbath-keeping became a heavy burden to the pious Jew.

Jesus took sharp issue with the minutiae of regulations that in his time had so buried the spirit and purpose of the Sabbath, and both by his teaching and his healing he restored to this day its original blessings (Mt. 12:1-13; Mk. 2:27,28; see also Charge of Sabbath-breaking, p. 268).

In the early Church the first day of the week, the day on which Jesus' resurrection had taken place, was called "the Lord's day," and in time this Sabbath replaced for Christians the Jewish Sabbath of the seventh day (Acts 20:7; I Cor. 16:2; Rev. 1:10).

Sabbatical Feasts

Feast of Trumpets or New Year Festival (Rosh Hashana) This was a lunar festival observed on the first day of Tishri, the first month of the civil year, the first new moon of the seventh month of the sacred year.* All work was suspended and the day was celebrated by a sacred convocation accompanied by the blowing of silver trumpets, as well as by special sacrificial offerings (Lev. 23:24,25; Num. 29:1-6; Ezra 3:6; Neh. 8:2). It was the most honored of the New Moon festivals.

New Moon

The appearing of the new moon marked the beginning of each month, and the occasion was observed by the

*Before the Exile the Hebrew civil calendar had begun in the autumn, but in post-exilic times an ecclesiastical calendar, following the Babylonian, was also adopted, which began in the spring with the vernal equinox, and the months were given new names. Both sacred and civil calendars were used.

Month of Sacred Year	Name of Month	Month of Civil Year
1	Abib or Nisan	7
2	Ziv or Iyyar	8
3	Sivan	9
4	Tammuz	10
5	Ab	11
6	Elul	12
7	Tishri or Ethanim	1
8	Bul or Marchesvan	2
9	Chisleu	3
10	Tebeth	4
11	Shebat	5
12	Adar	6
13	Veadar (leap year only)	

blowing of trumpets and by special burnt and peace offerings (Num. 10:10; 28:11-15; Is. 66:23; Amos 8:5).

Sabbatical Year

Following the sabbatical principle of a day of rest for man and beast, every seventh year was designated a sabbatical year of rest for the land, during which it was to lie fallow. Throughout the course of this year whatever the land yielded spontaneously was common property, to be shared with the poor and the stranger (Ex. 23:10,11; Lev. 25:1-7). The Law prescribed that in this seventh year Hebrew slaves were to be freed (Ex. 21:2; Deut. 15:12-18); Hebrew poor were to be released from payment on their loan debts during this period (Deut. 15:1-4); and the Law was to be read publicly to the people during the seven days of the Feast of Tabernacles (Deut. 31:10-13; Neh. 8). There is no evidence in the Old Testament that all these sabbatical ordinances were strictly adhered to; they were nevertheless held up before the nation as social ideals.

Year of Jubilee

Every fiftieth year, the one following a seventh sabbatical, was called the Year of Jubilee and was inaugurated on the tenth day of Tishri, the great Day of Atonement, with the sounding of the silver trumpets (Lev. 25:8-55). As with the sabbatical year, the land was to lie uncultivated; Hebrew slaves and their families were to be freed by their Hebrew owners. Every man's inheritance reverted to its original owner; if land was sold, the purchase price was governed by the number of years yet to run till Jubilee. Therefore land could not be sold in perpetuity, a regulation that prevented the acquisition of large estates and preserved the property inheritance of tribe and family. Although there are allusions to the Year of Jubilee by the prophets, there is no indication in Old Testament history that its provisions were faithfully observed.

National Feasts

Directly related to the agricultural seasons were the three great annual festivals every male Israelite was required to attend at the sanctuary: the Passover (and Feast of Unleavened Bread), the Feast of Weeks, and the Feast of Tabernacles (Ex. 23:14-17; Deut. 16:16). The first of these agricultural festivals saw the grain standing on the soil ready for harvesting; the second marked the full harvesting of the grain, the third observed the gathering in of the fruit of the land. Like the Sabbath, they were reckoned in relation to the sacred number seven. They were celebrated by feasting, singing, dancing, and processions. Their celebration was a strong unifying force among the tribes, strengthening the people's religious ties with the sanctuary, promoting gratitude to God for His providence, and blending the political and social interests of Israel. After the Temple was erected in Jerusalem these feasts were always observed in the holy city.

Passover

The solemn feast of Passover originated in Egypt under divine direction immediately preceding the tenth and last plague which took the life of the first-born of man and beast. To ensure preservation from this plague, the head of each Israelitish household killed a lamb or a kid—a male of the first year "without blemish"—and sprinkled its blood on the lintel, the upper beam, and the sideposts of the door of his dwelling. Its flesh was roasted whole and eaten with unleavened bread and bitter herbs; it was eaten in haste, for the Israelites were girded for the journey out of Egypt. That night the plague struck the life of the Egyptians' first-born but "passed over" the houses marked with the token of blood (Ex. 12:1-28).

The Passover became a commemorative institution to bring to Israel's remembrance both the preservation of its first-born and its deliverance from Egypt, a family feast celebrated from sunset to sunset on the fourteenth day of the month Abib (March-April), the first month of the sacred year, the seventh month of the civil year (Lev. 23:5; Num. 9:3). After the Exile this month was called Nisan (Es. 3:7).

According to Deuteronomy 16:2,5-7, the paschal lamb was no longer killed at home but sacrificed on the eve of Passover "in the place which the Lord shall choose to place his name there," and the fat and the blood given to the priests. The lamb was then taken home and eaten with unleavened bread (*mazzoth*) and bitter herbs. (Leaven was a lump of old, highly fermented dough added to fresh dough before it was kneaded to cause it to rise. Leaven thus became emblematic of corruption [Mt. 16:6,12; I Cor. 5:8] as well as of an all-pervading and transforming agent [Mt. 13:33].) This bread without leaven, heavy and unfermented, was called "the bread of affliction" to commemorate Israel's hasty departure from Egypt when the people did not linger to bake leavened loaves; the bitter herbs were to recall their rigorous bondage in Egypt. None of the flesh of the Passover lamb was left till morning. In this manner Jesus kept the Passover with his twelve apostles in an upper chamber in Jerusalem (Lu. 22:7-14; for Passover ritual in New Testament times see footnote, p. 311). No person having any bodily infirmity or ceremonial uncleanness could partake of this Passover meal, but could have a supplementary Passover on the fourteenth day of the following month (Num. 9:6-12).

The Old Testament makes mention of a number of memorial Passovers:

In the wilderness of Sinai (Num. 9:1-5)

Upon Israel's entrance into the Promised Land (Josh. 5:10)

Under King Hezekiah of Judah in his religious reforms (II Chron. 30)

Under King Josiah of Judah in his religious reforms (II Chron. 35:1-19)

Under Zerubbabel after completion of the Second Temple (Ezra 6:19,20)

Consistent with the whole Mosaic system, the paschal lamb was symbolic of the Messiah and his redeeming work. John the Baptist from the first called Jesus "the Lamb of God" (Jn. 1:29); Paul spoke of him as "Christ our passover . . . sacrificed for us" (I Cor. 5:7); Peter wrote of him as "a lamb without blemish and without spot" (I Pet. 1:19); and Revelation repeatedly applies the title "the Lamb" to Jesus Christ as the Savior who has redeemed men from the sins of the world (Rev. 5:6; 7:17; 14:1).

Closely associated with the Passover was the **Feast of Unleavened Bread**, which began the following day and was observed for seven days (Ex. 12:15-20; Lev. 23:6-14; Num. 28:17-25; Deut. 16:3,4,8). During this period all leaven was put out of the house. It was a happy occasion celebrating the opening of the reaping season, when the sickle was first put to the ripening grain. The first and seventh days were marked by religious convocations and all labor was suspended. The term *Passover* was often loosely applied to the whole festival period of eight days (Deut. 16:1-8; Lu. 22:1).

At this festival a sheaf of the newly ripened grain (a wave sheaf) was brought to the sanctuary and waved before the altar by the priest, thus consecrating the harvest to God. Throughout these seven days the people ate unleavened bread, and daily the priests offered for the congregation, according to Levitical law, the sacrifices of two young bullocks, a ram, and seven lambs without blemish, as well as required meal and drink offerings.

Feast of Weeks

The second annual festival, the Feast of Weeks, was also called the Feast of Harvest, the Day of Firstfruits (Ex. 34:22a; Lev. 23:15-22; Num. 28:26-31; Deut. 16:9-11). This one-day festival of rejoicing fell on the sixth of Sivan (third sacred month, May-June), the fiftieth day from the first day of Passover, and closed the reaping season of the grain harvest. On this day of holy convocation two baked loaves made of newly harvested grain, wave loaves that contained leaven, were brought to the sanctuary and waved before the Lord. These were accompanied by burnt offerings and meal and drink offerings.

In the New Testament this Day of Firstfruits is called **Pentecost**—its name derived from the Greek *pentecoste*, "fiftieth." The first Pentecost mentioned in the New Testament fell fifty days from Jesus' resurrection; it marked the outpouring of the Holy Ghost upon his disciples and the "birthday" of the Christian Church (Acts 2:1), of which Jesus Christ was "the firstfruits of them that slept" (I Cor. 15:20).

Feast of Tabernacles

This feast, also called the Feast of Ingathering (Sukkoth), was the third great annual feast. It was a joyous autumn festival that lasted seven days and marked the harvesting of the fruit of the land—its grapes, figs, and olives. It opened with a holy convocation on the fifteenth day of Tishri or Ethanim (seventh month of the sacred year, September-October), and on each day of the feast special sacrifices were offered at the sanctuary (Ex. 23:16b; Lev. 23:34-36; Num. 29:12-38; Deut. 16:13-15). Every seventh (sabbatical) year the Law was read publicly to the people during the seven days of the feast (Deut. 31:10-13).

The people observed this festival by dwelling in booths (temporary shelters) made of leafy branches erected on the rooftops, in the streets, or in the open fields as a reminder to each generation that their forefathers had lived in tents during the forty years' sojourn in the wilderness (Lev. 23:39-43; Neh. 8:16). Later, an eighth day of holy convocation was added to celebrate the entrance into Canaan (Lev. 23:36).

By Jesus' day part of the ritual of this feast was the pouring of water from the Pool of Siloam on the brazen altar to symbolize the divine provision of water afforded the Israelites in the wilderness (see p. 279).

Lesser Feasts

Feast of Purim

Held on the fourteenth and fifteenth days of Adar (the twelfth month of the sacred year, February-March), this festival commemorated the preservation of the Jews in Persia from the conspiracy of Haman, the king's prime minister, through the timely intervention of Queen Esther (Es. 9:20-32; Josephus, *Antiquities of the Jews,* xi, 6.13).

Feast of Wood Offering

A one-day festival was held on the fifteenth day of Abib (Nisan), when the people brought wood to the Temple that there might be a continuous supply for the fire that burned perpetually on the altar (see

Nehemiah 10:34; Josephus, *Wars of the Jews,* xi, 17.6).

Feast of Dedication or Feast of Lights (Hanukkah)

This feast commemorated the purification and rededication of the Temple by Judas Maccabaeus in 165 B.C. after its desecration by the Syrian king Antiochus Epiphanes. It was an eight-day period of national rejoicing which began on the twenty-fifth day of Chisleu (the ninth sacred month, November-December). Josephus called this feast "Lights" because it was observed by special illumination of the Temple, synagogues, and private homes (Jn. 10:22; I Macc. 4:52-59; Josephus, *Antiquities of the Jews,* xii, 7.7; see also p. 280).

Fasts

The custom of fasting existed among the Hebrews from early Bible times as a religious discipline or as a token of grief. The one who fasted abstained from food and drink, and often afflicted himself by rending his garments, sitting in sackcloth, and pouring ashes on his head. The purpose of fasting was to foster penitence and humility of soul; its exercise was regarded as efficacious in warding off evil and in invoking divine favor. The devout employed it as a means of seeking closer communion with God (Ps. 35:13,14; 69:10,11). Fasting was practiced in times of personal or national calamity or mourning, as at the death of King Saul and his sons (I Sam. 31:13), at Job's affliction (Job. 2:8,11-13), at Jonah's prophecy of Nineveh's fall (Jon. 3:4-10).

As the tendency toward formal fasting increased without proper inward repentance, the Hebrew prophets rebuked the mere outward conformity and laid emphasis on moral and spiritual regeneration as the true fast of the heart (Is. 58:1-7). Joel admonished: "Rend your heart, and not your garments" (Joel 2:13).

The practice of individual fasting increased after the Exile and by the first century A.D. the Pharisees fasted at least twice weekly (Lu. 18:12). To Jesus such formalism had little merit since it was often hypocritical, practiced to win the approval of men; he taught his followers to fast in secret in true humility and prayer, enjoining a spiritual discipline of mind and heart that would have its reward from the Father (Mt. 6:16-18). He commended a fasting from materialistic thinking, which would enable men to do the works he did, as on the occasion when he answered the apostles' question why they had failed to heal the lunatic child: "This kind can come forth by nothing, but by prayer and fasting" (Mk. 9:29). Questioned why his disciples did not fast, Jesus answered: "Can the children of the bridechamber fast, while the bridegroom is with them? as long as they have the bridegroom with them, they cannot fast. But the days will come, when the bridegroom shall be taken away from them, and then shall they fast in those days" (Mk. 2:19,20).

To Paul fasting meant abstaining from evil, even from its appearance (I Th. 5:22; compare Ja. 4:7). He commended the "godly sorrow [that] worketh repentance to salvation not to be repented of" (II Cor. 7:10; see also vv. 9,11).

Day of Atonement

On the tenth day of Tishri one national yearly fast, the Day of Atonement (Yom Kippur), was enjoined on all Israelites by Mosaic Law. It was a high Sabbath, a day of national humiliation on which the people neither ate nor drank, refrained from all work, and assembled for a holy convocation. They were to "afflict" their souls and repent in sorrow for their sins of the past year (Lev. 23:26-32).

On this occasion the high priest made solemn yearly atonement for the sins of the people, for the priesthood, and for the cleansing of the sanctuary (Lev. 16; Num. 29:7-11). This was the one day of the year on which he could enter the Holy of Holies, "within the veil." For this ceremony he first bathed in preparation, and clothed himself in the simple linen tunic and sash of a Levitical priest, since he was atoning for his own sins as well as those of the nation.

For himself and his house (that is, the priests) the high priest brought a young bullock for a sin offering and a ram for a burnt offering; for the people he chose two young male goats as a sin offering and a ram for a burnt offering, and cast lots for the goats—one to be used as a sacrifice, the other as a scapegoat. Then he killed his bullock at the altar of burnt offering, and while the blood was being received into a vessel he entered the Holy of Holies carrying a censer of live coals and a bowl of incense; there he poured the incense onto the coals, causing a fragrant cloud to rise before the Ark of the Covenant. Next he brought the blood of the bullock within the veil, sprinkled it once on the mercy seat of the Ark and seven times before it, thus making atonement for himself and the priesthood.

Outside the sanctuary, he killed the sacrificial goat and—entering within the veil for the third time—sprinkled its blood on the mercy seat as before, thus effecting figuratively the reconciliation of Israel with God.

So that God's presence and righteousness might remain with the nation, the high priest then sprinkled the mingled blood of the bullock and the goat seven times on the altar of incense in the Holy Place to cleanse it from the defilement of sinful men to which it had been subject during the past year. And by repeating this atoning ritual on the horns of the altar of burnt offering in the Court of the Congregation, he cleansed this altar also.

After this he laid his hands on the head of the scapegoat and solemnly confessed over it all the transgressions of the people (by this symbolic act transferring them to the animal); then it was led away into the desert and released. (After the Exile this ritual changed, the scapegoat being taken to a high rock twelve miles from Jerusalem and thrust over to its death.)

Divesting himself of his plain linen garments, the high priest bathed and resumed his priestly vestments. He then offered the two rams as burnt offerings for himself and the people, thereby consecrating himself and the people to God's service.

No reference is made in the Old Testament to the observance of the Day of Atonement—only to its institution by Moses. It is mentioned in the New Testament as "the fast" (Acts 27:9). It remains today the greatest of Jewish fasts, observed in penitence and prayer.

As with other sacrificial figures of the Mosaic system, Jesus also fulfilled the types of atonement prefigured by this day, not in the Old Testament form of a temporary cancellation or "covering" for sin by vicarious sacrifice, but in the destruction of sin itself by his own immaculate life and sacrifice, thus providing the true way of reconciliation with God (compare Jn. 1:29; I Jn. 2:2). The author of Hebrews identifies Jesus Christ as our holy and undefiled high priest, who has "entered . . . into heaven itself, now to appear in the presence of God for us" (Heb. 9:24), having made atonement "once for all" (Heb. 10:10) by the sinless sacrifice of himself (Heb. 9:7-12).

Lesser Fasts

After the Exile lesser national fasts were designated, principal among them the fasts of the fourth, fifth, seventh, and tenth months, days of observing national calamities which had befallen Judah (Zech. 8:19). The *fast of the fourth month* commemorated the fall of Jerusalem (Jer. 39:2; 52:6,7); the *fast of the fifth month* memorialized the destruction of the Temple by Nebuchadnezzar (Jer. 52:12-14; Zech. 7:3,4); the *fast of the seventh month* marked the anniversary of the murder of Gedaliah at Mizpah (II Ki. 25:25,26; Jer. 41:1-3); the *fast of the tenth month* recalled the opening of the siege of Jerusalem by Nebuchadnezzar (II Ki. 25:1; Jer. 39:1).

NOTEWORTHY FASTS OF SCRIPTURE:

Moses' fast of forty days on the mount before he received the Decalogue the second time (Ex. 34:28)

David's fast of seven days in intercession for his son, child of Bath-sheba (II Sam. 12:16-20)

Elijah's fast of forty days in despair over Israel's defection (I Ki. 19:8)

Judah's fast under King Jehoshaphat (II Chron. 20:3)

Daniel's two fasts for the restoration of Judah, the second a fast of three full weeks of mourning (Dan. 9:3-19; 10:2,3)

Esther's three-day fast and that of her people before she petitioned to the king (Es. 4:16)

Ezra's fast and that of the remnant in preparation for the return journey from Babylon to Jerusalem (Ezra 8:21-23)

Ezra's fast over the backsliding of the returned remnant of Judah in resuming a forbidden relationship with the heathen (Ezra 10:6)

Nehemiah's sorrowful fast over the desolation of the remnant in Jerusalem (Neh. 1:4)

Jesus' fast of forty days in the wilderness in preparation for his ministry (Mt. 4:2)

Paul's penitent fast of three days in Damascus after his conversion (Acts 9:9)

The Antiochan church's fast preceding Paul's first missionary journey (Acts 13:1-3)

Language

The languages spoken in southwestern Asia were Semitic, the name given to the tongues spoken by the descendants, real or attributed, of Shem.

The dialects of this Semitic family may be divided into three main branches: 1. The *Northern* or Aramaean, to which the Chaldee and Syriac belong. 2. The *Southern*, of which the Arabic is the most important, and which also includes the Ethiopic. 3. The *Central*, which comprises the Hebrew and the dialects spoken by the other inhabitants of Palestine, such as the Canaanites and Phoenicians.[5]

The **Hebrew** spoken by the early Israelites was close kin to the dialects of Canaan and Phoenicia. "The language of Canaan" (Is. 19:18) and "the Jews' language" (Is. 36:11,13) are the only terms by which the Old Testament mentions the Hebrew tongue.

The Hebrew language occupied a place all its own in the history of Israel. While developed contiguous to other peoples and languages, it maintained a purity quite marvelous. Outside races, however, gradually edged their way into Israel's life, language, customs, and religion. The classical period of Hebrew writing, from the eighth to the fifth century B.C., gave way before the impact of the Aramaic sweep to the south.[6]

All the books of the Old Testament are written in classical Hebrew with the exception of a few portions written in Chaldee or Biblical Aramaic (Gen. 31:47; Ezra 4:8-6:18; 7:12-26; Jer. 10:11; Dan. 2:4-7:28).

During the Exile Jewish captives adopted the **Aramaic** language of their Babylonian conquerors. This tongue was already in general use in southeastern Asia, northern Syria, and Mesopotamia. Aramaic gradually replaced Hebrew as the popular language in Palestine, until finally Hebrew was used only by scholars. Jesus spoke Galilean Aramaic.

The introduction of the **Greek** language into southwestern Asia came with the conquests of Alexander the Great. From 330 B.C. to 330 A.D. it was the *koine*, the international form of Greek spoken throughout the Graeco-Roman Empire. Those who adopted Hellenism spoke this vernacular tongue. Its use in Egypt by the Jews of the Dispersion resulted in the translation of the Hebrew Old Testament into Greek (the Septuagint, *ca.* 250-50 B.C.). Jesus undoubtedly spoke this common Greek as well as Aramaic, since he grew up in the midst of a large Greek-speaking population in Galilee and later many of his audiences included Gentiles. The New Testament itself was written in Greek.

Glossary

Semite

A term employed both ethnologically and linguistically. (1) It is used of the descendants of Shem, eldest son of Noah, who overspread southwestern Asia (Gen. 10:21-31). Among the ancient Shemitic or Semitic peoples were the Arabs, Babylonians, Assyrians, Phoenicians, Aramaeans or Syrians, Canaanites (or Amorites), Hebrews, and the like. (2) Anthropology has shown that these peoples were not so much a racial unit as a linguistic one, the uniting factor being that they all spoke some branch of the Semitic languages.

Hebrews

The chosen people were variously called Hebrews, Israelites, and Jews, but each name holds a different shade of meaning. The Hebrews were an Aramaean branch of the Semites who migrated from lands east of the Euphrates and settled mainly in Canaan. The etymology of the word *Hebrew* is obscure. It may have been derived from Eber, the third generation of the line of Shem, the eponymous ancestor of Abram (Gen. 10:21-24). (Some identify the Hebrews with the Habiri, a warlike people mentioned in the Tell el-Amarna letters who may have been the first wave of the Hebrew conquest of Canaan.) It may have been derived from the adverb *eber*, "beyond," "across," "on the other side." It was first applied to Abram by the Canaanites as denoting the people who came from the other side of the Euphrates (Gen. 14:13). This Hebraic division included the Israelites and Edomites (descendants of Abraham), as well as the Ammonites and Moabites (descendants of Lot), but the term early became the distinctive name by which foreigners knew this Semitic people (Gen. 39:17; I Sam. 4:6).

Israelites

The descendants of the patriarch Jacob (Israel; Gen. 32:28); the Children of Israel; the national name of the twelve tribes collectively; the chosen or covenant people; Jews. This was a term used by the Hebrews of themselves. Figuratively, an Israelite is a Christian.

Jews

This term at first denoted the inhabitants of the Kingdom of Judah (II Ki. 16:6). The exiles in Babylon were called Jews because they had come from Judah. After their return to Palestine this name applied in popular usage to all Israelites. Its broader designation also included those who embraced the Judaic religion.

Gentile

The word *Gentile* stems from the Hebrew *goy* (plural *goyim*) meaning literally "people," "nation," "nations," that is, non-Hebrews. The Greek equivalent in the New Testament is *ethnos*. According to Genesis 10:2-5, the goyim were descended from the seven sons of Japheth, Noah's third son.

The Authorized Version of the Old Testament often uses the word *Gentile* in the sense of "heathen"; the Revised Version more precisely translates it "nations." The Authorized Version of the New Testament occasionally translates this word from the Greek *Hellen*, Greek-speaking persons (Jn. 7:35; I Cor. 10:32); the Revised Version replaces this with the word *Greeks.*

The Jews applied the term *Gentile* to all peoples of non-Jewish faith, those not of "the circumcision," who therefore had no part in the worship, sacred rites, and Abrahamic promises special to Israel.

3

Old Testament History

The Old Testament is a composite record that preserves the legendary narratives, history, and sacred writings of Israel. It opens with a record of creation by a supreme, omnipotent God (Elohim) and unfolds to view a universe and man imaging forth the Creator's goodness and power. It proceeds at once to another account of creation, in which the Creator is called Lord God (Jehovah-Elohim), that depicts mankind under conditions of physical life; it narrates the appearance of evil in the world, the sin of Adam, his fall, and the subsequent state of his demoralized offspring. The record immediately advances to disclose God's mercy as shown to the Adamic race in His promise of redemption, a promise to be fulfilled in "the seed of the woman" that appeared centuries later as the Messiah, "God's anointed."

Through modern archeology we have obtained much fragmentary evidence of man's existence on the earth for many thousands of years. Some scholars, following Archbishop Ussher (who lived from 1580 to 1656 and whose chronology of the Bible was printed in the English Authorized Version), date Adam as 4004 B.C.; the man who existed before that time they usually term prehistoric man—man before written history. As more time passes, we may be able through continued archeological and geological research more precisely to date certain events and periods of Old Testament history. But in any case such modifications will in no way detract from the importance and meaning of those events. (Dates given in this volume conform to the major body of accepted traditional scholarship.)

The history of the race of Adam is presented in the line of Seth (Adam's third son) as that line passed through centuries of gradual moral and spiritual development—from the patriarchs to the covenant nation of Israel and from the Law to the Prophets. Throughout this Old Testament history, despite individual and national failings and apostasies, an advancing knowledge of God and a strengthening

Excavation of the Flood level at Ur: a fallen wall of clay bricks found below the Flood deposit. The University Museum, University of Pennsylvania.

conviction of His goodness are clearly traceable, together with a rising hope of what His Messiah might accomplish in the overthrow of evil when his righteous kingdom should prevail.

The covenant idea, "I will take you to me for a people, and I will be to you a God" (Ex. 6:7), is the varied and oft-repeated vehicle by which God's gracious relationship to Israel is made known. This covenant relationship, imperfectly effected by the Law and by the Prophets, is shown to be perfectly mediated by the historic Christ of the New Testament, the promised Messiah of the Old.

Briefly to follow the course of Israelite history as Scripture presents it, one begins with Adam, the first human being designated in the Bible, and traces it through the line of his third son Seth to the patriarch Noah, tenth in line of descent from Adam. Noah lived in the fertile alluvial valley between the Tigris and the Euphrates rivers. Because of Noah's righteousness in the midst of great wickedness God preserved him and his family during the Deluge that devastated Baby-

lonia, and God's covenant made earlier with mankind in Adam was renewed with Noah.

Noah had three sons—Shem, Ham, and Japheth. The principal stream of Old Testament history narrows to the Shemite line, and is traced through Shem to Terah and his son Abram. When the divine command and promise came to Abram, living in Ur of the Chaldees—"Get thee out of thy country . . . unto a land that I will shew thee. . . . I will make of thee a great nation . . . and in thee shall all families of the earth be blessed" (Gen. 12:1-3)—he left Babylonia and journeyed with Terah, Sarai his wife, and Lot his brother's son to Haran in Mesopotamia. There he remained about twenty-five years until the death of his father and then journeyed on to Beth-el in Canaan, but finding famine in the land, he crossed the Sinai Peninsula into Egypt. Forced by circumstances to leave Egypt, Abram returned to Canaan, and at its borders he separated from Lot. Lot settled in the plain east of Jordan; Abram, promised the land of Canaan, dwelt at Hebron west of the Dead Sea.

When Abram, faithful and righteous, was ninety-nine years old, God's promise of posterity was fulfilled in the birth of Isaac; Abram's name was changed to Abraham and Sarai's to Sarah. Isaac married Rebekah, and to them were born the twins Esau and Jacob. Jacob obtained the birthright and blessing of the first-born through deception, thereby incurring his brother's hatred. Isaac sent Jacob to Padan-aram in Mesopotamia to take a wife from the daughters of his mother's people. On his way Jacob tarried at Beth-el and here God renewed with him the covenant He had made with Abraham and Isaac. Jacob married Leah and Rachel, daughters of his uncle Laban, and by them and their two handmaids fathered twelve sons. After the birth of Joseph, his eleventh son and Rachel's first-born, at God's command Jacob returned to Canaan. As he journeyed he stopped at Peniel; there through prayer and spiritual transformation of his nature, his name was changed to Israel. His sons later headed the twelve tribes of Israel and were known as the Children of Israel.

Near Beer-sheba in Canaan Rachel bore Jacob his twelfth son, Benjamin. When his favorite, Joseph, was seventeen, Jacob sent him on an errand to his brothers shepherding their flocks at Shechem. The jealous brothers sold him to passing caravan merchants headed for Egypt, telling their father that he was dead. In Egypt Joseph was sold to Potiphar, a captain of Pharaoh's guard. Faithful in his duties, he soon rose to the position of overseer of his master's house. However, as a result of the malice of Potiphar's wife Joseph was imprisoned for two years, but God was with him, and when he successfully interpreted two dreams for Pharaoh as foretelling seven years of plenty followed by seven years of famine, the monarch made him premier of Egypt. During the years of abundant crops Joseph supervised the storage of grain as provision against the coming dearth.

The famine extended even into Canaan, and in time all Joseph's brothers except Benjamin came down into Egypt to buy grain. They did not know Joseph but he recognized them and sent them back for his younger brother. When they returned with Benjamin he revealed his identity, effected a compassionate reconciliation, and sent for his father and the brothers'

Pottery figurines discovered during excavations of the Flood level at Ur. The University Museum, University of Pennsylvania.

The world's oldest wall, from the pre-pottery Neolithic Age, revealed by excavations at Jericho. These are the walls encircled by Joshua and his army (Josh. 6). Jericho Excavation Fund.

families; the house of Jacob or Israel (some seventy people) settled in Goshen in Lower Egypt.

For more than four centuries the Israelite families multiplied; then a hostile Pharaoh, fearing their number and strength, enslaved them. In time the prophet Moses was raised up as the deliverer of the covenant people to free them from bondage and lead them to the promised land of Canaan. Mighty miracles attended Israel's exodus from Egypt. Moses led his people across the Red Sea to Mount Sinai in the southern part of the Sinai Peninsula. Here God (Jehovah) renewed His covenant, this time with the nation of Israel, and through Moses gave them His law. Israel also received civil laws and ordinances and a religious system of sacrificial worship embodied in a Tabernacle and a priesthood.

After a year's encampment at Sinai Israel journeyed north to Kadesh-barnea in the Negeb desert and twelve spies were sent into Canaan for forty days to assess its strength. Only two, Joshua and Caleb, brought back a good report, urging Israel to go forward to take the land. But the people were afraid of the Canaanites, and because they did not go forward they were condemned to wander for forty years in the Negeb wilderness, a year for a day. Here they learned needed discipline and reliance on the providence of God. At the close of the Wandering they encamped for a brief period in the plains of Moab east of the Dead Sea, there to be reminded of God's great covenant and law and to receive the promise of a God-sent Messiah.

Joshua, Moses' successor, led the Israelites across the Jordan into Canaan. Under his military leadership Israel captured the southern stronghold of Jericho. For the next twenty-four years Joshua successfully led the Israelites against the armies of the Canaanites until Canaan was subdued. At the close of his life Joshua allotted the land to the twelve tribes, commanding the Israelites to adhere to the worship of the one God.

During the ensuing period of the Judges—some 350 years—the people lapsed often into idolatry, tempted by the polytheism around them. They came under the oppression of the nations whose gods they served; periodically in their distress they turned to God for help, and judges were raised up to deliver them.

When Samuel, fifteenth and last of the judges, grew old, the people demanded a king, so Samuel, obedient to divine direction, anointed Saul Israel's first king. Later Saul was rejected for disobedience; upon Saul's death David, son of Jesse of the tribe of Judah, became king, reigning the first seven years over

Sarepta (Zarephath), the village in which Elijah found sanctuary in the house of a widow for three years during Ahab's reign in Israel. Here he multiplied oil and meal for his protector and raised her son from the dead. Excavation conducted by a University of Pennsylvania group. The University Museum, University of Pennsylvania.

The Pools of Solomon. Above: one of the pools at
low-water level. Jordan Tourism Office, New York.
Right: the first pool below the Saracen castle is 380
feet long, 25 feet deep, 229 feet wide at its west end
and 236 feet at the east. The second pool, about 50
yards below the first, is 423 feet long, 38 feet deep,
229 wide on the west and 236 on the east. Opposite
page: the lowest pool (248 feet from the middle
pool) is 582 feet long, 50 feet deep, 148 feet wide on
the west and 207 feet wide on the east. Water from
adjacent springs flows into the pools through under-
ground conduits; there are also surface channels that
collect rainwater. An aqueduct from the lower pool
carries water four miles to Bethlehem and to a point
directly under the Temple area in Jerusalem, ten
miles distant. R. E. M. Bain, photographer; from
Earthly Footsteps of The Man of Galilee (1894).

Judah with his capital at Hebron. He conquered Jebusite Jerusalem, made it the capital, united all the tribes, and ruled over the United Kingdom for thirty-three years. David "walked before [God] in truth, and in righteousness" and God renewed His covenant with the house of David.

Solomon succeeded his father David. Under Solomon's rule the kingdom reached a state of great prosperity and renown, and by the erection of a magnificent Temple in Jerusalem the worship of Jehovah was centralized and strengthened. However, through extravagance Solomon's reign became tyranny, and at his death in 933/932 B.C. the tribes revolted: ten tribes formed the northern Kingdom of Israel; the two that remained loyal to the house of David formed the southern Kingdom of Judah.

These two kingdoms, Judah and Israel, existed side by side for the next two centuries. From its inception Israel went after other gods, while Judah remained true to the worship of Jehovah. Sixty years after the division of the United Kingdom, the great period of Hebrew prophecy began in the ministries of Elijah and Elisha and flowered during the succeeding

four hundred years in the labors of the writing prophets, both Major and Minor. These spiritual seers continually admonished their people to eschew idolatry and to obey the moral and ethical law of Sinai, and gave witness to the presence and power of God in the affairs of the nation. Israel, ignoring the warning of its prophets, became wholly apostate; in 722 B.C. it was carried into Assyrian captivity and its people scatter-

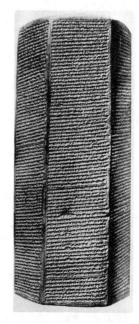

Sennacherib's prism. This hexagonal clay tablet (5½ inches at the base and approximately 15 inches high) records the siege of Jerusalem in 701 B.C., during the reign of Hezekiah: "Forty-six of his strong-walled cities I besieged and took. Himself like a caged bird I shut up in Jerusalem, his royal city. Earthworks I threw up against him; the one coming out of the city gate I turned back to his misery." Courtesy of the Oriental Institute, University of Chicago.

Cyrus' cylinder. This baked-clay cylinder bears a decree of the Persian king Cyrus, granting religious tolerance to his conquered peoples. As a result Jewish exiles were permitted to return to Jerusalem and rebuild their Temple. Courtesy of the Trustees of the British Museum.

ed, never again to be united. Although idolatry was widespread in Judah, this kingdom continued for another century and a half, its national life prolonged by periods of religious reform by godly kings and prophets. Finally, however, Judah's sin was also judged. Nebuchadnezzar, ruler of the Neo-Babylonian Empire, swept across the Fertile Crescent north of the Arabian Desert and, in three deportations, took the citizens of Judah captive. With the last deportation, in 586 B.C., Jerusalem was razed to the ground.

During the long exile Judah's faith was tried and a purer monotheism evolved; its loyalty to God was exemplified in the lives of Daniel and his three Hebrew companions. The Messianic people remained in Babylonian captivity until Cyrus, Persian conqueror of Babylon, released them in 538 B.C. and a willing remnant returned to their own land. Zerubbabel's expedition of 50,000 exiles to Jerusalem marked the first stage of the Restoration. The Temple was rebuilt and Mosaic worship restored. Eighty years later a second expedition of 7000 went back under the priestly leader Ezra. He was soon followed by Nehemiah, who directed his energies to the rebuilding of the walls of Jerusalem. Through the radical reforms instituted by Ezra and Nehemiah both the church and state were rehabilitated; a strict monotheism emerged, and with it the inception of Judaism. Old Testament history ceases with the book of Malachi, although more than four hundred years were to elapse before the advent of the Messiah (see p. 92).

A chronological outline of the Old Testament begins on page 73. It is given in progressive stages to show the continuous chain of events from Adam to Nehemiah and falls naturally into six historical periods. It is presented on a rising scale to suggest the extent of revelation. With this purpose in mind, the outline is to be read from the bottom of each page upward.

RESTORATION

CAPTIVITIES

Divided Kingdom
United Kingdom
CANAAN   Period of the Judges

WILDERNESS WANDERING

SOJOURN IN EGYPT

FAMILY HISTORY OF THE AGES BEFORE MOSES

OUTLINE OF OLD TESTAMENT HISTORY

God's covenant, the divine promise to men of redemption and salvation, is made first with "the seed of the woman." It is renewed with mankind through Noah, established with "His chosen," through Abraham. This covenant is conditioned only by the righteousness, obedience, and faith of men.

NOTE:
The Messianic promises
God's covenant

Read chart upward line by line

Family History of the Generations before Moses

Edenic period

4004 B.C. (Ussher) **ADAM**

First Account of Creation—God(Elohim) "created" the universe, and man in His image, by His word Gen. 1-2:4a

Second Account of Creation—The Lord God (Yahweh) "formed" mankind and beast out of the dust of the ground Gen. 2:4b-25
Adam, first human being according to Biblical record—progenitor of mankind—Eve, his wife—the Temptation and Fall—their expulsion from garden of Eden Gen. 3
The seed of the woman—the promise of the Redeemer (first Messianic prophecy) (Genesis 3:14, 15 sometimes called the Adamic Covenant)
"I will put enmity between thee and the woman, and between thy seed and her seed; it shall bruise thy head, and thou shalt bruise his heel."

3874 B.C. (Ussher) **SETH**

Birth of Cain and Abel, sons of Adam and Eve—Cain slays his brother Abel—"And the Lord set a mark upon Cain." Gen. 4, 5
Birth of Seth, Adam's third son—to Seth is born a son Enos—"then began men to call upon the name of the Lord."
Genealogies from Adam to Noah: the line of Seth (the Messianic line) and the line of Cain (worldly line)
Translation of Enoch (father of Methuselah) "And Enoch walked with God: and he was not; for God took him." (See Heb. 11:5)

2948 B.C. (Ussher) **NOAH**

Son of Lamech—tenth in line of descent from Adam—Noah's sons: Shem, Ham, and Japheth Gen. 5:28-8:22
The wickedness of the world—"But Noah found grace in the eyes of the Lord."
God warns Noah of a coming flood as judgment on the world—He commands him to build an ark to the saving of his house
The Flood—rain for forty days, waters rise—in fifth month ark rests on Mount Ararat
Noah sends forth a raven—he sends forth a dove three times—third time it "returned not again unto him any more."
Noah and his family leave the ark after one year (twelve lunar months) and ten days—he builds an altar to God

God establishes His Covenant with Noah and his Seed ((Noahic Covenant) Gen. 8:21-9:17
Noah plants a vineyard—is drunken and mocked by Ham—Noah curses Canaan (Ham's offspring), blesses Shem and Japheth

The Tower of Babel—"The Lord did there confound the language of all the earth. . . ." Gen. 11:1-9

2170 B.C. ? **ABRAHAM**

"Get thee out . . . unto a land that I will shew thee." Abram journeys from Ur to Haran (Abram) son of Terah in line of Shem—the call of Abram—God's command and promise Gen. 11:27-13:18

Journeys to Egypt—sent out of Egypt by Pharaoh—Abram separates from Lot—Lot goes to Sodom After twenty-five years, with Sarai his wife and nephew Lot, he journeys to Canaan

God's great covenant with Abram—A land and a seed (Abrahamic Covenant)

Abram dwells in Hebron—rescues Lot—is blessed by Melchizedek Gen. 14 (See Heb. 7)

God confirms his covenant with Abram Gen. 15

Sarai is barren—gives her handmaid Hagar to Abram—birth of Ishmael by Hagar Gen. 16

God renews the Covenant—Names changed to Abraham and Sarah Gen. 17:1-18:16
God reveals Himself to Abraham as the "Almighty God" (El Shaddai)
Circumcision is instituted as a token of the covenant
Abraham entertains three angels who confirm the coming of a son by Sarah
God's judgment on Sodom is revealed—Abraham pleads for Sodom
Sodom, Gomorrah destroyed—Lot and daughters saved Gen. 18:17-19:38

2070 B.C. **ISAAC**

Rightful heir, born to Abraham and Sarah Gen. 21
Hagar and Ishmael cast out—Hagar is comforted
Trial of Abraham's faith Gen. 22
Offering of Isaac—blessing to Abraham

OUTLINE OF OLD TESTAMENT HISTORY (Continued)

The terms *the sons of Jacob* and *the house of Jacob* designate Jacob's natural line of posterity; after Jacob's purifying experience and his change of name to Israel at Peniel, his sons and their descendants are also called *the children of Israel.*

While Israel comes to apply to the nation as a whole, the name often carries with it a deeper spiritual signification in that it denotes those who, like Jacob, give a spiritual response. Isaiah writes "The Lord sent a word into Jacob, and it hath lighted upon Israel" (Is. 9:8).

Read chart upward line by line

Family History of the Generation before Moses—Cont.

Sojourn in Egypt 430 years

---

until Shilob come...."
"The sceptre shall not depart from Judab...
From the tribe of Judab the Messiab is to come
Israel's prophecies to his twelve sons   Gen. 49

Jacob bestows the first blessing upon Ephraim, the second-born
Jacob acknowledges Joseph's sons, Manasseh and Ephraim, as his own
House of Israel settles in Goshen in Egypt—prospers and multiplies
"I will go down with thee... also surely bring thee up again...."
"Fear not to go down... I will there make of thee a great nation...."
Israel journeys into Egypt—House of Israel, seventy in number   Gen. 46-48

1880 B.C.

Joseph reveals his identity—"God sent me before you to preserve you a posterity...."
Joseph's brethren journey twice to Egypt to buy corn   Gen. 42-45

Joseph made ruler over Egypt by Pharaoh—seven years of plenty and seven years of famine
Sold to Potiphar—falsely accused, imprisoned two years—interprets Pharaoh's dreams
Favored son—hated by brethren who sell him to slave traders—carried into Egypt   Gen. 37, 39-41

ca. 1920 B.C.
JOSEPH

Benjamin, Rachel's second son, is born—Rachel dies in travail   Gen. 35:16-20

God renews His Covenant with Israel (Jacob) at Beth-el   Gen. 35:9-15

Jacob is reconciled with Esau—Jacob's sons avenge the defilement of their sister Dinah by Shechem, the Hivite
Jacob wrestles at Peniel—His name is changed to Israel—No longer a supplanter but "a prince" with God   Gen. 32-34

Joseph born to Rachel—Jacob desires to return to his own land—his worldly policy—he departs secretly   Gen. 30:22-31:55
Sons born to Jacob: six by Leah; two by Bilhah, Rachel's handmaid; two by Zilpah, Leah's handmaid   Gen. 30:1-21
Serves Laban for seven years to marry Rachel his younger daughter—is given Leah—serves another seven years for Rachel   Gen. 29

God renews the Abrahamic Covenant with Jacob at Beth-el—The vision of Jacob's ladder—Jacob's vow

Jacob journeys to Padan-aram to take a wife of his mother's people—"Thou shalt not take a wife of the daughters of Canaan."   Gen. 28

Jacob, aided by Rebekah, obtains patriarchal blessing by deception—Isaac later confirms the blessing to Jacob   Gen. 27:1-28:4
Esau at age of forty marries two Hittite women—"Which were a grief of mind unto Isaac and to Rebekah."   Gen. 26:34,35

God renews the Abrahamic Covenant with Isaac—"I will perform the oath which I sware unto Abraham thy father...."   Gen. 26

Esau sells his birthright as the elder to Jacob for a mess of pottage—"Thus Esau despised his birthright."
Younger twin of Esau—born to Isaac and Rebekah—Rebekah had been told: "Two nations are in thy womb... and the elder shall serve the younger."   Gen. 25:20-34

2010 B.C.
JACOB (ISRAEL)

Abraham, after death of Sarah, marries Keturah—she bears him sons—Abraham dies—"Abraham gave all that he had unto Isaac."
Abraham sends his servant to relatives in Mesopotamia to seek a wife for his son Isaac—Rebekah is chosen   Gen. 24:1-25:10

OUTLINE OF OLD TESTAMENT HISTORY (Continued)

Abraham, Isaac, and Jacob knew God as "most high God" and as "God Almighty." To Moses God declares Himself "JEHOVAH," "I AM THAT I AM." With the revelation of Himself as self-existent and ever-present comes the disclosure of His imperative law.

Under the covenant promise, "I will take you to me for a people, and I will be to you a God," Israel takes the decisive and progressive step of separating itself from the worship of many gods, and identifies itself with the worship of the One God. However, the realization of the magnitude of the covenant promise and of the law of "I AM THAT I AM" is to dawn upon Israel but slowly, as it learns "precept upon precept; line upon line . . . here a little, and there a little."

Read chart upward line by line

Sojourn in Egypt

1530 B.C. MOSES

Children of Israel increase greatly in number and in power—"and the land was filled with them." Ex. 1

Fearing their increase, a Pharaoh who knew not Joseph oppresses and enslaves them

Pharaoh decrees the destruction of all newborn Hebrew male children—"Every son that is born ye shall cast into the river. . . ."

Born to Amram and Jochebed, of tribe of Levi—is hidden in an ark of bulrushes—found by Pharaoh's daughter—reared as her son Ex. 1

Moses, at the age of forty, slays an Egyptian—flees into Midian—keeps the flocks of Jethro, priest of Midian, for forty years—marries Zipporah

1450 B.C.

God's call to Moses at the burning bush—God identifies Himself as the God of Abraham . . . of Isaac . . . of Jacob"

Moses is commissioned to deliver the Children of Israel from bondage and to lead them to "a good land" (Canaan)

God reveals Himself as "I AM THAT I AM" (Jehovah)—God's message to Israel—two signs given to Moses—Aaron, his brother, appointed to assist him

God renews His Covenant to Children of Israel by His Name Jehovah—"I will take you to me for a people, and I will be to you a God. . . ."

Moses and Aaron demand that Pharaoh release the Israelites—"Thus saith the Lord God . . . Let my people go. . . ." Ex. 5:1-15:21

Pharaoh refuses—imposes greater burdens—"Who is the Lord, that I should obey his voice. . . ?"

Ten plagues—Pharaoh's heart is hardened—"Against all the gods of Egypt I will execute judgment: I am the Lord."

The Passover is instituted (before tenth plague)—first-born of Israel sanctified to God (after tenth plague)

The exodus of the Children of Israel from Egypt—God guides them by a pillar of cloud and a pillar of fire.

Pharaoh pursues—Israel passes through the Red Sea on dry ground—Egyptians are overthrown

At Mount Sinai

The journey to Sinai—people murmur for water—Moses sweetens bitter waters of Marah Ex. 15:22-18:27

At Sin the people murmur for bread—miraculously fed with manna (daily manna for forty years except Sabbaths)

Water from the rock—Israel defeats Amalekites at Rephidim under Joshua's command, while Moses prays

Government of people burdens Moses—Jethro counsels him to appoint judges—Moses accepts his counsel

Israelites encamp at Mount Sinai for nearly a year Ex. 19

God renews His Covenant with the Nation of Israel (Mosaic Covenant) Ex. 20:1-24:8

Moses on mount forty days—receives the Ten Commandments on two tables of stone Ex. 24:9-31:18

Receives the pattern for a Tabernacle and the command to institute a priesthood

The Sabbath designated as a sign of God's "perpetual covenant" with Israel

Idolaters worship the golden calf—Moses breaks the tables of stone Ex. 32-34

Idolaters punished—Moses' great prayer of intercession—he sees God's glory

God renews His Covenant—Moses on mount another forty days

Idolatry expressly forbidden—the Decalogue given a second time

Tabernacle erected, Ark of the Covenant in Holy of Holies Ex. 35-40

Aaron and sons set apart for priestly service

(Leviticus elaborates Mosaic system of religious worship)

Numbering of people at Sinai Num. 1-4

Tribe of Levi set apart for priestly service

Additional laws—consecration of Levites Num. 5-8

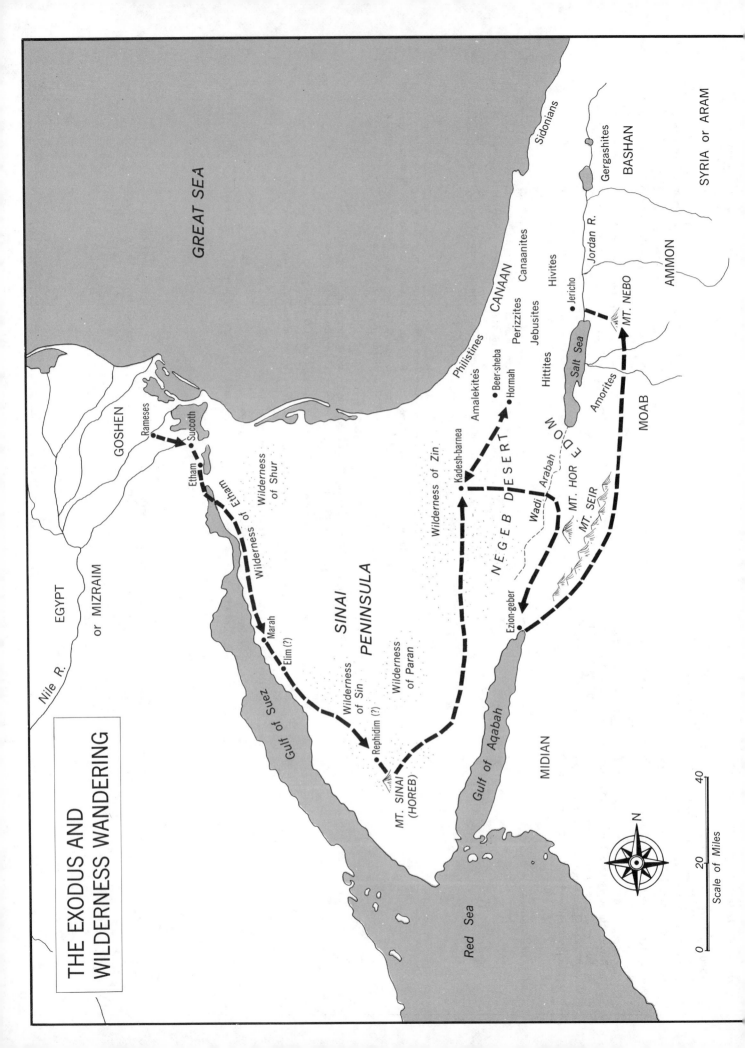

THE EXODUS AND
WILDERNESS WANDERING

GREAT SEA

EGYPT

Nile R.

or MIZRAIM

GOSHEN

Rameses
Succoth
Etham
Etham

Wilderness of Ethan

Wilderness of Shur

Wilderness of Sin

Marah
Elim (?)

SINAI
PENINSULA

Wilderness
of Paran

Rephidim (?)

Wilderness of Sin (?)

MT. SINAI
(HOREB)

Gulf of Suez

Gulf of Aqabah

MIDIAN

Red Sea

Wilderness of Zin

NEGEB DESERT

Kadesh-barnea

Amalekites

Beer-sheba
Hormah

Philistines

CANAAN

Perizzites

Jebusites

Hittites

Canaanites

Hivites

Salt Sea

Jericho

Sidonians

Gergashites

BASHAN

SYRIA or ARAM

Jordan R.

AMMON

MT. NEBO

MOAB

EDOM

Amorites

MT. HOR

MT. SEIR

Wadi Arabah

Ezion-geber

N

0   20   40
Scale of Miles

Faith, discipline, and obedience are now required of the Children of Israel. They must not only journey onward to the Promised Land to claim their inheritance but must advance in knowledge of the One God and His law that they may possess that land.

They do not press forward. They do not trust. Instead they wander in the wilderness for forty years. They murmur and murmur. They remain under God's ever-watchful care because they are the covenant people, and in each "year" for a "day" they learn discipline and gain trust and spiritual strength to endure.

Moses exhorts Israel: "Thou shalt remember all the way which the Lord thy God led thee these forty years in the wilderness, to humble thee, and to prove thee, to know what was in thine heart, whether thou wouldst keep his commandments, or no" (Deut. 8:2).

Read chart upward line by line

Conquest of Canaan

In Plains of Moab

Wandering in the Wilderness (40 years)

MOSES

Passover observed—manna ceases

Israel enters Canaan—Jordan waters are divided
Joshua sends spies to Jericho—Rahab shelters them
"As I was with Moses, so I will be with thee."
Succeeds Moses as leader of Israel Josh. 1-5 (See Deut. 31:23)

1410-1386 B.C.
JOSHUA

Moses' death—"his eye was not dim, nor his natural force abated."
—God said, "This is the land which I sware unto Abraham."
Moses, from Mount Nebo, views all the promised land Deut. 34
Moses' song—his blessing of the twelve tribes Deut. 32,33

God Renews His Covenant With the New Generation of Israel Deut. 29-31
—"The Lord thy God will raise up unto thee a Prophet from the midst of thee."
Moses' Prophecy of the Messiah Deut. 18:15, 18

Moses reviews the years of wandering—exhorts Israel to obedience to the law and covenant
Moses' closing addresses to new generation before their entrance into Canaan Deut. 1-28

Forty-eight cities, including six cities of refuge, are promised to Levites Num. 35
A list of Israel's forty-two journeys—Moses' warnings against idolatrous Canaanites Num. 33
Midianites defeated—tribes of Reuben and Gad speak for an inheritance on east side of Jordan Num. 31,32
Moses, at God's command, appoints Joshua his successor—"a man in whom is the spirit." Num. 27
Second numbering of Israel by Moses—not a man of first numbering remains save Caleb and Joshua Num. 26

Israelites commit whoredom and idolatry with Moab—Phinehas is zealous for Israel—the people punished Num. 25, Deut. 4:3
Balaam's Messianic Prophecy—"There shall come a Star out of Jacob, and a Sceptre shall rise out of Israel."
Balaam entertains an angel—"I have received commandment to bless: and he hath blessed; and I cannot reverse it."
Israel encamps in plains of Moab—Balak, king of Moab, sends for Balaam, a heathen prophet, to curse Israel Num. 22-24

People are rebellious—plagued by fiery serpents—the brazen serpent—Israel defeats Amorites and king of Bashan Num. 21
Moses sins in smiting rock for water—rebuked for unbelief—Israelites refused passage through Edom—Aaron's death—Eleazar succeeds him
After thirty-eight years of wandering Israel again arrives at Kadesh-barnea (Deut. 2:14)—people murmur for water
The budding of Aaron's rod—Aaron's priestly authority is established—duties of priests and Levites
Rebellion of Korah, Dathan, Abiram, and 250 men against Moses and Aaron—destruction of rebels—a plague against murmurers Num. 16-20

("Yea, forty years didst thou sustain them in the wilderness, so that they lacked nothing; their clothes waxed not old, and their feet swelled not." Neh. 9:21)
The Children of Israel are condemned to wander for forty years—"Each day for a year, shall ye bear your iniquities, even forty years."
Ten spies give an evil report—Caleb and Joshua give a good report—"Let us go up at once, and possess it."—The people murmur rebelliously
Israel encamps at Kadesh-barnea in wilderness of Paran—Moses sends twelve men to spy out the land of Canaan—they make a forty days' search Num. 13, 14

The sedition of Miriam (Moses' sister) and Aaron—Miriam becomes leprous but is healed through Moses' prayer
Moses appoints seventy elders—"I [God] will take of the spirit which is upon thee, and will put it upon them; and they shall bear the burden of the people with thee."
People crave food other than manna—Moses talks with God—"Have I not found favour in thy sight, that thou layest the burden of all this people upon me?"
Israelites journey from Sinai to Kadesh-barnea—guided by a pillar of cloud by day and of fire by night Num. 9-12

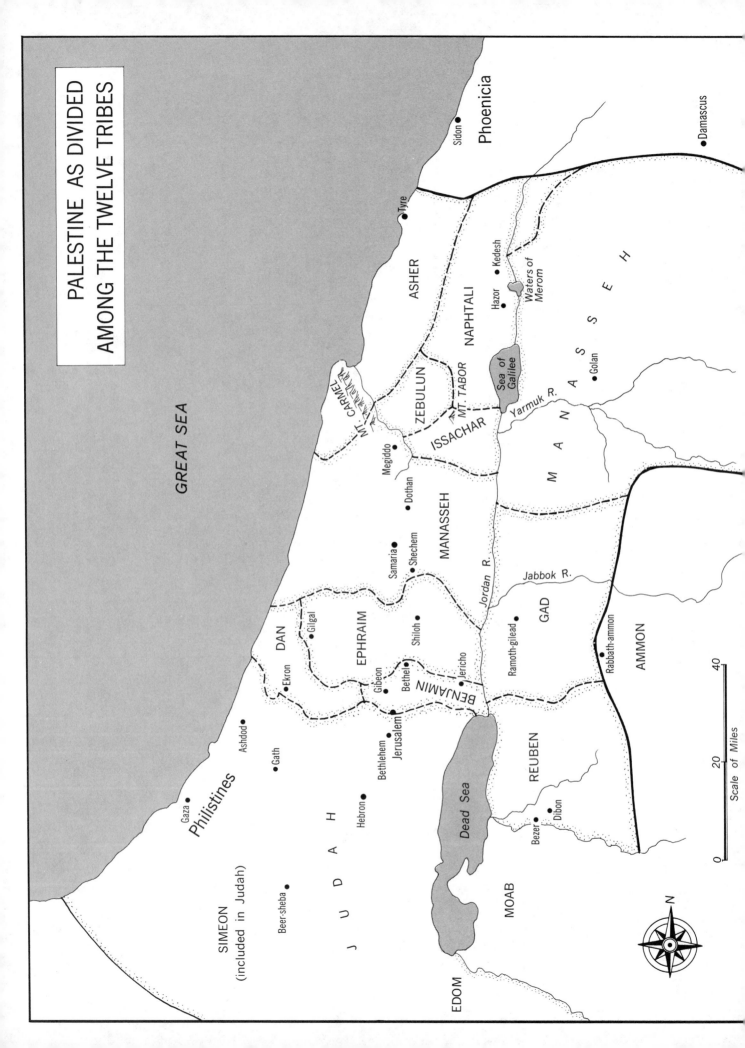

PALESTINE AS DIVIDED AMONG THE TWELVE TRIBES

GREAT SEA

Phoenicia

Sidon

Damascus

Tyre

ASHER

Kedesh

Hazor

Waters of Merom

NAPHTALI

MT. CARMEL

MT. TABOR

ZEBULUN

Sea of Galilee

ISSACHAR

Golan

Yarmuk R.

Megiddo

M A N A S S E H

Dothan

MANASSEH

Samaria

Shechem

Jabbok R.

DAN

Jordan R.

Gilgal

GAD

EPHRAIM

Ekron

Gibeon

Shiloh

Ramoth-gilead

Bethel

Jericho

Rabbath-ammon

Bethlehem

BENJAMIN

AMMON

Ashdod

Jerusalem

Gath

REUBEN

Dead Sea

Philistines

Gaza

Hebron

Bezer

Dibon

J U D A H

SIMEON
(included in Judah)

Beer-sheba

MOAB

EDOM

N

0   20   40

Scale of Miles

OLD TESTAMENT HISTORY (Continued)

The twelve tribes of Israel take possession of their heritage under the command of Joshua. At the close of his life he admonishes them, "Choose you this day whom ye will serve," and Israel responds, "The Lord our God will we serve, and his voice will we obey."

Learning to maintain this right choice becomes a painful experience for the Children of Israel after the leadership of Joshua ceases. Again and again they lapse into flagrant idolatry. They go "a whoring after other gods," thus breaking their oath of the covenant. Their idolatry brings them under the oppression of many enemies, and in their desolation they cry to God. Judges are repeatedly raised up to deliver them from servitude. Out of these crises grows tribal cooperation, which prepares the way for a more united Israel. The prophetic voice is revived in Samuel, the last of the judges.

Read chart upward line by line

God's Covenant Is Renewed with Israel by Joshua at Shechem—The tribes remain faithful "all the days of the elders that overlived Joshua" Josh. 24

Joshua's last exhortation to Israel—his warning against idolatry—"Keep and . . . do all that is written in the book of the law of Moses." Josh. 23

Tabernacle is set up at Shiloh (remains there until last days of Samuel)—Forty-eight cities, including six cities of refuge, are given to Levites

Caleb, at eighty-five, claims his inheritance as promised by Moses—"As yet I am as strong this day as I was in the day that Moses sent me. . ."
The land, though not fully subdued, is distributed among the twelve tribes as their inheritance—(This duty was included in Joshua's commission) Josh. 13-22
The capture of Jericho—conquest of Canaan by Joshua under God's direction—Joshua's many battles in which thirty-one kings are defeated Josh. 5:13-12:24

JOSHUA — *ca. 40 years*

Period of the Judges (300-350 years—ca. 1370-1028 B.C.)

OTHNIEL — Servitude of eighteen years under Mesopotamians—Othniel, brother of Caleb, judges and delivers Israel—land rests forty years Ju. 3:5-11

Israel's desertion of God's covenant through idolatry brings them under bondage—"They . . . corrupted themselves . . . in following other gods." Some Canaanite nations are left in the land to test Israel—the wickedness of the new generation Ju. 1:1-3:4
(Dates of judges uncertain—some of these tribal leaders possibly contemporary or local in their rule)

EHUD — Servitude of eighteen years under Moabites—Ehud delivers Israel—land rests eighty years Ju. 3:12-30

SHAMGAR — Delivers Israel from Philistines Ju. 3:31

DEBORAH, BARAK — Servitude of twenty years under Canaanites—Deborah, with Barak, delivers Israel—land rests forty years Ju. 4,5

GIDEON — Servitude of seven years under Midianites—Gideon is called of God to deliver Israel—given three signs of assurance Ju. 6-8
The sifting of his army from thirty-two thousand to three hundred to three hundred—his victory—country in quietness forty years

Abimelech sets himself up unlawfully as king at Shechem—three years of tyranny—Jotham's parable Ju. 9

TOLA — Judges Israel twenty-three years Ju. 10:1,2

JAIR — Judges Israel twenty-two years Ju. 10:3-5

JEPHTHAH — Servitude of eighteen years under Philistines, Ammonites—he delivers Israel, judges six years Ju. 10:6-12:7

IBZAN — Judges Israel seven years Ju. 12:8-10

ELON — Judges Israel ten years Ju. 12:11,12

ABDON — Judges Israel eight years Ju. 12:13-15

SAMSON — Servitude of forty years under Philistines—Samson judges Israel twenty years Ju. 13-16
He wars with the Philistines—is enticed and betrayed by Delilah, a Philistine woman

(Book of Ruth thought to be connected with period of Judges)
A period of lawlessness—"Every man did that which was right in his own eyes." Ju. 17-21

1088 B.C. ELI
High priest of the Tabernacle at Shiloh—judges Israel forty years 1 Sam. 1-6
Samuel, child of promise, ministers to Eli—called of God four times
Philistines capture Ark of the Covenant—death of Eli
Philistines, oppressed by presence of the Ark, return it
Samuel given prophecy of fall of Eli's house—established as a prophet

1048 B.C. SAMUEL
Brings about a religious revival at Mizpeh 1. Sam. 7
The Philistines attack and are defeated
Schools of the prophets are established
Judges Israel from Ramah
Judges yearly in Beth-el, Gilgal, Mizpeh

79

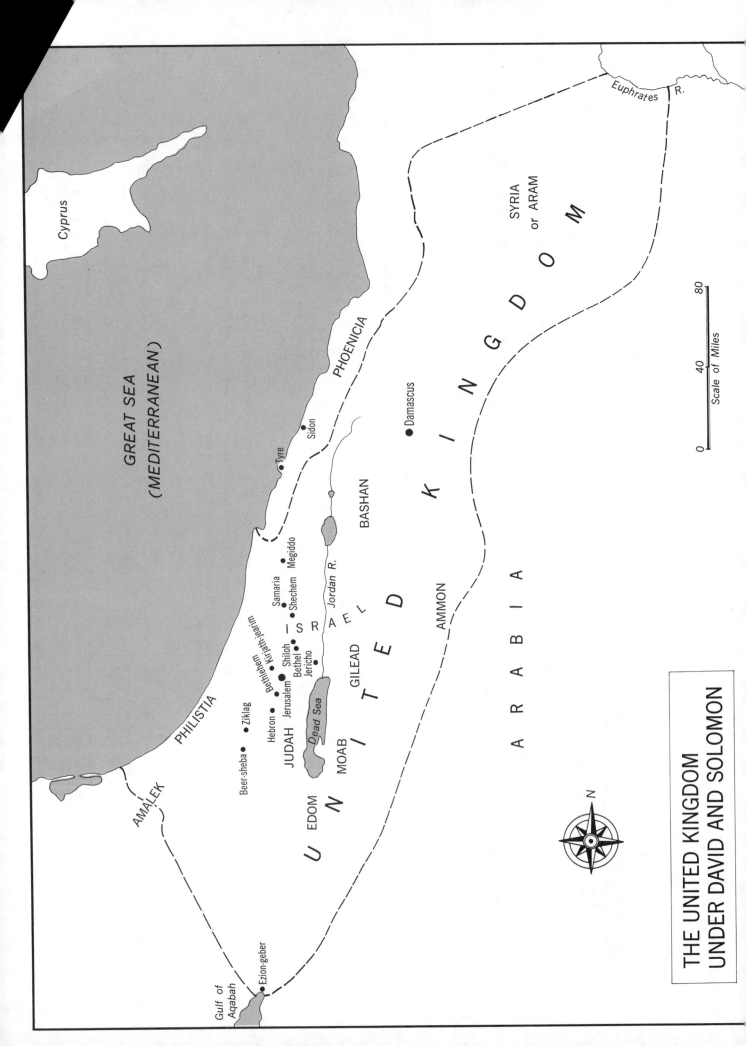

Cyprus

GREAT SEA
(MEDITERRANEAN)

Euphrates R.

SYRIA
or ARAM

K I N G D O M

PHOENICIA

• Sidon

• Tyre

• Damascus

BASHAN

Jordan R.

Megiddo •

Samaria •
• Shechem

I S R A E L

Kirjath-jearim •
Bethlehem •

Shiloh •
Bethel •
• Jericho

AMMON

GILEAD

Jerusalem •

U N I T E D

A R A B I A

Hebron •

Beer-sheba • • Ziklag

JUDAH

Dead Sea

MOAB

PHILISTIA

EDOM

AMALEK

N

Gulf of Aqabah

• Ezion-geber

80

40

Scale of Miles

0

THE UNITED KINGDOM
UNDER DAVID AND SOLOMON

OUTLINE OF OLD TESTAMENT HISTORY (Continued)

The period of the Judges, which provided only intermittent government, has shown Israel's dire need for a continuous godly leadership. When Saul, Israel's first king, is rejected for disobedience, God gives Israel, in the person of David, a moral and spiritual leadership that unites and strengthens the nation.

The keynote of David's long reign lies in his love for God. David cherishes God's covenant; in turn God makes a covenant with the house of David and the Messianic promise comes into clearer focus. God sets "a light ... in Jerusalem," a light so strong that from this "rod of Jesse," of the tribe of Judah, is to stem "The BRANCH"—the Messiah-King himself.

Read chart upward line by line

United Kingdom (1006-933/32 B.C.)

His kindness to Jonathan's son Mephibosheth
David subdues many enemy nations
Expansion of kingdom II Sam. 8-10; I Chron. 18, 19

(For its Messianic application see Acts 2:30)
It includes a seed, a throne, a kingdom "forever"
God Makes His Covenant with David (Davidic Covenant)

God promises David his son will build His temple
He purposes to build a temple for the Ark II Sam. 7; I Chron. 17

David appoints Levites as ministers, porters, priests, and musicians
Jerusalem becomes the religious center of the nation
He gathers 30,000 men to bring the Ark to Jerusalem II Sam. 6; I Chron. 13, 15, 16

David twice defeats the Philistines II Sam. 5:17-25; I Chron. 14:8-17
David conquers Jerusalem (Zion)—makes it his capital II Sam. 5:6-16; I Chron. 11:4-47

"Thou shalt feed my people Israel, and thou shalt be a captain over Israel."
David anointed king over all the tribes (reigns 33 years) II Sam. 5:1-5; I Chron. 11:1-3; 12:23-40

=== NOW BEGINS THE PERIOD OF THE UNITED KINGDOM, THE UNITED TWELVE TRIBES ===

Abner deserts to David but is slain by Joab—David mourns for Abner—Ish-bosheth is slain
A long war between the house of Saul and the house of David—Joab captains David's army
Ish-bosheth, Saul's son, made king over remaining tribes by Abner, captain of Saul's army
David anointed king over tribe of Judah—at thirty years of age—reigns at Hebron seven years II Sam. 2-4

1013-973 B.C. DAVID

Saul defeated—three sons slain—falls on his own sword—David sorrows
Saul at war with Philistines—consults the witch of Endor I Sam. 28-31; II Sam. 1; I Chron. 10

David flees to Gath—dwells at Ziklag in the land of the Philistines a year and four months I Sam. 27; I Chron. 12:1-22
Outlawed by Saul, David gathers 600 men—pursued by Saul and his army—David twice spares Saul's life—Samuel's death I Sam. 20-26

David marries Michal, daughter of Saul—Saul again tries to kill David—aided by Michal, David escapes and flees to Samuel in Ramah
Jonathan and David make a covenant—David is set over Saul's army—Saul's jealousy—he twice attempts to slay David I Sam. 18, 19
A Philistine army gathers against Israel—David slays the Philistine champion Goliath I Sam. 17

Samuel, under God's direction, goes to Bethlehem to anoint a new king, David, son of Jesse of tribe of Judah I Sam. 16

Samuel sends Saul to destroy Amalek—Saul does not fully obey—he spares king and withholds spoil—God rejects him for disobedience I Sam. 15
Saul's son Jonathan leads attack on Philistine garrison—Saul's oath—his life saved by the people from his father's oath
Saul wars with Philistines—arrogates to himself priestly office—Samuel rebukes him I Sam. 13, 14

1028-1013 B.C. SAUL

A Benjamite, anointed king by Samuel—delivers Jabeshgilead—confirmed king at Gilgal—Samuel chides Israel for ingratitude I Sam. 9-12

Beginning of the Monarchy

SAMUEL

Samuel warns the people of the manner of government under a king—they answer, "Nay; but we will have a king over us."
God comforts Samuel—"They have not rejected thee, but they have rejected me, that I should not reign over them."
Samuel, aged, makes his sons judges—Israel, dissatisfied with their sinful rule, desires a king—"Now make us a king to judge us like all the nations." I Sam. 8

(Transitional period from rule of Judges to establishment of monarchy)

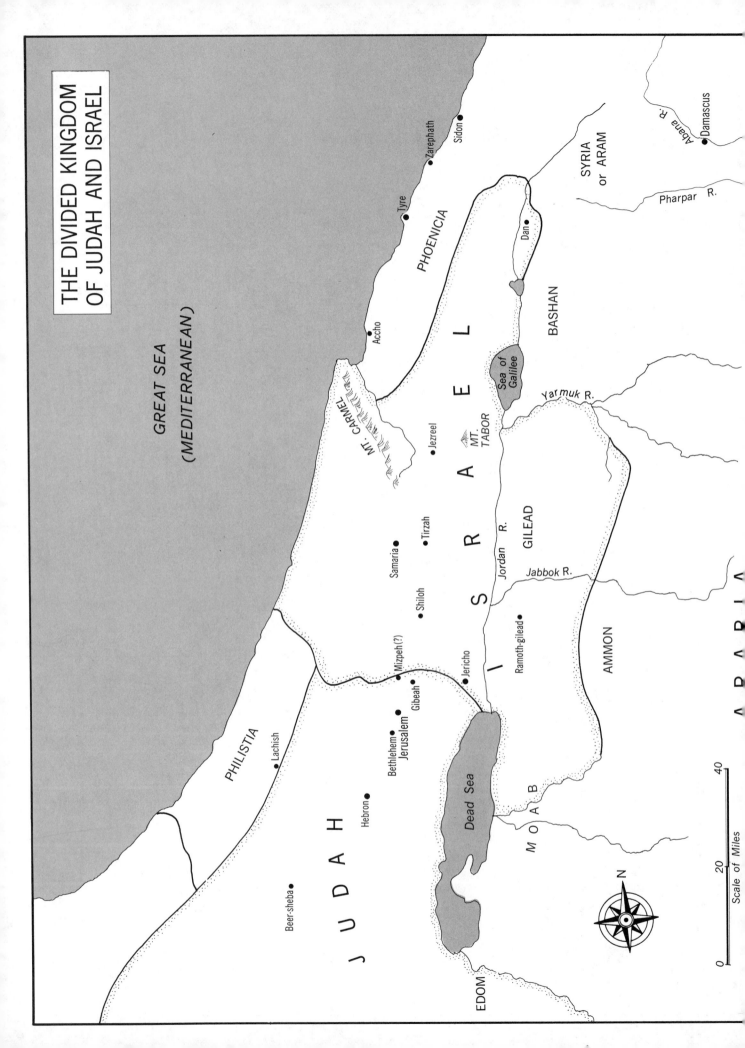

THE DIVIDED KINGDOM
OF JUDAH AND ISRAEL

GREAT SEA
(MEDITERRANEAN)

PHOENICIA

Damascus

Abana R.

SYRIA
or ARAM

Pharpar R.

Sidon

Zarephath

Tyre

Dan

BASHAN

Accho

Sea of
Galilee

Yarmuk R.

MT. CARMEL

Jezreel

MT.
TABOR

I   S   R   A   E   L

Tirzah

Samaria

Jordan R.

GILEAD

Shiloh

Jabbok R.

Mizpeh(?)

Ramoth-gilead

Jericho

AMMON

Bethlehem

Gibeah

Jerusalem

Lachish

PHILISTIA

Dead Sea

J U D A H

Hebron

M   O   A   B

Beer-sheba

EDOM

A R A B I A

N

0   20   40

Scale of Miles

OUTLINE OF OLD TESTAMENT HISTORY (Continued)

Under the reigns of David and his son Solomon, the kingdom moves forward in power, wealth, and prestige. Solomon's magnificent Temple rises as a great monument to Israel's worship of God. Despite his wisdom, Solomon, unable to withstand the temptations of wealth and temporal power, violates God's covenant by turning to worldliness and idolatry. Judgment falls on Solomon in that the kingdom will be rent. But "a light" is to remain in Jerusalem. God's word is: "Howbeit I will not rend away all the kingdom; but will give one tribe to thy son for David my servant's sake, and for Jerusalem's sake which I have chosen" (I Ki. 11:13).

Read chart upward line by line

United Kingdom—Cont.

973-933/32 B.C.
SOLOMON

Jeroboam flees to Egypt—Solomon's death
Solomon therefore seeks Jeroboam's life
Ahijah prophesies ten tribes will defect to Jeroboam

He sets Jeroboam the Ephraimite over house of Joseph
Many adversaries spring up against Solomon

"I will surely rend the kingdom from thee."
Solomon's disobedience and idolatry violate God's covenant
"His wives turned away his heart after other gods."
Solomon's many heathen wives and concubines I Ki. 11; II Chron. 9:29-31

Sought and honored for his wisdom by other kings—visit of queen of Sheba
Builds many cities—his riches, navy, horses, chariots I Ki. 9:10-10:29; II Chron. 8, 9

God Renews the Davidic Covenant with Solomon—A warning I Ki. 9:1-9; II Chron. 7:12-22

Dedication of the Temple—A RENEWAL OF GOD'S COVENANT WITH ISRAEL

Solomon builds the Temple (969 B.C., see I Ki. 6:1)—Seven years in construction
Imposes forced labor on his people to carry out his building projects
Makes a league with Hiram of Tyre for timber and stone for the Temple I Ki. 5-8; II Chron. 2:1-7:11

Solomon enlarges his kingdom—his reign one of peace—his great wisdom and fame I Ki. 4
God appears to him in a vision at Gibeon—prays for wisdom—his judgment concerning a babe
He consolidates the kingdom—Adonijah and Joab are slain—marries Pharaoh's daughter
Solomon succeeds David as king—reigns over United Kingdom forty years I Ki. 2:12-3:28; II Chron. 1

David's charge to Solomon—"serve [God] with a perfect heart . . . willing mind." I Ki. 2:1-11; I Chron. 28, 29
Solomon anointed king—David organizes Temple worship: priestly orders, singers, etc. I Ki. 1:32-53; I Chron. 23-27

Adonijah, son of David, usurps the kingdom—David renews his oath to Bath-sheba to make Solomon his successor I Ki. 1:5-31
He amasses wood, stone, and precious metals—charges Solomon to build the Temple I Chron. 22
Repentant, he purchases the threshingfloor of Araunah (Ornan) to build an altar to God—it becomes future site of the Temple
David commands Joab to number the people—penalty, choice of three plagues—David chooses three days' pestilence II Sam. 24; I Chron. 21

(David's Psalms and Prophecies concerning the Messiah and His Mission [See *A Condensation of the Psalms,* p. 204; *Messianic Prophecies,* p. 337])

He rejoices in God's everlasting covenant—he professes his faith in God's promises II Sam. 23
David's psalm of thanksgiving for deliverance—"The Lord is my rock, and my fortress, and my deliverer." II Sam. 22; Ps. 18
David battles the Philistines—his people enjoin him: "Thou shalt go no more out with us to battle, that thou quench not the light of Israel."
Sheba, a Benjamite, heads a revolt among the tribes—tribe of Judah supports David—Sheba slain II Sam. 20, 21
Absalom conspires against David—David flees from Jerusalem—Absalom slain by Joab—David mourns for Absalom—he returns to Jerusalem at people's entreaty
Joab takes Ammonite city of Rabbah—Amnon, son of David, defiles his sister Tamar—Absalom, son of David, slays Amnon and flees II Sam. 12:26-19:43; I Chron. 20

A son, Solomon, is born to David and Bath-sheba—"And the Lord loved him."
His sin is judged—the child dies—David arises, cleanses himself, and worships in the sanctuary
By parable of the ewe lamb the prophet Nathan causes David to perceive his sin—David confesses—he prays, fasts, and lies upon the earth seven days
David commits adultery with Bath-sheba—he occasions the death of her husband Uriah in battle—Bath-sheba becomes David's wife and bears him a son II Sam. 11:1-12:25; Ps. 51

DAVID

OUTLINE OF THE OLD TESTAMENT (Continued)

The Kingdom of Judah, though often backsliding, adheres to the worship of God. Significant periods of religious reformation, beginning with Asa, prolong its life and enable monotheism to survive. Note the four godly kings.

The measure of Judah's godly kings: "He did that which was right in the sight of the Lord, and walked in the ways of David his father."

Read chart upward line by line

The Kingdom of Israel, the ten rebellious tribes, establishes a counter-worship. Sin and idolatry permeate the nation and cause its eventual destruction.

The measure of Israel's wicked kings: "He . . . walked in the way of Jeroboam, and in his sin."

(SOUTHERN KINGDOM) KINGDOM OF JUDAH

915-875 B.C. ASA

Asa, angry, imprisons Hanani
Prophet Hanani reproves Asa's league

Dismantles Ramah, which Baasha had built
He leagues with Ben-hadad I of Syria
Asa wars with Baasha of Israel over Ramah . . . .

Asa Renews God's Covenant with Judah

Many from Israel return to Judah to worship
Great Religious Reformation

Asa's prayer to God—he overthrows the Ethiopians
A great Ethiopian army under Zerah invades Judah
Ten years of peace—Asa strengthens his kingdom
"Asa did that which was good and right. . . ."
Destroys idolatry—"took away . . . high places. . . ."
(A godly king) Son of Abijam 1 Ki. 15:9-24; II Chron. 14:1-16:10

917-915 B.C. ABIJAM

Abijam, declaring his cause to be right, defeats Jeroboam . . . .
(Abijah) Son of Rehoboam—reigns wickedly—wars with Jeroboam
1 Ki. 15:1-8; II Chron. 13

933/32-917 B.C. REHOBOAM

Punished under the yoke of Shishak of Egypt, Judah repents
Rehoboam and his people, after three years, revert to idolatry
Others, faithful, come from Israel to Jerusalem to worship
Priests and Levites of Israel leave their cities and resort to Judah
"Ye shall not go up, nor fight . . . for this thing is from me."
Judah is forbidden by God through Shemaiah to war against Israel
Rehoboam assembles an army to force the ten tribes to return
Tribes of Judah and Benjamin remain faithful to the House of David
1 Ki. 12:20-24; 14:21-31; II Chron. 11, 12

(Line of David, Messianic line, continues unbroken in Judah)

(NORTHERN KINGDOM) KINGDOM OF ISRAEL

887 B.C. ZIMRI

Zimri destroys himself by fire
Deposed by Elah's captain Zimri
Reigns one week at Tirzah
Zimri destroys House of Baasha
1 Ki. 16:11-20

888-887 B.C. ELAH

Slain by Zimri, his servant
Son of Baasha—reigns wickedly
1 Ki. 16:6-10

911-888 BAASHA

Doom of Baasha's house foretold by Jehu
Ben-hadad I of Syria attacks Israel
Baasha builds Ramah to confine Judah
Baasha and Asa of Judah war continuously . . . .

"walked in the way of Jeroboam. . . ."
He reigns wickedly at Tirzah, the capital
Baasha destroys the House of Jeroboam
1 Ki. 15:16-21,27-34; 16:1-7; II Chron. 16:1-6

912-911 B.C. NADAB

Slain by Baasha, who usurps the throne
"in the way of his father, and in his sin. . . ."
Son of Jeroboam—reigns wickedly 1 Ki. 15:25-28

933/32-912 B.C. JEROBOAM I

Jeroboam is defeated by Abijam, king of Judah
Ahijah foretells child's death and fall of Jeroboam dynasty,
His son being sick, Jeroboam inquires of the prophet Ahijah

Jeroboam's hand is withered—restored by the prophet
Prophecy against Jeroboam's idolatrous altar—altar is rent
The Levites and lawful priests of Israel return to Judah
"He made . . . priests of the lowest of the people. . . ."
He institutes an unlawful and unholy priesthood not of the Levites

"This thing became a sin: for the people went to worship. . . ."
Sets up two golden calves at Beth-el and Dan as symbols of Jehovah
Jeroboam deliberately breaks Israel's religious ties with Jerusalem
Made king of Israel by the ten rebellious tribes 1 Ki. 12:20-14:20;
II Chron. 11:14,15;13:1-20

(Line of succession to throne of Israel is broken repeatedly)

933/932 B.C. — NOW BEGINS THE PERIOD OF THE DIVIDED KINGDOM, JUDAH AND ISRAEL

Ten tribes revolt against Rehoboam, when Rehoboam rejects the counsel of the elders and arrogantly refuses Jeroboam's demand
Jeroboam appears before Rehoboam as a spokesman for the people to demand relief from the heavy tribute of forced labor laid on them by Solomon
Rehoboam, Solomon's son, is heir to the throne—all Israel comes to Shechem intending to make him king 1 Ki. 12:1-19; II Chron. 10

OUTLINE OF OLD TESTAMENT HISTORY (Continued)

In Judah a great religious reformation takes place under Jehoshaphat, and the kingdom prospers. However, three times he makes an "affinity," with apostate Israel, and his son marries Athaliah, daughter of Ahab and Jezebel of Israel.

Israel, though apostate, has not been deserted or cast off. The great prophets Elijah and Elisha are raised up to draw perverse Israel back to God.

Read chart upward line by line

Read chart upward line by line

Kings of Israel (Cont.)

Elisha causes iron to swim
Gehazi's sin and leprosy
Elisha heals Naaman's leprosy
Feeds 100 men with 20 loaves
Elisha heals poisoned pottage
Elisha raises her son from death
Elisha promises son to Shunammite
Elisha multiplies widow's oil
Elisha obtains water—Moabites overcome
Judah and Edom come to Israel's aid
Mesha of Moab rebels against Israel
Heals Jericho's waters—judges irreverence
Receives a double portion of the Spirit
Elisha succeeds Elijah as prophet
Translation of Elijah—Witnessed by Elisha
"He cleaved unto the sins of Jeroboam. . . ."
(Joram) Son of Ahab—reigns wickedly
II Ki. 1:17-6:7

853-843 B.C. JEHORAM

Elijah twice calls fire from heaven to consume them
Ahaziah thrice sends soldiers to apprehend Elijah
Elijah foretells king's death for seeking Baal-zebub
Son of Ahab and Jezebel—reigns wickedly
I Ki. 22:48-53; II Ki. 1; II Chron. 20:35-37

854-853 B.C. AHAZIAH

Ahab seeks Judah's aid against Syrians—slain in battle
Jezebel, by murder, obtains Naboth's vineyard for Ahab
Syrians under Ben-hadad II besiege Samaria—twice defeated
Elijah casts his mantle upon Elisha—Elisha follows him
Elijah is commissioned to anoint Hazael, Jehu, and Elisha
Elijah at Mount Horeb hears the "still small voice"
Slays prophets of Baal—obtains rain—flees from Jezebel's threat
Elijah reproves Ahab—his challenge to Israel at Mount Carmel
Elijah hides at Cherith—sent to Zarephath—raises widow's son
Elijah prophesies a drought (three years) because of Ahab's idolatry
Elijah, a prophet—Labors to lift Israel's standard of religion
Ahab introduces Baal worship in Israel—great apostasy
Ahab marries Jezebel, Zidonian princess and ardent worshiper of Baal
"a light thing for him to walk in the sins of Jeroboam. . . ."
Son of Omri—Israel's most wicked king—"He did very abominably. . . ."
I Ki. 16:29-22:40; II Chron. 18

876-854 B.C. AHAB

Omri builds city of Samaria—makes it the capital of Israel
"He walked in all the way of Jeroboam . . . and in his sin. . . ."
Made king by army—reigns wickedly at Tirzah I Ki. 16:16-28

887-876 B.C. OMRI

KINGDOM OF ISRAEL

Kings of Judah (Cont.)

Marries Athaliah of Israel
(Joram) Son of Jehoshaphat
II Ki. 8:16-18; II Chron. 21:5,6

851-844 B.C. JEHORAM

Miraculous help by prophet Elisha
Jehoshaphat aids Israel against Moabites
II Ki. 3:5-27

Reproved by prophet Eliezer for this alliance
Joins Ahaziah of Israel in building ships
"The battle is not your's, but God's."
King and people pray—miraculous deliverance
Judah is invaded by the Moabites and Ammonites
Places judges in Judah and a council in Jerusalem
Journeys through his kingdom to establish godly worship
He joins Ahab against Syrians—reproved by prophet Jehu
Jehoshaphat makes an alliance with King Ahab of Israel
He sends the Levites throughout Judah to teach Mosaic Law
He promotes the religious education of the people
"He took away the high places . . . out of Judah."
He continues the reformative work of his father Asa
He strengthens his kingdom—reigns well and prospers
"He walked in the first ways of his father David. . . ."
(A godly king) Son of Asa 1 Ki. 15:24; 22:1-50; II Chron. 17-20

875-851 B.C. JEHOSHAPHAT

Dies in the forty-first year of his reign
"Yet in his disease he sought not to the Lord, but to the physicians."
Asa is diseased in his feet 1 Ki. 15:23,24; II Chron. 16:12-14

Asa oppresses some of the people (at the time he imprisons Hanani)
II Chron. 16:10

KINGDOM OF JUDAH

85

OUTLINE OF OLD TESTAMENT HISTORY (Continued)

The idolatry of Israel, seeping into Judah, corrupts the kingdom, and two generations of Judah's kings walk "in the ways of the house of Ahab."

"Howbeit the Lord would not destroy the house of David, because of the covenant that he had made with David. . . ." II Chron. 21:7

Read chart upward line by line

Dynasty succeeds dynasty, but there is no "hearing ear" among Israel's kings.

Read chart upward line by line

Kings of Israel (Cont.)

800-785 B.C. JEHOASH
- Jehoash plunders Jerusalem
- He soundly defeats Judah
- Jehoash provoked to war by Amaziah
- Jehoash defeats Syrians three times
- Elisha dies—his bones revive a dead man
- Elisha foretells victories over Syria
- "departed not from . . . sins of Jeroboam" (Joash) Son of Jehoahaz—reigns wickedly II Ki. 13:10-25; 14:8-16; II Chron. 25:17-24

816-800 B.C. JEHOAHAZ
- By prayer Jehoahaz brings relief to his kingdom
- Jehoahaz oppressed by Hazael
- "followed the sins of Jeroboam. . . ." Son of Jehu—reigns wickedly II Ki. 10:35; 13:1-9

843-816 B.C. JEHU
- Hazael of Syria oppresses all Israel east of Jordan
- "But Jehu took no heed to walk in the law. . . ."
- Jehu is promised his dynasty will reign four generations
- "From the sins of Jeroboam . . . Jehu departed not. . . ."
- Fails to remove the golden calves from Beth-el and Dan
- He exterminates Baal worship in Israel
- He also slays brethren of Ahaziah of Judah
- With bloody zeal Jehu destroys the whole house of Ahab
- Orders death of Jezebel—her body eaten by dogs (cf. I Ki. 21:23)
- Usurps the kingdom II Ki. 9:30-10:36; II Chron. 22:7-9
- Ahaziah visits Jehoram at Jezreel—Jehu slays both kings
- Jehoram and Ahaziah war against Hazael—Jehoram is wounded
- Jehu is proclaimed king by his army captains
- Elisha commands that Jehu destroy the house of Ahab
- Elisha sends a prophet to anoint Jehu king of Israel (cf. I Ki. 19:16)
- Hazael slays Ben-hadad, his master—seizes the throne of Syria
- Ben-hadad ill—Elisha prophesies Hazael will rule Syria (cf. I Ki. 19:15)
- Elisha's prophecy of plenty fulfilled in sudden flight of Syrian army
- Ben-hadad II again besieges Samaria—great famine
- Syrian army smitten with blindness at Elisha's word—army dismissed in peace
- Elisha reveals to Jehoram imminent war plans of Syrian king II Ki. 6:8-8:16,25-29; 9:1-28; II Chron. 22:5-9

JEHORAM

KINGDOM OF ISRAEL

Kings of Judah (Cont.)

798-780 B.C. AMAZIAH
- By conspiracy Amaziah is slain
- Jerusalem plundered by Jehoash
- Ignominiously defeated by Israel
- Provokes Jehoash of Israel to war
- Amaziah worships idols of the Edomites
- Begins reign well—defeats Edomites
- Son of Jehoash II Ki. 14:1-20; II Chron. 25

837-798 B.C. JEHOASH
- Jehoash slain by his servants
- Jehoash appeases Hazael with Temple treasures
- Hazael of Syria comes against Jerusalem
- Kills Jehoiada's son Zechariah for his rebuke
- Jehoash turns to idolatry after Jehoiada's death
- Jehoash repairs the Temple in Jerusalem
- Jehoiada restores true worship of God
- People destroy Baal's temple and its images
- **Jehoiada Renews God's Covenant with Judah**
- Jehoash reigns righteously during life of Jehoiada
- Athaliah is slain at Jehoiada's order
- (Joash) Son of Ahaziah—crowned at age of seven by Jehoiada II Ki. 11:21-12:21; II Chron. 23, 24

843-837 B.C. ATHALIAH
- Joash hidden in Temple six years by Jehosheba and Jehoiada
- Joash saved by Jehosheba, wife of high priest Jehoiada
- Slays all the royal seed except grandson Joash
- Usurps throne II Ki. 11:1-20; II Chron. 22:10-23:15

844-843 B.C. AHAZIAH
- Ahaziah visits Jehoram in Israel—slain by Jehu
- Ahaziah joins Jehoram of Israel in war against Syrians
- "walked in . . . ways of . . . Ahab . . . his mother was his counsellor. . . ."
- Youngest son of Jehoram and Athaliah—reigns wickedly II Ki. 8:25-29; 9:16-29; II Chron. 22:1-9

JEHORAM
- Dies of an incurable disease—"He . . . departed without being desired."
- Philistines and Arabians ravage his kingdom and his house
- A written message of warning against him (ascribed to Elijah)
- Edom and Libnah, a city of Judah, revolt against his rule
- Slays all his royal brothers—Athaliah's evil influence
- Causes Judah "to go a whoring, like to the whoredoms of the house of Ahab. . . ." II Ki. 8:18-24; II Chron. 21

KINGDOM OF JUDAH

OUTLINE OF OLD TESTAMENT HISTORY (Continued)

During the next three hundred fifty years the Major and Minor Prophets appear, some in Judah, others in Israel, to thunder forth God's judgment on unrighteousness, to exhort the nation to repentance, yet at the same time to comfort the righteous with the promise of salvation through the Messiah.

Read chart upward line by line

As Israel refuses to heed its prophets and to reform, its corruption and degeneracy culminate in the nation's downfall. "Israel hath cast off the thing that is good. . . ." Hos. 8:3

Israel, carried captive into Assyria, is scattered, never again to be united . . . .

Kings of Israel (Cont.)

733-722 B.C. HOSHEA
- Heathen peoples colonize Israel
- Israel carried captive to Assyria
- Samaria falls to Sargon of Assyria
- Conspires with Egypt—is imprisoned
- Pays tribute to Shalmaneser of Assyria
- Usurps throne II Ki. 15:30; 17; 18:9-12

- Pekah slain by Hoshea
- He deports many Israelites to Assyria
- Tiglath-pileser invades northern Israel

736-733 B.C. PEKAH
- At warning of prophet Oded, captives are returned
- Brings many captives of Judah to Israel
- Pekah, with Rezin, wars against Ahaz of Judah
- With Rezin of Syria, wars against Jotham of Judah
- Reigns wickedly—follows "the sins of Jeroboam"
- Usurps throne II Ki. 15:25,27-31; 16:5; II Chron. 28:5-15

737-736 B.C. PEKAHIAH
- Slain by Pekah, a captain of his army
- "He departed not from the sins of Jeroboam. . . ."
- Son of Menahem—reigns wickedly II Ki. 15:22-26

743-737 B.C. MENAHEM
- Tiglath-pileser III of Assyria invades Israel—exacts tribute
- "He departed not . . . from the sins of Jeroboam. . . ."
- Usurps throne—reigns wickedly II Ki. 15:14,16-22

744 B.C. SHALLUM
- Usurps throne one month—slain by Menahem II Ki. 15:10,13-15

744 B.C. ZACHARIAH
- Slain by Shallum—(fall of house of Jehu)
- "He departed not from the sins of Jeroboam. . . ."
- Son of Jeroboam II—reigns wickedly II Ki. 14:29; 15:8-12

785-745 B.C. JEROBOAM II
- Hosea comforts Israel with God's promises of mercy and reconciliation
- Hosea, a prophet—Declares judgment on nation's whoredom Bk. of Hosea
- Amos pronounces judgments on Israel and Judah—prophesies captivities
- Amos, a prophet—A Judaean Bk. of Amos
- Jonah, a prophet (Book of Jonah probably written at a later date)
- Jeroboam recovers lost territories of Israel—great material prosperity
- "He departed not from all the sins of Jeroboam. . . ."
- Son of Jehoash—reigns wickedly II Ki. 14:23-29

KINGDOM OF ISRAEL

Kings of Judah (Cont.)

- Hezekiah refuses to serve Assyria
- Ahaz's son Hezekiah co-rules (?) II Ki. 18:1-10

735-720 B.C. AHAZ
- *Blessings of the Messianic Kingdom*
- Isaiah's prophetic labors Is. 11-36
- He closes the doors of the Temple
- Ahaz sins in worshiping gods of Damascus
- He meets Tiglath-pileser III at Damascus
- Ahaz buys Assyria's aid with Temple treasures
- Micah continues to prophesy
- *Isaiah Prophesies Sign of the Coming Messiah*
- Isaiah warns against such an alliance Is. 7-10
- Ahaz seeks aid of Assyria (See II Chron. 28:16-19)
- Great slaughter and many captives taken
- Kings of Israel and Syria attempt to depose Ahaz
- "walked in the way of the kings of Israel"
- Son of Jotham—reigns wickedly II Ki. 16; II Chron. 28

740-735 B.C. JOTHAM
- Pekah of Israel and Rezin of Syria war against Judah
- Micah, a prophet—Begins his labors Bk. of Micah
- Isaiah continues to prophesy
- He subdues the Ammonites and exacts tribute
- "Howbeit he entered not into the temple of the Lord."
- Jotham reigns well—prospers and becomes powerful
- Son of Azariah—accedes to throne II Ki. 15:7,32-38; II Chron. 27

780-740 B.C. AZARIAH
- Isaiah's call and vision of God's glory—the promise of a remnant
- *Isaiah Prophesies the Coming of the Messianic Kingdom*
- Isaiah, a prophet—Great patriot and statesman Is. 1-6
- Azariah's son Jotham becomes regent
- Angry at rebuke, Azariah is smitten with leprosy
- He transgresses by usurping the priestly office—rebuked by priests
- "But when . . . strong, his heart was lifted up to his destruction. . . ."
- "As long as he sought the Lord, God made him to prosper."
- (Uzziah) Son of Amaziah—begins his reign well—strengthens his kingdom II Ki. 14:21,22; 15:1-7; II Chron. 26

KINGDOM OF JUDAH

OUTLINE OF OLD TESTAMENT HISTORY (Continued)

Great religious reforms take place in Judah during the reigns of Hezekiah and Josiah, but these periodic movements do not succeed in expunging Judah's pleasure in idolatry.

Jeremiah warns: "Thine own wickedness shall correct thee, and thy backslidings shall reprove thee: know therefore and see that it is an evil thing and bitter, that thou hast forsaken the Lord thy God, and that my fear is not in thee, saith the Lord God of hosts."

Read chart upward line by line

The Kingdom of Judah

720-692 B.C. HEZEKIAH
(A godly king) Son of Ahaz—in first month he opens the Temple which his father had closed II Ki. 18-20; II Chron. 29-32; Is. 36-39
"He did that which was right in the sight of the Lord, according to all that David his father did."
Great religious reformation—Temple is cleansed and sacrificial worship restored—king invites Judah and former Israel to observe the Passover at Jerusalem
God's Covenant Is Renewed—People return home to destroy their idols—the tithes due the Levites are restored
Sennacherib of Assyria invades Judah—sends his army officer Rab-shakeh to demand Jerusalem's surrender
Hezekiah prays and sends for Isaiah—Isaiah prophesies against Sennacherib—Jerusalem is delivered and Assyrian army smitten
Hezekiah's sickness—by his prayer his life is lengthened by fifteen years
Unwisely shows treasures of kingdom to king of Babylon—reproved by Isaiah who foretells Judah's captivity in Babylon
Isaiah prophesies restoration of Judah—*Prophesies the Messiah, His Church, His Redemption, His Glory* Is. 40-66

Micah Prophesies the Coming Messiah Mic. 5

692-638 B.C. MANASSEH
Son of Hezekiah—reigns wickedly—reintroduces idolatry—builds altars to Baal II Ki. 21:1-18; II Chron. 33:1-20
Places a graven image in the Temple—practices heathen abominations
Carried captive to Babylon by king of Assyria—he humbles himself before God
He is restored to his kingdom—cleanses Jerusalem of idolatry

638 B.C. AMON
Son of Manasseh—reigns wickedly—"trespassed more and more." II Ki. 21:18-26; II Chron. 33:21-25
Amon is slain by his servants, who in turn are slain by the people

638-608 B.C. JOSIAH
(A godly king) Son of Amon—reigns at the age of eight II Ki. 22:1-23:30; II Chron. 34, 35
Begins "to seek after the God of David" (in eighth year of his reign)
Zephaniah, a prophet—Pronounces judgment on Judah Bk. of Zephaniah
Zephaniah sees Judah's retribution for sin as a foreshadowing of the Day of the Lord
Great religious reformation (in twelfth year)—Destroys idolatry throughout Judah
Jeremiah, a prophet—His call and heavy message against Judah Jer. 1:1,2; 3:6
Josiah repairs the Temple (in eighteenth year)—Book of the Law found in Temple
Terrified by curses of Mosaic Law, he humbles himself—seeks prophetess Huldah
Calls a solemn assembly in Jerusalem—Book of the Law read to the people
God's Covenant Is Renewed—"all the people stood to the covenant"
"all his days they departed not from following the Lord. . . ."
Nahum, a prophet—Foretells fall of Nineveh Bk. of Nahum
He pronounces judgment on Assyria for its violence and sin
Jeremiah rebukes Judah for playing the harlot (as did Israel)
Josiah provokes Necho, king of Egypt—slain at Megiddo

608 B.C. JEHOAHAZ
(Shallum) Son of Josiah—reigns wickedly 23:30-34; II Chron. 36:1-4; Jer. 22:10-12
Jehoahaz deposed by Necho—carried into Egypt

═══ KINGDOM OF JUDAH CONTINUES ALONE FOR NEARLY A CENTURY AND A HALF ═══

OUTLINE OF OLD TESTAMENT HISTORY (Continued)

In Judah the judgment can no longer be stayed; the nation is taken into captivity in Babylon, there to be purged of its idolatry. "The Lord God of their fathers sent to them by his messengers, rising up betimes, and sending; because he had compassion on his people, and on his dwelling place: But they mocked the messengers of God, and despised his words, and misused his prophets, until the wrath of the Lord arose against his people, till there was no remedy." II Chron. 36:15,16

Even so, the reforms initiated by the godly kings and the teachings of the prophets are so deeply implanted that the essence of spiritual religion will be sustained throughout Judah's captivity.

Read chart upward line by line

Land of Judah under Babylonian Rule

Jeremiah prophesies their punishment

"We will not hearken unto thee."

The people follow idolatrous gods of Egypt

The people disbelieve—they carry Jeremiah to Egypt

Jeremiah assures people of safety if they remain in Judah

Gedaliah slain—the remnant purpose to escape to Egypt

Jeremiah chooses to remain with remnant in Judah

Gedaliah appointed governor over poor left in Judah

(Mourning for Jerusalem, see Bk. of Lamentations)

Nebuchadnezzar frees Jeremiah from prison II Ki. 25:22-26; Jer. 39:10-44:30

=== 586 B.C.—FALL OF THE KINGDOM OF JUDAH ===

Third deportation—Judah is carried captive to Babylon

Jerusalem and Temple plundered—city burned and walls leveled

Jerusalem falls to Nebuchadnezzar—Zedekiah taken captive to Babylon

Zedekiah imprisons Jeremiah for his dire prophecies

Nebuchadnezzar besieges Jerusalem—lifts siege temporarily to war with Egypt Jer. 37:1-39:9

Ezekiel begins to prophesy among the captives of Judah in Babylon

Prophesies the New Covenant—"I will put my law in their inward parts, and write it in their hearts. . . ."

Jeremiah prophesies restoration of the remnant—prophesies the Messiah Jer. 23; 24; 30:1-34:22

Zedekiah rebels against Nebuchadnezzar—refuses Jeremiah's counsel—Jeremiah suffers continued persecution Jer. 20

597-586 B.C. ZEDEKIAH (Mattaniah) Son of Josiah—reigns wickedly II Ki. 24:17-25:21; II Chron. 36:10-21; Jer. 21; 27:12-28:17; 52:1-30

Jeremiah comforts the captives—encourages them to endure and to wait for restoration Jer. 29

Second Deportation of Captives—Jehoiachin and 10,000 men, including Ezekiel, carried captive to Babylon

Nebuchadnezzar besieges Jerusalem again—strips the Temple of all its treasures

597 B.C. JEHOIACHIN (Coniah, Jeconiah) Son of Jehoiakim—reigns wickedly three months II Ki. 24:8-16; 25:27-30; II Chron. 36:8-10; Jer. 22:24-30; 52:31-34

Habakkuk, a prophet—Predicts the fall of Chaldea (Babylon)—pronounces judgment upon Chaldea for its violence and sin

First Deportation of Captives—Daniel, a prince of Judah, is among the captives Dan. 1:3-6

Jehoiakim rebels against Babylon—Nebuchadnezzar besieges Jerusalem—Jehoiakim carried captive to Babylon

606 B.C.

Jeremiah's prophetic labors—his life endangered—his warnings unheeded—his roll of prophecies burned by king—prophecies redictated

Jeremiah prophesies Judah's seventy years' captivity—He foretells God's judgments against heathen nations Jer. 22:13-19; 25:1-27:11; 35; 36; 45-49

(In 606 B.C. Nineveh, capital of Assyria, falls to Nebuchadnezzar, marking rise of new Babylonian Empire)

Jehoiakim exacts tribute of his people for Egypt—becomes a vassal of Nebuchadnezzar, king of Babylon

608-597 B.C. JEHOIAKIM (Eliakim) Brother of Jehoahaz and son of Josiah—placed on throne by Necho of Egypt—reigns wickedly II Ki. 23:34-24:6; II Chron. 36:4-8; Dan. 1:1,2

Kingdom of Judah

OUTLINE OF OLD TESTAMENT HISTORY (Continued)

God's great Messianic plan of redemption is in no way altered by the fall of Judah or its captivity in Babylon. God's covenant with His chosen people remains unbroken; there is a righteous remnant to be saved and restored.

In exile rebellious Judah mourns for beloved Jerusalem and the Temple. In the fiery furnace of affliction the nation looks inward to effect a deeper repentance and a purer monotheism, strengthened by the wisdom and example of faithful leaders. On release from captivity, only those willing to strive for the rebuilding and restoration of Zion—"a willing remnant"—undertake the return journey to Jerusalem.

Read chart upward line by line

Restoration Period

536-515 B.C.
ZERUBBABEL

Royal decree stops work for fifteen years
They send a malicious letter to King Artaxerxes
Samaritans then vindictively hinder the building

Zerubbabel and chief Jews refuse their help
Samaritans (adversaries) offer aid in building Temple
Foundation of the Temple laid in second year of return
Temple altar set up in seventh month—sacrificial worship resumed

They take with them the sacred vessels of the Temple restored by Cyrus
Zerubbabel leads a willing remnant of Jews to Judaea (about 50,000)
Son of Shealtiel—in Messianic line—appointed governor of Judaea Ezra 1-4 (Mt. 1:12)

====== BEGINNING OF THE RESTORATION ======

The Exile (Captivity) of Judah in Babylon

536 B.C.
End of Judah's captivity
The people make preparation for their return to Jerusalem

538 B.C.
Cyrus issues proclamation for rebuilding of Temple in Jerusalem II Chron. 36:22,23; Ezra 1:1-4
(Cyrus of Persia conquers Babylon in 539 B.C.)

His vision of seventy weeks—*Foretells Time of Messiah's Coming and of His Cutting Off*
Daniel prays for restoration of Jerusalem and the sanctuary
Daniel's Apocalyptic Visions: rise of four Gentile kingdoms, superseded by Christ's kingdom Dan. 2; 7-12

Princes conspire against Daniel—his miraculous delivery from lions' den—king's decree honoring God
Darius the Mede rules (identity not known in secular history)—Daniel placed next in power to king

Daniel alone is able to interpret handwriting; the kingdom is to fall—Belshazzar slain this same night
King Belshazzar desecrates Temple vessels at an impious feast—the mysterious handwriting on the wall

Daniel interprets Nebuchadnezzar's second dream—king's madness and return to sanity—king's pride is humbled
Daniel's three companions cast into a fiery furnace for refusing obeisance to king's golden image—God delivers them

Daniel interprets Nebuchadnezzar's forgotten dream of a great image of gold, silver, bronze, iron, and clay—Daniel promoted
Daniel and three companions, chosen to king's court, abstain from defilement by refusing to eat the king's food—they excel in wisdom
A prophet—A captive of first deportation (contemporary with Jeremiah and Ezekiel) Dan. 1-6

606-536 B.C.
DANIEL

Obadiah, a prophet—Predicts doom of Edom for violence against Judah and for its unholy joy over Jerusalem's fall Bk. of Obadiah

Ezekiel's vision of the ideal temple—"And, behold, the glory of the Lord filled the house." Ezek. 40-48

His vision of the valley of dry bones—his symbol of two sticks—the promise of an everlasting covenant of peace
Ezekiel prophesies restoration of a remnant of Judah, their purification and reformation Ezek. 33-39

Prophesies judgments against heathen nations Ezek. 25-32

He prophesies destruction of Jerusalem—sees in a vision that God's glory has departed from it (Ezek. 11:23)
As a watchman he speaks to "the whole house of Israel"—sternly teaches rebellious Judah their captivity is result of their breach of God's covenant
Prophet-priest—A captive of second deportation—receives his call and commission (Ezek. 1-3)—his many apocalyptic visions Ezek. 4-24

====== JUDAH'S SEVENTY YEARS' EXILE IN BABYLON (Reckoned from first deportation in 606 B.C. to Jews' return to Judah in 536 B.C.) ======

592-570 B.C.
EZEKIEL

OUTLINE OF OLD TESTAMENT HISTORY (Continued)

With the building of the Second Temple and the possession of the Pentateuch, the written law, the returned remnant of Judah experiences a fresh spiritual impetus. The nation's unity is centered no longer in the monarchy but in the Judaic ecclesiastical system, which for the next four centuries is to nurture a strict monotheism.

Israel now stands waiting for the coming of the Messiah. "Behold, I will send my messenger, and he shall prepare the way before me: and the Lord, whom ye seek, shall suddenly come to his temple, even the messenger of the covenant, whom ye delight in: behold, he shall come, saith the Lord of hosts." Mal. 3:1

Read chart upward line by line

═══════ 432 B.C.—CLOSE OF OLD TESTAMENT HISTORY AND PROPHECY ═══════

"Behold, he shall come, saith the Lord...."
Malachi Prophesies the Advent of the Messiah
Strives to deepen the nation's love for God's covenant
Malachi condemns the sins of the priests and people
Malachi, a prophet—Last to restored remnant Bk. of Malachi

432 B.C.   (Foundation of Judaic ecclesiastical system is firmly laid)
433 B.C.   He returns to Jerusalem to enforce severe measures of reform
Nehemiah recalled to Persia—mixed marriages and abuses of Law appear

Israel's Ancient Covenant Renewed by the Nation
Ezra and Nehemiah teach the Law to the people from the Pentateuch
Ezra reappears in Jerusalem with Pentateuch (the Five Books of the Law) Neh. 8-13

The wall finished in fifty-two days — "for the people had a mind to work"
Nehemiah restores civil authority and institutes social reforms
Enemies conspire to stop the work—Nehemiah prays, sets a watch, arms his workmen
Sent to Jerusalem as governor of Judaea—encourages the people to rebuild the city's walls
445 B.C.   Cupbearer to Artaxerxes—learns of the distress of the remnant in Jerusalem Neh. 1-7
NEHEMIAH

He calls an assembly at Jerusalem—the men repent and give up their foreign wives
Ezra corrects religious abuses—mourns people's sin of intermarriage with idolatrous neighbors
Ezra leads a willing remnant to Jerusalem—second expedition of about 7000 Jews
458 B.C.   Artaxerxes' decree to Ezra: "all . . . minded of their own freewill to go up to Jerusalem, go with thee."
EZRA   Priest and scribe during reign of Artaxerxes I Longimanus of Persia Ezra 7-10

Jews remaining in Persia are saved from extermination by Esther, Jewish queen of King Ahasuerus (Xerxes) Bk. of Esther
ca. **483 B.C.**

Joel, a prophet—Foretells the Day of the Lord and the outpouring of the Spirit upon all men (Joel's date is uncertain)

Second Temple is dedicated—Priestly and Levitical offices are reestablished—Passover observed
515 B.C.

Darius finds Cyrus' decree and confirms it—forwards the building by contributions from his treasury
Tatnai is informed of Cyrus' decree—sends a letter to King Darius of Persia (Darius Hystaspes?) that search be made in archives
Zerubbabel and Jeshua commence again to build the Temple—Tatnai, Persian governor, questions their right to build Ezra 5:2-6:22

Zechariah Foretells the Messiah and the Glory of His Messianic Kingdom—"I will bring forth my servant the BRANCH."
Zechariah, a prophet—A contemporary of Haggai—also promotes building of the Temple—his many apocalyptic visions Bk. of Zechariah

Haggai prophesies the glory of this Second Temple—pronounces God's blessing on Zerubbabel, who stands as a signet of Israel's hope
Encourages Zerubbabel and his priest Jeshua—rouses people to action—"Is it time for you . . . to dwell in your cieled houses, and this house lie waste?"
ZERUBBABEL   Haggai, a prophet—In 520 B.C. rebukes the restored and divided remnant for neglecting to build the Temple Ezra 5:1; Bk. of Haggai

The Restoration Period

The Bible is silent regarding Jewish history from the time of Nehemiah and Malachi to the Advent of the Messiah, a period of more than 400 years during which great historical changes were taking place not only in Palestine but in the nations around it.

For historical data bearing on Palestine during this intertestamental period we must turn to secular sources. Five ruling powers rose to dominance, one after the other, each making an impact on the culture, religious development, and political fortunes of the Messianic people (see also pp. 213-15).

ALEXANDER THE GREAT

356-323 B.C.

336 B.C.—Alexander the Great, son of Philip of Macedon, reigns at age of twenty

334—Begins conquest of Persian Empire in Asia and Syria

332—Invades Egypt—founds city of Alexandria

331—Conquers Persia

327—Invades India

323—Dies in Babylon—his Macedonian Empire is divided among his generals—those territories which affect Biblical history are those given to Ptolemy (who received Egypt and Palestine and was founder of the dynasty of the Ptolemies) and to Seleucus (who received Asia Minor, Syria, and Persia, and was founder of the dynasty of the Seleucids)

Alexander the Great was a pupil of the great Greek philosopher Aristotle. He was twenty years of age when he began his conquest of the eastern world. In the short span of thirteen years he marched his army through Asia Minor, Syria, Palestine, Egypt, Medo-Persia, north to the Caspian Sea, through Parthia, and across the Indus river into India.

Brilliant though his exploits were, his great contribution to world history was the spread of Greek culture (*Hellenism*) and the Greek language over the Near East, thus uniting East and West (a most important preparation for the advent of Jesus Christ and the reception of Christianity).

". . . he, first of all men, was ready to transcend national differences, and to declare, as St. Paul was to declare, that there was neither Greek nor barbarian."[1]

THE PTOLEMIES

323-198 B.C.

323-285 B.C.—Ptolemy I (Soter)—a Macedonian, Alexander's general

320—Takes Jerusalem—carries a number of Jews to Egypt—favorable treatment of the Jews draws many to city of Alexandria—he founds the Library of Alexandria

285-247—Ptolemy II (Philadelphus)—Septuagint Version (LXX), translation of Hebrew Scriptures into Greek, is begun

247-222—Ptolemy III invades Syria

222-205—Ptolemy IV (Philopater)

205-181—Ptolemy V (Epiphanes)—is defeated by Antiochus III of Syria in 200 B.C.

198—Palestine passes into control of Syrian kings

In the division of Alexander's Empire, Egypt and Palestine fell to Ptolemy who was to found in Egypt the dynasty of the Ptolemies.

Ptolemy I founded the great Library of Alexandria, which became a flourishing seat of learning in the arts, sciences, and literature. It contained upward of seven hundred thousand manuscripts. About 250 B.C. under Ptolemy II seventy devout Jews of Alexandria began the translation of the Hebrew sacred writings into the Greek language for Greek-speaking Jews; completion required about two centuries. This version was known as the Septuagint Version or LXX. This was a further invaluable contribution in preparing the world for Christianity.

The Scriptures were henceforth to permeate the Greek-speaking world, proclaiming to that world the One God and the expectation of a Messianic king.

SYRIAN KINGS (SELEUCIDS)	MACCABEES (Hasmonaeans)	THE ROMANS
198-163 B.C.	167-63 B.C.	From 63 B.C.

SYRIAN KINGS (SELEUCIDS)

198-163 B.C.

198 B.C.—Antiochus III (The Great) of the Seleucid dynasty, ruling from 223-187, wrests Palestine and Coele-Syria from the Egyptian king, Ptolemy V

189—Loses Asia Minor to the Romans

187-175—Seleucus IV rules

175-163—Antiochus IV (Epiphanes) forces Hellenistic culture on the Jews—attempts to destroy the Jewish religion

168—Defiles the Temple in Jerusalem

167—Jews revolt against Syrian rule under the leadership of Mattathias, a priest of the house of Hashmon, provoked by the persecutions of Antiochus IV

The Seleucid dynasty established after the death of Alexander did not bear heavily upon the history of Palestine until Antiochus III defeated Ptolemy V and seized Palestine and Coele-Syria (the valley between the Lebanon and the Anti-Lebanon mountain ranges).

After the accession of Antiochus IV (Epiphanes) bitter persecution of the Jews ensued. He deliberately attempted extermination of Jewish religion in order to establish Hellenism. He instituted pagan worship, and defiled the Temple by offering a sow upon its alter. (Daniel 8:13 speaks of "the transgression of desolation." This defilement is a type of "the abomination of desolation" [Mt. 24:15].) Circumcision, Sabbath-keeping, and possession of copies of the Law were forbidden on pain of death. He slew thousands of the Jews. These persecutions and cruelties roused the Jews to revolt and led to the rise of the Maccabean family.

MACCABEES (Hasmonaeans)

167-63 B.C.

167 B.C.—Mattathias and sons revolt against Antiochus IV

166-160—Judas Maccabaeus—cleanses Temple—restores Jewish worship—institutes Feast of Dedication (165)

160-143—Jonathan Maccabaeus

143-135—Simon Maccabaeus—obtains independence for Jewish state from Antiochus VII—governorship and high priesthood bestowed on Maccabean house by the Jews

135-105—John Hyrcanus I, son of Simon—rise of Pharisaic and Sadducean sects

105-69—Reigns of: Aristobulus I, Alexander Jannaeus (rule marked by civil war between Pharisees and Sadducees), and Queen Alexandra, with son Hyrcanus II as high priest

69-63—Aristobulus II deposes his brother Hyrcanus II—civil war—appeal to Pompey

---

The aged priest Mattathias rose in rebellion against cruelties of Antiochus IV, and with his five sons led a religious revolt. The Jews rallied to the cause and from the hills fought guerrilla fashion against the Syrians.

Judas Maccabaeus, succeeding his father, thrice defeated Antiochus IV. He purified the Temple of pagan pollutions, set up a new altar, and restored the worship of the One God. He instituted the Feast of Dedication to mark restored Jewish worship.

Judas' successors won political independence from Syria and obtained for the Maccabean house the high priesthood. For nearly one hundred years Judaea experienced a period of freedom from oppression.

In 63 B.C. two brothers of the Maccabean house, Aristobulus II and Hyrcanus II, warred with each other over the right of succession; their appeal to the Roman general Pompey opened the door to Roman rule in Palestine.

THE ROMANS

From 63 B.C.

63 B.C.—Pompey, Roman general, captures Jerusalem—Palestine passes to Roman rule

63-40—Hyrcanus II reinstated as high priest and governor

47—Antipater, procurator of Judaea under Julius Caesar

47—Herod the Great, son of Antipater, governs Galilee

44—Julius Caesar assassinated—Antony receives Palestine

40-4—Herod the Great made king of Judaea by Antony (this is the Herod ruling at time of Jesus' birth, see p. 223)

27 B.C.-14 A.D.—Augustus Caesar reigns as Roman Emperor

4 B.C.-39 A.D.—Herod Antipas, son of Herod the Great, made tetrarch of Galilee and Peraea (ruling at time of Jesus' public ministry)

14-37 A.D.—Tiberias, Emperor

26-36—Pontius Pilate, procurator of Judaea under Tiberias

The Roman Republic founded in 300 B.C. was nearing its end when Pompey captured Jerusalem. At this time Palestine came under Roman rule and Rome henceforth exacted yearly tribute of the Jews but granted them religious liberty and a degree of political freedom.

The Republic was succeeded by the First Triumvirate (Julius Caesar, Pompey, and Crassus, 60 B.C.) and the Second Triumvirate (Octavianus, Antony, and Lepidus, 43 B.C.). Antony, who inherited Palestine at the death of Caesar, made Herod the Great king of Judaea and the Herodian house wielded a strong influence in Palestine for three-quarters of a century.

The Triumvirates of the Roman State were in turn succeeded by emperor rule, and Augustus Caesar (Octavianus) became the first Roman emperor. Law and justice distinguished his reign and a world at peace marked the long-awaited coming of Jesus Christ—"the Saviour of the world."

THE PLUMBLINE

A plumbline or a plummet is a heavy weight suspended from a line. This instrument is used by carpenters in building to test verticality—to determine the accuracy and precision of their work. Figuratively the word means "to test." Amos used the plumbline as a figure to teach Israel that God's judgments were just, impartial, and exacting: "Behold, the Lord stood upon a wall made by a plumbline, with a plumbline in his hand. And the Lord said unto me, Amos, what seest thou? And I said, A plumbline. Then said the Lord, Behold, I will set a plumbline in the midst of my people Israel: I will not again pass by them any more" (Amos 7:7,8). Isaiah said of God's justice: "Judgment also will I lay to the line, and righteousness to the plummet: and the hail shall sweep away the refuge of lies, and the waters shall overflow the hiding place" (Is. 28:17).

In the Old Testament the Law and the prophets set the plumbline of righteousness; in the New Testament Jesus set the plumbline of his example and gospel. Consecration, obedience, and love of God bring men's lives into alignment with God's will and purpose.

The Scriptural illustrations below show thought and action brought into line with divine demand.

God said to Abram, "Walk before me, and be thou perfect."
"And Abram fell on his face" Gen. 17:1,3

"God called unto him [Moses] "
Moses said, "Here am I." Ex. 3:4

"the Lord came, and stood, and called"
Samuel said. "Thy servant heareth." I Sam. 3:10

"the angel . . . said, Arise and eat"
Elijah "arose . . . did eat . . . and went" I Ki. 19:7,8

The Lord said, "Whom shall I send?"
Isaiah said, "Here am I; send me." Is. 6:8

God said, "Son of man . . . eat this roll, and go speak"
Then did I [Ezekiel] eat it . . ." Ezek. 1:1,3

"power of the Highest shall overshadow"
Mary said, "Be it unto me according to thy word." Lu. 1:35,38

"the star . . . went before them [the Magi] "
"till it came and stood over where the young child was" Mt. 2:9

"Jesus tarried . . . in the temple"
"wist ye not that I must be about my Father's business?" Lu. 2:43,46,49

"I [Jesus] send the promise of my Father"
"tarry ye . . . until ye be endued with power from on high" Lu. 24:49

"a light from heaven . . . and . . . a voice"
Saul asked, "What wilt thou have me to do?" Acts 9:3,4,6

See also:

"rose up, and went" . . . . Gen. 22:3	"Be ye therefore perfect" . . . . Mt. 5:48
"Here am I" . . . . Gen. 22:11	"they that were ready" . . . . Mt. 25:10
"Here am I" . . . . Gen. 46:2	"served God . . . night and day" . . . . Lu. 2:37
"face to face" . . . . Ex. 33:11	"sitting at the feet of Jesus" . . . . Lu. 8:35
"look straight before thee" . . . . Pr. 4:25	"hath chosen that good part" . . . . Lu. 10:42
"eye to eye" . . . . Is. 52:8	"a manchild . . . to rule" . . . . Rev. 12:5

4

Great Old Testament Characters

Any Bible reader needs to be thoroughly familiar with the outstanding characters of Old Testament history. These great men, among them Abraham, Moses, David, Isaiah, Nehemiah, are its soul and conscience, and their lives form fascinating links in the chronicle of human development. These were men who communed consciously with the Almighty. They caught glimpses of the divine nature and purpose. They heard God's voice when He spoke. They acted in consonance with His commands, and their actions had a strong impact on their people and on the mainstream of religious history.

The obedience of one man—Noah—to the divine command "Make thee an ark" preserved the spiritual seed of the woman of Genesis 3:15. The obedience of Abraham to the directive "Get thee out of thy country . . . unto a land that I will shew thee" started mankind on a search for truth with a new awareness of God's covenant relationship with man. Moses' compliance with God's command "Come now . . . that thou mayest bring forth my people . . . out of Egypt" resulted in a world being given the revelation of God's moral and spiritual law.

Though they reached great heights of spiritual insight and trust in God, these pioneers of faith were thoroughly human; their biographies, so clearly drawn by Old Testament writers, reveal not only their virtues but also their frailties and defects. "These characters are indeed specimen characters, models, as it were, for all time for the study of the Science of Man."[1] They blazed a trail of faith which has quickened the pace of mankind's spiritual journey. They are our friends; and we cannot be too grateful that the strength of their faith and vision and the lessons of their lives have come down to us in our Bible.

Each character presentation contains (1) a list of the events of the man's life for quick reference; (2) a brief study of the man and his period of history; and (3) Scriptural passages that show the measure of the man. In presenting these characters in this manner, the history of the Old Testament is linked together and shows a continuous chain of growing revelation.

Gen. 2:6-5:5

Adam: "make," "produce," "red," "ruddy," "soil," "ground"

Adam, the Biblical name given first human being—according to second account of creation (Gen. 2), Adam is formed of the dust of the ground by Jehovah

Placed in the garden of Eden—forbidden to eat of the tree of the knowledge of good and evil

Lord God forms every living creature out of the ground—brings them to Adam that he may name them

Eve, Adam's wife, is formed from Adam's rib

The temptation—serpent deceives Eve—fall of man—serpent cursed

The seed of the woman (first promise of the Redeemer)

Mankind's punishment

Expulsion of Adam and Eve from Eden

Adam's sons: Cain and Abel—Cain slays Abel

Seth, third son, is born—"then began men to call upon the name of the Lord"

Adams's days, 930 years

ADAM is the Scriptural name for the first human being, the person designated as the progenitor of the human race. He is identified with the fall of man, and stands, figuratively, for original sin.

Genesis sets forth two records of creation. A study of the sources reveals that they were drawn from two different documents: the first account (Gen. 1:1-2:4a) from the Priestly Code, the second (Gen. 2:4b ff.) from the Jehovistic Document. The second account "is written from the naive and primitive standpoint of legendary tradition, which dealt only with man's reception of physical life."[2] According to the first record, Elohim created; according to the second, Yahweh (Jehovah, Lord God) formed. (See pp. 145, 146.)

The name *Adam* first appears in chapter 2. It is, in the main, a collective noun pertaining to man, mankind, rather than to a single individual. Some consider this narrative of Adam an allegory; others look upon it as a literal account.

Formed by the Lord God out of "the dust of the ground," who "breathed into his nostrils the breath of life," man became a living soul. He was placed in the garden of Eden "to dress it and to keep it." Adam was shown the tree of life and the tree of the knowledge of good and evil. Of the latter he was commanded not to eat, "for in the day that thou eatest thereof thou shalt surely die." Here appears the first indication of a moral choice.

But Adam was alone. In the creation of the animal kingdom which followed there was found no "help meet for him," so the Lord God "caused a deep sleep to fall upon Adam" and from his rib He formed woman. This human pair, of the same flesh, differing from all other pairs, were one, and dwelt in Eden in a state of innocence.

The narration continues with the appearance of a talking serpent ("representing the spirit of revolt from God"[3]) to tempt, to deceive, and to rob them of their innocence by the invitation to eat of the tree of the knowledge of good and evil. The serpent promised: "Ye shall not surely die: for God doth know that in the day ye eat thereof, then your eyes shall be opened, and ye shall be as gods, knowing good and evil." They partook of the forbidden fruit; their eyes were opened, they discovered they were naked, and in fear and shame "hid themselves from the presence of the Lord God." Here appears the first exercise of moral choice, of the human will to be obedient or disobedient, and the first faint stirrings of conscience.

On this sin of disobedience fell divine judgment and expulsion from paradise, but close upon this judgment came the promise of a Redeemer. This promise laid the foundation of the whole Biblical system of redemption, and gave to Adam and his posterity a hope of salvation (Gen. 3:15). "And I will put enmity between thee [the serpent] and the woman, and between thy seed and her seed; it shall bruise thy head, and thou shalt bruise his heel."

> All that this passage tells us is that this Redeemer will be a member of the Adamic race in need of salvation. . . . The nature of His person and work cannot be surmised by this passage and these are to appear step by step throughout the coming centuries. But we now know that He will be a member of our race, and the Biblical system will be the filling out and unfolding of this gracious promise.[4]

Adam named his wife *Eve,* "the mother of all living." Adam and Eve had three sons: Cain, Abel, and Seth. Cain means "a lance;" Abel means "a vapor," "a breath" (inspiration); Seth means "substituted," "appointed," "compensation." Cain, in jealousy, slew his brother Abel who had offered a more pleasing offering to Jehovah, the firstlings of his flock in contrast to Cain's fruit of the ground (see I Jn. 3:12). Eve bore another son, Seth, in whom the spiritual seed was renewed, "For God, said she, hath appointed me another seed instead of Abel." Seth lived to carry forward the Messianic line, for after the birth of Seth's son Enos, "then began men to call upon the name of the Lord" (Gen. 4:26).

Two genealogical lines are given in Genesis, one of Cain and the other of Seth. Cain's is a worldly line whose record ceases about the time of the Deluge. Salvation is to run in the line of Seth, for from this lineage was to come "the seed of the woman." In Luke's Gospel the human genealogy of Jesus is traced back to Enos, to Seth, and to Adam, showing the historical fulfillment of the original promise (see Genealogies, pp. 114, 224).

The Apostle Paul compared the first Adam to the last Adam, and contrasted the effects of the sin of Adam with the effects of the perfect obedience of Christ.

"The first Adam was made a living soul; the last Adam was made a quickening spirit. . . . The first man is of the earth, earthy: the second man is the Lord from heaven" (I Cor. 15:45,47).

"(. . . if by one man's offence death reigned by one; much more they which receive abundance of grace and of the gift of righteousness shall reign in life by one, Jesus Christ.) Therefore as by the offence of one judgment came upon all men to condemnation; even so by the righteousness of one the free gift came upon all men unto justification of life. For as by one man's disobedience many were made sinners, so by the obedience of one shall many be made righteous" (Rom. 5:17-19).

A measure of the man

"And the Lord God formed man of the dust of the ground, and breathed into his nostrils the breath of life; and man became a living soul" (Gen. 2:7).

"Adam and his wife hid themselves from the presence of the Lord God" (Gen. 3:8).

"I was afraid, because I was naked; and I hid myself" (Gen. 3:10).

"The woman whom thou gavest to be with me, she gave me of the tree, and I did eat" (Gen. 3:12).

"Because thou hast hearkened unto the voice of thy wife, and hast eaten of the tree, of which I commanded thee, saying, Thou shalt not eat of it: cursed is the ground for thy sake; in sorrow shalt thou eat of it all the days of thy life; Thorns also and thistles shall it bring forth to thee; and thou shalt eat the herb of the field; In the sweat of thy face shalt thou eat bread, till thou return unto the ground; for out of it wast thou taken: for dust thou art, and unto dust shalt thou return" (Gen. 3:17-19).

"Therefore the Lord God sent him forth from the garden of Eden, to till the ground from whence he was taken" (Gen. 3:23).

"If I covered my transgressions as Adam, by hiding mine iniquity in my bosom. . . ." (Job 31:33).

97

Gen. 5:28-9:29

Noah: "rest," "quiet," "comfort"

Noah, son of Lamech, a patriarch*
    tenth in line of descent from
    Adam through Adam's son Seth
The wickedness of the world
The Lord God purposes to destroy
    man and all living creatures, "for
    it repenteth me that I have made
    them"
Noah, a preacher of righteousness,
    finds grace
Noah's three sons: Shem, Ham, and
    Japheth
Noah builds an ark at God's com-
    mand—Noah's wife, his sons and
    their wives, and two of every kind
    of living creature go into the ark
The Flood—rain for forty days and
    forty nights—ark rests upon
    Mount Ararat—waters on earth a
    year and ten days**—Noah sends
    forth a dove three times
Noah and his family leave the ark—he
    builds an altar and makes sacrifice
    to the Lord
God's everlasting covenant established
    with Noah and his seed, tokened
    by a rainbow
Becomes a husbandman—plants a vine-
    yard—becomes drunken—mocked
    by his son Ham—Noah curses
    Canaan, Ham's son—blesses Shem
    and Japheth
His days, 950 years

*Patriarch: the father of a race, a family or
a tribe; a term particularly used of heads of
families in pre-Mosaic times.

**"A year of 360 days is implied in the
history of the Flood (Gn. 6-8), but no
satisfactory explanation has yet been given
of the scheme of years and chronology in
the genealogical account of antediluvian
times (Gn. 5)." [5]

NOAH, one of the patriarchs of the pre-Mosaic period, was the son of Lamech and grandson of Methuselah in the line of Seth, the Messianic line. He was associated with the period of the Flood or Deluge.

The early narratives of Genesis, one of which pertains to Noah, were woven from legends and traditions of a far-distant past enveloped in the shadows of antiquity. These stories, recounted by word of mouth from generation to generation around the campfires of a nomadic people, were not set down in writing for many centuries. The story of Noah as the hero of the Deluge is based upon ancient Babylonian legends.

It dates from at least B.C. 3000, and it would pass through a long course of oral repetition before it reached the Hebrew form. And herein is seen the religious value of the latter. The genius of the Hebrew race under Divine inspiration gradually stripped it of all its crude polytheism, and made it the vehicle of spiritual truth. [6]

The Bible states that the wickedness of man was great in the earth but that Noah found grace in the eyes of the Lord. Noah was "a just man . . . and Noah walked with God." He begat three sons: Shem, Ham, and Japheth. God said to Noah: "The end of all flesh is come before me. . . . Make thee an ark . . . pitch it within and without with pitch . . . with thee will I establish my covenant; and thou shalt come into the ark, thou, and thy sons, and thy wife, and thy sons' wives with thee. And of every living thing of all flesh, two of every sort." Noah obeyed; "according to all that God commanded him, so did he." The Deluge was upon the face of the earth (the then-known world) for a year and ten days (acc. to the Priestly Code, Gen. 7:11; 8:14).

The archeological findings of the nineteenth and twentieth centuries verify the authenticity of the Biblical record with relation to the Flood. Sir Charles Marston in his book *New Bible Evidence* states that attention should be given to the evidence of the Flood, both in the cuneiform writings of Babylonia and Assyria alluding to the Flood and in the actual Flood deposits; that these deposits were found almost simultaneously by Dr. Langdon's expedition at Kish near Babylon in 1928-1929 and by Dr. Woolley excavating at Ur of the Chaldees, farther south, about half-way between Baghdad and the Persian Gulf. Dr. Woolley writes of his discovery:

The shafts went deeper, and suddenly the character of the soil changed. Instead of the stratified pottery and rubbish we were in perfectly clean clay, uniform throughout, the texture of which showed that it had been laid there by water. The workmen declared that we had come to the bottom of everything, to the river silt. . . . I sent the men back to work to deepen the hole. The clean clay continued without change . . . until it had attained a thickness of a little over 8 feet. Then, as suddenly as it had begun, it stopped, and we were once more in layers of rubbish full of stone implements . . . and pottery. . . .

The great bed of clay marked, if it did not cause, a break in the continuity of history. . . .

No ordinary rising of the rivers would leave behind it anything approaching the bulk of this clay bank; 8 feet of sediment imply a very great depth of water, and the flood which deposited it must have been of a magnitude unparalleled in local history. That it was so is further proved by the fact that the clay bank marks a definite break in the continuity of the local culture; a whole civilization which existed before it is lacking above it and seems to have been submerged by the waters.

Taking into consideration all the facts, there could be no doubt that the flood of which we had thus found the only possible evidence was the Flood of Sumerian history and legend, the Flood on which is based the story of Noah.[7]

When the waters receded, the ark rested on Mount Ararat. Noah's first act, the building of an altar, was one of thanksgiving for the mercy of God in the protection and safety of himself and his family. In turn, God established His covenant with Noah and his seed (all mankind), promising that a like judgment would not be repeated and that the natural law of the seasons would be perpetuated: "While the earth remaineth, seedtime and harvest, and cold and heat, and summer and winter, and day and night shall not cease." The rainbow became the token of this covenant. Noah is sometimes called the second father of the human race, for according to Scriptural history the whole earth was peopled with his descendants.

Noah became a husbandman and drank of the wine of his vineyard. Ham, entering his father's tent, found him drunken and naked, and told his brethren. Shem and Japheth looked not, but covered their father's nakedness. When Noah "awoke" from his intoxication and knew what Ham had done, he cursed Canaan (Ham's offspring) and blessed Shem and Japheth. Noah said, "God shall enlarge Japheth, and he shall dwell in the tents of Shem; and Canaan shall be his servant."

Noah is seldom thought of as a prophet, yet his curse of Canaan foreshadowed the subjection of the Canaanites to the Israelites (descendants of Shem); and through Shem the Messianic line was to run. The blessing to Japheth foreshadowed the inclusion of the Gentiles (descendants of Japheth [Gen. 10:2-5]) in the blessings of the Messiah and his gospel.

The Apostle Peter, writing nearly twenty-five hundred years later, drew a lesson in patient trust and assurance of salvation from the life of the patriarch Noah:

"... when once the longsuffering of God waited in the days of Noah, while the ark was a preparing, wherein few, that is, eight souls were saved by water. The like figure whereunto even baptism doth also now save us (not the putting away of the filth of the flesh, but the answer of a good conscience toward God,) by the resurrection of Jesus Christ" (I Pet. 3:20,21).

A measure of the man

"He [Lamech] called his name Noah, saying, This same shall comfort us concerning our work and toil of our hands, because of the ground which the Lord hath cursed" (Gen. 5:29).

"Noah found grace in the eyes of the Lord" (Gen. 6:8).

"Noah was a just man and perfect in his generations, and Noah walked with God" (Gen. 6:9).

"According to all that God commanded him, so did he" (Gen. 6:22).

"The Lord said unto Noah, Come thou and all thy house into the ark; for thee have I seen righteous before me in this generation" (Gen. 7:1).

"Though these three men, Noah, Daniel, and Job, were in it [the land], they should deliver but their own souls by their righteousness, saith the Lord God" (Ezek. 14:14).

"By faith Noah, being warned of God of things not seen as yet, moved with fear, prepared an ark to the saving of his house; by the which he condemned the world, and became heir of the righteousness which is by faith" (Heb. 11:7).

Gen. 11:27-25:10

Abraham: "father of a multitude"

Abram, son of Terah of the line of Seth—born in Ur of the Chaldees

Marries his half sister Sarai

Abram is called of God—God's covenant or promise of a land and a seed

He journeys to Haran with Terah, Sarai, and Lot, his brother's son

He journeys to Canaan, taking Sarai and Lot—builds altars at Shechem and Beth-el

Driven by famine, he goes into Egypt—conceals his relationship to Sarai—sent out of Egypt by Pharaoh—returns to Beth-el

Abram separates himself from Lot— God renews the promise of a land and a seed—Abram dwells at Hebron and builds an altar there

Rescues Lot from captivity

Abram is blessed by Melchizedek, king of Salem

God renews the covenant—Abram is promised a son

Sarai is barren—gives her handmaid Hagar to Abram—Hagar bears his son Ishmael

Covenant is renewed thirteen years later—Abram's name is changed to Abraham, Sarai's to Sarah— circumcision is instituted as a token of the covenant

Abraham is promised a son, Isaac, of Sarah—he entertains three angels

His prayer for men of Sodom

He sojourns in Gerar—he conceals from Abimelech his relationship to Sarah

Isaac is born—Hagar and Ishmael expelled—Abraham's covenant with Abimelech

The trial of Abraham's faith—the offering of Isaac

Dwells in Beer-sheba—Sarah's death and burial

Abraham obtains Rebekah as a wife for Isaac

Abraham marries Keturah—she bears him six sons

His days, 175 years

ABRAHAM (Abram) the

patriarch was the father and founder of the Hebrew nation. He is identified with the period which marked the inception of God's covenant with the Hebrews.

Abraham was in the direct line of Shem through Shem's son Arphaxad, and was thus in the natural line of the Messiah (see Genealogies, pp. 114, 224). Abram, as he was first called, was the son of Terah, born in Ur of the Chaldees. Abram married Sarai, his half sister, who was barren.

Genesis 12:1-3 records God's call to the nomad Abram and His covenant with him. How momentous was this call the centuries were to reveal. Upon his obedience lay the destiny of his race. God said, "Get thee out of thy country, and from thy kindred, and from thy father's house, unto a land that I will shew thee: And I will make of thee a great nation, and I will bless thee, and make thy name great . . . in thee shall all families of the earth be blessed."

Abram left the moon-worshiping city of Ur and journeyed to Haran in Mesopotamia, where he lived till the death of his father. At the age of seventy-five he went to Canaan, taking with him Sarai, his nephew Lot whom he greatly loved, and vast possessions of flocks and herds. Finding famine in the land he went down into Egypt; expelled from Egypt by its Pharaoh, he came again into Canaan. There he and Lot separated. "The land was not able to bear them . . . for their substance was great, so that they could not dwell together." Abram said, "Let there be no strife, I pray thee, between me and thee, and between my herdmen and thy herdmen; for we be brethren." So Lot chose the plain of Jordan to the east, and Abram dwelt in Canaan at Hebron ("union," "association"). Though they parted in peace, this separation was a necessary step in the patriarch's progress, for the worldly propensities of Lot's character, as seen in Lot's subsequent history, were not to hinder the divine purpose for which Abram had been called. God's injunction, "Get thee out of thy country, and from thy kindred," had at last been fully carried out.

After the separation from Lot, God showed Abram the fullness of the land He had promised him, saying, "Lift up now thine eyes, and look from the place where thou art northward, and southward, and eastward, and westward: For all the land which thou seest, to thee will I give it, and to thy seed for ever." (Note the prerequisite and the bestowal, "Lift up now thine eyes," and "all that thou seest.")

The author of the Epistle to the Hebrews defines the ultimate purpose of Abram's call and the spiritual nature of his inheritance: "By faith Abraham, when he was called to go out into a place which he should after receive for an inheritance, obeyed; and he went out, not knowing whither he went. . . .For he looked for a city which hath foundations, whose builder and maker is God" (Heb. 11:8,10).

When Abram was ninety-nine, God confirmed the covenant: "I am the Almighty God; walk before me, and be thou perfect. . . .As for me, behold, my covenant is with thee, and thou shalt be a father of many nations. . . .And I will give unto thee, and to thy seed after thee . . . all the land of Canaan" (Gen. 17:1,4,8). As the sign of this covenant circumcision was instituted. At this time also Abram's name was changed to Abraham and Sarai's to Sarah. In the heat of the day three angels appeared to Abraham. He ran to meet them, entertained them, and these angels confirmed to Abraham and to Sarah the coming of their son.

The Noahic covenant had pertained to the family of mankind, but the covenant made with Abraham and his seed designated a people chosen out of this family of mankind, selected and set apart to forward the divine plan of redemption. (See The Covenant between God and Men, p. 148.)

> The *covenant* (v.4) with Abraham is made the starting point of all Israel's religious history. As developed in the teachings of priest and prophet it has become one of the most fruitful of all religious ideas.[8]

The spiritual experience of Abraham and Sarah, implied in the change of names, is reflected in the promise and birth of a son, Isaac, to Sarah in her ninetieth year. Ishmael, Abraham's son by his concubine wife Hagar, was cast out at Sarah's word so that the legitimate son by promise would be the heir of the covenant (compare Gal. 4:23). Abraham was assured, "In Isaac shall thy seed be called."

Chapter 22 of Genesis records the testing of Abraham in the offering of Isaac, a soul-searching trial of Abraham's faith. God said, "Abraham," and he answered, "Behold, here I am." And he was told, "Take now thy son, thine only son Isaac, whom thou lovest . . . and offer him . . . for a burnt offering." Isaac was heir to the promises of the covenant, and to sacrifice this son would appear to nullify that covenant. Nevertheless Abraham's faith and loyalty endured. He "rose up early in the morning . . . and went unto the place of which God had told him"—a three-day journey to Mount Moriah. As he laid Isaac on the altar his hand was stayed by a voice from heaven, "Lay not thine hand upon the lad . . . now I know that thou fearest [reverest] God, seeing thou hast not withheld . . . thine only son from me." His trust in God's goodness was rewarded, and his son's life was preserved. Lifting up his eyes he saw a ram caught in a thicket, and this he substituted as his sacrifice. He named the place Jehovah-jireh, "In the mount of the Lord it shall be seen [RV it shall be provided]." Again came the promise, "In thy seed shall all the nations of the earth be blessed, because thou hast obeyed my voice."

As a result of the implicit faith and unswerving obedience of this patriarch his descendants became the people destined to bring forth the Messiah.

Jesus said, "Your father Abraham rejoiced to see my day: and he saw it, and was glad" (Jn. 8:56).

Paul taught that all who believe in Christ are Abraham's children and heirs of the Abrahamic covenant: "Now to Abraham and his seed were the promises made. He saith not, And to seeds, as of many; but as of one, And to thy seed, which is Christ. . . .if ye be Christ's, then are ye Abraham's seed, and heirs according to the promise" (Gal. 3:16,29).

A measure of the man

"I [God] know him, that he will command his children and his household after him, and they shall keep the way of the Lord, to do justice and judgment; that the Lord may bring upon Abraham that which he hath spoken of him" (Gen. 18:19).

"Abraham gave all that he had unto Isaac" (Gen. 25:5).

"He received the sign of circumcision, a seal of the righteousness of the faith which he had yet being uncircumcised: that he might be the father of all them that believe. . . ." (Rom. 4:11).

"He staggered not at the promise of God through unbelief; but was strong in faith, giving glory to God; And being fully persuaded that, what he had promised, he was able also to perform" (Rom. 4:20,21).

"And so, after he had patiently endured, he obtained the promise" (Heb. 6:15).

"By faith he sojourned in the land of promise, as in a strange country. . . . For he looked for a city which hath foundations, whose builder and maker is God" (Heb. 11:9,10).

"By faith Abraham, when he was tried, offered up Isaac: and he that had received the promises offered up his only begotten son. . . . Accounting that God was able to raise him up, even from the dead; from whence also he received him in a figure" (Heb. 11:17,19).

"Was not Abraham our father justified by works, when he had offered Isaac his son upon the altar? . . . And the scripture was fulfilled which saith, Abraham believed God, and it was imputed unto him for righteousness: and he was called the Friend of God" (Ja. 2:21,23).

Gen. 25:21-37:35; 42:1-50:13
Jacob: "heel-catcher," "supplanter"
Israel: "having power" (as a prince)

Jacob, younger son of Isaac and Rebekah and twin brother of Esau—born near Beer-sheba
Jacob purchases valued birthright from Esau—later obtains the blessing of his father by deception—Esau threatens to slay Jacob
Jacob journeys to Padan-aram to obtain a wife—his vision at Beth-el—God confirms to him the Abrahamic covenant
He serves Laban, his uncle, seven years for his daughter Rachel—is deceived and given to wife her elder sister Leah—serves another seven years for Rachel
Jacob begets Reuben, Simeon, Levi, Judah, Issachar, and Zebulun, of Leah; Dan and Naphtali of Bilhah, Rachel's maid; Gad and Asher of Zilpah, Leah's maid; Joseph of Rachel
His cunning policy and secret departure from Laban after twenty years of service
Jacob's wrestling at Peniel—his name is changed to Israel—his friendly meeting with Esau
Jacob's sons avenge defilement of their sister Dinah
Jacob dwells at Beth-el—he builds an altar and God blesses him
Benjamin, Rachel's second son, is born (Jacob's twelfth)—Rachel dies in travail
Jacob's favorite son, Joseph, is sold to merchants by his brethren and carried into Egypt—Jacob mourns
He twice sends his sons to Egypt because of famine in Canaan—they come before Joseph, now premier of Egypt
Jacob and his sons settle in Egypt
His blessings to his sons
He requests burial in Canaan
His days, 147 years

JACOB,

a patriarch, was the second son of Isaac and Rebekah and the grandson of Abraham. He fathered the twelve tribes of Israel and was connected with the period which marked the beginning of the history of the Children of Israel.

Not only were the righteousness and great faith of his grandfather part of Jacob's human heritage, but so also was the righteousness of his father Isaac, whose life shows an unfailing reliance on God and an obedience to the Abrahamic covenant renewed with him (Gen. 26:2-5). Isaac waited in faith for the coming of a son as his wife Rebekah remained barren for twenty years; but he entreated the Lord for her, and she conceived and bore twins, Esau the elder and Jacob the younger.

Before the birth of these children Rebekah had been told: "Two nations are in thy womb, and two manner of people . . . and the elder shall serve the younger." This prophecy foreshadowed the rivalry between Esau and Jacob as brothers, and between their descendants as nations, Edom and Israel (Num. 20:20,21; II Sam. 8:14). Esau was "a cunning hunter, a man of the field." Jacob was "a plain [quiet] man, dwelling in tents," leading the life of a herdsman. "Isaac loved Esau . . . but Rebekah loved Jacob."

The character of this patriarch is clearly portrayed, both his weaknesses and his strength, showing the inner conflict between the base desires of his nature and the inherent good. He shrewdly bought the birthright of the first-born from Esau, taking advantage of his brother's momentary hunger (see First-born, p. 40). According to prophecy the birthright had been promised to Jacob, and would have fallen to him in a divinely natural way; but in his strong desire to possess it he went even further and employed fraudulent measures to deceive his aging father and obtain the paternal blessing which would confirm the birthright. Although Esau also received a blessing, he vowed to kill his brother.

Later Isaac confirmed the blessing to Jacob and charged him to take a wife from the daughters of Laban, his mother's brother in Padan-aram. (Esau, at forty, had married two Hittite wives, "which were a grief of mind unto Isaac and to Rebekah.") Thus Jacob was sent beyond the reach of Esau's hatred.

Journeying to Padan-aram (a region of Mesopotamia east of the Euphrates) Jacob stopped at Beth-el where he lay down to sleep. His rest was troubled, fleeing as he was from his own thoughts and from the wrath of Esau. But he was given new hope. In a vision he beheld a ladder "set up on the earth, and the top of it reached to heaven: and behold the angels of God ascending and descending on it." He learned that he was not alone; that God was with him. Here at Beth-el God renewed the covenant he had made with Abraham and with Isaac.

Jacob faithfully served Laban for seven years that he might marry his younger daughter Rachel. "And they seemed unto him but a few days, for the love he had to her." But on the wedding night Laban gave his elder daughter Leah to Jacob. He who had deceived now drew to himself deception. Jacob was later given Rachel, but for her he had to labor another seven years.

For twenty years Jacob served his uncle faithfully under rigorous conditions (Gen. 31:38-42), but after the birth of Joseph, his eleventh son and Rachel's first-born, he desired to return to his own country. Laban was loath to let him go because he had prospered through Jacob's labors. Only grudgingly did Laban accord Jacob his wages, but Jacob craftily multiplied his flocks and herds at Laban's expense and became wealthy. Finally, at God's command, Jacob departed with his family, fleeing secretly by night. Laban pursued, but God forbade him to harm Jacob and the two made a covenant of friendship.

"Jacob went on his way, and the angels of God met him." Heartened, he sent messengers of reconciliation to Esau. But, still fearful of his brother's revenge, he spent a long night in prayer, and "there wrestled a man with him until the breaking of the day." In this spiritual experience his self-will yielded, his nature was changed and the true birthright became his through grace. The angel said, "Thy name shall be called no more Jacob, but Israel: for as a prince hast thou power with God and with men, and hast prevailed" (Gen. 32:28). Jacob called the name of the place Peniel, "for I have seen God face to face, and my life is preserved."

> "As the name was to the Hebrews the symbol or expression of the nature, the change of name is significant of the moral change in the patriarch himself; he is no longer Jacob the Supplanter, the Crafty one, the Overreacher, but Israel the Perseverer with God, who is worthy also to prevail": cp. Hos. 12:4. [9]

On the morrow the brothers were reconciled. Having seen God "face to face," he could now say to Esau, "I have seen thy face, as though I had seen the face of God, and thou wast pleased with me."

Leah gave Jacob six sons; her handmaid Zilpah gave him two; Rachel's handmaid Bilhah bore him two; and then Rachel, long barren, mothered his two favorite sons, Joseph and Benjamin (see also The Twelve Sons of Jacob, p. 150). These twelve sons of Jacob (Israel) headed the twelve tribes who became known as the Children of Israel or, collectively, as Israel—heirs of God's covenant made with Abraham, Isaac, and Jacob.

Nearly thirty years after his return to Canaan, and at a time when his son Joseph as prime minister governed Egypt, Jacob and his sons migrated to Egypt. Even as he went God assured him, "Fear not to go down into Egypt; for I will there make of thee a great nation: I will go down with thee into Egypt; and I will also surely bring thee up again" (Gen. 46:3,4).

At the close of his life Jacob blessed each of his twelve sons (see Prophecies of Jacob to His Twelve Sons, p. 152). The prophecy to his fourth son Judah was Messianic, designating the tribe of Judah as the one divinely chosen to bring forth the Messiah.

A measure of the man

"Jacob was a plain [ASV quiet] man. . . ." (Gen. 25:27)

"Thy brother [Jacob] came with subtilty, and hath taken away thy blessing" (Gen. 27:35).

"Is not he rightly named Jacob? for he hath supplanted me [Esau] these two times: he took away my birthright; and, behold, now he hath taken away my blessing" (Gen. 27:36).

"Jacob awaked out of his sleep, and he said, Surely the Lord is in this place; and I knew it not" (Gen. 28:16).

"Jacob served seven years for Rachel; and they seemed unto him but a few days, for the love he had to her" (Gen. 29:20).

"With all my power I have served your father [Laban]. And your father hath deceived me, and changed my wages ten times; but God suffered him not to hurt me" (Gen. 31:6,7).

"Jacob said, O God of my father Abraham, and God of my father Isaac . . . I am not worthy of the least of all the mercies, and of all the truth, which thou hast shewed unto thy servant. . . ." (Gen. 32:9,10).

"Thy name shall be called no more Jacob, but Israel: for as a prince hast thou power with God and with men, and hast prevailed" (Gen. 32:28).

"The Lord sent a word into Jacob, and it hath lighted upon Israel" (Is. 9:8).

"He [the Lord] shall cause them that come of Jacob to take root: Israel shall blossom and bud, and fill the face of the world with fruit" (Is. 27:6).

Gen. 30:22-24; 37; 39-50
Joseph: "increaser," "adding"

Son of Jacob and Rachel—born in Padan-aram—favored of his father

Hated by his brethren—his two dreams

Sent by Jacob to his brethren feeding their flocks at Dothan—sold by them to traveling merchants—carried into Egypt

Sold to Potiphar, a captain of Pharaoh's guard—becomes overseer in Potiphar's house—Potiphar's wife, failing to entice him, causes his imprisonment

Finds favor with the keeper of the prison—interprets dreams for the prisoners

Two years later Joseph interprets two dreams for Pharaoh foretelling coming famine—gives Pharaoh wise counsel

Joseph is set over Egypt by Pharaoh—marries Asenath, daughter of Potipherah, priest of On

Fills storehouses of Egypt during seven years of plenty in preparation for seven years of famine

His two sons, Manasseh and Ephraim, are born

He is merciful to his brethren who twice journey to Egypt to buy grain—he reveals himself to them and forgives them

He establishes his father and the families of his brethren in the region of Goshen in northeast Egypt

His two sons receive Jacob's blessing—Ephraim, the second-born, is given the first blessing

Joseph and his brethren bury their father in Hebron

After Jacob's death Joseph's brethren bow before him, still fearing his revenge, but he comforts them with assurances of kindness

His days, 110 years

JOSEPH, a patriarch, was the son of Jacob (Israel) and Rachel. He was associated with the period of preservation of the Children of Israel in Egypt.

Joseph was the eleventh son of Jacob, but the first son of the loved mother Rachel. "Israel loved Joseph more than all his children, because he was the son of his old age," and he gave to this favorite son a coat of many colors. "When his brethren saw that their father loved him more than all his brethren, they hated him, and could not speak peaceably unto him." Joseph, young, innocent, and without guile, confided freely to his brothers his strange dreams—dreams which prefigured his pre-eminence among them. "And they hated him yet the more. . . ."

He was seventeen years of age when Jacob sent him to his brothers who were feeding their flocks at Shechem and at Dothan. As he drew near they conspired to kill him, but Reuben, the eldest, restrained them from shedding blood. So Joseph was cast into a pit and, during Reuben's absence, sold for twenty pieces of silver to merchants traveling to Egypt. Dipping his coat in the blood of a kid, his brothers brought it to their father; and Jacob, believing their evil report, mourned his son as dead. Figuratively Joseph's coat, given to him by a loving father, may be likened to the seamless robe of Christ. As Joseph was stripped of his coat of many colors by the hatred of his brethren and it was returned with blood, so did Jesus' own nation strip him of his seamless robe and stain it with the blood of rejection and crucifixion.

Joseph was taken to Egypt and sold to Potiphar, an officer of Pharaoh, who soon advanced him to the position of chief steward of his house, for he saw that Joseph's God was with him. Potiphar's wife, attracted to Joseph, daily attempted to entice him. His refusal to yield to temptation showed his high moral standard and spiritual integrity: "There is none greater in this house than I . . . how then can I do this great wickedness, and sin against God?" But she falsely accused him, and he was thrown into prison, where he remained for two years. Yet there was no bitterness or recrimination on Joseph's part at this injustice; rather, he turned to serving his fellow prisoners and found favor with the prison keeper.

Pharaoh had two dreams that none of the wise men of Egypt could explain. The first dream was of seven lean cows which devoured seven fat ones; the second was of seven thin ears of corn which devoured seven full ears. Hearing of Joseph's wisdom and skill in interpreting dreams for fellow prisoners, Pharaoh sent for him. Joseph disclaimed any personal ability, saying, "It is not in me: God shall give Pharaoh an answer of peace." He interpreted the two dreams as one, as foretelling seven years of abundance to be followed by seven years of famine, and counseled Pharaoh to appoint a man to oversee the storing up of one-fifth of the crops during the plenteous years to meet the coming dearth. Pleased with this plan, Pharaoh chose Joseph to administer it, for he saw that he was "a man in whom the Spirit of God is."

Joseph was thirty when he stood before Pharaoh. He was made ruler of all Egypt, superseded in power only by Pharaoh himself. During seven plentiful years "the earth brought forth by handfuls," and when the famine was felt in adjacent countries only Egypt had a surplus of food to sell.

When hunger spread into Canaan, Joseph's brothers journeyed to Egypt to buy corn; "Joseph knew his brethren, but they knew not him." He did not make himself known but roughly accused them of being spies and imprisoned them for three days. Then he sent them home with a supply of food (hiding their purchase money in their bags); but he held one of them (Simeon) as hostage, demanding that they bring back to him their youngest brother.

Upon their return with Benjamin, Joseph revealed his identity and all the brothers were reunited. He stilled their fear and remorse for the evil they had done him. Of a generous and tender spirit himself, he comforted them: "God sent me before you to preserve you a posterity . . . and to save your lives by a great deliverance. So now it was not you that sent me hither, but God" (Gen. 45:7,8). Joseph sent for his father and the families of his brethren, seventy in all, and settled them in Goshen, a tract of land east of the Nile Delta suitable for pasturage. Thus Jacob's posterity, now known as the Children of Israel, were preserved to advance the great Messianic purpose of God. After the death of Jacob the brothers, still fearful of Joseph's vengeance, bowed down before him to ask pardon, and again he forgave them (see Gen. 37:7). In many respects Joseph's life is considered typical of the Messiah's.

Joseph had two sons by his Egyptian wife Asenath, Manasseh and Ephraim. Their grandfather Jacob before his death gave each his blessing, adopting them as his own but setting Ephraim the second-born before Manasseh (prophetically declaring the pre-eminence of the tribe of Ephraim). By so doing he acknowledged Joseph as his first-born and gave him the double portion, the inheritance of the eldest. Ephraim and Manasseh headed tribes which later shared in the division of the territory in Canaan, inheriting the birthright of the house of Joseph. On the basis of this birthright the tribe of Ephraim disputed the claim of the tribe of Judah for ascendancy in Israel.

Jacob's prophecy to Joseph showered with blessings this son who had so unfailingly placed his reliance on the providence of God: "Joseph is a fruitful bough . . . by a well; whose branches run over the wall: The archers have sorely grieved him, and shot at him, and hated him: But his bow abode in strength, and the arms of his hands were made strong by the hands of the mighty God of Jacob; (from thence is the shepherd, the stone of Israel:) Even by the God of thy father, who shall help thee; and . . . shall bless thee with blessings of heaven above. . . . The blessings of thy father . . . shall be . . . on the crown of the head of him that was separate from his brethren" (Gen. 49:22-26).

"The Lord was with Joseph, and he was a prosperous man; and he was in the house of his master the Egyptian. And his master saw that the Lord was with him, and that the Lord made all that he did to prosper in his hand" (Gen. 39:2,3).

"The Lord was with Joseph, and shewed him mercy, and gave him favour in the sight of the keeper of the prison. And the keeper . . . committed to Joseph's hand all the prisoners that were in the prison; and whatsoever they did there, he was the doer of it" (Gen. 39:21,22).

"Forasmuch as God hath shewed thee all this, there is none so discreet and wise as thou art: Thou shalt be over my house, and according unto thy word shall all my people be ruled: only in the throne will I [Pharaoh] be greater than thou" (Gen. 41:39,40).

"Joseph made haste; for his bowels did yearn upon his brother: and he sought where to weep; and he entered into his chamber, and wept there. And he washed his face, and went out, and refrained himself. . . ." (Gen. 43:30,31)

"So now it was not you that sent me hither, but God: and he hath made me a father to Pharaoh, and lord of all his house, and a ruler throughout all the land of Egypt" (Gen. 45:8).

"Joseph said unto them [his brethren], Fear not: for am I in the place of God? But as for you, ye thought evil against me; but God meant it unto good, to bring to pass, as it is this day, to save much people alive. Now therefore fear ye not: I will nourish you, and your little ones. And he comforted them, and spake kindly unto them" (Gen. 50:20,21).

Ex. 2-20; 24-40; Books of
Leviticus, Numbers, Deuteronomy

Moses: Heb. "drawing out"
Egypt. "born"

Son of Amram and Jochebed, of tribe of Levi—hidden in bulrushes to escape the death decree of Pharaoh

Adopted by Pharaoh's daughter—lives at Egyptian court till the age of forty

Slays an Egyptian—attempts to mediate between two of his countrymen

Flees to Midian—tends Jethro's flocks for forty years—marries Zipporah, daughter of Jethro

God's call to Moses at the burning bush on Mount Horeb—commissioned to deliver Israel from Egyptian bondage—given two signs

Stands before Pharaoh with Aaron, his brother—his great cry—the ten plagues

Passover instituted

The Exodus—Red Sea is divided before Israelites—the people given manna—water flows from the rock—successful battle at Rephidim

At Mount Sinai Moses receives Decalogue written on two tablets of stone, also various civil and religious laws—Israel worships golden calf—Moses breaks the tablets—Decalogue given again

Tabernacle erected—tribe of Levi consecrated to priesthood—Passover becomes a commemorative institution

Israel journeys to Kadesh-barnea—twelve spies sent into Canaan—unfavorable report causes people to fear to enter—Israel condemned to wander forty years

Moses governs Israel forty years in the wilderness—seventy elders chosen to aid him—under God's providence he brings Israel to Canaan's borders

His last addresses to Israel

From Mount Nebo Moses sees the Promised Land

His days, 120 years

MOSES was the mighty lawgiver

of Israel, the nation's first great leader, statesman, and prophet. He is identified with the period of the Exodus and the Wilderness Wandering, and with the inception of the Law.

The family of Jacob which had settled in Egypt in Joseph's day multiplied greatly during the following four centuries until their very number became a threat to the Egyptians. Fearing the strength of this Hebrew people, Pharaoh (probably Rameses II) enslaved them and made them "to serve with rigour," and even decreed the death of all their newborn male children. At this time the child Moses was born to Amram and Jochebed of the tribe of Levi. Hidden in the bulrushes of the Nile to escape the king's mandate, the child was rescued by Pharaoh's daughter and adopted as her son.

Moses' life may be divided into three periods of forty years each: forty years in Egypt, forty in Midian, and forty in the Wilderness of the Wandering.

Though he was reared in the splendor of the Egyptian court and versed in Egyptian wisdom, Moses' heart was with his people. One day in defense of a Hebrew, he slew an Egyptian (his first effort, a human endeavor, to aid his people). The following day he tried to settle a violent quarrel between two Hebrews, but his attempt to mediate justice was rejected. Pharaoh sought to kill him, but Moses fled into Midian, east of the Gulf of Aqabah.

> These two incidents prove that neither were the Israelites yet ready to go out of Egypt, nor Moses prepared to be their leader (James 1:20). It was by the staff and not the sword—by the meekness, and not the wrath of Moses that God was to accomplish that great work of deliverance.[10]

For forty years Moses remained in Midian. He married Zipporah, daughter of Jethro, priest of Midian, and tended the flocks of his father-in-law. During these quiet years in the desert he attained the meekness and spiritual maturity which fitted him to undertake the great task that lay before him, that of leading his people out of Egypt to the promised land of Canaan.

God's call came to Moses at Mount Horeb. Beholding the marvel of a bush burning with fire yet not consumed, he turned aside to see. "When the Lord saw that he turned aside to see, God called unto him out of the midst of the bush," and identified Himself as the God who had made His covenant with the patriarchal fathers: "I am . . . the God of Abraham, the God of Isaac, and the God of Jacob. . . . I have surely seen the affliction of my people which are in Egypt. . . . And I am come down to deliver them. . . ." "I will send thee unto Pharaoh, that thou mayest bring forth my people . . . out of Egypt." Moses was doubtful of his ability but God promised, "Certainly I will be with thee."

Then to Moses was given a fuller revelation of the nature of God than had heretofore been known. God had declared Himself to Abraham as "the Almighty," but to Moses he declared Himself as Jehovah, as the "I AM THAT I AM," the Self-Existent One—"the living God." To strengthen Moses' confidence and to provide Israel with convincing testimony of Moses' commission, he was given two visible signs of divine power—the turning of his rod into a serpent and the healing of the leprous hand.

Moses returned to Egypt. With Aaron his brother acting as spokesman, he demanded the release of the Hebrews. Pharaoh refused, and at Moses' word ten plagues struck at the Egyptians to force their release (see Ten Plagues, p. 149). After the tenth plague Pharaoh let them go, but immediately regretting his action he pursued them. Israel fled to the Red Sea and before Moses' uplifted rod the sea was divided and Israel passed over on dry ground. Thus by a mighty deliverance the power of the God of Israel was manifested.

At Mount Sinai God's covenant was renewed, this time with the nation of Israel. On the mount Moses saw God's wondrous power and glory, and in conscious communion with Him he was given a further revelation of the divine nature in the Decalogue—the laws of His covenant, whose moral and spiritual principles laid the foundation of the religious and social life of the nation (see The Law, p. 157).

To Moses was also divinely communicated a religious system, sacrificial and ceremonial in form, one whose every institution typified and prefigured the redemptive work of Israel's coming Messiah. A Tabernacle was erected and an Aaronic priesthood ordained (see Tabernacle, p. 159; Priesthood, p. 52).

During the next forty years of the Wilderness Wandering the great lawgiver governed Israel. Under his inspired leadership they were miraculously provided with manna from heaven and water from the rock, and disciplined to a reliance on God. He led them to the borders of Canaan where he gave his last counsels to the new generation about to enter the Promised Land. He rehearsed God's mercies to Israel and restated the Law with its basic principles. The covenant was again ratified with the nation and the people were warned to obey God's laws and keep themselves separate from idolatrous nations and their abominations.

With prophetic insight Moses foretold the coming of Israel's Messiah: "I [God] will raise them up a Prophet from among their brethren, like unto thee, and will put my words in his mouth. . . . And it shall come to pass, that whosoever will not hearken unto my words which he shall speak in my name, I will require it of him" (Deut. 18:18,19; compare Jn. 1:45; Acts 3:22,23).

From the hill of Pisgah on Mount Nebo in Moab Moses saw all the Promised Land. God said, "I have caused thee to see it with thine eyes, but thou shalt not go over thither." The record closes with the tribute, "There arose not a prophet since in Israel like unto Moses, whom the Lord knew face to face." This prophet appears once again in Scriptural history, being present "in glory" at the Transfiguration of Jesus (Lu. 9:30,31).

A measure of the man

"Moses was content to dwell with the man [Jethro, priest of Midian] . . . ." (Ex. 2:21)

"The Lord spake unto Moses face to face, as a man speaketh unto his friend" (Ex. 33:11).

"When Moses came down from mount Sinai . . . Moses wist not that the skin of his face shone while he talked with him [God] " (Ex. 34:29).

"Now the man Moses was very meek, above all the men which were upon the face of the earth" (Num. 12:3).

"With him will I speak mouth to mouth, even apparently, and not in dark speeches; and the similitude of the Lord shall he behold. . . ." (Num. 12:8)

"Moses was an hundred and twenty years old when he died: his eye was not dim, nor his natural force abated" (Deut. 34:7).

"By a prophet the Lord brought Israel out of Egypt, and by a prophet was he preserved" (Hos. 12:13).

"Moses verily was faithful in all his house, as a servant, for a testimony of those things which were to be spoken after. . . ." (Heb. 3:5)

"By faith Moses, when he was come to years, refused to be called the son of Pharaoh's daughter; Choosing rather to suffer affliction with the people of God, than to enjoy the pleasures of sin for a season; Esteeming the reproach of Christ greater riches than the treasures in Egypt: for he had respect unto the recompence of the reward. By faith he forsook Egypt, not fearing the wrath of the king: for he endured, as seeing him who is invisible" (Heb. 11:24-27).

Ex. 17:9-14; 24:13-18; 32:17; 33:11; Num.
11:28,29; 13; 14; 26:65; 27:15-23; Deut.
1:38; 3:21-28; 31:7-23; 34:9; Bk. of Joshua

Joshua: "Jehovah is salvation"

Joshua (Hoshea, Oshea) son of Nun, of
   tribe of Ephraim
Commands armies of Israel at Reph-
   idim in their first battle after the
   Exodus—defeats the Amalekites
Attends Moses at Mount Sinai
His zeal for Moses and the office of
   prophecy
One of twelve tribal spies appointed
   by Moses to search the land of
   Canaan—he and Caleb alone give a
   good report and urge the people
   to take the land—preservation of
   these two is promised
Joshua is appointed to succeed Moses
   at close of the Wilderness Wander-
   ing
God's commands and promises to
   Joshua
Joshua sends men to spy out Jericho
Before the Ark of the Covenant the
   waters of Jordan are cut off—
   Israel crosses Jordan on dry
   ground into Canaan
Rite of circumcision renewed
The manna ceases
Joshua, under divine direction, be-
   sieges Jericho—its walls fall
Israel is defeated at Ai—the trespass of
   Achan—Ai is conquered and burn-
   ed
Joshua's league with Gibeon—five
   kings war against Gibeon—Joshua
   goes to its aid—sun and moon
   stand still at his word
Joshua conquers kings of central and
   northern Palestine
He divides Canaan among the tribes of
   Israel
Tabernacle set up at Shiloh
Appoints cities of refuge and Levitical
   cities
His two final solemn addresses—
   renewal of the covenant
His days, 110 years

JOSHUA was Moses' immediate successor

and a great military hero. He was connected with the period of the conquest of Canaan and with the division of the territory among the tribes of Israel.

The early history of Joshua's life shows him to have been a man of considerable military, religious, and political stature, eminently qualified to succeed Moses. From the time of the Exodus he stood in close relationship to the great lawgiver. He was selected by Moses to command the armed forces of Israel against the Amalekites, and with the prayerful support of Moses he won a brilliant victory (Ex. 17:8-13). He was personal minister to Moses and privileged to attend him on Mount Sinai (Ex. 24:13; 32:17), and had charge of the early Tent of Meeting (Ex. 33:7-11).

Moses chose him as one of the twelve tribal representatives sent from Kadesh-barnea to search out the land of Canaan. (According to Numbers 13:16 his name was changed by Moses from Oshea to Jehoshua, Joshua.)

The spies found Canaan a good land, but ten of them reported that its cities were walled, its inhabitants were giants, warlike and strong, and the whole was surrounded by hostile tribes. The people wept and determined to return to Egypt. The other two, Joshua and Caleb, urged them to be courageous and take possession of their inheritance (Num. 13; 14): "The land . . . is an exceeding good land. If the Lord delight in us, then he will bring us into this land, and give it us. . . . Only rebel not ye against the Lord, neither fear ye the people of the land . . . their defence is departed from them, and the Lord is with us." The people still feared to go forward and would have stoned them, but the appearance of the Shekinah glory in the Tabernacle and the divine displeasure stayed their hand. For their disobedience and lack of faith Israel was condemned to wander in the wilderness forty years, a year for each day of the forty-day search. The spies who brought back the negative report died by plague, but the lives of Joshua and Caleb were preserved; and of all the Israelites over twenty years of age numbered by Moses at Sinai these two alone were permitted to enter the Promised Land because they "wholly followed the Lord" (Num. 26:63-65; 32:12).

Toward the close of the Wandering Moses appointed Joshua his successor in solemn ceremony, putting some of his own "honour" upon him (Num. 27:20).

When Joshua assumed the leadership of Israel after the death of Moses, God gave him this promise of assurance: "There shall not any man be able to stand before thee all the days of thy life: as I was with Moses, so I will be with thee: I will not fail thee, nor forsake thee." This promise was followed by His imperatives:
   "Be strong and of a good courage. . . ."
   "Divide for an inheritance the land. . . ."
   "Observe to do according to all the law. . . ." (Josh. 1:6,7)
Joshua's authority was confirmed and sustained from the outset by God's supporting power. Before the Ark of the Covenant (the symbol of God's presence) the waters of the Jordan were divided so that the

Israelites crossed over on dry ground.

Israel's national life in Canaan began with an act of religious dedication. Joshua caused all those born in the wilderness to be sanctified by circumcision; then the Passover was observed. And on the morrow after the people had eaten of the produce of the land, the manna that had providentially fed them in the wilderness ceased.

Joshua's whole conquest of Canaan was under divine direction. Before him lay the stronghold of Jericho, which barred their passage into the land. As Joshua pondered how best to besiege its massive walls, an angel, "the captain of the Lord's host," appeared to him and imparted the plan by which he should take the city. Obediently each day for six days the armies of Israel marched in silence around the city—first the armed men, then seven priests blowing trumpets, then priests bearing the sacred Ark of the Covenant, then more armed men. On the seventh day they compassed the city seven times; finally, at the long blast of the trumpet and the loud shout of all the people, the walls fell flat and each man walked straight into the city.

For the next twenty-four years Joshua fought the idolatrous nations within the land—the Hittites, Amorites, Canaanites, Perizzites, Hivites, and Jebusites. An intrepid general, he led the armies of Israel to victory over a confederation of kings of southern Palestine and defeated an alliance of northern kings, chasing them as far north as Zidon in Phoenicia. The enemy was overcome "in the mountains, and in the valleys, and in the plains, and in the springs, and in the wilderness" (Josh. 10-12). "He left nothing undone of all that the Lord commanded Moses" (Josh. 11:15).

Although the land, particularly northern Palestine, was not wholly subdued by the close of his life, Joshua divided the territory by lot among the twelve tribes, including the tribes of Manasseh and Ephraim but excluding Levi. In lieu of land this priestly tribe was given forty-eight cities of which six were appointed cities of refuge (see Levitical cities, pp. 45, 54).

In his final addresses Joshua emphatically warned his nation to keep itself separate, socially and religiously, from the idolatrous Canaanites left in the land, lest they fall into apostasy and lose their heritage.

"Be ye . . . very courageous to keep and to do all . . . the law of Moses. . . . That ye come not among these nations . . . neither make mention of the name of their gods . . . neither serve them. . . . But cleave unto the Lord your God. . . . Else if ye do in any wise go back, and cleave unto the remnant of these nations . . . and shall make marriages with them. . . . Know for a certainty that the Lord your God will no more drive out any of these nations from before you; but they shall be snares and traps unto you, and scourges in your sides, and thorns in your eyes, until ye perish from off this good land which the Lord your God hath given you" (Josh. 23:6-8,12,13).

Israel long felt the influence of Joshua's incorruptible spiritual leadership: "Israel served the Lord all the days of Joshua, and all the days of the elders that overlived Joshua" (Josh. 24:31).

A measure of the man

"Moses rose up, and his minister Joshua: and Moses went up into the mount of God" (Ex. 24:13).

"Joshua the son of Nun, a man in whom is the spirit. . . ." (Num. 27:18)

"Moses . . . took Joshua, and set him before Eleazar the priest, and before all the congregation: And he laid his hands upon him, and gave him a charge, as the Lord commanded by the hand of Moses" (Num. 27:22,23).

"Joshua the son of Nun was full of the spirit of wisdom; for Moses had laid his hands upon him: and the children of Israel hearkened unto him. . . ." (Deut. 34:9)

"Only be thou strong and very courageous, that thou mayest observe to do according to all the law . . . turn not from it to the right hand or to the left, that thou mayest prosper whithersoever thou goest" (Josh. 1:7).

"This book of the law shall not depart out of thy mouth; but thou shalt meditate therein day and night, that thou mayest observe to do according to all that is written therein: for then thou shalt make thy way prosperous, and then thou shalt have good success" (Josh. 1:8).

"On that day the Lord magnified Joshua in the sight of all Israel; and they feared him, as they feared Moses, all the days of his life" (Josh. 4:14).

"The Lord was with Joshua; and his fame was noised throughout all the country" (Josh. 6:27).

"Choose you this day whom ye will serve . . . but as for me and my house, we will serve the Lord" (Josh. 24:15).

I Sam. 1:1-13:15; 15; 16; 19:18-24; 25:1

Samuel: "heard of God"

Son of Hannah and Elkanah an Ephraimite—a child of prayer

Dedicated to the service of God—possibly a Nazarite by his mother's vow—from early childhood serves at Shiloh under Eli the high priest

The call of Samuel—he is apprised of God's judgment on Eli's house—he grows in grace—established as a prophet

Israel wars with Philistines—the Ark of the Covenant is captured—death of Eli and his sons—Ark is returned—kept at Kirjath-jearim

Samuel judges the people at Mizpah—their repentance—through his prayer Israel wins a miraculous victory over the Philistines

He dwells at Ramah—organizes bands of prophets at Ramah, Beth-el, Gilgal, Mizpah—makes yearly circuit to judge the people

When Samuel is old his sons govern corruptly—Israel demands a king—Samuel is grieved—warns Israel of the despotism an earthly king would impose

Samuel anoints Saul—Saul is made king at Gilgal

Samuel twice rebukes Saul for disobedience and prophesies his rejection

He is divinely directed to go to Bethlehem to anoint David as king in Saul's place

Samuel's home at Ramah becomes a refuge for David when he flees from Saul's wrath

Samuel's days, about 98 years

SAMUEL, the first great prophet

since Moses, was the last of the judges. He was associated with the closing period of the Judges and with the transition from the judgeship to the monarchy.

To review history: following the death of Joshua came the long period of the Judges, 300 to 350 years, when the new generation of the tribes of Israel was settling itself in Canaan. Under Joshua the Israelites had sworn "The Lord our God will we serve, and his voice will we obey" (Josh. 24:24); but in the years of transition from a nomadic to an agricultural way of life they adopted many Canaanitish customs and were continually attracted to forbidden heathen rites so that they became guilty of a flagrant compromise of monotheism with the polytheism of the Canaanites and border nations. The wickedness of the Israelites in communing with them resulted, intermittently, in years of servitude to the nations whose gods they worshiped. When oppression became too great to bear, Israel "cried unto the Lord," acknowledging its sin; and each time a judge was raised up to deliver Israel from bondage.

The more important of the judges (there were fifteen in all) were Othniel, Ehud, Shamgar, Deborah, Gideon, Jephthah, Samson, and Samuel. Aside from the periodic ministrations of the judges there was little lawful government or national unity. Only in times of crisis did the tribes unite sufficiently to throw off the enemy yoke. The prevailing spirit of disobedience and disunity is summed up in the last verse of Judges: "In those days there was no king in Israel: every man did that which was right in his own eyes."

> They [the judges] were not merely deliverers of the state from a foreign yoke, but destroyers of idolatry, foes of pagan vices, promoters of the knowledge of God, of religion, and of morality; restorers of theocracy in the minds of the Hebrews, and powerful instruments of Divine Providence in the promotion of the great design of preserving the Hebrew constitution, and, by that means, of rescuing the true religion from destruction.[11]

Samuel came when the moral and spiritual values of the nation were at low ebb and Israel had almost ceased to tend the lamp of her divine destiny. He was the son of Hannah and Elkanah, a child of prayer, dedicated to God before his birth. His mother had been barren, and she prayed, "O Lord of hosts, if thou wilt . . . give unto thine handmaid a man child, then I will give him unto the Lord all the days of his life." Her prayer was answered, and in gratitude Hannah kept her vow. When the child was weaned she took him to the sanctuary at Shiloh, there to minister unto the Lord before Eli the high priest. "And the word of the Lord was precious in those days; there was no open vision."

The prophetic call came to Samuel while he was still a boy (probably about the age of twelve). The Lord appeared to him in a vision. Three times He called, "Samuel," and each time Samuel thought Eli was speaking; but when God called the fourth time Samuel, instructed by Eli, answered, "Speak; for thy servant heareth." The purity of his mother's motive and prayer, the steadfast keeping of her vow, his service in a priestly environment—all these factors had prepared the child's willing mind for listening. To him was revealed God's judgment on Eli's house because of the high priest's failure to restrain the immoralities and irreligious feastings of his sons at the sanctuary. "And Samuel grew, and the Lord was with him, and did let none of his words fall to the ground. And all Israel from Dan even to Beer-sheba knew that Samuel was established to be a prophet of the Lord." His rise to authority as a prophet marked the recession of priestly influence as the prime moral power in Israel, bringing prophecy to the fore as the instrument by which God would communicate His will to men.

Twenty-five years later the judgment on the house of Eli was fulfilled in the death of Eli's sons by the Philistines and by the death of Eli himself. Samuel then became a judge of Israel. He assembled the people at Mizpah and exhorted them to turn from strange gods and return to the worship of Jehovah. Upon their repentance his prayer brought a miraculous victory over the Philistines and an era of peace.

With Samuel is seen for the first time the establishment of prophecy as an institution in Israel, whereby certain men, known as "sons of the prophets," gathered together in bands for prayer and spiritual communion, "men, whose hearts God had touched." These schools were located at Ramah, where Samuel lived, at Beth-el, Gilgal, and at Mizpah; Samuel made a yearly circuit to these centers to judge the people.

The prophets' service to their people cannot be overestimated, for as a theocratic nation Israel was dependent upon its seers for divine guidance. The prophets stood at the side of Israel's kings, actively participating in the government of the kingdom, making evident God's omnipotence and omnipresence by their wisdom and miracles. Their unswerving righteousness exerted a vast influence on the moral and spiritual life of the nation.

When Samuel was old he gave the government into the hands of his sons, but the people were dissatisfied with their rule; they demanded a king that they might be "like all the nations." Samuel was grieved but God said, "Hearken unto the voice of the people in all that they say unto thee: for they have not rejected thee, but they have rejected me, that I should not reign over them." He warned Israel of the danger of choosing an earthly king but yielded to their demand; and at God's direction anointed Saul, a Benjamite, as king. Before resigning his judgeship he reproved Israel for ingratitude for the deliverances it had experienced under God's kingship, yet assured the nation of God's continuing mercy if both they and the king would walk in His commandments.

When Saul was later rejected as king, Samuel went under divine direction to Bethlehem secretly to anoint David king. This great leader died at Ramah after a long life of loyalty to God and patriotic service to his nation.

A measure of the man

"For this child I [Hannah] prayed; and the Lord hath given me my petition.... Therefore also I have lent him to the Lord; as long as he liveth he shall be lent to the Lord" (I Sam. 1:27,28).

"Samuel ministered before the Lord, being a child, girded with a linen ephod" (I Sam. 2:18).

"Samuel grew, and the Lord was with him, and did let none of his words fall to the ground. And all Israel from Dan even to Beer-sheba knew that Samuel was established to be a prophet of the Lord ... for the Lord revealed himself to Samuel in Shiloh. ..." (I Sam. 3:19-21)

"Samuel judged Israel all the days of his life" (I Sam. 7:15).

"A man of God ... an honourable man. ..." (I Sam. 9:6)

"Samuel said unto all Israel ... I am old and grayheaded ... and I have walked before you from my childhood unto this day. Behold, here I am: witness against me before the Lord, and before his anointed: whose ox have I taken? or whose ass have I taken? or whom have I defrauded? whom have I oppressed? or of whose hand have I received any bribe to blind mine eyes therewith? and I will restore it you. And they said, Thou hast not defrauded us, nor oppressed us, neither hast thou taken ought of any man's hand" (I Sam. 12:1-4).

"As for me, God forbid that I should sin against the Lord in ceasing to pray for you: but I will teach you the good and the right way: Only fear the Lord, and serve him in truth with all your heart: for consider how great things he hath done for you" (I Sam. 12:23,24).

I Sam. 16-31; II Sam. 1-24; I Ki.
1:1-2:11; I Chron. 11-29

David: "well-beloved"

Youngest son of Jesse of tribe of Judah—born in Bethlehem—as a youth he shepherds his father's flocks

Anointed as future king of Israel by prophet Samuel

Called to King Saul's court as a musician

Israel and Philistines at war—David slays Goliath

David and Saul's son Jonathan make a covenant of friendship

David commands Saul's armies—marries Saul's daughter Michal

Saul's jealousy of David's popularity forces David to become a fugitive—David and his band of warriors are pursued by Saul—he twice spares Saul's life

Marries Abigail, widow of Nabal

Defeats the Amalekites

Saul is defeated by Philistines—takes his own life

David becomes king of Judah, rules at Hebron seven and a half years—war between houses of David and Saul

David becomes king of all Israel—conquers Jebusite Jerusalem and makes it his capital—rules 33 years—many wars of conquest

Brings Ark of the Covenant to Jerusalem—God's covenant with David

His sin with Bath-sheba—Nathan's parable—David's repentance and pardon

Birth of his son Solomon

Absalom, David's son, conspires for the throne—killed by Joab, captain of David's army—David's grief

David disobediently numbers the people—prepares for building of Temple

His son Adonijah and Joab conspire for the throne

Solomon is anointed king

David's charge to Solomon

He appoints the priesthood into courses or orders

His days, 70 years

DAVID, second ruler of Israel, was destined to become Israel's greatest king. He was associated with the period of the United Kingdom.

David, the youngest of the eight sons of Jesse, of the tribe of Judah, was a shepherd boy caring for his father's sheep in the hills of Bethlehem when the prophet Samuel came, at God's bidding, to anoint him Israel's future king; and "the Spirit of the Lord came upon David from that day forward."

His qualities of courage and trust in God were early evident. When a lion and a bear took the lambs of the flock, David delivered the lambs from their mouths and slew both the lion and the bear. His tender solicitude for the sheep was later manifested in his care of his Father's flock of Israel which was entrusted to him (II Sam. 5:2), thus prefiguring the true Shepherd of Israel.

According to one account (I Sam. 16:14-23) David was already known to King Saul as an accomplished harpist and as a man of war when the king sent for him to serve at his court that his troubled mind might be soothed with music. According to another record (I Sam. 17:1-18:2) David was unknown to Saul until he appeared as a shepherd youth before the king's army as it stood in battle array against the army of the Philistines. For forty days their champion, a nine-foot giant named Goliath, had paraded himself morning and evening, boastfully defying Israel's army. Fearlessly David took up the challenge, declaring, "Thou comest to me with a sword . . . but I come to thee in the name of the Lord of hosts, the God of the armies of Israel, whom thou hast defied." Using only the weapon he had proved, a shepherd's slingshot, he killed the Philistine giant with a single stone.

Saul set David over his armies and David became a great warrior and a national hero. He also became the king's son-in-law, marrying his daughter Michal. But David was so loved by the people, by Saul's son Jonathan (who had made a covenant of undying friendship with him), and by Michal that Saul feared the loss of his kingdom. In envy and fury he "became David's enemy continually," and repeatedly attempted to kill him, forcing David to flee.

For nearly six years David was a fugitive. Around him gathered a band of men, the distressed and the discontented. Twice during these years David had the opportunity to take Saul's life in revenge, but he spared it, restraining his men with the words "Destroy him not: for who can stretch forth his hand against the Lord's anointed, and be guiltless?" Finally he and his warriors sought refuge from Saul's pursuit in Philistia.

After the death of Saul, the tribe of Judah anointed David their king. Like Joseph, he was thirty years of age when he was placed in this high position. For seven and a half years he ruled Judah with his capital at Hebron. Then the other tribes of Israel accepted his leadership and he was anointed king of all Israel. (Note the three anointings: by Samuel, by Judah, by Israel [I Sam. 16:13; II Sam. 2:4; 5:3].) Then followed an important stage in the nation's history: David conquered Jebusite Jerusalem, made it the capital, and for thirty-three years governed the United Kingdom, consolidating it and extending its borders by many wars and victories. "And David executed judgment and justice unto all his people."

One of David's earliest acts as king of all Israel was to bring the Ark of the Covenant to the capital, thus moving the seat of worship from Shiloh to Jerusalem. His placing of this sacred object in a tabernacle on Mount Zion, one of the four hills upon which the city was built, made the mount sacred to the Hebrews. Jerusalem itself became known as "the city of God," "the Zion of the Holy One of Israel." David's kingdom and reign were from the beginning identified with monotheism.

David greatly desired to build a temple for the Ark, but was stayed from so doing by the word of the prophet Nathan. However, God made a covenant with David: he was promised a posterity, a throne, and an everlasting kingdom (II Sam. 7:11-16), and comforted with the assurance that his son would build the temple to His name. It was on this Davidic covenant that Israel's later hope for a Messianic king was based. In time Paul preached, "Of this man's seed hath God according to his promise raised unto Israel a Saviour, Jesus" (Acts 13:23).

When David sinned in his love for Bath-sheba and caused the death of her husband Uriah, Nathan's parable of the ewe lamb awoke him to the error of his deed with respect to himself and the nation (II Sam. 11; 12). Because David so truly loved God, this sin assumed enormous proportions, a transgression that would have been ignored by one less righteous. He acknowledged, "I have sinned against the Lord" (see Ps. 51), but the child of this adulterous union was nevertheless taken from him. The "godly sorrow [which] worketh repentance to salvation" (II Cor. 7:10) was David's experience, for from the purging and spiritual growth he experienced came the fruit of greater wisdom (as evidenced in the birth of his son Solomon, who was destined to succeed him).

He who had been taken from the sheepcote and lifted to royalty to a high degree exemplified righteousness, humility, moral and spiritual courage, an unwavering reliance on God, mercy toward his enemies, and true kingship. He prayed often for divine direction: he inquired of the Lord; he sought His face that His law might be the law of Israel. He ever acknowledged God as Israel's true sovereign, a fact of which later kings lost sight.

David, who could truly sing "The Lord is my shepherd," was called "the sweet psalmist of Israel," and to him are attributed seventy-five of the hymns in the book of Psalms. A study of these reveals the character of this man who served God with his whole heart; who meditated much on God's love and goodness; and who, through his own prayerful search for God, had a profound effect on Israel. His songs of joy, praise, and thanksgiving are a part of the great literature of the world.

A measure of the man

"The Lord hath sought him a man after his own heart...." (I Sam. 13:14; Acts 13:22).

"... cunning in playing, and a mighty valiant man, and a man of war, and prudent in matters, and a comely person, and the Lord is with him" (I Sam. 16:18).

"David ... the man who was raised up on high, the anointed of the God of Jacob, and the sweet psalmist of Israel, said, The Spirit of the Lord spake by me, and his word was in my tongue. The God of Israel said, the Rock of Israel spake to me, He that ruleth over men must be just, ruling in the fear of God" (II Sam. 23:1-3).

"David ... walked, in integrity of heart, and in uprightness...." (I Ki. 9:4)

"I will love thee, O Lord, my strength. The Lord is my rock, and my fortress, and my deliverer; my God, my strength, in whom I will trust; my buckler, and the horn of my salvation, and my high tower" (Ps. 18:1,2).

"I will bless the Lord at all times: his praise shall continually be in my mouth" (Ps. 34:1).

"I delight to do thy will, O my God: yea, thy law is within my heart" (Ps. 40:8).

"He chose David also his servant, and took him from the sheepfolds: From following the ewes great with young he brought him to feed Jacob his people, and Israel his inheritance" (Ps. 78:70,71).

"Hath not the scripture said, That Christ cometh of the seed of David, and out of the town of Bethlehem, where David was?" (Jn. 7:42)

GENEALOGY FROM ADAM TO DAVID

This chart—drawn from genealogical records in Genesis, Numbers, and First Chronicles—traces the Messianic line over a period of approximately 3000 years and shows the direct line of descent from Adam to David.

Names in italics designate: (1) those that correspond to ancient land divisions and peoples, or (2) Biblical progenitors of primitive nations which sprang from the immediate descendants of Noah (see box below).

──────── Messianic line   **Woman

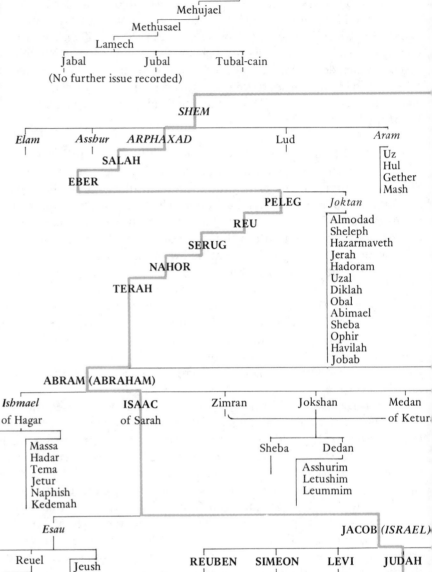

Abel

Cain

Enoch

Irad

Mehujael

Methusael

Lamech

Jabal   Jubal   Tubal-cain
(No further issue recorded)

SHEM

Elam   Asshur   ARPHAXAD   Lud   Aram

SALAH   Uz
EBER   Hul
Gether
Mash

PELEG   *Joktan*
REU   Almodad
SERUG   Sheleph
NAHOR   Hazarmaveth
TERAH   Jerah
Hadoram
Uzal
Diklah
Obal
Abimael
Sheba
Ophir
Havilah
Jobab

ABRAM (ABRAHAM)

Ishmael   ISAAC   Zimran   Jokshan   Medan
of Hagar   of Sarah   of Ketur

Nebajoth   Massa   Sheba   Dedan
Kedar   Hadar   Asshurim
Adbeel   Tema   Letushim
Mibsam   Jetur   Leummim
Mishma   Naphish
Dumah   Kedemah

Esau   JACOB (ISRAEL)

Eliphaz   Reuel   Jeush   REUBEN   SIMEON   LEVI   JUDAH
Jaalam
Teman   Nahath   Korah   of Leah
Omar   Zerah
Zepho   Shammah   Hanoch   Jemuel   Gershon
Gatam   Mizzah   Phallu   Jamin   Kohath
Kenaz   Hezron   Ohad   Merari
Amalek   Carmi   Jachin
Zohar
Shaul

Er   Onan   Shelah

Land Divisions

SHEM (Semites) . . . . Upper
                                    and Middle Asia
HAM (Hamites) . . . . Africa
                                    and S.W. Arabia
JAPHETH (Gentiles) . . . . Europe
                                    and part of Asia

ARAM . . . . Syria, Mesopotamia
ARPHAXAD . . . . North Assyria
ASSHUR . . . . Assyria
CANAAN . . . . Canaan
CUSH . . . . Ethiopia
ELAM . . . . Persia
MIZRAIM . . . . Egypt
NIMROD . . . . . . Babylonia (Chaldea)
PHUT . . . . Libya

Main Tribal Origins

Amalek . . . . Amalekite
Ben-ammi . . . . Ammonite
Casluhim . . . . Philistine
Esau . . . . Edomite
Gomer . . . . Cimmerian,
                                    Gaul, Celt
Heth . . . . Hittite
Ishmael . . . . Ishmaelite
Jacob (Israel) . . . . Israelite
Javan . . . . Ionian, Greek
Joktan . . . . Primitive Arab
Kenaz . . . . Kenezite
Madai . . . . Mede, Aryan (Indo-
                European, Indo-Iranian)
Magog . . . . Scythian
Meshech . . . . Moschi
Midian . . . . Midianite
Moab . . . . Moabite
Sidon . . . . Zidonian
Tiras . . . . Thracian
Tubal . . . . Tibareni

PROBABLE SETTLEMENTS OF NOAH'S DESCENDANTS

114

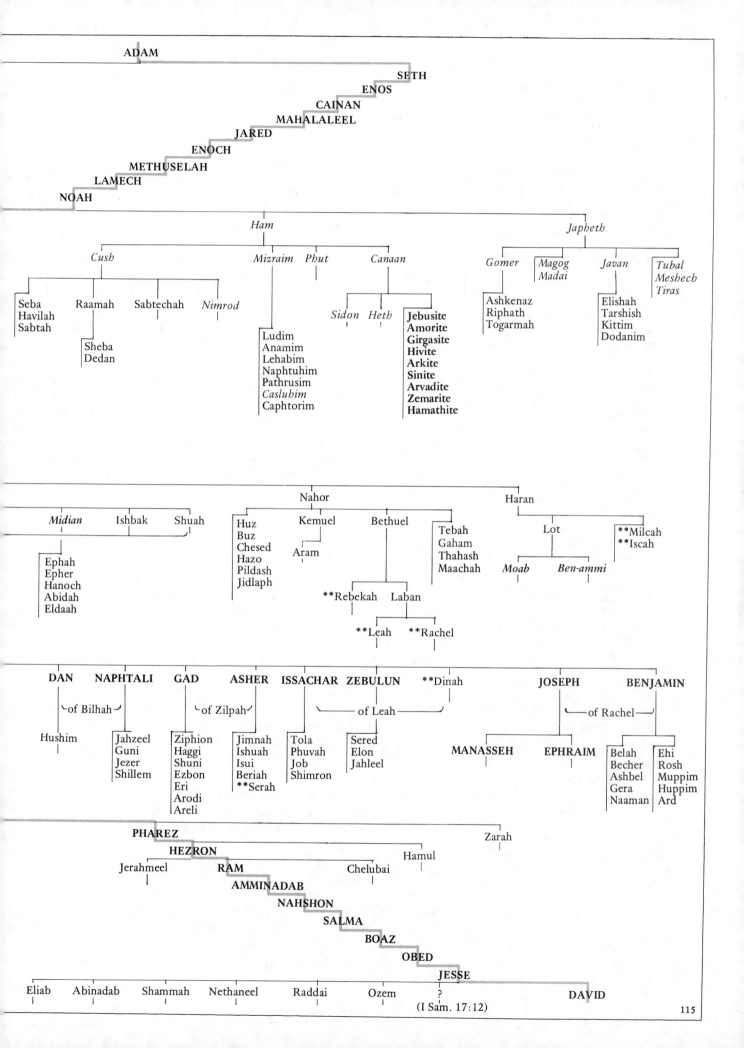

II Sam. 12:24,25; I Ki. 1-11; I Chron.
23:1; 28; 29; II Chron. 1-9

Solomon: "the peaceful"

Son of David and Bath-sheba—named
  Jedidiah by the prophet Nathan
Solomon is anointed king—David's
  charge to Solomon
Marries Pharaoh's daughter
He prays for an understanding heart—
  his wise judgment between two
  mothers
He fortifies and consolidates his king-
  dom—a reign of peace—makes
  foreign alliances—promotes extensive trade with other nations
His extraordinary wisdom and wealth
His preparation and building of the
  Temple in Jerusalem—his league
  with King Hiram of Tyre—
  dedication of the Temple
He builds palaces for himself and the
  queen
God renews the Davidic covenant with
  Solomon—warns him to eschew
  idolatry
Solomon builds a chain of chariot and
  storehouse cities—builds Israel's
  first merchant fleet
The three annual feasts of Mosaic Law
  are observed—Solomon continues
  appointments of the courses of
  the priests and Levites according
  to the order established by David
Visit of the queen of Sheba
Solomon takes to himself seven hundred wives and three hundred
  concubines—worships their
  foreign gods
Judgment on his apostasy: his kingdom to be divided—adversaries
  Hadad and Rezon arise—Solomon
  seeks to kill Jeroboam because of
  Ahijah's prophecy that Jeroboam,
  and not his own son Rehoboam,
  would reign over ten tribes of his
  kingdom
Solomon reigns 40 years

SOLOMON was the son of David
and Bath-sheba. He succeeded David as king of the United Kingdom and
was associated with a period of great prosperity in Israel and with the
building of the Temple in Jerusalem.

David chose Solomon as his heir. Shortly before his death he gave
Solomon the charge "to build an house for the sanctuary."

Solomon's reign of forty years may be divided into two periods: the
rise of his kingdom to prominence and economic strength, and the
deterioration of his own life by excessive indulgence and religious
apostasy.

Solomon started his reign well. He loved the Lord and walked "in
the statutes of David his father." He made a pilgrimage to the high place
at Gibeon to sacrifice and seek divine guidance. Deeply impressed by the
responsibilities of kingship, he prayed humbly for an understanding heart
to judge his people wisely. God answered, "Lo, I have given thee a wise
and an understanding heart. . . . And I have also given thee that which
thou hast not asked, both riches, and honour." The words "I *have* given
thee" state an eternal truth—that God's gifts are God-endowed "from the
foundation of the world" (compare Ps. 8:4-6). So long as Solomon used
these gifts in God's service—and he did for many years—his nation
prospered. Had Solomon fully discerned that the wisdom, riches, and
honor given him were spiritual gifts, he would not have misused them
later for his own glorification and self-indulgence.

His reign was one of peace, for David had subjugated Israel's border
enemies and his powerful neighbors Assyria and Egypt were at rest. He
built military garrisons and storehouses throughout his kingdom and
maintainted a strong, well-provisioned army which included 12,000
horsemen and 1400 chariots. Unlike his predecessors he made numerous
foreign alliances with nations from the Euphrates to the Nile, and
extended trade and commerce to a degree never before known to Israel.
Solomon owned huge copper mines and refineries in the Arabah rift near
the port of Ezion-geber at the head of the Gulf of Aqabah; his merchants
controlled the caravan routes between Arabia and the north; his Red Sea
navy sought the gold of Ophir and the wealth of East Africa and India,
and his Mediterranean fleet joined the Phoenician ships of Hiram to bring
silver, tin, lead, and iron from Tarshish (Tartessus) in Spain. His control
over his own subjects was strengthened by a reorganization of the land
into twelve districts so he might tax the people for the support of the
royal household—a reorganization that ignored tribal boundaries and
tribal rights.

Part of Solomon's vast building program was the erection of many
splendid buildings, among them the Temple, a palace for himself, and
another for his Egyptian wife. He inaugurated the policy of forced labor
by levying the services of Israelites and non-Israelites alike by tens of
thousands (I Ki. 5:13-18); this oppressive measure engendered a
discontent which eventually disrupted the kingdom.

Solomon's great contribution to Israel's religious history was the building of the Temple, which established Jerusalem as the center of Israel's worship and exalted Jehovah above the Baal gods of Canaan. This magnificent structure, begun in the fourth year of his reign, took seven years to construct. "The house, when it was in building, was built of stone made ready before it was brought thither: so that there was neither hammer nor axe nor any tool of iron heard in the house, while it was in building." With prayerful ceremony this sanctuary was dedicated (see Temple, p. 162). A second time God appeared to Solomon, as He had at Gibeon, and renewed the Davidic Covenant, explicitly enjoining obedience to that covenant (I Ki. 9:4-7).

The wisdom of Solomon brought him great renown. "There came of all people to hear the wisdom of Solomon, from all kings of the earth, which had heard of his wisdom." Among them was the queen of Sheba. It was said of Solomon that "he spake three thousand proverbs: and his songs were a thousand and five." Of the writings ascribed to him by antiquity or written in his name there remain the books of Proverbs, Ecclesiastes, and the Song of Solomon, which contain exquisite jewels of wisdom and instruction in righteousness, and which weigh the values of human life, its travail and fleeting pleasures.

As Solomon fulfilled his ambitions for the kingdom and became satiated with worldly success, he was drawn into idolatry, self-gratification, and sensuality. "He had seven hundred wives, princesses, and three hundred concubines: and . . . his wives turned away his heart after other gods." He worshiped the Phoenician goddess Ashtoreth and built high places for Chemosh and Molech, gods of the Moabites and the Ammonites. His disobedience brought disaster to the kingdom (I Ki. 11:11-13):

"The Lord said . . . Forasmuch as . . . thou hast not kept my covenant and my statutes . . . I will surely rend the kingdom from thee, and will give it to thy servant. Notwithstanding in thy days I will not do it for David thy father's sake: but I will rend it out of the hand of thy son. Howbeit I will not rend away all the kingdom; but will give one tribe to thy son for David my servant's sake, and for Jerusalem's sake which I have chosen."

Rehoboam, Solomon's only son by his Ammonite wife Naamah, was weak, foolish, and arrogant. Immediately after Rehoboam's accession to the throne, God's judgment on Solomon's sin was effected. The kingdom was divided, and "there was none that followed the house of David, but the tribe of Judah only." Later the tribe of Benjamin joined in forming the southern Kingdom of Judah (I Ki. 12:20,21).

Jesus made two indirect references to Solomon:

"Consider the lilies of the field, how they grow; they toil not, neither do they spin: And yet I say unto you, That even Solomon in all his glory was not arrayed like one of these" (Mt. 6:28,29).

"The queen of the south shall rise up in the judgment with this generation, and shall condemn it: for she came from the uttermost parts of the earth to hear the wisdom of Solomon; and, behold, a greater than Solomon is here" (Mt. 12:42).

"Solomon loved the Lord, walking in the statutes of David his father: only he sacrificed and burnt incense in high places" (I Ki. 3:3).

"Give therefore thy servant an understanding heart to judge thy people, that I may discern between good and bad. . . ." (I Ki. 3:9)

"God gave Solomon wisdom and understanding exceeding much, and largeness of heart, even as the sand that is on the sea shore. And Solomon's wisdom excelled the wisdom of all the children of the east country, and all the wisdom of Egypt" (I Ki. 4:29,30).

"I purpose to build an house unto the name of the Lord my God, as the Lord spake unto David my father, saying, Thy son, whom I will set upon thy throne in thy room, he shall build an house unto my name" (I Ki. 5:5).

"The Lord magnified Solomon exceedingly in the sight of all Israel, and bestowed upon him such royal majesty as had not been on any king before him in Israel" (I Chron. 29:25).

"But king Solomon loved many strange women . . . women of the Moabites, Ammonites, Edomites, Zidonians, and Hittites; Of the nations concerning which the Lord said . . . Ye shall not go in to them. . . ." (I Ki. 11:1,2)

"It came to pass, when Solomon was old, that his wives turned away his heart after other gods: and his heart was not perfect with the Lord his God. . . ." (I Ki. 11:4)

"And Solomon did evil in the sight of the Lord; and went not fully after the Lord, as did David his father" (I Ki. 11:6).

I Ki. 17-19; 21:17-29; II Ki. 1:1-2:11;
II Chron. 21:12-15

Elijah: "Jehovah is God"

A Tishbite of Gilead—Prophet to Israel

Elijah prophesies against King Ahab for his wicked reign—foretells a drought

He flees to the brook Cherith—is fed by ravens

God sends him to the widow of Zarephath—he miraculously multiplies her meal and oil—raises her son from death

After a three-year drought Elijah appears before Ahab and again reproves him

His challenge to the prophets of Baal—his prayer brings fire upon the altar—he slays the prophets of Baal

By prayer he obtains rain

Queen Jezebel threatens his life—he flees to Beer-sheba—his discouragement in the wilderness—is comforted by an angel—journeys to Mount Horeb—hears the "still small voice"

Commissioned to anoint Hazael, Jehu, and Elisha, who are destined to effect downfall of apostate house of Ahab

Casts his mantle on Elisha, signifying his appointment to the prophetic office

Elijah denounces Ahab and Jezebel for taking possession of Naboth's vineyard by violence—he prophesies their doom—Ahab is slain at Ramoth-gilead (I Ki. 22), Jezebel eaten by dogs (II Ki. 9:30-36)

Elijah twice brings fire from heaven in judgment against King Ahaziah—prophesies king's death—King Jehoram also earns Elijah's censure

Elijah, constantly companioned by Elisha, takes leave of the sons of the prophets at Gilgal, Beth-el, and Jericho—divides Jordan with his mantle and crosses over with Elisha

His translation into heaven

ELIJAH was the first great prophet of the northern Kingdom of Israel. He is identified with the period in Hebrew history in which the prophets began to appear as dominant figures to combat widespread apostasy and raise the ethical standard of Israel's religious worship.

The social discontent generated under Solomon reached its climax at the accession of Solomon's son Rehoboam to the throne. The kingdom was split when ten of the twelve tribes revolted against Rehoboam's rule (I Ki. 12). This rift was an important event in Israel's history. The United Kingdom was divided (933/32 B.C.): the tribes of Judah and Benjamin formed the southern Kingdom of Judah, continuing loyal to the house of David; the remaining ten tribes formed the northern Kingdom of Israel. These two monarchies went on side by side for the next two centuries.

Jeroboam, first king of the Northern Kingdom, fearing the return of his subjects to Judah, where the Temple was located, deliberately established a counter-worship and a counter-priesthood idolatrous in character (I Ki. 12:26-33). He set up two golden calves as symbols of Jehovah, one in Beth-el and the other in Dan, "and this thing became a sin: for the people went to worship." For the next two hundred years Israel walked in "the sins of Jeroboam."

Ahab, seventh king of Israel, was one of its most apostate rulers (I Ki. 16:30,31). Ahab's wife Jezebel was a Phoenician princess of Tyre, a fanatic champion of her native deity Baal, and through her influence Tyrian Baal worship with its gross immoralities was introduced into Israel. It flourished widely and threatened to smother the faint monotheism which still remained.

During this period of almost total apostasy the great prophet Elijah suddenly appeared to pronounce God's judgment on Ahab's sinful conduct: "As the Lord God of Israel liveth, before whom I stand, there shall not be dew nor rain these years, but according to my word." Of his preparation and call to the prophetic office there is no record, but his words "before whom I stand" show his authorization and mark him as a chosen servant of God. From the beginning miracles accompanied his ministry.

To protect him from Ahab's wrath God commanded, "Get thee hence"; so Elijah hid himself in the wilderness by the brook Cherith, there to be fed by ravens. At God's further command, "Arise, get thee to Zarephath," he found refuge in the home of an impoverished widow. There, by a miracle of grace—the multiplying of her meal and oil—he and her household were fed during the many days of famine. Through his prayer her son was restored to life.

After three years of a most disastrous drought, Elijah was told "Go, shew thyself unto Ahab." Courageously he appeared before the king and denounced him for his iniquity in worshiping Baal. Elijah called for an assembly of Israel and of the prophets of Baal at Mount Carmel that he might prove beyond doubt which was the true God. He questioned, "How long halt ye between two opinions? if the Lord be God, follow him: but if Baal, then follow him." He challenged the 450 prophets of Baal to prepare a sacrifice and call down on their altar a sign of fire from their god. All day they called but there was no answer. Then Elijah, appealing only once to his God, was answered by a consuming fire on his altar. The people were compelled to acknowledge "The Lord, he is the God."

Elijah commanded that all the prophets of Baal be slain, thereby incurring the implacable hatred of Jezebel. He fled for his life far south into the wilderness; but then, greatly discouraged over his failure to halt Israel's apostasy, he desired to die. But twice an angel aroused him from sleep, saying, "Arise and eat." Physically and spiritually sustained, he journeyed for forty days to Horeb (Sinai), the mount of God's self-revelation to Moses. There before him on the mount were displayed the mighty forces of earth (as later before John on Patmos), "but the Lord was not in the wind . . . the earthquake . . . the fire." After these Elijah heard "a still small voice" (Heb. "a sound of gentle stillness")—a divine force more potent than all he had just witnessed. By this experience he also learned, as had Moses, that violence is not the divine method of combating evil.

He was not permitted to lay down his work, but told to return and press on in the assurance that his labors would not be fruitless. He was bidden to appoint Hazael king over Syria, Jehu king over Israel, and Elisha his own successor—three men later instrumental in destroying the Baal worship Elijah had discredited and struggled to exterminate (I Ki. 19:15-17).

After at least five more years of faithful service this great prophet was translated, taken up into heaven in "a chariot of fire," an event witnessed by his successor Elisha.

> It was in the wicked Antediluvian Age that Enoch was translated, an expression of God's commendation of holiness. And now in the Prophetical Age, so far away from God, is this repetition of this great truth. . . .
>
> That this Elijah continued to exist was abundantly established by his appearance, centuries afterwards, in the Mount of Transfiguration. There with Moses, the great representative of the Law, and Elijah the representative of the Prophets, is Jesus the fulfillment of the Law and the Prophets.[1][2]

Ardent zeal and fervor were Elijah's prominent characteristics. He made his own high moral standard the ethical standard of the nation. He is a type of prophet for all time, as Malachi testified: "Behold, I will send you Elijah the prophet before the coming of the great and dreadful day of the Lord: And he shall turn the heart of the fathers to the children, and the heart of the children to their fathers, lest I come and smite the earth with a curse" (Mal. 4:5,6).

The function of spiritual cleansing that Elijah typified was later seen in the ministry of John the Baptist, who came "in the spirit and power of Elias [Elijah], to turn the hearts of the fathers to the children, and the disobedient to the wisdom of the just; to make ready a people prepared for the Lord [Messiah]" (Lu. 1:17).

A measure of the man

"Now by this [raising of widow's son] I know that thou art a man of God, and that the word of the Lord in thy mouth is truth" (I Ki. 17:24).

"Elijah the prophet . . . said, Lord God of Abraham, Isaac, and of Israel, let it be known this day that thou art God in Israel, and that I am thy servant, and that I have done all these things at thy word" (I Ki. 18:36).

"He requested for himself that he might die; and said, It is enough; now, O Lord, take away my life; for I am not better than my fathers" (I Ki. 19:4).

"I have been very jealous for the Lord God of hosts: for the children of Israel have forsaken thy covenant, thrown down thine altars, and slain thy prophets with the sword; and I, even I only, am left; and they seek my life, to take it away" (I Ki. 19:10).

"It came to pass, as they [Elijah and Elisha] still went on, and talked, that, behold, there appeared a chariot of fire, and horses of fire, and parted them both asunder; and Elijah went up by a whirlwind into heaven" (II Ki. 2:11).

"Jesus . . . said . . . Elias truly shall first come, and restore all things" (Mt. 17:11).

At the Transfiguration: "Behold, there talked with him [Jesus Christ] two men, which were Moses and Elias: Who appeared in glory, and spake of his decease which he should accomplish at Jerusalem" (Lu. 9: 30,31).

I Ki. 19:19-21; II Ki. 2-9; 13:14-21

Elisha: "God is my salvation"

A son of Shaphat

He is anointed by Elijah—leaves all to serve him

Witnesses Elijah's translation—takes up Elijah's mantle—receives double portion of his spirit—divides Jordan—is acknowledged Elijah's successor by the prophetic guilds

Elisha heals bitter waters of Jericho

Moab rebels against Israel—King Jehoram seeks aid of King Jehoshaphat of Judah and of king of Edom—Elisha's prayers bring water and promise of victory—Moabites smitten

Multiplies the widow's oil

Promises a son to Shunammite—raises her son from death

He renders poisoned pottage harmless—feeds a hundred men with twenty loaves—heals Naaman's leprosy—Gehazi, Elisha's servant, is smitten with leprosy at the prophet's word for coveting gain from Naaman which Elisha had refused

Causes iron axe head to swim

Discloses to King Jehoram battle plans of Syrian king—Syrian army, sent to seize Elisha, is smitten with blindness at Elisha's word—army is led to Samaria—their sight is restored—army dismissed in peace

Samaria besieged by Syria—great famine—Elisha'a life threatened by king—his prophecy of plenty fulfilled as Syrian army flees

Hazael kills King Ben-hadad II of Syria and reigns, according to Elisha's prophecy

Elisha anoints Jehu king of Israel—Jehu accomplishes destruction of Ahab's house and the death of Jezebel

Years later Elisha prophesies to King Jehoash three victories over the Syrians

Elisha's death at 90—his bones restore a dead man to life

ELISHA, the second great prophet in the Kingdom of Israel, was Elijah's successor. His work was accomplished during a period of continued apostasy in which, nevertheless, the blessings of God's grace were manifested to Israel.

Elisha's ministry began when Elijah, at divine direction, cast his mantle upon him. The prophet had been directed, "Elisha . . . shalt thou anoint to be prophet in thy room" (I Ki. 19:16). Elisha was "plowing with twelve yoke of oxen before him, and he with the twelfth" when the call came. At once he left his work, his family and home, to minister to Elijah.

Five years or more of consecrated preparation for his calling were accorded him under the tutelage of Elijah (the latter years of Ahab's reign, those of Ahaziah's, and possibly the early years of Jehoram's). He was known as that prophet "which poured water on the hands of Elijah." Elisha also profited by the religious education afforded him through association with the schools of the prophets.

On the way to the place of his translation Elijah bade farewell to these schools. He went with Elisha from Gilgal ("circle"). He said, "Tarry here . . . for the Lord hath sent me to Beth-el ['house of God'] ." A second time he commanded, "Tarry here . . . for the Lord hath sent me to Jericho ['place of fragrance'] ." A third time Elijah said, "Tarry, I pray thee, here; for the Lord hath sent me to Jordan [type of immortality] ." Each time Elisha answered, "As the Lord liveth, and as thy soul liveth, I will not leave thee." How close the unity of purpose and rapport of thought of these two God-directed men! "And they two went on . . . they two stood by Jordan . . . they two went over on dry ground . . . they still went on, and talked."

Elijah said, "Ask what I shall do for thee, before I be taken away from thee." The desire of his faithful disciple was to be worthy of inheriting the prophetic office from his great master: "I pray thee, let a double portion of thy spirit be upon me." Elijah answered, "Thou hast asked a hard thing: nevertheless, if thou see me when I am taken from thee, it shall be so unto thee; but if not, it shall not be so." Then occurred the glorious translation of Elijah. Elisha saw it, and received that for which he had prayed. Divesting himself of his own garments, ·tearing them in two pieces, he took up the mantle that had fallen to him from Elijah.

He immediately exercised the divine authority vested in him, smiting the waters of Jordan with the mantle so that its waters parted and he passed over on dry ground. The same great love that enabled Elisha to go beyond Jordan with Elijah also brought him back to shepherd Israel. The sons of the prophets at once acknowledged his right of succession. "He tarried at Jericho . . . went up from thence unto Beth-el . . . from thence to mount Carmel ['fruitful field,' 'harvest'] , and . . . returned to Samaria."

Elisha labored for approximately fifty years under four of the kings of Israel: Jehoram, Jehu, Jehoahaz, and Jehoash. Like Elijah, he was the mouthpiece of God's will, voicing the divine displeasure at the iniquitous conduct of secular rulers or bringing divine aid when these rulers turned to God for succor.

In the reign of Jehoram, during an invasion by the Moabites, the prophet wrought a miracle for the king and his confederates (Jehoshaphat and the king of Edom) whereby water in abundance was supplied to their thirsty armies and the Moabites were enticed into their hands (II Ki. 3:5-27).

On another occasion Elisha, through spiritual perception, aided Jehoram by warning him in advance of the battle plans of Israel's Syrian enemy. The Syrian king, learning of this, sent his army by night to capture the prophet; when Elisha's servant awoke in the morning to find the city compassed by the enemy, he feared for his master's safety. But Elisha said, "Fear not: for they that be with us are more than they that be with them"; he asked God to open the eyes of his servant that he might see that "the mountain was full of horses and chariots of fire round about." At his word God smote the Syrian army with blindness and Elisha led them to the city of Samaria. There, at his prayer, their eyes were opened and they found themselves in the power of the king of Israel. Following the prophet's humane recommendation, the king fed his enemies and dismissed them in peace. Throughout the whole train of events Elisha acted with such wisdom and mercy that no violence ensued, and the lives of both friend and foe were preserved (II Ki. 6:8-23).

A third time he aided this king by prophesying the end of a severe famine in Samaria caused by the siege of the city by Ben-hadad's Syrian army, and through divine intervention the enemy was routed (II Ki. 6:24-7:20).

The many miracles of Elisha's ministry, all of which took place after he received the double portion of the Spirit, evidenced the grace, mercy, and goodness of God, working blessings to men in the common walks of life.

At Jericho he purified the waters of a spring;
He multiplied the widow's oil to the saving of her house;
He comforted the Shunammite woman with the promise of a son;
He raised her son from the dead;
He rendered poisoned pottage harmless;
With twenty loaves he fed a hundred men;
He healed Naaman the Syrian of leprosy, but punished his own
    servant Gehazi for abusing his master's name;
He caused an iron axe head to float;
Elisha's bones restored a dead man to life.

Elisha fulfilled two of the commissions given Elijah at Horeb: to appoint Hazael king of Syria and to anoint Jehu king of Israel (II Ki. 8:7-13; 9:1-10). Through Hazael's wars against Israel, Israel was weakened; through Jehu the house of Ahab was totally destroyed, the wickedness of Jezebel against God's prophets was avenged, and Baal worship was exterminated in the Kingdom of Israel.

Elisha's life evidenced and foreshadowed the grace and practical love of humanity that so fully characterized the life of Jesus Christ.

Elijah "found Elisha ... who was plowing with twelve yoke of oxen before him, and he with the twelfth: and Elijah passed by him, and cast his mantle upon him" (I Ki. 19:19).

"Elisha said, I pray thee, let a double portion of thy [Elijah's] spirit be upon me" (II Ki. 2:9).

"Elisha saw it [Elijah's translation], and he cried, My father, my father, the chariot of Israel, and the horsemen thereof" (II Ki. 2:12).

"He took up also the mantle of Elijah that fell from him. ..." (II Ki. 2:13)

"When the sons of the prophets ... saw him, they said, The spirit of Elijah doth rest on Elisha. And they ... bowed themselves to the ground before him" (II Ki. 2:15).

"Here is Elisha the son of Shaphat, which poured water on the hands of Elijah" (II Ki. 3:11).

"Behold now, I [the Shunammite] perceive that this is an holy man of God, which passeth by us continually" (II Ki. 4:9).

"Fear not: for they that be with us are more than they that be with them" (II Ki. 6:16).

When the king of Israel said to Elisha of the Syrian prisoners, "My father, shall I smite them?" Elisha answered, "Thou shalt not smite them: wouldest thou smite those whom thou hast taken captive with thy sword and with thy bow? set bread and water before them, that they may eat and drink, and go to their master" (II Ki. 6:21,22).

ASA & JEHOSHAPHAT

I Ki. 15:8-24; II Chron. 14-16

Asa: "physician," "healer"

Asa, godly king—succeeds his father Abijam (Abijah) as third king of Judah

His reign is contemporary with the reigns of Jeroboam, Nadab, Baasha, Elah, Zimri, Omri, and Ahab, kings of Israel

Destroys idolatry and commands Judah to seek God and to keep His law

Strengthens his kingdom—obtains victory over the Ethiopians through prayer

Asa and his people make a solemn covenant with God at Jerusalem —long peace

War with Baasha of Israel

His league with Syria—reproved for his defection

Diseased in his feet—fails to seek God's help—his death

Reigns 41 years

JEHOSHAPHAT   Reformation in Judah

I Ki. 15:24; 22:2-50; II Ki. 3:6-27; II Chron. 17:1-21:1

Jehoshaphat: "Jehovah judges"

Jehoshaphat, godly king—succeeds his father Asa

His reign contemporary with reigns of Ahab, Ahaziah, and Jehoram, kings of Israel

He continues religious reforms of Asa—sends Levites to teach the Law in Judah

He fortifies his cities—his kingdom prospers

His league with Ahab to fight against Ramoth-gilead

Reproved by the prophet Jehu for his alliance with Ahab

Reappoints religious teachers for the people and reorganizes judiciary system

Kingdom invaded by Ammonites and Moabites—nation fasts—miraculous victory

Makes a league with Ahaziah to send ships to Tarshish—ships wrecked

Reigns 25 years

were "godly" kings of the southern Kingdom of Judah. Their reigns were responsible for important periods of reformation in Judah's history.

The United Kingdom had been divided into two kingdoms at the death of Solomon: the Kingdom of Judah and the Kingdom of Israel. The tribe of Judah, to which the tribe of Benjamin soon joined itself, constituted the southern kingdom.

Jacob's prophecy, centuries earlier, had designated the tribe of Judah as the one from which the Messiah would come (Gen. 49:8-12). David was of this tribe, and God's covenant had been renewed with David and his house. Although the Kingdom of Israel had the greater portion of territory and the majority of the population, the divinely appointed line of descent lay with the Kingdom of Judah. (It is interesting to note that through all the vicissitudes of Judah's coming history of nearly three and a half centuries the Davidic line was never broken, while in rival Israel the line of succession was broken repeatedly.)

The religious sanction also remained with Judah. The Temple, dedicated to the worship of Jehovah, stood in Jerusalem, Judah's capital, and the Levitical priesthood instituted by Moses was maintained in Judah; while in Israel its first king Jeroboam established a counter-worship, setting up two golden calves as symbols of Jehovah, one in Beth-el and the other in Dan, and a base unlawful priesthood (I Ki. 12:28-31).

The calf-worship of Israel never penetrated Judah but the worship of God was often corrupted by the inroads of other heathen cults. Both kingdoms went through centuries of idolatry and religious decline. Judah's idolatry, however, never reached the total apostasy of Israel's. Outstanding periods of reformation under Asa, Jehoshaphat, Hezekiah, and Josiah made a strong imprint on the nation's life span. The goodly reigns of these kings, whereby idolatry was partially rooted out and Judah's covenant with God renewed, gave a fresh, healthful impetus to monotheistic worship and lengthened its national life almost a century and a half beyond that of the Kingdom of Israel.

ASA was the first of the four "godly" kings, the great-grandson of Solomon and third king of Judah, reigning over forty years. "Asa did that which was right in the eyes of the Lord," as did his forefather David. At the beginning of his reign he launched a vigorous religious reform: expelled the sodomites from the land, destroyed the idols, and even deposed his grandmother for her worship of an Asherah; but he was unable wholly to suppress worship on heathen high places (I Ki. 15:14; see High Places, p. 50). During ten years of peace he strengthened the kingdom, fortified its cities, and enlarged his army.

When a great Ethiopian army invaded Judah, Asa prayerfully relied on God for help. As he returned triumphantly from his pursuit of the enemy, the prophet Azariah warned, "The Lord is with you, while ye be with him; and if ye seek him, he will be found of you; but if ye forsake him, he will forsake you." He urged the king to continue his reformative work; so Asa again purged Judah of its idols and climaxed his efforts with a solemn renewal of the ancient covenant with God.

In the latter part of his reign Asa fell from grace when he made an alliance with Ben-hadad I of Syria, seeking his help against Baasha of Israel. When the prophet Hanani rebuked him for his failure to rely on God, "Asa was wroth with the seer, and put him in a prison house; for he was in a rage with him because of this thing." In the thirty-ninth year of his reign Asa was diseased in his feet, "yet . . . he sought not to the Lord, but to the physicians. And Asa slept with his fathers. . . ."

JEHOSHAPHAT, son

of Asa, was the second of the four "godly" kings. "The Lord was with Jehoshaphat, because he walked in the first ways of his father David, and sought not unto Baalim." Immediately upon his accession to the throne he began a religious revival, as had his father, to cleanse Judah of its idolatry, sodomy, groves, and high places. Moreover he sent Levites into every city to teach the people the law of the Lord. Having lifted its religious standard, Judah prospered and was at peace with neighboring nations.

Jehoshaphat even made peace with King Ahab of Israel, ending the long period of hostility which had existed between the two kingdoms. This peace was further strengthened by the marriage of his son Jehoram to Athaliah, daughter of Ahab and Jezebel; but this alliance later proved injurious for it introduced Tyrian Baal worship into Judah. Jehoshaphat was persuaded by Ahab into an imprudent league to wrest the city of Ramoth-gilead from the Syrians. The battle was disastrous; Ahab was killed and Jehoshaphat almost lost his life. On the king's return the prophet Jehu reproved him: "Shouldest thou help the ungodly, and love them that hate the Lord? therefore is wrath upon thee from before the Lord."

Rededicating himself to Judah's welfare, Jehoshaphat journeyed personally throughout his kingdom, reappointing teachers for religious instruction of the people. He also reorganized local courts of justice, appointing judges in every fortified city and establishing a supreme court in Jerusalem composed of priests, Levites, and elders to review cases appealed from local courts. Though his reforms were sweeping, "the high places were not taken away: for as yet the people had not prepared their hearts unto the God of their fathers" (II Chron. 20:33).

A crisis in Jehoshaphat's reign occurred when the Moabites and Ammonites invaded Judah (II Chron. 20). The king turned unreservedly to God and called on Judah to fast with him. He prayed, "O our God . . . we have no might against this great company . . . neither know we what to do: but our eyes are upon thee." The answer came, "Be not afraid nor dismayed by reason of this great multitude; for the battle is not your's, but God's." Singers to praise "the beauty of holiness" were sent before the army, and when they began to sing, the Lord caused the enemy to destroy itself.

Toward the close of his reign Jehoshaphat made a league with another wicked king of Israel (Ahaziah), an economic one to build merchant ships; but this alliance was denounced by the prophet Eliezer and its failure foretold. His reign lasted twenty-five years.

A measure of the man

"Asa did that which was right in the eyes of the Lord, as did David his father. . . . But the high places were not removed: nevertheless Asa's heart was perfect with the Lord all his days" (I Ki. 15:11,14).

"When Asa heard . . . the prophecy of Oded the prophet, he took courage, and put away the abominable idols out of all the land of Judah and Benjamin . . . and renewed the altar of the Lord. . . ." (II Chron. 15:8)

"Hanani the seer came to Asa king of Judah, and said unto him, Because thou hast relied on the king of Syria, and not relied on the Lord thy God, therefore is the host of the king of Syria escaped out of thine hand. . . . Herein thou hast done foolishly: therefore from henceforth thou shalt have wars" (II Chron. 16:7,9).

"The Lord was with Jehoshaphat, because he walked in the first ways of his father David, and sought not unto Baalim; But sought to the Lord God of his father, and walked in his commandments, and not after the doings of Israel" (II Chron. 17:3,4).

"He had riches and honour in abundance" (II Chron. 17:5).

"Nevertheless there are good things found in thee, in that thou hast taken away the groves out of the land, and hast prepared thine heart to seek God" (II Chron. 19:3).

"He walked in the way of Asa his father, and departed not from it, doing that which was right in the sight of the Lord. Howbeit the high places were not taken away: for as yet the people had not prepared their hearts unto the God of their fathers" (II Chron. 20:32,33).

II Ki. 19; 20; II Chron. 26:22; 32:20-22;
Book of Isaiah

Isaiah: "Jehovah is salvation"

Son of Amoz—resides in Jerusalem

Isaiah prophesies for Kingdom of Judah during reigns of the kings Azariah (Uzziah), Jotham, Ahaz, and Hezekiah

His vision of God's glory comes to him in the last year of Uzziah's reign—his call to preach to an unrepentant people—God's promise of a remnant

Isaiah warns Ahaz against an alliance with Rezin of Syria and Pekah of Israel to fight Assyria—Syria and Israel turn against Ahaz and attack Judah (II Ki. 16:5)—Isaiah comforts Ahaz with prophecies of their downfall—foretells the Advent of the Messiah

When Ahaz turns for aid to Tiglath-pileser III of Assyria, Isaiah prophesies Assyria will invade Judah

He repeatedly warns Judah of judgment for its corruption, wickedness, pride, yet comforts his people with prophecies of the Messiah and his kingdom and with promise of a faithful remnant

He pronounces God's judgment on heathen nations

Isaiah aids Hezekiah's great religious reform

(Northern Kingdom of Israel carried captive to Assyria by Sargon in 722 B.C.)

Isaiah pronounces judgment against Sennacherib, son of Sargon, when he attempts to invade Judah—his prayers, joined with Hezekiah's, save Jerusalem

He foretells Hezekiah's recovery from sickness

Isaiah, hearing that Hezekiah has shown his treasures to Babylonian envoys, predicts the captivity of Judah

His labors, 40 years

ISAIAH was the first of the Major
Prophets, chief among the writing prophets, and his work marked the crest of the first great wave of Hebrew prophecy.

The prophetic movement instituted by Samuel and exemplified so strikingly by Elijah and Elisha was moving toward a fuller flowering in the labors and writings of the four Major Prophets and of the twelve Minor Prophets (for their dates and books see pp. 17-19). For four centuries (*ca.* 800-400 B.C.) the prophets were the outstanding men of the nation, its religious leaders, true patriots, and statesmen. The divine will was voiced through them; they were God's messengers, constantly reminding Israel of her destiny as the covenant people. By precept and living parable they exhorted the people of both the northern and southern kingdoms to a true moral repentance, foreseeing the doom of these kingdoms if they did not return to God. Their prophecies against oppressing heathen nations extended encouragement to the afflicted masses. These great seers, beholding God's eternal order above and beyond the world of their day, divested Israel's religion of its national character by revealing His impartial justice, and showed its principles and ethics to be universal. They knew Him as merciful, just, and righteous, the God of all nations.

Isaiah appears to have been of noble birth. He lived in Jerusalem and was an eminent statesman in the royal court (740-701 B.C.) under four of the kings of Judah: Uzziah, Jotham, Ahaz, and Hezekiah. Isaiah received his call to the office of prophet in early manhood, during the last year of Uzziah's reign (Is. 6). He was accorded a transcendent vision of God's glory and majesty that lifted him to spiritual heights. "I saw . . . the Lord sitting upon a throne, high and lifted up, and his train filled the temple. . . . And one [of the seraphim] cried . . . Holy, holy, holy, is the Lord of hosts: the whole earth is full of his glory" (compare Rev. 4:2,8).

His vision also cast him into the depths of despair: "Woe is me! for I am undone; because I am a man of unclean lips, and I dwell in the midst of a people of unclean lips. . . . Then flew one of the seraphims unto me, having a live coal in his hand. . . . And he laid it upon my mouth, and said, Lo, this hath touched thy lips; and thine iniquity is taken away, and thy sin purged." Hearing God's question "Whom shall I send?" Isaiah answered, "Here am I; send me." This revelation of God's holiness, sovereignty, and omnipresence became the wellspring of his life; and his utter dedication to God's service held him in unceasing communion with "the Holy One of Israel."

Under Uzziah and Jotham, Judah had prospered and grown fat. Ahaz inherited a kingdom outwardly strong but inwardly corrupt, riddled with vice and social evils (Is. 2:7,8; 3:14,15; 5:11,12,23). Isaiah vehemently rebuked his nation for its oppression of the poor, excessive indulgences, idolatry, formalism of worship, "vain oblations," pronouncing God's judgments on these evils.

Isaiah came at a time when the Assyrian Empire was at the height of its power and was pressing on the small neighboring states of Syria and Israel. These two sought the aid of Ahaz, but Isaiah counseled against such a confederacy and foretold the fall of Syria and Israel (Is. 7:1-9). When Ahaz made an alliance with Assyria, Isaiah prophesied its near-fatal results to Judah (II Ki. 16:5-8; Is. 8:5-12).

To Hezekiah's great reformation (see next page) Isaiah gave full support. He urged Hezekiah, as he had Ahaz, to refrain from foreign alliances, but with less success. For three years he walked half-naked and barefoot like a captive through Judah to warn the nation against reliance on Egypt and Ethiopia (Is. 20; 30; 31). In 701 B.C. Sennacherib of Assyria invaded Judah and threatened Jerusalem. Isaiah upheld Hezekiah in this crisis and through their prayers the city was delivered (Is. 36; 37; compare 10:24-27; 14:24-27; 17:12-14; 31:8,9), but later when Hezekiah allied himself with Babylon, Isaiah foretold Judah's captivity (Is. 39).

During these trying political times Isaiah comforted Judah with the promise of a God-sent Messiah, Immanuel (Is. 7:14; 28:6), and revealed the sublime nature of this Redeemer (Is. 9:6,7; 11:1-5). He enlarged his prophecies to predict the fall of the tyrant Assyria, to enumerate the blessings of the Messianic kingdom, to foretell the return of a faithful remnant of the covenant people and the calling of the Gentiles (Is. 10-12). At the same time he repeatedly warned Judah of judgment for its sins (Is. 1-5; 29). To strengthen the nation's faith he uttered ten "burdens" or judgments against heathen nations (Is. 13-23), and predicted the breaking up of the old world order (Is. 24-27). The righteous would be exalted in Zion and "see the king in his beauty," and "the ransomed of the Lord" would dwell in Messiah's kingdom (Is. 33; 35).

While the earlier prophecies of Isaiah look toward the captivities (Is. 1-39), his later prophecies, the work of his maturer years, look beyond the Exile to the glorious restoration of the covenant people (Is. 40-66). (Because of the change of style and theme in these latter writings, many modern scholars consider them the work of a Second Isaiah [Is. 40-55] and a Third Isaiah [Is. 56-66].) From the new standpoint the prophet saw the future as if it were present (as did John in his Apocalypse). His prophecies were full of comfort to a people whose "warfare is accomplished," whose "iniquity is pardoned." The wisdom and saving power of God are proclaimed and the restoration of Judah is assured, Cyrus being the instrument for their deliverance (Is. 40-48). God's mercy and tender love to the restored are stressed (Is. 54-59).

Isaiah foresaw the Messiah's First Advent in suffering and humiliation. Whereas he had previously spoken of Messiah's kingship, he now emphasized the Messiah's office as the "servant" of God whose mission was not alone to Israel but to the whole world (Is. 42:1-4; 49:1-10; 50:4-9; 52:13-53:12). He also foresaw the Messiah's Second Advent in judgment and glory (Is. 63:1-4). He painted a glowing picture of the inclusion of the Gentiles in the spiritual inheritance of Israel, and saw the glory of a new Jerusalem and of a new heaven and a new earth (Is. 60-66).

A measure of the man

"O house of Jacob, come ye, and let us walk in the light of the Lord" (Is. 2:5).

"I will wait upon the Lord, that hideth his face from the house of Jacob, and I will look for him. Behold, I and the children whom the Lord hath given me are for signs and for wonders in Israel from the Lord of hosts, which dwelleth in mount Zion" (Is. 8:17,18).

"The Lord said, Like as my servant Isaiah hath walked naked and bare-foot three years for a sign and wonder upon Egypt and upon Ethiopia. . . ." (Is. 20:3)

"A grievous vision is declared unto me. . . . Therefore are my loins filled with pain: pangs have taken hold upon me, as the pangs of a woman that travaileth: I was bowed down at the hearing of it; I was dismayed at the seeing of it" (Is. 21:2,3).

"Therefore said I, Look away from me; I will weep bitterly, labour not to comfort me, because of the spoiling of the daughter of my people. For it is a day of trouble, and of treading down, and of perplexity by the Lord God of hosts in the valley of vision. . . ." (Is. 22:4,5)

"O Lord, thou art my God; I will exalt thee, I will praise thy name; for thou hast done wonderful things; thy counsels of old are faithfulness and truth" (Is. 25:1).

"With my soul have I desired thee in the night; yea, with my spirit within me will I seek thee early: for when thy judgments are in the earth, the inhabitants of the world will learn righteousness" (Is. 26:9).

II Ki. 18-20; II Chron. 29-32;
Is. 36-39; Jer. 26:17-19

Hezekiah: "strengthened of Jah"

Hezekiah, godly king, succeeds his father Ahaz

Begins at once to restore true religion —commands Levites to sanctify themselves and the Temple

Nation observes solemn Passover— people destroy idols throughout Judah

Hezekiah rebels against Assyria, refusing to pay tribute—builds an aqueduct to supply Jerusalem with water—makes alliances with Ethiopia and Egypt

Hezekiah's sickness and prayer—his life is lengthened

Sennacherib of Assyria invades Judah —Hezekiah sends tribute—Sennacherib's army threatens Jerusalem—Isaiah prophesies against Sennacherib—army miraculously smitten by a plague

Hezekiah shows his treasures to Babylonian envoys—Isaiah rebukes him and prophesies Judah's captivity

Reigns 29 years

JOSIAH   **Reformation in Judah**

II Ki. 21:24; 22:1-23:30;
II Chron. 34; 35

Josiah: "Jah supports"

Josiah, godly king, succeeds his wicked father Amon

In faith and piety he destroys idolatry, abominations, and witchcraft throughout Judah and Samaria— prophet Jeremiah aids in reform

Repairs the Temple—book of the law is found—fearing judgment he consults the prophetess Huldah— renews the covenant—solemn Passover observed

Opposes Pharaoh-necho of Egypt—is slain in battle at Megiddo

Reigns 31 years

HEZEKIAH & JOSIAH were the last two of

the four "godly" kings who instituted important reformations in the southern Kingdom of Judah.

HEZEKIAH, son of Ahaz and thir-

teenth king, came to the throne (723 B.C.?) when Judah was in a deplorable state of apostasy. His father had worshiped Baalim and the gods of Syria, subjected Judah to abominable Canaanitish rites, and finally closed the doors of the Temple in Jerusalem.

Immediately upon his accession Hezekiah, aided by the prophets Isaiah and Micah, began religious reforms. "He in the first year of his reign, in the first month, opened the doors of the house of the Lord," and enjoined the Levitical priesthood to cleanse the Temple and sanctify it for its proper use. He said, "It is in mine heart to make a covenant with the Lord God of Israel." Eight days were needed to cleanse the sanctuary, and eight days to cleanse the outer court and restore the sacred vessels. When all this was done he called Judah to Jerusalem to observe the Passover. His proclamation was extended even to Israelitish brethren of the Northern Kingdom, and many humbled themselves, and came. The consecrating effect of its observance was felt in every corner of the kingdom; the people returned to their villages to destroy their idolatrous altars and high places. Hezekiah's next reform extended to the reorganization of Temple service: priests and Levites were appointed in their courses (orders) and the people commanded to pay the Mosaic tithes so the priesthood might be encouraged in its religious duties. His concern for the welfare of his subjects and his persevering efforts to promote the cause of true religion rank him as one of Judah's most righteous kings.

Under Hezekiah's leadership Judah prospered. He regained the cities of Philistia that Ahaz had lost, and threw off the yoke of Assyria by refusing to pay Shalmaneser V the yearly tribute Ahaz had rendered to Tigalth-pileser III. (In 722 B.C. Sargon II, Shalmaneser's successor, invaded the Kingdom of Israel and, according to Sargon's own inscription, deported more than 27,000 of its leading citizens to Assyria [II Ki. 18:9-11].) To strengthen Judah against Assyria, Hezekiah refortified Jerusalem and built an acqueduct to bring water within its walls. He made alliances with Ethiopia and Egypt, measures that Isaiah sternly rebuked (Is. 18:1-5; 20; 30:1-5; 31:1-3).

Hezekiah's reliance on God was manifest in his personal experience when he fell mortally ill. Turning to God (as King Asa had not), he was healed and his life lengthened by fifteen years.

Sargon's successor, Sennacherib, after invading Judah's border cities, marched against the capital (*ca.* 701 B.C.), and in a blasphemous letter demanded its surrender. Hezekiah, acknowledging God's supremacy over all the kingdoms of the earth, prayed for deliverance. It was revealed to Isaiah that God would defend the city, and that night an "angel of the Lord" smote the Assyrian camp with death and Jerusalem was delivered.

Hezekiah erred when he showed the treasures of his kingdom to ambassadors from Babylon. For this Isaiah rebuked him and foretold Judah's captivity in Babylon.

JOSIAH, son of Amon, was the

sixteenth and last of the "godly" kings (638-608 B.C.). His grandfather Manasseh, son of Hezekiah, had ruled for fifty-five years. Manasseh had reverted to heathen abominations but, carried captive by the Assyrians and imprisoned in Babylon, he later repented and returned to Jerusalem to correct the evils of his earlier reign. Manasseh's wicked son Amon ruled only two years.

Josiah was eight years old when he came to the throne; at sixteen he began to seek God diligently—he "walked in all the way of David his father, and turned not aside to the right hand or to the left." He was not quite twenty when he declared open warfare on idolatry.

At twenty-six he turned to the repair of the Temple. During the restoration the book of the law ("the legislative kernel" of our Deuteronomy, chaps. 5-26, 28; or, according to some critics, the Deuteronomic Code, chaps. 12-26) was found by Hilkiah the high priest. When Josiah heard its commandments and its curses pronounced on disobedience, he was greatly dismayed. Hoping to avert these fearful dooms, he humbly sought counsel of the prophetess Huldah and was comforted by her assurance that because of his contrition judgment would not fall on the kingdom during his lifetime.

Josiah summoned the people to Jerusalem. In solemn assembly he read aloud the book of the law and made a covenant with God to uphold its commandments and statutes, and caused the people to stand to the covenant. He then set out on a sweeping reform to bring Judah's religious worship into line with the Mosaic standard. The Temple was thoroughly cleansed of cultic practices, and idolatrous priests were removed. Josiah himself journeyed throughout Judah and even throughout Samaria (former Kingdom of Israel) and in his presence all altars were broken down, the graven images beaten into powder, and the groves (cultic poles of Asherah) cut down. So drastic were his measures that Baalism was abolished and worship at high places wholly destroyed. His labors were supported by the zeal of the prophet Jeremiah. Josiah also caused the Passover to be kept in strict conformity with Mosaic ordinances and on a scale unprecedented since the days of Samuel. For more than a decade the struggle for reform went on. It was far-reaching in its effects, for it buttressed the people in their knowledge of Mosaic Law and was to nurture spiritual religion during the coming years of exile in Babylon.

In 608 B.C., as Necho of Egypt marched his armies to war against the Assyrians, Josiah unwisely opposed their passage through Palestine and was slain at Megiddo.

The four reformative movements in the Southern Kingdom under its godly kings and prophets, by which Judah was periodically halted in its religious lapses, preserved and sustained the seed of righteousness, while apostate Israel, whose kings gave no heed to its God-sent prophets, went unrepentant to its doom. These vital revivals explain why Judah, after a limited captivity that burned away the dross of idolatry, was given renewed opportunity to return to the land of its destiny to carry forward its Messianic mission.

Hezekiah "did that which was right in the sight of the Lord, according to all that David his father did" (II Ki. 18:3).

"He clave to the Lord, and departed not from following him, but kept his commandments, which the Lord commanded Moses" (II Ki. 18:6).

"In those days was Hezekiah sick unto death. . . . Then he . . . prayed unto the Lord, saying, I beseech thee, O Lord, remember now how I have walked before thee in truth and with a perfect heart, and have done that which is good in thy sight. And Hezekiah wept sore" (II Ki. 20:1-3).

"In every work that he began in the service of the house of God, and in the law, and in the commandments, to seek his God, he did it with all his heart, and prospered" (II Chron. 31:21).

"In the eighth year of his [Josiah's] reign, while he was yet young, he began to seek after the God of David his father: and in the twelfth year he began to purge Judah and Jerusalem from the high places, and the groves, and the carved images, and the molten images" (II Chron. 34:3).

"Because thine heart was tender, and thou didst humble thyself before God, when thou heardest his words against this place, and against the inhabitants thereof, and humbledst thyself before me, and didst rend thy clothes, and weep before me; I have even heard thee also, saith the Lord. Behold, I will gather thee to thy fathers . . . in peace, neither shall thine eyes see all the evil that I will bring upon this place, and upon the inhabitants of the same" (II Chron. 34:27,28).

II Chron. 35:25; 36:12; Books of
Jeremiah and Lamentations

Jeremiah: "Jah will rise"

Son of Hilkiah (a priest of Anathoth)

Prophesies during the reigns of Josiah, Jehoahaz, Jehoiakim, Jehoiachin, Zedekiah

Jeremiah's call to the office of prophet

He rebukes Judah's persistent idolatry —warns nation to repent—preaches God's judgments on their sins

Jeremiah takes an active part in Josiah's great religious reformation

His life is threatened during King Jehoiakim's reign by hostility of people, priests, princes, and the king himself because of his direful predictions—foretells destruction of Jerusalem and seventy years' captivity of Judah in Babylon— foretells return of a remnant

God commands Jeremiah to write his prophecies that all Judah may hear—in a rage King Jehoiakim burns the roll of prophecies—roll rewritten

(Nineveh, capital of Assyria, falls to Nebuchadnezzar, king of Babylon)

Judah becomes a vassal of Nebuchadnezzar—first deportation of captives to Babylon

During King Jehoiachin's reign Nebuchadnezzar loots Jerusalem— second deportation of captives to Babylon

During King Zedekiah's reign Jeremiah prophesies Chaldean victory—is imprisoned

Jerusalem is captured by Nebuchadnezzar—Judah is carried captive to Babylon (third deportation)

Jeremiah remains in Jerusalem with a small remnant of Judah—when they revolt against Babylonian rule he is compelled to go with them to Egypt—continues his labors

Prophesies over 40 years

JEREMIAH, the second of the

Major Prophets, came three-quarters of a century after Isaiah. He also was associated with the great period of Hebrew prophecy. He prophesied during the closing years of Judah's history as a monarchy, beginning under King Josiah's godly reign and continuing until after the fall of Jerusalem (586 B.C.).

The call of Jeremiah was as distinct and clear as that of Isaiah: "The word of the Lord came unto me, saying . . . before thou camest forth out of the womb I sanctified thee, and I ordained thee a prophet unto the nations. Then said I, Ah, Lord God! behold, I cannot speak: for I am a child. But the Lord said unto me, Say not, I am a child: for thou shalt go to all that I shall send thee, and whatsoever I command thee thou shalt speak. Be not afraid of their faces: for I am with thee to deliver thee. . . . Then the Lord put forth his hand, and touched my mouth. And the Lord said unto me, Behold, I have put my words in thy mouth. See, I have this day set thee over the nations and over the kingdoms, to root out, and to pull down, and to destroy, and to throw down, to build, and to plant" (Jer. 1:4-10).

Now knowing himself God's messenger to Judah, Jeremiah fearlessly undertook the great task of "rooting out" and "pulling down." He relentlessly exposed Judah's iniquities in defiling God's goodness. Israel had been punished for its whoredom, "Yet," said Jeremiah, "her treacherous sister Judah feared not, but went and played the harlot also" (Jer. 3:8).

His resolve to carry out his mission in spite of all opposition was strengthened by the assurance of God's presence: "I have made thee this day a defenced city, and an iron pillar, and brasen walls against the whole land . . . they shall fight against thee; but they shall not prevail against thee; for I am with thee." Because he dared to declare calamitous judgments against the priests, the Temple, the people, and even Jerusalem itself, his life was repeatedly in danger. The men of his village of Anathoth plotted to kill him (Jer. 11:21). His family dealt treacherously with him (Jer. 12:6). He was persecuted by the priests and false prophets, beaten, and subjected to the humiliating indignity of imprisonment in the stocks (Jer. 26:8; 20:2). Their mockery and derision of God's word wrought agony in his soul. Jeremiah's own spirit would have failed him, but so imbued was he with the Spirit and with pitying love for his people that he wrote: "Then I said, I will not make mention of him [God], nor speak any more in his name. But his word was in mine heart as a burning fire shut up in my bones, and I was weary with forbearing, and I could not stay" (20:9).

Jeremiah's prophetic voice rang even more insistently in the streets of Jerusalem against Judah's disobedience during the wicked reigns of

Jehoahaz and Jehoiakim. For twenty-three years Jeremiah had warned his nation not to provoke God to their "own hurt." Now he predicted Judah's captivity: "This whole land shall be a desolation . . . and these nations shall serve the king of Babylon seventy years" (Jer. 25:11). When he foretold the destruction of their sacred sanctuary the Temple and of Jerusalem their holy city, all rose up, crying, "Thou shalt surely die."

Assyrian power was broken when Nebuchadnezzar of Babylon conquered Nineveh in 606 B.C. The same year he invaded Judah, placed it under tribute, and carried captive to Babylon King Jehoiakim and some of the nobility, including Daniel (first deportation [II Chron. 36:6; Dan. 1:2,3,6]).

Jeremiah, hindered on every side, was commanded of God to write all of his prophecies of judgment in a book in the hope that Judah would yet hear, "that they may return every man from his evil way; that I may forgive their iniquity and their sin." Jeremiah dictated these prophecies to his faithful friend Baruch, who read the roll publicly on several occasions; but King Jehoiakim dishonored these by slashing and burning the roll. Under divine direction Jeremiah commanded Baruch to rewrite it and, undaunted, added "many like words" (Jer. 36).

In Jehoiachin's reign Jeremiah was a sorrowful witness to the pillaging of the Temple by Nebuchadnezzar and to the second deportation (of ten thousand captives) to Babylon (597 B.C.), the king and Ezekiel among them (II Ki. 24:14,15; Ezek. 1:1,2).

Zedekiah was the last king of Judah. He too refused to heed Jeremiah's warnings, even casting the prophet ignominiously into a miry dungeon (Jer. 38:6-13). He rebelled against Babylon and in 586 B.C. Jerusalem fell to Nebuchadnezzar and the city was razed. Jeremiah saw the destruction of the Temple, the tragic desolation of Jerusalem, and the third and final deportation of captives to Babylon (II Ki. 25:11).

Because Jeremiah had repeatedly counseled his nation to submit to God's chastisement by the hand of Babylon, Nebuchadnezzar did not harm him, but permitted him to remain with a remnant in Judah. When this remnant, discrediting his prophecy of safety in Judah, fled to Egypt, he was compelled to go with them. The record of his life closes while he was still prophesying in Egypt.

As Jeremiah had worked "to root out, and to pull down," so he also strove "to build, and to plant." Like Isaiah, he assured Judah of God's love and forgiveness, comforting them with God's gracious promises of a return from captivity, a restoration of their glory, and the coming of the Messiah, "the Branch" (Jer. 32:37-33:26).

He perceived the terrible failure of external religion to effect a genuine repentance. He saw that God's law must be written in the heart, and consequently he foretold a *new covenant* when men would take individual responsibility for obedience: "Behold, the days come, saith the Lord, that I will make a new covenant with the house of Israel, and with the house of Judah . . . I will put my law in their inward parts, and write it in their hearts; and will be their God, and they shall be my people" (Jer. 31:31,33). The new covenant was to find its fulfillment in Jesus Christ and his gospel (Heb. 8:6-13).

A measure of the man

"Oh that my head were waters, and mine eyes a fountain of tears, that I might weep day and night for the slain of the daughter of my people!" (Jer. 9:1)

"But if ye [Judah] will not hear it, my soul shall weep in secret places for your pride; and mine eye shall weep sore, and run down with tears, because the Lord's flock is carried away captive" (Jer. 13:17).

"Woe is me, my mother, that thou hast borne me a man of strife and a man of contention to the whole earth! I have neither lent on usury, nor men have lent to me on usury; yet every one of them doth curse me. . . . O Lord, thou knowest: remember me, and visit me, and revenge me of my persecutors; take me not away in thy longsuffering: know that for thy sake I have suffered rebuke. Thy words were found, and I did eat them; and thy word was unto me the joy and rejoicing of mine heart: for I am called by thy name, O Lord God of hosts" (Jer. 15:10,15,16).

"I am in derision daily, every one mocketh me" (Jer. 20:7).

"But the Lord is with me as a mighty terrible one: therefore my persecutors shall stumble, and they shall not prevail. . . ." (Jer. 20:11)

"Mine heart within me is broken because of the [false] prophets; all my bones shake; I am like a drunken man, and like a man whom wine hath overcome, because of the Lord, and because of the words of his holiness" (Jer. 23:9).

". . . the word of the Lord hath come unto me, and I have spoken unto you, rising early and speaking; but ye have not hearkened" (Jer. 25:3).

Book of Ezekiel

Ezekiel: "God strengthens"

Priest and prophet, son of Buzi

Ezekiel is taken captive to Babylon by Nebuchadnezzar during reign of Jehoiachin (second deportation)

He resides with a colony of Jewish exiles at Tel-abib near the river Chebar

His vision of God's glory in the fifth year of his captivity—his call to preach to captive Judah—is filled with the Spirit—is commissioned as spiritual guardian of the whole house of Israel

Repeatedly by symbolic actions, dramatic imagery, and visions he preaches the rejection of Judah and the fall of Jerusalem as a consequence of Judah's iniquities

He preaches to a rebellious people—shows the exiles the true meaning of their captivity—gives them hope and prophesies the saving of a remnant

Ezekiel pronounces God's dire judgments upon the neighboring nations of Ammon, Moab, Edom, Philistia, and the cities of Tyre and Sidon—also a series of five judgments against Egypt

Ezekiel is recommissioned a guardian of the nation after the fall of Jerusalem—rebukes the unfaithful leaders (shepherds of Israel)

Comforts his people with prophecies of restoration and redemption

His apocalyptic vision of a holy Jerusalem and an ideal temple (chaps. 40-48)

He prophesies for 22 years

EZEKIEL was the third of

the Major Prophets. He was connected with the period of Judah's Babylonian captivity.

There was a striking difference between the fall of Israel and that of Judah. Israel was dispersed, never again to be united. Judah was not scattered but as an entity was to endure a seventy-year captivity (Jer. 25:11; 29:10). The Kingdom of Israel had begun with revolt and corrupted its religious worship from its inception. Judah was to be cleansed and drawn closer to God; from Judah a righteous remnant was to be saved and restored.

Ezekiel was a priest by birth and training, and lived in Jerusalem. He had an intimate knowledge of Temple worship and had undoubtedly been influenced as a young man by the preaching of Zephaniah and Jeremiah. Ezekiel was taken to Babylon by Nebuchadnezzar in 597 B.C. in the second deportation of captives (Ezek. 1:2; compare II Ki. 24:15). In the fifth year of his captivity he had a remarkable vision of God's glory in which he received his call to be a prophet (Ezek. 1:1-3:21).

He was told, "Son of man, I send thee to the children of Israel, to a rebellious nation that hath rebelled against me . . . son of man, hear what I say unto thee; Be not thou rebellious like that rebellious house: open thy mouth, and eat that I give thee." A roll (book) written with "lamentations, and mourning, and woe" was given him. "So I opened my mouth, and he caused me to eat that roll." Facing an obstinate people, Ezekiel was strengthened by the assurance "Behold, I have made thy face strong against their faces. . . . As an adamant harder than flint have I made thy forehead: fear them not, neither be dismayed at their looks, though they be a rebellious house."

For seven days he sat silent and "astonished" in the colony of Hebrew exiles at the river Chebar. At the end of this time he was further commissioned as a spiritual guardian of his people: "Son of man, I have made thee a watchman unto the house of Israel: therefore hear the word at my mouth, and give them warning from me." It was his responsibility to warn the captives of the necessity to reform their ways and endure their chastisement. If he failed to do so, he would be held accountable for their deaths. After a fresh vision of God's glory he was instructed to preach only under divine impulsion (Ezek. 3:22-27).

Ezekiel's ministry lasted for twenty-two years (592-570 B.C.); his early preaching was contemporary with Jeremiah's. By stern and vigorous measures he endeavored to rouse the captives from their bitterness of spirit and mournful longings for their homeland. In the first six years of his ministry the whole burden of his message was God's coming judgment upon Jerusalem for apostasy. He depicted its siege and destruction by signs of the tile, prolonged lying on his side, the defiled bread, and the sharp knife, impressing upon the captives the inevitability of its fall (Ezek. 4-7). In a series of visions he foretold the sin and doom of Jerusalem (Ezek. 8-11). Lying prophets decrying the truth of Ezekiel's warnings were reproved (Ezek. 12-14); and by the figures of a vine-branch, a wretched infant, two eagles and a vine, and a lioness' whelps, the rejection and desolation of Jerusalem were vividly portrayed (Ezek. 15-19). Ezekiel made greater use of the apocalyptic method of writing than did any other Old Testament prophet except Daniel (see Apocalyptic Writing, p. 490).

Ezekiel's great contribution to the development of religious thought was individual responsibility. Through God's reproof of the unjust proverb of sour grapes (Ezek. 18) he taught the personal relationship of man to God and man's moral accountability for his own conduct. A man was to be judged for his own thoughts and actions, and was not to suffer for the sins of others. "The soul that sinneth, it shall die. The son shall not bear the iniquity of the father, neither shall the father bear the iniquity of the son: the righteousness of the righteous shall be upon him, and the wickedness of the wicked shall be upon him." God would mercifully pardon the wicked man who turned from his wickedness: "He shall surely live, he shall not die." Conversely, should the righteous turn away from his righteousness, "for his iniquity that he hath done shall he die."

The prophet made only one reference to his personal life. On the evening of the opening day of the siege of Jerusalem his beloved wife died. His personal grief was made subordinate to his prophetic labors as an object lesson to Judah. As he was forbidden to mourn her death, so the captives were forbidden to weep over Jerusalem; they were to accept their nation's chastisement and let their mourning be for purification (Ezek. 24).

Ezekiel was recommissioned "a watchman" after the fall of Jerusalem in 586 B.C. (Ezek. 33). He was to "blow the trumpet" of warning. The same demand for a change of heart, enunciated so often before the city's fall (Ezek. 3:17-21; 18:5-29), was still imperative: "Say unto them, As I live, saith the Lord God, I have no pleasure in the death of the wicked; but that the wicked turn from his way and live: turn ye, turn ye from your evil ways; for why will ye die, O house of Israel?" His prophecies took on a new note of comfort. The captives were assured that if Israel were not to be spared, the heathen nations were in far graver danger (Ezek. 25-32). Ezekiel foretold the happy restoration of a spiritually regenerated remnant to their own land. By his two visions, one of the resurrection of dry bones and the other of the uniting of two sticks, the dead hope of Israel was revived, for God would again put His Spirit within His people, unite Judah and Israel, destroy the enemy armies of Gog and Magog, and establish the promised Messianic kingdom (Ezek. 36-39).

Fourteen years later, in the twenty-fifth year of his captivity, Ezekiel, while in the Spirit, envisioned an ideal community of restored people and an ideal temple with a priesthood undefiled (Ezek. 40-48). In this sanctuary the Shekinah glory was seen (Ezek. 44:4; compare 10:18; 11:23). And from this sanctuary issued life-giving waters that flowed out to heal and bless the whole world. The lofty concept of spiritual religion held by this priestly prophet contributed richly to the re-establishment and maintenance of Jewish theocratic worship after the Exile.

A measure of the man

"Now it came to pass . . . as I was among the captives . . . that the heavens were opened, and I saw visions of God" (Ezek. 1:1).

"The word of the Lord came expressly unto Ezekiel . . . and the hand of the Lord was there upon him" (Ezek. 1:3).

"Moreover he [Lord God] said unto me, Son of man, eat that thou findest; eat this roll, and go speak unto the house of Israel. . . . Son of man, cause thy belly to eat, and fill thy bowels with this roll that I give thee. Then did I eat it; and it was in my mouth as honey for sweetness" (Ezek. 3:1,3).

"Son of man, all my words that I shall speak unto thee receive in thine heart, and hear with thine ears. And go, get thee to them of the captivity . . . and tell them, Thus saith the Lord God; whether they will hear, or whether they will forbear. Then the spirit took me up, and I heard behind me a voice of a great rushing, saying, Blessed be the glory of the Lord from his place. . . . So the spirit lifted me up, and took me away, and I went in bitterness, in the heat of my spirit; but the hand of the Lord was strong upon me" (Ezek. 3:10-12,14).

"Son of man, I have made thee a watchman unto the house of Israel: therefore hear the word at my mouth, and give them warning from me" (Ezek. 3:17).

"Son of man, behold, I take away from thee the desire of thine eyes with a stroke: yet neither shalt thou mourn nor weep, neither shall thy tears run down. . . . So I spake unto the people in the morning: and at even my wife died; and I did in the morning as I was commanded" (Ezek. 24:16,18).

Book of Daniel

Daniel: "God is my judge"

As a youth of noble birth he is carried captive to Babylon in the first deportation

Appointed to king's service—he and his three companions early manifest devotion to God—they refuse to eat the delicacies of the king's table—the good result

Through prayer Nebuchadnezzar's forgotten dream of a great image broken by a stone is revealed to Daniel—he interprets it as a prophetic vision of four world empires which are to be succeeded by the Messianic kingdom

Daniel is made ruler of province of Babylon and chief of the king's governors

(Daniel's three companions refuse to worship the golden image set up by Nebuchadnezzar—they are cast into a fiery furnace—their miraculous delivery)

Daniel interprets Nebuchadnezzar's dream of a great tree—the king's madness and restoration

Daniel, at King Belshazzar's impious feast, interprets the handwriting on the wall—Belshazzar slain

Darius the Mede sets Daniel over the kingdom—the king's decree—Daniel disregards the decree—is cast into the lions' den—his miraculous deliverance

His apocalyptic vision of four beasts (kingdoms) and of the kingdom of God—vision of ram and he-goat—his prayer for restoration of Jerusalem—vision of seventy weeks—final visions to "the time of the end"

Daniel lives till at least third year of Cyrus, Persian conqueror of Babylon

DANIEL was the fourth and last of

the Major Prophets. He, like Ezekiel, was associated with the period of Exile. (Some scholars assign the writing of the book of Daniel to the sixth century B.C., others to the second, *ca.* 164 B.C.)

Daniel, a Jewish youth of either royal or noble blood, was carried captive to Babylon by Nebuchadnezzar in 606 B.C. during the reign of Jehoiakim. He lived during the whole of the seventy years' captivity, surviving till the days of Cyrus, the Persian conqueror of Babylon.

It was a custom in Oriental nations to choose the elite among captives of war to serve in the king's court. Daniel and his three countrymen, Hananiah, Mishael, and Azariah, were among those selected to be trained as the king's attendants and taught the Aramaic-Babylonian language and mysteries of the Chaldean sages. Their names were changed to Belteshazzar, Shadrach, Meshach, and Abed-nego, Babylonian names that honored the king's gods.

The first challenge to Daniel's faith came when he was commanded to eat the food served at the king's table, but he "purposed in his heart that he would not defile himself" with the king's meat or wine (Dan. 1). This refusal was actuated by a devout loyalty to Mosaic Law (Lev. 11). Granted permission to adhere to a simple fare of pulse (lentils) and water, he and his friends exercised this self-discipline for three years. At the end of this time they stood before the king, and none was found equal to them in appearance or health. "As for these four children, God gave them knowledge and skill in all learning and wisdom: and Daniel had understanding in all visions and dreams."

Daniel's ability and wisdom were manifest when he recalled and interpreted for Nebuchadnezzar a dream the king had forgotten, one that none of his Babylonian astrologers and soothsayers was able to explain even under threat of death (Dan. 2). Being numbered among the wise men, Daniel and his companions were in danger. Through their earnest prayers the secret was revealed to Daniel. Like Joseph (Gen. 41:16), he disclaimed any wisdom of his own, declaring "There is a God in heaven that revealeth secrets."

This was the dream: the king had seen a great and terrible image in human form, with a head of gold, the breast and arms of silver, the belly and thighs of brass, the legs of iron, the feet of iron and clay. The feet of this image were crushed by a stone "cut out without hands" from the mountainside, and the image was broken in pieces. The stone itself "became a great mountain, and filled the whole earth." Daniel interpreted this dream as representing four world kingdoms, which would rise and fall; but beyond these he saw another, the Messianic kingdom which God would establish. "In the days of these kings shall the God of heaven set up a kingdom, which shall never be destroyed: and the kingdom shall not be left to other people, but it shall break in pieces and consume all these kingdoms, and it shall stand for ever." The king acknowledged Daniel's God as "a God of gods," and promoted the seer to the position of governor of Babylon and master of the royal astrologers.

A second time Daniel interpreted a dream for Nebuchadnezzar (Dan. 4). The king had seen a tree of great height and majesty. An angel commanded that it be cut down, its stump bound with a metal hoop, and that it be left with the beasts of the field for seven years. The tree, Daniel explained, represented the king, who would be deprived of his reason and made to live like a beast till he knew "that the most High ruleth in the kingdom of men, and giveth it to whomsoever he will." Courageously Daniel urged Nebuchadnezzar to repent of his sins, but after a twelve-month respite judgment fell on the Babylonian monarch for his inordinate pride. At the end of the prescribed time the king's sanity returned and he humbly acknowledged God "the King of heaven."

During the reign of Belshazzar Daniel occupied a position of honor. At an impious feast given by this ruler Daniel was called to interpret a mysterious handwriting that had appeared on the wall of the banquet room (Dan. 5). He found the writing to be a judgment on Belshazzar, predicting the end of the Babylonian Empire and the rise of the Medo-Persian. The same night Belshazzar was slain and the Babylonian Empire fell to Darius the Mede (unidentifiable in secular history).

Darius, like the preceding Babylonian kings, soon recognized Daniel's moral excellence and made him one of three high officials who supervised the princes set over the 120 satrapies of his kingdom (Dan. 6). When Darius planned to promote him further, the jealous princes plotted against Daniel. Knowing Daniel's practice of daily prayer, they induced Darius to make a royal statute, effective for thirty days, that no petition be made to any god or man except to the king himself on penalty of death. This decree failed to sway Daniel's allegiance to God; he continued to pray three times a day "as he did aforetime." Though cast into a den of lions, he was not harmed, and the following morning he was able to say, "O king, live for ever. My God hath sent his angel, and hath shut the lions' mouths, that they have not hurt me: forasmuch as before him innocency was found in me; and also before thee, O king, have I done no hurt."

Throughout his whole career Daniel's example of unswerving fidelity to God was a tower of strength to a captive people, a shining example of obedience and trust to future generations.

The prophetic visions accorded Daniel in the last years of the Exile (Dan. 7-12) are apocalyptic in character and may be read with profit in relation to the book of Revelation. In the symbolic vision of four great beasts and the coming of the "Son of man" who stood before the "Ancient of days," the seer depicted the rise and fall of four world empires to be succeeded by the kingdom of the people of God (Dan. 7; compare chap. 2). This prediction was further amplified by the vision of the ram, the he-goat, and the little horn, and its interpretation by the angel Gabriel (Dan. 8). Daniel saw far beyond time and deep into reality. As he prayed for the restoration of his people and of Jerusalem, Gabriel informed him that seventy weeks were decreed until the time of Messiah's coming (Dan. 9). And finally he was comforted by a vision of future events down to the end of the age—to the deliverance of God's people by His angel Michael (Dan. 10-12).

A measure of the man

"Daniel purposed in his heart that he would not defile himself. . . ." (Dan. 1:8)

"There is a man in thy [Belshazzar's] kingdom, in whom is the spirit of the holy gods; and in the days of thy father light and understanding and wisdom, like the wisdom of the gods, was found in him; whom the king Nebuchadnezzar thy father . . . made master of the magicians, astrologers, Chaldeans, and soothsayers. . . ." (Dan. 5:11)

"This Daniel was preferred above the presidents and princes, because an excellent spirit was in him. . . ." (Dan. 6:3)

"Then the presidents and princes sought to find occasion against Daniel concerning the kingdom; but they could find none occasion nor fault; forasmuch as he was faithful, neither was there any error or fault found in him" (Dan. 6:4).

"I set my face unto the Lord God, to seek by prayer and supplications, with fasting, and sackcloth, and ashes: And I prayed unto the Lord my God, and made my confession. . . ." (Dan. 9:3,4)

"Fear not, Daniel: for from the first day that thou didst set thine heart to understand, and to chasten thyself before thy God, thy words were heard. . . ." (Dan. 10:12)

"O man greatly beloved, fear not: peace be unto thee, be strong, yea, be strong. And when he had spoken unto me, I was strengthened. . . ." (Dan. 10:19)

"Go thou thy way till the end be: for thou shalt rest, and stand in thy lot at the end of the days" (Dan. 12:13).

Ezra 1-6; Neh. 7:6-73; 12:1-9;
Book of Haggai; Zech. 4
Zerubbabel: "born at Babylon"

Zerubbabel (N.T. Zorobabel), son of Shealtiel (Salathiel)—of royal house of David—an ancestor of the Messiah

Cyrus' proclamation brings to an end the captivity of Judah

Zerubbabel leads the first expedition from Babylon to Jerusalem, thus marking the return of the remnant and the beginning of the Restoration—the sacred vessels of the Temple, which had been taken from Jerusalem by Nebuchadnezzar, are carried with them

Zerubbabel rules as governor of Judah

Temple altar is set up—the foundation of the Temple laid

Adversaries (the Samaritans) hinder its building for sixteen years—by a letter of complaint to Cyrus' successor they obtain a decree which halts the reconstruction

Zerubbabel, encouraged by the prophets Haggai and Zechariah, rouses the people to resume the work

Tatnai, Persian governor of the territory west of the Euphrates, questions their right to rebuild—informed of Cyrus' decree, he requests the new king, Darius, to have a search made for this decree in the Babylonian archives—it is found

Darius makes a new decree authorizing the rebuilding of the Temple

Four years later the Temple is completed and dedicated

ZERUBBABEL was the leader of

the first expedition of Jews who returned to Jerusalem from Babylonian exile. He was associated with the early period of the Restoration and the rebuilding of the Temple.

The prophets had taught that certain great empires were instruments of the divine will: by means of Assyria Israel was punished; by means of Babylon Judah was chastised; in like manner Medo-Persia became an instrument in effecting the restoration of the Jews to their own land that they might fulfill their Messianic destiny.

In 539 B.C. Cyrus, king of Persia, conquered Babylon. Isaiah had prophesied of him, "Thus saith the Lord.... He is my shepherd, and shall perform all my pleasure: even saying to Jerusalem, Thou shalt be built; and to the temple, Thy foundation shall be laid" (Is. 44:28). A year later Cyrus issued a proclamation: "The Lord God of heaven hath given me all the kingdoms of the earth; and he hath charged me to build him an house at Jerusalem, which is in Judah. Who is there among you of all his people? his God be with him, and let him go up to Jerusalem ... and build the house of the Lord God of Israel" (Ezra 1:1-3).

Zerubbabel, son of Shealtiel (I Chron. 3:17) and grandson of King Jehoiachin, was born in captivity. Nothing is known of his life in Babylon. Under his leadership, in 536 B.C., about 50,000 Jews, a "willing" remnant, made the return journey to Jerusalem (800 to 900 miles, four months of travel), taking with them the sacred vessels of the Temple which Nebuchadnezzar had carried away. The Messianic line—in the person of Zerubbabel—is thus seen in the Restoration (see Genealogies of Jesus Christ, p. 224).

> The return of the captives is, in a way, the rebirth of the nation.... The prophets continually kept before the nation that the Exile would not signify the cessation, but an interruption of their national career, that they were still the chosen people of Jehovah through whom His redemptive plans would be accomplished. Micah announced that the Messiah should be born in Bethlehem, not in Babylon, Persia, or any other state, hence the return to their inheritance.... The expedition of Zerubbabel to Jerusalem is the beginning of the last stage of their career that is to issue in the crowning fact of their selection from among the nations. It is the time of preparation for the coming of the world's Redeemer. It was necessary therefore that their religious institutions be established and central to these is the Temple, and thus for another five centuries will be foreshadowed the High Priest of the new covenant, the Lamb of God.[13]

Zerubbabel had been appointed governor of Judah by Cyrus (Hag. 1:1). Under his supervision and that of Joshua (Jeshua) the high priest, the altar of burnt offering was set up and sacrificial worship according to Mosaic Law was resumed. The second year after their return the foundation of the Second Temple was laid (535 B.C.). Neighboring Samaritans offered to help the Jews in its construction, but their aid was refused. (These people were a mixed race, descendants of the Israelites left in the land after the fall of Israel who had intermarried with the Assyrian colonists brought into Samaria. Their religion was a mixed religion: in part the worship of Jehovah and in part the worship of idols.) Zerubbabel answered, "Ye have nothing to do with us to build an house unto our God; but we ourselves together will build unto the Lord God of Israel." His emphatic repudiation of their services caused a schism between Samaritans and Jews that continued for centuries (Jn. 4:9).

Although the Samaritans could not change Cyrus' decree, which granted the Jews permission to rebuild their Temple, for the next sixteen years they employed every means at their command to hinder the work. Seeing the Jews were also beginning to rebuild Jerusalem's walls, they finally sent a malicious letter to Cyrus' successor (Cambyses), accusing the Jews of seditious motives, and succeeded in obtaining a decree that halted all work until the second year of King Darius.

At this critical moment in Israel's restoration history the prophets Haggai and Zechariah appeared on the scene and roused the apathetic remnant by their timely, inspired prophecies. Haggai upbraided the remnant for their negligence and procrastination: "Is it time for you, O ye, to dwell in your cieled houses, and this house lie waste?" (Hag. 1:4). His message was: "I am with you, saith the Lord" (Hag. 1:13), and His promise: "I will shake all nations, and the desire of all nations shall come: and I will fill this house with glory. . . . The glory of this latter house shall be greater than of the former" (Hag. 2:7,9). The people, infused with a new spirit of dedication began again to rebuild the Temple (520 B.C.).

The Persian satrap Tatnai questioned their right to rebuild, but when he was informed of Cyrus' decree he sent a letter to King Darius requesting verification. The record was found in the royal archives. Darius not only commanded that there be no hindrance to the work, but also gave further impetus to the Jews' hopes by contributing to it from his own treasury.

The prophecies of Haggai and Zechariah strengthened the authority of Zerubbabel and Joshua, for to the prophets these two typified the Messianic hope of the nation. Haggai said, "O Zerubbabel, my servant . . . saith the Lord . . . [I] will make thee as a signet: for I have chosen thee" (Hag. 2:23). Zechariah declared, "Not by might, nor by power, but by my spirit, saith the Lord of hosts. Who art thou, O great mountain? before Zerubbabel thou shalt become a plain: and he shall bring forth the headstone thereof with shoutings, crying, Grace, grace unto it" (Zech. 4:6,7). In apocalyptic visions Zechariah saw Joshua placed in charge of the Temple (Zech. 3), and foresaw by the figures of the golden candlestick and the two olive trees (Zerubbabel, the Davidic prince; Joshua, the priest—precursors of the two witnesses of Rev. 11) the completion of the Temple and the restoration of spiritual worship (Zech. 4).

In a little over four years the Second Temple was finished and dedicated (515 B.C.) [see Temple p. 163]. His contribution to this work of reconstruction was so great that this Temple is often referred to as Zerubbabel's Temple.

Ezra 7-10; Neh. 8-12

Ezra: "help"

Renowned priest and scribe

Ezra is commissioned by Artaxerxes I (Longimanus) of Persia to lead a second expedition of Jewish exiles, a willing remnant, from Babylon to Jerusalem

He is given silver and gold from the king and people to buy offerings for the altar and given a letter authorizing him to draw on the royal treasury for things needful for the Temple, to set up judges to enforce religious and civil law, and to claim exemption from taxes for those in service of the Temple

Before leaving, Ezra sends out a call for Levites to join the expedition—he proclaims a fast and the Jews pray for protection and guidance—they reach Jerusalem safely after a four-month journey

On his arrival he is informed of the mixed marriages that the people, priests, and Levites have made with their idolatrous neighbors—his great grief—his prayer of confession for their sin

Assembles the people at Jerusalem to demand the correction of this violation of Mosaic Law—the people repent and annul their foreign marriages

(A thirteen-year period of silence in Ezra's history—this he may have spent in Babylon at work on the final redaction of the Pentateuch)

Ezra joins Nehemiah in Jerusalem in reformative work—he instructs the people in the law of Moses from the Pentateuch

EZRA was the leader of the second expedition of Jews who returned to Judah from Babylonian exile. His life-work was identified with the period of the Restoration and the re-establishment of Mosaic Law.

In captivity, Judah, deprived of temple worship and suffering the loss of the beloved city of Jerusalem, turned with deeper insight to the spiritual wealth it still possessed—its heritage of the Law and of the Prophets, and its covenant history as God's people. A class of learned Jews, pious men known as *sopherim* or scribes, came into prominence toward the close of the Exile and during the early Restoration period. Formerly, scribes had been literary men who had served as kings' secretaries and historians but these sopherim were men who had become students of the Law. Dedicating themselves to preserving their nation's history and oral and written law codes, these scholars painstakingly gathered and collated all the material at hand. Thus Hebrew Scripture began to take form, and it is believed that Ezra contributed in large measure to this work.

Ezra was a priest born in Babylonian captivity, a lineal descendant of Aaron through his son Phineas. He was "a ready scribe in the law of Moses" and "had prepared his heart to seek the law of the Lord, and to do it, and to teach in Israel statutes and judgments" (Ezra 7:6,10). Greatly concerned for the religious welfare of the returned remnant in Jerusalem, he received permission from the Persian king Artaxerxes in 458 B.C. to go to Jerusalem to instruct the Jews in their sacred Law (Ezra 7).

Artaxerxes commissioned him to lead a fresh band of exiles: "All they of the people of Israel, and of his priests and Levites, in my realm, which are minded of their own freewill to go up to Jerusalem, go with thee."

Fourteen hundred and ninety-six men with their families responded to the call, but when Ezra discovered no Levites among them, ministers needed for temple service, he would not leave until he found some willing to make the journey, and 38 Levites and 220 Nethinim (temple servants) were added to their number. With them went considerable treasure: temple vessels taken by Nebuchadnezzar and freewill offerings of silver and gold from the king and his Jewish subjects. Before starting on this hazardous journey the caravan, now totaling about 7000, prayed for divine protection. "I proclaimed a fast there, at the river Ahava, that we might afflict ourselves before our God, to seek of him a right way for us, and for our little ones, and for all our substance. For I was ashamed to require of the king a band of soldiers and horsemen to help us against the enemy in the way: because we had spoken unto the king, saying, The hand of our God is upon all them for good that seek him; but his power and his wrath is against all them that forsake him." Without military strength or escort, but under "the hand of [their] God" they came safely to Jerusalem (Ezra 8).

Invested by royal decree with absolute authority to appoint magistrates to judge according to Mosaic Law as well as that of the king, Ezra at once began the work of reform (Ezra 9). He was horrified to learn that during the almost eighty-year period since the first expedition mixed marriage was again being practiced in Jerusalem: "The people of Israel, and the priests, and the Levites, have not separated themselves from the people of the lands. . . . For they have . taken of their daughters for themselves, and for their sons: so that the holy seed have mingled themselves with the people of those lands." To this zealous priest this affinity with strangers was a heinous sin, a flagrant violation of the Mosaic covenant which corrupted Judah's separateness and purity of worship (Ex. 34:15,16; Deut. 7:3,6). "When I heard this thing, I rent my garment and my mantle, and plucked off the hair of my head and of my beard, and sat down astonished." He prayed fervently for Israel's forgiveness, blushing for the ingratitude of the remnant to the God who had so mercifully delivered them from captivity, ashamed that they had used this "little space" of "grace" for their own trespasses when it should have been to them a season of "reviving."

Those who heard Ezra's impassioned confession gave him the immediate task of correcting this evil, pledging their support. A proclamation was sent throughout Judah, calling the remnant together to make a covenant with God to put away their heathen wives and the children born of them. All assembled at Jerusalem within three days under penalty of confiscation of their property and of excommunication from the congregation. With weeping they complied with this stern measure, and within three months divorced their foreign wives (Deut. 24:1). In this way the Jewish community preserved its separateness from other peoples and protected its distinctive monotheistic religion from corrupting external influences.

The record is silent concerning the next thirteen years of Ezra's life. Whether he returned to Babylon or remained in Jerusalem is not known, but when Nehemiah came to Jerusalem in 445 B.C. Ezra became his co-worker in the reformative movement that Nehemiah inaugurated. He appeared at the Feast of Trumpets as a leader among the priests and Levites, bringing with him the Book of the Law, which had reached its final canonical form (Five Books of Moses, Pentateuch, see p. 4). For seven days the Law was read aloud and explained to the people (Neh. 8). By demanding a stern and unswerving adherence to its principles, Ezra thus began that firm establishment of the Jewish ecclesiastical system which became so marked a feature of the next 450 years of Jewish history.

Ezra's is an austere and commanding figure, which has left a lasting impression upon the religious life of the Jewish people. Ezra is the true founder of Judaism. By investing the Law with a sanctity and influence that it had never before possessed, and making it the possession of the entire community, he endowed the Jewish people with a cohesive power which was proof against all attacks from without.[14]

". . . Ezra the priest, the scribe of the law of the God of heaven. . . ." (Ezra 7:21)

"Blessed be the Lord God of our fathers, which hath put such a thing as this in the king's heart, to beautify the house of the Lord which is in Jerusalem: And hath extended mercy unto me before the king, and his counsellors. . . . And I was strengthened as the hand of the Lord my God was upon me. . . ." (Ezra 7:27,28)

"At the evening sacrifice I arose up from my heaviness; and having rent my garment and my mantle, I fell upon my knees, and spread out my hands unto the Lord my God, And said, O my God, I am ashamed and blush to lift up my face to thee, my God: for our iniquities are increased over our head, and our trespass is grown up unto the heavens" (Ezra 9:5,6).

"Then Ezra rose up from before the house of God . . . he did eat no bread, nor drink water: for he mourned because of the transgression of them that had been carried away" (Ezra 10:6).

"Ezra the priest brought the law before the congregation both of men and women, and all that could hear with understanding. . . . And he read therein . . . from the morning until midday, before the men and the women . . . and the ears of all the people were attentive unto the book of the law" (Neh. 8:2,3).

Book of Nehemiah

Nehemiah: "comforted of Jehovah"

Son of Hachaliah and brother of Hanani

Cupbearer to King Artaxerxes (Longimanus) of Persia

Nehemiah mourns over the affliction of remnant in Jerusalem—his humble prayer

Artaxerxes appoints him governor and commissions him to rebuild the walls of Jerusalem—he journeys to Jerusalem with letters of authority from the king

By night Nehemiah secretly surveys the broken walls—rouses his people to rebuild

Enemies, led by Sanballat, Tobiah, and Geshem, conspire to prevent the work

The deplorable condition of the poor—Nehemiah causes the rich, who were exacting exorbitant rates of interest from the needy, to make restitution

The wall is finished in fifty-two days

Nehemiah's religious reforms: enforcement of Sabbath laws, determining of genealogies, teaching the Law to the people with the help of Ezra, celebration of Feast of Tabernacles

A national fast and repentance—Judah renews and seals the covenant with God

By lot one man out of every ten in the land is chosen to live in Jerusalem

Dedication of the wall—the offices of priests and Levites appointed

Nehemiah governs twelve years

He returns to Persia—a year later returns to Jerusalem to correct religious abuses

Brings about many reforms to compel obedience to Mosaic Law—purifies the priesthood—enforces the covenant's prohibition against mixed marriages

NEHEMIAH was a great Jewish

patriot and statesman. He was identified with the period of the Restoration—with the rebuilding of Jerusalem's walls and, like Ezra, with the firm establishment of the Jewish ecclesiastical system.

Nehemiah was cupbearer to King Artaxerxes in the winter palace at Shushan in Persia. Word was brought to him that the returned remnant in Jerusalem was in great affliction and reproach, and that the city's walls were still broken down. He was plunged into a grief that lasted many days. After fasting and prayer he determined to go to Jerusalem; and he petitioned the king for permission to repair its walls and gates. His request was granted and the king appointed him governor (Tirshatha) of Judah.

He reached Jerusalem in 445 B.C. Three days after his arrival he rode secretly by night around the city to inspect its ruined walls and burned gates. Then he urged, "Come, and let us build up the wall of Jerusalem, that we be no more a reproach." Willingly the people "strengthened their hands for this good work."

As Samaritan adversaries had hindered Zerubbabel in the reconstruction of the Temple, so now the Samaritans, Ammonites, and Arabians led by Sanballat, Tobiah, and Geshem tried to prevent the fortifying of the city. At first they laughed with scorn but Nehemiah confidently declared, "The God of heaven, he will prosper us." The gates and towers were rapidly repaired and in a short time "all the wall was joined together unto the half thereof: for the people had a mind to work." When mockery failed the adversaries united to fight against them, but Nehemiah armed his workmen and set a watch day and night. "They which builded on the wall, and they that bare burdens . . . every one with one of his hands wrought in the work, and with the other hand held a weapon." With urgency all labored from early morning until the stars appeared at night, not putting off their clothes except for washing.

Next, Nehemiah's enemies Sanballat and Geshem tried to entice him to meet with them outside the walls, but he refused. Four times they sought him; four times he gave the same reply, "I am doing a great work, so that I cannot come down: why should the work cease, whilst I leave it, and come down to you?" A fifth time they tried to intimidate Nehemiah with an open letter which insinuated that he and the Jews were planning to rebel against the king. He answered, "There are no such things done as thou sayest, but thou feignest them out of thine own heart"; and turning to God in prayer, beseeched: "Now . . . O God, strengthen my hands." The adversaries' final attempt to stop the work was to make Nehemiah fear for his life. One of Nehemiah's own countrymen was bribed to induce him to flee for safety into the Holy Place of the Temple (a violation of the Law for a layman), but Nehemiah refused, perceiving it as the guile of the enemy.

In fifty-two days the wall was finished, and it was formally dedicated with great joy (Neh. 12:27-43). With the strengthening of Jerusalem's walls, a portion of Judah's reproach was taken away.

Even as the walls were being rebuilt Nehemiah began the work of social and religious reform, erecting in his people's hearts the greater wall of spiritual Zion, Israel's true defense. He rebuked the practice of usury; the nobles were oppressing their own countrymen, causing them to lose or mortgage their lands and homes and to sell their children into slavery for debts. He shamed the rulers into abandoning this evil, citing his own example of long service without compensation. The management and defense of Jerusalem were placed in the hands of two trusted compatriots, Hanani and Hananiah. The genealogies of the returned remnant and place of residence were recorded. Every tenth man throughout the province was chosen by lot to reside in Jerusalem to supplement the city's population and provide for its protection and growth (Neh. 7; 11). Contemporary with Nehemiah was the prophet Malachi, who raised his voice against the social and religious abuses of the day and encouraged the devout with an express promise of Messiah's coming (Mal. 3:1; 4:2).

Nehemiah's efforts to enforce obedience to Mosaic Law were aided by Ezra the scribe, who, after thirteen years of apparent absence, had returned to Jerusalem bringing with him a copy of the written Law. Nehemiah called a great public assembly on the first day of the seventh month, the Feast of Trumpets, and for seven days, from morning to midday, Ezra and the Levites read the Law to the people and interpreted it (Neh. 8). The remnant wept when they heard it; there was a moral awakening. A national fast was held at which the people publicly confessed their sins and renewed their covenant, swearing an oath and sealing it in writing to obey all the obligations of Mosaic Law—to walk in God's law, to abstain from foreign marriages, to discontinue sacrilegious buying and selling on the Sabbath, to pay the Temple tax, to bring in the required firstfruits, and to tithe to the Levites (Neh. 9; 10).

After twelve years as governor Nehemiah returned to Persia (433 B.C.). In his absence the people soon violated their covenant oath, the Sabbath and the priesthood were profaned, and mixed marriages began again; so the following year he made a second journey to Jerusalem to enforce drastic reform measures. He came armed with a new commission that gave him power to regulate every detail relating to the Jewish religion and state. He compelled the Jews to fulfill their oath, corrected the abuses of the priesthood, and banned all commercial pursuits that violated the Sabbath. With almost frenzied zeal Nehemiah impressed on the Jews the great evil of mixed marriages: "I contended with them, and cursed them, and smote certain of them, and plucked off their hair, and made them swear by God, saying, Ye shall not give your daughters unto their sons, nor take their daughters unto your sons, or for yourselves." They were a separate people, set apart by God's covenant, and must so remain (Neh. 13).

From first to last Nehemiah was a man of piety and of prayer. When his work was finished Jerusalem was once more a fortified city, rebuilt and thriving, and the Mosaic ecclesiastical system of the Jewish Church was well established. The strict adherence of the covenant people to monotheism during the next four centuries prepared the way for the Advent of the Messiah.

A measure of the man

"When I heard these words . . . I sat down and wept, and mourned certain days, and fasted, and prayed before the God of heaven. . . ." (Neh. 1:4)

". . . there was come a man to seek the welfare of the children of Israel" (Neh. 2:10).

"Moreover from the time that I was appointed to be their governor in the land of Judah . . . that is, twelve years, I and my brethren have not eaten the bread of the governor. But the former governors . . . were chargeable unto the people, and had taken of them bread and wine . . . yea, even their servants bare rule over the people: but so did not I, because of the fear of God" (Neh. 5:14,15).

"Yea, also I continued in the work of this wall, neither bought we any land: and all my servants were gathered thither unto the work" (Neh. 5:16).

"I said, Should such a man as I flee? and who is there that, being as I am, would go into the temple to save his life? I will not go in" (Neh. 6:11).

"Remember me, O my God, concerning this, and wipe not out my good deeds that I have done for the house of my God, and for the offices thereof" (Neh. 13:14).

"I . . . said unto them [merchants], Why lodge ye about the wall? if ye do so again, I will lay hands on you. From that time forth came they no more on the sabbath" (Neh. 13:21).

"Remember me, O my God, for good" (Neh. 13:31).

Airview of the ruin-mounds of Shushan (Susa), for many centuries the capital of ancient Elam and later one of the three capitals of the Persian Empire. It was the home of King Ahasuerus and Queen Esther, the scene of Daniel's vision during the reign of Belshazzar, and the site of the royal palace in which Nehemiah served as Artaxerxes' cupbearer. The pillar containing the Code of Hammurabi was discovered here in 1901-1902. Courtesy of the Oriental Institute, University of Chicago.

5

Correlation –
Old Testament Subjects

The Bible is a record covering thousands of years showing the Hebrews' developing concept of God and their deepening religious beliefs. As a result, various aspects of their theology gained new meanings and significance as centuries passed.

Extensive concordance study of Scriptural passages shows the correlation and growth of these advancing ideas and is rewarding. Since, however, it is sometimes not possible for the Bible student to do all the independent research he would like to pursue, this chapter of correlated studies offers a quick but comprehensive grasp of important Old Testament subjects. These studies cover a variety of topics—from the two accounts of Creation to the Miracles of the Old Testament; from Moses' Blessings to the Silences of Biblical history. All of these throw light on Hebrew history and culture and make possible a fuller understanding of the spiritual riches of the Bible.

It has been said that "Scripture is best interpreted by Scripture." On this basis related Bible passages have been traced and correlated. Many of these subjects are presented in chart form to point up what the Scriptures themselves say, to guide the reader toward his own comparison and analysis, and to encourage him to explore other topics for himself. To illustrate: the chart entitled "The Covenant between God and Men" graphically carries the covenant from its Edenic promise to its fulfillment in Revelation, both in its historic aspect for the people of Israel and in its universal application to the spiritual Israel of faith. "Biblical Terms for Satan" gives the reader at a glance, in the very names of this personified evil, the growing recognition of its awful nature.

Some of the material relates to the Old Testament only; some is correlated with the New to show mutual relationships and advancing religious concepts. Old Testament promises, imagery, and types translate themselves into higher spiritual terms and fuller meanings.

Names of God

From earliest times the worship of most primitive peoples was polytheistic. The belief in many gods expressed itself in the deification of the forces and laws of nature to which men felt themselves helplessly subject. They conceived of these forces as separate powers, each wielding a beneficial or an adverse influence, spirits whose favor was sought through gifts or whose anger was appeased through propitiatory sacrifices and offerings. The deep-seated longings of men for security and for escape from evil, privation, and oppression found visible expression in the ceremonial worship of countless deities, idols, and nature objects, and also in the innumerable practices of primitive customs and taboos (see Worship, p. 47).

In Bible times the whole Middle East was polytheistic. From the Semites of this region came the Hebrew people, the one ethnic group that developed the idea of monotheism. The refinement of this idea evolved over the centuries, and it was a revolutionary step in the world's religious history when the nation of Israel dedicated itself to the One God, and that One invisible. The Israelites' early concept of Him was anthropomorphic (see p. 145). Only by degrees did they comprehend His omnipotence, omnipresence, goodness, and love. By the close of Old Testament history (ca. 432 B.C.), although still conceiving of God as a Being capable of wrath, jealousy, and vengeance, they worshiped Him as a merciful Redeemer, Lawgiver, Judge, Provider, Physician, Husband, Father. He was the "Holy One" who dwelt in heaven, whose wisdom and justice governed the affairs of men.

Tracing some of the principal Old Testament names for God from the English translations back to their Hebrew equivalents, several are prominent: Elohim; Yahweh; Adonai; shortened forms in poetry such as El, Yah or Jah; compounded terms such as El Shaddai, El Elyon, Jehovah-Elohim, Adonai-Jehovah. The names in themselves were distinctively interpretive of the divine character of the Deity and conveyed a specific message to the Hebrew.

ELOHIM: God, the Strong One, the Creator. Its root meaning is not known, but the name denotes excellence, dignity, majesty, strength.

Elohim comes from the word Eloah, a deity; and in the midst of widespread polytheism or belief in many gods the Israelites called their deity Elohim, a plural form of Eloah, exalting Him as the Creator of all, in whom every superior and excellent attribute was combined. In Genesis, chapter 1, it is Elohim who creates, and the plural form is seen in verse 26: "Let us make man in our image, after our likeness: and let them have dominion."

EL: God, Mighty One, Strong One, "God the Omnipotent." This Hebraic syllable appears in several combining forms in proper names: Elihu, Elisha, Elisabeth, Daniel, Israel, etc.; in sacred locale such as Beth-el and Peniel.

EL ELYON: Most High God, the Most High. He is "possessor of heaven and earth." This name first occurs in Genesis 14:18.

EL SHADDAI: Commonly translated God Almighty or The Almighty. "Shaddai is the All-bountiful." It first appears in Genesis 17:1 when God's covenant was affirmed with Abraham and he was assured of God's all-sufficiency. This title is much used in the book of Job.

ADONAI: Lord, Master. This title first occurs in Genesis 15:2 as the compound name Adonai-Jehovah (Lord God). Adonai conveyed the meaning of ruler of the world.

YAHWEH (JAHWEH, JEHOVAH): Lord, the Self-Existent, the Eternal. God revealed Himself to Moses as Jahweh—"I AM THAT I AM"—the living God, who is and will be eternally (Ex. 3:14). Under this name the covenant was made with the tribes of Israel, and Jehovah thus became the national name of Israel's God. In Genesis 2:4f. it is Jehovah-Elohim (Lord God) who forms.

Such reverence and sanctity were attached to this name that it was never voiced. When quoted from the written text Adonai was usually substituted. Vowel points of Adonai were eventually affixed to the Hebrew consonants of Yahweh, and by this hybrid method the Anglicised name Jehovah was evolved (ca. 1518 A.D.).

JAH: A contracted form of Jahweh used principally in poetry. This syllable appears in several combining forms: in the striking example of the Hebrew word hallelujah, "praise ye the Lord," which occurs so frequently in the Psalms; and in proper names such as Elijah, Isaiah, Jeremiah, Zephaniah.

The New Testament uses two Greek terms for God: Theos (a deity, God) and Kurios (God, Lord, Master). The name Jesus used most frequently to indicate God's relation to man was Father (Greek Pater). Abba, a transliterated vocative form of the Aramaic word for "father," appears three times in the New Testament as the name for God (Mk. 14:36; Rom. 8:15; Gal. 4:6). Jesus taught that God is One—his Father, our Father. In the Son was God's perfect nature fully expressed and God's love for man fully manifested.

Creation:
First Account

The first account of creation, found in Genesis 1:1-2:4a, is a record of the creative power of God. "The Bible begins with the truth of God, that God is, that there is one God, that He is the Creator of the universe, that the latter is not self-existent. The same is true of man. He was not only made by God, but in the image of God, the supreme creative act of God."[1] This marvelous account of creation by an unknown writer is from the Elohistic Document (E) incorporated in the Priestly Code (500-450 B.C.), the law code generally agreed by scholars to have supplied the framework of the first five books of the Bible, the Pentateuch (see p. 4).

In this first account the Deity is called Elohim—the Strong One, the Eternal. This Elohistic record was given precedence over an earlier Yahwistic account (J) (Gen. 2:4b-25; see p. 145) by the compilers of the Pentateuch; it sounded the highest keynote of spiritual truth and so was chosen to open the book of Genesis. The theology of this account was greatly advanced over the viewpoint of preceding documents (J,D,H), being devoid of the baser elements of polytheism, anthropomorphism, and remnants of ancient mythology. It served further to enlighten a culturally developed people sensitive to deep religious truths.

It was Elohim who created the universe and man. It was the Spirit of Elohim that moved "upon the face of the waters." Creation required only God's Word. "He spake, and it was done; he commanded, and it stood fast" (Ps. 33:9). Elohim, a plural form (see p. 142), implied the Trinity, the Godhead, whose Word and work are continuous in development and revelation throughout the Biblical record.

> In this first chapter of the Bible we see how creation is referred to God which enables us to explain the universe fundamentally on a rational basis, in terms of spirit and not in terms of matter. Everywhere are the marks of design, and design signifies a designer. Everything belongs to an order of effects and these signify a cause, and in this case the First Cause.[2]

The first chapter of Genesis records three acts of creation, the number specially indicative of divine completeness and perfection.

- "God created the heaven and the earth"
  - "God created . . . every living creature"
    - "God created man in his own image"

CREATION: FIRST ACCOUNT

Genesis 1-2:4a

"In the beginning God [Elohim] created the heaven and the earth."

"And the earth was without form, and void; and darkness was upon the face of the deep. And the Spirit of God moved upon the face of the waters."

God divided the light from the darkness
God divided the waters from the waters
God made lights to divide day from night

The word "let" appears fourteen times
"And it was so" six times
"God saw that it was good" six times
"God saw that it was very good" once

First Day	Second Day	Third Day	Fourth Day	Fifth Day	Sixth Day		Seventh Day
LIGHT	**HEAVEN**	**EARTH, SEAS, SEED**	**TWO GREAT LIGHTS STARS**	**MOVING CREATURE WINGED FOWL**	**LIVING CREATURE**	**MAN**	**REST, BLESSING, SANCTIFICATION**

First Day — LIGHT

"God said, Let there be light: AND THERE WAS LIGHT.

"And *God saw the light, that it was good:* and God divided the light from the darkness.

"And God called the light Day, and the darkness he called Night."

Second Day — HEAVEN

"And God said, Let there be a firmament in the midst of the waters, and let it divide the waters from the waters.

"AND GOD MADE THE FIRMAMENT, and divided the waters which were under the firmament from the waters which were above the firmament: *and it was so.*

"And God called the firmament HEAVEN."

Third Day — EARTH, SEAS, SEED

"And God said, Let the waters under the heaven be gathered together unto one place, and let the dry land appear: *and it was so.*

"AND GOD CALLED THE DRY LAND EARTH; and the gathering together of the waters called he SEAS: and *God saw that it was good.*

"And God said, Let the earth bring forth grass, the herb yielding seed, and the fruit tree yielding fruit after his kind, whose seed is in itself ... *and it was so.*

"AND THE EARTH BROUGHT FORTH ... WHOSE SEED WAS IN ITSELF, after his kind: and *God saw that it was good.*"

Fourth Day — TWO GREAT LIGHTS STARS

"And God said, Let there be lights in the firmament of the heaven to divide the day from the night; and let them be for signs ... seasons ... days ... years:

"And let them be for lights ... to give light upon the earth: *and it was so.*

"AND GOD MADE TWO GREAT LIGHTS; the greater light to rule the day, and the lesser light to rule the night: HE MADE THE STARS also.

"And God set them in the firmament ... to give light upon the earth, And to rule over the day and over the night, and to divide the light from the darkness: and *God saw that it was good.*"

Fifth Day — MOVING CREATURE WINGED FOWL

"And God said, Let the waters bring forth abundantly the moving creature that hath life, and fowl that may fly above the earth in the open firmament of heaven.

"AND GOD CREATED great whales, and EVERY LIVING CREATURE THAT MOVETH, WHICH THE WATERS BROUGHT FORTH abundantly, after their kind, and EVERY WINGED FOWL after his kind: and *God saw that it was good.*

"And God blessed them, saying, Be fruitful and multiply, and fill the waters in the seas, and let fowl multiply in the earth."

Sixth Day — LIVING CREATURE

"And God said, Let the earth bring forth the living creature after his kind ... *and it was so.*

"AND GOD MADE THE BEAST OF THE EARTH after his kind, and CATTLE after their kind, and EVERYTHING THAT CREEPETH upon the earth after his kind: and *God saw that it was good.*"

Sixth Day — MAN

"And God said, Let us make man in our image, after our likeness: and let them have dominion over ... all the earth....

"SO GOD CREATED MAN IN HIS OWN IMAGE ... male and female created he them.

"And God blessed them, and God said ... Be fruitful, and multiply, and replenish the earth, and subdue it: and have dominion over the fish of the sea, and over the fowl of the air, and over every living thing that moveth upon the earth.

"And God said, Behold, I HAVE GIVEN you every herb bearing seed ... and every tree, in the which is the fruit ... yielding seed; to you it shall be for meat.

"And to every beast of the earth, and to every fowl of the air, and to every thing that creepeth upon the earth, wherein there is life, I HAVE GIVEN every green herb for meat: *and it was so.*

"AND GOD SAW EVERY THING THAT HE HAD MADE, AND, BEHOLD, IT WAS VERY GOOD."

Seventh Day — REST, BLESSING, SANCTIFICATION

"Thus the heavens and the earth were finished, and all the host of them."

"And on the seventh day God ended his work which he had made; and he RESTED on the seventh day from all his work which he had made.

"AND GOD BLESSED THE SEVENTH DAY, AND SANCTIFIED IT....

"These are the generations of the heavens and of the earth when they were created...."

Creation:
Second Account

The second account of creation, as given in Genesis 2:4b-25, is, like the first, from the Priestly Code. It is drawn from the Yahwistic Document (J), written about 850 B.C. by an unknown author of the southern Kingdom of Judah. In this second account the Deity is called Yahweh (Jehovah), the Self-existent One. This Yahwistic account was given a secondary position by the priestly editors of the Pentateuch although it predates the Elohistic because it was apparently regarded as inferior in concept to the lofty theology of the former (see p. 143).

The Yahwist made his creation story the start of Israel's patriarchal history and presented Yahweh, Israel's nationalistic Deity, as the creator of the whole human race. In the background of this account lie primitive religious elements that the Hebrews had absorbed into their own folklore from the Babylonian, Chaldean, and Canaanite cultures of that early world. The story of creation, the Flood, and perhaps that of the Tower of Babel were oral tales that had their source in Babylonia. These early cultures cherished legends of creation wherein power was attributed to the mysterious forces of nature. These forces were personified as powers of good and evil, light and darkness, pitted against each other. Some of these early beliefs found their way into the Yahwistic account.

By 850 B.C. the Hebrews had emerged from the quagmire of polytheism, but vestiges of it still clung to Jehovistic worship. Inasmuch as heathen gods had been given visible form, it was not strange that the Hebrews first thought of their invisible God in anthropomorphic terms, as knowing evil as well as good and as possessing human attributes, passions, and manlike characteristics. So personalized was He that they spoke of His face (Ex. 33:20), His mouth (Num. 12:8), His arm (Ex. 15:16), His hand (Ex. 7:5); so localized was He that they thought of Him as hidden in "thick darkness" (Ex. 20:21), dwelling in the Tabernacle in the midst of His people (Ex. 15:17). He was described as walking in the garden (Gen. 3:8), as repenting His actions (Gen. 6:6); as jealous (Deut. 4:24), vengeful (Lev. 26:21), angry (Deut. 6:15).

The Yahwistic account differs markedly from the Elohistic in manner, order, and character. In the first account, Elohim *created;* in the second, Yahweh *formed.* In the Elohistic version, man was created *last* and in the *divine likeness;* in the Yahwistic, man was formed *first* and of *"dust."* In the first account, all was the creative work of God; in the second, Jehovah shared with Adam the characterization of His creation. This second account is a record of the beginning of physical life and its imperfections.

> The intention of the writer is evidently to give an answer to the question: How did sin and misery find their way into the world? As is natural among Orientals he put his reply into narrative form; and though it is generally accepted that the details are to be interpreted symbolically rather than literally, yet they are in marvellous agreement with the real facts of human nature and experience.[3]

CREATION: SECOND ACCOUNT
Genesis 2:4b-25

"... in the day that the Lord God [Jehovah-Elohim] made the earth and the heavens, And every plant of the field before it was in the earth, and every herb of the field before it grew: for the Lord God had not caused it to rain upon the earth, and there was not a man to till the ground.

"But there went up a mist from the earth, and watered the whole face of the ground."

MAN

"And the Lord God formed man of the DUST OF THE GROUND, and breathed into his nostrils the breath of life; and MAN BECAME A LIVING SOUL."

EDEN

"And the Lord God planted a garden eastward in Eden [Heb. *pleasure*, delight]; and there he put the man whom he had formed [to dress it and to keep it].

"AND OUT OF THE GROUND made the Lord God to grow every tree that is pleasant to the sight, and good for food; THE TREE OF LIFE also in the midst of the garden, and THE TREE OF KNOWLEDGE OF GOOD AND EVIL.

"And a river went out of Eden to water the garden; and from thence it was parted, and became into four heads [rivers Pison, Gihon, Hiddekel, and Euphrates]. . . .

"The Lord God commanded the man . . . Of every tree of the garden thou mayest freely eat: BUT OF THE TREE OF THE KNOWLEDGE OF GOOD AND EVIL, THOU SHALT NOT EAT OF IT: for in the day that thou eatest thereof thou shalt surely die."

BEAST AND FOWL

"And the Lord God said, It is not good that the man should be alone; I will make him an help meet for him. . . .

"OUT OF THE GROUND the Lord God formed every beast of the field, and every fowl of the air; and brought them unto Adam [Heb. *ruddy*, i.e. *a human being*] to see what he would call them:

"AND WHATSOEVER ADAM CALLED every living creature, THAT WAS THE NAME THEREOF.

"And Adam gave names to all cattle, and to the fowl of the air, and to every beast of the field;

"but for Adam there was not found an help meet for him."

WOMAN

"And the Lord God caused a DEEP SLEEP to fall upon Adam, and he slept;

"and he took one of his ribs, and closed up the flesh instead thereof; And the rib, which the Lord God had taken from man, made he a woman, and brought her unto the man.

"And ADAM SAID, This is now bone of my bones, and flesh of my flesh: SHE SHALL BE CALLED WOMAN, because she was taken out of Man.

"Therefore shall a man leave his father and his mother, and shall cleave unto his wife: and they shall be one flesh.

"And they were both naked, the man and his wife, and were not ashamed."

THE RECORD OF THE FALL OF MAN

according to Genesis, chapter 3

SERPENT "more subtil than any beast of the field which the Lord God had made." ("The serpent . . . representing the spirit of revolt from God. . . ."[4] Cf. Jn. 8:44)

TEMPTATION "And the serpent said unto the woman, Ye shall not surely die: For God doth know that in the day ye eat thereof [of the tree of the knowledge of good and evil], then your eyes shall be opened, and ye shall be as gods, knowing good and evil."

 Original sin "And when the woman saw that the tree was good for food, and that it was pleasant to the eyes, and a tree to be desired to make one wise, she took of the fruit thereof, and did eat, and gave also unto her husband with her; and he did eat."

FALL
Shame "And the eyes of them both were opened, and they knew that they were naked. . . ." ("divested of purity and innocence")

EXAMINATION
Fear, deception "Adam and his wife hid themselves from the presence of the Lord God. . . . And the Lord God called unto Adam . . . Where art thou? And he said, I heard thy voice . . . I was afraid, because I was naked; and I hid myself."

 Evasion and blame The man said, "The woman whom thou gavest to be with me she gave me of the tree, and I did eat."

 Confession of guilt The woman said, "The serpent beguiled me, and I did eat."

JUDGMENT
To the serpent "Thou art cursed above all cattle . . . above every beast . . . dust shalt thou eat all the days of thy life: And I will put enmity between thee and the woman, and between thy seed and her seed; it shall bruise thy head and thou shalt bruise his heel."

 To the woman "I will greatly multiply thy sorrow and thy conception. . . ."

 To the man "Cursed is the ground for thy sake; in sorrow shalt thou eat of it all the days of thy life. . . . dust thou art, and unto dust shalt thou return."

EXPULSION "The Lord God sent him forth from the garden of Eden, to till the ground from whence he was taken."

(This is the pattern of every temptation and sin: the desire to be as a god; the desire to know both good and evil; dissatisfaction; love of self; disobedience; fear, deception; evasion of responsibility. Still today every man finds himself confronted with some phase of this "original sin.")

THE FULFILLMENT OF THE PROMISE OF THE REDEEMER

The angel said: "Fear not, Mary: for thou hast found favour with God. And, behold, thou shalt . . . bring forth a son, and shalt call his name JESUS." Mary responded: "Behold the handmaid of the Lord; be it unto me according to thy word." Lu. 1:30,31,38

"This sacred moment, which marks the beginning of our Lord's incarnate life, should be contrasted with Gen. 3:6. There the disobedience of a woman brought sin and death into the world. Here the obedience of a woman brought salvation, reversing the effect of the Fall."[5]

Edersheim calls Jesus "the Unsinning, Unfallen Man."[6]

Note the contrasts:
Original sin — original promise
In disfavor — in favor
Fallen man — unfallen man

Adam to Jesus

THE PROMISE OF THE REDEEMER

The original promise of the gospel (Gen. 3:15)—a Savior for fallen man—is made to Adam and his posterity, a promise to be fulfilled in the Advent of Jesus: "And I will put enmity between thee and the woman, and between thy seed and her seed; it shall bruise thy head, and thou shalt bruise his heel." The offspring of the woman, as it relates to the promise, is called "the seed," whose work it is to bruise the serpent's head—to destroy the power and works of Satan (Heb. 2:14; Rom. 16:20).

THE COVENANT BETWEEN GOD AND MEN

God's promise to mankind of redemption was made through His covenant, the manifestation of His love and grace, and in turn men were to render obedience (see p. 47). This covenant relationship, as seen in His dealings with His chosen people Israel, underlies Old Testament history and theology and is summed up in Exodus 6:7: "I will take you to me for a people, and I will be to you a God." The covenant idea began to be explicit historically in the call of Abraham and was confirmed on a grander scale with the nation of Israel at Sinai. The fuller meaning of the promise "I will be to you a God" unfolded gradually through many Old Testament mediators, to be fulfilled perfectly in Christ (Immanuel or "God with us") in his first and second Advents.

	Promise of a Redeemer and of Redemption	Preservation	A Seed and a Land	A Holy Nation	A House and a Kingdom	Promise of Redemption through Christ	Full Redemption and Salvation through Christ	CONSUMMATION OF GOD'S COVENANT
	ADAMIC COVENANT	NOAHIC COVENANT	ABRAHAMIC COVENANT	MOSAIC OR SINAITIC COVENANT	DAVIDIC COVENANT	NEW COVENANT FORETOLD –ITS MEDIATOR–	NEW COVENANT	

ADAMIC COVENANT
(Promise of a Redeemer and of Redemption)

"The Lord God said unto the serpent, Because thou hast done this, thou art cursed above all cattle, and above every beast of the field; upon thy belly shalt thou go, and dust shalt thou eat all the days of thy life:

"And I will put enmity between thee and the woman, and between thy seed and her seed; it shall bruise thy head, and thou shalt bruise his heel." Gen. 3:14,15

NOAHIC COVENANT
(Preservation)

"I . . . will not again curse the ground any more for man's sake. . . . While the earth remaineth, seedtime and harvest, and cold and heat, and summer and winter, and day and night shall not cease." Gen. 8:21,22

"I establish my covenant with you, and with your seed after you; And with every living creature that is with you . . . from all that go out of the ark . . . neither shall all flesh be cut off any more by the waters of a flood. . . .

"I do set my bow in the cloud, and it shall be for a token of a covenant between me and the earth. And it shall come to pass, when I bring a cloud over the earth, that the bow shall be seen in the cloud." Gen. 9:9-15

ABRAHAMIC COVENANT
(A Seed and a Land)

"I will establish my covenant between me and thee and thy seed after thee in their generations for an everlasting covenant, to be a God unto thee, and to thy seed after thee.

"And I will give unto thee, and to thy seed after thee, the land wherein thou art a stranger, all the land of Canaan, for an everlasting possession; and I will be their God." Gen. 17:7,8

Promise to Abram: Gen. 12:1-3
Renewal: Gen. 13:14-17
Confirmed: Gen. 15:17,18
Covenant with Abraham: Gen. 17:1-11
Confirmed to Isaac: Gen. 26:2-5
Confirmed to Jacob: Gen. 28:13-15

MOSAIC OR SINAITIC COVENANT
(A Holy Nation)

Promise to Moses for Israel: Ex. 6:7,8

"After the tenor of these words I [the Lord] have made a covenant with thee and with Israel. . . . And [Moses] wrote upon the tables the words of the covenant, the ten commandments." Ex. 34:27,28

Mosaic covenant: Ex. 19-32, 34. Constituted of three related parts: Decalogue (20:1-26); judgments (21:1-24:11); ordinances (24:12-31:18).

This national covenant became the Law which governed Israel and set it apart from heathen nations.

Renewal of covenant before entrance into Canaan: Deut. 29, 30

Renewal by Joshua: Josh. 24:14-27

DAVIDIC COVENANT
(A House and a Kingdom)

"I will set up thy seed after thee, which shall proceed out of thy bowels, and I will establish his kingdom. . . . I will be his father, and he shall be my son. . . . And thine house and thy kingdom shall be established for ever before thee: thy throne shall be established for ever." II Sam. 7:12,14,16 (I Chron. 17:11-14)

Renewal of Davidic covenant with Solomon: I Ki. 9:1-9 (II Chron. 7:17-22)

Renewal under Jehoiada, high priest, during reign of Jehoash: II Ki. 11:17 (II Chron. 23:16)

Renewal by King Hezekiah: II Chron. 29:10

Renewal by King Josiah: II Ki. 23:2,3 (II Chron. 34:30-32)

Renewal under Ezra: Neh. 9:38-10:39

NEW COVENANT FORETOLD –ITS MEDIATOR–
(Promise of Redemption through Christ)

Isaiah: "I the Lord have called thee [my servant, Christ] in righteousness, and will hold thine hand, and will keep thee, and give thee for a covenant of the people, for a light of the Gentiles. . . ." Is. 42:6

Jeremiah: "The days come, saith the Lord, that I will make a new covenant with the house of Israel, and with the house of Judah. . . . I will put my law in their inward parts, and write it in their hearts; and will be their God, and they shall be my people." Jer. 31:31,33

Malachi: "The Lord, whom ye seek, shall suddenly come to his temple, even the messenger of the covenant, whom ye delight in: behold, he shall come, saith the Lord of hosts." Mal. 3:1

NEW COVENANT
(Full Redemption and Salvation through Christ)

"This is the covenant that I [the Lord] will make with the house of Israel after those days. . . . I will put my laws into their mind, and write them in their hearts: and I will be to them a God, and they shall be to me a people: And they shall not teach every man his neighbour, and every man his brother, saying, Know the Lord: for all shall know me, from the least to the greatest. For I will be merciful to their unrighteousness, and their sins and their iniquities will I remember no more." Heb. 8:10-12

"Now hath he [Jesus] obtained a more excellent ministry, by how much also he is the mediator of a better covenant which was established upon better promises." Heb. 8:6

CONSUMMATION OF GOD'S COVENANT

"And I [John] heard a great voice out of heaven saying, Behold, the tabernacle of God is with men, and he will dwell with them, and they shall be his people, and God himself shall be with them, and be their God.

"And God shall wipe away all tears from their eyes; and there shall be no more death, neither sorrow, nor crying, neither shall there be any more pain: for the former things are passed away." Rev. 21:3,4

THE TEN PLAGUES
(Exodus, chapters 7-12)

This term applies to the series of judgments that fell upon the Egyptians when Pharaoh refused to release the Israelites from bondage. The word *plague* means "a judgment," "a beating," "a smiting."

Moses said to Pharaoh, "Thus saith the Lord God of Israel, Let my people go, that they may hold a feast unto me in the wilderness" (5:1; cf. 4:22,23). But Pharaoh answered, "Who is the Lord, that I should obey his voice to let Israel go? I know not the Lord, neither will I let Israel go" (5:2).

Read chart across

Cry for release	Plague	Egypt smitten / Israel spared	Pharaoh's heart
"Let my people go, that they may serve me.." 7:16	1. Plague—Waters Turned to Blood	"And the magicians of Egypt did so with their enchantments..." 7:22; 8:7	"Pharaoh's heart was hardened, neither did he hearken..." 7:22
"Let my people go, that they may serve me." 8:1	2. Plague—Frogs		With "respite, he hardened his heart, and hearkened not..." 8:15
	3. Plague—Lice		"Pharaoh's heart was hardened, and he hearkened not..." 8:19
"Let my people go, that they may serve me." 8:20	4. Plague—Swarms of Flies	No swarms of flies in "the land of Goshen, in which my people dwell." 8:22	He "hardened his heart at this time also, neither would he let the people go." 8:?
"Let my people go, that they may serve me." 9:1	5. Plague—Murrain of Beasts	"The cattle of the children of Israel died not one." 9:6	"The heart of Pharaoh was hardened, and he did not let the people go." 9:7
	6. Plague—Boils		"The Lord hardened the heart of Pharaoh, and he hearkened not..." 9:12
"Let my people go, that they may serve me." 9:13	7. Plague—Hail	"Only in the land of Goshen ... was there no hail." 9:26	"He sinned yet more, and hardened his heart... neither would he let the children of Israel go..." 9:34,35
"Let my people go, that they may serve me." 10:3	8. Plague—Locusts		"The Lord hardened Pharaoh's heart, so that he would not let the children of Israel go." 10:20
	9. Plague—Thick Darkness	"All the children of Israel had light in their dwellings." 10:23	"The Lord hardened Pharaoh's heart, and he would not let them go." 10:27

Passover instituted: "It is the sacrifice of the Lord's passover, who passed over the houses of the children of Israel..." chap. 12

| | 10. Plague—Firstborn Slain | "I will pass over you and the plague shall not be upon you to destroy you..." 12:13 | "There was a great cry in Egypt; for there was not a house where there was not one dead. And [Pharaoh] called for Moses and Aaron by night, and said, Rise up, and get you forth from among my people, both ye and the children of Israel; and go, serve the Lord, as ye have said." 12:30,31 |

"Against all the gods of Egypt I will execute judgment..." 12:13

Pharaoh's first two offers of compromise refused: "Sacrifice to your God in the land," "sacrifice ... only ye shall not go very far away." 8:25,28

His third offer refused: "Go now ye that are men." 10:11

His fourth offer refused: "Only let your flocks and your herds be stayed." 10:24

NOTE:
—The seven cries for Israel's release
—Pharaoh's first arrogant refusal and his last defeated cry
—The magicians' imitations of the first two plagues
—The unyielding hardness of Pharaoh's heart
—The immunity granted the Children of Israel

149

THE TWELVE SONS OF JACOB
(Genesis 29; 30; 35:16-18)

The lives of the twelve sons of Jacob are important to an understanding of Israel's national history because they and their descendants were heirs to the sacred covenant God made with Abraham, Isaac, and Jacob (see Covenants, p. 47). The "seed" promised to Abraham was multiplied in Jacob, and from his posterity emerged the Messianic nation.

The background of the birth of each son is of special interest. Their father Jacob was the son of Isaac and Rebekah and grandson of Abraham. At Isaac's command, Jacob journeyed from Canaan to Padan-aram to marry one of the daughters of his uncle Laban. He worked for Laban for seven years as a dowry price for the younger daughter Rachel, whom he dearly loved. When his years of service were finished, Jacob, through deception, was given Laban's elder daughter Leah. Later Rachel also became his wife, but for her he had to serve an additional seven years. Leah bore him children while Rachel, his favorite, remained barren for many years. Each sister, to obtain offspring, offered her handmaid to Jacob as a secondary wife. Of these four wives Jacob fathered twelve sons.

The influences of tribal customs—the marrying first of the elder daughter, polygamy, the desire for numerous progeny, the substitution of handmaids as secondary wives—left their mark on these children. Added to these potent factors were the emotional pressures of human relationships—Jacob's strong love for Rachel, his hatred of Leah, the shame of barrenness, the sisters' rivalry for their husband's affection. These psychological forces were later reflected in the characters of the sons and their tribal offspring.

Reuben	"see ye a son"	of Leah
Simeon	"favorable hearing"	of Leah
Levi	"attached," "a joining"	of Leah
Judah	"celebrated"	of Leah
Dan	"judge"	of Bilhah (Rachel's handmaid)
Naphtali	"my wrestling"	of Bilhah
Gad	"fortune," "troop"	of Zilpah (Leah's handmaid)
Asher	"happy," "blessed"	of Zilpah
Issachar	"he will bring reward"	of Leah
Zebulun	"habitation"	of Leah
Joseph	"increaser," "adding"	of Rachel
Benjamin	"son of my right hand"	of Rachel

REUBEN   *Background: "[Jacob] loved ... Rachel more than Leah. ... when the Lord saw that Leah was hated, he opened her womb: but Rachel was barren."*

Leah said, "Surely the Lord hath looked upon my affliction; now therefore my husband will love me."

SIMEON   Leah said, "Because the Lord hath heard that I was hated, he hath therefore given me this son also."

LEVI   Leah said, "Now this time will my husband be joined unto me, because I have born him three sons."

JUDAH   Leah said, "Now will I praise the Lord. . . . and left bearing."

DAN (of Bilhah)	*Background: Rachel, grieving for her barrenness, envied Leah, and said to Jacob, "Give me children, or else I die." Jacob was angered and asked, "Am I in God's stead?" So Rachel, following an Oriental custom practiced in the event of barrenness, gave her handmaid Bilhah to Jacob to wife, with the intent of adopting any children as her own.* Rachel said, "God hath judged me, and hath also heard my voice, and hath given me a son."
NAPHTALI (of Bilhah)	Rachel said, "With great wrestlings have I wrestled with my sister, and I have prevailed."
GAD (of Zilpah)	*Background: The bitter rivalry between the sisters still persisted, for when Leah saw that Rachel had succeeded in giving her husband children through her handmaid and that she herself had ceased bearing, she gave her handmaid Zilpah to Jacob.* Leah said, "A troop cometh."
ASHER (of Zilpah)	Leah said, "Happy am I, for the daughters will call me blessed."
ISSACHAR	*Background: Reuben, at the time of wheat harvest, gathered mandrakes from the field as a present for his mother Leah (the eating of mandrakes by women was believed to promote conception). Rachel bartered with her sister for them, so Leah said to Jacob, "Thou must come in unto me; for surely I have hired thee with my son's mandrakes."* Leah said, "God hath given me my hire."
ZEBULUN	Leah said, "God hath endued me with a good dowry; now will my husband dwell with me, because I have born him six sons." ("Afterwards she bare a daughter, and called her name Dinah.")
JOSEPH	*Background: "And God remembered Rachel, and God hearkened to her, and opened her womb."* Rachel said, "God hath taken away my reproach. . . . The Lord shall add to me another son."
BENJAMIN	*Background: After the birth of Joseph, Jacob returned with his wives and family to his own country. Behind the birth of Rachel's second son lay the memory of the constant struggle of competition with her husband's other wives, bitterness over her father's greed and injustice (Gen. 31:14-16), her reluctance to surrender old household gods (Gen. 31:19,34,35; 35:4), the long journey from Padan-aram to Bethlehem (Ephrath). "And Rachel travailed, and she had hard labour."* "And it came to pass, as her soul was in departing, (for she died) that she called his name Ben-oni ['son of my sorrow']: but his father called him Benjamin."

JACOB'S PROPHECIES TO HIS TWELVE SONS

(Genesis, chapter 49)

Jacob proved worthy of God's call, reaching a spiritual maturity in his transforming experience at Peniel, for it was said of him "as a prince hast thou power with God and with men, and hast prevailed" (see Jacob, p. 102). His sons became the heirs of this purifying experience. Just before his death in Egypt he gave his patriarchal blessing to each of his twelve sons, "every one according to his blessing." Because of his own regeneration, his prophecies show his clear assessment of their characters—of propensities unworthy of propagation, and of enduring qualities worthy of nurture.

"Jacob called unto his sons, and said, Gather yourselves together, that I may tell you that which shall befall you in the last days. Gather yourselves together, and hear, ye sons of Jacob; and hearken unto Israel your father."

To REUBEN	"Reuben, thou art *my* firstborn, *my* might, and the beginning of *my* strength, the excellency of dignity, and the excellency of power:
	"Unstable as water, thou shalt not excel; because thou wentest up to thy father's bed; then defiledst thou it. . . ." (See Gen. 35:22)
To SIMEON To LEVI	"Simeon and Levi are brethren; instruments of cruelty are in their habitations.
	"O my soul, come not thou into their secret; unto their assembly, mine honour, be not thou united: for in their anger they slew a man, and in their selfwill they digged down a wall.
	"Cursed be their anger, for it was fierce; and their wrath, for it was cruel: I will divide them in Jacob, and scatter them in Israel." (See Gen. 34:24-31)
To JUDAH	*This is considered a Messianic prophecy; the Redeemer of men was to come through the line of Judah. In the book of Revelation Jesus Christ is called "the Lion of the tribe of Juda" (Rev. 5:5).*
	"Judah, thou art he whom thy brethren shall praise: thy hand shall be in the neck of thine enemies; thy father's children shall bow down before thee. Judah is a lion's whelp: from the prey, my son, thou art gone up: he stooped down, he couched as a lion, and as an old lion. . . .
	"The sceptre shall not depart from Judah, nor a lawgiver from between his feet, until Shiloh come; and unto him shall the gathering of the people be. . . ."
To ZEBULUN	"Zebulun shall dwell at the haven of the sea; and he shall be for an haven of ships; and his border shall be unto Zidon."

To ISSACHAR	"Issachar is a strong ass couching down between two burdens: And he saw that rest was good, and the land that it was pleasant; and bowed his shoulder to bear, and became a servant unto tribute."
To DAN	"Dan shall judge his people, as one of the tribes of Israel. Dan shall be a serpent by the way, an adder in the path, that biteth the horse heels, so that his rider shall fall backward."
To GAD	"Gad, a troop shall overcome him: but he shall overcome at the last."
To ASHER	"Out of Asher his bread shall be fat, and he shall yield royal dainties."
To NAPHTALI	"Naphtali is a hind let loose: he giveth goodly words."

To JOSEPH

Just before his prophecies to his twelve sons, Jacob blessed Joseph's two sons Manasseh and Ephraim, taking them as his own (Gen. 48). By this act Joseph, as the first son of Rachel, was given the position of the first-born with a double portion of the inheritance. "I have given to thee one portion above thy brethren . . ." (vs. 22). In bestowing the blessing, Jacob placed Ephraim, the second-born, before Manasseh. Later Manasseh and Ephraim headed tribes that received Joseph's inheritance in the Promised Land.

"Joseph is a fruitful bough, even a fruitful bough by a well; whose branches run over the wall:

"The archers have sorely grieved him, and shot at him, and hated him: But his bow abode in strength, and the arms of his hands were made strong by the hands of the mighty God of Jacob; (from thence is the shepherd, the stone of Israel:) Even by the God of thy father, who shall help thee; and by the Almighty, who shall bless thee with blessings of heaven above, blessings of the deep that lieth under, blessings of the breasts, and of the womb:

"The blessings of thy father have prevailed above the blessings of my progenitors unto the utmost bound of the everlasting hills: they shall be on the head of Joseph, and on the crown of the head of him that was separate from his brethren."

To BENJAMIN

"Benjamin shall ravin as a wolf: in the morning he shall devour the prey, and at night he shall divide the spoil."

MOSES' BLESSINGS TO THE TWELVE TRIBES
(Deuteronomy, chapter 33)

Centuries had elapsed since Jacob's prophecies to his twelve sons. Their posterity, the Children of Israel, had multiplied into twelve great tribes, and had been led out of Egypt under the guidance of their leader Moses. They had received the covenant and the Law and were aware of their destiny as the chosen people of God. As they stood ready to enter the Promised Land, Moses pronounced a prophetic blessing on each tribe which, like Jacob's prophecies, marked a salient trait of the tribe's history or character.

"This is the blessing, wherewith Moses the man of God blessed the children of Israel before his death."

To REUBEN	"Let Reuben live, and not die; and let not his men be few [RV omits the "not" in the second clause]."
To SIMEON	*(Simeon is not here mentioned, and later this tribe was absorbed into that of Judah. However, some scholars hold to the opinion that the second clause of the above verse relates to Simeon.)*
To JUDAH	"Hear, Lord, the voice of Judah, and bring him unto his people: let his hands be sufficient for him; and be thou an help to him from his enemies."
To LEVI	*Background: At Sinai the tribe of Levi was chosen from among the Children of Israel for priestly service. (See Ex. 32:26-29; Num. 1:49-53; 3:5-12; Mal. 2:4-6.)* "Let thy Thummim and thy Urim be with thy holy one, whom thou didst prove at Massah, and with whom thou didst strive at the waters of Meribah; Who said unto his father and to his mother, I have not seen him; neither did he acknowledge his brethren, nor knew his own children: for they have observed thy word, and kept thy covenant [see Ex. 32:25-28]. "They shall teach Jacob thy judgments, and Israel thy law: they shall put incense before thee, and whole burnt sacrifice upon thine altar. "Bless, Lord, his substance, and accept the work of his hands: smite through the loins of them that rise against him, and of them that hate him, that they rise not again."
To BENJAMIN	"The beloved of the Lord shall dwell in safety by him; and the Lord shall cover him all the day long, and he shall dwell between his shoulders."
To JOSEPH	*Background: Thirteen tribes of Israel entered Canaan, if Ephraim and Manasseh (tribes of the sons of Joseph) are counted as separate tribes. However, the land was later divided among twelve tribes by Joshua (Josh. 13-21), the original number "twelve"*

thus being preserved since the priestly tribe of Levi received Levitical cities and tithes in lieu of territory.

"Blessed of the Lord be his land, for the precious things of heaven, for the dew, and for the deep that coucheth beneath, And for the precious fruits brought forth by the sun, and for the precious things put forth by the moon, And for the chief things of the ancient mountains, and for the precious things of the lasting hills, And for the precious things of the earth and fulness thereof, and for the good will of him that dwelt in the bush: let the blessing come upon the head of Joseph, and upon the top of the head of him that was separated from his brethren.

"His glory is like the firstling of his bullock, and his horns are like the horns of unicorns: with them he shall push the people together to the ends of the earth: and they are the ten thousands of Ephraim, and they are the thousands of Manasseh."

To ZEBULUN
To ISSACHAR

"Rejoice, Zebulun, in thy going out; and, Issachar, in thy tents. They shall call the people unto the mountain; there they shall offer sacrifices of righeousness: for they shall suck of the abundance of the seas, and of treasures hid in the sand."

To GAD

"Blessed be he that enlargeth Gad: he dwelleth as a lion, and teareth the arm with the crown of the head. And he provided the first part for himself, because there, in a portion of the lawgiver, was he seated; and he came with the heads of the people, he executed the justice of the Lord, and his judgments with Israel."

To DAN

"Dan is a lion's whelp; he shall leap from Bashan."

To NAPHTALI

"O Naphtali, satisfied with favour, and full with the blessing of the Lord: possess thou the west and the south."

To ASHER

"Let Asher be blessed with children; let him be acceptable to his brethren, and let him dip his foot in oil. Thy shoes shall be iron and brass; and as thy days, so shall thy strength be."

Moses declared the happiness of Israel in having the omnipotent and eternal God as its protector: "There is none like unto the God of Jeshurun [a poetical name for Israel], who rideth upon the heaven in thy help, and in his excellency on the sky. The eternal God is thy refuge, and underneath are the everlasting arms: and he shall thrust out the enemy from before thee; and shall say, Destroy them. Israel then shall dwell in safety alone: the fountain of Jacob shall be upon a land of corn and wine; also his heavens shall drop down dew. Happy art thou, O Israel: who is like unto thee, O people saved by the Lord, the shield of thy help, and who is the sword of thy excellency!"

A NEW NAME

Personal names were significant to the Hebrews, and Biblical names often suggested the character of the person. Many Hebrew names are compounds containing the name of God, as seen in the use of the syllables El, Jah (iah), and Ab.

A name bestowed by parents conveyed something of their hopes for the child as well as their religious sentiments, or suggested some trait of the child's nature. Under Jewish custom a man's name was often changed following a deep religious experience or a public profession of religion. The new name, earned or bestowed, implied a moral and spiritual change in character, a new status, a sign of divine approval or favor.

Of the righteous who take hold of God's covenant it is written: "Even unto them will I [God] give in mine house and within my walls a place and a name better than of sons and of daughters: I will give them an everlasting name, that shall not be cut off" (Is. 56:5).

Read chart upward line by line

and I will write upon him MY NEW NAME." Rev. 3:12
and THE NAME OF THE CITY OF MY GOD. . .
"I will write upon him THE NAME OF MY GOD,

and in the stone A NEW NAME written. . . ." Rev. 2:17

"HIM THAT OVERCOMETH"   "I . . . will give him a white stone,

DISCIPLES	CHRISTIANS "followers of Christ" Acts 11:26; II Cor. 5:17; II Tim. 2:19
SAUL	PAUL (Roman cognomen) "small," "little" Acts 13:9
JOSES	BARNABAS "the son of consolation" Acts 4:36
SERVANTS	FRIENDS Jn. 15:15
TWELVE DISCIPLES	APOSTLES "those sent forth" Lu. 6:13
JOHN, JAMES	BOANERGES "sons of thunder" Mk. 3:17
SIMON BAR-JONA	PETER (CEPHAS) "a rock," "stone" Jn. 1:42; Mt. 16:18

KING OF KINGS, AND LORD OF LORDS Rev. 19:16
THE WORD OF GOD Rev. 19:13
THE LAMB OF GOd Jn. 1:29; Rev. 5:6

JESUS   MESSIAS, THE CHRIST "the anointed one" Jn. 1:41

SOLOMON	JEDIDIAH "beloved of Jehovah" II Sam. 12:25
OSHEA	JOSHUA (JEHOSHUA) "Jehovah his help" Num. 13:16
JACOB	ISRAEL "who prevails with God" Gen. 32:28
SARAI	SARAH "princess of the multitude" Gen. 17:15
ABRAM	ABRAHAM "the father of a great multitude" Gen. 17:5

(The new name and its meaning)

The Law: Three Stages

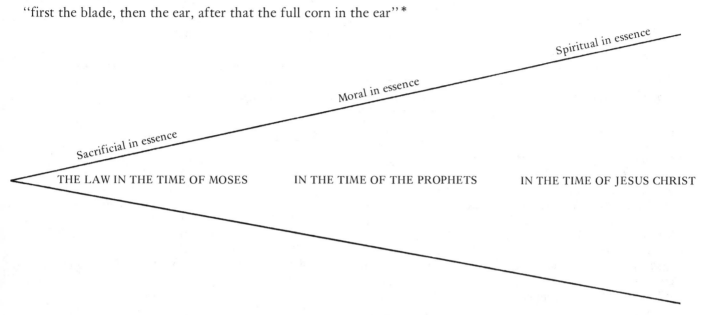

"first the blade, then the ear, after that the full corn in the ear" *

Spiritual in essence

Moral in essence

Sacrificial in essence

THE LAW IN THE TIME OF MOSES   IN THE TIME OF THE PROPHETS   IN THE TIME OF JESUS CHRIST

In Moses' Time

The national life of Israel began at Sinai. Up to the time of Moses the Hebrews had been governed by tribal law and the social mores of their race but at Sinai, law, as promulgated by Moses, was given a religious basis. God was declared the source of moral and spiritual law. As the Law of God, this law proved a potent force in regulating the religious and social life of Israel and in welding the people together as a nation. In the Old Testament law almost invariably means Mosaic Law. It is the development of both oral and written legislation that proceeded from the covenant made with Israel when God took them to Him as His people (Ex. 19-32, 34), and is contained in a body of statutes in the last four books of the Pentateuch. The Law, coming as it did to a people unversed in religious discipline and national unity, began the training of a nation in righteousness. Its purpose was to guide and instruct Israel, and to enforce the standard of worship "till the seed should come to whom the promise [of salvation] was made."

Moses, recognized as the first great leader of Israel, was also its first great lawmaker. The conscience of his people needed to be quickened, righteousness and sin defined, idolatry exterminated, and obedience to God emphasized.

God's law was first given to Israel in the Ten Commandments, which embodied both moral and spiritual law. The Decalogue established a covenant relation between a holy God and a chosen people. In subsequent law as it developed under Moses, a sacrificial system of worship was initiated to make atonement for sin. Punishment was imposed for transgression of the Law; blessing was promised for obedience. The Mosaic system set up a priesthood and prescribed the regulations of ceremonial observance for the priestly order and for the people (see Mosaic System, p. 51).

Under the Prophets

The period of the Prophets was an important phase in the developing conception of God as omnipotent and of His law as universal. Through the prophets and their teachings a higher standard of worship evolved.

The prophets saw the necessity of writing the Law upon the heart to effect repentance and a true communion. They laid stress on the moral principles of the Mosaic Law while yet looking to a new covenant to be inaugurated when the Messiah should come.

"To what purpose is the multitude of your sacrifices unto me? saith the Lord. . . . Bring no more vain oblations. . . . cease to do evil; Learn to do well. . . ." Is. 1:11-17

"I will put my law in their inward parts, and write it in their hearts. . . ." Jer. 31:33

*Mk. 4:28

"For I desired mercy, and not sacrifice; and the knowledge of God more than burnt offerings." Ho. 6:6

The Law, as given by Moses and carried forward by the prophets, reached its fulfillment in Jesus Christ.

In Jesus' Time

With the Advent of the Messiah, the Law, as type and "shadow of good things to come," was superseded by "the very image." As the Lamb of God Jesus made atonement for the sins of the world, by the offering of himself "once for all," not by the old means of vicarious sacrifice: "Think not that I am come to destroy the law, or the prophets: I am not come to destroy, but to fulfil" (Mt. 5:17). He did not set aside the teachings of Mosaic Law or of the prophets, but he filled them full of the spirit of love (Jn. 1:17). The Law was no longer a restraining force from without to be kept through fear of punishment, but an animating purifying power from within. Jesus brought to law-keeping the highest incentive, the spiritual motive of love for God and men:

"Thou shalt love the Lord thy God with all thy heart, and with all thy soul, and with all thy mind. . . . Thou shalt love thy neighbour as thyself. On these two commandments hang all the law and the prophets." Mt. 22:37,39,40

Paul understood clearly the place of the Law in the divine plan of redemption and perceived that the old dispensation of the Law had been superseded by the new dispensation of grace:

"Wherefore then serveth the law? It was added because of transgressions, till the seed should come to whom the promise was made; and it was ordained by angels in the hand of a mediator. . . . Wherefore the law was our schoolmaster to bring us unto Christ, that we might be justified by faith. But after that faith is come, we are no longer under a schoolmaster." Gal. 3:19,24,25

"Love worketh no ill to his neighbour: therefore love is the fulfilling of the law." Rom. 13:10.

The Remnant

In Israel's history the term *remnant* referred specifically to the Jews who came back to Jerusalem from Babylonian captivity (536 B.C.). Chastened and cleansed of polytheism, they returned a willing "holy nation," the nucleus or living substance of a more dedicated Israel. The redeemed, and therefore the new, Israel represents throughout all time a pledge of the salvation of the righteous.

The remnant also designates the small portion, the residue, who endure and remain faithful to their calling as "the chosen," steadfastly hopeful of deliverance. Psalm 126:5,6 describes them:

"They that sow in tears shall reap in joy. He that goeth forth and weepeth, bearing precious seed, shall doubtless come again with rejoicing, bringing his sheaves with him."

Isaiah spoke of the remnant as "a tenth . . . the holy seed" (Is. 6:13), and prophesied:

"It shall come to pass in that day, that the remnant of Israel, and such as are escaped of the house of Jacob, shall no more again stay upon him that smote them; but shall stay upon the Lord, the Holy One of Israel, in truth. The remnant shall return, even the remnant of Jacob, unto the mighty God. For though thy people Israel be as the sand of the sea, yet a remnant of them shall return: the consumption decreed shall overflow with righteousness." Is. 10:20-22

"The remnant that is escaped of the house of Judah shall again take root downward, and bear fruit upward." Is. 37:31

Jeremiah also prophesied of the remnant which would be saved:

"I [God] will gather the remnant of my flock out of all countries whither I have driven them, and will bring them again to their folds; and they shall be fruitful and increase." Jer. 23:3

Ezra the scribe alluded to God's mercy to the returned captives of Judah:

"Now for a little space grace hath been shewed from the Lord our God, to leave us a remnant to escape, and to give us a nail in his holy place, that our God may lighten our eyes, and give us a little reviving in our bondage." Ezra 9:8

Referring to his Jewish compatriots who had embraced Christianity, Paul wrote:

"Even so . . . at this present time also there is a remnant according to the election of grace." Rom. 11:5

John alludes in the Apocalypse to the righteous remnant of mankind which remains faithful to Christ's teachings:

"The dragon was wroth with the woman, and went to make war with the remnant of her seed, which keep the commandments of God, and have the testimony of Jesus Christ." Rev. 12:17.

The Tabernacle

During the Israelites' encampment in the wilderness of Sinai at the beginning of their national career, God called Moses up to Mount Sinai and commanded: "Speak unto the children of Israel, that they bring me an offering: of every man that giveth it willingly with his heart ye shall take my offering. . . . And let them make me a sanctuary; that I may dwell among them" (Ex. 25:2,8).

As Moses communed with God he was given the "pattern" for the Tabernacle and its sacred furniture—a pattern that was to typify in all its features the highest ideal of holiness (Ex. 25-31; compare Heb. 8:5). The people responded liberally with the needed materials, and under Moses' supervision the Tabernacle was erected in a period of about nine months (Ex. 35-40). It was called the Sanctuary, the House of the Lord, the Dwelling, the Tent of the Congregation, the Tent of Meeting (RV), the Tabernacle of Testimony.

In contrast to the great stone temples of Egypt this was a simple structure. The Tabernacle proper was

Above: Tabernacle uncovered. *A,* The Holy Place. *B,* The Holy of Holies. *Popular and Critical Bible Encyclopaedia. Below:* Israel's camp in the wilderness. The twelve tribes surrounded the Tabernacle, the Levites encircling it.

a large tent 30 cubits long, 10 cubits wide, and 10 cubits high (cubit about 18 in.). It stood within a court 100 cubits long and 50 cubits wide, fenced in by five-foot curtains of linen hung on pillars. Three sides of the Tabernacle were made of a framework of boards of acacia wood over which were spread (1) a covering of linen embroidered with cherubim, (2) a covering of goats'-hair cloth, (3) a covering of red-dyed rams' skins, and (4) a covering of badgers' skins (RV sealskins). The fourth side, the entrance to which faced east, had five pillars behind which was a screen richly worked in blue, purple, and scarlet. This oblong structure was partitioned into two chambers, the Holy Place and the Holy of Holies, by a veil, a handwoven curtain of fine linen, blue, purple, and scarlet, embroidered with figures of cherubim.

The Tabernacle represented God's dwelling place among His covenant people, and stood to Israel as a visible symbol of His presence. Upon its completion, a sign of the divine presence was manifested in the Shekinah glory—"A cloud covered the tent of the congregation, and the glory of the Lord filled the tabernacle."

The Tabernacle became the center of Israel's life, for with its erection a religious system was instituted to govern the nation in its covenant relation with God. A priestly order was founded and a detailed ceremonial and sacrificial worship was introduced. Every particular of this system typified and foreshadowed the work of the Messiah who was to come.

This portable sanctuary accompanied the Israelites throughout the forty years of their Wilderness Wandering. The Levites (see p. 54) were charged with its transportation and care, and with its erection each time the tribes pitched their tents. It was always placed in the center of the encampment, surrounded by three tribes to the east (camp of Judah), three tribes to the south (camp of Reuben), three tribes to the west (camp of Ephraim), and three tribes to the north (camp of Dan) (Num. 2).

159

THE TABERNACLE

Every feature of the Tabernacle from the Court of the Congregation to the Holy of Holies evidenced an increasing degree of sanctity—its dimensions, priesthood, furniture, and sacrificial ritual.

THE COURT OF THE CONGREGATION

Length . . . . 100 cubits
Breadth . . . . 50 cubits
Height of fence . . . . 5 cubits
(cubit about 18 in.)

The people were permitted to worship only in this outer court.

ITS FURNITURE

Brazen Altar (Altar of Burnt Offering) (See p. 49.)
Laver of Brass (bowl for ablutions of priests) (See p. 162.)

Upon the Brazen Altar the priests offered a lamb morning and evening for Israel, and officiated at the sacrificial offerings of the people. (See Sacrifice, p. 55.)

THE HOLY PLACE

Length . . . . 20 cubits
Breadth . . . . 10 cubits
Height . . . . 10 cubits
(A veil hung between Holy Place and Holy of Holies)

The priests alone entered the Holy Place.

The priests were the lineal descendants of Aaron, first high priest and brother of Moses. (See Aaronic priesthood, p. 52.)

ITS FURNITURE

Golden Altar (Altar of Incense) (See p. 49.)
Golden Candlestick
Table of Shewbread (See p. 49.)

Upon the Golden Altar the priests made an offering of incense morning and evening.

They supplied the oil for a continual light on the Golden Candlestick.

THE HOLY OF HOLIES

Length . . . . 10 cubits
Breadth . . . . 10 cubits
Height . . . . 10 cubits

Only the high priest entered the Holy of Holies and then but once a year, on the Day of Atonement. The high priest was the lineal descendant of Aaron through his son Eleazer and through Eleazer's son Phinehas.

ITS FURNITURE

Ark of the Covenant (symbolizing the very presence of God) (See p. 161.)

On the Day of Atonement the high priest sprinkled the blood of a bullock on the Mercy Seat of the Ark of the Covenant in atonement for his sins and those of the priests, and the blood of a goat for the sins of the people. (See p. 62.)

After Israel's conquest of Canaan under the leadership of Joshua, the Tabernacle was placed in Shiloh, a town in the territory of Ephraim, where it remained the religious center of worship until the death of the high priest Eli (Josh. 18:1; I Sam. 4:12-18).

The order of sanctuary worship typified the increasing degree of holiness the worshiper must attain in his approach to the throne of grace: from—the Court, to Holy Place, to Holy of Holies.

Conversely, from the throne of grace flowed the omnipotent goodness of God to the worshiper: from—Holy of Holies, to Holy Place, to the Court.

The Tabernacle is spoken of in Hebrews as "a figure for the time then present," one which had been superseded by a truer worship of God in Jesus Christ. The author of Hebrews and other New Testament writers used the Tabernacle as a spiritual type and figure: of the Church (Heb. 8:2; Rev. 21:2,3), of heaven (Heb. 9:24), of Christ's office and work (Heb. 9:7-14), of true worship (Heb. 10:19-22), of the body (II Cor. 5:1; II Pet. 1:13,14).

Ark of the Covenant

(Ex. 25:10-22)

The Ark of the Covenant was a chest of acacia (shittim) wood, two and one-half cubits in length, one and one-half cubits in breadth and height, inlaid and overlaid with gold. It was also known as "the ark of God" and "the ark of the testimony." It contained the two tables of the Law (Deut. 10:5), a pot of manna (Ex. 16:33), and Aaron's rod which had budded (Num. 17:10).

The lid was made of pure gold and was called the "mercy seat." On this lid two cherubim of beaten gold, figures representing celestial beings, faced each other. They looked toward the mercy seat, with their wings outstretched to cover it. The wings of the cherubim typified the throne of God and the mercy seat was regarded as His footstool (I Chron. 28:2; Ps. 132:7). In this manner God's presence in the midst of His people was symbolized.

> "There I will meet with thee, and I will commune with thee from above the mercy seat, from between the two cherubims which are upon the ark of the testimony. . . ." Ex. 25:22

The Ark was the sole object in the Holy of Holies of the Tabernacle. To this innermost sanctuary the high priest alone had access, and he could enter only once a year on the Day of Atonement to sprinkle the blood of the sin offerings on the mercy seat for the propitiation of his own sins and those of the nation.

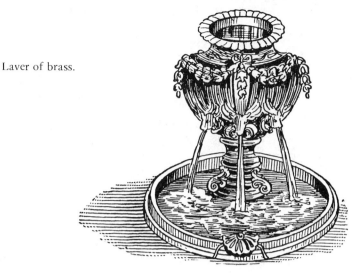

Laver of brass.

The Israelites regarded the Ark with the utmost reverence. When transported, it was wrapped in the veil of the Tabernacle and borne by the Kohathites (a family of the Levites) by means of two staves, for because of its sanctity this holy symbol was never to be touched by human hands (Num. 4:15; II Sam. 6:6,7). It preceded the tribes in their marches in the wilderness (Num. 10:33). Regarded as the presence of Jehovah Himself, it was carried into battle by the armies of Israel to insure victory.

History records:

Before the Ark the waters of the Jordan separated (Josh. 3).

It was carried by the Israelites as they marched around the walls of Jericho (Josh. 6).

It rested in the Tabernacle at Shiloh till the days of Samuel (I Sam. 4:4).

In Samuel's time the Ark was captured by the Philistines and carried to Ashdod to the temple of Dagon, a Philistine god, where its presence caused the head and hands of the idol Dagon to break in pieces, and the Philistines were so oppressed that at the end of seven months they returned it to the Israelites with a trespass offering. It was placed in the house of Abinadab in Kirjath-jearim where it remained for many years (I Sam. 4:6,7; 6:21; 7:1,2).

Ark of the Covenant with the mercy seat. Illustrations pages 160, 161, from *Popular and Critical Bible Encyclopaedia.*

When David became king over the United Kingdom, one of his earliest acts was to bring the Ark to Jerusalem and set it in a tent that he had pitched on Mount Zion (II Sam. 6; I Chron. 13, 15).

It was finally installed in the Holy of Holies of Solomon's Temple (I Ki. 8:1-11). No further historical mention is made of it, and it apparently did not appear in the Second Temple or in Herod's Temple.

The Temple

Solomon's Temple

969-962 B.C.   (I Ki. 5-8; II Chron. 2-7)

King David had erected a tabernacle in Jerusalem on the site of the threshing floor of Araunah to house the Ark of the Covenant, but it became his ardent desire to build a more permanent structure to glorify God and foster the best of the religious principles of Israel's worship. However, because David was a man of war, his son Solomon was chosen to build the Temple. David charged: "Take heed now; for the Lord hath chosen thee to build an house for the sanctuary: be strong, and do it." He gave Solomon "the pattern of all that he had by the spirit," together with treasures and costly materials which he had amassed for its building (I Chron. 22, 28).

Ground plan of Solomon's Temple. *New Standard Bible Dictionary.*

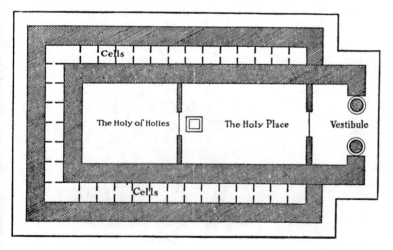

Solomon began construction of the Temple on Mount Zion (Moriah) in the fourth year of his reign, and it took seven years to complete. Sparing no cost, Solomon ordered precious cedar and cypress wood from King Hiram of Tyre (Lebanon) and engaged Tyrian masons and craftsmen skilled in the arts of metalwork, woodcarving, and the manufacture of dyed tapestries. To carry out his formidable project he imposed a levy of 30,000 Israelites to serve in shifts of 10,000 one month out of three, and sent them to Lebanon to fell timber. The logs were floated down the coast to the harbor of Joppa and transported overland to Jerusalem. One hundred fifty thousand Canaanite laborers were sent to the mountains to quarry stone for the foundations and walls.

"The house, when it was in building, was built of stone made ready before it was brought thither: so that there was neither hammer nor axe nor any tool of iron heard in the house, while it was in building" (I Ki. 6:7). It was a magnificent structure of white limestone. Its internal pattern was that of the Tabernacle, although the dimensions were double in length and width (60 by 20 cubits) and triple in height (30 cubits). (Whether the cubit used was the regular cubit of 17½ inches or the royal of 20½ inches is not clear.) The Temple proper was surrounded on three sides by a low three-storied building and fronted on the east by a stately porch or vestibule the width of the building and 10 cubits deep. The whole Temple rested on a raised platform. The interior of the house was lined with cedar, overlaid with gold, and elaborately adorned with figures of cherubim, palms, and flowers.

The Temple furniture was similar to that of the Tabernacle except that the brazen altar and brazen laver in the outer (general) court were much larger than those of the Tabernacle. The brazen laver or "brazen sea" (also called the "molten sea" because of its size), was an enormous bowl of brass (bronze) 17½ feet in diameter and 8¾ feet in depth, capable of holding 16,000 to 20,000 gallons of water, the whole resting on twelve oxen of cast bronze (for description see I Ki. 7:23-26). There were ten additional lavers for washing portions of the burnt offerings, ten seven-branched candlesticks, and ten tables of shewbread. Doors of solid olive wood shielded the heavily embroidered veil before the inner sanctuary.

At its solemn dedication the Shekinah glory filled the Temple as it had the Tabernacle upon its dedication. The Temple established Jerusalem as the center of Israel's worship and elevated Israel's God in the eyes of neighboring nations. It stood for nearly four hundred years until its destruction by Nebuchadnezzar in 586 B.C.

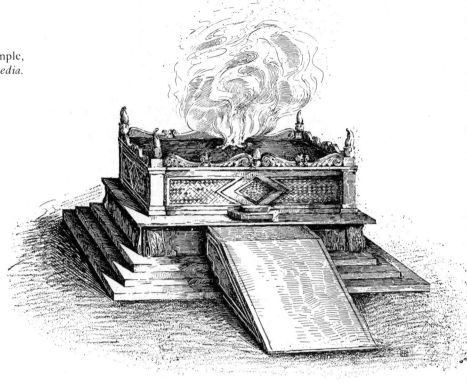

Second Temple (Zerubbabel's Temple)

535-516 B.C.

(Ezra 3-6; Bk. of Haggai; Zech. 4)

The Second Temple was begun under the direction of Zerubbabel shortly after the return of the Jews from captivity in Babylon. Although its building had been authorized by Cyrus, the Persian king, neighboring adversaries succeeded in halting the work for sixteen years. The prophets Haggai and Zechariah roused the people to action, and in 520 B.C. building was resumed by Zerubbabel. Four years later this structure was dedicated.

The appointments of the Second Temple were simple, entirely lacking the splendor that had marked Solomon's, as the people were poor and the city was still in ruins. No accurate description of this edifice exists. It was probably patterned on the first; but its architects, influenced perhaps by Ezekiel's vision of an ideal temple (Ezek. 40-43), added a second court. Only a veil hung between the Holy Place and the Holy of Holies. The Holy of Holies was empty, as the Ark of the Covenant had disappeared either at the looting of Solomon's Temple by Shishak of Egypt (*ca.* 930 B.C.) or by Nebuchadnezzar. This Temple was in existence for over five hundred years until replaced by Herod's Temple.

Herod's Temple

19 B.C.-62/64 A.D.   (Jn. 2:20)

Herod the Great, king of Judaea, to enhance the glory of his reign and win the favor of his Jewish subjects, rebuilt the Temple with great splendor. Its general plan remained the same as that of its predecessors but the Temple area was enlarged to include additional courts, cloisters, porches, and terraces. The main portion was constructed within ten years (19-9 B.C.) but it was not entirely finished until 62/64 A.D.

According to Josephus the Temple proper was completed within a year and a half by a corps of a thousand specially trained Levites and priests. It was made of white marble, embellished in the front with plates of gold. Between the Holy Place and the Holy of Holies hung a veil made of two parallel curtains. Below, on a series of terraces approaching the sanctuary, lay the marble-paved court of the priests, the court of Israel, the court of the women, and the cloisters north and south of these courts. The whole was enclosed by a wall 60 feet in height, having four gates on the north, four on the south, and one on the east—the latter probably the "Beautiful Gate." A great outer court known as the Court of the Gentiles surrounded the Temple. Along its western, northern, and eastern sides ran double rows of covered marble columns. The eastern colonnade was named Solomon's Porch. Particularly magnificent was the Royal Porch or colonnade to the south constructed of four rows of monolithic Corinthian columns, 162 in all, forming a nave and two aisles. The two side aisles were 30 feet in breadth and 50 feet in height, while the nave was 45 feet in breadth and 100 feet in height. The roofing was adorned with sculptured panels of cedar. The Court of the Gentiles was open to all foreigners but the Temple proper was accessible only to the Jews. Any Gentile

163

164

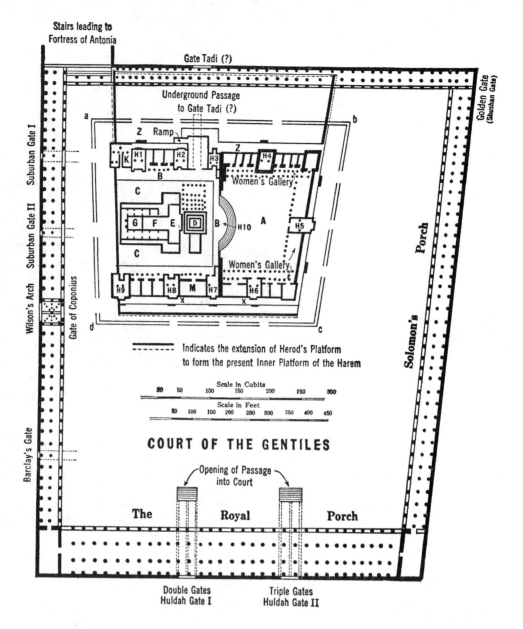

Plan of Herod's Temple and courts. a, b, c, d, The surrounding balustrade. X, Y, Z, The terrace. A, Court of the women, B, B, B, Court of Israel. C, C, C, Court of the priests. D, Altar of burnt offering. E, F, G, porch, Holy Place, and Holy of Holies. H, 1-9 gates of the sanctuary, 10, the 'upper gate.' Reproduced from *Expository Times*, Vol. 20 [1908-1909], p. 25, by permission of T. and T. Clark, Edinburgh.

who ventured into this sacred enclosure was subject to the death penalty.

This was the Temple to which Jesus came, the one he cleansed, the one in which he taught and healed, and whose destruction he prophesied (Mt. 24). The veil of this Temple was "rent in twain" on the day of Crucifixion. In 70 A.D., scarcely six years after its completion, Herod's Temple was totally destroyed by the Romans in the siege of Jerusalem.

Temple worship had no part in early Christian religion, but many of its aspects were closely woven into Christian thought as spiritual type and figure.

New Testament writers employed the term temple, as did Jesus, for the body (I Cor. 3:17; 6:19; II Cor. 6:16; compare Jn. 2:19,21) and to Christian believers individually and collectively (Eph. 2:20, 21; I Pet. 2:5).

The book of Revelation contains some of the imagery of Temple worship: priests (5:9,10; 7:14,15; 20:6), pillar (3:12), golden candlesticks (1:12,13,20; 11:3,4), golden altar (8:3; 9:13), Ark of the Covenant (11:19), temple (11:1; 15:5,8; 21:22). Its author used these types and symbols in their highest significations until, in Revelation 21, the symbols disappear and "GOD AND THE LAMB" are revealed as the temple of the New Jerusalem.

Satan

Satan is the Scriptural name for the evil force that from the beginning of time set itself against God. The name in Hebrew means "to lie in wait," "to oppose," and in Greek "accuser," "devil." Throughout the Bible the spirit of evil is portrayed in (1) its general influence as revolt against the divine will and (2) its specific character as personified evil.

The Old Testament offers little clarification of the nature of evil; in the New all the facets of its malicious character are seen to be what they really are. The early Hebrews believed in various kinds of evil spirits, a belief that stemmed from the animism of neighboring primitive peoples who attributed pain, sorrow, disease, and disaster to devils. Not until the time of the Captivity did the idea of one supreme evil spirit, lord over all orders of demons, emerge. This concept of a Satanic kingdom, with roots in the elaborate angelology and demonology of the Persians, grew in the Jewish apocalyptic and apocryphal literature of the intertestamental period.

In the Old Testament the spirit of evil is first depicted as a subtly beguiling talking serpent. A "satan" tempts David to number Israel (I Chron. 21:1). In the book of Job evil is personified as Satan "going to and fro in the earth," and being given divine permission to afflict Job physically. In Isaiah (14:12-14) Satan is Lucifer, self-willed ego, wholly antagonistic to God. In Zechariah (3:1,2 RV marg.) he appears as "The Adversary," testifying against Joshua the high priest before the angel of the Lord.

The New Testament reflects a general belief in Satan (Devil)—the Pharisees called him "Beelzebub, the prince of the devils"—and his agents; the physical ills and disorders (devils, unclean spirits) Jesus cast out were regarded as the work of Satan. Jesus' teachings display his awareness of this conception. He addressed Satan by name in his Temptation (Mt. 4:10), spoke of him as falling from heaven (Lu. 10:18), and as "the prince of this world" (Jn. 14:30). Jesus exposed Satan as "a murderer from the beginning . . . a liar, and the father of it" (Jn. 8:44), whose full judgment would come through the Comforter, the Spirit of truth (Jn. 16:7,8,11).

Paul repeatedly warned the Church of Satan's divisive wiles and drew aside the curtain to rouse Christians to put off the carnal mind: "What concord hath Christ with Belial?" (II Cor. 6:14,15).

John defined the spirit of evil as "antichrist," the enemy of Christ's gospel. In Revelation Satan is identified as the "great red dragon" and as "that old serpent . . . which deceiveth the whole world" (12:9). In this final warfare of good and evil Satan is cast out of heaven, his armies annihilated, he and his agents are consumed in "the lake of fire," and God's kingdom stands unopposed.

The Adversary in action:

beguiles	Gen. 3:13	blinds the mind	II Cor. 4:4
provokes	I Chron. 21:1	buffets	II Cor. 12:7
entices	II Chron. 18:20	hinders	I Th. 2:18
binds with infirmity	Lu. 13:16	snares	I Tim. 3:7
perverts	Acts 13:10	devours	I Pet. 5:8

PRINCIPAL BIBLICAL TERMS FOR SATAN

OLD TESTAMENT

SERPENT — "The serpent was more subtil than any beast of the field. . ." Gen. 3:1 (Typifies seductive, crafty, malicious influence)

SATAN — Satan is described as "going to and fro in the earth," and as "walking up and down in it." Job 1:7

Satan is also described as "standing" before the angel of the Lord "at his right hand to resist. . ." Zech. 3:1 (cf. Ps. 109:6)

LUCIFER — "How art thou fallen from heaven, O Lucifer, son of the morning! how art thou cut down to the ground, which didst weaken the nations!" Is. 14:12

"For thou hast said in thine heart, I will . . . I will . . . I will . . . I will . . ." Is. 14:13,14

"I will ascend into heaven,
I will exalt my throne above the stars of God.
I will sit also upon the mount of the congregation. . . .
I will ascend above the heights of the clouds;
I will be like the most High."

NEW TESTAMENT

TEMPTER — "When the tempter came to him [Jesus], he said, If thou be the Son of God. . . ." Mt. 4:3

BEELZEBUB — "Beelzebub the prince of the devils" Mt. 12:24

THE WICKED ONE, ENEMY — "The tares are the children of the wicked one; The enemy that sowed them is the devil. . . ." Mt. 13:38,39

SATAN — Jesus said, "Get thee behind me, Satan. . ." Lu. 4:8 — "I [Jesus] beheld Satan as lightning fall from heaven." Lu. 10:18

DEVIL — "Ye are of your father the devil, and the lusts of your father ye will do." Jn. 8:44

MURDERER — "He was a murderer from the beginning, and abode not in the truth, because there is no truth in him." Jn. 8:44

LIAR — "When he speaketh a lie, he speaketh of his own: for he is a liar, and the father of it." Jn. 8:44

THE PRINCE OF THIS WORLD — "The prince of this world cometh, and hath nothing in me [Jesus]." Jn. 14:30

SATAN — "And the God of peace shall bruise Satan under your feet shortly." Rom. 16:20

THE GOD OF THIS WORLD — "The god of this world hath blinded the minds of them which believe not. . . ." II Cor. 4:4

BELIAL — "And what concord hath Christ with Belial?" II Cor. 6:15

THE PRINCE OF THE POWER OF THE AIR — "The prince of the power of the air, the spirit that now worketh in the children of disobedience" Eph. 2:2

DEVIL — "Him that had the power of death, that is, the devil. . ." Heb. 2:14

"He that committeth sin is of the devil; for the devil sinneth from the beginning." I Jn. 3:8

ADVERSARY — "Your adversary the devil, as a roaring lion, walketh about, seeking whom he may devour." I Pet. 5:8

ANTICHRIST — "Who is a liar but he that denieth that Jesus is the Christ? He is antichrist, that denieth the Father and the Son." I Jn. 2:22

"Every spirit that confesseth not that Jesus Christ is come in the flesh is not of God: and this is that spirit of antichrist. . . ." I Jn. 4:3

"The spirit of error" I Jn. 4:6

ABADDON, APOLLYON ("Destroyer") — "A king . . . which is the angel of the bottomless pit. . . ." Rev. 9:11 (cf. Rev. 9:1; Is. 14:12-19)

DRAGON, OLD SERPENT, DEVIL, SATAN — "The great dragon was cast out, that old serpent, called the Devil, and Satan, which deceiveth the whole world. . . ." Rev. 12:9

THE ACCUSER — "The accuser of our brethren is cast down, which accused them before our God day and night." Rev. 12:10

DECEIVER — "And the devil that deceived them was cast into the lake of fire and brimstone. . . ." Rev. 20:10

Old Testament Miracles

The Old Testament abounds in miraculous signs and wonders that visibly attested the supremacy and might of the invisible God whom Israel worshiped. Patriarchs and prophets were accorded revelations of His nature and majesty and given unmistakable signs of His presence. The prophets' messages to the people were often accompanied by signs and wonders, for those who had not been the direct recipients of divine revelations must likewise be made to believe; and the miracles constituted a language that indisputably declared the supremacy of spiritual power.

The dominion of Israel's God was distinctively shown in the setting aside of the laws of nature as understood at that time or in their subservience to His higher law and purpose. Extraordinary signs in the physical world that evidenced His divine intervention and that could not be accounted for or explained on the basis of natural law were viewed as miracles.

Calamitous happenings to an individual, to Israel, or to her idolatrous neighboring nations, whereby extreme hardship or suffering ensued, were often interpreted in Scripture as signs of divine judgment on human iniquity. The still somewhat anthropomorphic concept of God held by Hebrew prophets and writers, reflecting the prevailing viewpoint of their day, led them to attribute such untoward acts to the "anger of the Lord," or to His wrath or vengeance. To a degree, such teaching checked wickedness and idolatry, chastened the rebellious spirit of the Israelites, forced repentance, and silenced men to awe and reverence of a righteous God.

Repeatedly, in every stage of the nation's history, God's love for His chosen people was manifest; and miracles were most in evidence when Israel's holy men walked in close communion with God. Although the majority were performed in the times of Moses, Joshua, Elijah, Elisha, and Daniel, miracles were not confined to their periods of history.

The miracles were of great diversity: of supremacy, presence, guidance, judgment, protection, deliverance, mercy, provident care, healing, raising from the dead, divine approbation.

Signs of God's Supremacy

"Thou art the God that doest wonders: thou hast declared thy strength among the people." Ps. 77:14

Moses' Rod and Leprous Hand

The changing of Moses' rod into a serpent and its return to its former state, and the changing of his hand into a leprous one with its restoration to wholeness were the two signs given to Moses as evidence to Israel that his commission to deliver them was from God (Ex. 4:1-8).

Aaron's Rod Became a Serpent

God's power was displayed to Pharaoh in the turning of Aaron's rod into a serpent. God's pre-eminence was further shown when Aaron's rod swallowed the serpents produced by Pharaoh's magicians (Ex. 7:9-13).

The Ten Plagues

To force Pharaoh to release the Children of Israel from bondage, Egypt, at Moses' word, was smitten with plagues: rivers turned to blood, plague of frogs, of lice, of flies, murrain of cattle, plague of boils, of hail, of locusts, of darkness, and the death of the first-born (Ex. 7-12; see also Chart, p. 156).

Dividing of the Red Sea

A mighty way of escape from Egypt was provided the

Israelites when Moses lifted up his rod over the sea, for God caused a strong east wind to part its waters and make the sea bed dry land (Ex. 14:21-31).

Dividing of the Jordan

When Israel's priests brought the Ark of the Covenant to the brink of the Jordan, its waters were cut off and Israel passed over on dry ground. This miracle was a sign that God's presence and power were with Joshua as they had been with Moses (Josh. 3:7-17).

Fall of Jericho's Walls

Under Joshua's leadership Israel besieged Jericho. Bearing the Ark of the Covenant, they marched around the city once each day for six days and seven times on the seventh. At their shout the walls fell, giving Israel their first victory in the Promised Land (Josh. 6:1-20).

Sun and Moon Stayed

At Joshua's word the sun and moon stood still for a whole day while Israel vanquished her enemies at Gibeon (Josh. 10:12-14).

Elijah's Sign to Determine the True God

At Mount Carmel the prophet Elijah challenged the priests of Baal to call down fire from their god upon their altar, but their prayers were not answered. Elijah's prayer to the living God brought a fire from heaven upon his altar, a fire which "consumed the burnt sacrifice, and the wood, and the stones, and the dust, and licked up the water that was in the trench" (I Ki. 18:17-39).

Dividing of the River Jordan by Elijah

The prophet smote the waters with his mantle and, accompanied by Elisha, passed over on dry ground (II Ki. 2:8).

Dividing of the Jordan by Elisha

The Prophet Elisha smote the waters with Elijah's mantle; the waters parted, and he crossed over Jordan on dry land (II Ki. 2:13,14).

Elisha Caused Iron to Float

As the sons of the prophets were building a new home by Jordan, an axehead borrowed by one of the workmen fell into the water. Elisha, by the exercise of spiritual power, caused it to float and it was thereby recovered (II Ki. 6:1-7).

Signs of God's Guidance

"My presence shall go with thee, and I will give thee rest." Ex. 33:14

The Burning Lamp

The ratification of God's covenant with Abram was signified by the sign of "a smoking furnace, and a burning lamp" which passed between the pieces of Abram's sacrifice (Gen. 15; see Fire, p. 55).

The Burning Bush

At Mount Horeb an angel appeared to Moses in a flame of fire out of a burning bush; and though the bush burned, it was not consumed. By this sign Jehovah made known His presence and power to Moses (Ex. 3:1-6).

The Pillar of Cloud and of Fire

During the Exodus from Egypt the Israelites were guided and guarded by a pillar of cloud by day and of fire by night. However, to the Egyptians who pursued them the cloud was one of darkness which stood between them and Israel. Upon the completion of the Tabernacle at Mount Sinai a cloud by day and a pillar of fire by night covered the sanctuary. During the forty years of the Wilderness Wandering when this cloud remained on the Tabernacle, the people did not journey; but when it lifted, they went forward (Ex. 13:20-22; 14:19,20; 33:9,10; 40:34-38; Num. 9:15-22).

Aaron's Sacrifices Consumed by the Fire of the Lord

The initial offerings of Aaron as high priest were consumed by a fire from the Lord, signifying divine acceptance of the Aaronic priesthood (Lev. 9:22-24).

Budding of Aaron's Rod

Following the rebellion of Korah and his company against the Aaronic priesthood, Moses placed twelve rods before the Ark of the Covenant to represent the twelve tribes of Israel. Overnight Aaron's rod, which represented the tribe of Levi, budded, blossomed, and bore fruit, a sign confirming the tribe of Levi to priestly service and the choice of Aaron and his family to the priesthood (Num. 17:1-11).

Words of Balaam's Ass

The Mesopotamian soothsayer Balaam was summoned by Balak, king of Moab, to come and curse Israel who had encamped in his land, but God forbade him to do so. Enticed by the promise of riches he finally went.

As he rode, three times God's angel stood in his path to deter him, but only when God caused Balaam's ass to speak did Balaam perceive the angel and turn from his perversity (Num. 22:21-34).

Gideon's Offering Consumed by Miraculous Fire Gideon, feeling unworthy of the angel's commission to him to deliver Israel from the Midianites, asked for a sign that God was speaking to him. He was given a sign of grace when his sacrifice was consumed by fire at the angel's touch (Ju. 6:11-23).

Double Sign Relating to Gideon's Fleece By two further signs—first of dew on a fleece of wool and not on the earth; second, of dew on the earth and not on the fleece—Gideon was given assurance that under his leadership Israel would defeat the Midianites and the Amalekites (Ju. 6:36-40).

Manoah's Sacrifice Consumed by the Fire of the Lord Manoah's offering made in thanksgiving for the angel's promise of a son (Samson) to his barren wife was consumed by a miraculous flame (Ju. 13:15-21).

A Warning Sign of Thunder and Rain Israel's desire for a king in the place of God, their real King, was granted in the crowning of Saul, though this wickedness had displeased God. Samuel, by the sign of a thunderstorm at the time of wheat harvest (a season when the sky was usually cloudless and a storm extremely rare), warned Israel and its king against the danger of apostasy and disobedience (I Sam. 12:16-19).

David's Sacrifice Consumed by the Fire of the Lord David's offering made at the threshing floor of Ornan (Araunah) was consumed by fire from heaven. He received it as a sign of divine forgiveness of his sin in numbering the people and as a revelation of the site for the Temple which he proposed to build (I Chron. 21:18-22:1).

Solomon's Sacrifice Consumed by the Fire of the Lord At the dedication of the Temple in Jerusalem fire from heaven consumed King Solomon's burnt offering as token of divine approval (II Chron. 7:1-3).

Signs of Divine Judgment

"Let all the earth fear the Lord: let all the inhabitants of the world stand in awe of him." Ps. 33:8

The Deluge The known world of Noah was judged for its wickedness by a flood of vast proportions, whose waters remained on the face of the ground for a year and ten days and "all flesh" was destroyed. Only Noah, a righteous man who found grace in God's sight, and his family, together with the animals and fowl taken into the ark which God had commanded him to build, were preserved to replenish the earth (Gen. 6:5-8:19).

Confusion of Tongues at Babel The descendants of Noah, who spoke one common language, determined to build for themselves in the plain of Shinar a city, a name, and a temple-tower which would "reach unto heaven." By divine intervention their language was confused so that the imaginings of their hearts were defeated (Gen. 11:1-9).

Destruction of Sodom and Gomorrah The iniquitous sodomy of the inhabitants of Sodom and Gomorrah drew down from heaven a judgment of brimstone and fire, and these two cities were totally destroyed (Gen. 19:24,25).

Lot's Wife Became a Pillar of Salt When Lot and his family were mercifully saved from the fate of Sodom and Gomorrah, they were commanded, "Look not behind thee," but Lot's wife disobeyed and was turned into a pillar of salt (Gen. 19:15-17,26).

Destruction of Pharaoh's Army in the Red Sea The Egyptians who pursued the Israelites into the Red Sea as they crossed over on the dry bed of the sea were drowned when Moses caused its waters to return to their place (Ex. 14:23-28).

Destruction of Nadab and Abihu Two sons of Aaron the high priest were struck by fire from heaven for presuming on the high priest's office of offering incense in the Holy of Holies and of offering fire in their censers other than that taken from the brazen altar (Lev. 10:1-3).

Fire of Judgment at Taberah Fire from the Lord consumed those Israelites who complained of the hardships of the Wilderness

Wandering. At Moses' intercessory prayer the fire was quenched (Num. 11:1-3).

Provision of Quail and Subsequent Plague

On their way from Sinai to Kadesh-barnea the Israelites, dissatisfied with the manna God had given them, longed for the Egyptian delicacies of the table. God punished them for "lusting" by surfeiting them with a month's diet of quail. These migratory birds were swept over the camp by a strong wind. Intemperate indulgence resulted in a great plague (Num. 11:4-10,18-23,31-34).

Death of the Ten Spies

Ten of the twelve spies sent to Canaan by Moses to search out the land brought back an adverse report which caused Israel not only to murmur against their God-appointed leader but also to fear to take the land. These spies "died by the plague before the Lord" (Num. 14:36,37).

Judgment upon Korah, Dathan, Abiram, and Their Company

These Levites, aspiring to higher priestly privileges, rebelled against the ecclesiastical authority of Moses and Aaron. An earthquake swallowed up the three impious leaders with their families and tents, and the two hundred and fifty men of their company were consumed by fire from the Lord (Num. 16:1-35).

Destruction of Israelites Who Complained against Moses and Aaron

A plague struck the people who unreasonably blamed Moses for the severe judgment which fell on Korah and his company. The plague was stayed by the high priest's offering of incense as an atonement for this sin (Num. 16:41-49).

The Brazen Serpent

Because the discouraged Israelites in the wilderness murmured against God and Moses, venomous serpents were sent to plague them. Upon the people's repentance, Moses prayed for deliverance; and, at God's command, set up on a standard a serpent made of brass. Those who voluntarily and in faith looked up at it were healed (Num. 21:4-9; cf. Jn. 3:14,15).

Dagon's Fall

In the time of Israel's high priest Eli, the Philistines captured the sacred Ark of the Covenant and placed it in Ashdod in the temple of their god Dagon. Its presence caused the fall and destruction of the idol Dagon (I Sam. 5:1-5).

Philistines Smitten with Pestilence

The Ark of the Covenant in the hands of the Philistines proved a curse to them, and they were plagued with emerods to compel its return to Israel (I Sam. 5:6-12).

The Reapers of Beth-shemesh Smitten

Seventy men of this town of Judah died for their irreverence in looking into the Ark of the Covenant (I Sam. 6:19). (The excessive number of 50,070 is regarded by many scholars as a gloss in the text. The Septuagint gives the number as "seventy.")

Death of Uzzah

When the Ark of the Covenant was transported from Kirjath-jearim to Jerusalem at David's command, it was set on a new cart; and as Uzzah, its driver, touched the Ark to steady it (an act specifically forbidden by Mosaic Law, Num. 4:15), "God smote him there for his error" (II Sam. 6:6,7).

Jeroboam's Altar Rent and His Hand Withered

At the word of the prophet from Judah the idolatrous altar set up at Beth-el by apostate King Jeroboam was split asunder, and when the king lifted his hand against the prophet, it withered and stiffened in midair. At the prophet's prayer it was restored (I Ki. 13:1-6).

Disobedient Prophet Slain

The prophet sent to rebuke King Jeroboam was warned by a divine injunction to have no dealings with the inhabitants of the apostate northern Kingdom of Israel. But he was deceived into accepting the hospitality of a lying prophet of that kingdom. As he was returning home to Judah he was slain by a lion for his disobedience (I Ki. 13:7-26).

Destruction of the Mockers of Elisha

Bears destroyed the irreverent children who derided the prophet (II Ki. 2:23,24).

Gehazi Smitten with Leprosy

Motivated by greed, Gehazi, servant of Elisha, abused his master's name and office by accepting the gifts of Naaman the Syrian leper, just healed by the prophet. Confronted with his error by Elisha, Gehazi compounded his sin by lying, and was punished with leprosy (II Ki. 5:20-27).

Uzziah Smitten with Leprosy

King Uzziah of Judah trespassed upon the priestly office by entering the Holy Place of the Temple and offering incense on its Golden Altar. As he stood angry and unrepentant at the rebuke of the priests, leprosy "rose up in his forehead" (II Chron. 26:16-21).

Nebuchadnezzar's Madness and Restoration   The pride of Nebuchadnezzar, king of the mighty empire of Babylonia, was humbled as he underwent seven years of madness and the loss of his kingdom "till he knew that the most high God ruled in the kingdom of men" (Dan. 4:28-37; 5:21).

Handwriting on the Wall
During an impious feast Belshazzar, last king of Babylonia (according to secular sources prince regent), saw the fingers of a disembodied hand which wrote mysterious words on the wall. By this inscription, interpreted by Daniel, he was judged for his pride and idolatry, and "found wanting." That same night he was slain and his kingdom fell to the Medes (Dan. 5).

Protection and Deliverance

"The angel of the Lord encampeth round about them that fear him, and delivereth them." Ps. 34:7

Sodomites Smitten with Blindness
When sodomites tried to force their way into Lot's house to seize his two guests, these two, in reality angelic messengers, smote them with blindness so that they were confused and frustrated in their wicked purpose (Gen. 19:1-11).

Protection of the Chosen People during the Ten Plagues in Egypt   The Hebrews experienced immunity from the plagues of flies, murrain of cattle, hail, darkness, and death of the first-born (Ex. 8:22; 9:6,26; 10:23; 12:12,13).

Dividing of the Red Sea
(See Signs of God's Supremacy, p. 167.)

Israel's Victory at Rephidim
Israel's forces, led by Joshua, defeated the Amalekites in their first battle in the wilderness. They were aided by the intercessory prayer of Moses, signified in the steady holding of up Moses' hands by Aaron and Hur as he held aloft the rod of God (Ex. 17:8-13).

Elijah Twice Delivered from Ahaziah's Soldier Bands   When Elijah prophesied the death of King Ahaziah of Israel because of his idolatry, the king sent soldiers to apprehend him, but at the word of the prophet they were destroyed by fire from heaven (II Ki. 1:10,12).

Water Obtained for the Thirsting Armies of Israel, Judah, and Edom and Victory Promised   Through spiritual inspiration Elisha counseled the three kings of this confederate army at war with Moab to dig trenches in the then dry valley of Edom, and these were miraculously filled with water, though neither wind nor rain was seen. Moabites overcome (II Ki. 3:5-20).

Syrian Army Smitten with Blindness—Their Sight Restored   At the prayer of Elisha God smote with blindness the Syrian army sent to capture him. The prophet then led this army to Samaria where, at his prayer, their eyes were opened and they found themselves in the stronghold of Israel. In accord with Elisha's counsel Israel fed its enemy and sent them back peaceably to their own country (II Ki. 6:8-23).

Syrian Army of King Ben-hadad Put to Flight   God caused the Syrians besieging Samaria, whose siege had caused severe famine in the city, to hear the sound of many horses and chariots. Believing the king of Israel had received strong reinforcements, the enemy fled in panic (II Ki. 7:6,7).

Deliverance of Jerusalem from Sennacherib's Army   When Sennacherib of Assyria threatened to invade Jerusalem, King Hezekiah with implicit faith resorted to prayer. He was assured by Isaiah that Jerusalem would not fall to the enemy although it would suffer a two-year siege. At the end of that time the Assyrian army was struck with a sudden plague by "the angel of the Lord," and Jerusalem was delivered (II Ki. 19:14-36).

Overthrow of Judah's Enemies through Jehoshaphat's Prayer   When the Moabites, Ammonites, and inhabitants of Mount Seir (Edomites) invaded Judah, the people obeyed King Jehoshaphat's command to fast and pray. Trustfully marching to battle the following day, preceded by singers who praised "the beauty of holiness," Judah found she did not have to fight, as her enemies had destroyed each other (II Chron. 20:1-24).

Deliverance from the Fiery Furnace
Shadrach, Meshach, and Abed-nego, companions of Daniel in captivity in Babylon, in unswerving loyalty to God refused to worship the golden image set up by King Nebuchadnezzar, and so were cast into a fiery furnace. They walked unharmed in the flames and beside them appeared another whose form was "like the Son of God." They were brought forth unscathed; not a hair of their head was singed, "nor the smell of fire had passed on them" (Dan. 3:1-27).

Daniel's Deliverance from a Lion's Den Because of a conspiracy of his jealous enemies in King Darius' court, Daniel was thrown into a lion's den. But his loyalty to and faith in God and his innocency of any wrong to his king preserved him from the ravenous beasts (Dan. 6:1-23).

Jonah's Deliverance from the Belly of the Whale The prophet Jonah was commissioned by God to warn wicked Nineveh, the capital of Assyria, of coming judgment, but he disobeyed and fled to Tarshish by sea. When a storm arose he was thrown overboard by the superstitious crew of the ship and swallowed by a great fish. Three days and three nights Jonah was in its belly, and at his repentance God caused the fish to disgorge him upon dry land (Jon. 1:15-2:10).

God's Care

"The Lord is good to all: and his tender mercies are over all his works." Ps. 145:9

Hagar and Her Son Provided with Water The bondmaid Hagar and her son Ishmael cast out by Abraham suffered from thirst in the wilderness, but God opened Hagar's eyes to see a nearby well so that the life of her son was saved (Gen. 21:14-20).

Bitter Waters of Marah Sweetened En route from the Red Sea to Sinai, the Israelites encamped at Marah. They found its spring bitter, but Moses under divine guidance cast a tree into the waters and they were purified (Ex. 15:22-25).

Quails Providentially Sent When the people murmured for want of food, "at even the quails came up, and covered the camp" (Ex. 16:11-13).

Manna in the Wilderness Bread came from heaven in the form of manna; the Israelites gathered an omer (one-tenth of an ephah, an ephah being a little less than a bushel) for each person every morning for five days of the week, and on the sixth day double in preparation for the Sabbath. This supply of manna continued throughout the forty years of the Wilderness Wandering (Ex. 16:11-35; Josh. 5:12).

Water from the Rock at Rephidim When the people thirsted for water God commanded Moses to strike a rock in Horeb (the Horeb range bordering Rephidim), and water gushed forth (Ex. 17:1-7).

Water from the Rock at Meribah in Kadesh The rebellious Israelites blamed Moses and Aaron for lack of water. In anger Moses struck the rock twice to obtain water, whereas he had been commanded by God only to speak to it, thereby failing to sanctify God in the eyes of the people (Num. 20:1-13; 27:14; Deut. 32:51). (Some scholars believe this to be the same event as that of Ex. 17.)

Samson's Thirst Quenched in Answer to Prayer Shortly after Samson's slaughter of a thousand Philistines with the jawbone of an ass, he prayed for water; and in answer a spring burst out of the ground (Ju. 15:18,19). (The word "jaw" in verse 19 designates a locality, Lehi meaning "jawbone"; cf. verse 17.)

Elijah Fed by Ravens at Cherith Elijah, directed to hide at the brook Cherith from the anger of King Ahab of Israel because of the prophet's prediction of a drought, was divinely provided morning and evening with bread and meat brought him by ravens, till the time the brook dried up (I Ki. 17:2-7).

Elijah Sustained at Zarephath; the Multiplying of the Widow's Meal and Oil Divinely directed to Zarephath in Phoenicia to seek out a widow of that city appointed to support him during the drought and consequent famine, Elijah caused her meager stock of meal and oil to be multiplied continuously; thus sustaining him, the widow, and her son till the three-year drought was ended (I Ki. 17:8-16).

Elijah by Prayer Obtained Rain Elijah at Mount Carmel prayed for rain to end Israel's three-year drought. Eight times he sent his servant to observe the sky before the first sign of cloud appeared and this was followed by a great rain (I Ki. 18:41-45).

Elijah Fed by an Angel Fearing Queen Jezebel's threat against his life, Elijah fled into the wilderness beyond Beer-sheba; there, discouraged over his inability to check Israel's apostasy, he desired to die. God's tender care for him was manifested when twice he was awakened from sleep by an angel who provided him with food and drink; and he "went in the strength of that meat forty days and forty nights unto Horeb the mount of God" (I Ki. 19:2-8).

Jericho's Unwholesome Waters Healed Elisha cast a cruse (earthenware

CORRELATION—OLD TESTAMENT SUBJECTS 173

saucer) of salt into the unhealthy waters of Jericho's spring, accompanying this symbolic act of purification with the pronouncement that God had healed its waters (II Ki. 2:19-22).

Widow's Oil Multiplied
A prophet's widow whose two sons were to be sold for her husband's debt, was aided by Elisha, who miraculously multiplied her one pot of oil. Selling the oil, she was able not only to pay the debt but to sustain herself and her sons with the remainder (II Ki. 4:1-7).

Healing of Poisoned Pottage
Elisha rendered harmless the poisonous herb which had been innocently added to the caldron of the food of the prophets (II Ki. 4:38-41).

Twenty Loaves of Bread Multiplied
Elisha fed one hundred men with twenty barley loaves, "and they did eat, and left thereof" (II Ki. 4:42-44).

Healings and Raisings

"He sent his word, and healed them, and delivered them from their destructions." Ps. 107:20

Healings of Barrenness
Isaac born to Sarah (Gen. 17:15-19; 21:1-3).
Children born to Abimelech's household (Gen. 20:17).
Esau and Jacob born to Rebekah (Gen. 25:21-26).
Joseph born to Rachel (Gen. 30:22-24).
Samson born to Manoah's wife (Ju. 13:2-24).
Samuel born to Hannah (I Sam. 1:1-20).
A son born to the Shunammite (II Ki. 4:8-17).

Healing of Jacob's Fear and of Esau's Hatred
Jacob had twice supplanted Esau, taking both his brother's birthright and his blessing (Gen. 27). For twenty years Jacob, although beyond the reach of Esau's wrath, feared his brother's revenge; while Esau, who had vowed to kill him, nursed his hatred. Through Jacob's transforming experience at Peniel his fear was dispelled, and the following morning when the brothers met, Jacob found Esau healed of his hatred (Gen. 32:3-33:11).

Healing of Miriam's Leprosy
Miriam led Aaron in a seditious attack against their brother Moses, and in punishment was struck with leprosy. She was healed through Moses' intercessory prayer (Num. 12:1-15).

Healing of Jeroboam's Withered Hand
A prophet of Judah pronounced judgment against King Jeroboam's idolatrous altar, and when the king lifted his hand against the prophet, it withered. At the prayer of the prophet his hand was restored (I Ki. 13:4-6).

Raising of the Widow's Son by Elijah
Through his ministrations and prayer the prophet restored to life the son of the widow of Zarephath (I Ki. 17:17-24).

Raising of the Shunammite's Son by Elisha
Upon the death of her child, a child born of promise (II Ki. 4:16), the Shunammite mother with great faith made a journey of over fifteen miles to Mount Carmel to seek Elisha's help. Through his prayer and ministrations the child was restored to life (II Ki. 4:18-37).

Healing of Naaman's Leprosy
Naaman, commander-in-chief of the Syrian army and a leper, hearing of the healing power of the prophet Elisha through a Hebrew slave girl of his wife, went to him for healing. Humbling himself to obey the prophet's simple command to wash in the Jordan, he was healed (II Ki. 5:1-15).

A Corpse Revived by Elisha's Bones
A dead man, placed in the sepulcher of Elisha, was restored to life when his body touched the bones of the prophet (II Ki. 13:21).

Healing of Hezekiah and Lengthening of His Life
King Hezekiah, informed of his imminent death by the prophet Isaiah, prayed for deliverance. His prayer was heard; he was healed through the ministration of Isaiah and promised that his life would be lengthened by fifteen years. The sign of this promise was the turning back of the shadow on the sundial ten degrees (II Ki. 20:1-11; II Chron. 32:24-26; Is. 38).

Healing of Job's Boils
Job, smitten with boils by Satan, was healed when he came to a proper understanding of God's might and majesty and when he humbled himself before his Creator (Job 2:7; 42:10).

Signs of Divine Approbation

"Keep thy heart with all diligence; for out of it are the issues of life." Pr. 4:23

The Translation of Enoch

"Enoch walked with God: and he was not; for God took him" (Gen. 5:24; cf. Heb. 11:5).

The Translation of Elijah

"Behold, there appeared a chariot of fire, and horses of fire . . . and Elijah went up by a whirlwind into heaven" (II Ki. 2:11).

Jerusalem

The name means "foundations of peace," "a peaceful possession," "vision of peace." Jerusalem is a mountain city situated 2500 feet above sea level on the edge of a rocky tableland at the summit of a Judaean mountain ridge. Only from the south, by way of Bethlehem, can it be approached by a slight and gradual ascent. The Mediterranean lies 33 miles to the west and the Dead Sea 14 miles to the east. The plateau is bounded by two main valleys, the Kidron to the east and the Hinnom to the south and west, and intersected by a smaller north-south valley known as the Tyropoeon.

Abram knew the city as Salem (Gen. 14:18), Joshua as Jebusi, the city of the Jebusites (Josh. 18:16), and David as Jerusalem. David captured Zion, the stronghold of the Jebusites, the rock escarpment on the southern tip of the eastern ridge (II Sam. 5:7). There he built his palace, causing Zion to be reverenced as "the city of David." It was sanctified when David brought the Ark of the Covenant to the Tabernacle which he erected in Zion (II Sam. 6:17). Later, when Solomon built the Temple on the site of the threshing floor of Araunah, a little distance to the north (Mt. Moriah; II Chron. 3:1), the name Zion was extended to include this area. Still later it came to designate the whole city of Jerusalem. Jerusalem thus became the center of Israel's religious worship, the capital of all of Judah's kings for more than four hundred years, and the home of many of its prophets. Hallowed by centuries of sacred history, Jerusalem was cherished as "the holy city," "the place that I [God] have chosen to set my name" (Neh. 1:9). Strife and corruption—political and ecclesiastical—figured large in its turbulent history. Often under attack by enemy nations, it was preserved many times by divine intervention. Twice it was razed: by Nebuchadnezzar in 586 B.C.; by the Romans in 70 A.D. It was an important scene of Jesus' labors, the city he "wept over" for its spiritual blindness.

To psalmist, priest, prophet, and New Testament writer Jerusalem and Zion had a spiritual significance:

"the city of our God, in the mountain of his holiness" (Ps. 48:1)

"Zion, the perfection of beauty" (Ps. 50:2)

"Thine eyes shall see Jerusalem a quiet habitation, a tabernacle that shall not be taken down; not one of the stakes thereof shall ever be removed, neither shall any of the cords thereof be broken." (Is. 33:20)

"Jerusalem which is above is free, which is the mother of us all." (Gal. 4:26)

"Ye are come unto mount Sion, and unto the city of the living God, the heavenly Jerusalem, and to an innumerable company of angels. . . ." (Heb. 12:22; see 11:10,16)

New Jerusalem

This term is found only in the book of Revelation and designates the city which "lieth foursquare," having none of the imperfections of its earthly counterpart. It is the spotless bride of Christ, "the Lamb's wife," "having the glory of God" (Rev. 21:2,9,11).

"I will write upon him [that overcometh] the name of my God, and the name of the city of my God, which is new Jerusalem, which cometh down out of heaven from my God. . . ." (Rev. 3:12)

Silences
of Biblical History

There are notable silences throughout Biblical history, often preparatory to some advancing step, to be gauged in import by their mighty fruit-bearing. These were not mere periods of passivity, but of patient active stillness and quiet growth.

Silence in Israel's history between the death of Joseph and the birth of Moses, between the close of the book of Genesis and the opening record of Exodus.

The Children of Israel, as the seed of Abraham, having been given the promise of a covenant by the Almighty God, were able to endure the heavy bondage of Egypt and to draw together in reliance upon their Deity.

> *The fruit of this silence:* Having reached a depth of sorrow and suffering wherefrom they greatly desired to be delivered, the Israelites were given a leader, Moses, who under divine guidance brought them out of Egypt.

Silence of forty years in Moses' life when he served Jethro, priest of Midian.

Moses, having been brought up in the Egyptian court, nevertheless was stirred by loyalty and love to defend his own people. Failing in his human attempts, he was forced to flee into Midian. There he was "content" to abide with Jethro and to tend Jethro's flocks until, after years of spiritual maturing, his continuing desire to aid his people ripened into an ability to hear God's voice and recognize divine direction. Thus he came "to the mountain of God, even to Horeb."

> *The fruit of this silence:* Having grown in meekness and grace, he was prepared to lead Israel out of Egypt's bondage and to reveal to them the nature of the One God and His Law.

Silence of nearly thirty-nine years in Joshua's life during the Wandering to the entrance into the Promised Land.

Joshua, having ministered to Moses and having been entrusted with the militant leadership and defense of Israel, grew through training and endurance in the qualities of wisdom, perception, patience, and spiritual courage.

> *The fruit of this silence:* Having become a worthy successor to Moses, Joshua infused his people with courage to march into Canaan, to rely on God's help against the enemy, and to gain possession of their inheritance.

Silence as Elijah stood on Mount Horeb.

Elijah, having slain the priests of Baal and having fled for his life into the wilderness, desired to die. But, sustained twice by the ministrations of an angel, he journeyed on to Mount Horeb, and standing on the mount in obedience to God's command, he beheld the ferocity of the wind, the earthquake, and the fire.

The fruit of this silence: Having witnessed the impotence of these raging forces, and perceiving that the Lord was not "in" them, Elijah was enabled to hear the "still small voice," to continue fearlessly his work of rooting out idolatry in Israel, and to rise to his own translation.

Silence of nearly ten years in Elisha's life—from his call by Elijah to the beginning of his own ministry.

Elisha was plowing in his father's field when Elijah cast his mantle upon him. He immediately followed the prophet and ministered to him during the reigns of three of Israel's kings.

The fruit of this silence: Having developed his spiritual talents under the tutelage of the great reformer, Elisha was ready to walk beyond Jordan with him, to behold his translation, wear his mantle, and put into active use the "double portion" of the Spirit. His miracles were as remarkable as those of Elijah, and the healings attributed to his ministry are more numerous than those of any other Old Testament figure.

Silence of more than four centuries from Malachi, the last of the Old Testament prophets, to John the Baptist, the forerunner of Jesus Christ.

The willing remnant of Judah which had endured the purifying trial of captivity in Babylon, had returned to its homeland determined to rebuild Jerusalem and to re-establish its adherence to monotheism.

The fruit of this silence: Having rooted out the great temptation to idolatry, and having rededicated itself, this faithful remnant moved toward the fulfillment of the purpose for which the whole nation had been chosen—the advent of Israel's Messiah.

Silence of thirty years in the life of John the Baptist from his birth "till the day of his shewing unto Israel."

This child of promise born to Elisabeth and Zacharias "grew, and waxed strong in spirit." At an early age he withdrew from the world, lived in the desert, and made ready for the performance of his office as "the prophet of the Highest" and as "the voice of one crying in the wilderness."

The fruit of this silence: At the appointed time, having prepared himself, John went forth to "preach the baptism of repentance for the remission of sins"; to proclaim "The kingdom of heaven is at hand"; and to bear witness to Jesus as the Messiah or Christ, "the Lamb of God, which taketh away the sin of the world."

Silence in Jesus' life from his infancy to his appearance in the Temple at the age of twelve.

"The child grew, and waxed strong in spirit, filled with wisdom: and the grace of God was upon him." At twelve, in company with Mary and Joseph, Jesus went down to Jerusalem for the Feast of the Passover. After the close of the feast they found him in the Temple questioning the doctors of the Law, astonishing them with his understanding and his answers.

The fruit of this silence: Having grown in grace and having reached the legal age when he could come to Jerusalem as "a servant of the Law," Jesus took this opportunity to declare openly his sonship with God and the purpose for which he had come into the world—"I must be about my Father's business."

Silence of eighteen years in Jesus' life from the age of twelve to the beginning of his ministry at the age of thirty.

These were "silent years" of maturing for his divine mission. "Jesus increased in wisdom and stature, and in favour with God and man."

The fruit of this silence: Jesus was ready for the inauguration of his ministry, for the commendation of his heavenly Father, and for the authorization which came at his baptism: "This is my beloved Son, in whom I am well pleased."

Silence between Jesus' last discourse on Tuesday of the week preceding Resurrection and his command to Peter and John on Thursday to prepare the Passover.

In the quiet sanctuary of Bethany, Jesus rested in prayer before facing Gethsemane and Calvary.

The fruit of this silence: Having girded himself in communion with God, he went forth in the sublime faith and knowledge of the divine power which was his as the Son to endure what lay before him.

Silences of Jesus during his arraignments before Herod and Pontius Pilate.

Before Herod "he answered him nothing"; before Pilate "Jesus gave him no answer." His bearing was indicative of deep reserves of endurance, meekness, and spiritual knowledge.

The fruit of this silence: Pilate, having questioned him again, "Knowest thou not that I have power to crucify thee, and have power to release thee?" Jesus answered with authority, "Thou couldest have no power at all against me, except it were given thee from above," and proved his assertion three days later by his resurrection.

Silence of three days in the tomb.

Jesus had said: "Love your enemies. . . ."—"This is life eternal, that they might know thee the only true God, and Jesus Christ, whom thou hast sent."—"I and my Father are one."—"I am the resurrection, and the life. . . ."

The fruit of this silence: Victory over death and the grave, and his triumphant glorious appearing on Resurrection morning.

Silence in Saul's life when he went into Arabia shortly after his conversion.

Paul (Saul) had experienced the new birth by the grace of Jesus Christ. Destined to be an apostle to the Gentiles, he gave searching thought to the relation of Jesus to the Old Testament Law and Messianic promises.

The fruit of this silence: Having reached the unshakable conviction that Jesus was the fulfillment of the Law and the Prophets, Paul embraced Christianity in its fullness and became its greatest exponent.

Silence of some seven years in Paul's early ministry when he went out from Tarsus to preach in the regions of Syria and Cilicia.

Paul expounded Christ's gospel as it was being revealed to him "by the Spirit" to those who knew neither the Mosaic Law nor Jesus Christ.

The fruit of this silence: Many basic Christian principles having been clarified and developed in his thought, he was now seasoned for the greater work which lay before him in the Gentile world.

Silence of two years in Paul's life while he was held prisoner in Caesarea by Felix, the Roman procurator.

Paul turned to a deep contemplation of the Church in its ideal and universal meaning and to the strengthening of the faith of its adherents.

The fruit of this silence: Having perceived the Church not only as a society of believers but as "the body of Christ," Paul also poured forth in his Prison Epistles the riches of his revelations concerning the true nature of the Church.

Silence in John's life from his early activities in the Church to the time of his writings.

This beloved disciple, having labored faithfully among the churches for more than half a century and having risen to a demonstrable knowledge of love and sonship which the Master's life and words had revealed to him, reached a high measure of "the stature of the fulness of Christ."

The fruit of this silence: John grew in discipleship to receive and record the Revelation of Jesus Christ and to see the New Jerusalem wherein God and the Lamb reign supreme.

Silence in heaven for "about the space of half an hour," after the opening of the seventh seal (Rev. 8:1).

The fruit of this silence: The prophetic judgments of God on all that is ungodly.

6

A Study
of Job

The Book of Job, a dramatic poem of superlative beauty, is grouped along with Proverbs and Ecclesiastes as the Wisdom Literature of the Old Testament. Date and authorship are uncertain. Some scholars consider it the oldest book of the Bible, written at a very early date; others place it at a date between David and Isaiah (973-740 B.C.); still others assign it to a period nearer the Exile. Modern criticism takes the view that several portions of the book, particularly the speeches of Elihu (chaps. 32-37) are later interpolations.

Job is a quest for the answer to suffering—a problem that has perplexed men since the beginning of time.

Its theme: Why does a righteous man suffer?
Corollary questions:

> How will he endure under trial?
> Is God's government of the world just?
> Is there hope beyond the grave?

The book depicts the doctrine of original sin—a doctrine not canceled out until the Messiah taught the perfection of man as the son of God (Mt. 5:48). Throughout the book it becomes apparent that the preponderance of evidence is shifting from Job's side to God's side, and from Satan's arrogant assumption of power to the revelation of God's supremacy.

The whole assumes somewhat the form of a trial—Satan's charges, Job's complaint, the accusations and exhortations of his friends, his repeated assertion of his innocence, the speeches of the Almighty and His vindication of Job. Many terms suggestive of a court trial appear repeatedly: case (cause), defense (order one's cause), argument; complaint, judge, witness, law, surety; testify, plead for and against; condemn, acquit, pardon.

Job, a righteous man, is forced by loss and suffering to sift all his thoughts, test his faith, and come to a proper understanding of his Creator. Struggling with the inherent sinfulness and weakness of human nature, Job swings between hope and despair as he prays for deliverance. His experience might be likened to what takes place on a threshing floor: the continuous round of trampling sheaves of ripe grain, the breaking up, the fanning out of the chaff, the sifting and gathering of the kernels.

Not understanding the reason for his affliction—Satan is tempting him—Job draws false conclusions as to the source of his suffering. His three friends who come to console him assert God is punishing him for sin, an argument he refutes passionately. Like them, he ascribes his affliction to God but, knowing his own integrity, feels his punishment is unjust. The empty arguments of his friends fail to convince him of guilt or of God's justice, and he refuses to resign himself to unmerited suffering. So evident to his senses are the injustices and inconsistencies of human experience that he even impugns God's moral government of the world. Repeatedly he attempts to call the Almighty to account—while at the same time his ingrained trust in God's righteousness continually asserts itself—until out of the whirlwind of his thoughts he is humbled to a clearer recognition of his Creator's greatness and goodness. God then vindicates Job's righteousness and restores his health and prosperity.

Job's anguished questions could only have their full answer in the teachings and mission of Jesus Christ, the perfect Son whom God later so completely vindicated. But Job did arrive at an exalted sense of trust based on faith and revelation, as did all the Old Testament patriarchs and prophets who pressed on in faith, not yet having received the promise (Heb. 11:39).

Job is written primarily in dialogue; the prologue and epilogue alone are prose; the dialogues are all poetry. In this study the speeches of the participants have been presented in dialogue form and have been somewhat abridged to make the major points more graphic.

Prologue
Debate: Job and His Three Friends

First Cycle	*Second Cycle*	*Third Cycle*
Eliphaz and Job	Eliphaz and Job	Eliphaz and Job
Bildad and Job	Bildad and Job	Bildad and Job
Zophar and Job	Zophar and Job	

Elihu's Discourse
Dialogue: God and Job
Epilogue

Prologue

Job was a pious patriarch of the land of Uz (located by some scholars in the northwestern section of the Arabian Desert). "That man was perfect and upright, and one that feared God, and eschewed evil."

He was a prosperous man, with a large family and much wealth. "There were born unto him seven sons and three daughters. His substance also was seven thousand sheep, and three thousand camels, and five hundred yoke of oxen, and five hundred she asses, and a very great household; so that this man was the greatest of all the men of the east."

His piety was such that after his sons feasted in their houses he took care to sanctify them, offering burnt offerings for them continually: "It may be that my sons have sinned, and cursed God in their hearts."

> ***THE ADVERSARY (AV SATAN) PRESENTS HIMSELF BEFORE GOD***. *"Now there was a day when the SONS OF GOD came to present themselves before the LORD, and SATAN came also among them."*

GOD: Whence cometh thou?

SATAN: From going to and fro in the earth, and from walking up and down in it.

GOD: Hast thou considered my servant Job, that there is none like him in the earth, a perfect and an upright man, one that feareth God, and escheweth evil?

SATAN: Doth Job fear God for nought? Hast not thou made an hedge about him, and about his house, and about all that he hath on every side? thou hast blessed the work of his hands, and his substance is increased in the land.

   But put forth thine hand now, and touch all that he hath, and he will curse [RV renounce] thee to thy face.

GOD: Behold, all that he hath is in thy power; only upon himself put not forth thine hand.

> ***JOB'S LOSS***. *His livestock is stolen, his sheep destroyed by lightning, his camels carried away by the Chaldeans, his servants slain. His sons and daughters die when a great wind causes his eldest son's house to collapse upon them as they feast. JOB grieved; he "rent his mantle, and shaved his head, and fell down upon the ground, and worshipped."*

JOB: Naked came I out of my mother's womb, and naked shall I return thither: the Lord gave, and the Lord hath taken away; blessed be the name of the Lord.

"In all this Job sinned not, nor charged God foolishly."

> ***THE ADVERSARY AGAIN PRESENTS HIMSELF BEFORE GOD***. *"Again there was a day when the SONS OF GOD came to present themselves before the Lord, and SATAN came also among them to present himself before the Lord."*

GOD: From whence comest thou?

SATAN: From going to and fro in the earth, and from walking up and down in it.

GOD: Hast thou considered my servant Job . . . still he holdeth fast his integrity, although thou movedst me against him, to destroy him without cause.

SATAN: Skin for skin, yea, all that a man hath will he give for his life. But put forth thine hand now, and touch his bone and his flesh, and he will curse thee to thy face.

GOD: Behold, he is in thine hand; but save his life.

JOB'S AFFLICTION. So SATAN smote JOB's body with boils "from the sole of his foot unto his crown. And he took him a potsherd to scrape himself withal; and he sat down among the ashes."

JOB'S WIFE: Dost thou still retain thine integrity? curse [RV renounce] God, and die.

JOB: Thou speakest as one of the foolish [RV (marg.) impious] women speaketh. What? shall we receive good at the hand of God, and shall we not receive evil?

"In all this did not Job sin with his lips."

JOB'S THREE FRIENDS COME TO MOURN WITH AND COMFORT HIM: ELIPHAZ the Temanite (a descendant of Teman, a grandson of Esau), BILDAD the Shuhite (a descendant of Shuah, a son of Abraham), and ZOPHAR the Naamathite of Naamah (a tribe about which nothing is now known). "They sat down with him upon the ground seven days and seven nights, and none spake a word unto him: for they saw that his grief was very great."

Debate: Job and His Three Friends

[Chapters 3-31]

JOB'S COMPLAINT (chap. 3). JOB curses the day he came forth from the womb, and thereby was destined to sorrow, oppression, misery, and despair. He longs for death.

JOB: Let the day perish wherein I was born, and the night in which it was said, There is a man child conceived. . . . As for that night, let darkness seize upon it; let it not be joined unto the days of the year. . . . Why died I not from the womb? . . .

Wherefore is light given to him that is in misery, and life unto the bitter in soul; Which long for death, but it cometh not. . . . Why is light given to a man whose way is hid, and whom God hath hedged in? . . .

For my sighing cometh before I eat, and my roarings are poured out like the waters. For the thing which I greatly feared is come upon me, and that which I was afraid of is come unto me.

First Cycle of Speeches

The calamities of Job are so great his three friends conclude that his afflictions show him guilty of a sin of some sort, a sin he is compounding by his complaints against God. They doubt Job's piety and his integrity.

> ***ELIPHAZ' FIRST SPEECH** (chaps. 4, 5). ELIPHAZ reproves JOB for his despair. If Job is upright, will not God preserve him? (chap. 4).*

ELIPHAZ: If we assay to commune with thee, wilt thou be grieved? but who can withhold himself from speaking? Behold, thou hast instructed many, and thou hast strengthened the weak hands. . . . But now it is come upon thee, and thou faintest; it toucheth thee, and thou art troubled.

Is not this thy fear, thy confidence, thy hope, and the uprightness of thy ways? Remember, I pray thee, who ever perished, being innocent? or where were the righteous cut off?

Even as I have seen, they that plow iniquity, and sow wickedness, reap the same. By the blast of God they perish. . . .

> *To humble Job he tells of an awesome vision in which he was shown God's righteousness and man's insignificance.*

Now a thing was secretly brought to me, and mine ear received a little thereof. . . . Fear came upon me. . . . Then a spirit passed before my face; the hair of my flesh stood up: It stood still, but I could not discern the form thereof: an image was before mine eyes, there was silence, and I heard a voice, saying, Shall mortal man be more just than God? shall a man be more pure than his maker?

Behold, he put no trust in his servants; and his angels he charged with folly: How much less in them that dwell in houses of clay, whose foundation is in the dust, which are crushed before the moth? They are destroyed from morning to evening: they perish for ever without any regarding it.

> *ELIPHAZ warns JOB against foolish, rash complaint and urges him to commit his cause to a just and righteous God. He assumes Job's sinfulness: because Job is suffering, he must be suffering as the result of some great sin. He urges Job to accept God's chastening and cites the benefits of His correction (chap. 5).*

Call now, if there be any that will answer thee; and to which of the saints wilt thou turn? For wrath killeth the foolish man, and envy slayeth the silly one. I have seen the foolish taking root: but suddenly I cursed his habitation. . . .

I would seek unto God, and unto God would I commit my cause: Which doeth great things and unsearchable; marvellous things without number. . . .

He taketh the wise in their own craftiness: and the counsel of the froward is carried headlong. . . . But he saveth the poor from the sword, from their mouth, and from the hand of the mighty. . . .

Happy is the man whom God correcteth: therefore despise not thou the chastening of the Almighty: For he maketh sore, and bindeth up: he woundeth, and his hands make whole. He shall deliver thee in six troubles: yea, in seven there shall no evil touch thee. . . . And thou shalt know that thy tabernacle shall be in peace; and thou shalt visit thy habitation, and shalt not sin.

JOB'S REPLY (chaps. 6, 7). JOB shows that his grief weighs on him heavily; his complaint is not without cause. He longs for the comfort of death. The words of his friends are without solace and he reproves their unkindness. He asks them to reconsider their unjust judgment (chap. 6).

JOB: The arrows of the Almighty are within me, the poison whereof drinketh up my spirit: the terrors of God do set themselves in array against me. . . . The things that my soul refused to touch are as my sorrowful meat.

Oh that I might have my request. . . . Even that it would please God to destroy me; that he would let loose his hand, and cut me off! Then should I yet have comfort . . . let him not spare; for I have not concealed the words of the Holy One. . . .

To him that is afflicted pity should be shewed from his friend; but he forsaketh the fear of the Almighty. My brethren have dealt deceitfully as a brook, and as the stream of brooks they pass away; Which are blackish by reason of the ice, and wherein the snow is hid: What time they wax warm, they vanish. . . .

For now ye are nothing; ye see my casting down, and are afraid. . . .

Teach me, and I will hold my tongue: and cause me to understand wherein I have erred. How forcible are right words! but what doth your arguing reprove? . . .

Look upon me; for it is evident unto you if I lie. Return, I pray you, let it not be iniquity; yea, return again, my righteousness is in it.

In great physical suffering and dread, JOB complains of his undeserved misery and justifies his desire for death. Why is God preoccupied with testing man? Why does He not forgive—if there has been sin—since man is so small in His sight? Job cannot reconcile his suffering with the idea of God as "the preserver of men" (chap. 7).

Is there not an appointed time to man upon earth? are not his days also like the days of an hireling? . . . I [am] made to possess months of vanity, and wearisome nights are appointed to me. When I lie down, I say, When shall I arise, and the night be gone? and I am full of tossings to and fro unto the dawning of the day. My flesh is clothed with worms and clods of dust; my skin is broken, and become loathsome. My days are swifter than a weaver's shuttle, and are spent without hope. O remember that my life is wind: mine eye shall no more see good. . . .

Therefore I will not refrain my mouth; I will speak in the anguish of my spirit; I will complain in the bitterness of my soul. . . .

When I say, My bed shall comfort me, my couch shall ease my complaint; Then thou scarest me with dreams, and terrifiest me through visions: So that my soul chooseth strangling, and death rather than my life. . . .

What is man, that thou shouldest magnify him? and that thou shouldest set thine heart upon him? And that thou shouldest visit him every morning, and try him every moment? . . .

I have sinned [RV If I have sinned]; what shall I do unto thee, O thou preserver of men? why hast thou set me as a mark against thee . . . And why dost thou not pardon my transgression, and take away mine iniquity?

BILDAD'S FIRST SPEECH (*chap. 8*). *BILDAD picks up the thread of Eliphaz' argument—Job is suffering because he is a sinner. He discourses on God's justice and the fate of hypocrites. Looking to JOB to repent, he prophesies Job's restoration.*

BILDAD: How long wilt thou speak these things? and how long shall the words of thy mouth be like a strong wind? Doth God pervert judgment? or doth the Almighty pervert justice? . . .

If thou wouldest seek unto God betimes, and make thy supplication to the Almighty; If thou wert pure and upright; surely now he would awake for thee, and make the habitation of thy righteousness prosperous. . . .

Can the rush grow up without mire? can the flag grow without water? Whilst it is yet in his greenness, and not cut down, it withereth before any other herb. So are the paths of all that forget God; and the hypocrite's hope shall perish. . . .

Behold, God will not cast away a perfect man, neither will he help the evildoers: Till he [RV He will yet] fill thy mouth with laughing, and thy lips with rejoicing.

JOB'S REPLY (*chaps. 9, 10*). *JOB, while acknowledging God's justice, feels himself helpless to contend for his innocence before the invisible God whose might is so manifest throughout His creation. He asserts that God's justice is arbitrary against the innocent, and he knows of no "daysman" (mediator, arbiter) to intercede for him before God (chap. 9).*

JOB: I know it is so of a truth: but how should man be just with God [RV (marg.) before God]? If he will contend with him, he cannot answer him one of a thousand. He is wise in heart, and mighty in strength: who hath hardened himself against him, and hath prospered? . . .

Behold, he taketh away, who can hinder him? . . . God will not withdraw his anger, the proud helpers do stoop under him. How much less shall I answer him, and choose out my words to reason with him? Whom, though I were righteous, yet would I not answer, but I would make supplication to my judge.

If I had called, and he had answered me; yet would I not believe that he had hearkened unto my voice. For he breaketh me with a tempest, and multiplieth my wounds without cause. He will not suffer me to take my breath, but filleth me with bitterness. If I speak of strength, lo, he is strong: and if of judgment, who shall set me a time to plead? If I justify myself, mine own mouth shall condemn me: if I say, I am perfect, it shall also prove me perverse. . . .

This is one thing, therefore I said it, He destroyeth the perfect and the wicked. . . .

If I say, I will forget my complaint, I will leave off my heaviness, and comfort myself: I am afraid of all my sorrows, I know that thou wilt not hold me innocent. If I be wicked, why then labour I in vain? . . . For he is not a man, as I am, that I should answer him, and we should come together in judgment. Neither is there any daysman betwixt us, that might lay his hand upon us both.

Let him take his rod away from me, and let not his fear terrify me: Then would I speak, and not fear him; but it is not so with me.

JOB remonstrates earnestly with GOD about his affliction as he continues to seek the reason for his trial. He cannot believe the Creator takes pleasure in destroying the work of His own hands, and he asserts his innocence in the midst of his perplexity (chap. 10).

My soul is weary of my life; I will leave my complaint upon myself; I will speak in the bitterness of my soul. I will say unto God, Do not condemn me; shew me wherefore thou contendest with me. Is it good unto thee that thou shouldest oppress, that thou shouldest despise the work of thine hands, and shine upon the counsel of the wicked? . . .

Thou knowest that I am not wicked; and there is none that can deliver out of thine hand. Thine hands have made me and fashioned me together round about; yet thou dost destroy me. Remember, I beseech thee, that thou hast made me as the clay; and wilt thou bring me into dust again? . . .

If I be wicked, woe unto me; and if I be righteous, yet will I not lift up my head. I am full of confusion; therefore see thou my affliction; For it increaseth. Thou huntest me as a fierce lion. . . . Wherefore then hast thou brought me forth out of the womb? . . .

Are not my days few? cease then, and let me alone, that I may take comfort a little, Before I go whence I shall not return, even to the land of darkness and the shadow of death. . . .

ZOHPAR'S FIRST SPEECH *(chap. 11). ZOPHAR unfeelingly reproves JOB for affirming his innocence: does Job presume, from the imperfection of his human nature, to fathom the wisdom of the Infinite? God knows Job's sin even if Job does not.*

ZOPHAR: Should a man full of talk be justified? . . . For thou hast said, My doctrine is pure, and I am clean in thine eyes. But oh that God would speak, and open his lips against thee. . . . Know therefore that God exacteth of thee less than thine iniquity deserveth.

Canst thou by searching find out God? canst thou find out the Almighty unto perfection? . . . If he cut off, and shut up, or gather together, then who can hinder him? For he knoweth vain men: he seeth wickedness also; will he not then consider it?

ZOPHAR urges JOB to put away iniquity and enumerates the blessings of repentance.

If thou prepare thine heart, and stretch out thine hands toward him; If iniquity be in thine hand, put it far away, and let not wickedness dwell in thy tabernacles. For then shalt thou lift up thy face without spot; yea, thou shalt be stedfast, and shalt not fear. . . . And thine age shall be clearer than the noonday; thou shalt shine forth, thou shalt be as the morning.

JOB'S REPLY *(chaps. 12-14). JOB scorns the stale commonplaces mouthed by his friends. Their arguments have brought him neither comfort nor enlightenment, nor resolved his confusion over what appear to him marked inconsistencies in God's government of the world (chap. 12).*

JOB: No doubt but ye are the people, and wisdom shall die with you. But I have understanding as well as you; I am not inferior to you. . . .

I am as one mocked of his neighbour, who calleth upon God, and he answereth him: the just upright man is laughed to scorn. . . . The tabernacles of robbers prosper, and they that provoke God are secure; into whose hand God bringeth abundantly. . . .

Behold, he breaketh down, and it cannot be built again: he shutteth up a man, and there can be no opening. . . . With him is strength and wisdom: the deceived and the deceiver are his. He leadeth counsellors away spoiled, and maketh the judges fools. . . . He increaseth the nations, and destroyeth them: he enlargeth the nations, and straiteneth them again. He taketh away the heart of the chief of the people of the earth, and causeth them to wander in a wilderness where there is no way.

JOB holds his friends' defense of God's actions worthless and brands their arguments lies. He even calls their arguments wicked—a deceitful attempt to gain favor with GOD. JOB turns from his friends to plead his cause before God. Still convinced in his heart of God's righteousness (although he has been arguing against it) JOB turns to Him, certain that He will justify his innocence (chap. 13).

Surely I would speak to the Almighty, and I desire to reason with God.

But ye are forgers of lies, ye are all physicians of no value. . . . Will ye speak wickedly for God? and talk deceitfully for him? Will ye accept his person? will ye contend for God? . . . He will surely reprove you, if ye do secretly accept persons. Your remembrances [RV memorable sayings] are like unto ashes, your bodies [RV defences] to bodies of clay.

Hold your peace, let me alone, that I may speak, and let come on me what will. Wherefore do I . . . put my life in mine hand? Though he slay me, yet will I trust in him: but I will maintain mine own ways before him. He also shall be my salvation: for an hypocrite shall not come before him. . . .

Behold now, I have ordered my cause [prepared my defense]; I know that I shall be justified. . . . Only do not two things unto me: then will I not hide myself from thee. Withdraw thine hand far from me: and let not thy dread make me afraid [see 9:34]. Then call thou, and I will answer: or let me speak, and answer thou me. How many are mine iniquities and sins? make me to know my transgression and my sin. Wherefore hidest thou thy face, and holdest me for thine enemy?

Contemplating the frailty and sinful nature of mortal man, JOB entreats GOD's forbearance in this life and voices a hope for His favor beyond the grave (chap. 14).

Man that is born of a woman is of few days, and full of trouble. He cometh forth like a flower, and is cut down: he fleeth also as a shadow, and continueth not. And dost thou open thine eyes upon such an one, and bringest me into judgment with thee? Who can bring a clean thing out of an unclean? not one. Seeing his days are determined, the number of his months are with thee, thou hast appointed his bounds that he cannot pass; Turn from him, that he may rest, till he shall accomplish, as an hireling, his day. . . .

O that thou wouldest hide me in the grave, that thou wouldest keep me secret, until thy wrath be past, that thou wouldest appoint me a set time, and remember me! If a man die, shall he live again? all the days of my appointed time will I wait, till my change come. Thou shalt call, and I will answer thee: thou wilt have a desire to the work of thine hands.

Second Cycle of Speeches   [Chapters 15-21]

Job's three friends, unable to draw from Job an admission of guilt, continue more vehemently their argument that the wicked are punished by God. This Job denies.

ELIPHAZ' SECOND SPEECH *(chap. 15). ELIPHAZ sharply condemns JOB for impiety and rebukes him for presuming to reject the wisdom of his elders.*

ELIPHAZ: Should a wise man utter vain knowledge. . . . Should he reason with unprofitable talk? or with speeches wherewith he can do no good? . . . Thine own mouth condemneth thee, and not I. . . .

What understandest thou, which is not in us? With us are both the grayheaded and very aged men, much elder than thy father. Are the consolations of God small with thee? . . . Why doth thine heart carry thee away? . . . That thou turnest thy spirit against God, and lettest such words go out of thy mouth?

Using Job's own words, ELIPHAZ enlarges on the sinfulness of man, and as a warning rehearses the fears and doom of the wicked.

What is man, that he should be clean? and he which is born of a woman, that he should be righteous? Behold, he putteth no trust in his saints; yea, the heavens are not clean in his sight. How much more abominable and filthy is man, which drinketh iniquity like water? . . .

The wicked man travaileth with pain all his days, and the number of years is hidden to the oppressor. A dreadful sound is in his ears: in prosperity the destroyer shall come upon him. . . . Trouble and anguish shall make him afraid. . . .

He shall not be rich, neither shall his substance continue, neither shall he prolong the perfection thereof upon the earth. . . .

Let not him that is deceived trust in vanity: for vanity shall be his recompence. It shall be accomplished before his time, and his branch shall not be green. He shall shake off his unripe grape as the vine, and shall cast off his flower as the olive.

JOB'S REPLY *(chaps. 16, 17). JOB complains bitterly of the unmerciful indictment by his friends; he complains also of God's hostile treatment of him, further compounded by the mockery of his professed friends (chap. 16).*

JOB: I have heard many such things: miserable comforters are ye all. . . .

I also could speak as ye do: if your soul were in my soul's stead, I could heap up words against you, and shake mine head at you. But I would strengthen you with my mouth, and the moving of my lips should assuage your grief. . . .

But now he [God] hath made me weary: [RSV he has] made desolate all my company. And thou hast filled me with wrinkles . . . and my leanness . . . beareth witness to my face. He teareth me in his wrath, who hateth [RV persecuted] me: he gnasheth upon me with his teeth. . . .

They have gaped upon me with their mouth; they have smitten me upon the cheek reproachfully; they have gathered themselves together against me. God hath delivered me to the ungodly, and turned me over into the hands of the wicked.

I was at ease, but he hath broken me asunder: he hath also taken me by my neck, and shaken me to pieces, and set me up for his mark. His archers compass me round about. . . . He breaketh me with breach upon breach, he runneth upon me like a giant.

> *Though standing in "the shadow of death," JOB maintains his innocence and cries out to the earth not to conceal his innocent blood. In a moment of perception he asserts that his witness is in heaven, but he longs for someone who might plead his case.*

My face is foul with weeping, and on my eyelids is the shadow of death; Not for any injustice in mine hands: also my prayer is pure. O earth, cover not thou my blood, and let my cry have no place.

Also now, behold, my witness is in heaven, and my record is on high [RV he that voucheth for me is on high]. My friends scorn me: but mine eye poureth out tears unto God. O that one might plead for a man with God, as a man pleadeth for his neighbour!

> *JOB pleads with GOD to be a surety for him. He is facing death and his friends have failed him. He continues to question where his hope lies, seeing before him only the grave. His speech concludes on a note of despair (chap. 17).*

My breath is corrupt, my days are extinct, the graves are ready for me. Are there not mockers with me? and doth not mine eye continue in their provocation?

Lay down now, put me in a surety with thee [RV Give now a pledge, be surety for me with thyself]; who is he that will strike hands with me? For thou hast hid their heart from understanding: therefore shalt thou not exalt them. . . .

He [God] hath made me also a byword of the people. . . . Mine eye also is dim by reason of sorrow, and all my members are as a shadow. . . .

My days are past, my purposes are broken off, even the thoughts of my heart. . . . If I wait, the grave is mine house: I have made my bed in the darkness. . . . And where is now my hope? as for my hope, who shall see it? They [RV It] shall go down to the bars of the pit [RV Sheol], when our rest together is in the dust.

BILDAD'S SECOND SPEECH *(chap. 18). BILDAD rebukes JOB's words (which to him are presumptuous) and comfortlessly reiterates the awful calamities of the wicked.*

BILDAD: How long will it be ere ye make an end of words? . . . Wherefore are we counted as beasts, and reputed vile in your sight? He teareth himself in his anger [RV Thou that tearest thyself in thine anger]: shall the earth be forsaken for thee? and shall the rock be removed out of his place?

Yea, the light of the wicked shall be put out, and the spark of his fire shall not shine. . . . The steps of his strength shall be straitened, and his own counsel shall cast him down. . . . His confidence shall be rooted out of his tabernacle, and it shall bring him to the king of terrors. . . . His roots shall be dried up beneath, and above shall his branch be cut off. His remembrance shall perish from the earth, and he shall have no name in the street. He shall be driven from light into darkness, and chased out of the world.

> *JOB'S REPLY (chap. 19). JOB charges that his friends are cruel. Granted that he may have erred, nevertheless with all their words they have not yet shown him his error. He maintains that God's severity to him is unjust and has estranged him from friends and kinsmen who once held him in esteem. He craves the pity of his three companions, not their condemnation.*

JOB: How long will ye vex my soul, and break me in pieces with words? . . . And be it indeed that I have erred, mine error remaineth with myself. . . .

Know now that God hath overthrown me, and hath compassed me with his net. Behold, I cry out of wrong, but I am not heard: I cry aloud, but there is no judgment. He hath fenced up my way that I cannot pass, and he hath set darkness in my paths. He hath destroyed me on every side. . . . He hath also kindled his wrath against me, and he counteth me unto him as one of his enemies. . . .

He hath put my brethren far from me, and mine acquaintance are verily estranged from me. My kinsfolk have failed, and my familiar friends have forgotten me. . . .

My bone cleaveth to my skin and to my flesh, and I am escaped with the skin of my teeth.

Have pity upon me, have pity upon me, O ye my friends; for the hand of God hath touched me. Why do ye persecute me as God. . . ?

> *JOB's hope turns again to God; he declares his conviction that his Vindicator lives and "at the latter day" will justify him, and that he himself will see his justification. He warns his three reprovers that judgment will fall upon them.*

I know that my redeemer [RV (marg.) vindicator] liveth, and that he shall stand at the latter day upon the earth: And though after my skin worms destroy this body, yet in my flesh shall I see God: Whom I shall see for myself, and mine eyes shall behold, and not another. . . .

Be ye afraid of the sword: for wrath bringeth the punishments of the sword, that ye may know there is a judgment.

> *ZOPHAR'S SECOND SPEECH (chap. 20). Taking no note of Job's words of hope for vindication, ZOPHAR returns to the theme that the wicked man is punished by God—that the sinner's joy will be short, his life fleeting as a dream, and his ill-gotten wealth lost.*

ZOPHAR: I have heard the check of my reproach, and the spirit of my understanding causeth me to answer.

Knowest thou not this of old, since man was placed upon earth, That the triumphing of the wicked is short, and the joy of the hypocrite but for a moment? Though his excellency mount up to the heavens, and his head reach unto the clouds; Yet he shall perish for ever. . . . He shall fly away as a dream, and shall not be found. . . .

He hath swallowed down riches, and he shall vomit them up again:

God shall cast them out of his belly. . . . That which he laboured for shall he restore, and shall not swallow it down: according to his substance shall the restitution be, and he shall not rejoice therein. . . .

The heaven shall reveal his iniquity; and the earth shall rise up against him. The increase of his house shall depart, and his goods shall flow away in the day of his wrath.

This is the portion of a wicked man from God, and the heritage appointed unto him by God.

JOB'S REPLY (chap. 21). To JOB neither BILDAD's nor ZOPHAR's arguments concerning the punishment of the wicked are valid. He refutes their contentions by the evidence of common observation: frequently the wicked enjoy unbroken prosperity, health, and long life, even when they defy God. The question of God's moral government of the world still puzzles and dismays him since godly and ungodly alike die.

JOB: Suffer me that I may speak. . . . As for me, is my complaint to man? and if it were so, why should not my spirit be troubled? . . . Even when I remember I am afraid, and trembling taketh hold on my flesh.

Wherefore do the wicked live, become old, yea, are mighty in power? Their seed is established in their sight with them. . . . Their houses are safe from fear, neither is the rod of God upon them. . . . They send forth their little ones like a flock, and their children dance. . . . They spend their days in wealth, and in a moment go down to the grave. Therefore they say unto God, Depart from us; for we desire not the knowledge of thy ways. What is the Almighty, that we should serve him? and what profit should we have, if we pray unto him? . . . How oft is the candle of the wicked put out! and how oft cometh their destruction upon them! . . .

Shall any teach God knowledge? seeing he judgeth those that are high. One dieth in his full strength, being wholly at ease and quiet. . . . And another dieth in the bitterness of his soul, and never eateth with pleasure. They shall lie down alike in the dust, and the worms shall cover them.

Behold, I know your thoughts, and the devices which ye wrongfully imagine against me. . . . How then comfort ye me in vain, seeing in your answers there remaineth falsehood?

Third Cycle of Speeches   [Chapters 22-31]

Job has not altered his position. He has rejected the charge of wickedness, maintaining his integrity. Eliphaz, unable to refute Job's reasoning, ignores his speech and now accuses Job of specific offenses that would merit such calamities as he is suffering. Bildad speaks briefly of the majesty of God; Zophar remains silent.

ELIPHAZ' THIRD SPEECH (chap. 22). ELIPHAZ asserts that God does not profit by a man's goodness, neither does He lose by a man's sin. Convinced that God does not punish a man for his piety, ELIPHAZ dogmatically repeats his claim that Job is a sinner. He proceeds—without basis—to accuse JOB of oppressing the poor, the widow, and the fatherless.

ELIPHAZ: Can a man be profitable unto God, as he that is wise may be profitable unto himself? Is it any pleasure to the Almighty, that thou art righteous? or is it gain to him, that thou makest thy ways perfect? Will he reprove thee for fear of thee? will he enter with thee into judgment?

Is not thy wickedness great? and thine iniquities infinite? For thou hast taken a pledge from thy brother for nought, and stripped the naked of their clothing. Thou hast not given water to the weary to drink, and thou hast withholden bread from the hungry. . . . Thou hast sent widows away empty, and the arms of the fatherless have been broken. Therefore snares are round about thee, and sudden fear troubleth thee. . . .

ELIPHAZ softens his indictment with promises of God's mercy if JOB will repent.

Acquaint now thyself with him, and be at peace: thereby good shall come unto thee. . . . If thou return to the Almighty, thou shalt be built up, thou shalt put away iniquity far from thy tabernacles. . . .

For then shalt thou have thy delight in the Almighty, and shalt lift up thy face unto God. Thou shalt make thy prayer unto him, and he shall hear thee, and thou shalt pay thy vows. Thou shalt also decree a thing, and it shall be established unto thee: and the light shall shine upon thy ways.

JOB'S REPLY (chaps. 23, 24). JOB longs for access to God, whom he still cannot find. He reaffirms his confidence in God's goodness and justice (chap. 23).

JOB: Oh that I knew where I might find him! that I might come even to his seat! I would order my cause before him. . . . I would know the words which he would answer me, and understand what he would say unto me.

Will he plead against me with his great power? No; but he would put strength in me. There the righteous might dispute with him; so should I be delivered for ever from my judge.

Behold, I go forward, but he is not there; and backward, but I cannot perceive him: On the left hand . . . but I cannot behold him: he hideth himself on the right hand, that I cannot see him: But he knoweth the way that I take: when he hath tried me, I shall come forth as gold.

JOB reasserts his integrity, in answer to the groundless charges of Eliphaz. He is still unable to account for his affliction.

My foot hath held his steps, his way have I kept, and not declined. Neither have I gone back from the commandment of his lips; I have esteemed the words of his mouth more than my necessary food.

But he is in one mind, and who can turn him? and what his soul desireth, even that he doeth. For he performeth the thing that is appointed for me: and many such things are with him. Therefore am I troubled at his presence: when I consider, I am afraid of him.

JOB complains again of God's moral ordering of the world, perplexed that God—seeing the wicked shamelessly oppress the widow, the fatherless, the poor, and commit violent crimes openly—permits the wicked to flourish unpunished. He voices his belief that they will be judged (chap. 24).

Why, seeing times are not hidden from the Almighty, do they that know him not see his days?

Some remove the landmarks; they violently take away flocks. . . . They drive away the ass of the fatherless, they take the widow's ox for a pledge. They turn the needy out of the way. . . . They cause him to go naked without clothing, and they take away the sheaf from the hungry; Which make oil within their walls, and tread their winepresses, and suffer thirst. Men groan from out of the city, and the soul of the wounded crieth out: yet God layeth not folly to them. . . . The murderer . . . killeth the poor and needy, and in the night is as a thief. The eye also of the adulterer waiteth for the twilight. . . .

Though it be given him [the wicked] to be in safety, whereon he resteth; yet his [God's] eyes are upon their ways. They are exalted for a little while, but are gone and brought low; they are taken out of the way as all other. . . .

And if it be not so now, who will make me a liar, and make my speech nothing worth?

BILDAD'S THIRD SPEECH (chap. 25). Like Eliphaz, BILDAD—unable to refute it—ignores Job's argument. Instead, he declares God's omnipotence and man's insignificance.

BILDAD: Dominion and fear are with him, he maketh peace in his high places. Is there any number of his armies? and upon whom doth not his light arise?

How then can man be justified with God? or how can he be clean that is born of a woman? . . . yea, the stars are not pure in his sight. How much less man, that is a worm? . . .

JOB'S REPLY (chaps. 26-31). JOB rejects BILDAD's harsh words as of no help but he acknowledges God's power to be infinite and unsearchable (chap. 26).

JOB: How hast thou helped him that is without power? how savest thou the arm that hath no strength? How hast thou counselled him that hath no wisdom? . . .

Hell is naked before him [God], and destruction hath no covering. He stretcheth out the north . . . and hangeth the earth upon nothing. He bindeth up the waters in his thick clouds. . . . He holdeth back the face of his throne, and spreadeth his cloud upon it. He hath compassed the waters with bounds, until the day and night come to an end. . . . By his spirit he hath garnished the heavens. . . .

Lo, these are parts of his ways: but how little a portion is heard of him? but the thunder of his power who can understand?

Emphatically JOB rejects again the false arguments of his opponents and asserts that as long as he lives he will hold to the position that he is innocent. This brings him a measure of hope and peace (27:1-26).

As God liveth, who hath taken away my judgment; and the Almighty, who hath vexed my soul; All the while my breath is in me, and the spirit of God is in my nostrils; My lips shall not speak wickedness, nor my tongue utter deceit.

God forbid that I should justify you: till I die I will not remove mine integrity from me. My righteousness I hold fast, and will not let it go: my heart shall not reproach me so long as I live.

(Verses 7-23 of chapter 27 are in the tone of the three friends. They may be a part of Zophar's speech, of which there is no record in the third cycle, or they may be Job's statement of the fate of hypocrites, which Job admits but which he feels has no application to him since he continues righteously to call upon God.)

JOB longs to understand the divine wisdom which governs human affairs. This he knows cannot be mined like the treasures of the earth, or found in the sea, or bought for gold. It is to be found in God; man finds it in loving God and shunning evil (chap. 28).

JOB: Surely there is a vein for the silver, and a place for gold where they fine it. Iron is taken out of the earth, and brass is molten out of the stone. . . .

But where shall wisdom be found? and where is the place of understanding? Man knoweth not the price thereof; neither is it found in the land of the living. The depth saith, It is not in me. . . . It cannot be gotten for gold, neither shall silver be weighed for the price thereof . . . for the price of wisdom is above rubies. . . .

Whence then cometh wisdom? and where is the place of understanding? . . . God understandeth the way thereof, and he knoweth the place thereof. . . . And unto man he said, Behold, the fear of the Lord, that is wisdom; and to depart from evil is understanding.

JOB ruminates on the false charges made by ELIPHAZ. He mourns for his former position of honor among his fellow men (chap. 29).

Oh that I were as in months past, as in the days when God preserved me; When his candle shined upon my head, and when by his light I walked through darkness; As I was in the days of my youth, when the secret of God was upon my tabernacle. . . .

When I went out to the gate through the city, when I prepared my seat in the street! The young men saw me, and hid themselves: and the aged arose, and stood up. . . . The nobles held their peace, and their tongue cleaved to the roof of their mouth. When the ear heard me, then it blessed me; and when the eye saw me, it gave witness to me: Because I delivered the poor that cried, and the fatherless, and him that had none to help him. The blessing of him that was ready to perish came upon me: and I caused the widow's heart to sing for joy.

I put on righteousness, and it clothed me: my judgment was as a robe and a diadem. I was eyes to the blind, and feet was I to the lame. I was a father to the poor: and the cause which I knew not I searched out. And I brake the jaws of the wicked, and plucked the spoil out of his teeth. . . .

My root was spread out by the waters, and the dew lay all night upon my branch. . . . Unto me men gave ear, and waited, and kept silence at my counsel. . . . I chose out their way, and sat chief, and dwelt as a king in the army, as one that comforteth the mourners.

JOB bemoans his present humiliation and suffering as despair again overtakes him (chap. 30).

But now they that are younger than I have me in derision, whose fathers I would have disdained to have set with the dogs of my flock. . . . now am I their song, yea, I am their byword. . . .

And now my soul is poured out upon me; the days of affliction have taken hold upon me. . . . By the great force of my disease is my garment changed. . . . He hath cast me into the mire, and I am become like dust and ashes.

I cry unto thee, and thou dost not hear me: I stand up, and thou regardest me not. Thou art become cruel to me: with thy strong hand thou opposest thyself against me. . . . When I looked for good, then evil came unto me. . . . My bowels boiled, and rested not. . . . My skin is black upon me, and my bones are burned with heat.

JOB again avows the integrity of his whole life—a life that vindicates him from all the charges made or insinuated by his opponents. His personal conduct has been blameless: he has been faithful to his wife, just to his servants, kind to the poor; he has not made wealth his hope or committed secret idolatry; neither has he been vengeful or inhospitable. He has nothing to hide (chap. 31).

Doth not he see my ways, and count all my steps? . . . Let me be weighed in an even balance, that God may know mine integrity.

If my step hath turned out of the way. . . . If mine heart have been deceived by a woman. . . . If I did despise the cause of my manservant or of my maidservant, when they contended with me. . . . If I have withheld the poor from their desire, or have caused the eyes of the widow to fail; Or have eaten my morsel myself alone, and the fatherless hath not eaten thereof. . . . If I have seen any perish for want of clothing. . . . If I have lifted up my hand against the fatherless, when I saw my help in the gate: Then let mine arm fall from my shoulder blade, and mine arm be broken from the bone. For destruction from God was a terror to me, and by reason of his highness I could not endure. If. . . . If. . . . If. . . .

Oh that one would hear me! behold, my desire is, that the Almighty would answer me, and that mine adversary had written a book. Surely I would take it upon my shoulder, and bind it as a crown to me. I would declare unto him the number of my steps; as a prince would I go near unto him.

If my land cry against me . . . or [I] have caused the owners thereof to lose their life: Let thistles grow instead of wheat, and cockle instead of barley.

The words of Job are ended.

"So these three men ceased to answer Job, because he was righteous in his own eyes" (32:1).

Elihu's Discourse

Elihu, son of Barachel the Buzite, who has not been mentioned before but who has evidently been listening to the arguments of Job and his three friends, comes forward to reason with Job. He is a young man, with a higher conception of God and a more merciful attitude toward Job than those of Job's dogmatic friends. He is angry with Job because Job "justified himself rather than God," and with Job's friends "because they had found no answer, and yet had condemned Job" (32:2-5).

Elihu feels himself divinely commissioned as a messenger to speak to Job "in God's stead." His arguments fail to advance much beyond those of Job's other accusers. Like them he accepts the premise that Job is a sinner and urges his submission to the chastening of a just God—a chastening designed to discipline and purify and bless men. Elihu points out to Job that his own doubts and rebellion are hindering his deliverance from affliction and admonishes him to "stand still, and consider the wondrous works of God." Elihu's eloquent words regarding the majesty of the Almighty are designed to persuade Job to trust his Creator.

He alternately addresses the three friends and Job.

> *ELIHU has waited for his elders to speak; now he offers himself as the mediator (daysman) for whom Job had longed and presents his qualifications (32:6-33:7).*

ELIHU: I am young, and ye are very old; wherefore I was afraid, and durst not shew you mine opinion. I said, Days should speak, and multitude of years should teach wisdom. But there is a spirit in man: and the inspiration of the Almighty giveth them understanding. Great men are not always wise: neither do the aged understand judgment. Therefore I said, Hearken to me; I also will shew mine opinion.

Behold, I gave ear to your reasons, whilst ye searched out what to say . . . and, behold, there was none of you that convinced Job, or that answered his words: Lest ye should say, We have found out wisdom: God thrusteth him down, not man. Now he hath not directed his words against me: neither will I answer him with your speeches.

> *"They were amazed, they answered no more: they left off speaking. . . ."*

Wherefore, Job, I pray thee, hear my speeches. . . . My words shall be of the uprightness of my heart: and my lips shall utter knowledge clearly. The spirit of God hath made me, and the breath of the Almighty hath given me life. If thou canst answer me, set thy words in order before me, stand up. Behold, I am according to thy wish in God's stead: I also am formed out of the clay. Behold, my terror shall not make thee afraid, neither shall my hand be heavy upon thee.

> *ELIHU rebukes JOB for his charge against God and remonstrates with him that God need not account to man for His ways. He declares that God instructs and chastens men to repentance for their preservation—by warning vision or by suffering and the ministry of a messenger (33:8-33).*

Surely thou hast spoken in mine hearing, and I have heard the voice of thy words, saying, I am clean without transgression, I am innocent. . . . Behold, he findeth occasions against me, he counteth me for his enemy. . . .

Behold, in this thou art not just: I will answer thee, that God is greater than man. Why dost thou strive against him? for he giveth not account of any of his matters.

For God speaketh once, yea twice, yet man perceiveth it not [Moffatt, God has one mode of speech; yes, and if man heeds it not, another].

In a dream, in a vision of the night. . . . Then he openeth the ears of men, and sealeth their instruction, That he may withdraw man from his purpose, and hide pride from man. He keepeth back his soul from the pit, and his life from perishing by the sword.

He is chastened also with pain upon his bed. . . . Yea, his soul draweth near unto the grave, and his life to the destroyers. If there be a messenger with him, an interpreter, one among a thousand, to shew unto man his uprightness: Then he is gracious unto him, and saith, Deliver him from going down to the pit: I have found a ransom. His flesh shall be fresher than a child's: he shall return to the days of his youth: He shall pray unto God, and he will be favourable unto him: and he shall see his face with joy: for he will render unto man his righteousness.

Elihu refers to himself as the Divinely-sent (ch. 32:8; 33:6) "messenger," the "interpreter" to explain to Job and vindicate God's righteousness; such a one Eliphaz had denied that Job could look for (ch. 5:1), and Job (ch. 9:33) had wished for such a "daysman" or umpire between him and God. . . . Elihu, the God-sent mediator of a temporal deliverance (vv. 24-26), is a type of the God-man Jesus Christ the Mediator of *eternal* deliverance: "the *messenger* of the covenant" (Malachi 3:1).[1]

He looketh upon men, and if any say, I have sinned, and perverted that which was right, and it profited me not; He will deliver his soul from going into the pit, and his life shall see the light. Lo, all these things worketh God oftentimes with man, To bring back his soul from the pit, to be enlightened with the light of the living.

> *ELIHU contends that Job puts himself on the side of the wicked when he questions God's justice. He defends God's government of the world by declaring that the omnipotent God cannot be unjust and calls on JOB to humble himself. He accuses JOB of the added sin of rebellion in arraigning God's justice (chap. 34).*

Job hath said, I am righteous: and God hath taken away my judgment. Should I lie against my right? . . . What man is like Job, who drinketh up scorning like water? Which goeth in company with the workers of iniquity. . . . For he hath said, It profiteth a man nothing that he should delight himself with God. . . .

Far be it from God, that he should do wickedness; and from the Almighty, that he should commit iniquity. For the work of a man shall he render unto him, and cause every man to find according to his ways. . . .

Wilt thou condemn him that is most just? . . .

Surely it is meet to be said unto God, I have borne chastisement, I will not offend any more: That which I see not teach thou me: if I have done iniquity, I will do no more. Should it be according to thy mind? he will recompense it, whether thou refuse, or whether thou choose; and not I. . . .

Job hath spoken without knowledge, and his words were without wisdom. My desire is that Job may be tried unto the end because of his answers for wicked men. For he addeth rebellion unto his sin . . . and multiplieth his words against God.

> *ELIHU enlarges on Job's presumption. He reasons that because God is so exalted Job must not make comparison between his righteousness and God's. He maintains, as had Eliphaz (22:2,3), that God is not touched by either Job's sin or his righteousness but that Job injures himself by his sin or benefits himself and his fellow men by his righteousness (35:1-8).*

Thinkest thou this to be right, that thou saidst, My righteousness is more than God's? For thou saidst, What advantage will it be unto thee? and, What profit shall I have, if I be cleansed from my sin?

I will answer thee. . . . Look unto the heavens, and see; and behold the clouds which are higher than thou. If thou sinnest, what doest thou against him? . . . If thou be righteous, what givest thou him? or what receiveth he of thine hand? Thy wickedness may hurt a man as thou art; and thy righteousness may profit the son of man.

> *ELIHU asserts that the cry of the oppressed often seems to go unanswered because the oppressed do not turn with humble faith to their Creator. Job's cause (judgment) is before God; therefore Job must wait patiently and with trust (35:9-16).*

By reason of the multitude of oppressions they make the oppressed to cry. . . . But none saith, Where is God my maker, who giveth songs in the night. . . . Surely God will not hear vanity, neither will the Almighty regard it.

Although thou sayest thou shalt not see him, yet judgment is before him; therefore trust thou in him. But now, because it is not so, he hath visited in his anger. . . . Therefore doth Job open his mouth in vain. . . .

> *ELIHU declares that God is just in His ways, and the purpose of His discipline is to turn men from sin. He warns JOB that his rebellion and his longing for death are hindering the flow of God's blessings (36:1-21).*

Suffer me a little, and I will shew thee that I have yet to speak on God's behalf. I will . . . ascribe righteousness to my Maker. . . . he that is perfect in knowledge is with thee. Behold, God is mighty, and despiseth not any: he is mighty in strength and wisdom. . . . He withdraweth not his eyes from the righteous: but with kings are they on the throne; yea, he doth establish them for ever, and they are exalted.

And if they be bound in fetters, and be holden in cords of affliction; Then he sheweth them their work, and their transgressions that they have exceeded. He openeth also their ear to discipline, and commandeth that they return from iniquity. If they obey and serve him, they shall spend their days in prosperity, and their years in pleasures. But if they obey not, they shall perish by the sword, and they shall die without knowledge. . . . He delivereth the poor in his affliction, and openeth their ears in oppression.

Even so would he have removed thee out of the strait into a broad place, where there is no straitness; and that which should be set on thy table should be full of fatness. But thou hast fulfilled the judgment of the wicked: judgment and justice take hold on thee. . . . Desire not the night [death], when people are cut off in their place. Take heed, regard not iniquity: for this hast thou chosen rather than affliction.

As ELIHU's discourse draws to a close he enjoins JOB to magnify the marvelous works of God. His eloquence mounts as he declares the majesty and might of God in the wonders of the heavens, all of which testify to His righteous government of the world; men should therefore revere and trust Him (36:22-37:24).

Behold, God exalteth by his power: who teacheth like him? Who hath enjoined him his way? or who can say, Thou hast wrought iniquity?

Remember that thou magnify his work, which men behold. Every man may see it; man may behold it afar off. . . .

Can any understand the spreadings of the clouds, or the noise [RV thunderings] of his tabernacle? . . . great things doeth he, which we cannot comprehend. For he saith to the snow, Be thou on the earth; likewise to the small rain, and to the great rain of his strength. . . .

It [the cloud] is turned round about by his counsels: that they may do whatsoever he commandeth them upon the face of the world in the earth. He causeth it to come, whether for correction, or for his land, or for mercy.

Hearken unto this, O Job: stand still, and consider the wondrous works of God. Dost thou know when God disposed them. . . . Dost thou know the balancings of the clouds. . . . Hast thou with him spread out the sky. . . ?

With God is terrible majesty. Touching the Almighty, we cannot find him out: he is excellent in power, and in judgment, and in plenty of justice: he will not afflict. Men do therefore fear him. . . .

Dialogue
God and Job

[Chapters 38:1-42:6]

Job makes no reply to Elihu, but Elihu's words have given him inspiration. Whereas heretofore he had thought of God as afar off and unapproachable, Job now hears God's voice addressing him out of the whirlwind and he rises to a clearer comprehension of his Creator.

GOD'S FIRST SPEECH (38:1-40:2). Here begins Job's great moment of enlightenment. GOD is about to vindicate JOB, but first He must bring His servant to a realization and acknowledgment of His omnipotence and omniscience. In language of superlative grandeur GOD reproves and silences JOB. His challenging questions cause JOB to look anew at the phenomena of the universe in which he lives and to ask if he could himself have made any of them or even "understand how they were created" (38:1-38).

GOD: Who is this that darkeneth counsel by words without knowledge? Gird up now thy loins like a man; for I will demand of thee, and answer thou me.

Where wast thou when I laid the foundations of the earth? . . .

Who hath laid the measures thereof, if thou knowest? . . .

Whereupon are the foundations thereof fastened? or who laid the corner stone thereof; When the morning stars sang together, and all the sons of God shouted for joy?

Or who shut up the sea with doors. . . . And said, Hitherto shalt thou come, but no further: and here shall thy proud waves be stayed?

Hast thou commanded the morning since thy days. . . ?

Hast thou entered into the springs of the sea? . . .

Have the gates of death been opened unto thee? . . .

Hast thou perceived the breadth of the earth? . . .

Where is the way where light dwelleth? and as for darkness, where is the place thereof. . . ?

Hast thou entered into the treasures of the snow? . . .

By what way is the light parted. . . ?

Who hath divided a watercourse for the overflowing of waters . . . ?

Hath the rain a father? . . . Out of whose womb came the ice? and the hoary frost of heaven, who hath gendered it? . . .

Canst thou bind the sweet influences of Pleiades, or loose the bands of Orion? Canst thou bring forth Mazzaroth in his season? or canst thou guide Arcturus with his sons?

Knowest thou the ordinances of heaven? canst thou set the dominion thereof in the earth?

Canst thou lift up thy voice to the clouds, that abundance of waters may cover thee?

Canst thou send lightnings, that they may go, and say unto thee, Here we are?

Who hath put wisdom in the inward parts? or who hath given understanding to the heart? . . .

GOD continues to challenge JOB. Had his wisdom brought into being the wonders of animate creation or given them their life-giving instincts? GOD's questioning brings JOB to a further recognition of the Creator's providential care and goodness (38:39-39:30).

Wilt thou hunt the prey for the lion? or fill the appetite of the young lions. . . ? Who provideth the raven his food? . . .

Knowest thou the time when the wild goats of the rock bring forth? or canst thou mark when the hinds do calve? . . .

Who hath sent out the wild ass free? . . .Whose house I have made the wilderness, and the barren land his dwellings. . . .The range of the mountains is his pasture, and he searcheth after every green thing.

Will the unicorn [RV wild-ox] be willing to serve thee, or abide by thy crib? . . .

Gavest thou the goodly wings unto the peacocks? or wings and feathers unto the ostrich? . . .

Hast thou given the horse strength? hast thou clothed his neck with thunder? . . .

Doth the hawk fly by thy wisdom, and stretch her wings toward the south?

Doth the eagle mount up at thy command, and make her nest on high?

GOD now demands an answer from JOB (40:1,2).

Shall he that contendeth with the Almighty instruct him? he that reproveth God, let him answer it.

JOB'S FIRST ANSWER (40:3-5). The disclosure of God's greatness and care for all His creatures humbles Job and convinces him of his ignorance and presumption in impugning God's government of the world.

JOB: Behold, I am vile [RV of small account] ; what shall I answer thee? I will lay mine hand upon my mouth. Once have I spoken; but I will not answer: yea, twice; but I will proceed no further.

GOD'S SECOND SPEECH (chaps. 40:6-41:34). Again GOD speaks out of the whirlwind (40:6-14).

GOD: Gird up thy loins now like a man: I will demand of thee, and declare thou unto me. Wilt thou also disannul my judgment? wilt thou condemn me, that thou mayest be righteous? Hast thou an arm like God? or canst thou thunder with a voice like him?
     Deck thyself now with majesty and excellency; and array thyself with glory and beauty. Cast abroad the rage of thy wrath. . . . Look on every one that is proud, and bring him low; and tread down the wicked in their place. Hide them in the dust together; and bind their faces in secret. Then will I also confess unto thee that thine own right hand can save thee.

GOD declares His control over the gigantic creatures of the earth and sea. If man cannot subdue these, how can he call to account the Creator Himself (40:15-41:34)?

Behold now behemoth, which I made with thee; he eateth grass as an ox. Lo now, his strength is in his loins. . . . He moveth his tail like a cedar. . . . His bones are as strong pieces of brass. . . . He is the chief of the ways of God: he that made him can make his sword to approach unto him.
    Canst thou draw out leviathan with an hook? or his tongue with a cord which thou lettest down? Canst thou put an hook into his nose? . . . Will he make a covenant with thee? wilt thou take him for a servant for ever? . . .
    Canst thou fill his skin with barbed irons? or his head with fish spears? Lay thine hand upon him, remember the battle, do no more. Behold, the hope of him is in vain: shall not one be cast down even at the sight of him? None is so fierce [courageous] that dare stir him up: who then is able to stand before me? Who hath prevented me [RV first given unto me] , that I should repay him? whatsoever is under the whole heaven is mine.
    I will not conceal his parts, nor his power, nor his comely proportion. Who can discover the face of his garment? or who can come to him with his double bridle? Who can open the doors of his face? his teeth are terrible round about. . . . The sword of him that layeth at him cannot hold: the spear, the dart, nor the habergeon. . . .

Upon earth there is not his like; who is made without fear. He beholdeth all high things: he is a king over all the children of pride.

JOB'S SECOND ANSWER (42:1-6). Contritely JOB acknowledges God's omnipotence, and his heart and mind are at peace (compare Ps. 51:17; Is. 66:2). Realizing now how badly qualified he was to judge, even in regard to what had happened to himself, he candidly admits that he was guilty of the charge brought against him by the Almighty (38:2; 34:5).

Job had prayed "Oh that I knew where I might find him! that I might come even to his seat!" (23:3; compare Ps. 9:4). His continuous inner wrestling and questioning have brought him an answer to his search; he now has a clear and sensible perception of God's being and goodness.

JOB: I know that thou canst do every thing, and that no thought can be withholden from thee [RV And that no purpose of thine can be restrained].

Who is he that hideth counsel without knowledge [God's question to him (38:2)]? therefore have I uttered that I understood not; things too wonderful for me, which I knew not.

Hear, I beseech thee, and I will speak: I will demand of thee, and declare thou unto me [God's words to him (38:3; 40:7)]. I have heard of thee by the hearing of the ear: but now mine eye seeth thee.

Wherefore I abhor myself [RV (marg.) *loathe* my words], and repent in dust and ashes.

Epilogue

[Chapter 42:7-17]

GOD'S VINDICATION OF JOB. Satan's charge has been disproved. Job has been afflicted, perplexed, tormented by human reasoning and the almost overwhelming evidence before his senses until he even longed for death; at no time has he renounced God. Upon Job's acknowledgment "now mine eye seeth thee" and his retraction of his rash words, God speaks on Job's behalf and vindicates his integrity.

> *God reproves Job's three friends for their false estimate of Job as a sinner and a hypocrite, and then commands them to humble themselves. He bids JOB to pray for them.*

GOD: My wrath is kindled against thee [Eliphaz], and against thy two friends: for ye have not spoken of me the thing that is right, as my servant Job hath.

Therefore take unto you now seven bullocks and seven rams, and go to my servant Job, and offer up for yourselves a burnt offering; and my servant Job shall pray for you: for him will I accept [receive with favor] : lest I deal with you after your folly. . . .

> *"So Eliphaz . . . and Bildad . . . and Zophar . . . went, and did according as the Lord commanded them."*

> *GOD'S RESTORATION OF JOB. JOB forgives his friends; GOD restores JOB to health, usefulness, and honor, and blesses him with a double recompense.*

"The Lord also accepted Job. And the Lord turned the captivity of Job, when he prayed for his friends: also the Lord gave Job twice as much as he had before.

"Then came there unto him all his brethren, and all his sisters, and all they that had been of his acquaintance before, and did eat bread with him in his house . . . every man also gave him a piece of money . . . and an earring of gold.

"So the Lord blessed the latter end of Job more than his beginning: for he had fourteen thousand sheep, and six thousand camels, and a thousand yoke of oxen, and a thousand she asses. He had also seven sons and three daughters. . . .

"After this lived Job an hundred and forty years, and saw his sons, and his sons' sons, even four generations."

> "Behold, we count them happy which endure. Ye have
> heard of the patience [Moffatt, stedfastness] of Job,
> and have seen the end of the Lord [New English Bible,
> how the Lord treated him in the end] ; that the Lord is
> very pitiful, and of tender mercy." (Ja. 5:11)

7

A Condensation of the Psalms

The book of Psalms is a beautiful collection of lyric poetry whose title signifies "praises." Many of these psalms, set to music, became the hymnbook of the Hebrew nation. They range in authorship from Moses (Ps. 90) and David to the psalmists of the Restoration period, and cover in time close to a thousand years of Israel's history. This collection was early divided into five sections: Pss. 1-41, 42-72, 73-89, 90-106, 107-150, each closing with a doxology. Of its 150 psalms, 75 are attributed to David or compiled in his name. The Hallel ("praise"), Pss. 113-118, was sung at the Passover, Feast of Weeks, and Feast of Tabernacles. Songs of Degrees or Ascents, Pss. 120-134, were sung by pilgrims journeying to Jerusalem for the annual festivals.

The Psalms rehearse continually the blessings of God's love to Israel. They are the passionate outpourings of the human heart in praise and trust to an omniscient God; the devotional prayers of the penitent, the doubtful, the fearful who sought comfort, guidance, and protection; the supplications of the godly and the upright who walked in integrity and craved deliverance from sin and the wickedness of men. And they reveal the profound meditations of those who loved the law of God and strove to obey its precepts.

Throughout the Psalms the voice of prophecy is heard, portraying Christ in his sufferings, resurrection, ascension, church, and kingdom. Those considered peculiarly Messianic are Pss. 2, 16, 22, 40, 45, 69, 72, 110, and 118, but in many others may be seen the pattern of the Godlike man that is fulfilled in Jesus Christ (see Lu. 24:44).

To observe the main theme of each poem is to see Psalms as "a mirror of the life of the soul, not of Israel merely, but of humanity."[1] Because these poems are cries of the soul to God out of the depths of human anguish, and songs from the heights of pure joy and inspiration, they touch a responsive chord in every one of us. "The Psalms should be studied in the light of eternal truth, and the local significance should be lost in the universal."[2]

The substance of each psalm has been pointed up to enable the reader to see quickly its timeless truths so applicable to present-day experience. The psalms have been arranged in groups of ten for convenient reading. An asterisk (*) indicates a psalm written by or attributed to David.

PSALM 1. The happiness of the godly. The unhappiness of the ungodly.
PSALM 2. God's Anointed (Christ) to reign over the whole earth with an iron rod.
*PSALM 3. The security of God's protection.
*PSALM 4. The godly man's happiness and safety are secure in God.
*PSALM 5. God does not show favor to the wicked, but blesses and defends the righteous.
*PSALM 6. A prayer for mercy and healing in time of affliction.
*PSALM 7. Prayer of a man of integrity for deliverance from his enemies.
*PSALM 8. God's excellent glory is magnified by His works. Man is crowned with glory, honor, and dominion.
*PSALM 9. A song of praise for God's righteous judgment.
*PSALM 10. Prayer for surcease from grievous ways of the wicked.

*PSALM 11. A prayer of trust in God in time of trial.
*PSALM 12. Prayer of entreaty for God's help when the wicked walk on every side.
*PSALM 13. A prayer of trust in divine mercy, though the answer be delayed.
*PSALM 14. The corruption of the foolish man.
*PSALM 15. Description of a righteous man, a dweller in Zion.
*PSALM 16. Supplication to God for preservation. The godly man's heritage of joy and everlasting life (see Acts 2:25-31).
*PSALM 17. A confident prayer of an innocent heart for God's protection.
*PSALM 18. A song of thanksgiving for God's deliverance and mercy.
*PSALM 19. God's works show His glory, His perfect law, His grace.
*PSALM 20. A prayer of faith in God's help and salvation.

*PSALM 21. A king's joyous prayer of thanksgiving for God's many blessings.
*PSALM 22. A cry of distress, yet of sublime trust in God (see Mt. 27:46).
*PSALM 23. The great Shepherd and His loving constant care.
*PSALM 24. God's sovereignty. The pure in heart dwell in His holy place.
*PSALM 25. A confident prayer for forgiveness, mercy, and deliverance.
*PSALM 26. A declaration of integrity and a prayer for redemption.
*PSALM 27. Fearless faith upheld by the power and goodness of God.
*PSALM 28. An earnest prayer for help. Rejoicing in God's answer.
*PSALM 29. The majesty, power, and glory of the voice of God.
*PSALM 30. Thanksgiving for healing and deliverance from death.

*PSALM 31. Confident prayer in time of trouble. God's mercy and goodness.
*PSALM 32. The blessedness of God's forgiveness of sins.
PSALM 33. The upright shall praise God's goodness and creative power.
*PSALM 34. God is to be praised and trusted. Preservation of the righteous.
*PSALM 35. Prayer of a righteous man for his enemies' confusion.
*PSALM 36. The transgressions of the wicked. The excellence of God's loving-kindness to the upright in heart.
*PSALM 37. The transitory estate of the wicked and his end. The patience and preservation of the righteous and his end.
*PSALM 38. A submissive prayer for mercy under chastisement for sin.

*PSALM 39. The vanity of mortal life. Hope in God.
*PSALM 40. The blessings of trust in God. Obedience to His will
is the rightful sacrifice (see Heb. 10:7).

*PSALM 41. Prayer to God for succor from suffering and from malice of enemies.
PSALM 42. The thirst of the soul for the living God.
PSALM 43. A prayer for light and truth and God's guidance.
PSALM 44. A prayer for deliverance by a faithful nation under reproach.
PSALM 45. A song of rejoicing over the King's marriage (see Rev. 19:7,8).
PSALM 46. God is the refuge and strength of His people.
PSALM 47. Praise to God, the enthroned King of all the earth.
PSALM 48. The everlasting glory of Zion, the city of God.
PSALM 49. Folly of trusting in riches for redemption of the soul.
PSALM 50. The true spirit of sacrifice, which God enjoins.

*PSALM 51. The confession of a contrite heart; a prayer for forgiveness of sins, for
purity, and for restoration to grace.
*PSALM 52. The boastful, deceitful wicked are destroyed, while the righteous abide.
*PSALM 53. The folly and corruption of men who say there is no God.
*PSALM 54. Prayer for help and defense against enemies who oppress.
*PSALM 55. Mourning over the treachery of a friend. Comfort in prayer and
in certainty of God's care.
*PSALM 56. Complete trust and reliance on God in time of fear.
*PSALM 57. A fixed faith in God's mercy and truth amid calamities.
*PSALM 58. Prayer for destruction of unjust judges that God's judgment
may be manifest.
*PSALM 59. Prayer for deliverance from enemies. God a sure defense.
*PSALM 60. A prayer for God's presence and help in battle.

*PSALM 61. A prayer of confidence in God and a vow to serve Him continually.
*PSALM 62. God is the rock of man's salvation—his refuge and strong defense.
*PSALM 63. The soul that thirsts is satisfied in God; it joyfully praises Him.
*PSALM 64. Prayer for preservation from the secret devices of the wicked.
*PSALM 65. Praise for God's blessings and benefits to man and the earth.
PSALM 66. Praise and honor to God for His mighty works toward men.
PSALM 67. A prayer that all nations of the earth worship God.
*PSALM 68. Praise to "Jah" for the excellence and strength of His
presence and for His gracious providence to Israel.
*PSALM 69. A cry for deliverance from the mire of grief and affliction
over unmerited reproach (see Mt. 27:34,48; Jn. 15:25).
*PSALM 70. A cry for speedy deliverance from the wicked.

PSALM 71. Prayer of an aged man for strength and quickening against the trials of
old age. His hope and confident trust in God's deliverance.
*PSALM 72. Prayer for the righteous and enduring reign of the ideal King (Christ).
PSALM 73. The psalmist is tempted to envy the prosperity of the wicked; but his
conclusion is "It is good for me to draw near to God."
PSALM 74. Prayer to God that He remember His covenant people and restore His
holy sanctuary desolated by the adversary.
PSALM 75. Thanksgiving that God puts down the proud, exalts the righteous.
PSALM 76. An exhortation to revere God for His victorious judgments.

PSALM 77. A struggle to maintain faith. Comfort is found in remembering
God's power and mercy.

PSALM 78. A new generation warned to be not stubborn or rebellious
but to keep steadfastly God's law and covenant.

PSALM 79. A lament over the desolation of Jerusalem and a prayer
for forgiveness and removal of reproach.

PSALM 80. Prayer to the great Shepherd of Israel for salvation.

PSALM 81. A call to praise and obey the God who has succored Israel, for His benefits
fall not to the obstinately willful.

PSALM 82. A reproof of unjust judgment. Prayer for God's justice.

PSALM 83. A plea that God confound the enemies of Israel.

PSALM 84. The soul's longing to abide in the sanctuary of the living God.

PSALM 85. Prayer that God's mercy and salvation be shown to His people.

*PSALM 86. A trusting prayer for the continuance of God's mercies.

PSALM 87. A song of the glory of Zion and of those born in her.

PSALM 88. Supplication for deliverance from the darkness of death.

PSALM 89. Praise for the blessings and mercies of God's covenant,
and prayer for their renewal in time of reproach.

PSALM 90. God's everlastingness and the fleeting days of a man.
Prayer to use the days wisely that the works of
a man's hands may endure.

PSALM 91. The safety and security of him who trusts, whose habitation is "the
secret place of the most High."

PSALM 92. Praise to the most High for His great works and for His goodness.

PSALM 93. A song of praise of God's majesty, power, and holiness.

PSALM 94. Prayer for God's vengeance on the wicked and His merciful
upholding of the righteous.

PSALM 95. Praise to God for the works of His hands, and exhortation to
harden not the heart against Him.

PSALM 96. A call to all nations to praise and honor God and to give to
Him the glory due His righteous reign.

PSALM 97. Psalm of rejoicing that God is above all gods and that His
righteousness is manifest.

PSALM 98. A song of rejoicing that all the ends of the earth have
seen the salvation of God.

PSALM 99. An exhortation to exalt God in Zion, for He is great
and holy, and He answers prayer.

PSALM 100. A glad song of praise to God the Creator.

*PSALM 101. A vow to walk faithfully before God with a perfect heart.

PSALM 102. Prayer of one overwhelmed by affliction. He takes comfort in remembering
the mercy and eternity of God.

*PSALM 103. A hymn of praise and gratitude for God's loving-kindness.

PSALM 104. Meditation on the manifold works of the Creator and His tender
care over all.

PSALM 105. Rehearsal of God's blessings to Israel, His covenant people.

PSALM 106. Rehearsal of Israel's rebellions and God's deliverances.

PSALM 107. A call to praise God for His deliverance of the children
of men from their many distresses.

*PSALM 108. A prayer of praise, and a plea to God whose help alone
can bring victory over the enemy.
*PSALM 109. Prayer that the deceitful wicked be put to confusion.
*PSALM 110. The Priest-King and his reign (see Mt. 22:44; Heb. 5:6).

PSALM 111. An exhortation to praise God for His glorious and enduring works.
PSALM 112. The blessedness of the upright man who fears God.
PSALM 113. God is to be universally praised. His mercy to the poor.
PSALM 114. A hymn of praise for God's mighty deliverance of Israel.
PSALM 115. The omnipotence of God and the impotence of idols.
PSALM 116. Psalmist's gratitude to God for the deliverance of his soul
from death. A profession of love and consecration.
PSALM 117. A call to the nations to praise God for His mercy.
PSALM 118. Praise for the saving and enduring goodness of God. The
coming of Christ typified (see Mt. 21:9,42).
PSALM 119. Prayerful joyful meditation on the law of God—His way,
His word, His testimonies, precepts, statutes,
commandments, judgments, and ordinances—and on
the blessings which flow from obedience to them.
PSALM 120. Cry of distress for surcease from deceitful tongues.

PSALM 121. God the Creator is the keeper and preserver of His people.
*PSALM 122. A song of rejoicing for Jerusalem and a prayer for its peace.
PSALM 123. Confident prayer to God for deliverance from the scorn of men.
*PSALM 124. Thanksgiving to God for deliverance from enemies.
PSALM 125. God is round about those who trust Him.
PSALM 126. Joyous thanksgiving for restoration after captivity.
PSALM 127. All labor not of God is vain. Children are God's gift.
PSALM 128. The happiness of him who loves God and walks in His ways.
PSALM 129. Thankfulness to God that affliction has not prevailed.
PSALM 130. A supplicating cry for God's forgiving love, attended
by hope and patience.

*PSALM 131. Childlike humility and trust in God.
PSALM 132. A prayer for God's favor to Zion, His chosen habitation.
*PSALM 133. Blessing on brethren who dwell together in unity.
PSALM 134. A call to those who watch in the sanctuary by night to bless God,
and a prayer that God bless them.
PSALM 135. Praise to God for His mighty power. The vanity of idols.
PSALM 136. Praise to the God of gods "for his mercy endureth for ever."
PSALM 137. A psalm of mourning of those in captivity far from Zion.
*PSALM 138. Song of thanksgiving to God for answered prayer.
*PSALM 139. Song of praise to the omniscient and omnipresent Creator.
Man the marvelous work of His hands.
*PSALM 140. Prayer for deliverance from the treachery of enemies.

*PSALM 141. The psalmist's supplication that his prayer be found worthy of acceptance,
and that he be protected from the wicked.
*PSALM 142. A cry to God for refuge in time of trouble.
*PSALM 143. An earnest supplication for God's favor, guidance, and grace.

*PSALM 144. Prayer that the mighty hand of God deliver His servant from the
hand of wicked strangers.
*PSALM 145. The goodness, greatness, and sure mercies of God are extolled.
His kingdom is glorious and everlasting.
PSALM 146. Song of praise to God, the true helper of men.
PSALM 147. Praise to God, whose understanding and power are infinite.
PSALM 148. The whole universe is exhorted to praise its Creator.
PSALM 149. The children of Zion are exhorted to joy in their King,
who beautifies the meek with salvation.
PSALM 150. "Let every thing that hath breath praise the Lord."

The burst of praise—the hallelujahs, *"praise ye Jah"*—of the closing psalm exhorts:

"Praise ye the Lord. Praise God. . . . Praise him. . . . Praise
him. . . . Praise him. . . . Praise him. . . . Let every thing
that hath breath praise the Lord. Praise ye the Lord."

Part III

NEW
TESTAMENT

8

Life and Ministry of Jesus

Acquaintance with Israel's history from the time of Malachi to the time of the Gospel record is indispensable to the study of the life of Jesus Christ. It was an epoch through which there were at work strong underlying forces that shaped the political and religious atmosphere of the world into which Jesus came. The irresistible tides of Graeco-Roman civilization were felt all around the Mediterranean basin and touched the fortunes of the small land of Judaea to provide the setting for Christ's coming.

Old Testament history ceases with Nehemiah's second journey to Jerusalem (432 B.C.), and Old Testament prophecy ceases with the book of Malachi about the same time. Between the close of the Old Testament record and the birth of Jesus more than four hundred years elapsed, but the Bible is silent regarding Jewish history during this intertestamental period. From other sources, however, we know that the fortunes of Palestine suffered severely under foreign conquerors.

When Old Testament history closed, the Jews in Judah were under protective Persian control, as they had been since their release from captivity in 536 by Cyrus, the Persian conqueror of Babylon. For another two hundred years they remained subjects of the Persian Empire—until the brilliant young Macedonian general Alexander the Great wrested the control of Palestine from Persia in 333-331 B.C. during his spectacular conquest of Asia. Alexander brought the great civilizing influence of Hellenism and for the first time the small Jewish state of Judaea (the territory corresponding to old Kingdom of Judah) came into contact with Western ideas of Greek culture and literature. These Hellenistic ideas spread rapidly throughout the Near East and had a marked bearing on the subsequent history of the Jewish nation. Alexander and his successors treated the Jews well and encouraged them to settle in Greek colonies outside the borders of Palestine. The Greek language came into general use all through the eastern Mediterranean basin, including Palestine. With the division of Alexander's eastern kingdom among his generals at his death (323 B.C.), Palestine and Egypt fell under the rule of the Greek Ptolemies for a little more than a century. Palestine then passed briefly to the Hellenizing Seleucid kings of Syria (thirty-one years), thence to political independence under the Jewish house of the Maccabees (Hasmoneans). (See p. 93.)

Political Scene

The rise of Maccabean power began when Antiochus IV (Epiphanes), one of the Syrian kings (175-163 B.C.), tried to force Judaea into complete subjection to his rule. Up to this time the Jews had successfully resisted Greek ideas and retained tenaciously through custom and Judaic law their own racial and cultural identity, inspired by the strong religious belief in a covenant relationship with God that promised them future national greatness. Antiochus attempted to Hellenize the Jews by imposing pagan cults and culture and to wipe out Jewish theocratic worship. He ordered the destruction of all the copies of the Law and forbade under penalty of death the sacred covenant practices of circumcision, Sabbath-keeping, and religious feasts (see Customs). In 168 B.C. he desecrated the Temple at Jerusalem by offering a sow to Olympian Zeus on a Greek altar erected over the Brazen Altar ("the abomination that maketh desolate" of Daniel 9:27 and 11:31; Mt. 24:15). (Mosaic Law branded swine as unclean [Lev. 11:7].) Thousands of faithful Jews who resisted his edicts perished cruelly at his command.

With righteous zeal Mattathias, an aged priest, and his five sons led a guerrilla revolt, a struggle that was to last approximately twenty-five years. Judas Maccabaeus, the third son, captured Jerusalem in 165 B.C. and destroyed Antiochus' idolatrous altar. With this purification of the Temple the Feast of Dedication (Hanukkah) was instituted and Judaic worship restored. After the deaths of Judas and his younger brother Jonathan, Simon succeeded to leadership and by treaty with Syria won for the Jews the political independence of Judaea in 142 B.C. This new Jewish state conferred on Simon and his descendants the leadership of the nation and the office of high priest.

At Simon's death his son John Hyrcanus succeeded as ruler and high priest. Ruling for thirty-one years (135-105 B.C.), he brought the Jewish state to great prosperity and power, adding to Judaea the territories of Samaria, Idumaea, and Galilee. He settled Galilee with Jews of pure Jewish blood and won it to a patriotic Judaism. Peraea, a division of Palestine east of the Jordan, also fell under his influence and became predominantly Jewish.

Two distinct religious parties came into view in Palestine at this time, the Pharisees and the Sadducees; the first were champions of pure Judaism and highly popular with the people while the second, the priestly party, embraced the cultural influences of Hellenism and took no part in the early Maccabean struggle (see pp. 217-218). Toward the close of his rule John Hyrcanus withdrew his support from the Pharisees to favor the more aristocratic Sadducean party. These two sects became open enemies and during the reign of John's third son Alexander Jannaeus (104-78 B.C.) there was bitter fighting between them.

The successors of John Hyrcanus set themselves up as kings and became tyrannical and corrupt. During the reign of Aristobulus II, grandson of John Hyrcanus (69-63 B.C.), the Herodian house began its advance to power under the able and energetic Antipater, governor of Idumaea. (Idumaea or Edom was a territory south of Judaea peopled after the fall of Jerusalem by descendants of the Edomites. This territory was conquered by John Hyrcanus and its inhabitants compelled to adopt Judaism.) To further his own interests Antipater curried favor with Hyrcanus II, high priest and brother of Aristobulus II. When Aristobulus and Hyrcanus warred over the throne, Antipater supported the latter. The two brothers, each seeking to settle the dispute in his own favor, appealed to Pompey, the Roman general who had a year earlier annexed Syria to the Roman Empire (64 B.C.) and was now stationed at Damascus. Pompey ordered them to maintain peace, but Aristobulus rebelled; Judaea was thus drawn into the stream of Roman history. Pompey marched against him and, after a costly siege, defeated him at Jerusalem in 63 B.C. The Maccabean state was overthrown, and through the civil strife of these two brothers the Jews lost their liberty and became subject to the Romans. Palestine was added to the Roman Empire and the Jews were forced to pay annual tribute to Rome.

Pompey reinstated Hyrcanus as high priest, making him ruler without the title of king, to reign over the Jewish regions of Judaea (with Idumaea), Galilee, and Peraea.

Hyrcanus was a weak governor, and his crafty advisor Antipater soon became the more powerful of the two. With the aid of Pompey's legions, Hyrcanus and Antipater survived successive revolts by those who still championed Aristobulus' cause. However, in 49 B.C. civil war broke out between Pompey and Julius Caesar, and the following year Pompey was defeated and died in Egypt. Antipater quickly shifted his allegiance to Caesar, hastening to solicit his good will by coming to Caesar's aid at a desperate moment in his Egyptian campaign. In gratitude Caesar granted to the Jews of Egypt, Syria, and Phoenicia their religious freedom and privileges—they were allowed to observe the Sabbath laws, worship in their synagogues, and contribute without restriction to the Temple treasury. As a special favor Caesar permitted the refortification of Jerusalem (which had been dismantled by John Hyrcanus under pressure from Syria) and exempted Judaean Jews from supplying troops for military service. These privileges were soon extended to the Jews of Asia Minor, allowing them to observe unhindered their ancient customs. Antipater won Roman citizenship for himself; in 47 B.C. he became procurator of Judaea and virtual ruler of Palestine. Although he had procured important concessions for the Jews, they hated him for his Idumaean origin (see Gen. 27:41), his usurpation of Maccabean power, and his consistent allegiance to Rome.

Herod the Great, son of Antipater, like his father served the interests of Rome. Antipater had made him governor of Galilee (47 B.C.) and later Julius Caesar appointed him procurator of Coele-Syria—the territory between the Lebanon and Anti-Lebanon ranges. When the Maccabean house attempted to re-establish the kingship under Antigonus II, son of Aristobulus II, Herod went to Rome to appeal to Mark Antony and Octavianus (great-nephew and heir of Julius Caesar), members of the Second Triumvirate. They made Herod king of Judaea (40 B.C.), but upon his return to Palestine he was forced to wage a bloody battle to unseat Antigonus; and not until 37 B.C. did he occupy the palace at Jerusalem.

During his long reign (40-4 B.C.) Herod proved an able, although despotic and cruel, governor. To promote his influence and prestige and to make his position legitimate in the eyes of the Jews Herod allied himself to the Maccabean house by marrying Mariamne (the second of his five wives), granddaughter of Hyrcanus II, but the Jews continued to hate him as they had hated his father. In the years following, driven by fanatic jealousy and fear for his throne, one by one he murdered his enemies within the Maccabean house; he even murdered Mariamne and their two sons. In view of this it becomes less difficult to understand the terror that gripped Herod when he learned toward the close of his life that the King of the Jews had been born or to account for the cruelty he employed in the massacre of the Innocents (Mt. 2).

Herod's political fortunes were advanced by his slavish devotion to Rome. When Augustus Caesar (Octavianus) became Roman Emperor in 27 B.C., he

Another of Herod the Great's Copper Coins. Obverse: lettering around a helmet. Reverse: Macedonian shield, with disk surrounded by rays. *The Jewish Encyclopedia.*

found in Herod a staunch supporter to guard the eastern boundaries of the Empire: Augustus gave him cities, large land grants, and lifelong favor. By 20 B.C. Herod's kingdom included Judaea, Samaria, Galilee, Trachonitis, Batanaea, Auranitis, Gaulanitis, and Peraea. During Augustus' peaceful reign Herod strengthened his realm, gave Roman order to its cities and towns, and made the roads safe for travel and commerce.

Although half-Jewish himself (Herod's father, Antipater, had been forced by John Hyrcanus to become religiously a Jew), Herod treated the Greek population of his kingdom with marked partiality, embarking upon a vast building program. He constructed the sumptuous harbor city of Caesarea nearly seventy miles northwest of Jerusalem on the Mediterranean, protecting it with a massive breakwater; by making skillful use of the tides, he provided the city with water for flushing the streets. (By the time of Herod Agrippa, Caesarea had become the official residence of the Roman governors.) Herod rebuilt much of the city of Samaria (Sebaste) and erected throughout his domain numerous theaters, amphitheaters, stadiums, and aqueducts. Hellenistic culture was encouraged, and many temples to Roman and Greek gods were erected throughout Palestine (but not in Judaea where, according to Josephus, such temples were forbidden). His allegiance to Caesar obliged him to break many of the customs and laws of the Jews, and his punishment of any civil disobedience—small or great—was severe. To conciliate the Jews of Judaea he painstakingly rebuilt their Temple out of gleaming white marble overlaid with gold, adding to it the imposing Court of the Gentiles (see p. 163), but his flagrant acts of paganism continually antagonized the Jews and defeated his generosity. This was the Herod who was ruling when Jesus was born.

Religious Scene

While Palestine was subjected to the various political crises of the intertestamental period, gradual changes were also taking place in the religious life of the Jewish nation. At the beginning of this period, some eighty years after the return of Judah from captivity

Copper Coin of Herod the Great. Obverse: a tripod with tray; on either side a palm branch. Reverse: lettering surrounding a wreath, in which is an X. *The Jewish Encyclopedia.*

215

in Babylon, Ezra and Nehemiah (458-445 B.C.) found that, although sacrificial temple worship had been re-established by the zealots and puritans who had returned with Zerubbabel, the people had grown lax in their adherence to monotheism and had failed to preserve their separateness from their polytheistic neighbors. These two great patriots determined to maintain for Judah its Jewish nationality and individuality. This could best be done only by a rigid observance of the distinctive Mosaic social and religious practices by which the Jews had been governed for centuries. As a result of their efforts the Priestly Code, embodied in the Pentateuch, was adopted by the nation and the ritualistic system of Judaism with its strict observance of Mosaic Law came into being. A dedicated priestly control dominated every aspect of national life; monotheism stood pre-eminent and became a national instinct in the church-state.

Side by side with this ritualistic system of worship existed a synagogue worship consisting of prayer, meditation, and Scriptural study. The synagogue was an institution that probably originated among the Jews during the Exile. Transplanted to Judaea upon the captives' return, it flourished in every city and village. The Jews of the Diaspora (Dispersion) —those who through the vicissitudes of poverty, war, slavery, or political adversity had settled throughout the pre-Roman world—continued synagogue worship in the lands of their adoption and ardently adhered to and disseminated the Judaism of their fathers.

> It [the synagogue system] was essentially decentralized, since synagogs were encouraged everywhere. It was intensely democratic, instead of autocratic. Its main purpose was ethical and practical—intended to dominate all common life. It exalted the function of the prophet rather than that of the priest; and so it magnified the idea of Scriptures, which were the records of prophetic teaching and interpretation, as well as the action of preachers and interpreters of its own day. It became the home of what there was of popular education.... Its accent fell upon instruction rather than upon worship, tho the latter was not neglected in the rather elaborate scheme of prayers.[1]

Another important contribution to the religious life of the nation during the intertestamental period was the gradual compilation and completion of Hebrew Scripture: the addition to the Pentateuch of two other major groups of sacred literature—the Prophets and the Writings (see p. 4)—although this literature was not formally accepted as canonical until the first century A.D. The Prophets and the Writings, as well as the Law, became the textbooks of the synagogues and strengthened the faith of the pious under foreign domination and during bitter internal dissension. With the widening use of Greek it was inevitable that the Scriptures should be translated into that language for the use of the Jews of the Dispersion. About 250 B.C.

a Greek version, the Septuagint or LXX (traditionally believed to have been prepared by seventy scholars), was begun by the Jews of Alexandria, Egypt, under the patronage of Ptolemy Philadelphus and was finished around 50 B.C. It included the Law, the Prophets, and the Writings, as well as fourteen books which are today termed the *Apocrypha* (see p. 5). This important version, used by all Greek-speaking Jews, spread the truths and Messianic hopes of the Old Testament throughout the Greek-speaking world. All this helped prepare for the coming of Christ.

In the Maccabean period, as the priesthood became political and aristocratic, it lost touch with the aspirations of the Jew, its influence waned, and the religious education of the people passed into the hands of the scribes and Pharisees, zealous guardians of Judaism. With the rise of the Pharisaic party, which fought vigorously against the Hellenism introduced into Palestine, an intense devotion to legalistic Judaism developed; a minutely detailed oral law emerged and piety became the chief concern of the individual. In time the casuistry of the scribes and Pharisees hedged the Jew about with a multitude of restrictive regulations regarding his every action—night and day— from which his conscience was never free (see p. 268). Worship ceased to be a communion with God. It had been replaced by a supersensitive obedience to the letter of the Law.

Scribes

The group of men known as the scribes played a large part in intertestamental religious history. The early scribes of the Old Testament were kings' secretaries and clerks, but the priestly scribes (called *sopherim*) who rose to prominence toward the close of the Exile, among them Ezra (see p. 136), were a class of pious, learned Jews dedicated to the study, exposition, and preservation of Mosaic Law. Because of their efforts the sacred writings of the nation were collated and edited, and through the centuries thereafter scribes painstakingly transcribed all copies of the Scriptures and explained their meaning.

During the rule of the Maccabees lay scribes or scholars, in close sympathy with the Pharisees, appeared side by side with the priestly *sopherim*. They began to assume undue authority for the interpretation of the Law, adding many regulations to cover minor details of daily life. Their chief concern was with the Law's minute exposition down to every word and letter; so great was their emphasis on the letter that the moral law tended to be obscured and almost buried under their sophistry. In time they created a whole new collection of traditional oral law and their opinions were handed down as law itself.

> Eventually in the second century of our era this tradition came to be reduced to written form. We call the

results the rabbinical literature. This huge mass of interpretation of the Scripture, the fruit of the devoted efforts of hundreds of different scholars, was gradually ordered and codified in two forms: (a) Cast in the form of running commentaries on the written law, called Midrashim or Midrashes; (b) systematically classified on the basis of a list of subjects, called "orders"—this came to be known as Mishnah. As the years went by, several Mishnahs—all containing the same six orders of material—arose. Gradually one of them, popularly ascribed to Judah the Patriarch, gained pre-eminent, almost canonical, rank. It then came to be the basis for further study and interpretation. The results of this process were the Talmuds, which sought to interpret and explain the Mishnah. Of the two Talmuds, the one called the Babylonian and completed in the sixth century eventually gained priority. It consists of the whole of the Mishnah, quoted literally section by section in the original Hebrew, each section being followed by the new interpretative material. This material, written in Aramaic after the editing of the Mishnah, is known as the "Gemara."[2]

In New Testament times the scribes' influence as lawyers and magistrates was great, and many of these "doctors of the law" sat in the Sanhedrin, the governing body of the Jews. "The scribes built up a great edifice of regulations based on the Law until these became an intolerable burden. And it was this edifice Jesus swept away, when he came with a religion of the spirit and of liberty."[3]

Pharisees

By Jesus' day there were four principal philosophical parties in Palestine (Pharisees, Sadducees, Essenes, Zealots) that influenced the religious life of the Jews. Of these four the Pharisees were dominant. Numbering between 6000 and 7000, they were a religious sect who in the second century B.C. (during the Maccabean period) separated themselves from the encroaching Hellenistic influences imposed by the Syrian king Antiochus Epiphanes and rallied to the defense of Judaism in order to preserve the monotheism of the nation and the purity of the Mosaic Law. The name *Pharisees* derives from a Hebrew word meaning "the separated ones." As patriotic and pious churchmen, devoted teachers and preachers of the Law, themselves strict observers of the principles of Judaism, they strove to set an example of virtue, concord, and public-spiritedness and to keep alive the religious spirit of the chosen nation. Their interests centered in the synagogue, and by their efforts every child and adult was taught the Law (first five books of Moses, Torah, Pentateuch). In addition to the written Law these religious leaders taught the scribal opinions and interpretations of the Law—an "oral law" that finally came to control every phase of daily life. They also recognized the books of the Prophets and the Writings (Hagiographa) as sacred literature and taught them in the synagogues.

They adhered to a belief in angels and to the doctrine of the resurrection of the dead (Acts 23:8). The Jewish historian Josephus (37-?100 A.D.) wrote:

> They also believe that souls have an immortal vigor in them, and that under the earth there will be rewards or punishments, according as they have lived virtuously or viciously in this life; and the latter are to be detained in an everlasting prison, but that the former shall have power to revive and live again; on account of which doctrines they are able greatly to persuade the body of the people. . . .[4]

During the decadence of the period of the later Maccabean kings and the oppressive rule of the Romans the Pharisees revived the prophetic hope for a Messianic king and kingdom. "It was they who, for the most part, prepared the ground for Christianity by taking the Messianic idea and working it into the very texture of common consciousness."[5]

When the New Testament record opens the Pharisees were numerous in Palestine and their prestige and influence were supreme among the people. Their earlier purpose had become obscured and they had grown arrogantly exclusive, proud of their piety and given to overemphasis on the externals of the Law and "the tradition of the elders." All of this led to hypocrisy, corruption, and spiritual dullness. The Pharisees and scribes were in continual conflict with Jesus' teachings and with his healing works on the Sabbath. His rebuke of them was severe: "The scribes and the Pharisees sit in Moses' seat. . . . Woe unto you, scribes and Pharisees, hypocrites!" (Mt. 23:2,14).

Sadducees

The Sadducees were a Jewish party that also originated in the second century B.C. during the Maccabean period. Their few members were drawn from the priestly families of Jerusalem and the aristocratic lay families of Judaea. Unlike the Pharisees, they did not separate themselves from the Hellenistic influences pervading Palestine, and their interests became more political than religious. In favor with the Maccabean house, they gained the high priesthood and controlled the Temple and its worship. In Jesus' day they held the balance of power in the Sanhedrin (see p. 219).

Their conservative acceptance of the written law (Pentateuch) only and their rejection of the oral law and traditions so carefully fostered by the Pharisees kept the two parties constantly at variance, but at times the Sadducees found it expedient to accede to Pharisaic practices to curry favor with the people. Some of their views were diametrically opposed to those of the Pharisees; they denied the resurrection of the dead with its rewards and punishments and the existence of angels (Mt. 22:23; Acts 23:8). Their opposition to Jesus was aroused toward the close of his public ministry when the momentum of his work endangered their ecclesiastical and political status in Jerusalem; this hostility, a factor contributing to his crucifixion, continued as sporadic persecution of the early Apostolic Church. Jesus warned his disciples: "Beware of the leaven [doctrine] of the Pharisees and of the Sadducees" (Mt. 16:6).

Essenes

In the Maccabean period certain Jews—the Essenes—felt impelled to a devoutness even greater than the piety practiced by the Pharisees. These men formed themselves into a monastic brotherhood and withdrew from the pleasures and evils of the outside world to practice a rigid asceticism. Many of them lived as celibates in isolated communal colonies in the Dead Sea region, although many were said to reside in small communities in the cities and villages of Palestine. They numbered about four thousand, according to Philo and Josephus. New members were added by proselyting and by the adoption of children. They supported themselves by the simplest manual labor, principally agriculture, and shared all things. This sect revered Moses and was devoted to the study of the Law, but, eschewing animal sacrifices, was barred from Temple worship. Adhering to the highest ethical ideals, they were strongly opposed to slavery and war. Avoiding all sensual defilement, they sought the highest possible purity. They believed in the soul's immortality; their chief concern was life after death.

No New Testament reference is made to the Essenes, but the historians Pliny, Philo, Josephus, and Eusebius mention them. They disappeared as a sect early in the second century A.D. The discovery in 1947 of the Dead Sea Scrolls in the arid limestone caves of the Qumran Wady in the Wilderness of Judaea, a little more than a mile from the northwest shore of the Dead Sea, focused attention of Biblical scholars on this little-known religious sect, for one of the scrolls was a code which appears to have governed these ascetics. (Its rules and principles are called The Manual of Discipline by Millar Burrows in *The Dead Sea Scrolls,* pp. 371-389.) Awakened interest led archeologists to the examination of a long-standing nearby ruin called Khirbet Qumran. In 1951, after careful excavation, the ruin proved to be part of the main Essene community.

Zealots

This party, an offshoot of the Pharisees, was composed of patriotic and fanatical Jewish resisters to Roman domination of Palestine. There had long been dissatisfied agitators in the land, restless under cruel and corrupt Roman governors, but at the time of the Roman census of Quirinius (*ca.* 6 A.D.) they became a loosely formed sect under the leadership of Judas of Galilee (Acts 5:37). Acknowledging God as their only Ruler and Lord, the Zealots considered subservience to Rome and the payment of tribute a betrayal of Israel's theocratic constitution, and for this principle they were willing to fight to the death. In time this party deteriorated into bands of lawless guerrillas and seditionists, terrorizing the people of their own country. Zealots played a memorable part in the Jewish rebellion of 66 and in the fanatical defense of Jerusalem before its fall in 70 A.D. In 72 in a last stand against the Romans 960 Zealots all died in the mountain fortress of Masada, killing one another rather than submit to the might of Rome.

The Sectarian Manual of Discipline, one of the Dead Sea Scrolls of Qumran. The Shrine of the Book. The Israel Museum, Jerusalem.

Excavation of Khirbet Qumran, an Essene community, as seen from the hills, with the Dead Sea in the background. By courtesy of the Israel Department of Antiquities and Museums.

Sanhedrin

The Sanhedrin was the supreme ecclesiastical court of the Jews, a judicial council composed of seventy members in addition to the high priest. The time of its origin is uncertain. Its seeds are seen in the appointment of seventy elders by Moses (Num. 11:16,17), also in the group of judges set up by King Jehoshaphat (II Chron. 19:5-11). It is probable that this particular tribunal began its existence as a senate in Jerusalem in the third century B.C., during the period of Greek supremacy (II Macc. 1:10; Josephus, *Antiq.* xii 3.3; Acts 5:21). It was called *Sanhedrin* for the first time under the Maccabean Hyrcanus II by Josephus (*Antiq.* xiv 9.3).

At first composed of eminent priests, Levites, and Jewish aristocracy (later known as Sadducees), by Jesus' day its members, appointed for life, were drawn from the scribes and elders of the Pharisaic party as well. "Chief priests, scribes, and elders" is the New Testament designation for this council. Though its functions had been religious, political, and civil in the time of the Maccabees and Herod the Great, under the Roman procurators its authority as a court of justice was limited to religious matters and confined to Judaea. In effect its pronouncements nevertheless influenced all Jewry.

Its council chamber was the Hall of Hewn Stones bordering on the Temple area. The members sat in a semicircle and were presided over by the high priest. Attended by two court scribes and faced by three rows of scholars, they debated and passed judgment on all questions of Jewish law and considered cases sometimes submitted by local councils of outlying towns.

When a man was on trial for his life, the Sanhedrin's high duty was to act in his defense, to judge him innocent until proved guilty, and to expend every effort to save him. Many times it fell short of this high ideal. This council could pronounce sentence of death on any Jew guilty of the crimes of blasphemy, Sabbath-breaking, or heresy, but the execution of such sentence was subject to the approval of the Roman procurator. It was a corrupt and politically minded Sanhedrin that bent Pilate to its will and

219

brought about the crucifixion of Jesus and which so intolerantly persecuted the early Christian Church.

The Messianic Hope

A scholar has said "Take Christ out of the Old Testament and the whole structure falls apart." The word *Messiah* originates in the Hebrew *Messias* "anointed one" (Greek, *Christos,* Christ), and designated to the Hebrew mind a God-appointed deliverer and ideal king who would free Israel from the oppression of heathen enemies, exalt it to a position of honor and glory, and usher in an unending reign of righteousness and peace. The hope of such a deliverer sprang from the Israelites' knowledge of themselves as the chosen people of Jehovah and from their trust in the ultimate triumph of the One God.

The name *Messiah* does not appear before the book of Daniel, but the idea of a personal Messiah runs throughout the Old Testament. The early Messianic prophecies in their orderly development are clearer to us in the light of Israel's history than they were to the early Hebrews, for the original Messianic expectation was at first nebulous, proceeding no further than the hope for political power and supremacy. The promise of a deliverer is implicit in Genesis 3:15 in the seed of the woman who is to bruise the serpent's head. Universal in scope, it points to the salvation of all mankind from evil and its concomitants. This redeemer was destined to spring from the tribe of Judah (Gen. 49:10). Just prior to Israel's entrance into Canaan Baalam prophesied of Israel: "There shall come a Star out of Jacob, and a Sceptre shall rise out of Israel" (Num. 24:17). Moses, Israel's first great leader, foretold the coming of a prophet greater than himself: "The Lord thy God will raise up unto thee a Prophet from the midst of thee, of thy brethren, like unto me; unto him ye shall hearken" (Deut. 18:15). God's covenant with the house of David marked the expectation that deliverance would come through the seed of David, Israel's first righteous king (II Sam. 7:12-16).

Not until the period of Israel's prophets (800-400 B.C.), however, did the Messianic hope begin to take definite shape. Failure of the Davidic dynasty to maintain its greatness, and the subsequent oppressions, wars, sorrows, and suffering of the people attendant upon the division of the kingdom turned the pious to God. Israel's great prophet Isaiah began to teach a higher conception of the popular hope and to stress the moral and spiritual character of the Messiah God would send, whose sole concern would be to establish righteousness and justice among his people: "There shall come forth a rod out of the stem of Jesse, and a Branch shall grow out of his roots: and the spirit of the Lord shall rest upon him, the spirit of wisdom and understanding, the spirit of counsel and might, the spirit of knowledge and of the fear of the Lord . . . with righteousness shall he judge the poor, and reprove with equity for the meek of the earth . . . and with the breath of his lips shall he slay the wicked" (Is. 11:1,2,4).

The same prophet held forth to Israel the promise of Immanuel (Is. 7:14), portrayed with inspiration the divine majesty of his nature, and foretold a glorious new age of peace: "His name shall be called Wonderful, Counsellor, The mighty God, The everlasting Father, The Prince of Peace. Of the increase of his government and peace there shall be no end, upon the throne of David, and upon his kingdom, to order it, and to establish it with judgment and with justice from henceforth even for ever. The zeal of the Lord of hosts will perform this" (Is. 9:6,7). Jeremiah and Ezekiel encouraged the nation in this same high concept, prophesying of "a righteous Branch, and a King," "one shepherd" (Jer. 23:5,6; Ezek. 34:23). The passages relating to the suffering servant (Is. 53), so familiar today, were not regarded as Messianic until so seen by New Testament writers. The prophecy of Micah (5:2), designating Bethlehem as the locale of the Messiah's birthplace, was later fulfilled to the letter.

The Messianic expectation of the Anointed One is also to be seen in the Psalms. His sufferings, resurrection, ascension, priesthood, kingship and pre-eminence are foretold (see Messianic Prophecies, p. 337). The hope of redemption as set forth in the prophetic and poetic writings was not always connected with the figure of a Messiah, God Himself being frequently presented as the Deliverer from idolatry, war, sin, and death (Jer. 3:22; Mic. 4:1-4; Is. 25:8; 43:25).

The remnant of Judah returned from exile in Babylon with a hope for the restoration and glory of the nation—albeit a dim and distant hope, since they were still under foreign domination. This hope was almost extinguished three and a half centuries later when the Syrian king Antiochus Epiphanes attempted to exterminate the Judaic religion and force Hellenism on the Jews. The short period of Jewish independence under the priest-kings of the Maccabees failed to bring to realization the high political and religious aspirations of the nation. Their reigns were corrupt and were succeeded by the despotism of Herod the Great and the increasing tyranny of Rome. Thus the more puritanical element of the nation sought refuge and comfort in the prophetic Messianic expectation of a Deliverer springing from the house of David, and the idea of a personal Messiah gained in popular appeal.

This concept was encouraged by a whole new type of pseudepigraphal and apocalyptic religious literature that came into being from the beginning of the Maccabean period (mainly from 165 B.C. to 120 A.D.), the work of lay writers among the Pharisees of

Palestine and the Jews of the Dispersion. (Pseudepigrapha ["writings under assumed names"]: III and IV Maccabees, Enoch, Testaments of the Twelve Patriarchs, Jubilees, Letter of Aristeas, Sibylline Oracles, Psalms of Solomon, Zadokite Fragments, Assumption of Moses, II Enoch, II and III Baruch, Martyrdom of Isaiah, and the Books of Adam and Eve. Fourth Ezra is sometimes classed with this group and is the same as II Esdras, chaps. 3-14.) Although none of these books attained canonical status, they contributed much to strengthen the nation's trust in God and to help the individual Jew retain his faith. Drawing on Old

Recent excavation of Masada has uncovered the summer palace of King Herod the Great. This ancient fortress town on the western bank of the Dead Sea was the scene of the Zealots' last stand against the Romans. Israel Government Tourist Office.

Hills around Bethlehem.

Testament prophecy, the authors of these books amplified the teachings of the prophets as to the final destiny of the Jewish nation and of the world in general on the Day of Judgment when God's righteousness and justice would be vindicated; as a result a Jewish eschatology (doctrine relating to the last or final things) gradually took shape to express Jewish hopes and beliefs.

Two threads may be traced through this new body of literature: one nationalistic in tone pertaining to this world, the other transcendental and universal relating to the world to come. The principal theme was the establishment of the ideal kingdom of God. Their authors, despairing over the evil and distress in their times, looked to the future for the consummation of the sublime hope. Writing in apocalyptic language—in vivid symbolic images such as those of various beasts and birds and projecting a belief in angels and demons—they contrasted the kingdoms of the earth in which evil, death, and sin prevailed with the kingdom of God, which was wholly good; and they evolved great world pictures portraying successive stages or epochs involved in the bringing in of the eternal kingdom.

There was a great advance in the doctrine of the resurrection of the dead, a subject touched on only briefly in the Old Testament and then chiefly as it related to Israel (Is. 26:19; Ezek. 37; Dan. 12:2; Hos. 6:2; 13:14). The individual responsibility of a man for his own thoughts and acts (which Jeremiah and Ezekiel had preached) was extended to the resurrection of the individual dead. There was to be a resurrection for both the righteous and the wicked, the former to be raised to everlasting life and paradisaic bliss, the latter to awake to everlasting shame and punishment.

As the Messianic hope strengthened, it was natural that the personal Messiah and his work should occupy a permanent and central position in this developing eschatology. In some of these apocalyptic writings the concept of him is a transcendent one. He is described in the book of Enoch[6] (I Enoch 37-72) as an angelic being and is alluded to by the title of "the Son of Man" (a term that appears in Dan. 7:13, which Jesus later appropriated to himself) and by the title "Anointed One." He appears as a pre-existent heavenly Messiah and is called "the Righteous One" and "the Elect One." His place is beside the Ancient of Days (compare Dan. 7:13) "under the wings of the Lord of spirits," and he is given power to judge men and to reveal "the treasures of that which is hidden." Before him "unrighteousness shall disappear as a shadow, and have no continuance." In the Psalms of Solomon (Chap. 17)[7] he is designated "the son of David," "a righteous king, taught of God" who would purge Jerusalem of heathen conquerors and "make it holy as of old." Of his judgment is written: "At his rebuke nations shall flee before him, And he shall reprove sinners for the thoughts of their heart." The advent of this Messiah was to usher in the Messianic Age in which wars and idolatry would cease and all men would turn to God and with a new heart would keep His new covenant.

These writings had a profound influence on national thought, were imbedded in the Jews' educational background, and formed the eschatological beliefs of New Testament times. (See Jesus' discourse on Signs of Christ's Coming and Last Judgment [Mt. 24-25], pp. 306-310.)

Such was the political and religious situation in Palestine at the time of Jesus' birth. The Jewish nation, early instituted under theocratic government and possessed of a proud history, was restless and rebellious under the Roman yoke. Their hopes ran high for a king of their own, a powerful monarch who would deliver them from their oppressors; but when their King came, a suffering Messiah rather than a reigning one, they did not know him.

Jesus' Early Years

From the life and work of Jesus the Christ, known to us in his coincidence as the Son of God and the Son of man, stems the religion of Christianity, whose living principles are today an ever-operative force in the spiritualization of mankind. The great purpose of his mission was to reveal on earth "as it is in heaven" the kingdom of God, the spiritual realm of perfection, and to establish in the hearts and minds of men the reign and sovereignty of God. His whole motivation was love for God and love for man. This Son came out from the Father with an all-inclusive knowledge of the goodness of the Creator. He came into the world with an all-inclusive knowledge of the kingdom that he might awaken men to their rightful knowledge and possession of it, teaching "Behold, the kingdom of God is within you." "As my Father hath taught me, I speak these things."

Every event in Jesus' life was essential to the fulfillment of his mission and to the accomplishment of his proof of resurrection and ascension, pertinent and imperative to the salvation of "every one of us." Starting from this point of view, this study treats the principal events of Jesus' life in their orderly unfoldment, continuity, and mounting significance. The Gospels have been quoted freely and deliberately by the author that the reader may hear for himself the Word that shines through the words.

Erasmus, the great Biblical scholar of Rotterdam, once said that the New Testament pages "will give you Christ Himself . . . in an intimacy so close that He would be less visible to you if He stood before your eyes." No one of the four Gospels—Matthew, Mark, Luke, John—gives a full account of Jesus' life, but the interwoven harmony of all four preserves the record of his earthly sojourn and chronicles the fulfillment of his mission. (These Gospels in their relation to each other as literature are charted on p. 21.)

The birth of Jesus marked the beginning of the Christian era, but not until the sixth century A.D. was modern chronological dating introduced. At that time Dionysius Exiguus, a scholar and monk of the Western Church, published his calculation of dates, counting Jesus' birth as the starting point. However, his computations involved an error of several years and the date of Jesus' birth actually falls between 7 and 4 B.C.

In the advent of Jesus, the Messiah of the Old Testament became "the Christ" of the New and the promise of the seed of the woman (Gen. 3:15) was at last realized. Paul wrote, "When the fulness of the time was come, God sent forth his Son, made of a woman, made under the law, To redeem them that were under the law, that we might receive the adoption of sons" (Gal. 4:4,5).

The coming of the Son of God in the flesh has been called the Incarnation, and the divine Word made flesh has been called the incarnate Son. "The Incarnation means the presence of the Divine in the human. . . ."[8] Isaiah had foretold the divine nature of this Messiah: "The government shall be upon his shoulder: and his name shall be called Wonderful, Counsellor, The mighty God, The everlasting Father, The Prince of Peace" (Is. 9:6). Yet he had also foretold Christ's earthly sufferings: "He is despised and rejected of men; a man of sorrows, and acquainted with grief" (Is. 53:3).

John opens his gospel record: "In the beginning was the Word, and the Word was with God, and the Word was God. . . . In him was life; and the life was the light of men. . . . And the Word was made flesh, and dwelt among us, (and we beheld his glory, the glory as of the only begotten of the Father,) full of grace and truth" (Jn. 1:1,4,14). A sublime description of the incarnate Son—THE WORD WAS MADE FLESH . . . AND WE BEHELD HIS GLORY.

> The Word is God's self-revealing activity within God himself before the world was, distinguished but not separated from God (vv. 1,2) within the creation of all things (v. 3), and within the animation and illumination of man (v. 4). . . .[9]

The Gospel of Matthew and the Gospel of Luke give genealogies of Jesus. Matthew carries Jesus' genealogy forward from Abraham, the father of the Hebrew race, to Joseph, a direct descendant of David and the reputed father of Jesus, showing Jesus as the son of Abraham, the covenant seed in whom all the nations of the world would be blessed, and the son of David, to whose house God had promised an everlasting kingship. Matthew traces Jesus' royal descent from David's son Solomon, thereby showing his right to be called King of the Jews and the promised Messiah of his nation (Ps. 80:3,4; Is. 11:1; Jer. 23:5).

(Scholars agree that Matthew's genealogy is an artificial arrangement with some omissions of links in the line of generation. As an aid to memory, it was grouped into three general divisions—from Abraham to David, David to the Exile, and from the Exile to Jesus. There are fourteen generations listed from Abraham through David, fourteen from David through Josias, and fourteen from Jeconias to Jesus.)

GENEALOGIES OF JESUS CHRIST

According to Matthew 1:1-16 and Luke 3:23-38

Matthew gives the genealogy of Joseph, reputed father of Jesus, carrying the line forward from Abraham, father of the Hebrew race.

Luke gives the genealogy of Mary (although Joseph's name is substituted), carrying the line back to Adam.

ADAM
SETH
ENOS
CAINAN
MALELEEL
JARED
ENOCH
MATHUSALA
LAMECH
NOE
SEM
ARPHAXAD
CAINAN
SALA
HEBER
PHALEC
RAGAU
SARUCH
NACHOR
THARA

ABRAHAM . . . . **ABRAHAM**

Matthew		Luke
ISAAC	. . . .	ISAAC
JACOB	. . . .	JACOB
JUDAS	. . . .	JUDA
PHARES	. . . .	PHARES
ESROM	. . . .	ESROM
ARAM	. . . .	ARAM
AMINADAB	. . . .	AMINADAB
NAASSON	. . . .	NAASSON
SALMON	. . . .	SALMON
BOOZ	. . . .	BOOZ
OBED	. . . .	OBED
JESSE	. . . .	JESSE
DAVID	. . . .	DAVID

SOLOMON
ROBOAM
ABIA
ASA
JOSAPHAT
JORAM
OZIAS
JOATHAM
ACHAZ
EZEKIAS
MANASSES
AMON
JOSIAS
JECHONIAS

NATHAN
MATTATHA
MENAN
MELEA
ELIAKIM
JONAN
JOSEPH
JUDA
SIMEON
LEVI
MATTHAT
JORIM
ELIEZER
JOSE
ER
ELMODAM
COSAM
ADDI
MELCHI
NERI

SALATHIEL . . . . SALATHIEL
ZOROBABEL . . . . ZOROBABEL

ABIUD
ELIAKIM
AZOR
SADOC
ACHIM
ELIUD
ELEAZAR
MATTHAN
JACOB
JOSEPH

RHESA
JOANNA
JUDA
JOSEPH
SEMEI
MATTATHIAS
MAATH
NAGGE
ESLI
NAUM
AMOS
MATTATHIAS
JOSEPH
JANNA
MELCHI
LEVI
MATTHAT
HELI
JOSEPH (Mary)

. . . . JESUS CHRIST . . . .

Luke carries Jesus' genealogy back from Joseph to Seth the founder of the Messianic line and to Adam—from the genesis of mankind—showing him to be not only the son of Abraham, but the Son of Man, and therefore Savior to the whole human race. Although the line of descent is through David, it is not through the kingly line of Solomon, but through David's son Nathan. According to Scripture the Messiah was to be the actual descendant of David according to the flesh (II Sam. 7:12-19; Acts 2:30; Rom. 1:3). This prophecy was fulfilled in Jesus as the son of Mary, daughter of Heli and a descendant of David.

The genealogy given in Matthew is the genealogy of Joseph, the reputed father of Jesus, his father in the eyes of the law. The genealogy given in Luke is the genealogy of Mary, the mother of Jesus, and is the human genealogy of Jesus Christ in actual fact. The Gospel of Matthew was written for Jews. All through it Joseph is prominent, Mary is scarcely mentioned. In Luke, on the other hand, Mary is the chief personage in the whole account of the Saviour's conception and birth. Joseph is brought in only incidentally and because he was Mary's husband. In all of this, of course, there is a deep significance.

In Matthew, Jesus appears as the Messiah. In Luke He appears as "the Son of Man," our Brother and Redeemer, who belongs to the whole race and claims kindred with all kinds and conditions of men. So in Matthew, the genealogy descends from Abraham to Joseph and Jesus, because all the predictions and promises touching the Messiah are fulfilled in Him. But in Luke the genealogy ascends from Jesus to Adam, because the genealogy is being traced back to the head of the whole race and shows the relation of the second Adam to the First. . . .

Mary was a descendant of David through her father, Heli. It is true that Luke 3:23 says that Joseph was the son of Heli. The simple explanation of this is that Mary being a woman her name according to Jewish usage could not come into the genealogy, males alone forming the line, so Joseph's name is introduced in the place of Mary's, he being Mary's husband. Heli was his father-in-law, and so Joseph is called the son of Heli, and the line thus completed. While Joseph was son-in-law of Heli, according to the flesh he was in actual fact the son of Jacob (Matthew 1:16).

Two genealogies are absolutely necessary to trace the lineage of our Lord and Saviour Jesus Christ, the one the royal and legal, the other the natural and literal; and these two genealogies we find—the legal and royal in Matthew's Gospel, the Gospel of law and kingship; the natural and literal in Luke's, the Gospel of humanity.

We are told in Jeremiah 22:30 that any descendant of Jeconiah could not come to the throne of David. Joseph was of this line, and while Joseph's genealogy furnishes the royal line for Jesus, his son before the law, nevertheless Jeremiah's prediction is fulfilled to the very letter, for Jesus (strictly speaking) was not Joseph's descendant and therefore was not of the seed of Jeconiah. If Jesus had been the son of Joseph in reality, He could not have come to the throne, but He is Mary's son through Nathan, and can come to the throne

legally by her marrying Joseph and so clearing His way legally to it.

As we study these two genealogies of Jesus carefully and read them in the light of Old Testament prediction, we find that so far from constituting a reason for doubting the accuracy of the Bible they are rather a confirmation of the minutest accuracy of that Book. . . . We need no longer stumble over the fact of two genealogies, but discover and rejoice in the deep meaning in the fact.[10]

The term *Son of man* was used by Jesus himself more than eighty times. But while Matthew and Luke trace Jesus' genealogy back as the Son of man and indicate his essential humanity, John, although he quotes Jesus' use of the title, never calls him the Son of man in his Gospel, and he gives no human genealogy. John gives the spiritual genealogy, calling Jesus "the only begotten of the Father" and "the Son of God," denoting his divine nature and origin. (And John declares that those who believe on Christ are likewise "born, not of blood, nor of the will of the flesh, nor of the will of man, but of God" [Jn. 1:13].)

Jesus appeared to the world for only a few years, yet his appearing changed the whole course of human history.

In thirty years Jesus completed his individual preparation for his great calling.

In three years he laid the foundation for the kingdom of God on earth and gave the perfect example of sonship for every follower.

In three days he crowned his universal life purpose of redemption by overcoming death and the grave.

In forty days he revealed his complete dominion over matter in preparation for the final victory of ascension above matter.

Birth and Infancy of Jesus

Events of marked significance surrounded the birth and early years of Jesus, from the angel's first announcement to Zacharias to the safe return of Joseph, Mary, and Jesus to Nazareth from Egypt.

Announcement to Zacharias   Lu. 1:5-25

The Gospel narrative opens in the Temple in Jerusalem with an angel's announcement to Zacharias of the coming of a son to his wife Elisabeth. According to Old Testament prophecy, the Messiah was to be preceded by his forerunner: "Behold, I will send my messenger, and he shall prepare the way before me:

and the Lord, whom ye seek, shall suddenly come to his temple, even the messenger of the covenant, whom ye delight in: behold, he shall come, saith the Lord of hosts" (Mal. 3:1).

Zacharias was a priest of the order of Abia (Abijah, eighth of the twenty-four courses, see p. 55); Elisabeth was of the ancient priestly line of Aaron, and up to this time she had been barren. This devout couple, well advanced in years, lived in the hill country of Judaea. "They were both righteous before God, walking in all the commandments and ordinances of the Lord blameless." In their hearts was a deep reverence, a purity wherein the spirit of God and the presence of angels could abound.

As Zacharias was executing his priestly office within the Holy Place of the Temple—and on this day it had been determined by lot that he should perform the sacred ritual of sprinkling incense on the Golden Altar, a special privilege that fell to a priest only once during his lifetime—an angel appeared at the right side of the altar. Zacharias was troubled at his appearing, but the angel said, "Fear not . . . for thy prayer is heard; and thy wife Elisabeth shall bear thee a son, and thou shalt call his name John." (This promised child was later known as John the Baptist.)

The promises continued one by one as Zacharias listened: "Thou shalt have joy and gladness; and many shall rejoice at his birth. For he shall be great in the sight of the Lord, and shall drink neither wine nor strong drink; and he shall be filled with the Holy Ghost [New Testament term for the Holy Spirit, the Spirit of God, see p. 375], even from his mother's womb. And many of the children of Israel shall he turn to the Lord their God. And he shall go before him in the spirit and power of Elias [AV New Testament form of the name Elijah], to turn the hearts of the fathers to the children, and the disobedient to the wisdom of the just; to make ready a people prepared for the Lord."

"Whereby shall I know this?" asked Zacharias. The angel answered, "I am Gabriel [Dan. 8:15,16; 9:21], that stand in the presence of God; and am sent to speak unto thee, and to shew thee these glad tidings." Doubting Gabriel's words, Zacharias asked for a sign. This he was given—he was told that because of his unbelief he would be struck dumb until the day these things should occur; and when he came out of the Temple he was unable to speak, to the astonishment of those in the courtyard.

As soon as his Temple duties had been accomplished, Zacharias returned to his own house in Judaea. "And after those days his wife Elisabeth conceived, and hid herself five months, saying, Thus hath the Lord dealt with me in the days wherein he looked on me, to take away my reproach among men" (see Barrenness, p. 41).

Annunciation to Mary

Lu. 1:26-38

While Zacharias and Elisabeth were anticipating the birth of their son, in the Galilean town of Nazareth to the north a related event was transpiring in the life of Mary, a cousin of Elisabeth. Mary was a virgin, a young daughter of Heli and a lineal descendant of King David through his son Nathan. She was betrothed to an Israelite named Joseph, a carpenter of Nazareth, a righteous and just man probably much her senior. According to Matthew, Joseph was of noble blood and could trace his line of descent from King David through David's royal son Solomon.

> It needs not surprise us that the representative of such an illustrious ancestry should be found in a station so obscure. . . . The vicissitudes of the Jewish nation for century after century; its deportation to Babylon, and long suspension of national life; its succession of high-priestly rulers, after the return; its transition to the Asmonean line, and, finally, the reign of the Idumean house of Herod, with all the storm and turmoil which marked so many changes, had left, to use the figure of Isaiah [53:2], only a root in a dry ground, a humble citizen of Nazareth, as the heir of its ancient royalty.[11]

Six months after the angel Gabriel had spoken to Zacharias he appeared to Mary: "Hail, thou that art highly favoured, the Lord is with thee: blessed art thou among women." She was troubled at this greeting, but he said, "Fear not, Mary: for thou hast found favour with God. And, behold, thou shalt conceive in thy womb, and bring forth a son, and shalt call his name JESUS [Joshua = Savior]. He shall be great, and shall be called the Son of the Highest: and the Lord God shall give unto him the throne of his father David: And he shall reign over the house of Jacob for ever; and of his kingdom there shall be no end." Isaiah had prophesied "Behold, a virgin shall conceive, and bear a son, and shall call his name Immanuel" (Is. 7:14; compare Mt. 1:22,23). For centuries every Jewish woman had yearned to mother the Messiah, and now this God-given privilege was bestowed on this young pure-minded maiden who had waited with the same hope as her forebears.

This generation was of God, not of man, for when Mary questioned "How shall this be, seeing I know not a man?" the angel answered, "The Holy Ghost shall come upon thee, and the power of the Highest shall overshadow thee: therefore also that holy thing which shall be born of thee shall be called the Son of God." The angel then revealed to her that her kinswoman Elisabeth had also found favor with God and six months earlier had conceived a son whose birth was to be associated with these glad tidings.

Mary's ready response evidenced her worthiness

for so sacred an honor, "Behold the handmaid of the Lord; be it unto me according to thy word."

> His [Jesus'] coming into the world is mediated by His mother's faith responsive to, and receptive of, the grace of God (Lu. 1:30-38). If He was Son of God at all, He did not begin to be so at any given age—at twelve (Lu. 2:49), or at the Baptism (Mk. 1:11), or at the Transfiguration (9:7), or at the Resurrection (Acts 13:33; Rom. 1:4). He never was anything else. It is in harmony with that unique relation to God and man which is of the essence of His consciousness, that there should be something unique in the mode of His entrance into the world as well as in that of His leaving it.[12]

At once and in haste, Mary journeyed to Elisabeth's home in Judaea, nearly a hundred miles from Nazareth. As she went she treasured in her heart the angel's message. When Elisabeth heard Mary's greeting, the child within her stirred and she too was filled with the Holy Ghost. Her spiritual insight told her that here was the mother of Israel's Messiah, and with great elation she welcomed Mary: "Blessed art thou among women, and blessed is the fruit of thy womb. And whence is this to me, that the mother of my Lord should come to me? For, lo, as soon as the voice of thy salutation sounded in mine ears, the babe leaped in my womb for joy. And blessed is she that believed: for there shall be a performance of those things which were told her from the Lord."

In answer to Elisabeth, Mary poured forth a song of praise "My soul doth magnify the Lord. . . ." (Lu. 1:46-55). This song—the Magnificat—so like that of Hannah (I Sam. 2:1-10) yet so far surpassing it, expressed the wealth of her deep religious thought and spiritual exaltation and mirrored her joy in having part in the great Messianic purpose of God. "The whole hymn is a mosaic of Old Testament imagery and language, and shows a mind so coloured by the sacred writings of her people that her whole utterance becomes, spontaneously, as by a second nature, an echo of that of prophets and saints."[13]

To protect the sacred secret of her child's conception Mary lingered with Elisabeth, but at the end of three months she returned to her own house, for during the period of betrothal, which might last as long as a year, the bride-to-be continued to live in the home of her parents.

Birth of John the Baptist
Lu. 1:57-80

Meanwhile Elisabeth gave birth to her son, and in accordance with Mosaic Law on the eighth day after his birth the child was circumcised, the rite admitting him into the privileges and duties of the covenant of Abraham. On this day, so important to every Jewish household, Elisabeth's cousins and neighbors came to rejoice with her and to celebrate the naming of the child. When they would have given the boy his father's name Elisabeth objected, "Not so; but he shall be called John." Zacharias, deprived of the power of speech for many months, asked for a waxed tablet and wrote, in accord with the angel's word, "His name is John." His tongue was immediately freed. No longer in doubt, he praised God and prophesied the future dignity and mission of the child as the forerunner of Israel's Messiah.

> "Blessed be the Lord God of Israel; for he hath visited and redeemed his people, And hath raised up an horn of salvation for us in the house of his servant David. . . .
> "And thou, child, shalt be called the prophet of the Highest: for thou shalt go before the face of the Lord to prepare his ways;
> "To give knowledge of salvation. . . . To give light to them that sit in darkness . . . to guide our feet into the way of peace."

In consonance with the angel's prophecy the child was brought up by his parents as a Nazarite. *Nazarite* means "separated" and refers to one who consecrated himself to the service of God by abstinence from the wine of the grape and every other kind of intoxicating drink, by permitting no razor to touch the hair of his head, and by avoiding ceremonial defilement with relation to food and to the dead (Num. 6:1-21). A man (or a woman) might take the Nazarite vow voluntarily as often as he wished, being free to set its length of observance. But John, like Samson and Samuel, was consecrated by his parents before birth, and so remained a Nazarite all his life. These words from Luke are all that are recorded of John's early years: "the hand of the Lord was with him," and "the child grew, and waxed strong in spirit, and was in the deserts till the day of his shewing unto Israel."

Announcement to Joseph
Mt. 1:18-25

When Joseph found that Mary was to bear a child, he decided to divorce her. A Jewish betrothal was virtually as binding as marriage and could be annulled only by a legal bill of divorcement. Joseph's kindness prompted him to plan to do this quietly to save her disgrace. Had he done so publicly it might have subjected her to the Mosaic penalty of stoning (Jn. 8:5). As Joseph deliberated, an angel came to him in a dream, saying, "Fear not to take unto thee Mary thy wife: for that which is conceived in her is of the Holy Ghost. And she shall bring forth a son, and thou shalt call his name JESUS: for he shall save his people from their sins." When Joseph awoke, he put aside his misgivings and took Mary as his wife.

Advent of Jesus
Lu. 2:1-20

As Mary awaited in Nazareth the birth of her child, a proclamation issued from distant Rome touched her life and that of Joseph in a strange way. Augustus ordered a census that he might methodically levy taxes on all the peoples of his Empire. Roman subjects registered in the places of their residence, but Jews were enrolled in the cities of their birth according to families and tribes. This circumstance required Joseph to report to Bethlehem, since he belonged to the house of David of the tribe of Judah. Joseph took Mary with him on the sixty-nine-mile journey to Bethlehem in Judaea. Thus were they brought to the prophetically appointed place for the birth of Israel's Messiah.

Having traveled slowly, no doubt chiefly on foot, they found the town crowded; there was no room in the inn or khan, the lodging place provided for strangers. A place was made for them where the household animals were tethered, and in this humblest of surroundings Mary was delivered of her first-born son. Seven hundred years earlier Isaiah had prophesied "Unto us a child is born, unto us a son is given" (Is. 9:6). He for whom Israel had patiently watched and waited had now appeared.

Again there came an announcement by an angel, this time to shepherds watching over their flock by night in the fields of Bethlehem. Note in the very language of the announcement this touching of heaven and earth as the Word was made manifest to a waiting world: "Lo, *the angel of the Lord came upon them,* and *the glory of the Lord shone round about them:* and they were sore afraid. And the angel said . . . Fear not: for, behold, *I bring you good tidings* of great joy, *which shall be to all people.* For UNTO YOU IS BORN THIS DAY in the city of David A SAVIOUR, WHICH IS CHRIST THE LORD. And *this shall be a sign unto you; Ye shall find the babe* wrapped in swaddling clothes, lying in a manger. And suddenly there was with the angel a multitude of the heavenly host praising God, and saying, *Glory to God in the highest,* and *on earth peace,* good will toward men."

The shepherds hastened to the manger and saw the babe, as the angel had said, and they spread word of the Savior's birth. The shepherds' story was greeted with astonishment "but Mary kept all these things, and pondered them in her heart."

Presentation in the Temple
Lu. 2:21-39

On the eighth day the infant was circumcised and called Jesus, the name divinely communicated to both Mary and Joseph. After forty days Mary traveled with Joseph the six miles from Bethlehem to Jerusalem to make her purification offerings in the Temple. Mosaic Law regarded a woman as unclean after childbirth—forty days for a son, eighty days for a daughter—and required the sacrifice of a lamb for a burnt offering and a pigeon for a sin offering at the end of that time to effect a cleansing. The humble circumstances of Jesus' parents are indicated in Mary's offering of two turtledoves, as a woman of little means could substitute a pigeon or turtledove for the burnt offering (Lev. 12).

Then the child was "presented" to the Lord and the five-shekel redemption price for the first-born son was paid to the priests of the sanctuary (see p. 41). In Jerusalem was a just and devout Jew named Simeon who was expectantly awaiting the Messiah, because to him had come the promise of the Holy Ghost "that he should not see death, before he had seen the Lord's Christ." Guided by the Spirit he came to the Temple and looked with clear vision on the child. Taking him in his arms, he blessed God and gave witness to the Christ and his mission: "Mine eyes have seen thy salvation, Which thou hast prepared before the face of all people; A light to lighten the Gentiles [Is. 42:6; 60:1-3], and the glory of thy people Israel." Simeon's prophecy defined the blessing—a light to all men, and a glory to those transformed by his truth (see Jn. 8:12; II Cor. 4:4).

Simeon's added words foretold strong resistance to this light, for this pure Messianic standard, a measuring rod for the quality of men's thoughts, would cause great overturning in the world: "Behold, this child is set for the fall and rising again of many in Israel; and for a sign which shall be spoken against . . . that the thoughts of many hearts may be revealed [Moffatt, destined to be a Sign for man's attack—to bring out the secret aims of many a heart]."

While Simeon was still speaking, an aged prophetess named Anna, who had faithfully served God night and day in the Temple, "gave thanks likewise unto the Lord, and spake of him to all them that looked for redemption in Jerusalem." Thus these two representatives of the true Israel gave prophetic witness to the nation of the newborn Messiah.

Visit of the Magi
Mt. 2:1-12

Shortly after Jesus' presentation in the Temple, certain Magians or wise men of the Orient reached Jerusalem after a long journey from Persia (according to legend, three kings known as Melchior, Gaspar, and Balthasar). They were of a learned and priestly caste whose religion, similar to Zoroastrianism, included the expectation of a savior. They asked, "Where is he that is born King of the Jews? for we have seen his star in the east, and are come to worship him."

When King Herod heard of their question, he was instantly apprehensive for the security of his throne and demanded of the scribes and priesthood where

Christ should be born. They cited the prophecy of Micah made some seven hundred years earlier: "In Bethlehem of Judaea." Herod directed the Magi to Bethlehem, cunningly asking that they bring him word when they had found the child so he too might worship him, though he was really planning the child's destruction.

"And, lo, the star, which they saw in the east, went before them, till it came and stood over where the young child was." Thus led, they found him; they "fell down, and worshipped him: and when they had opened their treasures they presented unto him gifts; gold, and frankincense, and myrrh." As the Christ child had received the homage of Israel in the adoration of the shepherds, now he received at the hands of these priestly pilgrims the first homage of the Gentile world. Warned in a dream not to return to Herod, the Magi then returned to their own country by another route. Their obedience proved a protection to the child and their gifts a provision for his imminent flight into Egypt.

Strangely—or was it strange?—the religious leaders of the Jewish nation, well versed in Old Testament prophecy, made no move to seek out the Christ child although the shepherds had reported what they had heard and seen, Simeon and Anna had spoken plainly in the Temple, Micah's prophecy had been brought to mind, and the Magi's visit indicated that the Messiah's time was at hand.

Flight into Egypt and Return
Mt. 2:13-23

As the Magi departed, an angel also warned Joseph in a dream: "Arise, and take the young child and his mother, and flee into Egypt, and be thou there until I bring thee word: for Herod will seek the young child to destroy him." Obediently, by night—perhaps the same night—Joseph took his little family into Egypt (according to tradition, the city of On [Heliopolis]), there to remain for many months. Egypt was a Roman province outside Herod's jurisdiction; many Jews of the Dispersion resided there.

Herod did not treat the Magi's words lightly. When he found that they had thwarted him in his attempt to find the child, he was enraged; he ordered the slaying of all male children under two years of age at Bethlehem and the places nearby. This act was in character; Herod already had killed a number of his own household to retain his grip on the throne.

Old Testament history records a similar account of the tyranny of a ruler against the Messianic people. In the days just prior to the birth of Moses, the Pharaoh of Egypt, fearing the increase and growing strength of the Children of Israel, had commanded his Hebrew subjects, "Every son that is born ye shall cast into the river" (Ex. 1:22). Moses had been rescued

from this decree by Pharaoh's own daughter and reared as her son. As Moses was spared for the deliverance and guidance of the generations of Israel, so Jesus was placed beyond the reach of the destroyer and protected that he might carry out his Messianic mission for the world.

Egypt proved a haven to Joseph and his family until after the death of Herod. Joseph was then divinely commanded, "Arise, and take the young child and his mother, and go into the land of Israel: for they are dead which sought the young child's life." Archelaus, cruel as his father Herod, was ruling as ethnarch in Judaea; but Joseph—journeying in quiet bypaths far from Jerusalem—brought Mary and Jesus safely to Nazareth in Galilee. In this manner was fulfilled the deeper meaning of Hosea's prophecy "Out of Egypt have I called my son" (compare Hos. 11:1; see also p. 540).

Childhood to Manhood
Lu. 2:40-52

Jesus' childhood and youth were spent in the small secluded city of Nazareth nestled in the hollow of a mountain ridge bordering on the northern side of the Plain of Esdraelon. The nearby slopes were covered with terraced gardens and the chief occupation of its inhabitants was agriculture. From the brow of the hill where the city was built there was a magnificent view of Palestine. From this vantage point Jesus as a child could have seen stretching to the south and west the fertile Esdraelon, the great granary of Palestine, the terrible scene in the past of many of Israel's wars and the battlefield of her conquerors, Egyptian, Assyrian, Chaldean, Greek, and Roman; to the west the Carmel range and the azure waters of the Mediterranean; and to the east beyond Jordan the rocky highland region of Gilead. From this hilltop he could also have traced the Via Maris, the Way of the Sea (Mt. 4:15), the great caravan route running north and south from Damascus to Egypt, and another extending west to east from the seacoast town of Ptolemais (Accho) to the Decapolis region beyond Jordan. Sheltered Nazareth was nevertheless part of the busy life of Galilee, tolerantly cosmopolitan as the result of its broad interests and contact with Greek and Roman influences.

Jesus was not the only child in the household; there were four brothers and several sisters in the family group (Mk. 6:3). (Three viewpoints regarding the "brethren" of Jesus have been held through the centuries: that Joseph had children by a former wife; that Mary bore other children after the birth of Jesus; that these were his kinsmen.) Luke describes the entire span of Jesus' childhood in one brief verse, embracing his physical growth and budding spiritual development in a few words: "The child grew, and waxed strong in spirit, filled with wisdom: and the grace of God was upon him." In Joseph's home was a deep love for God and a strict observance of all the Mosaic ordinances. Joseph proved a faithful guardian of the child he was privileged to foster; under his careful guidance Jesus was nurtured, cherished, educated, and trained in a knowledge of the Scriptures.

> The Jewish Law earnestly impressed upon parents, especially upon fathers, the duty of instructing their children in the knowledge of God, His mighty acts and His laws, and also of disciplining them in religion and morality. . . . It was the home in Nazareth that opened to Jesus the avenues of knowledge, and first put Him in possession of the treasures of the OT. It also seems certain that in His home there was a type of family life which made fatherhood stand to Him henceforward as the highest manifestation of a love beneficent . . . and all-forgiving.[14]

Jesus was undoubtedly educated in the manner of all Jewish boys. From infancy a Hebrew boy learned simple prayers from his mother; at the age of five he began to commit to memory the commandments and statutes of Mosaic Law, at six he attended the synagogue school for Scriptural instruction by the rabbis. Sabbath and weekday services thoroughly familiarized him with the Law and the Prophets and impressed on him the duties, privileges, and glory of being an Israelite. At the age of thirteen he became a "son of the Law" or "servant of the Law," bound to observe the Jewish fasts and religious feasts, to attend public worship, and to learn a trade.

> But whatever the Boy Jesus may have learned as a child or boy in the house of His mother, or in the school of the synagogue, we know that His best teaching was derived from immediate insight into His Father's will. . . . The calm, untroubled seclusion of the happy valley, with its green fields and glorious scenery, was eminently conducive to a life of spiritual communion; and we know how from its every incident—the games of its innocent children, the buying and selling in its little market-place, the springing of its perennial fountain, the glory of its mountain lilies in their transitory loveliness, the hoarse cry in their wind-rocked nest of the raven's callow brood—He drew food for moral illustration and spiritual thought.[15]

Aramaic was the native tongue of Galilee, the language Jesus spoke; he also knew the classical Hebrew of Scripture, as some of his quotations indicate (Mk. 12:29,30; Lu. 22:37; Mt. 27:46). Probably he was familiar with Greek, a language common in Galilee among the foreign population.

In the Temple at Twelve

When Jesus was twelve, Joseph and Mary took him to Jerusalem for the Feast of the Passover (see p. 60). As he eagerly joined the thousands of pilgrims who had come to this annual eight-day gathering, his mind must have been filled with all that he had learned, reverence

Street of arches in Old Jerusalem leading to Herod's Palace. *The Jewish Encyclopedia.*

and dedication stirring within him as he went in the company of his parents to observe its solemn ceremonies.

At the close of the feast Joseph and Mary joined other Galilean villagers, relatives, and friends traveling homeward. After a day's journey they discovered that Jesus was not in the company of his cousins and friends. Hastily the two returned to Jerusalem to search for him, and after three days they found him—not in the market places, in the busy streets, or at the city's gates, but in the Temple—"sitting in the midst of the doctors [of the Law], both hearing them, and asking them questions" (the rabbinical method of teaching was by question and answer). Jesus was engrossed with this opportunity to learn from the leading religionists of his nation, and they in turn were amazed at his intelligence and at the answers he gave.

Approaching Jesus, Mary chided him on the basis of human relationship: "Son, why hast thou thus dealt with us? behold, thy father and I have sought thee sorrowing." But he countered with the question "How is it that ye sought me? wist ye not that I must be about my Father's business?" Wycliffe translates this "Wist ye not that in those things which be of my Father, it behooveth me to be? [spelling modernized]." The first recorded words of Jesus, even at this early age, declare his true Sonship and relationship to

God. But Joseph and Mary did not understand the deeper meaning of his statement. Although conscious of his higher Sonship, he returned to Nazareth with them and remained subject to their authority until he reached maturity.

There is no further record of Joseph after this journey to Jerusalem, and according to tradition he died during Jesus' early manhood.

Eighteen Years at Nazareth

Eighteen silent years elapsed before Jesus emerged into public life. "In these years He 'began to do' long before He 'began to teach.' They were the years of . . . a sinless youth, a sinless manhood, spent in that humility, toil, obscurity, submission, contentment, prayer, to make them an eternal example to all our race."[16] The Gospels give no details of these years, but in the light of Jesus' awareness of his divine mission they must have been filled with prayer, study of the Scripture, and revelation in preparation for that mission. He gained a profound knowledge of the Old Testament books and later drew on their riches to sustain him in temptation, strife, and suffering. He understood their Messianic prophecies as did no other. During these years his daily occupation, like that of Joseph, was carpentry, a trade that disciplined him in work and service and one he doubtless practiced until his departure from Nazareth. One brief verse in Luke bridges the history of this period from childhood to maturity: "And Jesus increased in wisdom and stature, and in favour with God and man."

Opening Events of Jesus' Ministry

By 26 A.D. the political scene had changed. Augustus partitioned Palestine after Herod the Great's death in 4 B.C., following the divisions Herod had stipulated in his will. Herod's son Archelaus was made ethnarch of Samaria, Judaea, and northern Idumaea. Herod Antipas, another son, received Galilee and Peraea; a third son, Philip, received the regions of Ituraea, Gaulanitis, Trachonitis, Auranitis, and Batanaea. After ten years of misgovernment Archelaus was supplanted by a Roman procurator. In 26 the procurator was Pontius Pilate; the Roman emperor was Tiberias, Augustus' successor. The high priests of the Jewish hierarchy in Jerusalem at this time were Annas and Caiaphas.

Ministry of John the Baptist   Mt. 3:1-12; Mk. 1:1-8; Lu. 3:1-20

The preaching of John the Baptist prefaced the opening of Jesus' public ministry and stirred afresh the Messianic hope. As the birth of John had preceded

that of Jesus by six months, so his ministry preceded that of Jesus by the same length of time, and he began his labors probably in the summer of 26 A.D. The last of the prophets, he closed the prophetic period; the forerunner of Jesus Christ, he stood at the threshold of a new order, introducing the dispensation of grace and announcing the imminent presence of the promised Messiah.

John was in the barren hills of the wilderness of Judaea when he received his call to preach, a call as compelling as that of Isaiah or of Jeremiah. The Fourth Gospel attests: "There was a man sent from God, whose name was John. The same came for a witness, to bear witness of the Light, that all men through him might believe. He was not that Light, but was sent to bear witness of that Light" (Jn. 1:6-8).

A child of promise and a Nazarite from birth, John was disciplined and sanctified to his office. His clothes were as simple as those of the early prophets, a camel's-hair tunic and wide leather belt, and his food was locusts and wild honey. Sternly calling the nation to repentance, he startled them with the message: "Repent ye: for the kingdom of heaven is at hand"— words never before proclaimed. (The word *repentance* is a translation of the Greek *metanoyah*, meaning "to think differently," "to have another mind," "to feel contrition and desire to amend.") John's audiences were chiefly circumcised Jews dissatisfied with the ceremonial forms of worship. To them he preached a new kind of purification, "the baptism of repentance for the remission [forgiveness] of sins," administering the rite of baptism or immersion in water. This washing by water was the sign and seal of a moral cleansing in preparation for spiritual regeneration. Baptism had up to this time been employed only for Gentile proselytes; it was a practice foreign to the Jews, who considered that as members of the chosen race they needed no cleansing.

The Jews understood from the writings of the Prophets that an Elijah was to precede the Messianic King (Mal. 4:5). The common people welcomed John, and eager crowds came from Jerusalem and all parts of Judaea to confess their sins and be baptized in the Jordan. When John saw many Pharisees and Sadducees come to the baptism, he read their hearts and warned against unrepentance and a reliance for salvation on their physical descent from Abraham: "O generation of vipers, who hath warned you to flee from the wrath to come? Bring forth therefore fruits meet for repentance [Weymouth, let your lives prove your change of heart]: And think not to say within yourselves, We have Abraham to our father: for I say unto you, that God is able of these stones to raise up children unto Abraham. And now also the axe is laid unto the root of the trees: therefore every tree which bringeth not forth good fruit is hewn down, and cast into the fire."

Desiring to know how to put their repentance into action, the people asked, "What shall we do then?" John's answer turned their thought to practical acts of brotherhood and to just dealings with their fellow men.

To the people he said: "He that hath two coats, let him impart to him that hath none; and he that hath meat, let him do likewise."

To the publicans: "Exact no more than that which is appointed you."

To the soldiers: "Do violence to no man, neither accuse any falsely; and be content with your wages."

When the people speculated as to whether or not he was the Christ, John laid no claim to the title but proclaimed instead the coming of another prophet superior to himself: "I indeed baptize you with water unto repentance; but he that cometh after me is mightier than I, whose shoes I am not worthy to bear: he shall baptize you with the Holy Ghost, and with fire: Whose fan is in his hand, and he will throughly purge his floor, and gather his wheat into the garner; but he will burn up the chaff with unquenchable fire."

John's ministry, confined mainly to the region of the Jordan, continued for about fifteen months. The latter portion was contemporary with Jesus' Judaean ministry, but was abruptly terminated by imprisonment and martyrdom (see pp. 242, 271).

Baptism of Jesus

Mt. 3:13-17; Mk. 1:9-11; Lu. 3:21-23

When Jesus reached the age of thirty, the age at which under Mosaic Law a priest entered upon his office, he came from his home in Nazareth to the Jordan to be baptized by John. In the eighteen years since he had spoken the prescient words "I must be about my Father's business," he had quietly matured. He was now ready to assume his office as Savior of the world.

Jesus was "without sin." John immediately recognized his excellence and protested: "I have need to be baptized of thee, and comest thou to me?" Needing no repentance himself but conforming to the new order by which men were seeking to prepare for the kingdom, Jesus humbled himself and placed himself on the side of sinners that he might fulfill the work of righteousness and mediation for which he had been sent. He answered the Baptist: "Suffer it to be so now: for thus it becometh us to fulfill all righteousness." These first recorded words of the man Jesus are indicative of the "wisdom and stature" that were his from the start of his mission.

So John baptized him, and this deliberate act inaugurated Jesus' public ministry, an outward sign of consecration. But to Jesus himself was given the heavenly sign of the Holy Ghost. As he came up out of the water, "lo, the heavens were opened unto him, and he saw the Spirit of God descending like a dove, and lighting upon him: And lo a voice from heaven, saying, This is my beloved Son, in whom I am well pleased." This baptism by the Spirit gave testimony to his readiness, and conferred upon him the signet of divine approbation. Jesus was filled anew with the Holy Ghost and equipped for the stupendous work that lay ahead. John too witnessed this divine baptism and later confirmed it (Jn. 1:32-34).

The Temptation

Mt. 4:1-11; Mk. 1:12,13; Lu. 4:1-13

Jesus' temptation immediately followed his baptism. Returning from the Jordan, he "was led by the Spirit into the wilderness." Impelled by the conviction that his ministry was at hand and with resolution crystallized, here in the lonely mountain wilds of Judaea he fasted and prayed for forty days. The kingdom he was to found on earth, a spiritual kingdom, could only be made visible by its establishment in the hearts of men, and through communion with his Father Jesus sought the means and methods by which this was to be accomplished. So fully endowed was he with the Holy Ghost that he was able to appraise rightly the things of God and the things of the world; and when Satan presented to him three phases of worldly temptation, he withstood and overcame each one.

After forty days Jesus was hungry, and the tempter said, "If thou be the Son of God, command that these stones be made bread."

Jesus answered: "It is written, Man shall not live by bread alone, but by every word that proceedeth out of the mouth of God" (compare Deut. 8:3).

Then the devil took him up and set him on a pinnacle of the Temple and said, "If thou be the Son of God, cast thyself down: for it is written, He shall give his angels charge concerning thee."

Jesus answered: "It is written again, Thou shalt not tempt the Lord thy God" (compare Deut. 6:16).

Again, the devil took him up into a high mountain, and in a moment of time showed him all the kingdoms of the world and their glory, and said, "All these things will I give thee, if thou wilt fall down and worship me."

Jesus answered: "Get thee behind me, Satan: for it is written, Thou shalt worship the Lord thy God, and him only shalt thou serve" (compare Deut. 6:13).

The devil said, "If . . . if . . . if" in the attempt to introduce into his thought a doubt as to his true identity.

The tempter's whole object during the forty days evidently was to get Him to distrust the heavenly testimony

In such a tranquil spot as this on the bank of the Jordan, Jesus was baptized. Israel Government Tourist Office.

borne to Him at His baptism as THE SON OF GOD—to persuade Him to regard it as but a splendid illusion—and, generally, to dislodge from His breast the consciousness of His Sonship.[17]

In this struggle the Devil tried to tempt Jesus to debase his spiritual power so that his Messianic mission might fail; but Jesus made no compromise with Satan. He would not misuse that power for personal glorification, nor was he deluded into founding or furthering his kingdom by political power or policy. The Savior put Satan behind him from the outset, and in whatever form evil appeared throughout his ministry, "the prince of this world" could find nothing in him.

> The three temptations are addressed to the three forms in which the disease of sin makes its appearance on the soul—to the solace of sense, and the love of praise, and the desire of gain (I John 2:16).[18]

> Assuming that in the Baptism Jesus accepted the Messianic call, the possibilities of the ensuing ordeal of temptation were three—that He should recoil from the task, that He should misconceive it, or that, rightly apprehending it, He should adopt wrong methods.[19]

> The first bypath down which he was tempted to turn was the plan of concentrating on the effort to make life smoother and more comfortable for himself and his followers.... Again, he was tempted to offer the people a "sign," such as that of leaping safely from a pinnacle of the Temple. But in his thought every gift with which he was equipped was meant to help men, not to dazzle them. Moreover, almost till the last day of his life Jesus is represented as taking steps to evade any danger that threatened to bring his work to a premature close.
> The fact that Jesus was speaking figuratively in describing his temptations is made especially clear in the third narrative, which represents him as being offered, at the price of homage to Satan, the lordship over all earthly kingdoms which he viewed from a high mountain. The peculiar subtlety of this suggestion lay in this: that it might easily be made to appear that a long life of popularity and earthly power would provide far greater opportunity for beneficent work and lofty teaching than a short life largely spent in controversy and ending in a violent death.[20]

With Jesus' words "Get thee behind me, Satan," the Devil left him, and "angels came and ministered unto him." Satan did not openly renew the attack until Jesus' first announcement of his coming humiliating death, when Peter protested "Be it far from thee, Lord: this shall not be unto thee" (Mt. 16:21-23). But Satan was finally vanquished in Jesus' struggles at Gethsemane and at Calvary.

Jesus was the perfect Son in all things. He alone, through his pure love for God and man, maintained a spiritual discipline of thought which refused entry to Satan's arguments. He proved the kingdom of God

within him to be an impregnable fortress. Even before he began to preach the kingdom, he proved its power and presence in his own experience. According to Edersheim, the three forty-day fasts—of Moses (Ex. 24:18), of Elijah (I Ki. 19:8), and of Jesus—present interesting points of comparison and contrast:

> Moses fasted in the middle, Elijah at the end, Jesus at the beginning of His ministry. Moses fasted in the Presence of God; Elijah alone; Jesus assaulted by the Devil. Moses had been called up by God; Elijah had gone forth in the bitterness of his own spirit; Jesus was driven by the Spirit. Moses failed after his forty days' fast, when in indignation he cast the Tables of the Law from him; Elijah failed before his forty days' fast; Jesus was assailed for forty days and endured the trial. Moses was angry against Israel; Elijah despaired of Israel; Jesus overcame for Israel.[21]

John the Baptist's Testimony

Jn. 1:19-34

About this time the Sanhedrin (see p. 219) decided to investigate the Baptist's new religious movement, which was drawing such great crowds of followers and exciting all Judaea with the hope of a Messiah. They sent priests and Levites to John, who was baptizing at Bethabara (a ford on the east side of the Jordan twelve miles south of the Sea of Galilee), to ask "Who art thou?"

John answered their question explicitly: "I am not the Christ.... I am not [Elijah].... I am the voice of one crying in the wilderness, Make straight the way of the Lord, as said the prophet Esaias [Isaiah]." Literally he was not Elijah (Elias), but in figure he was (Mt. 17:11,12). So they questioned, "Why baptizest thou then?" Again referring to his office as forerunner, John replied, "I baptize with water: but there standeth one among you, whom ye know not; He it is, who coming after me is preferred before me, whose shoe's latchet I am not worthy to unloose."

On the following day as he saw Jesus coming toward him, radiant from his victory over Satan in the wilderness, John declared to his followers: "Behold the Lamb of God, which taketh away the sin of the world. This is he of whom I said, After me cometh a man which is preferred before me: for he was before me. And I knew him not: but that he should be made manifest to Israel, therefore am I come baptizing with water." John did not testify of Christ as a conquering Messiah or as the Lion of the tribe of Judah; he spoke of him as the Lamb of God, a sacrificial offering, whose work would be that of atonement.

To confirm his identification of Jesus as the God-sent Messiah, John revealed that God had told him of the sign by which he would know him: "I saw the Spirit descending from heaven like a dove, and it

The Judaean Wilderness. This endless sand map of wadi and hillock, dune and escarp, flows down to the Dead Sea, which lies beneath its haze in the distance, with the massif of the Moab mountains rising on its far side. Photograph by Manoug. Jordan Tourism Office—New York.

abode upon him. And I knew him not: but he that sent me to baptize with water, the same said unto me, Upon whom thou shalt see the Spirit descending, and remaining on him, the same is he which baptizeth with the Holy Ghost." Joyously John assured his listeners that he had seen this visible sign, declaring, "I saw, and bare record that this is the Son of God."

First Disciples

Jn. 1:35-51

The next day as John the Baptist conversed with two of his disciples, Andrew and John,* he saw Jesus

*Andrew is identified as Simon Peter's brother, but the second disciple, though unnamed, has been identified by most scholars as John, later one of the twelve apostles. Characteristically, John does not mention his own name in his Gospel (Jn. 1:35,40).

passing by and, pointing him out to them, said again, "Behold the Lamb of God!" When they heard these words they instantly followed Jesus, and thus began for each of them a life of following. Their first meeting with the Savior was natural and simple. His direct "What seek ye?" went straight to the heart of their motive and to the quality of their desire, requiring them to search within. When the two asked, "Master, where dwellest thou?" Jesus invited, "Come and see." So "they came and saw where he dwelt, and abode with him that day: for it was about the tenth hour." What they heard in that *tenth* hour is not known, but as he shared with them the treasures of his consciousness they *saw* where he dwelt—"in the secret place of the most High"—and became convinced that the Messiah Israel had long awaited was before them.

Andrew hastened to tell his brother Simon "We have found the Messias" and to bring him to Jesus. Sensing at once his potential, Jesus gave Peter a new surname: "Thou art Simon the son of Jona: thou shalt be called Cephas."

Having gathered these three young Galilean disciples, Jesus started for Galilee and on the way found Philip of Bethsaida. "Follow me," he said. Philip at once sought Nathanael to tell him the joyous news: "We have found him, of whom Moses in the law, and the prophets, did write, Jesus of Nazareth, the son of Joseph." Nathanael looked askance at the idea that the Messiah could come from such a locale: "Can there any good thing come out of Nazareth?" His incredulous attitude reflected a current Judaean concept of the inferiority of Galilee to Judaea because of its mixed population of Jews and strangers. Philip repeated the Master's invitation, "Come and see."

As Nathanael approached, Jesus said, "Behold an Israelite indeed, in whom is no guile!" (*Strong's Concordance,* guile: [fig.] *wile:*—craft, deceit, guile, subtilty.) When Nathanael asked "Whence knowest thou me?," Jesus answered, "Before that Philip called thee, when thou wast under the fig tree, I saw thee." In quick faith Nathanael accepted him, "Rabbi, thou art the Son of God; thou art the King of Israel." Jesus asked, "Because I said unto thee, I saw thee under the fig tree, believest thou? thou shalt see greater things than these. . . . Verily, verily, I say unto you, Hereafter ye shall see heaven open, and the angels of God ascending and descending upon the Son of man." The heavens had been opened to Jesus at baptism; now he promised this same blessing to his new disciples.

Affirmations such as "we have found the Messias," "we have found him, of whom Moses . . . and the prophets, did write," and "thou art the Son of God . . . the King of Israel" had never before been made. For these humble Galileans there was no doubt concerning this man.

First Miracle
Water into Wine   Jn. 2:1-11

After a three-day journey Jesus came with his new disciples to a marriage in Cana of Galilee, one at which his mother was also present. A Jewish marriage was a time of great rejoicing, an event that broke the pattern of everyday life, marked by a marriage feast that usually lasted seven days. It was customary to serve wine throughout the celebration, but at this particular wedding feast the supply had been exhausted. Mary turned to her son, "They have no wine." Detaching himself from family ties and personal relationships as he had at the age of twelve, Jesus answered: "Woman [a term of respect], what have I to do with thee? mine hour is not yet come."

> When he [Jesus] had returned from His first Temple-visit, it had been . . . to "be subject to His Parents." That period was now ended, and a new one had begun—that of active consecration of the whole life to His "Father's business." And what passed at the marriage-feast marks the beginning of this period. We stand on the threshold, over which we pass from the old to the new—to use a New Testament figure: to the marriage-supper of the Lamb.

> Viewed in this light, what passed at the marriage in Cana seems like taking up the thread, where it had been dropped at the first manifestation of His Messianic consciousness. . . . What He had first uttered as a Child, on His first visit to the Temple, that He manifested forth when a Man, entering on His active work—negatively, in His reply to His Mother; positively, in the "sign" He wrought.[22]

Even though Jesus had said "Mine hour is not yet come," Mary unhesitatingly instructed the servants, "Whatsoever he saith unto you, do it." At hand, probably near the door in readiness for the many ceremonial cleansings obligatory on the Jew, stood six large earthenware or stone jars, each capable of holding about nine gallons of water. Jesus commanded, "Fill the waterpots with water," and the servants filled them to the brim. Then he said, "Draw out now, and bear unto the governor of the feast." And when the servants poured they found that the water had been transformed into wine. When the "governor," an honored guest in charge of the festivities, tasted it, he said to the bridegroom, "Every man at the beginning doth set forth good wine; and when men have well drunk, then that which is worse: but thou hast kept the good wine until now."

This turning of the water into wine, a miracle of grace and compassion, revealed the Father's presence and bounty and gave the first public evidence of Jesus' divine nature and power. It prefigured Jesus' whole ministry, in which he poured forth without measure the rich wine of his Father's love. "This beginning of miracles did Jesus in Cana of Galilee, and manifested forth his glory; and his disciples believed on him."

A curve of the Galilean shore line. Israel Government Tourist Office.

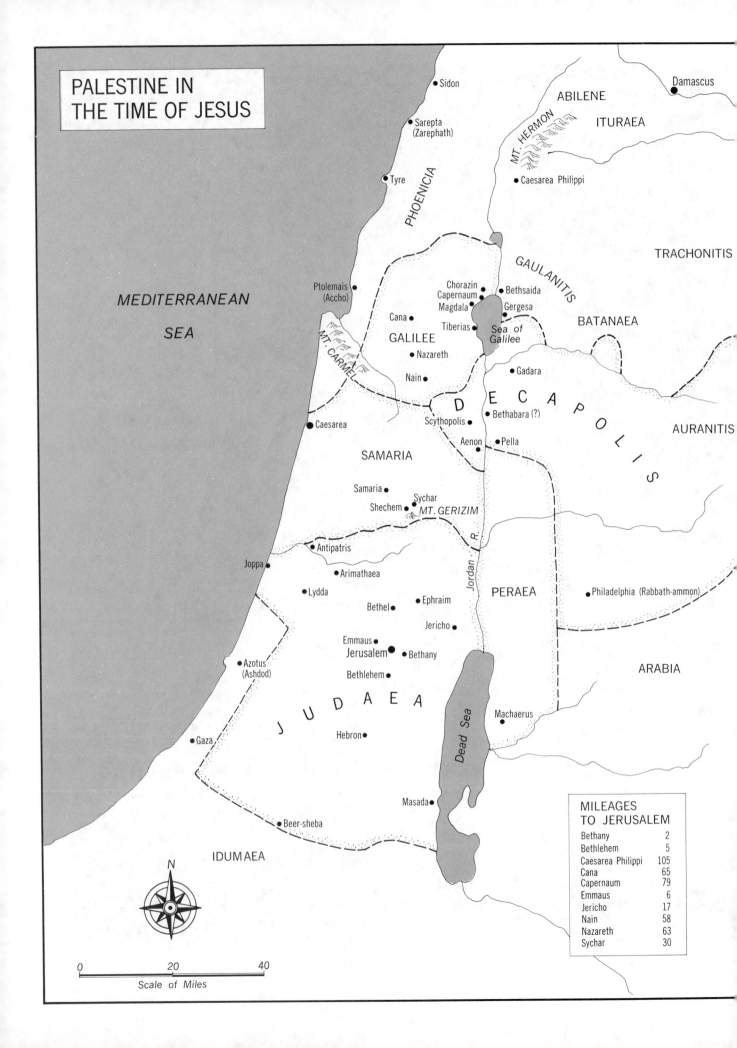

PALESTINE IN
THE TIME OF JESUS

MEDITERRANEAN

SEA

Sidon

ABILENE

Damascus

ITURAEA

MT. HERMON

Sarepta
(Zarephath)

PHOENICIA

Caesarea Philippi

Tyre

TRACHONITIS

GAULANITIS

Ptolemais
(Accho)

Chorazin
Capernaum   Bethsaida
Magdala   Gergesa

BATANAEA

Cana

Tiberias

Sea of
Galilee

GALILEE

MT. CARMEL

Nazareth

Nain

Gadara

D E C A P O L I S

AURANITIS

Caesarea

Scythopolis

Bethabara (?)

SAMARIA

Aenon   Pella

Samaria

Sychar

Shechem   MT. GERIZIM

Antipatris

Joppa

Arimathaea

Jordan R.

PERAEA

Philadelphia (Rabbath-ammon)

Lydda

Bethel   Ephraim

Jericho

Emmaus
Jerusalem   Bethany

ARABIA

Azotus
(Ashdod)

Bethlehem

J U D A E A

Machaerus

Gaza

Hebron

Dead Sea

Masada

IDUMAEA

Beer-sheba

N

MILEAGES TO JERUSALEM	
Bethany	2
Bethlehem	5
Caesarea Philippi	105
Cana	65
Capernaum	79
Emmaus	6
Jericho	17
Nain	58
Nazareth	63
Sychar	30

0   20   40

Scale of Miles

Public Ministry

Jesus' public career falls naturally into these periods of ministry—Judaean, Galilean, Perean, and Passion Week—and covers in point of time three years, 27-30 A.D.

He was now about his Father's business—to establish on earth the kingdom of heaven, the sovereignty of God. His purpose was to reveal the Father and the Son and bring redemption from sin. Through preaching, healing, and the power of his own example he made known the realities and presence of the kingdom and the love and will of his Father—"I speak that which I have seen with my Father" (Jn. 8:38). This kingdom, he taught, was "at hand" (Mk. 1:15), one "not of this world" but spiritual (Jn. 18:36), not a place but a power "within you" (Lu. 17:21), one that could only be attained by a new birth (Jn. 3:5) and by obedience to the commands of Christ. It was the Father's good pleasure to give men this kingdom (Lu. 12:32); its truths would set them free from sin and suffering of every sort (Jn. 8:32).

He made many illuminating statements concerning this kingdom: its appearing so small as to be like seed; so natural in evolving as to be like nature's growth; so priceless as to be like a pearl; so transforming as to be like leaven. Its spiritual nature became increasingly evident as his ministry progressed: it was a realm of Spirit, for he taught that "God is Spirit."

> The Kingdom of God, a spiritual and moral kingdom, was to be established upon the earth. It was the nature of this kingdom, first, to transform the individual, second, to dominate and purify the world. Such a kingdom could not be founded from without. . . . The only means of establishing such a kingdom as he had been commissioned to found was to win to its support individuals who felt its truth and power, waiting patiently until those adherents should attain such numbers and strength as would leaven humanity entire, and transform the whole into the ideal society of perfected individuals.
>
> This plan of Jesus is the most remarkable ever conceived. Rome had united the Mediterranean world by an all-conquering idea of universal political dominion, and men had marveled at the accomplishment of the impossible. Yet how much greater was Jesus' idea of uniting the whole world by the ties of religion into a universal spiritual brotherhood, a union not external, political and selfish, but internal, religious, humanitarian. An invisible kingdom which, planted in a small and obscure country, should expand till it embraced all countries, all men, all time. Such was Jesus' idea of the Kingdom of God. . . . Jesus determined upon this plan with full confidence that it was God's will, and with full assurance of its ultimate success. The accomplishment of it he set about with a resolution which carried him through hardships, isolation, reproach, opposition, martyrdom. . . .
>
> Jesus' own life was the embodiment of his conception of the kingdom, an ideal realization of God's perfect will for men, and so a concrete and living illustration of his teaching.[23]

Jesus came into the world fully prepared and qualified to bring this kingdom to earth. Isaiah had said of the promised Immanuel: "Butter and honey shall he eat, that he may know to refuse the evil, and choose the good" (Is. 7:15). Hebrews states of him: "Thou hast loved righteousness, and hated iniquity; therefore God, even thy God, hath anointed thee with the oil of gladness above thy fellows" (Heb. 1:9).

God had appointed him. "Behold my servant, whom I uphold; mine elect, in whom my soul delighteth; I have put my spirit upon him: he shall bring forth judgment to the Gentiles" (Is. 42:1). "Who verily was foreordained before the foundation of the world, but was manifest in these last times for you. . . ." (I Pet. 1:20).

God had equipped him. "God giveth not the Spirit by measure unto him" (Jn. 3:34).

God had commissioned him. "The Spirit of the Lord God is upon me; because the Lord hath anointed me to preach good tidings unto the meek; he hath sent me to bind up the brokenhearted, to proclaim liberty to the captives, and the opening of the prison to them that are bound; To proclaim the acceptable year of the Lord, and the day of vengeance of our God. . . ." (Is. 61:1,2).

God had certified him. "This is my beloved Son, in whom I am well pleased" (Mt. 3:17). "Jesus of Nazareth, a man approved of God among you by miracles and wonders and signs, which God did by him in the midst of you. . . ." (Acts 2:22).

In carrying out his mission Jesus gloriously fulfilled the threefold office of Prophet, Priest, and King foretold of his Messiahship—"(a) A prophet to enlighten, warn, and instruct (John vi:14; iii:2). (b) A priest to sympathize, intercede, and make atonement for his people (Is. liii; Heb. vii). (c) A king to reign in, rule over, protect, deliver, and bless them (Zech. xiv:9; Ps. ii:6)."[24]

Jesus' public ministry revealed the magnitude of the nature of Christ as he marked the way of the kingdom.

Judaean Ministry

Following the marriage in Cana Jesus went to Capernaum (in Galilee) and from there to Jerusalem to attend the Passover, probably in the spring of 27 A.D. This visit to Jerusalem marked the beginning of his ministry in Judaea.

Much of the land of Judaea was wilderness. Its central portion rose 1500 to 1800 feet above sea level in a rugged mountainous tableland cut by numerous gorges and valleys. To the east the land dropped sharply into the desert strip of the Jordan-Dead Sea rift; to the west it sloped gradually into the lowlands toward the Mediterranean. Flocks of sheep grazed its stony hills, and where possible the mountainsides were terraced for cultivation of vineyards and olive groves. Judaea's inhabitants were intensely patriotic Jews who fiercely resented the rule of Rome. The region was also the stronghold of Pharisaism and the home of Rabbinism (see Rabbis, p. 250); here the spirit of Mosaic religion had been all but lost in meaningless ritual and punctilious observance of formal rules of conduct.

During his Judaean ministry—an approximately nine-month period that John's Gospel alone records—Jesus cleansed the Temple, set before the people his Messianic claims, and began his preaching of the kingdom; but the Jewish religious leaders, jealous of their ecclesiastical control over the people, opposed him instantly. Seeking hearts more humble, he left Jerusalem to preach for a time in the Judaean hills and his disciples baptized those who believed (Jn. 4:2), but when he felt the resentment and hostility of the Pharisees he turned toward Galilee.

First Cleansing
of the Temple
Jn. 2:13-22

Jesus was now ready to begin his Messianic labors. The time was propitious; his first disciples had been selected and the Feast of the Passover was at hand. So he journeyed to Jerusalem, for he could have opened his public ministry in no more fitting place than the citadel of the nation's religion, within the very confines of the Temple itself.

His first public act—cleansing the Temple—was both authoritative and startling. Entering the courts of the sanctuary, his gaze rested on a scene shockingly like that of a noisy, crowded market place. Droves of sheep, goats, and oxen were being herded into pens between the arched columns of the Court of the Gentiles; cages of doves were stacked nearby. The din of merchants filled the air as they bargained with the thousands of pilgrims from all parts of Palestine over the sale of sacrificial offerings; and, to add to the desecration, a thriving trade was going on at the moneychangers' stalls as foreign coin was exchanged into half-shekels for the Temple tax. These abuses within the Temple precincts had been fostered with the tacit consent of the priests because of the profits accruing to the Temple treasury. Rebuking this profanation of his Father's house, Jesus made a scourge or lash of small cords and drove out those who sold sheep and oxen and doves. He overthrew the tables of the moneychangers, commanding, "Take these things hence; make not my Father's house an house of merchandise." They could not understand him as with divine zeal he swept all before him.

By this striking, fearless act Jesus focused upon himself the attention of the nation. The Jewish rulers at once approached him. Who was this Galilean stranger who had stepped out of obscurity? He was obviously not one of the Levitical priesthood; he was unknown to them as a rabbi. Though their consciences were doubtless pricked, they were angry because their prestige had suffered a severe blow; yet, feeling the silent approval of Jesus' act by those watching, they dared not reprove him. So in half-concealed antagonism they asked a sign of his authority. In veiled language Jesus promised them the "sign" of resurrection, foretelling at the very outset of his ministry the victorious fruition of his work: "Destroy this temple, and in three days I will raise it up." It was as if he had said "I am the immortal Son of God, and in time you shall know this." Assuming he meant Herod's Temple, they countered: "Forty and six years was this temple in building, and wilt thou rear it up in three days?" The Apostle John noted later that Jesus was referring to "the temple of his body."

Jesus began at once to preach the good news of the kingdom of God to the common people. Many were attracted to him during this feast, not only because of his words but also because he performed miracles such as they had never seen before, and they believed in him (Jn. 2:23). But among the Pharisees hostility to this new teacher sprang up almost immediately.

First Discourse
The New Birth
Jn. 3:1-21

Nicodemus was among those early drawn to the Galilean. While Jesus was still in Jerusalem this prominent and wealthy member of the Pharisaic party and a ruler of the Jews (a member of the Sanhedrin) sought an interview. Desiring to hear of the new teachings from the lips of the Teacher himself, he came to the house in which Jesus was staying. Sincere in his search for the truth, he was at the same time concerned about his position, and to avoid criticism or censure by other members of the council he came in the darkness of night.

Out of this timid visit came Jesus' great discourse on the new birth. Nicodemus began cautiously: "Rabbi, we know that thou art a teacher come from God: for no man can do these miracles that thou doest, except God be with him." Jesus went at once to the core of the matter, demanding complete discipleship: "I say unto thee, Except a man be born again, he cannot *see* the kingdom of God."

> **Born again**—or, as it were, *begin life anew* in relation to God; his manner of thinking, feeling, and acting with reference to spiritual things, undergoing a *fundamental and permanent revolution.* **cannot see**—can have no part in.... **the kingdom of God**—whether in its beginnings here (Luke 16:16), or its consummation hereafter. (Matthew 25:34; Ephesians 5:5).[25]

Perplexed, Nicodemus asked, "How can a man be born when he is old? can he enter the second time into his mother's womb, and be born?" Prone to literal interpretation of the Scriptures through his Pharisaic training, he failed to grasp the fact that Jesus was speaking of spiritual regeneration. Had Jesus used the figure of the new birth in reference to Gentile proselytes, his words might have been intelligible to his visitor; but because Nicodemus was a Jew, a member of the chosen people and therefore in his own eyes already justly entitled to the kingdom, he did not realize that the words applied to him.

Startling Nicodemus with an answer that brushed aside all preconceived ideas of Jewish rights to citizenship in the kingdom, Jesus bluntly set forth the fundamental and indispensable qualification for access to it: "I say unto thee, Except a man be born of water and of the Spirit, he cannot *enter* into the kingdom of God. That which is born of the flesh is flesh; and that which is born of the Spirit is spirit. Marvel not that I said unto thee, Ye must be born again." His statement struck at the very foundations of ritualistic religion, requiring a twofold purification—first of repentance, then of regeneration. Jesus continued: "The wind bloweth where it listeth, and thou hearest the sound thereof, but canst not tell whence it cometh, and whither it goeth: so is every one that is born of the Spirit." By this allusion to the mystery of the movements of the wind he illustrated the mystery of the regenerating power of the Spirit.

Nicodemus, still not understanding, asked, "How can these things be?" As a religious teacher he should have known the transforming power of God in the hearts of men, as taught in the Old Testament; the "night" of Nicodemus' thought may be glimpsed in Jesus' rebuke: "Art thou a master of Israel, and knowest not these things? . . . If I have told you earthly things, and ye believe not, how shall ye believe, if I tell you of heavenly things?" Jesus asserted the divine origin of his teachings and urged Nicodemus to accept in faith the truths he was telling him: "No man hath ascended up to heaven, but he that came down from heaven, even the Son of man which is in heaven."

Jesus revealed many fundamental facts concerning the kingdom as he closed his discourse with Nicodemus: the way of salvation through the sufferings and triumphs of the Son of man; the gift of eternal life to those who believe; the love of God in sending His only begotten Son, not to condemn but to save; and the condemnation of those who willfully turn away from the Light which is come into the world. "And as Moses lifted up the serpent in the wilderness, even so must the Son of man be lifted up: That whosoever believeth in him should not perish, but have eternal life. For God so loved the world, that he gave his only begotten Son, that whosoever believeth in him should not perish, but have everlasting life. . . ."

Although Jesus' words had made a deep impression on Nicodemus, he did not at this time make an open avowal of discipleship.

(A full list of Jesus' discourses appears on p. 336.)

John the Baptist's
Further Testimony

Jn. 3:22-36

When Jesus left Jerusalem for the nearby villages of Judaea, many people followed him and were baptized in his name by his disciples. John's disciples therefore protested to John, baptizing at the springs of Aenon. Far from regarding Jesus a rival, however, the Baptist gladly testified again to Jesus' pre-eminence: "A man can receive nothing, except it be given him from heaven. Ye yourselves bear me witness, that I said, I am not the Christ, but that I am sent before him. He that hath the bride is the bridegroom: but the friend of the bridegroom, which standeth and heareth him, rejoiceth greatly because of the bridegroom's voice: this my joy therefore is fulfilled. He must increase, but I must decrease.

"He that cometh from above is above all. . . . And what he hath seen and heard, that he testifieth. . . . For he whom God hath sent speaketh the words of God: for God giveth not the Spirit by measure unto him. The Father loveth the Son, and hath given all things into his hand. He that believeth on the Son hath everlasting life: and he that believeth not the Son shall not see life; but the wrath of God abideth on him."

Second Discourse
Water of Life

Jn. 4:1-42

Some months later, in the winter of 27 A.D., Jesus and his small band of disciples set out for Galilee. Two main reasons had prompted his departure from Judaea. The opposition of the Pharisees was increasing as Jesus' revolutionary teachings attracted new adherents. His success even greater than John's, it was of primary importance to Jesus that there be no premature clash with this religious party. According to the Synoptists, Jesus left when he heard that the Baptist had been imprisoned by Herod Antipas for daring to denounce the immorality of Antipas' marriage to Herodias, the wife of Herod's brother Philip (Mt. 4:12; 14:3; Mk. 6:17; Lu. 3:19,20). (Josephus says that John was sent to the castle of Machaerus, a fortress-prison in Peraea east of the Dead Sea built by the Maccabean ruler Alexander Jannaeus, refortified by Herod the Great and used as one of his residences.)

En route to Galilee Jesus and his companions passed through Samaria, a region of racially mixed population. The Samaritans were a people who had sprung from both Assyrian and Israelitish origins through intermarriage after the northern kingdom of Israel was invaded and colonized by Assyria. Samaritan religious practice was mixed—partly the worship of Jehovah, partly worship of idols. On Judah's return from Captivity (536 B.C.) the Samaritans had offered their assistance in the rebuilding of the Second Temple, but because of the impurity of their religion the help had been summarily refused and a schism arose between the Jews and the Samaritans. Although their worship remained Jewish in form and they adopted the Pentateuch as their sacred Scripture, in 432 B.C. the Samaritans erected a rival temple on Mount Gerizim near Shechem, one later destroyed by John Hyrcanus. This schism was still in existence in the time of Jesus; so intense was the antipathy

ead Sea by
oonlight, near
ericho, with
ountains of
oab in distance.
ordan Tourism
ffice—New
ork.

etween the Jews and Samaritans that the strict Jew regarded even setting foot in Samaria a defilement.

It was about midday when Jesus approached Sychar (near Shechem); being "wearied with his journey" he rested at Jacob's Well while his disciples went into the city to obtain food. His weariness was undoubtedly occasioned less by physical fatigue than by the weight upon his spirit of the resistance of the Pharisees and the recent disheartening news of John's imprisonment. As Jesus awaited the disciples' return, a

Samaritan woman approached to draw water, and his meeting with her presented the first opportunity to teach in Samaria.

Jesus asked a small favor—"Give me to drink"—thus opening the way for his rendering a great service to her. Aware that he was a Jew, she was surprised at his request and demurred. "With His wondrous skill in using even the smallest and commonest trifles to lead to the highest and worthiest truths, He [lifted] her thoughts to matters infinitely above the mere wants of the body."[26] He said, "If thou knewest the gift of God, and who it is that saith to thee, Give me to drink; thou wouldest have asked of him, and he would have given thee living water.... Whosoever drinketh of this water shall thirst again: But whosoever drinketh of the water that I shall give him shall never thirst; but the water that I shall give him shall be in him a well of water springing up into everlasting life" (compare Jn. 7:37). The water he offered, spiritual life, alone could satisfy perpetually the deep longings of the soul. Eagerly the woman asked, "Sir, give me this water, that I thirst not, neither come hither to draw."

At her entreaty Jesus at once roused her conscience, laying bare the immorality of her life; to receive this gift of God required a purification. At this point, perceiving he was a prophet, the woman interposed the age-old bitterly disputed question concerning the place where God should be worshiped—at Mount Gerizim or in Jerusalem. Jesus lifted her thought above localized worship and thus lessened the longstanding animosity: "Woman, believe me, the hour cometh, when ye shall neither in this mountain, nor yet at Jerusalem, worship the Father. Ye worship ye know not what: we know what we worship: for salvation is of the Jews. But the hour cometh, and now is, when the true worshippers shall worship the Father in spirit and in truth: for the Father seeketh such to worship him. God is a Spirit: and they that worship him must worship him in spirit and in truth." (Most later translators working from the Greek render this passage "God is Spirit.")

"Words like these marked an epoch in the spiritual history of the world; a revolution in all previous ideas of the relation of man to his Maker."[27] Not accepting his answer, and still looking to the future, she said, "I know that Messias cometh, which is called Christ: when he is come, he will tell us all things." He replied, "I that speak unto thee am he"—Jesus' first open declaration of Messiahship.

The disciples, returning from the city, were amazed to find the Master deep in conversation with a hated Samaritan, but they asked no questions. Leaving her waterpot at the well, the woman hurried to spread the news to the men in the city: "Come, see a man, which told me all things that ever I did: is not this the Christ?"

During his first discourse Jesus had lifted a man's thought step by step to the necessity of regeneration within. In the second he lifted a woman's thought to the desire for the living water of Christ. The first had taken place at night; the second occurred at midday. According to gospel history Nicodemus did not emerge from that long night to confess his faith (except for one brief moment [Jn. 7:50-52]) until after Jesus' crucifixion, when he came openly to assist Joseph of Arimathaea in preparing Jesus' body for burial (Jn. 19:39,40). The woman of Samaria ran quickly in the clear light of that same day to summon others to hear and judge for themselves.

When the disciples offered Jesus the food they had purchased, he said, "I have meat to eat that ye know not of.... My meat is to do the will of him that sent me, and to finish his work." While they had been gone he had won his first adherent in Samaria, and through her he was already winning more; this was true refreshment and sustenance. These firstfruits of his teaching in Samaria presaged to him a great harvest, and he told his disciples, "Say not ye, There are yet four months, and then cometh harvest? behold, I say unto you, Lift up your eyes, and look on the fields; for they are white already to harvest."

At the invitation of those who believed, Jesus remained in Sychar for two days. Many others were convinced by his preaching—"Now we believe ... for we have heard him ourselves, and know that this is indeed the Christ, the Saviour of the world."

Galilean Ministry

Jesus' return to Galilee in the winter of 27 A.D. marked the beginning of his Galilean ministry, and for the next twenty-three months he made Galilee the principal field of his labors. This province in the northern part of Palestine was a rich land, with its fertile Plain of Esdraelon, the swift-flowing Upper Jordan, and the Sea of Galilee (also known as Lake of Chinnereth, Lake of Gennesaret, Sea of Tiberias). Fish from the Sea of Galilee was in Jesus' time a major asset in the economic life of Palestine as well as a chief source of subsistence. Well-watered by numerous streams, Galilee produced grain and fruits in abundance; its thriving trade routes tapped the busy commerce of Egypt, Arabia, and Syria. Well-built Roman military roads also traversed the region.

Galilee possessed a large Gentile population of many nationalities—Phoenicians, Arabs, Syrians, Greeks, Romans. It also possessed a faithful Jewish population, descendants of those patriotic Jews brought in long before by John Hyrcanus. Because Galilee numbered among its inhabitants many of foreign extraction (Is. 9:1) and because the speech of its Jews was marked by linguistic peculiarities, Judaeans looked upon Galileans with condescension. The people were industrious, vigorous, and—Josephus says—"inured to war from their infancy. . . . The cities lie here very thick, and the very many villages there are here are every where so full of people by the richness of their soil, and the very least of them contained above fifteen thousand inhabitants."[28] Galilee was more liberal in outlook and less narrowly nationalistic in spirit than Judaea because of its wider contacts with the Greek and Roman world, and its people were to prove more receptive to the new teachings of Jesus. Here Jesus was not under the jurisdiction of the Sanhedrin in Jerusalem, nor was he so exposed to the observation of the scribes and Pharisees.

Jesus made the port city of Capernaum his headquarters. Capernaum, on the northwest shore of the Sea of Galilee, was situated on the direct caravan route from Damascus to Egypt. Of considerable size and importance, it contained a customs station, military post, and the official residence of Herod Antipas' representative. Capernum means the *field of repentance, city of comfort, city of compassion, city of consolation.* Jesus "came and dwelt in Capernaum." From here he made many circuits throughout Galilee to preach the gospel of the kingdom and to confirm his words by notable miracles of healing.

First Period
of the Galilean Ministry

When Jesus came into Galilee, the Galileans received him readily, for many had witnessed his works at the Passover in Jerusalem in the spring of 27 A.D. It was natural for him to begin his preaching in the synagogues, where ready and eager audiences of both men and women were to be found. The synagogue was the center of Jewish religious and social life, a place of worship and a school for instruction in the Scriptures for both children and adults. By Jesus' time Jerusalem had more than four hundred fifty synagogues, and every village had at least one—where ten male Jews resided it was obligatory to form a congregation. The synagogue's Sabbath order of service was presided over by a ruler or rabbi: it called for prayer, the reading of portions of the Law and the Prophets, and an exposition of Scripture by a member of the congregation or a distinguished visitor. Jesus was often invited to give the exposition, so much of his early teaching was done in the synagogues.

He opened his ministry in Galilee with the ringing announcement "The time is fulfilled, and the kingdom of God is at hand: repent ye, and believe the gospel" (Mk. 1:15). He came "in the power of the Spirit . . . and there went out a fame of him through all the region round about" (Lu. 4:14). He traveled through the villages and towns, substantiating his message by many miracles.

These first six months in Galilee were marked by great success and popularity, but Jesus' words and miracles eventually roused the fears of the entrenched religious teachers—the Pharisees and the scribes—who became alarmed by both his revolutionary teachings and his disregard of traditional law. They soon brought against him serious accusations of blasphemy and Sabbath-breaking.

Healing
of Nobleman's Son   Jn. 4:46-54

The first recorded event of Jesus' Galilean ministry—the healing of the son of an officer of Herod Antipas' court—took place in Cana (see p. 358). This is the first specific healing mentioned in the Gospels and a significant one because it was accomplished at a distance. It made known a basic truth—the Word of God had a saving power whether the Savior himself was present or absent.

This officer's son was dying at Capernaum. Hearing that Jesus had come into Galilee, he went to Cana to beseech "Sir, come down ere my child die." Jesus did not come down; instead he commanded "Go

thy way; thy son liveth." The man returned to Capernaum to find that his son had been healed in the same hour Jesus had spoken these words to him. Thus this influential man and his whole household were brought into the faith.

Jesus' Miracles

Let us here consider Jesus' miraculous works, for healing was a characteristic and vital part of the gospel he taught. The Old Testament pages attest the healing power of the Spirit through the faith of Israel's righteous men and prophets (see Miracles of the Old Testament, p. 167). So when the people saw Jesus manifest this same power in restoring men to immediate wholeness they recognized that he was worthy to be called a prophet (Lu. 7:16; Jn. 9:17). His spiritual power was of a magnitude never seen before; suffering and sinning humanity was drawn irresistibly to him, for the salvation he offered embraced body as well as soul. One scholar has said that his miracles of healing were the outreaching of tenderness to the human need.

The power Jesus exerted came from God; he himself called it "the Spirit of God" (Mt. 12:28); it was his by divine authority as the Son of God, and as the Son of man he maintained its possession by his life of unbroken communion with God. His unceasing prayer, coupled with undeviating obedience to the will of God, was the essence of that communion. He consistently disclaimed any power of his own to work miracles: "The Son can do nothing of himself, but what he seeth the Father do: for what things soever he doeth, these also doeth the Son likewise. For the Father loveth the Son, and sheweth him all things that himself doeth."

> Jesus . . . could appeal to his miraculous powers as evidences of His Divine mission, and often did so. . . . Even in the wilderness He had refused to exert them, under any circumstances, either for His natural wants, or for His personal ends, and He adhered to this amazing self-restraint through His whole career. . . . No more sublime spectacle can be conceived than boundless power, kept in perfect control, for ends wholly unselfish and noble.[29]

Frederick Farrar says: "All Christ's miracles are revelations also."[30] To men they are revelations because they reveal a spiritual force that transcends the known laws of the physical world; to Jesus they were the natural effect of his accurate knowledge of God and the laws of His kingdom, giving evidence of the concord and order of that kingdom, which he was establishing on earth.

Although these miracles were seen by many (most of them took place in public), they were not wonder-

One of the four sources of the Jordan River flowing out of a basalt cliff on the western slope of Mount Hermon. Israel Government Tourist Office.

done solely for the purpose of attracting men. Jesus spoke of them as attesting his Messiahship: "The works that I do in my Father's name, they bear witness of me" (Jn. 10:25). They were undeniable proofs of the truth of his teachings and the direct result of the power of the Word in the affairs of men. In his answer to the Baptist's question "Art thou he that should come?," Jesus pointed to his healing works: "The blind receive their sight, and the lame walk, the lepers are cleansed, and the deaf hear, the dead are raised up, and the poor have the gospel preached to them" (Mt. 11:5).

Jesus' miracles may be generally classified as (1) those of healing and (2) those of supremacy over the forces of nature.

Specific Miracles of Healing

From the inception of his ministry Jesus proclaimed that "the kingdom of heaven is at hand," and his devotion of time and effort to healing human ills shows clearly that such untoward conditions have no place in the kingdom (compare Rev. 21:4). Sick minds and bodies were made whole; sinners were forgiven; hearts were chastened; men, women, and children were restored to useful lives. These cures were sometimes occasioned by individual faith, sometimes by the faith or love of a friend, sometimes by Jesus' compassion. Often his commands required of those who sought his help the seemingly impossible—"Rise, take up thy bed and walk"; "Stretch forth thine hand"—but immediately and unquestioningly he was obeyed.

Out of the vast number of physical healings Jesus performed, only a few specific ones were recorded by the Gospel writers. These include cures of blindness, dumbness, deafness, paralysis, atrophy, leprosy, fever, insanity, epilepsy, deformity, adultery, greed, as well as raisings from the dead. His healings are cited in the succeeding narrative in order of their occurrence. (A list of Jesus' miracles appears on p. 335; see also The Healing Work of Jesus, p. 358.)

Miracles of Supremacy

Not only did Jesus heal the sick and raise the dead; he also manifested his dominion over the forces of nature and its phenomena. Through prayer—his affirmation and understanding of God's omnipotence—he exercised the power of the Spirit as the occasion demanded: when a lesson was requisite, when protection and sustenance were urgent, when mortality needed to be vanquished.

Jesus proved his control over the elements of nature:
Turning water into wine at the wedding feast (Jn. 2:1-11).
Stilling the tempest (Mt. 8:23-27; Mk. 4:35-41; Lu. 8:22-25).

Walking on the sea (Mt. 14:24-33; Mk. 6:47-52; Jn. 6:16-21).
Withering the fruitless fig tree (Mt. 21:18-20; Mk. 11:12-14,20).

He drew upon the beneficence and providence of God to meet immediate need:
Providing the great draft of fishes at the call of the four disciples (Lu. 5:1-11).
Feeding five thousand with five loaves and two fishes (Mt. 14:13-21; Mk. 6:34-44; Lu. 9:11-17; Jn. 6:1-14).
Feeding four thousand with seven loaves and a few fishes (Mt. 15:32-38; Mk. 8:1-9).
Obtaining tribute money from the fish's mouth (Mt. 17:24-27).
Providing the second great draft of fishes after Resurrection (Jn. 21:1-11).

Jesus banished time and space, and transcended the substance of matter:
"Immediately the ship was at the land whither they went" (Jn. 6:21).
Suddenly vanishing from the sight of two disciples at Emmaus (Lu. 24:31).
Suddenly appearing among the apostles although "the doors were shut" (Jn. 20:19; 20:26).

Jesus "abolished death, and . . . brought life and immortality to light":
When he overcame death and rose again (Mt. 28:1-7; Mk. 16:1-7; Lu. 24:1-8; Jn. 20:1-10).
When, by his appearances during the forty days after Resurrection, he supplied evidence of his continuing existence (Acts 1:3).
When he ascended (Mk. 16:19; Lu. 24-51; Acts 1:9-11).

The Master did not reserve to himself the power to work miracles, but taught his followers its universal availability. He enjoined them to do the works he did, and his teachings imparted the knowledge and faith to follow his example. A principal prerequisite to attainment was faith in him: "I say unto you, He that believeth on me, the works that I do shall he do also" (Jn. 14:12). Hand in hand with this were such other essentials as love, humility, prayer, watching, and obedience to the moral and spiritual precepts of his gospel.

First Rejection at Nazareth
Lu. 4:16-30

From Cana Jesus went to Nazareth, the first visit to his home since the opening of his ministry. Reports of his new doctrine and of his healing power had preceded him, and on the Sabbath when he went to the synagogue he had attended from boyhood he was invited by the presiding rabbi to read from the Prophet Isaiah. Jesus selected the Messianic passage: "The Spirit of the Lord is upon me, because he hath anointed me to preach the gospel to the poor; he hath sent me to heal the brokenhearted, to preach deliverance to the captives, and recovering of sight to the blind, to set at liberty them that are bruised, To preach the acceptable year of the Lord" (Is. 61:1,2). His choice and use of this passage indicated his comprehensive knowledge of the Old Testament, for he read only that portion uniquely applicable to his present ministry, making no mention of the prophet's words concerning "the day of vengeance."

Closing the book, he affirmed, "This day is this scripture fulfilled in your ears." Startled by his claim to Messiahship, his friends and neighbors asked each other "Is not this Joseph's son?" They had known him so long in his humble beginnings that they could not believe his claim to Messiahship. Aware of their incredulity, Jesus said, "Ye will surely say unto me this proverb, Physician, heal thyself: whatsoever we have heard done in Capernaum, do also here in thy country.... Verily I say unto you, No prophet is accepted in his own country." He rebuked them by reciting two instances in the lives of Israel's great prophets when their messages, ignored by Israel, were heeded by foreigners: Elias (Elijah) by the widow of Sarepta (Zarephath); Eliseus (Elisha) by Naaman the Syrian.

Those who had known him from boyhood reacted with anger and violence. They "thrust him out of the city, and led him unto the brow of the hill whereon their city was built, that they might cast him down headlong." Luke records no miracle of healing on this visit, but he does make note of Jesus' miraculous escape from Nazareth, for "passing through the midst of them [he] went his way"—one of many advancing steps toward his own resurrection.

Call of the Four
Great Draft of Fishes   Mt. 4:18-22; Mk. 1:16-20; Lu. 5:1-11

After his rejection at Nazareth, Jesus settled in Capernaum and inaugurated a positive course of action. Although the first disciples had been with Jesus at the Passover and during his Judaean ministry, he apparently went alone to Nazareth while for a time they resumed their former occupation of fishing. (Fishing was one of the chief industries of Capernaum, as it was of several other cities that dotted the densely populated shores of the Sea of Galilee, among them Chorazin, Bethsaida, Magdala, Gergesa, Tarichea, and Sinnabris. Several thousand small fishing craft sailed the waters of the lake, and the many varieties of fish

caught and sold fresh, pickled, or dried, formed an important part of the Palestinian diet. Common sights were those of fishermen casting their nets in the early morning hours and spreading them out to dry in the warm afternoon sun. Such Galileans were courageous, intelligent, enterprising men, and by the very nature of their livelihood were given to that meditation during their long hours on the water that would make them receptive students of the Word.)

The Master now extended a definite call to four who had joined him earlier in his ministry—a summons that in its simplicity demanded the highest service. As he walked along the shore of the Sea of Galilee Jesus found Simon and Simon's brother Andrew casting their nets. "Follow me," he said, "and I will make you fishers of men." Matthew records "They straightway left their nets, and followed him." A little farther along he saw James and John, partners of Simon and Andrew, mending their nets. He spoke to them; "they immediately left the ship and their father, and followed him."

According to Luke, the call of the Four came on a day Jesus preached to the people from Simon Peter's boat. He said to Simon, "Launch out into the deep, and let down your nets for a draught." Simon answered, "Master, we have toiled all the night, and have taken nothing: nevertheless at thy word I will let down the net." Having done so, he and Andrew caught so many fish that their net broke. They summoned their partners James and John, nearby in another vessel; the catch was so large that both boats began to sink. Humbled by this miracle, Simon kneeled at the Master's feet, saying, "Depart from me; for I am a sinful man, O Lord," but Jesus only drew him closer with the promise of a new and higher vocation: "Fear not; from henceforth thou shalt catch men." And, when the four had brought their small craft to land, "they forsook all, and followed him."

As the priests of Israel more than a millennium earlier, standing in the waters overflowing the banks of the Jordan, had anticipated the blessings of the Promised Land, so now these first disciples, standing in the shallows of the Galilean Sea, saw before them a glorious calling. They did not fully comprehend the magnitude of that calling, but Jesus did, and he foresaw their successful ministry and its far-reaching effects.

Widening Fame
and Opposition

Much transpired in the ensuing months—late spring and early summer of 28 A.D. Jesus healed the man with the unclean spirit, Simon's mother-in-law, the leper, and the paralytic (Mt. 8:14-17; 9:1-8; Mk. 1:21-2:12; Lu. 4:33-44; 5:12-26; see also pp. 359-360). He called Matthew the publican, a taxgatherer, to discipleship; he preached in the synagogues of Galilee and was "glorified of all." As his fame spread multitudes came to him bringing their sick and diseased, and he healed them.

Jesus had now become a national figure. Crowds from Galilee, Decapolis, Jerusalem, Judaea, and Peraea flocked to hear his simple gospel of love and to believe on him. The Pharisees and scribes had soon grown apprehensive and resistant; their own long-established rabbinical authority was jeopardized. Jesus faced fantastic odds. The rabbis of his day claimed sole jurisdiction of religious teaching. (*Rabbi* means "my master," a title respectfully given to scholars of the Law who had graduated from rabbinical schools such as the famous ones of Hillel and Schammai. Their lives were devoted to the study and teaching of the Torah and to memorizing the great body of oral traditions that interpreted the Law [see p. 216]. This last task alone was a tremendous one and only the greatest rabbis fully achieved it.) The rabbis wielded an amazing power over the people, for their interpretations of the Law, which dictated practically every detail of daily life, were revered equally with, if not above, Scripture itself; and they constantly added new doctrines and refinements. By the time of Jesus the conscientious Jew could find little peace of mind in his anxious attempt to obey their endless array of regulations.

> They or their nominees filled every office, from the highest in the priesthood to the lowest in the community. They were the casuists, the teachers, the priests, the judges, the magistrates, and the physicians of the nation. . . . No one could be born, circumcised, brought up, educated, betrothed, married, or buried—no one could celebrate the Sabbath or other feasts, or begin a business, or make a contract, or kill a beast for food, or even bake bread, without the advice or presence of a Rabbi.[31]

Jesus did not hesitate to set aside rabbinical teachings that conflicted with his gospel; he was breaking down their whole materialistic system, hence he posed a real threat to their jealously guarded and hitherto invulnerable position and incurred their bitter antagonism.

Discourse
The Son and the Father   Jn. 5:19-47

It had been some months since Jesus had been in Judaea; in early summer of 28 A.D. he made a brief visit to Jerusalem to attend one of the national feasts (unidentified by the Gospel writer) and once more to proclaim his message in the city whose Pharisaic teachers had rejected it. The growing acceptance in Galilee of his new doctrine had not escaped the attention of the Jewish authorities in Jerusalem and his every word and act had been reported. His first known act in Jerusalem on this visit was the healing at the public pool of Bethesda of the man who had been an invalid for thirty-eight years. This startling cure on the Sabbath and his deliberate command that the man carry his bed on the Sabbath (Jn. 5:1-16) gave the Jerusalem hierarchy a pretext to move against him. They charged him with Sabbath-breaking and sought to kill him.

In the face of official persecution Jesus boldly defended his right to good works: "My Father worketh hitherto, and I work." His claim to divine Sonship, already attested to in Galilee, instantly caused his Jerusalem hearers to add the charge of blasphemy, so they "sought the more to kill him" (Jn. 5:17,18). Supporting his prerogative of Sonship and explaining the work of the Father and of the Son more fully, he said, "The Son can do nothing of himself, but what he seeth the Father do. . . . For the Father loveth the Son, and sheweth him all things that himself doeth." No thought of rivalry was present in the aim and spirit of his works—only a perfect unity and accord with his Father.

In his defense he further asserted that the Father had given him power to quicken and to judge (which he had just done in his healing of the chronic invalid): "As the Father raiseth up the dead, and quickeneth them; even so the Son quickeneth whom he will. For the Father judgeth no man, but hath committed all judgment unto the Son: That all men should honour the Son, even as they honour the Father." That quickening, he explained, was even now at hand: "I say unto you, He that heareth my word, and believeth on him that sent me, hath everlasting life, and shall not come into condemnation; but is passed from death unto life."

He continued, citing the indisputable testimony of four witnesses, although only two were required by Jewish law: of John the Baptist, of his own works, of the Father Himself, and of the Scriptures. He closed his discourse: "Ye will not come to me, that ye might have life. I receive not honour from men. . . . Do not think that I will accuse you to the Father: there is one that accuseth you, even Moses, in whom ye trust. For had ye believed Moses, ye would have believed me: for he wrote of me."

Jesus' opponents raised no hand against him, and soon after the feast he returned from Jerusalem to Galilee, there to heal in the synagogue on the Sabbath a man with a withered hand (Mt. 12:9-14; Mk. 3:1-6; Lu. 6:6-11; see p. 360). This Sabbath healing aroused such violent opposition on the part of the Pharisees and scribes that they met in council to find some way to destroy him. When Jesus heard of this, "he withdrew himself from thence" (see Swelling Tide of Hatred, p. 352).

Site of Pool of Bethesda, Jerusalem. Excavations within the compound of the Crusader Church of St. Anne have reached down to the level of the Pool of Bethesda of Jesus' time. Jordan Tourism Office—New York.

Second Period
of the Galilean Ministry

The effects of the open break with the Jewish rulers in Jerusalem were felt in Galilee; from this time on they watched Jesus' every act with suspicion and perverted his words. Jesus no longer taught freely in the synagogues, but drew his audiences away from the villages to the mountains and to the seaside. Up to this time only seven of Jesus' disciples have been known to us by name: Andrew, Peter, John, James, Philip, Nathanael, and Matthew. But in the second Galilean period, which covered about ten months (summer of 28 A.D. to April of 29), the Master began deliberate organizing of his closest followers in the choice of twelve apostles. Definite instruction and practical training followed. In his incomparable Sermon on the Mount Jesus set forth the underlying principles of the kingdom of God and proceeded fearlessly in the face of still-rising hostility to impress these truths on his audience by parables, by discourses, and by miracles. Toward the close of this second Galilean period many adherents, disillusioned in Jesus as their hope for a popular leader, began to turn away.

Choosing
the Twelve Apostles
Mk. 3:13-19; Lu. 6:12-16

In midsummer 28, to avoid the persecution of the scribes and Pharisees who dominated the synagogues, Jesus ceased to teach in the cities and came down along the shore of the Sea of Galilee. He was thronged by people from Galilee, Judaea, Idumaea, Peraea, even from the Phoenician cities of Tyre and Sidon to the north, people drawn to him by the reports of his remarkable cures. He healed the sick, the diseased, the palsied, the epileptic, and preached to them of the kingdom.

Pressed by their many demands, he saw that the time had come to choose from among his many disciples a few he could thoroughly train to help him in his labors. His earnest preparation for this important step is evident in the brief account of this event. "He went out into a mountain to pray, and continued all night in prayer to God. And when it was day, he called unto him his disciples: and of them he chose twelve, whom also he named apostles." The word *apostle* means "one commissioned" or "one sent" and signifies a delegate as well as a messenger.

The old order of the Law was past, supplanted by the teachings of grace. The twelve apostles superseded in type the twelve tribes of Israel of the Old Testament, representing a new spiritual Israel in whose hearts and minds God's law would be written and God's covenant would be kept.

No one can know all the qualities Jesus sought in those he chose or all the qualifications they possessed, but promising and worthy they must have been to deserve such honor.

These men came from various walks of life: some had been prosperous fishermen, one was an affluent tax collector of Roman revenues, another a guerrilla fighter sworn to oppose Roman rule; the occupations of the others are not recorded. They were vigorous, intelligent young men, and—with the exception of Judas Iscariot—all were native to the province of Galilee. They had probably been educated as children in the synagogue schools, but none was steeped in the ecclesiastical doctrines then prevalent. They were humble, teachable men, hungry of soul, convinced from the moment they met Jesus that he was the Messiah, and without reservation they willingly left all—livelihood, family, home—to follow him. All embodied in varying degrees two fundamental requisites—faith and obedience—requirements Jesus later taught as essential to true discipleship.

The New Testament biographies of the apostles are scant and vary in detail. They nevertheless establish some facts about the lives of most of them and thereby help round out the narrative of Jesus' ministry.

Simon Peter or Cephas	"hearing"; "rock," "stone"
Andrew, Peter's brother	"manly"
James, son of Zebedee	(from O.T. name Jacob)
John, son of Zebedee	"Jehovah is gracious"
Philip	"lover of horses"
Bartholomew or Nathanael	"son of Tolmai"; "given of God"
Matthew or Levi	"gift of Jehovah"; "a joining"
Thomas or Didymus	"a twin" or "double"
Simon Zelotes	"hearing"; "a Zealot"
James the Less	(from O.T. name Jacob)
Thaddaeus	"that praises and confesses"
or Lebbaeus	"a man of heart"
or Judas	(from O.T. name Judah)
Judas Iscariot	"man of Kerioth"

Simon Peter

Simon was the son of Jona (Bar-jona), a native of Bethsaida who resided in Capernaum with his wife and mother-in-law. A fisherman, with his brother Andrew he was in partnership with James and John and their father Zebedee. He became one of Jesus' earliest and most ardent disciples, one of the chosen Four. At their first meeting the Master immediately perceived the latent possibilities of the man and called him Cephas, the Aramaic word for "rock," or Peter, from the Greek *petros* (Jn. 1:42). From the outset Peter showed outstanding qualities of leadership and his name always appears first in the list of the apostles. In temperament he was generous and impulsive; of a quick and inquiring mind, he asked the Master more questions than did any of the others. He was one of the three (with James and John) chosen to be present with Jesus at the raising of Jairus' daughter, at the Transfiguration, and in the group apart in the Garden of Gethsemane.

At all times Peter manifested a quick, fervent zeal and a boundless enthusiasm for Jesus' work. When Jesus gave his great discourse on the bread of life, many Jews turned away. As Jesus questioned the Twelve, "Will ye also go away?" Peter answered loyally, "Lord, to whom shall we go? thou hast the words of eternal life" (Jn. 6:67,68).

When his clear insight enabled him to declare of Jesus "Thou art the Christ, the Son of the living God," Jesus blessed him for his perception and promised him a stewardship in his Church: "I say . . . unto thee, That thou art Peter, and upon this rock I will build my church; and the gates of hell shall not prevail against it. And I will give unto thee the keys of the kingdom of heaven" (Mt. 16:16-19).

Once Jesus sharply rebuked Peter for his misunderstanding of the necessity of the cross as a part of the Messianic mission: "Get thee behind me, Satan: thou art an offence unto me: for thou savourest not the things that be of God, but those that be of men" (Mt. 16:23).

When Jesus spoke of giving up material possessions for treasure in heaven, Peter asked, "Behold, we have forsaken all, and followed thee; what shall we have therefore?" Jesus replied: "Ye which have followed me, in the regeneration when the Son of man shall sit in the throne of his glory, ye also shall sit upon twelve thrones, judging the twelve tribes of Israel. And every one that hath forsaken houses, or brethren, or sisters, or father, or mother, or wife, or children, or lands, for my name's sake, shall receive an hundredfold, and shall inherit everlasting life" (Mt. 19:27ff.).

Jesus foresaw a severe testing time for Peter, and at the Last Supper he said, "Simon, Simon, behold, Satan hath desired to have you, that he may sift you as wheat: But I have prayed for thee, that thy faith fail not: and when thou art converted, strengthen thy brethren." Impetuously Peter affirmed, "Lord, I am ready to go with thee, both into prison, and to death." Jesus, knowing Peter's untried faith, predicted, "I tell thee, Peter, the cock shall not crow this day, before that thou shalt thrice deny that thou knowest me" (Lu. 22:31ff.).

At his Master's arrest Peter was quick to draw his sword, but at Jesus' command he sheathed it. As the soldiers bound Jesus and led him to the house of the high priest for trial, Peter followed "afar off." Then "he sat with the servants, and warmed himself at the fire," and before the crowing of the cock he

vehemently denied Jesus three times. Even as Peter made the third denial, Jesus turned and looked at him; Peter, instantly filled with remorse, "went out, and wept bitterly" (Mt. 26:75). The pain of guilt lifted when Jesus accorded him a special appearance after Resurrection. Later the three denials were canceled and he was restored to favor; and, strengthened by Christ's love and grace, he was entrusted with the mission "Feed my sheep" (Jn. 21:16).

To the fulfillment of this charge Peter dedicated the remainder of his life. At Pentecost he made the first statement of Christian doctrine for the Church. His mission of preaching and healing was mainly to the Jews, and with courageous faith he gave the early Christians eminent leadership. He is the author of two epistles of the New Testament, First and Second Peter. (For a more detailed account of his later life, see The Work of the Twelve Apostles, p. 374.)

Andrew

Andrew was Simon Peter's brother, also a fisherman. That he was a searcher after truth is evident. He first appears as a disciple of John the Baptist, but when John pointed to Jesus and called him the Lamb of God he immediately followed Jesus. He was the first to say "We have found the Messias," as he brought his brother to Jesus. Andrew was one of the Four called by the Master at the beginning of the Galilean ministry. At the feeding of the five thousand Andrew reported to Jesus, "There is a lad here, which hath five barley loaves, and two small fishes: but what are they among so many?" (Jn. 6:9). With Peter, James, and John, Andrew earnestly questioned Jesus at the Mount of Olives about the destruction of the Temple and heard his words concerning the fall of Jerusalem and his Second Coming. Nothing is known of Andrew's apostolic ministry.

James

Son of Zebedee and Salome and elder brother of John. James' home was probably Bethsaida. His father was a prosperous Galilean fisherman with his own hired servants; his mother was one of the faithful women who later ministered to Jesus in Galilee (Mk. 15:41). (It would appear that Salome was the sister of the Virgin Mary; *if so* James and John were cousins of Jesus [compare Mt. 27:56; Mk. 15:40; Jn. 19:25].) James and John were in partnership with Peter and Andrew. The four were eager disciples of Jesus and were so united in spirit and service that the accounts of their association with him are always closely intertwined. Slain by Herod Agrippa I in 44 A.D. during persecution of the Christian Church, James was the first of the apostles to suffer martyrdom (Acts 12:1,2).

John

This younger brother of James, son of Salome and Zebedee, was also a fisherman. He was originally a disciple of John the Baptist (an inference drawn from Jn. 1:35,40), and like Andrew he followed Jesus at once. He and James, two of the Four, were mending their nets when Jesus called them to the ministry.

At the time these two were chosen to be among the Twelve Jesus gave them the name Boanerges, "sons of thunder" (Mk. 3:17). Only brief glimpses of their untempered zeal appear in the Gospel story. On one occasion John reported to Jesus, "We saw one casting out devils in thy name; and we forbad him, because he followeth not with us," but Jesus replied, "Forbid him not: for he that is not against us is for us" (Lu. 9:49,50). On another occasion John and James desired that Jesus bring down fire upon certain inhospitable Samaritans, but he rebuked them: "Ye know not what manner of spirit ye are of. For the Son of man is not come to destroy men's lives, but to save them" (Lu. 9:55,56).

As Jesus journeyed to Jerusalem to face death these two brothers asked for the positions of honor at his right and left hand in his kingdom. When he replied "Ye know not what ye ask: can ye drink of the cup [the cross] that I drink of? and be baptized with the baptism that I am baptized with?" they answered, "We can" (Mk. 10:38,39; compare Mt. 20:20,21).

Like Peter, James and John stood in special favor with Jesus in the inner circle of three—present with him at the raising of Jairus' daughter, at the Transfiguration, and in Gethsemane.

Of a strong and loving nature, John gave the Master a deep, unselfish loyalty and received in return Jesus' special love. He is identified as "that disciple whom Jesus loved." He was so close to Jesus in spirit that at the Last Supper he reclined in the place of honor at his right hand—"leaning on Jesus' bosom." Alone of all the apostles John stood faithfully at the cross, and to him Jesus entrusted his mother. He outran Peter to the tomb on Resurrection morning. Without evidence of Jesus' resurrection other than the discarded grave clothes, "he saw, and believed." As Jesus stood on the shore of the Sea of Galilee at his third appearance to the apostles, John was the first to recognize him. When Peter questioned Jesus of John, "What shall this man do?" the answer was "If I will that he tarry till I come, what is that to thee? follow thou me" (Jn. 21:21,22).

John stood with Peter as a co-leader and "pillar" in the Apostolic Church. After the fall of Jerusalem in 70 A.D. he lived, according to tradition, at Ephesus, where he labored as pastor in the churches of Asia Minor. As the last surviving apostle he served as mentor to the Church, helping to guard and guide its purity and spiritual integrity. Banished to the isle of Patmos by the Roman emperor Domitian (ca. 95 A.D.), he there received the marvelous visions and prophecies of the Apocalypse. Five books of the New Testament came from his pen: the Fourth Gospel; First, Second, Third John; and the book of Revelation. Some current opinion holds that the last four were written not by this John but by an unknown writer called John the Elder. There is, however, much internal evidence to indicate that they could have been written by no one but this apostle.

Philip

A native of Bethsaida, according to tradition a charioteer. The name Philip (from the Greek *philippos*) means "a lover of horses," perhaps indicating the character of the man, for a trainer of horses usually possesses restraint, steadiness, and self-control. Philip was the first disciple to whom Jesus spoke the significant words "Follow me." He hastened to tell Nathanael that he and Peter and Andrew had found Israel's long-awaited Messiah.

At the feeding of the five thousand—Jesus' first miracle of its kind—Philip's comprehension of the illimitable power of God was tested by Jesus' question "Whence shall we buy bread, that these may eat?" His answer showed he entertained no expectation of divine aid in meeting the need of the multitude: "Two hundred pennyworth of bread is not sufficient for them, that every one of them may take a little" (Jn. 6:5,7).

At the Last Supper Philip petitioned, "Lord, show us the Father, and it sufficeth us." His request for a visible manifestation of God indicated his lack of a full understanding of the complete oneness of Christ's nature with the Father's. Jesus replied, "Have I been so long time with you, and yet hast thou not known me, Philip? he that hath seen me hath seen the Father; and how sayest thou then, Shew us the Father?" (Jn. 14:8,9). The last Biblical mention of Philip is of his presence in the upper room with those who before Pentecost awaited the descent of the Holy Ghost (Acts 1:13).

Bartholomew (Nathanael)

This apostle was a native of Cana in Galilee. In the Synoptic Gospels he is called Bartholomew (son of Tolmai); in the Fourth Gospel he is named Nathanael. When Philip informed him he had found the Messiah, a man called Jesus from Nazareth, Nathanael hesitated, remarking innocently, "Can there any good thing come out of Nazareth?" Jesus' commendation of Nathanael was immediate—"Behold an Israelite indeed, in whom is no guile!"—as he discerned the wholesome character of the man—without artifice, cunning, deceit, treachery, or wile. The moment Nathanael heard Jesus' words he acknowledged,

"Rabbi, thou art the Son of God; thou art the King of Israel." Nathanael was one of the seven apostles fishing on the Sea of Galilee to whom Jesus appeared after Resurrection. Beyond this no Scriptural record remains.

Matthew

Matthew, also known as Levi in the Gospels of Mark and Luke, was the seventh disciple specially called by the Master early in the Galilean ministry. He was the son of Alphaeus and probably a man of considerable wealth, for he held the lucrative position at Capernaum of a publican or collector of Roman tax revenues. The Jews classed publicans with the worst kind of sinners—traitors, renegades, murderers—and looked on them with the utmost contempt and hate, not only because they were in the employ of a foreign government, but also because they frequently extorted excessive fees from their own people. Publicans were socially ostracized, forbidden to enter the Temple or the synagogue, participate in public prayers, fill offices in courts of law, or give testimony.

But how differently Jesus regarded the publican Matthew, and how instant his measure of Matthew's character: "He saw a *man* . . . sitting at the receipt of custom" and said to him "Follow me" (Mt. 9:9). Without a backward glance Matthew "left all, rose up, and followed him" (Lu. 5:28). Jesus' mission embraced all classes of men; he did not hesitate to choose Matthew, seeing in him fitness for discipleship. With joy Matthew made Jesus a feast in his own house to which a great company of other publicans were invited (Lu. 5:29). Nothing is known of his apostolic labors.

Some scholars attribute the authorship of the Gospel of Matthew to Matthew himself; others are of the opinion that if he was not the author of the entire book he certainly contributed substantially to it.

Thomas

The first mention of this apostle is at his appointment as one of the Twelve. In the Synoptics he is called Thomas, while in John he is also identified as Didymus, a twin. The four events that bring Thomas into view toward the close of Jesus' ministry show him to have been a man of courage and loyalty but slow to attain sure understanding and faith.

Thomas, in the face of grave danger to Jesus, bravely offered to accompany him to Bethany at the time of Lazarus' sickness, saying to the other apostles, "Let us also go, that we may die with him" (Jn. 11:16). Thomas refused to believe the apostles' report of Jesus' resurrection without tangible personal evidence: "Except I shall see in his hands the print of the nails, and put my finger into the print of the nails, and thrust my hand into his side, I will not believe." His doubt was removed eight days later when Jesus showed him the proof he sought, saying, "Be not faithless, but believing." Strengthened and comforted, Thomas acknowledged, "My Lord and my God" (Jn. 20:25ff.). He was one of the seven apostles who breakfasted with Jesus at the Sea of Galilee during his third appearance after Resurrection. Nothing further is known of his life.

Simon Zelotes

Only the appointment of this apostle as one of the Twelve is recorded. Matthew and Mark designate him "the Canaanite"; Luke identifies him as "Zelotes." His name indicates that he was a Zealot, a member of a party of patriotic and fanatical Jewish resisters to Roman rule over Palestine (see also p. 218). His appointment implied a willing submission to lay aside the sword of war for "the sword of the Spirit." Cunningham Geikie says of him, "No name is more striking in the list than that of Simon the Zealot, for to none of the Twelve could the contrast be so vivid between their former and their new position."[32]

James

This apostle was the son of Mary and Alphaeus (Cleophas, according to Jn. 19:25) and brother of Joses. He was called James "the less" (little, small, or RSV "the younger"), perhaps because of his stature or youth, to distinguish him from James the son of Zebedee. His mother was one of the devoted women who ministered to Jesus in Galilee and who was present at the cross and at the tomb on Resurrection morning. Of his apostleship nothing is known.

Thaddaeus (Lebbaeus, Judas)

Matthew calls him Thaddaeus and Lebbaeus, Luke designates him Judas (John further adds "not Iscariot"), but little is known about him. A single saying is attributed to him: at the Last Supper, when Jesus told his apostles he was going away, Judas asked a forthright question concerning the visible manifestation of Christ's kingdom—"Lord, how is it that thou wilt manifest thyself unto us, and not unto the world?" (Jn. 14:22)—showing that he had not yet fully grasped the spiritual nature of that kingdom.

Judas Iscariot

This Judas, from the town of Kerioth in southern Judaea (the only Judaean among the apostles), was the son of a Simon about whom nothing is recorded. His name always occurs last in the lists of the Twelve. Judas' motives for following Jesus appear to have been mixed: he began with affection for the Master, yet underneath was a strain of ambition and greed, worldly and political.

Judas Iscariot was treasurer of the apostle band; and at the supper in Bethany, as Mary anointed Jesus' feet with a costly ointment, he asked, "Why was not this ointment sold for three hundred pence, and given to the poor?" John commented later: "This he said, not that he cared for the poor; but because he was a thief, and had the bag, and bare what was put therein" (Jn. 12:5,6).

Jesus' insight was not at fault in choosing Judas; in selecting such a man he was holding out to all men the hope of regeneration and salvation. He knew what evil propensities were struggling for ascendency in the human nature of the man, but he also knew that as Judas heard the truth of his teachings and served him there would be continuous opportunity for spiritual growth. He waited patiently for a change in Judas. If Judas chose to give up these propensities his heart and spirit would soften; if not, they would harden slowly but inexorably. Less than a year after Judas' appointment as an apostle Jesus made indirect reference to his character: "Have not I chosen you twelve, and one of you is a devil?" (Jn. 6:70).

Judas' disappointed hopes for a temporal Messianic kingdom and his mercenary desires impelled him to betray his Master; to this end he covenanted with Jesus' enemies for a paltry thirty pieces of silver—about nineteen dollars in today's terms. At the Last Supper the Master identified him as his betrayer, adding, "It had been good for that man if he had not been born" (Mt. 26:24). When Judas failed to resist Satan and the last vestige of moral conscience was darkened, Jesus let him go. Within a few hours Judas guided armed Levites of the Temple guard as well as a band of Roman soldiers to the garden of Gethsemane to effect Jesus' arrest, betraying him with a kiss.

Judas had become irked by the very standard of apostleship he had at first espoused, for it unmasked his failings, and when that irritation hardened into resistance he himself was betrayed by his own weaknesses. Repentance came too late and, having set in motion a flood of events he was powerless to stop, he hanged himself (Mt. 27:5; compare Acts 1:18).

His place was later filled by a disciple named Matthias, who had been a follower of Jesus from the beginning (Acts 1:15-26).

The task before the Twelve was stupendous. Their mission, laden with promise, must not fail. Through them was to come not only the promulgation of Christ's gospel but also the founding of his Church. From the time of their selection Jesus carefully taught and trained them, showing by his example "the way, the truth, and the life." They were henceforth privileged to hear his inspired words, to witness his wondrous deeds, to mark his voluntary and perfect obedience to the Father's will, to partake of his loving spirit, to be with him daily, to do the works he did, and to grow into a more mature comprehension of his Messiahship and glory.

At first Jesus took the Twelve with him wherever he went. Later, he sent them out on an evangelizing mission, preparing them for future service. Times of severe testing lay ahead; there was much to learn and so short a time in which to learn it. Peter's faith faltered, Thomas doubted, Judas turned traitor. The weak places of their faith needed to be strengthened so there would be no breach in the wall of their discipleship.

With the exception of Judas Iscariot, so far as we know, these faithful delegates fulfilled in their lives the great trust Jesus laid upon them. According to the spirit of each, they served him with love and loyalty. They needed no greater authority; they asked for none beyond the Holy Spirit that had been promised them. They preached boldly in the name of Jesus Christ and their inspired devotion to his cause established the new Christian movement firmly. Persecuted, examined before the Sanhedrin, scourged and imprisoned, they rejoiced to be "counted worthy to suffer shame for his name." No more glorious testimony could be given of them than that they had been chosen by the Master, and men "took knowledge of them, that they had been with Jesus."

Opposite page: The Horns of Hattin: twin peaks overlooking the Sea of Galilee and the Plain of Gennesaret. This lovely natural amphitheater is the traditional site of Jesus' Sermon on the Mount. Photograph: Israel Government Tourist Office.

The Sermon on the Mount

Mt. 5-7; Lu. 6:20-49

Eager crowds now attended Jesus' every move. As he came down from his mountain retreat after his selection of the Twelve, he was met on a hillside plateau by a great multitude. They had streamed out from the cities and villages of Galilee, Judaea, and the region of Decapolis; they had come even from far-off Tyre and Sidon, bringing their sick and diseased, and with compassion Jesus healed them all.

To them he delivered his great discourse concerning the kingdom, since termed the Sermon on the Mount. (The title has been applied at least since the time of Augustine [*ca.* 394 A.D.]. Some modern scholars are of the opinion that the two records of this sermon as found in Matthew and Luke are two different accounts of

257

the same event; that the discourse in Luke appears in its original form, while Matthew's is a compilation and careful grouping of many of Jesus' teachings about the kingdom. Other scholars believe they were given on two different occasions.) According to Matthew, Jesus "went up into a mountain: and when he was set, his disciples came unto him" (The site has been tentatively identified as the Horns of Hattin, a hill in the plateau country west of Tiberias.) Here under the open sky he expounded the principles of the kingdom of heaven on earth, the character and life of its citizens, and their fundamental duties. He also defined the moral and spiritual laws that constitute its government, and dealt with "things new and old." The Law of Sinai was completed in the new commands of love and grace.

Jesus' sermon showed an open break with Judaism; he drew a sharp line between the ritualistic righteousness of his day and the dynamic moral and spiritual righteousness of the kingdom to be exemplified in the new life of his followers.

> For the first time in the history of religion, a communion is founded without a priesthood, or offerings, or a Temple, or ceremonial services; without symbolical worship or a visible sanctuary. There is an utter absence of everything external or sensuous: the grand spiritual truths of absolute religious freedom, love, and righteousness, alone are heard.[33]

This discourse is sometimes called Jesus' ordination address to his apostles, but it was directed to all his hearers and is applicable throughout all time to every new disciple.

Duties of Citizenship in the Kingdom

Beatitudes (Mt. 5:3-12)

Jesus began with promises of happiness and blessedness to the citizens of the kingdom. The Beautitudes, as these blessings are now called, express the essential spirit of the kingdom and open its gates to all men. Jesus named the cardinal virtues required of citizenship in the kingdom and specified the rewards for those who qualified:

Blessed are the poor in spirit

Blessed are they that mourn

Blessed are the meek

Blessed are they which do hunger and thirst after righteousness [right-mindedness]

Blessed are the merciful

Blessed are the pure in heart

Blessed are the peacemakers

Blessed are they which are persecuted for righteousness' sake . . . when men shall revile you, and persecute you, and shall say all manner of evil against you falsely, for my sake—

> their's is the kingdom of heaven
>
> they shall be comforted
>
> they shall inherit the earth
>
> they shall be filled

they shall obtain mercy

they shall see God

they shall be called the children [RSV sons] of God

their's is the kingdom of heaven. . . . Rejoice, and be exceeding glad: for great is your reward in heaven: for so persecuted they the prophets which were before you. . . .

Significantly, Jesus made mention not of a temporal kingdom that would fulfill the nation's current Messianic hope of conquering a world but rather of a spiritual kingdom attainable only through humility, righteousness, trial, and persecution.

Duties of Its Citizens to the World (Mt. 5:13-16)
As citizens of the kingdom, Christ's followers were to set an example whose vitality and goodness would turn men to God.

"Ye are the salt of the earth: but if the salt have lost his savour, wherewith shall it be salted? . . .

"Ye are the light of the world. A city that is set on an hill cannot be hid. . . . Let your light so shine before men, that they may see your good works, and glorify your Father which is in heaven."

The Moral and Spiritual Law of the Kingdom

Its Righteousness Contrasted with Traditional Teachings (Mt. 5:17-48)
Jesus taught of a higher righteousness under the kingdom's law of love. He did not set aside Mosaic Law or leave it in the letter; he transformed it by the spirit of love and called on his followers to keep its moral and spiritual requirements in this same spirit, warning "except your righteousness shall exceed the righteousness of the scribes and Pharisees, ye shall in no case enter into the kingdom of heaven." His every declaration was in contradistinction to the cold letter of traditional law and the sacrosanct formalism of the rabbis. Conscious of himself as the fulfillment of the Law, his words *"I say unto you"* carried a superior authority, superseding what the ancients had said. He extended law-keeping to the self-discipline of surmounting impure thoughts and hateful feelings; these, according to the law of the kingdom, come under condemnation as surely as extreme offenses. The children of the kingdom were to strive to be perfect "even as your Father which is in heaven is perfect." (Note the contrasts.)

"It was said by them of old time, Thou shalt not kill; and whosoever shall kill shall be in danger of the judgment:

"But I say unto you, That whosoever is angry with his brother without a cause shall be in danger of the judgment: and whosoever shall say to his brother, Raca ['O empty one'], shall be in danger of the council: but whosoever shall say, Thou fool, shall be in danger of hell fire.

"It was said by them of old time, Thou shalt not commit adultery:

> *"But I say unto you,* That whosoever looketh on a woman to lust after her hath committed adultery with her already in his heart."

"It hath been said, Whosoever shall put away his wife, let him give her a writing of divorcement:

> *"But I say unto you,* That whosoever shall put away his wife, saving for the cause of fornication, causeth her to commit adultery: and whosoever shall marry her that is divorced committeth adultery."

"It hath been said, An eye for an eye, and a tooth for a tooth:

> *"But I say unto you,* That ye resist not evil; but whosoever shall smite thee on thy right cheek, turn to him the other also.
>
> "And if any man will sue thee at the law, and take away thy coat, let him have thy cloke also. And whosoever shall compel thee to go a mile, go with him twain. . . ."

"It hath been said, Thou shalt love thy neighbour, and hate thine enemy.

> *"But I say unto you,* Love your enemies, bless them that curse you, do good to them that hate you, and pray for them which despitefully use you, and persecute you; That ye may be the children of your Father which is in heaven: for he maketh his sun to rise on the evil and on the good, and sendeth rain on the just and on the unjust. For if ye love them which love you, what reward have ye? do not even the publicans the same? . . ."

The Righteousness Required in the Kingdom, and Its Reward (Mt. 6:1-7:12) Jesus specified clearly what the citizens of his kingdom must and must not do. The desire to do the will of God rather than to impress men should be the incentive to true righteousness, and righteous deeds were to be done "in secret"—sincerely and unostentatiously. The duty of the seekers of the kingdom was to love God in single-minded service, to lay up spiritual treasures. They were not to let the anxieties of daily life distract them in their search, but to trust in God's care. They were not to judge the faults of others and overlook the greater faults within themselves. And always they were to pray, to "ask . . . seek . . . knock." God would assuredly answer their prayers.

In this portion of his sermon Jesus contrasted the righteous action with its opposite so his listeners could not fail to catch his meaning. (Note the contrasts.)

Charity. "Take heed that ye do *not* your alms [RV righteousness] before men, to be seen of them: otherwise ye have no reward of your Father which is in heaven. . . .

> "But when thou doest alms, let not thy left hand know what thy right hand doeth: That thine alms may be in secret: and thy Father which seeth in secret himself shall reward thee openly."

Prayer. "When thou prayest, thou shalt *not* be as the hypocrites are: for they love to pray standing in the synagogues and in the corners of the streets, that they may be seen of men [see p. 293]. Verily I say unto you, they have their reward.

"But thou, when thou prayest, enter into thy closet, and when thou hast shut thy door, pray to thy Father which is in secret; and thy Father which seeth in secret shall reward thee openly.

"But when ye pray, use *not* vain repetitions, as the heathen do: for they think that they shall be heard for their much speaking. Be not ye . . . like unto them: for your Father knoweth what things ye have need of, before ye ask him.

"After this manner therefore pray ye." The *Lord's Prayer* is in two parts: the first relates to God—His nature, His kingdom, His will; the second relates to the needs of men. In the realization of the first lies the fulfillment of the second.

"Our Father which art in heaven, Hallowed be thy name. Thy kingdom come. Thy will be done in earth, as it is in heaven. Give us this day our daily bread. And forgive us our debts, as we forgive our debtors. And lead us not into temptation, but deliver us from evil: For thine is the kingdom, and the power, and the glory, for ever. Amen." (The most ancient manuscripts do not include this doxology.)

Forgiveness. "If ye forgive men their trespasses, your heavenly Father will also forgive you:

"But if ye forgive *not* men their trespasses, neither will your Father forgive your trespasses."

Secret Fasting. "When ye fast, be *not*, as the hypocrites, of a sad countenance: for they disfigure their faces, that they may appear unto men to fast. Verily I say unto you, They have their reward.

"But thou, when thou fastest, anoint thine head, and wash thy face; That thou appear not unto men to fast, but unto thy Father which is in secret: and thy Father, which seeth in secret, shall reward thee openly."

Wealth. "Lay *not* up for yourselves treasures upon earth, where moth and rust doth corrupt, and where thieves break through and steal:

"But lay up for yourselves treasures in heaven, where neither moth nor rust doth corrupt, and where thieves do not break through nor steal: For where your treasure is, there will your heart be also."

Single-mindedness. "The light of the body is the eye: if . . . thine eye be single, thy whole body shall be full of light.

"But if thine eye be evil, thy whole body shall be full of darkness. If therefore the light that is in thee be darkness, how great is that darkness!

"No man can serve two masters: for either he will hate the one, and love the other; or else he will hold to the one, and despise the other. Ye cannot serve God and mammon."

Trust in God's Care. "Take *no* thought, saying, What shall we eat? or, What shall we drink? or, Wherewithal shall we be clothed? (For after all these things do the Gentiles seek:) for your heavenly Father knoweth that ye have need of all these things.

"But seek ye first the kingdom of God, and his righteousness; and all these things shall be added unto you. . . ."

Intelligent Behavior. "Judge *not,* that ye be not judged. For with what judgment ye judge, ye shall be judged: and with what measure ye mete, it shall be measured to you again. And why beholdest thou the mote [splinter] that is in thy brother's eye, but considerest not the beam that is in thine own eye? . . .

"First cast out the beam out of thine own eye; and then shalt thou see clearly to cast out the mote out of thy brother's eye."

"Give *not* that which is holy unto the dogs, neither cast ye your pearls before swine, lest they trample them under their feet, and turn again and rend you."

Diligence in Prayer. "Ask, and it shall be given you; seek, and ye shall find; knock, and it shall be opened unto you: For every one that asketh receiveth; and he that seeketh findeth; and to him that knocketh it shall be opened. . . ."

True Religion. "All things whatsoever ye would that men should do to you, do ye even so to them: for this is the law and the prophets."

In this succinct admonition, often called the *Golden Rule,* Jesus summed up the positive universal principle of brotherhood—the "royal law" of the kingdom (Ja. 2:8).

The New Way of Life Enjoined (Mt. 7:13-27)

Jesus closed his sermon with a series of admonitions. His followers would not find the way to the kingdom an easy one since it demanded self-discipline and self-denial, but it would lead to eternal life. His followers would know the professing Christian from the practicing one by his works. And if they would be wise and secure they would build their lives on his spiritual teachings.

Choose the Right Path. "Enter ye in at the strait [RV narrow] gate:

"for wide is the gate, and broad is the way, that leadeth to destruction, and many there be which go in thereat:

"Because strait is the gate, and narrow is the way, which leadeth unto life, and few there be that find it."

Be on Guard against False Teachers. "Beware of false prophets, which come to you in sheep's clothing, but inwardly they are ravening wolves. Ye shall know them by their fruits. Do men gather grapes of thorns, or figs of thistles?

"Even so every good tree bringeth forth good fruit; but a corrupt tree bringeth forth evil fruit. A good tree cannot bring forth evil fruit, neither can a corrupt tree bring forth good fruit. Every tree that bringeth not forth good fruit is hewn down, and cast into the fire. Wherefore by their fruits ye shall know them."

Have a Living Faith. "Not every one that *saith* unto me, Lord, Lord, shall enter into the kingdom of heaven;

but he that *doeth* the will of my Father which is in heaven. . . ."

Build on the Rock of Christ. "Whosoever *heareth* these sayings of mine, *and doeth them,* I will liken him unto a wise man, which built his house upon a rock: And the rain descended . . . the floods came

... the winds blew, and beat upon that house; and it fell not: for it was founded upon a rock.

"And every one that *heareth* these sayings of mine, *and doeth them not*, shall be likened unto a foolish man, which built his house upon the sand: And the rain descended ... the floods came ... the winds blew, and beat upon that house; and it fell: and great was the fall of it."

Jesus' words struck home; his audience sensed a ring of truth and authority foreign to the teachings of their rabbis.

As he had "set himself" on the mount, and his disciples had come to him, so he "set" the kingdom on a mount and his followers must seek it.

Jesus' Testimony of the Baptist
Mt. 11:2-19; Lu. 7:18-35

Jesus continued journeying that summer among the cities and villages of Galilee. Wherever he went multitudes followed him. He had given them the doctrine of the kingdom; again he demonstrated the power of that doctrine. In Capernaum he encountered the marvelous faith of a Roman centurion and healed his servant (Mt. 8:5-13; Lu. 7:1-10; see p. 361). He startled all Galilee with the raising of the widow's son at Nain (Lu. 7:11-16; see p. 370). In awe the people declared, "A great prophet is risen up among us"; "God hath visited his people." And he restored the sight and speech of a man both blind and dumb (Mt. 12:22-29; compare Lu. 11:14; see p. 361).

Reports of these miracles spread rapidly and word reached even John the Baptist in Peraea. Languishing for months in prison, this fiery preacher, cut off in the prime of his career and shut away from the free and open life of the wilderness, sent messengers to Jesus to ask "Art thou he that should come? or look we for another?"—an unexpected question from one who had once testified with conviction "Behold the Lamb of God!"

Jesus' answer to John brings to mind passages of Isaiah (Is. 35:5; 61:1) that pointed to Christ's healing and saving mission: "Go and shew John again those things which ye do hear and see: The blind receive their sight, and the lame walk, the lepers are cleansed, and the deaf hear, the dead are raised up, and the poor have the gospel preached to them." And he added "Blessed is he, whosoever shall not be offended in me," which Weymouth translates: "Blessed is every one who does not stumble and fall because of my claims."

After the departure of John's messengers Jesus spoke to the people in defense of the Baptist. John was no "reed shaken with the wind." He was a prophet, "yea ... more than a prophet," being Christ's forerunner prophesied by Malachi (Mal. 3:1). Jesus acknowledged John as greatest of those born of woman, but went on to say, "Notwithstanding he that is least in the kingdom of heaven is greater than he"—greater was the lowliest disciple who followed Christ in faith and loyalty.

Discourse
Woes on Impenitent Cities
Invitation to the Weary
Mt. 11:20-30

Addressing himself to the still-resistant listeners in the crowd, who would heed neither John nor himself, Jesus upbraided his generation and the unrepentant cities of Chorazin, Bethsaida, and Capernaum from which they had come: "Woe unto thee ... for if the mighty works, which were done in you, had been done in Tyre and Sidon, they would have repented long ago in sackcloth and ashes."

Changing the tone, he praised the wisdom of the Father who had hidden spiritual truths from intellectual and worldly minds and unveiled them to babes. In language clearer than ever before Jesus spoke of himself in relation to the Father, for though rejected by Chorazin, Bethsaida, and Capernaum, questioned by John, and maligned by the rabbis, he was known to the Father, and to him had been committed the things of the kingdom: "All things are delivered unto me of my Father: and no man knoweth the Son, but the Father; neither knoweth any man the Father, save the Son, and he to whomsoever the Son will reveal him."

Then, with a compassion that embraced both friends and enemies, he issued to all an invitation to come to him to learn of God: "Come unto me, all ye that labour and are heavy laden, and I will give you rest. Take my yoke upon you, and learn of me; for I am meek and lowly in heart, and ye shall find rest unto your souls. For my yoke is easy [Weymouth: my yoke is good], and my burden is light."

Parables
Second Galilean Period

The Pharisees and scribes were now openly hostile to Jesus as they felt their influence waning, and they seized every opportunity to oppose his doctrines and contradict his words. This caused Jesus to change his mode of teaching; he began to instruct the people by means of parables—anecdotal illustrations of his point.

The Biblical parable has been defined as "an earthly story with a heavenly meaning." This method of instruction was a tactful and impressive means of setting forth clearly and impersonally great spiritual truths. Jesus' analogies engaged the attention of the common people as well as that of his more learned listeners and induced them to dwell upon and retain the kernel of his teachings. His parables tested and sifted his audiences—to ears unprepared to hear the message was obscure; to the hearing ear it was lucid.

All of Jesus' parables are replete with meaning; their interpretation cannot be set within bounds for many implications and applications are possible. In simple, graphic language he spoke of the sower, the seed, the net, the bread, the candle, the vineyard, the shepherd, making familiar objects and activities of daily life symbolic, giving them spiritual counterparts to make the realities of the kingdom more intelligible and persuasive to his listeners. He so illumined the course of nature and human life, so delicately balanced the natural law with the spiritual truth, and so imbued his words with "the seed" of revelation that the parable has throughout all time become peculiarly his own.

> To the parables of our Lord there is nothing in all language to be compared, for simplicity, grace, fulness, and variety of spiritual teaching. They are adapted to all classes and stages of advancement, being understood by each according to the measure of his spiritual capacity.[34]

To the multitudes Jesus spoke in parables; only to his disciples did he expound them (Mk. 4:34). When the disciples asked "Why speakest thou unto them in parables?" Jesus answered: "Because it is given unto you to know the mysteries of the kingdom of heaven, but to them it is not given. For whosoever hath, to him shall be given, and he shall have more abundance: but whosoever hath not, from him shall be taken away even that he hath. Therefore speak I to them in parables: because they seeing see not; and hearing they hear not, neither do they understand." He then emphasized the special privilege that was theirs: "Blessed are your eyes, for they see: and your ears, for they hear. For verily I say unto you, That many prophets and righteous men have desired to see those things which ye see, and have not seen them; and to hear those things which ye hear, and have not heard them" (Mt. 13:10ff.).

(A list of Jesus' recorded parables appears on p. 336.)

Parable
Two Debtors
Lu. 7:41-50

The parable of the two debtors was spoken in the house of Simon, a Pharisee, where Jesus had been invited to dine: there was not yet an open break between him and the Pharisees, and he taught—as always—wherever there was an inquiring mind. As he reclined at dinner, a woman—easily recognizable as a despised sinner—slipped unnoticed into the room. Standing at the foot of his couch she began to wash his feet with her tears, to wipe them with her unbound hair, and to sprinkle them with a precious ointment. Simon instantly disapproved, feeling that Jesus could be no prophet if he permitted such a woman as this social outcast to approach him. A Pharisee would have repulsed her contemptuously, fearful of the pollution of her touch. Aware of his cold disdain, Jesus reproved Simon for his self-righteousness; but like the prophet Nathan who showed David his sin, he used a parable to cause Simon to judge himself.

"There was a certain creditor which had two debtors: the one owed five hundred pence, and the other fifty. And when they had nothing to pay, he frankly forgave them both." Jesus questioned Simon, "Tell me therefore, which of them will love him most?" After Simon's reluctant admission "I suppose that he, to whom he forgave most," Jesus emphasized the lesson of forgiveness by throwing into bold relief the contrition of the woman who "loved much" and the disrespect of his host who "loved little." "Seest thou this woman? I entered into thine house, thou gavest me no water for my feet: but she hath washed my feet with tears, and wiped them with the hairs of her head. Thou gavest me no kiss: but this woman since the time I came in hath not ceased to kiss my feet. My head with oil thou didst not anoint: but this woman hath anointed my feet with ointment. Wherefore I say unto thee, Her sins, which are many, are forgiven; for she loved much: but to whom little is forgiven, the same loveth little."

Turning to the woman still waiting in penitence, Jesus said, "Thy sins are forgiven. . . . Thy faith hath saved thee; go in peace." (See Healing of Penitent Sinner, p. 368.)

LIFE AND MINISTRY OF JESUS 265

Parables of the Kingdom

The time was ripening for a fuller revelation of the mysteries of the kingdom—"things which [had] been kept secret from the foundation of the world." Therefore on a day that enthusiastic crowds converged on him at the Sea of Galilee—crowds so great that he retreated into a small boat to speak to those who lined the shore—Jesus told eight parables of the kingdom, depicting its intrinsic nature.

The Sower and the Seed   Mt. 13:1-23; Mk. 4:1-20; Lu. 8:4-15

Jesus was well aware that not all who heard his gospel would appropriate its truths, and the parable of the sower is an apt illustration of his own ministry in planting the kingdom. It was also a teaching to his disciples, who would soon go out to spread the seed of his gospel among all people. Just as the soil of the Galilean fields and hills varied from stony shallowness to depth and richness, so they would find that the soil of the human heart differed in quality and capacity to effect spiritual growth.

"Behold, a sower went forth to sow; And when he sowed, some seeds fell by the way side, and the fowls came and devoured them up:

"Some fell upon stony places, where they had not much earth: and forthwith they sprung up, because they had no deepness of earth: And when the sun was up, they were scorched; and because they had no root, they withered away.

"And some fell among thorns: and the thorns sprung up, and choked them:

"But other fell into good ground, and brought forth fruit, some an hundredfold, some sixtyfold, some thirtyfold."

When his disciples asked the meaning of this parable Jesus interpreted it in the most explicit terms, explaining the spiritual meaning phrase by phrase. They would encounter the casual listener, the momentarily enthusiastic, the pleasure-loving, the care-ridden and worldly. But only in the receptive soil of a good heart, the "good ground," would the seed, the Word, remain alive to be nourished and cultivated to yield its spiritual harvest—coming, as Paul says, "unto the measure of the stature of the fulness of Christ."

"The sower soweth the word" (Mk.); ("The seed is the word of God" [Lu.]).

"And these are they by the way side, where the word is sown; but when they have heard, Satan cometh immediately, and taketh away the word that was sown in their hearts" (Mk); ("lest they should believe and be saved" [Lu.]).

"And these are they likewise which are sown on stony ground; who, when they have heard the word, immediately receive it with gladness; And have no root in themselves, and so endure but for a time: afterward, when affliction or persecution ariseth for the word's sake, immediately they are offended" (Mk.); ("which for a while believe, and in time of temptation fall away" [Lu.]).

"And these are they which are sown among thorns; such as hear the word, And the cares of this world, and the deceitfulness of riches, and the lusts of other things entering in, choke the word, and it becometh unfruitful" (Mk.); ("and bring no fruit to perfection" [Lu.]).

"And these are they which are sown on good ground; such as hear the word, and receive it, and bring forth fruit, some thirtyfold, some sixty, and some an hundred" (Mk); ("keep it, and bring forth fruit with patience" [Lu.]).

Natural Growth of the Seed   Mk. 4:26-29

In the parable of the seed Jesus taught, by reference to a law of nature, the natural invisible life-giving energy of the truths of the kingdom at work in the lives of men. A marvel is the new life of the Christian that, supplied by the Spirit, spontaneously develops and transforms him into spiritual maturity.

"So is the *kingdom of God*, as if a man should cast seed into the ground; And should sleep, and rise night and day, and the seed should spring and grow up, he knoweth not how. For the earth bringeth forth fruit of herself; first the blade, then the ear, after that the full corn in the ear. But when the fruit is brought forth, immediately he putteth in the sickle, because the harvest is come."

Tares and Wheat   Mt. 13:24-30, 36-43

While Jesus' parable of the sower illustrates the planting of the kingdom, the parable of the tares and wheat illustrates its harvesting. By similitude Jesus once more presented a foreview of the kingdom's progressive development on earth, growing among all classes of men and under varying social conditions. (Some interpret this development as the evolving of the visible Church.) Although the good seed had been sown, Jesus foresaw that Satan, whose attempt from the beginning of time had been to set up a reign counter to God's (Is. 14:13,14), would attempt to displace this heavenly kingdom by planting the spurious seed of evil "while men slept."

"The *kingdom of heaven* is likened unto a man which sowed good seed in his field: But while men slept, his enemy came and sowed tares among the wheat, and went his way." Tares are noxious weeds which in their early sprouting bear a close resemblance to the grain. The householder said "An enemy hath done this." In answer to his servants' question "Wilt thou then that we go and gather them up?" he answered "Nay; lest while ye gather up the tares, ye root up also the wheat with them. Let both grow together until the harvest: and in the time of harvest I will say to the reapers, Gather ye together first the tares, and bind them in bundles to burn them: but gather the wheat into my barn."

The disciples sought an explanation and again Jesus interpreted concisely, relating the parable to himself and his mission. His parable admonished vigilance, wisdom, righteousness, and patient endurance to the end—until "that Wicked be revealed" and cast out.

> "He that soweth the good seed is the Son of man;
> "The field is the world;
> "the good seed are the children of the kingdom;
> "but the tares are the children of the wicked one;
> "The enemy that sowed them is the devil;
> "the harvest is the end of the world;
> "and the reapers are the angels."

> "As therefore the tares are gathered and burned in the fire; so shall it be in the end of this world. The Son of man shall send forth his angels, and they shall gather out of his kingdom all things that offend, and them which do iniquity; And shall cast them into a furnace of fire: there shall be wailing and gnashing of teeth. [The outgathering]
> "Then shall the righteous shine forth as the sun in the kingdom of their Father." [The ingathering]

Both the outgathering of the wicked and the ingathering of the righteous are prophetically described in the book of Revelation.

Mustard Seed　　　Mt. 13:31,32; Mk. 4:30-32; Lu. 13:18,19

In his parable of the mustard seed, proverbially the smallest of all seeds which yet produces a plant of relatively vast size, Jesus both unveiled and veiled the fact that even "a grain" of the truth of the kingdom contains a divine energy and indestructible vitality, so that from its humblest beginnings it expands to embrace and bless the world.

> "The *kingdom of heaven* is like to a grain of mustard seed, which a man took, and sowed in his field: Which indeed is the least of all seeds: but when it is grown, it is the greatest among herbs, and becometh a tree, so that the birds of the air come and lodge in the branches thereof."

Leaven　　　Mt. 13:33; Lu. 13:20,21

The parable of the mustard seed portrayed the outward manifestation of the kingdom and its blessings in the lives of men; Jesus' parable of the leaven described its invisible workings. As leaven is the fermenting element that causes dough to rise and become light, so the leaven of Christian truth would ultimately permeate the world's thought to regenerate and transform the individual and society.

> "The *kingdom of heaven* is like unto leaven, which a woman took, and hid in three measures of meal, till the whole was leavened."

Hidden Treasure　　　Mt. 13:44

The kingdom was at hand—it had come. Jesus urged each man to recognize and evaluate it rightly. His parable of the hidden treasure pertains to the priceless value of the kingdom for the one who perceives its worth and makes it his own. In this analogy the kingdom was found unexpectedly and without a search, but to obtain what he had found he joyfully relinquished all other possessions to establish a just claim to it.

> "The *kingdom of heaven* is like unto treasure hid in a field; the which when a man hath found, he hideth, and for joy thereof goeth and selleth all that he hath, and buyeth that field."

The Pearl　　　Mt. 13:45,46

Jesus' parable of the pearl of great price is closely related to the parable of the hidden treasure in its central thought of the inestimable worth of the kingdom. Here, however, the kingdom was found as the result of fervent desire and long and earnest search; in this instance also it was obtained in the same way—only when all else had been renounced.

> "The *kingdom of heaven* is like unto a merchant man, seeking goodly pearls: Who, when he had found one pearl of great price, went and sold all that he had, and bought it."

The Dragnet　　　Mt. 13:47-50

The final parable of this series is that of the dragnet. It may be likened somewhat to the parable of the tares and wheat, dealing as it does with the same point but presenting it in another aspect and laying the burden of emphasis on the future separation of the wicked and the just. The dragnet, an object familiar in Jesus' day, was an immense net sometimes a quarter of a mile or more long which, paid out from a vessel in a large semicircle near the shore, swept the bottom of the sea and caught all the fish within its compass.

Jesus' figurative use of the dragnet was indicative of the all-embracing ministry of God's kingdom, which reaches out to draw all men irresistibly under its influence.

"The *kingdom of heaven* is like unto a net, that was cast into the sea, and gathered of every kind: Which, when it was full, they drew to shore, and sat down, and gathered the good into vessels, but cast the bad away.

"So shall it be at the end of the world: the angels shall come forth, and sever the wicked from among the just, And shall cast them into the furnace of fire: there shall be wailing and gnashing of teeth" (see Rev. 20:11-15).

At the conclusion of these parables Jesus asked the people: "Have ye understood all these things?" "Yea, Lord," they answered. Then he said: "Therefore every scribe which is instructed unto the kingdom of heaven is like unto a man that is an householder, which bringeth forth out of his treasure things new and old."

Accusations against Jesus

It will be useful here to examine the accusations repeatedly brought against Jesus by the Pharisees, the scribes, and eventually the Sadducees. These were couched in religious terms until almost the last, when political charges were raised. The accusations of a religious nature can be grouped under four general headings: blasphemy, Sabbath-breaking, improper religious conduct, madness and alliance with Satan.

Sometimes Jesus rebuked those who made such charges, allowed a silence to speak for him, or withdrew from the scene; but in every instance he acted to avoid any danger that would bring his mission to an untimely end. Occasionally, however, he deliberately challenged restrictive rabbinical traditions. As he dealt with these accusations he imparted many essential Christian truths.

Charge of Blasphemy

To blaspheme is to slander, defame, or dishonor the character of God, to speak evil of His holy name or person. Jesus' repeated claim to Sonship with God and to possession of God's divine attributes of power were blasphemous in the eyes of the scribes and Pharisees. To them this unknown Galilean was usurping the prerogatives of God. According to Mosaic Law the crime of blasphemy was punishable by death (Lev. 24:16).

When Jesus healed the palsied man, saying, "Son, thy sins be forgiven thee," the scribes said to themselves, "Why doth this man thus speak blasphemies? who can forgive sins but God only?" But he substantiated his claim by healing the man, making evident the fact that he did have this power (Mk. 2:5-12). (Later the Christian Church pronounced forgiveness in the name of Christ.)

When Jesus declared to the Jews, following his healing of the infirm man, "My Father worketh hitherto, and I work," they sought to kill him, enraged that he spoke in such familiar terms of God, "making himself equal with God" (Jn. 5:17,18).

When Jesus later asserted "I and my Father are one," the Jews took up stones to stone him. He reasoned with them: "Many good works have I shewed you from my Father; for which of those works do ye stone me?" They answered, "For a good work we stone thee not; but for blasphemy; and because that thou, being a man, makest thyself God." Jesus cited Scriptural authority for his affirmation of unity with the Father, asking: "Is it not written in your law, I said, Ye are gods? [Ps. 82:6] If he called them gods, unto whom the word of God came, and the scripture cannot be broken; say ye of him, whom the Father hath sanctified, and sent into the world, Thou blasphemest; because I said, I am the Son of God?" Calling their attention to his works, he justified his claim: "If I do not the works of my Father, believe me not. But if I do, though ye believe not me, believe the works: that ye may know, and believe, that the Father is in me, and I in him." But again they tried to take him (Jn. 10:30-39).

When he cast a devil out of the man who was dumb, the Pharisees and the scribes abandoned discretion and bared their enmity openly: "This fellow doth not cast out devils, but by Beelzebub the prince of the devils." Jesus instantly exposed the fallacy of their reasoning, "If Satan cast out Satan, he is divided against himself; how shall then his kingdom stand?" Turning the accusation against them, he asserted that *they* were the blasphemers since they were denying the power of God: "He that is not with me is against me; and he that gathereth not with me scattereth abroad. . . . All manner of sin and blasphemy shall be forgiven unto men: but the blasphemy against the Holy Ghost shall not be forgiven . . . neither in this world, neither in the world to come" (Mt. 12:24-32).

At Jesus' trial before the Sanhedrin, the high priest Caiaphas demanded, "Art thou the Christ, the Son of the Blessed?" When Jesus answered, "I am: and ye shall see the Son of man sitting on the right hand of power, and coming in the clouds of heaven," the council formally accused him of blasphemy and condemned him to death (Mk. 14:61-64).

Charge of Sabbath-breaking

The Hebrew Sabbath of the Old Testament was Israel's most sacred religious institution, a sign of its covenant relation with God. It was a day of cessation from labor, a holy day of worship in accordance with the Fourth Commandment, and under Mosaic Law its nonobservance was punishable by death (Ex. 31:14). By New Testament times the scribes and Pharisees had laid upon the observance of this day a burden of minute regulations.

No feature of the Jewish system was so marked as its extraordinary strictness in the outward observance of the Sabbath, as a day of entire rest. The scribes had elaborated, from the command of Moses, a vast array of prohibitions and injunctions, covering the whole of social, individual, and public life, and carried it to the extreme of ridiculous caricature. Lengthened rules were prescribed as to the kinds of knots which might legally be tied on Sabbath. The camel-driver's knot and the sailor's were unlawful, and it was equally illegal to tie or to loose them. A knot which could be untied with one hand might be undone. A shoe or sandal, a woman's cup, a wine or oilskin, or a flesh-pot might be tied. A pitcher at a spring might be tied to the body-sash, but not with a cord.

It was forbidden to write two letters, either with the right hand or the left, whether of the same size or of different sizes, or with different inks, or in different languages, or with any pigment . . . or anything that can make marks. . . . But they might be written on any dark fluid, on the sap of a fruit-tree, on road-dust, on sand, or on anything in which the writing did not remain. . . .

The quantity of food that might be carried on Sabbath from one place to another was duly settled. It must be less in bulk than a dried fig: if of honey, only as much as would anoint a wound; if water, as much as would make eyesalve; if paper, as much as would be put in a phylactery; if ink, as much as would form two letters.

To kindle or extinguish a fire on the Sabbath was a great desecration of the day, nor was even sickness allowed to violate Rabbinical rules. It was forbidden to give an emetic on Sabbath, to set a broken bone, or put back a dislocated joint, though some Rabbis, more liberal, held that whatever endangered life made the Sabbath law void, "for the commands were given to Israel only that they might live by them."

. . .From the decline of the sun on Friday, to its setting, was Sabbath-eve. . . . All food must be prepared, all vessels washed, and all lights kindled, before sunset. . . . The refinements of Rabbinical casuistry were, indeed, endless. To wear one kind of sandals was carrying a burden, while to wear another kind was not. One might carry a burden on his shoulder, but it must not be slung between two. It was unlawful to go out with wooden sandals or shoes which had nails in the soles, or with a shoe and a slipper, unless one foot were hurt. . . .

In an insincere age such excessive strictness led to constant evasions by Pharisees and Sadducees alike. To escape the restrictions which limited a journey on Sabbath to 2,000 cubits from a town or city, they carried food on Friday evening to a spot that distance beyond the walls, and assumed, by a fiction, that this made that spot also their dwelling. They could thus, on the Sabbath, walk the full distance to it, and an equal distance beyond it, this journey being only the legal distance from the fictitious place of residence![35]

When Jesus ignored or took issue with these irksome and spiritually unnecessary restrictions he was accused of Sabbath-breaking. This offense was a flagrant sin in their eyes, second only to that of the blasphemy of his Messianic claim.

On a Sabbath Jesus healed the man who had been an invalid for thirty-eight years, ordering him to take up his bed and walk. When the man obeyed, the Jews reprimanded him: "It is the sabbath day: it is not lawful for thee to carry thy bed." Learning that it was Jesus who had so commanded, they tried to kill Jesus (Jn. 5:10-16).

When his disciples picked ears of corn on the Sabbath as they went through the cornfields, the Pharisees asked, "Why do they on the sabbath day that which is not lawful?" Jesus replied with a query: "Have ye never read what David did, when he had need, and was an hungred, he, and they that were with him? How he went into the house of God . . . and did eat the shewbread, which is not lawful to eat but for the priests, and gave also to them which were with him?" "The sabbath was made for man, and not man for the sabbath: Therefore the Son of man is Lord also of the sabbath," he said. Matthew adds to this account Jesus' words: "Or have ye not read in the law, how that on the sabbath days the priests in the temple profane the sabbath, and are blameless? But I say unto you, That in this place is one greater than the temple" (Mt. 12:1-6; Mk. 2:24-28).

One Sabbath as Jesus taught in the synagogue, he saw a man with a withered hand. The Pharisees and scribes challenged: "Is it lawful to heal on the sabbath days?"; among the Pharisees healing practices were prohibited on the Sabbath unless a life were in actual danger. Jesus asked: "What man shall there be among you, that shall have one sheep, and if it fall into a pit on the sabbath day, will he not lay hold on it, and lift it out? How much then is a man better than a sheep?" He summarized: "Wherefore it is lawful to do well on the sabbath days" and, turning to the man, healed him (Mt. 12:10-13).

This same charge of unlawful healing was made when Jesus healed the woman who had been crippled for eighteen years (Lu. 13:14).

When Jesus effected on a Sabbath day the marvelous healing of the man born blind, the Pharisees argued among themselves, some saying "This man is not of God, because he keepeth not the sabbath day," others saying "How can a man that is a sinner do such miracles?" (Jn. 9:16).

Although the rabbis were increasingly incensed at Jesus' continued infraction of their Sabbath prohibitions, they never brought a formal charge of Sabbath-breaking against him; the mercy of his works and the sympathy and approval of the people restrained them.

Charge of Improper Religious Conduct

By New Testament times the conduct of the Jew was under constant rabbinical scrutiny. As a member of God's holy Israel he was to keep himself holy. He therefore felt impelled to obey every Mosaic law and each scribal regulation. If he did not, the penalty was both exclusion from religious worship and social ostracism. The intent of these legislations was the prevention of sin and defilement. Contact with any unclean thing caused defilement and the Law therefore made distinctions as to what was "clean" and "unclean." The Law forbade the worship of idols, social contact with the heathen, the eating of the flesh of unclean animals (Lev. 11; Deut. 14:2-21). Certain purificatory rites were enjoined for women after childbirth (Lev. 12), after contact with a human corpse (Num. 19:11-22) or the bodies of dead animals (Lev. 5:2), for lepers (Lev. 14), for discharges of the body (Lev. 15), and for certain unavoidable contaminations.

By Jesus' day the catalogue of unclean things that could cause ritual defilement had grown out of all bounds through the casuistry of the Pharisees. Ceremonial rites of purification had been highly elaborated, extending even to the washing of hands, the preparation of foods, the washing of food vessels, and so on. The spirit of the Law was entombed in hollow ritual.

When this new teacher from Galilee failed to conform to the trivia of rabbinical regulations relating to purification or to keep his person withdrawn from those individuals whose presence was considered polluting, the scribes and Pharisees accused him of irreligious conduct. Jesus' teachings abolished the need for ceremonial purification and changed the emphasis from outward cleanliness to inward purity of mind and heart.

"Why," the Pharisees and scribes asked critically, "walk not thy disciples according to the tradition of the elders, but eat bread with unwashen hands?" (See p. 273). Jesus rebuked them: "Well hath Esaias prophesied of you hypocrites ... This people honoureth me with their lips, but their heart is far from me. Howbeit in vain do they worship me, teaching for doctrines the commandments of men. For laying aside the commandment of God, ye hold the tradition of men, as the washing of pots and cups: and many other such like things ye do. ... Full well ye reject the commandment of God, that ye may keep your own tradition. ... There is nothing from without a man,

that entering into him can defile him: but the things which come out of him, those are they that defile the man" (Mk. 7:5-15).

A similar charge of improper conduct was implied when Jesus dined at a Pharisee's house and, to his host's astonishment, sat down to eat without ceremonially washing his hands. Jesus responded, "Now do ye Pharisees make clean the outside of the cup and the platter; but your inward part is full of ravening and wickedness. Ye fools, did not he that made that which is without make that which is within also?" (Lu. 11:39,40).

"Why eateth your Master with publicans and sinners?" the apostles were asked when the Pharisees saw Jesus at the feast of Matthew the publican. Publicans were considered apostate because of their close association with the Gentiles, so the rabbis (who held themselves aloof from social outcasts lest they become polluted) were shocked that a teacher of his stature would let himself be seen in such company (see also p. 255). To Jesus, fear of pollution weighed not at all in the scale of mercy, and his response was "They that be whole need not a physician, but they that are sick. But go ye and learn what that meaneth, I will have mercy, and not sacrifice" (Mt. 9:11-13; compare Hos. 6:6).

The fear of contamination that so troubled the Pharisees did not mar the ministry of Jesus, who restored to health the socially ostracized who had need. On one occasion Jesus put out his hand and touched a leper before healing him (Mt. 8:3), and later he did not hesitate to approach and touch the bier of a dead man in Nain and restore him to life (Lu. 7:14).

"Why do the disciples of John and of the Pharisees fast, but thy disciples fast not?" This question referred mainly to the fasts religious Jews imposed upon themselves voluntarily. To chasten the soul one sat sorrowful of face in sackcloth and ashes (see p. 61). Some of the Pharisees fasted as frequently as twice a week to impress others with their piety. Jesus taught that with the kingdom of heaven at hand this was not a time for mourning: "Can the children of the bridechamber fast, while the bridegroom is with them? as long as they have the bridegroom with them, they cannot fast. But the days will come, when the bridegroom shall be taken away from them, and then shall they fast in those days" (Mk. 2:18-20).

He went on to teach by two short parables—the new patch on an old garment, the new wine in old bottles—that his new religion could not be added or adapted to the ritualistic forms of Judaism: "New wine must be put into new bottles." "The joy of the kingdom does not go well with fasting. There must be congruity between faith and form. The new faith must make its own new forms."[36] Jesus instructed his followers in the Sermon on the Mount to shun the frequently empty ceremonial display of mourning or humility, and instead to fast in secret (Mt. 6:16-18).

Charge of Madness and of Alliance with Satan

Jesus' enemies could not deny the validity of his miraculous works. Infuriated at their own inability to counteract his teachings or duplicate his healings, they resorted to slander and insinuation, declaring he was mad.

Jesus was attracting such crowds during the second period of his Galilean ministry that wherever he went people pressed him so continually he scarcely had time to eat. His zeal in the face of the Pharisees' hostility must have appeared fanatical to some, so that at one point his friends—and perhaps his relatives—concerned for his safety, "went out to lay hold on him: for they said, He is beside himself." But the scribes who had come from Jerusalem interpreted his fervor maliciously, claiming that he was in league with the devil: "He hath Beelzebub, and by the prince of the devils casteth he out devils." Jesus warned them in the strongest of terms that to call the power by which he acted diabolical was to commit the unpardonable sin of blasphemy against the Holy Ghost, "because they said, He hath an unclean spirit" (Mk. 3:21,22,28-30).

There was division among his listeners at his extraordinary statement, in his discourse on the Good Shepherd, that he would lay down his life but would take it again at his Father's command. Many said, "He hath a devil, and is mad; why hear ye him?" Others, remembering his healing of the man born blind, said, "These are not the words of him that hath a devil. Can a devil open the eyes of the blind?" (Jn. 10:20,21).

These accusations precipitated recurrent crises, but each served only to advance the undeniable truth that this was the Son of God, speaking God's word with power. The enmity of the Pharisees, scribes, and Sadducees, however, hardened into relentless resistance, and repeatedly they sought to destroy him:
—"watched" to find accusation against him
  —"murmured" at his reception of sinners
    —"sent forth spies" to find treason in his words
      —"assembled together"
        —"consulted" to take him by subtlety
          —"covenanted" with Judas
            —"delivered him to Pilate" for judgment
              —"were instant with loud voices" to crucify

The succeeding weeks of Jesus' Galilean ministry were marked by a number of startling miracles. His apostles were filled with amazement by his stilling of a storm—"What manner of man is this, that even the winds and the sea obey him!" (Mt. 8:27). He restored to sanity the demoniac of Gadara (Mt. 8:28-34; Mk. 5:1-20; Lu. 8:26-39; see p. 362); at Capernaum he healed the woman with an issue of blood and raised the daughter of Jairus (Mt. 9:18-26; Mk. 5:21-43; Lu. 8:40-56; see pp. 362, 370).

Second Rejection at Nazareth
Mt. 13:54-58; Mk. 6:1-6

As Jesus set out from Capernaum for Nazareth he healed two blind men and a dumb demoniac (Mt. 9:27-34). On this second visit to his own village, this time accompanied by the Twelve, Jesus again taught in the synagogue. Word of his miracles had preceded him, but the Nazarenes still failed to see beyond the old associations and refused to credit his Messiahship. They asked, "From whence hath this man these things? and what wisdom is this which is given unto him, that even such mighty works are wrought by his hands? Is not this the carpenter, the son of Mary, the brother of James, and Joses, and of Juda, and Simon? and are not his sisters here with us?"

Jesus repeated what he had said at his first rejection, "A prophet is not without honour, but in his own country, and among his own kin, and in his own house." It is recorded that he "could there do no mighty work, save that he laid his hands upon a few sick folk, and healed them." Knowing the futility of further appeal he left Nazareth, never to return. (One is inclined too often to think of Jesus' "mighty work" as only healings and spectacular miracles when his real "mighty work" was greater than any of these. His whole ministry was dedicated to the proving of his sonship with God and the deathlessness of life—and each day he was carrying forward that proof, for all mankind, to the final issues of resurrection and ascension. His disbelieving fellow townsmen cut themselves off from his blessings and failed to contribute to the strengthening of his life work.)

Commissioning of the Twelve
Mt. 9:35-11:1; Mk. 6:7-13; Lu. 9:1-6

From Nazareth Jesus and his apostles continued a circuit of Galilee, relying for food and shelter mainly on traditional Hebrew hospitality (see p. 44). Certain women who had been healed also accompanied the little band and ministered to its daily needs from their own resources. Among these were Mary Magdalene; Joanna, the wife of Herod's steward Chuza; Susanna; Salome; and Mary, wife of Cleophas and mother of James the Less.

As Jesus journeyed, the wretched, the poor, the sick gathered about him for healing, and when he saw that they were as sheep without a shepherd, he was filled with compassionate love for them. The Twelve as a group had been closely associated with him now for more than six months and had had the continuous benefit of his personal teaching. They were ready for active service; so, providing for the present and preparing for the future, Jesus commissioned them to preach and to heal. This new and further step in the organization of the kingdom was far-reaching in importance and significance, although at the time it went almost unnoticed by the political and religious authorities.

Jesus' plan was to send the Twelve before him on an evangelizing mission. Invested with his power and authority, they went out "two and two," facing without him the demands of any situation they might encounter. With great care he instructed them where they were to go, what they were to preach, and what they were to do. He limited this mission to the Jewish population of Galilee: "Go not into the way of the Gentiles, and into any city of the Samaritans enter ye not: But go rather to the lost sheep of the house of Israel."

His message was to be their message: "As ye go, preach, saying, The kingdom of heaven is at hand." Their works were to be patterned on his: "Heal the sick, cleanse the lepers, raise the dead, cast out devils." The spirit of their giving was to be as generous and selfless as his: "Freely ye have received, freely give." They were admonished to make no provision for their journey, "for the workman is worthy of his meat," and to enter only the homes and villages which welcomed them.

He fortified them against the persecution they would experience both now and when their mission was more universal in scope. Though brought before councils and kings, the Spirit would teach them what to answer. Jesus spelled out the cost of discipleship— the hatred of men, even of immediate families—but comforted them with the reminder of the enmity and slander he, their Master, had endured. Above all, he assured them that God would reward their courageous service (Mt. 10:16-42).

These formidable challenges did not deter them. During the next three or four months the apostles traveled through the villages of Galilee (according to Josephus, some two hundred forty), preaching and healing everywhere.

They rejoined Jesus somewhere in the neighborhood of Capernaum to report what had been accomplished, but as soon as their presence was known the people gathered in such numbers that the apostles had neither privacy to talk to him nor leisure to eat. Seeing that the Twelve needed sustenance and rest, Jesus pointed out the wisdom of proper self-care: "Come ye yourselves apart into a desert place, and rest a while" (Mk. 6:30-32; Lu. 9:10). Quietly they withdrew to a small plain near Bethsaida, some six miles away,

crossing the tip of the Sea of Galilee by boat. Seclusion was doubly desirable—not only because of the press of the multitudes but also because word had just been received from the Baptist's disciples that John had been beheaded by Herod Antipas (Mt. 14:13). It was rumored, too, that Herod was inquiring if Jesus were the Baptist risen from the dead (Mt. 14:1,2).

Feeding the Five Thousand   Mt. 14:13-23; Mk. 6:33-46; Lu. 9:10-17; Jn. 6:1-15

There was little opportunity for seclusion; the people, anticipating Jesus' destination, outran him along the shore. Touched anew by their eagerness to hear, Jesus again fed their spiritual hunger and healed their sick. Though "the day was now far spent" they lingered to hear more, until the Twelve urged, "This is a desert place. . . . Send them away, that they may go into the country round about . . . and buy themselves bread: for they have nothing to eat."

But Jesus vetoed their suggestion, answering, "They need not depart; give ye them to eat." Turning to Philip he asked, "Whence shall we buy bread, that these may eat?" He said this "to prove him: for he himself knew what he would do." When they told him of the meager supply on hand of but five loaves and two fishes, Jesus commanded that they bring these to him and seat the people. Matthew numbers them "five thousand men, beside women and children," and Mark reports "they sat down in ranks, by hundreds, and by fifties (a description that certainly suggests an eyewitness report).

Jesus then took the loaves and fishes and, "looking up to heaven, he blessed, and brake, and gave the loaves to his disciples, and the disciples to the multitude." The few brief phrases "he himself knew what he would do," "looking up to heaven," and "when he had given thanks" (Jn. 6:11) bespeak his prayer and the source to which he looked for the fulfillment of their needs. He confidently drew on the infinite resources of God, and his knowledge of God's beneficence abundantly multiplied the few loaves and fishes so that when the apostles had distributed them to the people all were filled, and twelve baskets of fragments remained. (These baskets [kophinos] were the handbaskets in which the Hebrews carried their provisions when traveling.)

Moses had fed his people in the wilderness with manna; it was a rabbinical teaching that Israel's Messiah would do the same. The five thousand, seeing this great miracle, were convinced that here was their Messianic King: "This is of a truth that prophet that should come into the world." The expectation of the Messianic kingdom at once excited them. Here was a man, they thought, who could do all things that Moses did—let us make him king! With him at their head they would surely throw off Roman tyranny. Jesus had long since overcome the temptation to wield worldly power as a means to his ends, so when he "perceived that they would come and take him by force, to make him a king," he immediately sent his apostles by boat toward Capernaum to take them away from this dangerous excitement; dispersed the multitude; and himself quietly withdrew "into a mountain apart to pray."

Walking on the Sea   Mt. 14:24-33; Mk. 6:47-52; Jn. 6:16-21

While Jesus remained in prayer, the apostles' progress across the open stretch of water was hindered by storm—"the wind was contrary." The significance of the miracle of the feeding of the five thousand was for a time eclipsed in their minds by the commotion they had just witnessed. Although it was night, from his mountain top Jesus "saw" them toiling at their oars. Between three and six o'clock in the morning (the fourth watch of the night) Jesus came to them, "walking on the sea"—giving proof of his dominion over still another form of matter.

The apostles thought they were seeing an apparition, but immediately he reassured them: "Be of good cheer; it is I; be not afraid." When Peter realized it was the Master, his faith rose to new heights. That he caught a glimpse of this dominion and was eager to exercise it himself is obvious from the Biblical narrative, for at Jesus' invitation, "Come," he "walked on the water, to go to Jesus"; he walked until he looked at the turbulent waves, then his faith failed and he began to sink. Jesus immediately caught him by the hand, saying, "O thou of little faith, wherefore didst thou doubt?" And "when they were come into the ship, the wind ceased." A new reverence pervaded the hearts of the Twelve and they avowed, "Of a truth thou art the Son of God."

John alone records another startling miracle coincident with this event: "Then they willingly received him into the ship: and immediately the ship was at the land whither they went."

Discourse
Christ the Bread of Life   Jn. 6:22-71

The next day when some of the multitude Jesus had fed discovered he was gone, they pursued him to Capernaum and found him in the synagogue. Aware of their motive, he chided, "Ye seek me, not because ye saw the miracles but because ye did eat of the loaves, and were filled." He deliberately discouraged their hopes though he foresaw that he would lose much of his popularity; and, as he had turned the Samaritan woman's thought from the water of Jacob's Well to

the "water of life," so he now turned their thought from the bread which perishes to the "bread of life," urging "Labour not for the meat which perisheth, but for that meat which endureth unto everlasting life, which the Son of man shall give unto you: for him hath God the Father sealed."

When they asked "What shall we do, that we might work the works of God?" he answered "This is the work of God, that ye believe on him whom he hath sent."

Some among them, possibly scribes and Pharisees from Judaea, challenged—"What sign shewest thou then, that we may see, and believe thee?"—and reminded him of the heavenly manna Moses had given Israel. In reply Jesus declared himself, the Christ, to be the real bread of life: "Moses gave you not that bread from heaven; but my Father giveth you the true bread from heaven. For the bread of God is he which cometh down from heaven, and giveth life unto the world." When some of his listeners petitioned "Lord, evermore give us this bread," he declared plainly "I am the bread of life: he that cometh to me shall never hunger." At his assertion that he came from heaven his hearers muttered among themselves, for was he not the son of Joseph and Mary of Nazareth? But he patiently pointed out that those taught of God would understand the truth of his words.

Speaking now almost entirely in the first person, he reiterated his claim that faith in the Son would give a man everlasting life: "I am that bread of life. Your fathers did eat manna in the wilderness, and are dead. This is the bread which cometh down from heaven, that a man may eat thereof, and not die. I am the living bread which came down from heaven: if any man eat of this bread, he shall live for ever: and the bread that I will give is my flesh, which I will give for the life of the world. . . . He that eateth my flesh, and drinketh my blood, dwelleth in me, and I in him. As the living Father hath sent me, and I live by the Father: so he that eateth me, even he shall live by me."

"How can this man give us his flesh to eat?" they asked. They should have understood him, for the figurative meaning of eating and drinking was familiar to his Jewish listeners. The words nevertheless confused them; they could not see that he meant they must acknowledge that he came from God, that his teachings therefore were from God, and that they must take into their own lives these truths and into their hearts the same spirit of love that motivated him. Still seeing only the person of the man Jesus, many found his words "an hard saying." "Doth this offend you?" asked Jesus. "What and if ye shall see the Son of man ascend up where he was before? It is the spirit that quickeneth; the flesh profiteth nothing: the words that I speak unto you, they are spirit, and they are life."

This discourse marked a crisis in Jesus' ministry—a decisive break with the people, for from this time on many disciples turned away. Their short-lived enthusiasm dissipated when it became clear that Jesus' aims were immeasurably beyond nationalistic hopes. His season of popularity with the people was over.

When Jesus asked his apostles, "Will ye also go away?" Peter voiced their unshaken loyalty: "Lord, to whom shall we go? thou hast the words of eternal life."

Discourse
Traditions of the Elders Mt. 15:1-20; Mk. 7:1-23

The break with the people was followed by a clash between Jesus and hostile Pharisees and scribes sent up from Jerusalem to harass him. They found fault when they saw Jesus' disciples were not observing the prescribed Judaic ritual of washing their hands before eating.

> The legal washing of the hands before eating was especially sacred to the Rabbinist; not to do so was a crime as great as to eat the flesh of swine. . . .
>
> It was laid down that the hands were first to be washed clean. The tips of the ten fingers were then joined and lifted up so that the water ran down to the elbows, then turned down so that it might run off to the ground. Fresh water was poured on them as they were lifted up, and twice again as they hung down. The washing itself was to be done by rubbing the fist of one hand in the hollow of the other. When the hands were washed before eating they must be held upwards; when after it, downwards, but so that the water should not run beyond the knuckles. The vessel used must be held first in the right, then in the left hand; the water was to be poured first on the right, then on the left hand, and at every third time the words repeated: "Blessed art Thou who hast given us the command to wash the hands."
>
> . . . Hand-washing before prayer, or touching anything in the morning, was as rigidly observed, for evil spirits might have defiled the hands in the night. To touch the mouth, nose, ear, eyes, or the one hand with the other, before the rite, was to incur the risk of disease in the part touched. The occasions that demanded the observance were countless: it must be done even after cutting the nails, or killing a flea. The more water used, the more piety. . . . If one had not been out it was enough to pour water on the hands; but one coming in from without needed to plunge his hands into the water, for he knew not what uncleanness might have been near him while in the streets, and this plunging could not be done except in a spot where there were not less than sixty gallons of water.[37]

The Pharisees asked: "Why do thy disciples transgress the tradition of the elders?" Jesus retorted: "Why do *ye* also transgress the commandment of God by your tradition?," purposely taking issue with their superficial superstitious concept of what constituted

Washing of the hands before and after eating. *Popular and Critical Bible Encyclopaedia.*

defilement. He openly rebuked this ceremonialism, branding them hypocrites; they were teaching as the Law their own doctrines: "For laying aside the commandment of God, ye hold the tradition of men, as the washing of pots and cups: and many other such like things ye do." He pinpointed one of these errors—their hypocritical use of the oath Corban to avoid fulfilling their filial duty—thus making "of none effect" the Fifth Commandment (Mk. 7:10-13). (Corban originally meant a sacrificial offering to God [Lev. 1:2], but by Jesus' time it had become the mere mouthing of a vow.)

Turning to the people, Jesus spoke with authority: "Hearken unto me every one of you, and understand: There is nothing from without a man, that entering into him can defile him: but the things which come out of him, those are they that defile the man."

The disciples later reported the Pharisees' displeasure at his words. Jesus was ready with his answer: "Every plant, which my heavenly Father hath not planted, shall be rooted up. Let them alone: they be blind leaders of the blind. And if the blind lead the blind, both shall fall into the ditch."

When they asked for an explanation of this new principle of what constituted real defilement, he replied, "Are ye also yet without understanding? Do not ye yet understand, that whatsoever entereth in at the mouth goeth into the belly, and is cast out into the draught? But those things which proceed out of the mouth come forth from the heart; and they defile the man. For out of the heart proceed evil thoughts, murders, adulteries, fornications, thefts, false witness, blasphemies: These are the things which defile a man: but to eat with unwashen hands defileth not a man."

With this incident the second Galilean period closed.

Third Period of the Galilean Ministry

This period of approximately seven months began in early summer 29 A.D. and was spent largely in journeys that took Jesus and the Twelve beyond the borders of his own province. Galilee was no longer a fruitful field for evangelization because of the gradual disaffection of the people and the open breach with the Pharisees. For a short while Jesus went north to the coastal cities of Phoenician Tyre and Sidon. Slowly making his way homeward, he went east and south by a circuitous route, passing through Decapolis, a region that included the territory of a league of ten cities originally colonized by the Greeks after Alexander's conquest. These prosperous cities were independently administered but subject to Roman authority, and among their racially mixed inhabitants Jesus found an eager audience.

Again withdrawing from Galilee, this time to the Gentile city of Caesarea Philippi about thirty-five miles north of Capernaum, he turned his full attention to the further training of the apostles and to the strengthening of their faith and understanding of his Messiahship. During this journey came the experience of his transfiguration and his revealing announcements to the disciples of his coming death and resurrection.

After returning to Capernaum, Jesus continued on to Jerusalem to attend the Feast of Tabernacles. Despite the mounting hostility of the Pharisees and Sadducees, he stood boldly in the Temple to teach that he was the Light of the world and the bearer of the truth which sets men free. The Pharisees and chief priests sent officers to seize him, but they could not, "because his hour was not yet come."

Feeding the Four Thousand

Mt. 15:29-38; Mk. 8:1-9

A journey into the Gentile territory of Tyre and Sidon, northwest of Galilee, opened the third period of Jesus' Galilean ministry (Mt. 15:21; Mk. 7:24). These proud Phoenician cities, mentioned often in the Old Testament for their wealth and commerce, were situated some twenty miles apart on the Mediterranean coast. Here Jesus hoped for privacy and time for quiet communion with his apostles, but his fame had preceded him and even here the people sought him out. Mark says "he could not be hid." Shortly after the healing of the Syrophoenician woman's daughter (Mt. 15:22-28; Mk. 7:25-30; see p. 363), he turned eastward, crossed the headwaters of the Jordan, and journeyed slowly through the non-Jewish district of Decapolis to the Sea of Galilee. Here he healed a deaf man who also had a speech impediment (Mk. 7:31-37; see p. 363). For some months he preached, gathering considerable numbers of adherents. His compassion embraced the new lambs of his flock and he healed their lame, blind, dumb, and maimed.

At the close of this circuit Jesus spent three days preaching to a crowd of four thousand; before dismissing them, he said to his apostles, "I will not send them away fasting, lest they faint in the way." As he had fed five thousand in Galilee, so here he fed four thousand. He commanded his listeners to sit on the ground and, taking the seven loaves and the few small fishes that were at hand, he "gave thanks, and brake, and gave to his disciples . . . and they did set them before the people. . . . So they did eat, and were filled: and they took up of the broken meat that was left seven baskets." (These baskets [Gk. *spuris*] were the storage hampers used by Gentiles, containers of the size in which Paul made his escape from a window in Damascus [Acts 9:25; compare p. 391].)

Pharisees Require a Sign

Mt. 15:39-16:12; Mk. 8:10-21

Shortly after feeding the four thousand Jesus and his apostles embarked for Magdala, a city on the west shore of the Sea of Galilee. Back once more among the Jews, the Master was again subjected to Pharisaic skepticism. The rabbis sought of him some supernatural sign, shutting their minds to the numerous miracles he had already performed. Jesus' patience was tried by such obduracy and he "sighed deeply in his spirit." His words, his miracles, seemed lost. His rebuke was sharp: "O ye hypocrites, ye can discern the face of the sky; but can ye not discern the signs of the times [events that pointed, in accord with Old Testament prophecy, to the presence of the Messiah among them]? A wicked and adulterous generation seeketh after a sign; and there shall no sign be given unto it, but the sign of the prophet Jonas [the sign of resurrection]" (compare Mt. 12:39-41).

After the Pharisees' stubborn refusal to accept his miracles as sufficient evidence of his claims, Jesus left for Bethsaida, making the ten-mile journey by boat. His spirit was soon tried again, this time by the obtuseness of his own apostles, whose faith was clouded by the Pharisees' resistant attitude.

As the apostles left the boat at Bethsaida they discovered they had brought with them only one loaf of bread. He—who had just given them a "sign from heaven" in the feeding of the four thousand—immediately uttered a warning; they were forgetting the lesson he had taught of God's bounty always at hand: "Take heed and beware of the leaven of the Pharisees and of the Sadducees." They did not grasp his meaning, thinking he spoke of bread leaven. Jesus reminded them of the two feedings of the multitudes. His questions, put in rapid succession, were a rebuke which quickened their perception.

"Why reason ye, because ye have no bread?"
"Perceive ye not yet, neither understand?"
"Have ye your heart yet hardened?"
"Having eyes, see ye not?"
"Having ears, hear ye not?"
"Do ye not remember?"
"When I brake the five loaves among five thousand, how many baskets full of fragments took ye up?"
"When the seven among four thousand, how many baskets full of fragments took ye up?"
"How is it that ye do not understand?"

At last the apostles realized that the leaven to which he referred was "the doctrine" of the Pharisees and Sadducees—the teachings that deadened trust in God.

Peter's Confession concerning Christ
Mt. 16:13-20; Mk. 8:27-30; Lu. 9:18-21

After healing a blind man at Bethsaida (Mk. 8:22-26; see p. 364), Jesus again went away from the contentious atmosphere of Galilee, this time setting out northward with his apostles for Caesarea Philippi at the foot of majestic, snowcapped Mount Hermon in the Anti-Lebanon range. As they walked together, he questioned them to determine how much they understood of his real spiritual nature. He had already been called the Messiah or Christ and he had often implied that fact; now he sought their clear and open avowal. Pausing along the way he asked, "Whom do men say that I the Son of man am?" They enumerated the differing opinions current among the people: John the Baptist, Elijah, Jeremiah, one of the prophets. Despite all his miracles and preaching it was evident that few thought of him with certainty as the Messiah.

Desiring from them a higher concept of himself, he persisted: "But whom say ye that I am?" Instantly Simon Peter spoke for them all: "*Thou art the Christ, the Son of the living God.*" Commending his perception, Jesus said, "Blessed art thou, Simon Bar-jona: for flesh and blood hath not revealed it unto thee, but my Father which is in heaven." Peter's confession marked a milestone in the advancing understanding of the Twelve. They openly acknowledged Jesus not as a great prophet, not as a national Messiah, but as truly "the Christ of God." Stirred to a greater comprehension that the *living* Son of the *living* God was with them, they realized that for them there

could be no empty profession of faith, no *dead* works.

At this direct acknowledgment Jesus proceeded for the first time to speak of his Church and to ground it on the solid rock of the truth Peter had voiced: "I say also unto thee, That thou art Peter, and upon this rock I will build my church; and the gates of hell shall not prevail against it."

> **My church**, with emphasis on the *My*, signifying that the Church is not a human but a divine institution. In this passage the Church is identified with the Kingdom of Heaven.[38]

It was inevitable that a new institution should arise to carry forward his gospel, for the Temple and synagogue had proved unequal to the task. That Peter clearly understood the foundation rock of this Church to be the Christ is seen in his early preaching after Pentecost and in his writings (Acts 4:10-12; I Pet. 2:4-8).

"I will give unto thee the keys of the kingdom of heaven," Jesus promised, "and whatsoever thou shalt bind [forbid] on earth shall be bound [forbidden] in heaven: and whatsoever thou shalt loose [permit] on earth shall be loosed [permitted] in heaven"—the stewardship of the mysteries of the kingdom, later extended to all the apostles (Mt. 18:18). Their understanding of truth would guide them in upholding the heavenly standard in all things.

First Foretelling of Death and Resurrection
Mt. 16:21-28; Mk. 8:31-9:1; Lu. 9:22-27

Almost immediately his teachings took on a new and somber note. Having drawn from the Twelve their deep conviction of himself as the Christ, Jesus deemed them ready to face his disclosure of the sufferings that lay before him and he now announced for the first time his coming death and resurrection. He knew that the future held persecution for him and testing almost beyond endurance for his apostles, so he began carefully to buttress their faith and prepare them to meet the "stumbling block" of the cross: "The Son of man must suffer many things, and be rejected of the elders and chief priests and scribes, and be slain, and be raised the third day."

Peter, always the first to speak, rejected this startling new conception: "Be it far from thee, Lord: this shall not be unto thee." The idea of a suffering Messiah, wholly inconsistent with the Jewish hope of a triumphant King, was inconceivable to Peter. With the same command with which Jesus had silenced Satan in the wilderness, the Master instantly reproved Peter: "Get thee behind me, Satan: thou art an offence unto me: for thou savourest not the things that be of God, but those that be of men." This was the voice of temptation from one of his own trying again to turn him from fulfilling his mission according to the divine plan of salvation—from giving proof of life eternal. He was willing to suffer for mankind and "[pour] out his soul unto death," for in time he would see "the travail of his soul, and . . . be satisfied" (Is. 53:11,12).

The uncovering of a state of thought that shrank from persecution and suffering presented the Master with an opportunity to teach the apostles an essential requirement of discipleship—his followers must be willing to face and endure suffering, to surrender all for Christ, that they might gain the kingdom. As he was obediently taking up his cross, so they must take up theirs: "If any man will come after me, let him deny himself, and take up his cross, and follow me. For whosoever will save his life shall lose it: and whosoever will lose his life for my sake shall find it."

He told them that though they would see him subjected to shame and humiliation, they would also see him manifested in glory: "For the Son of man shall come in the glory of his Father with his angels; and then he shall reward every man according to his works." They were not to be reluctant to place him first in their lives: "Whosoever . . . shall be ashamed of me and of my words in this adulterous and sinful generation; of him also shall the Son of man be ashamed, when he cometh in the glory of his Father with the holy angels."

He closed this foreshadowing of his death and resurrection with the assurance that some of those present would see the establishment of the kingdom: "I tell you of a truth, there be some standing here, which shall not taste of death, till they see the kingdom of God."

The apostles had so recoiled at the idea of their Messiah's suffering and death that his declaration that he would rise the third day passed almost unheeded. They doubtless held the current general belief of the future resurrection of the dead, a doctrine accepted and taught by the Pharisees, but that Jesus meant a resurrection that would bring him among them again was beyond their immediate credence.

The Transfiguration   Mt. 17:1-13; Mk. 9:2-13; Lu. 9:28-36

The Master did not leave the apostles long in contemplation of suffering and sorrow. Six or eight days after Peter's confession he took Peter, James, and John, the most enlightened of the Twelve, beyond Caesarea Philippi "up into an high mountain"— probably Mount Hermon. There, to strengthen their faith, he accorded them a glimpse of his innate glory as the Son of God. As he prayed, he was transfigured before them, his whole being illumined. "His face did shine as the sun, and his raiment was white as the light" (Mt.). "The fashion of his countenance was altered, and his raiment was white and glistering" (Lu.). (See II Pet. 1:16-18.)

> The light . . . shone not *upon* Him *from without*, but *out of* Him *from within*. . . .[39]

With his passion now full in view, the very appearance of Jesus was transfigured. For a little while the veil was lifted (Mk. 9:2f.) and the three favored disciples—Peter, James, and John—saw him in the glory of his utter consecration to the will of God, that will that was leading him to Calvary.[40]

As Jesus stood radiant, Moses and Elijah also appeared with him "in glory," and the three apostles were privileged to hear them talk "of his decease which he should accomplish at Jerusalem"—a conversation which taught the disciples that the experience which lay before their Master was not a fate he was powerless to resist but a voluntary task he was willing to undertake. Luke records that at one point the apostles slept, but "when they were awake, they saw his glory, and the two men that stood with him."

> He had taken the three with Him, to overcome their dread of His death and repugnance to the thought of it, as unbefitting the Messiah; to strengthen them to bear the sight of His humiliation hereafter; and to give them an earnest of the glory into which He would enter after His decease. . . Their presence [that of Moses and Elijah] . . . was a symbol that the Law and the Prophets henceforth gave place to a higher Dispensation; but they had also another mission. They had passed through death, or, at least, from life, and knew the triumph that lay beyond mortality to the faithful servants of God. Who could speak to Him as they, of His decease which He should accomplish at Jerusalem, and temper the gloom of its anticipation? Their presence spoke of the grave conquered, and of the eternal glory beyond.[41]

"Lord, it is good for us to be here," Peter exclaimed, "if thou wilt, let us make here three tabernacles [booths]; one for thee, and one for Moses, and one for Elias." While he was still speaking, a luminous cloud overshadowed them—not the thick cloud of Sinai but the Shekinah of God's presence— and they heard a voice commanding, "This is my beloved Son, in whom I am well pleased; hear ye him." The three apostles prostrated themselves in awe, but Jesus touched them, saying, "Arise, and be not afraid"; and as they "lifted up their eyes, they saw no man, save Jesus only."

Peter, James, and John had seen not only the Son of man, but also the Son of God, coincident. The "Christ of God" Peter had declared was radiantly revealed for a moment unconditioned by time or flesh.

> Among its intended lessons may be the following:— First, to teach that, in spite of the calumnies which the Pharisees had heaped on Jesus, the old and new dispensations are in harmony with each other. To this end the author and the restorer of the old dispensation talk with the

founder of the new. . . . Secondly, to teach that the new dispensation was superior to the old. Moses and Elias appear as inferior to Jesus, not merely since their faces did not, so far as we know, shine like the sun, but chiefly because the voice from the excellent glory commanded to hear *him*, in preference to them. Thirdly, to gird up the energies of Jesus for the great agony which was so soon to excruciate him. Fourthly, to comfort the hearts of the disciples, who, being destined to see their master, whom they had left all to follow, nailed to a cross, to be themselves persecuted, and to suffer the want of all things, were in danger of despair. But by being eyewitnesses of his majesty they became convinced that his humiliation, even though he descended into the place of the dead, was voluntary, and could not continue long.[42]

> Its value is symbolic. Silence regarding it is enjoined by Jesus, and practiced by the disciples until the Resurrection, with which it is closely connected in significance. The problem of the transfigured body of Jesus and of the Resurrection body is the same. . . .
> *The great lesson for the disciples* was that the dreadful shame of His cross was really glory, and that all suffering is ultimately radiant with heavenly beauty, being perfected in Christ. Peter's suggestion of the three tents is an attempt to materialize and make permanent the vision, to win the crown without the cross. The vision vanished, and they saw "Jesus only." It was real, but only a glimpse and foretaste. By loyalty once more to the Master, in the common ways of life to which they returned, the disciples would come to share the eternal glory of the Risen Lord.[43]

As they came down from the mountain Jesus directed them: "Tell the vision to no man, until the Son of man be risen again from the dead" (Mt. 17:9). They obeyed, but they pondered among themselves the meaning of his words. Matthew alone includes the word "again" as part of Jesus' statement. It indicates that this was for Jesus a resurrection (compare Mt. 26:32), and his transfigured appearance on Resurrection morning gave sustained and tangible evidence of the glory earlier manifested at his Transfiguration.

Second Foretelling of Death and Resurrection
Mt. 17:22,23; Mk. 9:30-32; Lu. 9:43-45

The following day when Jesus rejoined the other nine apostles, who had waited at the foot of the mountain, he healed the lunatic child they had failed to cure during his absence (Mt. 17:14-21; Mk. 9:14-29; Lu. 9:37-43; see p. 364).

As they passed unobtrusively through the countryside on their way homeward to Capernaum, Jesus a second time impressed on the Twelve the imminence of his death and resurrection, turning their attention again to the ordeal awaiting him—to the depths he must plumb before he could enter into his full glory:

"The Son of man is delivered into the hands of men, and they shall kill him; and after that he is killed, he shall rise the third day." He urged "Let these sayings sink down into your ears."

Still they remained in ignorance of his meaning. They were saddened, "but they understood not that saying, and were afraid to ask him."

Jesus' Payment of Tribute
Mt. 17:24-27

Shortly after their return to Capernaum Peter was accosted by collectors of the Temple tax, who asked, "Doth not your master pay tribute?" (This tribute was the didrachme—a half-shekel, worth about thirty-three cents, the only silver coin of the Jews—demanded under Mosaic Law and dutifully paid by every male Israelite over the age of twenty.) Regarded as a "ransom for his soul," the tax went toward the maintenance of the Temple and its services (Ex. 30:11-16). It was payable from the first of Adar (March), but was usually collected close to Passover, between the fifteenth and twenty-fifth of Adar, by moneychangers (sent out by the Sanhedrin) who set up their tables in every town in which Jews resided. For a nominal fee these men exchanged foreign currencies into the prescribed half-shekel.

During Passover they set up their tables in the Temple court for the convenience of the thousands of pilgrims, who deposited their money in one of thirteen trumpet-shaped boxes that stood in the Temple treasury, the Court of the Women.

Jesus' payment of this tax may have been overdue, as he had been almost constantly traveling and had not attended the preceding Passover. He was not opposed to Temple worship, as his cleansing of the Temple indicated, nor is there any indication in the Gospels that he had not paid this tax the two years before. To the tax collector's question Peter, acting on his own initiative, replied, "Yea," in quick defense of the Master, unaware that any principle was involved. Jesus, conscious of all matters that related to himself and his work, knew what had transpired; as Peter came into the house where Jesus was staying Jesus put a question to him before Peter could broach the subject: "What thinkest thou, Simon? of whom do the kings of the earth take custom or tribute? of their own children, or of strangers?" At Peter's reply, "Of strangers," Jesus declared, "Then are the children free."

> It was not customary for kings to take tribute from, or tax, their own children, and therefore, as Lord of the temple, and Son of the King of heaven, he was exempt from this tax; nevertheless, as he was to fulfil all righteousness as a Jew, he conformed to the custom.[44]

Having made clear to Peter by this simile his exemption from human impositions, Jesus commanded, "Notwithstanding, lest we should offend them, go thou to the sea, and cast an hook, and take up the fish that first cometh up; and when thou hast opened his mouth, thou shalt find a piece of money: that take, and give unto them for me and thee." Matthew, the former collector of Roman taxes, alone records this incident.

Discourse
Humility and Forgiveness   Mt. 18; Mk. 9:33-50; Lu. 9:46-50

As the apostles had walked with Jesus on the road to Capernaum they had pushed aside his reiterated prophecy of his death; instead they began arguing among themselves as to who would be greatest in the kingdom of heaven, each vying for the highest position in the government of the kingdom. Jesus did not allow this error of rivalry to remain unchallenged. When they reached his headquarters in Capernaum he sat down to instruct the Twelve concerning their true office and service: "If any man desire to be first, the same shall be last of all, and servant of all." He took a little child and, lifting him up in his arms, said to them: "Verily I say unto you, Except ye be converted, and become as little children, ye shall not enter into the kingdom of heaven. Whosoever therefore shall humble himself as this little child, the same is greatest in the kingdom of heaven."

> Conversion must be thorough; not only must the heart be turned to God in general, and from earthly to heavenly things, but in particular, except ye be converted from that carnal ambition which still rankles within you, into that freedom from all such feelings which ye see in this child, ye have neither part nor lot in the kingdom at all; and he who in this feature has most of the child, is highest there.[45]

He spoke of the duties of Christian brotherhood. His disciples were to avoid giving offense, to avoid causing any of his "little ones"—the innocent, the youthful, the immature—to stumble or to sin; they were to eschew by strict self-discipline all that would lead to evil. Every effort was to be made to save those who had left the right path.

Jesus gave clear directives concerning the spirit that should animate them should it be necessary to discipline a fellow Christian: "If thy brother shall trespass against thee, go and tell him his fault between thee and him alone: if he shall hear thee, thou hast gained thy brother. But if he will not hear thee, then take with thee one or two more, that in the mouth of two or three witnesses every word may be established. And if he shall neglect to hear them, tell it unto the church: but if he neglect to hear the church, let him be unto thee as an heathen man and a publican."

Jesus promised his Church the answer to their prayers: "If two of you shall agree on earth as touching any thing that they shall ask, it shall be done for them of my Father which is in heaven. For where two or three are gathered together in my name, there am I in the midst of them."

Peter asked the question, "How oft shall my brother sin against me, and I forgive him? till seven times?" Rabbinical law declared a threefold forgiveness was sufficient, but Jesus swept away all limits: "I say not unto thee, Until seven times: but, Until seventy times seven," and emphasized his point with an unforgettable parable (the only one attributed to the third period of the Galilean ministry).

Parable of the Unmerciful Servant (Mt. 18:23-35) "The kingdom of heaven [is] likened unto a certain king, which would take account of his servants." One servant who owed the king ten thousand talents could not pay. The king thereupon commanded that he and his household be sold for payment. When the servant petitioned, "Lord, have patience with me, and I will pay thee all," the king compassionately forgave him his debt. But the same servant went out to seek by violence from a fellow servant the trifling sum of one hundred denarii, and when that one could not pay and importuned, "Have patience with me, and I will pay thee all," the servant, without pity, cast him into prison. When the king heard what that servant had done he was angry and had him imprisoned until he should pay all that he owed.

A talent was computed at approximately one thousand dollars, and ten thousand talents (ten million dollars) indicated a fabulous debt. One hundred denarii amounted to twenty dollars, a denarius equaling about twenty cents. The first servant, therefore, refused to forgive what approximated one five-hundred-thousandth of what he himself had been forgiven. Forgiveness had come to the first petitioner as the result of a prayer for mercy, but when he failed to extend the same charity to his fellow man he cut himself off from that mercy.

"So likewise," Jesus warned, "shall my heavenly Father do also unto you, if ye from your hearts forgive not every one his brother their trespasses."

> Jesus nowhere says that God treats lightly the unfilial and unfraternal spirit—which, in the gospel, is the essence of sinfulness.[46]

By this parable Jesus illustrated how small is the debt man is asked to forgive his fellow man, and how enormous the debt the Father willingly forgives the children of men.

In all the precepts of this vital discourse Jesus

Tower of David, located near the Jaffa Gate entrance to the old walled city of Jerusalem. The lower part of this massive masonry, dating back to the days of King Herod, must have been a familiar sight to Jesus and his disciples. Israel Government Tourist Office.

nourished his Church; and these fundamental Christian principles had direct bearing on its subsequent harmony and brotherhood.

Feast of Tabernacles   Jn. 7:1-8:59

It was autumn (29 A.D.) and the eight-day harvest Feast of Tabernacles (one of the three great annual feasts observed in Jerusalem, see p. 61) was at hand. Jesus' Galilean ministry was over; the break with the people and the Pharisees had not lessened. Jesus had not assumed the kingship over his nation as the people had hoped, and the religious leaders stubbornly resisted the spiritual demands of the kingdom.

More than a year and a half had elapsed since Jesus' last visit to Jerusalem. He had stayed away from the national feasts because on his last visit the Jews had tried to kill him, accusing him of blasphemy and Sabbath-breaking. Jesus' brothers urged him to attend the feast with them, but he demurred: "I go not up yet unto this feast; for my time is not yet full come," but later he did go (in secret to escape public attention, for he knew that his enemies were still seeking to kill him). It required resolute courage to return to Jerusalem to face a powerful, hostile priesthood and a half-believing people, and to assert more forcibly his Messianic claim. The Sanhedrin hoped he would come so he would be within their reach. They searched everywhere for him at the feast, but not until the fourth day did Jesus suddenly appear and, pressed with the urgency of his message, teach openly in the Temple.

He spoke so authoritatively that the people asked, "Do the rulers know indeed that this is the very Christ . . . When Christ cometh, will he do more miracles than these which this man hath done?"

On each day of this festival the people had lived outdoors in leafy booths—on housetops, in the streets of the city, and on hillsides—to commemorate their wilderness wandering; each morning the priests had drawn water from the Pool of Siloam to pour out on the altar as a reminder of God's provision of water in the wilderness, and had made the required sacrifices. Daily the people had marched in procession around the altar (seven times on the seventh day), carrying in the left hand a citron and in the right a palm branch intertwined with willow and myrtle. Each evening under the great light of the huge candelabra in the Court of the Women they danced and sang in joyous revelry. It was on the last day of the feast, the "great day" that celebrated Israel's entrance into Canaan so abundant in its springs of water, that Jesus lifted the symbolism of the pouring out of water to its full significance. Whereas the priests had poured water, through him would pour the Holy Spirit. On the ears of the multitude fell his arresting voice, "If any man thirst, let him come unto me, and drink. He that believeth on me, as the scripture hath said, out of his belly shall flow rivers of living water." As he had offered the water of life to the woman of Samaria, so now he urged his nation to partake of the living water of the Spirit.

Some of his hearers cried, "Of a truth this is the Prophet"; "This is the Christ." When the Pharisees and Sadducees heard these comments they were goaded into action, realizing the threat to their security. They sent Temple officers to seize Jesus; but the soldiers found themselves unable to obey the order, reporting, "Never man spake like this man."

Discourse
The Light of the World
Jn. 8:12-30

As the day drew to a close the great candelabra in the Court of the Women were lighted for the final festivities. Either on this night in the blaze of this illumination or early the following morning after the healing of the woman taken in adultery (Jn. 8:2-11; see p. 369), Jesus made another appeal to the people: "I am the light of the world: he that followeth me shall not walk in darkness, but shall have the light of life." With this announcement Christ proclaimed himself the pure Light of truth that dispels the world's darkness of sin and ignorance (Is. 42:6; 60:1-3; Lu. 2:32).

This teaching was immediately challenged by the Pharisees. Jesus justified his statement by Jewish law: "Though I bear record of myself, yet my record is true: for I know whence I came, and whither I go. . . . It is also written in your law, that the testimony of two men is true [Deut. 17:6; 19:15]. I am one that bear witness of myself, and the Father that sent me beareth witness of me." He rested with confidence on the testimony of these two divine witnesses.

They asked, "Where is thy Father?" Jesus replied, "Ye neither know me, nor my Father: if ye had known me, ye should have known my Father also."

The conflict grew sharper as Jesus warned his listeners that they would perish if they did not believe in him as their God-sent Savior: "I go my way, and ye shall seek me, and shall die in your sins: whither I go, ye cannot come." Ignoring his warning, they fastened only on that part of his statement that he was going beyond their reach, so Jesus explained, "Ye are from beneath; I am from above: ye are of this world; I am not of this world. I said therefore unto you, that ye shall die in your sins: for if ye believe not that I am he, ye shall die in your sins."

Still it was as though he spoke another language, for they questioned, "Who art thou?" Patiently he answered, "Even the same that I said unto you from the beginning. . . . When ye have lifted up the Son of man, then shall ye know that I am he, and that I do nothing of myself; but as my Father hath taught me, I speak these things. And he that sent me is with me: the Father hath not left me alone; for I do always

those things that please him." His words were spoken with such conviction and power that many of the Jews of Jerusalem believed.

Discourse
Spiritual Freedom
Jn. 8:31-59

Jesus' discourse on spiritual freedom followed as a natural sequence his discourse on the light of the world. Turning to those who were persuaded he was the Messiah, he instructed them more fully concerning the saving power and freedom his teachings conferred on those who live according to them: "If ye continue in my word, then are ye my disciples indeed; And ye shall know the truth, and the truth shall make you free."

Some countered "We be Abraham's seed, and were never in bondage to any man." They were thinking of nationalism; he of freedom from the thralldom of sin. His reply explained this deeper concept: "Whosoever committeth sin is the servant of sin. And the servant abideth not in the house for ever: but the Son abideth ever. If the Son therefore shall make you free, ye shall be free indeed." Pointing out the inconsistency of their claim to be Abraham's seed while they tried to kill him, a man who had told them the truth, he said, "If ye were Abraham's children, ye would do the works of Abraham. . . . Ye do the deeds of your father."

When some contended "We have one Father, even God," Jesus replied, "If God were your Father, ye would love me: for I proceeded forth and came from God; neither came I of myself, but he sent me. Why do ye not understand my speech? even because ye cannot hear my word." With fearsome clarity he denounced them as children of the devil who were following willingly and willfully their own sinful desires: "Ye are of your father the devil, and the lusts of your father ye will do. He was a murderer from the beginning, and abode not in the truth, because there is no truth in him. When he speaketh a lie, he speaketh of his own: for he is a liar, and the father of it. . . . If I say the truth, why do ye not believe me? He that is of God heareth God's words: ye therefore hear them not because ye are not of God."

Furiously they threw at him the epithet *Samaritan* and accused him of having a devil. Patiently Jesus replied, "I have not a devil; but I honour my Father, and ye do dishonour me. And I seek not mine own glory: there is one that seeketh and judgeth." They had been forced by his works to acknowledge that he possessed a measure of divine power, but they refused to admit that he was the Christ and accord him the dignity and honor due the Son.

Bringing them back to the subject of his discourse—spiritual freedom—Jesus promised the reward of immortality to those who continued in his teachings: "If a man keep my saying, he shall never see death." At this mention of immortality the Jews retorted, "Now we know that thou hast a devil. Abraham is dead, and the prophets; and thou sayest, If a man keep my saying, he shall never taste of death. Art thou greater than our father Abraham, which is dead? and the prophets are dead: whom makest thou thyself?" Jesus answered, "If I honour myself, my honour is nothing: it is my Father that honoureth me. . . . Your father Abraham rejoiced to see my day: and he saw it, and was glad."

Immediately they seized on the literal point that his obvious age precluded his having seen Abraham. There was only one answer he could give: his divine pre-existence. Even though he knew this truth would be misunderstood, Jesus unhesitatingly gave it: "I say unto you, Before Abraham was, I am." This assertion of his eternal existence was a further revelation of the nature of the Christ and explained many of the statements he had already made about himself.

> You see me, indeed, now a man like yourselves, and I appear to you of as late origin and as short a life, but before all generations I had a being with him, who told the Israelites his name was, I AM.[47]

Instantly his words were branded the height of blasphemy. Enraged that he dared to employ the same sacred term as that used by God when He revealed Himself as Jehovah to Moses (Ex. 3:14), the Jews picked up stones to stone him to death; "but Jesus hid himself, and went out of the temple, going through the midst of them, and so passed by."

Healing
of Man Born Blind
Jn. 9

Either on this day or the following Sabbath Jesus, despite Sabbath restrictions against healing, restored the sight of a beggar born blind by anointing his eyes and sending him to wash in the Pool of Siloam—the only healing recorded during this visit to Jerusalem (see p. 365). It was a practical illustration that the "Christ was the light of the world in a double sense, opening the understanding as well as the eyes of mankind."

Word of this astounding miracle on the Sabbath spread rapidly; the restored man was brought before the chief Pharisees and asked to recount his cure. The council was soon hopelessly divided: some said "This man is not of God, because he keepeth not the sabbath day," while others argued in perplexity "How can a man that is a sinner do such miracles?" Turning again to the man, they asked his opinion of Jesus. He answered without hesitation: "He is a prophet."

The Pharisees refused to believe the beggar had

been born blind; they sent for his parents and questioned them closely, hoping to minimize or refute the miracle. But his parents would admit only that he was their son and that he had been born blind. They feared to say more because before the feast the authorities had threatened to expel from the synagogue any who acknowledged Jesus as Christ—a dreaded censure that spelled social and religious ostracism.

Frustrated in their attempt to discredit the healing, the Pharisees then ordered the man to ascribe it to God, claiming Jesus was a sinner. But the man reaffirmed that Jesus had healed him. Again they interrogated him. The man answered, "I have told you already, and ye did not hear . . . will ye also be his disciples?" In abusive language they accused him of being Jesus' disciple; they were disciples of Moses; as for Jesus, they did not know his origin. (They had been told repeatedly that he was sent from God, but to acknowledge his claim was to admit that he superseded Moses, an admission that would have undermined their authority.) In astonishment the healed man exclaimed, "Why herein is a marvellous thing, that ye know not from whence he is, and yet he hath opened mine eyes. Now we know that God heareth not sinners: but if any man be a worshipper of God, and doeth his will, him he heareth. Since the world began was it not heard that any man opened the eyes of one that was born blind. If this man were not of God, he could do nothing." Angered at the temerity of the beggar (whom they regarded as a sinner since they believed blindness was a punishment for wickedness), the Pharisees excommunicated him. However, the door of the kingdom of heaven was still open to this son of Abraham, for Jesus later sought him out and revealed himself to him as the Messiah, and the man instantly believed.

Discourse
The Good Shepherd
Jn. 10:1-21

After the confession of faith by the healed man, Jesus remarked to the crowd standing by: "For judgment I am come into this world, that they which see not might see; and that they which see [Phillips, think they can see] might be made blind." Some of the Pharisees asked, "Are we blind also?" Jesus answered that their blindness was willful, for they claimed to possess light, yet they stubbornly rejected God's Messiah: "If ye were blind, ye should have no sin: but now ye say, We see; therefore your sin remaineth."

The incredible blindness of the Pharisees gave rise to Jesus' discourse on the Good Shepherd. Their words and acts illustrated their unfitness to teach or interpret God's love to men. What sort of shepherds could these religious leaders be for the flock of Israel?

Jesus had already proved himself a true shepherd. He had come not to shut men out from God's mercy but to open to them the door of the kingdom: he had come not to condemn men for sin but to save them from it.

In the metaphorical language of two interwoven parables he drew a sharp contrast between a good shepherd and a hireling.

"He that entereth not by the door into the sheepfold, but climbeth up some other way, the same is a thief and a robber.

"But he that entereth in by the door is the shepherd of the sheep.

"To him the porter [doorkeeper] openeth; and the sheep hear his voice: and he calleth his own sheep by name, and leadeth them out. And when he putteth forth his own sheep, he goeth before them, and the sheep follow him: for they know his voice.

"And a stranger will they not follow, but will flee from him: for they know not the voice of strangers."

A peculiar, inherent characteristic of sheep is their loyalty to one shepherd; their response to his voice only; their complete dependence on his care, for unlike other creatures they are unable to protect or fend for themselves. During the day the shepherd led his flock to pasturage and water, watched that none strayed or fell, and cared for the young; at night he tended their wounds and passed them under his rod or stout wooden staff into a sheepfold, a walled enclosure or natural cave, and guarded the door against marauders and the attacks of predators.

Realizing that the Pharisees did not understand this parable, Jesus now spoke in the first person and identified himself as both the Good Shepherd of his Father's flock and the Door of the Sheepfold. By him alone could men enter the kingdom:

"I am the door of the sheep [the way into the sheepfold].

"All that ever came before me are thieves and robbers: but the sheep did not hear them.

"I am the door: by me if any man enter in, he shall be saved, and shall go in and out, and find pasture.

"The thief cometh not, but for to steal, and to kill, and to destroy:

"I am come that they might have life, and that they might have it more abundantly.

"I am the good shepherd: the good shepherd giveth his life for the sheep.

"But he that is an hireling . . . whose own the sheep are not, seeth the wolf coming, and leaveth the sheep, and fleeth: and the wolf catcheth them, and scattereth the sheep. The hireling fleeth, because he is an hireling, and careth not for the sheep.

"I am the good shepherd, and know my sheep, and am known of mine. As the Father knoweth me, even so know I the Father: and I lay down my life for the sheep."

As he spoke of the sacrifice he would make he envisioned a flock, a fold, a church that would embrace all men, all nations, Jew and Gentile.

"Other sheep I have, which are not of this fold: them also I must bring, and they shall hear my voice; and there shall be one fold, and one shepherd."

His closing words indicated his wholly voluntary sacrifice of himself, actuated by perfect love for the Father and by the desire to fulfill His will: "Therefore doth my Father love me, because I lay down my life, that I might take it again. No man taketh it from me, but I lay it down of myself. I have power to lay it down, and I have power to take it again. This commandment have I received of my Father."

This was a mysterious statement to his hearers; some thought he was mad, and even those who believed him wondered. Its meaning did not become clear until after his death and resurrection.

Feast of Dedication

Jn. 10:22-42

Whether Jesus stayed in Jerusalem after the Feast of Tabernacles or left Judaea is not known, but two months later he was again in Jerusalem, this time to attend the Feast of Dedication (see p. 61), "and it was winter." (Some Gospel harmonies place Jesus' attendance at the Feast of Dedication in the Peraean ministry.)

As he walked in Solomon's Porch, the east portico of the Temple, the Jewish authorities immediately converged on him to demand, "If thou be the Christ, tell us plainly." Jesus replied, "I told you, and ye believed not: the works that I do in my Father's name, they bear witness of me. But ye believe not, because ye are not of my sheep." He went on to tell his attackers that his sheep were the believers he had won and these he could never lose, because they were given him by his omnipotent Father. Their safety was assured, for his work was really the Father's work. "I give unto them eternal life; and they shall never perish, neither shall any man pluck them out of my hand. My Father, which gave them me, is greater than all; and no man is able to pluck them out of my Father's hand. I and my Father are one."

At his absolute statement of oneness with the Father the Jews were infuriated. They picked up stones, as they had at the Feast of Tabernacles, intending to stone him for blasphemy. He checked them with a quotation from their own Scripture, in which the term *gods* had been applied to the judges of Israel (Ps. 82:6), then asked, "Say ye of him, whom the Father hath sanctified, and sent into the world, Thou blasphemest; because I said, I am the Son of God?" Again Jesus cited his works as evidence of his divinity: "If I do not the works of my Father, believe me not. But if I do, though ye believe not me, believe the works: that ye may know, and believe, that the Father is in me, and I in him." The repeated linking of his name with God's only angered the Jewish religious hierarchy more. An attempt was made to seize him, but he escaped and returned to Galilee.

View across the Kidron Valley to the
Mount of Olives east of Jerusalem.
Jordan Tourism Office
New York

Peraean Ministry

Early in the winter of 29-30 A.D. Jesus left Galilee, never to return. He knew "the time was come that he should be received up," but he "stedfastly set his face to go to Jerusalem" whatever the cost (Lu. 9:51). He journeyed slowly by way of Peraea (called in the New Testament the land "beyond Jordan"), a narrow district east of the Jordan extending roughly from the Sea of Galilee to the Dead Sea—the most picturesque part of Palestine, with thickly wooded hills and well-watered fruitful valleys. Brought under Jewish domination during the rule of the Maccabees, Peraea remained predominantly Jewish until the time of Roman rule under the Herods.

Jesus now began to evangelize this semi-Gentile region as he moved toward Jerusalem. Most of the events attributed to this period are recorded in Luke's Gospel; he provides a number of Jesus' important discourses and parables not found elsewhere in the Gospels, but is silent regarding Jesus' exact route through Peraea or the cities visited.

As the Master observed the signs of his coming rejection, his discourses became more forceful, his parables more pointed, and he accelerated his warnings to the nation of judgment to come for disbelief. He lamented for Jerusalem; like the husbandman in the parable of the barren fig tree he patiently labored over this "barren" nation, pressing on to instill in humble hearts the requirements of discipleship. There was so much to tell, so little time in which to tell it. Toward the close of this period of about four months he went to Bethany (in Judaea) to raise Lazarus from the dead. He then went to Ephraim in northern Judaea; from there he traveled again into Peraea; and then—by way of Jericho—to Jerusalem.

Commissioning
of the Seventy
Lu. 10:1-24

As Jesus left Galilee for the last time, he started south through Samaria. Repulsed by the inhospitality of a Samaritan village, he changed his course, fording the Jordan (probably near Scythopolis), and chose a road running south through Peraea (Mt. 19:1; Mk. 10:1; Lu. 9:51-56).

Knowing his time was short, he felt the necessity of spreading the gospel to as many as possible. He increased the number of his missionaries, appointing seventy disciples (in addition to the Twelve) and sent them in advance by twos into the cities of Peraea, where there were many non-Jews as well as Jews. "The harvest truly is great," he said, "but the labourers are few: pray ye therefore the Lord of the harvest, that he would send forth labourers into his harvest."

> The Jews held, agreeably to Gen. 10, that the human race was made up of 70 peoples, 14 descended from Japhet, 30 from Ham, and 26 from Shem.[48]

> He [Jesus] determined, therefore, to send out no fewer than seventy, which, in Jewish opinion, was the number of the nations of the world. The lesson could not be doubtful. It was a significant announcement that, for the first time in the history of man, a universal religion was being proclaimed.[49]

His careful instructions to the Seventy were similar to those given the apostles. They too were to heal the sick and to preach that the kingdom of God is at hand; the command to go only to the house of Israel was omitted.

The journey of the Seventy was not an extended one. On their return they reported with joy—"Lord, even the devils are subject unto us through thy name." While they exulted in the immediate fruits of their mission, Jesus perceived the deeper significance of their accomplishment and confided it to them: "I beheld Satan as lightning fall from heaven [Moffatt, Yes, I watched Satan fall from heaven like a flash of lightning]" (compare Rev. 12:9-12). He saw the sway of Satan broken as his own messengers wielded the power of his teaching, and he foresaw the ultimate triumph of the kingdom.

He not only confirmed their power to heal, but also assured them of authority over all the forces of evil: "Behold, I give unto you power to tread on serpents and scorpions, and over all the power of the enemy: and nothing shall by any means hurt you" (compare Ps. 91:13,14). He also directed their thought to the higher attainment and ever-enduring reward: "Notwithstanding in this rejoice not, that the spirits are subject unto you; but rather rejoice, because your names are written in heaven" (compare Heb. 12:23; Rev. 21:27).

On this same occasion Jesus "rejoiced in spirit" "I thank thee, O Father, Lord of heaven and earth, that thou hast hid these things from the wise and prudent, and hast revealed them unto babes."

Visit to Bethany
Lu. 10:38-42

Not long after the return of the Seventy, Jesus made a short visit into Judaea to the home of Mary and Martha and their brother Lazarus. These three lived in Bethany, a village on the eastern slope of the Mount of Olives, two miles from Jerusalem. This is the first mention of Jesus' friendship with this family.

Of the two sisters Mary was the more earnest disciple. Jesus found her an eager listener, for she "sat at Jesus' feet, and heard his word," while "Martha was cumbered about much serving." At Martha's complaint that Mary did not help, he gently chided: "Martha, Martha, thou art careful and troubled about many things: But one thing is needful: and Mary hath chosen that good part, which shall not be taken away from her."

Discourse
Prayer
Lu. 11:1-13

Once during his Peraean ministry, as Jesus was praying, the disciples asked, "Lord, teach us to pray, as John also taught his disciples." In response he taught them a prayer that was a communion with the Father and a petition for His grace, a desire for His kingdom, a yielding to divine will, and a trust in Him to meet daily needs of soul and body. This prayer of our Lord (found in the Sermon on the Mount [Mt. 6:9-13]) appears in Luke's Gospel, possibly in its original form.

He followed the prayer with the brief parable of the importunate friend (Lu. 11:5-8), illustrating how perseverance in prayer brings its answer. As a man does not turn away from the persistent request of a friend in need or a father give his children a stone when asked for bread, so their heavenly Father will not refuse a suppliant, but will give the highest gift of all—the Holy Spirit—to those who ask.

Discourse
Blasphemous Pharisees and Scribes
Lu. 11:15-54

Even in Peraea Jesus was not free from the hostility of his enemies, who continued to dog his footsteps. The healing of a dumb man possessed of a devil precipitated a controversy among the Pharisees who witnessed it (Lu. 11:14; compare Mt. 12:22; see p. 361). Some charged that Jesus was casting out devils by Beelzebub; others asked for a spectacular "sign from heaven."

The accusation that he was in league with Satan drew from Jesus a strong refutation and a warning discourse. "Every kingdom divided against itself is brought to desolation; and a house divided against a house falleth. If Satan also be divided against himself, how shall his kingdom stand? ... But if I with the finger of God cast out devils, no doubt the kingdom of God is come upon you." And by the short parable of the binding of the strong man (Lu. 11:21,22; compare Mt. 12:29) he taught that Christ is stronger than Satan and can despoil him of his goods, warning, "He that is not with me is against me: and he that gathereth not with me scattereth."

By another short parable—that of the man with an unclean spirit (Lu. 11:24-26; compare Mt. 12:43-45)—Jesus likened the Pharisaic consciousness, which dared to suggest that his healing work was done in alliance with Satan, to the awful condition of a man's mind that had been emptied of a foul spirit but—because nothing pure and good had been put in its place—the foul spirit had returned, bringing with it "seven other spirits more wicked than himself." Jesus observed: "The last state of that man is worse than the first."

One commentator says of these two parables:

> In the one case, Satan is *dislodged by Christ,* and so *finds, in all future assaults, the house* preoccupied; *in the other, he merely goes out and comes in again, finding the house "EMPTY" (Matthew 12:44) of any rival, and all ready* to welcome him back. This explains the important saying that comes in *between the two parables,* v. 23. *Neutrality in religion there is none.* The absence of positive attachment to Christ involves hostility to Him.[50]

Referring to their insistence on a sign from heaven, Jesus called them a wicked generation and told them (as he had the Pharisees of Galilee) that no sign would be given but that of Jonah: "As Jonas was a sign unto the Ninevites, so shall also the Son of man be to this generation." The queen of Sheba (who had come from far away to hear Solomon) and the Ninevites (who had repented at the preaching of Jonah) would condemn this generation at the judgment, for, "behold, a greater than Solomon is here ... behold, a greater than Jonas is here."

On the same day that Jesus answered the attacks of the Pharisees he was invited to eat with some of them at one of their homes—probably a light midday meal. His host expressed surprise when his guest sat down to eat without performing the traditional ablutions. The time for plain speaking had come. Unhesitatingly Jesus exposed Pharisaic hypocrisy, upbraiding those present for their foolish adherence to the endless ritual of the washing of hands and food utensils: "Now do ye Pharisees make clean the outside of the cup and the platter; but your inward part is full of ravening and wickedness. Ye fools, did not he that made that which is without make that which is within also?" He urged these greedy men to dispense charity to the needy in a spirit of love—thus they would be truly clean within and without: "Rather give alms of such things as ye have; and, behold, all things are clean unto you."

Jesus went on to rebuke the hypocrisy of their punctilious tithing while they failed miserably in their greater duty to the moral law. "Woe unto you, Pharisees! for ye tithe mint and rue and all manner of herbs, and pass over judgment and the love of God: these ought ye to have done, and not to leave the other undone."

When the scribes who were also present heard themselves included in the strong denunciation of the Pharisees "as graves which appear not, and the men that walk over them are not aware of them," they protested, since to them nothing held greater defilement than a corpse or a grave. Their hypocrisy was scathingly exposed. These lawyers who had taken upon themselves the clarification of the Law had instead imposed on the nation a merciless yoke of traditional scribal law. Jesus charged that while their forebears had killed God's prophets, they were killing the spirit of prophecy, shutting the door of the kingdom and taking away "the key of knowledge" from men.

Jesus' indictment marked an open rift with these two parties and incited them to fanatic determination somehow to entrap him.

Discourse
Trust in God's Care
Watchfulness: Christ's Coming   Lu. 12

As Jesus left the Pharisee's house he was at once surrounded by a crowd so great that its members trampled each other. Still filled with righteous indignation, he proceeded first to warn his disciples to avoid hypocrisy: "Beware ye of the leaven of the Pharisees, which is hypocrisy. For there is nothing covered, that shall not be revealed; neither hid, that shall not be known." He exhorted them to proclaim their faith openly—had he not just given them a notable example of courage?—to trust God's care in all circumstances, and to be unafraid of what men could do to them for their confession of Christ. "I say unto you my friends, Be not afraid of them that kill the body, and after that have no more that they can do. But I will forewarn you whom ye shall fear: Fear him, which after he hath killed hath power to cast into hell; yea, I say unto you, Fear him." And with great simplicity he told them that He who valued the smallest sparrow valued the very hairs of their heads and would not forget them (compare Mt. 10:28-31).

Acknowledging him before men was vitally important: "Whosoever shall confess me before men, him shall the Son of man also confess before the angels of God: But he that denieth me before men shall be denied before the angels of God." Should they be accused for their faith before the tribunals of men, the Holy Ghost would teach them what to answer.

When a listener interrupted to ask if Jesus would act as judge in a matter of inheritance, he warned against covetousness with the parable of the rich fool (Lu. 12:16-21; see p. 288), and against preoccupation with self-preservation (Lu. 12:22-24; compare Mt. 6:25-34). Guiding them away from the concerns of daily life, he urged the people to seek their spiritual inheritance, the kingdom whose treasures are imperishable, and reminded them in three short parables that they were to be as servants continually watchful and prepared.

Parable of the Watchful Servants

In the first (Lu. 12:35-38) he said, "Let your loins be girded about, and your lights burning; and ye yourselves like unto men that wait for their lord, when he will return from the wedding; that when he cometh and knocketh, they may open unto him immediately." Those vigilant servants who could joyously open the door instantly to hail that return—regardless the hour—would be honored by the lord of the house at a repast at which he himself would serve them. Christ would exalt the faithful and himself serve them at the feast of heaven.

Parable of the Goodman of the House

Because his coming would be secret and sudden, like that of a "thief," this second parable (Lu. 12:39,40; compare Mt. 24:43,44) warned them to watch and not be like the goodman (householder) who failed to guard his house and allowed it to be broken into.

Parable of the Faithful and Faithless Stewards

Peter asked, "Lord, speakest thou this parable unto us, or even to all?" Jesus responded indirectly with a third parable (Lu. 12:42-48; compare Mt. 24:45-51) implying that he referred to those who would minister to his Church. This parable contrasted a faithful steward with an unfaithful one. The former wisely performed the duties of caring for the master's household during his master's absence; the latter neglected his responsibilities, indulged himself, and abused his fellow servants. Of the faithful steward Jesus remarked, "Of a truth I say unto you, that he will make him ruler over all that he hath"; and of the unfaithful steward, who knew his master's wishes and yet was disobedient, "That servant . . . shall be beaten with many stripes." To the servant who did not carry out his duties because he lacked knowledge of his lord's will, the penalty was less severe.

On a note of urgency Jesus foretold the conflict and division his gospel would engender (Lu. 12:49-59): "I am come to send fire on the earth; and what will I, if it be already kindled?" He foresaw that the spirituality of his gospel would in time destroy all the world's evil. In full consciousness of the cup of sorrow he would have to drink to finish his mission, he was now anxious to hasten its accomplishment. In this solemn moment he confided to them the weight upon his spirit: "I have a baptism to be baptized with; and how am I straitened till it be accomplished!"

Referring again to the purging effect of his gospel on the lives of men, Jesus warned that it would bring conflict that would sever even men's closest relationships: "Suppose ye that I am come to give peace on earth? I tell you, Nay; but rather division: For from henceforth there shall be five in one house divided, three against two, and two against three. The father shall be divided against the son, and the son against the father; the mother against the daughter, and the daughter against the mother; the mother in law against her daughter in law, and the daughter in law against her mother in law."

In the closing words of the discourse Jesus appealed to his hearers to choose now the salvation he offered, else they would remain in bondage to the world until they had paid "the very last mite" (Lu. 12:54-59).

Parables of the Peraean Ministry

At this point let us examine the principal parables of Jesus during his Peraean ministry. They had differing subjects: grace, redemption, salvation, Christian conduct, warning, judgment. With one exception (Mt. 20:1-16) they are found only in Luke's Gospel. These memorable parables had direct application to the nation as well as to the individual; they are not only effective concrete illustrations of Jesus' gospel, but when seen in their order and mounting significance they are also strong links in the chain of his spiritual logic, amplifying his teachings of the Sermon on the Mount.

Good Samaritan   Lu. 10:25-37

Somewhere near the beginning of the Peraean ministry Jesus spoke the parable of the Good Samaritan. When a certain lawyer tested Jesus—"Master, what shall I do to inherit eternal life?"—Jesus caused him to answer his own question out of the Law. The man replied that one must love God with all his heart and his neighbor as himself. When Jesus then responded, "This do, and thou shalt live," the lawyer began to justify himself: "And who is my neighbour?" Like most of the Jews of his time, he held a circumscribed view of his fellow man, seeing only the Israelite as his neighbor.

> This very question, like Peter's (Mt. xviii:21), was one involving a wrong condition of mind. He who asked, "Whom shall I love?" proved that he did not understand what love meant; for he wished to have it known beforehand where he should be at liberty to stop, while the very essence of love is, that it has no limit, except in its own inability to proceed further, that it is a debt which we must be forever paying (Rom. xiii:8).[51]

Jesus answered the lawyer's question with a parable. "A certain man went down from Jerusalem to Jericho, and fell among thieves, which stripped him of his raiment, and wounded him, and departed, leaving him half dead." Three travelers saw him as they journeyed: the first two, a priest and a Levite, "came and looked on him, and passed by on the other side"; but the third, a Samaritan, "came where he was" and with compassion bound up his wounds, poured in wine to cleanse and oil to heal, put him on his own beast and "brought him to an inn, and took care of him." The following day, as he departed, the Samaritan directed the innkeeper to tend the wounded man, promising to defray the cost.

Jesus' choice of travelers was trenchant. The priest and the Levite were respected religionists of the lawyer's own nation, while the Samaritan was both cursed and hated by the Jews; yet only the Samaritan, moved by the true spirit of brotherhood, practiced the mercy and benevolence that should have sprung naturally from the other two. Jesus implied that one's neighbor is the man in need, wherever he may be, but his principal emphasis was on the necessity of un-qualified neighborliness. "Which now of these three, thinkest thou, was neighbour unto him that fell among the thieves?" asked Jesus. And when the lawyer admitted, "He that shewed mercy on him," Jesus enjoined, "Go, and do thou likewise."

Throughout his ministry this was the quality of love Jesus exemplified toward suffering humanity, robbed of its spiritual heritage, stripped of righteousness, wounded by transgressions. Christ bound up the brokenhearted, healed the sick, and abundantly poured the balm of the Spirit into the human heart.

Importunate Friend

This parable (Lu. 11:5-8) is treated in the discourse on prayer (see p. 285).

Rich Fool
Lu. 12:16-21

One of Jesus' important discourses to a large audience was interrupted by a petty personal request from one of his listeners: "Master, speak to my brother, that he divide the inheritance with me." Following his invariable rule, Jesus refused to pass judgment in a civil matter; understanding the underlying motive behind the man's petition, he rebuked self-gratification: "Take heed, and beware of covetousness: for a man's life consisteth not in the abundance of the things which he possesseth."

He emphasized the point with the parable of the rich fool: "The ground of a certain rich man brought forth plentifully: And he thought within himself, saying, What shall I do, because I have no room where to bestow my fruits?" He thought to pull down his barns and build greater that he might store his surplus and say to his soul, "Soul, thou hast much goods laid up for many years; take thine ease, eat, drink, and be merry." But God said to him, "Thou fool, this night thy soul shall be required of thee: then whose shall those things be, which thou hast provided?"

Jesus summed up the futility of such worldly reasoning: "So is he that layeth up treasure for himself, and is not rich toward God." He did not condemn normal thrift, industry, comfort, or even wealth; he did condemn self-indulgence and trust in perishable material possessions, sins detrimental to the natural yearnings of the soul toward God. Always the burden of the Master's message was that men should concern themselves with the kingdom of God and set about the laying up of "treasures in heaven" (Mt. 6:20; Lu. 12:33).

Barren Fig Tree
Lu. 13:6-9

When Jesus was informed and questioned about Pilate's slaying of certain Galileans (possibly for suspected sedition), as they were offering sacrifices, he touched on the viewpoint common among the Jews that great calamities were inflicted in divine vengeance as punishment for great sin (Lu. 13:1-5): "Suppose ye that these Galileans were sinners above all the Galileans, because they suffered such things? . . . Or those eighteen, upon whom the tower in Siloam fell, and slew them (an incident about which nothing is known), think ye that they were sinners above all men that dwelt in Jerusalem? I tell you, Nay: but, except ye repent, ye shall all likewise perish."

A forceful parable of warning to his nation followed this exhortation to repent. "A certain man had a fig tree planted in his vineyard; and he came and sought fruit thereon, and found none. Then said he unto the dresser of his vineyard, Behold, these three years I come seeking fruit on this fig tree, and find none: cut it down; why cumbereth it the ground?" Israel had been set apart from the nations, spiritually nourished and cared for through the Law and the Prophets, yet had failed to bring forth the fruit of faith in the season of its Messiah's advent. Jesus' compassionate long-suffering for his nation is evident in the answer of the gardener: "Lord, let it alone this year also, till I shall dig about it, and dung it: And if it bear fruit, well: and if not, then after that thou shalt cut it down."

The warning of this parable was later illustrated in the miracle of the withering of the fruitless fig tree (see pp. 301-302), and openly stated in the Master's teaching, at the Last Supper, "If a man abide not in me, he is cast forth as a branch, and is withered" (Jn. 15:6).

Wedding Guest   Lu. 14:7-11

Once when Jesus dined as a guest in the house of a prominent Pharisee, he noted how the Pharisees and scribes elbowed each other for the choice seats at the tables (the custom was for each guest to seat himself according to his own estimate of his social standing unless escorted to his seat by the host). Without hesitation Jesus rebuked their self-exaltation and pretension to honor: "When thou art bidden of any man to a wedding, sit not down in the highest room; lest a more honourable man than thou be bidden of him; And he that bade thee and him come and say to thee, Give this man place; and thou begin with shame to take the lowest room. But when thou art bidden, go and sit down in the lowest room; that . . . he may say unto thee, Friend, go up higher: then shalt thou have worship in the presence of them that sit at meat with thee." George A. Buttrick comments: "Under the guise of a lesson in table manners, Jesus explains that in heaven's household humility is a lovely and essential grace." [52]   Jesus' concluding statement on the value of humility was "For whosoever exalteth himself shall be abased; and he that humbleth himself shall be exalted."

In New Testament times it was often the custom for an entire village, including the handicapped and the poor, to be invited to an elaborate feast. Perhaps it was with this charitable practice in mind that Jesus went on to teach of the true hospitality of a host—not a generosity that included one's friends and brethren capable of repaying the invitation, but rather a mercy that extended to the poor, the maimed, and the blind who might never repay (Lu. 14:12-14). Such hospitality would have full recompense "at the resurrection of the just."

Great Supper   Lu. 14:15-24; compare Mt. 22:1-14

When one of the men who sat at the table heard Jesus speak of the recompense that would come at the resurrection of the righteous, it brought to his mind the great feast which the Jews anticipated at the opening of the Messianic kingdom. Believing that every righteous son of Abraham would participate (compare Mt. 8:11), he observed piously, "Blessed is he that shall eat bread in the kingdom of God."

Jesus' answer was designed to shake the complacent attitude of this man and of those who shared the same idea. In figurative language he told them the kingdom had come; the feast was already prepared by the Son's presence among them, but they were refusing the Father's invitation to participate. "A certain man made a great supper, and bade many: And sent his servant at supper time to say to them that were bidden, Come; for all things are now ready. And they all with one consent began to make excuse." No one refused outright, but each put first his own interests and cares.

One said, "I have bought a piece of ground, and I must needs go and see it."

Another said, "I have bought five yoke of oxen, and I go to prove them."

Another said, "I have married a wife, and therefore I cannot come."

Then the master of the house, angered by the slights to his invitation, commanded his servant, "Go out quickly into the streets and lanes of the city, and bring in hither the poor, and the maimed, and the halt, and the blind." And these physically and spiritually needy willingly came. When he heard there was yet room at his table the host said to his servant, "Go out into the highways and hedges, and compel them to come in, that my house may be filled." The invitation to those in "the highways and hedges" outside the city foreshadowed the extension of Christ's gospel to the world and the inclusion of Gentiles in the kingdom.

Turning from the parable to his own mission and openly calling that supper his own, Jesus spoke of those who refused to receive his teaching: "I say unto you, That none of those men which were bidden shall taste of my supper." (Compare Rev. 19:9: "Blessed are they which are called unto the marriage supper of the Lamb.")

Counting Cost
of Discipleship   Lu. 14:25-35

Crowds of people followed Jesus as he journeyed through Peraea, some drawn to him because of his popularity and their hope of worldly benefits, some curious, some believing, some half-believing. In the strongest terms he enjoined them to take serious thought about the exacting requirements of "following" him, for he wanted as disciples only those who sought him with spiritual motives. "If any man come to me, and hate [*Strong's Concordance*, love less] not his father, and mother, and wife, and children, and brethren, and sisters, yea, and his own life also, he cannot be my disciple. And whosoever doth not bear his cross, and come after me, cannot be my disciple" (compare Mt. 10:37-39). A man must put his allegiance to Christ above all human affections; yea, he must put it before life itself.

To follow him in the Way required complete self-abnegation; to underline his point Jesus urged, in a twofold parable, that every professing disciple consider most earnestly the cost of enduring to the end, lest his work count for nothing. "Which of you, intending to build a tower, sitteth not down first, and counteth the cost, whether he have sufficient to finish it? Lest haply, after he hath laid the foundation, and is not able to finish it, all that behold it begin to mock him, Saying, This man began to build, and was not able to finish."

Continuing, Jesus admonished his would-be followers to remember that in this world the odds against them would be great. They must first ask themselves if their faith was sufficient to enable them to stand against the foe or if they would be forced to compromise: "Or what king, going to make war against another king, sitteth not down first, and consulteth whether he be able with ten thousand to meet him that cometh against him with twenty thousand? Or else, while the other is yet a great way off, he sendeth an ambassage, and desireth conditions of peace."

Jesus concluded this parable with a warning to his followers to exercise a living faith: "So likewise, whosoever he be of you that forsaketh not all that he hath, he cannot be my disciple. Salt is good: but if the salt have lost its savour, wherewith shall it be seasoned? It is neither fit for the land, nor yet for the dunghill; but men cast it out." One commentator notes: " 'The salt which has lost its savour' is here the discipleship which refuses to make the sacrifices which Christ demands (vv. 26,27,33)."[53]

Lost Sheep
Lu. 15:1-7

On one occasion the Pharisees and scribes were incensed when many publicans and sinners came to hear Jesus speak. They looked haughtily on these degraded outcasts of their nation as outside the duties of their ministry, whereas Jesus regarded the saving of sinners as an integral part of his. To them it was

pollution to be with such people, but this great teacher loved them; he hesitated neither to associate publicly with them nor to eat at their tables, claiming them for his kingdom.

When the Pharisees and scribes complained, "This man receiveth sinners, and eateth with them," Jesus told three parables that challenged their bigoted and arrogant exclusiveness and illustrated the precious value to the Father of every "lost" or repentant sinner and the joy in heaven over his return to spiritual life. "The first two parables set forth mainly the *seeking* love of God; while the third describes to us rather the rise and growth of repentance responsive to that love."[54]

The first parable was a pastoral one; the loss of a single sheep that had wandered from the flock was of vital concern to the shepherd and he spared no effort in the search for his own. "What man of you, having an hundred sheep, if he lose one of them, doth not leave the ninety and nine in the wilderness, and go after that which is lost, until he find it? And when he hath found it, he layeth it on his shoulders, rejoicing. And when he cometh home, he calleth together his friends and neighbours, saying unto them, Rejoice with me; for I have *found* my sheep which was lost."

Jesus drew an analogy. "I say unto you, that likewise joy shall be in heaven over one sinner that repenteth, more than over ninety and nine just persons, which need no repentance."

Lost Piece of Silver
Lu. 15:8-10

The second parable, with its simple domestic setting, restated the truth of the first and emphasized again that all should participate in the joy of others' good. "Either what woman having ten pieces of silver, if she lose one piece, doth not light a candle, and sweep the house, and seek diligently till she find it? And when she hath found it, she calleth her friends and her neighbours together, saying, Rejoice with me; for I have *found* the piece which I had lost."

Again he concluded, "Likewise, I say unto you, there is joy in the presence of the angels of God over one sinner that repenteth."

Prodigal Son
Lu. 15:11-32

The narrative of the prodigal son is one of Jesus' most beautiful and poignant parables. This time the sinner was a beloved son who had gone astray—claimed his inheritance before the rightful time and willfully left his father's house.

"A certain man had two sons. . . . And he divided unto them his living. And not many days after the younger son gathered all together, and took his journey into a far country, and there wasted his substance with riotous living." Only when he was reduced to dire want in body and soul—to the extremity of hiring himself out to feed swine and craving their food—did he come to himself. Remembering that the servants in his father's house fared far better, he determined, "I will arise and go to my father, and will say unto him, Father, I have sinned against heaven, and before thee, And am no more worthy to be called thy son: make me as one of thy hired servants."

"And he arose, and came to his father." He made the long journey back from that "far country." "But when he was yet a great way off, his father saw him, and had compassion, and ran, and fell on his neck, and kissed him." Humbly this repentant son confessed his guilt and desired only that he be made a servant within his father's house. But his father received him with love and joy and honor, and commanded all the household to rejoice: "Bring forth the best robe, and put it on him; and put a ring on his hand, and shoes on his feet: And bring hither the fatted calf, and kill it; and let us eat, and be merry: For this my son was dead, and is alive again; he was lost, and is *found.*"

The elder son was angry that his prodigal brother had been lovingly received and welcomed with a feast. Thinking only of his faithful labors in his father's service through many years, unaware of the purging through which his brother had passed, he would not rejoice. He saw not a brother but a sinner. The father gently reminded him of the inheritance already his: "Son, thou art ever with me, and all that I have is thine." He added, "It was meet [fitting] that we should make merry, and be glad: for this thy brother was dead, and is alive again; and was lost, and is found."

The implication was clear in this vignette of parental love. God regards every man as His son; and though a mortal may sin, in God's sight a man never loses his status as a son. Although he is seemingly lost for a time to the Father—and even to himself—when he turns in repentance from sin he finds himself forgiven and restored to favor. If there was great joy at the return of one prodigal son, should Jesus' proud listeners begrudge the teaching of the gospel of God's love to humanity's outcasts or deny to repentant sinners their place in the kingdom?

> Only of another Elder Brother [Jesus] was it true that he never disobeyed one of the Father's commands, and that all that the Father had was his (cf. Jn. 17:10); he did not grudge his brethren their welcome home, but went into the far country (cf. 19:12) to live with them and die for them, to show them what home was like.[55]

Unjust Steward   Lu. 16:1-13

The parable of the unjust steward, told by Jesus to his disciples, differed from many of his other parables in both approach and subject matter. In it a dishonest steward was rebuked by his master for abusing his office and wasting the wealth entrusted to his care but commended for the diligence he exercised in protecting his selfish personal interests. From the practices of the worldly minded Jesus drew a lesson for the "children of light."

"A certain rich man . . . called [his steward], and said . . . give an account of thy stewardship; for thou mayest be no longer steward. Then the steward said within himself, What shall I do? for my lord taketh away from me the stewardship: I cannot dig; to beg I am ashamed. I am resolved what to do, that, when I am put out of the stewardship, they may receive me into their houses." So he sent for each one of his master's debtors, and asked the first, "How much owest thou unto my lord?" He answered, "An hundred measures of oil." The steward commanded him to "sit down quickly, and write fifty." To another he asked, "How much owest thou?" and that one answered, "An hundred measures of wheat." To him the steward said, "Take thy bill, and write fourscore." The rich man "commended the unjust steward, because he had done wisely: for the children of this world are in their generation wiser than the children of light."

> It must not be supposed that our Saviour here meant to commend the practice of deceit and breach of trust. He only recommended the same attention to our heavenly interest as the unjust steward had shewed to his worldly advantage.[56]

While the worldly used the things of this world and the privileged responsibilities afforded them to their own selfish purposes, Jesus' followers must use theirs for the one high purpose of winning the kingdom; so he urged upon his hearers a right and wise stewardship in the new dispensation. "He that is faithful in that which is least is faithful also in much: and he that is unjust in the least is unjust also in much. If therefore ye have not been faithful in the unrighteous mammon [deceitful riches], who will commit to your trust the true riches? And if ye have not been faithful in that which is another man's, who shall give you that which is your own? No servant can serve two masters. . . . Ye cannot serve God and mammon." (Judas Iscariot is a classic example of the truth of this parable.)

Unable to refute his teaching, covetous Pharisees standing by sneered at Jesus, suspecting correctly that this parable was directed toward them. His blow at the sin of the love of money struck too close to home, and the more the gospel standard was accepted the more their deficiencies were exposed. Jesus rebuked them sharply: "Ye are they which justify yourselves before men; but God knoweth your hearts: for that which is highly esteemed among men is abomination in the sight of God. The law and the prophets were until John: since that time the kingdom of God is preached, and every man presseth into it. . . ." (Lu. 16:14-16)

Rich Man and Lazarus
Lu. 16:19-31

To make the immediate truth of his words still clearer to the insolent, unbelieving Pharisees, Jesus gave the parable of Dives ("rich man") and Lazarus, for the Pharisees, relying on their wealth and Abrahamic descent, were not pressing into the kingdom as were the humble. This parable held the sharpest reproof of the unfeeling rich who could countenance, without any stirrings of conscience, the misery of the poor daily before their eyes. Speaking in the eschatological terms of his day, Jesus carried the moral of this highly figurative narrative from the visible world to the invisible.

"There was a certain rich man, which was clothed in purple and fine linen, and fared sumptuously every day: And there was a certain beggar named Lazarus, which was laid at his gate, full of sores, And desiring to be fed with the crumbs which fell from the rich man's table: moreover the dogs came and licked his sores." Lazarus died and "was carried by the angels into Abraham's bosom." The rich man also died, and "in hell [Gr. *Hades,* Heb. *Sheol:* the underworld] he lift up his eyes, being in torments, and seeth Abraham afar off, and Lazarus in his bosom." Hopefully relying on his Abrahamic descent, the rich man sought Abraham's mercy, though he himself had showed none, asking that Lazarus be sent to relieve his suffering. Abraham reminded him that he had been blessed in his lifetime, and Lazarus had had a life of hardship; that now Lazarus was comforted; "and beside all this, between us and you there is a great gulf fixed: so that they which would pass from hence to you cannot; neither can they pass to us, that would come from thence."

The rich man then prayed that Abraham send Lazarus to his five brothers to save them; but Abraham said, "They have Moses and the prophets; let them hear them." But he remonstrated, "Nay, father Abraham: but if one went unto them from the dead, they will repent." Abraham replied, "If they hear not Moses and the prophets, neither will they be persuaded, though one rose from the dead."

> It ought never to be forgotten, that it is not the primary purpose of the parable to teach the fearful consequences which will follow the abuse of wealth and contempt of the poor, but the fearful consequences of unbelief, of having the heart set on this world, and refusing to believe in that invisible world, here known only to faith, until by a miserable and too late experience the existence of such an unseen world has been discovered. The sin of Dives in its roots is unbelief: the squandering on self, and contempt of the poor, are only the forms which it takes. His unbelief also shows itself in supposing that his brethren, while refusing to give heed to the sure word of God, would heed a ghost. This is of the very essence of unbelief, that it gives that credence to portents which it refuses to the truths of God.[57]

Later another Lazarus did come from the dead, but the nation did not hear (Jn. 11), nor did Jesus Christ's own signal resurrection awaken them.

Unprofitable Servant
Lu. 17:7-10

To the apostles' "Increase our faith," Jesus answered: "If ye had faith as a grain of mustard seed, ye might say unto this sycamine tree [black mulberry], Be thou plucked up by the root, and be thou planted in the sea; and it should obey you." Knowing they needed to manifest a continuous obedience to the will of God, he taught them more about the stringent requirements of discipleship by means of a parable of an unprofitable servant, one that pertained to unremitting selfless service. The faith they so greatly desired would be advanced and strengthened by persistent willing performance of duty.

At first this parable seems harsh and peremptory. "Which of you, having a servant [bond servant] plowing or feeding cattle, will say unto him by and by, when he is come from the field, Go and sit down to meat? And will not rather say unto him, Make ready wherewith I may sup, and gird thyself, and serve me, till I have eaten and drunken; and afterward thou shalt eat and drink? Doth he thank that servant because he did the things that were commanded him? I trow not. So likewise ye, when ye shall have done all those things which are commanded you, say, We are unprofitable [unmeritorious] servants: we have done that which was our duty to do."

"So likewise ye." Servants were accorded no special merit for discharging their appointed tasks; neither should Jesus' disciples be vainglorious of their achievements; nor should they look for cessation from their labors for the kingdom. "There is no respite: a man can never say, 'For an hour I am not under obligation.' However honorably he may live, or imagine himself to live, the only verdict he can render is, 'I have done only my duty.' "[58]

Importunate Widow,
or Unjust Judge
Lu. 18:1-8

In the background of this parable is Jesus' teaching concerning the coming of the kingdom (Lu. 17:20-37). When the Pharisees asked the time of its coming Jesus told them plainly it was here and now—an invisible spiritual kingdom "within" the hearts of men—but its full revelation he related to his Second Advent. Warning that the coming of the Son of man would bring sudden judgment on a heedless world, he stressed the necessity for unceasing prayer.

To urge that "men ought always to pray, and not to faint," he told the parable of the importunate widow. (Poor widows were often pitiable objects in Hebrew society, even though protected and provided for in some measure by special Mosaic legislation [Deut. 24:17,19; 26:12; 27:19]. To exercise kindness and mercy to widows was an esteemed virtue certain to ensure a blessing [Job 31:16; Is. 1:17; Jer. 7:6,7; 22:3,4].) This parable carries its impact by comparison and contrast, and teaches the lesson of persistence. If an unjust judge would finally yield to the importunities of a helpless widow, how much more surely would a just God hear the prayers of His elect and avenge wrongs done them?

"There was in a city a judge, which feared not God, neither regarded man: And there was a widow in that city; and she came unto him, saying, Avenge me of mine adversary. And he would not for a while: but afterward he said within himself, Though I fear not God, nor regard man; Yet because this widow troubleth me, I will avenge her, lest by her continual coming she weary me." Although the judge kept putting her off, the woman continued to press her claims until at last he rendered judgment in her favor.

Jesus ended the proverb: "Hear what the unjust judge saith. And shall not God avenge his own elect, which cry day and night unto him, though he bear long with them? I tell you that he will avenge them speedily. Nevertheless when the Son of man cometh, shall he find faith on the earth?"

Pharisee and Publican   Lu. 18:9-14

The parable of the Pharisee and the publican was perhaps given while Jesus was still on the subject of prayer. It taught that true prayer must come from a humble heart and was directed toward "certain which trusted in themselves that they were righteous, and despised others."

It was customary for the Jew of Jesus' day to pray at set hours (to repeat his "prayers of the phylacteries"* morning and evening, except on Sabbaths and feast days); wherever he was he stood facing

*Phylacteries were small square leather bags or pouches (tephillin) fashioned from the skin of a clean animal, which contained certain Scriptural passages written on small rolls (Ex. 13:1-16; Deut. 6:4-9; 11:13-21). These, fastened to leather bands, were worn at prayer time, one on the forehead and one on the inside of the upper left arm near the heart. Whether the wearing of these phylacteries was an actual practice in earlier Israelitish history is not known, but it is certain that it had become an established Judaic institution by the second century B.C. Phylacteries were highly venerated, and were regarded as a protection against demons and the "evil eye." (The only New Testament reference to them is found in Matthew 23:5.)

Jerusalem in an attitude of reverence with eyes cast down. His prayers were often audible, and the overly devout Pharisee frequently made lengthy supplications "standing in the synagogues and in the corners of the streets" to attract the admiration of others. In the Sermon on the Mount Jesus had already rebuked such ostentatious praying (Mt. 6:5,6).

"Two men went up into the temple to pray; the one a Pharisee, and the other a publican. The Pharisee stood and prayed thus with himself, God, I thank thee, that I am not as other men are," and extolled his virtues, both moral and religious; but the publican "standing afar off, would not lift up so much as his eyes unto heaven, but smote upon his breast, saying, God be merciful to me a sinner." One spoke arrogantly, the other contritely.

Jesus commended the humility of the publican and condemned the self-righteousness of the Pharisee, "I tell you, this man went down to his house justified rather than the other: for every one that exalteth himself shall be abased; and he that humbleth himself shall be exalted." As in the parable of the good Samaritan, Jesus' choice of characters was intentional. His vivid contrast between the two and his bold commendation of the prayer of a sinner could not fail to antagonize the religious leaders and make them aware of the great gulf between their teachings and his.

Laborers
in the Vineyard   Mt. 20:1-16

The parable of the laborers in the vineyard followed immediately the incident of the rich young ruler's refusal to give up his great possessions to follow Jesus and Peter's consequent question, "Behold, we have forsaken all, and followed thee; what shall we have therefore?" (Mt. 19:16-30). Jesus promised that they would be enthroned in his kingdom and also that "every one" who left all for him would receive a hundredfold blessing and the infinite recompense of everlasting life. But by way of warning he declared, "Many that are first shall be last; and the last shall be first." It was not their province to judge themselves first, for his followers would receive their due according to heaven's appraisal. To correct the calculating "What shall we have?," Jesus told this parable:

"The kingdom of heaven is like unto a man that is an householder, which went out early in the morning to hire labourers into his vineyard. And when he had agreed with the labourers for a penny a day, he sent them into his vineyard." At the third hour the householder found others "standing idle in the marketplace," and these he hired. Again at the sixth, ninth, and even the eleventh hour he found others;

these also he sent to his vineyard, saying, "Whatsoever is right, that shall ye receive." At evening every man was recompensed a penny, "beginning from the last unto the first." Those who had entered the vineyard early in the morning complained because they did not receive more, having "borne the burden and heat of the day." They were told that the wage was just and equitable, "Didst not thou agree with me for a penny?" They were further told, "Is it not lawful for me to do what I will with mine own? Is thine eye evil, because I am good?"

Jesus' closing statement (which some versions omit) reiterated his earlier warning: "So the last shall be first, and the first last: for many be called, but few chosen."

Those who served in the Father's vineyard from early morning had no cause for murmuring, for serving was a recompense in itself and they who were called were spared the differing degrees of frustration, delay, and remorse of "standing idle in the marketplace."

> [This] parable, amid its other lessons, involved the truth that, while all who serve God should not be defrauded of their just and full and rich reward, there could be in heaven no murmuring, no envyings, no jealous comparison of respective merits, no base strugglings for precedency, no miserable disputings as to who had performed the maximum of service, or who had received the minimum of grace.[59]

> He who works in my kingdom for the sake of a reward hereafter may do his work well, but he honors me less than others who trust in me without thinking of future gain. The spirit in which you labour for me gives your service its value.[60]

(The life of Paul, the final apostle to be called by Jesus Christ, is a signal illustration of that of a man who did not enter the vineyard until the "eleventh hour" and yet received full recompense. Paul said: "Last of all he was seen of me also, as of one born out of due time. . . . and his grace which was bestowed upon me was not in vain; but I laboured more abundantly than they all: yet not I, but the grace of God which was with me" [I Cor. 15:8,10].)

Ten Pounds
Lu. 19:11-27

The parable of the ten pounds was given at the very close of the Peraean ministry on the occasion of the feast in Zacchaeus' house in Jericho or shortly thereafter. A joyous hope ran high among Jesus' listeners because he was on his way to Jerusalem, and many of them were anticipating the immediate appearance of the kingdom. Instead, Jesus knew he was soon to be rejected in Jerusalem. His parable was a poignant statement pervaded by sadness that some of his own nation, failing to make use of the truth he, their Messiah, had given them, were themselves to be rejected.

"A certain nobleman went into a far country to receive for himself a kingdom, and to return. And he called his ten servants, and delivered them ten pounds, and said unto them, Occupy till I come. But his citizens hated him, and sent a message after him, saying, We will not have this man. to reign over us." The nobleman, "when he was returned, having received the kingdom," called each servant to him for an accounting. Jesus illustrated his point with the fate of three of the ten: the servant who had increased one pound to ten was made ruler of ten cities, another the ruler of five. Concerning the servant who had made no use of his opportunity, the nobleman ordered: "Take from him the pound, and give it to him that hath ten pounds. . . . For I say unto you, That unto every one which hath shall be given; and from him that hath not, even that he hath shall be taken away from him." And of the citizens who had refused his reign, he said, "Bring hither, and slay them before me."

So imminent was the experience of the cross that Jesus scarcely veiled his message: the coming of the kingdom would be delayed. He was leaving the world to go to the Father. Before his departure he was entrusting an equal measure of spiritual knowledge to his followers and commanding that it be put to use. He knew that after his ascension disbelievers would refuse to serve him. But at his Second Coming in glory—"having received the kingdom" from his Father —there would be an accounting of every man's work: a royal reward for the faithful who improved their opportunities, the loss of the gift to those who failed to use it, and swift judgment on those who rejected him.

Raising of Lazarus
Jn. 11:1-44

During the few months Jesus was in Peraea, in addition to his teaching, he healed on the Sabbath the woman stooped for eighteen years and the man with dropsy (Lu. 13:10-17; 14:1-6; see p. 366). Then, toward the close of this period, he went to Bethany where he worked the spectacular miracle that precipitated the events of Passion Week. Many months earlier, far from Judaea he had raised from the dead the son of the widow of Nain and the daughter of Jairus. Now, in full view of unbelieving Jerusalem, Jesus restored to life his friend Lazarus, a man of a family prominent in Jerusalem.

The Master was still in Peraea when he received word from Mary and Martha that their brother Lazarus ("he whom thou lovest") was sick. At once he informed the apostles, "This sickness is not unto death, but for the glory of God, that the Son of God might be glorified thereby." He did not, however, start immediately for Bethany, but remained in prayer two days where he was. "He desired not only to manifest His power to His friends, but to make a signal appeal to impenitent Jerusalem, by working a miracle which would attest His Messiahship beyond all question."[61]

When he did determine to go, the apostles were worried for his safety, remembering that the Pharisees had tried to stone him on his last visit to Jerusalem scarcely two months before. Jesus confided, "Our friend Lazarus sleepeth; but I go, that I may awake him out of sleep." But seeing they thought he spoke of Lazarus as taking rest in sleep, he stated plainly, "Lazarus is dead." "And I am glad for your sakes that I was not there," he added, "to the intent ye may believe"—that your faith may be strengthened. By the time he reached Bethany Lazarus had been in the grave four days and his family and friends were in deep mourning.

> In that sultry climate burial followed immediately on death, and it sometimes happened that a swoon was mistaken for death, and the buried man came to life again. The Jewish belief was that the soul hovered about the sepulchre for three days, fain to re-animate its clay. On the fourth day decomposition set in, and hope was then abandoned. Jesus arrived on the fourth day, and there was no doubt of the reality of Lazarus' death and of the ensuing miracle. It was not a recovery from a trance, but a veritable resurrection.[62]

Martha went out to meet Jesus, "but Mary sat still in the house." Martha greeted him, "Lord, if thou hadst been here, my brother had not died." When he comforted her, "Thy brother shall rise again," she replied, "I know that he shall rise again in the resurrection at the last day." Lifting her thought above the common Jewish hope of a future resurrection, he who had declared himself the water of life and the bread of life now revealed himself—the Christ—as the present quickening power of all resurrection: "I am the resurrection, and the life: he that believeth in me, though he were dead, yet shall he live: And whosoever liveth and believeth in me shall never die." (Peter and Paul in their Christian ministry proved the quickening power of this truth: Peter in the raising of Dorcas, Paul in the raising of Eutychus.) Jesus questioned Martha, "Believest thou this?" And she affirmed, as had the woman of Samaria, "Yea, Lord: I believe that thou art the Christ, the Son of God, which should come into the world."

Mary, like Martha, greeted him with the words "Lord, if thou hadst been here, my brother had not died." Jesus, seeing her and her friends weeping, "groaned in the spirit, and was troubled." He asked, "Where have *ye* laid him?" Upon their answer, "Come and see," he wept, not—as they thought—in sorrow for Lazarus but in compassion for their unbelief. They led him to the grave, probably a tomb hewn in the limestone rock of the hillside. Before its entrance a heavy circular stone had been rolled, as was the custom for protection against profanation of the dead

and defilement of the living. Giving no heed to the Jewish belief of ceremonial pollution from contact with the dead, Jesus commanded, "Take *ye* away the stone." Martha remonstrated, "Lord, by this time he stinketh: for he hath been dead four days." Seeking a deeper faith and a more expectant hope, Jesus reminded her, "Said I not unto thee, that, if thou wouldest believe, thou shouldest see the glory of God?"

Then "*they* took away the stone." In absolute conviction Jesus prayed out loud, "Father, I thank thee that thou hast heard me. And I knew that thou hearest me always: but because of the people which stand by I said it, that they may believe that thou hast sent me." "Lazarus, come forth," he summoned; when Lazarus, still swathed in graveclothes, came out of the tomb, Jesus commanded, "Loose him, and let him go."

Sanhedrin's Plot against Jesus

Jn. 11:45-54,57

On witnessing this extraordinary miracle many of those who had come to weep with the family were constrained to believe in Jesus, but some hastened to report to the rulers that Jesus was again in Judaea working great miracles, even to the raising of the dead. The Pharisees, alarmed lest Jesus' movement sweep all before it, met in council with the Sadducees to take action: "What do we? for this man doeth many miracles. If we let him thus alone, all men will believe on him: and the Romans shall come and take away both our place and nation." Jesus' whole concern was that men might believe in the Son of God; theirs, in defiance of God's will, was that men should not believe.

Caiaphas, high priest and official head of the Sanhedrin, cut them short. "Ye know nothing at all, Nor consider that it is expedient for us, that one man should die for the people, and that the whole nation perish not." By such callous reasoning he justified their determination to maintain the religious and political *status quo.* These ecclesiastics were certain that if the people rose up to proclaim Jesus as king the Romans would strike swiftly, the hierarchy would fall, and the Jewish nation itself might cease to exist. From that day the Pharisees and the Sadducees united to bring about Jesus' downfall and death. The Sanhedrin issued a decree that if anyone knew his whereabouts, he was to report it immediately that they might arrest Jesus.

"Jesus therefore walked no more openly among the Jews; but went thence unto a country near to the wilderness"—a withdrawal with his disciples to Ephraim, a city some fifteen miles north of Jerusalem.

Leaving Ephraim after a few weeks, perhaps for reasons of safety, Jesus went again to Peraea, taking a circuitous route northward and eastward along the borders of Samaria and Galilee, and crossing the Jordan (probably at Scythopolis). Somewhere along the way he heard a heart-rending cry for mercy from a company of ten lepers (Lu. 17:11-19; see p. 366). These outcasts, suffering from one of the most dread diseases of the East, were forbidden by law to approach their countrymen but must announce their presence with the cry, "Unclean, unclean!" The Savior responded, "Go shew yourselves unto the priests" (Lev. 14). "And ... as they went, they were cleansed." Only one of the ten—a Gentile, a Samaritan—had sufficient gratitude to return to kneel at Jesus' feet and give thanks to God. All were cleansed in body, only one in soul.

Discourse
Coming of the Kingdom and of the Son of Man   Lu. 17:20-18:8

In Peraea Jesus was continually harassed by the rabbis, whose hostility was daily growing more bitter. Repeatedly they attempted to compromise him with the authorities. On one of the last days of his journey toward Jerusalem they confronted him with the question of when the kingdom of God would come. The Jewish expectation was that a powerful temporal monarch would free the nation from Roman domination and establish a Jewish empire with its capital at Jerusalem. If they could prove he was fomenting political revolution there would be grounds for civil action.

Correcting the prevalent erroneous view concerning the kingdom, Jesus explained that it was far different from what they were expecting—it was neither political nor temporal; it was a moral and spiritual kingdom the establishment of which had already begun: "The kingdom of God cometh not with observation: Neither shall they say, Lo here! or, lo there! for, behold, the kingdom of God is within you."

Later, addressing only the disciples, Jesus linked the consummation of the kingdom with his Second Coming: "As the lightning, that lighteneth out of the one part under heaven, shineth unto the other part under heaven; so shall also the Son of man be in his day." As to the time, his prophecy was indefinite; he said only that that day could not come prior to his sufferings and rejection. But he warned that it would come suddenly and devastatingly on a worldly generation as judgment had struck in the days of Noah and Lot, and when it did come it would separate the prepared from the unprepared. They asked, "Where, Lord?" and his answer was enigmatic: "Wheresoever the body is, thither will the eagles be gathered together."

> As birds of prey scent out the carrion, so wherever is found a mass of incurable moral and spiritual corruption, there will be seen alighting the ministers of Divine judgment. . . .[63]

Jesus closed this discourse with an admonition to pray persistently and not to lose heart, illustrating his point with the parable of the importunate widow who persevered in prayer and faith until she obtained justice (see p. 292).

Jesus' Answer to Pharisees concerning Divorce   Mt. 19:3-12; Mk. 10:2-12

While Jesus was still in Peraea, the Pharisees, taking advantage of the custom of the day to appeal to any rabbi on disputed religious questions, tried to maneuver him into some contradiction of Mosaic Law that might arouse popular feeling against him.

They chose the controversial subject of divorce, a corruptive practice for which he had rebuked them some two months earlier (Lu. 16:14-18): "Is it lawful for a man to put away his wife for every cause [Weymouth, whenever he chooses]?" This was a delicate question beset by many complexities. Under Mosaic Law a husband was granted the right to dissolve the marriage and send his wife back to her family with a written bill of divorcement if "she find no favour in his eyes, because he hath found some uncleanness in her" (Deut. 24:1,2). The two rival rabbinical schools of Hillel and Shammai held sharply divergent views as to the interpretation of this passage: that of Hillel sanctioned divorce for any cause, however trivial, where a wife's dispostion or faults might displease her husband; that of Shammai sanctioned it only on the grounds of adultery. The opinions of both schools were regulating its current practice among the Jews. Furthermore, when this question was posed Jesus was in Peraea, the domain of Herod Antipas, the tyrant who had imprisoned and beheaded John the Baptist for his denunciation of Herod's conduct in divorcing his wife to marry his niece Herodias.

Giving the moral question of divorce the weight it deserved, Jesus directed his listeners' thought not to the Mosaic institution that permitted it but to the ordained constitution of marriage given in their Scripture (Gen. 2:24). "What therefore God hath joined together, let not man put asunder," he told them.

The Pharisees' next question was natural: "Why did Moses then command to give a writing of divorcement, and to put her away?" He explained that

Mosaic Law did not abrogate the sacred primitive provision, but made a concession to ease the marriage bond in order to prevent greater evils: "Moses because of the hardness of your hearts suffered you to put away your wives: but from the beginning it was not so." He rendered his judgment: "Whosoever shall put away his wife, except it be for fornication, and shall marry another, committeth adultery: and whoso marrieth her which is put away doth commit adultery." This principle, which restrained excessive divorce, had already been laid down in the Sermon on the Mount (Mt. 5:32). According to Mark's Gospel, Jesus' condemnation of this social evil was unqualified, forbidding divorce without exception (compare Lu. 16:18), but this absolute he confided only to his disciples in private. (By teaching the sanctity of marriage Jesus raised woman to a higher and more respected position in family life; she was not chattel to be put aside lightly.)

Alone with the Master, the disciples commented that if a man were bound to his wife as Jesus had said, then it seemed to them it was not good to marry. "All men cannot receive this saying," he replied, "save they to whom it [Weymouth, the grace] is given." He mentioned three cases where the unmarried state—celibacy—was better: "There are some eunuchs, which were so born from their mother's womb: and there are some eunuchs, which were made eunuchs of men: and there be eunuchs, which have made themselves eunuchs for the kingdom of heaven's sake. He that is able to receive it, let him receive it."

Third Foretelling of Death and Resurrection   Mt. 20:17-19; Mk. 10:32-34; Lu. 18:31-34

The time of the Passover season was approaching as Jesus began his last journey to Jerusalem, going from Peraea by way of Jericho and Bethany. Foreseeing the outcome of the swelling tide of hatred directed against him (see p. 352), he fully understood what this visit held in store. On two previous occasions he had explicitly predicted his coming death and resurrection: "the Son of man must suffer many things," and "the Son of man shall be delivered into the hands of men." This visit would bring to a climax the seething forces of evil, but it would also bring into view the greater forces of spiritual love and power which as the Christ he possessed. He knew that men could not make assault on his eternal life as the Son of God; they could only touch that which was of his "earthly house of this tabernacle."

The whole situation was under his control. He set the time; he chose the hour. He knew he was ready. Months before had come his prophecy, "I lay down my life for the sheep. . . . I have power to lay it down,

and I have power to take it again." He did not avoid the experience, evade it, flee from it; he faced it with calm resolution.

As he walked with his apostles, "Jesus went before them: and they were amazed; and as they followed, they were afraid." So weighted with significance was this journey that the Master took them aside a third time to teach them again, "Behold, we go up to Jerusalem; and the *Son of man* shall be betrayed unto the chief priests and unto the scribes, and they shall condemn him to death, and shall deliver him to the Gentiles to mock, and to scourge, and to crucify him: and the third day he shall rise again." For the first time mention was made of the part the Gentiles would play in his humiliation and crucifixion. But still they understood none of the things he told them.

> As Jesus went on his way to Jerusalem—the Jerusalem that killed her prophets and stoned the messengers God sent her—he no longer walked with his disciples as of old in friendly intercourse. He walked in front of them, alone, the physical distance between them faintly shadowing forth the gulf that separated his thought from theirs (Mk. 10:32). Following after, the disciples were amazed and frightened at the changed mood of their Master. When he did speak to them, it was of the fate that awaited him in Jerusalem.[64]

So far were the apostles from comprehending the terrible import of his words that James and John asked for the posts of honor in his coming kingdom: "Grant unto us that we may sit, one on thy right hand, and the other on thy left hand, in thy glory." Jesus answered: "Ye know not what ye ask: can ye drink of the cup that I drink of? and be baptized with the baptism that I am baptized with?" It was as though he had said, "Can you withstand such suffering and humiliation as I must endure?" They said, "We can." Then Jesus told them: "Ye shall indeed drink of the cup that I drink of; and with the baptism that I am baptized withal shall ye be baptized: But to sit on my right hand and on my left hand is not mine to give; but it shall be given to them for whom it is prepared" (Mk. 10:37ff.; compare Mt. 20:20ff.). (James later laid down his life as the first martyr of the apostle band [Acts 12:1,2], and John throughout the first century faithfully labored in the Church and triumphantly endured the persecutions directed against it.)

The other apostles were indignant at the request of the two, but Jesus reminded them again that their mission, like his, was to be one of selfless service: "Whosoever will be great among you, shall be your minister: And whosoever of you will be the chiefest, shall be servant of all. For even the Son of man came not to be ministered unto, but to minister, and to give his life a ransom for many" (Mk. 10:43-45).

Conversion of Zacchaeus
Lu. 19:1-10

Crossing the Jordan from Peraea, Jesus approached the city of Jericho in the verdant plain of the Jordan valley, six miles northwest of the Dead Sea. On its outskirts he healed the blind beggar Bartimaeus who called out to him for help (Mt. 20:29-34; Mk. 10:46-52; Lu. 18:35-43; see p. 367).

As Jesus walked through the streets of Jericho, crowds surrounded him; for some this was the first glimpse of the miracle-working Galilean. In Jericho lived Zacchaeus, a wealthy publican who, like the rest, was eager to see Jesus. A short man, he ran ahead of the crowd and climbed into a sycomore-fig tree to wait for Jesus to pass. When the Master reached the tree he looked up and said, "Zacchaeus, make haste, and come down; for to day I must abide at thy house." Zacchaeus climbed quickly down and welcomed him to his house, but some of the crowd grumbled because Jesus went to be the guest of a publican. Publicans were hated for their service to Rome and classed as sinners; they were also hated for their extortionary practices against the people of their own nation.

What Jesus said to his host that day is not known, but Zacchaeus' heart was wholly changed. So complete was the transformation that Zacchaeus offered to redress all his wrongs: "Behold, Lord, the half of my goods I give to the poor; and if I have taken any thing from any man by false accusation, I restore him fourfold."

Jesus blessed him: "This day is salvation come to this house, forsomuch as he also is a son of Abraham. For the Son of man is come to seek and to save that which was lost."

Anointing of Jesus by Mary of Bethany
Mt. 26:6-13; Mk. 14:3-9; Jn. 12:1-8

John notes in his Gospel that six days before Passover Jesus came to Bethany, sixteen miles southwest of Jericho. There his friends made him a supper in the home of Simon the leper; and Mary, Martha, and Lazarus were present. Only one special incident is mentioned—a tender display of outpouring love in which Mary anointed Jesus' feet with spikenard (a costly aromatic oil extracted from the nard plant) and wiped them with her hair. "And the house was filled with the odour of the ointment."

Judas Iscariot objected. "Why was not this ointment sold for three hundred pence [approximately sixty dollars], and given to the poor?" Jesus alone knew the significance of Mary's act: "Ye have the poor with you always, and whensoever ye will ye may do them good: but me ye have not always. She hath done what she could: she is come aforehand to anoint my body to the burying." He commended her pure love: "Wheresoever this gospel shall be preached throughout the whole world, this also that she hath done shall be spoken of for a memorial of her."

The Week Preceding Resurrection (Passion Week)

Jesus at last entered Jerusalem openly as the Messianic King. Heretofore he had come quietly, even secretly, taking steps to avoid any open clash with the religious leaders that might have ended his mission prematurely. Now he took the offensive. Jesus' every act during the week was done in the knowledge that his crucifixion was imminent.

The Master moved through these final days with absolute authority, no longer muting his message in the citadel of his enemies. Unopposed he cleansed the Temple of its corruption and, standing acclaimed in its courts, taught the people. Once and for all he silenced the specious reasoning of the religious leaders and assailed them with a withering denunciation. But chiefly his efforts during this last week were directed toward strengthening the faith of his apostles—foretelling the destruction of all evil, the continuity and spread of his gospel, his Second Advent, and the coming of the Comforter. With sublime equanimity he faced the mockery of two unjust trials and endured the dread humiliation and suffering of the cross.

From men who walked with Jesus and treasured his every word and deed have come intimate details of this week. Of such significance to man's salvation are these that they are recounted in detail day by day, sometimes hour by hour. We know much of what Jesus thought: his sorrow over his nation's impenitence, his unswerving fidelity to the spiritual and the ideal in every conflict with his foes, his anguish of soul concerning his betrayer. We are permitted to hear his intercessory prayers for his disciples and for his Church, to glimpse his agony of soul, and to sense his complete surrender of will in Gethsemane. Finally, we feel something of his inviolable peace throughout the trials, and his sublime forgiving love and trust on the cross; we are aware above all of his absolute conviction that he would endure and triumph.

Sunday

The first day of the week, now called Sunday, was a day of triumph in which Jesus was openly acknowledged Israel's God-sent Messiah. It was Passover season and hundreds of thousands of pilgrims had come to the Holy City from Galilee, Judaea, Peraea, and foreign lands to celebrate the great annual festival. (According to Josephus [*Wars of the Jews*, vi, 9.3], writing in the first century A.D., at least 2.7 million persons came annually to Jerusalem to observe the Passover.) Jesus calmly and deliberately chose this moment when national and religious fervor was at its peak to enter Jerusalem publicly and thus formally present his claim as the Christ.

Word spread rapidly that Jesus was in Bethany—only two miles away—and was coming to Jerusalem. The recent raising of Lazarus had stirred great excitement among the Jerusalem Jews and many were anticipating his arrival. Some attending the feast, who had heard the gospel from the Master's own lips or been healed by him, were anxious to see him again. Others, who had never seen him, were eager for a sight of this remarkable being. The hope of what he might do filled their minds—would he dare to speak openly inasmuch as the hierarchy had only recently issued orders for his arrest? would he set up the kingdom and assume the kingship? would he free them from Roman tyranny? When Jesus appeared on this day he was greeted with wild enthusiasm as the son of David—the Messiah-King.

Triumphal Entry   Mt. 21:1-11; Mk. 11:1-11; Lu. 19:29-44; Jn. 12:12-19

Sunday morning Jesus left Bethany with his apostles, accompanied by a following of Galilean and Peraean pilgrims, by Jews who had seen him raise Lazarus, and by guests who had been at the Sabbath feast in Bethany. As he approached Bethphage near the Mount of Olives he sent two of his disciples into the village. There they would find tied by the side of the road a young donkey that had never been ridden. He would this day enter Jerusalem in consonance with Zechariah's prophecy (9:9): "Behold, thy King cometh unto thee, meek, and sitting upon an ass, and a colt the foal of an ass." Heretofore he had entered on foot; this time he would ride on an ass—the symbol of Jewish royalty as well as an emblem of peace. When the apostles returned with the colt they threw their cloaks onto its back and Jesus mounted.

Jesus' route took him south of the Mount of Olives into the well-traveled caravan road from Jericho to Jerusalem; and when word reached the city that he was on his way, a great crowd surged out, joined by thousands of the pilgrims encamped outside the city's walls. They threw their outer garments in his pathway and strewed palm fronds before him (signs of special honor), shouting, "Hosanna [save now] to the son of David: Blessed is he that cometh in the name of the Lord; Hosanna in the highest" (compare Ps. 118:25,26). As the procession began the rocky descent toward Jerusalem, the southeastern corner of the city and the Temple flashed briefly into view and the acclaim became a chant.

> It was a triumph in wondrous contrast with that of earthly monarchs. No spoils of towns or villages adorned it; no trains of captives destined to slavery or death; the spoil of His sword and His spear were seen only in trophies of healing and love—for the lame whom He had cured ran before, the dumb sang His praises, and the blind, sightless no longer, crowded to gaze on their benefactor.[65]

The popular ovation alarmed the leading Pharisees of the Sanhedrin who had mingled with the crowd, and they said to each other, "Perceive ye how ye prevail nothing? behold, the world is gone after him." Some of them demanded, "Master, rebuke thy disciples." But he refused. "I tell you that, if these should hold their peace, the stones would immediately cry out."

The road began a rugged ascent to a ledge of smooth rock. In an instant the proud city, with its gleaming Temple courts, white flat-roofed houses, and tall palm trees, came into full view of the winding procession. The chants of praise grew louder at this vista of magnificence; Jesus, seeing instead an impenitent city that would not relinquish its hopes for a temporal king and kingdom, wept for it: "If thou hadst known, even thou, at least in this thy day, the things which belong unto thy peace! but now they are hid from thine eyes." The Jews of Jerusalem and its hierarchy had stood at the threshold of spiritual opportunity throughout his ministry; had their sight been clear, they would have understood that God had indeed visited His people in the person of His Son.

Jesus foresaw Jerusalem's tragic fate—"The days shall come upon thee, that thine enemies shall cast a trench about thee, and compass thee round, and keep thee in on every side, And shall lay thee even with the ground, and thy children within thee; and they shall not leave in thee one stone upon another; because thou knewest not the time of thy visitation" (Lu. 19:43,44)—a prophecy fulfilled to the letter in the fall of the city in 70 A.D. (see p. 468).

The road curved north and then west over the bridge that spanned the deep rocky declivity of the

Kidron Valley, which ran along the east wall of the city. In the river bed below, dry many months of the year, raced the brook Kidron swollen by winter rains. The procession entered Jerusalem through the east gate, today called St. Stephen's Gate, and wound its way along narrow streets festive with flags and banners for the Passover feast. Inhabitant and pilgrim alike asked "Who is this?" The crowds replied "This is Jesus the prophet of Nazareth of Galilee."

Jesus went first to the Temple, leaving the people to disperse. In silent appraisal he "looked round about upon all things" (Mk. 11:11)—a moral and spiritual measurement of the sanctuary—and found them wanting. And, because evening was approaching and because the chief priests and Pharisees were still conspiring to take his life, Jesus withdrew from Jerusalem to safety outside the city's walls, to Bethany, and lodged there that night and each succeeding night.

Monday

Monday was a day of undisputed public demonstration of the Master's authority. He moved among the people as the recognized Messiah. On this day he pronounced judgment against the barren fig tree and in the presence of the Passover crowds a second time cleansed the Temple of its abuses. Unmolested, he taught openly in the courtyard of the Temple, so many rallying to his cause so enthusiastically that the Sanhedrin dared not touch him yet.

Barren Fig Tree Cursed   Mt. 21:18,19; Mk. 11:12-14

As the Master returned to Jerusalem from Bethany this Monday morning, he was hungry. "He saw a fig tree in the way . . . and found nothing thereon, but leaves only. . . ." It was not the season for figs, but nevertheless a productive tree should have borne some early figs or given promise of a later harvest. The fruit of this tree appears before its leaves; one in full leaf without fruit is thus considered barren for the season. Fruitlessness was anathema to the Master, so he said to the fig tree: "Let no fruit grow on thee henceforward for ever." This act had deep significance; Jesus had indeed hungered through nearly three years of ministry to be recognized by his own nation as their promised Messiah, yet their professed love of God had borne no fruit of faith. The import of this incident is heightened by the fact that several months earlier in Peraea Jesus had told the prophetic parable of the barren fig tree (Lu. 13:6-9; see p. 288). In it the master of the vineyard had said, "Behold, these three

years I come seeking fruit on this fig tree, and find none: cut it down; why cumbereth it the ground?" "That word [to the fig tree] did not *make* the tree barren, but sealed it up in its own barrenness."[66]

Second Cleansing
of the Temple   Mt. 21:12-17; Mk. 11:15-19; Lu. 19:45-48

Upon entering Jerusalem Jesus' first overt act was to cleanse the Temple. Nearly three years before he had purged it as a warning, but the Temple authorities had not during the intervening years corrected the corruption he had exposed. Now he purged it again, this time as a judgment. Rebuking the avarice of the priests, he demanded scathingly, "Is it not written, My house shall be called of all nations the house of prayer? but ye have made it a den of thieves." As he had found the fig tree barren, so he found the Temple barren of its proper fruits.

Jesus spent the remainder of Monday teaching in the Temple courts. And when the common people present saw his fearlessness and heard his reprimand of the Temple authorities, they forgot for the moment their dread of the Sanhedrin and brought to him their lame and blind. With growing jubilation they witnessed one extraordinary healing after another as he made his Father's house a true house of prayer, till the Temple rang with praise and even the children cried "Hosanna to the son of David."

The scribes and chief priests, angered at this popular demonstration, remonstrated, "Hearest thou what these say?" Jesus answered, "Yea; have ye never read, Out of the mouth of babes and sucklings thou hast perfected praise?" While the rulers went away to devise some means of destroying him, he left the Temple and quietly returned to Bethany.

Tuesday

On Tuesday Jesus concluded his public teaching to his nation, making a last appeal for Israel's repentance. The day was marked by repeated controversy and conflict with the religious authorities. The Sanhedrin had had time to reflect on the events of the preceding day: as guardians of the Temple their prestige had suffered woefully, their wealth had been threatened, and with increasing fear they realized that so long as this man was at large their ecclesiastical and even their political position under Rome was imperiled. They reassembled their scattered forces for a verbal attack on Jesus. First they questioned his rabbinical authority, then each party in turn—the Pharisees, Sadducees, and scribes—put to him a seemingly innocuous question, hoping to implicate him. But each time they failed to involve him and themselves suffered loss of prestige. Instead Jesus challenged his questioners, warning of the consequences of rejecting him; and when they refused to repent, Jesus publicly denounced them as hypocrites and fools. Their frustration and fury resulted in a secret conspiracy with Judas against his life. This day ended with a somber discourse in which Jesus prophesied to his apostles the destruction of the Temple, the fall of Jerusalem, and God's final judgment on the world's ungodliness.

Fig Tree Withered
Mt. 21:20-22; Mk. 11:20-26

Tuesday morning as Jesus and the Twelve again came along the road from Bethany to Jerusalem, they saw the fruitless fig tree dried up from the roots—Jesus' only miracle of judgment. When Peter exclaimed, "Master, behold, the fig tree which thou cursedst is withered away," Jesus replied, "Have faith in God. For verily I say unto you, That whosoever shall say unto this mountain, Be thou removed, and be thou cast into the sea; and shall not doubt in his heart . . . he shall have whatsoever he saith." The reply must at first have seemed almost irrelevant, but in reality he was teaching them an added lesson: that unwavering faith and trust in God would remove any obstacle, however great, that might stand in the way of their labors for the kingdom. He taught them also that this faith must be coupled with love and forgiveness for their fellow men, else their prayers would not be answered: "And when ye stand praying, forgive, if ye have ought against any: that your Father also which is in heaven may forgive you your trespasses."

Questioning of Jesus' Authority
Mt. 21:23-27; Mk. 11:27-33; Lu. 20:1-8

Jesus went directly to the Temple to teach the people once more. He was accosted almost immediately by a delegation from the Sanhedrin, who demanded, "By what authority doest thou these things? and who gave thee this authority?" Jesus countered their question with one of his own, "I will also ask of you one question, and answer me, and I will tell you by what authority I do these things. The baptism of John, was it from heaven, or of men? answer me."

With this question these masters of Israel suddenly found themselves both on the defensive and in a serious quandary. They had failed to respond to the teachings of the Baptist, though the people had flocked to him. They argued among themselves: "If we shall say, From heaven; he will say, Why then believed ye him not? But and if we say, Of men; all the people will stone us: for they be persuaded that John was a prophet." They had no intention of according Jesus recognition, but to deny John as a God-sent prophet would rouse the anger of the people. Their prestige as teachers of the Law was more important to them than truth. A straight answer would endanger their position; on the other hand, to admit before the people that they could not discern the Baptist's spiritual stature would cover them with shame. Therefore they replied evasively. "We cannot tell." Because of their dishonest answer Jesus refused further discussion: "Neither do I tell you by what authority I do these things."

Parable Two Sons
Mt. 21:28-32

Jesus knew his time was short; now without concern for the consequences his words would produce, he boldly challenged before all who were present the moral right of the chief priests, scribes, and Pharisees to teach their nation. He told three parables, unmistakable in meaning, in which he reproved priestly hypocrisy and iniquity and warned the nation of the fearful aftermath of rejecting him.

In the first parable he stripped them of all pretension as qualified leaders and teachers: "A certain man had two sons; and he came to the first, and said, Son, go work to day in my vineyard. He answered and said, I will not: but afterward he repented, and went. And he came to the second, and said likewise. And he answered and said, I go, sir: and went not." Jesus asked, "Whether of them twain did the will of his father?" And they said, "The first," by their own admission condemning themselves.

Jesus related his words to his listeners: "Verily I say unto you, That the publicans and the harlots go into the kingdom of God before you. For John came unto you in the way of righteousness, and ye believed him not: but the publicans and the harlots believed him: and ye, when ye had seen it, repented not afterward, that ye might believe him."

Parable The Vineyard
Mt. 21:33-46; Mk. 12:1-12; Lu. 20:9-19

In the second parable Jesus exposed the enormity of the wickedness of the nation's leaders in resisting the will of God and in repudiating His prophets and His Son. He drew upon the beautiful language of the Old Testament parable of Isaiah 5:1-7. "There was a certain householder, which planted a vineyard, and hedged it round about, and digged a winepress in it, and built a tower, and let it out to husbandmen, and went into a far country: And when the time of the fruit drew near, he sent his servants to the husbandmen, that they might receive the fruits of it. And the husbandmen took his servants, and beat one, and killed another, and stoned another. Again, he sent other servants ... and they did unto them likewise. But last of all he sent unto them his son, saying, They will reverence my son. But when the husbandmen saw the son, they said among themselves, This is the heir; come, let us kill him, and let us seize on his inheritance. And they caught him, and cast him out of the vineyard, and slew him."

Turning to the chief priests and scribes, Jesus asked, "What shall therefore the lord of the vineyard do?" According to Mark and Luke, he answered his own question. "He shall come and destroy these husbandmen, and shall give the vineyard to others." The implication was clear: the kingdom of God would be taken from their keeping and would pass into the stewardship of others. That they understood his meaning was apparent in their answer: "God forbid."

Jesus resumed his interpretation of the parable: "Did ye never read in the scriptures, The stone which the builders rejected, the same is become the head of the corner: this is the Lord's doing, and it is marvellous in our eyes?" Here he identified himself with the Stone, the Old Testament figure for the Messiah or Christ of Psalms 118:22,23, Isaiah 28:16, and Daniel 2:34,35. They had rejected the cornerstone of the kingdom; now they were rejected. "Therefore say I unto you, The kingdom of God shall be taken from you, and given to a nation bringing forth the fruits thereof. And whosoever shall fall on this stone shall be broken: but on whomsoever it shall fall, it will grind him to powder."

Parable
Marriage of the King's Son   Mt. 22:1-14

Jesus' third parable restated and amplified the warning of the second, and emphasized his royalty and dignity as God's Son. Underlying this vivid parable was Christ's conviction that the Father's plan of redemption, though rejected by His chosen people, would assuredly be accomplished; there would be others who would accept the Father's invitation and so prove worthy to partake of His grace and truth.

"The kingdom of heaven is like unto a certain king, which made a marriage for his son. . . ." Summoned by the royal servants to the wedding, his subjects would not come. The king sent other servants to tell of the bountiful preparation and provision—"all things are ready: come unto the marriage." But the invited still "made light of" this great privilege and thoughtlessly went their own ways. Some not only

ignored the royal command but also committed treason by mistreating and killing the king's servants. "When the king heard thereof, he was wroth: and he sent forth his armies, and destroyed those murderers, and burned up their city," a judgment fulfilled historically in the fall of Jerusalem in 70 A.D.

Though the guests chosen had not proved worthy, the wedding feast was ready and waiting, so the king sent his servants to find new guests. They went out "into the highways, and gathered ... both bad and good"—including without discrimination all who would come.

When the king came in to greet his guests, he found among them a man without a wedding garment; he rebuked his unpreparedness and insensibility to this special opportunity. "Friend, how camest thou in hither not having a wedding garment?" And the man was speechless! "Bind him hand and foot," the king commanded, "and take him away, and cast him into outer darkness." Jesus concluded, "Many are called, but few are chosen."

> It was customary in the east, while the weather was hot, to offer a change of raiment to every guest invited, by way of refreshment, and their garments were suited to the occasion of the festival. Now as a change of raiment had undoubtedly been offered to this man, as well as the rest, and he neglected or refused to put it on, the king had reason to be offended at his unsuitable appearance.
>
> The application of this parable is certainly very plain; whoever receives the gospel receives the wedding-garment of true holiness, to be worn by every one that expects to be admitted to the marriage of the Lamb; and whoever presents himself without this, connected with his faith in Christ, will be cast into darkness.[67]

The morning's teaching was clear. Jesus' enemies knew he spoke of them, but their fear of the people kept them from taking any overt action against him. Even so, within the hour they were again plotting violence.

Pharisees' Question
about Tribute   Mt. 22:15-22; Mk. 12:13-17; Lu. 20:20-26

Defeated in their attempt to implicate Jesus on the ecclesiastical charge of teaching without proper rabbinical authority, the Pharisees—joined by the Herodians (a minor political party supporting Herod's dynasty)—tried next to involve him under civil law. Hoping to trick him into some damaging statement which would bring him under the jurisdiction of the Roman governor, they sent out spies who asked, "Is it lawful for us to give tribute unto Caesar, or no?" Should he oppose the Roman tax he could be accused of rebellion.

Jesus was neither deceived by their craftiness nor

thrown off guard; calling for a Roman coin, he pointed out Caesar's image on its face and said, "Render to Caesar the things that are Caesar's, and to God the things that are God's." This lifted the issue far above human dispute into a realm of reasoning where there was no conflict between a man's obligation to men and a man's debt to God. Startled by his words, the Pharisees fell silent and went away.

Sadducees' Question about Resurrection
Mt. 22:23-33; Mk. 12:18-27; Lu. 20:27-40

Jesus was approached next by some of the aristocratic and influential Saducean priesthood. Heretofore they had paid scant attention to him and his claims. Now they determined to discredit him and at the same time cast doubt on the cherished beliefs of their rivals, the Pharisees, by a cunningly devised question pertaining to the resurrection of the dead, one they were positive he could not answer.

The Pharisees taught the resurrection of the body, the immortality of the soul, and future reward and punishment. Although a few rabbis entertained a spiritual conception of this future state, the majority held the materialistic view that the present body would be reanimated exactly as it had been before death, with all its carnal desires and imperfections. Men would continue to eat, drink, marry wives, and beget children. The Sadducees believed in no future state whatever and called the doctrine of resurrection absurd—they found no support for it in the Pentateuch, the only portion of Scripture they considered binding.

The Sadducees introduced their question by citing Mosaic Law (Deut. 25:5): "Master, Moses wrote unto us, If a man's brother die, and leave his wife behind him, and leave no children, that his brother should take his wife, and raise up seed unto his brother." Then they posed the case of a woman who had been married in turn to seven brothers, each of whom had died leaving her childless; and then she herself had died: "Therefore in the resurrection whose wife shall she be of the seven?"—a facetious query, in the answer to which they hoped to find basis for ridicule.

"Ye do err, not knowing the scriptures, nor the power of God," answered Jesus, dealing with the matter seriously. "The children of this world marry, and are given in marriage: But they which shall be accounted worthy to obtain that world, and the resurrection from the dead, neither marry, nor are given in marriage: Neither can they die any more: for they are equal unto the angels; and are the children of God, being the children of the resurrection." Jesus' reply refuted the current conception of bodily resurrection and revealed that it is to a higher plane of existence the dead are raised.

He then went on to disprove the Sadducees' adamant belief that there is no immortality. By testimony from Moses—whose authority alone they accepted—Jesus showed that Moses himself believed in resurrection and immortality: "And as touching the dead, that they rise: have ye not read in the book of Moses, how in the bush God spake unto him, saying, I am the God of Abraham, and the God of Isaac, and the God of Jacob? He is not the God of the dead, but the God of the living: ye therefore do greatly err."

His questioners could find nothing more to say.

Scribes' Question about the Great Commandment
Mt. 22:34-40; Mk. 12:28-34

When the scribes saw that the Sadducees had been reduced to silence, one of them inquired, "Master, which is the great commandment in the law?" Jesus answered from Scripture: "Thou shalt love the Lord thy God with all thy heart, and with all thy soul, and with all thy mind. This is the first and great commandment. And the second is like unto it, Thou shalt love thy neighbour as thyself. On these two commandments hang all the law and the prophets" (compare Deut. 6:5; Lev. 19:18). Although the scribe had asked for one great commandment, Jesus gave him two and declared their inseparability. All the Law was summarized in two concise commands; in both exist one basic imperative—"thou shalt love."

The scribe was completely satisfied with this interpretation, and exclaimed, "Well, Master, thou hast said the truth: for there is one God; and there is none other but he: And to love him with all the heart . . . and to love his neighbour as himself, is more than all whole burnt offerings and sacrifices." The scribe's discerning comment brought quick commendation from Jesus: "Thou art not far from the kingdom of God."

In these controversies, as in all others, Jesus proved himself a master teacher. He met his opponents' questions practically, but in every instance he also lifted their thought to a higher plane. They could not find a shred of evidence against him on either civil or religious grounds, "and no man after that durst ask him any question."

Jesus' Irrefutable Question
Mt. 22:41-46; Mk. 12:35-37; Lu. 20:41-44

While the deputation of priests and rabbis was still present in the Temple, Jesus made one more attempt to prevail upon them to exchange their earthly view of the Messiah for a more spiritual one, as they had never comprehended the twofold nature of the Savior God had sent them. Now he put the question "What think ye of Christ [the promised and expected Messiah]? whose son is he?"

In consonance with the common Jewish expectation, they quickly replied, "The son of David"—so different an answer from Peter's (Mt. 16:16). Their reply was scripturally correct regarding the Messiah's human lineage, but Jesus was not satisfied to let them think the Messiah was merely the son of David. So, quoting to them the Messianic passage from Psalm 110, he asked, "How then doth David in spirit call him Lord [Moffatt, How is it then that David is inspired to call him *Lord*?], saying, "The Lord [God] said unto my Lord [Messiah], Sit thou on my right hand, till I make thine enemies thy footstool? If David then call him Lord, how is he his son?" This scriptural authority clearly indicated Christ's superiority to David; he antedated David. The Christ was far more than the Son of man; he pre-existed as the Son of God, ruling in power with Him.

The ecclesiastics could not answer. Although their eschatological beliefs had prepared them to some extent for the truth that their Savior would be more than human, yet they could not see or would not admit this man as the fulfillment of their Messianic hope. They had cried "Blasphemy!" whenever he asserted that he was the Son of God; having rejected him, they remained obdurate. By contrast, "the common people heard him gladly."

The New Testament writers understood this twofold nature—the humanity and divinity of Christ—and the spirituality of his kingdom, and inculcated these teachings in the early Church (Jn. 1:1,14; Acts 2:22-36; Rom. 1:3,4; I Tim. 3:16; Heb. 1:1-3).

Discourse
Pharisees and Scribes   Mt. 23; Mk. 12:38-40; Lu. 20:45-47

Jesus now took the offensive against the scribes and Pharisees. Addressing his disciples and the crowd in the Temple, he pronounced a withering judgment on these hypocritical teachers: "The scribes and the Pharisees sit in Moses' seat: All therefore whatsoever they bid you observe, that observe and do; but do not ye after their works: for they say, and do not. For they bind heavy burdens and grievous to be borne, and lay them on men's shoulders; but they themselves will not move them with one of their fingers."

As he had whipped out the buyers and sellers from the Temple, so he now whipped out all that pertained to the Pharisaic sins of oppression, pride, blind erudition, ostentation, and greed. His opening

denunciation was a terrible indictment, "Woe unto you, scribes and Pharisees, hypocrites! for ye shut up the kingdom of heaven against men: for ye neither go in yourselves, neither suffer ye them that are entering to go in." Eight times Jesus declared, "Woe unto you, scribes and Pharisees, hypocrites! . . . Ye compass sea and land to make one proselyte, and when he is made, ye make him twofold more the child of hell than yourselves."

He called them "fools" and "blind guides," denouncing the casuistry of their swearing of oaths, their punctilious attention to trifles while neglecting the moral requirements of the Law, their extortions and excesses. He termed them "whited sepulchres, which indeed appear beautiful outward, but are within full of dead men's bones, and of all uncleanness"; he charged that while they claimed to honor the ancient prophets, they were in fact persecuting and killing the prophets of their own day. Branding them a "generation of vipers," he foretold their doom—"the damnation of hell."

Jesus met only hardness of heart and cold hostility, but he lamented compassionately for the whole house of Israel, addressing it by a name that represented to every Jew all that was distinctive and precious in his religion. "O Jerusalem, Jerusalem, thou that killest the prophets, and stonest them which are sent unto thee, how often would I have gathered thy children together, even as a hen gathereth her chickens under her wings, and ye would not! Behold, your house is left unto you desolate." They themselves had shut out the divine Light, and without the Christ their religion was empty of meaning. They had not come *to* him; therefore he must go *from* them. He concluded significantly: "For I say unto you, Ye shall not see me henceforth, till ye shall say, Blessed is he that cometh in the name of the Lord." Not until they could see and acknowledge him "whom they pierced" as the Messiah sent from God would they be blessed by his grace and salvation (see Zech. 12:10; Rom. 11:26; II Cor. 3:15,16).

Gentiles Seek Jesus   Jn. 12:20-36

Even as Jesus grieved for Jerusalem, his heart was gladdened by a new development. His apostles Andrew and Philip came to him with the message that some of the Greek proselytes to the Jewish faith had asked to see him. These were men who had come to Jerusalem for the Passover. Jesus recognized instantly that these were serious seekers after truth, whose inquiry foreshadowed the wider spread of the gospel. The door of faith was opening to the Western world and through it to all humanity. The time was now at hand for him to demonstrate his complete dominion over death—the last enemy of mankind. Some months earlier he had said "My time is not yet full come." Now his answer to Andrew and Philip was: "The hour is come, that the Son of man should be glorified."

His thought turned to his imminent crucifixion. He alluded to it delicately, likening his sacrifice to a planting and a harvest: "Except a corn of wheat fall into the ground and die, it abideth alone: but if it die, it bringeth forth much fruit." His answer disclosed the manner of his glorification—the surrender of his human life, which was to result in resurrection. He went on to encourage his followers to the same spirit of self-renunciation, promising it would lead to glory: "He that loveth his life shall lose it; and he that hateth his life in this world shall keep it unto life eternal. If any man serve me, let him follow me . . . him will my Father honour."

The path to his exaltation lay through humiliation; that he should shrink from dying at the hands of sinful men was humanly natural. He prayed aloud: "Now is my soul troubled; and what shall I say? Father, save me from this hour: but for this cause came I unto this hour. Father, glorify thy name." While he recoiled at the impending shadow of the cross, he shrank immeasurably more from the thought of any failure on his part to fulfill the Father's plan; but his instant acknowledgment that his sacrifice could only glorify God banished the momentary uncertainty that he would not endure. This inner struggle was a forerunner of the mental agony of Gethsemane.

As he was speaking, a voice from heaven—the same that had spoken at his Baptism and Transfiguration—was heard: "I have both glorified it, and will glorify it again." Some of the crowd thought they heard thunder; others thought an angel spoke to him. "This voice came not because of me, but for your sakes," Jesus explained. "Now is the judgment of this world: now shall the prince of this world be cast out [a judgment of doom on Satan's kingdom to come simultaneously with Jesus' 'hour' of glorification]. And I, if I be lifted up from the earth, will draw all men unto me."

Puzzled, the people asked, "We have heard out of the law [Old Testament] that Christ abideth for ever: and how sayest thou, The Son of man must be lifted up? who is this Son of man?" (compare Ps. 110:4; Is. 9:7; Dan. 2:44; 7:13,14). Jesus did not explain; they would not have understood; rather he urged them to believe in him: "Yet a little while is the light with you. Walk while ye have the light, lest darkness come upon you . . . believe in the light, that ye may be the children of light."

Jews' Rejection of Jesus

Jn. 12:37-50

The Master's public teaching was finished. Though he had a large following among the common people, the nation as a whole still refused to accept him, and the secret disciples he had won among the rulers dared not admit their faith openly for fear of excommunication by the Pharisees. The nation's unbelief is summed up by John in the words of Isaiah: "Lord, who hath believed our report? and to whom hath the arm of the Lord been revealed? . . . He hath blinded their eyes, and hardened their heart; that they should not see with their eyes, nor understand with their heart, and be converted, and I should heal them" (see Is. 53:1; 6:10).

He left the Temple, never to enter its precincts again, warning that rejection of him was essentially a rejection of God and that such denial would come under judgment: "He that rejecteth me, and receiveth not my words, hath one that judgeth him: the word that I have spoken, the same shall judge him in the last day."

Discourse
Destruction of Jerusalem
Signs of Christ's Coming
Last Judgment

Mt. 24-25; Mk. 13; Lu. 21:5-38

As they were leaving the Temple the apostles drew Jesus' attention to its magnificent buildings, still in construction. The Temple was a gleaming structure of white marble and plated gold; according to Josephus some of its massive slabs were 35 to 60 feet long, seven and a half feet high, and nine feet broad. All of this gave an impression of strength and impregnability. But Jesus did not look on this spectacular beauty with eyes of admiration. Had not the Temple rejected its true high priest (Heb. 8)? Instead, "As for these things which ye behold, the days will come, in the which there shall not be left one stone upon another, that shall not be thrown down."

Through the east gate Jesus and the Twelve left Jerusalem. Descending the steep side of the Kidron ravine, they crossed over and climbed the stony ascent of the Mount of Olives. From its summit the city spread before them, the huge dome of the sanctuary shining in the last rays of the setting sun. Peter, James, John, and Andrew asked Jesus privately for an explanation of his recent words about the Temple: "Tell us, when shall these things be? and what shall be the sign of thy coming, and of the end of the world [RV (marg.) the consummation of the age]?"

Underlying this question were centuries of Jewish inquiry as to the final condition of man and the world—eschatological views that reflected developing

Jewish reasoning on the end of the present world order, the coming of the Messianic kingdom, the resurrection of the dead, judgment of the righteous and the wicked, and the consummation of all things (see Messianic Hope, p. 220). An accepted part of these beliefs, fostered by apocalyptic Jewish writers of the intertestamental period and briefly alluded to in the Old Testament, was the idea that the Messianic age would be preceded by a time of travail and by cataclysmic events. It was therefore natural that Jesus' answer should make use of these current ideas and terms when imparting his own moral and spiritual views on the many phases of this important subject.

Heretofore Jesus had made only veiled reference to his Second Coming (*Parousia*, a Greek term denoting Christ's future advent [Mt. 24:3,27,37,39]); the apostles' twofold question had brought the topic to the fore. He now began to teach them the "when" and the "what" of his Coming, but he spoke in apocalyptic language of the signs that would precede it. The time period relating to each was intentionally indefinite and the order of events mentioned not necessarily chronological; they were signs of the end of the present world age, which would mark the birth pangs of the Messianic Age. The first portion of his discourse might be said to fall into four parts: (1) False Christs (Mt. 24:4-8; Mk. 13:5-8; Lu. 21:8-11); (2) Persecution, Apostasy, World-wide Preaching (Mt. 24:9-14; Mk. 13:9-13; Lu. 21:12-19); (3) Fall of Jerusalem, the Great Tribulation (Mt. 24:15-22; Mk. 13:14-20; Lu. 21:20-24); (4) Coming of the Son of Man (Mt. 24:23-36; Mk. 13:21-32; Lu. 21:25-33; see Lu. 17:22-24).

False Christs

The Jews expected that their Messiah would restore Israel's greatness, subdue the Gentile nations, and establish the triumphant reign of God over the earth. The chief reason for their rejection of Jesus was political: he had not fulfilled these hopes. Consequently Jesus foresaw the rise of false claimants to the Messiahship after his departure, so he began his answer with a warning: "Take heed that no man deceive you. For many shall come in my name, saying, I am Christ; and shall deceive many." (Several of the false Christs who soon arose are mentioned in Acts—Theudas, Judas of Galilee, and "the Egyptian" [Acts 5:36,37;21:38]—and referred to by Josephus [*Antiquities of the Jews*, xx, 5.1; *Wars of the Jews*, ii, 8.1; *Antiq.* xx, 8.6].) He drew a graphic picture of the unrest and upheaval to occur before the full splendor of the kingdom could be made manifest: "Ye shall hear of wars and rumours of wars: see that ye be not troubled: for all these things must come to pass, but

the end is not yet. For nation shall rise against nation ... and there shall be famines, and pestilences, and earthquakes, in divers places. All these are the beginning of sorrows [RV of travail]."

Persecutions, Apostasy, World-wide Preaching

He forewarned the disciples of conflict, external and internal, against his Church: persecutions civil and ecclesiastical, hatred, betrayal of brother by brother, son by father, parents by children. He prophesied that the love of many for Christ would "wax cold," but promised that "He that shall endure unto the end, the same shall be saved." While believers were enduring the period of apostasy, the gospel was to be preached "in all the world for a witness ... and then shall the end come."

Fall of Jerusalem, the Great Tribulation

Becoming more precise in his predictions, Jesus forecast the historical event that was imminent in the apostles' lifetime—the destruction of Jerusalem, which would be attended and followed by a period of great distress and suffering. This would transpire (according to Matthew and Mark) when the "abomination of desolation" should "stand in the holy place" (Mt.), "standing where it ought not" (Mk.)—a desecration of the Temple greater than that of Antiochus Epiphanes spoken of by Daniel (Dan. 8:13; 11:31; compare I Macc. 1:35-67; see also p. 214). Luke alone quotes Jesus as saying "When ye shall see Jerusalem compassed with armies, then know that the desolation thereof is nigh" (Lu. 21:20).

This prophecy has been interpreted by scholars as referring to the desecration of the Temple by the Zealots in 66-67 A.D., its profanation by the presence of the ensigns of the Roman army in the Holy Place, or (because of its apocalyptic imagery) to a form of antichrist.

In the period of tribulation to follow, the infant Church would be in jeopardy. Jesus told them that when Jerusalem became the arena of conflict his followers were to escape to safety: "Then let them which are in Judaea flee to the mountains. ... For these be the days of vengeance, that all things which are written may be fulfilled ... for there shall be great distress in the land, and wrath upon this people. And they shall fall by the edge of the sword, and shall be led away captive into all nations: and Jerusalem shall be trodden down of the Gentiles, until the times of the Gentiles be fulfilled" (Lu.). (Compare Rom. 11:25,26.) "Then shall be great tribulation, such as was not since the beginning of the world to this time, no, nor ever shall be. And except those days should be shortened, there should no flesh be saved: but for the elect's sake those days shall be shortened" (Mt.).

Within the lifetime of some of the apostles these prophecies began to be fulfilled: in the flight of the apostles and the Jerusalem church to Pella in Peraea in 66 A.D., in the siege and fall of Jerusalem to the Romans in 70 (see p. 468), in the harsh enslavement of those who survived, in the predominance of the Gentile role in the spreading of the gospel. The great tribulation of which Jesus spoke as beginning in his generation still goes on in human experience, for prophetic history has not yet been fully consummated; but in Christ's promise that the time would be shortened, Christians have long found, and can still find, comfort.

The Coming of the Son of Man

Because the final coming of the Son of man would not be immediate, Jesus repeated his warning concerning false Christs and their deceiving works. His coming in the Spirit would not be secret or localized, but open and manifest—"For as the lightning cometh out of the east, and shineth even unto the west; so shall also the coming of the Son of man be." These things had been told them for their protection, to put them on guard against the doctrines of spurious leaders. Jesus therefore added this admonition: "Take ye heed: behold, I have foretold you all things." It was essential that his apostles and the Church understand that these signs were not to be feared but to be recognized as signs of overturning "until he come whose right it is" (Ezek. 21:27).

Rapidly he summarized the last signs to precede his Coming: "There shall be signs in the sun, and in the moon, and in the stars; and upon the earth distress of nations, with perplexity; the sea and the waves roaring; Men's hearts failing them for fear, and for looking after those things which are coming on the earth: for the powers of heaven shall be shaken."

That the apostles' faith might remain strong, Jesus immediately led their thought beyond the tribulation and overturning to the saving sign of his coming in glory: "Then shall appear the sign of the Son of man in heaven: and then shall all the tribes of the earth mourn, and they shall see the Son of man coming in the clouds of heaven with power and great glory." Coincident with Christ's coming his angels would sound the trumpet to assemble the whole body of faithful believers: "He shall send his angels with a great sound of a trumpet, and they shall gather together his elect from the four winds, from one end of heaven to the other" (compare I Th. 4:16,17).

Because his words (in Matthew 24) relating to the "when" of his Coming have a metaphorical as well as a historical meaning, interpretations of them have great latitude:

"the end is not yet" (v. 6)

"these are the beginning" (v. 8)

"then shall the end come" (v. 14)

"When ye ... shall see the abomination of desolation ... stand in the holy place. ... Then let them which be in Judaea flee into the mountains" (vv. 15,16)

"then shall be great tribulation ... but for the elect's sake those days shall be shortened" (vv. 21,22)

"Immediately after the tribulation of those days shall the sun be darkened, and the moon shall not give her light, and the stars shall fall from heaven, and the powers of the heavens shall be shaken: And then shall appear the sign of the Son of man in heaven" (vv. 29,30)

Parable of the Fig Tree and Young Leaves

To encourage his followers to press on during the dark hours before his Second Advent, by the parable of a fig tree Jesus translated the signs of tribulation into symbols of hope, for as this tree putting forth leaves portends summer, so these signs would mark his return: "When these things begin to come to pass, then look up, and lift up your heads; for your redemption draweth nigh." With absolute conviction he reaffirmed that all he had spoken would come to pass, but revealed that even he did not know the exact time: "Heaven and earth shall pass away, but my words shall not pass away. But of that day and hour knoweth no man, no, not the angels of heaven, but my Father only."

The two questions [concerning the Parousia] that are really left open are those of the time and the manner. The view that seems best to cover the admittedly wide diversity of the N.T. teaching on the question may be stated as follows: (1) He has already returned in that life of the Spirit which sprang up among believing men, best exemplified in the Church. (2) He is still in process of returning according as men see more clearly and apply more consistently what he can mean for the world. (3) He is yet to return in still greater power as men surrender more completely to his Spirit. (4) There will be a final consummation in the recognition of his universal Lordship, described by Paul as the time when "all things shall have been made subject to Christ" (see I Cor. 15:23-28).[68]

The second portion of this discourse also falls into four sections: (1) Admonitions to Watch (Mt. 24:37-51; Mk. 13:33-37; Lu. 21:34-36); (2) Parable of the Ten Virgins (Mt. 25:1-13); (3) Parable of the Talents (Mt. 25:14-30); (4) Description of Last Judgment (Mt. 25:31-46). Here Jesus further emphasized the paramount necessity of preparation for "that day" and "that hour" of the Coming he had just prophesied. It would come suddenly and swiftly—a day of judgment, a day of redemption of the righteous and of vengeance to the wicked.

Admonitions to Watch

Using parable language, Jesus urged his disciples, and by implication his Church, to constant vigilance that they might "be accounted worthy to escape all these things that shall come to pass, and to stand before the Son of man."

"If the goodman of the house had known in what watch the thief would come, he would have watched, and would not have suffered his house to be broken up. Therefore be ye also ready: for in such an hour as ye think not the Son of man cometh."

"Who then is a faithful and wise servant," Jesus asked, "whom his lord hath made ruler over his household, to give them meat in due season [to feed the church of God, Acts 20:28]?" He answered his own question with the parable of the faithful and unfaithful servants who were summarily rewarded according to their service (Mt. 24:46-51; compare Lu. 12:42-46).

Parable of the Ten Virgins

Vigilance was not enough; Jesus therefore warned them yet more emphatically "against the peril of the drowsy life and the smouldering lamp."[69] Individual preparation was also essential, for to see Christ in his glory each of his followers must be enlightened and ready. He compared his Second Advent to the happy occasion of a marriage during which the bridesmaids went out to welcome the bridegroom as he came to the marriage feast. "Then shall the kingdom of heaven be likened unto ten virgins, which took their lamps, and went forth to meet the bridegroom. And five of them were wise, and five were foolish. They that were foolish took their lamps, and took no oil with them: But the wise took oil in their vessels with their lamps."

All were virgins. All possessed lamps. All went forth to meet the bridegroom, but the bridegroom did not come immediately. All slept. All heard the midnight cry: "Behold, the bridegroom cometh; go ye out to meet him." All arose and trimmed their lamps; all were willing to meet the bridegroom, but not all were ready. The foolish had made no provision for the delay and were unaware of their defection until the test of endurance came. Their oil was exhausted and they could not borrow from the wise: "Go ye rather to them that sell, and buy for yourselves." While they went to do that which should already have been done, the bridegroom came; "and they that were ready went in with him to the marriage: and the door was shut." As the wise man of Matthew 7:24 built his house on a rock to withstand the adversities of life, so the wise virgins laid up strong reserves of spiritual character to

endure the delay of the bridegroom's coming. Too late the foolish virgins came again, beseeching "Lord, Lord, open to us," only to receive the answer "Verily I say unto you, I know you not."

> ... the real difference between the two classes who profess to love the Lord's appearing is a *radical* one—the possession by the one class of *an enduring principle of spiritual life,* and the want of it by the other.[70]

The Master desired that all enter the kingdom; he foresaw the burden of disappointment, sorrow, and remorse of those on whom the door would be shut. He closed this parable with the warning "Watch therefore. . . ."

Parable of the Talents

The parable of the ten virgins represents the servants of Christ as awaiting his coming; this parable represents them as active in his service. Laying stress on the interval of absence before the Second Advent, Jesus emphasized the disciples' duty to make full use of their natural abilities and of their moral and spiritual capabilities.

"The kingdom of heaven is as a man travelling into a far country, who called his own servants, and delivered unto them his goods." He gave eight talents—"to every man according to his several ability"—to one five, to another two, and to another one (see Talent, p. 278). After a long time the servants' master returned and demanded an accounting; he found that while seven talents had been put to use and multiplied, one had been buried in the earth. The two servants who had doubled their talents received the blessing "Well done, thou good and faithful servant: thou hast been faithful over a few things, I will make thee ruler over many things: enter thou into the joy of thy lord." To the fearful servant who returned his talent unused came the rebuke "Thou wicked and slothful servant. . . . Take therefore the talent from him, and give it unto him which hath ten talents. . . . And cast ye the unprofitable servant into outer darkness."

The teaching was plain. Though each man's gift was distinctive and peculiar to him, each was afforded the same measure of privilege, opportunity, and responsibility for service to Christ in the establishment of his kingdom on earth. Those who proved faithful to Christ's demands and appropriated their gifts for good were accorded the full measure of Christ's love and joy, while he who allowed his talent to lie dormant lost it, excluding himself from the joy of the kingdom. Paul later wrote "Be instant in season, out of season . . . do the work of an evangelist, make full proof of thy ministry" (II Tim. 4:2,5).

Description of the Last Judgment

Jesus passed now to the subject of the final judgment that would take place at the end of the age or present world order (a judgment later to be fully developed and portrayed prophetically in Revelation). Again he clothed his message in parable form—the parable of the sheep and the goats. As the exalted King-Messiah, supreme in power and attended by the radiant hosts of heaven, the Son of man would judge the righteous and the wicked according to their works. From his position of majesty he would honor all those worthy to inherit the kingdom and invite them to partake of its joys; upon the wicked he would pronounce the retribution of "everlasting punishment."

"When the Son of man shall come in his glory, and all the holy angels with him, then shall he sit upon the throne of his glory: And before him shall be gathered all nations: and he shall separate them one from another, as a shepherd divideth his sheep from the goats: And he shall set the sheep on his right hand, but the goats on the left."

To those on his right hand the King said: "Come, ye blessed of my Father, inherit the kingdom prepared for you from the foundation of the world: For I was an hungred, and ye gave me meat: I was thirsty, and ye gave me drink: I was a stranger, and ye took me in: Naked, and ye clothed me: I was sick, and ye visited me: I was in prison, and ye came unto me. . . . Inasmuch as ye have done it unto one of the least of these my brethren, ye have done it unto me."

To those on his left hand: "Depart from me, ye cursed, into everlasting fire, prepared for the devil and his angels. . . . Inasmuch as ye did it not to one of the least of these, ye did it not to me. And these shall go away into everlasting punishment: but the righteous into life eternal."

The severe judgment pronounced on the wicked at Christ's Coming is not an arbitrary one on the part of the Judge; it is the punishment men have brought upon themselves by their failure to love God and practice brotherhood, whereas the righteous have earned redemption and eternal life by their practice of the love of Christ.

The liberal view of modern theology is that the eschatological outlook of Jesus [regarding the kingdom] was borrowed from, or accommodated to, temporary forms of Jewish thought, and that the valuable and enduring element is the conception of the Kingdom as entering into the life of mankind in this world, growing in range and power, and destined to permeate society and all its institutions with its Divine spirit. From this point of view the Second Coming, the central event of the history, is to be understood as a spiritual return which has been taking place in the events of history from Pentecost down to the present hour. Similarly the Last Judgment is interpreted as a continuous process which runs parallel with the history of nations and churches.[71]

The Conspiracy   Mt. 26:1-5, 14-16; Mk. 14:1,2,10,11; Lu. 22:1-6

After Jesus had finished these tremendous eschatological revelations, his thought reverted to his coming death. Aware of the wickedness fermenting in the minds of his enemies and of the fact that his time was now very short, he confided to the apostles the time of his betrayal: "Ye know that after two days is the feast of the passover, and the Son of man is betrayed to be crucified."

Perhaps even as he was speaking, the chief priests, scribes, and elders met in the house of the high priest Caiaphas to plot Jesus' death. But they must take him without arousing the populace. This could not be easily accomplished, for the city was crowded with pilgrims and strangers who regarded the Galilean either as a great prophet or as the promised Messiah. There were no open grounds for attack—his righteousness was above reproach—but from Jesus' own band a disloyal apostle provided a way to apprehend him. Judas Iscariot, seething with dissatisfactions heretofore latent, stole away from the apostles sometime during that evening and, bargaining with the chief priests, agreed to betray his Master for thirty pieces of silver (an amount equivalent to about nineteen dollars, the price of a slave; see Ex. 21:32; Zech. 11:12,13). From that moment he watched for an opportunity to betray Jesus when the people were not there. This act set in motion a series of events from which there was no turning back.

Judas, the only Judean of the Twelve, may have joined the group in the first place from political motives, and the betrayal may have been due to personal disappointment. But this in nowise excuses Judas. For weeks and months he lived in the presence of Jesus and had the greatest opportunity ever offered to any man to come to a proper understanding of the true nature of the kingdom of God. So far was Judas from being a victim of divine predestination that the utmost God could do to save a man—show him Jesus Christ—was done for him. Judas destroyed himself physically because he came to realize that he had already destroyed himself morally. . . . The idea that he was a necessary step in God's plan to save the world is utterly false. Jesus was not crucified because Judas betrayed him. He went to Jerusalem expressly to suffer death, and he made no effort to escape it once he was convinced it was the Father's will.[72]

Wednesday

The Gospels are silent concerning Wednesday, which Jesus apparently spent in complete seclusion in Bethany. This day of rest has been called "a Sabbath to His Soul." It has its analogy in Revelation (8:1) in the "silence in heaven about the space of half an hour" that followed the opening of the seven seals. That it was a day filled with prayer and communion and a full realization of his oneness with the Father was attested by Jesus' serenity on the two succeeding days as he bade farewell to his beloved apostles and submitted heroically to the death of the cross.

Thursday

The next day, Thursday, marked Jesus' last day with his own, and was one of fellowship and intimate communion with them. At its close he observed the Passover and instituted a new sacrament. He summarized for the apostles the essence of his ministry; however, even in his final discourses he continued to speak almost wholly by figure and parable. Jesus' closest companions still apprehended little of what lay ahead. Thinking only of their need—"[loving] them unto the end"—he strengthened them for the terrible hours of coming crisis, leading them as far into the holy of holies of his consciousness as they could follow. Far from being left without hope, they were encouraged by his certainty of ultimate triumph and by his promise of another Comforter, "the Spirit of truth," which would remain with them forever.

Last Supper   Mt. 26:17-35; Mk. 14:12-31; Lu. 22:7-38; Jn. 13-17

The Passover Meal

This feast was to be held in the early evening of this Thursday, and it was necessary to make ready for it before sunset.* At noon all labor ceased, and every family in Jerusalem and environs was engaged in its preparation: the paschal lamb was slain; its sacrificial parts—the blood and the fat—were taken to the

*There is a question as to whether Jesus observed the actual Passover meal on this day as the Synoptics state or an anticipatory one because of his coming death, for, according to John, the Passover did not take place until Friday (Jn. 18:28).

Temple to be presented at the altar, while the remainder was to be eaten in the home with unleavened bread and bitter herbs (see Feasts, p. 60).

"Where wilt thou that we prepare for thee to eat the passover?" Jesus' apostles asked. Since Bethany was considered within the limits of Jerusalem, the Passover could have been observed in Bethany, but he chose to observe it in the Holy City. The true Lamb of God would close his mission where it had begun and there eat with his disciples the paschal lamb, which prefigured in type his sacrifice for "the sinfulness of human sin." He directed Peter and John to "Go into the city to such a man, and say unto him, The Master saith, My time is at hand; I will keep the passover at thy house with my disciples" (Mt.) "And he will shew you a large upper room furnished and prepared: there make ready for us" (Mk.).

The Passover meal began shortly after six o'clock; only the Twelve were present with him.* As they reclined on low couches at the table (see Meals, p. 44), Jesus, with the sorrowful and yet glorious knowledge that he was soon to leave them, said, "With desire I have desired to eat this passover with you before I suffer."

Sometime during this supper a contention arose among the apostles. Unable properly to evaluate the Master's triumphs and confidences of this week and not yet having relinquished their hopes of a worldly Messianic kingdom, they began to argue as to who should be greatest—a subject that should never have intruded itself into this sacred hour. Jesus silenced them with a question: "Whether is greater, he that sitteth at meat, or he that serveth? is not he that sitteth at meat? but I am among you as he that serveth." He promised each would receive a kingdom and a throne, and be accorded the honor of eating and drinking at his table in his kingdom because they had served with him throughout the many trials of his ministry.

Jesus enforced the lesson of selfless service with a symbolic act. He took a towel, and girding himself, washed the feet of each of his apostles. Peter shrank from this act of humility on the Master's part (feet-washing was the function of a slave), but Jesus pointed out the true significance of his act: "What I do thou knowest not now; but thou shalt know hereafter. . . . If I wash thee not, thou hast no part

*The probable order of the Passover feast: (1) The first cup of wine was blessed. (2) The hands were washed and a prayer offered. (3) Bitter herbs dipped in vinegar and fruit juice were eaten, and the paschal lamb was placed on the table. (4) The father of the house was asked by the eldest son to explain the meaning of the Passover (Ex. 12:26,27). (5) The second cup of wine was blessed. (6) The first part of the Hallel was sung (Pss. 113, 114). (7) The lamb was eaten, with unleavened bread and thank offerings. (8) The third cup of wine (the cup of blessing) was blessed. (9) The fourth cup of wine was served. (10) The second part of the Hallel was sung (Pss. 115-118).

with me." When Peter realized that he meant purification of heart, he welcomed the cleansing. Mindful that he had just washed the feet of his betrayer, Jesus added, "Ye are clean, but not all." Only Judas could have understood these words. Jesus continued, "Know ye what I have done to you? . . . If I then, your Lord and Master, have washed your feet; ye also ought to wash one another's feet. For I have given you an example, that ye should do as I have done to you."

As the paschal supper proceeded Jesus was troubled about Judas, and he declared, "One of you shall betray me." Sorrowfully, one by one, they asked, "Lord, is it I?" Finally he answered: "He that dippeth his hand with me in the dish, the same shall betray me . . . woe unto that man . . . it had been good for that man if he had not been born" (Mt.). "He it is, to whom I shall give a sop, when I have dipped it" (Jn.). Dipping a thin piece of bread into the main dish, he gave it to Judas Iscariot; after that Satan entered into Judas. Jesus had been aware that Judas was conspiring against him, yet he had continued to cherish him as his disciple until, at this feast, Judas showed himself barren of any response.

At once Jesus dismissed him: "That thou doest, do quickly." John records that none of the others knew for what purpose this was said. Judas immediately went out, and "it was night"—not only a point in time but also a spiritual darkness in Judas.

Institution of the Lord's Supper

The observance of the Passover meal was now concluded. Jesus' homage to the ritual of this ancient ceremony had been given for the last time. Reverently turning from the past, Jesus instituted a new spiritual communion in the presence of the faithful eleven. Using bread and wine as symbols of that communion, he took bread, blessed it, broke it, and gave it to his apostles with the words "Take, eat; this is my body [Luke adds 'which is given for you']." Then he took the cup, gave thanks, and gave it to them, saying, "Drink ye all of it; For this is my blood of the new testament [new covenant], which is shed for many [RV poured out for you] for the remission of sins" (Mt.). "This do in remembrance of me" (Lu.). "And they all drank of it," dedicating themselves to the new covenant he was inaugurating (Heb. 8:8-10; 10:5-9). Thus simply did the Master set the pattern of a sacrament that would continually bring to the mind of the Christian his supreme offering of selfless love. This sacrament has since been called the Lord's Supper or the Eucharist.

In the intimacy of this Last Supper Jesus did indeed commune with them, and give of his "body," continuing to pour out that life-giving stream of truth and love that had animated his whole ministry and would inspire theirs.

With the traitor no longer in their midst, Jesus opened his heart to these closest friends, sharing unrestrainedly what was uppermost in his thought—that he was going to the Father. Though the time was a sad one because he was leaving them, it was nevertheless an exalting one as he drew them nearer to himself and to each other in bonds of love and as he spoke freely of his unique relationship to God.

In the hour that followed Jesus revealed that his parting from them was imminent, and that the sorrowful experience before him was in reality a glorification of both himself and the Father: "Now is the Son of man glorified, and God is glorified in him." He looked with anticipation to his return to the Father, which would follow his overcoming of the cross, a triumph in which he would magnify the Father and the Father would exalt him; and in this joy the suffering and humiliation of the cross would become as a thing of no account. He urged them to the practice of love:

> "Little children, yet a little while I am with you. Ye shall seek me: and as I said unto the Jews, Whither I go, ye cannot come; so now I say to you. A *new* commandment I give unto you, That ye love one another; *as I have loved you, that ye also love one another.* By this shall all men know that ye are my disciples, if ye have love one to another."

For the moment they did not heed the new commandment, thinking only of their separation from him. In dismay Peter asked: "Lord, whither goest thou?" and Jesus replied, "Whither I go, thou canst not follow me now; but thou shalt follow me afterwards." Peter protested: "Lord, why cannot I follow thee now? I will lay down my life for thy sake." "Wilt thou lay down thy life for my sake?" Jesus asked searchingly. "I say unto thee, The cock shall not crow, till thou hast denied me thrice."

Knowing that the loyalty of this impetuous disciple would soon be tested, Jesus comforted him. "Simon, Simon, behold, Satan hath desired to have you, that he may sift you as wheat: But I have prayed for thee, that thy faith fail not: and when thou art converted, strengthen thy brethren." He knew the depths of Peter's love, but he knew his faith was still vulnerable. He knew also that Peter would be chastened, that he would falter but not fail. "Lord, I am ready to go with thee, both into prison, and to death," Peter asserted vehemently. Having loved and served the Master, he could not conceive of any ordeal that would cause him to forsake him. (According to Matthew, this assertion of loyalty was made later, on the walk to Gethsemane, by the other apostles as well.)

Discourse
Christ the Way
the Truth, the Life Jn. 14

Perceiving that the separation loomed large in their thought, Jesus admonished them to trust:

"Let not your heart be troubled: ye believe in God, believe also in me. In my Father's house are many mansions: if it were not so, I would have told you. I go to prepare a place for you. And if I go ... I will come again, and receive you unto myself; that where I am, there ye may be also. And whither I go ye know, and the way ye know."

Thomas protested: "Lord, we know not whither thou goest; and how can we know the way?" In one succinct statement Jesus summarized his lifework for Thomas and clarified anew the oneness of the Father and the Son.

"I am the way, the truth, and the life; no man cometh unto the Father, but by me. If ye had known me, ye should have known my Father also: and from henceforth ye know him, and have seen him."

Philip, too, failing still fully to understand the like nature of God and His Christ, entreated: "Lord, shew us the Father, and it sufficeth us." Jesus answered patiently. "Have I been so long time with you, and yet hast thou not known me, Philip? he that hath seen me hath seen the Father; and how sayest thou then, Shew us the Father? Believest thou not that I am in the Father, and the Father in me? the words that I speak unto you I speak not of myself: but the Father that dwelleth in me, he doeth the works."

From queries such as these of Peter, Thomas, and Philip, Jesus saw his disciples' need for continued help and instruction. His next words reassured them that his and the Father's love would always be with them. It was only within this hour of parting that he told them of the Comforter (Paraclete; from the Gk. *parakletos* "advocate," "helper"), which would replace his human presence. Henceforth his presence would be in their hearts as a living force, strengthening them with grace and power.

"He that believeth on me, the works that I do shall he do also; and greater works than these shall he do; because I go unto my Father. And whatsoever ye shall ask in my name, that will I do, that the Father may be glorified in the Son. . . .

"If ye love me, keep my commandments. And I will pray the Father, and he shall give you another Comforter, that he may abide with you for ever; Even the Spirit of truth; whom the world cannot receive, because it seeth him not, neither knoweth him: but ye know him; for he dwelleth with you, and shall be in you. . . . Yet a little while, and the world seeth me no more; but ye see me: because I live, ye shall live also."

Judas (not Iscariot) asked earnestly, "Lord, how is it that thou wilt manifest thyself unto us, and not unto the world?" Jesus explained it was because they loved him and were receptive to his teachings. "If a man love me, he will keep my words: and my Father will love him, and we will come unto him, and make our abode with him." Here again is his assertion that the Father and the Son are inseparable. (The same truth is seen in its fulfillment in Revelation in the relationship of God and the Lamb [Rev. 21:22,23; 22:3].)

Carrying his revelation further, Jesus now spoke of the office of the Comforter in the Father's plan. As the Father had sent the Son to represent Him, so the Father would send the Holy Ghost to continue His Son's work and interpret his teachings to generations to come. The meaning of all that the Son had imparted would in due time be fully understood as men grew in spiritual stature.

"These things have I spoken unto you, being yet present with you. But the Comforter, which is the Holy Ghost, whom the Father will send in my name, he shall teach you all things, and bring all things to your remembrance, whatsoever I have said unto you."

Jesus urged his apostles not to look on his departure with sorrow, but rather with peace, joy, and expectant hope, for his return to the Father would mark the perfect completion of his work.

"Peace I leave with you, my peace I give unto you: not as the world giveth, give I unto you. Let not your heart be troubled, neither let it be afraid. Ye have heard how I said unto you, I go away, and come again unto you. If ye loved me, ye would rejoice, because I said, I go unto the Father: for my Father is greater than I."

There remained before him one more task to accomplish for the world—the overcoming of Satan's last temptation, death.

"Hereafter I will not talk much with you: for the prince of this world cometh, and hath nothing in me. But that the world may know that I love the Father; and as the Father gave me commandment, even so I do. Arise, let us go hence."

Discourse
The Vine and the Branches   Jn. 15

Even as Jesus urged them to gird their thought and hasten toward the experience with him—"Arise, let us go hence"—he did not bring his confidences to an end. He pressed on to tell them more. Using the appropriate figure of a vine and its branches, he emphasized the paramount truth that to bear the fruit of the Spirit his disciples must continue to live in closest union with him, Christ. As branches of a vine are pruned to vitalize them for greater fruitfulness, so they too must be willing to let all unworthiness be stripped away to quicken them to greater spiritual fruit. If not, they would be barren and useless.

"I am the true vine, and my Father is the husbandman. Every branch in me that beareth not fruit he taketh away: and every branch that beareth fruit, he purgeth it, that it may bring forth more fruit. . . .

"I am the vine, ye are the branches: He that abideth in me, and I in him, the same bringeth forth much fruit: for without me ye can do nothing. If a man abide not in me, he is cast forth as a branch, and is withered. . . . Herein is my Father glorified, that ye bear much fruit; so shall ye be my disciples."

Feeling his apostles now responsive, he gave to love a new dimension.

"This is my commandment, That ye love one another, *as I have loved you.* Greater love hath no man than this, that a man lay down his life for his friends. Ye are my friends, if ye do whatsoever I command you. . . . Ye have not chosen me, but I have chosen you, and ordained you, that ye should go and bring forth fruit, and that your fruit should remain. . . ."

Up to this time the world's hatred had been focused chiefly on him, but Jesus knew that that enmity would now be directed against these, his representatives. He well knew how men reacted under hatred of truth. So Jesus again forewarned of persecution. But he also assured his disciples that the illuminating presence of the Comforter and their own authoritative witness to the truth would triumph over the world's hatred.

"If the world hate you, ye know that it hated me before it hated you. If ye were of the world, the world would love his own: but because ye are not of the world, but I have chosen you out of the world, therefore the world hateth you. . . . If they have persecuted me, they will also persecute you. . . . But all these things will they do unto you for my name's sake, because they know not him that sent me. . . ."

Discourse
His Going and Returning   Jn. 16

They sat sad and silent as Jesus explained the necessity of his departure.

"It is expedient for you that I go away: for if I go not away, the Comforter will not come unto you; but if I depart, I will send him unto you."

It was better for them that Christ's personal presence should be withdrawn, in order that His spiritual presence might be nearer to them than ever, or, rather, might for the first time truly begin. This would be effected by the coming of the Holy Ghost, when He who was now "with" them, would be ever "in" them.[73]

In this Comforter his followers would have an Advocate whose coming would indict the world on three counts:

"Of sin, because they believe not on me; Of righteousness, because I go to my Father, and ye see me no more; Of judgment, because the prince of this world is judged."

He will **convince** it **of righteousness**, for whereas his enemies thought that Jesus was discredited by the shameful death on the Cross, it would become evident that his death was a return to the Father, who had welcomed him as "the Holy and Righteous One" (cf. Acts 3:14; 2:36; 5:30-32). The Resurrection cancels the shame of the Cross and vindicates the righteousness of Jesus.[74]

The work of the Advocate was also to reveal the "many things" Jesus had to leave unsaid.

"I have yet many things to say unto you, but ye cannot bear them now. Howbeit when he, the Spirit of truth is come, he will guide you into all truth: for he shall not speak of himself; but whatsoever he shall hear, that shall he speak: and he will shew you things to come. He shall glorify me: for he shall receive of mine, and shall shew it unto you."

The Master now encouraged them with the promise that their sorrow would be brief and that it would be followed by a lasting joy, for they would see him again.

"A little while, and ye shall not see me: and again, a little while, and ye shall see me, because I go to the Father. . . . Ye shall weep and lament, but the world shall rejoice: and ye shall be sorrowful, but your sorrow shall be turned into joy. . . . I will see you again, and your heart shall rejoice, and your joy no man taketh from you."

He further declared that in that day when they were taught by the Spirit of truth they would find they could pray directly to the Father, and through the Comforter's teachings understand all that he had been telling them.

"These things have I spoken unto you in proverbs: but the time cometh, when I shall no more speak unto you in proverbs, but I shall shew you plainly of the Father. At that day ye shall ask in my name: and I say not unto you, that I will pray the Father for you: For the Father himself loveth you, because ye have loved me, and have believed that I came out from God. I came forth from the Father, and am come into the world: again, I leave the world, and go to the Father."

As he affirmed this truth the apostles responded quickly: "Lo, now speakest thou plainly, and speakest no proverb [parable] . . . by this we believe that thou camest forth from God." But Jesus, foreseeing their terrified desertion within the hour, searched their thought again with a penetrating question: "Do ye now believe? Behold, the hour cometh, yea, is now come, that ye shall be scattered, every man to his own, and shall leave me alone: and yet I am not alone, because the Father is with me." And he concluded his discourse with a promise of victory:

"These things have I spoken unto you, that in me ye might have peace. In the world ye shall have tribulation: but be of good cheer; I have overcome the world."

Jesus' Intercessory Prayer   Jn. 17

The Savior brought his hour of communion to a close with a threefold prayer of intercession. He prayed for himself, for his apostles, and for his future followers.

For himself: "Father, the hour is come; glorify [Wycliffe, clarify] thy Son, that thy Son also may glorify thee: As thou hast given him power over all flesh, that he should give eternal life to as many as thou hast given him. . . . I have glorified thee on the earth: I have finished the work which thou gavest me to do. And now, O Father, glorify thou me with thine own self with the glory which I had with thee before the world was."

For his apostles: "Holy Father, keep through thine own name those whom thou hast given me, that they may be one, as we are. . . . I pray not that thou shouldest take them out of the world, but that thou shouldest keep them from the evil [RV the evil one]. . . . Sanctify them through thy truth: thy word is truth. As thou hast sent me into the world, even so have I also sent them into the world. And for their sakes I sanctify myself, that they also might be sanctified through the truth."

For his future disciples: "Neither pray I for these alone, but for them also which shall believe on me through their word; That they all may be one; as thou, Father, art in me, and I in thee, that they also may be one in us: that the world may believe that thou hast sent me. And the glory which thou gavest me I have given them; that they may be one, even as we are one: I in them, and thou in me, that they may be made perfect in one. . . ."

When they had sung a psalm, they left the upper room to make their way toward the Mount of Olives. Shortly before Thursday midnight Jesus crossed the valley of the Kidron with his apostles and approached the garden of Gethsemane.

Friday

Friday was a day of suffering. It began with Jesus' agonizing struggle in Gethsemane as he awaited his impending crucifixion. From victorious prayer he went forth to face arrest by his enemies; to be tried without mercy or justice, once by the Jewish authorities, once by the Roman; to be subjected to indignity and mockery; and to be crucified like a common thief. Voluntarily he laid down his life that "he might take it again" in his Father's good time.

In Garden
of Gethsemane

Mt. 26:30,36-46; Mk. 14:26, 32-42; Lu. 22:39-46; Jn. 18:1

In the dark hours of Friday morning Jesus came to Gethsemane ("oil press"), a small grove of olive trees at the foot of the Mount of Olives. At its entrance he directed eight of the apostles "Sit ye here, while I go and pray yonder." He advanced beyond the eight in every sense of the term—into a realm they were yet unaware of. He took with him into the garden Peter, James, and John, the three of his disciples who could at that point in time walk with him a bit further in understanding. With his thought weighted by the coming crisis of the cross, he confided, "My soul is exceeding sorrowful, even unto death: tarry ye here, and watch with me."

Withdrawing even from these three, he went "a little farther"—"about a stone's cast." As he had gone many times to a mountain top to pray, so now he went "farther" to a new altitude of consecration and self-surrender. At the beginning of his ministry he had faced the temptation of Satan and repudiated worldly policy; now in Gethsemane he faced the temptation of avoiding the cross. Three times he kneeled down with his face to the ground and prayed for strength and willingness to do the Father's will. The first time he said, "O my Father, if it be possible, let this cup pass from me: nevertheless not as I will, but as thou wilt." An angel appeared "strengthening him," but "being in an agony he prayed more earnestly: and his sweat was

These ancient olive trees in the Garden of Gethsemane (if not the originals then their offshoots) still stand sentinel, silent testimonials to the scene of the Master's agony on the eve of his crucifixion.

as it were great drops of blood falling down to the ground." While he prayed, the apostles slept. When he found them sleeping, he said to Peter: "What, could ye not watch with me one hour? Watch and pray, that ye enter not into temptation: the spirit indeed is willing, but the flesh is weak." These three, so dear and so close to him, failed to grasp this crucial opportunity to stand by him and uphold his cause.

Withdrawing again, his entreaty mounted in earnestness and self-immolation: "O my Father, if this cup may not pass away from me, except I drink it, thy will be done." When he turned again to the three for the support of their prayers, he found them asleep once more. Mark appends the definitive statement "for their eyes were heavy," while Luke explains they were "sleeping for sorrow." (At the Transfiguration they had been "heavy with sleep.") And a third time from his lips came the same intense cry: as the Son of

These venerable trees reproduce for the visitor today the seclusion and simplicity of the traditional site of Gethsemane.

man he entreated that the cup pass from him; as the Son of God he acknowledged "Thy will be done."

The conflict was over, the temptation overcome. He said to his apostles: "Sleep on now, and take your rest: it is enough, the hour is come; behold, the Son of man is betrayed into the hands of sinners. Rise up, let us go; lo, he that betrayeth me is at hand."

Betrayal and
Arrest   Mt. 26:47-56; Mk. 14:43-52; Lu. 22:47-53; Jn. 18:2-12

While Jesus was still speaking of the betrayer, Judas Iscariot appeared at the gate of the garden leading a company of Levites of the Temple guard provided by the Sanhedrin and with them Roman officers appointed to keep order during the arrest. Judas had little difficulty finding his Master, for Jesus often came to this quiet sanctuary for prayer, but lest he escape in the darkness of the morning hour the force had been provided lanterns and torches, swords and staves.

Jesus went forward. "Whom seek ye?" "Jesus of Nazareth." At his calm, fearless "I am he," they recoiled for a moment in confusion. A kiss (the usual salutation by a disciple to a rabbi) had been agreed upon by Judas and the chief priests as the sign of identification—an infamous abuse of his apostleship—so Judas approached and greeted him, "Master, master," and kissed him. Judas' moment of triumph was shattered by Jesus' penetrating question which forced Judas to look within himself at the awful evil he was perpetrating, "Friend, wherefore art thou come?" "Judas, betrayest thou the Son of man with a kiss?"

Jesus' immediate concern was for the safety of the apostles—"If therefore ye seek me, let these go their way"—but as the soldiers seized Jesus, Peter resisted, drew his sword, and cut off the ear of Malchus, the high priest's servant. Strong in the spiritual freedom he had just won in Gethsemane, Jesus reproached Peter: "Put up thy sword into the sheath: the cup which my Father hath given me, shall I not drink it?" (Jn.) ". . . all they that take the sword shall perish with the sword. Thinkest thou that I cannot now pray to my Father, and he shall presently give me more than twelve legions of angels? But how then shall the scriptures be fulfilled, that thus it must be?" (Mt.) (One Roman legion numbered about 6000 infantry. Jesus undoubtedly used the figure of twelve legions, representing an overwhelming force, to teach Peter that God's help superior to all else, was ever available.)

In the midst of the violence of arrest he touched the ear of Malchus and healed him, his love still reaching out to forgive an enemy. This compassionate act also shielded Peter and the other apostles from the danger of retaliation and seizure. The prophecy of desertion made only a few hours before came to pass, for as the soldiers bound Jesus to take him away, all the apostles forsook him and fled.

Jewish Ecclesiastical Trial

Jesus before Annas

(Jn. 18:13-23) Jesus faced two trials: one Jewish, the other Roman. The Jewish trial before the Sanhedrin was ecclesiastical; the Roman trial before Pilate was civil and political. The Sanhedrin had almost complete jurisdiction over the religious life of the Jew and could pronounce the sentence of death upon anyone guilty of certain violations of Mosaic Law, particularly those of blasphemy, Sabbath-breaking, and heresy (see p. 219). Jesus was arraigned before this powerful body as a blasphemer and false prophet who was drawing the people away from orthodox rabbinical teachings.

The Jewish trial, in which Jesus was taken before Annas, Caiaphas, and the Sanhedrin, began long before dawn. According to John's Gospel he was brought first to the palatial residence of Caiaphas in Jerusalem to face an unofficial hearing before Caiaphas' father-in-law Annas. Peter and another disciple, who had fled only to a safe distance from the soldiers, retraced their steps and followed Jesus, still at a distance. "That disciple [John] was known unto the high priest, and went in with Jesus into the palace." Matthew records: "Peter followed him afar off unto the high priest's palace." But John returned to speak to the serving maid at the door so Peter might be admitted into the building's courtyard.

Annas had been high priest from 7 to 15 A.D., but had long since been deposed by the Romans. He had, however, succeeded by political influence and intrigue in keeping the office within his family, and had continued to wield great power even though his son-in-law was titular high priest. Devoid of legal authority, he nevertheless examined Jesus about his disciples and his doctrine in the attempt to obtain some incriminating statement.

Jesus refused to answer Annas' questions: "I spake openly to the world; I ever taught in the synagogue, and in the temple, whither the Jews always resort; and in secret have I said nothing. Why askest thou me? ask them which heard me." At this answer one of the Temple guards struck him for insolence. Annas then sent him to Caiaphas, who awaited his arrival in another part of the building.

Jesus before Caiaphas

(Mt. 26:57-75; Mk. 14:53-72; Lu. 22:54-65; Jn. 18:24-27) Jesus was held under close guard in a room above the courtyard while as many as possible of the members of the Sanhedrin were hastily summoned, for rabbinical law required the presence of at least twenty-three for a quorum. Although the trial they were about to hold had a semblance of legal form, it ruthlessly violated the established rules for the just trial of prisoners. Their purpose, which should have been to work for the prisoner's acquittal, was in this case wholly bent upon his destruction. The law provided that a capital trial could not be held at night or immediately preceding a feast day or the Sabbath; the prisoner was to be adjudged innocent until at least two witnesses had testified and their testimony had been confirmed, and if the prisoner were proven guilty the judges were still required to fast and pray for a full day before pronouncing sentence. This preliminary trial was thus a mockery from the outset, a malicious perversion of justice.

As the members of the Sanhedrin sat cross-legged in a semicircle, the high priest in the center, Jesus was placed bound before them. As he stood entirely at their mercy—or so they thought in their ignorance—they examined witness after witness, trying to find those whose testimony agreed. At last they found two false witnesses who, misquoting his statement in the Temple nearly three years before, testified: "We heard him say, I will destroy this temple that is made with hands, and within three days I will build another made without hands" (see Jn. 2:19-21). But even their testimony was not in full agreement, so no indictment could be made.

Instead of releasing Jesus, Caiaphas further violated the legality of the trial by asking a direct question that would cause the prisoner to testify against himself. "Answerest thou nothing? what is it which these witness against thee?" But Jesus "held his peace, and answered nothing." Frustrated in his attempt to obtain conclusive evidence but still determined to incriminate Jesus, Caiaphas put a second direct question, to which he demanded an answer: "I adjure thee by the living God, that thou tell us whether thou be the Christ, the Son of God." This was even more dangerous to Jesus' case, for it concerned his claim to Messiahship, one the hierarchy had been resisting with every weapon at their command.

Jesus need not have complied. Nevertheless he did answer—"I am," and added without restraint a further claim to honor: "Ye shall see the Son of man sitting on the right hand of power, and coming in the clouds of heaven." Instantly the elated high priest charged him with blasphemy: "What further need have we of witnesses? behold, now ye have heard his blasphemy. What think ye?" The Sanhedrin concurred: "He is guilty of death." Gloating over their success, they subjected Jesus to the personal indignities he had foretold: they spat in his face, and blindfolded and struck him—some with their fists, others with their open palms—and taunted: "Prophesy unto us, thou Christ, Who is he that smote thee?"

During this trial Peter sat with the household servants and officers of the guard in the courtyard below, awaiting the outcome. As he warmed himself by the fire that had been kindled against the cold night air, a maidservant recognized him and asked: "Art not thou also one of his disciples?" Suddenly frightened, Peter disclaimed any knowledge of his Master: "I am not," and withdrew to the gateway of the courtyard. Questioned a second time, he denied with an oath. The third time he began to curse and to swear "I know not the man." At his third denial a rooster crowed, and "the Lord turned, and looked upon Peter." Peter remembered his Master's words; his

Sanhedrin in session. Before this Council Jesus' ecclesiastical trial took place, and before it the apostles faced arraignment for preaching in Jesus' name. *Popular and Critical Bible Encyclopaedia.*

remorse was immediate and terrible. "He went out, and wept bitterly."

Jesus before the Sanhedrin

(Mt. 27:1,2; Mk. 15:1; Lu. 22:66-71) Driven by the pressure of time, the Sanhedrin hastened formally to legalize its action of the preceding night. Ignoring the Judaic regulation that a day intervene before trial and pronouncement of a capital sentence, it convened in full shortly after daybreak—before Jerusalem was awake—to ratify the death sentence. This meeting was held in its own chambers, the Hall of Hewn Stones within the Temple area. Jesus was arraigned before the council and interrogated again—"Art thou the Christ? tell us." His answer: "If I tell you, ye will not believe: And if I also ask you, ye will not answer me, nor let me go." Calmly he reaffirmed his coming glorification, a declaration they had branded blasphemous the night before. "Hereafter shall the Son of man sit on the right hand of the power of God." These words from his own lips were all they wanted to hear: "What need we any further witness?" Before the highest governing body of the Jews Jesus thus formally asserted his Messiahship, and the ruling council thus formally rejected their Messiah by pronouncing his claim blasphemous.

The Sanhedrin could pronounce the death sentence but it could not carry it out without the authorization of the Roman governor; so, still in the early morning hours, Jesus was bound and taken before Pontius Pilate.

Meanwhile the traitor had had time to reflect on the enormity of his offense. Gone were the excitement and glamor of priestly recognition. Shunned and alone, Judas awaited the outcome of the trial. When he saw the Master actually led away, he rushed frightened and conscience-stricken to the Temple to return the blood money to the Sanhedrists. "I have sinned in that I have betrayed the innocent blood!" But Judas was no longer of use to the priests; now he was only an odious reminder of their own corruption. "What is that to us? see thou to that" was their contemptuous retort. Judas' remorse came too late to turn back the tide of events he had set in motion. He threw the thirty silver shekels to the marble pavement, and went out and hanged himself (Mt. 27:3-10; compare Acts 1:18).

Roman Civil Trial

Jesus before Pilate

(Mt. 27:2,11-14; Mk. 15:1-5; Lu. 23:1-5; Jn. 18:28-38) The ecclesiastical trial was over. Before Jesus lay a civil trial that would also result in tragic injustice. The man he faced was Pilate, Roman Procurator appointed by the Emperor Tiberius as governor of the troublesome and restless province of Judaea. Pilate regarded his Jewish subjects with contempt, and his rule was marked by corruption and cruelty. He made no attempt to understand the Jewish mind and continually offended the Jews by his disregard of their theocratic beliefs; he was therefore unable to cope with their fanatic fervor. They had successfully bested him several times—on one occasion forcing him to remove the imperial image of Caesar (to them an emblem of idolatry) from the standards of the Roman troops in Jerusalem, on another occasion forcing him to take down from Herod's palace in Jerusalem tablets bearing prayers to the Emperor. The animosity that existed between the Jewish priesthood and the Roman governor lay close to the surface.

Pilate had come from his official residence at Caesarea to maintain order at the Passover feast, and he was in the Praetorium, hall of judgment, in the Castle of Antonia when the chief priests brought Jesus to him between six and nine o'clock on this decisive Friday morning. Still piously observant of Judaic ceremonialism, they would not enter the hall itself for fear of defilement, since it was a heathen building not purged of leaven for the feast—an uncleanness that would have prevented their eating the Passover (see footnote, p. 311). Pilate came out to inquire what the accusation against their prisoner was. At first they reported Jesus an evildoer. Pilate, not unaware of the nature of Jesus' activities, would have dismissed the case to their jurisdiction—"Take ye him, and judge him according to your law." When they answered "It is not lawful for us to put any man to death," he saw clearly their determination to obtain a death sentence. They then brought the charge of treason: "We found this fellow perverting the nation, and forbidding to give tribute to Caesar, saying that he himself is Christ a King." This was not the charge on which the Sanhedrin had condemned him, but they knew Pilate

would give no credence to the religious indictment of blasphemy; he would naturally be vitally concerned if Jesus were a threat to Rome.

Pilate went back into the palace to question Jesus and to determine for himself whether this political charge was true. "Art thou the King of the Jews?" he asked. Jesus answered: "Sayest thou this thing of thyself, or did others tell it thee of me?" He disarmed Pilate's fears of treason with the explanation that his claim to kingship pertained to a spiritual kingdom—"My kingdom is not of this world: if my kingdom were of this world, then would my servants fight, that I should not be delivered to the Jews: but now is my kingdom not from hence."

His reply caused Pilate to ask again: "Art thou a king then?" Jesus responded: "Thou sayest that I am a king. To this end was I born, and for this cause came I into the world, that I should bear witness unto the truth. Every one that is of the truth heareth my voice." Not comprehending the quality of the man but idly curious as to his philosophy, Pilate queried, "What is truth?" Jesus made no reply. After this Pilate brought Jesus into the open court and reported to the Sanhedrin: "I find in him no fault at all."

Seeing that Pilate was about to acquit him, the Sanhedrin hurled many other accusations; to strengthen their original charge they added the allegation of sedition, saying he was stirring up the Jews from Galilee to Judaea. Jesus stood silent. The governor was amazed at his silence: "Answerest thou nothing? behold how many things they witness against thee."

Jesus before Herod

(Lu. 23:6-12) Pilate now realized with alarm that the case was assuming serious proportions. His attention was caught by the name *Galilee*, a province not under his jurisdiction, and he asked if the prisoner were a Galilean. He knew Herod Antipas, tetrarch of Galilee, was in Jerusalem for the Passover season, and learning Jesus belonged to Herod's jurisdiction, Pilate sent Jesus to him. Herod (son of Herod the Great, who had attempted to slay the Messiah at birth) was glad to see Jesus. Having heard many reports about him, he hoped to see him perform a miracle in his presence, but Jesus remained completely silent under the questioning of this dissolute ruler. Herod's curiosity quickly turned to anger; he and his soldiers treated Jesus with contempt and mockery, and after arraying him in a bright-colored robe, returned him to the Roman governor. By his action he implicated himself morally in the condemnation of Jesus; on this day he and Pilate, formerly enemies, became friends.

Jesus before Pilate

(Mt. 27:15-31; Mk. 15:6-20; Lu. 23:13-25; Jn. 18:38-19:16) Forced now to make some decision,

Pilate summoned the Jewish authorities to the judgment seat, which stood in the large open pavement, Gabbatha, in front of the Praetorium. Hoping to end the matter quickly and at the same time to placate these powerful Jews, he announced to the chief priests and to the rapidly gathering crowd: "I, having examined him before you, have found no fault in this man touching those things whereof ye accuse him: No, nor yet Herod. . . . I will therefore chastise him, and release him."

Pilate could have acquitted Jesus, but he feared the wrath of the Jewish rulers. He decided to appeal to the gathering crowd for a sign of mercy, hoping to gain the people's support and thus defeat the avowed intention of the Sanhedrin. It was the Roman governor's custom to release one prisoner of their choice to the people during the Passover season; and he was holding in chains an insurrectionist named Barabbas, a robber and murderer. "Whom will ye that I release unto you? Barabbas, or Jesus which is called Christ?" he asked. Before Pilate's proposal could make an impact on the minds of the people, the chief priests raised a cry for Barabbas, and soon a concerted shout arose: "Away with this man, and release unto us Barabbas." (The Sinaitic Syriac and Armenian New Testament versions, Moffatt's translation, and an RSV footnote give the name as Jesus Bar-Abbas. If this was the man's full name, as it might have been, the fact sharpens the contrast between the murderer Jesus Bar-Abbas [the son of the father, i.e., Rabbi] and Jesus the Messiah [the Son of the Father] .)

While Pilate sat in the judgment seat and heard with dismay the mounting furor, his wife sent a disturbing message—"Have thou nothing to do with that just man: for I have suffered many things this day in a dream because of him." As he hesitated, the cry of the mob for Barabbas became more insistent. Torn between his wish to pacify the Jews and his desire to save Jesus, Pilate vacillated. "What shall I do then with Jesus which is called Christ?" As with one voice came the cry: "Crucify him, crucify him." Again he appealed for some sign of mercy: "Why, what evil hath he done? I have found no cause of death in him: I will therefore chastise him, and let him go." But the mood of the crowd had now been fanned into fury, and they were "instant with loud voices, requiring that he might be crucified."

Mindful of his failures in the past to change the Jewish mind, Pilate saw that he could break down neither their implacable hatred nor their determination to destroy Jesus. Throwing off the responsibility, he took a basin of water and washed his hands before them, declaring: "I am innocent of the blood of this just person: see ye to it." The people cried: "His blood be on us, and on our children." So Pilate released Barabbas and surrendered Jesus to a detachment of Roman soldiers for scourging, a customary punishment before crucifixion. The soldiers took Jesus into the Praetorium and called the rest of their cohort together to make sport of him. As judge, Pilate watched. The prisoner was flogged cruelly with a whip of leather thongs that had been knotted or tipped with lead. The soldiers mockingly clothed Jesus in a scarlet mantle, placed a plaited thorn crown on his head and a reed in his right hand, and knelt before him taunting: "Hail, King of the Jews!" Adding indignity to indignity, they spat on him, and struck him on the head.

Pilate brought the prisoner out before the crowd once more, still hoping for some compassionate response, but his appeal went unheeded amid shouts of "Crucify him, crucify him." At this fresh outcry, Pilate yielded to their desires even though he continued to maintain "I find no fault in him."

Elated at their success, the chief priests blurted out to the governor their actual charge against Jesus: "We have a law, and by our law he ought to die, because he made himself the Son of God." Frightened by this disclosure, Pilate returned to the judgment hall to examine Jesus further: "Whence art thou?" But Jesus did not answer. When Pilate demanded, "Speakest thou not unto me? knowest thou not that I have power to crucify thee, and have power to release thee?" he did answer, since he could not allow this claim to pass unchallenged. "Thou couldest have no power at all against me, except it were given thee from above: therefore he that delivered me unto thee hath the greater sin." (Three days later at Resurrection he gave sublime proof of this statement.)

In great alarm Pilate again tried to reason with the Jews until they said to him, "If thou let this man go, thou art not Caesar's friend: whosoever maketh himself a king speaketh against Caesar." At this threat to his political position and his own interest, Pilate again yielded. He who had so often corrupted power to his own ends found himself impotent to perform the one act of justice he truly desired. His decision was a blot on Rome's imperial justice.

Bringing Jesus before the people for the last time, he mounted the judgment seat, saying: "Behold your King!" The maddened crowd shouted, "Away with him, away with him, crucify him." With the question "Shall I crucify your King?" Pilate capitulated and pronounced the death sentence.* Jesus' rejection was complete. The leaders of the nation had repudiated their Messiah; now they disowned their King—"the King that cometh in the name of the Lord."

---

*Josephus says that charges were brought against Pilate by the Samaritans before Vitellius, governor of Syria in 35 A.D. for the wanton slaughter of certain of their number. Vitellius ordered him to Rome for trial before the Emperor Tiberias, but Tiberias died before Pilate reached the capital. Pilate's further history is not known, but according to tradition he committed suicide.

Crucifixion   Mt. 27:31-56; Mk. 15:20-41;
                                  Lu. 23:26-49; Jn. 19:17-37

The site of the crucifixion was Golgotha (Lat. Calvary), a slight rise of land outside the city walls. As Jesus was led along the road in the forenoon of Friday, he carried his own cross, aided at the last by Simon of Cyrene. The scarlet mantle had been replaced by his own plain garments. He was flanked by four Roman soldiers and preceded by a herald bearing a tablet that named his crime. The way was long, the streets were narrow and crowded with hostile or silent spectators; the cross was heavy, and as he bent beneath its weight the women of Jerusalem wept in sorrow. With his ever-present compassion, Jesus turned to say: "Daughters of Jerusalem, weep not for me, but weep for yourselves, and for your children. . . . For if they do these things in a green tree, what shall be done in the dry?"

At Golgotha Jesus was offered vinegar mixed with gall, a potion customarily given to criminals before execution; but after tasting it he refused to drink. "A single touch of humanity was permitted during these preparations—the offer of a draught of the common sour wine drunk by the soldiers, mingled with some stupefying bitter drug, usually myrrh. . . . But Jesus would take nothing to cloud His faculties, even though it might mitigate His pain."[75]

Jesus was stripped of all but his loincloth and nailed to the cross, a thief to his right and another to his left; above his head was placed Pilate's inscription in Hebrew, Latin, and Greek: JESUS OF NAZARETH THE KING OF THE JEWS.

Crucifixion, this cruel and degrading form of capital punishment practiced by the Greeks and Romans, was inflicted only on slaves and criminals. The experience of the cross has been called Jesus' "humiliation," but it was in truth men's humiliation for it was they who stooped to shame, not he. The soldiers at the foot of the cross, insensitive to his suffering, divided his garments among them and cast lots for his seamless robe, fulfilling the Hebrew prophecy "They parted my raiment among them, and for my vesture they did cast lots" (compare Ps. 22:18).

To add to the desecration of this hour the chief priests, scribes, and elders ridiculed Jesus with the very charges made against him at the trial: "Thou that destroyest the temple, and buildest it in three days, save thyself. If thou be the Son of God, come down from the cross. . . . He saved others; himself he cannot save. If he be the King of Israel, let him now come down from the cross, and we will believe him. He trusted in God; let him deliver him now, if he will have him: for he said, I am the Son of God." And the thieves who hung beside him "cast the same in his teeth."

As Jesus hung on the cross he made a number of statements, sometimes termed "the seven last words." His first words were *"Father, forgive them; for they know not what they do"* (Lu. 23:34). Deserted by his disciples and repudiated by the world's hatred of all he represented, no bitter or rebellious expression escaped him. Only pure love for God and man could have prompted so selfless a prayer.

One of the malefactors who hung beside him reviled him; but the other rebuked such rashness and confessed his own guilt: "We receive the due reward of our deeds: but this man hath done nothing amiss." "Lord, remember me when thou comest into thy kingdom," he entreated. With calm assurance Jesus promised: *"Verily I say unto thee, To day shalt thou be with me in paradise"* (Lu. 23:43). The criminal had barely turned from his evil deeds, had admitted his sin only a moment before, yet Jesus was sensitive to this sinner's cry for help. Here was the first suppliant of the cross! Even before Jesus' own triumph was apparent came its first redemptive victory. The thief had not earned paradise or its peace, but through Christ's forgiveness and grace he at once stood on its threshold.

Jesus' mother, with Mary Magdalene and two other faithful women, stood near the cross in the company of John (Jn. 19:25). John's love for his Master had outweighed fear for himself; he alone of the eleven was so close to the Master's spirit that he could love enough to stand at his cross. Seeing Mary and John, Jesus said, *"Woman, behold thy son!"* and to John, *"Behold thy mother!"* (Jn. 19:26,27). No single duty or responsibility, human or divine, had Jesus ever neglected; he made provision for his mother by entrusting her to the care of John and at the same time honored the beloved apostle who had qualified. Jesus bestowed on him an outward sign of inward sonship, an act foreshadowing the spiritual sonship John later beheld and declared in his writings.

According to John's Gospel Jesus was crucified at the sixth hour, or noon (Jn. 19:14); according to Mark it was the third hour, nine o'clock in the morning (Mk. 15:25). From the sixth to the ninth hour (twelve to three o'clock) a strange darkness fell over the land and at the ninth hour Jesus cried out in a loud voice: *"Eli, Eli, lama sabachthani? . . . My God, my God, why hast thou forsaken me?"* (Mt. 27:46), the first words of the Twenty-second Psalm. Jesus had reached the heights of exaltation at his Transfiguration; he touched the depths of anguish at his Crucifixion. The burden of the world's blindness and opposition pressed upon him, and mankind's future hope of salvation lay cradled in this crucial moment. Up to this point he had vanquished every evil assault of "the

Aerial view of the Old City, Jerusalem. Center right shows the Temple area. The Moslem Dome of the Rock marks the former site of Solomon's Temple. To its right lies the deep wadi of the Kidron Valley. Jordan Tourism Office—New York.

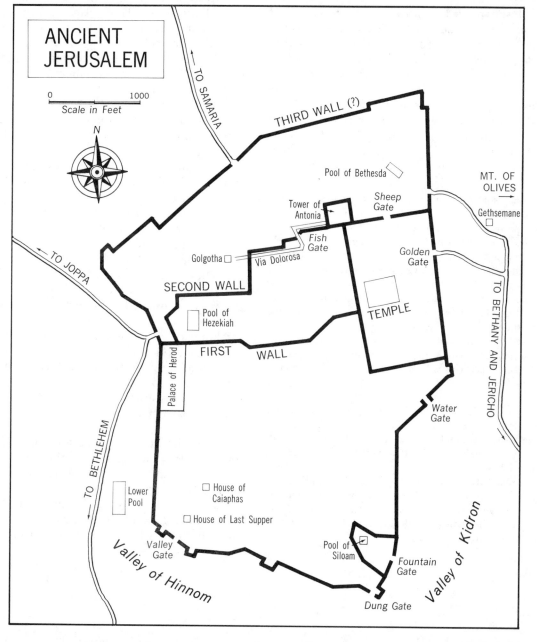

ANCIENT JERUSALEM

0   1000
Scale in Feet

N

TO SAMARIA

THIRD WALL (?)

Pool of Bethesda

MT. OF OLIVES

Sheep Gate

Tower of Antonia

Gethsemane

Fish Gate

Golgotha   Via Dolorosa

Golden Gate

TO JOPPA

SECOND WALL

TEMPLE

Pool of Hezekiah

Palace of Herod

FIRST   WALL

Water Gate

TO BETHLEHEM

Lower Pool

House of Caiaphas

House of Last Supper

TO BETHANY AND JERICHO

Pool of Siloam

Valley Gate

Fountain Gate

Valley of Hinnom

Dung Gate

Valley of Kidron

prince of this world." Were he to fail to overcome the last onslaught of Satan, all for which he had labored would be lost. His whole lifework of service for the Father and for his fellow men appeared to hang in the balance as he bore the strain of this hour, but in patient suffering he endured.

"I thirst" (Jn. 19:28). This Jesus said, "knowing that all things were now accomplished, that the scripture might be fulfilled" (compare Ps. 69:21). His enemies had already given him the vinegar and gall of insolence and scorn. While the soldiers held to his mouth a sponge filled with wine vinegar, his Father alone was slaking his true thirst for righteousness. In the depths of this almost bottomless pit of travail he was sustained with the water of Life.

A triumphant cry now sprang from his lips: *"It is finished"* (Jn. 19:30). His love had been tried to the last fiber of endurance—and had endured. He was proving to men, though they did not yet understand it, that the prince of this world had found "nothing" in him.

Then Jesus prayed *"Father, into thy hands I commend my spirit"* (Lu. 23:46). This prayer was the ultimate in obedience, expressing a sublime trust that out of what appeared to be overwhelming defeat would come, in God's own time, a glorious victory and resumption of his work. With this last declaration he "bowed his head, and gave up the ghost."

Jesus' first and last words on the cross affirmed the divine relationship of Father and Son and maintained it untarnished. This was the real spiritual victory which he had won.

> The outstanding feature of His life was its deliberate and unceasing submission to the will of His Father in every point. . . . His life was, all through, the complete representation, the perfect realization, of the will of God. . . . The sinful passions of man, which could not bend Christ to yield to them, rose against Him in hatred, and put Him to death. Thus, on the part of men, the Crucifixion was a murder. But on the part of Christ, the death of the Cross was the culmination of His righteous life, the crowning act of assent to the will of God. It was a "death unto sin." It was the refusal of sin carried to its last and victorious extremity.
>
> Looked at in this way, then, the death of Christ was the perfect display of righteousness, the complete achievement of union with the Divine will, the absolute condemnation of human sin.[76]

> Jesus had seen clearly the necessary outcome of this journey to Jerusalem. . . . Deliberately he planned the Jerusalem visit, and calmly he placed himself into the hands of those who sought his life. His teaching would thus be consummated and glorified. . . .
>
> Jesus realized that his own death at the hands of the Jews did not mean the destruction of his work nor the failure of his cause. . . . The Kingdom of God would live and triumph, notwithstanding his death—indeed, in a measure because of his death. . . .

Nor would he by that experience which men call death lay down the work of his life. He knew that shortly, in God's own good time, he would resume it (Matt. xvi:21,25; comp. Hos. vi:2). The soul which draws its life from God forever lives. "There is no death: what seems so is transition." The crucifixion was an incident in the life of an immortal being. What we term death is but the point at which the relation of the living soul to the physical body changes from that to which we are accustomed. Jesus lived and Jesus lives. He did not die. Shall we deny immortality to him, when we hold to it for ourselves? The Christian does not die: he rises to a larger, better life. Jesus "brought life and immortality to light." He taught us that there is no death, but only transition to a higher sphere of existence.[77]

The unnatural pall of darkness over the land during the hours of crucifixion was not the only marvel which took place in the physical world around Jesus. At his death the veil in the Temple, the two great tapestried curtains of purple and gold (said to have been 60 feet long and 30 feet wide, each the thickness of the palm of the hand) that hung 18 inches apart between the Holy Place and the Holy of Holies, was "rent in twain from top to the bottom," a sign to men that henceforth they would have free access to the Father through the atoning sacrifice of His Son (Heb. 10:19-22). One commentary remarks: ". . .that thick veil which for so many ages had been the dread symbol of *separation between God and guilty men* was, without a hand touching it, mysteriously 'rent in twain from top to bottom'—'the Holy Ghost this signifying, that the way into the holiest of all was now made manifest!' . . . Before, it was death *to go in,* now it is *death to stay out.*"[78] (In the Revelation that Jesus Christ later gave to John, "the temple of God was opened in heaven" and the seer beheld "the ark of his testament [covenant]," the Old Testament tabernacle symbol of the presence of God, without a concealing veil [Rev. 11:19].)

Only Matthew records that the earth quaked and the rocks nearby were split, and many tombs of the saints were opened. The Roman centurion and the soldiers with him at the cross who witnessed the earthquake and the things which had happened exclaimed: "Truly this was the Son of God." The multitude slowly returned to Jerusalem, beating their breasts as, sobered and guilt-stricken, they began to comprehend the enormity of the crime to which they had given assent.

The Sabbath began at sundown. This was a high Sabbath, the opening day of the Feast of Unleavened Bread; so that the bodies of Jesus and the two with him should not hang on the cross after sunset (Deut 21:23) the Jews asked of Pilate that the prisoners' legs be broken, a Roman method of hastening death, and that the bodies be taken down. So the soldiers broke the legs of the two thieves, but when they saw that Jesus was already dead "they brake not his legs." However, a soldier took his spear and pierced Jesus' side, and "forthwith came there out blood and water." Thus Scripture was again fulfilled: "A bone of him shall not be broken" (compare Ex. 12:46; Ps. 34:20); "They shall look on him whom they pierced" (compare Ps. 22:16; Zech. 12:10).

Burial

Mt. 27:57-61; Mk. 15:42-47; Lu. 23:50-56; Jn. 19:38-42

It was almost evening and burial must take place before the Jewish Sabbath began. Joseph of Arimathaea, a highly respected member of the Sanhedrin who had long been a secret disciple of Jesus and who had not consented to the sentencing, summoned his courage and went openly to Pilate to ask for Jesus' body. With the procurator's permission, Joseph took the body from the cross and, assisted by the Nicodemus who had sought out Jesus by night at the beginning of his ministry, prepared it for burial, winding it in linen sprinkled with spices. Joseph's own tomb hewn out of rock was near at hand—"a new sepulchre, wherein was never man yet laid." There they placed Jesus' body. A great stone was rolled before its entrance, and Mary Magdalene and many other women who had followed him from Galilee marked where the body was entombed. Thus tragically the work and life of Jesus the Christ appeared to end.

Saturday

Saturday was for Jesus' enemies one of apprehension as they waited for the close of the Jewish Sabbath to take further precautionary measures to ensure the certainty of his death. Remembering his remarkable miracles and fearing his possible resurrection and its consequences since he had said, "After three days I will rise again," the Sanhedrin deliberately took steps to thwart it.

Sealing of the Tomb

Mt. 27:62-66

Immediately after sunset some of the council hurried to Pilate to ask that a Roman guard seal the sepulcher until the third day to prevent Jesus' disciples from stealing his body by night and claiming his resurrection, for then, said they, "The last error shall be worse than the first." Pilate gave them authority; so they sealed the stone (stretching across it a strong cord whose ends were made fast by clay stamped with an official impress) and stationed Roman soldiers to stand guard.

The Forty Days
from Resurrection
to Ascension

Three days after Crucifixion Jesus rose from the dead. The veil of the flesh had been rent. The Father brought him forth triumphant as His forever-living witness. He totally vindicated His Son and crowned his Messiahship with immortality. Ten meetings of Jesus with his disciples occurred in the next forty days, during which he "shewed himself alive after his passion by many infallible proofs" and further instructed them in "the things pertaining to the kingdom of God." As the Risen Christ he taught them step by step the full significance of his resurrection in relation to his Messiahship, and prepared them for the higher glory of his ascension.

Resurrection

No "stone" set or sealed by the authority of men could keep the Christ entombed, and early in the morning on the first day of the week came Jesus' glorious resurrection. The four Gospels report with restraint and simplicity the events surrounding the Resurrection, letting this miracle speak eloquently for itself. There was no human witness to Jesus' resurrection, only the angelic declaration of that fact. Peculiar to Matthew is the record that "the angel of the Lord descended from heaven, and came and rolled back the stone from the door, and sat upon it. His countenance was like lightning, and his raiment white as snow: And for fear of him the keepers did shake, and became as dead men." Jesus had been in the tomb three days. The Jews reckoned days from sundown to sundown; thus he was in the tomb part of Friday, all of Saturday, and part of the following day. On this first day of the week Jesus Christ walked through the open door as the one "alive for evermore" (Rev. 1:18), proving his power over death for himself and for us. He walked away from mortality—the tomb—into eternal life.

> Had the Ruler of the Universe given no sign when the spotless and loving Christ was made away with by His murderers, the problem of evil would have been well-nigh overwhelming, and faith in the supremacy of a moral order would have lacked one of its strongest supports.[79]

The Resurrection, confirmed by Jesus' subsequent appearances, revived the fainting faith of the apostles and filled them with renewed spiritual strength and confidence. His physical presence convinced them of his resurrection and he became to them the Risen Christ. This rising gave incontrovertible evidence of the truth of his teachings and authenticated every precept he had uttered. From the inception of the Church his followers made this dynamic of resurrection the focal point of all Christian hope and ministry.

The Empty Tomb

Mt. 28:1-8; Mk. 16:1-8;
Lu. 24:1-8; Jn. 20:1-10

Toward dawn on the first day of the week, Mary Magdalene, Mary the mother of James, Salome, and the other women—those who had stood at the cross—came to the tomb with spices to anoint the body of Jesus. They asked one another: "Who shall roll us away the stone from the door?" But when they reached the tomb they found the stone already rolled away. When the women entered the tomb they found it empty of the body of Jesus. Instead, an awaiting angel asked: "Why seek ye the living among the dead?" (Lu.). "Ye seek Jesus, which was crucified. He is not here: for he is risen, as he said" (Mt.). "Go quickly, and tell his disciples that he is risen from the dead; and, behold, he goeth before you into Galilee; there shall ye see him."

Mary Magdalene ran to tell Peter and John. "They have taken away the Lord out of the sepulchre, and we know not where they have laid him." The two disciples hurried to the tomb to see for themselves. John outran Peter, looked in and saw the linen clothes, but did not enter. Peter went in "and seeth the linen clothes lie, And the napkin, that was about his head, not lying with the linen clothes, but wrapped together in a place by itself." When John did enter, "he saw, and believed," reading correctly the meaning of the empty graveclothes. He returned to Jerusalem with the dawning conviction that his Master had risen; but Peter went away "wondering in himself at that which was come to pass."

At birth the Christ child had been wrapped in swaddling clothes. After Resurrection the linen wrappings that swathed the body of Jesus for burial were laid aside in quiet order. He had himself removed the strictures of mortal life with which he had been bound.

Report of Roman Guard

Mt. 28:11-15

The Roman guard came into the city to report to the chief priests the startling events of the morning. The Sanhedrin met in hurried conclave; their precautionary measures had failed and the question now was how to prevent the people from believing that Jesus had risen from the dead and was therefore all he had professed himself to be. Denial was the only course open to them, so with a large sum of money they bribed the soldiers to spread a false report: "Say ye, His disciples came by night, and stole him away while we slept." For a Roman soldier to sleep while on guard was a capital offense, but the Sanhedrin promised that if the matter came to the attention of Pilate they would persuade him to grant immunity. So the soldiers "took the money, and did as they were taught: and this saying is commonly reported among the Jews until this day."

Justin Martyr, who flourished about A.D. 170, says, in his 'Dialogue with Trypho the Jew,' that the Jews dispersed the story by means of special messengers sent to every country.[80]

Ten Appearances during Forty Days

That Jesus was seen by his disciples during the forty days following his resurrection is a fact carefully authenticated and verified by the Gospel writers. By tarrying on earth the Master gave proof of his resurrection. Ten appearances are specifically recorded as having occurred during this period, five of these taking place on the day of Resurrection.

In each of these five appearances he sounded out the understanding of those to whom he appeared. He found them slow to believe. The acceptance for centuries of the inevitability of death was so predominant that the realization of his living presence was almost beyond their grasp. To them he appeared, disappeared, reappeared, but the glory of his true being, glimpsed by Peter, James, and John at the Transfiguration, they all began to understand more clearly. At first they could only recognize his presence briefly—sometimes when they were together, sometimes when alone; but with each reappearance, they gained a stronger conviction of the reality of his resurrection and of his unquestionable victory over the flesh.

There has been much discussion among theologians regarding the mode of Jesus' existence after his resurrection. The Gospels specifically state that his appearance was such that his followers often did not recognize him at once. Mary Magdalene did not know him; the two disciples walking to Emmaus did not know him, nor did the seven apostles at the Sea of Galilee.

There are two sets of notices [concerning the risen Christ's manner of existence] which are not easily combined in an intelligible conception. On the one hand, there are several statements which create the impression that Jesus resumed the same mode of bodily existence which was interrupted at His death upon the cross. The story of the empty tomb (Mk. 16:1-8) meant that the body which had hung upon the cross was revivified. That it was a body of flesh and blood, capable of being handled, and sustained by food and drink—not an apparition of a spiritualistic kind—is a point which is specially emphasized in details of the narratives (Jn. 20:27, Lu. 24:30). On the other hand, it is far from being a normal life in the body. His face and form have a strange aspect. He appears suddenly in the midst, the doors being shut (Jn. 20:26), and as suddenly vanishes out of their sight (Lu. 24:31). To this series belong the references of St. Paul, who places the appearance to himself on a level with the others, and speaks of Christ as possessing a body which is not of flesh and blood, but has been transfigured and glorified (I Co. 15:50, Ph. 3:21).

The explanation of the phenomena, according to Schleiermacher, is that in the one set of statements we have the matter described from the side of the risen Christ, in the other an account of the impression which He made on the disciples (*Leben Jesu*). Others conceive that while after the Resurrection He existed as a spiritual being, He yet assumed material substance and form at special moments for special purposes (Rothe, *Theologische Ethik*). The primitive theory probably was that after the Resurrection His mode of existence was the same as during the ministry, with an augmentation of the power over His body which He even then possessed (Mk. 6:45-50), and that only at the Ascension was the body transformed. Some modern theologians hold that the body was raised from the grave as a spiritual body, others that it was gradually spiritualized in the period between the Resurrection and the Ascension.[81]

1. To Mary Magdalene

Mk. 16:9-11; Jn. 20:11-18

On Resurrection morning, after Mary Magdalene had told Peter and John of the disappearance of Jesus' body, she returned weeping to the tomb. She had not grasped the angel's message that her Master was risen. "As she wept, she stooped down, and looked into the sepulchre"; and saw two angels guarding the place where the body had lain. They asked: "Woman, why weepest thou?" In anguished grief she answered: "Because they have taken away my Lord, and I know not where they have laid him." Still not perceiving the significance of their question, she turned away. As she did so, Jesus stood before her, but she "knew not that it was Jesus."

At once he led her thought beyond the man Jesus to the Risen Christ and his first words to her were like those of the angels—"Woman, why weepest thou? whom seekest thou?" Mary, supposing him to be the gardener, entreated: "Sir, if thou have borne him hence, tell me where thou hast laid him, and I will take him away." Jesus addressed her by name. This time she knew him. In gladness she cried, "Rabboni [my great master]."

As she approached to assure herself of his physical presence, Jesus stopped her: "Touch me not; for I am not yet ascended to my Father: but go to my brethren, and say unto them, I ascend unto my Father, and your Father; and to my God, and your God." He carefully guarded the victory he had just won, allowing neither human joy nor affection to hold him in the flesh. His whole spiritual impulsion was upward—to rise to his full stature as the ascended Christ, thus completing his earthly mission. His words "*my* Father, and *your* Father" and "*my* God, and *your* God" implied significantly that his union with the Father would be a blessing to them and that the God-given power he manifested was theirs also. As his resurrection was to men "the resurrection, and the life," so his ascension above matter would be to them ascension and life.

Mary hastened to the mourning apostles to tell them she had seen Jesus and had talked with him, but they did not believe her.

2. To the Women

Mt. 28:9,10; Lu. 24:9-11

As the other women went from the sepulcher on Resurrection morning to carry the angel's message to the apostles, Jesus met them; and at his "All hail" they fell at his feet to worship him. "Be not afraid," he reassured them. This admonition was familiar to them, for these words had been spoken to the Twelve when Jesus walked on the water, and to Peter, James, and John at the Transfiguration. He confirmed the angel's message. "Go tell my brethren that they go into Galilee, and there shall they see me." In awe and joy they ran to tell the disciples, but "their words seemed to them as idle tales."

3. To Two Disciples

Mk. 16:12,13; Lu. 24:13-35

In the afternoon of this same momentous day Cleopas, a disciple, with another whose name is not known, walked along the road to Emmaus, a town about seven miles distant from Jerusalem. As they talked of the events of the past three days, Jesus drew near and journeyed with them. "But their eyes were holden that they should not know him."

"What manner of communications are these that ye have one to another, as ye walk, and are sad?" Jesus questioned. Cleopas replied: "Art thou only a stranger in Jerusalem, and hast not known the things which are come to pass there in these days?" Jesus persisted: "What things?" They told him they had been talking of Jesus of Nazareth, a great prophet and teacher, a mighty worker of miracles. The priests and rabbis had condemned him and caused him to be crucified, though his followers had hoped he would be the Messiah who would redeem Israel. But now it was the third day following his death. Some of the women of their company had startled them with a report that they had visited the tomb at daybreak and found the body gone. The women declared also that they had had a vision of angels who said that Jesus was alive. These two disciples had themselves gone to the tomb and found it empty, but Jesus they had not seen.

Their unbelief brought quick reproof: "O fools, and slow of heart to believe all that the prophets have spoken: Ought not Christ to have suffered these things, and to enter into his glory?" Then "beginning at Moses and all the prophets, he expounded unto them in all the scriptures the things concerning himself." Quoting passage after passage, he traced the Old Testament prophecies of the Messiah and his kingdom, making plain that the whole spirit and content of the Scriptures foretold a suffering Messiah, whose kingdom was a spiritual kingdom to be manifested by precisely the way of loving self-sacrifice the Nazarene had taken. How illumined were the Messianic passages of Scripture as they walked with him, not alone from Jerusalem to Emmaus, but from Moses and the prophets to Christ and his glory.

Nearing the village, Cleopas and his companion urged: "Abide with us: for it is toward evening." As Jacob had maintained his hold on the angel until he received a blessing, so these two constrained the Stranger to remain with them; they yearned to hear more. While he broke bread with them, "their eyes were opened, and they knew him; and he vanished out of their sight." With sudden elation they realized they had been communing with the Master: "Did not our heart burn within us, while he talked with us by the way, and while he opened to us the scriptures?" They had not at first recognized him, yet the Word he had spoken had filled them with inspiration and comfort. "So, then, they had learned to the full the Resurrection-lesson—not only that He was risen indeed, but that it needed not His seen Bodily Presence, if only He opened up to the heart and mind all the Scriptures concerning Himself.... This is the great lesson concerning the Risen One, which the Church fully learned in the Day of Pentecost."[8 2] They hastily returned to Jerusalem to testify to the apostles that they had seen Jesus.

4. To Peter
Lu. 24:34 (I Cor. 15:5)

Cleopas and his companion found the apostles with other disciples gathered together, but before they could relate their thrilling news they were greeted with joyous testimony—"The Lord is risen indeed, and hath appeared to Simon." But what passed between the Master and Peter at this appearance is not told us. Jesus' prayer for the strengthening of Peter's faith (Lu. 22:32) and Peter's love for Christ had brought him through the dark days of remorse and purging. This penitent apostle, sorrowing over the bitter memory of his denial, must indeed have been comforted by the appearance vouchsafed him on this Resurrection day.

5. To the Apostles (Thomas Absent)
Mk. 16:14; Lu. 24:36-48; Jn. 20:19-25

The same evening, as the apostles (except Thomas, Jn. 20:25) met together behind closed doors because of their fear of the authorities, Jesus suddenly stood among them. His first words were "Peace be unto you," but they were terrified; they thought he was an apparition. Despite the fact that the apostles had thrice seen their Master raise the dead and had heard his own promise that he would himself rise again, they could neither wholly credit the testimony of those who had seen him nor readily admit the evidence of his physical presence even when he stood before them. He "upbraided them with their unbelief and hardness of heart"; showed them his hands and his feet: "Handle me, and see; for a spirit hath not flesh and bones, as ye see me have"; and before them all he ate fish and honeycomb. This tangible proof of his bodily presence convinced the apostles of his resurrection. They yielded up their disbelief with their realization of his victory over death, and their souls were flooded with joy.

He had explained the Old Testament prophecies of the suffering Messiah to the two disciples on the road to Emmaus; now he expounded them again to the apostles, clarifying God's Messianic plan of redemption: "Thus it is written, and thus it behoved Christ to suffer, and to rise from the dead the third day: And that repentance and remission of sins should be preached in his name among all nations, beginning at Jerusalem. And ye are witnesses of these things." (This manner of teaching—of drawing on Old Testament prophecies which related to Christ—was later adopted by the apostles and Paul in the early Church for the propagation of the gospel.)

Again Jesus blessed them: "Peace be unto you: as my Father hath sent me, even so send I you." As his Father had authorized him, so he authorized them to carry forward his work. Then "he breathed on them, and saith unto them, Receive ye the Holy Ghost"—imparting to them symbolically the earnest of his own spirit, a token of that power which was to appear in its fullness at Pentcost.

There is no gospel record of any ministry to the common people or of any physical healings by Jesus on this day or during the ensuing forty days, but Matthew records that the mighty power of his resurrection was felt—that from the tombs opened by the earthquake at Jesus' crucifixion "many bodies of the saints which slept arose, And came out of the graves after his resurrection, and went into the holy city, and appeared unto many" (Mt. 27:52,53), a foreshadowing of the resurrection of all men.

6. To the Apostles (Thomas Present)
Jn. 20:26-29

Eight days elapsed before the apostles saw their Master again. As they were gathered together in Jerusalem, once more he appeared among them, although the doors were closed. Thomas had been absent at Jesus' previous appearance; he had not been convinced by the report of the others. "Except I shall see in his hands the print of the nails, and put my finger into the print of the nails, and thrust my hand into his side, I will not believe," he had asserted.

Jesus acted at once to dispel Thomas' doubt by permitting him to touch his wounded hands and side, saying "Be not faithless, but believing." Convinced at last, Thomas acknowledged "My Lord and my God." Continuing to teach, not alone for Thomas but for future followers, Jesus responded: "Because thou hast seen me, thou hast believed: blessed are they that have not seen, and yet have believed"; he sought faith that rested on spiritual insight and conviction.

7. To Seven Apostles   Jn. 21:1-23

Jesus' next appearance took place in Galilee. The apostles at his bidding had returned to their home province to await his coming. One evening as seven of them—Simon Peter, Thomas, Nathanael, James, John, and two others—stood by the Sea of Galilee, uncertain what to do since he had not yet come, Peter decided to go fishing. They all agreed to go with him, "and that night they caught nothing." When morning dawned Jesus stood on the shore, but they did not know him. When he asked: "Children, have ye any meat?" they answered, "No." "Cast the net on the right side of the ship, and ye shall find," he commanded. Obediently they made the cast and found the waters teeming with fish, their net so full they could scarcely drag it along. John, seeing the miraculous abundance where before there seemed to be nothing, was the first to recognize the presence of the Christ. "It is the Lord," he exclaimed to Peter. And Peter instantly girded his fisherman's coat about him and swam ashore.

As the others dragged the full net the short distance to land they saw fish and bread laid ready on a fire of coals and heard Jesus say: "Bring of the fish which ye have now caught." Peter drew the net up on the beach, and "for all there were so many [a hundred fifty-three], yet was not the net broken." Jesus gave of his, they brought of theirs. "Come and dine," he invited, and none dared ask "Who art thou? knowing that it was the Lord." The Master's invitation marked a joyful reunion and communion. The apostles came to this morning repast with a renewed awareness of divine power, and Christ fed them afresh.

By the living parable of the great draft of fishes nearly three years before Jesus had illustrated to his first disciples their coming ministry. In that experience they had toiled all night in vain, but at his word they trustfully let down their net and launched out into the deep to gather the firstfruits of their faith. Their net broke, however, and they could not retain all they had caught. In the ensuing years Jesus had carefully taught and trained them to be "fishers of men," but after Resurrection, foundering without his personal leadership, they returned to their old occupation of fishing, and that night—as before—they had caught nothing. When at his word they again trustfully let down their net, they instantly gathered fruits of their faith and obedience, and this time they lost nothing of the fullness of their labors. This miracle made a marked impression on the apostles. It quickened them to the responsibilities and possibilities of their fast-approaching ministry; it was a new summons to their high calling. Henceforth they must launch out to use the power of the resurrected Christ.

The glad morning meal was finished but more special teaching was needed. So seldom was Jesus with them now in person that every word he uttered was doubly precious. He addressed to Peter a searching threefold question and afforded him, in the presence of the others, the opportunity to cancel the three denials by which this apostle had so dishonored the Christ and his own apostleship. He knew Peter's devotion, but it was imperative that Peter himself look to the very core of his own being to see whether he truly put Christ above all else. Jesus asked "Lovest thou me *more than these*? . . . Lovest thou *me*? . . . *Lovest* thou me?" (Two Greek words for *love* are used here: *agapao*, which appears in Jesus' first two questions; *phileo* in his third question and in Peter's three answers.)

> Phileo . . . *have affection* for (denoting *personal* attachment, as a matter of sentiment or feeling; while [*agapao*] is wider, embracing especially the judgment and the *deliberate* assent of the will as a matter of principle, duty and propriety).[83]

In the old dispensation God had set a "plumbline" of justice and righteousness in the midst of His people; in the new dispensation Jesus set for Christians this plumbline of love and consecration. Each time the question was asked, Peter affirmed his love; each time Jesus gave him the charge to shepherd his flock: "Feed my lambs. . . . Feed my sheep. . . . Feed my sheep." The three denials were annulled, and a contrite apostle was wholly forgiven and restored to favor. A warning followed the thrice-repeated charge to Peter—his service would lead to martyrdom—but the Master sealed him to himself with an explicit "Follow me."

Seeing his friend John standing nearby, Peter asked: "Lord, and what shall this man do?" Jesus answered: "If I will that he tarry till I come, what is that to thee? follow thou me." (John adds a note to this incident: "Then went this saying abroad among the brethren, that that disciple should not die: yet Jesus said not unto him, He shall not die; but, If I will that he tarry till I come, what is that to thee?") After Pentecost Peter faithfully discharged his Master's trust and suffered willingly for the Church.

8. To the Apostles and Others

Mt. 28:16-20;
Mk. 16:15-18 (I Cor. 15:6)

Jesus' fourth appearance to the apostles took place on a mountain top in Galilee. (Others may have been present, for Paul notes in his writings that Jesus was seen on one occasion by more than five hundred brethren.) Now the Christ gave them their final commission, referring to himself in the most absolute sense—from the standpoint of his place in the Godhead: "All power is given unto me in heaven and in earth. Go ye therefore, and teach all nations, baptizing them in the name of the Father, and of the Son, and of the Holy Ghost: Teaching them to observe all things whatsoever I have commanded you." This high commission opened with the grandeur and assurance of his authority—"all power . . . in heaven and in earth"—and emphasized the universal nature of their labors in the Church they were to found. All that he was and had he placed at their command. In his name they were to go forth to make disciples of all nations, baptizing them into the nature and grace of God, His Son, and the Holy Spirit.

To encourage them to undertake this mission and to carry it out, he pledged: "Lo, I am with you alway, even unto the end of the world." Always, by means of the Holy Spirit, he would be with them and those who would continue after them to the consummation of the age, till his gospel was established triumphant throughout the world.

To every believer Jesus Christ promised the same signs of Christian healing that had accompanied his own ministry: "These signs shall follow them that believe; In my name shall they cast out devils; they shall speak with new tongues; They shall take up serpents; and if they drink any deadly thing, it shall not hurt them; they shall lay hands on the sick, and they shall recover."

9. To James

(I Cor. 15:7)

"After that, he was seen of James," the Lord's brother. Only Paul, himself at one time an obstinate disbeliever, mentions the appearance to James. James had not believed in Jesus' Messiahship during the ministry, but he became a convert after this resurrection appearance. He later occupied an active and authoritative place in the early Apostolic Church in Jerusalem, the only member of Jesus' family known to advance his cause publicly (Gal. 1:19).

10. To the Apostles

Mk. 16:19; Lu. 24:49-53
(Acts 1:4-11; I Cor. 15:7)

Forty days after resurrection Jesus again met with his apostles in Jerusalem. In this interval he had trans-

formed to joy and certainty every state of consciousness among them which needed assurance—the sorrowing and despairing, the bewildered, the agonizing, the terrified, the doubtful, the hesitant, and the resistant. It was fitting and significant that the final stage of his personal ministry should close in Jerusalem, and that the outpouring of the Spirit soon to occur should take place in Zion (Is. 2:3). During this fifth and last appearance to all his apostles he commanded them to remain in Jerusalem till they were baptized with the Holy Ghost: "Behold, I send the promise of my Father upon you: but tarry ye in the city of Jerusalem, until ye be endued with power from on high" (compare Acts 1:4,5).

The question of the kingdom was still before the apostles' thought: "Lord, wilt thou at this time restore again the kingdom to Israel?" Jesus replied: "It is not for you to know the times or the seasons, which the Father hath put in his own power." But his further words implied that the full coming of the kingdom awaited the spread of the gospel over the whole earth: "But ye shall receive power, after that the Holy Ghost is come upon you: and ye shall be witnesses unto me both in Jerusalem, and in all Judaea, and in Samaria, and unto the uttermost part of the earth."

When he had finished all these sayings, he walked with his apostles to the Mount of Olives—"he led them out as far as to Bethany." At Bethany they had witnessed his miracle of the raising of Lazarus. From Bethany he had gone forth to his triumphal entry into Jerusalem. From Bethany he had gone forth to the communion of the Last Supper, to Gethsemane, to Golgotha—and to the glory of Resurrection. In the searching light and perspective of these events Bethany takes on a spiritual dimension. "As far as to Bethany" indicates the spiritual altitude to which Christ led his apostles and to which they were able to walk with him.

Ascension

Mk. 16:19; Lu. 24:50,51 (Acts 1:9-11)

Then came that transcendent step, when Jesus Christ passed beyond the sight of men. As he stood with his apostles on the summit of Olivet "he lifted up his hands, and blessed them. And . . . while he blessed them, he was parted from them, and carried up into heaven." His words at the Last Supper had been "Now I go my way to him that sent me." His departure from the world of matter and of the flesh was fulfilled in the manifest act of the Ascension. The lifted hands betokened not only a blessing but also a ceaseless pouring out of love and grace. Parting from those to whom he was entrusting the dedicated purpose of his lifework, his blessing came not alone from his farewell benediction but also from his own perfect exemplification of selfless obedience.

In Acts Luke further records: "while they beheld,

he was taken up; and a cloud received him out of their sight." The apostles had briefly glimpsed Christ's glory at Transfiguration; they had seen his changed form after Resurrection; but the full glory of Ascension they could not perceive through human sight. Even as they looked upward, two angels stood by them: "Ye men of Galilee, why stand ye gazing up into heaven? this same Jesus, which is taken up from you into heaven, shall so come in like manner as ye have seen him go into heaven." Angels had announced the Savior's birth; now angels attended his departure from the earth and confirmed his word of a glorious Second Coming (Mt. 24:30). With joy the eleven returned to Jerusalem to await the baptism of the Holy Ghost.

The angels' promise rests not on time, for when the Christian disciple walks, through prayer, faith, and overcoming to the spiritual heights of Olivet, he will see Christ "come in like manner"—in power and glory—as the apostles saw him go. The Ascension fulfilled Jesus' own words: "What and if ye shall see the Son of man ascend up where he was before?" (Jn. 6:62) and was the natural and final step in his overcoming of the world. Mark's Gospel records the great truth of the Master's Ascension in these words: "He was received up into heaven, and sat on the right hand of God"—in his rightful place of highest honor and power, to reign with his Father in heaven and on earth. While his visible being went beyond human sight, his invisible presence remains with us, and his words "Lo, I am with you alway" echo down the ages as the Christ-spirit continues to redeem and regenerate the lives of mankind.

Jesus' Miracles

OPENING OF PUBLIC MINISTRY

Turning of Water into Wine (Jn. 2:1-11)

GALILEAN MINISTRY (First Period)

Healing of Nobleman's Son (Jn. 4:46-54)
Draft of Fishes (Lu. 5:1-11)
Healing of Man with the Unclean Spirit (Mk. 1:21-28; Lu. 4:31-37)
Healing of Peter's Wife's Mother (Mt. 8:14,15; Mk. 1:29-31; Lu. 4:38,39)
Healing of a Leper (Mt. 8:2-4; Mk. 1:40-45; Lu. 5:12-14)
Healing of a Paralytic (Mt. 9:2-8; Mk. 2:3-12; Lu. 5:17-26)
Healing of an Infirm Man (Jn. 5:1-15)
Healing of a Man with a Withered Hand (Mt. 12:9-13; Mk. 3:1-5; Lu. 6:6-10)

GALILEAN MINISTRY (Second Period)

Healing of the Centurion's Servant (Mt. 8:5-13; Lu. 7:1-10)
Raising of the Widow's Son (Lu. 7:11-16)
Healing of a Penitent Sinner (Lu. 7:36-50)
Healing of Man Both Blind and Dumb (Mt. 12:22; Lu. 11:14?)
Stilling the Tempest (Mt. 8:23-27; Mk. 4:35-41; Lu. 8:22-25)
Healing of the Gadarene Demoniac (Mt. 8:28-34; Mk. 5:1-20; Lu. 8:26-39)
Raising of Jairus' Daughter (Mt. 9:18,19,23-26; Mk. 5:22-24, 35-43; Lu. 8:41,42,49-56)
Healing of a Woman Having an Issue of Blood (Mt. 9:20-22; Mk. 5:25-34; Lu. 8:43-48)
Healing of Two Blind Men (Mt. 9:27-31)
Healing of a Dumb Demoniac (Mt. 9:32-34)
Feeding of the Five Thousand (Mt. 14:13-21; Mk. 6:34-44; Lu. 9:11-17; Jn. 6:1-14)
Walking on the Sea (Mt. 14:24-33; Mk. 6:47-52; Jn. 6:16-21)
Ship Immediately at its Destination (Jn. 6:21)

GALILEAN MINISTRY (Third Period)

Healing of Syrophenician Woman's Daughter (Mt. 15:21-28; Mk. 7:24-30)
Healing of a Man Deaf and Stuttering (Mk. 7:32-37)
Feeding of the Four Thousand (Mt. 15:32-38; Mk. 8:1-9)
Healing of a Blind Man (Mk. 8:22-26)
Healing of an Epileptic Boy (Mt. 17:14-21; Mk. 9:14-29; Lu. 9:37-43)
Coin in the Fish's Mouth (Mt. 17:24-27)
Healing of an Adulterous Woman (Jn. 8:2-11)
Healing of a Man Born Blind (Jn. 9:1-41)

PERAEAN MINISTRY

Healing of a Stooped Woman (Lu. 13:10-17)
Healing of a Man with Dropsy (Lu. 14:1-6)
Raising of Lazarus (Jn. 11:1-46)
Healing of Ten Lepers (Lu. 17:11-19)
Healing of a Blind Beggar (Mk. 10:46-52; Lu. 18:35-43; cf. Mt. 20:29-34)
Healing of Zacchaeus (Lu. 19:1-10)

PASSION WEEK

Barren Fig Tree Withered (Mt. 21:18-20; Mk. 11:12-14, 20,21)
Healing of Malchus' Ear (Lu. 22:49-51)

AFTER CRUCIFIXION

Jesus' Resurrection (Mt. 28:1-7; Mk. 16:1-7; Lu. 24:1-8; Jn. 20:1-10)
Vanishing from Sight (Lu. 24:31)
Sudden Appearances to the Apostles through Closed Doors (Jn. 20:19,26)
Draft of Fishes (Jn. 21:1-11)
Jesus' Ascension (Mk. 16:19; Lu. 24:50,51; Acts 1:9-11)

Jesus' Parables

GALILEAN MINISTRY

New Cloth on Old Garment (Mt. 9:16; Mk. 2:21; Lu. 5:36)
New Wine in Old Bottles (Mt. 9:17; Mk. 2:22; Lu. 5:37-39)
House Built on Rock and on Sand (Mt. 7:24-27; Lu. 6:47-49)
Two Debtors (Lu. 7:41-50)
Sower and the Seed (Mt. 13:1-23; Mk. 4:1-20; Lu. 8:4-15)
The Natural Growth of the Seed (Mk. 4:26-29)
Tares and Wheat (Mt. 13:24-30, 36-43)
Mustard Seed (Mt. 13:31, 32; Mk. 4:30-32; Lu. 13:18,19)
Leaven (Mt. 13:33; Lu. 13:20,21)
Hidden Treasure (Mt. 13:44)
Pearl (Mt. 13:45,46)
Dragnet (Mt. 13:47-50)
Unmerciful Servant (Mt. 18:23-35)

PERAEAN MINISTRY

Good Samaritan (Lu. 10:25-37)
Importunate Friend (Lu. 11:5-8)
Rich Fool (Lu. 12:16-21)
Watchful Servants (Lu. 12:35-38)
Goodman of the House (Lu. 12:39,40; cf. Mt. 24:43,44)
Faithful and Faithless Stewards (Lu. 12:42-48; cf. Mt. 24:45-51)

Barren Fig Tree (Lu. 13:6-9)
Wedding Guest (Lu. 14:7-11)
Great Supper (Lu. 14:15-24)
Counting the Cost of Discipleship (Lu. 14:28-35)
Lost Sheep (Lu. 15:1-7)
Lost Piece of Silver (Lu. 15:8-10)
Prodigal Son (Lu. 15:11-32)
Unjust Steward (Lu. 16:1-13)
Rich Man and Lazarus (Lu. 16:19-31)
Unprofitable Servant (Lu. 17:7-10)
Importunate Widow, or Unjust Judge (Lu. 18:1-8)
Pharisee and Publican (Lu. 18:9-14)
Laborers in the Vineyard (Mt. 20:1-16)
Ten Pounds (Lu. 19:11-27)

PASSION WEEK

Two Sons (Mt. 21:28-32)
The Vineyard, or Wicked Husbandmen (Mt. 21:33-46; Mk. 12:1-12; Lu. 20:9-19)
Marriage of the King's Son (Mt. 22:1-14)
Fig Tree and Young Leaves (Mt. 24:32,33; Mk. 13:28,29 Lu. 21:29-31)
Household and Porter Watching (Mk. 13:34-36)
Ten Virgins (Mt. 25:1-13)
Talents (Mt. 25:14-30)

Jesus' Discourses

JUDAEAN MINISTRY

New Birth (Jn. 3:1-21)
Water of Life (Jn. 4:4-26)

GALILEAN MINISTRY (First Period)

The Son and the Father (Jn. 5:19-47)

GALILEAN MINISTRY (Second Period)

Sermon on the Mount (Mt. 5-7; Lu. 6:20-49)
Woes upon Impenitent Cities, Christ's Invitation to the Weary (Mt. 11:20-30)
Christ the Bread of Life (Jn. 6:22-71)
Against Traditions of the Elders (Mt. 15:1-20; Mk. 7:1-23)

GALILEAN MINISTRY (Third Period)

Humility and Forgiveness (Mt. 18; Mk. 9:33-50; Lu. 9:46-50)
Christ the Light of the World (Jn. 8:12-30)

Spiritual Freedom (Jn. 8:31-59)
The Good Shepherd (Jn. 10:1-18)

PERAEAN MINISTRY

Prayer (Lu. 11:1-13)
Denunciation of Blasphemous Pharisees and Scribes (Lu. 11:15-54)
Trust in God's Care, Watchfulness for Christ's Coming (Lu. 12)
Coming of the Kingdom of God and of the Son of Man (Lu. 17:20-18:8)

PASSION WEEK

Denunciation of Pharisees and Scribes (Mt. 23; Mk. 12:38-40; Lu. 20:45-47)
Destruction of Jerusalem, Signs of Christ's Coming, Last Judgment (Mt. 24-25; Mk. 13; Lu. 21:5-38)
Christ the Way, the Truth, the Life (Jn. 14)
The Vine and the Branches (Jn. 15)
His Going and Returning (Jn. 16)

**PRINCIPAL MESSIANIC PROPHECIES OF OLD TESTAMENT
FULFILLED IN NEW TESTAMENT**

THE FIRST PROMISE OF THE REDEEMER

Gen. 3:15	Seed of the woman	Gal. 4:4,5; Rev. 12:5

THE MESSIAH'S NAME AND NATURE

Ps. 2:7; Is. 9:6	Son of God	Mt. 16:16; Lu. 1:32-35; Heb. 5:5
Is. 7:14	Son of man	Mt. 1:23; 16:13; Heb. 2:16
Deut. 18:15,18	Prophet	Jn. 1:45; 6:14; Acts 3:22
Ps. 110:4	Priest	Heb. 6:20; 7:15-17, 24-26
Ps. 2:6; Jer. 23:5,6	King	Lu. 19:38; Jn. 1:49
Is. 40:11; Ezek. 34:23	Shepherd	Jn. 10:11-16; I Pet. 2:25
Is. 9:6	Prince of Peace	Acts 5:31; Eph. 2:14,15
Is. 7:14	Immanuel (God with us)	Mt. 1:23
Is. 7:15; 53:9	Without sin	Heb. 4:15; I Pet. 2:22
Is. 9:2; 42:6; Mal. 4:2	A light	Jn. 1:9; 8:12
Ps. 110:1	Pre-eminence	Mt. 28:18; Heb. 1:2-8; I Pet. 3:22

HIS LINEAGE

Gen. 12:3; 22:18	Of Abraham	Mt. 1:1; Lu. 3:34; Gal. 3:16
Gen. 17:19; 26:4	Of Isaac	Mt. 1:2; Rom. 9:6-8
Gen. 28:13,14; Num. 24:17	Of Jacob	Mt. 1:2; Lu. 3:34
Gen. 49:10; Mic. 5:2	Of tribe of Judah	Mt. 2:6; Lu. 3:33; Rev. 5:5
Ps. 89:3,4; Is. 9:7; Jer. 23:5	Of Davidic throne	Mt. 1:1; Lu. 1:32; Rev. 22:16

HIS PRESENCE AMONG MEN

Mic. 5:2	Nativity in Bethlehem	Mt. 2:6; Lu. 2:4-7; Jn. 7:42
Dan. 9:22-25; Mal. 3:1	Time of his coming	Mt. 11:10; Mk. 1:15; Gal. 4:4
Is. 7:14	Born of a virgin	Mt. 1:18,23; Lu. 1:26-35
Ho. 11:1	Called out of Egypt	Mt. 2:15,19,20
Ps. 45:7; Is. 11:2; 61:1	Anointed of God	Lu. 4:18; Acts 10:38; Heb. 1:9
Ps. 69:9; Is. 56:7	Zeal for the house of God	Mt. 21:12,13; Jn. 2:13-17
Is. 35:4-6; 61:1; Mal. 4:2	Healing work	Mt. 4:23,24; 11:4,5
Is. 9:1,2	Ministry in Galilee	Mt. 4:13-16
Ps. 118:22; Is. 53:3	Rejection	Mt. 21:42; Jn. 1:11; Acts. 4:11
Zech. 9:9	Triumphal entry	Mt. 21:1-10; Jn. 12:12-16
Ps. 41:9; Zech. 11:12	Betrayal	Mt. 26:14-16; Jn. 13:18-30
Ps. 27:12; Is. 53:7	Trials	Mk. 14:53-65; 15:1-15
Is. 53:7	Silence under accusation	Mt. 26:62,63; 27:12-14; Lu. 23:9
Ps. 69:4; 109:3-5	Hated without a cause	Jn. 15:23-25
Is. 53:4-6,11	Suffering for others' sins	Mt. 27:27-31; I Pet. 3:18
Ps. 22:16; Zech. 12:10	Crucifixion	Lu. 23:33; Jn. 19:37; Acts 2:23
Is. 53:8,9,12	Death with malefactors	Mk. 15:27,28; Lu. 23:33
Ps. 69:21	Gall and vinegar	Mt. 27:34,48
Ps. 22:18	Lots cast for his vesture	Mt. 27:35
Num. 9:12; Ps. 34:20	No bone broken	Jn. 19:33,36
Ps. 16:8-11	Resurrection	Mt. 28:5-9; Acts 1:3; 2:24-32
Ps. 68:18; 110:1	Ascension	Mk. 16:19; Lu. 24:50,51

HIS ETERNAL PRESENCE AND POWER

Is. 32:15; Joel 2:28,29	The Holy Spirit, Comforter	Jn. 14:16; Acts 2:4,16,17
Ps. 40:6-8	His sanctifying sacrifice	Mt. 20:28; Heb. 9:24-26; 10:5-14
Is. 53:4-6,10,11	Forgiveness of sins	Mt. 26:28; Lu. 24:47; Acts 10:43
Is. 25:7,8; Ho. 13:14	Death conquered	I Cor. 15:20-23,54-57; II Tim. 1:10
Ps. 118:22; Is. 28:16	Cornerstone	Eph. 2:20; I Pet. 2:4-7
Is. 42:1-7; 49:6; 60:1-3	A light to all nations	Lu. 2:30-32; Acts 26:22,23; 28:28
Dan. 2:44; 7:13,14	His everlasting kingdom	Col. 1:13; Rev. 11:15; 12:10

A Harmony of the Gospels

	Matthew	Mark	Luke	John
EARLY LIFE OF JESUS				
Prologue				1:1-18
Luke's preface			1:1-4	
Genealogies of Jesus	1:1-17		3:23-48	
The announcement to Zacharias			1:5-25	
The annunciation to Mary			1:26-38	
Mary's visit to Elisabeth			1:39-56	
Birth of John the Baptist			1:57-80	
The announcement to Joseph	1:18-25			
Birth of Jesus in Bethlehem			2:1-20	
Circumcision			2:21	
Presentation in the Temple			2:22-39	
Visit of the wise men	2:1-12			
Flight to Egypt and return	2:13-23			
From Childhood to Manhood at Nazareth			2:40	
In the Temple at age of twelve			2:41-51	
Eighteen silent years			2:52	
Opening Events of His Ministry				
Ministry of John the Baptist	3:1-12	1:1-8	3:1-18	
Baptism of Jesus	3:13-17	1:9-11	3:21-23	
Temptation of Jesus	4:1-11	1:12,13	5:1-13	
John the Baptist's testimony				1:19-28
Jesus the Lamb of God				1:29-34
The first disciples				1:35-51
The first miracle—water made wine				2:1-11
PUBLIC MINISTRY				
Judaean Ministry				
In Jerusalem at the Passover:				
First cleansing of the Temple				2:13-22
First discourse: the new birth				3:1-21
Jesus' disciples baptize in Judaea				3:22; 4:1,2
John the Baptist's further testimony				3:23-36
John the Baptist imprisoned by Herod	4:12	1:14	3:19,20	
In Samaria:				
Second discourse: water of life				4:1-42
Galilean Ministry (First Period)				
Preaching and fame	4:12-17	1:14,15	4:14,15	4:43-45
Healing of the nobleman's son				4:46-54
First rejection at Nazareth, his escape			4:16-30	
Jesus dwells in Capernaum	4:13-16		4:31	
Call of the Four, great draft of fishes	4:18-22	1:16-20	5:1-11	
Healing of man with unclean spirit		1:21-28	4:31-37	
Healing of Peter's wife's mother	8:14-17	1:29-34	4:38-41	
Preaching and healing in Galilee	4:23-25	1:35-39	4:42-44	
Healing of a leper	8:1-4	1:40-45	5:12-16	
Healing of a paralytic	9:1-8	2:1-12	5:17-26	
Accusation of blasphemy				
The call of Matthew (Levi)	9:9-13	2:13-17	5:27-32	
Question about observance of fasting	9:14-17	2:18-22	5:33-39	
Parable of new cloth on old garment	9:16	2:21	5:36	
Parable of new wine in old bottles	9:17	2:22	5:37-39	

	Matthew	Mark	Luke	John
In Jerusalem:				
Healing of infirm man at Pool of Bethesda				5:1-15
Accusation of blasphemy				5:16-18
Discourse: the Son and the Father				5:19-47
In Galilee:				
Disciples pluck grain on Sabbath	12:1-8	2:23-28	6:1-5	
Healing of a man with a withered hand	12:9-14	3:1-6	6:6-11	
Widening fame	12:15-21	3:7-12		

Galilean Ministry (Second Period)

	Matthew	Mark	Luke	John
The choosing of the twelve apostles		3:13-19	6:12-19	
Discourse: the Sermon on the Mount	5-7		6:20-49	
Parable of house built on rock, on sand	7:24-27		6:47-49	
Healing of centurion's servant	8:5-13		7:1-10	
Raising of the widow's son at Nain			7:11-17	
Answer to John the Baptist's question	11:2-30		7:18-35	
Discourse: Woes on impenitent cities, Christ's invitation to the weary	11:20-30			
Healing of a penitent sinner			7:36-50	
Parable of two debtors			7:41-50	
Women minister to Jesus			8:1-3	
Healing of a man blind and dumb	12:22-45	3:20-30	(11:14?)	
Accusation of the Pharisees; blasphemy against the Holy Ghost				
Jesus declares his true kindred	12:46-50	3:31-35	8:19-21	
Parables of the kingdom of heaven: sower, seed, tares, mustard seed, leaven, hidden treasure, pearl, dragnet	13:1-53	4:1-34	(8:4-18; (13:18-21	
Stilling the tempest	(8:18, (23-27	4:35-41	8:22-25	
Healing of the Gadarene demoniac	8:28-34	5:1-20	8:26-39	
Raising of Jairus' daughter	9:18-26	5:21-43	8:40-56	
Healing of a woman with issue of blood	9:20-22	5:25-34	8:43-48	
Healing of two blind men	9:27-31			
Healing of dumb demoniac	9:32-34			
Second rejection at Nazareth	13:54-58	6:1-6		
Commissioning of the Twelve	(9:35- (11:1	6:7-13	9:1-6	
The martyrdom of John the Baptist	14:1-12	6:14-29	9:7-9	
Feeding of the five thousand	14:13-23	6:30-46	9:10-17	6:1-14
People would make him a king				6:15
Walking on the sea; the ship immediately at the land	14:24-36	6:47-56		6:16-21
Discourse: Christ the bread of life				6:22-71
Discourse: against traditions of elders	15:1-20	7:1-23		

Galilean Ministry (Third Period)

	Matthew	Mark	Luke	John
Journey to Tyre and Sidon:				
Healing of Syrophenician's daughter	15:21-28	7:24-30		
Return by way of Decapolis:				
Multitudes healed	15:29-31			
Healing of man deaf and stuttering		7:31-37		
Feeding of the four thousand	15:32-38	8:1-9		
Pharisees and Sadducees demand a sign	(15:39- (16:12	8:10-21		
Healing of a blind man		8:22-26		

339

	Matthew	Mark	Luke	John
Journey to Caesarea Philippi:				
Peter's confession concerning Christ	16:13-20	8:27-30	9:18-21	. . . .
Jesus' first foretelling of his				
death and resurrection	16:21-28	8:31-9:1	9:22-27	. . . .
The Transfiguration	17:1-13	9:2-13	9:28-36	. . . .
Healing of an epileptic boy	17:14-21	9:14-29	9:37-43	. . . .
In Galilee:				
Jesus' second foretelling of				
his death and resurrection	17:22,23	9:30-32	9:43-45	. . . .
Coin in the fish's mouth	17:24-27	. . . .	. . . .	. . . .
Discourse: humility and forgiveness	18:1-35	9:33-50	9:46-50	. . . .
Parable of the unmerciful servant	18:23-35	. . . .	. . . .	. . . .
In Jerusalem at Feast of Tabernacles	. . . .	. . . .	. . . .	7:1-13
Teaching in the Temple	. . . .	. . . .	. . . .	7:14-8:2
Healing of woman taken in adultery	. . . .	. . . .	. . . .	8:3-11
Discourse: Christ the light of the world	. . . .	. . . .	. . . .	8:12-30
Discourse: spiritual freedom	. . . .	. . . .	. . . .	8:31-59
Healing of a man born blind	. . . .	. . . .	. . . .	9:1-41
Discourse: the good shepherd	. . . .	. . . .	. . . .	10:1-21
In Jerusalem at Feast of Dedication	. . . .	. . . .	. . . .	10:22-42
Accusation of blasphemy				
Peraean Ministry				
Final departure from Galilee to Peraea	19:1,2	10:1	9:51-56	. . . .
Teaches immediacy of discipleship	8:19-22	. . . .	9:57-62	. . . .
Sending forth of the Seventy	. . . .	. . . .	10:1-24	. . . .
Parable of the good Samaritan	. . . .	. . . .	10:25-37	. . . .
Visit to Mary and Martha at Bethany	. . . .	. . . .	10:38-42	. . . .
Discourse: prayer	. . . .	. . . .	11:1-13	. . . .
Parable of importunate friend	. . . .	. . . .	11:5-8	. . . .
Discourse: denunciation of Pharisees	. . . .	. . . .	11:15-54	. . . .
Discourse: trust in God's care,				
watchfulness for Christ's coming	. . . .	. . . .	12:1-59	. . . .
Parable of the rich fool	. . . .	. . . .	12:16-21	. . . .
Parable of the watchful servants	. . . .	. . . .	12:35-38	. . . .
Parable of the goodman of the house	. . . .	. . . .	12:39,40	. . . .
Parable of faithful and faithless stewards	. . . .	. . . .	12:42-48	. . . .
Preaching on repentance	. . . .	. . . .	13:1-5	. . . .
Parable of the barren fig tree	. . . .	. . . .	13:6-9	. . . .
Healing of a stooped woman	. . . .	. . . .	13:10-17	. . . .
Answers question as to who shall be saved	. . . .	. . . .	13:22-30	. . . .
Jesus' reproof of Herod and Jerusalem	. . . .	. . . .	13:31-35	. . . .
At dinner in chief Pharisee's house:				
Healing of a man with dropsy	. . . .	. . . .	14:1-6	. . . .
Parable of the wedding guest	. . . .	. . . .	14:7-11	. . . .
Virtue of hospitality to the poor	. . . .	. . . .	14:12-14	. . . .
Parable of the great supper	. . . .	. . . .	14:15-24	. . . .
Three requirements for discipleship	. . . .	. . . .	14:25-27	. . . .
Parable of counting cost of discipleship	. . . .	. . . .	14:28-35	. . . .
Teaching on saving of sinners:				
Parable of the lost sheep	. . . .	. . . .	15:1-7	. . . .
Parable of the piece of silver	. . . .	. . . .	15:8-10	. . . .
Parable of the prodigal son	. . . .	. . . .	15:11-32	. . . .

	Matthew	Mark	Luke	John
Teachings of warning:				
Parable of unjust steward	. . . .	. . . .	16:1-17	. . . .
Parable of rich man and Lazarus	. . . .	. . . .	16:19-31	. . . .
Teaching on forgiveness, faith, service	. . . .	. . . .	17:1-10	. . . .
Parable of the unprofitable servant	. . . .	. . . .	17:7-10	. . . .
Raising of Lazarus at Bethany	. . . .	. . . .	. . . .	11:1-46
Sanhedrin's plot to kill Jesus	. . . .	. . . .	. . . .	11:47-53
Jesus' withdrawal to Ephraim, thence through				
borders of Samaria and Galilee to Peraea	. . . .	. . . .	17:11	11:54
Healing of ten lepers	. . . .	. . . .	17:12-19	. . . .
Discourse: coming of the kingdom of God				
and of the Son of man	. . . .	. . . .	17:20-18:8	
Parable of the importunate widow	. . . .	. . . .	18:1-8	
Parable of Pharisee and publican	. . . .	. . . .	18:9-14	
Concerning divorce and marriage	19:3-12	10:2-12		
Blessing little children	19:13-15	10:13-16	18:15-17	
Instructions to a rich young ruler	19:16-22	10:17-31	18:18-30	
Dangers of wealth, rewards of selfless				
service	19:23-30			
Parable of laborers in the vineyard	20:1-16	. . . .		
Jesus' third foretelling of his				
death and resurrection	20:17-19	10:32-34	18:31-34	
The ambition of James and John	20:20-28	10:35-45	. . . .	
Healing of a blind beggar (or of two men)	20:29-34	10:46-52	18:35-43	
Healing of Zacchaeus at Jericho	. . . .	. . . .	19:1-10	
Parable of the ten pounds	. . . .	. . . .	19:11-28	
Jesus' enemies lie in wait for him	. . . .	. . . .	. . . .	11:55-57
Anointing of Jesus by Mary of Bethany	26:6-13	14:3-9	. . . .	12:1-11

PASSION WEEK

Sunday

	Matthew	Mark	Luke	John
Triumphal entry into Jerusalem	21:1-11	11:1-11	19:29-44	12:12-19

Monday

	Matthew	Mark	Luke	John
Barren fig tree cursed	21:18,19	11:12-14	. . . .	. . . .
Second cleansing of the Temple	21:12-17	11:15-19	19:45-48	. . . .

Tuesday

	Matthew	Mark	Luke	John
Fig tree withered	21:20-22	11:20-26	. . . .	
Questioning of Jesus' authority	21:23-27	11:27-33	20:1-8	. . . .
Parables of warning to the nation:				
Of two sons	21:28-32			
Of the vineyard or the wicked husbandmen . .	21:33-46	12:1-12	20:9-19	
Of marriage of king's son	22:1-14	. . . .	. . . .	
Three questions by Jewish parties	22:15-40	12:13-34	20:20-40	. . . .
Jesus' irrefutable question about Christ	22:41-46	12:35-37	20:41-44	
Discourse: denunciation of				
Pharisees and scribes—eight woes	23:1-39	12:38-40	20:45-47	
Widow's mites		12:41-44	21:1-4	. . . .
Greeks (Gentiles) seek Jesus	. . . .	. . . .	. . . .	12:20-36
Rejection of Christ by the Jews	. . . .	. . . .	. . . .	12:37-50
Jesus foretells destruction of the Temple	24:1,2	13:1,2	21:5,6	. . . .
Olivet Discourse: destruction of Jerusalem,				
signs of Christ's Coming, Last Judgment	(24:3- (25:46	13:3-37	21:7-38	. . . .

341

	Matthew	Mark	Luke	John
Parables of warning to his disciples:				
Of fig tree and young leaves	24:32,33	13:28,29	21:29-31	. . . .
Of household and porter watching	. . . .	13:34-36	. . . .	. . . .
Of the ten virgins	25:1-13	. . . .	. . . .	. . . .
Of the talents	25:14-30	. . . .	. . . .	. . . .
Description of Last Judgment	25:31-46	. . . .	. . . .	. . . .
Conspiracy of chief priests and Judas	(26:1-5, (14-16	(14:1,2, (10,11	22:1-6	. . . .

Wednesday
    (The record is silent) . . . .

Thursday

	Matthew	Mark	Luke	John

Last Supper: observance of Passover,
    washing of disciples' feet, naming of
    betrayer, instituting of Lord's Supper,
    foretelling of Peter's denial . . . .
	26:17-35	14:12-31	22:7-38	13-17
				14:1-31

Discourse: Christ the way, truth, life	. . . .	. . . .	. . . .	14:1-31
Discourse: the vine and the branches	. . . .	. . . .	. . . .	15:1-27
Discourse: his going and returning	. . . .	. . . .	. . . .	16:1-33
Intercessory prayer	. . . .	. . . .	. . . .	17:1-26

Friday

	Matthew	Mark	Luke	John
In Gethsemane, his thrice-repeated prayer	(26:30, (36-46	(14:26, (32-42	22:39-46	18:1
Betrayal and arrest	26:47-56	14:43-52	22:47-53	18:2-12
Healing of Malchus' ear	. . . .	. . . .	22:51	. . . .
Jewish ecclesiastical trial:				
Before Annas, father-in-law of Caiaphas	. . . .	. . . .	. . . .	18:13-23
Before Caiaphas and Sanhedrin	26:57-75	14:53-72	22:54-65	18:24-27
Peter's denial				
Before Sanhedrin	27:1,2	15:1	22:66-71	. . . .
Judas hangs himself (cf. Acts 1:16-20)	27:3-10	. . . .	. . . .	. . . .
Roman civil trial:				
Before Pilate	(27:2, (11-14	15:1-5	23:1-5	18:28-38
Before Herod (Antipas)	. . . .	. . . .	23:6-12	. . . .
Before Pilate	27:15-31	15:6-20	23:13-25	(18:39- (19:16
Crucifixion at Golgotha (Calvary)	27:32-56	15:21-41	23:26-49	19:17-37

Seven last sayings: Lu. 23:34,43;
        Jn. 19:26,27; Mt. 27:46 (Mk. 15:34);
        Jn. 19:28,30; Lu. 23:46				

Darkness, earthquake; veil of Temple rent . . .	27:50-54	15:33,38	23:44,45	. . . .
Burial in the tomb	27:57-61	15:42-47	23:50-56	19:38-42

Saturday

	Matthew	Mark	Luke	John
Sealing of tomb, guard set	27:62-66	. . . .	. . . .	. . . .

THE FORTY DAYS FROM RESURRECTION TO ASCENSION

Resurrection:

	Matthew	Mark	Luke	John
The empty tomb	28:1-8	16:1-8	24:1-8	20:1-10
The guards' report to Sanhedrin	28:11-15	. . . .	. . . .	. . . .

	Matthew	Mark	Luke	John
Ten Appearances of Jesus during Forty Days:				
To Mary Magdalene	. . . .	16:9-11	. . . .	20:11-18
To the women	28:9,10	. . . .	24:9-11	. . . .
To two disciples on road to Emmaus	. . . .	16:12,13	24:13-35	. . . .
To Peter (I Cor. 15:5)	. . . .	. . . .	24:34	. . . .
To apostles, Thomas absent (I Cor. 15:5)	. . . .	16:14	24:36-48	20:19-25
To apostles, Thomas present	. . . .	. . . .	. . . .	20:26-31
To seven apostles at Sea of Galilee	. . . .	. . . .	. . . .	21:1-23
Great draft of fishes				
The morning repast				
Peter's restoration to grace				
To apostles (and five hundred disciples)				
(I Cor. 15:6)	28:16-20	16:15-18	. . . .	. . . .
To James (I Cor. 15:7)				
To all the apostles				
Promised the baptism of the Holy Ghost	. . . .	. . . .	24:49	. . . .
(Acts 1:4-8; I Cor. 15:7)				
Ascension	. . . .	16:19	24:50-53	. . . .
Two angels forecast Christ's				
Second Coming (Acts 1:9-11)				
Apostles go forth to preach, teach, heal	. . . .	16:20	. . . .	. . . .

9

Correlation – Jesus

It is from John's Gospel that we see most clearly the two-fold nature of Christ—in his pre-existence as the Word of God (1:1; 17:5) and in his appearance to humanity in the man Jesus (1:14,18). Christ Jesus' words reveal his knowledge of himself as both divine and human, the Son of God, the Son of man. As the *Son of God,* "the only begotten of the Father," he knew a relationship that existed in the beginning—"before the world was," and the divinity of his nature is evidenced in the power and glory of his life.

> "I and my Father are one." Jn. 10:30. "Before Abraham was, I am." Jn. 8:58
> "I came forth from the Father, and am come into the world: again, I leave the world, and go to the Father." Jn. 16:28
> "All things that the Father hath are mine." Jn. 16:15
> "I am the light of the world." Jn. 8:12. "I am the bread of life." Jn. 6:35

As the *Son of man* (a term Jesus used of himself some eighty times), he indicated his relationship to the human race. His human nature was at all times coincident with his divine nature, enabling him to do the works of his Father.

> "The Son of man came not to be ministered unto, but to minister, and to give his life a ransom for man." Mk. 10:45
> "No man hath ascended up to heaven, but he that came down from heaven, even the Son of man which is in heaven." Jn. 3:13
> "God sent not his Son into the world to condemn the world; but that the world through him might be saved." Jn. 3:17

The topical studies in this section relate to certain aspects of Jesus' life that are specially helpful to an understanding of his words and works. Some correlate Jesus' prescient words, others accent focal points in his ministry. These have been charted to afford a quick but comprehensive grasp of the subject.

JESUS' FOREKNOWLEDGE OF EVENTS

Repeatedly Jesus taught "The Son of man must suffer many things." As the Son of man he foreknew his coming rejection and sufferings. In the face of one prophetic declaration after another, it becomes clear that from only one source—his heavenly Father—could there pour out sufficient strength and love to enable him to walk steadfastly forward.

Of Crucifixion and Resurrection

"Therefore doth my Father love me, because I lay down my life, that I might take it again. No man taketh it from me, but I lay it down of myself. I have power to lay it down, and I have power to take it again. This commandment have I received of my Father." Jn. 10:17,18

"Behold, we go up to Jerusalem; and the *Son of man* shall be betrayed unto the chief priests and unto the scribes, and they shall condemn him to death, And shall deliver him to the Gentiles to mock, and to scourge, and to crucify him: and the third day he shall rise again." Mt. 20:18,19 (Three times he prophesied this.)

Jesus said of Mary of Bethany, "She hath done what she could: she is come aforehand to anoint my body to the burying." Mk. 14:6,8 (Six days before Jesus' last Passover)

"The hour is come, that the *Son of man* should be glorified. Verily, verily, I say unto you, Except a corn of wheat fall into the ground and die, it abideth alone: but if it die, it bringeth forth much fruit." Jn. 12:23,24

Of Betrayal

"The *Son of man* shall be betrayed into the hands of men. . . ." Mt. 17:22

"Ye know that after two days is the feast of the passover, and the *Son of man* is betrayed to be crucified." Mt. 26:2

Jesus said to his apostles, "Ye are clean, but not all. For he knew who should betray him. . . ." Jn. 13:10,11

"Verily, verily, I say unto you, that one of you shall betray me. . . . He it is, to whom I shall give a sop, when I have dipped it. And when he had dipped the sop, he gave it to Judas Iscariot. . . ." Jn. 13:21,26

"Judas, betrayest thou the *Son of man* with a kiss?" Lu. 22:48

Of Desertion by Apostles

"All ye shall be offended because of me this night: for it is written, I will smite the shepherd, and the sheep shall be scattered." Mk. 14:27

"Behold, the hour cometh, yea, is now come, that ye shall be scattered, every man to his own, and shall leave me alone: and yet I am not alone, because the Father is with me." Jn. 16:32

Of His Hour	"They sought to take him: but no man laid hands on him, because his hour was not yet come." Jn. 7:30

"Now is my soul troubled; and what shall I say? Father, save me from this hour: but for this cause came I unto this hour." Jn. 12:27

"Now before the feast of the passover, when Jesus knew that his hour was come that he should depart out of this world unto the Father. . . ." Jn. 13:1

"Father, the hour is come; glorify thy Son, that thy Son also may glorify thee. . . . I have glorified thee on the earth: I have finished the work which thou gavest me to do. And now, O Father, glorify thou me with thine own self with the glory which I had with thee before the world was." Jn. 17:1,4,5

"He went forward a little, and fell on the ground, and prayed that, if it were possible, the hour might pass from him." Mk. 14:35

"Behold, the hour is at hand, and the *Son of man* is betrayed into the hands of sinners." Mt. 26:45

Of Rejection

"And he began to teach them, that the *Son of man* must suffer many things, and be rejected . . . ." Mk. 8:31

"Did ye never read in the scriptures, The stone which the builders rejected, the same is become the head of the corner. . . ." Mt. 21:42

"O Jerusalem, Jerusalem, thou that killest the prophets, and stonest them which are sent unto thee, how often would I have gathered thy children together, even as a hen gathereth her chickens under her wings, and ye would not!" Mt. 23:37

Jesus' teaching of his rejection is embodied also in many of his parables.

The parable of the barren fig tree: "A certain man had a fig tree planted in his vineyard; and he came and sought fruit thereon, and found none. Then said he unto the dresser of his vineyard, Behold, these three years I come seeking fruit on this fig tree, and find none: cut it down; why cumbereth it the ground?" Lu. 13:6-9

The parable of the rich man and Lazarus: "If they hear not Moses and the prophets, neither will they be persuaded, though one rose from the dead." Lu. 16:19-31

The parable of the ten pounds: A certain nobleman went into a far country to receive a kingdom. He commanded his servants, "Occupy till I come. But his citizens hated him, and sent a message after him, saying, We will not have this man to reign over us." Lu. 19:11-27

The parable of the two sons: When they were sent to work in the vineyard, one said, "I will not: but afterward he repented, and went." The other said, "I go, sir: and went not." Mt. 21:28-32

The parable of the marriage of the king's son: "They [the guests] would not come . . . they made light of it, and went their ways. . . ." Mt. 22:1-10

The parable of the vineyard: "Those husbandmen said among themselves, This is the heir; come, let us kill him. . . ." "What shall therefore the Lord of the vineyard do? he will come and destroy the husbandmen, and will give the vineyard unto others." Mk. 12:1-11

Of Endurance and Victory	"Destroy this temple, and in three days I will raise it up. . . . But he spake of the temple of his body." Jn. 2:19,21

"Behold, I cast out devils, and I do cures to day and to morrow, and the third day I shall be perfected. Nevertheless I must walk to day, and to morrow, and the day following: for it cannot be that a prophet perish out of Jerusalem." Lu. 13:32,33

"Yet a little while, and the world seeth me no more; but ye see me: because I live, ye shall live also. At that day ye shall know that I am in my Father, and ye in me, and I in you." Jn. 14:19,20

"Be of good cheer; I have overcome the world." Jn. 16:33

"And now I am no more in the world. . . ." Jn. 17:11

On the cross: "To day shalt thou be with me in paradise." Lu. 23:43
On the cross: "Father, into thy hands I commend my spirit. . . ." Lu. 23:46
On the cross: "It is finished. . . ." Jn. 19:30

"All power is given unto me in heaven and in earth." Mt. 28:18

Of the Comforter

"I will pray the Father, and he shall give you another Comforter, that he may abide with you for ever; Even the Spirit of truth; whom the world cannot receive, because it seeth him not, neither knoweth him: but ye know him; for he dwelleth with you, and shall be in you. I will not leave you comfortless: I will come to you." Jn. 14:16-18

"The Comforter, which is the Holy Ghost, whom the Father will send in my name, he shall teach you all things, and bring all things to your remembrance, whatsoever I have said unto you." Jn. 14:26

"Nevertheless I tell you the truth; It is expedient for you that I go away: for if I go not away, the Comforter will not come unto you; but if I depart, I will send him unto you. . . . I have yet many things to say unto you, but ye cannot bear them now. Howbeit when he, the Spirit of truth, is come, he will guide you into all truth: for he shall not speak of himself; but whatsoever he shall hear, that shall he speak: and he will shew you things to come." Jn. 16:7,12,13

Of Ascension

"What and if ye shall see the *Son of man* ascend up where he was before?" Jn. 6:62

"Ye have heard how I said unto you, I go away, and come again unto you. If ye loved me, ye would rejoice, because I said, I go unto the Father: for my Father is greater than I." Jn. 14:28

"Now I go my way to him that sent me. . . ." Jn. 16:5

To Mary Magdalene Jesus said, "Touch me not; for I am not yet ascended to my Father: but go to my brethren, and say unto them, I ascend unto my Father, and your Father; and to my God, and your God." Jn. 20:17

Of His Second Coming	"The *Son of man* shall come in the glory of his Father with his angels; and then he shall reward every man according to his works." Mt. 16:27
	"And then shall they see the *Son of man* coming in the clouds with great power and glory. And then shall he send his angels, and shall gather together his elect from the four winds, from the uttermost part of the earth to the uttermost part of heaven. . . . But of that day and that hour knoweth no man, no, not the angels which are in heaven, neither the Son, but the Father." Mk. 13:26,27,32
	"I go to prepare a place for you. And if I go and prepare a place for you, I will come again, and receive you unto myself. . . ." Jn. 14:2,3

Of Pre-eminence	"What think ye of Christ? whose son is he? They say unto him, The son of David. He saith unto them, How then doth David in spirit call him Lord, saying, The Lord said unto my Lord, Sit thou on my right hand, till I make thine enemies thy footstool? If David then call him Lord, how is he his son?" Mt. 22:42-45
	"When the *Son of man* shall come in his glory, and all the holy angels with him, then shall he sit upon the throne of his glory: And before him shall be gathered all nations. . . ." Mt. 25:31,32
	"Hereafter shall the *Son of man* sit on the right hand of the power of God." Lu. 22:69

Of His Church	When Peter declared, "Thou art the Christ, the Son of the living God," Jesus said, "And I say also unto thee, That thou art Peter, and upon this rock I will build my church; and the gates of hell shall not prevail against it." Mt. 16:16,18
	"Verily, verily, I say unto you, He that believeth on me, the works that I do shall he do also; and greater works than these shall he do; because I go unto my Father." Jn. 14:12
	"For where two or three are gathered together in my name, there am I in the midst of them." Mt. 18:20

Of the Universality of His Mission	"Other sheep I have, which are not of this fold: them also I must bring, and they shall hear my voice; and there shall be one fold, and one shepherd." Jn. 10:16
	"Go ye into all the world, and preach the gospel to every creature. He that believeth and is baptized shall be saved. . . ." Mk. 16:15,16
	"Thus it is written, and thus it behoved Christ to suffer, and to rise from the dead the third day: And that repentance and remission of sins should be preached in his name among all nations, beginning at Jerusalem." Lu. 24:46,47

Questions Asked by Jesus

During his three years of public ministry Jesus asked many searching questions, all well fitted to the situation and to the need of his listeners. The purpose of many of his interrogations was to increase individual spiritual understanding; the intent of others was to startle his listeners into self-examination and self-purification.

Listed here are the major questions put by Jesus; although presented without their background, each contains a vital lesson.

Concerning His Mother

"How is it that ye sought me? wist ye not that I must be about my Father's business?" Lu. 2:49 (In Temple at age of twelve)

"Woman, what have I to do with thee?" Jn. 2:4 (At marriage in Cana)

"Who is my mother? and who are my brethren?" Mt. 12:48

The Sermon on the Mount

"If ye love them which love you, what reward have ye? do not even the publicans the same? And if ye salute your brethren only, what do ye more than others? do not even the publicans so?" Mt. 5:46,47 (Lu. 6:32-34)

"Is not the life more than meat, and the body than raiment?" Mt. 6:25

"Which of you by taking thought can add one cubit unto his stature?" Mt. 6:27 (Lu. 12:25) Luke adds: "If ye then be not able to do that thing which is least, why take ye thought for the rest?" Lu. 12:26

"Why take ye thought for raiment? . . . if God so clothe the grass of the field, which to day is, and to morrow is cast into the oven, shall he not much more clothe you, O ye of little faith?" Mt. 6:28,30 (Lu. 12:28)

"Why beholdest thou the mote that is in thy brother's eye, but considerest not the beam that is in thine own eye?" Mt. 7:3 (Lu. 6:41) Luke includes the question: "Can the blind lead the blind? shall they not both fall into the ditch?" Lu. 6:39

"Or what man is there of you, whom if his son ask bread, will he give him a stone? Or if he ask a fish, will he give him a serpent? If ye then, being evil, know how to give good gifts unto your children, how much more shall your Father which is in heaven give good things to them that ask him?" Mt. 7:9-11 (Lu. 11:11-13)

"Do men gather grapes of thorns, or figs of thistles?" Mt. 7:16

"Why call ye me, Lord, Lord, and do not the things which I say?" Lu. 6:46 (Mt. 7:21)

To His Disciples

"Say not ye, There are yet four months, and then cometh harvest? . . ." Jn. 4:35 (To his early disciples)

"Is a candle brought to be put under a bushel, or under a bed? and not to be set on a candlestick?" Mk. 4:21

"Why are ye fearful, O ye of little faith?" Mt. 8:26 (Mk. 4:40; Lu. 8:25) (At stilling of the storm)

"If they have called the master of the house Beelzebub, how much more shall they call them of his household?" Mt. 10:25 (At commissioning of Twelve)

"Will ye also go away?" Jn. 6:67 (As some leave him)

"Whom do men say that I the Son of man am? . . . But whom say ye that I am?" Mt. 16:13,15 (Mk. 8:27,29; Lu. 9:18,20)

"What is a man profited, if he shall gain the whole world, and lose his own soul? or what shall a man give in exchange for his soul?" Mt. 16:26 (Mk. 8:36,37)

"How think ye? if a man have an hundred sheep, and one of them be gone astray, doth he not leave the ninety and nine, and goeth into the mountains, and seeketh that which is gone astray?" Mt. 18:12

"Salt is good: but if the salt have lost his saltness, wherewith will ye season it?" Mk. 9:50 (Lu. 14:34)

"Suppose ye that I am come to give peace on earth?" Lu. 12:51

"If therefore ye have not been faithful in the unrighteous mammon, who will commit to your trust the true riches? And if ye have not been faithful in that which is another man's, who shall give you that which is your own?" Lu. 16:11,12 (Following parable of unjust steward)

"Shall not God avenge his own elect, which cry day and night unto him, though he bear long with them?" Lu. 18:7 (Following parable of importunate widow)

"When the Son of man cometh, shall he find faith on the earth?" Lu. 18:8

"Who then is a faithful and wise servant, whom his lord hath made ruler over his household, to give them meat in due season?" Mt. 24:45

"Whether is greater, he that sitteth at meat, or he that serveth? is not he that sitteth at meat? but I am among you as he that serveth." Lu. 22:27 (At the Last Supper)

"Know ye what I have done to you?" Jn. 13:12 (At washing of disciples' feet)

"When I sent you without purse, and scrip, and shoes, lacked ye any thing?" Lu. 22:35

"Why sleep ye? rise and pray, lest ye enter into temptation." Lu. 22:46 (At Gethsemane)

"Why are ye troubled? and why do thoughts arise in your hearts?" Lu. 24:38 (At first appearance after Resurrection)

"Children, have ye any meat?" Jn. 21:5 (At third appearance after Resurrection as apostles were fishing)

To Individual Apostles

"What seek ye?" Jn. 1:38 (To his first two disciples)

"O thou of little faith, wherefore didst thou doubt?" Mt. 14:31 (To Peter after his attempt to walk on the water)

"Ye know not what ye ask: can ye drink of the cup that I drink of? and be baptized with the baptism that I am baptized with?" Mk. 10:38 (Mt. 20:22) (To James and John)

"Wilt thou lay down thy life for my sake?" Jn. 13:38 (To Peter)

"Have I been so long time with you, and yet hast thou not known me, Philip? he that hath seen me hath seen the Father; and how sayest thou then, Shew us the Father? Believest thou not that I am in the Father, and the Father in me?" Jn. 14:9,10

"Simon, sleepest thou? couldest not thou watch one hour?" Mk. 14:37 (Mt. 26:40; Lu. 22:46)

"Judas, betrayest thou the Son of man with a kiss?" Lu. 22:48

"Thinkest thou that I cannot now pray to my Father, and he shall presently give me more than twelve legions of angels?" Mt. 26:53

"The cup which my Father hath given me, shall I not drink it?" Jn. 18:11

"Simon, son of Jonas, lovest thou me more than these? . . . lovest thou me? . . . lovest thou me?" Jn. 21:15-17 (To Peter)

"If I will that he [John] tarry till I come, what is that to thee? follow thou me." Jn. 21:22 (To Peter)

To Seekers of Healing

"Wilt thou be made whole?" Jn. 5:6 (To the impotent man)

"What is thy name?" Mk. 5:9 (Lu. 8:30) (To the Gadarene demoniac)

"Who touched me?" Lu. 8:45 (Mk. 5:31) (To woman with issue of blood)

"Why make ye this ado, and weep?" Mk. 5:39 (To those who mourned Jairus' daughter)

"Believe ye that I am able to do this?" Mt. 9:28 (To two blind men)

"Dost thou believe on the Son of God?" Jn. 9:35 (To man born blind)

"Were there not ten cleansed? but where are the nine?" Lu. 17:17 (To one of the ten lepers)

To Individuals

"If I have told you earthly things, and ye believe not, how shall ye believe, if I tell you of heavenly things?" Jn. 3:12 (To Nicodemus)

"Can the children of the bridechamber mourn, as long as the bridegroom is with them?" Mt. 9:15 (To disciples of John the Baptist)

"What is written in the law? how readest thou?" Lu. 10:26 (To a lawyer)

"Man, who made me a judge or a divider over you?" Lu. 12:14 (To a covetous man)

"I am the resurrection, and the life: he that believeth in me, though he were dead, yet shall he live: And whosoever liveth and believeth in me shall never die. Believest thou this?" Jn. 11:25,26 (To Martha)

"Why callest thou me good?" Mt. 19:17 (Mk. 10:18; Lu. 18:19)

"Where is the guestchamber, where I shall eat the passover with my disciples?" Lu. 22:11 (Mk. 14:14) (To the goodman of the house)

"If they do these things [crucify me] in a green tree, what shall be done in the dry?" Lu. 23:31 (As Jesus carried his cross)

"Woman, why weepest thou? whom seekest thou?" Jn. 20:15 (To Mary Magdalene at the tomb)

"O fools, and slow of heart to believe all that the prophets have spoken: Ought not Christ to have suffered these things, and to enter into his glory?" Lu. 24:25,26 (To two disciples on way to Emmaus)

To Pharisees, Scribes, Sadducees

Concerning the Charge of Blasphemy "Wherefore think ye evil in your hearts? For whether is easier, to say, Thy sins be forgiven thee; or to say, Arise, and walk?" Mt. 9:4,5 (Mk. 2:8,9; Lu. 5:22,23) (At healing of man sick of the palsy)

"If Satan cast out Satan, he is divided against himself; how shall then his kingdom stand? And if I by Beelzebub cast out devils, by whom do your children cast them out? . . . Or else how can one enter into a strong man's house, and spoil his goods, except he first bind the strong man? . . ." Mt. 12:26-29 (Mk. 3:23-27; Lu. 11:18-22) (At healing of a man blind and dumb)

Concerning the Charge of Sabbath-breaking "Is it lawful to do good on the sabbath days, or to do evil? to save life, or to kill?" Mk. 3:4 (Lu. 6:9) (At a healing on the Sabbath)

His Denunciatory Questions to a Non-hearing and Unrepentant Generation "How can ye believe, which receive honour one of another, and seek not the honour that cometh from God only?" Jn. 5:44 (At Jerusalem at Passover)

"If ye believe not his [Moses'] writings, how shall ye believe my words?" Jn. 5:47

"Why doth this generation seek after a sign? . . ." Mk. 8:12

"Why do ye not understand my speech? even because ye cannot hear my word." Jn. 8:43

"Which of you convinceth me of sin? And if I say the truth, why do ye not believe me?" Jn. 8:46

"Did ye never read in the scriptures, The stone which the builders rejected, the same is become the head of the corner: this is the Lord's doing, and it is marvellous in our eyes?" Mt. 21:42 (Mk. 12:10,11; Lu. 20:17)

"Ye serpents, ye generation of vipers, how can ye escape the damnation of hell?" Mt. 23:33

To the People

"What went ye out into the wilderness to see? A reed shaken with the wind? But what went ye out for to see? A man clothed in soft raiment? . . . But what went ye out for to see? A prophet? . . ." Mt. 11:7-9 (Lu. 7:24-26) (Concerning John the Baptist)

"Doth this offend you [Jesus' declaration of himself as the bread of life]? What and if ye shall see the Son of man ascend up where he was before?" Jn. 6:61,62

"Are not five sparrows sold for two farthings, and not one of them is forgotten before God?" Lu. 12:6

"Ye hypocrites, ye can discern the face of the sky and of the earth; but how is it that ye do not discern this time? Yea, and why even of yourselves judge ye not what is right?" Lu. 12:56,57 (Mt. 16:3)

"Which of you, intending to build a tower, sitteth not down first, and counteth the cost, whether he have sufficient to finish it? . . . Or what king, going to make war against another king, sitteth not down first, and consulteth whether he be able with ten thousand to meet him that cometh against him with twenty thousand?" Lu. 14:28,31 (Cost of discipleship)

SWELLING TIDE OF HATRED AGAINST JESUS

"The hatred of Christ's enemies grows with His self-revelation."[1] Almost from the opening of Jesus' ministry there was active resistance to his work—resistance which quickly flared into open hostility. His enemies employed every means at their disposal to make his work of none effect. Sometimes Jesus withdrew beyond the reach of their malice; other times he answered their accusations directly; occasionally he was silent. Wisdom, spiritual insight, and power characterized all his words and actions, and safeguarded him until his hour was come to be glorified.

Read chart column by column

	Opposition at first cleansing of Temple	First rejection at Nazareth	Accusation
Jesus said, "He that hateth me hateth my Father also. If I had not done among them the works which none other man did, they had not had sin: but now have they both seen and hated both me and my Father." Jn. 15:23,24	Jesus opened his ministry by cleansing the Temple, thereby challenging the corrupt religious practices of his day. The rulers demanded, "What sign shewest thou unto us, seeing that thou doest these things?" Jn. 2:18	"And all they in the synagogue, when they heard these things, were filled with wrath, And rose up, and thrust him out of the city, and led him unto the brow of the hill whereon their city was built, that they might cast him down headlong." Lu. 4:28,29	"Therefore the Jews sought the more to kill him, because he not only had broken the sabbath [by healing the impotent man], but said also that God was his Father, making himself equal with God." Jn. 5:18
Jesus said, "I must walk to day, and to morrow, and the day following: for it cannot be that a prophet perish out of Jerusalem." Lu. 13:33 ". . . almost till the last days of his life Jesus is represented as taking steps to evade any danger that threatened to bring his work to a premature close."[2]	Jesus answered, "Destroy this temple, and in three days I will raise it up. . . . But he spake of the temple of his body." Jn. 2:19,21	"But he passing through the midst of them went his way. . . ." Lu. 4:30	Jesus answered, "The Son can do nothing of himself, but what he seeth the Father do: for what things soever he doeth, these also doeth the Son likewise." Jn. 5:19

Accusation	Opposition of Jews to his teachings	Threat of danger in Jerusalem	Threat of stoning	Accusation and threat of stoning
Jesus healed the man with the withered hand on the Sabbath, despite Pharisaic prohibition against Sabbath healing. Mt. 12:13 "Then the Pharisees went out, and held a council against him, how they might destroy him." Mt. 12:14 "They were filled with madness; and communed one with another what they might do to Jesus." Lu. 6:11	"After these things [teaching of himself as the living bread from heaven] Jesus walked in Galilee: for he would not walk in Jewry, because the Jews sought to kill him. "Now the Jews' feast of tabernacles was at hand." Jn. 7:1,2	"Many of the people believed on him, and said, When Christ cometh, will he do more miracles than these which this man hath done? "The Pharisees heard that the people murmured such things concerning him; and the Pharisees and the chief priests sent officers to take him." Jn. 7:31,32	Jesus said, "Your father Abraham rejoiced to see my day: and he saw it, and was glad. . . . Verily, verily, I say unto you, Before Abraham was, I am. "Then took they up stones to cast at him. . . ." Jn. 8:58,59	Jesus said, "I and my Father are one. "Then the Jews took up stones again to stone him." They said, ". . . we stone thee . . . for blasphemy; and because that thou, being a man, makest thyself God." Jesus answered, ". . . believe the works: that ye may know, and believe, that the Father is in me, and I in him. "Therefore they sought again to take him. . . ." Jn. 10:30-39
"But when Jesus knew it, he withdrew himself from thence. . . ." Mt. 12:15	Jesus said, "I go not up yet unto this feast; for my time is not yet full come . . . then went he also up unto the feast, not openly, but as it were in secret." Jn. 7:8,10	Jesus said, "Yet a little while am I with you, and then I go unto him that sent me. Ye shall seek me, and shall not find me: and where I am, thither ye cannot come." Jn. 7:33,34	"But Jesus hid himself, and went out of the temple, going through the midst of them, and so passed by." Jn. 8:59	"But he escaped out of their hand, And went away again beyond Jordan . . . and there he abode." Jn. 10:39,40

Treachery of the Pharisees

As Jesus openly rebuked Pharisaic hypocrisy, "the scribes and the Pharisees began to urge him vehemently, and to provoke him to speak of many things:

"Laying wait for him, and seeking to catch something out of his mouth, that they might accuse him." Lu. 11:53,54

Imminent danger

The Sanhedrin held a council: "If we let him thus alone, all men will believe on him: and the Romans shall come and take away both our place and nation."

Caiaphas said, "It is expedient for us, that one man should die for the people, and that the whole nation perish not.

"Then from that day forth they took counsel together for to put him to death." Jn. 11:47-53

Rising hostility of Sanhedrin

At the close of his ministry Jesus cleansed the Temple again. He charged the authorities: "Is it not written, My house shall be called of all nations the house of prayer? but ye have made it a den of thieves.

"The scribes and chief priests heard it, and sought how they might destroy him: for they feared him, because all the people was astonished at his doctrine." Mk. 11:17,18

Malicious plotting

"And the chief priests and the scribes ... sought to lay hands on him; and they feared the people: for they perceived that he had spoken this parable against them. . . .

"They watched him, and sent forth spies, which should feign themselves just men, that they might take hold of his words, that so they might deliver him unto the power and authority of the governor." Lu. 20:19,20

Conspiracy

The Sanhedrin co[...]ed to kill Jesus bu[...] said, "Not on the [...] day, lest there [...] uproar among [...] people."

"Then one of [...] twelve, called Ju[...] cariot, went unt[...] chief priests, An[...] ... What will ye [...] me, and I will [...] him unto you? [...] they covenanted [...] him for thirty pie[...] silver.

"And from that ti[...] sought opportuni[...] betray him." [...] 26:5,14-16

"He began to say unto his disciples . . . Beware ye of the leaven of the Pharisees, which is hypocrisy. For there is nothing covered, that shall not be revealed. . . ." Lu. 12:1,2

"Jesus therefore walked no more openly among the Jews; but went thence unto a country near to the wilderness. . . ." Jn. 11:54

"And when even was come, he went out of the city." Mk. 11:19

"But he perceived their craftiness, and said ... Why tempt ye me? ... they could not take hold of his words before the people: and they ... held their peace." Lu. 20:23,26

Before the San[...] plotted with [...] Jesus had said, [...] know that after [...] days is the feast [...] passover, and the S[...] man is betrayed [...] crucified." Mt. 26[...]

Betrayal and arrest	Prejudgment at Jewish trial	Scourging and mockery at Roman trials	Humiliation and crucifixion	Resurrection belied
…das, one of the …ve, came, and with … a great multitude … swords and staves, … the chief priests … elders of the …ple. … he that betrayed … gave them a sign, …g, Whomsoever I … kiss, that same is …hold him fast. And … he came to Jesus, … said, Hail, master; …issed him. . . . … came they, and …hands on Jesus, and … him.'' Mt. …7-50	All the council "sought for witness against Jesus to put him to death; and found none." The high priest asked, "Art thou the Christ, the Son of the Blessed?" When Jesus replied affirmatively and foretold his coming in glory, the high priest cried, "What need we any further witnesses? Ye have heard the blasphemy: what think ye? And they all condemned him to be guilty of death." Mk. 14:55,61-64	The chief priests accused Jesus, "We found this fellow perverting the nation, and forbidding to give tribute to Caesar, saying that he himself is Christ a King." Lu. 23:2 "Pilate asked him . . . Answerest thou nothing?" Mk. 15:4 "When Herod saw Jesus . . . he questioned with him in many words. . . . "Herod with his men of war set him at nought, and mocked him, and arrayed him in a gorgeous robe, and sent him again to Pilate." Lu. 23:8,9,11 "Then Pilate . . . took Jesus, and scourged him." Jn. 19:1	"And he bearing his cross went forth into a place called . . . Golgotha: Where they crucified him, and two other with him, on either side one, and Jesus in the midst." Jn. 19:17,18 "They that passed by reviled him, wagging their heads, And saying . . . If thou be the Son of God, come down from the cross. Likewise also the chief priests mocking him, with the scribes and elders, said, He saved others; himself he cannot save. . . . "The thieves also, which were crucified with him, cast the same in his teeth." Mt. 27:39-44	To prevent Jesus' resurrection the chief priests demanded permission of Pilate to seal the tomb. "Pilate said . . . Ye have a watch: go your way, make it as sure as ye can. So they went, and made the sepulchre sure, sealing the stone, and setting a watch." Mt. 27:65,66 After Resurrection the chief priests bribed the Roman watch to discredit this miracle: "Say ye, His disciples came by night, and stole him away while we slept. . . . So they took the money, and did as they were taught: and this saying is commonly reported among the Jews until this day." Mt. 28:13,15
… forbade Peter to …is sword: "Think-…hou that I cannot …pray to my Father, … he shall presently … me more than … legions of an-…" Mt. 26:53	Jesus answered, "I am: and ye shall see the Son of man sitting on the right hand of power, and coming in the clouds of heaven." Mk. 14:62	To chief priests "he answered nothing." Mk. 15:3 To Pilate, Jesus "yet answered nothing." Mk. 15:5 To Herod, Jesus "answered him nothing." Lu. 23:9	Jesus prayed, "Father, forgive them; for they know not what they do." "Father, into thy hands I commend my spirit. . . ." Lu. 23:34,46	Two angels present at the sepulchre on Resurrection morning said to the women, "Why seek ye the living among the dead? He is not here, but is risen." Lu. 24:5,6

355

TYPES OF WOMANHOOD

In this top section certain women of the Old and New Testaments have been used as figurative types of ideal womanhood or motherhood. As one traces the Scriptural record a higher standard of true womanhood is seen evolving—through God's mercy, favor, and grace; through woman's maternal care, consecration, prayer, righteousness, purity, and travail.

This purer standard was clearly manifest in the Virgin Mary who mothered the long-promised Savior. In the book of Revelation womanhood is the type used by John to portray the spiritual quality of thought which brings forth the "man child," and which enables mankind to come into perfect union with Christ.

Read top section upward

Read bottom section downward

In this section certain women of Scripture are used as the antitheses of true womanhood and motherhood. On a descending scale is seen the corruption of womanhood through a love of evil, lust, seduction, idolatry, inordinate ambition, hatred, and greed—depravity that has its end in judgment and destruction.

(THE LAMB'S WIFE) "I . . . saw the holy city . . . coming down from God . . . prepared as a bride adorned for her husband." Rev. 19:7; 21:2
"The marriage of the Lamb is come, and his wife hath made herself ready." Rev. 19:7; 21:2

(THE WOMAN IN TRAVAIL) "She brought forth a man child . . . her child was caught up unto God, and to his throne."
"A great wonder in heaven; a woman clothed with the sun . . . the moon under her feet. . . ." Rev. 12:1,5

MARY "That which is conceived in her is of the Holy Ghost." Mt. 1:20
"A virgin shall be with child. . . ."—"Behold the handmaid of the Lord. . . ." Mt. 1:23; Lu. 1:38

ELISABETH At Mary's salutation "the babe leaped in her womb; and Elisabeth was filled with the Holy Ghost." Lu. 1:41

HANNAH Hannah said, "For this child I prayed. . . . as long as he liveth he shall be lent to the Lord." I Sam. 1:27,28

RUTH Ruth said to Naomi, "Intreat me not to leave thee . . . thy people shall be my people, and thy God my God." Ru. 1:16

DEBORAH "A prophetess . . . she judged Israel at that time."—"I Deborah arose . . . a mother in Israel." Ju. 4:4; 5:7

RACHEL "God remembered Rachel [who was barren] . . . And she . . . bare a son; and said, God hath taken away my reproach." Gen. 29:31; 30:22,23

SARAH God said, "Yea, I will bless her, and she shall be a mother of nations; kings of people shall be of her." Gen. 17:16 (cf. Heb. 11:11)

EVE God said, "It [the woman's seed] shall bruise thy head [the serpent's head]. . . ." Gen. 3:15

EVE "Took of the fruit [of tree of knowledge of good and evil] . . . gave also unto her husband . . . and he did eat." Gen. 3:6

POTIPHAR'S WIFE "Cast her eyes upon Joseph; and she said, Lie with me. . . . she spake to Joseph day by day. . . ." Gen. 39:7,10

DELILAH The Philistines said: "Entice him [Samson], and see wherein his great strength lieth . . . that we may bind him." Ju. 16:5
"She pressed him daily with her words . . . so that his soul was vexed unto death; That he told her all his heart. . . ." Ju. 16:16,17

JEZEBEL "Jezebel slew . . . prophets of the Lord. . . ."—"The prophets of Baal . . . eat at Jezebel's table." I Ki. 18:13,19

ATHALIAH (Mother of King Ahaziah) "His mother was his counsellor to do wickedly." II Chron. 22:3
(Jezebel's daughter) "She . . . destroyed all the seed royal of the house of Judah [except Joash]." II Chron. 22:10

HERODIAS "Had a quarrel against [John Baptist], and would have killed him. . . ."—Caused his beheading Mk. 6:17-28

SAPPHIRA With her husband sinned in withholding part of their means and "lied" to the Holy Ghost. Acts 5:1-10

(THE GREAT WHORE) "BABYLON THE GREAT, THE MOTHER OF HARLOTS AND ABOMINATIONS OF THE EARTH" Rev. 17:5
"She shall be utterly burned with fire: for strong is the Lord God who judgeth her." Rev. 18:8

Changing Concepts
of Womanhood

Among ancient peoples a woman was regarded as a man's chattel or a husband's possession, the result of centuries of custom that had become accepted law (see Hebrew Society, p. 36). This was true of Semitic women. Hebrew Scripture taught, however, that woman was made to be "an help meet" for man, a companion suitable to his nature (Gen. 2:20); thus from early times Hebrew wives were accorded considerably more liberty and given more protection than their contemporaries in other Eastern nations. Mosaic Law discouraged polygamy and concubinage and held generally to monogamous marriage; and Hebrew wives and mothers held a respected place in the social structure of the family. Their status was further enhanced as such women of virtue and faith as Sarah, Miriam, Deborah, Ruth, Hannah, Abigail, and Esther rose to positions of influence, honor, and dignity.

> No literature of any age offers a finer ideal of the Wife and Mother than this Hebrew poem [Pr. 31], written not less than two thousand five hundred years ago. . . . The picture of loving fidelity, ceaseless industry, prudence, management, charity, thrift, wisdom, self-respect; of noble reverence, rising from the husband on earth to God above, and of motherly virtues towards her children, must have kindled high aspirations in many a Jewish wife.[3]

The Gospels give only two specific teachings of Jesus regarding the status of woman: that which protected her virtue (Mt. 5:32) and that which upheld the marriage covenant (Mk. 10:2-12). Nevertheless, Jesus' concept of the worth of every human being as a child of the one Father by its very nature gave a new dignity to woman.

The truths of the kingdom applied to all, and Jesus numbered women as well as men among his followers (although relatively few are named by the Gospel writers), and he freely exercised his healing power on their behalf. The record shows Jesus' second discourse was to the woman of Samaria at Jacob's Well. He healed Simon's mother-in-law, the stooped woman, the woman with the issue of blood, the Canaanite's daughter, and raised Jairus' daughter from the dead. He forgave the social outcast who anointed his feet with her tears as he dined at Simon's house, and also forgave the adulterous woman who was about to be stoned. He regarded with dignity and affection Lazarus' sisters Mary and Martha, appreciating the capabilities of the homemaker Martha and the spiritual perception of the more gentle Mary. Even as he hung on the cross he provided for his mother by placing her in the care of John. The privileged first to whom Jesus showed himself alive after Resurrection were Mary Magdalene and other faithful women who had come to the sepulcher to mourn.

In synagogue worship women had not been permitted to play a role in the order of service, but were segregated from the men of the congregation. In the evolution of the early Church, however, women held a new status; they were no longer wholly excluded from participation in the community of church worship. The spiritually intuitive among them welcomed the gospel and responded to the call to spread it. Their influence began at once to be felt. Dorcas of Joppa was known for her good works. Mary, mother of John Mark, offered her house as a meeting place for the Christians of Jerusalem, as did Lydia to the Christians in Philippi. Priscilla was Paul's invaluable helper in the churches of Corinth, Ephesus, and Rome; and Phebe of Cenchrea was entrusted to deliver to the church at Rome Paul's important Epistle to the Romans.

The teachings of Christianity opened the way for a fuller acknowledgment of the rights and equality of women, and their leavening effect is seen in the freedoms enjoyed by the modern woman.

HEALING WORK OF JESUS

The Gospels record more than a score of specific healings wrought by Jesus during his public ministry. These healings extended over a wide range of human afflictions, physical, mental, and moral. He cured sick and disabled bodies; healed paralysis, congenital deformities, chronic and contagious diseases; impaired faculties, insanity; sin, immorality; and he raised the dead.

These healings have been correlated from the several Gospels so that the reader may readily gain insight into Jesus' mode of spiritual healing. In many instances the accounts indicate not only the distressing bodily conditions of those who approached Jesus for help but also their mental state—the fears, doubts, superstitious beliefs that needed to be cast out, and the faith, repentance, obedience that responded to Christ's healing touch.

Jesus was always compassionate, his healings instant. His commands were brief but imperative. A close scrutiny of these healings shows that he demanded action on the part of the one he addressed. He often gave the command "rise" or "arise," and when obeyed it was followed by positive and immediate results. (Rise means, in part, "move upward . . . reach a higher level . . . Syn. ascend, mount." [4])

Observe Jesus' commands. Observe the effect in its natural sequence as indicated by the word "and." (*And* is defined: "along with or together with . . . added to or linked to . . . express the general relation of connection or addition, esp. accompaniment, participation, combination, contiguity, continuance, simultaneity, sequence." [5])

HEALING OF THE NOBLEMAN'S SON

"fever" (healed at a distance)   Jn. 4:46-54

Jesus' outstanding command: "Go thy way. . . ."

> "Jesus came again into Cana of Galilee, where he made the water wine. And there was a certain nobleman, whose son was sick at Capernaum."

> "When he heard that Jesus was come out of Judaea into Galilee, he went unto him, and besought him that he would come down, and heal his son: for he was at the point of death."

> The nobleman said, "Sir, come down ere my child die."

> Jesus did not "come down," but he said, "Go thy way; thy son liveth."

"*And* the man believed the word that Jesus had spoken unto him, *and* he went his way."

The healing took place "at the seventh hour," "the same hour, in the which Jesus said unto him, Thy son liveth."

HEALING OF MAN WITH UNCLEAN SPIRIT

Jesus' command to the unclean spirit: "Hold thy peace, and come out of him."

"Straightway on the sabbath day he entered into the synagogue, and taught. And they were astonished at his doctrine: for he taught them as one that had authority, and not as the scribes."

"There was in their synagogue a man with an unclean spirit. . . ."

The man cried out, "Let us alone; what have we to do with thee, thou Jesus of Nazareth? art thou come to destroy us? I know thee who thou art, the Holy One of God."

"Jesus rebuked him, saying, Hold thy peace, and come out of him."

"*And* when the devil had thrown him in the midst, he came out of him, *and* hurt him not."

HEALING OF PETER'S WIFE'S MOTHER

"When they were come out of the synagogue, they entered into the house of Simon and Andrew, with James and John."

"But Simon's wife's mother lay sick of a fever, and anon they tell him of her."

Jesus "stood over her, and rebuked the fever. . . ."
"He . . . took her by the hand, and lifted her up. . . ."

"*and* it left her: *and* immediately she arose and ministered unto them."

HEALING OF A LEPER

Jesus' command: "Be thou clean."

"There came a leper and worshipped him. . . ."

The leper beseeched, "Lord, if thou wilt, thou canst make me clean."

"Jesus, moved with compassion, put forth his hand, and touched him, and saith unto him, I will; be thou clean."

"*And* as soon as he had spoken, immediately the leprosy departed from him, *and* he was cleansed."

It was required: "Tell no man. . . ."
        "Go, and shew thyself to the priest. . . ."
        "Offer for thy cleansing. . . ."

HEALING OF THE PARALYTIC

Jesus' command: "Arise, and take up thy bed, and go thy way into thine house."

"Men brought in a bed a man which was taken with a palsy. . . . because of the multitude, they went upon the housetop, and let him down through the tiling with his couch . . . before Jesus."

Jesus, seeing their faith, said, "Man, thy sins are forgiven thee." "Arise, and take up thy bed, and go thy way into thine house."

"*And* immediately he rose up before them, *and* took up that whereon he lay, *and* departed to his own house, glorifying God."

HEALING OF THE INFIRM MAN

Jesus' command: "Rise, take up thy bed, and walk."

At the pool of Bethesda "lay a great multitude of impotent folk . . . waiting for the moving of the water" for healing.

"A certain man . . . there . . . had an infirmity thirty and eight years."

"When Jesus saw him lie . . . he saith unto him, Wilt thou be made whole?"

He answered, "Sir, I have no man . . . to put me into the pool: but while I am coming, another steppeth down before me."

Jesus said, "Rise, take up thy bed, and walk."

"*And* immediately the man was made whole, *and* took up his bed, *and* walked. . . ."

"Afterward Jesus findeth him in the temple. . . ."

It was required: "Sin no more, lest a worse thing come unto thee."

HEALING OF THE MAN WITH A WITHERED HAND

Jesus' commands: "Rise up, and stand forth in the midst."
                 "Stretch forth thine hand."

Jesus "entered into the synagogue . . . and there was a man whose right hand was withered."—"They watched him, whether he would heal him on the sabbath day. . . ."

"But he knew their thoughts, and said to the man . . . Rise up, and stand forth in the midst."

"*And* he arose *and* stood forth."

Jesus said, "It is lawful to do well on the sabbath days." He commanded the man, "Stretch forth thine hand."

"*And* he did so: *and* his hand was restored whole as the other."

Jesus' command: "Go thy way...."

There came to Jesus a centurion (a Roman military officer, a Gentile) "beseeching him, And saying, Lord, my servant lieth at home sick of the palsy, grievously tormented."

Jesus said, "I will come and heal him."

> (According to Luke's Gospel the centurion sent elders of the Jews. "They besought him instantly, saying, That he was worthy.... For he loveth our nation, and he hath built us a synagogue.")

The centurion answered: "Lord, I am not worthy that thou shouldest come under my roof: but speak the word only, and my servant shall be healed. For I am a man under authority, having soldiers under me: and I say to this man, Go, and he goeth; and to another, Come, and he cometh; and to my servant, Do this, and he doeth it."

"When Jesus heard it, he marvelled, and said to them that followed, Verily I say unto you, I have not found so great faith, no, not in Israel."

Jesus said to the centurion, "Go thy way; and as thou hast believed, so be it done unto thee."

"*And* his servant was healed in the selfsame hour."

THE HEALING OF A MAN BLIND AND DUMB

"Then was brought unto him one possessed with a devil, blind and dumb...."

"*and* he healed him, insomuch that the blind and dumb both spake and saw."

"And all the people were amazed, and said, Is not this the Son of David?

"But when the Pharisees heard it, they said, This fellow doth not cast out devils, but by Beelzebub the prince of the devils.

"And Jesus knew their thoughts, and said unto them, Every kingdom divided against itself is brought to desolation; and every city or house divided against itself shall not stand: And if Satan cast out Satan, he is divided against himself; how shall then his kingdom stand? And if I by Beelzebub cast out devils, by whom do your children cast them out? therefore they shall be your judges.

"But if I cast out devils by the Spirit of God, then the kingdom of God is come unto you.

"Or else how can one enter into a strong man's house, and spoil his goods, except he first bind the strong man? and then he will spoil his house."

THE HEALING OF THE GADARENE DEMONIAC

"many devils" (insanity)   Mt. 8:28-34; Mk. 5:1-20; Lu. 8:26-39

Jesus' command: "Come out of the man, thou unclean spirit."

"There met him . . . a certain man, which had devils long time, and ware no clothes, neither abode in any house, but in the tombs." —"No man could bind him. . . . neither could any man tame him."

"But when he saw Jesus afar off, he ran and worshipped him, And cried . . . What have I to do with thee, Jesus, thou Son of the most high God? . . . For he said unto him, Come out of the man, thou unclean spirit."

Jesus asked, "What is thy name?"

He answered, "My name is Legion: for we are many."

"The devils besought him, saying, Send us into the swine. . . . And forthwith Jesus gave them leave."

"*And* the unclean spirits went out, and entered into the swine: *and* the herd ran violently down a steep place into the sea . . . and were choked in the sea."

"*And* [the people] found the man . . . sitting at the feet of Jesus, clothed, *and* in his right mind: and they were afraid."

HEALING OF THE WOMAN HAVING AN ISSUE OF BLOOD

"an issue of blood"   Mt. 9:20-22; Mk. 5:25-34; Lu. 8:43-48

Jesus' command: "Go in peace, and be whole of thy plague."

The woman, diseased with an issue of blood for twelve years, "had suffered many things of many physicians, and had spent all that she had, and was nothing bettered, but rather grew worse."

"The woman . . . came behind him, and touched the hem of his garment: For she said within herself, If I may but touch his garment, I shall be whole."

"*and* immediately her issue of blood stanched." Jesus said, "Daughter, thy faith hath made thee whole; go in peace, and be whole of thy plague."

HEALING OF TWO BLIND MEN

"blind"   Mt. 9:27-31

Two blind men cried, "Thou son of David, have mercy on us."

Jesus said to them, "Believe ye that I am able to do this?"

They answered, "Yea, Lord."

"Then touched he their eyes, saying, According to your faith be it unto you."

"*And* their eyes were opened. . . ." It was required: "See that no man know it."

HEALING OF DUMB DEMONIAC

"dumb"

Mt. 9:32-34

"They brought to him a dumb man possessed with a devil."

"*And* when the devil was cast out, the dumb spake. . . ."

HEALING OF SYROPHENICIAN WOMAN'S DAUGHTER

"unclean spirit" (healed at a distance)

Mt. 15:21-28; Mk. 7:24-30

Jesus' command: "Go thy way. . . ."

"A certain woman [a Greek and a Syrophenician], whose young daughter had an unclean spirit, heard of him, and came and fell at his feet."

She cried, "Have mercy on me, O Lord, thou son of David; my daughter is grievously vexed with a devil."

"But he answered her not a word."

"And his disciples came and besought him, saying, Send her away; for she crieth after us."

"But he answered and said, I am not sent but unto the lost sheep of the house of Israel."

"Then came she and worshipped him, saying, Lord, help me."

Jesus said, "Let the children first be filled: for it is not meet to take the children's bread, and to cast it unto the dogs."

She answered, "Yes, Lord: yet the dogs under the table eat of the children's crumbs."

Jesus said, "For this saying go thy way; the devil is gone out of thy daughter."—"O woman, great is thy faith: be it unto thee even as thou wilt."

"*And* her daughter was made whole from that very hour."

HEALING OF A MAN DEAF AND STUTTERING

"deaf," "an impediment in his speech"

Mk. 7:32-37

Jesus' command: "Be opened."

"They bring unto him one that was deaf, and had an impediment in his speech; and they beseech him to put his hand upon him."

"He took him aside from the multitude, and put his fingers into his ears, and he spit, and touched his tongue. . . ."

Jesus "looking up to heaven . . . saith unto him . . . Be opened."

"*And* straightway his ears were opened, *and* the string of his tongue was loosed, *and* he spake plain."

HEALING OF A BLIND MAN

Jesus "made him look up."

"They bring a blind man unto him, and besought him to touch him."

"He took the blind man by the hand, and led him out of the town; and when he had spit on his eyes, and put his hands upon him, he asked him if he saw ought."

"*And* he looked up, and said, I see men as trees, walking."

"After that he [Jesus] put his hands *again* upon his eyes, and made him look up. . . ."

"*and* he was restored, *and* saw every man clearly."

The following healings are recorded as having occurred after Jesus' Transfiguration.

HEALING OF AN EPILEPTIC BOY

Jesus' commands: "Bring him unto me."
"Dumb and deaf spirit . . . come out . . . enter no more into him."

"There came to him a certain man, kneeling down to him, and saying, Lord, have mercy on my son [mine only child]: for he is lunatick, and sore vexed. . . . And I brought him to thy disciples, and they could not cure him."

Jesus reproved a faithless generation, and said, "Bring him unto me."

"And when he saw him, straightway the spirit tare him; and he fell on the ground, and wallowed foaming."

Jesus asked the father, "How long is it ago since this came unto him?" He answered, "Of a child. . . . but if thou canst do any thing, have compassion on us, and help us."

Jesus said, "If thou canst believe, all things are possible to him that believeth." With tears the father said, "Lord, I believe; help thou mine unbelief."

"Jesus . . . rebuked the foul spirit . . . Thou dumb and deaf spirit, I charge thee, come out of him, and enter no more into him."

"And the spirit . . . rent him sore, and came out of him: and he was as one dead; insomuch that many said, He is dead. But Jesus took him by the hand, and lifted him up. . . ."

"*and* he arose."—"*and* the child was cured from that very hour."

"Then came the disciples to Jesus apart, and said, Why could not we cast him out?"

Jesus answered, "Because of your unbelief."—"This kind can come forth by nothing, but by prayer and fasting."

Jesus' command: "Go, wash. . . ."

"As Jesus passed by, he saw a man which was blind from his birth. And his disciples asked him, saying, Master, who did sin, this man, or his parents, that he was born blind?"

Jesus answered, "Neither hath this man sinned, nor his parents: but that the works of God should be made manifest in him. I must work the works of him that sent me, while it is day. . . . As long as I am in the world, I am the light of the world."

"When he had thus spoken, he spat on the ground, and made clay of the spittle, and he anointed the eyes of the blind man with the clay. . . .'"

Jesus said, "Go, wash in the pool of Siloam. . . ."

"He went his way therefore, and washed, *and* came seeing."

In the healings prior to this, moral and spiritual changes are implied. In this healing the man's faith and his enlightenment as to God's Messiah are also recorded.

The neighbors asked, "How were thine eyes opened?" He said, "A man . . . called Jesus . . . anointed mine eyes . . . and I went and washed, and I received sight."

The Pharisees questioned him about his healing but some would not believe his testimony, for they regarded Jesus as a sinner for having healed on the Sabbath. They questioned further, "What sayest thou of him [Jesus], that he hath opened thine eyes?"

He answered, "He is a prophet."

Still refusing to believe, they questioned his parents, "Is this your son, who ye say was born blind? how then doth he now see?" The parents, fearing excommunication from the synagogue should they acknowledge Jesus as Christ, testified only to his identity but evaded the ensnaring query, saying, "He is of age; ask him."

The Pharisees called the man born blind and demanded, "Give God the praise: we know that this man [Jesus] is a sinner."

He answered, "Whether he be a sinner or no, I know not: one thing I know, that, whereas I was blind, now I see."

Again they asked, "What did he to thee?" He replied, "I have told you already, and ye did not hear: wherefore would ye hear it again? will ye also be his disciples? Then they reviled him . . . Thou art his disciple; but we are Moses' disciples. We know that God spake unto Moses: as for this fellow, we know not from whence he is."

The man answered, "Why herein is a marvellous thing, that ye know not from whence he is, and yet he hath opened mine eyes. . . . If this man were not of God, he could do nothing." And they cast him out, saying, "Thou wast altogether born in sins, and dost thou teach us?"

Jesus, hearing this, found the man, and asked: "Dost thou believe on the Son of God? He answered . . . Who is he, Lord, that I might believe on him? . . . Jesus said unto him, Thou hast both seen him, and it is he that talketh with thee."

The man said, "Lord, I believe. *And* he worshipped him."

Jesus said, "For judgment I am come into this world, that they which see not might see; and that they which see might be made blind. And some of the Pharisees . . . said unto him, Are we blind also?"

HEALING OF THE STOOPED WOMAN

"bowed together" (on the Sabbath, in synagogue)   Lu. 13:10-17

Jesus' command: "Called her to him. . . ."

> "There was a woman [a daughter of Abraham] which had a spirit of infirmity eighteen years, and was bowed together, and could in no wise lift up herself."

> "When Jesus saw her, he called her to him, and said unto her, Woman, thou art loosed from thine infirmity."

> "And he laid his hands on her. . . ."

"and immediately she was made straight, *and* glorified God."

HEALING OF MAN WITH DROPSY

"dropsy" (on the Sabbath)   Lu. 14:1-6

> "As he went into the house of one of the chief Pharisees to eat bread on the sabbath day . . . they watched him. And, behold, there was a certain man before him which had the dropsy."

> Jesus asked, "Is it lawful to heal on the sabbath day?"

> "And they held their peace."

"And he took him, and healed him, and let him go; And answered them . . . Which of you shall have an ass or an ox fallen into a pit, and will not straightway pull him out on the sabbath day?"

> "And they could not answer him again to these things."

HEALING OF TEN LEPERS

"leprosy"   Lu. 17:11-19

Jesus' command: "Go shew yourselves unto the priests."

> "There met him ten men that were lepers, which stood afar off."

> "They lifted up their voices . . . Jesus, Master, have mercy on us."

> Jesus said: "Go shew yourselves unto the priests."

"And . . . as they went, they were cleansed."

"And one of them, when he saw that he was healed, turned back, *and* with a loud voice glorified God, *And* fell down on his face at his feet, giving him thanks: and he was a Samaritan."

> *Jesus' command to the Samaritan: "Arise, go thy way. . . ."*

>> Jesus asked, "Were there not ten cleansed? but where are the nine? There are not found that returned to give glory to God, save this stranger."

> "Arise, go thy way: thy faith hath made thee whole."

HEALING OF THE BLIND BEGGAR BARTIMAEUS

Jesus' commands: ". . . commanded him to be called."
           "Receive thy sight. . . ."

(Matthew records the healing of two blind men.)

"As he went out of Jericho with his disciples and a great number of people, blind Bartimaeus . . . sat by the highway side begging."—"And hearing the multitude pass by, he asked what it meant. And they told him, that Jesus of Nazareth passeth by."

"When he heard that it was Jesus . . . he began to cry out, and say, Jesus, thou son of David, have mercy on me. And many charged him that he should hold his peace: but he cried the more a great deal, Thou son of David, have mercy on me."

"And Jesus stood still, and commanded him to be called."

"And they call the blind man, saying unto him, Be of good comfort, rise; he calleth thee."

"*And* he, casting away his garment, rose, *and* came to Jesus."

Jesus asked, "What wilt thou that I should do unto thee?"

The blind man said, "Lord, that I might receive my sight."

Jesus replied, "Receive thy sight: thy faith hath saved thee."

"*And* immediately he received his sight, *and* followed him, glorifying God. . . ."

HEALING OF MALCHUS' EAR

Jesus' command to Peter: "Put up again thy sword into his place. . . ."

"Judas then, having received a band of men and officers from the chief priests and Pharisees, cometh thither with lanterns and torches and weapons."

Judas said, "Master, master; and kissed him." (Sign of betrayal)

"Then came they, and laid hands on Jesus, and took him."

"Then Simon Peter having a sword drew it, and smote the high priest's servant, and cut off his right ear. The servant's name was Malchus."

Jesus said, "Suffer ye thus far."—"Put up again thy sword into his place: for all they that take the sword shall perish with the sword. Thinkest thou that I cannot now pray to my Father, and he shall presently give me more than twelve legions of angels? But how then shall the scriptures be fulfilled, that thus it must be?"

"The cup which my Father hath given me, shall I not drink it?"

"*And* he touched his ear, *and* healed him."

(Luke alone records the healing.)

*Three specific moral healings are included
in this study of Jesus' healing work.*

HEALING OF A PENITENT SINNER

Jesus' command: "Go in peace."

Jesus "went into the Pharisee's house, and sat down to meat."

"And, behold, a woman in the city, which was a sinner,* when she knew that Jesus sat at meat in the Pharisee's house, brought an alabaster box of ointment, And stood at his feet behind him weeping, and began to wash his feet with tears, and did wipe them with the hairs of her head, and kissed his feet, and anointed them with the ointment."

"Now when the Pharisee . . . saw it, he spake within himself, saying, This man, if he were a prophet, would have known who and what manner of woman this is that toucheth him: for she is a sinner."

"And Jesus answering said unto him, Simon, I have somewhat to say unto thee. And he saith, Master, say on."

> "There was a certain creditor which had two debtors: the one owed five hundred pence, and the other fifty. And when they had nothing to pay, he frankly forgave them both. Tell me therefore, which of them will love him most?"
>
> "Simon answered . . . I suppose that he, to whom he forgave most."
>
> "And he said unto him, Thou hast rightly judged."

"And he turned to the woman, and said unto Simon, Seest thou this woman?"

"I entered into thine house, thou gavest me no water for my feet: but she hath washed my feet with tears, and wiped them with the hairs of her head."

"Thou gavest me no kiss: but this woman since the time I came in hath not ceased to kiss my feet."

"My head with oil thou didst not anoint: but this woman hath anointed my feet with ointment."

"Wherefore I say unto thee, Her sins, which are many, are forgiven; for she loved much: but to whom little is forgiven, the same loveth little."

"*And* he said unto her, Thy sins are forgiven. . . . Thy faith hath saved thee; go in peace."

---

*This woman is sometimes identified with Mary Magdalene "out of whom [Jesus] had cast seven devils" (Mk. 16:9; Lu. 8:2). But many scholars feel that there is no ground for this identification unless the nature of the seven devils is considered to be a moral malady rather than a physical affliction, nor any valid reason for identifying her with Mary of Bethany, sister of Martha and Lazarus, who also anointed Jesus' feet.

Jesus' command: "Make haste, and come down. . . ."

"Jesus . . . passed through Jericho. And . . . there was a man named Zacchaeus, which was the chief among the publicans, and he was rich. And he sought to see Jesus . . . and could not for the press, because he was little of stature. And he ran before, and climbed up into a sycomore tree to see him: for he was to pass that way."

"When Jesus came to the place, he looked up, and saw him, and said unto him, Zacchaeus, make haste, and come down; for to day I must abide at thy house."

"And he made haste, and came down, and received him joyfully. . . ."

"*And* Zacchaeus stood, and said . . . Lord, the half of my goods I give to the poor; and if I have taken any thing from any man by false accusation, I restore him fourfold."

"*And* Jesus said . . . This day is salvation come to this house, forsomuch as he also is a son of Abraham. For the Son of man is come to seek and to save that which was lost."

HEALING OF THE ADULTEROUS WOMAN*

Jesus' command to the woman: "Go, and sin no more."

"Early in the morning [Jesus] came again into the temple. . . . And the scribes and Pharisees brought unto him a woman taken in adultery. . . . They say unto him, Master, this woman was taken in adultery, in the very act. Now Moses in the law commanded us, that such should be stoned: but what sayest thou?. . ."

"But Jesus stooped down, and with his finger wrote on the ground, as though he heard them not. So when they continued asking him, he lifted up himself, and said unto them, He that is without sin among you, let him first cast a stone at her. And again he stooped down, and wrote on the ground."

"They which heard it, being convicted by their own conscience, went out one by one, beginning at the eldest, even unto the last. . . ."

"When Jesus had lifted up himself, and saw none but the woman, he said unto her, Woman, where are those thine accusers? hath no man condemned thee?"

"She said. No man, Lord."

"*And* Jesus said . . . Neither do I condemn thee: go, and sin no more."

---

*The healing of the adulterous woman is the only specific healing recorded as having taken place in the Temple. According to modern scholars, this account (Jn. 7:53-8:11) was not a part of the original Gospel of John, but being historically sound was inserted at a later date.

JESUS' FOUR RAISINGS FROM THE DEAD

The three raisings from the dead which Jesus accomplished during his ministry—each under differing and increasingly difficult conditions—strengthened and prepared Jesus for his own supreme demonstration of the eternality of life.

Read chart down for individual subject
Read across for comparison

THE RAISING OF
JAIRUS' DAUGHTER

THE RAISING OF
THE WIDOW'S SON

"Now when he came nigh to the gate of the city [Nain], behold, there was a dead man carried out, the only son of his mother, and she was a widow. . . .

"And when the Lord saw her, he had compassion on her. . . ."

Jairus, a ruler of the synagogue, came to Jesus and "fell at his feet, And besought him greatly, saying, My little daughter lieth at the point of death: I pray thee, come and lay thy hands on her, that she may be healed; and she shall live."

"But as he went the people thronged him."

"There cometh one from the ruler of the synagogue's house, saying to him, Thy daughter is dead; trouble not the Master."

The raising of widow's son and raising of J daughter came w the second perio Jesus' Galilean n try and before Transfiguration.

The raising of La came within the p of Jesus' Peraean istry and after Transfiguration.

Jesus said to the mother, "Weep not."

"And he came and touched the bier: and they that bare him stood still."

Jesus said to the father, "Fear not: believe only, and she shall be made whole."

Jesus said to the people making a noise, "Give place: for the maid is not dead, but sleepeth. And they laughed him to scorn."—"And he put them all out. . . ."

Jesus said, "Young man, I say unto thee, Arise."

"And he that was dead sat up, and began to speak. And he delivered him to his mother."

"He . . . took her by the hand, and called, saying, Maid, arise."

"And straightway the damsel arose, and walked; for she was of the age of twelve years."

"And the fame hereof went abroad into all that land."

"They glorified God, saying . . . a great prophet is risen up . . . God hath visited his people." Lu. 7:11-16

Mt. 9:18,19,23-26
Mk. 5:22-24,35-43
Lu. 8:41,42,49-56

THE RAISING OF LAZARUS

...w a certain man was sick, named Lazarus, of ...any.... Therefore his sisters sent unto ...us]...."

...s said to his apostles, "This sickness is not ...o death, but for the glory of God, that the ...of God might be glorified thereby....

...abode two days still in the same place ...re he was.... after that he saith ... Our ...d Lazarus sleepeth; but I go, that I may ...ke him....

...en Jesus came ... he had lain in the grave ...days already."—"by this time he stink-...."

...said to Mary and friends: "Where have ye ...im?" He "cometh to the grave ... a cave, ...stone lay upon it. Jesus said, Take ye away ...stone.... Then they took away the ...."

...prayed, "Father, I thank thee that thou ...heard me...."

...cried, "Lazarus, come forth."

> "And he that was dead came forth, bound hand and foot with grave-clothes: and his face was bound about with a napkin."

...s saith unto them, Loose him, and let him

> "Then many of the Jews ... believed on him.

> "But some ... went their ways to the Pharisees, and told them what things Jesus had done.... Then from that day forth they took counsel together for to put him to death."

Jn. 11:1-46,53

THE RAISING OF JESUS HIMSELF

"And when they were come to the place, which is called Calvary, there they crucified him...." Lu. 23:33

"Now in the place where he was crucified there was a garden; and in the garden a new sepulchre, wherein was never man yet laid. There laid they Jesus...." Jn. 19:41,42

> Jesus was crucified on the sixth day of the week (Friday) and his resurrection occurred on the first day of the following week (Sunday).

"The angel of the Lord descended from heaven, and came and rolled back the stone from the door...." (leaving it an "open door"—See Heb. 10:20; Rev. 3:8)

"They [the women] came unto the sepulchre ... found the stone rolled away ... entered in, and found not the body...."

The angel said, "He is not here: for he is risen, as he said."

Simon Peter "went into the sepulchre, and seeth the linen clothes lie, And the napkin, that was about his head, not lying with the linen clothes, but wrapped together in a place by itself."

> "To whom [the apostles] also he shewed himself alive after his passion by many infallible proofs, being seen of them forty days, and speaking of the things pertaining to the kingdom of God."

Mt. 28:1-10
Mk. 16:1-11
Lu. 24:1-12
Jn. 20:1-18
Acts 1:3

Jesus Christ said, "I am the resurrection, and the life: he that believeth in me, though he were dead, yet shall he live: And whosoever liveth and believeth in me shall never die, Believest thou this?" Jn. 11:25,26

JESUS' TRAINING OF HIS TWELVE APOSTLES

Jesus said to his apostles: "Blessed are the eyes which see the things that ye see: For I tell you, that many prophets and kings have desired to see those things which ye see, and have not seen them; and to hear those things which ye hear, and have not heard them" (Lu. 10:23,24). The greatest privilege that could be accorded men was theirs—that of being chosen to walk with the Master. This privilege carried with it a great responsibility, for they were the ones who would promulgate his healing gospel. To this end he patiently instructed them in the truths of the kingdom and, by word and example, taught them the power of God until they were trained, disciplined, and qualified to fulfill their apostolic office.

They were not only commissioned, they were recommissioned; not only given access to the kingdom, but appointed a kingdom; not only promised the Holy Ghost, but given the Holy Ghost.

	CALLED, CHOSEN, ORDAINED	COMMISSIONED TO ISRAEL	GIVEN ACCESS TO THE KINGDOM
In the first year of his ministry Jesus called four disciples, and in the second year he chose twelve apostles: Simon Peter Andrew James John Philip Bartholomew (Nathanael) Matthew (Levi) Thomas (Didymus) Simon Zelotes James (the Less) Thaddaeus (Judas, Lebbaeus) Judas Iscariot (See character studies, pp. 252-256)	Jesus "went out into a mountain to pray, and continued all night in prayer to God. And when it was day, he called unto him his disciples: and of them he chose twelve, whom also he named apostles. . . ." Lu. 6:12,13 "He ordained twelve, that they should be with him, and that he might send them forth to preach, And to have power to heal sicknesses, and to cast out devils." Mk. 3:14,15	"These twelve Jesus sent forth, and commanded them, saying, Go not into the way of the Gentiles, and into any city of the Samaritans enter ye not: But go rather to the lost sheep of the house of Israel. "And as ye go, preach, saying, The kingdom of heaven is at hand. "Heal the sick, cleanse the lepers, raise the dead, cast out devils: freely ye have received, freely give." Mt. 10:5-8 Jesus' further instructions Mt. 10:9-42	Jesus asked his disciples, "Whom do men say that I the Son of man am?" And again "Whom say ye that I am?" "And Simon Peter answered and said, Thou art the Christ, the Son of the living God. "And Jesus . . . said unto him, Blessed art thou, Simon Bar-jona: for flesh and blood hath not revealed it unto thee, but my Father which is in heaven. "And I say also unto thee, That thou art Peter, and upon this rock I will build my church; and the gates of hell shall not prevail against it. "And I will give unto thee the keys of the kingdom of heaven. . . ." Mt. 16:13-1
	Mt. 10:1-4; Mk. 3:13-19; Lu. 6:12-16	Mk. 6:7-13; Lu. 9:1-6	Mk. 8:27-30; Lu. 9:1 21

RECOMMISSIONED TO ALL NATIONS

APPOINTED A KINGDOM

PROMISED THE HOLY GHOST

(At the Lord's Supper)

"And I will pray the Father, and he shall give you another Comforter, that he may abide with you for ever; even the Spirit of truth. . . .

"I will not leave you comfortless: I will come to you. . . .

"But the Comforter, which is the Holy Ghost, whom the Father will send in my name, he shall teach you all things, and bring all things to your remembrance, whatsoever I have said unto you." Jn. 14:16-18,26

"But when the Comforter is come, whom I will send unto you from the Father, even the Spirit of truth, which proceedeth from the Father, he shall testify of me: And ye also shall bear witness, because ye have been with me from the beginning." Jn. 15:26,27

n. 14-16

(At the Lord's Supper)

"Ye are they which have continued with me in my temptations.

"And I appoint unto you a kingdom, as my Father hath appointed unto me; That ye may eat and drink at my table in my kingdom, and sit on thrones judging the twelve tribes of Israel." Lu. 22:28-30
(See Mt. 19:28)

(Jesus' prayer for the apostles' sanctification)

"Holy Father, keep through thine own name those whom thou hast given me, that they may be one, as we are. . . .

"Sanctify them through thy truth: thy word is truth.

"As thou hast sent me into the world, even so have I also sent them into the world.

"And for their sakes I sanctify myself, that they also might be sanctified through the truth." Jn. 17:11,17-19

(At one of Jesus' appearances to the apostles after Resurrection)

"All power is given unto me [Jesus Christ] in heaven and in earth. Go ye therefore, and teach all nations, baptizing them in the name of the Father, and of the Son, and of the Holy Ghost:

"Teaching them to observe all things whatsoever I have commanded you: and, lo, I am with you alway, even unto the end of the world." Mt. 28:18-20

(Before his Ascension)

"Being assembled together with them, [Jesus] commanded them that they should not depart from Jerusalem, but wait for the promise of the Father. . . . ye shall be baptized with the Holy Ghost not many days hence. . . .

"Ye shall receive power, after that the Holy Ghost is come upon you: and ye shall be witnesses unto me both in Jerusalem, and in all Judaea, and in Samaria, and unto the uttermost part of the earth." Acts. 1:4,5,8

"Then returned they unto Jerusalem from the mount called Olivet. . . .

"And when they were come in, they went up into an upper room. . . . These all continued with one accord in prayer and supplication, with the women, and Mary the mother of Jesus, and with his brethren." Acts 1:12-14

(At Pentecost, ten days after Jesus' Ascension)

"And when the day of Pentecost was fully come, they were all with one accord in one place.

"And suddenly there came a sound from heaven as of a rushing mighty wind, and it filled all the house where they were sitting.

"And there appeared unto them cloven tongues like as of fire, and it sat upon each of them.

"And they were all filled with the Holy Ghost, and began to speak with other tongues, as the Spirit gave them utterance." Acts. 2:1-4

10

The Work of the Twelve Apostles

"Ye shall receive power, after that the Holy Ghost is come upon you: and ye shall be witnesses unto me both in Jerusalem, and in all Judaea, and in Samaria, and unto the uttermost part of the earth."   Acts 1:8

His Church continued the work Jesus had begun. The organization of that Church in a world that had just rejected the Master fell to the twelve apostles. This was a stupendous task, and they were unlettered men according to the standards of the day—men who had not been educated in the rabbinical schools. But they were well-trained spiritually through their long and close association with Jesus, and their teaching adhered to the basic truths of his Messiahship and Resurrection. The power of the Holy Ghost was clearly evident in their teaching and healing work, and authenticated the truths of the gospel message.

The only contemporary record of the early Church during the first thirty-three years of its existence (30-63 A.D.), with the exception of a few brief allusions in Paul's Epistles, is found in the New Testament book known to us as The Acts of the Apostles. Written by Luke, Acts is a continuation of the history of Christianity begun in the Gospel of Luke. It does record the acts of the apostles—of Peter and John, of Paul, and the work of other prominent evangelists. The account, vivid in its simplicity, gives a picture of the origin and growth of the Church in Jerusalem, its spread into Palestine, and its extension to Asia Minor and the continent of Europe.

Acts 1   After Resurrection Jesus had confirmed his former promise to his apostles of the gift of the Holy Spirit when he "breathed on them" and said, "Receive ye the Holy Ghost" (Jn. 20:22). He had commanded them: "Tarry ye in the city of Jerusalem, until ye be endued with power from on high" (Lu. 24:49). Just before his Ascension he repeated his promise: "Ye shall be baptized with the Holy Ghost not many days hence." Returning to Jerusalem from the Mount of Olives, the eleven withdrew to an "upper room" to pray and to await in joyous expectation the fulfillment of that pledge.

The apostles were joined by other disciples, among them Jesus' mother, his brothers, and the faithful women who had accompanied him in Galilee, until their total was about a hundred twenty. The inner circle of the Twelve having been broken by Judas Iscariot's defection, Peter proposed the appointment of another apostle to fill Judas' place. From among the disciples who had traveled with Jesus from his Baptism to his Resurrection two men were nominated, Joseph and Matthias; after prayer for guidance, the whole assembly cast lots and Matthias was chosen.

Acts 2   Birth of the Church

The momentous occurrence of the descent of the Holy Ghost came on the Day of Pentecost, ten days after Jesus' Ascension. Pentecost was a Jewish harvest festival, a day of dedication of the firstfruits of the grain harvest to the Divine Giver, observed fifty days after Passover. This particular Pentecost fell on the fiftieth day from Jesus' Resurrection, marking the birthday of the Christian Church.

The inpouring of the power of the Spirit to the minds of the disciples came swiftly and suddenly. As they were gathered together "with one accord in one place," they heard "a sound from heaven." To Elijah the sound from heaven had been as "a still small voice"; to the apostles it was "as of a rushing mighty wind" filling the house in which they waited. Light accompanied the coming of this divine influence; they saw "cloven tongues like as of fire" rest on the head of each one. All were "filled with the Holy Ghost, and began to speak with other tongues, as the Spirit gave them utterance."*

Word of this extraordinary event spread rapidly and soon a crowd gathered, many of whom were Jews of the Dispersion who had resettled in Jerusalem or had come to the Holy City for the feast—men from Persia, Mesopotamia, Arabia, Asia Minor, Africa, Crete, and Rome. These were amazed because each man, whatever his nationality, heard the disciples speak the truth of God in his own tongue. Language differences were overcome as they shared the inspiration of the Spirit. "We may see in this event, which seemed to obliterate the barriers of nationality and language, a reversal of the separation and confusion of tongues (Gen. 11)." [1]

Some of the devout asked the meaning of this phenomenon; others mocked the speakers, accusing them of being filled with new wine. Peter, as spokesman for the other apostles, instantly denied this slanderous charge. He declared that what they were hearing was in reality the language of inspiration, the outpouring of the Holy Spirit long ago foretold by the prophet Joel: "It shall come to pass in the last days, saith God, I will pour out of my Spirit upon all flesh: and your sons and your daughters shall prophesy" (compare Joel 2:28-32).

He linked this Pentecostal outpouring to Jesus of Nazareth, whose life and ministry among them had been attested by miracles and signs. He stingingly reproached them for the crucifixion of Jesus but added that God had raised him to life, not allowing His Holy One to suffer corruption, even as David had prophesied (Ps. 16:8-11). He asserted that he and the others were eyewitnesses to Jesus' resurrection. He testified to Jesus' ascension and glorification and explained that this gift of the Holy Ghost as seen by them at Pentecost had been bestowed by the ascended Christ. "Therefore let all the house of Israel know assuredly, that God hath made that same Jesus, whom ye have crucified, both Lord and Christ."

Cut to the heart his listeners asked: "What shall we do?" "Repent," Peter answered, "and be baptized every one of you in the name of Jesus Christ for the remission of sins, and ye shall receive the gift of the Holy Ghost." Three thousand were baptized that day, the firstfruits of the Pentecostal gospel harvest.

Baptism had been employed by John the Baptist as a symbolic rite of purification; it had been practiced by Jesus' apostles during his ministry; now in accordance with one of his final commands, to baptize in his name (Mt. 28:19), it was adopted by the nascent Church to mark the acceptance of believers. It signified not only repentance but initiation into the new moral and spiritual way of life in Christ.

The Church in Jerusalem

The apostles, having a clearer realization of their part in Christ's continuing mission and now equipped with the power of the Holy Ghost, the promised Comfort-

---

*Spirit of God and Holy Spirit are Old Testament terms for the invisible divine presence and power as seen in the affairs of men. Holy Ghost is the New Testament designation, a translation from Greek.

The Holy Ghost is first mentioned in connection with those whose lives touched the birth of the child Jesus: with John the Baptist (Lu. 1:15), the Virgin Mary (Lu. 1:35), Elisabeth (Lu. 1:41), Zacharias (Lu. 1:67), Simeon (Lu. 2:25). Jesus was "child of the Holy Ghost" (Mt. 1:18); he was embued with a fresh influx of the Holy Ghost at baptism (Lu. 3:22); and this Spirit which "filled" his being enabled him to triumph over Satan at the Temptation and to preach and heal with irresistible power.

Jesus defined the Holy Ghost as the "Comforter," the "Spirit of truth," emanating from the Father and the Son (Jn. 14:16,17,26; 15:26), an ever-present continuing power unfolding truth to men (Jn. 16:8,13,14). To the Church the "Spirit of God" and the "Spirit of Christ" were one (Rom. 8:9), the divine force that gave Christianity its substance and impetus. The Holy Ghost so guided the early Church that the book of Acts has sometimes been called "the Gospel of the Holy Ghost."

er, went forward with confidence to preach Jesus as the Messiah. Basic to their assurance was the Master's resurrection and ascension which verified the truths of all he had taught. They were the natural leaders and teachers of the new religion. Among them Peter was acknowledged chief and called upon to play a prominent role. Jesus' charge "Feed my sheep" still echoed in Peter's mind; it was he who first used "the keys of the kingdom" in opening the door of faith to the Jews on the Day of Pentecost (and later to the Gentiles in the house of Cornelius). Through the power of the Holy Ghost the apostles performed many miracles, and the unique characteristic of healing that had accompanied Jesus' ministry continued to be a distinguishing mark of his Church.

The growth of the new sect was enthusiastic and rapid, springing out of the conviction of Jesus' resurrection. Many now accepted him as the long-awaited Messiah and were constant in listening to the apostles' teachings. This embryo Christian society was called *ecclesia*, a Greek word meaning "an assembly of called-out ones." Although these new adherents still went to the Temple and the synagogue to worship, they were united by a new and deeper sense of love and brotherhood, and soon groups began to meet in one another's homes for prayer and "breaking of bread." Although this eating together may have included the communion of the Lord's supper, its major purpose was fellowship. A new community life evolved as believers sold their possessions and shared all in a common purpose.

Acts 3   The healing power the apostles had practiced when they were with Jesus (Lu. 9:6) continued in the early Church and helped authenticate their mission. Typical of their work was the healing of a man more than forty years old, a beggar lame from birth. Daily he had been carried by his friends to the Temple and placed near the Beautiful Gate to beg alms of those who entered. As Peter and John passed him one day on their way to prayer, he asked for money. They paused, and Peter, seeing his need for physical healing and eager to share his spiritual wealth, said, "Look on us." As the man waited for the usual alms Peter spoke again: "Silver and gold have I none; but such as I have give I thee: In the name [by the power] of Jesus Christ of Nazareth rise up and walk" (*arise*, the active command Jesus so often gave). Peter stretched out his hand to the outcast and lifted him up; immediately the man's feet and ankle bones became strong; he stood, and walked. Leaping for joy and praising God, he entered with them into the Temple.

Many, assembled for evening prayer, saw the man walking and running. Realizing that a miracle had taken place, they excitedly surrounded the three.

"Why marvel ye at this?" Peter protested, "or why look ye so earnestly on us, as though by our own power or holiness we had made this man to walk?" Seizing the opportunity, he explained that the healing came from God through His Son Jesus and was the natural result of faith in Christ. He was God's Holy One and the Prince of life whom they had denied and killed but whom God had raised from the dead. Peter urged his listeners to repent so that this sin, committed in ignorance, might be wiped out.

He reminded them of Moses' warning command concerning disbelief in their coming Messiah: "A prophet shall the Lord your God raise up unto you of your brethren, like unto me; him shall ye hear in all things whatsoever he shall say unto you. And it shall come to pass, that every soul, which will not hear that prophet, shall be destroyed from among the people" (compare Deut. 18:15,18,19). He declared that they, the children of the prophets and heirs of the Abrahamic covenant, were the first to be given the blessing of the Risen Christ.

Acts 4   While Peter and John were teaching the people, the priests, the Sadducees, and the captain of the Temple guard suddenly appeared. They were incensed to find the apostles proclaiming the resurrection of Jesus, for the doctrine of the resurrection of the dead was one they rejected. Unless such teaching was repressed it would effectually undermine the already unpopular Sadducean ideas, so the captain quickly arrested the two. But Peter's speech and the lame man's healing had already convinced the people, and five thousand converts were added to the church that day.

Peter and John were imprisoned and held overnight; the following morning they were brought before the Sanhedrin. "By what power, or by what name, have ye done this?" the council demanded. Peter fearlessly repeated what he had preached to the people—that through the name of Jesus Christ, whom they themselves were responsible for crucifying but whom God had resurrected, the man had been healed. He announced for the ears of the nation: "This is the stone which was set at nought of you builders, which is become the head of the corner. Neither is there salvation in any other: for there is none other name [Moffatt, nor even a second Name] under heaven given among men, whereby we must be saved." His judges were startled at so bold an answer from one rabbinically untrained; they realized that these men had been the close associates of Jesus and would be dangerous if allowed further to spread his teachings.

The members of the Sanhedrin hurriedly deliberated what action to take. The miracle could not be denied, since by now all the city knew of it; nor did they dare punish these men for an obviously good deed. The only course open to them was to resort to threats. They therefore warned Peter and John not to teach again in the name of Jesus, but the apostles were not to be intimidated: "Whether it be right in the sight of God to hearken unto you more than unto God, judge ye. For we cannot but speak the things which we have seen and heard." The council found no justifiable reason for punishment, so after further threats the two were released.

Peter and John reported to the brethren the Sanhedrin's order, but this injunction, far from breaking their ranks, served only to unite the church. With one voice they prayed that courage be given them to speak in Jesus' name and that divine power accompany their preaching with healing. A sign was immediately given: the place in which they were assembled was shaken and all felt a fresh inpouring of the Holy Ghost. Spiritually strengthened, they went forth to speak God's message with boldness.

The spirit of brotherhood and unity continued in the new society to a remarkable degree. Many willingly sold their lands and houses and brought the money to the apostles for distribution, so there was not a needy man among them. One of those who gave up his possessions was Joses, a Cyprian Levite whom the Twelve renamed Barnabas. He became a preacher, an apostle of the Church, and Paul's co-worker on his first missionary journey.

Acts 5   Not all the members were equal to this spirit of self-sacrifice, however. One couple, Ananias and Sapphira, sold some property, and with his wife's full knowledge Ananias withheld a portion of the money for themselves. Peter detected this duplicity and he rebuked him: "Ananias, why hath Satan filled thine heart to lie to the Holy Ghost, and to keep back part of the price of the land?. . .thou hast not lied unto men, but unto God." At these words Ananias fell dead at the apostle's feet. Three hours later Sapphira came in, unaware of her husband's death; and when Peter questioned her, she too lied. "How is it that ye have agreed together to tempt the Spirit of the Lord?" he asked; "behold, the feet of them which have buried thy husband are at the door, and shall carry thee out." She too fell dead. This swift judgment on religious hypocrisy struck awe in the hearts of the whole Christian community.

The new cause prospered as miracles and signs continued to accompany the apostles' preaching. Their healing work, particularly Peter's, was so successful that great numbers of men and women believed; and the people of Jerusalem and the neighboring villages brought their sick and laid them in the streets in the hope that Peter's shadow at least might fall on them. And they all were healed.

This success aroused the anger and jealousy of the high priest and the Sadducean party; they seized the Twelve and put them in the common prison. But hate and malice could not stop the Word. That night an angel opened the prison doors and freed them, saying, "Go, stand and speak in the temple to the people all the words of this life." The following morning when the high priest Caiaphas sent for the prisoners, the Temple officers reported that they could not be found, although the prison doors were still shut and the guards on duty.

Then came the astonishing news that the apostles were in the Temple again teaching the people. At this, the captain himself went with his officers and brought them to the council room, being careful to rearrest them without violence for fear of being stoned by the people. Caiaphas charged: "Did not we straitly [strictly] command you that ye should not teach in this name? and, behold, ye have filled Jerusalem with your doctrine, and intend to bring this man's blood upon us." (So quickly had they forgotten their eager willingness at Jesus' trial to take upon themselves the curse of his innocent blood [Mt. 27:25].) Peter answered fearlessly: "We ought to obey God rather than men." As at his previous arraignment, he testified that the Jesus they had slain God had exalted as Prince and Savior of Israel. "We are his witnesses of these things; and so is also the Holy Ghost, whom God hath given to them that obey him."

Infuriated, the Sanhedrin determined to kill the apostles, but at this point a note of caution was sounded. One of the Pharisees of the council, the eminent and respected rabbi Gamaliel, advised against so rash an act. He cautioned the council to move slowly against these followers of Jesus, recalling two earlier revolutionary movements—one led by Theudas and the other by Judas of Galilee—the impact of which had dissipated after these leaders had been killed, without any action instigated by the Sanhedrin against their adherents. "Refrain from these men, and let them alone: for if this counsel or this work be of men, it will come to nought: But if it be of God, ye cannot overthrow it; lest haply ye be found even to fight against God."

Reluctantly his fellow members agreed. But before the prisoners were released the Sanhedrin had them beaten; again they warned them not to speak in the name of Jesus. This was the apostles' first taste of persecution. They left the council rejoicing that they had been found worthy to suffer shame and humiliation for Jesus' name (compare Mt. 5:11,12; Lu. 21:12). Flouting the Sanhedrin's prohibition, they preached every day—openly in the Temple and privately in homes.

Acts 6, 7   Within two or three years many converts—both men and women—

were added to the Church. From the first, women had eagerly accepted the gospel, responded to the call to spread its truths, and by their ennobling influence steadily advanced the cause of Christianity. Jesus had given woman a higher standing than she had heretofore enjoyed; this was evident at once in her new status in the early Church.

The Jerusalem church had a rapidly multiplying membership of both Hebrew- and Greek-speaking Jews, the former outnumbering the latter. A difficulty arose when the Hellenists complained that their widows were being discriminated against by Hebrew Christians in the daily distribution of provisions. To rectify this situation the apostles called a meeting and suggested the appointment of seven men—men honest, wise, "full of the Holy Ghost"—to oversee the fair and charitable distribution of food and other necessities. The apostles themselves desired to be free to devote their full time and efforts to prayer and preaching. This proposal found enthusiastic approval. Seven spiritually minded men were chosen to supervise the dispensing of church charity—Stephen, Philip, Prochorus, Nicanor, Timon, Parmenas, and Nicolas—and these the Twelve formally inducted by the laying on of hands.

> The "laying on of hands" usually symbolizes the bestowal of the Holy Spirit, which at the very beginning seems to have been connected with this rite rather than with baptism (see Acts 19:5-6 and ... 8:17). The rite is taken over from the O.T., where it symbolizes the establishment of some vital connection between two persons, and the transference of some power or responsibility from the one to the other. Thus Moses, when appointing Joshua his successor, laid his hands on him, by which act he "put some of his honor upon him" (Num. 27:23,20). So the apostles in Acts frequently do in healing, confirming, and ordaining. [2]

Their Greek names suggest that these seven men were probably Hellenic (Greek-speaking) Jews, with the exception of Nicolas, a convert from Antioch in Syria. (These seven are traditionally regarded as the first "deacons" of the Church. However, their office differed from that of the deacons appointed in the latter half of the first century A.D. [I Tim. 3:8-12].) This was the first organizational step taken by the Apostolic Church and it promoted harmony and unity in the Christian community.

The first attack on the Church had come from the Sadducees; the second, which resulted in the death of Stephen (ca. 32 A.D.), was brought about by conservative Hellenistic Jews who feared the new teachings. Stephen, a mature and ardent Christian, possessed in rich measure both the spirit and the power of the Holy Ghost. He not only carried out the stewardship to which he had been appointed but also soon achieved an almost apostolic prominence as he healed and preached with great effectiveness. Being a Greek-speaker, he appears to have taught the gospel mainly in the Jerusalem synagogues of foreign colonists—the Libertines (Jews freed from Roman slavery), Cyrenians and Alexandrians of northern Africa, and men from Cilicia and the province of Asia. (It is entirely probable that Saul of Tarsus, the zealous young pupil of Gamaliel, was among Stephen's antagonists in the Cilician synagogue.)

Stephen's teachings drew him into bitter controversy with some of his listeners. He was so eloquent in defense of the new faith that they were unable to resist his reasoning or the Christlike spirit he manifested. They became alarmed by the threat his teaching posed to the Law of Moses (to accept Christ as Savior virtually nullified ceremonial law and implied its eventual abandonment), and determined to silence him. Resorting to the world's weapons, they bribed men to spread a rumor that his teachings which exalted Jesus as pre-eminent were blasphemous, taking glory away from Moses and from God. Stephen was seized, arraigned before the Sanhedrin, and accused by the suborned witnesses: "This man ceaseth not to speak blasphemous words against this holy place, and the law: For we have heard him say, that this Jesus of Nazareth shall destroy this place, and shall change the customs which Moses delivered us" (the crime charged against Jesus [Mk. 14:58] and later against Paul [Acts 21:28]). But Stephen stood serene, even while this accusation was being made against him, his face alight with an inner radiance "as it had been the face of an angel."

When questioned by the high priest, Stephen began an impassioned plea to make his judges understand that Jesus of Nazareth was the God-sent Messiah. He opened his defense with an account of Israel's history from the time of Father Abraham to the Wilderness Wandering to show how God's love and grace had continually sustained His people. He gave full honor to the great prophet Moses, but went on "to remind his Moses-worshipping audience of the grand testimony of their faithful lawgiver, that *himself was not the last and proper object of the Church's faith, but only a humble precursor and small model of Him to whom their absolute submission was due."* [3] Stephen declared: "This is that Moses, which said unto the children of Israel, A prophet shall the Lord your God raise up unto you of your brethren, like unto me; him shall ye hear. This is he, that was in the church in the wilderness with the angel which spake to him in the mount Sina, and with our fathers: who received the lively oracles [the Law] to give unto us: To whom our fathers would not obey, but thrust him from them, and in their hearts turned back again into Egypt."

As for the Temple his opponents claimed he was

defaming, Stephen told his judges (now its privileged overseers) that it was an error to consider it the final dwelling place of God. This he did first by reciting the progressive history of the sanctuary from a movable Tabernacle in the wilderness to the structure erected by Solomon in Jerusalem, then by quoting from Isaiah: "Howbeit the most High dwelleth not in temples made with hands; as saith the prophet, Heaven is my throne, and earth is my footstool: what house will ye build me? saith the Lord: or what is the place of my rest? Hath not my hand made all these things?" (compare Is. 66:1,2).

Abruptly Stephen's tone changed to one of scathing rebuke of his judges, now as obstinate in resisting God as their forebears had been: "Ye stiffnecked and uncircumcised in heart and ears, Ye do always resist the Holy Ghost: as your fathers did, so do ye. Which of the prophets have not your fathers persecuted? and they have slain them which shewed before of the coming of the Just One; of whom ye have been now the betrayers and murderers: Who have received the law by the disposition of angels, and have not kept it."

An instant uproar spread through the assembly hall and Stephen's judges gnashed their teeth at him (grating the teeth was a Jewish form of expressing rage). But he, "full of the Holy Ghost," looked up and cried: "I see the heavens opened, and the Son of man standing on the right hand of God." This was too much for his enemies. With a loud outcry they stopped their ears against this assertion of Jesus' glorification, which seemed to them a final blasphemy (compare Mt. 26:65). Not waiting to condemn him formally or to obtain the necessary Roman permission for execution, they rushed upon him in a body and dragged him outside the city walls to stone him; and the witnesses, whose hands were to be the first to stone him (Deut. 17:7), "laid down their clothes at a young man's feet, whose name was Saul. . . . And Saul was consenting unto his death." (This is our first introduction to Saul–Paul, as we later know him.)

While the stones rained upon him, Stephen entreated "Lord Jesus, receive my spirit." Kneeling down, he prayed: "Lord, lay not this sin to their charge" (both prayers much like those of Jesus on the cross), and with these words he died.

Acts 8   The Extension of the Church into Palestine Stephen's martyrdom precipitated a period of cruel persecution. Very shortly after Stephen's murder the young Pharisee Saul appears to have been given almost unrestricted authority by the chief priests to destroy the Christian Church. With blind rage and fanatic zeal he forced his way into every house in which he suspected there were Christians, committed men and women to prison, and caused many to be put to death. Their lives in danger, their homes no longer safe even for secret meetings, many believers fled into Judaea and Samaria, but the apostles remained in Jerusalem. Far from crushing the Church, this persecution identified its faith; wherever these fugitives scattered they preached the gospel, thus extending the new movement throughout Palestine.

The dispersion brought Philip the Evangelist, colleague of Stephen, to the city of Samaria. Philip was one of the seven appointed by the apostles to administer charity. Being Hellenistic, he had few of the national prejudices of Hebrew-speaking Jews toward the Samaritans and so felt no antipathy toward them. These people of mixed descent, who followed the Pentateuch as their sole code, warmly received his preaching of Christ, and his ministry was marked by many healings and conversions, "and there was great joy in that city."

Many of Samaria's citizens were followers of Simon (Magus), a sorcerer who delighted them with magical arts and to whom they attributed divine power; but after seeing Philip's miracles they transferred their allegiance to Jesus Christ and were baptized. Simon also was attracted to this new religion, and was baptized. When the apostles in Jerusalem heard of these conversions, they sent Peter and John to visit the Samaritans; through their prayers and the laying on of the apostles' hands the new believers received the gift of the Holy Ghost. The ministry of Paul to the Gentile world was foreshadowed by the admittance of this racially mixed group into the Church.

Simon remained in the company of Philip, amazed at his miracles of healing, so different from the tricks by which he had duped the people; when he saw the power of the Spirit after the laying on of the apostles' hands, he offered Peter money for this power. Peter's reprimand was instant: "Thy money perish with thee, because thou hast thought that the gift of God may be purchased with money. Thou hast neither part nor lot in this matter: for thy heart is not right in the sight of God. Repent therefore of this thy wickedness, and pray God, if perhaps the thought of thine heart may be forgiven thee. For I perceive that thou art in the gall of bitterness, and in the bond of iniquity." In great fear Simon begged the apostle to pray that God's judgment for this sin be averted.

Peter and John returned to Jerusalem, preaching in many Samaritan villages along the way. Philip, however, was directed by an angel to travel southward to the road that ran down from Jerusalem to Gaza. In faith he obeyed, not knowing the object of his journey; in the desert he met an Ethiopian eunuch of high office, a convert to Judaism, returning home in his chariot from a religious pilgrimage to Jerusalem. This man had charge of the treasures of Candace, queen of the Ethiopians. The inner voice of the Spirit commanded Philip to join him, and as Philip drew near, he heard him reading aloud the prophecy of the suffering Servant from the book of Isaiah (53:7,8). "Understandest thou what thou readest?" Philip asked. The Ethiopian invited him into his chariot to explain this puzzling passage; as they rode, Philip, using the passage as his text, told him of Jesus, the fulfillment of this prophecy.

Eagerly the Ethiopian accepted the gospel; when they reached an oasis, he said: "See, here is water; what doth hinder me to be baptized?" Confessing his faith in Jesus as the Son of God, he went down with Philip into the water and Philip baptized him. As they came up out of the water Philip was "caught away" by the Spirit (compare I Ki. 18:12; II Ki. 2:16); the Ethiopian, now sealed in discipleship, went his way rejoicing, to carry the gospel into northern Africa. Philip found himself at Azotus, the old Philistine city of Ashdod; from there he journeyed on to preach in the coastal cities as far north as Caesarea.

Acts 9   The next important recorded event is the *conversion of Saul (Paul)*, *ca.* 33/34 A.D., on his way to Damascus to persecute Christians of that distant city. This is followed by his ministry in Damascus, his brief visit to Jerusalem, and his return to his native Tarsus in Cilicia (vv. 1-30). Saul's conversion, so important in its issues for the Church, and his subsequent ministry to the Gentile nations are discussed in the Life and Ministry of Paul, p. 389.

Luke's record of the expansion of the Apostolic Church in Palestine from this point on follows only the activities of Peter. With Saul's conversion persecution of the Church slackened, and by 40 A.D. many churches had sprung up in Judaea, Samaria, and Galilee, the regions of Jesus' ministry. Early in the second decade of the Church's history Peter was sent out by the parent church in Jerusalem to visit these clusters of believers. He came to see the Christians at Lydda, a town in the Maritime Plain, and was taken to the bedside of a man who had been a paralytic for eight years. "Aeneas," he said, "Jesus Christ maketh thee whole: arise, and make thy bed." Aeneas immediately arose from his bed, healed. Many of the townspeople of Lydda and nearby Sharon, hearing of this remarkable healing, were converted.

At the coastal city of Joppa (modern Jaffa), Tabitha (Dorcas), a woman of the church much loved for her charitable works, fell ill and died. Her friends laid her out in an upper room; knowing that Peter was at Lydda, some ten miles distant, they sent two men to implore him to come at once. When he arrived, he was taken to the upper room—now filled with grieving friends who tearfully showed him various garments her hands had made. But Peter "put them all forth," as Jesus himself had done at the raising of Jairus' daughter. Kneeling, he prayed. Then, turning to her, he said: "Tabitha, arise." She opened her eyes; seeing Peter, she sat up. Calling in her friends, he returned her to them alive. Word of this miracle was soon on everyone's lips, and many more embraced the new faith.

Acts 10:1-11:18   Peter remained in Joppa for some days in the house of Simon the tanner, and while he was there a new and important chapter began for the Church with the baptism of Cornelius. Cornelius was a Roman centurion stationed at Caesarea, forty miles north of Joppa. This Gentile was a convert to Judaism, a man who feared God, gave generously to the poor, and devoted much time to religious worship. Praying one day, he saw in a vision an angel, who said: "Cornelius . . . Thy prayers and thine alms are come up for a memorial before God. And now send men to Joppa, and call for one Simon, whose surname is Peter: He lodgeth with one Simon a tanner . . . he shall tell thee what thou oughtest to do." At once Cornelius dispatched two of his servants and a soldier with the message.

The following day as they were approaching the city, Peter went to the housetop to pray. It was noon and he suddenly became very hungry; while food was being prepared he, too, had a vision. He saw heaven open and a great sheet lowered to the earth by its four corners. In it were all kinds of beasts, reptiles, and birds. A voice commanded: "Rise, Peter; kill, and eat." Peter answered: "Not so, Lord; for I have never eaten any thing that is common or unclean [undedicated, unholy]." The voice came again: "What God hath cleansed, that call not thou common." After the voice had spoken to him a third time the sheet was gathered up into heaven.

The meaning of this vision was obscure to Peter, and while he puzzled about it, Cornelius' messengers came to the gate. The Spirit directed the apostle: "Behold, three men seek thee. Arise. . .and go with them, doubting nothing: for I have sent them." The next morning, accompanied by some of the Christians from Joppa, he set out for Caesarea. The following day he found the centurion waiting with his close friends and relatives. As he went into the house Cornelius threw himself down at Peter's feet, but the apostle would not permit this personal homage; lifting him up, he said: "Stand up; I myself also am a man."

For Peter and his companions to enter the house of a Roman was a radical departure from the Jewish practice of segregation. This putting aside of an age-old custom is apparent in his greeting: "Ye know how that it is an unlawful thing for a man that is a Jew to keep company, or come unto one of another nation; but God hath shewed me that I should not call any man common or unclean. Therefore came I unto you without gainsaying, as soon as I was sent for: I ask therefore for what intent ye have sent for me?"

Cornelius related how he had been divinely directed to send for Peter; now he and his friends were waiting to hear what God had commanded Peter to tell them. The meaning of the apostle's vision now became clear to him. The two visions were one in purpose: to make plain to the Church by this special revelation that God's salvation was for all men. No longer was the non-Jew to be regarded unworthy of God's grace. No longer were the Mosaic ceremonial distinctions of "clean" and "unclean" meats (Lev. 11) to debar the Jew from social intercourse and table-fellowship with the non-Jew. Peter declared: "Of a truth I perceive that God is no respecter of persons: But in every nation he that feareth him, and worketh righteousness, is accepted with him." The gospel message of salvation, which he had shared only with "the circumcision," he now imparted to Cornelius and his friends. While he was still speaking of the forgiveness of sins to whoever believes in Jesus, the Holy Ghost fell on them all; they spoke with tongues, as had the disciples at Pentecost, and praised God. Peter's Jewish companions were astonished to see this gift of the Spirit bestowed equally on the Gentiles.

By this sign of divine approbation it was evident that these men had been accepted in God's sight and should not be shut out from the Church. Remembering Jesus' words relating to spiritual baptism ("ye shall be baptized with the Holy Ghost" [Acts 1:5; 11:16]), Peter said: "Can any man forbid water, that these should not be baptized, which have received the Holy Ghost as well as we?" and at his command they were baptized.

The Jerusalem church was critical of Peter for his transgression of Jewish law in associating with non-Jews and eating at their table, but when he had given them a full explanation of all that had occurred they approved his conduct and acknowledged that God had granted the same grace to the Gentiles He had granted the Jews. The conversion of Cornelius established for the Church the principle of equality for all segments of its membership—a mark of the universality of Christ's gospel—but it remained for Paul rather than Peter and the other apostles to carry the gospel to the non-Jewish nations.

Acts 11:19-30 Extension of the Church beyond Palestine

Luke digresses: he turns from Peter's work to record the carrying of the gospel beyond Palestine, the establishing of the Gentile church at Antioch in Syria, and the early ministries of Barnabas and Saul (see p. 392).

Acts 12 The Church Persecuted by Herod

In 44 A.D. the church in Jerusalem was again subjected to persecution, this time political. After the recall of Pontius Pilate to Rome (36 A.D.) Judaea had been governed briefly by new procurators, first by Marcellus and then by Marullus. In 41 Herod Agrippa I, grandson of Herod the Great, was made king of all Palestine by the Roman Emperor Claudius. Although educated in Rome and Hellenistic in his sympathies, Herod Agrippa was half-Jewish and upon occasion found it politically expedient to support the Judaic interests of his subjects. In the third year of his rule, to curry favor with the Jews he harassed the growing Christian sect by striking at some of its leaders. At his order the Apostle James, brother of John, was beheaded.

When Herod saw that this act gratified the Jews, he had Peter arrested and imprisoned about the time of the Feast of Unleavened Bread, intending to execute him at its close. Sixteen soldiers were assigned to guard the prisoner, four for each watch of the night; he was securely chained by the wrists to two and the other two were stationed at the door. Church members prayed fervently for his release but their faith was tested to the utmost through the remaining days of the feast, for their prayers were not answered quickly. When they were, however, events transpired so rapidly that Peter thought it was a vision.

During the early morning hours, shortly before Herod planned to send for him, Peter lay asleep between the two soldiers. An angel appeared at his side, awakened him, and a light shone in the cell. "Arise up quickly," commanded the angel. As Peter did so, the chains fell from his hands. Again the angel spoke: "Gird thyself, and bind on thy sandals." Peter obeyed. "Cast thy garment about thee, and follow me." Peter followed him, and unseen they passed the first and second guards of the prison. As they approached the great iron gate leading to the city, it swung open of itself and they went out. When they were safely beyond pursuit, the angel suddenly left Peter. Only then did he realize he was free and that it was not a dream: "Now I know of a surety, that the Lord hath sent his angel, and hath delivered me out of the hand of Herod, and from all the expectation of the people of the Jews." (See Example of Deliverance through Prayer, p. 550.)

He went to the house of Mary, the mother of John Mark, where he knew many of the faithful would be gathered. Mary was a well-to-do Christian woman whose home was a chief meeting place for the early disciples. So dim had grown the hope for Peter's life that when he knocked on the door they could not believe at first that it was he. Peter stayed only long enough to describe to them his marvelous deliverance and to ask them to inform James (Jesus' brother), apparently the acting head of the Church. Then, to insure the disciples' safety and his own, he left the city.

With the death of Herod Agrippa in 44 A.D. political persecution against the Church in Palestine ceased for a time. The vicious attacks it had endured since inception—the persecution of the apostles by the Sanhedrin, the attempted suppression of the gospel, the death of Stephen, the sufferings of Christians under Saul's cruelties, the martyrdom of James, the imprisonment of Peter—only served to bind its members together more closely and make its cause prosper.

Here the Biblical record of the activities of the Twelve in Palestine under Peter's leadership ceases and Luke turns from their work to chronicle the ministry of Paul among the non-Jewish nations—a ministry that carried Christ's gospel to the far reaches of the Graeco-Roman world.

APOSTOLIC CHURCH, 30-63 A.D.

When Jesus commissioned his apostles and sent them out to spread his teachings, he stated clearly that their mission was to be a universal one (Acts 1:8). The unique history of their work in the early Apostolic Church is preserved in the Acts of the Apostles—"so mightily grew the word of God and prevailed." This important record covers a period of a little more than thirty years of missionary work. It was natural that Christ's Church should first take root in the regions in which he had preached. It was also natural that it should be established by the apostles he had chosen and trained.

Under the leadership of Peter the apostles carried the gospel to the Jewish nation but, bound by the traditions of centuries, they hesitated to approach the Gentiles. Therefore Paul was specially called as an apostle to the Gentiles. By his efforts and his extensive missionary journeys he succeeded in promulgating the teachings of Jesus Christ throughout the Roman Empire north of the Mediterranean and in firmly establishing numerous Christian churches from Asia Minor to Rome.

THE GROWTH OF THE CHURCH IN JERUSALEM	SPREAD TO PALESTINE, SYRIA, AND CILICIA	EXTENSION TO ASIA MINOR, MACEDONIA, GREECE, ROME
Acts. 2:1-8:4	Acts 8:5-12:25	Acts 13-28
The outpouring of the Holy Ghost, the Holy Spirit, on the apostles at Pentecost —founding of the church	Fleeing Christians preach in Judaea and Samaria	The acts of Paul and Barnabas on first journey into Asia Minor—"opened the door of faith unto the Gentiles" Acts 14:27
Acts of Peter and John	Acts of Philip the Evangelist, of Peter, of John	The acts of Paul and Silas on second journey: into Asia Minor, Macedonia, and Greece—"churches established in the faith, and increased in number daily" (Acts 16:5)—Paul begins to write his Epistles
Acts of the Twelve—they preach boldly in the name of Jesus—convert and baptize thousands—they carry on the healing work of the Master	Conversion of Saul (Paul)—his acts in Damascus, Jerusalem, Syria, and Cilicia (Gal. 1:21)	
Repeated imprisonment of the apostles by the Sanhedrin	Conversion of Cornelius, a Gentile, by Peter	Continued acts of Paul on his third journey: into Asia Minor, Macedonia, and Greece
The Christian community evidences a strong spirit of fellowship and unity— seven deacons appointed	Growth of the church in Syrian Antioch with a Jewish and Gentile membership —acts of Barnabas and Saul	Paul's two-year imprisonment at Caesarea, 58-60 A.D.
Acts of Stephen, one of the seven deacons—his martyrdom	Herod Agrippa I persecutes Christians in Jerusalem, killing Apostle James and imprisoning Peter—Peter's deliverance— the Jerusalem church grows and prospers	Paul's first imprisonment at Rome— continued preaching and teaching, 61-63 A.D.
Great persecution of infant church by Saul—many flee from Jerusalem for safety		
The outpouring of the Holy Ghost on the church in Jerusalem (fulfillment of Joel 2:28,29)	The outpouring of the Holy Ghost on the Gentiles (forwarding world-wide Christianity)	Christ's gospel is widely disseminated in the Roman Empire

APOSTOLIC HEALING

Just before his ascension Jesus had said to his disciples, "Go ye into all the world, and preach the gospel to every creature. . . . And these signs shall follow them that believe; In my name shall they cast out devils; they shall speak with new tongues; They shall take up serpents; and if they drink any deadly thing, it shall not hurt them; they shall lay hands on the sick, and they shall recover" (Mk. 16:15-18).

Though the Master was no longer with them in person, the Holy Spirit which had filled him now animated them and empowered them to carry out his command, for Mark records they preached everywhere, "the Lord working with them, and confirming the word with signs following" (Mk. 16:20). Acts makes clear these were not isolated incidents but that multitudes were healed (5:12,16). Acts also makes clear that the divine power to heal was not confined to the Twelve but was given to other consecrated Christians, according to Jesus' promise. Stephen, Philip the Evangelist, and the apostles Barnabas and Paul exercised it in great measure in their ministries (6:8; 8:6,7; 14:3; 28:9).

A number of specific healings are recorded of Peter and Paul. Note the commands (so similar to those of Jesus) and their natural sequence.

HEALING OF THE LAME MAN—BY PETER

"lame" from birth   Acts 3:1-10 (See 4:7-22)   In Jerusalem

Peter's commands: "Look on us."

"In the name of Jesus Christ . . . rise up and walk."

"A certain man [above forty years of age] lame from his mother's womb was carried, whom the laid daily at the gate of the temple which is called Beautiful, to ask alms. . . . Who seeing Peter and John about to go into the temple asked an alms."

Peter with John said, "Look on us."

"He gave heed . . . expecting to receive something of them."

Peter said, "Silver and gold have I none; but such as I have give I thee: In the name of Jesus Christ . . . rise up and walk."

"And he took him by the right hand, and lifted him up. . . ."

"*and* immediately his feet and ankle bones received strength. *And* he leaping up stood, and walked, and entered with them into the temple, walking, and leaping, and praising God."

HEALING OF AENEAS—BY PETER

"palsy"   Acts 9:32-35   At Lydda

Peter's command: "Arise, and make thy bed."

At Lydda, Peter "found a certain man named Aeneas, which had kept his bed eight years, and was sick of the palsy."

Peter said, "Aeneas, Jesus Christ maketh thee whole: arise, and make thy bed."

"*And* he arose immediately."

HEALING OF THE CRIPPLED MAN—BY PAUL

"impotent in his feet"   Acts 14:8-10   At Lystra

Paul's command: "Stand upright on thy feet."

> "There sat a certain man at Lystra, impotent in his feet, being a cripple from his mother's womb, who never had walked."

> "The same heard Paul speak. . . ."

> "Paul . . . stedfastly beholding him, and perceiving that he had faith to be healed, Said with a loud voice, Stand upright on thy feet."

"*And* he leaped and walked."

HEALING OF DAMSEL WITH SPIRIT OF DIVINATION—BY PAUL

"spirit of divination"   Acts 16:16-18   At Philippi

Paul's command: "I command thee [the spirit] in the name of Jesus Christ to come out of her."

> "As we [Paul, Silas, Luke] went to prayer, a certain damsel possessed with a spirit of divination met us, which brought her masters much gain by soothsaying."

> She "followed Paul and us, and cried. . . . These men are the servants of the most high God, which shew unto us the way of salvation. And this did she many days."

> "But Paul, being grieved, turned and said to the spirit, I command thee in the name of Jesus Christ to come out of her."

"*And* he came out the same hour."

HEALING FROM VIPER'S BITE—BY PAUL

serpent bite   Acts 28:1-6   At Melita

> "When Paul had gathered a bundle of sticks, and laid them on the fire, there came a viper out of the heat, and fastened on his hand."

> "When the barbarians saw the venomous beast hang on his hand, they said among themselves, No doubt this man is a murderer, whom, though he hath escaped the sea, yet vengeance suffereth not to live."

> "And he shook off the beast into the fire. . . ."

"*and* felt no harm."

> "Howbeit they looked when he should have swollen, or fallen down dead suddenly: but after they had looked a great while, and saw no harm come to him, they changed their minds, and said that he was a god."

"The father of Publius [in whose home Paul lodged] lay sick of a fever and of a bloody flux. . . ."

"Paul entered in, and prayed, and laid his hands on him. . . ."

"*and* healed him."

RAISINGS FROM THE DEAD BY THE APOSTLES

THE RAISING OF DORCAS BY PETER

Acts 9:36-42

"There was at Joppa a certain disciple named . . . Dorcas . . . full of good works and almsdeeds. . . .

"And it came to pass . . . that she was sick, and died: whom when they had washed, they laid her in an upper chamber."

They sent for Peter "desiring him that he would not delay to come to them.

"Then Peter arose and went with them . . . they brought him into the upper chamber: and all the widows stood by him weeping. . . .

"But Peter put them all forth, and kneeled down, and prayed; and turning him to the body said, Tabitha, arise.

"And she opened her eyes: and when she saw Peter, she sat up. And he gave her his hand, and lifted her up, and . . . presented her alive."

THE RAISING OF PAUL FROM STONING

Acts 14:19,20

"There came thither certain Jews from Antioch and Iconium, who persuaded the people, and, having stoned Paul, drew him out of the city, supposing he had been dead.

"Howbeit, as the disciples stood round about him, he rose up,

"and came into the city: and the next day he departed with Barnabas to Derbe."

THE RAISING OF EUTYCHUS BY PAUL

Acts 20:7-12

"Upon the first day of the week when the disciples came together to break bread, Paul preached unto them . . . and continued his speech until midnight.

"And there were many lights in the upper chamber. . . .

"And there sat in a window a certain young man named Eutychus being fallen into a deep sleep: and as Paul was long preaching, he sunk down with sleep, and fell down from the third loft, and was taken up dead.

"And Paul went down, and fell on him, and embracing him said, Trouble not yourselves; for his life is in him. . . .

"And they brought the young man alive, and were not a little comforted."

11

Life and Ministry of Paul

The Scriptural biography of Paul the apostle, the great missionary to the Gentile world, is found only in the book of Acts. Its author, Luke, the writer of the Gospel of Luke, was a trusted companion of Paul, and much of Acts is an eyewitness account. The record of the life and work of this great figure is condensed into eighteen short chapters (9-28). It is supplemented and enriched by Paul's own writings, which recount certain events in his life and give the reader further insight into his motives, aspirations, and quality of thought—his striving for perfection, his absorbing love for Christ Jesus, and the ripening development of his conception of Christianity as a universal religion. These two sources give us a clear view of the scope of his work. They are of vital interest to the followers of Christ, preserving as they do for the Church in all ages his dynamic life, words, and doctrines. Paul's conversion on the road to Damascus marked the dawn of a new day for Christianity and proved to be the greatest event of early Christian history.

The world of Paul, a Jew, was Graeco-Roman. He was the first effective spokesman through whom the gospel was addressed to this Gentile world. Reverence for Roman and Greek gods was waning; the human heart was crying out for more satisfying wisdom than superstition and human intellect could provide. Classic Greek culture had long since passed; Roman power was dedicated to world conquest and materialism; and the Jews, who had waited centuries for the Messiah, failed to know him when he came. An indelible imprint was soon to be made upon these three civilizations by this first and greatest of Christian missionaries—a Jew yet a Roman citizen, raised in a strongly Greek environment, fluent in the Greek tongue as well as in Aramaic and Hebrew. Paul was familiar with these cultures, and with understanding and resolute purpose he presented the gospel of Jesus Christ to their diverse nationalities.

388

Early Life

Paul was born probably between 1 and 5 A.D., in Tarsus, capital of the Roman province of Cilicia in Asia Minor. Tarsus—in Paul's words, "no mean city"—was an important commercial center on the great east-west trade route that ran through the narrow pass in the Taurus Mountains from western Asia Minor to Syria and the Far East. It was also a cosmopolitan university city, a distinguished seat of Greek learning and philosophy.

His Hebrew name was Saul (he is so called in the Biblical record until his first missionary journey), his Roman cognomen Paulus, "the little one." He was of the tribe of Benjamin, the only tribe of the twelve besides Judah that remained faithful to the house of David. His family was of the Dispersion—faithful Jewish religionists who for political or economic reasons had left Palestine to settle in Tarsus about 171 B.C. but whose affections were still passionately centered in their homeland. We have no information concerning his mother and know only that his father was a Pharisee and a Roman citizen, thus presumably a man of position and wealth (Acts 23:6). The privilege of Roman citizenship descended to Paul from his father; how it came to him is not known; it could have been purchased or granted for a service to some influential Roman. (This citizenship later proved of inestimable value, affording Paul the protection of Roman civil law as he journeyed throughout the Roman Empire as an apostle to the Gentiles. It saved him from flogging by Roman soldiers in Jerusalem and afforded justice when Festus, Roman governor of Judaea, would have put Paul at the mercy of the Sanhedrin.

Every Jewish boy learned a trade; for young Saul it was tentmaking, a trade he later practiced in Thessalonica, in Corinth, and in Ephesus to support himself and his fellow missionaries (I Th. 2:9; Acts 18:3; 20:34).

Although his early boyhood was spent in a city celebrated for its Greek learning, Saul's education was thoroughly Hebraic, probably obtained in a synagogue school. His family sent him to Jerusalem, most likely at the age of thirteen, to study to become a rabbi. He received his rabbinical training under Gamaliel, one of Judaism's most distinguished teachers of the Law. (This was the Gamaliel who counseled forbearance when the Sanhedrin would have killed Peter and the other apostles for preaching that Jesus was the Messiah.) Paul himself says he was taught "according to the perfect manner of the law of the fathers."

He proved a brilliant student, well versed in Mosaic Law, the Prophets, and the Writings and proficient in their exposition (Gal. 1:14). Like all Hellenistic Jews he used the Septuagint, the Greek translation of the Old Testament, but he was also familiar with the original Hebrew. Apparently unaffected by Gamaliel's liberalism, the young Saul became a violently intolerant religionist, intent on maintaining Judaic traditions and living as the strictest of Pharisees (Acts 26:5).

It appears that after Saul had completed his rabbinical studies in his twenties, he returned to Tarsus for a period; there is no indication in any of his writings that he ever saw Jesus or was present in Palestine during Jesus' public ministry.

When Saul returned to Jerusalem Christianity had taken root in Palestine and the Church, through the preaching of the apostles, had become an entity in Jerusalem. From Peter's first preaching on the Day of Pentecost, the number of adherents to the sect of the Nazarenes (as Christians were first called) grew phenomenally (see, for example, Acts 2:41,47; 4:4). The Sanhedrin found itself powerless to silence the apostles' preaching or to prevent their healing. As Christianity flourished, additional teachers came to the fore, Stephen the powerful evangelist among them (see p. 378). Stephen carried the gospel into the Jerusalem synagogues of foreign colonists, where it met heated opposition from the Pharisees. Saul, being a Greek-speaking Jew, undoubtedly heard Stephen preach in the Cilician synagogue the startling Christian claims of Jesus' Messiahship. As a zealous and able champion of the Pharisaic party, whose supreme duty it was to guard the sanctity of Judaism against all encroachments, Saul may well have taken part in bitter debates with Stephen.

Acts 7:58-8:4   It is in the violent scene of Stephen's murder at Jerusalem that Saul—as a passive persecutor of the infant Church—entered apostolic history (see p. 379). He stood in the inner circle of the angry mob that surrounded Stephen and guarded the clothes of those who stoned him: "When the blood of thy martyr Stephen was shed," he later said, "I also was standing by, and consenting unto his death, and kept the raiment of them that slew him" (Acts 22:20).

Yet even at the moment he was approving this cruelty, Saul could not help hearing Stephen's prayer, "Lord Jesus, receive my spirit," and his cry, "Lord, lay not this sin to their charge" (compare Lu. 23:34). These prayers burned themselves indelibly on his mind; although Paul never mentions them they may have been the first "prick" to goad his conscience (compare Acts 9:5). "We cannot dissociate the martyrdom of Stephen from the conversion of Paul. The spectacle of so much constancy, so much faith, so much love, could not be lost. It is hardly too much to say with Augustine, that 'the Church owes Paul to the prayer of Stephen.'"[1]

Stephen's martyrdom opened the floodgates of animosity against the rising sect, and a great persecution of Christians followed—one in which Saul with blind ardor now took a prominent part. With the tacit approval of the Sanhedrin he "made havock of the church"—he beat Christians in the synagogues; in fury he entered house after house in which suspected Christians were hiding and dragged men and women off to prison, and at their trials gave testimony that led to their deaths. Many fled from Jerusalem into Judaea and Samaria, but he hunted them out and "punished them oft in every synagogue, and compelled them to blaspheme; and being exceedingly mad against them . . . persecuted them even unto strange cities" (Acts. 26:9-11).

But out of the Church's suffering came that very extension of Christianity its enemies tried to prevent, for those who fled from Jerusalem into Judaea and Samaria, and even beyond Palestine, preached the gospel wherever they went, and it took root quickly. In time Philip the Evangelist, Peter, and John firmly established Christianity in Samaria, Ashdod (Azotus), and the cities of the Sharon plain—Caesarea, Joppa, and Lydda (see p. 379).

Acts 9:1-30   Saul's Conversion. Saul did not restrict his fanatic cruelties to Jerusalem. Intent on the destruction of Christians everywhere, he decided to go to Damascus, capital of Syria, 130 miles to the northeast. He asked the high priest for letters of introduction to Damascan synagogues—documents that would give him authority to arrest any man or woman of the new faith he might find there and to bring them chained to Jerusalem for trial. Saul was probably at least thirty when he undertook this journey—such authority would not have been delegated to a younger man.

During this journey took place Saul's conversion, the great turning point of his life. By divine intervention Saul was turned from the mad course he was pursuing and set right. The word *convert* means "turn," "turn back." One of the earliest dates given for his conversion is 33/34 A.D., at least three years after the ascension of Jesus. (The event is described three times in Acts.)

As he journeyed there suddenly shone around him and his party a light from heaven. They all fell to the earth, and Saul heard a voice saying "Saul, Saul, why persecutest thou me?" "Who art thou, Lord?" he questioned. "I am Jesus whom thou persecutest." Using the metaphor of a recalcitrant animal injuring itself against an oxgoad—the long pole with a sharp point used to prod oxen while plowing—the Jesus of his vision continued, "It is hard for thee to kick against the pricks." In astonishment and fear Saul asked, "Lord, what wilt thou have me to do?" His surrender to Christ was immediate and complete. The Lord said, "Arise, and go into the city, and it shall be told thee what thou must do." Saul's companions were speechless; they heard the voice, but saw no one. Saul "arose from the earth"; when he opened his eyes he could see nothing, and his companions led him to Damascus.

The revelation of Christ to Saul had come as a blinding vision of light. The full force of his misguided zeal smote him. In an anguish of remorse he fasted and prayed: "He was three days without sight, and neither did eat nor drink." His penitence was deep, piercing, regenerative: "The recollections of his early years,—the passages of the ancient Scriptures which he had never understood,—the thought of his own cruelty and violence,—the memory of the last looks of Stephen,—all these crowded into his mind, and made the three days equal to long years of repentance."[2]

At the end of that time the Lord appeared in a vision to a Damascus Christian named Ananias, commanding him to go to the house of one Judas in the street called Straight; there he would find Saul at prayer and expecting him, for Saul in a vision had seen Ananias coming in and laying his hand upon him that he might receive his sight. When Ananias protested the danger of exposing himself to this enemy of Christianity (Saul's reputation had preceded him), he was told that Saul was now "a chosen vessel" to bear the gospel to both the Gentiles and the Jews. Finding Saul, Ananias laid his hands on him and said, "Brother Saul, the Lord, even Jesus, that appeared unto thee in the way as thou camest, hath sent me, that thou mightest receive thy sight, and be filled with the Holy Ghost." Saul immediately received his sight: "there fell from his eyes as it had been scales"; and he "arose, and was baptized." He had experienced the new birth of which Jesus had spoken to Nicodemus, and his nature was transformed.

From the beginning Saul had acted sincerely, fully convinced that by his violent defense of Judaism he was championing God's plan of salvation. "I verily thought with myself, that I ought to do many things contrary to the name of Jesus of Nazareth" (Acts 26:9). But now he knew he had been fighting against God's Anointed. He realized the enormity of his sin in persecuting Christians and was humbled by the mercy of God, who had forgiven him so much. He perceived he was being saved neither because of his Jewish ancestry nor as a righteous Pharisee, but—although a sinner—as a man precious in God's sight. In Saul's conversion is seen the gospel of Jesus Christ in action, God's gift of grace and redemption.

Later in his life Paul revealed more of the facts regarding this extraordinary occurrence. Before King

"The street called Straight" runs westward from the East Gate of Damascus. In 1881 when this engraving was printed, it was also called "the Sultan's Highway" by Mohammedans. Picture Collection, New York Public Library.

Agrippa he disclosed that on the road to Damascus the risen Christ had given him his commission: "I have appeared unto thee for this purpose, to make thee a minister and a witness both of these things which thou hast seen, and of those things in the which I will appear unto thee; Delivering thee from the people, and from the Gentiles, unto whom now I send thee, To open their eyes, and to turn them from darkness to light, and from the power of Satan unto God, that they may receive forgiveness of sins, and inheritance among them which are sanctified by faith that is in me" (Acts 26:16-18). In an address to the Jews of Jerusalem Paul disclosed that Ananias had confirmed this commission: "The God of our fathers hath chosen thee, that thou shouldest know his will, and see that Just One, and shouldest hear the voice of his mouth. For thou shalt be his witness unto all men of what thou hast seen and heard" (Acts 22:14,15).

This journey to Damascus, which so revolutionized Saul's personal life, altered the course of history; the destructive zeal of his loyalty to Judaism was now transformed into constructive service for Christ. This single conversion opened wide Christ's redemptive gospel to the Gentile world.

Saul's call was explicit: he was to be the apostle to the Gentiles. His eyes had been opened; now he was to open their eyes. Thus would Jesus' prophecy be advanced: "Other sheep I have, which are not of this fold: them also I must bring, and they shall hear my voice; and there shall be one fold, and one shepherd" (Jn. 10:16). Paul subsequently fulfilled his commission to the Gentiles with singular success, carrying Christ's gospel to Asia Minor, Greece, and even to imperial Rome.

Later, when his apostolic authority was challenged by dissenting voices in the churches, he frequently felt obliged to defend his calling: "Am I not an apostle? ... have I not seen Jesus Christ our Lord?" (I Cor. 9:1); "Paul, an apostle of Jesus Christ by the will of God" (Col. 1:1); "an apostle, (not of men, neither by man, but by Jesus Christ, and God the Father....)" (Gal. 1:1); "Paul, a servant of Jesus Christ, called to be an apostle" (Rom. 1:1).

Saul was called by Jesus Christ after the Ascension. In his writings Paul rarely omitted the title *Christ* when referring to Jesus; most of his references were to "Jesus Christ," "the Lord Jesus Christ," and "Christ Jesus." When he carried his gospel to the Gentiles, he who knew Christ was acquainting the Gentile with Christ, "not after the flesh, but after the Spirit" (see II Cor. 5:16).

Luke records that Saul, in the first glow of his new vision, "straightway ... preached Christ in the synagogues, that he is the Son of God" (Acts 9:20). Paul himself, however, reports in his Epistle to the Galatians that almost at once he went into Arabia.

there to remain for "a season"—perhaps some part of three years (Gal. 1:15-18). This was a significant period of Saul's life, passed over without comment by Luke, but it was natural that this intellectual should seek solitude and meditation fully to understand the transforming experience that had come to him.

> It is difficult to conceive of any change more total, any rift of difference more deep, than that which separated Saul the persecutor from Paul the Apostle; and we are sure that—like Moses, like Elijah, like our Lord Himself, like almost every great soul in ancient or modern times to whom has been entrusted the task of swaying the destinies by moulding the convictions of mankind . . . he would need a quiet period in which to elaborate his thoughts, to still the tumult of his emotions, to commune in secrecy and in silence with his own soul. It was necessary for him to understand the Scriptures; to co-ordinate his old with his new beliefs. [3]

The same clear understanding Jesus had imparted to his apostles when he "opened" the Scriptures to them after Resurrection was imparted by revelation to Saul in the quiet of the desert of Arabia (Gal. 1:11, 12). Living with the regenerating change within himself and adjusting all earlier rabbinical beliefs and Scriptural knowledge to the revelation granted him, Saul gave profound thought to the relation of Jesus to the Old Testament Law and to the Messianic prophecies. He yielded to the truth that Jesus was the fulfillment of the Messianic promises and reached the unshakable conviction that Jesus was the incarnate Son of God. From this point on Saul embraced Christianity without reservation.

Upon his return from Arabia he preached with marked success in the synagogues of Damascus. He grew in influence among the Christian disciples and routed all the arguments of the Jews by his proofs that Jesus was "very Christ." His brilliant rabbinical and Pharisaic learning was now employed to expound the teachings he had once branded heretical. Soon he was faced with the bitter hostility of the Jews whose cause he had ceased to advocate; their antagonism reached such a pitch that, watching day and night at the gates of the city, they plotted to kill him. But Saul's friends helped him escape from Damascus by lowering him in a large basket by night through a window in the city wall (II Cor. 11:32,33).

So Saul came again to Jerusalem—now as a captive of Christ and armed with a new and glorious commission. He attempted to join the Christian disciples, but they all were afraid of him, doubting he was really a believer. Barnabas, an early convert who had contributed his possessions to the new Christian community (Acts 4:36,37), took Saul to the apostles and apprised them of Saul's conversion and of his fearless preaching of Christ at Damascus. Saul stayed with Peter fifteen days but saw none of the other apostles except James, the Lord's brother (Gal. 1:18,19).

Having been accepted as one of the brethren, Saul boldly preached Christ and argued with the Greek-speaking Jews. "Here was a man of education and ability, whose convictions became so strong that he willingly—nay gladly—forfeited the good will of all his old friends, forfeited his social position and all of his worldly prospects, by espousing the cause and the name of the Christ."[4] His preaching aroused controversy and resistance among his former compatriots, who now regarded him as a renegade and an enemy. Praying in the Temple, he was accorded another vision of Jesus Christ, who declared to him again his wider mission: "Make haste, and get thee quickly out of Jerusalem: for they will not receive thy testimony concerning me" (Acts 22:18). He remonstrated, feeling sure that the testimony of one who had completely reversed his position would be convincing, but the command came again, "Depart: for I will send thee far hence unto the Gentiles" (Acts 22:21).

Saul's field of labor was not to be Jerusalem or Palestine. And when the Hellenistic Jews tried to kill him, solicitous Christian brethren in the Jerusalem church sent him far away to his native city of Tarsus.

Saul now needed to be seasoned for the enormous task before him. Though Acts records nothing of his missionary activities during the next seven years, we learn from Galatians that he began at once to preach to the Gentiles in nearby Cilicia and Syria, and that favorable word of the zealous labors of this former persecutor of Christ had spread to the churches of Judaea (Gal. 1:21-24).

Cut off from the supervision of the apostles and the parent church in Jerusalem, Saul was significantly left free during these formative years of his ministry to clarify "by the Spirit" the gospel as it was being revealed to him. His preaching took form through practical experience and was strengthened through spiritual revelation and conviction. As he addressed himself to the Gentiles, who had little or no knowledge of Mosaic Law or of Jesus, he developed the Christian principles of redemption and salvation he was later to expound with such effectiveness.

Saul apparently underwent many physical and mental hardships during this Cilician and Syrian period, some of which probably took place before Luke met him; Luke makes no reference to them. Five times he was beaten with thirty-nine stripes by the Jews,* three times he was scourged by the Romans, three times he experienced shipwreck; repeatedly in city and village he was in danger from his own

---

*Mosaic Law stipulated, "Forty stripes he may give him, and not exceed" (Deut. 25:3); but customarily only thirty-nine were administered in order to remain within the Law.

unbelieving countrymen as well as from the heathen; often he endured hunger and thirst, exposure and cold (II Cor. 11:24-27).

During these years of Saul's preaching in southeast Asia Minor the apostles were keeping guard over the churches of Palestine. They had confined their ministry to the Jews, but the conversion of the Roman centurion Cornelius (Acts 10), which took place during this period, startled the church in Jerusalem into a recognition that the Gentiles also were to be partakers of Christ's grace.

Acts 11:19-30   Following Stephen's martyrdom many of the Christian Jews driven from Jerusalem by Saul's persecution traveled as far as Phoenicia, Cyprus, Cyrene in northern Africa, and Antioch in Syria. It was natural that some of these fugitives should be drawn to their Jewish countrymen already settled in these foreign lands and that they should proclaim the gospel to them. But when others who were Greek-speaking Jews reached Antioch, they began to preach to the Greeks also. As a result great numbers of Greek converts were won. This innovation of addressing uncircumcised Gentiles was an important advance in the spread of Christianity and led to the founding of the first Gentile church.

Antioch lay 300 miles north of Jerusalem. The city had been founded about 300 B.C. by Alexander's general Seleucus I Nicator and named in honor of his father Antiochus; with the Roman conquest it had become the capital of the province of Syria and the third largest city of the Roman Empire, with a population of over 500,000 of various nationalities, including a flourishing Jewish colony. Its seaport of Seleucia 20 miles to the west gave it access to Mediterranean commerce, while its caravan routes brought trade from Arabia and Mesopotamia. Here the Jews enjoyed equal civil and commercial privileges with the Syrian, Greek, and Roman population. Antioch was a notoriously vice-riddled city, but it was destined to become the second capital of Christianity during the apostolic era.

The church in Jerusalem sent the Greek-speaking Jew Barnabas to Antioch to investigate the new practice of preaching to Gentiles. Barnabas was well qualified for the task: "he was a good man, and full of the Holy Ghost and of faith" who later received the title of apostle (Acts 14:14). Seeing that God's grace was attendant on the new movement, he rejoiced in this fellowship of Jew and non-Jew, and gave the Antiochan church encouragement and guidance. However, as Barnabas observed its rapid growth he saw the need for another minister. Himself a broad-minded Jew of the Dispersion, he desired the aid of a helper who had a sympathetic spirit toward Gentiles, one of

wider culture and unprejudiced viewpoint than might be found among his colleagues in the Jerusalem church. Remembering the convert Saul whom he had championed in Jerusalem (Acts 9:27), word of whose preaching in Syria and Cilicia had reached the churches of Judaea, and recalling Saul's zeal and courage, he went to Tarsus to find him and brought him to Antioch. Together they labored for a full year (44-45 A.D.), and their work was crowned with great success. So frequently was the Greek word *Christos* heard in the city's streets that the name *Christian* was conferred on the followers of the new faith.

About this time certain Christian teachers came to Antioch from Jerusalem, among them the prophet Agabus. His prediction of an imminent famine in Judaea caused the Antiochan church to send its co-pastors, Barnabas and Saul, on the 300-mile journey to the Holy City with contributions for their brethren. Arriving in Jerusalem on their errand of mercy, they found this church had suffered greater calamity than that of famine—the martyrdom of the apostle James and the imprisonment of Peter by Herod Agrippa I (Acts 12). But Peter had been spared through the prayers of the church, and with the death of Herod in August 44, political persecution ceased for a time.

Acts 12:25   Barnabas and Saul returned to Antioch, probably in 46 A.D. They brought with them John Mark (Mk. 14:51?), a relative of Barnabas and son of a prominent Christian woman, Mary, in whose house the Jerusalem church had gathered to pray for Peter's release from prison.

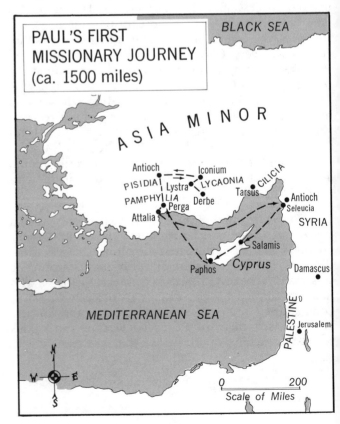

PAUL'S FIRST MISSIONARY JOURNEY (ca. 1500 miles)

On the island of Cyprus Saul's name was changed to Paul. These pillars are remnants of a temple to Zeus at the upper end of the forum in Salamis, a city on the east coast of Cyprus, visited by Paul and Barnabas. Religious News Service Photo.

First Missionary Journey

47-48 A.D.

Started from Syrian Antioch to Seleucia
Salamis, Paphos (on Cyprus)
Perga (in district of Pamphylia, Asia Minor)
Antioch (in district of Pisidia)
Iconium, Lystra, Derbe (in district of Lycaonia)
Returned to Lystra, Iconium, Antioch, Perga
Attalia (in Pamphylia)
Syrian Antioch

Acts 13 Not long after Saul's trip to Jerusalem—his second as a Christian—the church in Antioch was directed by the Holy Ghost, "Separate me Barnabas and Saul for the work whereunto I have called them." So the two apostles, supported by the prayers of the church and "sent forth by the Holy Ghost," departed for Asia Minor to promulgate the gospel. This missionary journey into the country west and north of Cilicia marked the widening scope of the early Church. In route it was a circuit—they started from Antioch in Syria and returned to Antioch in Syria. Saul considered this Gentile city, so happily situated at the crossroads to the West, eminently fitted to be his headquarters. From its mixed Christian community sprang foreign missions, for while Jerusalem was the center of the Christian movement under the apostles, it was too circumscribed by centuries of Judaism to serve as the center of a universal faith.

In 47 Barnabas and Saul sailed from Seleucia, the port of Antioch, to the seaport of Salamis on the island of Cyprus, 60 miles off the coast of Syria, taking Mark with them. They began their preaching in the synagogues, for many Jews of the Dispersion had made their homes on Cyprus. (They would find synagogues in almost every city and village throughout the Roman Empire.) Traveling 100 miles westward across the island, they arrived at Paphos, the capital, where they met the Roman proconsul Sergius Paulus, who had in his retinue a sorcerer, a Jewish exorcist and false prophet called Elymas. The proconsul was eager to hear the gospel, but Elymas opposed Saul, trying to keep the Roman from listening.

This opening incident revealed what lay before Saul repeatedly—perversion versus conversion—and Saul faced it down. Saul looked piercingly at Elymas and said, "O full of all subtilty and all mischief, thou child of the devil, thou enemy of all righteousness, wilt thou not cease to pervert the right ways of the Lord? . . . the hand of the Lord is upon thee, and thou shalt be blind, not seeing the sun for a season." Immediately Elymas was struck with blindness. (Luke does not record what took place at the end of that "season.") Sergius Paulus, witnessing this astonishing event, was converted.

With this incident Saul's name was changed to Paul. The change in his name is significant. From the outset of his mission to the Roman Empire he was known by his Roman name, and with this experience at Paphos he appears to have assumed leadership of the group. "As 'Abram' was changed into 'Abraham,' when God promised that he should be the 'father of many nations;' as 'Simon' was changed into 'Peter,' when it was said, 'On this rock I will build my church;'—so 'Saul' is changed into 'Paul,' at the moment of his first great victory among the Heathen."[5]

Leaving Cyprus, Paul and his companions sailed north to Attalia on the mainland of Asia Minor, up the Cestrus River seven miles to the inland city of Perga in the Roman district of Pamphylia. Here Mark suddenly left them to return to Jerusalem. Paul considered Mark's departure a desertion of their cause (Acts 15:38).

The two apostles journeyed north toward Antioch in Pisidia; toiling through the rugged mountain passes of the Taurus they emerged on the great central plateau of Asia Minor. This Antioch, also founded by Seleucus Nicator, was a flourishing city situated on the great trade route running east to Syria and west to Ephesus on the Aegean Sea; it was the center of Roman civil and military authority for the surrounding territory. Here Paul found a colony of friendly Jews and was invited to preach at their synagogue service. Luke carefully records the substance of this speech, the first detailed account of Paul's preaching to prospective converts. Paul proclaimed, as had Peter, that Jesus was the suffering and glorified Messiah

393

promised in the Scriptures; he rehearsed the history of Israel, the promise of a Savior through the seed of David, the fulfillment of that promise in Jesus, the condemnation and crucifixion of Jesus by his own nation, and Jesus' glorious resurrection from the dead. He closed his sermon with the assertion: "Be it known . . . that through this man is preached unto you the forgiveness of sins: And by him all that believe are justified from all things, from which ye could not be justified by the law of Moses." This he followed with a strong warning against unbelief, couched in the words of Habakkuk, that however startling his message might be, yet if they disbelieved as their fathers had disbelieved the prophecy of Chaldean destruction, they would perish (Hab. 1:5).

After the meeting had broken up, the devout Gentile proselytes of the congregation begged Paul to preach the Word again on the following Sabbath; many in the synagogue talked further with the apostles, who urged them to put their trust in God's grace. The next Sabbath almost the whole city gathered to listen. So great was the crowd that the leaders of the synagogue, angry and envious, interrupted him again and again with contradictions and abusive taunts. This was a crisis. Seeing the Jews' rejection of his message of a free salvation and determined that the Gentiles should hear, Paul made the courageous decision to appeal directly to the receptive Gentiles in the audience. His rebuke to his resistant countrymen was strong: "It was necessary that the word of God should first have been spoken to you: but seeing ye put it from you, and judge yourselves unworthy of everlasting life, lo, we turn to the Gentiles." The Gentiles listened readily and accepted the gospel, and many became Christians.

Soon all the region adjacent to Antioch had heard of Christ, but the apostles' Jewish detractors, fervid in their defense of what they felt to be their exclusive heritage, fought the new teaching, stirred up the influential men and women of the city, and drove Paul and Barnabas out. Shaking the dust of Antioch from their feet as a testimony against their adversaries (Lu. 9:5), they set out for Iconium, while the infant church they had left behind, filled with joy, stood firm.

Acts 14   Iconium, 80 miles southeast on the same trade route as Pisidian Antioch, was the prosperous capital of the district of Lycaonia. Here the same thing happened: Paul and Barnabas made many Jewish and Greek converts, but again they were confronted by the animosity of the religious leaders within the Jewish community. However, they remained here a long time, preaching and attesting to the power of the gospel by many miracles. But the city was ultimately divided into two factions, those who sided with the apostles and those who held with the Jews; and when hostile Jews and Greeks both banded together to stone them, the two fled to Lystra, 18 miles to the south.

In Lystra Paul effected a miracle similar to that performed by Peter (Acts 3:1-10). A man crippled from birth, "who never had walked," sat in the audience and heard Paul speak. "He had faith to be healed," and Paul, perceiving this, commanded: "Stand upright on thy feet." And the man both "leaped and walked." The people at once thought Barnabas and Paul were gods, calling Barnabas Jupiter, and Paul Mercury, because he was the principal speaker. The priest of the temple of Jupiter brought oxen and garlands, intending to offer sacrifice. When the apostles realized the interpretation that had been placed upon the healing, they ripped their clothes (a characteristic Jewish sign of grief and abhorrence) and rushed out into the crowd, exclaiming, "Sirs, why do ye these things? We also are men . . . and preach unto you that ye should turn from these vanities unto the living God." Their agitated appeal barely checked this act of idolatry.

The Jews of Antioch and Iconium, not content with driving the apostles from their own cities, came to Lystra and poisoned public opinion against them. Here Paul suffered physical violence; he was stoned and dragged out of the city apparently dead. But the disciples rallied to his side and he revived. He "arose" and went into the city, and the next day left with Barnabas for Derbe.

At Derbe, 30 miles southeast of Lystra, they preached again and won many believers. Then, disregarding the danger that threatened at the hands of their enemies, they retraced their steps to Lystra, Iconium, and Antioch to strengthen and sustain the faith of the new converts. Paul and Barnabas ordained elders in each church—the first known organizational measure taken by Paul—and encouraged its members to withstand persecution: "We must through much tribulation enter into the kingdom of God."

Passing once more through Pisidia and Pamphylia to Perga, Paul and Barnabas sailed from Attalia and returned to Antioch in Syria. They had been away about eighteen months and had traveled some 1500 miles by land and sea. These faithful missionaries called the church together and "rehearsed all that God had done with them, and how he had opened the door of faith unto the Gentiles."

Acts   15:1-35   The Council of Jerusalem (49/50 A.D.). About a year and a half after Paul and Barnabas had returned to Syrian Antioch the Church faced dissension from within. A question arose so serious that the future of Christianity as a universal faith weighed upon it: Were

Gentile converts to be forced under the yoke of Mosaic legalism in order to become Christians?

From the first, the two apostles had laid down no requirements for Gentile conformity to Mosaic Law, nor had they demanded that Gentiles be circumcised; and in the Antioch church Jews and Gentiles dwelt side by side in an unusual degree of fellowship, the Jews having set aside to some extent their ingrained habits of social segregation from peoples of other nations. But this unity was disrupted by Judaic Christians who came up from Jerusalem and asserted that salvation was not possible without the prescribed circumcision.

Paul and Barnabas at once took issue with this doctrine because it tended to put Christianity under the bondage of Judaism and denied salvation through faith in Christ. Circumcision had been observed by the Hebrews from the time of Abraham as a symbol of purity and as a token of God's covenant (Gen. 17:10-14). Baptism by water had been inaugurated by John the Baptist; baptism by the Spirit had come with Jesus. To Paul, therefore, circumcision was no longer a sign of the covenant; the higher figure of baptism had superseded it: "In Christ Jesus neither circumcision availeth any thing, nor uncircumcision, but a new creature" (Gal. 6:15; see Col. 2:11,12).

There was so much argument that the church sent Paul, Barnabas, and Titus (one of Paul's uncircumcised Greek converts) to Jerusalem to confer with the Twelve and the elders of the parent church in an effort to settle this vital matter. In the course of their journey they visited the churches in Phoenicia and Samaria, telling them of the Gentiles' eager reception of Christianity. In Jerusalem they reported to the apostles and the church concerning the success of their preaching to the Gentiles, together with the controversial question to which it had given rise. Some of the Pharisaic sect stood up in the assembly and agreed with the Judaizers' point of view, insisting on the necessity of circumcising Gentile converts and also demanding the keeping of the Mosaic practices of segregation, fasting, abstention from unclean meats, and the like. Although this controversy had started as an attack on Paul's procedure among the Gentiles, it brought to the fore for future ages the far larger question of liberty versus literalistic bondage to the Law. It was a question too big for immediate decision; a meeting was called in order that the subject might be thoroughly debated.

But before the council convened Paul took pains to meet privately with the leaders of the Jerusalem church in an atmosphere free of bias or emotional pressures to explain and defend more fully the gospel he preached. Only from his letter to the Galatians do we learn of this private conference and read from his own hand how prayerfully he prepared for it and how

assiduously and with what strength and independence of thought he contended for the safeguarding of Gentile Christians (Gal. 2:1-5). "I went up by revelation, and communicated unto them that gospel which I preach among the Gentiles, but privately to them which were of reputation, lest by any means I should run, or had run, in vain."

Although pressure was brought to bear to circumcise Titus, he would not allow it, for to sanction this practice would have been to lose the liberty that the Christian gains in Christ. Paul refused to compromise even for a moment what later developed in his writings as cardinal doctrines of the gospel—the doctrines of grace and justification by faith in Jesus Christ. He was not awed by the prominence of the leaders of the Jerusalem church, nor was he swayed from his convictions because of them. He neither knew nor cared what their exact office was—God was not impressed with a man's status—and he found that they added nothing new to his gospel (Gal. 2:6).

At the open conference that followed, the rightness of Paul's position was conceded by James, Peter, and John. When they saw that "he that wrought effectually in Peter to the apostleship of the circumcision, the same was mighty in [Paul] toward the Gentiles," he was accorded equal standing with Peter and the other apostles, and his and Barnabas' mission to the Gentiles was fully acknowledged by the Jerusalem church (Gal. 2:7-9).

Peter upheld and endorsed Paul's stand, reminding the assembly of the lesson God had taught them by the conversion of Cornelius and his friends—that non-Jews whose hearts were ready were given the gift of the Holy Ghost even as were they and that there was no difference between the Jew and the Gentile, for God had purified the hearts of the Gentiles by faith. Rhetorically he questioned those who were holding out for the rite of circumcision: "Why tempt ye God, to put a yoke upon the neck of the disciples, which neither our fathers nor we were able to bear? But we believe that through the grace of the Lord Jesus Christ we shall be saved, even as they." Then the assembly listened attentively while Barnabas and Paul recounted the experiences of their missionary journey to Asia Minor and the miracles God had wrought among the Gentiles.

James, head of the church, confirmed Peter's position, showing it to be in harmony with Amos' prophecy relating to the inclusion of the Gentiles in the Messianic blessing (see Amos 9:11,12). He then gave for the Church the authoritative and historic decision that removed Christianity from the category of a Jewish sect to its true status as a universal religion. It exempted Gentiles from the burden of Mosaic Law but at the same time laid down for them four prohibitions against practices particularly abhorrent to the Jews: eating food that had been offered to idols, sexual immorality, eating the flesh of strangled animals, and drinking blood.

Letters were drawn up containing the council's decision, with an affectionate commendation of Barnabas and Paul and the acknowledgment that they were men who had hazarded their lives to spread the gospel. These letters were written for the churches of Syria and Cilicia. The Jerusalem church sent Judas Barsabas and Silas, enlightened Christian teachers, back to Antioch with Barnabas and Paul to confirm this decree orally.

The troubled Antioch church eagerly assembled to meet its returning delegates and the Jerusalem emissaries, and was overjoyed to hear that the principle of salvation by faith had been upheld. Judas soon returned to Jerusalem, but Silas, drawn by the vision of a wider ministry that included the Gentiles, chose to remain in Antioch.

> Paul, in fact, by the intensity of his convictions, the enlightenment of his undersanding, the singleness of his purpose, had made himself completely master of the situation. He had come to the very forefront in the guidance of the Church. The future of Christianity rested with the Gentiles, and to the Gentiles the acts and writings of Paul were to be of greater importance than those of all the other Apostles. His Apostolate had been decisively recognised. He had met Peter and John, and even the awe-inspiring brother of the Lord, in conference, and found himself so completely their equal in the gifts of the Holy Ghost, that it was impossible for them to resist his credentials. He had greatly enlarged their horizon, and they had added nothing to him. He had returned from Jerusalem more than ever conscious of himself, conscious of his own power, clear in his future purposes. He inspired into the Church of Antioch his own convictions with a force which no one could resist.[6]

Although the council had settled the question of freedom from Mosaic legalism for Gentile Christians and established the equality of Jewish and Gentile members within the Church, the continued observance of the Law by Jewish Christians was taken for granted. It was natural therefore that some Judaic beliefs should still constitute a social barrier which kept the Jew from mingling freely with his Gentile brethren. The exclusiveness practiced by generations of Jews could not be so easily or quickly eradicated, and sometimes complications arose. One such occasion occurred later when Peter visited Antioch (the exact date is not known) and for a while ate with Gentile believers; but when certain Jews came from the Jerusalem church, Peter temporized. Afraid of being censured, he withdrew from the company of the Gentiles. Peter's behavior fell far short of the spirit of the gospel and of the stand he had professed at the council, and because his example influenced Barnabas and others to segregate themselves also, Paul again rose to the defense of the principle of Christian freedom and openly rebuked his fellow apostle. Paul wrote of this experience: "When Peter was come to Antioch, I withstood him to the face, because he was to be blamed. . . . I said unto Peter before them all, If thou, being a Jew, livest after the manner of Gentiles . . . why compellest thou the Gentiles to live as do the Jews?" (Gal. 2:11, 14).

Despite this strong rebuke Peter held Paul in deep respect and affection; in his Second Epistle he referred to him as "our beloved brother Paul" (II Pet. 3:15).

PAUL'S SECOND MISSIONARY JOURNEY
(ca. 3500 miles)

EUXINE OR BLACK SEA

ILLYRICUM

Adriatic Sea

ITALY

MACEDONIA

Philippi
Neapolis

Amphipolis
Thessalonica
Berea

Apollonia

Troas

MYSIA

BITHYNIA

ASIA MINOR

CAPPADOCIA

GALATIA

Antioch

Iconium

Lystra

TAURUS MTS.

Derbe

CILICIA

Tarsus

Antioch

SYRIA

Aegean
Sea

ACHAIA
(GREECE)

Athens

Corinth
Cenchrea

Ephesus

ASIA

PHRYGIA

Cyprus

Crete

MEDITERRANEAN SEA

Caesarea
Jerusalem

N

100   200
Scale of Miles

Second Missionary Journey

51-54 A.D.

Started from Syrian Antioch through Cilicia
Derbe, Lystra
Regions of Phrygia and Galatia
Troas (seaport in province of Mysia)
Neapolis (seaport of Macedonia)
Philippi, Thessalonica, Berea (in Macedonia)
Athens, Corinth (in Achaia)
From Cenchrea to Ephesus (in province of Asia)
Caesarea, Jerusalem (in Palestine)
Returned to Syrian Antioch

Acts 15:36-41   Paul was now free to contemplate another journey. The mother church in Jerusalem had acknowledged and approved his authority as an apostle to the Gentiles. Therefore in 51 A.D., at the age of about forty-seven, he turned his attention to the infant churches he had founded in Asia Minor, and proposed to Barnabas that they visit each one to check on their well-being. Barnabas wanted to take Mark as their companion, but Paul objected—Mark had left them early on the first journey. Because his love for Christ came first, Paul would allow nothing—not even a strong personal relationship—to impede his mission.

The most resolute courage, indeed, was required for the work to which St. Paul was now publicly pledged. He would not associate with himself in that work one who had already

The Cilician Gates, a series of sharp defiles in the Tauru Mountains, used by Paul on hi missionary journeys. Throug this pass ran an ancient trad route from the Euphrates to th uplands of Asia Minor. Courtes of the Oriental Institute, Unive sity of Chicago.

shown a want of constancy. This was the occasion of what must have been a most painful difference between him and his comrade in the faith and in past perils, Barnabas (Acts 15:35-40).[7]

The disagreement was so sharp that the two friends separated. Barnabas and Mark sailed to Cyprus; Paul chose Silas to accompany him on this second missionary journey. Silas (Silvanus) was already a man of seasoned Christian character and was, like Paul, a Roman citizen (Acts 16:37). Luke makes no further mention of Barnabas and Mark. Only from Paul's letters do we learn of the continuing missionary work of Barnabas (I Cor. 9:6); later, when Mark had reached greater Christian maturity, Paul found his help of comfort and value (Col. 4:10,11; II Tim. 4:11).

Paul's second journey, like his first, was a circuit; he started from Antioch in Syria and returned there three years later. Led by the Spirit, his work expanded greatly in scope and importance as he crossed Asia Minor and carried the gospel into southeast Europe. This time he and Silas went overland, first through the already-evangelized territory of Syria and Cilicia (Gal. 1:21-23), then on across the Taurus mountain chain to visit the churches of Derbe, Lystra, Iconium, and Antioch in Pisidia, founded on his first journey three years earlier.

Acts 16   Only one incident is told of Paul's stay in Lystra—his meeting with young Timotheus, who, with his mother, had apparently been converted on the apostle's first visit. In the interim Timotheus (Timothy) had proved himself a disciple of blameless character, already held in high regard by the churches of Lystra and Iconium. Seeing in him great promise, Paul wished to take him along, and the brethren of Lystra readily concurred. So with the laying on of hands by Paul and the elders Timothy

was ordained (I Tim. 4:14; II Tim. 1:6; see p. 378).

Because Timothy was half Jew (his father was a Greek), Paul had him submit to circumcision before their departure. Although he had fought determinedly for the principle of Gentile freedom from circumcision, Paul kept the Law in this instance in tolerance of the Jewish viewpoint so that no door be shut against his effort to reach his countrymen. Christianity did not interfere with Jewish customs, and inasmuch as this young man was not a pure Gentile, as was Titus, this was not so much a religious question as a social and racial one. Paul himself occasionally observed certain Jewish customs such as the keeping of vows (Acts 18:18; 21:23-26), though he did not deem them essential to salvation (see I Cor. 9:19-23).

Timothy became Paul's faithful helper on this journey and later his chief companion on the third journey. Through the ensuing years Timothy was to be entrusted with missions of the highest importance, and Paul's letters show the esteem and affection in which he held him: "my own son in the faith" (I Tim. 1:2) "Timothy, my dearly beloved son" (II Tim. 1:2).

All along the way Paul, Silas, and Timothy delivered the letters containing the decision reached at the council in Jerusalem, and thus the unity of the churches was strengthened and membership increased daily. The three spent many weeks proclaiming the gospel in the regions of Phrygia and Galatia. Galatia was originally a north-central Asia Minor region inhabited largely by descendants of Gauls of northern Italy and France who had invaded this territory early in the third century B.C. In Paul's day Galatia was a large Roman province that included not only this region having the cities of Ancyra, Pessinus, and Tavium, but also portions of the districts of Phrygia, Lycaonia, and Pisidia. Whether the churches of Galatia were founded at this time is not clear from Luke's account (Acts

The ruins of Philippi, Greece, where Paul preached his first sermon to the Gentiles. Here Lydia, a wealthy woman of Thyatira, became the first Christian convert in Europe and the first Christian community in Europe was organized. Religious News Service Photo.

16:6), but it is probable they were.*

Traveling westward, they were forbidden by the Holy Ghost to preach in the province of Asia to the west or in the province of Bithynia to the north—so they continued on to the Mysian port of Troas (near the site of ancient Troy) on the Aegean Sea. Thus Paul, divinely directed, was prevented from further preaching at this time in Asia Minor and led toward another field of labor.

At Troas Paul had a vision of a Macedonian who entreated "Come over into Macedonia, and help us." He responded at once to this summons to bring the gospel to the continent of Europe. He stood on the threshold of enlarged opportunity; ahead of him was not merely a short journey across the Aegean, but also a decisive step into the Western world, the seat of highly advanced Hellenic culture and the home of Roman justice, the most enlightened law of the day.

After the vision they made every effort to get passage on a ship to Macedonia, convinced that the Lord had called them to preach the gospel there. At this point in the record Luke introduces himself as a member of Paul's company (16:10). Luke was almost certainly a Gentile—according to Eusebius he was a native of Syrian Antioch, and Paul's grouping of Luke's name in his letters with those of other Gentile fellow laborers heightens the implication that this new disciple was a Gentile (Col. 4:12-14). We also learn that Luke was a doctor; Paul called him "the beloved physician." His two books, the Gospel of Luke and the Acts of the Apostles, show him to have been a man of education and a skilled reporter of marked literary ability. He became an intimate friend of Paul and his faithful biographer for the next eleven years.

Sailing from Troas across the northern tip of the Aegean, the little group landed at Neapolis in Macedonia, the region north of Greece in the present Balkan Peninsula. They journeyed inland to the nearby city of Philippi, an important Roman colony on the great Via Egnatia from Rome to Asia. There was no synagogue in Philippi, so on the first Sabbath they went to a meeting place outside the city gate near a river where Jews and converts to Judaism often met for prayer. There Paul addressed the gathering, in this case one wholly of women. Among his hearers was Lydia, formerly of Thyatira in Asia Minor, a dealer in cloth—a "seller of purple"—who became Paul's first European convert. Already a proselyte to the Jewish faith, Lydia was instantly receptive to the gospel, and with her whole household, family and slaves alike, was baptized into the Christian faith. She extended to Paul and his companions the hospitality of her home, which upon her insistence they accepted.

On another occasion as they went again to the place of public prayer a young slave girl "possessed with a spirit of divination [clairvoyance]," who brought her owners much profit by fortune-telling, followed them, crying out, "These men are the servants of the most high God, which shew unto us the way of salvation." She had persisted in this for many days; on this day Paul rebuked the spirit, "I command thee in the name of Jesus Christ to come out of her." And the spirit of divination "came out" the same hour. Her masters, furious because she was now useless as a source of income, seized Paul and Silas and dragged them into the forum before the Roman praetors, and, capitalizing on anti-Jewish prejudice,

*Galatians 4:13 indicates that Paul had made two visits to the Galatians before he wrote to them on his third journey. Its phrase "at the first" (literally "at the former time") has led some scholars to interpret it as meaning the visits made on his second and third journeys (Acts 16:6; 18:23); others feel it refers to the visits made on his first and second journeys (Acts 13:14-14:24; 16:6).

charged that these Jews were troubling the city, teaching customs which they, as Roman citizens, could not lawfully accept or practice.

When a crowd joined in the accusation, the magistrates ordered that Paul and Silas be stripped and publicly flogged; then the two were handed over to a jailer who threw them into a dark inner prison and fastened their feet in stocks. But nothing could quench the spirit and courage of these dedicated disciples. They prayed; their faith and joy, transcending physical suffering and prison chains, rose in hymns of praise to God at the midnight hour. The other prisoners listened with surprise to such a sound in a Roman dungeon and the heaviness of their own hearts was lightened. Almost simultaneously "there was a great earthquake, so that the foundations of the prison were shaken: and immediately all the doors were opened, and every one's bands were loosed."

The keeper, wakened suddenly from sleep, saw with terror that the prison doors were open and he drew his sword to kill himself. If the prisoners had escaped, under Roman law he would face inevitable death. But Paul shouted: "Do thyself no harm: for we are all here." In gratitude and relief, sensing the goodness of these men and the presence of a higher power, the jailer called for a light and fell trembling at the feet of the apostles. Bringing them out of the dungeon, he asked, "Sirs, what must I do to be saved?" "Believe on the Lord Jesus Christ," they replied, "and thou shalt be saved, and thy house," explaining to him the grace of Christ.

The jailer had been callous and indifferent to the physical plight of his prisoners before; now his heart was flooded with compassion and he hastened to wash their wounds; then he and his household were baptized. Treating them as guests, he brought Paul and Silas into his house and fed them, rejoicing in his newfound faith.

Nor was this all. In the morning the magistrates reversed their hasty decision and sent officers to release Paul and Silas. Paul refused to be dismissed in this offhand manner, however. He demanded justice. After such public indignity and insult it was important that their innocence be made known. Their rights as Roman citizens had been flagrantly violated: the forbidden scourge had been applied to their persons

Roman scourges. *International Standard Bible Encyclopedia.*

and they had suffered imprisonment without any kind of trial. The praetors themselves must come and free them. The magistrates were alarmed when they heard Paul's charge, realizing they had committed one of the greatest of crimes under Roman law, thus placing their own lives in jeopardy. They hurried to the jail to beg the two to leave. The wrong having been openly acknowledged, Paul and Silas consented to go, but before departing from Philippi they reported the comforting news of their release to Lydia and the others. The remarkable circumstances of these prison events, together with the apostles' forbearance toward the magistrates, did much to advance the cause of Christianity in Philippi. "Thus it was that a woman, a girl and a man became the nucleus of the first church in Europe, and the bringing of the Gospel to Europe was begun in a prison experience." [8]

Acts 17 Paul and Silas traveled on through Amphipolis and Apollonia to Thessalonica, which lay about a hundred miles southwest on the Via Egnatia, but Timothy and Luke apparently remained at Philippi to continue working in the new church.

Thessalonica (now Salonika) was the capital of Macedonia, a wealthy seaport on the Thermaic Gulf and a "free city" under the autonomous rule of local officials called politarchs. Its importance made it a highly favorable center for the dissemination of the gospel. Despite the treatment he and Silas had received at Philippi, Paul at once began to preach of Christ (I Th. 2:2). On three successive Sabbaths he went to the synagogue and attempted to reason with the Jews, pointing out from Scripture that their promised Messiah was one who must suffer, die, and rise again, and that Jesus was this Messiah. During these three weeks his forceful preaching won a large number of converts, both men and women, some from among the Jews and many from among the Greeks.

But again, as on the first journey, opposition arose. The devout of the synagogue felt impelled to safeguard their religious beliefs. Jealous Jews gathered some of the unprincipled idlers of the market place, started a riot, and stormed the house of Jason, in which Paul and his friend were lodging. When the apostles could not be found, the angry crowd seized Jason and some of the brethren, brought them before the politarchs, charging, "These that have turned the world upside down are come hither also; Whom Jason hath received: and these all do contrary to the decrees of Caesar, saying that there is another king, one Jesus." But the officials demanded only a bail bond from Jason and the others and let them go.

Because Paul and Silas were still in great danger, the new disciples sent them off secretly that night to Berea, 50 miles to the southwest. But the church

The rocky plateau of the ancient Acropolis (the "Upper City") overlooks modern Athens. The Parthenon (center), temple of the virgin goddess Athena, and the elegant Erechtheum, on its left, date from the 5th century B.C. In the background, Lycabettus Hill rises almost 1000 feet high. Greek National Tourist Office.

which had been founded in Thessalonica took root and flourished, so much so that within a few months of his departure Paul wrote of them: "Ye were ensamples to all that believe in Macedonia and Achaia. For from you sounded out the word of the Lord not only in Macedonia and Achaia, but also in every place your faith to God-ward is spread abroad; so that we need not to speak any thing" (I Th. 1:7,8).

In the populous Macedonian city of Berea Paul and Silas continued their ministry, and Timothy soon joined them. The Jews of the Berean synagogue were more open-minded than those of Thessalonica; they accepted the gospel "with all readiness of mind, and searched the scriptures daily, whether those things were so." When Paul's enemies in Thessalonica learned he was preaching God's message in Berea they pursued him, and incited a riot there. Paul was again forced to flee. Christian friends at once sent Paul to the Aegean seacoast. To insure his safety the men who accom-

panied him went with him by ship all the way to Athens, a sea journey of more than 300 miles. They returned to Berea with Paul's urgent message that Silas and Timothy, whom he had left behind to aid new converts, should rejoin him as quickly as possible.

While Paul waited in Athens he surveyed his surroundings with interest; this was his first visit to the celebrated metropolis of Achaia (southern Greece). In the fifth century B.C. the Athenian city-state had attained eminence as a great democracy and as the center of Greek philosophy and art; Pericles, Socrates, Plato, and Aristotle, among others, had given it lasting glory. Even under Roman government in Paul's day Athens remained the cultural and intellectual center of the Empire.

The name Athens came from that of the warlike goddess Athena (Minerva) whose magnificent temple, the Parthenon, dominated the city's fortified citadel, the craggy hill of the Acropolis. Athena was con-

401

sidered not only the protector of her people but also the patron deity of the arts. The Acropolis, covered with temples and statues of gods and heroes, was a museum of architectural and sculptural splendor, approached from the west through the magnificent marble gateway of the Propylaea. Close to the Parthenon stood the Erechtheum or temple of King Erechtheus, the Temple of Zeus, and the Temple of the Wingless Victory. Images of wood, stone, marble, bronze adorned every public building and lined the streets; every Greek god in Olympus found a place in the city's *agora* (market place or public square). The Greek traveler Pausanias reported that there were more gods in Athens than in all the rest of Greece put together. The worship of these many gods testified to the religious sentiment of the Athenians—to a paganism diametrically opposed to the spirit of Christianity.

Paul, a Jew whose former religion forbade the representation of the human body in any form, was not impressed with the city's art and sculpture; rather his soul was shocked and horrified to see the city completely given over to idolatry. Following his usual practice, he preached in the synagogue, but he also debated daily with Greek philosophers of the city's agora. Some of them, desiring to hear more of his novel ideas, invited him to Areopagus, the city court of Athens, to question: "May we know what this new doctrine . . . is? For thou bringest certain strange things to our ears: we would know therefore what these things [Jesus and the resurrection] mean." (Luke tersely describes the intellectual temper of Athens: "For all the Athenians and strangers which were there spent their time in nothing else, but either to tell, or to hear some new thing.")

At Mars' Hill (Areopagus) Paul gave his now-famous discourse concerning the one true God. He was aware that he was addressing Gentile intellectuals, some Epicureans, others Stoics. The Epicureans were a sect of philosophers, followers of the school of Epicurus of Samos (341-270 B.C.), whose philosophy was popular in Asia Minor, Rome, and the Athens of Paul's day. Epicurus taught that happiness (pleasure) was the chief aim of existence, to be attained by prudence, honor, and justice. This happiness was to be found in a tranquil mind and a body free from pain. He sought to reach a state of thought unaffected by the changes and vicissitudes of life. Politics, business, and knowledge were eschewed as distractions to serenity of mind. Men lived in a universe formed and governed by the chance organization of atoms; there was no future life or immortality, for at the close of physical existence the soul and body would dissolve. In Epicurus' philosophy the gods played no part in the lives of men, being relegated to a sphere of their own outside the world. His doctrines freed men from the fear of death and from a superstitious fear of the gods.

The more noble of Epicurus' followers held to the higher ethics of his teachings, while the less refined reduced them to materialism and sensualism.

The Stoics were a sect of philosophers whose school had been founded in Athens by Zeno in 308 B.C. While the Epicureans denied the existence of a divine Being, the Stoics were pantheistic, seeing a divine Being in all nature, a nature pervaded and ordered by the animating spirit of reason. To them virtue was the supreme good, the chief aim of existence, to be obtained by conforming to the laws of nature. They were therefore under the necessity of submitting willingly to evil as well as to good. The soul was held to be corporeal, and at death would be burned or absorbed in God. By the exercise of reason and an austere morality, the wise man should be free from passions and unaffected by joy or grief, pleasure or pain. "He therefore lives a consistent, harmonious life, in conformity with the perfect order of the universe. He discovers this order by knowledge or wisdom. But the Stoics also defined this ideal as a system of particular duties, such as purity in one's self, love toward all men, and reverence toward God. In Stoic ethics, Greek philosophy reached the climax of its moral teaching."[9] In practice, however, the Stoics tended toward inordinate pride and egotism, and their pantheistic worship was inimical to the Gospel.

Mindful of these two philosophies, Paul spoke with exquisite tact and courtesy as he skillfully refuted the foundations of their hypotheses. He set the doctrine of a divine Creator and His creation against the atheistic theory that the world was formed by a chance organization of the atoms of matter, and the truth of the one God against the belief in many gods. And though he stood surrounded by heathen shrines of unexcelled beauty, he declared that this infinite God could not be worshiped materially.

"Ye men of Athens, I perceive that in all things ye are too superstitious [Phillips: in all respects an extremely religious people]. For as I passed by, and beheld your devotions, I found an altar with this inscription, TO THE UNKNOWN GOD. Whom therefore ye ignorantly worship, him declare I unto you. God that made the world and all things therein, seeing that he is Lord of heaven and earth, dwelleth not in temples made with hands; Neither is worshipped with men's hands, as though he needed any thing, seeing he giveth to all life, and breath, and all things; And hath made of one blood all nations of men for to dwell on all the face of the earth. . . . For in him we live, and move, and have our being; as certain also of your own poets* have said, For we are also his offspring. Forasmuch then as we are the offspring of God, we ought not to think that the Godhead is like unto gold

*Aratus and Cleanthes, Greek Stoics of third century B.C.

The Areopagus, or Mars' Hill, where Paul addressed the men of Athens. Picture Collection, New York Public Library.

or silver, or stone, graven by art and man's device. And the times of this ignorance God winked at; but now commandeth all men every where to repent: Because he hath appointed a day, in the which he will judge the world in righteousness by that man whom he hath ordained; whereof he hath given assurance unto all men, in that he hath raised him from the dead."

The Athenians gave Paul close attention until he spoke of the resurrection of the dead. He always testified of Jesus' resurrection, and each time it met with strong disbelief. The response at Mars' Hill was no exception. Some of these intellectuals scoffed at such an incredible idea; others said they would like to hear him at greater length. Paul himself was a man of the highest intellectual capacities, but he condemned intellectualism as an end in itself, without spiritual impetus. Later he wrote the Corinthians that while Christ's crucifixion was a "stumbling block" to the Jews, it was "foolishness" to the Greeks (I Cor. 1:22,23).

A few of his listeners were won over to Christianity, among them Dionysius, a member of the court of Areopagus, and Damaris, an Athenian woman. When he saw that on the whole the Athenians gave little credence to the truth of resurrection, Paul departed from Athens. Philippi, Thessalonica, Corinth, and Ephesus became great centers for the extension of Christianity; Athens, steeped in philosophic materialism, remained alien to the theology of Christianity, and Paul never returned there so far as is known.

Before Paul left Athens Timothy (and probably Silas) arrived from Berea with word that the Thessalonian converts needed help to withstand the persecution they were suffering at the hands of their own countrymen (I Th. 2:14); so although he felt great need of Timothy's presence and support, Paul's anxiety impelled him to send Timothy and Silas back to Thessalonica to comfort and strengthen the new church (I Th. 3:1-5).

Acts 18:1-22   Paul traveled on to Corinth, the Roman capital of Achaia, 40 miles west of Athens on the narrow isthmus joining the Peloponnesian peninsula with the mainland of Greece. Corinth had two deep-water ports: Cenchrea nine miles to the east on the Saronic Gulf, with access to the Aegean, and Lechaeum to the west on the Corinthian Gulf, leading into the Adriatic; its vast maritime trade had made it immensely wealthy. Greeks, Romans, large settlements of Jews, and resident strangers from many lands made up its cosmopolitan population. It was adorned with many splendid buildings, including the stadium of the great Isthmian games, the great Agora, and the notorious temple of Aphrodite with its thousand courtesans. Immorality and licentious extravagance were rife in this highly sophisticated city, yet Paul was to remain here for a year and a half and find it fertile ground for the message of Christianity.

Paul found lodging in the home of Aquila and Priscilla, a Jewish couple who had been expelled from Rome by the anti-Semitic edict of Claudius in 49 A.D. It is not known whether they had already heard of Christianity in Rome (according to the Roman historian Suetonius, the emperor's edict had resulted from agitation among the Jews over Christian teachings) or whether they were introduced to it in Corinth, but these two became Paul's staunch helpers. A warm friendship sprang up among them, a joy to the apostle the rest of his life. Paul supported himself by his own labor, that no shadow be cast on his motive or mission; since his hosts were also tentmakers, he

403

worked with them. His own words tell us how conscientiously he and his companions toiled at their trade: "Neither did we eat any man's bread for nought; but wrought with labour and travail night and day, that we might not be chargeable to any of you" (II Th. 3:8; compare II Cor. 11:9).

Every Sabbath Paul spoke in the Corinthian synagogue, winning over many Jews and Greeks to Christianity. His whole bearing and manner of approach to his subject were in marked contrast to those at Athens; he still felt the sting of Athenian indifference. Profiting by that discouraging experience, he refrained from all reference to Greek philosophies and confined himself wholly to the simple, unadorned message of the cross. Later he wrote to the Corinthians: "I . . . came not with excellency of speech or of wisdom, declaring unto you the testimony of God. For I determined not to know any thing among you, save Jesus Christ, and him crucified. . . . And my speech and my preaching was not with enticing words of man's wisdom, but in demonstration of the Spirit and of power. . . ." (I Cor. 2:1-4; compare 1:17,18).

Silas and Timothy now rejoined Paul at Corinth. Timothy brought good news of the steadfastness of the Thessalonian church under persecution (I Th. 3:6,7). He reported, however, that some members were troubled about certain gospel teachings, especially those relating to the Second Coming of Christ and the resurrection of the dead. Some were anxious about the fate of loved ones who had died since conversion. The prevalent Greek beliefs of that day held no hope of immortality; death was the end. Though living converts now had the hope of resurrection in Christ, what share would those who had died have in the glory of the Second Advent?

Although Paul longed keenly to see the Thessalonian brethren to comfort them in person, it was not safe for him to make the journey because of the animosity still directed against him by his Jewish adversaries in Macedonia (I Th. 2:17,18). The apostle poured out in writing what he would have said could he have come personally, marking the beginning of a new form of activity that was to hold great significance for the future development of the Church. His two letters to the Thessalonians are the first expositions of Christian theology we now possess. These show how, at first hand, Paul taught the gospel to the Gentiles some twenty years after Ascension.

In the first letter are seen the great doctrinal truths of election (1:4), the Trinity (1:1,5), the power of the Holy Ghost (1:5), conversion (1:9), the walk of the Christian (2:12; 4:1), sanctification (4:3,7; 5:22, 23), love (4:9), resurrection (4:14-18), the Day of the Lord (5:1-3), Christ's Second Coming (1:10; 2:19; 3:13; 4:13-17; 5:23). The doctrine of Christ's Coming, the Coming Jesus himself had foretold (Mt. 24:27-31),

is particularly developed in this Pauline epistle

First Epistle to the Thessalonians.

🐚 **Chapter 1** conveys the joy of Paul, Silas, an Timothy in the Thessalonians' conversion an allegiance to Christ, and commends them to a believers in Macedonia and Achaia as shinin examples of faith.

🐚 **Chapter 2** reminds the Thessalonians o the manner in which the gospel was imparted t them—courageously, truthfully, affectionately laboriously—and of their acceptance of it as th Word of God. Paul praises them for their fortitude under persecution, and longs to come t them.

🐚 **Chapter 3** explains his reason for sendin Timothy, expresses again his joy at Timothy' good report of their faith and love, and gives hi earnest prayer for their spiritual growth that the might be perfect in holiness before God at th Coming of Jesus Christ.

🐚 **Chapter 4:1-12** gives practical exhorta tions for the Christian's sanctification: mora purity, brotherly love, honest labor.

In 🐚 **Chapters 4:13-5:11** the apostle take up the subject of Christ's Second Coming t enlighten his readers concerning the state o believers who have died. They could have hop for their loved ones now gone, for with tha Coming would be resurrection, first for "the dea in Christ," then for living believers, all to b "caught up together" to be with Christ foreve The time of Christ's coming in judgment—"th day of the Lord"—is unknown, but it will b sudden; being children of light, believers shoul be vigilant and spiritually prepared for the salva tion to which God has appointed them.

🐚 **Chapter 5:12-28** gives further practica admonitions relating to their present Christian lif as they await the hope of Christ's Coming. Th letter closes with a farewell prayer and bene diction.

Paul was now deeply involved in his ministry i Corinth. "Pressed in the spirit," he continuall preached that Jesus was the promised Messiah. Th malevolence of the Jews that had driven him from cit to city now flared against him here, and when some i the synagogue went so far as to declare Jesus wa accursed—"anathema" (RV I Cor. 12:3)—Paul gave u his attempts to reach them. He shook his clothes t indicate he was through: "Your blood be upon you own heads; I am clean [Weymouth, not responsible] from henceforth I will go unto the Gentiles." Fro this time on he preached in the house of Justus,

Corinthian whose house adjoined the synagogue, and many Corinthians became Christians. Among the converts were the chief ruler of the synagogue, Crispus, with his family; Stephanas with his household; and Gaius, all of them baptized by Paul himself (I Cor. 1:14,16; 16:15). The little church grew, although it was harassed continually by clashes with unbelieving Jews.

In a night vision Paul was encouraged by the voice of Christ: "Be not afraid, but speak, and hold not thy peace: For I am with thee, and no man shall set on thee to hurt thee: for I have much people in this city." So trusting divine direction, he remained in Corinth.

Tidings had reached the apostle that the message in his first letter to the Thessalonians concerning Christ's Coming had been misunderstood. In view of his vivid description of that Coming, some believed it to be imminent. So he wrote again to correct this mistaken idea and detail certain circumstances which were to occur prior to that event, reminding them that this he had told them before.

Second Epistle to the Thessalonians

🙌 **Chapter 1** conveys Paul's joy and gratitude for the marked growth in faith of the Thessalonian church and for their endurance under persecution and trial. He sees in their suffering a token that God, who recompenses tribulation, will avenge His people at Christ's Coming. Paul prays that its members be accounted worthy of their calling.

🙌 **Chapter 2** warns them not to be deceived by any pretended revelation or by a message purported to be from him that Christ's Coming is immediate, explaining that the "day of Christ [RV day of the Lord]" is not yet here, for certain signs must precede that event. There will first be "a falling away [RSV rebellion]" that "that man of sin" who would exalt himself above God and usurp His place and power may be revealed (see Is. 14:12-14). Did they not remember that he had told them this when he was with them?

> **The rebellion** is, strictly speaking, within the church, but the outcome affects the world outside; and evil becomes blatant and dominant in the whole of the inhabited world. This apostasy was one feature of the picture of the future which Paul had drawn for the Thessalonians.
> **The man of lawlessness** is the very embodiment of this evil (cf. John 8:44; the devil "is a liar and the father of lies").[10]

This "mystery of iniquity [RV lawlessness]," Paul points out, is already at work in secret, but when the deceiving satanic nature of the Lawless One, under restraint at present, is fully understood, Christ will come in power and glory to destroy "that Wicked." The followers of the man of sin are doomed, while the followers of Christ are chosen to salvation. Therefore the Thessalonians are to be steadfast in the gospel truths they had been taught.

🙌 **Chapter 3** asks for their prayers that God's message may spread rapidly and its glory be displayed. Paul urges that they wait patiently for Christ's Coming and continue in welldoing. In strong language he reproves the disorderly and idle members of the church, reminding them of the example he and his fellow apostles had set for them. His apostolic benediction.

At the end of eighteen months of increasingly successful preaching in Corinth the animosity of the Jews there erupted in violence and civil action against Paul. His Jewish adversaries rose in a body, seized him, and dragged him before Gallio, the Roman proconsul of Achaia, with the charge "This fellow persuadeth men to worship God contrary to the law." But before Paul could speak a word in his own behalf Gallio refused even to hear the case, recognizing it as a quibble over Jewish theology, not an infringement of Roman law. The Greek bystanders, encouraged by Gallio's contemptuous snub of the accusers, turned on Sosthenes, head of the synagogue, and beat him in the presence of Gallio, but "Gallio cared for none of those things." This impartial Roman justice—in direct contrast to that Paul had received at Philippi—afforded him and the Corinthian church a measure of protection. Paul continued his evangelistic work unmolested for a while longer and the church spread into the surrounding region (Acts 18:18; Rom. 16:1).

In the spring of 54 A.D. Paul sailed from Cenchrea for Jerusalem, having made a vow he hoped to consummate on a coming feast day (perhaps Pentecost). Aquila and Priscilla, probably with others not named, accompanied him to Ephesus, a voyage eastward of eight to ten days across the Aegean Sea. Ephesus was on the west coast of the province of Asia, a province Paul had earlier bypassed under the direction of the Spirit. While his ship lay in harbor Paul preached briefly to his countrymen in the synagogue; when its members urged him to remain, he promised: "I will return again unto you, if God will." Then he sailed for Palestine, leaving Aquila and Priscilla in Ephesus to nurture the seed he had planted.

Paul landed at Caesarea in the summer of 54, traveled to Jerusalem (his fourth visit) and "saluted the church." From there he returned to Syrian Antioch. He had given three years to this second journey and traveled some 3500 miles by land and sea.

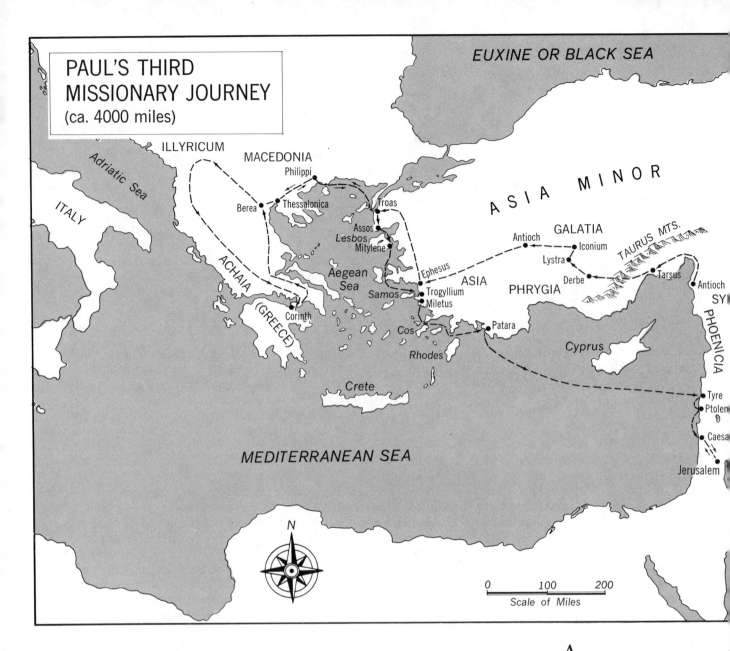

PAUL'S THIRD MISSIONARY JOURNEY
(ca. 4000 miles)

EUXINE OR BLACK SEA

ILLYRICUM MACEDONIA

ASIA MINOR

Adriatic Sea

ITALY

Philippi

Berea Thessalonica

Troas

GALATIA

TAURUS MTS.

Antioch Iconium

Assos
Lesbos
Mitylene

Lystra

ACHAIA

Aegean
Sea

Ephesus ASIA

Derbe

Tarsus

Antioch

PHRYGIA

SY

Corinth

Samos

Trogyllium
Miletus

PHOENICIA

(GREECE)

Cos

Rhodes

Patara

Cyprus

Crete

Tyre
Ptolem

MEDITERRANEAN SEA

Caesa

Jerusalem

N

0   100   200
Scale of Miles

Third Missionary Journey

54-58 A.D.

Started from Syrian Antioch
Galatia and Phrygia
Ephesus, Troas
Macedonia, Illyricum, Corinth
Returned through Macedonia to Philippi
Troas, Assos (in Mysia)
Mitylene (on Lesbos), island of Samos
Trogyllium, Miletus (Asian seaports)
Islands of Coos and Rhodes
Patara (in province of Lycia)
Tyre, Ptolemais (Phoenician seaports)
Caesarea, Jerusalem

Acts 18:23-28   Paul did
not remain long in Syrian Antioch after the close of
the second missionary journey. There was much still
to be done. The apostle was now about fifty; his
abilities were at their height and he was eager to pour
out the spiritual riches of the gospel to the Gentile
world. Leaving Antioch for the last time in the early
autumn of 54, he began his third and longest
missionary journey (a map distance of some 4000 to
4500 miles). His companions when he set out are not
known, but it is quite probable that Timothy was with
him, and possibly Titus. Silas' name disappears from
Luke's record. A ministry in Ephesus was Paul's first
objective since he had promised the Ephesian synagogue he would return. He went directly to Tarsus
412 miles from Antioch; from there he took an inland
route across Asia Minor to Ephesus. This enabled him
to revisit on the way the churches of Derbe, Lystra,
Iconium, and Antioch and to make a circuit through

406

Galatia and Phrygia to revisit the churches he had founded there on his second journey (see p. 398).

To gather contributions for the relief of the Christian poor in Judaea was Paul's second objective, and in Galatia he instituted for this purpose the organizational step of a weekly collection on the first day of the week (I Cor. 16:1-3). The churches of the Christian world later adopted this practice for their own maintenance and for charitable work.

While Paul was overseeing the Galatian and Phrygian churches, the Church gained an eloquent evangelist in the person of Apollos, a cultured Alexandrian Jew who came to Ephesus proclaiming the Messianic hope as taught by John the Baptist. Apollos preached repentance and baptism by water but was apparently ignorant of the baptism of the Holy Ghost. When Aquila and Priscilla heard him in the synagogue, they took him to their home and more fully explained "the way"—a term that had come into use as a designation for Christianity. (The repeated appearance of Priscilla's name in Luke's record underlines the fact that women were already taking active part in church work.) Apollos became a powerful exponent of the gospel. With the encouragement of the Ephesian brethren he extended his mission to Achaia and gave much help to Achaian Christians, convincing many by strong arguments and Scriptural proof that Jesus was the promised Messiah. Paul later found him a valuable co-worker: "I have planted, Apollos watered; but God gave the increase" (I Cor. 3:6; 16:12; Tit. 3:13).

Acts 19

Having completed the tremendous task of overseeing the churches of inner Asia Minor, Paul pushed on to Ephesus. He saw here in this Greek capital of Ionia, now the capital of the large province the Romans called Asia (the western region of modern Turkey), a potential center for the diffusion of Christianity. It was to prove one of the most important scenes of his labors. Ephesus was a celebrated metropolis situated at the mouth of the Cayster River, three miles inland from the Aegean. It had grown enormously wealthy as a result of the heavy trade which flowed into it from the interior of Asia Minor, from the north-south coastal roads, and from the sea lanes of the Mediterranean and the Aegean. Among its heterogeneous population of Asiatics, Ionian Greeks, Romans, and foreign traders was a large Jewish community. Ephesus was Hellenic in culture yet Oriental in religion: a city of astrology, incantations, sorcery, amulets, exorcisms, and every sort of magical imposture. Its principal religious cult was the worship of the Asiatic goddess Diana, whose magnificent temple stood at the head of the harbor. Licentiousness and vice were rampant in the city, and legalized prostitution flourished in the courts of Diana's temple.

The Diana of the Ephesians was neither the Greek goddess Artemis nor the Roman Diana (chaste goddess of the hunt), but a many-breasted Asiatic fertility goddess worshiped by the peoples of Asia Minor long before the development of Greek culture. "Originally a representative of the 'Earth-Goddess' type (familiar to the Aryans and to Mediterranean primitive religions), she was the great Asiatic nursing mother, the patroness of the sexual instinct, and the mother and nurse of gods, men, animals, and plants."[11] Diana's image, believed to have fallen from heaven (possibly a meteorite [Acts 19:35]), was enshrined in her temple. The temple of Paul's time, the fifth built on this site, was more massive than the Athenian Parthenon, and its 127 sixty-foot columns were lavishly carved and painted. For more than two centuries the wealth of Asia Minor had been poured into its building. (Its predecessor, destroyed by fire in 356 B.C., was considered one of the Seven Wonders of the Ancient World.)

Almost immediately upon his arrival in Ephesus Paul met twelve disciples of John the Baptist, strangers to the Christian community, who, like Apollos, were ignorant of baptism in the name of Jesus and of the inspiration of the Holy Spirit that accompanied it. But when Paul explained that John's baptism was one of repentance to prepare men for Christ, for John had preached that men were to believe on Jesus who was to come after him, they readily accepted baptism. When Paul laid his hands on them they were filled with spiritual inspiration.

Paul began his work in the synagogue, teaching there for three months, using argument and persuasion

A drawing of the statue of Diana of the Ephesians. The statue may be seen at the center rear of the photograph on page 413 showing the reconstruction of the temple to Diana at Ephesus. *Popular and Critical Bible Encyclopedia.*

to convince the congregation of the truths of the gospel. As in the past, there eventually arose angry resistance on the part of some, and when disbelievers spoke disparagingly of the new faith Paul openly separated himself and his converts from the synagogue and moved to the lecture hall of Tyrannus (probably a Greek teacher of philosophy). Here for two years Paul daily reasoned and instructed the Jews and Greeks and also went from house to house to explain the good news. He tells how earnestly he ministered to the Ephesians: "Ye know, from the first day that I came into Asia, after what manner I have been with you at all seasons, Serving the Lord with all humility of mind, and with many tears, and temptations, which befell me by the lying in wait of the Jews: And how I kept back nothing that was profitable unto you" (Acts 20:18-20).

His fame soon spread "so that all they which dwelt in Asia heard the word of the Lord Jesus, both Jews and Greeks." Churches were formed in the adjacent cities of Colossae, Hierapolis, and Laodicea through the efforts of Paul, Timothy, and the new converts Epaphras, Archippus, Appia, and Philemon. (Possibly to this period can also be attributed establishment of the churches of Smyrna, Pergamos, Thyatira, Sardis, and Philadelphia, mentioned in Revelation 1:11.)

God was glorified not only in Paul's preaching but also in his works of healing in the name of Jesus. So great was the people's faith in his ability to heal that they brought handkerchiefs and garments for him to touch and carried them to the sick, "and the disease departed from them, and the evil spirits went out o them."

One of the prevalent evils Christianity en countered in Ephesus was that of exorcism—the driving out of demons from the human body by mean of magic formulas, incantations, or repetition o certain names.

To get control over a demon, it was necessary to know its name (cp. Mark 5:9) or to invoke the name of a superio power or spirit. Josephus (*Ant.* VIII. ii.5) relates how an exorcist, named Eleazar, when expelling a demon in the presence of Vespasian, invoked the name of Solomon. The great magical Papyrus of the third century, in the Biblio theque Nationale of Paris, gives spells in which the names o Abraham, Isaac, and Jacob, and of Jesus, God of the Hebrews, are used. [12]

When itinerant Jews who practiced exorcism for profi saw the amazing miracles which followed Paul' utterance of the name *Jesus* they attempted to imitat him. The seven sons of the priest Sceva tried to driv an evil spirit out of a man with the incantation "W adjure you by Jesus whom Paul preacheth." But th man answered, "Jesus I know, and Paul I know; bu who are ye?" and, turning on them, overpowere them, so that the seven fled "naked and wounded."

This exposé of the profane use of Jesus' nam

discredited the practice of exorcism in Ephesus. Many who had used magical arts gave them up, brought their books of magic and publicly burned them—the total worth almost 50,000 pieces of silver ($10,000).

> **Their books,** i.e., documents inscribed with magical spells and charms. Such "Ephesian letters," as they were called, were famous the world over, and were credited with sovereign efficacy in averting ill luck. [13]

It was a striking victory for Christianity and for Paul. Luke records the rapid growth of the Church simply: "So mightily grew the word of God and prevailed."

While the gospel was triumphing in Ephesus Paul received disheartening word that some of the Christians in Corinth had lapsed into the immorality for which this Greek city was notorious, without rebuke from their fellow Christians.* This caused him much anxiety; this church, from which he had been absent for nearly three years, occupied a special place in his affection. (He had spent more than a year and a half in Corinth on his preceding journey both founding and working in this church, and it was one of major importance in Europe.) As its founder, Paul felt compelled to write its members to separate themselves from the world and be obedient to Christian principles, "not to company with fornicators." This letter has been lost, but Paul refers to it in a later one (I Cor. 5:9).

The message was received with poor grace. A few of the Corinthians misunderstood; they took him too literally and cut themselves off from contact with the outside world. Others continued their association with those of immoral or wicked conduct—both within and without the church—even eating with such persons either in private or at the communal meal (I Cor.

---

*Here we begin to see the first of the many serious church problems with which Paul had to deal as an apostle to the Gentiles:
Christian ethics
Christian fellowship and unity
Factions
Insubordination to apostolic authority
Worldliness
Asceticism
Judaism and its relation to converts
Circumcision
Segregation
Resurrection of the dead
Day of Christ
Personal ambitions
False teachers
False gospels, Greek philosophies, Gnosticism
Idolatry
Non-essentials
Fear of suffering and persecution
Proper use of spiritual gifts
Social question of slavery
Civil obedience
Place of women in the Church
Marriage, and its sanctity
Duties of a pastor

5:9-11; 8:9,10). Paul was somewhat cheered, however, by the arrival of three Corinthian friends (Stephanas, Fortunatus, and Achaicus) who by their faithfulness refreshed his spirit in an otherwise painful situation (I Cor. 16:17,18).

Another serious disorder in the Corinthian church was brought to Paul's attention—the rise of factions in the congregation (I Cor. 1:11). The members had divided themselves into four parties, each asserting allegiance to a favorite teacher: some to Paul, some to Apollos, others to Cephas (Peter), still others to Christ. Paul at once saw the danger—attachment to personalities would adulterate Christ's gospel. He sent Timothy and Erastus (possibly the same prominent official mentioned in Romans 16:23) as his emissaries overland through Macedonia to Corinth to remind this

Ruins of the Temple of Diana at Sardis (Turkey). Turkish Tourism and Information Office.

church, as its founder, of his example as a Christian teacher and of his methods of teaching, that this spirit of disruption might be healed (I Cor. 4:17).

Shortly after their departure Paul sent Titus and a companion to Corinth by sea with a letter, our First Corinthians (II Cor. 12:18). Titus' mission on this trip was not only to carry Paul's directives and aid in harmonizing the church, but evidently also to organize weekly collections for the poor of Jerusalem (I Cor. 16:1,2; II Cor. 8:6). By his apostolic persuasion and discipline Paul hoped to win that church back to loyalty to Christ before Timothy arrived there (I Cor. 16:10,11). Though the tone of the letter was occasionally severe, it was strongly loving: "I write not these things to shame you, but as my beloved sons I warn you. For though ye have ten thousand instructors in Christ, yet have ye not many fathers: for in Christ Jesus I have begotten you through the gospel. Wherefore I beseech you, be ye followers of me" (I Cor. 4:14-16).

First Epistle to the Corinthians

🕊 Chapters 1-4 are concerned with the divisive party spirit rending the Corinthian church. 🕊 Chapter 1 makes an appeal for unity, rebukes partisan divisions and the following of human leaders. Paul reminds the Corinthians that they were baptized in Christ's name and saved through his crucifixion. Should they be putting other names before Christ's? He reproves those who would boast of a worldly wisdom, showing that the cross of Christ alone is the power and wisdom of God; they should glory in God alone. In 🕊 Chapter 2 Paul further reminds his readers that he had come to them with but one thought—to let them be persuaded of the gospel message. He had not employed any eloquence of his own or worldly wisdom but had relied on the truths of the Spirit and the power of God to convince them, for he desired their faith to rest in that power. Among mature Christians he does speak wisdom, not a wisdom of this world but a wisdom of God that before had been hidden in mystery. Christians do know the blessings that God gives those who love Him—these have been revealed to them by the Spirit of God—and these things he speaks of in spiritual terms, "comparing spiritual things [truths] with spiritual." One who has "the mind of Christ" can discern these things. In 🕊 Chapter 3 he points out that because of their spiritual immaturity he had given them only the milk of the Word, nor does he yet find them strong enough to partake of the solid food of the truth. Does not their carnal-mindedness, manifest in envying, strife, and divisions, show them to be

spiritually immature? Ministers of the Word such as he and Apollos are only instruments of God to advance His Church. Jesus Christ is the one foundation, and Christians should take heed to build their lives thereon, for their work will be tried by fire. What they build is the temple of God and is to be kept undefiled. Let no one deceive himself and boast in human wisdom or in human teachers—"for all things are your's; Whether Paul, or Apollos, or Cephas, or the world, or life, or death, or things present, or things to come; all are your's; And ye are Christ's and Christ is God's." 🕊 Chapter 4 asks the Corinthians to consider what a teacher really is—a steward of the truths of God. As to the merits of Apollos and himself, Paul does not judge; God is the judge. He and Apollos furnish true examples of stewardship. With keen irony Paul rebukes the smug superiority of the Corinthians—the satisfaction in their human teachers and their "fancied spiritual attainments in knowledge"—contrasting it with the suffering and slander he and his fellow apostles are undergoing. As its founding father he lovingly entreats this church to follow his example; he is sending Timothy to remind them of his Christian conduct as a teacher. He promises to come shortly and warns that, if necessary, he will exercise his apostolic authority.

🕊 Chapter 5 rebukes the church for not exercising disciplinary measures in a case of gross immorality by one of its members—an instance that had not even disturbed its conscience—and demands the excommunication of the guilty person for his own good and that of the church. (Paul had already warned in a previous letter to have no association with immoral or sinful persons.) He now clarifies this point: he had not meant that they utterly forego contacts with such persons, for then they would be compelled to go wholly out of the world, but that they are not to "keep company" or even eat with any believer who has given himself over to fornication, covetousness, idolatry, drunkenness, reviling, or extortion. The church must purge itself.

🕊 Chapter 6 reprimands church members for the serious fault of litigating their quarrels with one another in secular courts before unbelievers instead of settling their disputes before an arbitrator chosen from among their own ranks. A deeper fault is pointed out—they should not have lawsuits with one another at all. It is better to suffer wrong than to wrong another. Did they not know that the unrighteous—fornicators, idolators, adulterers, perverts, thieves, drunkards, extortioners—would not inherit the kingdom of God? Such had been some of them, but through baptism they had been sanctified and cleansed of these errors and were now endeavoring to live pure lives. Enlarging on the subject of sanctification, Paul quotes a saying current among some of them: "[Ye say], all things are lawful unto me." The Corinthians apparently felt that though they no longer ate food consecrated to idols they were free to indulge the appetite. Paul refutes this view as one merely leading to another form of idolatry. He acknowledges that, granting all things are lawful to him (compare I Cor. 8:4), they are nevertheless not good for him, and he refuses to let himself be brought under their influence. He explains that the body is holy—it does not exist for gratification but for the service of Christ. The Corinthians are warned not to sin against their bodies, for their bodies are "members of Christ" and "temples" of the Spirit.

🔊 **Chapter 7** answers the Corinthians' apparent question on marriage, giving the apostle's views on marriage and celibacy, the duties of husband and wife, and his advice to both married and unmarried. Paul upholds marriage as an honorable estate, not a sin, regarding it as a necessity for mankind as a moral safeguard against fornication. He advises marriage as a general rule, to be mutually observed in love, but he recommends celibacy, which leaves a person freer of the cares of the world that one "may attend upon the Lord without distraction" (I Cor. 7; Eph. 5:22-33). To those married to unbelievers he recommends that they stay together if possible; if they cannot, let the unbelieving partner go in peace. As he counsels that the Christians force no break in the marriage relationship because of their calling to serve Christ, so he urges Christians not to rupture any other part of the social fabric of their lives—whether they be circumcised, uncircumcised, slave, married, unmarried—but that they continue in their present state, loving God and doing His will where they are.

🔊 **Chapters 8:1-11:1** answer the question of the propriety of eating meats that had been offered to idols. Those who have one God know that an idol is nothing. They know, too, that such meats in themselves can make men neither better nor worse. Nevertheless seasoned Christians should not put temptation in the way of a brother in the faith who does not have this knowledge and maturity, for if that one sees them eating in an idol's temple, will he not be influenced to do the same even though his conscience tells him he is sinning? Through a lack of wisdom and self-discipline they may cause a weaker brother—one "for whom Christ died"—to

perish. When they so sin against the brethren they sin against Christ. He points to the self-disciplined athlete of the Greek games to illustrate the abstinence required of Christians who are running the race of faith to gain not a perishable wreath but an "incorruptible" crown. Paul so runs, keeping his body in subjection. The Corinthians are warned against false confidence: were not some of their forefathers (all of them "baptized unto Moses" and nourished with spiritual meat and drink) tempted to idolatry and discontent, and as a result severely punished? He entreats his Corinthian friends to abstain from sacrificial feasts to idols. Do not the "cup" Christians bless and the "bread" Christians break mean communion with Christ? To eat the meats Gentiles offer to idols is wholly incompatible with their partaking of the Eucharist—"Ye cannot drink the cup of the Lord, and the cup of devils: ye cannot be partakers of the Lord's table, and of the table of devils" (I Cor. 10:21; compare Mt. 6:24). Therefore whatever they eat or drink or do let it be for the glory of God and the edification of others. "Be ye followers of me, even as I also am of Christ."

🔊 **Chapter 11:2-34** corrects those disorders in church worship that have come to Paul's attention. He rebukes the practice of women worshiping with unveiled heads at church services and of men worshiping with covered heads. Supporting his view by a general principle of subordination of woman to man and of man to Christ, he lays down a rule that women should cover their heads in church and that men should uncover theirs. (In Paul's time respectable women did not appear publicly unveiled in either Greece or the East.) He also rebukes the dissensions in church meetings and the abuse of the Lord's Supper, reminding them of the origin, significance, and sacredness of this meal.

In 🔊 **Chapter 12** he enlightens the Corinthian believers on the subject of "spiritual gifts." First of all, let it be understood that no one inspired by the Spirit of God blasphemes Christ, and no one acknowledges Jesus as Lord unless he is influenced by the Spirit. From the one Spirit comes the rich variety of talents they possess— spiritual wisdom and knowledge, faith, power to heal and to work miracles, inspired utterances, discernment of good and evil (compare I Jn. 4:1), languages and the interpretations of languages. All is the work of the one Spirit. Therefore they should not undervalue their own gift or envy another's. Every member with his special talent is as essential to the Church of Christ as each member of the body is to the whole human body.

"Just as the differences of powers and functions are a great advantage to the body, so the existence of different gifts benefits the Church. The position of each individual, his possession of this or that gift, has been ordered by God."[14] "Now ye are the body of Christ, and members in particular." It is right, however, for one to desire the best gifts, for one's spiritual growth and that of the Church. Having pointed out that envy, rivalry, and depreciation of others' spiritual gifts would not help the follower of Christ to reach the goal of spiritual perfection, Paul says, "I [show] unto you a more excellent way," and then he gives his glorious exposition on love (AV charity).

🙷 Chapter 13 has been called the New Testament psalm of love. It is a declaration of love in action. No gift, however excellent—neither prophecy, nor knowledge, nor faith—is anything without this pre-eminent grace. Paul describes this "way" which transcends all others (Moffatt's translation): "Love is very patient, very kind. Love knows no jealousy; love makes no parade, gives itself no airs, is never rude, never selfish, never irritated, never resentful; love is never glad when others go wrong, love is gladdened by goodness, always slow to expose, always eager to believe the best, always hopeful, always patient. Love never disappears." Love is everlasting; the gifts of prophecy, tongues, and knowledge are transitory, helpful now in our present state, but unneeded when at last we come into full communion with God.

In 🙷 Chapter 14 Paul urges church members first to cultivate this spirit of love, then to develop spiritual talents—particularly that of inspired preaching for the edification of the Church. (It appears that the Corinthian church prided itself in a gift of tongues which took the form of ecstatic utterances.) Paul did not forbid this phenomenon, but he did warn against its abuse. To speak in such a manner when there was no interpreter present would not edify the congregation. And let each speak one by one. Let women be silent. "Let all things be done decently and in order."

In 🙷 Chapter 15 Paul abruptly changes to a new subject. Having heard that some in the church were denying the resurrection of the body, he repeats the truth he had preached to them before, that Christ had risen from the dead, substantiating this fact with the eyewitness testimony of the Twelve and of the five hundred who had seen Jesus after the Resurrection. To deny the resurrection of the dead, Paul points out, is to deny Christ's resurrection, thereby making Christian faith useless—Christ's rising constitutes the pledge that all will rise. He discusses the manner of the resurrection and the nature of the resurrection body, using the analogy of seed and its fruit, showing the necessity for a transformation of the human nature to the spiritual, the laying aside of "the corruptible" for "the incorruptible," that sin and death may be overcome (vvs. 35-55); see p. 448. He rejoices that this victory can be won through Christ and exhorts the Corinthians to be steadfast and firm in faith.

🙷 Chapter 16 concerns the collection for the Christian brethren at Jerusalem, Paul's future plans to come to Corinth, his personal greetings and benediction.

About this time Paul appears to have made a second trip to Corinth, a short one by sea from Ephesus (not mentioned in Acts but implied in Second Corinthians 12:14; 13:1), one that left the apostle heavy-hearted. He appears, too, upon his return to Ephesus to have written the Corinthians another letter, severe in tone (II Cor. 2:3,4; 7:8), "out of much affliction and anguish of heart . . . with many tears," denouncing the false teachers in the area around Corinth and strongly defending his apostleship. (This third letter has not survived; some scholars hold that the tenth to the thirteenth chapters of our Second Corinthians are a portion of it.)

The apostle had been in Ephesus nearly three years and had seen Christianity firmly established in the province of Asia. Luke now gives his readers a glimpse into Paul's plan for the further evangelization of the Gentiles. He "purposed in the spirit, when he had passed through Macedonia and Achaia, to go to Jerusalem, saying, After I have been there, I must also see Rome." But there was still work to be done before he could leave: "I will tarry at Ephesus until Pentecost. For a great door and effectual is opened unto me, and there are many adversaries" (I Cor. 16:8,9).

Luke had made no mention of persecution in Ephesus up to this time other than the opposition that had forced Paul to move his seat of teaching from the synagogue to the school of Tyrannus. He does, however, record one trial Paul faced from Gentile enemies toward the end of his ministry in that city.

It will be remembered that the principal religious cult at Ephesus was the worship of Diana (see p. 407). An inevitable clash arose between this Diana-worship and Christianity. As the result of the depressing effect of Paul's preaching on Diana-worship, an uprising broke out among certain Ephesians whose livelihood was the making of silver models of Diana's great shrine. Demetrius, a silversmith, led the attack. He assembled his fellow craftsmen and harangued them:

Reconstruction of Temple of Diana, Ephesus. Drawings Collection Royal Institute of British Architects.

"Sirs, ye know that by this craft we have our wealth. Moreover ye see and hear, that not alone at Ephesus, but almost throughout all Asia, this Paul hath persuaded and turned away much people, saying that they be no gods, which are made with hands: So that not only this our craft is in danger to be set at nought; but also that the temple of the great goddess Diana should be despised, and her magnificence should be destroyed, whom all Asia and the world worshippeth."

The assembly of artisans, infuriated by this affront to Diana and this threat to their profits, broke into a chant: "Great is Diana of the Ephesians"; others soon took up the cry. Rioting began. The growing crowd rushed into the city's huge amphitheater (seating about 25,000), dragging with them Gaius and Aristarchus, two of Paul's Macedonian traveling companions. Paul wanted to enter the arena and speak to the people but his friends restrained him. As the crowd milled around in confusion—some shouting one thing, some another—the Jews, fearing that they would be accused of instigating this disturbance, sent forward a Jew named Alexander to clear them of possible blame. But the Ephesians drowned him out and for two hours shouted their praise of Diana.

Finally the recorder—the official responsible for law and order in the city—calmed the people, declaring that nothing could disturb the greatness of Diana, but adding that these preachers were not disreputable men who had broken any law: "Ye have brought hither these men . . . neither robbers of churches, nor yet blasphemers of your goddess. Wherefore if Demetrius, and the craftsmen . . . have a matter against any man, the law is open, and there are deputies." With these words he dismissed the assembly.

Luke is silent about other dangers to which Paul was exposed during his long stay in Ephesus, but Paul did recall these perils vividly in writing to the Corinthians and the Romans and spoke of his antagonists as having been as ferocious as wild beasts so that he was in constant danger of death: "We would not, brethren, have you ignorant of our trouble which came to us in Asia, that we were pressed out of measure, above strength, insomuch that we despaired even of life: But we had the sentence of death in ourselves, that we should not trust in ourselves, but in

Theater at Ephesus, 495 feet in diameter, capable of seating 25,000. Here occurred the riot led by Demetrius against Paul. A marble street 36 feet wide and 1735 feet long leads to the harbor, now silted up. Ewing Galloway.

God which raiseth the dead" (II Cor. 1:8,9; see I Cor. 15:30-32). Priscilla and Aquila are mentioned as having "laid down [RSV risked] their own necks" to save his life (Rom. 16:4).

Acts 20:1-3   Soon after the clash with Demetrius Paul parted warmly from his Christian friends, and in the early summer of 57 left Ephesus for Corinth. He traveled northward by way of Troas with Gaius and Aristarchus. He hoped Titus would meet him there with some word of the Corinthians' response to his stern letter, but when Titus did not arrive he had no peace of mind, and so went on to Macedonia (II Cor. 2:12,13).

On his first journey through Macedonia five years earlier persecution had restricted his efforts to the cities of Philippi, Thessalonica, and Berea. During his absence, however, the seed he had planted had taken firm root and now, meeting less resistance, Paul evangelized other cities of Macedonia, going as far northwest as the Roman province of Illyricum on the Adriatic coast. This circuit alone was at least 400 miles. Only a glimpse of his labors and triumphs is given us in the brief passages of Acts 20:2 and Romans 15:19.

Sometime during this period Titus rejoined him, bringing a favorable report of the Corinthian church. When Paul learned of their repentance and of their love for him, his spirit was lightened considerably (II Cor. 7:6,7). His faith in this church vindicated, Paul wrote its members again, justifying once more his apostolic ministry in an effort to end any remaining disloyalty to Christ—a letter that reveals the depths of his love and concern. Titus and two other faithful workers carried his message back to Corinth (II Cor. 8:16-19).

Second Epistle to the Corinthians

🙖 **Chapters 1:1-2:13** open with an apostolic greeting which includes thanksgiving for divine comfort and deliverance from some terrible trouble he had experienced in Asia which had brought him close to death, so nearly so that he had lost all hope of surviving. He asks their prayers for his continued preservation. He explains the reason for his delay in coming to them: he would not come in a rebuking spirit. He could not feel sorry for the severity of the letter he had written because it had made them repent, and he now gladly forgives the penitent offender he had previously censured (I Cor. 5:3-5). Let them also forgive the offender lest he be lost to the church. He reveals his past anxiety, for when he had come to Troas and Titus did not arrive with a report regarding them he had left a successful ministry in that city to press on to Macedonia.

🙖 **Chapters 2:14-6:10** relate the glory, joy, and sustaining inspiration of Paul's apostolic ministry. 🙖 **Chapter 2:14-17** tells of his successful work in Macedonia after he had received Titus' good news of the repentance of the Corinthian church. 🙖 **Chapters 3:1-4:6** answer the charges of Judaizing preachers who had impugned his doctrine and questioned Paul's credentials as an apostle. He declares he needs no letter of recommendation. The Corinthians are his best recommendation, indeed a letter of Christ, who through his labors have the Spirit of God written on their hearts, known and read by everyone. God has made him an able minister of the new covenant which is not a rigid written code (the letter which kills) but a spirit which is life-giving. He declares the ministry of condemnation (the Law of Moses) was glorious but asserts that the ministry of righteousness (the Gospel) exceeds it in glory. He speaks plainly, not as Moses who "veiled from them [the Children of Israel] the fact that the glory [of the old covenant] fades in Christ" (Moffatt). The covering that is still on their hearts can only be taken away in Christ. When men turn to the Lord—to Spirit—the veil will be lifted. In the presence of Spirit is liberty. And "we all" with unveiled faces, seeing the glory of Spirit, are being transformed into the same image "from glory to glory." He is preaching this gospel openly and honestly; it is not his gospel but Christ's, and he is Christ's servant. In 🙖 **Chapter 4:7-18** Paul asserts that this treasure, "the light of the knowledge of the glory of God" which comes through the life of Jesus, has been entrusted to him, a weak "earthen vessel," so all men may see that its power belongs to God. In his ministry he has been often hard pressed and suffered much, but divine power has sustained him and he ever holds to the glorious hope of resurrection. Therefore he is not discouraged; though these afflictions have weakened his body, his spirit has been constantly strengthened. His light and transitory suffering is winning for him a substantial and eternal glory. 🙖 **Chapter 5:1-10** continues Paul's expectation of immortality as he declares his confident hope of a spiritual body—"a house not made with hands, eternal in the heavens." His desire is always "to be absent" from the temporal frame and "to be present with the Lord," that he might be acceptable to him, for all must appear before Christ's judgment seat. 🙖 **Chapters 5:11-6:10** explain that because of this judgment that lies before all, he is laboring to persuade men, and love for Christ is his compelling motive. He is convinced that Jesus' death for all men made his death theirs, and this death was for the purpose of making the living live not to themselves but to the crucified and resurrected Christ. "Therefore if any man be in Christ, he is a new creature: old things are passed away; behold, all things are become new." This ministry of reconciliation of men to God through Christ has been given to him. He and his fellow workers come as ambassadors in Christ's stead, in all things endeavoring to be exemplary ministers—in patient endurance of afflictions and hardship, watchful prayer, blameless character, with spiritual power promoting and defending the truth.

In 🙖 **Chapters 6:11-7:1** Paul assures the Corinthians of his deep love for them and appeals for a similar affection from them. He has withheld nothing, but they have been restrained in their attitude toward him. He interrupts his appeal for mutual love to urge that they make no close ties of any kind with unbelievers because this might lead to compromise with or complicity in evil—for what fellowship has righteousness with unrighteousness, and what communion has light with darkness, and what agreement has the temple of God with idols? Are they not "the temple of the living God?" As such, it is imperative that they fulfill the Scriptural requirement to separate themselves from "the unclean thing"—from everything that might tempt them to idolatry and immorality.

Chapter 7:2-16 continues the apostle's plea for their love and reveals his intense relief and great joy at Titus' good report of their godly sorrow, which has resulted in genuine repentance over past errors and disloyalties. "Now I rejoice, not that ye were made sorry, but that ye sorrowed to repentance.... For behold this selfsame thing, that ye sorrowed after a godly sort, what carefulness it wrought in you, yea, what clearing of yourselves, yea, what indignation, yea, what fear, yea, what vehement desire, yea, what zeal, yea, what revenge! In all things ye have approved yourselves to be clear in this matter."

Chapters 8-9 enjoin liberality in the Corinthians' contributions for the Jerusalem church, teach the Christian grace of giving, and mention Titus' new mission to Corinth to collect their gifts.

In **Chapters 10-13** the tone becomes stern as Paul rebukes the Corinthians' revolt against him and as he vigorously vindicates his apostleship. (Because of this sharp change from a warm, friendly relationship with the church and the thankful relief that all was well [chaps. 1-9], scholars believe that these remaining chapters are a portion of the "severe" third letter [see p. 412].) **Chapter 10** is a defense of Paul's apostleship. In it he answers a slanderous charge that he is a coward when among them, but bold at a distance. In the meek and gentle spirit of Christ he begs them not to make it necessary for him to be stern when he comes, otherwise he is minded to speak plainly to those who believe him impelled by worldly motives. True he lives in the flesh, but he does not conduct his ministry on a merely human basis. In his warfare for Christ he does not use worldly weapons but spiritual weapons which are "mighty through God to the pulling down of strong holds"—deceptive theories, imaginings, and any rampart raised against the knowledge of God. He fights to bring "into captivity every thought to the obedience of Christ." They will find him bold to punish the disobedient. He refuses to compare himself with boastful teachers who are trying to take over his ministry; he knows that Corinth is included in his sphere of labor. Therefore he claims the Corinthians as his converts; in fact he entertains the hope that they will work with him in spreading the gospel to regions beyond Corinth. In **Chapter 11** Paul gives a forced commendation of himself—his zeal, love, humility—because he is anxious lest some may still be drawn away from their "espousal" to Christ by Judaizing teachers. As a Hebrew and an Israelite he is the equal of such teachers; as a minister of Christ he is far their superior—the numerous sufferings and perils he has undergone for the gospel and his daily "care" of the churches bear him witness. If he must "boast [RV glory]," it will be of the labors and reproaches he has sustained for the name of Christ. **Chapter 12:1-18** continues his unwilling recommendation of himself in which he relates an exalting vision that transported him to the realm of heaven; it also confides the humiliating trial of a bodily infirmity that had brought him to a greater reliance on Christ's grace. He rebukes the Corinthian church for compelling him to vindicate himself when so many signs of his apostleship are evident. In **Chapters 12:19-13:14** Paul explains that his appeal has not been in his own defense but for their edification, for he fears that when he comes to them he will still find errors and vices which have not been corrected so that severe measures may be necessary. He exhorts them to examine themselves to see if they are true believers: he desires only their perfection. Farewell greeting and benediction.

Only the apostle's affection for the Corinthian church and his desire to heal it had compelled him to confide the two heretofore untold personal experiences of chapter 12. His first confidence, a wonderful revelation of paradise which he had treasured silently for many years, is testimony to his own high attainment in communion with God: "I knew a man in Christ above fourteen years ago, (whether in the body, I cannot tell; or whether out of the body, I cannot tell: God knoweth;) such an one caught up to the third heaven. . . . How that he was caught up into paradise, and heard unspeakable words, which it is not lawful for a man to utter. Of such an one will I glory: yet of myself I will not glory, but in mine infirmities" (II Cor. 12:2-5). Dummelow paraphrases verses 2, 3, and 4:

(2) Fourteen years ago I experienced such a divine ecstasy that I knew not whether I was still in the flesh or whether I had been translated to another sphere. (3) I

repeat, I did not know in what state of being I was; (4) but I had a divine revelation which caused me unspeakable joy and taught me truths too deep for words to express. [15]

Paul's second confidence was of a different sort, a testimony to the power and grace of Christ. A bodily affliction had plagued him, or was possibly still plaguing him at times, but it had only served to keep him humble and to draw him closer to Christ, for in Christ he found strength for his weakness: "Lest I should be exalted above measure through the abundance of the revelations, there was given to me a thorn in the flesh, the messenger of Satan to buffet me. . . . For this thing I besought the Lord thrice, that it might depart from me. And he said unto me, My grace is sufficient for thee: for my strength is made perfect in weakness. Most gladly therefore will I rather glory in my infirmities, that the power of Christ may rest upon me" (II Cor. 12:7-9; compare Gal. 4:13,14).

Luke the physician never divulged the nature of this "thorn," nor did Paul. For years there had run through Paul's writings a recurrent note of sadness for his part in Stephen's martyrdom when he had stood by "consenting unto his death, and kept the raiment of them that slew him." Also there was continuing sorrow for his blind hatred and cruelty toward Christians before his conversion, indicated in his letter to the Galatians: "Ye have heard of my conversation in time past in the Jews' religion, how that beyond measure I persecuted the church of God, and wasted it" (Gal. 1:13; see Acts 26:9,10; I Tim. 1:13). The thorn in his flesh could well have had its roots in his regret and remorse. But this prick of conscience lessened as he found joy in selfless service and love of Christ and as he put the past behind him (Phil. 3:13,14). There are statements of Paul that imply a release: "The law of the Spirit of life in Christ Jesus hath made me free from the law of sin and death" (Rom. 8:2). "I can do all things through Christ which strengtheneth me" (Phil. 4:13).

Toward the close of 57 A.D., after Paul and his companions had finished gathering the Macedonian donations for the Jerusalem church and completed the circuit into Illyricum, they came southward through Greece to Corinth (Acts 20:3). Luke records nothing of the Corinthians' reception of their mentor; the difficulties that had so troubled the church were apparently fully resolved, and Paul's subsequent letters never alluded to any further discipline of its membership. Words he later wrote to the Galatians with reference to the Law could well be applied to his silence on this subject: "If I build again the things which I destroyed, I make myself a transgressor" (Gal. 2:18). We learn from his letters, however, that he renewed many friendships there (see Rom. 16:21-23).

Paul wintered three months in Corinth. During this time he not only taught in the metropolitan church but probably also visited the neighboring churches of Achaia. He concerned himself as well with completing the collection of contributions for the Christians of Palestine that Achaian Christians had been laying aside for more than a year and that now constituted a considerable sum (I Cor. 16:2; II Cor. 8:10; 9:2). The outstanding literary achievements of this brief period were his Epistle to the Galatians (some scholars place the writing at Ephesus prior to this Corinthian visit) and his Epistle to the Romans, the first letters to expound the great doctrines of the Christian system.

The occasion of Paul's circular letter to the churches of Galatia (see p. 398) was the disturbing news that Judaizing teachers were undermining his apostolic authority by claiming his dependence on others for his knowledge of the Master, since he had not known Jesus the man, and leading the Galatians away from the gospel Paul had taught them. Despite the ruling of the Council of Jerusalem, these teachers were insisting on the keeping of Judaic law, particularly the rite of circumcision, as necessary to the attainment of salvation. This led to controversy and bickering within the church.

The purpose of the Epistle to the Galatians was to counteract the insidious influence that taught reliance on the Law for salvation rather than on Christ's grace, and to bring the Galatian churches back to loyal adherence to the true gospel. In this letter are developed the great Christian doctrines of grace and justification by faith. Other basic truths of the gospel are briefly alluded to: the working of the Spirit in the believer (3:2,3,5; 5:22-25), the incarnation (4:4); the crucifixion (6:12,14).

Epistle to the Galatians

Chapters 1-2 affirm Paul's apostolic authority. He expresses his amazement that the Galatians have so soon turned away from the gospel of faith and grace he had taught them. He defends his gospel as having come to him not from men but by direct revelation from the risen Christ and asserts that at no time had he been dependent on the apostles for his apostolic training. In fact he had withdrawn to Arabia after his conversion, then returned to Damascus to preach; three years later he had visited Jerusalem briefly, seeing only Peter and James; after that he had preached in distant Syria and Cilicia, still free of supervision by the church in Jerusalem. He also cites the independent stand he had taken at the Council of Jerusalem for the freedom of Gentile believers from the bondage of the Law and the recognition of his coordinate apostleship by the Twelve. Far from being a subordinate apostle, he had even rebuked Peter on one occasion for compromising Christian principles by withdrawing from the table of the Gentiles at Antioch to eat with the Jews. Turning to the subject of salvation, Paul points out the inconsistency of expecting to be justified by the works of the Law when justification can come only by faith in Christ. He declares his own renunciation of the dead works of the Law and his sole reliance upon the living Christ.

🐦 **Chapter 3** explains Paul's doctrine of justification by faith (one of his clearest expositions of this subject, see p.451). He appeals to the Galatians' own experience: what legitimate reason could they give for turning to the works of the Law for salvation? Had they not already received the gift of the Spirit by faith: even as Abraham believed God and was justified by his faith? Because they are the children of faith, they are the children of Abraham and are blessed with faithful Abraham—acceptable to God. Those depending on the works of the Law (legalism) for salvation come under the curse of that law (Deut. 27:26)—but Christ has redeemed men from this curse that all, Jew and Gentile, might be justified (accepted) through faith. Paul maintains that just as a covenant made between men cannot be annulled or added to once it has been confirmed, so God's covenant made with Abraham and his seed—Christ—cannot be abrogated through the Law which came four hundred and thirty years later. The Law, added because of transgressions, came through a mediator (Moses) and was the "schoolmaster" to bring men to Christ. Christians, having been baptized into Christ, are already the children of God and so heirs of the Abrahamic promise.

🐦 **Chapter 4** continues the subject of justification by faith. Christ's redemptive work brings them as sons of God into their full heritage. The apostle makes a personal appeal to the Galatians to return to the gospel of faith. By the allegory of the bondwoman Hagar and her son Ishmael, born of the flesh, and the free woman Sarah (Abraham's wife) and her son Isaac, born by promise, he illustrates that Christ's followers are, figuratively, descendants of Sarah—accepted as sons and heirs. As Sarah was commanded to cast out the bondwoman and her son, so the Galatians are to turn away from the covenant of the Law that engenders bondage to the covenant of grace that makes free.

🐦 **Chapter 5** contains Paul's exhortation to stand fast in the liberty that is in Christ Jesus and "be not entangled again with the yoke of bondage." If Christians accept circumcision—in other words, bind themselves to legalism as essential to salvation—they become debtors to the whole Law, and Christ avails them nothing. It is by the Spirit, through faith, active in love, that Christians wait for the hope of righteousness. They had been doing well; what has hindered them from obeying the truth? They have been called to freedom; not for license but for serving one another in love, for the whole Law is fulfilled in the one precept "Thou shalt love thy neighbour as thyself." The backbiting and hatefulness they are manifesting toward each other will be their undoing. Instead, they are to be governed by Spirit; then they will not indulge the lusts of the flesh, since the flesh is the antithesis of the Spirit. He warns of the evils of the flesh and contrasts these with the virtues of the Spirit, against which there is no law, and concludes, "If we live in the Spirit, let us also walk in the Spirit."

In 🐦 **Chapter 6** Paul adds practical admonitions that will lead to a better spirit of brotherhood in the church—forbearance and loving correction of a brother at fault; compassionate help of others burdened by care or sorrow, so fulfilling the law of Christ; meek practice of one's Christian faith that each may have rejoicing within himself. He warns the Galatians not to be deceived—if they sow to the flesh they will reap corruption; if they sow to the Spirit they will reap life everlasting. If they do not weary in doing good, they will surely reap life's harvest. They are to do good to all men at every opportunity, especially to the followers of Christ. All this he has written them in his own handwriting. In a final appeal Paul bluntly states that the men who are urging circumcision upon them do it to present an outward show of zeal, but their real object is to escape the persecution Christians face when they take a stand for Christ. These very men who are circumcised do not keep the Law of Moses; they only want to exult in their power over Christians. God forbid that he should exult in anything except the cross of his Lord Jesus Christ, which means that the world is crucified to him and he to the world. In Christ neither circumcision nor uncircumcision is of any use, but a transformed nature. From now on let no man trouble him concerning his apostleship; he has scars that mark him as the servant of Christ. Apostolic benediction.

A sense of responsibility for the Christianization of the non-Jewish world weighed heavily on Paul. Asia Minor, Macedonia, and Achaia had heard the gospel, but the vast territory of the Roman Empire to the west still lay in almost total ignorance of Christ. He had long thought of a journey westward; he was now free to formulate his plans. He had planted the seed of Christianity in the great centers of Asia Minor and Greece; he now determined to evangelize Rome, the capital of the Western world. After the discharge of one remaining duty—the delivery of the contributions of the Macedonian and Achaian churches to the parent church in Jerusalem—he hoped to be on his way.

He would not be pioneering in the capital; a sturdy church whose faith was well known to Greek and Asian Christians already existed there (Rom. 1:8). This church in Rome had in all probability been founded by Jews and Jewish converts who had been in Jerusalem on the Day of Pentecost (Acts 2:10) and who had become adherents of the new faith after hearing Peter preach. In Paul's day its membership was predominantly Gentile, due partly to Claudius' edict banishing the Jews from Rome for a period and partly to the Jews' continued refusal to open their minds to Christianity.

From Corinth Paul wrote of his longing to see them that he might impart to them "some spiritual gift" which would further establish their faith, mentioning that he had intended many a time to come but thus far had been deterred. He had proclaimed the gospel to the Greek-speaking races and others; now he was ready and eager to proclaim it to them (Rom. 1:11-15).

The apostle desired Roman Christians to have from his own hand, before his arrival, a clear statement of the principal truths of the gospel as they had been revealed to him. In the background was his continued concern over the tenacity of Jewish unbelief and his preoccupation with the theme of justification, which he had expounded in his Epistle to the Galatians. His letter to the Romans is his greatest doctrinal work, more a treatise than a letter, a systematic development of the cardinal doctrines of the Christian system—salvation by grace and justification by faith as they related to both Jew and Gentile, an explanation of Israel's partial blindness to the gospel, and a practical guide to Christian life and service.

The Epistle is a revelation of the spiritual riches of his own experience, as well as a masterly delineation of a universal ideal. His touch is never firmer, his grasp never stronger, than when he lays bare in swift heart-searching sentences the meaning, the joys, the hopes, and the responsibilities of the new life in Christ. [16]

Although Romans is chronologically the sixth of Paul's extant letters, the importance of its contents accorded it first place among the Pauline Epistles in New Testament canon.

Epistle to the Romans

Chapter 1:1-17 gives Paul's introduction of himself to the Christians at Rome, relates his calling to preach, and conveys his burning desire to teach the gospel to them. His theme is the righteousness of God which comes to man by faith and leads to salvation. "The gospel of Christ ... is the power of God unto salvation to every one that believeth; to the Jew first, and also to the Greek. For therein is the righteousness of God revealed from faith to faith: as it is written, the just [RV righteous] shall live by faith."

Chapters 1:18-3:20 deal with God's wrath against all sin and against the unrighteousness of men—who, having learned of His "eternal power and Godhead," refuse to give Him honor. All the world lies under the guilt of sin and needs God's saving grace. The Gentiles by their wickedness are guilty, having violated their conscience; the Jews also are guilty, having violated revealed (Scriptural) law. Each will be judged according to the law he obeys. Paul warns the Jews not to feel secure in God's favor simply because they possess the Law, for they have flagrantly disobeyed its moral precepts and dishonored God. Circumcision will count for nothing in their salvation unless it is of the heart. He answers certain Jewish objections that might be raised (3:1-8), but concludes that Jew and Gentile alike are guilty of sin, confirming this indictment from the Scriptures (Ps. 14:1-3; 5:9; 10:7; 36:1; Is. 59:7,8). Justification before God cannot come through the works of the Law.

In Chapter 3:21-31 Paul returns to the theme of the righteousness that comes from God, obtainable through faith in His Son. Here he develops the doctrine of justification by faith: the forgiveness of sin through God's free, unmerited grace in the redemption (deliverance) that is found in Jesus Christ. By faith in Christ's propitiatory sacrifice the sins of the past are pardoned through God's forbearance, that God's righteousness might be demonstrated and He might be shown to be just and the justifier of those who believe in His Son. The one God saves all men alike through faith and not through the works of the Law. By this teaching is the Law made void? No, God's law is more fully established.

In Chapters 4-5 Paul illustrates this doctrine of justification by faith by the example of Abraham, who was himself justified by faith because he believed in God and His promises. Righteousness was imputed to him before he received circumcision; he and his seed became the heirs of God's promises through grace, not through the works of the Law. As such, Abraham is the "father" of all who seek righteousness by faith. In like manner is righteousness reckoned to those who believe in Him who raised Jesus from the dead. The next step in Paul's reasoning is logical, the natural happy effects of having been forgiven. Standing in a new relation to God, a state of grace to which Christ has given men access, believers have peace with God. They have a joyous hope of attaining divine perfection, an exultant faith that endures and triumphs in tribulation, and an assurance of God's love in that—while they were yet sinners—Jesus Christ died for their salvation. If men have been freed from guilt through his blood and reconciled to God, much more will they, being reconciled, be saved through union with the living Christ. Paul contrasts the sin of Adam with the grace of Jesus Christ. By Adam sin and death entered the world, "and so death passed upon all men, for that all have sinned." But God's free gift of grace, manifested in Jesus Christ, far outweighs the sin, bringing redemption to all and bestowing a righteousness that leads to everlasting life.

🕮 Chapters 6-8 deal with the sanctification of the believer. "How shall we, that are dead to sin, live any longer therein?" 🕮 Chapter 6 declares that the Christian, now justified, enters into a new life in Christ, being baptized into Christ's death and resurrection. He crucifies the "old man" of sin, refuses obedience to sin, and becomes the servant of righteousness, manifesting holiness. In 🕮 Chapter 7 Paul shows the Jew that the believer, having died to sin, is free from the Law through union with Christ. The Law was good in that it exposed the awful nature of sin, but it was not adequate to save from the power of sin. In Paul's own spiritual conflict with sin he had found that the Law that forbade sin had instead stirred it within him. Only in Christ had he found deliverance from sin's thralldom.   In 🕮 Chapter 8 he rejoices in the efficacy of divine grace, in the higher law of Spirit which releases men from the Law's condemnation and the power of sin—"the law of the Spirit of life in Christ Jesus hath made me free from the law of sin and death." (The term *the Spirit,* used only once previously in Romans as *Holy Ghost* [5:5], appears nineteen times in this chapter.) Walking in this Spirit men are no longer in bondage to the flesh or to the carnal-mindedness that leads to death, but are risen to a new life and accepted as the sons of God. The Spirit itself, together with their spirit, bears testimony to the glorious truth that they are the children of God, "heirs of God, and joint-heirs with Christ." All creation is earnestly awaiting the manifestation of the sons of God that the creation itself may be delivered from the law of decay. And even Christians, who have so much of the spirit of Christ within them, groan as they await the redemption of the body. They are sustained in this hope by the intercession of the Spirit itself, by God's foreordained purposes for His elect, and by the intercession of Christ. From the summit of inspiration Paul concludes his argument of justification by faith with the statement that there is nothing in this whole world—no suffering, or tribulation, or powers, or time, or space—that can separate men from the love of God and the love of Christ.

In 🕮 Chapters 9-11 Paul turns to a subject that has caused him much sorrow—the unbelief of his own nation that has been shutting them out from salvation. Their unbelief appears to exclude them from the elect. In these three chapters Paul reconciles God's covenant promises to Israel, His chosen, with His promises to the Gentiles; he explains that because of Israel's rejection of Christ, God's saving grace has been offered to the Gentiles, and when the Gentiles have come fully into the Church, Israel, no longer unbelieving, will also be brought in—"and so all Israel shall be saved." 🕮 Chapter 9 expresses the apostle's anguish over the rejection of Israel, for they are God's covenant people, to whom the promises came and from whom sprang the Messiah. This exclusion does not mean that God has broken His promises; rather, all through Israel's history God through His sovereign will and mercy has selected those best fitted to carry out the divine purpose. The prophet Hosea had foretold the calling of the Gentiles (Ho. 1:10; 2:23), and Isaiah had prophesied that only an elect remnant of Israel would be saved (Is. 10:22; 1:9). The Gentiles have attained righteousness and won acceptance because of their faith in Christ, while the Jews have not attained it and have been rejected because they sought it through the Law and not by faith. In 🕮 Chapter 10 Paul declares that his Jewish brethren, though zealous for God, have failed to understand the gift of righteousness which comes by faith, but have obstinately held to the Law, seeking a righteousness by their own merit. The simple and accessible way of faith is to acknowledge Jesus as Lord with one's tongue and believe Jesus' resurrection in one's heart. There is no distinction between Jew and Greek, for Christ is Lord of all and bestows the riches of his grace on all who seek him. Jesus' name is made known by preaching; indeed, it has been made known everywhere. The Gentiles, though not the covenant people, have heard and believed.. The Jews have had ample opportunity to hear the gospel message but have stubbornly refused to listen. In 🕊 **Chapter 11** the apostle declares his conviction that Israel nevertheless will at last be saved and welcomed into the kingdom. God has not utterly cast off His people. A remnant that is not blind, of whom Paul is one, has attained to the "election of grace," and Israel's lapse has only given opportunity for the conversion of the Gentiles. Paul likens the Gentiles to a "wild olive tree" grafted onto the cultivated olive tree of Israel that they might partake of the covenant promises. The Gentiles are not to boast over the fall of Israel, for Israel is the "root" through which the knowledge of God has come. The Gentiles should not believe they are preferred above Israel—the latter lost their place through unbelief. The Gentiles stand where they are by faith, and God will also break them off if they do not remain faithful. In time, when Israel turns from unbelief, God will again graft them into the kingdom and "so all Israel shall be saved." This section of the letter closes with a sudden burst of praise for God's infinite wisdom and mercy.

🕊 **Chapters 12-13** are devoted to practical admonitions for the Christian in his relation to the Church and to the world. Having experienced the saving mercy of God, the Christian's life must be consecrated as "a living sacrifice" to the service of God. In humility he must make use of whatever spiritual gifts he possesses and must manifest brotherly love and conduct both within and outside the Church. His duty to the state must be one of obedience to its rulers. Above all, love must be the motivating power of all his actions. Paul sums up his ethical teachings: "Love worketh no ill to his neighbour: therefore love is the fulfilling of the law."

🕊 **Chapters 14:1-15:13**, continuing the theme of Christian love, urge sympathetic forbearance toward those weaker in faith, a refraining from judgment and condemnation of those holding differing views. Why judge a brother when each shall stand before God's judgment seat and give account of himself? Rather, resolve not to hinder another's spiritual progress; let each one build up his weaker brother so that all "may with one mind and one mouth glorify God." Paul urges Jew and Gentile alike to welcome each other in brotherhood, as Christ had welcomed them, and so advance the glory of God.

In 🕊 **Chapters 15:14-16:27** Paul gives the reason for writing the Roman brethren—though he knows their hearts are already filled with goodness and spiritual knowledge, he feels constrained as the God-appointed minister to the Gentiles to put them in mind of the truths of the gospel that they may be acceptable to God, a worthy offering, sanctified by the Holy Ghost. He asks for their prayers for the successful consummation of his forthcoming visit to Jerusalem and for his safe journey to Rome. He expresses his heartfelt love to the church and to his many friends there. Benediction and prayer.

This letter was entrusted to Phebe, a deaconess (RV) or dispenser of charity, of the church in Cenchrea, who safeguarded it during the hazardous sea voyage to Italy and delivered it to the church at Rome (Rom. 16:1,2).

Acts 20:3-38   Having finished his mission to the Corinthian church, in the spring of 58 Paul planned to sail from Cenchrea to one of the ports of Palestine, then on to Jerusalem to deliver the churches' contributions; but at the last moment he learned that the Jews were plotting to kill him after his ship left port. Their hatred against this leader of Christianity had been fanned by his presence. What he had written to the Galatians and to the Romans he was undoubtedly preaching in Corinth. To hear him assert that "blindness in part is happened to Israel" (Rom. 11:25); "no man is justified by the law in the sight of God" (Gal. 3:11); "neither circumcision availeth any thing, nor uncircumcision" (Gal. 5:6); "there is neither Jew nor Greek . . . for ye are all one in Christ Jesus" (Gal. 3:28)—to have the cherished Jewish heritage offered to the Gentiles and the Mosaic system of salvation relegated to an inferior position—were more than Paul's adversaries could tolerate.

To protect his life Paul was forced to retrace his steps by land the long distance through Achaia and Macedonia, there to find a ship that would take him on his way to Jerusalem. Hundreds of miles were added to his homeward trip and many weeks to his time schedule, but this change in route afforded the churches of Macedonia a farewell meeting with him. He was accompanied by Timothy, Sopater of Berea, Trophimus and Tychicus of Roman Asia, Aristarchus and Secundus of Thessalonica, and Gaius of Derbe. Some of these were, no doubt, the elected treasurers entrusted with the Achaian contributions (I Cor. 16:3,4).

Luke and Paul were reunited at Philippi after nearly six years. Paul had left Luke there on his second journey, although he may have seen him several times as he passed through the city. These two remained in Philippi to celebrate the Passover while the others continued on to Troas in Asia Minor.

At the close of the feast Paul and Luke boarded ship; after five days' sail they landed at Troas and joined the others, remaining seven days. On the first day of the week, when the Troas church was gathered together to observe the communal feast which Jesus' last commandment had enjoined on his followers (Luke's first clear reference to the practice of meeting on the Lord's Day [compare I Cor. 16:2]), Paul discoursed till midnight in an upper room to the many who had come. In one of the windows sat a young man named Eutychus, and "as Paul was long preaching, he sunk down with sleep, and fell down from the third loft [upper story], and was taken up dead." Paul immediately went down to him, "embraced" him, and assured the others, "Trouble not yourselves; for his life is in him." He returned to the upper room and with the brethren partook of the Eucharist, ate of a common meal, and continued to talk until daybreak. So he departed, and "they brought the young man alive, and were not a little comforted."

Paul chose to take the straight 20-mile Roman road to Assos, while his companions took ship around Cape Lectum and picked him up later. Thirty miles farther down the coast of Asia Minor they touched at Mitylene, capital of the Aegean island of Lesbos; two days later they put in at the island of Samos but stayed the night at Trogyllium, an anchorage on the mainland opposite Samos; the following day they reached the seaport of Miletus, some 30 miles south of Ephesus. From here Paul summoned the ranking members of the Ephesian church to come to Miletus, for he was anxious to reach Jerusalem in time for Pentecost. Certain that this was the last time they would meet, Paul gave a moving farewell. He appealed to them to keep in mind the integrity and faithfulness with which the gospel had been brought to them so that they might follow his example. He must now press on, even though further suffering for Christ's cause awaited him. "Now ... I go bound in the spirit unto Jerusalem, not knowing the things that shall befall me there: Save that the Holy Ghost witnesseth in every city, saying that bonds and afflictions abide me. But none of these things move me, neither count I my life dear unto myself, so that I might finish my course with joy, and the ministry, which I have received of the Lord Jesus."

He entrusted the church to the care of its elders with a warning that they guard against false teachers from without and sectarian perverters from within. "I know that ye all ... shall see my face no more. Wherefore I take you to record this day, that I am pure from the blood of all men [Phillips: my conscience is clear as far as any of you is concerned]. For I have not shunned to declare unto you all the counsel of God [compare Ezek. 3:17-21]. Take heed therefore unto yourselves, and to all the flock, over the which the Holy Ghost hath made you overseers, to feed the church of God. ... For I know this, that after my departing shall grievous wolves enter in among you, not sparing the flock. Also of your own selves shall men arise, speaking perverse things, to draw away disciples after them. Therefore watch, and remember, that by the space of three years I ceased not to warn every one night and day with tears. And now, brethren, I commend you to God, and to the word of his grace, which is able to build you up, and to give you an inheritance among all them which are sanctified."

When he had finished speaking he knelt and prayed with them. They wept and embraced Paul, "sorrowing most of all ... that they should see his face no more."

Acts 21 The ship was waiting. When they had torn themselves away, Paul and his companions launched and, running before the wind, sailed south to the island of Coos, the following day 50 miles southeast to the island of Rhodes, and from Rhodes due east to Patara on the mainland in the province of Lycia. Changing ships, they sailed to Tyre in Phoenicia and, finding Christians there, remained with them for seven days while the ship unloaded its cargo. These brethren, foreseeing through spiritual intuition the dangers of Paul's forthcoming visit to Jerusalem, begged him not to go. However, when the ship was ready to leave, he sailed again, stopping for a day at Ptolemais (Accho), a Syrian seaport 30 miles south of Tyre, and the day following arrived at Caesarea in Palestine. Here he stayed in the home of Philip the Evangelist, one of the seven stewards appointed years before by the Twelve (see p. 379). During this visit Agabus, Paul's long-time friend, came from Judaea to see him. Agabus too foresaw the danger if Paul persisted in going on to Jerusalem. Taking Paul's sash and binding his own hands and feet to emphasize his warning, he predicted: "Thus saith the Holy Ghost, So shall the Jews at Jerusalem bind the man that owneth this girdle, and shall deliver him into the hands of the Gentiles."

This prophecy only tested Paul's courage and deepened his resolve. He was not unaware of the peril. While still at Corinth he had felt keen anxiety about this forthcoming visit; the Holy City would be filled with Jews from every land observing the Day of Pentecost, among them some who had shown bitter hatred of his teachings or who had repeatedly sought his life. His concern had been expressed in his earnest plea to the Christians in Rome to pray for his preservation: "I beseech you, brethren ... that ye strive together with me in your prayers to God for me; That I may be delivered from them that do not believe in Judaea; and that my service which I have for

Miletus. Here the Apostle Paul gave his moving farewell address to the elders of the Ephesus church. Turkish Tourism and Information Office.

Jerusalem may be accepted of the saints; That I may come unto you with joy by the will of God, and may with you be refreshed" (Rom. 15:30-32).

Much as Jesus had steadfastly set his face to go to Jerusalem, so Paul set his face to meet whatever perils lay ahead for him. He silenced his friends with the question "What mean ye to weep and to break mine heart? for I am ready not to be bound only, but also to die at Jerusalem for the name of the Lord Jesus." They acquiesced: "The will of the Lord be done."

After three days of traveling Paul and his company, now joined by friends from Caesarea, quietly entered Jerusalem, where they received a warm welcome from the Christian community. The next day he and the other delegates turned over to the mother church the donations of the Macedonian and Achaian churches (Acts 24:17). Then Paul made a detailed formal report to James and the elders "what things God had wrought among the Gentiles by his ministry" during the past four years; and his listeners praised God for the victories that had been won for Christianity.

Even as the elders rejoiced they told Paul that dangerous elements of discord existed in the Jerusalem church. A Pharisaic faction was stirring up hatred against Paul, informing Jewish Christians (the thousands of Jews who believed but still adhered to Mosaic Law, not yet having attained the fullness of Christian faith) that he was teaching Jews of the Dispersion to abandon the rite of circumcision and other Mosaic customs. This claim was false in that Paul had not detracted from the value of the Law to the Jew (compare Rom. 2:25; 3:1,2), but it was true in the sense that he taught that faith and life in Christ alone saved a man. The assembly pointed out that Paul's presence in the city could not be hidden; his every appearance in public would attract a crowd of spectators, many violently hostile. To disarm the hatred, they proposed that Paul take charge of four men who were already under a Nazarite vow, accompany them to the Temple for the remaining week of their vow, and pay all the costs of their offerings. By this act of piety he would thus prove to Jewish Christians that he was not opposed to the Law. Assent violated no religious principle for him (I Cor. 9:19,20), so he acceded to their request—a conciliatory gesture that proved almost disastrous to his future ministry. The crisis it precipitated delayed Paul's active service for several years and culminated in a journey to Rome in chains.

On Paul's seventh day in the Temple he was recognized by some of the Asian Jews. They seized him: "This is the man, that teacheth all men every where against the people, and the law, and this place: and further brought Greeks also into the temple, and hath polluted this holy place" (they assumed he had brought his Ephesian friend Trophimus into the sanctuary). The crowd closed in around Paul and forced him out of the Temple; the doors were shut, and they began to beat him with intent to kill.

Word of the uproar almost immediately reached Claudius Lysias, commandant of the Roman cohort stationed in the Tower of Antonia. (This structure was a portion of the palace repaired by Nehemiah [Neh. 2:8; 7:2], the home of former Maccabean priest-kings, and the edifice rebuilt and renamed by Herod the Great in honor of Mark Antony. It was large enough to garrison a Roman cohort, which at full strength numbered a thousand, 760 foot soldiers and 240 cavalrymen. Occupying a strategic position at the northwest corner of the Temple area, the highest of its four turrets overlooked the Temple courts and any disturbance was visible at once to the sentries on duty.)

Lysias was alarmed. Only seven weeks earlier, during the Feast of Passover, an Egyptian pseudo-Messiah had led four thousand men in an uprising against Jerusalem; the Roman governor Felix had routed them but the Egyptian had escaped. Was this another insurrection? The commandant, with his officers and at least two hundred soldiers, rushed to the spot. The Jews reluctantly ceased beating their victim. Lysias took Paul prisoner, ordered him bound with two chains, and demanded to know who he was and what he had done. Some of the enraged crowd shouted one accusation, some another. Because of the turmoil Lysias commanded that the prisoner be taken

into the Fortress, and the Roman soldiers literally had to carry Paul to protect him from his countrymen who followed shouting for his death. When they reached the stone steps that led into the Fortress, Paul asked permission of the commandant to speak to the people. This was granted when Lysias found Paul was not the Egyptian insurrectionist he had feared.

Acts 22   So Paul stood on the stairs and beckoned the crowd to come near, and when there was "a great silence" he spoke to them in Aramaic: "Hear ye my defence." They listened with close attention as Paul testified of his Jewish lineage, his training as a rabbi under the great Gamaliel, his zealous persecution of Christians, his conversion and call to apostleship, and the vision commissioning him to preach to the Gentiles. The racial and religious prejudices of his listeners were instantly inflamed by the word *Gentiles*. Infuriated that Paul had the temerity to declare heaven had shown equal favor to uncircumcised Gentiles—"heathen dogs" in the eyes of these sons of Abraham—they tossed off their outer cloaks (as at the stoning of Stephen), threw dust into the air, and screamed: "Away with such a fellow from the earth: for it is not fit that he should live." Only the presence of the Roman soldiers saved Paul from the death Stephen had suffered.

Lysias had understood neither Paul's Aramaic speech nor the reason for the crowd's violent reaction, so in accord with Roman custom he ordered that the prisoner be whipped to make him confess his crime. As the soldiers bared Paul's back and tied his hands behind him in readiness for the lash, he claimed his right as a Roman citizen to immunity from scourging: "Is it lawful for you to scourge a man that is a Roman, and uncondemned?" The centurion in charge hurriedly warned the commandant that his prisoner was a Roman. When Paul confirmed the fact to Lysias, the commandant responded, "With a great sum obtained I this freedom." Paul answered, "But I was free born." Lysias stopped the examination immediately, realizing he had committed a serious offense against Roman law. He kept Paul in custody to protect him, and the following day called the Sanhedrin into session to find out the charge against him.

Acts 23   Paul was taken before the council. Strong in his Christian dignity and integrity, he testified, "I have lived in all good conscience before God until this day." The high priest Ananias gave him no opportunity to say more, but ordered that they strike him on the mouth—not merely a most degrading insult, but also an abuse of judicial power (Jn. 7:51). Paul instantly protested: "God shall smite thee, thou whited wall: for sittest thou to judge me after the law, and commandest me to be smitten contrary to the law?"

The Sanhedrin consisted of both Pharisees and Sadducees; and knowing the Pharisees taught the resurrection of the dead while the Sadducees rejected this doctrine, Paul astutely enlisted Pharisaic support: "Men and brethren, I am a Pharisee, the son of a Pharisee: of the hope and resurrection of the dead I am called in question." In this one brief remark he pinpointed the reason for all the persecution he had experienced and for which he was even now on trial—the world's opposition to Christ as the true way to eternal life. His statement at once set the two parties against each other. The Pharisaic group rallied to his defense: "We find no evil in this man: but if a spirit or an angel hath spoken to him, let us not fight against God." The quarreling between the two factions became so violent that the Roman commandant feared Paul would be torn to pieces; he ordered his soldiers to take him from them by force and return him to the Fortress.

That night the Lord appeared to Paul in a vision and said, "Be of good cheer, Paul: for as thou hast testified of me in Jerusalem, so must thou bear witness also at Rome"—a promise from which he was to draw comfort during the following two years of imprisonment in Caesarea.

More than forty Jews, desperate and determined to put an end to this exponent of a gospel that undermined organized Judaism, swore that they would not eat or drink until they had killed Paul. They conspired with the chief priests of the Sanhedrin to gain access to Paul for questioning on the following day, but this conspiracy was uncovered by Paul's sister's son, who was living in Jerusalem and who reported it to his uncle. Paul in turn asked that his nephew be taken to Lysias, and when the commandant heard of the plot he counseled the youth to keep it secret.

Lysias acted swiftly to remove his controversial prisoner from Jerusalem. He commanded that a strong escort of 200 soldiers, 70 horsemen, and 200 spearmen be ready by nine o'clock that night; providing Paul with two spare horses, he sent him to Caesarea (65 miles away) to Felix, the Roman procurator of Judaea. The entire military guard accompanied Paul to Antipatris, about halfway to Caesarea; the foot soldiers then returned to Jerusalem and only the cavalry continued on with Paul. Lysias also wrote a letter to Felix in which he related the events of Paul's arrest, omitting mention of his own infraction of Roman law and claiming credit for saving the life of a Roman citizen. He stated he had taken the prisoner before the Jews' supreme court and found nothing deserving of death or imprisonment. "But when it was told me how that the Jews laid wait for the man, I sent straightway to thee, and gave commandment to his accusers also to say before thee what they had against him."

Thus ended Paul's third missionary journey of at least 4000 miles and his fifth visit to Jerusalem after conversion.

Acts 24   Imprisonment in Caesarea (58-60 A.D.)

Felix held Paul in Herod's judgment hall till his accusers arrived. After five days the high priest and the elders of the Sanhedrin reached Caesarea, bringing with them Tertullus, a well-trained orator. Tertullus presented the case against Paul, using every verbal weapon at his command. Ingratiatingly he addressed the procurator—"most noble Felix"—complimenting him on his "very worthy deeds ... done unto this nation by thy providence." He was apologetic: "That I be not further tedious unto thee, I pray thee that thou wouldest hear us of thy clemency a few words." He regretted that the Roman captain had taken Paul out of their jurisdiction: "We have found this man a pestilent fellow, and a mover of sedition among all the Jews throughout the world, and a ringleader of the sect of the Nazarenes: Who also hath gone about to profane the temple: whom we took, and would have judged according to our law."

Paul flatly denied the charges of sedition and profanation of the Temple: "They neither found me in the temple disputing with any man, neither raising up the people, neither in the synagogues, nor in the city: Neither can they prove the things whereof they now accuse me." He readily admitted he was a Nazarene—a Christian: "But this I confess unto thee, that after the way which they call heresy, so worship I the God of my fathers, believing all things which are written in the law and in the prophets: And have hope toward God, which they themselves also allow, that there shall be a resurrection of the dead, both of the just and unjust. And herein do I exercise myself, to have always a conscience void of offence toward God, and toward men."

Paul then laid bare the underlying complaint against him: "Touching the resurrection of the dead I am called in question by you this day." He was, in truth, on trial in defense of Christ's gospel. He who had been Christianity's ardent promulgator now became its great champion, and he was to continue to defend it fearlessly before the highest authorities of the Roman Empire.

Felix knew something of Christianity (Luke notes that he had "more perfect knowledge of that way"), so he was aware that the real charge against the prisoner related to religious differences with which Roman law had no concern. He realized it would be dangerous and certainly unjust to turn this man over to the fanatic Jewish hierarchy, yet he hesitated

Roman pillars mark the shore at Caesarea, the capital of Roman Judaea. This city was the principal port of Palestine in Paul's day. Here Paul was held prisoner for two years under Felix the governor, and from here he set sail for Rome. Israel Tourist Office.

through self-interest to offend these important personages. He deferred a decision on the ground that he wished to question Lysias more fully. Felix remanded Paul to the custody of a centurion, ordering that he be given a certain amount of liberty and that his friends be allowed to visit him.

Later the procurator, accompanied by his notorious Jewish wife Drusilla, sent for Paul to hear his explanation of Christianity. Felix, once a slave, freed by the Emperor Claudius, owed much in the way of duty to the sovereign state; but, according to the Roman historian Tacitus, his rule, far from showing a comparable mercy, was one of corruption and cruelty. Thus when Paul spoke fearlessly to him about righteousness, self-control, and the judgment soon to come, Felix, remembering no doubt his many breaches of justice and the immorality of his private life, became alarmed and dismissed him: "Go thy way for this time; when I have a convenient season, I will call for thee." Secretly hoping to receive a bribe from Paul, he talked with him frequently, but there never arrived the "convenient season" which might have brought him change of heart; his conscience never reached a penitent state.

Felix left Paul in prison for two full years. Three missionary journeys were behind the apostle. Thousands of Jews and Gentiles had been converted; the infant churches in Asia Minor, Macedonia, and Greece needed constant nourishment and guidance. During this period his time and thought must have been occupied with much prayer for the Church and meditation on its deeper meanings and mission. The fruit of his thought is reflected in the epistles later written from Rome.

Luke's last reference to himself was at the meeting with James in Jerusalem (Acts 21:18), but the details recorded of Paul's experiences in Jerusalem and Caesarea indicate that he was still nearby. It is quite probable that during the interval of Paul's imprisonment Luke sought out every available eyewitness to the life of Jesus and wrote his Gospel while awaiting his friend's release (see Lu. 1:1-3).

According to Josephus, at the end of the second year of Paul's imprisonment Felix was recalled to Rome by Nero to face charges of injustice brought against him by the Jews of Caesarea. He put Paul in chains before he left, hoping to curry favor with the Jews and thereby appease Jewish accusers at his own trial.

Acts 25   Porcius Festus succeeded Felix as procurator; three days after assuming office he went to Jerusalem to acquaint himself with this troublesome city now under his jurisdiction. The high priest and other Jewish leaders immediately tried to push their case against Paul, asking that he be brought to Jerusalem for trial, still planning to kill him along the way. But Festus would not grant this favor while still so new in office and answered that he would hold the prisoner for trial in Caesarea.

As soon as Festus returned from Jerusalem Paul was arraigned before him. The Jewish leaders repeated their charges of heresy, sacrilege, and treason; once again Paul denied them: "Neither against the law of the Jews, neither against the temple, nor yet against Caesar, have I offended any thing at all." Festus saw that the Jewish charges were not political, as he had

expected, but religious. He had the authority to set Paul free, but like Pilate and Felix he was not morally strong enough to render a judgment free of self-interest. Instead, "willing to do the Jews a pleasure," he asked the prisoner, "Wilt thou go up to Jerusalem, and there be judged of these things before me?"

Paul refused. He knew the futility of finding justice or mercy in any trial before the hostile Sanhedrin, even under the procurator's protection, and he was fully aware of the peril of assassination. Festus was vacillating and Paul realized he would not gain his freedom under this new Roman official, so he exercised the one special privilege of Roman citizenship still left open to him—the right of recourse to Caesar: "I stand at Caesar's judgment seat, where I ought to be judged: to the Jews have I done no wrong, as thou very well knowest. For if I be an offender, or have committed any thing worthy of death, I refuse not to die: but if there be none of these things whereof these accuse me, no man may deliver me unto them. I appeal unto Caesar." This appeal automatically removed the matter from Festus' jurisdiction to that of Nero, the supreme tribunal at Rome. Festus could only answer, "Unto Caesar shalt thou go."

Soon afterward Herod Agrippa II, great-grandson of Herod the Great, and his sister Bernice made a courtesy call on the new governor. Agrippa had been a favorite of the Emperor Claudius and was a friend of Nero. This last of the Herods ruled the tetrarchy of Herod Philip and the adjacent territory east and north of Galilee. During the visit Festus brought up the perplexing subject of his prisoner with his eminent guest, reviewed the history of the case, and discussed its puzzling aspects. At the hearing there had been none of the expected civil charges, only accusations concerning the Jews' religion and Paul's words of "one Jesus," who was dead but whom the prisoner maintained was alive; so finding no evidence of sedition, he had suggested a Jewish trial at Jerusalem under his protection. The prisoner had refused, demanding instead to be tried by Caesar. Agrippa's interest was aroused: "I would also hear the man myself."

To please his royal guest Festus arranged a hearing for the next day. With great pomp Agrippa and Bernice appeared in the auditorium, accompanied by Roman tribunes and others of high rank in Caesarea. Paul was brought in chained, and Festus asked Agrippa to help him decide what accusation his letter to the Emperor should contain when he sent the prisoner to Rome.

Acts 26   With Agrippa's permission Paul began his defense, making full and eloquent use of this rare opportunity not only to defend himself but also to proclaim the gospel to this king, the military commanders, and the civilians of high rank of Caesarea (compare Acts 9:15). He addressed Agrippa as one who, being partly Jewish himself, had a knowledge of Jewish customs and had heard of the agitating question Christianity posed for the Jew: "I think myself happy, king Agrippa, because I shall answer for myself this day before thee touching all the things whereof I am accused of the Jews."

As in his speech to his own people at Jerusalem, now he attested his Jewish heritage, his life as a Pharisee, his hope for the promised Messiah whose fulfillment he saw in the risen Jesus, his early persecution of Christians, and the vision that led to his conversion and call to apostleship among the Gentiles.

He testified also that he had been obedient to that vision and had labored in Damascus, Jerusalem, the coasts of Judaea, and finally among the Gentiles, but because he had taught repentance and salvation through Jesus his countrymen had seized him in the Temple and tried to kill him. These things had brought him to this day, but God's love and power had enabled him to endure: "Having therefore obtained help of God, I continue unto this day, witnessing both to small and great, saying none other things than those which the prophets and Moses did say should come: That Christ should suffer, and that he should be the first that should rise from the dead, and should shew light unto the people, and to the Gentiles."

Feeling that the prisoner's statements were becoming extravagant, the procurator broke in. "Paul, thou art beside thyself; much learning doth make thee mad." Paul's reference to the resurrection of the dead, a doctrine intelligible to Agrippa the Jew, was wholly unintelligible to this sophisticated Roman. "I am not mad, most noble Festus," Paul replied courteously, "but speak forth the words of truth and soberness. For the king knoweth of these things, before whom also I speak freely: for I am persuaded that none of these things are hidden from him; for this thing was not done in a corner."

Paul's sincerity and conviction had held Agrippa's close attention from the start, and Paul felt his words had fallen on sympathetic ears. Turning again to the king, he entreated, "King Agrippa, believest thou the prophets?" And without awaiting an answer, he declared, "I know that thou believest." This drew from Agrippa the half-admission "Almost thou persuadest me to be a Christian." In great earnestness and love the apostle responded and in his anwer included all of his distinguished audience: "I would to God, that not only thou, but also all that hear me this day, were both almost, and altogether such as I am, except these bonds." But Agrippa did not give assent; instead he rose. The hearing was ended.

Later Festus and Agrippa agreed privately that the prisoner was innocent. "This man," said Agrippa, "might have been set at liberty, if he had not appealed unto Caesar." On this note Paul's Caesarean imprisonment came to a close.

This Greek vase painting shows a merchant vessel running reefe in a gale. Merchant ships had no need to maneuver swiftly an could therefore afford to seek a favoring wind. Unlike th warships of the time, these ships—used peacefully for trade—ha neither sharp beak nor oars. From Margaret B. Synge, *A Boo of Discovery* (Putnam, 1920).

EUXINE OR BLACK SEA

ILLYRICUM (DALMATIA)

Adriatic Sea

MACEDONIA

Philippi

ITALY

ree Taverns

teoli

ASIA MINOR

Troas

TAURUS MTS.

ACHAIA

Nicopolis

Aegean Sea

Ephesus

Miletus

PAMPHYLIA

CILICIA

LYCIA

Corinth

Patmos

Myra

ADRIA

Sicily

Rhegium

Syracuse

Crete

Rhodes

Cyprus

PHOENICIA

Phenice

Sidon

Melita

Fair Havens

Tyre

Caesarea

MEDITERRANEAN SEA

N

Syrtis Major

100   200

Scale of Miles

Voyage to Rome and Imprisonments

60-63 A.D.

From Caesarea
Sidon (in Phoenicia)
Myra (in province of Lycia)
Fair Havens (on Crete)
Island of Melita
Syracuse (on Sicily)
Rhegium, Puteoli (seaports of Italy)
Rome

Acts 27   Although Paul made his voyage to Rome as a prisoner of Nero, his work was far from finished. Christ's prophecy two

years before—"thou [must] bear witness also at Rome"—was soon to be fulfilled in a journey entailing some 2500 miles. Paul was now about fifty-seven years old; still hopeful and vigorous, he looked forward eagerly to the consummation of this promise. With other prisoners, Paul was placed in the custody of Julius, a centurion of an Augustan cohort (possibly part of the imperial guard or of a body of troops assigned to some special service for the Emperor). They set sail from Caesarea in late August of 60 A.D. Paul's friends Luke and Aristarchus sailed with him.

Luke's detailed eyewitness account of this journey is one of the most vivid and dramatic portions of his biography of Paul, and gives an authentic record of first-century navigation and seamanship. "Entering into a ship . . . we launched, meaning to sail by the coasts of Asia. . . . And the next day we touched at Sidon [70 miles north of Caesarea]." Julius treated his

429

notable prisoner courteously and gave him freedom to visit Christian brethren at Sidon, a sign of the deference shown him throughout the long journey to Italy.

"We sailed under [the lee of] Cyprus, because the winds were contrary . . . over the sea of Cilicia and Pamphylia . . . to Myra, a city of Lycia. And there the centurion found a ship of Alexandria sailing into Italy; and he put us therein. And when we had sailed slowly many days . . . the wind not suffering us, we sailed under Crete . . . unto a place which is called The fair havens. . . ." Here they remained too long—until early in October, when navigation of the open Mediterranean becomes dangerous. (Between November and March all shipping was suspended.) Faced with the possibility of spending the winter in this small unprotected Cretan harbor, some wanted to press on to the larger, safer port of Phenice, only a few hours' sail to the west. Paul warned, "Sirs, I perceive that this voyage will be with hurt and much damage, not only of the lading and ship, but also of our lives." Neither the captain, the owner of the ship, nor the centurion Julius heeded his advice; when a light south wind rose they were deceived into thinking conditions were favorable, and so set sail.

They never reached Phenice. A sudden northeast storm became almost a typhoon. "And when the ship was caught, and could not bear up into the wind, we let her drive." They sheltered briefly in the lee of the island of Clauda to the south of Crete, and the captain seized the opportunity to hoist aboard the small boat they had been towing and to undergird the ship by repeatedly passing stout ropes tightly around its hull. To avoid being driven south onto the dreaded sandbars of the Syrtis Major, a gulf on the African coast, the crew lowered the mainsail partially to steady the ship, left up the small storm sail, and let the ship drift to leeward before the gale.

Another day passed; now in danger of foundering, they began to lighten the ship. The third day they lightened the vessel still more, passengers and prisoners alike helping the crew cut away and throw overboard some of the ship's gear. All seemed lost. They could not see the sky, and therefore could not take their position by the stars; the vessel was showing signs of heavy strain. The crew could do nothing. More days passed in fear, danger, and growing exhaustion. "When neither sun nor stars in many days appeared, and no small tempest lay on us, all hope that we should be saved was then taken away."

Paul alone did not despair. During a night of prayer God comforted him with the promise of a fulfilled destiny at Rome and the preservation of the lives of all on board. The following morning he gathered the men around him: "Sirs, ye should have hearkened unto me, and not have loosed from Crete, and to have gained this harm and loss. And now I exhort you to be of good cheer: for there shall be no loss of any man's life among you, but of the ship. For there stood by me this night the angel of God, whose I am, and whom I serve, Saying, Fear not, Paul; thou must be brought before Caesar: and, lo, God hath given thee all them that sail with thee. Wherefore, sirs, be of good cheer: for I believe God, that it shall be even as it was told me. Howbeit we must be cast upon a certain island."

About midnight on the fourteenth day of the storm, as they drifted helplessly in the central Mediterranean, the Sea of Adria below the Adriatic Sea, the crew took soundings and found they were nearing land. Fearful of running onto rocks, they "cast four anchors out of the stern, and wished for the day." The crew then plotted to save their own lives. Under cover of darkness they let down the small boat into the sea under pretext of casting anchors out of the foreship. Paul, sensing this treachery that would have left the ship unmanned and helpless, quietly warned Julius and the soldiers, "Except these abide in the ship, ye cannot be saved." To prevent the crew's escape the soldiers sprang into action and cut the ropes of the small boat, setting it adrift.

In full assurance of ultimate safety, in virtue of a DIVINE *pledge, to all in the ship, Paul speaks and acts throughout this whole scene in the exercise of a sound judgment as to the indispensable* HUMAN *conditions of safety; and as there is no trace of any feeling of inconsistency between these two things in his mind, so even the centurion, under whose orders the soldiers acted on Paul's views, seems never to have felt perplexed by the twofold aspect, Divine and human, in which the same thing presented itself to the mind of Paul. Divine agency and human instrumentality are in all the events of life quite as much as here.*[17]

While the day was dawning Paul urged the drenched group aboard to renew their strength for the ordeal that lay ahead, for they had eaten no regular meal for days: "Take some meat: for this is for your health: for there shall not an hair fall from the head of any of you." Then he took some bread, gave thanks, and began to eat. The others followed his example and were cheered. Bodies and spirits refeshed, they lightened the ship again, this time casting the cargo of wheat into the sea.

At daybreak they discovered a shoreline with a small inlet, and in this they grounded the ship. Its prow stuck fast in the mud while the stern, exposed to the violence of the waves, began to break up. The soldiers would have killed the prisoners to keep them from escaping but Julius stopped them. Instead he commanded that all who could swim make for the land, and the rest go ashore on loose pieces of

Two islets named St. Paul's Islands mark the entrance to St. Paul's Bay, Malta, the Melita of Bible times where Paul suffered shipwreck. Religious News Service Photo.

reckage; and all 276 persons on board landed safely the island of Melita (the Malta of today):

Paul was thus delivered from his fourth ship-reck. Even the tempest had not taken him seriously f course, but had carried him toward his desired stination, casting him onto a tiny dot of land to the uth of Italy. He could well have rejoiced in the ords of the Psalmist: "Surely the wrath of man shall aise thee: the remainder of wrath shalt thou strain." (See An Example of Enduring Trust, p. 547.)

Acts 28   The Maltese ceived the survivors with kindness and kindled a fire their comfort. As Paul gathered a bundle of sticks d laid them on the fire, "there came a viper out of e heat, and fastened on his hand." When the

islanders saw the serpent strike, they superstitiously concluded he was a murderer whom justice was avenging; but instantly Paul shook it off into the fire "and felt no harm" (compare Mk. 16:18). They watched him for a long time, but when his body did not swell and he did not die suddenly they decided instead that he was a god (compare Acts 14:11).

The viper had come out of the heat; it had been shaken back into the heat from which it had come. All the venom of past persecution by Paul's enemies was typified in the attack of the serpent. Throughout his ministry his enemies had attempted to pervert, para-lyze, and destroy the work he had been divinely called to do. At Damascus, Lystra, Thessalonica, Berea, Corinth, Ephesus, and Jerusalem assaults had been

431

made on his life; he had suffered repeated beatings and imprisonment; more than all else he had borne the poisonous attacks of malice and blasphemy against the gospel. Like the Master, the apostle had been subjected to a swelling tide of hatred. The Master had proved it all "of none effect," and Paul strove to do the same. His constant dwelling in Christ had in this instance at Malta given him immunity, and when he shook off the serpent he shook off, in figure, the hatred that had pursued him.

Publius, the "chief man" of Malta, lodged Paul and his companions hospitably for three days. (Malta was under the jurisdiction of the province of Sicily and *chief man* was the official title of the Maltese representative of the praetor of Sicily.) During his stay Paul healed Publius' father, sick of dysentery and fever. When others on the island heard of it, many who were diseased came and were healed. Although Paul's great work was that of preaching, teaching, and converting, he nevertheless fully obeyed the Master's command to heal. Luke makes general reference to the miracles that accompanied Paul's preaching (Acts 14:3; 19:11). Specifically, he had healed the crippled man at Lystra; cast the spirit of divination out of the slave girl of Philippi; raised Eutychus from the dead; rendered the viper's bite harmless. Paul fulfilled this vital part of his Christian ministry naturally and well (compare Mt. 10:8).

After three months, when navigation was again possible, Julius, his prisoner, and the rest of the company embarked on an Alexandrian wheat ship. After an 80-mile run they put in at Syracuse, the chief port of Sicily, for three days; touched for one day at Rhegium on the southwestern tip of Italy; and ended their sea journey at Puteoli, 180 miles farther north on the beautiful Bay of Naples. Here Paul was happy to find Christian brethren, and was invited to stay with them for seven days.

The apostle had left Palestine in the late summer of 60 A.D.; he began the last lap of his journey, the 130-mile trip to Rome, in the spring of 61. Traveling northward up the Italian peninsula, Paul and his party reached the Appian Way, the great Roman road running from Capua to the imperial city. Word of his arrival had reached the church in Rome. Two parties of Christian friends came down to welcome Paul, one meeting him at the Appii Forum (Market of Appius), 40 miles from Rome, the other awaiting him at a place called Three Taverns, 10 miles farther on. A surge of joy filled him at the warmth of their reception, "whom when Paul saw, he thanked God and took courage."

So it was with gratitude and fresh hope that this prisoner of Rome—in reality "a prisoner of Jesus Christ"—traveled the last few miles to enter the magnificent capital of the world's greatest empire. Julius delivered his charges to the prefect or captain of the Emperor's bodyguard, the Praetorian Guard, who had custody of those awaiting trial before the Emperor.

First Imprisonment in Rome (61-63 A.D.)

Because Paul was of the class of prisoners whose offense was not flagrant—and possibly through the intervention of Julius—he was permitted to live in his own rented house. Nevertheless he was under close military guard, chained night and day to a Roman soldier, his right hand fastened to the soldier's left.

Without delay Paul began his work in Rome. Three days after his arrival he sent for the elders of the synagogues. When they came he explained his presence in the city and the reason for his humiliating bonds: though he had committed no crime against his nation or its customs he had been delivered a prisoner to the Romans, who would have released him, but in order to save his life from his Jewish enemies he had been forced to appeal to Caesar; he was here to defend himself, not to make accusations against his people, but the real cause for his chains was that he preached Jesus as the Messiah, the fulfillment of Israel's hope. They listened courteously, then assured him they had heard no derogatory reports about him and would indeed be interested to have him explain his views, for they had heard much criticism of the Christian sect everywhere.

On an appointed day a large number came to his lodging, and all day Paul talked with them, telling them of "the kingdom of God, persuading them concerning Jesus, both out of the law of Moses, and out of the prophets." The reaction of his audience was divided: some believed, some did not. To the nonbelievers he gave a strong parting rebuke as they left: "Well spake the Holy Ghost by Esaias the prophet unto our fathers, Saying, Go unto this people, and say, Hearing ye shall hear, and shall not understand; and seeing ye shall see, and not perceive: For the heart of this people is waxed gross, and their ears are dull of hearing, and their eyes have they closed; lest they should see with their eyes, and hear with their ears, and understand with their heart, and should be converted, and I should heal them. Be it known therefore unto you, that the salvation of God is sent unto the Gentiles, and that they will hear it."

Luke concludes his biography on a triumphant note: "Paul dwelt two whole years in his own hired house, and received all that came in unto him, Preaching the kingdom of God, and teaching those things which concern the Lord Jesus Christ, with all confidence, no man forbidding him."

During these two years Paul maintained his correspondence. Only from his four prison epistles—Philemon, Colossians, Ephesians, Philippians—do we know something of his continued supervision of the distant churches he had founded. His friends and fellow laborers were a great comfort to him; they ran his errands, carried his messages, kept the lines of communication open. Among these were Timothy, Aristarchus, Mark (Marcus), Jesus (Justus), Luke, Epaphroditus of Philippi, Demas, Epaphras, Tychicus, Onesimus of Colossae, and the converts of Caesar's household.

He was careful to keep the churches informed of his welfare and plans, and was continually thankful for their concern for him. To the Colossians he wrote: "All my state shall Tychicus declare unto you" (Col. 4:7); to the Ephesians: "I have sent unto you [Tychicus] for the same purpose, that ye might know our affairs" (Eph. 6:22).

The four letters written from Rome reveal Paul's ripening conception of the true Church, and give to the Church some of his most profound theological teachings. With great versatility and insight he dealt with Christian truths and their practical application.

The first of Paul's prison letters was personal, written to his friend Philemon, a wealthy citizen of Colossae in Phrygia whom with his household Paul had led into Christianity (Philem. 1:19) and in whose home the church met. Philemon's slave Onesimus had apparently robbed his owner and then run away to Rome. Here he had met Paul and been converted. Paul prevailed upon him to return to his master, giving Onesimus a letter of intercession designed to win him pardon. The situation was a delicate one. Master and slave, now Christians, stood in a new relationship to each other. Paul handled this matter with consummate tact. This eloquent letter exemplifies Christian love in action.

Epistle to Philemon

With great courtesy and love Paul addresses Philemon, commending his Christian character and works which have given joy and refreshment to the apostle and to the Church. Paul informs Philemon he has gained a son and a helper in the slave Onesimus, whom he has converted to the faith. He longs to keep Onesimus with him in Rome, but this he cannot in conscience do without Philemon's willing consent. He could command his friend to do what is fitting, but as "Paul the aged . . . a prisoner of Jesus Christ" he chooses rather to entreat "for love's sake" that the slave be forgiven. He pleads that Onesimus be received not as a runaway servant but compassionately, "as a brother beloved," who, now

repentant and in Christ, should prove dearer and of greater service than previously.

> Paul believed that Onesimus since his conversion had a new master in Christ, and that this entitled him to be considered on a plane of Christian brotherhood (v. 16). This indirect attack on Roman slavery asserted the principle of spiritual equality in Christ—a principle that eventually destroyed the system of slavery.[18]

Paul even pledges to pay the slave's debt, yet at the same time gently reminds Philemon of his own great debt to him for the saving of his soul. The whole tone of the letter shows that Paul confidently expects Philemon will do more than he has asked. It closes with his greeting and apostolic blessing.

The second of Paul's prison letters, the Epistle to the Colossians, was occasioned by the visit of his convert Epaphras, the probable founder of the Gentile church in Colossae. Epaphras brought to Rome encouraging word of the church's healthy state, but at the same time reported the rise among its members of certain teachings which threatened its spiritual life. The nature of this heresy is not specifically mentioned but it appears to have been a form of early Gnosticism—a philosophic-religious movement that fused Greek philosophy, Oriental mysticism, and Judaism. The Gnostics laid claim to an ancient wisdom in spiritual things, both speculative and elaborate, a belief that angels had a part in the work of creation, acting as intermediaries between God and the world of matter and as being instrumental in aiding men to obtain freedom from the clutch of matter. Gnosticism included a rigorous asceticism coupled with a strict observance of Judaic ordinances.

> These philosophers combined the speculation of the Greek Pythagoras with Persian mysticism and Essenic Judaism. They held matter to be essentially evil. Hence the origin of the world was a grave problem since God was good. They conceived a series of intermediate agents or aeons to relieve God of the burden of the evil world. They at once had trouble with the person of Christ in their system when any of them accepted Christianity. They solved the matter by making Jesus one of the aeons. In morals they had two extremes. One went to license, the other to asceticism.[19]

Paul's message, carried by Tychicus, was a strong refutation of this heresy which assigned to Jesus a position of inferiority, and a clear explanation of Christ's true place in the Godhead and of his headship over the Church. Christ was pre-eminent, all that was needed for redemption.

Epistle to the Colossians

    Chapter 1:1-14 contains Paul's apostolic

greeting, his gratitude for the Colossians' faith, and his prayer for their continued spiritual progress.   ❧ **Chapter 1:15-23** develops the doctrine of the supremacy of Christ in the order of the universe, Christ's place in the Godhead, his pre-eminence in the Church, and his work of reconciliation.

"Who is the image of the invisible God"
"by him were all things created"
"he is before all things"
"by him all things consist"
"he is the head of the body, the church"
"the firstborn from the dead"

The remaining verses (24-29) of ❧ **Chapter 1** remind the Colossians of the apostle's labors and sufferings on their behalf that they who are Gentiles might know the riches of the gospel and understand the mystery hidden from past generations: the truth of the indwelling Christ—"Christ in you, the hope of glory."

❧ **Chapter 2** shows Paul's earnest concern that the Colossian church continue constant in the faith and be on guard against enticing Greek and Asiatic philosophies and man-made tradition. In Christ only is "all the fulness of the Godhead bodily"; in him is their completeness; in him is "the circumcision made without hands" which puts off the sins of the flesh; "buried with him in baptism" they have resurrection through faith. Christ has given them life and forgiven their sins through his victorious atoning work on the cross. Therefore they need not Mosaic ordinances, or mediation of angels, or asceticism, for in Christ are they dead to "the rudiments of the world."

❧ **Chapters 3:1-4:6** urge those who have risen with Christ to set their affection on spiritual things and to live in union with him. Christian living requires complete regeneration of character, putting off the evil habits of "the old man" and putting on a new nature in the likeness of God (see pp. 454-457). In this "new man" racial, religious, and social distinctions do not exist, Christ being "all, and in all." They are to appropriate such qualities of Christ as mercy, kindness, humility, meekness, forbearance, forgiveness, charity, peace, gratitude. Paul details the reciprocal duties of wives and husbands, children and fathers, servants and masters. He solicits their prayers for the furtherance of his preaching, and admonishes wisdom and graciousness in their dealings with the outside world.

❧ **Chapter 4:7-18** commends Tychicus, the bearer of the letter, and Onesimus who accompanies him, and sends greetings from Paul's fellow workers. His own greeting and benediction.

When Tychicus carried Paul's letter to the Colossians he also took with him a companion letter which is called the Epistle to the Ephesians. Some early manuscripts omit the words *at Ephesus* from the first verse of this letter. Because of this and because Paul had instructed the church of Colossae and the church of Laodicea (11 miles distant) to share their letters (Col. 4:16), many scholars consider this a Laodicean letter, or a circular one to the churches of the East. It contains neither personal greetings to friends in the Ephesian church nor any reference to its local church life despite his long stay in Ephesus. The omission of these things would tend to confirm the view that he was writing to a larger audience. Ephesians is therefore Paul's most impersonal communication; its character is of a treatise or homily that develops the subject of the union of all believers in Christ, both Jew and Gentile.

Although Paul had first regarded the Church as a great organized society of believers, he had come to see it as far more. He understood, and presented in this epistle, the idea of Church in its spiritual fulness and glory. As the human body is one coordinated whole, so the Church is one body—"the body of Christ"—consisting of all who hold fast to Christ, its Head (see p. 459). He unfolded, as John did later, the grandeur and fullness of God's eternal purpose to redeem all humanity through His Son. These lofty concepts give us glimpses into the "most holy place" of Paul's consciousness.

Epistle to the Ephesians

❧ **Chapter 1:1-14** contains Paul's brief apostolic greeting, and immediately breaks forth into a burst of praise for God's spiritual blessings which have come to men through Jesus Christ, for God's eternal purpose and grace in foreordaining believers to His holiness and praise, for world-wide redemption through His Son, and for the sealing of the believer by the Holy Spirit until his full redemption is accomplished.

❧ **Chapter 1:15-23** is Paul's prayer that Christians fully comprehend their calling, the rich glory of their inheritance, and the greatness of God's power toward them, seen in the working of His might in raising Christ from the dead and exalting him, giving him eternal dominion, and appointing him "head over all things to the church, Which is his body."

❧ **Chapter 2** declares the effects of God's love and grace through Christ, whereby men are saved from sin and quickened to spiritual life; and whereby the Gentiles have been brought into union with Christ along with the commonwealth of Israel. Through his sacrifice on the cross Christ Jesus has "broken down the middle wall of partition" between Jew and Gentile, reconciling both to God and giving them access to the Father. All men therefore are fellow citizens of the kingdom and of the household of God and, "fitly framed together," are built up into one living temple.

❧ Chapter 3:1-13 expounds "the mystery," hidden from past ages, that has been revealed to him—the Gentiles are to be saved and to be fellow heirs of God's promise through Christ. To him has been given the stewardship of this mystery that the Gentiles might know the inexhaustible riches and fellowship of Christ. ❧ Chapter 3:14-21 is the apostle's earnest prayer that the Father mightily strengthen them in the inner man by His Spirit so that Christ may dwell in their hearts by faith; that they, firmly grounded in love, may be able to attain to a full comprehension of the Father's love—in breadth, length, depth, height—and know the love of Christ; so they may be made complete.

❧ Chapters 4-6 deal with the edifying—building up—of the Church into a perfect unity with Christ (see p. 460), and set forth the life and service of the Christian. They give a more complete exposition of essential precepts relating to Christian character and duties than Paul had heretofore written. ❧ Chapter 4:1-16 urges believers to walk worthy of their great calling—in humility, meekness, patience, and forbearing love. They are to demonstrate spiritual unity and brotherhood, all having "one body . . . one Spirit . . . one hope. . . . One Lord, one faith, one baptism, One God and Father." Every individual gift of grace given through the munificence of Christ is to be used for the edifying and perfecting of God's people, till all men reach the stature of the perfect man, till all reach spiritual maturity, till the whole Church grows up into a perfect union with Christ, its Head. ❧ Chapters 4:17-6:9 exhort to Christlike living. Believers are to put off the old sinful manner of life and to put on the nature of Christ; to *walk* wisely as "children of light" in the way of truth which they have learned. Here Paul discusses the Spirit-motivated life and the duties of wives and husbands, children and fathers, servants and masters toward each other, of which the Church's relationship to Christ and Christ's relationship to his Church are prototypes. In ❧ Chapter 6:10-24 Paul calls on his readers to strengthen themselves in the Lord: to put on the "whole armour of God" that they may be able to resist the wiles of the devil, for they fight against the unseen forces of evil and spiritual wickedness. The believer must arm himself beforehand "to withstand in the evil day, and having done all to stand." His armor is truth, righteousness, peace, faith, salvation; his weapons the Word of God and prayer. Paul asks for their prayers on his behalf. Apostolic benediction.

Among Paul's friends was Epaphroditus of Philippi, who came to Rome to be of assistance and to bring financial aid from the Philippian church (Phil. 2:25). This church was the first the apostle had founded in Europe on his second missionary journey some ten years earlier, and it had always been warm and generous in its treatment of him (II Cor. 11:9; Phil. 4:15,16). While Epaphroditus was in the Roman capital, he fell sick and almost died. The Philippian congregation had heard of their messenger's illness; and Paul, knowing their anxiety for Epaphroditus' welfare and for his, sent him home, entrusting him with a comforting letter to the church.

Faithful from its inception, this church had earned the apostle's deepest regard and heartfelt love; it was his "joy and crown," having no grave defects of character, no disorders, no doctrinal errors to correct. To this beloved church he confided his innermost thoughts and further revealed his consuming love for Christ. This fourth prison epistle is Paul's most affectionate letter. Although he had been in chains more than two years—and perhaps even at this moment was awaiting trial—its tone is joyous and triumphant.

Epistle to the Philippians

❧ Chapter 1 opens with Paul's salutation to the whole assembly at Philippi, expresses his gratitude for their cooperation in spreading the gospel from the first day they heard it, and includes a prayer for their continued spiritual development. He rejoices that his Roman imprisonment, far from ending his work, has made the gospel known to the Emperor's bodyguard stationed in the Praetorium of the palace and has stimulated its spread among the Roman people. He affirms that his sole object, whether he suffers, lives or dies, is to glorify Christ. He discloses an inner conflict: he longs to depart from this world to be with Christ, but feels it needful for their sakes that he remain with them. Therefore he is confident he will regain his freedom and continue his ministry. Whether or not he comes to them, let their lives be worthy of Christ's gospel that he may know they are standing fast "in one spirit, with one mind." Let them never be terrified by their adversaries; their courage is a token of salvation, for they are privileged not only to believe in Christ but also to suffer for his sake.

❧ **Chapter 2** urges the Christian pattern of life—"Let this mind be in you, which was also in Christ Jesus"—and sets before his readers the Son's self-immolating example of meekness and service. They are to labor earnestly to "work out" their own salvation, knowing that God "worketh in" them, causing them to love His gracious will and enabling them to do it. They are to do everything without grumbling and contention that they may be blameless, the sons of God, shining as lights in the midst of a perverse nation, holding before the world the Word of Life. Thus will he be able to rejoice that his work has not been in vain. Paul plans to send Timothy to them shortly, for he has no one like him who will be so genuinely concerned for their well-being. He speaks of his hope for a speedy release that he too may come to them. He feels it necessary to send Epaphroditus now, his faithful fellow worker and their messenger, who longs to return home because of their anxiety when they heard he had been sick. Indeed, he had been sick almost to the point of death, but God had had mercy on his friend—and on himself also, sparing him an added sorrow. One commentator has paraphrased verse 27: "When God was merciful unto Epaphroditus, God was merciful unto me."

❧ **Chapter 3** warns the church to be on guard against the seducing Judaizers he scornfully calls dogs, evil workers, of the concision (mutilators of the flesh), and affirms that Christians represent the true circumcision, for they worship God in the spirit and have their joy in Christ Jesus. Paul declares that because of his own rigorous Jewish background he has had more cause than many to trust in legal righteousness, but renounced all he had gained through the Law, counting it worthless, that he might gain the righteousness of Christ. His whole life motive is to "win Christ . . . be found in him . . . know him, and the power of his resurrection, and the fellowship of his sufferings," so he might attain resurrection. He does not claim to have attained this perfection but he continually presses toward the goal and urges all Christians to do the same. Since their "conversation" (RV citizenship; Cruden's, behavior, or manner of life [3:20]) is in heaven, they are to watch for the Savior from heaven who will, in the exercise of his power, transform the fleshly body that it may be "fashioned like unto his glorious body" (compare Mk. 9:2).

❧ **Chapter 4** enjoins the church to steadfastness in Christ, to rejoicing, to prayer, to the continual meditation of true and good thoughts; they are to follow his example. Thus they will find "the peace of God, which passeth all understanding." Paul thanks the Philippian church for its thoughtful provision for his needs and for its sympathy and service through the years. He confides, however, that for his part he has learned to be content whatever his state, knowing his sufficiency is in Christ. Apostolic greeting and benediction.

In these last four epistles Paul spoke often of his imprisonment, but he endured this affliction patiently and even gladly, seeing it as profitable to the spread of the gospel: "The prisoner of Jesus Christ for you Gentiles" (Eph. 3:1); "I am an ambassador in bonds" (Eph. 6:20); "Remember my bonds" (Col. 4:18). "I would ye should understand, brethren, that the things which happened unto me have fallen out rather unto the furtherance of the gospel; So that my bonds in Christ are manifest in all the palace [of Caesar], and in all other places; And many of the brethren in the Lord, waxing confident by my bonds, are much more bold to speak the word without fear. Some indeed preach Christ even [through motives] of envy and strife . . . and some also of good will . . . notwithstanding, every way . . . Christ is preached; and I therein do rejoice. . . ." (Phil. 1:12-18).

During this imprisonment he had faced his own Gethsemane, yielding up his will—his longing to leave the world—to Christ's will that he remain to minister to the churches: "For to me to live is Christ, and to die is gain. But if I live in the flesh, this is the fruit of my labour: yet what I shall choose I wot not. For I am in a strait betwixt two, having a desire to depart, and to be with Christ; which is far better: Nevertheless to abide in the flesh is more needful for you" (Phil 1:21-24).

Like the merchant of Jesus' parable, Paul gave all for the pearl of great price: "I count all things but loss for the excellency of the knowledge of Christ Jesus my Lord: for whom I have suffered the loss of all things, and do count them but dung, that I may win Christ" (Phil. 3:8).

This man, who had written to the Corinthians "this corruptible must put on incorruption, and this mortal must put on immortality," ever held to the shining hope of transfiguration and resurrection: "For our conversation [RV citizenship] is in heaven; from whence also we look for the Saviour, the Lord Jesus Christ: Who shall change our vile body [RV the body of our humiliation], that it may be fashioned like unto his glorious body, according to the working whereby he is able even to subdue all things unto himself" (Phil. 3:20,21).

Paul constantly strove for a more perfect understanding of Christ: "Not as though I had already attained, either were already perfect: but I follow after, if that I may apprehend that for which also I am apprehended of Christ Jesus ... this one thing I do, forgetting those things which are behind, and reaching forth unto those things which are before, I press toward the mark for the prize of the high calling of God in Christ Jesus" (Phil. 3:12-14; compare I Cor. 13:12).

Further Journeying (63-67/68 A.D.)

History is silent regarding Paul's first trial in Rome before Nero, but there are indications within his three remaining letters, two to Timothy and one to Titus, that he was acquitted (*ca.* 63 A.D.), that he left the capital and continued his missionary labors for another four or five years (63-67?).* The testimony of Clement of Rome, Eusebius, Chrysostom, and Jerome bears this out. Scholars who accept these three epistles as genuinely Paul's feel they give Paul's own evidence of a further strenuous period of travel and of a second imprisonment in Rome, historical evidence that cannot be fitted into the record of Paul's life as it is recorded in the later chapters of Acts (20-28).**

His preceding letters had indicated his desire to revisit Asia Minor and Macedonia upon his release (Philem. 1:22; compare Phil. 1:26; 2:24). Paul's exact movements and itinerary during this period between imprisonments cannot now be traced. He had apparently abandoned his earlier plan to go to Spain (Rom. 15:24,28), since there is no record of any visit; instead he traveled east. Accompanying him from time to time were trusted companions who assisted him and supported his zeal. Some he assigned to key positions in the churches as he felt his own work drawing to a close. We read that Paul visited Crete (Tit. 1:5), leaving Titus to oversee its churches. Another journey took the apostle to Asia Minor, where he stationed Timothy at Ephesus to strengthen the church (I Tim. 1:3). He left his friend Trophimus sick at Miletus (II Tim. 4:20); his cloak and his parchments were entrusted to Carpus at Troas (II Tim. 4:12). Paul proceeded to Macedonia, where his First Epistle to Timothy was written (I Tim. 1:3). Erastus he left at Corinth (II Tim. 4:20). He may have wintered at Nicopolis in Achaia in 67, for he wrote to Titus that such was his intention and that he would send for

*Second Timothy 4:16,17 were interpreted by early church fathers as referring to Paul's first defense before Nero and subsequent release. Later scholars believe they may refer to an earlier trial.

**First and Second Timothy and Titus were early attributed to Paul, but modern scholarship questions his authorship on the grounds of historical difficulties, literary style, reference to increasing heresies, and advanced church organization.

Titus to come to him there (Tit. 3:12); or he may have been rearrested before this plan could be fulfilled.

In the doctrinal epistles (I and II Corinthians, Galatians, Romans) Paul had expounded the fundamental doctrines of Christianity; in the prison epistles (Philemon, Colossians, Ephesians, Philippians) he had shared his revelations of the Church both as a society among men and as the ideal and spiritual body of Christ; now, in his last letters (I Timothy, Titus, II Timothy)—the pastoral epistles—he dealt with the ecclesiastical organization of the churches and defined the work of a true pastor in the care of his flock.

In this closing period of his life Paul's great concerns were for the purity of church doctrine and for the conduct of church members. Unqualified teachers were beginning to make themselves heard. Instead of promoting the love that springs from a pure heart, a good conscience, and a sincere faith, these had turned to speculative discussions of Jewish genealogies and legends. The apostle's pastoral letters urged suppression of these errors and faithful adherence to wholesome teachings. They set out specific moral and spiritual qualifications for church officers, and prescribed rules for Christian conduct.

In 66/67 A.D. Paul wrote from Macedonia to his beloved Timothy in Ephesus (I Tim. 1:3). The great promise he had foreseen in this young disciple from their first meeting in Lystra had been fully justified. Timothy had been his companion on much of his second and third journeys, his trusted emissary to Corinth and the churches of Macedonia, and his comrade during a part of the Roman imprisonment. The riches of the apostle's thought were open to Timothy during these years of close association; it was his privilege to have had Paul's personal instruction and guidance, and to have been present when at least seven of the Pauline epistles were written (I and II Thessalonians, II Corinthians, Romans, Philippians, Philemon, Colossians).

Paul had left Timothy, now between thirty-five and forty, in charge of the Ephesian church. To supervise this important church, some of whose members were drifting away from the faith, was a formidable task. Paul's letter was timely, filled with the distilled wisdom of his years of experience. He gave Timothy apostolic guidance for the preservation of the gospel, guidelines for the appointment of church officers, specific rules for church discipline, and explicit instruction in Christian behavior. Interspersed with church matters were Paul's exhortations to Timothy himself that have, according to a nineteenth-century scholar, "ever since furnished a treasury of practical precepts for the Christian Church."

First Epistle to Timothy

The keynote is "that thou mayest know how thou oughtest to behave thyself in the house of God" (3:15). **Chapter 1** gives Paul's apostolic greeting to Timothy and charges the young pastor to rebuke those who are teaching incorrect doctrine and quibbling interpretations of the Law. The Law is good if used lawfully, enacted not so much for a righteous man as for the restraint of evildoers. Recalling the enormity of his own sin, Paul rejoices that through God's mercy and grace he has been forgiven and entrusted with Christ's gospel, and sees himself as a pattern of Christ's patient love to all believers. He exhorts Timothy to protect the purity of church doctrine, expressing confidence that Timothy will fulfill this trust in accordance with the prophecies made at his ordination, and will "war a good warfare" (compare I Tim. 4:14; II Tim. 1:6). He warns him not to wreck his faith by blasphemy as had Hymenaeus or by disobedience as had Alexander, associates the apostle had excommunicated (II Tim. 2:17,18; 4:14,15).

Chapter 2 gives directions concerning prayer and concerning the conduct and place of women in public worship. Prayer is to be offered for all men, including those high in government, that the Church might have peace, and that all men might be brought to a knowledge of the truth, since there is but one God and one mediator, Christ Jesus, who gave himself as a ransom for all. Prayer should be holy, offered in a spirit free of anger and dispute. Paul rules that women are to dress modestly and not embellish their persons with costly clothes and ornaments—their ornaments should be good works; in church they are to be silent and submissive, neither teaching in the congregation nor usurping the authority of the men (compare I Cor. 14:34,35; 11:2-15).

Chapter 3 lists the qualifications of church officers. A bishop, an elder, must be blameless in character; the character of deacons must likewise be irreproachable. Paul states these requisites to guide Timothy in his dealings with church members, for "the church of the living God [is] the pillar and ground of the truth." Here he exclaims in wonder at the "mystery of godliness" of this religion as manifested in the incarnate Christ.

Chapter 4 reiterates Paul's charge to Timothy to guard against false teachings of asceticism that do not promote spirituality and that are causing some to fall away from the faith—such teachings as prohibition of marriage and insistence on abstinence from certain kinds of food. As a good minister it is Timothy's duty to warn his congregation against these errors. General instructions of a personal nature follow: Timothy is to train himself in godliness, as godliness holds the promise of life now and of life to come; despite his youth he is to set an example of Christian excellence, applying himself to the public reading of Scripture, to exhortation, to teaching, to meditation. Thus he will save himself and those who hear.

Chapters 5-6 contain counsel on how to deal with various groups within the church: with the old and the young of both sexes; with widows and unmarried women; with elders, those meriting honor and those deserving reproof. Timothy is counseled to "lay hands suddenly on no man [ordain no one hastily]." Finally, he is advised as to the conduct of Christian slaves under both heathen and Christian masters. Paul cautions against false teachers who, in addition to their other wrong practices, are using religion as a means of gain. This admonition is followed by a warning against greed—"for the love of money is the root of all evil." Again there is an appeal to Timothy to follow righteousness and godliness, to persevere in the "good fight of faith" to which he has been called, and to keep spotless the gospel which has been committed to him. Apostolic benediction.

Shortly after Paul had written to Timothy he wrote to Titus, who had been left in charge of the churches in Crete. How or when Christianity was brought to the island is not known—perhaps by Jews who had heard Peter's sermon on the Day of Pentecost (Acts 2:11) or by Paul during his stay at Fair Havens (Acts 27:8,9). The Cretan churches were troubled by false teachers—Gnostic believers and Jewish converts who insisted on continued adherence to Jewish ordinances. In addition, the Cretans themselves had an unsavory reputation as liars and gluttons.

Titus, like Timothy, was a personal convert of Paul—termed by the apostle "mine own son after the common faith." He was the young Greek delegate Paul had taken to the Council of Jerusalem years before (Gal. 2:1,3), Paul's companion at Ephesus on the second missionary journey, and the co-worker entrusted with two important missions to Corinth (II Cor. 12:18; 8:6 and II Cor. 8:16-18). Paul always spoke of him with deep affection and high esteem (II Cor. 2:13; 8:22,23).

Paul's letter gives Titus authority to appoint pastors in the local churches of Crete and furnishes him with valuable spiritual guidance much like that given to Timothy.

Epistle to Titus

🕭 **Chapter 1** reminds Titus that he has been sent to Crete to "set in order the things that are wanting, and ordain elders in every city." Paul sets down the requisite qualifications for church officers: stewards of God must be blameless in character and possess a strong faith so they can encourage others with sound teaching and be equipped effectively to silence willful, conceited, deceitful teachers who are undermining the faith of whole families "for filthy lucre's sake."

🕭 **Chapter 2** is Paul's strong directive to instruct the various groups within the congregation—aged men and women, young men and women, servants, and believers in general—in Christian character and duties that are in accord with "sound doctrine." All are to live "soberly, righteously, and godly, in this present world" while awaiting the fulfillment of their hope of Christ's return in glory.

🕭 **Chapter 3** contains further exhortations. Titus is to remind believers to be obedient citizens of the state and to live in peace and brotherhood with those in the world around them. At one time they had been foolish, disobedient, hateful, sensuous, but God's mercy and grace had saved them through the regenerative power of the Holy Ghost, and now they must be "careful to maintain good works." Titus is warned to stand aloof from foolish and contentious discussions; to warn unteachable persons (heretics) twice, then have nothing more to do with them. Apostolic benediction.

Second Imprisonment in Rome (67/68 A.D.) In 64, during Paul's absence from the Roman capital, Rome caught fire and more than half the city was destroyed. The debauched, half-mad Nero was rumored to have set the fire. Perhaps to divert suspicion from him, blame was laid on the Christians of Rome. According to Tacitus, thousands were martyred with great cruelty—crucified, burned as torches, torn by beasts. Christians were henceforth recognized as a distinct body, separate from both Jews and pagans. During the next few years the hatred and suspicion of the whole Empire was directed more or less against this sect, and any event that brought its members to the attention of the Roman authorities only served to heighten that suspicion.

It was inevitable that in time so eminent a leader as Paul should be seized and imprisoned again at Rome. The exact charge against him is not known. The conditions of his incarceration the second time were far more severe than the first; he was not only chained night and day to a soldier but was also treated as a common criminal. Now nearing sixty-five, such treatment was a difficult trial for the apostle. He continued, however, to supervise the churches whenever and wherever possible, sending Crescens to Galatia; Titus to Dalmatia (the coastal region of Illyricum); Tychicus to Ephesus. Some of his Asian friends had fallen away. Amid this sense of desertion he had been greatly cheered by the visits of his Ephesian friend Onesiphorus, who had come to Rome and courageously and painstakingly searched him out. Of his close friends Luke alone was now with him to lighten his loneliness and alleviate the hardships of his environment. But he longed to see Timothy, and wrote him to come to Rome quickly.

This second letter, written at the close of nearly thirty-three years of labor for the Church, is the last of Paul's correspondence the world now possesses. At the Last Supper Jesus had consoled his sorrowing disciples, enlarging their understanding; now Paul, knowing his martyrdom was imminent, comforted and strengthened Timothy—and through him Christians everywhere. He renewed his charge to this dear comrade, confident that Timothy would carry on the gospel message in full measure.

Second Epistle to Timothy

🕭 **Chapter 1** conveys Paul's deep affection for Timothy and his longing to see him. The young preacher is reminded of his spiritual capabilities and urged to persevere with a fresh courage and zeal in professing the faith, for the spirit that had been given him was one not of fear but "of power, and of love, and of a sound mind." Paul calls on Timothy to suffer with him, willingly and without shame, the afflictions that come to a minister of the gospel, for their calling is holy and holds the hope of immortality. He charges him to safeguard the Christian truth committed to him, mentioning sadly the widespread disaffection and desertion of some of his own converts in the province of Asia, among them Phygellus and Hermogenes, but acknowledging gratefully the loyalty and aid of Onesiphorus of Ephesus, who had visited him in Rome.

In 🕭 **Chapter 2** Paul charges Timothy to recruit trustworthy men for the ministry and commit to them what he has received that they may be able to teach others. As "a good soldier of Jesus Christ" Timothy must resolutely endure hardship and suffering. A soldier does not entangle himself with the world's occupations so he may please his commanding officer. A man competing in athletic games does not win the prize unless he obeys the rules. The husbandman has the right to the first share of his crop. Let him mark well these three illustrations he has given and God will give him understanding. Let him always remember that Jesus was raised from the dead; for this teaching he himself suffers imprisonment, chained as a criminal, but "the word of God is not bound." He endures all these things for the sake of those called of God, that they may obtain salvation. He relies on the promise that those who die with Christ will live with him; that those who suffer with Christ will reign with him; that those who deny Christ, them will Christ deny; that even though men believe not, Christ "abideth faithful: he cannot deny himself." Timothy is admonished to be a sound workman, rightly handling the word of truth, shunning heretical doctrines. Thus he will be a vessel of honor fit for use in the household of God. Let him flee youthful lusts and aim for the virtues of righteousness, faith, love, and peace in the company of those having a like goal. Timothy is cautioned against participating in foolish discussions which only engender strife. Rather, a servant of the Lord must gently, patiently, meekly correct the errors of his opponents, hoping for their repentance.

In Chapter 3 Paul foretells "perilous times" of apostasy which will precede the Second Coming of Christ, when men will be lovers of self and indulge in the worst sort of evil, keeping up a form of religion but denying its power. Turn away from such persons. These reprobates resist the truth, but they cannot continue to do so with any more success than could the two Egyptian magicians (Jannes and Jambres, according to Jewish tradition) who resisted Moses in the plagues (Ex. 7:11). Paul reminds Timothy again of his gospel and of his own example of patience and love, and of the persecutions endured at Antioch, Iconium, and Lystra, yet God had delivered him from them all. All who live godly lives will know persecution. Paul urges Timothy to be faithful to the lessons he has learned from the Scriptures since childhood; in them is to be found a complete and sufficient guide to the man of God in all things relating to perfection.

 Chapter 4 gives Paul's final solemn charge to Timothy to be tirelessly zealous in his preaching of the gospel—"instant in season, out of season . . . endure afflictions, do the work of an evangelist, make full proof of thy ministry"—for times of apostasy lie ahead. His own ministry is finished and the time of his departure is near. Paul rests in the assurance that he has fought a

good fight and guarded the faith, and that "a crown of righteousness" is awaiting him, as it does all who are faithful. The apostle requests Timothy to come to Rome speedily and bring Mark with him, picking up on the way the cloak and parchments left at Troas. He informs Timothy that at his direction some of his fellow workers have gone into various fields of labor but speaks sorrowfully of others who have deserted him. In fact, he confides that no Christian friend had stood by him "at [his] first answer" (possibly a reference to a preliminary trial before the imperial court during his second imprisonment); nevertheless Christ had strengthened him so that he had been able to make a full proclamation of the gospel before all the Gentiles present. He closes on a triumphant note of absolute trust that Christ would "preserve [him] unto his heavenly kingdom." Greetings and apostolic benediction.

Paul's Martyrdom

The Biblical record of Paul's life ceases with this second letter to Timothy. It was the close of a career that had encompassed a phenomenal amount of travel for the time—of some 12,000 to 15,000 miles in the course of his missionary activities. According to the early church fathers Tertullian and Origen, this greatest of missionaries who did so much to mold Christian thought and articulate Christian doctrine died by the sword at Rome in 67 or 68 A.D., toward the end of Nero's reign.

In Paul's final letter to Timothy there shines through the strong character of this man who had "redeemed" the time. Though he had termed himself "Paul the aged," there was no letting down in his zeal, no carelessness in modes of thought, no diminishing of devotion and love for the Church; only a mounting vision and an invincible faith. God, who had strengthened him when all men had deserted him, would rescue him from every evil and bring him into His heavenly realm. Jesus had stood unmoved by the humiliation of rejection; Paul was not ashamed of the humiliation of imprisonment. He was at peace, for he had long since been persuaded that *nothing* could separate him from the love of God.

In the shadow of martyrdom Paul held a strong and exalted conviction of immortality. Immortality to him was not something still to be accomplished, but a truth already manifest and available to all in the life of Christ. His good fight of faith had assured him "a crown of righteousness."

PARALLELS IN THE LIVES OF PAUL AND JESUS

After conversion Paul dedicated himself to preaching and expounding the gospel of Christ. He sought to approximate the Master's love; thus the circumstances and experiences of his life parallel in many instances those of the life of Jesus.

The keynote of Paul's life is summed up in his own words: "For to me to live is Christ."

JESUS	PAUL
Submission to the Father's Will	
"I came down from heaven, not to do mine own will, but the will of him that sent me." Jn. 6:38	"Lord, what wilt thou have me to do?" Acts 9:6
True Genealogy	
"In the beginning was the Word, and the Word was with God, and the Word was God."	"As many as received him, to them gave he power to become the sons of God. . . . Which were born, not of blood, nor of the will of the flesh, nor of the will of man, but of God." Jn. 1:12,13
"And the Word was made flesh, and dwelt among us, (and we beheld his glory, the glory as of the only begotten of the Father,) full of grace and truth." Jn. 1:1,14	"Paul, an apostle, (not of men, neither by man, but by Jesus Christ, and God the Father. . . .)" Gal. 1:1
Minister and Apostle	
"For even the Son of man came not to be ministered unto, but to minister, and to give his life a ransom for many." Mk. 10:45	"I am ordained a preacher, and an apostle . . . a teacher of the Gentiles in faith and verity." I Tim. 2:7 (Acts. 26:16)
Universal Mission	
"A light to lighten the Gentiles, and the glory of thy people Israel." Lu. 2:32	"He is a chosen vessel unto me, to bear my name before the Gentiles, and kings, and the children of Israel." Acts 9:15
"Other sheep I have, which are not of this fold: them also I must bring, and they shall hear my voice; and there shall be one fold, and one shepherd." Jn. 10:16	"I [Christ] send thee [to the Gentiles], To open their eyes, and to turn them from darkness to light, and from the power of Satan unto God. . . ." Acts 26:17,18

Season of Solitude

Jesus, after baptism, withdrew into the solitude of the wilderness of Judaea to face his temptation and the requirements of his mission. Mt. 4:1-11	Paul, after conversion, withdrew into the solitude of Arabia to reflect upon his conversion and his call to apostleship. Gal. 1:15-17

One Gospel

"Jesus . . . said, My doctrine is not mine, but his that sent me. If any man will do his will, he shall know of the doctrine, whether it be of God, or whether I speak of myself." Jn. 7:16,17	"I certify you, brethren, that the gospel which was preached of me is not after man. For I neither received it of man, neither was I taught it, but by the revelation of Jesus Christ." Gal. 1:11,12

Early Hostility of Enemies

"All they in the synagogue. . . . rose up, and thrust him out of the city [Nazareth], and led him unto the brow of the hill . . . that they might cast him down headlong." Lu. 4:28,29	"The Jews took counsel to kill him. . . . And they watched the gates [of Damascus] day and night to kill him." Acts 9:23,24

The Effectual Working of God's Power

"The words that I speak unto you I speak not of myself: but the Father that dwelleth in me, he doeth the works." Jn. 14:10	"I laboured more abundantly than they all: yet not I, but the grace of God which was with me." I Cor. 15:10

Transfiguration

"After six days Jesus taketh with him Peter, and James, and John, and leadeth them up into an high mountain apart by themselves: and he was transfigured before them." Mk. 9:2	"I knew a man in Christ above fourteen years ago, (whether in the body, I cannot tell; or whether out of the body, I cannot tell: God knoweth;) such an one caught up to the third heaven." II Cor. 12:2-4

Preaching, Healing, Raising the Dead

"Jesus went about all the cities and villages, teaching in their synagogues, and preaching the gospel of the kingdom, and healing every sickness and every disease among the people." Mt. 9:35	"Long time . . . abode they [Paul and Barnabas] speaking boldly in the Lord, which gave testimony unto the word of his grace, and granted signs and wonders to be done by their hands." Acts 14:3
Jesus raised the widow's son Lu. 7:11-17	Paul raised from stoning Acts 14:19,20
He raised Jairus' daughter Lu. 8:41-56	Paul raised Eutychus Acts 20:7-12
He raised Lazarus Jn. 11:1-45	

JESUS	PAUL

The Object of Envy

"The Pharisees . . . said . . . Perceive ye how ye prevail nothing? behold, the world is gone after him." Jn. 12:19

"He [Pilate] knew that the chief priests had delivered him for envy." Mk. 15:10

"When the Jews saw the multitudes, they were filled with envy, and spake against those things which were spoken by Paul, contradicting and blaspheming." Acts 13:45

Accusation of Irreligious Conduct

The Pharisees charged: "This man is not of God, because he keepeth not the sabbath day." Jn. 9:16

"This is the man, that teacheth all men every where against the people, and the law, and this place: and further brought Greeks also into the temple, and hath polluted this holy place." Acts 21:28

Humiliation and Persecution

"Pilate therefore took Jesus, and scourged him." Jn. 19:1

"Then did they spit in his face, and buffeted him; and others smote him with the palms of their hands. . . ." Mt. 26:67

"Of the Jews five times received I forty stripes save one. Thrice was I beaten with rods, once was I stoned. . . ." II Cor. 11:24,25

"The high priest Ananias commanded them that stood by him to smite him on the mouth." Acts 23:2

Trial before Jewish Authorities

Before the high priest Caiaphas and Sanhedrin in Jerusalem Mt. 26:57-68

Before the high priest Ananias and Sanhedrin in Jerusalem Acts 22:30-23:10

Trial before Roman Authorities

Before Pilate Jn. 18:28-19:16
Before Herod Antipas Lu. 23:7-12
Before Pilate Lu. 23:13-24

Before Felix Acts 24
Before Porcius Festus Acts 25:1-12
Before Herod Agrippa II Acts 25:23-26:32

Accusation of Sedition and Treason

"We found this fellow perverting the nation, and forbidding to give tribute to Caesar, saying that he himself is Christ a King." Lu. 23:2

"We have found this man a pestilent fellow, and a mover of sedition among all the Jews throughout the world, and a ringleader of the sect of the Nazarenes." Acts 24:5

443

JESUS	PAUL

Subject to Worldly Policy

"Pilate, willing to content the people, released Barabbas unto them, and delivered Jesus . . . to be crucified." Mk. 15:15

"Felix, willing to shew the Jews a pleasure, left Paul bound." Acts 24:27 (cf. 25:9)

Accusation of Madness

"Many of them said, He hath a devil, and is mad; why hear ye him?" Jn. 10:20

"Festus said with a loud voice, Paul, thou art beside thyself; much learning doth make thee mad." Acts 26:24

Innocency

Pilate said, "I find in him no fault at all." Jn. 18:38

Festus and Herod Agrippa said, "This man doeth nothing worthy of death or of bonds." Acts 26:31

Willingness to Endure Suffering

"I lay down my life for the sheep." Jn. 10:15

"I endure all things for the elect's sakes. . . ." II Tim. 2:10

Crucifixion and Martyrdom

"Jesus knew that his hour was come that he should depart out of this world unto the Father. . . ." Jn. 13:1

"I am now ready to be offered, and the time of my departure is at hand." II Tim. 4:6

Faithful Accomplishment of Mission

"I have glorified thee on the earth: I have finished the work which thou gavest me to do." Jn. 17:4

"I have fought a good fight, I have finished my course, I have kept the faith." II Tim. 4:7

Expectation of Glorification

"Now, O Father, glorify thou me with thine own self with the glory which I had with thee before the world was." Jn. 17:5

"Hereafter shall ye see the Son of man sitting on the right hand of power, and coming in the clouds of heaven." Mt. 26:64

"Now I know in part; but then shall I know even as also I am known." I Cor. 13:12

"Henceforth there is laid up for me a crown of righteousness, which the Lord, the righteous judge, shall give me at that day. . . ." II Tim. 4:8

12

Paul's Doctrinal Teachings

Christ Jesus himself had done no writing. Through the preaching of the apostles and other evangelistic ministers the facts of Jesus' divine Sonship and ministry, his message of the kingdom, his crucifixion, resurrection, and ascension, and their significance were passed on by word of mouth to new believers in the Church. A short time after the birth of the Church some of Jesus' sayings began to be preserved and come into circulation, but for some two decades (30-52/53 A.D.), until Paul began to write, the Church had little in written form to guide its theology and conduct. Paul's letters, coming before the Gospels, were the first Christian literature to define and develop the doctrines of grace latent in the teachings of Jesus Christ and to apply them to the spiritual life of the Christian and the Church. His writings bridge the interval between Jesus' ascension and Christ's Revelation as given by John, with its prophetic fulfillment of Christ's Second Coming.

Paul's place in the early Church was tremendously important. His extensive missionary journeys to Asia Minor, Greece, and Rome vastly widened the scope of Christianity. His leadership and apostolic authority were dominant in the many churches he founded and supervised. His burning love and labors for Christ and his intellectual capacities as a theologian made his thinking a vital influence throughout the Christian world.

Paul's express calling by Christ was a continuation of the divine plan for the salvation of men. He was specially equipped to lift Christianity beyond the restrictions of Judaism into its true sphere of universal religion. In the process of planting the gospel in the cities and outposts of the Roman Empire Paul crystallized Christian doctrine for the Church. His letters developed so fully the spirit and depth of Christ's life and gospel that they inevitably became part of Christian Scripture. His terminology indicated the analytical quality of his thought as well as the distinct individuality of his approach to Christianity. He gave new meaning and application to Old Testament words and concrete form to Old Testament ideas that were precursors of Christian doctrine, expanding the significance of these terms by relating them to Christ.

> reconciliation
> atonement
> redemption
> salvation
> faith
> fellowship
> glory
> the way
> image of God, of His Son
> kingdom of God, of Christ
> grace of God, of Christ
> power of God, of Christ, and of the Holy Ghost

He also introduced many new words and phrases into the Christian vocabulary, among them:

> mortality, immortality
> corruptible, incorruptible
> carnally minded, spiritually minded
> fulness of God, fulness of Christ
> fellow citizens, fellow heirs
> predestined
> communion
> revelation
> edification
> justification
> sanctification
> spiritual wickedness
> spiritual body
> spiritual gifts
> spiritual understanding
> fruit of the Spirit
> mind of Christ
> Godhead

Salvation is in Jesus Christ! This was the Church's message to the world; its universality was given definite expression by Paul. He had experienced this salvation; it had revolutionized his life, giving him an entirely new concept of God and His Messiah. He perceived God's great love for man through the atoning work of His Son, and saw man no longer a sinner but a "new creature" in Christ. His absolute conviction that Jesus was the saving Christ was the heart of his unshakable faith. Reason coincided with faith when he understood the Father's plan of redemption, and his experience in Christ's service only deepened that faith. One definition of *experience* is "personal acquaintance with reality." Paul testified positively: "I *know* whom I have believed." The verb *know* appears many times in his writings.

The visions and revelations of the Spirit vouchsafed to Paul so illumined his consciousness that he reached the point where life in Christ became the only reality: "For to me to live is Christ" (Phil. 1:21). From that transcendent holy place of communion—the "paradise" of which he spoke in Second Corin-

thians (12:2-4)—he who thought after the manner of the Spirit, "comparing spiritual things with spiritual," beheld the path of glory that Christ Jesus had blazed for man up to the throne of God. Jesus' atoning work so translated itself in Paul's thought into the "new and living way" of salvation that, in terms of incarnation, crucifixion, resurrection, and ascension, he correlated that "way" to himself and to the Christian.

His basic doctrines are taken up here under the following headings:

> Incarnation
> Crucifixion and the Cross
> Resurrection and Glory
> Salvation by Grace
> Justification by Faith
> Sanctification

Incarnation

Paul stressed from the outset of his ministry the doctrine of the incarnation of Christ (see p. 391). His first testimony on behalf of Christianity was his affirmation in Damascus that Jesus "is the Son of God" and that "this is very Christ" (Acts 9:20,22). This was wholly in accord with the Messianic prophecy that Christ would come through the Abrahamic line in the seed of David. Paul understood that this Son, "the image of the invisible God," had come in the flesh that he might fulfill the divine purpose in destroying sin; that his coming was the evidence of God's love for humanity and the means of man's reconciliation and redemption.

> "Of this man's [David's] seed hath God according to his promise raised unto Israel a Saviour, Jesus." (Acts 13:23; compare Rom. 1:2-4)
>
> "When the fulness of the time was come, God sent forth his Son, made of a woman, made under the law, To redeem them that were under the law, that we might receive the adoption of sons." (Gal. 4:4,5)
>
> "For what the law could not do, in that it was weak through the flesh, God sending his own Son in the likeness of sinful flesh, and for sin, condemned sin in the flesh." (Rom. 8:3; compare Phil. 2:6,7)

The incarnation was the cornerstone of the Church's faith. Paul's writings developed this doctrine of the incarnate Christ, as did the writings of Peter and John (I Pet. 4:1; II Pet. 1:16-18; Jn. 1:14; I Jn. 1:1-3; 5:6). The indisputable fact of the historic Christ enabled the Church to withstand persistent persecution and the corrupting influence of the Gnosticism that would later deny his incarnation (I Jn. 4:2,3; II Jn. 1:7).

Crucifixion and the Cross

Paul referred to his gospel as "the preaching of the cross," seeing in "the blood of Christ" the efficacious means of reconciling men to God. The unity of God and man, disrupted by sin on the part of men, had been earnestly sought throughout Old Testament history in the vicarious sacrificial system established under Mosaic Law (see p. 55). But the blood of bulls and goats was not sufficient to take away sin and reunite man with God. Only the atoning work of Christ made reconciliation possible because it effected a purification in the hearts of men that led to a repentance and reformation which enabled them to do the will of God (Col. 1:20-23). Though hatred had put Christ Jesus on the cross, his outpouring love canceled and forgave all the world's sin, and thereby revealed the infinite love of the Father.

The devout Jew found the cross an obstacle to his acceptance of Jesus as Israel's Messiah because of the Mosaic curse upon any man whose dead body hung upon a tree (Deut. 21:23). To the non-Jew it was an obstacle also, for crucifixion was a stigma, an infamous mode of punishment inflicted on rebels and criminals by many mid-Eastern nations: Assyrians, Persians, Egyptians, and later the Greeks and Romans.

> "The preaching of the cross is to them that perish foolishness; but unto us which are saved it is the power of God . . . we preach Christ crucified, unto the Jews a stumblingblock, and unto the Greeks foolishness. . . ." (I Cor. 1:18,23)

Paul taught that the sinless Jesus, the perfect Son, by his submission to death for the sins of the world and his victory over it, purchased for the whole human race the means of freedom from the bondage of sin. Jesus' sacrifice on the cross was the ransom that nullified the penalties of God's violated law, opening the way of salvation through faith.

> "You, being dead in your sins and the uncircumcision of your flesh, hath he quickened together with him, having forgiven you all trespasses; Blotting out the handwriting of ordinances that was against us, which was contrary to us, and took it out of the way, nailing it to his cross. . . ." (Col. 2:13,14)
>
> "Christ hath redeemed us from the curse of the law, being made a curse for us: for it is written, Cursed is every one that hangeth on a tree: That the blessing of Abraham might come on the Gentiles through Jesus Christ; that we might receive the promise of the Spirit through faith." (Gal. 3:13,14)

The message of the cross, then, was not one of humiliation, but a glorious one of reconciliation and redemption. By his voluntary sacrifice Jesus made full atonement for sin, thus enabling the Christian believer to stand justified before God in a state of grace.

> "God commendeth his love toward us, in that, while we were yet sinners, Christ died for us. Much more then, being now justified by his blood, we shall be saved from wrath through him. For if, when we were enemies, we were reconciled to God by the death of his Son, much more, being reconciled, we shall be saved by his life. And not only so, but we also joy in God through our Lord Jesus Christ, by whom we have now received the atonement." (Rom. 5:8-11)

Jesus had warned his disciples that following him would entail cross-bearing, and Paul gladly took up the cross. To him it meant crucifying all that was unlike Christ. He demonstrated in his own life the power of the cross to overcome sin, and taught its practical meaning for everyone.

Of himself he said: "I die daily" (I Cor. 15:31).

"I am crucified with Christ: nevertheless I live; yet not I, but Christ liveth in me: and the life which I now live in the flesh I live by the faith of the Son of God, who loved me, and gave himself for me" (Gal. 2:20).

"God forbid that I should glory, save in the cross of our Lord Jesus Christ, by whom the world is crucified unto me, and I unto the world" (Gal. 6:14).

Of Christians he said: ". . . we are killed all the day long" (Rom. 8:36).

". . . our old man is crucified with him, that the body of sin might be destroyed, that henceforth we should not serve sin" (Rom. 6:6).

"They that are Christ's have crucified the flesh with the affections and lusts" (Gal. 5:24).

Resurrection and Glory

The doctrine of resurrection was a basic teaching of the Apostolic Church. In the Old Testament the great truth of immortality was shadowed forth in the translation of Enoch in the Antediluvian Age (Gen. 5:21-24; Heb. 11:5,6) and confirmed in the translation of Elijah in the Prophetic Age (II Ki. 2:1-12). Job's thought touched on it in hope; Psalms and the Prophets whispered it in prophecy (Job 14:13-15; 19:25-27; Ps. 17:15; 71:20; Is. 26:19; Dan. 12:2). Jewish eschatology of Jesus' day relating to resurrection of the dead and a future life was a development of the intertestamental period (see p. 92). The Pharisees (but not the Sadduceees) taught the hope of resurrection after the final Judgment. Their views, however, were in the main materialistic, their concept going no higher than the resuscitation of the body and the resumption of physical life, including procreation (see p. 304). The common Jewish belief in resurrection is seen in Martha's words to Jesus about her brother Lazarus: "I know that he shall rise again in the resurrection at the last day" (Jn. 11:24). With Jesus' overcoming of death and the revealed truth of his words "I am the resurrection, and the life" (Jn. 11:25), the teaching of resurrection took on new meaning and force. It immediately became a basic hope and element of Christian belief.

Though many had testified explicitly to Jesus' resurrection—the apostles, the five hundred, the two disciples on the road to Emmaus, the women—only Paul's personal experience at conversion, when the ascended Christ called him on the road to Damascus, convinced him that Jesus had indeed risen and was the living Savior. Henceforth Jesus' resurrection was to him incontrovertible fact, and his testimony regarding it was as emphatic as the eyewitness testimony of the Twelve.

Paul thereafter taught resurrection as the Christian's hope and as the goal of a new life, a goal crowned with divine glory and immortality. He did not teach it as a hope for the future alone but as the quickening power of the Spirit at work here and now in the Christian's daily life, enabling him to "put off the old man" and "put on the new."

Of himself he said: "I count all things but loss for the excellency of the knowledge of Christ Jesus my Lord ... that I may win Christ, and be found in him. ... That I may know him, and the power of his resurrection, and the fellowship of his sufferings, being made conformable unto his death; If by any means I might attain unto the resurrection of the dead" (Phil. 3:8-11).

Of Christians he said: "God hath both raised up the Lord, and will also raise up us by his own power" (I Cor. 6:14; compare Acts 17:31).

Paul's most explicit exposition on the subject of resurrection is contained in the fifteenth chapter of First Corinthians. It was an answer to the assertion of some in the Corinthian church that there was no resurrection of the dead. To deny resurrection, he declared, was to deny the resurrection of Jesus himself; to impugn Jesus' resurrection was to make Christian faith worthless. Rather, the Son's resurrection had given mankind a sure pledge of immortality—that in him all would rise.

"Now is Christ risen from the dead, and become the firstfruits of them that slept. For since by man came death, by man came also the resurrection of the dead. For as in Adam all die, even so in Christ shall all be made alive." (I Cor. 15:20-22)

Paul departed from the Pharisaic view of mere revivification of the physical body to teach that a man would be given a new body. He was familiar with the account of the transfiguration of Jesus' body that Peter, James, and John had beheld. He was familiar, too, with the apostles' testimony concerning the distinctive nature of the body of the risen Jesus at his appearances during the forty days between the Resurrection and the Ascension. Also at the time of his conversion Paul himself had seen the radiance of the risen Christ. Thus he was led to conclude that the risen body would be of a different character. Christ "shall fashion anew the body of our humiliation, that it may be conformed to the body of his glory" (RV Phil. 3:21).

In the same treatise (I Cor. 15) Paul expounded the nature of the resurrection body (vv. 35-57). When Jesus had prophesied the manner in which his glorification would be made manifest, he had used the metaphor of a grain of wheat which, sown in the ground, brings forth "much fruit" (Jn. 12:24). Paul employed the same example of the seed and the transforming law of nature to show the manner of resurrection, the preservation of identity and the new spiritual body with which a man will rise.

He began his exposition by propounding the rhetorical question "Some men will say, How are the dead raised up? and with what body do they come?"

"Thou fool, that which thou sowest is not quickened, except it die: And that which thou sowest, thou sowest not that body that shall be, but bare grain, But God giveth it a body as it hath pleased him, and to every seed his own body.

"All flesh is not the same flesh: but there is one kind of flesh of men, another flesh of beasts. . . . There are also celestial bodies, and bodies terrestrial: but the glory of the celestial is one, and the glory of the terrestrial is another.

"There is one glory of the sun, and another glory of the moon, and another glory of the stars: for one star differeth from another star in glory.

"So also is the resurrection of the dead.

"It is sown in corruption; it is raised in incorruption:

". . . sown in dishonour . . . raised in glory:

". . . sown in weakness . . . raised in power:

"... sown a natural body ... raised a spiritual body.

"There is a natural body, and there is a spiritual body.

"And so it is written, The first man Adam was made a living soul; the last Adam was made a quickening spirit. . . .

"The first man is of the earth, earthy: the second man is the Lord from heaven [RV the second man is of heaven].

"As is the earthy, such are they also that are earthy: and as is the heavenly, such are they also that are heavenly. And as we have borne the image of the earthy, we shall also bear the image of the heavenly."

Paul realized that, because the nature of the fleshly body was in such great contrast to that of the spiritual body, mortality could not lay hold of the spiritual realities of the kingdom of God. There must of necessity be a change. The perishable nature must clothe itself with the imperishable, a change that must begin on earth and be consummated in heaven. When the transformation is complete, the resurrection life will have been fully achieved and the sin which brought death into the world will have been overcome (compare Rom. 5:12). Through life in Christ men win this victory.

"Now this I say, brethren, that flesh and blood cannot inherit the kingdom of God; neither doth corruption inherit incorruption.

"Behold, I shew you a mystery; We shall not all sleep, but we shall all be changed, In a moment, in the twinkling of an eye, at the last trump: for the trumpet shall sound, and the dead shall be raised incorruptible, and we shall be changed. For this corruptible must put on incorruption, and this mortal must put on immortality.

"So when this corruptible shall have put on incorruption, and this mortal shall have put on immortality, then shall be brought to pass the saying that is written, Death is swallowed up in victory." (Compare II Cor. 5:4)

Paul envisioned the universal harvest of Christ's resurrection in its sequence and glory (I Cor. 15:23-28): first in Christ's rising; then in the resurrection of his followers at his Coming (compare I Th. 4:16,17); Christ's reign would continue until all enemies, including "the last enemy"—death—had been subdued; the Son would then deliver up the kingdom to the Father; and after that the Son himself would also become subject to Him "that God may be all in all" (the grand sequence seen in prophetic fulfillment in John's Apocalypse).

Salvation by Grace

In the Old Testament, *grace* denoted the favor or kindness of God to men, or of men toward each other; it also denoted beauty or comeliness. In the New Testament it had a much richer connotation. It signified the outpouring of God's love and mercy to men without regard to merit, a divine bestowal in and through His Son—"the sum of all blessing that comes from God through Christ: 'grace' the source, 'peace' the stream."[1] Grace is "the influence or spirit of God operating in man to regenerate or strengthen."[2]

No one was better equipped than Paul to understand God's grace or to expound its meaning, for no sinner had been a greater object of His mercy and pardon. Paul had been converted—"turned"—on the road to Damascus by what he afterward learned was God's grace. For the first time he found release from the burden of sin and condemnation under the Law, and experienced the forgiveness and reconciliation with God which comes through Christ. When he came to understand the magnitude of that saving grace, he gave it full emphasis in the Christian system. (The word *grace* is used more than a hundred times in his epistles.)

Paul defined *grace* as "the free gift" of God (Rom. 5:15), God's "kindness toward us through Christ Jesus" (Eph. 2:7), "the power of Christ" (II Cor. 12:9) which effects salvation (Eph. 3:7). To Paul the Spirit of God and the Spirit of Christ were one (Rom. 8:9). He perceived that Christ Jesus was not only the means of God's grace but that he was that grace embodied and exemplified—God's perfect manifestation of boundless love (Eph. 1:23; compare Jn. 1:14,16,17). Christ's grace was to him the regenerative divine influence which brings the sinner up from the depths of hell, reaches out to embrace all men, lifts humanity to the heaven of God's presence, and shows man his divinity (Eph. 3:17-19; Tit. 3:7). To Paul there was only one way—faith in Christ Jesus—by which to obtain this grace of God, for faith in Christ carried with it faith in the Father who had sent him.

Of himself he said: "I thank Christ Jesus our Lord, who hath enabled me, for that he counted me faithful, putting me into the ministry; Who was before a blasphemer, and a persecutor, and injurious: but I obtained mercy, because I did it ignorantly in unbelief. And the grace of our Lord was exceeding abundant with faith and love, which is in Christ Jesus" (I Tim. 1:12-14).

"By the grace of God I am what I am: and his grace which was bestowed upon me was not in vain;

but I laboured more abundantly than they all: yet not I, but the grace of God which was with me" (I Cor.15:10; compare Eph. 3:7,8).

"I do not frustrate the grace of God. . . ." (Gal. 2:21).

Of Christians he said: "God, who is rich in mercy, for his great love wherewith he loved us, Even when we were dead in sins, hath quickened us together with Christ, (by grace ye are saved;) And hath raised us up together, and made us sit together in heavenly places in Christ Jesus. . . . For by grace are ye saved through faith; and that not of yourselves: it is the gift of God" (Eph. 2:4-6,8).

The salutation of every epistle Paul wrote spoke "grace" and "peace" in a twofold way: from God the Father, and from Jesus Christ; and Paul's benedictions invoked the blessing of the manifested grace of the Son on all. This continued use of the word *grace,* far from being repetitious, gains in emphasis. These greetings and benedictions were unique to Paul, a mark of his authorship, employed by no other of the New Testament writers.

The Law Superseded

The Jew had been taught that salvation could be earned only by a righteousness obtainable through obedience to Mosaic Law (the legislation found in Exodus, Leviticus, Numbers, and Deuteronomy). To this the Pharisees and scribes had added a large body of traditional law (see pp. 216-217). The moral law of Sinai taught the meaning of sin and the need to overcome it, since sin came under divine condemnation. But the Mosaic sacrificial and ceremonial system brought no deliverance. Rather, it added a burden, for those who did not keep the whole Law came under its curse (Gal. 3:10). As a conscientious Pharisee Paul had been rigorously trained in its precepts. He had been faithful to his highest concept of righteousness but, zealous as he was in law-keeping, he had not been saved from sin or brought into spiritual life.

Having been saved by Christ, he was forced to re-examine the place of the Law in the divine plan of redemption. He knew that the Law was good insofar as it taught obedience and righteousness, but he saw it as a temporary and subsidiary provision, a preparatory dispensation to bring men to Christ. The righteousness the Law could not bestow was obtainable through Christ's grace. Paul at no time disparaged the Law, recognizing its blessings to Israel (Rom. 3-7), but once Christ had come "the works of the law" ceased to be the way to gain acceptance with God.

> "Christ is the end of the law for righteousness to every one that believeth." (Rom. 10:4)

> "But after that the kindness and love of God our Saviour toward man appeared, Not by works of righteousness which we have done, but according to his mercy he saved us, by the washing of regeneration, and renewing of the Holy Ghost; Which he shed on us abundantly through Jesus Christ our Saviour; That being justified by his grace, we should be made heirs according to the hope of eternal life." (Tit. 3:4-7)

Paul found substantiation in Scripture for his teaching of the primacy of faith over the works of the Law. The covenant with Abraham, "to be a God unto thee, and to thy seed after thee," had come by promise and was conditioned by the patriarch's faith. That covenant had been fulfilled in Jesus Christ. Pharisaic Law interpreted the covenant as pertaining only to the descendants of Abraham—"the circumcision"—but Paul, removing its application from the realm of biological descent, declared the promise that had been accepted in faith by Abraham was the inheritance of all who accepted Christ in faith; they thereby became the spiritual seed of Abraham (Gal. 3:7).

> "Now to Abraham and his seed were the promises made. He saith not, And to seeds, as of many; but as of one, And to thy seed, which is Christ. And this I say, that the covenant, that was confirmed before of God in Christ, the law, which was four hundred and thirty years after, cannot disannul, that it should make the promise of none effect. For if the inheritance be of the law, it is no more of promise: but God gave it to Abraham by promise.

> "Wherefore then serveth the law? It was added because of transgressions, till the seed should come to whom the promise was made. . . .

> "But the scripture hath concluded all under sin, that the promise by faith of Jesus Christ might be given to them that believe. But before faith came, we were kept under the law, shut up unto the faith which should afterwards be revealed. Wherefore the law was our schoolmaster to bring us unto Christ, that we might be justified by faith. But after that faith is come, we are no longer under a schoolmaster.

> "For ye are all the children of God by faith in Christ Jesus." (Gal. 3:16-19,22-26)

The new way of faith liberated the Jew from the legalism of Mosaic Law, with its burden of guilt and condemnation. But beyond this, Christ's redemptive grace was effectual in delivering all men from the natural law of sin and death (the carnal law of the flesh to which the whole Adamic race was subject). Paul himself had experienced a measure of spiritual power and freedom from sin (Rom. 7:14-25).

"There is therefore now no condemnation to them which are in Christ Jesus, who walk not after the flesh, but after the Spirit. For the law of the Spirit of life in Christ Jesus hath made me free from the law of sin and death.

"For what the law could not do, in that it was weak through the flesh, God sending his own Son in the likeness of sinful flesh, and for sin, condemned sin in the flesh: That the righteousness of the law might be fulfilled in us, who walk not after the flesh, but after the Spirit." (Rom. 8:1-4)

Justification by Faith

Closely allied to and implicit in the Christian doctrine of grace is the doctrine of justification by faith. To justify is "to show to be just," "to show to be righteous"; "to vindicate"; "to absolve from guilt." Hebrew Scripture taught that all men were guilty of sin, being the sons of Adam, and came under God's condemnation of sin. The Jew was acutely aware of sin and guilt, having received the moral law of the covenant. He had long sought vindication through the "works of the law"—through personal righteousness and good deeds—but his hope had not been realized, for he had not kept the Law's moral precepts and personal merit was not sufficient to wipe out sin.

The Christian sought vindication through faith in Jesus Christ and found it attainable. God's righteousness was manifested in Christ and through Christ's propitiatory sacrifice (which fulfilled in type the Jewish concept of atonement); and when a man through faith acknowledged the righteousness of Christ that righteousness was imputed to him and his past sins were forgiven. Justified, he was now acceptable to God, standing in a new relation to Him—in a state of grace. "God can justly declare a sinner righteous who has faith in Christ because his face is turned to the light; he is in sympathy with Christ, and desires to follow His example."[3]

Paul made clear the one requirement necessary to win this justification—faith in the Son of God. The faith that saved was the acceptance of Jesus Christ as that Son, through whom God's righteousness is manifested. "The firm foundation of faith is the essential supreme perfection of God; his unerring knowledge, immutable truth, infinite goodness, and almighty power."[4] Inasmuch as faith was the only condition, God's salvation was for all men, Jew and non-Jew. This requirement did not invalidate the Law but "set the principle that God's will must be done on a firmer basis."[5] Of all the New Testament writers Paul most clearly defined the doctrine of justification by faith. His two principal treatises on this subject are to be found in his epistles to the Romans (chaps. 3-5) and to the Galatians (2:15-3:29).

"Now we know that what things soever the law saith, it saith to them who are under the law: that every mouth may be stopped, and all the world may become guilty before God. Therefore by the deeds of the law there shall no flesh be justified in his sight: for by the law is the knowledge of sin.

"But now the righteousness of God without the law is manifested, being witnessed by the law and the prophets; Even the righteousness of God which is by faith of Jesus Christ unto all and upon all them that believe: for there is no difference: For all have sinned, and come short of the glory of God; Being justified freely by his grace through the redemption that is in Christ Jesus: Whom God hath set forth to be a propitiation [RSV expiation] through faith in his blood, to declare his righteousness for the remission of sins that are past, through the forbearance of God; To declare . . . at this time his righteousness: that he might be just, and the justifier of him which believeth in Jesus. . . . Therefore we conclude that a man is justified by faith without the deeds of the law." (Rom. 3:19-28)

As justification was not dependent on works of the Law, neither was it dependent on circumcision, the cherished practice of the covenant people. Using Abraham as a Scriptural illustration, Paul showed that the father of the Hebrew race had himself won justification by faith in God's covenant promise before circumcision was instituted, and therefore all who had faith were Abraham's seed and were justified through that faith.

"What saith the scripture? Abraham believed God, and it was counted unto him for righteousness. . . . How was it then reckoned? . . . Not in circumcision . . . he received the sign of circumcision, a seal of the righteousness of the faith which he had yet being uncircumcised: that he might be the father of all them that believe, though they be not circumcised; that righteousness might be imputed unto them also." (Rom. 4:3,10,11)

Sanctification

Paul's doctrine of sanctification (inner purification) was a necessary corollary of the teaching of justification. Sanctification completes justification and leads to holiness and perfection. The believer, having been forgiven his past sins and now made one with Christ through faith, is required to put off his former sinful manner of life. He must strive to become Christlike and to rid mind and body of fleshly affections and lusts, "for the risen life must begin in a very real sense here below if it is to be perfected hereafter (Col. 3:1)."[6]

As Jesus had declared for himself the great fact of pre-existence with the Father, so Paul grasped this great truth and declared it for Christians—"he [God] hath chosen us in him [Christ] before the foundation of the world, that we should be holy and without blame before him in love" (Eph. 1:4). All through Paul's writings runs his concept of what man is in God's image. (For Paul's delineation of that man and his teachings as to attaining the full stature of manhood in Christ, see charts on the Old Man, New Man, and Perfect Man, pp. 454-458).

Paul taught that growth in grace is effected through the agency of the Holy Spirit, the indwelling power that enables the believer to put on the spiritual graces of Christ until he reaches the perfection of manhood in Christ (compare Rom. 8:1-17; Eph. 4:13).

"... God hath from the beginning chosen you to salvation through sanctification of the Spirit and belief of the truth." (II Th. 2:13)

"Having therefore these promises, dearly beloved, let us cleanse ourselves from all filthiness of the flesh and spirit, perfecting holiness in the fear of God." (II Cor. 7:1)

The Life of the Christian

Paul had much to say about the life or "walk" of the Christian. It was plain that the follower of Christ, born again, must lead an entirely new life, for being in Christ he was "a new creature." To maintain this new state he now must grow into full manhood in Christ. He must eschew all evil and love the good; he must love his fellow man in the spirit of Christ and bring forth the fruits of the Spirit. Paul's epistles are full of instruction and rules relating to Christian conduct in personal life, in church life, and in the body politic.

"Walk worthy of the vocation wherewith ye are called" (Eph. 4:1), "in the Spirit" (Gal. 5:16), "in newness of life" (Rom. 6:4), "in love" (Eph. 5:2), "as children of light" (Eph. 5:8).

"Overcome evil with good." (Rom. 12:21)

"Have no fellowship with the unfruitful works of darkness, but rather reprove them." (Eph. 5:11)

"Follow after righteousness, godliness, faith, love, patience, meekness." (I Tim. 6:11)

"Set your affection on things above" (Col. 3:2), "fight the good fight of faith" (I Tim. 6:12).

"Be kindly affectioned one to another with brotherly love; in honour preferring one another.... As much as lieth in you, live peaceably with all men." (Rom. 12:10,18)

Paul's Discipleship

The Master's example and the demands of Christian discipleship became rules from which Paul did not swerve. What Paul preached he also exemplified in both spirit and action. He unfailingly endeavored to bring his life into line with Christ's and to adhere to his commands for Christian perfection. At all points his life after conversion was consistent with the gospel.

Jesus had taught a new birth (Jn. 3:5). Paul *was* born again. Jesus had yielded to the divine will at Gethsemane; Paul yielded to the divine will on the road to Damascus. Jesus had asked, "Dost thou believe on the Son of God?" (Jn. 9:35); Paul declared, "I know whom I have believed" (II Tim. 1:12).

Jesus had commanded, "As I have loved you ... love one another" (Jn. 13:34); Paul had loved selflessly: "I will very gladly spend and be spent for you" (II Cor. 12:15). Jesus had warned, "Watch and pray, that ye enter not into temptation: the spirit indeed is willing, but the flesh is weak" (Mt. 26:41). Paul was tempted by bodily suffering and mental anguish, but he reached a point in his experience where he could say "I can do all things through Christ which strengtheneth me" (Phil. 4:13).

Jesus had commanded the apostles: "Go ye into all the world, and preach the gospel to every creature" (Mk. 16:15); Paul, the apostle "born out of due time," carried out this commission faithfully: "I laboured more abundantly than they all" (I Cor. 15:10; compare Acts 26:22,23). And, in consonance with Jesus' promise "He that shall endure unto the end, the same shall be saved" (Mt. 24:13), Paul was able to say with confidence, "I have finished my course, I have kept the faith: Henceforth there is laid up for me a crown of righteousness" (II Tim. 4:7,8).

Paul left an indelible mark upon the world. Though martyred for his beliefs, his was a triumphant life. He was responsible for the spread of Christianity into the Mediterranean world in a string of organized churches from Syria to Rome, and, in a large measure, for the development and cohesive unity of the doctrines of the new religion. As a result of his correspondence the Church came into possession of a unique body of literature which has preserved those Christian doctrines and nourished its spiritual life. The religious philosophy of Christianity with its new note of love and brotherhood was destined to permeate the thinking of mankind, to affect the rise and fall of nations, and change the lives of countless millions. His message is not restricted to past ages. It is vital and vibrant in meaning for the Christian today.

13

Correlation–Christian and Church

The Apostle Paul, trained by years of promulgation and defense of the gospel of Christ, was the first of Jesus' followers to define for the Christian and the Church the nature of Christianity—its fundamental truths and precepts. He understood its redemptive regenerative power "not as the word of men, but as it is in truth, the word of God, which effectually worketh also in you that believe" (I Th. 2:13).

Paul had much to say about the life or "walk" of the Christian. The work of the Christian is to overcome "the world, the flesh, and the devil." To aid him in his warfare, Paul wrote in definitive terms of the nature of "the old man," "the new man," and "the perfect man" (subject matter developed by no other New Testament writer). His verbs are those of action: "believe," "follow," "put off," "put on," "strive," "fight," "watch," "edify," "pray," "overcome."

He defined that which is carnal as "the old man," "the body of sin." He threw a penetrating light upon the depraved and impenitent character of the old man, which must be put off, for every propensity is unworthy, negative, sinful, destructive. He defined the man who is being regenerated—experiencing the new birth—as "the new man, which is renewed in knowledge after the image of him that created him." He showed the progressive steps that follow the new birth, and pointed out the warfare in putting off the old and putting on the new. That the perfect man might stand forth to the apprehension of the Christian, Paul presented to view the man who has "the mind of Christ." When the "putting on" is complete, man is seen in his full stature, conformed to the image of God's son.

What relates to the Christian individually Paul applied to the edifying of the Church collectively; the Church's redemptive mission becomes clear; and the Church is seen as the very "body of Christ."

The material presented in chart form in this section is topical studies that correlate significant aspects of Paul's doctrines. Some of the charts are designed to be read from the bottom of the page upward, a further reminder of the progressive development of revelation and understanding.

"PUT OFF . . . THE OLD MAN"

"WHICH IS CORRUPT ACCORDING TO THE DECEITFUL LUSTS" Eph. 4:22

Paul writes: "Let no man deceive you by any means: for that day [the day of Christ] shall not come, except there come a falling away first, and that man of sin be revealed, the son of perdition; Who opposeth and exalteth himself above all that is called God. . . ." (II Th. 2:3,4).

Read chart downward line by line

"THE BODY OF SIN" Rom. 6:6

EVIL THINKING

"the god of this world hath blinded the minds of them which believe not" II Cor. 4:4
"the carnal mind is enmity against God" Rom. 8:7
"haters of God, despiteful . . . inventors of evil things" Rom. 1:30
"unto them that are defiled and unbelieving is nothing pure;
but even their mind and conscience is defiled" Tit. 1:15
"Perverse disputings of men of corrupt minds, and destitute
of the truth, supposing that gain is godliness" I Tim. 6:5
"fleshly wisdom" II Cor. 1:12 — "cunning craftiness" Eph. 4:14
"unthankful, unholy. . . . despisers of those that are good" II Tim. 3:2,3
"envy . . . evil surmisings" I Tim. 6:4

EVIL SPEAKING

"Their throat is an open sepulchre; with their tongues they have used deceit; the poison
of asps is under their lips: Whose mouth is full of cursing and bitterness" Rom. 3:13,14
"unruly and vain talkers and deceivers. . . . Whose mouths must be stopped, who subvert whole
houses, teaching things which they ought not, for filthy lucre's sake" Tit. 1:10,11
"profane and vain babblings, and oppositions of science falsely so called" I Tim. 6:20
"proud, knowing nothing, but doting about questions and strifes of words" I Tim. 6:4
"tattlers . . . busybodies, speaking things which they ought not" I Tim. 5:13
"doubletongued" I Tim. 3:8 — "Speaking lies in hypocrisy" I Tim. 4:2
"backbitings, whisperings" II Cor. 12:20 — "boasters" II Tim. 3:2
"anger, wrath, malice, blasphemy, filthy communication" Col. 3:8
"handling the word of God deceitfully" II Cor. 4:2
"their word will eat as doth a canker" II Tim. 2:17

EYES THAT SEE NOT

"their eyes have they closed; lest they . . . should be converted" Acts 28:27
"spirit of slumber, eyes that they should not see" Rom. 11:8
"Having the understanding darkened" Eph. 4:18
"no fear of God before their eyes" Rom. 3:18

"they will not endure sound doctrine; but after their own lusts shall they heap
    to themselves teachers, having itching ears; And they shall turn away their
    ears from the truth, and shall be turned unto fables." II Tim. 4:3,4
"giving heed to seducing spirits, and doctrines of devils" I Tim. 4:1

IMPENITENT HEART

"impenitent heart treasurest up . . . wrath against the day of wrath" Rom. 2:5
"Tribulation and anguish, upon every soul of man that doeth evil" Rom. 2:9
"lovers of their own selves . . . Without natural affection" II Tim. 3:2,3
"Traitors . . . lovers of pleasures more than lovers of God" II Tim. 3:4
"Having a form of godliness, but denying the power thereof" II Tim. 3:5
"own conceits" Rom 12:16 — "bitterness . . . anger . . . malice" Eph. 4:31
"covetousness" Eph. 5:3 — "greedy of filthy lucre" I Tim. 3:3
"covenantbreakers . . . implacable, unmerciful" Rom. 1:31
"spiritual wickedness in high places" Eph. 6:12
"reprobate concerning the faith" II Tim. 3:8
"hidden things of dishonesty" II Cor. 4:2
"unbelievers . . . infidel" II Cor. 6:14,15

UNSEEMLY CONDUCT

"rioting and drunkenness . . . chambering and wantonness . . . strife and envying" Rom. 13:13
"they learn to be idle, wandering about from house to house" I Tim. 5:13
"disobedient to parents" II Tim. 3:2 — "selfwilled . . . soon angry" Tit. 1:7
"serving divers lusts and pleasures, living in malice and envy,
    hateful and hating one another" Tit. 3:3
"whose God is their belly, and whose glory is in their shame,
    who mind earthly things" Phil. 3:19
"drunk with wine, wherein is excess" Eph. 5:18

UNFRUITFUL WORKS

"the works of the flesh are manifest, which are these; Adultery, fornication, uncleanness,
    lasciviousness, Idolatry, witchcraft, hatred, variance, emulations, wrath, strife,
    seditions, heresies, Envyings, murders, drunkenness, revellings, and such like" Gal. 5:19-21
"Their feet are swift to shed blood: Destruction and misery are in their ways" Rom. 3:15,16
"in works they deny him [God], being abominable . . . unto every good work reprobate" Tit. 1:16
"he that soweth to his flesh shall of the flesh reap corruption" Gal. 6:8
"filthiness of the flesh and spirit" II Cor. 7:1
"unfruitful works of darkness" Eph. 5:11
"the wages of sin is death" Rom. 6:23

Read chart upward line by line

"PUT ON THE NEW MAN, WHICH AFTER GOD IS CREATED IN RIGHTEOUSNESS AND TRUE HOLINESS"

"Be ye transformed by the renewing of your mind" Rom. 12:2

Read chart upward line by line

A CROWN "INCORRUPTIBLE"

"then shall I know even as also I am known" I Cor. 13:12

"then [we see] face to face" I Cor. 13:12

"when that which is perfect is come, then that which is in part shall be done away" I Cor. 13:10

"a perfect man . . . the measure of the stature of the fulness of Christ" Eph. 4:13

"hath made us meet to be partakers of the inheritance of the saints in light" Col. 1:12

"aged women . . . be in behaviour as becometh holiness . . . teachers of good things" Tit. 2:3

"aged men be sober, grave, temperate, sound in faith, in charity, in patience" Tit. 2:2

THE AGED ("aged"—senior, advanced, patriarchal, ripened and matured for use)

"Stand fast therefore in the liberty wherewith Christ hath made us free" Gal. 5:1

"thanks be to God, which giveth us the victory through . . . Jesus Christ" I Cor. 15:57

"it is required in stewards, that a man be found faithful" I Cor. 4:2

"Fight the good fight of faith, lay hold on eternal life" I Tim. 6:12

"every man that striveth for the mastery is temperate in all things" I Cor. 9:25

"press toward the mark for the prize of the high calling of God in Christ Jesus" Phil 3:14

"let us run with patience the race that is set before us" Heb. 12:1

"SO RUN, THAT YE MAY OBTAIN" I Cor. 9:24

"patient continuance in well doing" Rom. 2:7

"be strong in the grace that is in Christ Jesus" II Tim. 2:1

"Let your speech be alway with grace, seasoned with salt" Col. 4:6

"abound in love one toward another, and toward all men" I Th. 3:12

"be ye not unwise, but understanding what the will of the Lord is" Eph. 5:17

"let us not sleep, as do others; but let us watch and be sober" I Th. 5:6

"walk circumspectly, not as fools, but as wise, Redeeming the time" Eph. 5:15,16

"Rejoicing in hope; patient in tribulation; continuing instant in prayer" Rom. 12:12

"Examine yourselves, whether ye be in the faith; prove your own selves" II Cor. 13:5

"Put on the whole armour of God, that ye may be able to stand against . . . the devil" Eph. 6:11

"continue thou in the things which thou hast learned and hast been assured of" II Tim. 3:14

"Let this mind be in you, which was also in Christ Jesus" Phil. 2:5

"bringing into captivity every thought to the obedience of Christ" II Cor. 10:5

"thou, O man of God . . . follow after righteousness . . . faith, love, patience, meekness" I Tim. 6:11

YOUNG MAN

"Young men likewise exhort to be sober minded" Tit. 2:6

"exercise thyself . . . unto godliness" I Tim. 4:7 — "keep thyself pure" I Tim. 5:22

"be thou an example . . . in conversation, in charity, in spirit, in faith, in purity" I Tim. 4:12

"Flee also youthful lusts: but follow righteousness, faith, charity, peace" II Tim. 2:22

"earnestly desiring to be clothed upon with our house which is from heaven" II Cor. 5:2

"henceforth be no more children, tossed to and fro . . . with every wind of doctrine" Eph. 4:14

"WHEN I BECAME A MAN, I PUT AWAY CHILDISH THINGS" I Cor. 13:11

THE CHILD

"walk in the Spirit" Gal. 5:25 — "Walk, as children of light" Eph. 5:8

"Follow after charity, and desire spiritual gifts" I Cor. 14:1

"the creature . . . delivered . . . into the glorious liberty of the children of God" Rom. 8:21

"Be ye therefore followers of God, as dear children" Eph. 5:1

"Children, obey your parents in the Lord: for this is right" Eph. 6:1

"the heir, as long as he is a child, differeth nothing from a servant, though . . . lord of all" Gal. 4:1

"I SPAKE AS A CHILD, I UNDERSTOOD AS A CHILD, I THOUGHT AS A CHILD [Fig., an *immature* Christian]"

THE BABE

"thou standest by faith" Rom. 11:20

"If ye then be risen with Christ, seek those things which are above" Col. 3:1

"let us cleanse ourselves . . . perfecting holiness in the fear of God" II Cor. 7:1

"nourished up in the words of faith and of good doctrine" I Tim. 4:6

"I have fed you with milk, and not with meat: for hitherto ye were not able to bear it" I Cor. 3:2

"I, brethren . . . speak unto you . . . as unto carnal, even as unto babes in Christ" I Cor. 3:1

"after that ye believed, ye were sealed with that holy Spirit of promise" Eph. 1:13

BIRTHRIGHT "ye have received the Spirit of adoption, whereby we cry, Abba, Father" Rom. 8:15

"PUT ON THE NEW MAN" Eph. 4:24 — "PUT ON INCORRUPTION . . . PUT ON IMMORTALITY" I Cor. 15:53

"Know ye not that ye are the temple of God. . . ?" I Cor. 3:16

"grow up into him in all things, which is the head, even Christ" Eph. 4:15

"charity [love] edifieth" I Cor. 8:1 ("edify"—build, construct, establish)

"let every man take heed how he buildeth thereupon" I Cor. 3:10

THE ONLY FOUNDATION—JESUS CHRIST

Read chart upward line by line

THE SPIRITUAL NATURE OF THE PERFECT MAN

"a perfect man . . . the measure of the stature of the fulness of Christ" Eph. 4:13

GOD

"the head of Christ" I Cor. 11:3

CHRIST

"the head of every man" I Cor. 11:3

"in him dwelleth all the fulness of the Godhead
bodily. And ye are complete in him" Col. 2:9,10

THE PERFECT MAN

"whom he [God] did foreknow, he also did predestinate
to be conformed to the image of his Son" Rom. 8:29

"after the image of him that created him" Col. 3:10
"chosen . . . in him [God] before the foundation of the world" Eph. 1:4
"in him we live, and move, and have our being" Acts 17:28
"we are . . . his offspring" Acts 17:28
"there is a spiritual body" I Cor. 15:44
"fashioned like unto his glorious body" Phil. 3:21
"as is the heavenly, such are they also that are heavenly" I Cor. 15:48
"a building of God, an house not made with hands,
eternal in the heavens" II Cor. 5:1

He abides in "the kingdom of his dear Son" Col. 1:13
He has "the spirit which is of God" I Cor. 2:12
He has "the mind of Christ" I Cor. 2:16
He is "spiritually minded" Rom. 8:6
He has "the light of the knowledge of the glory of God
in the face of Jesus Christ" II Cor. 4:6
He has "the peace of God, which passeth all understanding" Phil. 4:7
He walks "in love" Eph. 5:2
He walks as a child "of light" Eph. 5:8
He understands "what the will of the Lord is" Eph. 5:17
He does "the will of God" Eph. 6:6
He is inseparable from "the love of Christ" Rom. 8:35
He is "glorified" Rom. 8:30
He is "incorruptible" I Cor. 15:52
He has "immortality" I Cor. 15:53
He has "eternal life" Rom. 6:23

THE TRUE CHURCH

"The Church has existed from all eternity as an idea in the mind of God (Eph. 3:3-11), the heritage prepared for Christ (Eph. 1:10,11)."[1]

Through God's grace and Paul's own labor in that grace, whereby he could truly compare "spiritual things with spiritual," he discerned Christ's Church not only as a visible society of believers in the world needing edification but also as the very "body of Christ," subject to Christ, its Head.

GOD

"the head of Christ" I Cor. 11:3

CHRIST

"Who is the image of the invisible God, the firstborn of every creature. . . . And he is before all things, and by him all things consist. And he is the head of the body, the church. . . ." Col. 1:15,17,18

CHURCH, "THE BODY OF CHRIST"

"an holy temple" Eph. 2:21
"the Israel of God" Gal. 6:16 (cf. 3:29)
"the city of the living God, the heavenly Jerusalem" Heb. 12:22
"the general assembly and church of the firstborn, which are written in heaven" Heb. 12:23

"Now concerning spiritual gifts, brethren, I would not have you ignorant. . . . Now there are diversities of gifts, but the same Spirit. And there are differences of administrations, but the same Lord. And there are diversities of operations, but it is the same God which worketh all in all." I Cor. 12:1,4-6

"For as the body is one, and hath many members, and all the members of that one body, being many, are one body: so also is Christ. For by one Spirit are we all baptized into one body, whether we be Jews or Gentiles, whether we be bond or free; and have been all made to drink into one Spirit." I Cor. 12:12,13

"Now ye are the body of Christ, and members in particular." I Cor. 12:27

"There is one body, and one Spirit, even as ye are called in one hope of your calling; One Lord, one faith, one baptism, One God and Father of all, who is above all, and through all, and in you all." Eph. 4:4-6

"Speaking the truth in love . . . grow up into him in all things, which is the head, even Christ: From whom the whole body fitly joined together and compacted by that which every joint supplieth, according to the effectual working in the measure of every part, maketh increase of the body unto the edifying of itself in love." Eph. 4:15,16

EDIFYING (BUILDING UP) OF THE CHURCH

Read chart upward line by line

GOD

"the head of Christ" I Cor. 11:3

CHRIST

"the head of the church" Eph. 5:23

THE CHURCH

THE SOCIETY OF CHRISTIAN BELIEVERS

"Which is his [Christ's] body" Eph. 1:23

HOLINESS—"ye have your fruit unto holiness" Rom. 6:22
GRACE—"the grace of God that bringeth salvation" Tit. 2:11
LOVE—"the love of Christ, which passeth knowledge" Eph. 3:19
PEACE—"the peace of God, which passeth all understanding" Phil. 4:7
HEALING—"the gifts of healing by the same Spirit" I Cor. 12:9
SUFFICIENCY—"ye, always having all sufficiency in all things" II Cor. 9:8
WISDOM—"Let the word of Christ dwell in you richly in all wisdom" Col. 3:16
POWER—"God hath . . . given us the spirit . . . of power, and of love, and of a sound mind" II Tim. 1:7
RIGHTEOUSNESS—"Being filled with the fruits of righteousness, which are by Jesus Christ" Phil. 1:11
LIGHT—"the light of the knowledge of the glory of God in the face of Jesus Christ" II Cor. 4:6
LIFE—"if Christ be in you . . . the Spirit is life because of righteousness" Rom. 8:10
SPIRIT OF GOD—"we have received . . . the spirit which is of God" I Cor. 2:12

"as ye are zealous of spiritual gifts, seek that ye may excel to the edifying of the church" I Cor. 14:12

SPIRITUAL GIFTS—"the manifestation of the Spirit is given to every man to profit withal" I Cor. 12:7

AMBASSADORS—"we are ambassadors for Christ" II Cor. 5:20
STEWARDS—"stewards of the mysteries of God" I Cor. 4:1
MINISTERS—"able ministers of the new testament [new covenant]" II Cor. 3:6
SERVANTS—"he that is called, being free, is Christ's servant" I Cor. 7:22
LABORERS—"we are labourers together with God" I Cor. 3:9
ELDERS—"Let the elders that rule well be counted worthy of double honour" I Tim. 5:17

DEACONS—"they that have used the office of a deacon well purchase . . . a good degree" I Tim. 3:13

APOSTLES, PROPHETS, EVANGELISTS, PASTORS, TEACHERS Eph. 4:11

VOCATION—"walk worthy of the vocation wherewith ye are called" Eph. 4:1

ELECT—"the elect of God, holy and beloved" Col. 3:12

PARTAKERS—"we are all partakers of that one bread" I Cor. 10:17

FELLOWCITIZENS—"ye are . . . fellowcitizens with the saints" Eph. 2:19

SAINTS—"them that are sanctified in Christ Jesus, called to be saints" I Cor. 1:2

FREEMEN—"he that is called in the Lord, being a servant, is the Lord's freeman" I Cor. 7:22

FELLOWHEIRS—"Gentiles . . . of the same body, and partakers of his promise in Christ" Eph. 3:6

HEIRS—"heirs of God, and joint-heirs with Christ" Rom. 8:16

BRETHREN—"brethren beloved of the Lord, because God hath . . . chosen you to salvation" II Th. 2:13

HOUSEHOLD—"ye are . . . of the household of God" Eph. 2:19 — "the household of faith" Gal. 6:10

MEMBERS—"ye are the body of Christ, and members in particular" I Cor. 12:27

TEMPLE—"ye are the temple of the living God" II Cor. 6:16

HABITATION—"In whom [Jesus Christ] ye also are builded together for an habitation of God" Eph. 2:22

HOUSE OF GOD—"which is the church of the living God, the pillar and ground of the truth" I Tim. 3:15

WORKMANSHIP—"we are his workmanship, created in Christ Jesus unto good works" Eph. 2:10

BUILDING—"ye are God's husbandry, ye are God's building" I Cor. 3:9

"Let all things be done unto edifying" I Cor. 14:26

But let every man take heed how he buildeth thereupon" I Cor. 3:10

"As a wise masterbuilder, I [Paul] have laid the foundation, and another buildeth thereon.

"In whom all the building fitly framed together groweth unto an holy temple in the Lord" Eph. 2:21

"JESUS CHRIST himself being the chief CORNER STONE" Eph. 2:20

"[YE] ARE BUILT UPON THE FOUNDATION OF THE APOSTLES AND PROPHETS" Eph. 2:20

Read chart upward line by line

Many of these Pauline passages which relate to man individually apply also to the Church collectively.

REDEMPTIVE HEALING MISSION OF THE CHRISTIAN CHURCH

Individual, Collective, Universal

Jesus Christ declared: "I am the way, the truth, and the life: no man cometh unto the Father, but by me." As Jesus' life and ministry revealed this Way, so his Church offers salvation to all men through this one redemptive Way. The mission of the Christian Church is the extension of this basic truth (as correlated from Paul's Epistles).

Read chart upward line by line

BLESSINGS ....
"Fruit of the Spirit is love, joy, peace, longsuffering, gentleness, goodness, faith, Meekness, temperance" Gal. 5:22,23
.... "Blessed be the God ... who hath blessed us with all spiritual *blessings* in heavenly places in Christ" Eph. 1:3

SALVATION ....
"For the grace of God that bringeth *salvation* hath appeared to all men" Tit. 2:11
.... "For God hath not appointed us to wrath, but to obtain *salvation* by our Lord Jesus Christ" I Th. 5:9

SANCTIFICATION ....
"God hath from the beginning chosen you to salvation through *sanctification* of the Spirit" II Th. 2:13
.... "Ye are washed ... *sanctified* ... justified in the name of the Lord Jesus, and by the Spirit of our God" I Cor. 6:11

ATONEMENT ....
"Whom [Christ Jesus] God hath set forth to be a propitiation through faith in his blood" Rom. 3:25
.... "We also joy in God through our Lord Jesus Christ, by whom we have now received the *atonement*" Rom. 5:11

REDEMPTION ....
"In whom [God's Son] we have *redemption* through his blood, even the forgiveness of sins" Col. 1:14
.... "Our Saviour Jesus Christ ... gave himself for us, that he might *redeem* us from all iniquity" Tit. 2:13,14

ABOLITION ....
"Our Saviour Jesus Christ ... hath *abolished* death" II Tim. 1:10
.... Christ "having *abolished* in his flesh the enmity, even the law of commandments contained in ordinances" Eph. 2:15

HEALING ....
"By the mercies of God ... present your bodies a living sacrifice, holy, acceptable unto God" Rom. 12:1
.... "God hath set some in the church ... apostles ... prophets ... teachers ... miracles ... gifts of *healings*" I Cor. 12:28

"As often as ye eat this bread, and drink this cup, ye do shew the Lord's death till he come" I Cor. 11:26

ACCESS . . . . "For through him [Christ Jesus] we both have *access* by one Spirit unto the Father" Eph. 2:18

MEDIATION . . . . "Christ . . . that is risen again, who is even at the right hand of God . . . maketh intercession for us" Rom. 8:34
. . . . "There is one God, and one *mediator* between God and men, the man Christ Jesus" I Tim. 2:5

RECONCILIATION . . . . "We pray you in Christ's stead, be ye *reconciled* to God" II Cor. 5:20
. . . . .God "hath *reconciled* us to himself by Jesus Christ, and hath given to us the ministry of *reconciliation*" II Cor. 5:18

JUSTIFICATION . . . . "Therefore being *justified* by faith, we have peace with God through our Lord Jesus Christ" Rom. 5:1
. . . . "By the righteousness of one [Jesus Christ] the free gift came upon all men unto *justification* of life" Rom. 5:18

UNITY . . . . "God is faithful, by whom ye were called unto the fellowship of his Son Jesus Christ our Lord" I Cor. 1:9
. . . . "One body . . . one Spirit . . . one hope. . . . One Lord, one faith, one baptism, One God and Father of all" Eph. 4:4-6

BAPTISM . . . . "He [God] saved us, by the washing of regeneration, and renewing of the Holy Ghost . . . through Jesus Christ" Tit. 3:5,6
. . . . "By one Spirit are we all *baptized* into one body . . . and have been all made to drink into one Spirit" I Cor. 12:13

CALLING . . . . "Who [God] hath saved us, and *called* us with an holy *calling* . . . according to his own purpose and grace" II Tim. 1:9
. . . . .God "*called* you by our gospel, to the obtaining of the glory of our Lord Jesus Christ" II Th. 2:14

GOSPEL . . . . "Our Saviour . . hath brought life and immortality to light through the *gospel*" II Tim. 1:10
. . . . "It [*the gospel* of Christ] is the power of God unto salvation to every one that believeth" Rom. 1:16

Read chart upward line by line

"CHRIST IS ALL, AND IN ALL" Col. 3:11

"YE ARE ALL ONE IN CHRIST JESUS" Gal. 3:28

Christ "hath broken down the middle wall of partition between us" Eph. 2:14

Jew	Greek
bond	free
male	female

Middle
wall
of
partition

463

The Israel of God

Old Testament

To the Hebrew prophets *Israel* signified not only the natural posterity of Jacob but also a spiritual entity—that segment of the nation faithful to God's covenant and law. "The Lord sent a word into Jacob, and it hath lighted upon Israel." (Is. 9:8) "The Lord hath redeemed Jacob, and glorified himself in Israel." (Is. 44:23)

New Testament

To Christians the *Israel of God* designates a spiritual Israel, those who follow Christ in faith, for such become the true seed of Abraham and so heirs of the Abrahamic covenant which was fulfilled in Jesus Christ.

Jesus foresaw a new Israel at the Last Day, a believing Israel, when he said to his apostles: "Ye which have followed me, in the regeneration when the Son of man shall sit in the throne of his glory, ye also shall sit upon twelve thrones, judging the twelve tribes of Israel" (Mt. 19:28).

Paul saw the true Israel not as confined to the descendants of Abraham or to those who kept the Mosaic Law, but as those who accepted Christ: "Even as Abraham believed God, and it was accounted to him for righteousness. Know ye therefore that they which are of faith, the same are the children of Abraham" (Gal. 3:6,7); "For in Christ Jesus neither circumcision availeth any thing, nor uncircumcision, but a new creature. And as many as walk according to this rule [of faith], peace be on them, and mercy, and upon the Israel of God" (Gal. 6:15,16).

John recorded the apocalyptic prophecy of the full salvation of the redeemed of all nations, spiritual Israel, typified in the sealing of "twelve thousand" of each of the twelve tribes, with the exception of Dan (Rev. 7)—the redeemed were stamped with the seal of the living God to mark their godliness and their exemption from His judgments on the ungodly. "Dan is omitted because Anti-Christ is to spring from him (compare Gen. 49:7). Manasseh is substituted for Dan, though he is already included under Joseph."[2] "There were sealed an hundred and forty and four thousand of all the tribes of the children of Israel [an apocalyptic number signifying completeness].... After this I beheld ... a great multitude, which no man could number, of all nations, and kindreds, and people, and tongues, stood before the throne, and before the Lamb, clothed with white robes, and palms in their hands...."

The true Israelite is a real Christian; collectively the true Israel is the Church, the people of God who serve Him continually.

Mysteries

In the New Testament there is a term used by Jesus, Paul, and John that is not found in Hebrew Scripture. It is the word *mystery*, whose Old Testament counterpart is the word *secret*. In Old Testament times God revealed Himself to mankind (specifically to His chosen people) under the Abrahamic covenant. The deep things of God were perceived only by His godly servants and prophets, and by them only in part, but what they did perceive became the spiritual heritage of the nation.

"The *secret* things belong unto the Lord our God: but those things which are revealed belong unto us and to our children for ever, that we may do all the words of this law." Deut. 29:29

"The *secret* of the Lord is with them that fear him; and he will shew them his covenant." Ps. 25:14; compare Pr. 3:32

"He revealeth the deep and *secret* things: he knoweth what is in the darkness, and the light dwelleth with him." Dan. 2:22

The same thought of divine revelation is found in the New Testament word *mystery*, for which the Greek word is *mysterion*—initiation into mysteries or secrets, into that which is hidden or concealed. In the New Testament context mysteries are revelations, "knowable secrets." Jesus used the term only once (with the overtone of wonderful things), when he said to his disciples: "Unto you it is given to know the *mystery* of the kingdom of God: but unto them that are without, all these things are done in parables: That seeing they may see, and not perceive; and hearing they may hear, and not understand; lest at any time they should be converted, and their sins should be forgiven them" (Mk. 4:11,12; compare Mt. 13:35). It was only the obtuseness of men and their love of the world that kept them from fully appreciating the spiritual truths he taught.

The word "mysteries" in Scripture is not used in its classical sense—of 'religious secrets,' nor yet of 'things incomprehensible, or in their own nature difficult to be understood'—but in the sense of 'things of purely Divine revelation,' and, usually, 'things darkly announced under the ancient economy, and during all that period darkly understood, but fully published under the Gospel' (I Corinthians 2:6-10; Ephesians 3:3-6,8,9). "The mysteries of the kingdom of heaven," then, mean those glorious Gospel truths which at that time only the more advanced disciples could appreciate, and they but partially.[3]

The word *mystery* appears in the Epistles of Paul more often than in any other portion of the New Testament. At his conversion Paul was indeed initiated into the knowledge of Jesus Christ; as he grew in spiritual stature, the mysteries of God—His divine will and purpose concerning Christ and his Church—were revealed to him. He never considered this knowledge a personal possession but rather a gift of the Spirit obtainable only through selfless love: "Though I have the gift of prophecy, and understand all mysteries, and all knowledge; and though I have all faith, so that I could remove mountains, and have not charity [RV love], I am nothing" (I Cor. 13:2).

Iniquity

"Let no man deceive you by any means: for that day [the day of Christ] shall not come, except there come a falling away first, and that man of sin be revealed, the son of perdition; Who opposeth and exalteth himself above all that is called God, or that is worshipped; so that he as God sitteth in the temple of God, shewing himself that he is God. . . .

"And now ye know what withholdeth that he might be revealed in his time. For the *mystery* of iniquity doth already work: only he who now letteth will let, until he be taken out of the way.

"And then shall that Wicked be revealed, whom the Lord shall consume with the spirit of his mouth, and shall destroy with the brightness of his coming: Even him, whose coming is after the working of Satan with all power and signs and lying wonders, And with all deceivableness of unrighteousness in them that perish; because they received not the love of the truth, that they might be saved." II Th. 2:3-10

The Hidden Wisdom of God

"Howbeit we speak wisdom among them that are perfect [ASV full-grown]: yet not the wisdom of this world, nor of the princes of this world, that come to nought: But we speak the wisdom of God in a *mystery*, even the hidden wisdom, which God ordained before the world unto our glory: Which none of the princes of this world knew: for had they known it, they would not have crucified the Lord of glory.

"But as it is written, Eye hath not seen, nor ear heard, neither have entered into the heart of man, the things which God hath prepared for them that love him. But God hath revealed them unto us by his Spirit: for the Spirit searcheth all things, yea, the deep things of God. For what man knoweth the things of a man, save the spirit of man which is in him? even so the things of God knoweth no man, but the Spirit of God." I Cor. 2:6-11; see I Tim. 3:9

Resurrection

"Now this I say, brethren, that flesh and blood cannot inherit the kingdom of God; neither doth corruption inherit incorruption.

"Behold, I shew you a *mystery;* We shall not all sleep, but we shall all be changed, In a moment, in the twinkling of an eye, at the last trump: for the trumpet shall sound, and the dead shall be raised incorruptible, and we shall be changed. For this corruptible must put on incorruption, and this mortal must put on immortality. So when this corruptible shall have put on incorruption, and this mortal shall have put on immortality, then shall be brought to pass the saying that is written, Death is swallowed up in victory." I Cor. 15:50-54; see I Th. 4:13-17

The Blindness of Israel: Conversion of the Gentiles

"I say then, Hath God cast away his people? God forbid.... God hath not cast away his people which he foreknew.... at this present time ... there is a remnant according to the election of grace. And if by grace, then is it no more of works: otherwise grace is no more grace....

"What then? Israel hath not obtained that which he seeketh for; but the election hath obtained it, and the rest were blinded ... unto this day.... I say then, Have they stumbled that they should fall? God forbid: but rather through their fall salvation is come unto the Gentiles, for to provoke them to jealousy [zeal]....

"For if the casting away of them be the reconciling of the world, what shall the receiving of them be, but life from the dead? For if the firstfruit be holy, the lump is also holy: and if the root be holy, so are the branches. And if some of the branches be broken off, and thou [Gentiles], being a wild olive tree, wert graffed in among them, and with them partakest of the root and fatness of the olive tree; Boast not against the branches.... Thou wilt say then, The branches were broken off, that I might be graffed in. Well; because of unbelief they were broken off, and thou standest by faith. Be not highminded, but fear: For if God spared not the natural branches, take heed lest he also spare not thee.... continue in his goodness: otherwise thou also shalt be cut off.

"And they also, if they abide not still in unbelief, shall be graffed in: for God is able to graff them in again.... For I would not, brethren, that ye should be ignorant of this *mystery,* lest ye should be wise in your own conceits; that blindness in part is happened to Israel, until the fulness of the Gentiles be come in. And so all Israel shall be saved...." Rom. 11:1-26

God's Will: His Divine Purpose in Christ

"Blessed be the God and Father of our Lord Jesus Christ, who hath blessed us with all spiritual blessings in heavenly places in Christ: According as he hath chosen us in him before the foundation of the world, that we should be holy and without blame before him in love....

"Having made known unto us the *mystery* of his will, according to his good pleasure which he hath purposed in himself: That in the dispensation of the fulness of times he might gather together in one all things in Christ, both which are in heaven, and which are on earth; even in him: In whom also we have obtained an inheritance, being predestinated according to the purpose of him who worketh all things after the counsel of his own will." Eph. 1:3,4,9-11

Joint-heirship of All Men in Christ's Riches

"... by revelation he made known unto me the *mystery.* ... Which in other ages was not made known unto the sons of men, as it is now revealed unto his holy apostles and prophets by the Spirit; That the Gentiles should be fellowheirs, and of the same body, and partakers of his promise in Christ by the gospel." Eph. 3:3-6

Christ's Love for His Church

"The husband is the head of the wife, even as Christ is the head of the church: and he is the saviour of the body....

"Husbands, love your wives, even as Christ also loved the church, and gave himself for it; That he might sanctify and cleanse it with the washing of water by the word, That he might present it to himself a glorious church, not having spot, or wrinkle, or any such thing; but that it should be holy and without blemish.... For no man ever yet hated his own flesh; but nourisheth and cherisheth it, even as the Lord the church: For we are members of his body, of his flesh, and of his bones.... This is a great *mystery*: but I speak concerning Christ and the church." Eph 5:23-32; compare Jn. 3:29; Rev. 19:6-8

The Indwelling Christ

"Whereof [for the church's sake] I am made a minister, according to the dispensation of God which is given to me for you, to fulfil the word of God; Even the *mystery* which hath been hid from ages and from generations, but now is made manifest to his saints: To whom God would make known what is the riches of the glory of this *mystery* among the Gentiles; which is Christ in you, the hope of glory." Col. 1:25-27; see Lu. 17:21

CORRELATION—CHRISTIAN AND CHURCH 467

Christ, the Incarnate Fullness of the Godhead

"For I would that ye knew what great conflict I have for you, and for them at Laodicea. . . . That their hearts might be comforted, being knit together in love, and unto all riches of the full assurance of understanding, to the acknowledgement of the *mystery* of God, and of the Father, and of Christ; In whom are hid all the treasures of wisdom and knowledge. . . . In him dwelleth all the fulness of the Godhead bodily. And ye are complete in him, which is the head of all principality and power." Col. 2:1-3,9,10

Godliness

"Without controversy great is the *mystery* of godliness: God [RV He who] was manifest in the flesh, justified in the Spirit, seen of angels, preached unto the Gentiles, believed on in the world, received up into glory." I Tim. 3:16

There are three mysteries in the book of Revelation, and John, using apocalyptic language, makes them "knowable secrets."

The Seven Stars

"I [John] was in the Spirit on the Lord's day, and heard behind me a great voice, as of a trumpet, Saying, I am Alpha and Omega, the first and the last. . . . And being turned, I saw seven golden candlesticks; And in the midst of the seven candlesticks one like unto the Son of man. . . . And he had in his right hand seven stars. . . . The *mystery* of the seven stars which thou sawest in my right hand, and the seven golden candlesticks. The seven stars are the angels of the seven churches: and the seven candlesticks which thou sawest are the seven churches." Rev. 1:10-13,16,20

The Mystery of God Finished

"The angel [with the little book] which [John] saw stand upon the sea and upon the earth lifted up his hand to heaven, And sware by him that liveth for ever and ever . . . that there should be time no longer: But in the days of the voice of the seventh angel, when he shall begin to sound, the *mystery* of God should be finished, as he hath declared to his servants the prophets. . . . And the seventh angel sounded; and there were great voices in heaven, saying, The kingdoms of this world are become the kingdoms of our Lord, and of his Christ; and he shall reign for ever and ever." Rev. 10:5-7; 11:15

The Great Whore

"There came one of the seven angels which had the seven vials, and talked with me . . . Come hither; I will shew unto thee the judgment of the great whore that sitteth upon many waters. . . .

"So he carried me away in the spirit into the wilderness: and I saw a woman sit upon a scarlet coloured beast, full of names of blasphemy, having seven heads and ten horns. And the woman was arrayed in purple and scarlet colour, and decked with gold . . . having a golden cup in her hand full of abominations and filthiness of her fornication: And upon her forehead was a name written, MYSTERY, BABYLON THE GREAT, THE MOTHER OF HARLOTS AND ABOMINATIONS OF THE EARTH. And I saw the woman drunken with the blood of the saints, and with the blood of the martyrs of Jesus. . . .

"And the angel said unto me . . . I will tell thee the *mystery* of the woman, and of the beast that carrieth her, which hath the seven heads and ten horns. The beast that thou sawest was, and is not; and shall ascend out of the bottomless pit, and go into perdition: and they that dwell on the earth shall wonder, whose names were not written in the book of life from the foundation of the world, when they behold the beast that was, and is not, and yet is. . . .

"The seven heads are seven mountains, on which the woman sitteth. And there are seven kings: five are fallen, and one is, and the other is not yet come; and when he cometh, he must continue a short space. And the beast that was, and is not, even he is the eighth, and is of the seven, and goeth into perdition.

"And the ten horns which thou sawest are ten kings, which have received no kingdom as yet; but receive power as kings one hour with the beast. These have one mind, and shall give their power and strength unto the beast. These shall make war with the Lamb, and the Lamb shall overcome them: for he is Lord of lords, and King of kings: and they that are with him are called, and chosen, and faithful.

"And he saith unto me, The waters which thou sawest, where the whore sitteth, are peoples, and multitudes, and nations, and tongues.

"And the ten horns which thou sawest upon the beast, these shall hate the whore, and shall make her desolate and naked, and shall eat her flesh, and burn her with fire. For God hath put in their hearts to fulfil his will, and to agree, and give their kingdom unto the beast, until the words of God shall be fulfilled.

"And the woman which thou sawest is that great city, which reigneth over the kings of the earth." Rev. 17

Apostolic Church, 61-96 A.D.
and Secular History

54-66 A.D.	66-70 A.D.	79-96 A.D.
54-68 A.D.—Nero, Roman Emperor	66 A.D.—Jerusalem church flees for safety to Pella in Peraea	79-81 A.D.—Titus, Roman Emperor
61-63—Paul imprisoned at Rome	66/67—Paul's epistles, *First Timothy, Titus*	81-96—Domitian, Roman Emperor (younger brother o[f] Titus)—Domitian enforce[s] cult of emperor worshi[p] throughout Roman Empir[e] —persecution of Christian[s] spreads to Asia Minor
ca. 61—*Epistle of James*	67/68—Paul's second imprisonment at Rome—his *Second Epistle to Timothy*	
ca. 62—*First Epistle of Peter*	67/68—Peter's martyrdom —Paul's martyrdom	
62—Martyrdom of James, head of Jerusalem church, by Pharisees and Sadducees	68-69—Galba, Otho, Vitellius, Roman Emperors	ca. 80-90—*Fourth Gospel* b[y] John
64—Burning of Rome—Nero persecutes the Christians of Rome	69-79—Vespasian, Roman Emperor	ca. 90—*First, Second, and Thir[d] Epistles of John*
ca. 66—*Second Epistle of Peter*	Before 70—*Synoptic Gospels, Acts, Jude, Hebrews*	95-96—Apostle John is banishe[d] to isle of Patmos
66—Palestinian Jews revolt against Rome—Vespasian leads Roman army against Galilee and Judaea	70—Fall of Jerusalem to Titus, son of Vespasian	ca. 96—*Book of Revelation* b[y] John

The apostolic history of the Church as recorded in Acts closes with the first imprisonment of Paul at Rome, 61-63 A.D. There are a few allusions in Paul's pastoral epistles that suggest another journey to Greece by that apostle before a second imprisonment, but these do not throw light on the state of the Church during that interval, and the other New Testament writers of the period between 61 and 96 A.D. deal with doctrine rather than church history. We must turn to secular sources for events that affected the Church between Paul's martyrdom and the time of the writing of John's Apocalypse.

During the first decade of this period the Jewish nation perished in the fall of Jerusalem in 70 A.D. Its end began in 66, when the Jews of Judaea and Galilee revolted against Roman rule, beginning their insurrection in Jerusalem. Cestius Gallus, governor of Syria, came down with his Roman legions to besiege the city but retreated in defeat. Nero then sent Vespasian, one

of his ablest generals, to crush the revolt. Jesus in h[is] Olivet discourse had forewarned the apostles: "Whe[n] ye shall see Jerusalem compassed with armies, the[n] know that the desolation thereof is nigh. Then l[et] them which are in Judaea flee to the mountains" (L[uke] 21:20,21). So before the Roman standards were at th[e] gates of Jerusalem, the Church fled for safety to Pell[a,] a Hellenistic city of Decapolis, east of the Jordan.

Vespasian fought Galilee and Judaea for almo[st] two years until he was recalled to Rome to [be] crowned Emperor after Nero's death. Titus succeed[ed] his father Vespasian as general of the army, and [in] April 70 laid siege to Jerusalem with an army of six[ty] thousand. This attack occurred during Passover wee[k] when thousands of pilgrims overflowed the cit[y.] Jerusalem was soon divided into angry factio[ns] fighting for control and, in the strife which followe[d] the city's granaries were destroyed by fire. Hunger w[as] rampant, and those who dared to search the hillsid[es] for food were crucified by Roman soldiers.

After many days of pounding with battering rams, the Romans breached the walls and took part of the city. In the ensuing weeks, upon the Jews' repeated and even scornful refusal to surrender, Titus stripped the hills of all houses and trees and built a wall, the height of a man and five miles in circumference, locking in well over a million inhabitants and strangers. A terrible famine ensued; bodies piled up in the streets; looting, betrayal of brother by brother, even cannibalism ravaged the city. So terrible was the Jews' suffering that Titus implored them to yield, but they continued their desperate resistance. One by one Jerusalem's strongholds were captured until, early in August 70, the Temple was assaulted and the soldiers gained entrance to its outer court. Titus wished to spare the sanctuary but after six days a soldier threw a blazing torch into its window and the sanctuary burst into flames. A dreadful carnage followed as thousands of priests, women, and children perished by fire and sword. The massive stones of the Temple, cracked by the intensity of the heat, soon fell into ruins. The lower city was set on fire but fanatic Zealots retreated to the upper city to fight on for almost a month more. When the siege was ended, after 134 days, more than a million Jews had been slain, and of the survivors nearly a hundred thousand were taken into slavery. Except for three towers and the western wall reserved to protect the Roman garrison, Jerusalem's walls were leveled and the city totally destroyed (compare Mic. 3:12; Lu. 19:43,44).

During the latter half of the first century A.D. the Church suffered rising persecution at the hands of Rome. By 64 Rome had come to regard Christians as troublemakers since clashes between Jews and Christians frequently disturbed the local peace. Hostility flared into violence when the half-mad Nero—to divert suspicion from himself—blamed Christians for the burning of Rome. The bloody persecution that followed was initially restricted to Christians at Rome, but Nero's edict against them set a precedent. Persecution spread to Asia Minor during Domitian's reign (81-96), when emperor worship became the imperial religion (see p. 490). Christians, regarding such worship as blasphemous, refused to bow the knee, and Domitian wrought a terrible vengeance upon them.

Not only was the Church endangered from without, but its life within was threatened by heretical doctrines of apostate teachers and by the spread of Oriental mysticism which tended to adulterate the purity of the gospel. Between 61 and 90 the General Epistles (James, I and II Peter, I, II, and III John, Jude) appeared, so-called because they were addressed to Christians in general. They were written to safeguard Christian doctrine, to steady Christian adherents to meet the impending crises of their day. In 96, at the height of Domitian's persecution, the Church was buttressed by the mighty Patmos vision of John's Apocalypse.

14

The Epistle to the Hebrews

Although this book is called "The Epistle of Paul the Apostle to the Hebrews" in the King James Version, it was written anonymously, and its authorship has therefore long been in question. Some scholars reject Paul's authorship entirely, others attribute this letter directly to his hand, while still others agree that if not written by Paul it is nevertheless Pauline in spirit and content. It is dated earlier than the destruction of Jerusalem, probably about 62-64 A.D. The Greek manuscripts generally have the name of Paul affixed to them. The author was known to the churches (Heb. 13:18,19), he called Timothy his brother (Heb. 13:23), his salutation from Italian Christians indicated he was still in Italy (Heb. 13:24), and his benediction of "grace be with you" followed the form used only by Paul (Heb. 13:25). By the second century A.D. authorship was attributed to Paul and in 419 the Fifth Council of Carthage formally included Hebrews among his fourteen Epistles.

Addressed to Hebrew Christians, its design is clear: to urge those who had embraced Christ's gospel to turn from Judaism and its ceremonial worship. The Jew found it difficult to perceive that the Mosaic forms were only types, "a figure for the time then present," that the old dispensation of the Law had come to an end, and that the Advent of Jesus Christ had inaugurated the new dispensation of grace. In this epistle the Hebrew Christian was assured that his new-found religion was not divorced from Mosaism but was Mosaism's perfect fulfillment. Whereas the Law was only "a shadow of good things to come," Christ is the substance. Hebrews is a remarkable legal brief in defense of Christianity—an inspired analytical presentation of the superiority of the new covenant over the old.

This epistle claims for Jesus, in a way no other book of the New Testament does, his rightful office of great high priest.

Jesus as Priest is the burden of the book. . . . The author uses the method of contrast to prove his great contention. He measures Jesus against every point of glory in the Old Testament Dispensation.[1]

As the Son, he stands superior to the prophets, to the angels, to Moses, and to the Aaronic priesthood. He serves in a heavenly sanctuary; he offers a better sacrifice. Through his humanity as well as his divinity he is seen as the perfect mediator of the new covenant. By rending the veil of the flesh he provided all men free access to God. His one sacrifice of himself was sufficient to cleanse men from sin and enable them to enter "into the holiest . . . by a new and living way."

Hebrews holds an important place in the structure of the New Testament. In the Gospels the Savior is seen primarily in his Messianic office of Prophet; in Hebrews in his Messianic office of High Priest; and in Revelation in his Messianic office of King.

The abridgment of Hebrews that follows shows the counterpoint between the Old and New Covenants. Text should be read in sequence whether it appears in left or right column.

OLD COVENANT

*God hath spoken unto the
fathers by the prophets*

God, who at sundry times and in divers manners spake in time past unto the fathers by the prophets, (1:1)

NEW COVENANT

God hath spoken unto us by His Son

Hath in these last days spoken unto us by his Son, whom he hath appointed heir of all things, by whom also he made the worlds; Who being the brightness of his glory, and the express image of his person [RV the very image of his substance], and upholding all things by the word of his power, when he had by himself purged our sins, sat down on the right hand of the Majesty on high; (1:2,3)

Christ's pre-eminence over the angels

Being made so much better than the angels, as he hath by inheritance obtained a more excellent name than they.

For unto which of the angels said he at any time, Thou art my Son, this day have I begotten thee? And again, I will be to him a Father, and he shall be to me a Son? And again, when he bringeth in the first begotten into the world, he saith, And let all the angels of God worship him. . . .

But unto the Son he saith, Thy throne, O God, is for ever and ever: a sceptre of righteousness is the sceptre of thy kingdom. Thou hast loved righteousness, and hated iniquity; therefore God, even thy God, hath anointed thee with the oil of gladness above thy fellows. . . .

But to which of the angels said he at any time, Sit on my right hand, until I make thine enemies thy footstool? (1:4-9,13)

OLD COVENANT

NEW COVENANT

The world in subjection to Christ Jesus

Therefore we ought to give the more earnest heed to the things which we have heard, lest at any time we should let them slip. . . . How shall we escape, if we neglect so great salvation; which at the first began to be spoken by the Lord, and was confirmed unto us by them that heard him. . . .

For unto the angels hath he not put in subjection the world to come, whereof we speak. . . . Thou hast put all things in subjection under his feet. . . . But now we see not yet all things put under him. (2:1,3,5,8)

The incarnate Son tastes of death for the salvation of all

But we see Jesus, who was made a little lower than the angels for the suffering of death, crowned with glory and honour; that he by the grace of God should taste death for every man. . . .

Forasmuch then as the children are partakers of flesh and blood, he also himself likewise took part of the same; that through death he might destroy him that had the power of death, that is, the devil; And deliver them who through fear of death were all their lifetime subject to bondage. For verily he took not on him the nature of angels; but he took on him the seed of Abraham. Wherefore in all things it behoved him to be made like unto his brethren, that he might be a merciful and faithful high priest in things pertaining to God, to make reconciliation for the sins of the people. For in that he himself hath suffered being tempted, he is able to succour them that are tempted. (2:9,14-18)

Christ Jesus more worthy than Moses

Wherefore, holy brethren, partakers of the heavenly calling, consider the Apostle and High Priest of our profession, Christ Jesus; Who was faithful to him that appointed him. . . . For this man was counted worthy of more glory than Moses, inasmuch as he who hath builded the house hath more honour than the house. (3:1-3)

Moses verily was faithful in all his house, as a servant, for a testimony of those things which were to be spoken after; (3:5)

But Christ as a son over his own house; whose house are we, if we hold fast the confidence and the rejoicing of the hope firm unto the end. (3:6)

OLD COVENANT

NEW COVENANT

A warning against unbelief—faith
assures entrance into God's rest

Wherefore (as the Holy Ghost saith, To day if ye will hear his voice, Harden not your hearts, as in the provocation, in the day of temptation in the wilderness.... So I sware in my wrath, They shall not enter into my rest.)

Take heed, brethren, lest there be in any of you an evil heart of unbelief, in departing from the living God.... For we are made partakers of Christ, if we hold the beginning of our confidence stedfast unto the end; While it is said, To day if ye will hear his voice, harden not your hearts, as in the provocation. (3:7,8,11-15)

For some, when they had heard, did provoke.... But with whom was he grieved forty years? was it not with them that had sinned.... And to whom sware he that they should not enter into his rest, but to them that believed not? So we see that they could not enter in because of unbelief. (3:16-19)

Let us therefore fear, lest, a promise being left us of entering into his rest, any of you should seem to come short of it.

For unto us was the gospel preached, as well as unto them: but the word preached did not profit them, not being mixed with faith in them that heard it. For we which have believed do enter into rest....

For he that is entered into his rest, he also hath ceased from his own works, as God did from his.

Let us labour therefore to enter into that rest, lest any man fall after the same example of unbelief. For the word of God is quick, and powerful, and sharper than any twoedged sword, piercing even to the dividing asunder of soul and spirit, and of the joints and marrow, and is a discerner of the thoughts and intents of the heart....

Seeing then that we have a great high priest, that is passed into the heavens, Jesus the Son of God, let us hold fast our profession.... Let us ... come boldly unto the throne of grace, that we may obtain mercy, and find grace to help in time of need. (4:1-3,10-16)

High priest of the
Levitical order

Every high priest taken from among men is ordained for men in things pertaining to God, that he may offer both gifts and sacrifices for sins: Who can have compassion

OLD COVENANT

on the ignorant, and on them that are out of the way; for that he himself also is compassed with infirmity.... And no man taketh this honour unto himself, but he that is called of God, as was Aaron. (5:1,2,4)

NEW COVENANT

Christ, high priest after the more excellent order of Melchisedec

So also Christ glorified not himself to be made an high priest but he that said unto him, Thou art my Son, to day have begotten thee. As he saith also in another place, Thou art a priest for ever after the order of Melchisedec [Ps. 110:4]... Though he were a Son, yet learned he obedience by the things which he suffered; And being made perfect, he became the author of eternal salvation unto all them that obey him; Called of God an high priest after the order of Melchisedec (5:5,6,8-10)

(In Chapter 5:11-6:20 the author reproves his readers for spiritual immaturity and urges them not to fall away to apostasy.)

For this Melchisedec ... priest of the most high God ... To whom also Abraham gave a tenth part of all; first being by interpretation King of righteousness, and after that also King of Salem, which is, King of peace; Without father, without mother, without descent, having neither beginning of days, nor end of life; but made unto the Son of God; abideth a priest continually (7:1-3)

If therefore perfection were by the Levitical priesthood, (for under it the people received the law,) what further need was there that another priest should rise after the order of Melchisedec, and not be called after the order of Aaron? (7:11)

For the priesthood being changed, there is made of necessity a change also of the law.... For it is evident that our Lord sprang out of Juda; of which tribe Moses spake nothing concerning the priesthood. And it is yet far more evident: for that after the similitude of Melchisedec there ariseth another priest, Who is made, not after the law of a carnal commandment, but after the power of an endless life. For he testifieth Thou art a priest for ever after the order of Melchisedec (7:12,14-17)

For there is verily a disannulling of the commandment going before for the weakness and unprofitableness thereof. (7:18)
For the law made nothing perfect, (7:19)

but the bringing in of a better hope did; by the which we draw nigh unto God. And inasmuch as not without an oath he was made priest: (7:19,20)

OLD COVENANT	NEW COVENANT

OLD COVENANT

(For those priests were made without an oath [7:21]

NEW COVENANT

but this with an oath by him that said unto him, The Lord sware and will not repent, Thou art a priest for ever after the order of Melchisedec:) By so much was Jesus made a surety of a better testament. (7:21,22)

They truly were many priests, because they were not suffered to continue by reason of death. (7:23)

But this man, because he continueth ever, hath an unchangeable priesthood. Wherefore he is able also to save them to the uttermost that come unto God by him, seeing he ever liveth to make intercession for them.

For such an high priest became us, who is holy, harmless, undefiled, separate from sinners, and made higher than the heavens; Who needeth not daily, as those high priests, to offer up sacrifice, first for his own sins, and then for the people's: for this he did once, when he offered up himself. (7:24-27)

For the law maketh men high priests which have infirmity; (7:28)

but the word of the oath, which was since the law, maketh the Son, who is consecrated for evermore. (7:28)

Christ the mediator of a new and better covenant

Now of the things which we have spoken this is the sum: We have such an high priest, who is set on the right hand of the throne of the Majesty in the heavens; A minister of the sanctuary, and of the true tabernacle, which the Lord pitched, and not man. (8:1,2)

For every high priest is ordained to offer gifts and sacrifices: wherefore it is of necessity that this man have somewhat also to offer. For if he were on earth, he should not be a priest, (8:3,4)

seeing that there are priests that offer gifts according to the law: Who serve unto the example and shadow of heavenly things, as Moses was admonished of God when he was about to make the tabernacle. . . . (8:4,5)

But now hath he obtained a more excellent ministry, by how much also he is the mediator of a better covenant, which was established upon better promises. (8:6)

For if that first covenant had been faultless, then should no place have been sought for the second. For finding fault with them, he saith, Behold, the days come, saith the Lord, when I will make a new covenant with the house of Israel and with the house

OLD COVENANT

NEW COVENANT

of Judah: Not according to the covenant that I made with their fathers in the day when I took them by the hand to lead them out of the land of Egypt; because they continued not in my covenant.... (8:7-9)

For this is the covenant that I will make with the house of Israel after those days, saith the Lord; I will put my laws into their mind, and write them in their hearts: and I will be to them a God, and they shall be to me a people: And they shall not teach every man his neighbour, and every man his brother, saying, Know the Lord: for all shall know me, from the least to the greatest. For I will be merciful to their unrighteousness, and their sins and their iniquities will I remember no more [cf. Jer. 31:33,34]. (8:10-12)

In that he saith, A new covenant, he hath made the first old. Now that which decayeth and waxeth old is ready to vanish away. (8:13)

The earthly sanctuary and its sacrifices

Then verily the first covenant had also ordinances of divine service, and a worldly sanctuary.

For there was a tabernacle made; the first, wherein was the candlestick, and the table, and the shewbread; which is called the sanctuary. And after the second veil, the tabernacle which is called the Holiest of all; Which had the golden censer, and the ark of the covenant....

Now ... the priests went always into the first tabernacle, accomplishing the service of God.

But into the second went the high priest alone once every year, not without blood, which he offered for himself, and for the errors of the people: The Holy Ghost this signifying, that the way into the holiest of all was not yet made manifest, while as the first tabernacle was yet standing: Which was a figure for the time then present, in which were offered both gifts and sacrifices, that could not make him that did the service perfect, as pertaining to the conscience.... (9:1-4,6-9)

OLD COVENANT

NEW COVENANT

*Christ serves in a heavenly sanctuary
and offers a better sacrifice*

But Christ being come an high priest of good things to come, by a greater and more perfect tabernacle, not made with hands, that is to say, not of this building; Neither by the blood of goats and calves, but by his own blood he entered in once into the holy place, having obtained eternal redemption for us. (9:11,12)

For if the blood of bulls and of goats, and the ashes of an heifer sprinkling the unclean, sanctifieth to the purifying of the flesh: (9:13)

How much more shall the blood of Christ, who through the eternal Spirit offered himself without spot to God, purge your conscience from dead works to serve the living God?

And for this cause he is the mediator of the new testament, that by means of death, for the redemption of the transgressions that were under the first testament, they which are called might receive the promise of eternal inheritance.

For where a testament is, there must also of necessity be the death of the testator. For a testament is of force after men are dead: otherwise it is of no strength at all while the testator liveth. (9:14-17)

Whereupon neither the first testament was dedicated without blood. . . . And almost all things are by the law purged with blood; and without shedding of blood is no remission.

It was therefore necessary that the patterns of things in the heavens should be purified with these; (9:18,22,23)

but the heavenly things themselves with better sacrifices than these. For Christ is not entered into the holy places made with hands, which are the figures of the true; but into heaven itself, now to appear in the presence of God for us. (9:23,24)

Christ's one sacrifice put away sin forever

Nor yet that he should offer himself often, as the high priest entereth into the holy place every year with blood of others. . . . but now once in the end of the world hath he appeared to put away sin by the sacrifice of himself. . . . So Christ was once offered to bear the sins of many; and unto them that look for him shall he appear the second time without sin unto salvation. (9:25-28)

*Sacrifices which
never take away sin*

For the law having a shadow of good things

OLD COVENANT

to come, and not the very image of the things, can never with those sacrifices which they offered year by year continually make the comers thereunto perfect. For then would they not have ceased to be offered? because that the worshippers once purged should have had no more conscience of sins. But in those sacrifices there is a remembrance again made of sins every year. For it is not possible that the blood of bulls and of goats should take away sins. (10:1-4)

Every priest standeth daily ministering and offering oftentimes the same sacrifices, which can never take away sins: (10:11)

NEW COVENANT

Wherefore when he cometh into the world, he saith, Sacrifice and offering thou wouldest not, but a body hast thou prepared me: In burnt offerings and sacrifices for sin thou hast had no pleasure. Then said I, Lo, I come (in the volume of the book it is written of me,) to do thy will, O God. . . . He taketh away the first, that he may establish the second.

By the which will we are sanctified through the offering of the body of Jesus Christ once for all. (10:5-7,9,10; compare Ps. 40:6-8)

But this man, after he had offered one sacrifice for sins for ever, sat down on the right hand of God; From henceforth expecting till his enemies be made his footstool. For by one offering he hath perfected for ever them that are sanctified. Whereof the Holy Ghost also is a witness to us: for after that he had said before, This is the covenant . . . I will put my laws into their hearts, and in their minds will I write them; And their sins . . . will I remember no more. Now where remission of these is, there is no more offering for sin. (10:12-18)

Let us enter the holiest by this new and living way

Having therefore, brethren, boldness to enter into the holiest by the blood of Jesus, By a new and living way, which he hath consecrated for us, through the veil, that is to say, his flesh; And having an high priest over the house of God; Let us draw near with a true heart in full assurance of faith, having our hearts sprinkled from an evil conscience, and our bodies washed with pure water. (10:19-22)

Warning against apostasy, and exhortation to hold fast the faith and patience

Let us hold fast the profession of our faith without wavering;

OLD COVENANT   **NEW COVENANT**

(for he is faithful that promised;) And let us consider one another to provoke unto love and to good works: Not forsaking the assembling of ourselves together ... but exhorting one another: and so much the more, as ye see the day approaching.

For if we sin wilfully after that we have received the knowledge of the truth, there remaineth no more sacrifice for sins, But a certain fearful looking for of judgment and fiery indignation, which shall devour the adversaries.

He that despised Moses' law died without mercy under two or three witnesses: Of how much sorer punishment, suppose ye, shall he be thought worthy, who hath trodden under foot the Son of God, and hath counted the blood of the covenant, wherewith he was sanctified, an unholy thing, and hath done despite unto the Spirit of grace? ... It is a fearful thing to fall into the hands of the living God. . . .

Cast not away therefore your confidence, which hath great recompense of reward. For ye have need of patience, that, after ye have done the will of God, ye might receive the promise. For yet a little while, and he that shall come will come, and will not tarry.

Now the just shall live by faith: but if any man draw back, my soul shall have no pleasure in him. But we are not of them who draw back unto perdition; but of them that believe to the saving of the soul. (10:23-31,35-39)

The operation of faith

Now faith is the substance of things hoped for, the evidence of things not seen. For by it the elders obtained a good report. Through faith we understand that the worlds were framed by the word of God, so that things which are seen were not made of things which do appear. (11:1-3) ["Faith is that by which the invisible becomes real and the future becomes present."[2]]

(The writer of Hebrews calls the glorious roll of Old Testament heroes, whose faith was the substance of their hope while as yet they knew only the promise.)

ABEL, by faith, "offered unto God a more excellent sacrifice than Cain."
ENOCH, by faith, "was translated that he should not see death."
NOAH, by faith, "prepared an ark to the saving of his house."
ABRAHAM, by faith, "when he was called to go out ... obeyed."
by faith, "sojourned in the land of promise."
by faith, "looked for a city ... whose builder and maker is God."
SARA, by faith, "was delivered of a child when she was past age." (11:4-11)

These all died in faith, not having received the promises, but having seen them afar off, and were persuaded of them, and embraced them, and confessed that they were strangers and pilgrims on the earth. For they that say such things declare plainly that they seek a country. And truly, if they had been mindful of that country from whence they came out, they might have had opportunity to have returned. But now they desire a better country ... an heavenly: wherefore God is not ashamed to be called their God: for he hath prepared for them a city. (11:13-16)

ABRAHAM, by faith, "when he was tried, offered up Isaac."
  ISAAC, by faith, "blessed Jacob and Esau concerning things to come."
    JACOB, by faith, "when he was a dying, blessed both the sons of Joseph."
      JOSEPH, by faith, "made mention of the departing of the children of Israel."
        MOSES, by faith, "was hid three months of his parents."
                by faith, "refused to be called the son of Pharaoh's daughter."
                by faith, "forsook Egypt, not fearing the wrath of the king."
                by faith, "kept the passover, and the sprinkling of blood."
          ISRAEL, by faith, "passed through the Red sea as by dry land."
                by faith, "the walls of Jericho fell down."
            RAHAB, by faith, "perished not with them that believed not."

GEDEON, BARAK, SAMSON, JEPHTHAE, DAVID, SAMUEL, and the PROPHETS,
    by faith, "subdued kingdoms, wrought righteousness, obtained promises."
    by faith, "stopped the mouths of lions, Quenched . . . fire, escaped . . . the sword."
    by faith, "out of weakness were made strong, waxed valiant in fight."
    by faith, "turned to flight the armies of the aliens."

WOMEN, by faith, "received their dead raised to life again."
  OTHERS, by faith, "were tortured, not accepting deliverance."
                by faith, "had trial of cruel mockings . . . scourgings . . . imprisonment."
                by faith, "were stoned . . . sawn asunder . . . slain with the sword."
                by faith, "wandered about in sheepskins . . . destitute, afflicted."
                by faith, "wandered in deserts . . . mountains . . . caves." (11:17-38)

These all, having obtained a good report through faith, received not the promise: God having provided some better thing for us, that they without us should not be made perfect. (11:39,40)

Exhortation to run the race unto perfection through
faith and through the grace that is in Jesus Christ

Wherefore seeing we also are compassed about with so great a cloud of witnesses, let us lay aside every weight, and the sin which doth so easily beset us, and let us run with patience the race that is set before us. . . ." (12:1)

Let US (by faith   "run with patience. . . . Looking unto Jesus the author and finisher
   and grace)   of our faith; who for the joy that was set before him endured
                                the cross, despising the shame, and is set down at the right
                                hand of the throne of God."

   (by faith   "consider him that endured such contradiction of sinners against
   and grace)   himself, lest ye be wearied and faint in your minds. Ye have
                                not yet resisted unto blood, striving against sin. And ye
                                have forgotten the exhortation. . . . My son, despise not thou
                                the chastening of the Lord. . . . For whom the Lord loveth
                                he chasteneth. . . . for our profit, that we might be
                                partakers of his holiness."

   (by faith   "lift up the hands which hang down, and the feeble knees;
   and grace)   And make straight paths for your feet, lest that which is lame be
                                turned out of the way; but let it rather be healed."

(by faith   "Follow peace with all men, and holiness, without which no man
and grace)   shall see the Lord."

(by faith   "[look] diligently lest any man fail of the grace of God; lest any
and grace)   root of bitterness springing up trouble you." (12:2-15)

OLD COVENANT   **NEW COVENANT**

"Ye are come . . . unto the city of the living God"

Ye are not come unto the mount that might be touched, and
that burned with fire, nor unto blackness, and darkness, and
tempest, And the sound of a trumpet, and the voice of words;
(12:18,19)

which voice they that heard intreated that
the word should not be spoken to them any
more: (For they could not endure that
which was commanded. . . .) (12:19,20)

But ye are come unto mount Sion . . .
   —unto the city of the living God, the heavenly Jerusalem
      . . .
   —to an innumerable company of angels,
   —To the general assembly and church of the firstborn,
      which are written in heaven . . .
   —to God the Judge of all . . .
   —to the spirits of just men made perfect . . .
   —to Jesus the mediator of the new covenant . . .
   —to the blood of sprinkling, that speaketh better things
      than that of Abel. (12:22-24)

Warning: refuse not obedience to the New Covenant

See that ye refuse not him that speaketh. For if they escaped
not who refused him that spake on earth, much more shall not
we escape, if we turn away from him that speaketh from
heaven:

Whose voice then shook the earth: but now he hath
promised, saying, Yet once more I shake not the earth only, but
also heaven.

And this word, Yet once more, signifieth the removing of
those things that are shaken, as of things that are made, that
those things which cannot be shaken may remain.

Wherefore we receiving a kingdom which cannot be moved,
let us have grace, whereby we may serve God acceptably with
reverence and godly fear: For our God is a consuming fire.
(12:25-29; see Hag. 2:6)

(Further admonitions concerning Christian graces. Benediction.
[13:1-25])

15

The First Epistle of John

The First Epistle of John (the first of three) was written in Ephesus about 90 A.D. Its thought, style, and language are so close to that of the Fourth Gospel that its authorship has traditionally been attributed to John the Apostle.

For more than half a century John had been "a link between the first and third generations of Christians," an active pastor preaching the gospel among the Jews of Palestine and later, in Asia Minor, among the Gentiles. In the latter days of his ministry the churches of Asia were unsettled by the inroads of Gnosticism, (Greek, *gnosis,* "knowledge"), a blend of Oriental mysticism, Essenic Judaism, and Hellenistic philosophy. The initiates of Gnosticism claimed possession of a special knowledge of truth higher than the revelation that came through Jesus Christ.

Gnosticism regarded spirit as good, matter as evil and the source of all evil, with no contact between good and evil. This premise of the sinfulness of matter led Gnostics into one of two paths. Maintaining that soul and body are separate entities, they regarded the soul as free of any evil the body might do (the teaching called *antinomianism*). This concept led some to extreme asceticism and others to gross immorality.

The point of central importance in this belief of the separateness of spirit and matter was the Gnostics' denial of the Incarnation. They admitted that Christ had come but denied the humanity of his person while on earth; they held Jesus Christ merely to have been a phantom or appearance and his life in the flesh and his sufferings on the cross to have been unreal. This belief (termed *docetism*) struck at the very core of Christianity.

John wrote his First Epistle as a strong rebuke to those (the "Gnostic Christians") who had espoused these insidious teachings. Out of his personal knowledge of Jesus he bore witness that Christ had indeed come in the flesh and that Jesus was the Son of God—"that which was from the beginning, which we have heard, which we have seen with our eyes . . . and our hands have handled, of the Word of life . . . which was with the Father, and was manifested unto us" (1:1,2). "Who is a liar but he that denieth that Jesus is the Christ? He is antichrist, that denieth the Father and the Son" (2:22).

For the Gnostics the pursuit of knowledge became a life-goal in itself, a "loveless intellectualism" that left them devoid of brotherly love or any sense of responsibility toward the unenlightened.

John uncompromisingly condemned the Gnostic viewpoint licensing sin. Sin was lawless (3:4). "Little children, let no man deceive you: he that doeth righteousness is righteous, even as he is righteous. He that committeth sin is of the devil; for the devil sinneth from the beginning" (3:7,8).

John warned the Church against those who professed a knowledge of God but did not practice the love of God: "He that saith, I know him, and keepeth not his commandments, is a liar, and the truth is not in him. . . . He that saith he is in the light, and hateth his brother, is in darkness even until now" (2:4,9). The Christian's revelation of God comes through Jesus Christ and is already his: "Let that therefore abide in you, which ye have heard from the beginning . . . ye need not that any man teach you" (2:24,27).

The theme of the whole epistle is love—"God is love" (4:16). John defined God's great love for man, man's love for God, and godly love one for another. The demand is that men should love one another.

John taught Christians that fellowship with God is a living union with His Son and with one another, and in so doing he reduced the immortal meanings of love and sonship to their essence.

THE NATURE OF GOD	"God is light, and in him is no darkness at all." I Jn. 1:5
	"God is love. . . ." I Jn. 4:16
	"The Spirit is truth." I Jn. 5:6
THE NATURE OF HIS SON JESUS CHRIST	"The Word of life . . . that eternal life, which was with the Father. . . ." I Jn. 1:1,2
	"An advocate with the Father, Jesus Christ the righteous." I Jn. 2:1
	"In him is no sin." I Jn. 3:5
THE DIVINE PURPOSE OF THE SON	"For this purpose the Son of God was manifested, that he might destroy the works of the devil." I Jn. 3:8
	"This is the record, that God hath given to us eternal life, and this life is in his Son." I Jn. 5:11
THE INCARNATION OF THE SON	"That which was from the beginning, which we have heard, which we have seen with our eyes, which we have looked upon, and our hands have handled, of the Word of life; (For the life was manifested, and we have seen it, and bear witness, and shew unto you that eternal life, which was with the Father, and was manifested unto us;). . . ." I Jn. 1:1,2

THE GODHEAD AND ITS WITNESS	"This is he that came by water and blood, even Jesus Christ; not by water only, but by water and blood. And it is the Spirit that beareth witness, because the Spirit is truth.
	"For there are three that bear record in heaven, the Father, the Word, and the Holy Ghost: and these three are one.
	"And there are three that bear witness in earth, the Spirit, and the water, and the blood: and these three agree in one.
	"If we receive the witness of men, the witness of God is greater; for this is the witness of God which he hath testified of his Son. He that believeth on the Son of God hath the witness in himself. . . ." Jn. 5:6-10
GOD'S COMMANDMENT TO BELIEVE ON HIS SON	"And this is his commandment, That we should believe on the name of his Son Jesus Christ. . . ." I Jn. 3:23
FELLOWSHIP WITH GOD AND WITH HIS SON	"That which we have seen and heard declare we unto you, that ye also may have fellowship with us: and truly our fellowship is with the Father, and with his Son Jesus Christ. And these things write we unto you, that your joy may be full." I Jn. 1:3,4
	"He that acknowledgeth the Son hath the Father also." I Jn. 2:23
	"If that which ye have heard from the beginning shall remain in you, ye also shall continue in the Son, and in the Father." I Jn. 2:24
	"We know that the Son of God is come, and hath given us an understanding, that we may know him that is true, and we are in him that is true, even in his Son Jesus Christ. This is the true God, and eternal life." I Jn. 5:20
THE SPIRITUAL NATURE OF THE SONS OF GOD	"If ye know that he is righteous, ye know that everyone that doeth righteousness is born of him." I Jn. 2:29
	"Beloved, now are we the sons of God, and it doth not yet appear what we shall be: but we know that, when he shall appear, we shall be like him; for we shall see him as he is. And every man that hath this hope in him purifieth himself, even as he is pure." I Jn. 3:2,3
	"Whosoever is born of God doth not commit sin; for his seed remaineth in him: and he cannot sin, because he is born of God. In this the children of God are manifest. . . ." I Jn. 3:9,10
	"And he that keepeth his commandments dwelleth in him, and he in him. And hereby we know that he abideth in us, by the Spirit which he hath given us." I Jn. 3:24
	"God is love; and he that dwelleth in love dwelleth in God, and God in him. Herein is our love made perfect, that we may have boldness in the day of judgment: because as he is, so are we in this world." I Jn. 4:16,17
	"He that hath the Son hath life. . . . These things have I written . . . that ye may know that ye have eternal life. . . ." I Jn. 5:12,13
	"We know that whosoever is born of God sinneth not; but he that is begotten of God keepeth himself, and that wicked one toucheth him not." I Jn. 5:18
THE FATHER'S LOVE FOR ALL HIS SONS	"Ye have an unction from the Holy One, and ye know all things." I Jn. 2:20
	"Behold, what manner of love the Father hath bestowed upon us, that we should be called the sons of God: therefore the world knoweth us not, because it knew him not." I Jn. 3:1

"In this was manifested the love of God toward us, because that God sent his only begotten Son into the world, that we might live through him." I Jn. 4:9

"Herein is love, not that we loved God, but that he loved us, and sent his Son to be the propitiation for our sins." I Jn. 4:10

THE SONS' LOVE FOR THE FATHER

"Whoso keepeth his word, in him verily is the love of God perfected: hereby know we what we are in him. He that saith he abideth in him ought himself also so to walk, even as he walked." I Jn. 2:5,6

"We love him [God], because he first loved us." I Jn. 4:19

"Whosoever believeth that Jesus is the Christ is born of God: and every one that loveth him that begat loveth him also that is begotten of him. By this we know that we love the children of God, when we love God, and keep his commandments. For this is the love of God, that we keep his commandments. . . ." I Jn. 5:1-3

BROTHERLY LOVE AND FELLOWSHIP

"If we walk in the light, as he is in the light, we have fellowship one with another, and the blood of Jesus Christ his Son cleanseth us from all sin." I Jn. 1:7

"Hereby perceive we the love of God, because he laid down his life for us: and we ought to lay down our lives for the brethren." I Jn. 3:16

"Beloved, let us love one another: for love is of God; and every one that loveth is born of God, and knoweth God." I Jn. 4:7

"Beloved, if God so loved us, we ought also to love one another. No man hath seen God at any time. If we love one another, God dwelleth in us, and his love is perfected in us." I Jn. 4:11,12

"This commandment have we from him, That he who loveth God love his brother also." I Jn. 4:21

ANTICHRIST (Denying God's love)

"Little children. . . . as ye have heard that antichrist shall come, even now are there many antichrists; whereby we know that it is the last time. They went out from us, but they were not of us; for if they had been of us, they would no doubt have continued with us: but they went out, that they might be made manifest that they were not all of us." I Jn. 2:18,19

"Who is a liar but he that denieth that Jesus is the Christ? He is antichrist, that denieth the Father and the Son." I Jn. 2:22

"Every spirit that confesseth not that Jesus Christ is come in the flesh is not of God: and this is that spirit of antichrist. . . . and even now already is it in the world." I Jn. 4:3

"He that believeth not God hath made him a liar; because he believeth not the record that God gave of his Son." I Jn. 5:10

OVERCOMING THE WORLD

"Ye are of God, little children, and have overcome them: because greater is he that is in you, than he that is in the world." I Jn. 4:4

"For whatsoever is born of God overcometh the world: and this is the victory that overcometh the world, even our faith. Who is he that overcometh the world, but he that believeth that Jesus is the Son of God?" I Jn. 5:4,5

"LOVE NOT THE WORLD"

As a loving pastor John warns the Christian against evil influences that would draw him away from the love of God: "Love not the world, neither the things that are in the world. If any man love the world, the love of the Father is not in him. For all that is in the world, the lust of the flesh, and the lust of the eyes, and the pride of life, is not of the Father, but is of the world. And the world passeth away, and the lust thereof: but he that doeth the will of God abideth for ever" (I Jn. 2:15-17).

A careful study of John's First Epistle shows that along with the apostle's fundamental teachings of the nature of God and His loving relationship to men is his underlying recognition of carnal elements of the human mind antagonistic to Christ; hence many of his positive statements of truth are intensified by a warning or denial against these opposing errors.

"Beloved, believe not every spirit, but try the spirits whether they are of God. . . . We are of God: he that knoweth God heareth us; he that is not of God heareth not us. Hereby know we the spirit of truth, and the spirit of error" (I Jn. 4:1,6).

The Spirit of Truth	The Spirit of Error
"If we walk in the light, as he is in the light, we have fellowship one with another, and the blood of Jesus Christ his Son cleanseth us from all sin." I Jn. 1:7	"If we say that we have fellowship with him, and walk in darkness, we lie, and do not the truth." I Jn. 1:6
"Hereby we do know that we know him, if we keep his commandments." I Jn. 2:3	"He that saith, I know him, and keepeth not his commandments, is a liar, and the truth is not in him." I Jn. 2:4
"He that loveth his brother abideth in the light, and there is none occasion of stumbling in him." I Jn. 2:10	"But he that hateth his brother is in darkness, and walketh in darkness, and knoweth not whither he goeth, because that darkness hath blinded his eyes." I Jn. 2:11
"He that acknowledgeth the Son hath the Father also." I Jn. 2:23	"Whosoever denieth the Son, the same hath not the Father. . . ." I Jn. 2:23
"Whosoever abideth in him sinneth not:" I Jn. 3:6	"whosoever sinneth hath not seen him, neither known him." I Jn. 3:6
"Let no man deceive you: he that doeth righteousness is righteous, even as he is righteous." I Jn. 3:7	"He that committeth sin is of the devil; for the devil sinneth from the beginning." I Jn. 3:8
"Whosoever is born of God doth not commit sin; for his seed remaineth in him: and he cannot sin, because he is born of God." I Jn. 3:9	"Whosoever doeth not righteousness is not of God, neither he that loveth not his brother." I Jn. 3:10

The Spirit of Truth	The Spirit of Error
"We know that we have passed from death unto life, because we love the brethren." I Jn. 3:14	"He that loveth not his brother abideth in death. Whosoever hateth his brother is a murderer: and ye know that no murderer hath eternal life abiding in him." I Jn. 3:14,15
"My little children, let us not love in word, neither in tongue; but in deed and in truth." I Jn. 3:18	"Whoso hath this world's good, and seeth his brother have need, and shutteth up his bowels of compassion from him, how dwelleth the love of God in him?" I Jn. 3:17
"We are of God: he that knoweth God heareth us; he that is not of God heareth not us." I Jn. 4:6	"They are of the world: therefore speak they of the world, and the world heareth them." I Jn. 4:5
"Love is of God; and every one that loveth is born of God, and knoweth God." I Jn. 4:7	"He that loveth not knoweth not God; for God is love." I Jn. 4:8
"There is no fear in love; but perfect love casteth out fear: because fear hath torment." I Jn. 4:18	"He that feareth is not made perfect in love." I Jn. 4:18
"This commandment have we from him, That he who loveth God love his brother also." I Jn. 4:21	"If a man say, I love God, and hateth his brother, he is a liar: for he that loveth not his brother whom he hath seen, how can he love God whom he hath not seen?" I Jn. 4:20
"He that believeth on the Son of God hath the witness in himself. . . ." I Jn. 5:10	"he that believeth not God hath made him a liar; because he believeth not the record that God gave of his Son." I Jn. 5:10

JOHN'S
BENEDICTION

"We know that we are of God . . . And we know that the Son of God is come, and hath given us an understanding, that we may know him that is true, and we are in him that is true, even in his Son Jesus Christ. This is the true God and eternal life.

"Little children, keep yourselves from idols. Amen." I Jn. 5:19-21

16

The Revelation of St. John the Divine

The book of Revelation, the only book of prophecy of the New Testament, known also as the Apocalypse, is a fitting close to the canon of Scripture, presenting Jesus Christ in his glory as "King of kings and Lord of lords." The word *revelation* (from Latin) means "to unveil," the drawing back of a covering to disclose the heretofore unknown. The word *apocalypse* (from Greek) means "uncovering."

> "The Revelation of Jesus Christ, which God gave unto him, to shew unto his servants things which must shortly come to pass; and he sent and signified it by his angel unto his servant John." (1:1)

This book is perhaps the least understood of all the books of the Bible. It is couched in apocalyptic language (see p. 490), although this in itself is not an insurmountable problem. Among the reasons for misunderstanding, other than the remarkable nature of the book's contents and the difficulty of its symbolism, is the tendency to take the apocalyptic language literally, not going beyond the symbolism to the basic spiritual truth, or to confine the symbolism to a single interpretation; or the tendency to give it a rigid historical interpretation, and by so doing to obscure the relevance of its message and hide the infinite interpretations it holds for all time and for each one of us.

Authorship

The writer of the book calls himself John and states that he is in exile in the isle of Patmos. He speaks with the authority of an apostle and as one known to the churches of the province of Asia. This John has been identified in the main with John the Apostle, who according to tradition had settled in Ephesus sometime

The barren spread-eagle isle of Patmos in the Aegean Sea, the Biblical scene of John's apocalyptic visions. Religious News Service Photo.

during the latter half of the first century and had resided there until the reign of Trajan (98-117 A.D.). To see that he was eminently qualified to impart the message of Revelation, one needs only to remember his intimate association with the Master Christian, his prominent place in the early Church, and his more than half a century of unceasing service. But above all, the spiritual tone of his Gospel and of his three Epistles show him to have been possessed of an exceptional insight into the nature and person of Christ. A strong argument for his authorship is the explicit testimony of the early Christian fathers (*ca.* 140-250 A.D.): Justin Martyr, Irenaeus, Tertullian, Clement of Alexandria, Origen, Hippolytus.

There is also evidence within the book itself that supports this view of the apostle's authorship. There are many language resemblances between Revelation and the Fourth Gospel and I, II, and III John. Certain words and phrases peculiar to Johannine writings are common to Revelation, such as "testimony," "witness," "true"; "keep," "overcometh"; "the water of life"; "the Word of God," and "the Lamb" (John's distinctive titles for Christ), the latter appearing nearly thirty times in Revelation. Those who reject John's authorship do so mainly on the ground that there is too great a dissimilarity in literary style and content from his other writings, while those who accept it hold that the divergences are a result of the fact that his subject matter is so different and his vision so transcendent that the writing could not follow his earlier style.

Time and Place of Writing

The time of writing was about 96 A.D. The place was

489

Patmos, a rocky barren island off the coast of southwestern Asia Minor, used by the Romans as a penal colony. According to Eusebius, John was banished to this island during the latter part of the reign of the Roman Emperor Domitian (81-96).

Spiritually matured through long experience and the ripening of Christ's love within him, with his life reduced to stark simplicity, surrounded for long days and nights by the grandeur of the infinite expanse of sea and sky, John was sensitively receptive to the voice and message of Christ.

Emperor Worship

Christians had been under increasing suspicion and harassment from the time of Nero, a harassment which had at first been confined to Rome but had gradually spread to Asia Minor. John's banishment was a result of the severe persecution Christians were suffering because of the imposed emperor or Caesar worship which prevailed throughout the Roman world during the reign of Domitian. (Tertullian [150-222 A.D.] records that during a persecution at Rome under Domitian, John in his ninetieth year was cast into a cauldron of boiling oil, from which he emerged unscathed.) The seeds of such emperor worship may be traced to the period immediately following the conquests of Alexander the Great (336-323 B.C.) when hero worship by his admirers elevated this Macedonian general almost to the position of a deity. As the Roman Empire became dominant, this practice of emperor worship was adopted, and in time its rulers were exalted to the position of gods; but, as in the case of Alexander, this deification took place after their deaths.

Domitian, however, swollen with arrogance and ambition, demanded the title "Lord and God" (*dominus et deus*) during his lifetime, and took harsh measures to force all his subjects to so acknowledge him. Emperor worship became the chief cult of the Empire, unifying its farflung provinces. From a polytheistic point of view no issue was involved, for bending the knee or burning incense in the emperor's honor was a matter of good manners; but to Jews and Christians this practice was blasphemous, a violation of religious principles. Jewish subjects had long been exempt from this Roman rite as an ethnic group whose religion forbade worship of other gods, but Christians were in a class apart because they refused to give their allegiance to but one Lord, Jesus Christ. The result was an inevitable clash between Christianity and Rome—in spirit, a battle between two kingdoms. Because of Christians' determined refusal to bow down, untold numbers were branded treasonous; tortured, and martyred in cruel ways. In the last four years of Domitian's rule, so fierce was the persecution that it foreshadowed to John a universal martyrdom.

Christian faith and allegiance might, at any moment, anywhere in the Empire, be tested as men and women were faced with the ordeal of choosing between Caesar and Christ. In this crisis John's Apocalypse burst upon the Church as a shining light to strengthen its trembling faith and hope.

Purpose

The ethical and universal purpose of Revelation, as with the messages of the prophets and the ministry of Jesus, was twofold—for the writer's day and for all time. "The permanent message of the book is its witness to the belief, which history has again and again proved to be true, that *spiritual and not material forces are in the end the strongest.*"[1] John wrote to give encouragement to a Church under fiery trial, to strengthen its followers to endure, to be "faithful unto death." His visions assured the Church that God's judgments would fall on all unrighteousness, and pointed with confident hope to the ultimate victory of Christ's kingdom which, in his prophecy, became an accomplished fact.

> The essential purpose of revelation is *life*: the gift of the life of God to the life of man. . . . The 'chief end of revelation' is not philosophy, though it has a philosophy profound and worthy. It is not doctrine, though it has a doctrine satisfying and inspiring. It is not enjoyment, though it has its experiences precious and lasting. It is not even morality, though it has its ethic unique and powerful. Christianity *has* all these, but *is* far more than them all. It is the religion of redemption, including salvation from sin, equipment for holiness, and provision for life to be lived in fellowship with God and for His glory. The 'chief end' of revelation is the union of God and man, and in that union the fulfilment of all God's purposes for the world.[2]

Apocalyptic Writing

Because of the vicious persecution of the Church, John's message must reach the world in a form that could be understood by those for whom it was intended and yet be expressed in such terms as to be unintelligible to those hostile to it. John chose to clothe his message in apocalyptic language, a style of writing that made large use of symbolism, vivid imagery, visions, and predictions containing an element of mystery. He drew repeatedly on the current Jewish belief in angelology; angels were employed as messengers of God to unveil His divine purpose and as instruments of divine judgment. Apocalypses conveyed encouragement to the afflicted in the form of great world pictures, vast panoramas depicting the destined fall and destruction of the forces of evil and the sure victory and reign of the forces of righteousness. This method was familiar to the Jews, for portions of Hebrew prophetical Scripture—of Isaiah, Jeremiah, Ezekiel, Joel, Zechariah, and particularly Daniel (chaps. 7-12)—were apocalyptic in character, as was much of the eschatological literature of the inter-testamental period. Such writings were most prevalent in times of imperialistic oppression, a literature of crises.

Jesus himself had employed the apocalyptic in his teachings of the kingdom (Mt. 16:27,28; Lu. 17:20-37) and of his Second Coming (Mt. 10:23; 26:64; Mk. 8:38; Lu. 12:40). He made extensive use of it in his Olivet discourse in speaking of the great tribulation which would precede the appearing of the Son of man, in describing his return in glory, the gathering of his elect, the Last Judgment (Mt. 24; 25:31-46; Mk. 13; Lu. 21:5-28).

Paul also made use of this style of writing in his reference to the man of sin (II Th. 2:1-12), as did Peter in speaking of the Day of the Lord (II Pet. 3:5-13), and John in reference to Antichrist (I Jn. 2:18-23):

It was therefore natural that John should use the thought forms so familiar to his day. Much of his symbolism and imagery was drawn from prophetic Scripture. Among his pictorial figures were the living creatures of Ezekiel; the horned beasts of Daniel; the red, black, white, and bay horses, the golden candle-stick, the two olive trees of Zechariah; the locusts of Joel; the trumpets, the measuring line, angelic beings, living waters. Fire as a descriptive symbol of divine power and judgment is employed repeatedly: the eyes of Christ are "as a flame of fire" (Rev. 1:14; 19:12), a censer filled with fire from the heavenly altar is cast on the earth and followed by God's flaming judgments (8:5 ff.), the feet of the angel with the open book are as "pillars of fire" (10:1), Babylon is judged by fire (18:8), God's enemies are devoured by fire (20:8,9), and in a "lake of fire" all evil is consumed (19:20; 20:10,14,15). All these symbols, and more, were adapted to John's use and infused with new meaning through the genius of his inspiration as he set forth the message imparted to him.

Theme

The grand theme of the book is the gradual victory of Christ over the world, the fulfillment of the promise of his Second Coming in exaltation and glory, and the bringing in of God's covenanted kingdom.

John's Apocalypse bears a close and unmistakable relationship to Jesus' Olivet discourse, foretelling in detail as it does the signs of Christ's coming in judgment. When Christ walked among men he had specifically foretold his Second Coming, one which was to carry with it universal salvation and blessing. He had stated plainly in the Olivet discourse and also before the Sanhedrin that the Son of man would come "in the clouds of heaven" and "with power and great glory." And at the Last Supper he had taught his disciples that though he was going away, he would

surely come again—he would send them the Comforter, the "Spirit of truth" discernible to men through faith and understanding (Jn. 14:16-18). Although Jesus' disciples did not fully understand the meaning of his promise, they did look for its fulfillment. The Apostolic Church felt Christ's presence in the influx of the Holy Ghost at Pentecost and watched with joyous expectation for his imminent return. Slowly, however, the Church came to understand that the final consummation of his Coming awaited the purification and preparation of the hearts of men.

The Day of the Lord

Coincident with Christ's Coming is "the day of the Lord" (AV) or "the day of Jehovah" (RV) foretold by the Old Testament prophets. During early prophetic history it denoted a day of judgment. Israel waited expectantly for the time when Jehovah would deliver the nation from oppression by foreign powers and would exalt it among the nations, and when He would sit in judgment on the heathen (Ps. 37:28,29).

As Israel grew in comprehension of the holiness of the One God and its covenant relation with Him, there dawned the realization that because God was a righteous Judge, all unrighteousness would pass under His rod. The prophets, emphasizing the moral law, called for reform and justice. The nation was made aware that they as well as the heathen must purge themselves of sin and apostasy. Every man was to be held accountable for his own deeds (Is. 2:12; Ezek. 18:20,30). The prophets predicted a fearful punishment on the unrighteous, but they also foresaw the glory and rule of the righteous in God's kingdom. Amos was the first to write of the Day of the Lord, terming it one of "darkness" (Amos 5:18); Joel described it as "great" and "terrible" (Joel 2:31).

This day pointed to one of vengeance on the wicked and of recompense to the godly; one of judgment on the nation and of judgment on the individual; one without definition of time, yet one ever at hand until the final judgment. "The great day of the Lord is near, it is near, and hasteth greatly.... That day is a day of wrath, a day of trouble and distress, a day of wasteness and desolation, a day of darkness and gloominess, a day of clouds and thick darkness...." (Zeph. 1:14,15).

Through the centuries this idea of a day of final judgment gathered momentum; it took a great leap forward in the pseudepigraphic apocalyptic literature of the first century B.C. and became one of the accepted eschatological beliefs of New Testament times.

Jesus' teachings strengthened this general belief in a final day of judgment. In the parable of the tares and the wheat (Mt. 13:24-30, 36-43), he foretold those who would be excluded from the kingdom and those

OVER-ALL VIEW OF THE BOOK OF REVELATION

"The Revelation of Jesus Christ . . . unto his
    servant John"

A Threefold Blessing:
    "Blessed is he that readeth . . . [blessed
    are] they that hear the words of this
    prophecy . . . [blessed are they that] keep
    those things which are written therein: for
    the time is at hand." Rev. 1:3

Read chart upward line by line

"Surely I come quickly."
Christ's Last Promise —

Epilogue

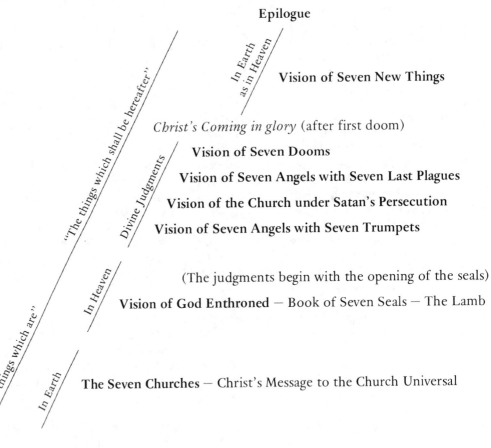

*In Earth
as in Heaven*

Vision of Seven New Things

Christ's Coming in glory (after first doom)

Vision of Seven Dooms

Vision of Seven Angels with Seven Last Plagues

Vision of the Church under Satan's Persecution

Vision of Seven Angels with Seven Trumpets

(The judgments begin with the opening of the seals)

Vision of God Enthroned — Book of Seven Seals — The Lamb

The Seven Churches — Christ's Message to the Church Universal

Vision of the Glorified Christ — Alpha and Omega in midst of seven candlesticks

Call of John on Patmos

Keynote: "Behold, he cometh with clouds; and every eye shall see him. . . ."

"And from Jesus Christ. . . ."
"And from the seven Spirits which are before his throne;
"From him which is, and which was, and which is to come;
John's Salutation to the Seven Churches: "Grace be unto you, and peace,

Introduction

"The things which shall be hereafter"

Divine Judgments

In Heaven

"The things which are"

In Earth

"The things which thou hast seen"

who would inherit it—*a gathering out and a gathering in.*

"The Son of man shall send forth his angels, and they shall gather out of his kingdom all things that offend, and them which do iniquity; And shall cast them into a furnace of fire. . . . Then shall the righteous shine forth as the sun in the kingdom of their Father."

This sifting process is again clearly seen in Jesus' prophetic description of the Last Judgment wherein all nations would stand before Christ, who in glory would sit as judge to separate the righteous from the unrighteous (Mt. 25:31-46).

"Then shall the King say unto them on his right hand, Come, ye blessed of my Father, inherit the kingdom prepared for you from the foundation of the world. . . .
"Then shall he say also unto them on the left hand, Depart from me, ye cursed, into everlasting fire, prepared for the devil and his angels."

Christ's twofold mission of "gathering out" and "gathering in" is clearly portrayed throughout the Book of Revelation, with these results:
1. That which is unworthy of redemption is cast out and destroyed.
2. That which is worthy of redemption is purified and redeemed.
3. That which was "from the beginning"— the imperishable things of God, true yesterday, today, and forever—stands untouched "from everlasting to everlasting."

Paul spoke more often of the Day of Christ than of the Day of the Lord, but the underlying truth was the same: there was to be a day of judgment, but it was Christ who would judge, he being the one ordained to this work by God (Acts 17:31).

Coincident with the sifting of the righteous and unrighteous is the final destruction of the Evil One. The first Scriptural promise of the Redeemer foretold the doom of the forces of evil—the bruising of the serpent's head by the seed of the woman (Gen. 3:15). The Wicked One had been a malicious opposer of the will of God from the beginning of time. With the record of his first personalized appearance as the tempter (Gen. 3) began Satan's long warfare to establish a kingdom opposed to God's kingdom, to preempt His divine power, and to thwart His redemptive merciful plan for mankind. Alluded to as Lucifer in Isaiah (14:13,14), he arrogantly asserted, "I *will* ascend into heaven, I *will* exalt my throne above the stars of God: I *will* sit also upon the mount of the congregation. . . . I *will* ascend above the heights of the clouds; I *will* be like the most High."

Christ at his First Advent struck Satan a mortal blow as he uncovered the nature of the usurper, branding him "a liar," "a murderer from the beginning" (Jn. 8:44); as he redeemed men from the bondage of sin, sickness, want, and death, and set before them his example of sinlessness. The report of the Seventy on their return from a successful healing mission drew from Jesus the prescient remark, "I beheld Satan as lightning fall from heaven" (Lu. 10:18). Paul wrote of "that Wicked. . . . whom the Lord shall consume with the spirit of his mouth, and shall destroy with the brightness of his coming" (II Th. 2:8). In Revelation Christ's Second Advent brings the utter destruction of Satan and his deceiving works, and the series of divine judgments reach their climax in the final judgment of Chapter 20:11-15.

"The Time is at Hand"

To the prophet Habakkuk of the Old Testament the word of the Lord had come, saying, "The vision is yet for an appointed time, but at the end it shall speak, and not lie: though it tarry, wait for it; because it will surely come, it will not tarry" (Hab. 2:3).

Jesus himself had said of the time of his Second Coming: "Of that day and that hour knoweth no man, no, not the angels which are in heaven, neither the Son, but the Father" (Mk. 13:32).

Regarding the question of the immediacy of Christ's Coming Paul had written to the Thessalonians: "Let no man deceive you by any means: for that day [of Christ] shall not come, except there come a falling away first, and that man of sin be revealed, the son of perdition" (II Th. 2:3). The author of Hebrews stated, "For yet a little while, and he that shall come will come, and will not tarry" (Heb. 10:37).

Now Revelation declares: "The time is at hand" (Rev. 1:3), and "Behold, he cometh . . . and every eye shall see him" (Rev. 1:7).

The Majesty of Christ

The Gospels record that at Jesus' ascension "he was received up into heaven and sat on the right hand of God." Where the Gospels close, the revelation of the glorified Christ opens. This revelation vouchsafed John gives Christ his rightful place in the Godhead. "The Godhead of the Father and of the Son and of the Holy Ghost is all one, the glory equal, the majesty co-eternal."[3] In Christ's First Advent he came in humiliation, in his Second he comes in exaltation. The glory of the Ascended One is vividly described. "His eyes were as a flame of fire . . . his feet like unto fine brass . . his voice as the sound of many waters. . . . his countenance was as the sun shineth in his strength." He appears as the Living One having "the keys of hell and of death," and walks in the midst of the churches as their spiritual mentor. He speaks to them as the "Amen, the faithful and true witness, the beginning of the creation of God."

As the revelation progresses he is seen as "the Lamb," and "KING OF KINGS, AND LORD OF LORDS." Like God the Alpha and Omega, Christ declares himself "the beginning and the end, the first and the last."

The Patmos vision was in reality a series of visions. John was commanded to write of "the things which thou hast seen," his vision of Christ (Rev. 1:1-20); "the things which are," Christ's messages to seven representative churches (2:1-3:22); "the things which shall be hereafter," the series of judgments that fall on Satan and his kingdom ending in the victory of God and the Lamb (4:1-22:21). John wrote from the altitude of inspiration, above the region of the senses, as his words indicate: "I was in the Spirit on the Lord's day, and heard behind me a great voice, as of a trumpet, Saying, I am Alpha and Omega. . . . And I turned to see the voice that spake with me. . . ." Three times John was commanded to "come up hither" (Rev. 4:1; 17:1; 21:9) and each time he made the transition to a higher plane of thought. From the realm of the temporal he looked *up to* the realm of the eternal; *out from* the realm of the eternal he looked upon the realm of the temporal; lastly, he saw *one* realm, Immanuel ("*God with us*"), and "time no longer."

Revelation affords the reader a boundless range of meaning, whatever the approach—historical, symbolic, or spiritual; through the centuries a search for its true significance has been earnest and continuous. Literal interpretation of the symbols tends to confine their meaning; to narrow down the interpretation of its

symbols to a past age is to strip this prophecy of its spiritual message for today and obscure its moral and spiritual implications.

To illustrate: some scholars designate the white, red, black, and pale horses of the seals of Chapter 6 the evils of conquest, war, famine, and death, and then hold these seals to have been fulfilled by various events in the first century of the Christian era. But the message in John's depiction of the uncovering of evil could quite as well be related to the social and political evils surfacing in the world today. They could also as well relate to the moral errors in individual human thought which need to be expunged: such as the white horse of personal domination, selfishness, racial prejudice; the red horse of greed, anger, envy, hate, lust, fear, suffering; the black horse of poverty, frustration, inadequacy, spiritual hunger; the pale horse of mortality, loss, grief, hopelessness, spiritual deadness, and so forth.

Similarly, the four winged creatures before the throne of God (Rev. 4) like a lion, a calf, a man, an eagle, "full of eyes before and behind . . . and . . within" cannot be confined to a single definition of cherubim, each having a specific characteristic. They can be interpreted as representing many spiritual attributes of heavenly being, which attributes the reader should determine for himself.

The author has intentionally given no personal interpretation to the symbols in order that the reader may be left free to gain his own inspiration and unfoldment. However, as an aid to the student an outline of Revelation has been given on the following pages. Also, a cross reference study of John's figurative terms showing probable Old Testament sources of much of his symbolism appears on page 508-521. By seeing the Old Testament usage one can gain deeper insight into these Hebraic thought forms and perceive John's more spiritual use of their rich imagery.

The outline is designed to be read upward, further to emphasize the ascending scale of revelation and the tremendous conquest of good over evil, culminating in the final supremacy of God's kingdom. Certain of the things John saw are emphasized by boldface type; references to Christ and certain salient points to be particularly noted are indicated by italic type.

SALUTATION AND PROLOGUE
(Revelation, chapter 1)

"The Things Which Thou Hast Seen"

The persecuted Church is strengthened by John's vision of the living glorified Christ and by the reassurance of his Second Coming.

"I [Jesus Christ] am he that liveth, and was dead; and, behold, I am alive for evermore, Amen; and have the keys of hell and of death." Rev. 1:18

Read chart upward line by line

Vision of the Glorified Christ

Call of John

PROLOGUE ON EARTH

to the Churches

John's Salutation

(Rev. 1)
Introduction

"And the seven candlesticks which thou sawest are the seven churches."

"The seven stars are the angels of the seven churches:"

"The mystery of the seven stars . . . in my right hand, and the seven golden candlesticks."

"Write the things which thou hast seen, and the things which are, and the things which shall be hereafter;"

"And have the keys of hell and of death."

"I am the first and the last: I am he that liveth, and was dead, and, behold, I am alive for evermore, Amen; Fear not;"

"And when I saw him, I fell at his feet as dead. And he laid his right hand upon me, saying unto me, Fear not;"

"And his countenance was as the sun shineth in his strength."

"And he had in his right hand seven stars: and out of his mouth went a sharp two-edged sword [cf. Rev. 19:15]:"

"And his feet like unto fine brass . . . and his voice as the sound of many waters."

"His head and his hairs were white . . . as snow; and his eyes were as a flame of fire [cf. Dan. 7:9; Rev. 19:12];"

"Clothed with a garment down to the foot [emblem of priesthood], and girt about the paps with a golden girdle."

"And being turned, I saw seven golden candlesticks; And in the midst . . . one like unto the Son of man,"

"I turned to see the voice that spake with me." (visible sound and audible light)

"Unto Ephesus, and unto Smyrna . . . Pergamos . . . Thyatira . . . Sardis . . . Philadelphia . . . Laodicea."

"And, What thou seest, write in a book, and send it unto the seven churches which are in Asia;"

"Saying, I am Alpha and Omega, the first and the last [this clause in AV is omitted in the oldest manuscripts]:"

"I was in the Spirit on the Lord's day, and heard behind me a great voice, as of a trumpet,"

"Was in the isle that is called Patmos, for the word of God, and for the testimony of Jesus Christ."

"I John, who also am your brother, and companion in tribulation, and in the kingdom and patience of Jesus Christ,"

"Which is, and which was, and which is to come, the Almighty."

"I am Alpha and Omega, the beginning and the ending, saith the Lord [oldest manuscripts read "Lord God"],"

"And all kindreds of the earth shall wail because of him. Even so, Amen."

"Behold, he cometh with clouds [cf. Acts 1:9,11]; and every eye shall see him, and they also which pierced him:"

"To him be glory and dominion for ever and ever [Gr. unto the ages of the ages]. Amen."

"Unto him that loved us, and washed us from our sins in his own blood, And hath made us kings and priests unto God and his Father;"

"And from Jesus Christ . . . the faithful witness . . . first begotten of the dead . . . prince of the kings of the earth."

"From him which is, and which was, and which is to come; and from the seven Spirits which are before his throne;"

"John to the seven churches which are in Asia: Grace be unto you, and peace,"

"Blessed is he that readeth, and they that hear the words of this prophecy, and keep those things which are written therein: for the time is at hand."

"And of all things that he saw."

"And he sent and signified it by his angel [messenger] unto his servant John: Who bear record of the word of God, and of the testimony of Jesus Christ,"

"The Revelation of Jesus Christ, which God gave unto him, to shew unto his servants things which must shortly come to pass;"

THE LETTERS TO THE SEVEN CHURCHES
(Revelation, chapters 2, 3)
"The Things Which Are"

Christ's message to the Church Universal:
Each letter commences with a description of Christ's glory.
Each letter states, "I know thy works."
Each letter contains a promise to "him that overcometh."
Each letter utters the call, "He that hath an ear, let him hear what the Spirit saith unto the churches."

Six churches are rebuked.
One church receives commendation.
In first three letters the behest to hear precedes the overcoming (hearing that one may overcome).
In last four letters the behest to overcome precedes the hearing (overcoming that one may hear).

Read chart upward line by line

EPHESUS (Rev. 2)

Christ speaks:
"I know thy works"
Rebuke ("because")
The Warning
The Call
The Promise

- "These things saith he that holdeth the seven stars in his right hand, who walketh in the midst of the seven golden candlesticks...."
- "Thy works...labour...patience, and how thou canst not bear them which are evil....And hast borne...hast laboured...hast not fainted...."
- "Nevertheless I have somewhat against thee, because [for the cause that] thou hast left thy first love."
- "Remember...from whence thou art fallen, and repent, and do the first works; or else I will come...quickly, and...remove thy candlestick...."
- "He that hath an ear, let him hear what the Spirit saith unto the churches...."
- "To him that overcometh will I give to eat of the tree of life, which is in the midst of the paradise of God."

SMYRNA

Christ speaks:
"I know thy works"
Rebuke
Encouragement
The Call
The Promise

- "These things saith the first and the last, which was dead, and is alive...."
- "Thy works...tribulation...poverty, (but thou art rich)"
- "I know the blasphemy of them which say they are Jews...but are the synagogue of Satan."
- "Fear none of those things which thou shalt suffer...be thou faithful unto death, and I will give thee a crown of life."
- "He that hath an ear, let him hear what the Spirit saith unto the churches...."
- "He that overcometh shall not be hurt of the second death."

PERGAMOS

Christ speaks:
"I know thy works"
Rebuke
The Warning
The Call
The Promise

- "These things saith he which hath the sharp sword with two edges...."
- "And where thou dwellest, even where Satan's seat is: and thou holdest fast my name, and hast not denied my faith...."
- "I have a few things against thee, because thou hast...them that hold the doctrine of Balaam...of the Nicolaitanes...."
- "Repent; or else I will come unto thee quickly, and will fight against them with the sword of my mouth."
- "He that hath an ear, let him hear what the Spirit saith unto the churches...."
- "To him that overcometh will I give to eat of the hidden manna...will give him a white stone...a new name written...."

THYATIRA

Christ speaks:
"I know thy works"
Rebuke
The Warning
The Promise
The Call

- "These things saith the Son of God, who hath his eyes like unto a flame of fire, and his feet are like fine brass...."
- "And charity...service...faith...patience...works; and the last to be more than the first."
- "Notwithstanding I have a few things against thee, because that woman Jezebel...to seduce my servants...."
- "I will cast...them that commit adultery with her into great tribulation, except they repent...."
- "He that overcometh...to him will I give power over the nations....I will give him the morning star [see Rev. 22:16]."
- "He that hath an ear, let him hear what the Spirit saith unto the churches."

SARDIS (Rev. 3)

Christ speaks:
"I know thy works"
Rebuke
The Warning
The Promise
The Call

- "These things saith he that hath the seven Spirits of God, and the seven stars...."
- "That thou hast a name that thou livest, and art dead."
- "Be watchful...strengthen the things...ready to die: for I have not found thy works perfect before God."
- "Repent...Thou hast a few...which have not defiled their garments...they shall walk with me in white...."
- "He that overcometh...shall be clothed in white raiment...I will confess his name...."
- "He that hath an ear, let him hear what the Spirit saith unto the churches."

PHILADELPHIA

Christ speaks:
"I know thy works"
Commendation
Encouragement
The Promise
The Call

- "These things saith he that is holy, be that is true, be that hath the key of David,
- "He that openeth, and no man shutteth; and shutteth, and no man openeth..."
- "I have set before thee an open door...for thou...hast kept my word, and...not denied my name."
- "Because thou hast kept the word...I also will keep thee from the hour of temptation."
- "Behold, I come quickly: hold fast that which thou hast, that no man take thy crown."
- "Him that overcometh will I make a pillar in the temple...and he shall go no more out."
- "And I will write upon him the name of my God...name of the city of my God...my new name."
- "He that hath an ear, let him hear what the Spirit saith unto the churches."

LAODICEA

Christ speaks:
"I know thy works"
Rebuke
The Warning
The Promise
The Call

- "...saith the Amen, the...true witness, the beginning of the creation of God...."
- "That thou art neither cold nor hot: I would thou wert cold or hot."
- "Because thou art lukewarm...I will spue thee out of my mouth."
- "Buy of me gold...white raiment...anoint thine eyes...be zealous...and repent."
- "To him that overcometh will I grant to sit with me in my throne...."
- "He that hath an ear, let him hear what the Spirit saith unto the churches...."

VISION OF GOD ENTHRONED, BOOK OF SEVEN SEALS, THE LAMB

(Revelation, chapters 4:1-8:1)

"The Things Which Shall be Hereafter"

The scene changes to heaven. The Church is comforted with a vision of God's omnipotence and glory and with the assurance that through His Christ the enemies of God will be judged and the godly will triumph.

"Thou [the Lamb] art worthy to take the book, and to open the seals thereof: for thou wast slain, and hast redeemed us to God by thy blood. . . ." Rev. 5:9

Read chart upward line by line

(Rev. 8:1)

Interludes

NATIONS WORSHIP REDEEMED OF ALL

"The Lamb . . . shall feed them, and shall lead them unto living fountains of waters. . . ."

"And he that sitteth on the throne shall dwell among them."

"Therefore are they before the throne . . . and serve [God] day and night in his temple."

"These . . . came out of great tribulation . . . *washed their robes . . . white in the blood of the Lamb.*"

A multitude out of all nations, clothed in white, is seen worshiping *God and the Lamb.*

(SPIRITUAL ISRAEL) (Rev. 7)
SEALING OF 144,000

"There were sealed [144,000] of all the tribes of . . . Israel." (cf. Rev. 14:1)

He cried: "Hurt not the earth . . . till we have sealed the servants of our God in their foreheads."

"And I saw another angel ascending from the east, having the seal of the living God:

"I saw four angels standing on the four corners of the earth, holding the four winds. . . ."

SIXTH SEAL

Shaking of earth and heaven — "For the great day of his wrath is come; and who shall be able to stand?"

FIFTH SEAL

They were told to rest for "a little season," till the full number of martyrs was completed.

The souls of the martyrs cry for vindication — White robes were given them.

FOURTH SEAL

A pale horse whose rider was named Death — "And Hell followed . . . power was given unto them . . . to kill. . . ."

THIRD SEAL

A black horse whose rider had a pair of balances in his hand — Famine followed him.

SECOND SEAL

A red horse whose rider had a great sword — "Power was given to him . . . to take peace from the earth. . . ."

FIRST SEAL (Rev. 6)

A white horse whose rider had a bow — "And he went forth conquering, and to conquer." (cf. Rev. 19:11)

(The judgments begin in the unveiling of the signs of tribulation which precede the Coming of Christ.)

THE LAMB

John heard angels sing praises to *God and the Lamb*. "The number . . . was ten thousand times ten thousand, and thousands of thousands. . . ."

"And hast made us unto our God kings and priests: and we shall reign on the earth."

"They sung a new song . . . Thou art worthy to take the book, and to open the seals . . . for thou . . . hast redeemed us to God by thy blood. . . ."

"He . . . took the book . . . And when he had taken the book, the four beasts and . . . elders fell down before the Lamb. . . ."

"**Lo, in the midst of the throne . . . stood a Lamb as it had been slain, having seven horns and seven eyes . . . the seven Spirits of God . . .**"

SEVEN SEALS BOOK OF (Rev. 5)

An elder said, "Weep not . . . the Lion of . . Juda, the Root of David, hath prevailed to open the book, and to loose the seven seals. . . ."

"No man in heaven, nor in earth . . . was able to open the book, neither to look thereon. And I wept much, because no man was found worthy. . . ."

"And I saw a strong angel proclaiming with a loud voice, Who is worthy to open the book, and to loose the seals thereof?"

"**And I saw in the right hand of him that sat on the throne a book written within and on the backside, sealed with seven seals.**"

Saying, Thou art worthy . . . to receive glory . . . honour . . . power: for thou hast created all things . . . for thy pleasure they are and were created."

"The four and twenty elders fall down . . . and worship him that liveth for ever . . . and cast their crowns before the throne,

"Saying, Holy, Holy, holy, Lord God Almighty, which was, and is, and is to come." (Three threefolds)

"And the four beasts had each of them six wings about him; and they were full of eyes within: and they rest not day and night,

"The first beast was like a lion . . . the second beast like a calf . . . the third beast had a face as a man . . . the fourth beast was like a flying eagle."

"Before the throne . . . a sea of glass like unto crystal . . . in the midst . . . and round about . . . were four beasts full of eyes before and behind."

"Out of the throne proceeded lightnings and thunderings and voices: and there were seven lamps of fire burning before the throne . . . the seven Spirits of God."

"Round about the throne . . . I saw four and twenty elders sitting, clothed in white raiment; and they had on their heads crowns of gold."

"**Behold, a throne was set in heaven, and one sat on the throne . . . and there was a rainbow round about the throne, in sight like unto an emerald.**"

"And immediately I was in the spirit. . . ."

GOD ENTHRONED (Rev. 4)

"Behold, a door was opened in heaven: and the first voice . . . said, Come up hither, and I will shew thee things which must be hereafter."

497

VISION OF SEVEN ANGELS WITH SEVEN TRUMPETS
(Revelation, chapters 8:2-11:19)

God's judgments continue against all that is ungodly in the earth, and though the judgments are severe they are tempered with mercy. The persecuted Church is comforted again, this time with the promise of the consummation of God's eternal purpose of salvation.

(Note the resistance of the ungodly to repentance.)

Read chart upward line by line

SEVENTH TRUMPET

"The temple of God was opened in heaven . . . there was seen . . . the ark of his testament. . . ."

"Because thou hast taken to thee thy great power, and hast reigned."

The elders worshiped: "We give thee thanks, O Lord God Almighty. . . ."

"And of his Christ; and he shall reign for ever and ever."

Voices in heaven: *"The kingdoms of this world are become the kingdoms of our Lord,*

"And the remnant were affrighted, and gave glory to the God of heaven."

"The same hour . . . a great earthquake . . . tenth part of the city fell . . . slain of men seven thousand. . . ."

"And they ascended up to heaven in a cloud; and their enemies beheld them."

"After three days and an half the spirit of life from God entered into them, and they stood. . . ."

"They that dwell upon the earth shall rejoice over them . . . because these two prophets tormented them. . . ."

When their testimony is finished, the beast out of the bottomless pit "shall . . . kill them."

"These are the two olive trees, and the two candlesticks standing before the God of the earth."

THE TWO WITNESSES

"I will give power unto my two witnesses, and they shall prophesy [1260] days, clothed in sackcloth.

(Rev. 11)

"And the holy city shall they tread under foot forty and two months." (cf. Lu. 21:24)

"But the court which is without the temple leave out . . . for it is given unto the Gentiles:

"Rise, and measure the temple of God, and the altar, and them that worship therein.

The angel said, "Thou must prophesy again before many peoples, and nations, and tongues, and kings."

"And it was in my mouth sweet as honey: and as soon as I had eaten it, my belly was bitter. . . ."

John was commanded, "Go and take the little book. . . . And I took the little book. . . . and ate it up;

Interludes

"But in the days . . . of the seventh angel, when he shall begin to sound, the mystery of God should be finished. . . ."

"The angel . . . lifted up his hand to heaven, And sware . . . that there should be time [ASV delay] no longer:

"He had in his hand a little book open . . . he set his right foot upon the sea . . . his left foot on the earth. . . ."

"I saw another mighty angel come down from heaven, clothed with a cloud: and a rainbow was upon his head. . . ."

(Rev. 10)

THE LITTLE BOOK

"And the rest of the men which were not killed by these plagues yet repented not of the works of their hands. . . ."

(Second Woe) Four angels of Euphrates and their armies loosed. Fire and brimstone from horses' mouths kill a third part of men. . . .

"The locusts were like . . . horses prepared unto battle . . . their faces were as the faces of men . . . their teeth . . . as . . . of lions."

They were given power as scorpions to torment for five months those "which have not the seal of God in their foreheads."

"And he opened the bottomless pit; and there arose a smoke. . . . And . . . out of the smoke locusts upon the earth. . . ."

(First Woe) "I saw a star fall from heaven unto the earth: and to him was given the key of the bottomless pit [Hades, Gr. abyss] ."

An angel said, "Woe, woe, woe, to the inhabiters of the earth by reason of the other voices of the trumpet . . . yet to sound!"

"The third part of the sun was smitten . . . the moon . . . the stars . . . the day shone not for a third part of it, and the night likewise."

"There fell a great star . . . upon the third part of the rivers . . . fountains . . . and the third part . . became wormwood. . . ."

"A great mountain burning with fire was cast into the sea. . . ." A third part became blood, a third of its life and ships destroyed.

"Hail and fire mingled with blood . . . were cast upon the earth: and the third part of trees . . . and . . . grass was burnt up."

SIXTH TRUMPET

(Rev. 9)

FIFTH TRUMPET

FOURTH TRUMPET

THIRD TRUMPET

SECOND TRUMPET

FIRST TRUMPET

(Rev. 8)

"The angel . . . filled it with fire of the altar, and cast it into the earth: and there were voices . . . thunderings . . . lightnings, and an earthquake."

"Another angel . . stood at the altar, having a golden censer. . . . And the smoke of the incense, which came with the prayers of the saints, ascended up before God. . . ."

"I saw the seven angels which stood before God; and to them were given seven trumpets."

WITH TRUMPETS

SEVEN ANGELS

VISION OF THE CHURCH UNDER SATAN'S PERSECUTION
(Revelation, chapters 12, 13)

The Church is comforted with a vision of the heavenly Messiah whom Satan, the great enemy of Christ and his Church, cannot destroy. Satan is conquered "in principle" when he is cast out of heaven, but the earth is to feel his wrath. His vile nature is personified in the blasphemous beasts which rise to persecute the saints. To endure, the Church is to exercise patience, faith, and spiritual wisdom.

Read chart upward line by line

WOMAN IN TRAVAIL (Rev. 12)

"There appeared a great wonder in heaven; a woman clothed with the sun, and the moon under her feet, and upon her head a crown of twelve stars."

"She being with child cried, travailing in birth, and pained to be delivered."

GREAT RED DRAGON

"There appeared another wonder in heaven . . . a great red dragon, having seven heads and ten horns, and seven crowns upon his heads."

"The dragon stood before the woman which was ready to be delivered, for *to devour her child as soon as it was born.*"

THE MAN CHILD

"*She brought forth a man child, who was to rule all nations with a rod of iron . . . her child was caught up unto God. . . .*"

"And the woman fled into the wilderness, where she hath a place prepared of God. . . ."

WAR IN HEAVEN

"There was war in heaven: Michael and his angels fought against the dragon; and the dragon fought and his angels,"

"And prevailed not: neither was their place found any more in heaven."

"And the great dragon was cast out, that old serpent . . . Devil . . . Satan, which deceiveth the whole world. . . ." (cf. II Jn. 1:7)

Song of Rejoicing and Woe

John heard a voice in heaven: "*Now is come salvation, and strength, and the kingdom of our God, and the power of his Christ:*

"*For the accuser of our brethren is cast down, which accused them before our God day and night.*" (cf. I Pet. 5:8)

"They overcame him by the blood of the Lamb . . . by the word of their testimony . . . they loved not their lives unto the death.

"Therefore rejoice, ye heavens, and ye that dwell in them."

(Third Woe) "Woe to the inhabiters of the earth and of the sea!

"For the devil is come down unto you, having great wrath, because he knoweth that he hath but a short time."

WOMAN AND REMNANT PERSECUTION OF

"When the dragon saw that he was cast unto the earth, he persecuted the woman which brought forth the man child."

"I . . . saw a beast rise up out of the sea, having seven heads . . . ten horns . . . upon his heads the name of blasphemy."

"To the woman were given . . . wings of a great eagle, that she might fly into the wilderness. . . ."

"The serpent cast out of his mouth water as a flood after the woman, that he might cause her to be carried away. . . ."

"And the earth helped the woman, and the earth opened her mouth, and swallowed up the flood. . . ."

"And the dragon was wroth with the woman, and went to make war with the remnant of her seed,

"Which keep the commandments of God, and have the testimony of Jesus Christ." (cf. Rom. 11:5)

BEAST OUT OF SEA (Rev. 13)

"And the dragon gave him his power, and his seat, and great authority."

"I . . . saw a beast rise up out of the sea, having seven heads . . . ten horns . . . upon his heads the name of blasphemy."

"He opened his mouth . . . to blaspheme [God's] name . . . tabernacle . . . them that dwell in heaven."

"It was given unto him to make war with the saints, and to overcome them: and power . . . over all . . . nations."

"All . . . upon the earth shall worship him, whose names are not written in the book of life. . . ."

Warning

"If any man have an ear, let him hear."

"*Here is the patience and the faith of the saints.*"
A call to endure. Sure retribution to persecutors of the saints.

BEAST OUT OF EARTH

"I [saw] another beast . . . out of the earth . . . he had two horns like a lamb . . . spake as a dragon."

"He . . . causeth the earth . . . to worship the first beast . . . deceiveth . . . by means of . . . miracles. . . ."

"Saying . . . they should make an image to the beast . . . he had power to give life unto the image. . . ."

"That [it] should . . . cause that as many as would not worship . . . should be killed."

"Causeth all . . . to receive a mark in their right hand, or in their foreheads." (contra. Rev. 7:2-4)

"That no man might buy or sell, save he that had the mark . . . the name . . . or the number. . . ."

A Call

"Here is wisdom. Let him that hath understanding count the number of the beast. . . ."

VISION OF SEVEN ANGELS WITH SEVEN LAST PLAGUES

(Revelation, chapters 14-16)

The Church, which has suffered severe persecution under the fierceness of her enemies but which has held out even to martyrdom against the mark of the beast, is further strengthened by a vision of the blessedness of those who follow the Lamb, a prophecy of the fall of Babylon, and a vision of God's salvation and judgment in the harvesting of the earth at Christ's Second Coming.

The divine judgments now continue in the pouring out of God's wrath upon all that is ungodly.

Read chart upward line by line

(Rev. 15, 16)

SEVEN LAST PLAGUES

SEVENTH VIAL

"There fell upon men a great hail out of heaven . . . and men blasphemed God . . ."

"Thunders . . . lightnings . . . earthquake . . . great Babylon came in remembrance before God. . . ."

Into the air — "There came a great voice . . . from the throne, saying, *It is done.*"

Warning

and keepeth his garments, lest he walk naked, and they see his shame."

The voice of Christ is heard: "*Behold, I come as a thief. Blessed is he that watcheth,*

SIXTH VIAL

"They . . . go forth unto . . . kings of the earth . . . to gather them to the battle [of Armageddon] ."

"I saw three unclean spirits . . . come out of the mouth of the dragon . . . beast . . . false prophet."

Upon Euphrates — "The water . . . dried up, that the way of the kings of the east . . . be prepared."

FIFTH VIAL

"They gnawed their tongues for pain, *And blasphemed the God of heaven . . . and repented not. . . .*"

Upon the seat of the beast — "And his kingdom was full of darkness. . . ."

FOURTH VIAL

Upon the sun — "Men were scorched . . . *and blasphemed . . . and they repented not to give [God] glory.*"

THIRD VIAL

Upon the rivers and fountains of waters — "And they became blood." "The judgment is declared just."

SECOND VIAL

Upon the sea — "And it became as the blood of a dead man: and every living soul died in the sea."

FIRST VIAL

Upon the earth — "There fell a . . . grievous sore upon the men which had the mark of the beast. . . ."

"And I heard a great voice out of the temple saying . . . Go your ways, and pour out the vials of the wrath of God upon the earth."

Preparation in heaven

"And the temple was filled with smoke from the glory of God . . . no man was able to enter . . . till the seven plagues . . . were fulfilled."

"The seven angels came out of the temple. . . . [were given] seven golden vials full of the wrath of God."

They hold the harps of God. "And they sing the song of Moses [Ex. 15:1-19] . . . and the song of the Lamb. . . ."

"I saw as it were a sea of glass mingled with fire: and them that had gotten the victory over the beast . . . stand on the sea of glass. . . ."

"I saw another sign in heaven . . . seven angels having the seven last plagues; for in them is filled up the wrath of God."

Interludes

IS GATHERED EARTH'S VINTAGE

"The angel thrust . . . gathered . . . and cast it into the great winepress of the wrath of God."

He cried, "Thrust in thy sharp sickle, and gather the clusters of the vine of the earth; for her grapes are fully ripe."

"Another angel came out of the temple . . . having a sharp sickle . . . another . . . from the altar, which had power over fire. . . ."

IS REAPED EARTH'S HARVEST

"And he that sat on the cloud thrust in his sickle on the earth; and the earth was reaped." (cf. Mk. 14:62)

"Another angel came out of the temple, crying . . . Thrust in thy sickle, and reap . . . for the harvest of the earth is ripe."

"Behold a white cloud . . . [on it] one sat like unto the Son of man . . . on his head a . . . crown . . . in his hand a sharp sickle."

Promise

"Write, Blessed are the dead which die in the Lord . . . saith the Spirit, that they may rest from their labours. . . ."

"Here is the patience of the saints: here are they that keep the commandments of God, and the faith of Jesus."

"He shall be tormented with fire and brimstone . . . and they have no rest day nor night, who worship the beast and his image. . . ."

A third angel: "If any man worship the beast . . . and receive his mark. . . . The same shall drink of the wine of the wrath of God . . ."

COMING JUDGMENTS

Another angel said: "Babylon is fallen . . . because she made all nations drink of the wine of the wrath of her fornication."

"Saying . . . give glory to [God] ; for the hour of his judgment is come: and worship him that made heaven . . . earth . . . sea. . . ."

"I saw another angel fly in the midst of heaven, having the everlasting gospel to preach unto them . . . on the earth. . . ."

EVERLASTING GOSPEL

(Rev. 14)

"These were redeemed . . . the firstfruits unto *God and to the Lamb.* And in their mouth was found no guile . . . are without fault. . . ."

"They sung . . . a new song before the throne. . . . These . . . were not defiled with women. . . . These are they which follow the Lamb. . . ."

CHURCH TRIUMPHANT FIRSTFRUITS OF

"Lo, a Lamb stood on the Mount Sion . . . with him an hundred forty and four thousand, having his Father's name written in their foreheads." (cf. Rev. 7:4-8)

500

VISION OF SEVEN DOOMS
(Revelation, chapters 17:1-20:15)

The first doom, the judgment of Babylon which has previously been announced (14:8), is now given in detail. John's epithets, "the great whore," and "THE MOTHER OF HARLOTS," who was arrayed in purple and scarlet, vividly describe her debauched character. "In one hour" this great city, typifying the seat of empire and all wickedness, worldliness, and heathenism is brought to utter desolation.

Read chart upward line by line

SEVEN DOOMS (Rev. 17)

"So he carried me away in the spirit into the wilderness. . . ."

"With whom the kings of the earth have committed fornication, and the inhabitants of the earth have been made drunk with the wine of her fornication."

"One of the seven angels . . . talked with me . . . Come hither; I will shew unto thee the judgment of the great whore that sitteth upon many waters:

THE GREAT WHORE
DESCRIPTION OF

"I saw a woman sit upon a scarlet coloured beast, full of names of blasphemy, having seven heads and ten horns."

"The woman was arrayed in . . . scarlet . . . decked with gold and precious stones . . . a golden cup in her hand full of abominations. . . ."

"Upon her forehead was a name written, MYSTERY, BABYLON THE GREAT, THE MOTHER OF HARLOTS AND ABOMINATIONS OF THE EARTH."

"And I saw the woman drunken with the blood of the saints, and . . . the blood of the martyrs of Jesus. . . ."

"The angel said . . . I will tell thee the mystery of the woman, and of the beast that carrieth her. . . ."

A Call

"Here is the mind which hath wisdom."

"They . . . shall wonder, whose names were not . . . in the book of life . . . when they behold the beast that was, and is not, and yet is."

"The beast that thou sawest was, and is not; and shall ascend out of the bottomless pit, and go into perdition. . . ."

"The seven heads are seven mountains. . . . there are seven kings. . . . the beast . . . is the eighth . . . and goeth into perdition."

"The ten horns . . . are ten kings, which have received no kingdom as yet; but receive power . . . one hour with the beast."

"These have one mind, and shall give their power and strength unto the beast. *These shall make war with the Lamb. . . .*"

"*The Lamb shall overcome them . . . be is Lord of lords, and King of kings* . . . they . . . *with him are called* . . . chosen . . . faithful."

"The waters which thou sawest, where the whore sitteth, are peoples, and multitudes, and nations, and tongues."

"The ten horns . . . shall hate the whore . . . make her desolate . . . eat her flesh, and burn her with fire."

"For God hath put in their hearts to fulfill his will . . . until the words of God shall be fulfilled."

"And the woman which thou sawest is that great city, which reigneth over the kings of the earth."

DOOM OF BABYLON (Rev. 18)

"**I saw another angel come down from heaven, having great power; and the earth was lightened with his glory.**"

"He cried mightily . . . Babylon the great is fallen . . . and is become the habitation of devils. . . ."

"For all nations have drunk of the wine of the wrath of her fornication,

"And the kings of the earth have committed fornication with her,

"And the merchants of the earth are waxed rich through the abundance of her delicacies."

Warning call

"I heard another voice from heaven, saying, Come out of her, my people,

"That ye be not partakers of her sins, and that ye receive not of her plagues."

"For her sins have reached unto heaven, and God hath remembered her iniquities."

"Reward her even as she rewarded you, and double unto her double according to her works. . . ."

"For she saith in her heart, I sit a queen, and am no widow, and shall see no sorrow."

"Her plagues [therefore shall] come in one day, death, and mourning, and famine. . . ."

"She shall be utterly burned with fire: for strong is the Lord God who judgeth her."

Earth mourns

"The kings of the earth, who . . . lived deliciously with her, shall . . . lament for her. . . ."

"The merchants . . . shall . . . mourn over her; for no man buyeth their merchandise any more. . . ."

"As many as trade by sea . . . cried . . . Alas . . . for in one hour is she made desolate."

VISION OF SEVEN DOOMS—Continued

As heaven rejoices over the doom of the harlot, the marriage of the Lamb is announced. His bride, "the holy city, new Jerusalem" (21:2), "arrayed in fine linen clean and white," is the antithesis of the great whore. Before the fulfillment of the marriage, Christ as "KING OF KINGS" leads his armies to victory over the beast, the false prophet, and the kings of the earth in the battle of Armageddon.

Satan is bound for a thousand years, and during this millennial period the saints reign with Christ.

Read chart upward line by line

DOOM OF BABYLON —*Continued*

"Rejoice over her, thou heaven, and ye holy apostles and prophets; for God hath avenged you on her."
"And a mighty angel took up a stone like a great millstone, and cast it into the sea, saying,
"Thus with violence shall that great city Babylon be thrown down, and shall be found no more at all."

FOUR ALLELUIAS (Rev. 19)

"I heard a great voice of much people in heaven, saying, Alleluia; Salvation . . . glory . . . honour . . . power, unto . . . our God:
"For true and righteous are his judgments: for he hath judged the great whore . . . and hath avenged the blood of his servants at her hand."
"And again they said, Alleluia. And her smoke rose up for ever and ever."
"And the four and twenty elders and the four beasts fell down and worshipped God . . . saying, Amen; Alleluia."
"And I heard as it were the voice of a great multitude . . . saying, Alleluia: for the Lord God omnipotent reigneth."

Heaven rejoices

Interludes

LAMB ANNOUNCED MARRIAGE OF THE

"Worship God: for the testimony of Jesus is the spirit of prophecy." (cf. Rev. 22:9)
"And he said unto me, See thou do it not: I am thy fellowservant, and of thy brethren that have the testimony of Jesus:
"And he saith unto me, These are the true sayings of God. And I fell at his feet to worship him."
"He saith unto me, Write, Blessed are they which are called unto the marriage supper of the Lamb."
"To her was granted that she should be arrayed in fine linen, clean and white: for the fine linen is the righteousness of saints."
"Let us . . . rejoice . . . give honour to him: for the marriage of the Lamb is come, and his wife hath made herself ready."

CHRIST'S COMING IN GLORY

"And be bath on his vesture and on his thigh a name written, KING OF KINGS, AND LORD OF LORDS." (cf. Rev. 19:16)
And he treadeth the winepress of the fierceness and wrath of Almighty God."
"Out of his mouth goeth a sharp sword, that with it he should smite the nations . . . be shall rule them with a rod of iron [cf. Rev. 12:5] :
And the armies which were in heaven followed him upon white horses, clothed in fine linen, white and clean."
"And he was clothed with a vesture dipped in blood: and his name is called The Word of God."
"His eyes were as a flame of fire, and on his head were many crowns; and he had a name written, that no man knew, but he himself."
"I saw heaven opened . . . behold a white horse . . . be that sat upon him was called Faithful and True . . . in righteousness he doth judge and make war."

BATTLE OF ARMAGEDDON

"I saw the beast . . . kings . . . their armies, gathered . . . to make war against him . . . on the horse, and . . . his army." (cf. Rev. 16:16)
"That ye may eat the flesh of kings . . . and the flesh of all men, both free and bond, both small and great."
"I saw an angel standing in the sun . . . he cried . . . to all the fowls . . . of heaven, Come . . . unto the supper of the great God;

DOOM OF FALSE PROPHET
DOOM OF BEAST

"The beast was taken, and with him the false prophet that wrought miracles before him,
"With which he deceived them that had received the mark of the beast, and them that worshipped his image."
"These both were cast alive into a lake of fire burning with brimstone."

DOOM OF KINGS

"And all the fowls were filled with their flesh."
"The remnant were slain with the sword of him that sat upon the horse. . . ." (cf. Rev. 17:14)

Millennium

"I saw an angel come down from heaven, having the key of the bottomless pit and a great chain. . . ." (Rev. 20)
"He laid hold on the dragon, that old serpent . . . Devil, and Satan, and bound him a thousand years,
"And cast him into the bottomless pit, and shut him up, and set a seal upon him,
"That he should deceive the nations no more, till the thousand years should be fulfilled:
"And after that he must be loosed a little season."

VISION OF SEVEN DOOMS—*Concluded*

At the close of the millennial period Satan gathers his forces to renew his attack on the Church, "the camp of the saints . . . and the beloved city," but the power of God utterly destroys them. The Last Judgment follows, in which every man is judged according to his works, and death and hell are annihilated, never again to present a vestige of reality.

Read chart upward line by line

(John now sees the seven *new* things of God.)

(GOD'S JUDGMENTS ARE OVER – SATAN'S POWER AND KINGDOM ARE AT AN END.)

UNBELIEVING DEAD
DOOM OF DEATH, HELL,

"And whosoever was not found written in the book of life was cast into the lake of fire." (cf. Rev. 21:8)

"And death and hell [Hades] were cast into the lake of fire. **This is the second death.**"

LAST JUDGMENT

"And they were judged every man according to their works."

"And the sea gave up the dead which were in it; and death and hell delivered up the dead which were in them:"

"And the dead were judged out of those things which were written in the books, according to their works."

"And another book was opened, which is the book of life [cf. Rev. 3:5; 13:8; 17:8; 20:15; 22:19] :"

"**And I saw the dead, small and great, stand before God: and the books were opened:**"

"**And there was found no place for them.**"

"And I saw a great white throne, and him that sat on it, from whose face the earth and the heaven fled away;"

DOOM OF SATAN

"And shall be tormented day and night for ever and ever."

"**The devil that deceived them was cast into the lake of fire and brimstone, where the beast and the false prophet are,**"

"And fire came down from God out of heaven, and devoured them."

"And they went up on the breadth of the earth, and compassed the camp of the saints about, and the beloved city:"

"The number of whom is as the sand of the sea."

"And shall go out to deceive the nations . . . in the four quarters of the earth, Gog and Magog, to gather them . . . to battle:"

DOOM OF GOG AND MAGOG

"And when the thousand years are expired, Satan shall be loosed out of his prison,"

"But they shall be priests of *God and of Christ*, and shall reign with him a thousand years."

A Call

"Blessed and holy is he that hath part in the first resurrection: on such the second death hath no power [cf. Rev. 20:14],"

"But the rest of the dead lived not again until the thousand years were finished. **This is the first resurrection.**"

Millennium

"And they [the saints and martyrs] lived and reigned with Christ a thousand years."

"Neither his image, neither had received his mark upon their foreheads, or in their hands;"

"And I saw the souls of them that were beheaded for the witness of Jesus, and for the word of God [cf. Rev. 6:9], and which had not worshipped the beast,"

(Rev. 20) "I saw thrones, and they sat upon them, and judgment was given unto them:"

VISION OF SEVEN NEW THINGS
(Revelation, chapters 21:1-22:5)

The former imperfect things have passed away. A new heaven and a new earth appear to John's view. New Jerusalem, "the Lamb's wife," is depicted as having the glory and power of God and the Lamb. From the mount of spiritual vision John beholds the consummated kingdom of God and the bliss of the redeemed in their union with God and His Christ.

Henceforth GOD AND THE LAMB reign together, Christ occupying his rightful place in the Godhead.

Read chart upward line by line

NEW LIGHT

"*But they which are written in the Lamb's book of life.*"
"*Neither whatsoever worketh abomination, or maketh a lie:*"
"*There shall in no wise enter into it any thing that defileth,*"

"The gates of it shall not be shut at all by day: for there shall be no night there."
"And the kings of the earth do bring their glory and honour into it."
"And the nations of them which are saved shall walk in the light of it:"
"For the glory of *God* did lighten it, *and the Lamb* is the light thereof."
"The city had no need of the sun, neither of the moon, to shine in it:"

NEW TEMPLE

"**I saw no temple therein: for the Lord God Almighty and the Lamb are the temple of it.**"

"And the twelve gates were twelve pearls . . . the street . . . was pure gold, as it were transparent glass."
"The foundations of the wall . . . were garnished with all manner of precious stones. . . ."
"The building of the wall of it was of jasper: and the city was pure gold, like unto clear glass."

"He measured the wall thereof, an hundred and forty and four cubits. . . ."
"The length and the breadth and the height of it are equal."
"And the city lieth foursquare . . . and he measured the city . . . twelve thousand furlongs [1500 miles]."
"And he that talked with me had a golden reed to measure the city, and the gates . . . and the wall thereof."

"The wall . . . had twelve foundations, and in them the names of the twelve apostles of the Lamb."
"On the east three gates; on the north three gates; on the south three gates; and on the west three gates."
"And names written thereon, which are the names of the twelve tribes of the children of Israel:"
"And had a wall great and high, and had twelve gates, and at the gates twelve angels,"

"Her light was like unto a stone most precious, even like a jasper stone, clear as crystal;"
"Descending out of heaven from God, Having the glory of God:"

New Jerusalem Description of

"And he carried me away in the spirit to a . . . high mountain, and shewed me that great city, the holy Jerusalem,"
"One of the seven angels having the vials said: "Come hither, I will shew thee *the bride, the Lamb's wife.*""

"And all liars, shall have their part in the lake which burneth with fire and brimstone: which is the second death."
"But the fearful, and unbelieving, and the abominable, and murderers, and whoremongers, and sorcerers, and idolaters,"

"*He that overcometh shall inherit all things; and I will be his God, and be shall be my son.*" (Immanuel, Is. 7:14; Mt. 1:23)
"I will give unto him that is athirst of the fountain of the water of life freely."
"He said unto me, *It is done. I am Alpha and Omega, the beginning and the end.*"
"He that sat upon the throne said, *Behold, I make all things new* . . . Write: for these words are true and faithful."

NEW PEOPLES

"And there shall be no more death, neither sorrow, nor crying, neither . . . any more pain: for the former things are passed away."
"And God himself shall be with them, and be their God. And God shall wipe away all tears from their eyes;"
"I heard a great voice . . . Behold, the tabernacle of God is with men, and he will dwell with them, and they shall be his people,"

NEW JERUSALEM

"**I John saw the holy city, New Jerusalem, coming down from God out of heaven,** prepared as a bride adorned for her husband." (cf. Rev. 3:12)

"I saw a new heaven and a new earth: for the first heaven and the first earth were passed away; and there was no more sea." (cf. Is. 65:17; 66:22)

(Rev. 21)
SEVEN NEW THINGS

NEW HEAVEN NEW EARTH

Christ thrice affirms his promise to the Church, "Behold, I come quickly" (Rev. 22:7,12,20).

Read chart upward line by line

John's benediction: "The grace of our Lord Jesus Christ be with you all. Amen."

John's prayer: "Amen. Even so, come Lord Jesus."

"Surely I come quickly." (Christ's third avowal of this promise.)

Warning

No man shall "add unto" or "take away from the words of the book of this prophecy."

A Gracious Invitation

"And let him that is athirst come. And whosoever will, let him take the water of life freely."

"The Spirit and the bride say, Come. And let him that heareth say, Come."

"I am the root and the offspring of David, and the bright and morning star."

"I Jesus have sent mine angel to testify unto you these things in the churches." (cf. Rev. 1:1)

"For without are dogs . . . sorcerers . . . whoremongers . . . murderers . . . idolaters, and whosoever loveth and maketh a lie."

"Blessed are they that do his commandments, that they may have right to the tree of life, and may enter . . . into the city."

"I am Alpha and Omega, the beginning and the end, the first and the last."

"Behold, I come quickly; and my reward is with me, to give every man according as his work shall be."

"And he that is righteous, let him be righteous still: and he that is holy, let him be holy still."

"He that is unjust, let him be unjust still: and he which is filthy, let him be filthy still:"

"He saith unto me, Seal not the sayings of the prophecy of this book: for the time is at hand."

He saith: "See thou do it not: for I am thy fellowservant, and of thy brethren the prophets . . . worship God."

"I John saw these things, and heard them. . . . I fell down to worship before . . . the angel which shewed me these things."

"Behold, I come quickly: blessed is he that keepeth the sayings of the prophecy of this book."

"And the Lord God of the holy prophets sent his angel to shew unto his servants the things which must shortly be done."

"And he [the angel] said unto me, These sayings are faithful and true:"

"And they shall reign for ever and ever."

"And there shall be no night there; and they need no candle, neither light of the sun; for the Lord God giveth them light:"

"And his servants shall serve him: And they shall see his face; and his name shall be in their foreheads."

"And there shall be no more curse: but *the throne of God and of the Lamb* shall be in it;"

"And yielded her fruit every month: and the leaves of the tree were for the healing of the nations."

"In the midst of the street . . . on either side of the river, was there the tree of life, which bare twelve manner of fruits,"

"He shewed me a pure river of water of life, clear as crystal, proceeding out of the throne of God and of the Lamb."

OF JESUS CHRIST
THE FINAL WITNESS

EPILOGUE

(Rev. 22)

PARADISE OF GOD

PANORAMA OF THE APOCALYPSE

JOHN SAW THE PERFECT ORDER OF THINGS IN HEAVEN
Rev. 4:1-5:8

"I saw in the right hand of him that sat on the throne a book written . . . sealed with seven seals. And I saw a strong angel proclaiming . . . Who is worthy to open the book, and to loose the seals thereof?"

One of the elders before the throne said, "Behold, the Lion of the tribe of Juda, the Root of David, hath prevailed to open the book. . . ."

"IN THE MIDST OF THE THRONE . . . STOOD A LAMB AS IT HAD BEEN SLAIN. . . ."

VISION OF BOOK OF SEVEN SEALS
Rev. 5:9-8:1

"Thou [The Lamb] art worthy to take the book, and to open the seals thereof: for thou wast slain, and hast redeemed us to God by thy blood out of every kindred, and tongue, and people, and nation. . . ."

God's judgments begin when THE LAMB looses the seven seals (thereby unveiling the forces of evil at work on the earth).

VISION OF SEVEN TRUMPETS
Rev. 8:2-11:19

"I saw . . . seven angels which stood before God; and to them were given seven trumpets."

"Another angel came and stood at the altar, having a golden censer . . . the angel took the censer, and filled it with fire of the altar, and cast it into the earth. . . . And the seven angels . . . prepared themselves to sound."

"Come up hither, and I will shew thee things which must be hereafter."

The circle of the earth

JOHN SAW JESUS CHRIST COME IN GLORY AND IN JUDGMENT
Rev. 1-3

"I was in the Spirit on the Lord's day, and heard. . . . And . . . I saw. . . ."

"I . . . heard . . . a great voice . . . Saying, I am ALPHA and OMEGA, the first and the last. . . ."

"I am he that liveth, and was dead; and, behold, I am alive for evermore, Amen; and have the keys of hell and of death."

John saw the order of things on the earth—works perfect and imperfect, godly and ungodly, righteous and unrighteous.

LETTERS TO THE SEVEN CHURCHES bear Christ's warnings and promises

1. White horse and its rider
2. Red horse and its rider
3. Black horse and its rider
4. Pale horse and its rider
5. Souls of the slain (the martyred)
6. Earthquake (Men hid from wrath of GOD AND THE LAMB.) "The great day of his wrath is come; and who shall be able to stand?"

Interludes:
REDEEMED OF ISRAEL sealed with seal of the living God in their foreheads

REDEEMED OF NATIONS worship GOD AND THE LAMB

7. Silence in heaven

1. 1/3 earth smitten
2. 1/3 sea smitten
3. 1/3 rivers and springs smitten
4. 1/3 part of heavenly bodies smitten
5. Opening of bottomless pit—locusts hurt only ungodly
6. 1/3 of men smitten "The rest of the men which were not killed by these plagues yet repented not of the works of their hands. . . ."

Interludes:
THE LITTLE BOOK
THE TWO WITNESSES

7. ("Time no longer"— the mystery of God finished)
Heaven now rejoices: "The kingdoms of this world are become the KINGDOMS OF OUR LORD, AND OF HIS CHRIST; and he shall reign. . . ."

"AND ONE SAT ON THE THRONE"
All That Is Ungodly and Unrighteous

VISION OF THE CHURCH PERSECUTED BY SATAN Rev. 12-14	VISION OF SEVEN LAST PLAGUES Rev. 15, 16	VISION OF SEVEN DOOMS Rev. 17-20		VISION OF SEVEN NEW THINGS Rev. 21, 22

VISION OF THE CHURCH PERSECUTED BY SATAN
Rev. 12-14

"There appeared a great wonder in heaven; a woman clothed with the sun, and the moon under her feet, and upon her head a crown of twelve stars.

1. Woman in travail
2. Red dragon
3. Man child
4. War in heaven, Satan cast out: "Now is come salvation, and strength, and the KINGDOM OF OUR GOD, AND THE POWER OF HIS CHRIST for the accuser . . . is cast down. . . ."

"Woe to the inhabiters of the earth and of the sea! for the devil is come down unto you, having great wrath. . . ."

"The dragon . . . persecuted the woman which brought forth the man child."

5. War with "remnant of her seed"
6. Beast out of sea
7. Beast out of earth
"He causeth all . . . to receive a mark in their right hand, or in their foreheads."

Interludes:
THE LAMB AND THE REDEEMED ON ZION
EVERLASTING GOSPEL
COMING JUDGMENTS
HARVEST OF EARTH
VINTAGE OF EARTH

VISION OF SEVEN LAST PLAGUES
Rev. 15, 16

"I saw another sign in heaven . . . seven angels having the seven last plagues; for in them is filled up the wrath of God.

"I looked, and, behold, the temple of the tabernacle of the testimony in heaven was opened: And the seven angels came out of the temple, having the seven plagues. . . .and no man was able to enter into the temple, till the seven plagues . . . were fulfilled."

1. Plague upon earth "grievous sore upon the men which had the mark of the beast. . . ."
2. Upon the sea
3. Upon the rivers and springs
4. Upon the sun "Men . . . blasphemed the name of God . . . and they repented not to give him glory."
5. Upon seat of beast "His kingdom was full of darkness; and they . . . blasphemed the God of heaven . . . and repented not of their deeds."
6. Upon Euphrates
7. Into the air Earthquake and hail, "and men blasphemed God. . . ."

VISION OF SEVEN DOOMS
Rev. 17-20

"One of the seven angels . . . talked with me . . . I will shew unto thee the judgment of the great whore that sitteth upon many waters: With whom the kings of the earth have committed fornication, and the inhabitants of the earth have been made drunk with the wine of her fornication."

"And the woman [on a scarlet colored beast] . . . is that great city, which reigneth over the kings of the earth."

1. Doom of Babylon

Interludes:
ALLELUIAS IN HEAVEN
MARRIAGE OF THE LAMB ANNOUNCED

CHRIST COMES IN GLORY AS "KING OF KINGS"—Battle of Armageddon
2. Doom of beast
3. Doom—false prophet
4. Doom of kings

MILLENNIUM: Satan is bound, saints reign with Christ

5. Doom—Gog and Magog
6. Doom of Satan

Earth and heaven vanish
GENERAL RESURRECTION
LAST JUDGMENT

7. Doom of death, hell, and unbelieving dead (those "not found written in the book of life")

"I saw a new heaven and a new earth. . . ."
"I . . . saw the holy city . . . coming down from God. . . ."

The circle of the earth

VISION OF SEVEN NEW THINGS
Rev. 21, 22

1. New Heaven
2. New Earth
3. New Jerusalem, the Lamb's Wife "The city lieth foursquare. . . ."
4. New Peoples "The tabernacle of God is with men, and he will dwell with them, and they shall be his people, and God himself shall be with them, and be their God."

"God shall wipe away all tears . . . there shall be no more death . . . sorrow, nor crying, neither . . . any more pain: for the former things are passed away. And he . . . said, Behold, I make all things new."

5. New Temple "The LORD GOD ALMIGHTY AND THE LAMB are the temple of it."
6. New Light "The glory of GOD did lighten it, AND THE LAMB is the light thereof."
7. Paradise of God "A pure river of water of life . . . proceeding out of the THRONE OF GOD AND OF THE LAMB."

"On either side . . . was there the tree of life. . . ."

"There shall be no more curse: but the THRONE OF GOD AND OF THE LAMB shall be in it; and his servants shall serve him."

Old Testament Terms
in the Apocalypse

In describing the grandeur of Christ's Revelation and the divine judgments of the terrible Day of the Lord upon all ungodliness, John drew freely on Hebrew Scripture for imagery and terminology. He used some of the prophetic language and apocalyptic symbolism of the Major and Minor Prophets, and employed many vivid figures of speech relating to events of Israel's history and to significant forms of its religious worship, but to these he gave a spiritual application and made them universal in scope. More than four hundred allusions to the Old Testament are to be found in Revelation.

Through cross-reference study the probable sources of some of John's imagery may be traced. To see them in their original settings throws light on their deeper meaning in Revelation. To aid the reader many of John's phrases and Old Testament correlatives have been set side by side. In pursuing this study it is helpful to read first the full Revelation verse or verses designated under each Revelation phrase before reading the Old Testament passages for comparison. (An occasional New Testament passage has been included where pertinent.)

The faithful witness (Rev. 1:5)

"Behold, I have given him [Messiah] for a witness to the people, a leader and commander to the people." Is. 55:4

"Jesus answered . . . To this end was I born, and for this cause came I into the world, that I should bear witness unto the truth." Jn. 18:37

He cometh with clouds; they shall see him whom they pierced, and shall wail (Rev. 1:7)

"I saw in the night visions, and, behold, one like the Son of man came with the clouds of heaven, and came to the Ancient of days, and they brought him near before him." Dan. 7:13

"Then shall appear the sign of the Son of man in heaven: and then shall all the tribes of the earth mourn, and they shall see the Son of man coming in the clouds of heaven with power and great glory." Mt. 24:30

"I will pour upon the house of David, and upon the inhabitants of Jerusalem, the spirit of grace and of supplications: and they shall look upon me whom they have pierced, and they shall mourn for him, as one mourneth for his only son. . . ." Zech. 12:10.

"One of the soldiers with a spear pierced his [Jesus'] side, and forthwith came there out blood and water." Jn. 19:34; cf. 19:37

Alpha and Omega (Rev. 1:8,11; cf. 21:6; 22:13)	(The first and last letters of the Greek alphabet. John employed these terms as titles for both God and Christ, "the beginning and the end, the first and the last," to indicate their eternal existence.)
	"Thus saith the Lord the King of Israel, and his redeemer the Lord of hosts; I am the first, and I am the last; and beside me there is no God." Is. 44:6; cf. 41:4
	"Hearken unto me, O Jacob and Israel, my called; I am he; I am the first, I also am the last." Is. 48:12
Seven golden candlesticks (Rev. 1:12)	"I have looked, and behold a candlestick all of gold, with a bowl upon the top of it, and his seven lamps thereon. . . ." Zech. 4:2; cf. Ex. 25:31-37
Hairs white like wool, eyes as a flame of fire, feet like fine brass, voice as the sound of many waters (Rev. 1:14,15)	"I beheld till the thrones were cast down, and the Ancient of days did sit, whose garment was white as snow, and the hair of his head like the pure wool. . . ." Dan. 7:9
	"I lifted up mine eyes . . . and behold a certain man clothed in linen. . . . His body also was like the beryl, and his face as the appearance of lightning, and his eyes as lamps of fire, and his arms and his feet like in colour to polished brass. . . ." Dan. 10:5,6
	"Behold, the glory of the God of Israel came from the way of the east: and his voice was like a noise of many waters: and the earth shined with his glory." Ezek. 43:2
Out of his mouth went a twoedged sword (Rev. 1:16)	"He hath made my mouth like a sharp sword; in the shadow of his hand hath he hid me, and made me a polished shaft. . . ." Is. 49:2
	"The word of God is quick, and powerful, and sharper than any twoedged sword, piercing even to the dividing asunder of soul and spirit. . . ." Heb. 4:12
He that hath an ear, let him hear (Rev. 2:7; cf. Mt. 11:15)	"Behold, a king shall reign in righteousness. . . . And the eyes of them that see shall not be dim, and the ears of them that hear shall hearken." Is. 32:1,3
	"And the man said unto me, Son of man, behold with thine eyes, and hear with thine ears, and set thine heart upon all that I shall shew thee. . . ." Ezek. 40:4
	On six different occasions Jesus admonished: "He that hath ears to hear, let him hear" (Mt. 11:15; 13:9,43; Mk. 4:23; 7:16; Lu. 14:35).
A new name (Rev. 2:17; cf. 3:12)	"Even unto them will I give in mine house and within my walls a place and a name better than of sons and of daughters: I will give them an everlasting name, that shall not be cut off." Is. 56:5; see 62:2
Jezebel (Rev. 2:20,21)	"There was none like unto Ahab, which did sell himself to work wickedness in the sight of the Lord, whom Jezebel his wife stirred up." I Ki. 21:25

Christ searches the reins and hearts (Rev. 2:23)	"I the Lord search the heart, I try the reins, even to give every man according to his ways, and according to the fruit of his doings." Jer 17:10
Nations shall be broken as a potter's vessel (Rev. 2:26,27)	"He [God] shall break it [Kingdom of Judah] as the breaking of the potter's vessel that is broken in pieces; he shall not spare. . . ." Is 30:14; cf. Jer. 19:11
The morning star (Rev. 2:28; cf. 22:16)	"There shall come a Star out of Jacob, and a Sceptre shall rise out of Israel. . . ." Num. 24:17
	"We have also a more sure word of prophecy; whereunto ye do well that ye take heed, as unto a light that shineth in a dark place, until the day dawn, and the day star arise in your hearts." II Pet. 1:19
Key of David (Rev. 3:7)	"The key of the house of David will I [God] lay upon his shoulder; so he shall open, and none shall shut; and he shall shut, and none shall open." Is. 22:22
Throne of God (Rev. 4:2)	"I saw . . . the Lord sitting upon a throne, high and lifted up, and his train filled the temple." Is. 6:1
Rainbow (Rev. 4:3)	"As the appearance of the bow that is in the cloud in the day of rain, so was the appearance of the brightness round about. This was the appearance of the likeness of the glory of the Lord." Ezek. 1:28; cf Gen. 9:13-17
Four winged beasts, threefold song of praise (Rev. 4:6-8)	"Out of the midst thereof [a fiery whirlwind] came the likeness of four living creatures. . . . And every one had four faces, and . . . four wings. . . . They four had the face of a man, and the face of a lion . . . the face of an ox . . . the face of an eagle. . . . And their rings were full of eyes round about them four." Ezek. 1:5,6,10,18
	"Above it [God's throne] stood the seraphims: each one had six wings with twain he covered his face, and with twain he covered his feet, and with twain he did fly. And one cried unto another, and said, Holy holy, holy, is the lord of hosts: the whole earth is full of his glory." Is 6:2,3
Book of seven seals (Rev. 5:1)	"When I looked, behold, an hand was sent unto me; and, lo, a roll of a book was therein . . . and it was written within and without: and there was written therein lamentations, and mourning, and woe." Ezek 2:9,10
Root of David (Rev. 5:5)	"In that day there shall be a root of Jesse, which shall stand for an ensign of the people; to it shall the Gentiles seek. . . ." Is. 11:10
The Lamb, having seven eyes (Rev. 5:6)	"He is brought as a lamb to the slaughter . . . for he was cut off out of the land of the living: for the transgression of my people was he stricken." Is. 53:7,8
	"The next day John seeth Jesus coming unto him, and saith

Behold the Lamb of God, which taketh away the sin of the world." Jn. 1:29

"Behold, I will bring forth my servant the BRANCH. For behold the stone that I have laid before Joshua; upon one stone shall be seven eyes . . . and I will remove the iniquity of that land in one day." Zech. 3:8,9; cf. 4:10

Kings and priests of God (Rev. 5:10)	"Ye shall be named the Priests of the Lord: men shall call you the Ministers of our God. . . ." Is. 61:6
Thousands of thousands (Rev. 5:11)	"The Ancient of days did sit . . . thousand thousands ministered unto him, and ten thousand times ten thousand stood before him. . . ." Dan. 7:9,10

White, red, black, and pale horses (Rev. 6:2-8)

"I saw by night, and behold a man riding upon a red horse . . . and behind him were there red horses, speckled, and white. . . . These are they whom the Lord hath sent to walk to and fro through the earth." Zech. 1:8,10

"Behold, there came four chariots out from between two mountains . . . of brass. In the first chariot were red horses; and in the second . . . black horses; And in the third . . . white horses; and in the fourth . . . grisled and bay horses. . . . These are the four spirits of the heavens, which go forth from standing before the Lord of all the earth." Zech. 6:1-3,5

"Thus saith the Lord God; How much more when I send my four sore judgments upon Jerusalem, the sword, and the famine, and the noisome beast, and the pestilence, to cut off from it man and beast?" Ezek. 14:21

Great day of His wrath (earthquake, sun became black, moon became as blood, stars fell, the heavens departed as a scroll, men hid) (Rev. 6:12-17)

"The day of the Lord is great and very terrible; and who can abide it?" Joel 2:11; cf. 1:15; Na. 1:6; Zeph. 1:14,15

"The earth shall quake before them; the heavens shall tremble: the sun and the moon shall be dark, and the stars shall withdraw their shining. . . . The sun shall be turned into darkness, and the moon into blood, before the great and the terrible day of the Lord come." Joel 2:10,31; cf. Hag. 2:6

"All the host of heaven shall be dissolved, and the heavens shall be rolled together as a scroll: and all their host shall fall down, as the leaf falleth off from the vine, and as a falling fig from the fig tree." Is. 34:4

"The loftiness of man shall be bowed down . . . and the Lord alone shall be exalted in that day. . . . And they shall go . . . into the caves of the earth, for fear of the Lord, and for the glory of his majesty, when he ariseth to shake terribly the earth." Is. 2:17-19; cf. Is. 13:6-10; Ezek. 38:19,20; Na. 1:5

Four winds of the earth (Rev. 7:1)

"Upon Elam will I bring the four winds from the four quarters of heaven, and will scatter them toward all those winds. . . ." Jer. 49:36

"I saw in my vision by night, and, behold, the four winds of the heaven strove upon the great sea." Dan. 7:2

Seal of the living God in foreheads of His servants (Rev. 7:2,3; cf. 14:1; 22:4)

"The Lord said unto him, Go through . . . the midst of Jerusalem, and set a mark upon the foreheads of the men that sigh and that cry for all the abominations that be done in the midst thereof. And to the others he said in mine hearing, Go ye after him through the city, and smite: let not your eye spare, neither have ye pity: Slay utterly old and young . . . but come not near any man upon whom is the mark; and begin at my sanctuary." Ezek. 9:4-6

The Lamb, as shepherd, leads the redeemed (Rev. 7:17)

"The Lord is my shepherd; I shall not want. He maketh me to lie down in green pastures: he leadeth me beside the still waters." Ps. 23:1,2

"They shall not hunger nor thirst; neither shall the heat nor sun smite them: for he that hath mercy on them shall lead them, even by the springs of water shall he guide them." Is. 49:10

"I will set up one shepherd over them, and he shall feed them, even my servant David. . . ." Ezek. 34:23

Trumpets (Rev. 8:2)

"Blow ye the trumpet in Zion, and sound an alarm in my holy mountain: let all the inhabitants of the land tremble: for the day of the Lord cometh, for it is nigh at hand. . . ." Joel 2:1; cf. Num. 10:2

Golden altar, incense, fire of the altar (Rev. 8:3-5)

"He [high priest] shall take a censer full of burning coals of fire from off the altar before the Lord, and his hands full of sweet incense beaten small, and bring it within the vail." Lev. 16:12; cf. Ex. 30:1,7,8

"He spake unto the man clothed with linen, and said, Go in between the wheels, even under the cherub, and fill thine hand with coals of fire from between the cherubims, and scatter them over the city." Ezek. 10:2

Voices, thunderings, lightnings (Rev. 8:5)

"The Lord also thundered in the heavens, and the Highest gave his voice . . . he sent out his arrows, and scattered them; and he shot out lightnings. . . ." Ps. 18:13,14

Hail and fire (Rev. 8:7)

"I [Lord God] will plead against him with pestilence and with blood; and I will rain upon him . . . and upon the many people that are with him, an overflowing rain, and great hailstones, fire, and brimstone." Ezek. 38:22

A great mountain burning with fire (Rev. 8:8)

"I am against thee, O destroying mountain, saith the Lord, which destroyest all the earth: and I will stretch out mine hand upon thee, and roll thee down from the rocks, and will make thee a burnt mountain." Jer. 51:25

Bitter waters of wormwood (Rev. 8:11)

"Thus saith the Lord of hosts . . . I will feed them, even this people, with wormwood, and give them water of gall to drink." Jer. 9:15; cf. 23:15

Devasting locusts
like unto horses having
the teeth of lions
(Rev. 9:3-11)

"He [the Lord] spake, and the locusts came . . . and that without number, And did eat up all the herbs in their land, and devoured the fruit of their ground." Ps. 105:34,35; cf. Ex. 10:1-15

"That which the palmerworm hath left hath the locust eaten; and that which the locust hath left hath the cankerworm eaten; and that which the cankerworm hath left hath the caterpiller eaten [all locusts in various stages of development] . . . . For a nation is come up upon my land, strong, and without number, whose teeth are the teeth of a lion. . . ." Joel 1:4,6

"The land is as the garden of Eden before them [locusts], and behind them a desolate wilderness; yea, and nothing shall escape them. The appearance of them is as the appearance of horses; and as horsemen, so shall they run. Like the noise of chariots on the tops of mountains shall they leap, like the noise of a flame of fire that devoureth the stubble, as a strong people set in battle array." Joel 2:3-5

Eating of the
little book; as
sweet as honey
(Rev. 10:8-11)

"Thy words were found, and I did eat them; and thy word was unto me the joy and rejoicing of mine heart. . . ." Jer. 15:16

"He [the voice] said unto me, Son of man . . . eat this roll, and go speak unto the house of Israel. So I opened my mouth, and he caused me to eat that roll. . . . Son of man, cause thy belly to eat, and fill thy bowels with this roll that I give thee. Then did I eat it; and it was in my mouth as honey for sweetness." Ezek. 3:1-3

Measuring reed
(Rev. 11:1)

"I lifted up mine eyes . . . and behold a man with a measuring line in his hand. Then said I, Whither goest thou? And he said unto me, To measure Jerusalem, to see what is the breadth thereof, and what is the length thereof." Zech. 2:1,2

"The hand of the Lord was upon me [Ezekiel], and brought me thither. In the visions of God brought he me into the land of Israel . . . and, behold, there was a man, whose appearance was like the appearance of brass, with a line of flax in his hand, and a measuring reed; and he stood in the gate [of the city]." Ezek. 40:1-3

Forty and two months
(Rev. 11:2)

(Three and a half years, the 1260 days of Revelation 11:3; 12:6; 13:5; see 12:14; Dan. 7:25; 12:7. In Jewish thought this time period was associated with one of tribulation and persecution: duration of famine in Elijah's day [I Ki. 18:1; Lu. 4:25] and of persecution of Jews under Antiochus Epiphanes, 168-165 B.C. [I Macc. 1:21-67; *Ant.* xii, 5.4].

Court outside the temple
(Rev. 11:2)

(See the Court of the Gentiles of Herod's Temple, p. 163.)

Two witnesses, two olive
trees, two candlesticks
(Rev. 11:3,4,10)

"At the mouth of two witnesses . . . shall the matter be established." Deut. 19:15; cf. Jn. 8:17,18

"I have looked, and behold a candlestick all of gold . . . And two olive trees by it, one upon the right side of the bowl, and the other upon the left side thereof. . . . Then said he [the angel], These are the two anointed ones, that stand by the Lord of the whole earth." Zech. 4:2,3,14

Three days and a half (Rev. 11:11)	("A definite for an indefinite period.")
God's two prophets revived and stood upon their feet (Rev. 11:11)	"Thus saith the Lord God; Come from the four winds, O breath, and breathe upon these slain, that they may live. So I prophesied as he commanded me, and the breath came into them, and they lived, and stood up upon their feet, an exceeding great army." Ezek. 37:9,10
The kingdom of God and of His Christ; his reign over all (Rev. 11:15)	"I saw in the night visions, and, behold, one like the Son of man came with the clouds of heaven, and came to the Ancient of days. . . . And there was given him dominion, and glory, and a kingdom, that all people, nations, and languages, should serve him: his dominion is an everlasting dominion, which shall not pass away, and his kingdom that which shall not be destroyed." Dan. 7:13,14; cf. vv. 18,27
Woman travailing in birth (Rev. 12:2)	"Like as a woman with child, that draweth near the time of her delivery, is in pain, and crieth out in her pangs; so have we been in thy sight, O Lord." Is. 26:17
	"Be in pain, and labour to bring forth, O daughter of Zion, like a woman in travail: for now shalt thou go forth out of the city. . . ." Mic. 4:10
Great red dragon (Rev. 12:3,9)	The "serpent" of Genesis 3:1.
	"In that day the Lord with his sore and great and strong sword shall punish leviathan the piercing serpent, even leviathan that crooked serpent [metaphorically, powers hostile to God's people]; and he shall slay the dragon that is in the sea." Is. 27:1; see Ezek. 29:3; 32:2
Dragon stood ready to devour the child (Rev. 12:4)	"Pharaoh charged all his people, saying, Every [Hebrew] son that is born ye shall cast into the river. . . ." Ex. 1:22; cf. Mt. 2:16
A man child (Rev. 12:5)	"Behold, a virgin shall conceive, and bear a son, and shall call his name Immanuel." Is. 7:14
	"Unto us a child is born, unto us a son is given: and the government shall be upon his shoulder: and his name shall be called Wonderful, Counsellor, The mighty God, The everlasting Father, The Prince of Peace." Is. 9:6
	"Before she travailed, she brought forth; before her pain came, she was delivered of a man child. . . . as soon as Zion travailed, she brought forth her children." Is. 66:7,8
Rod of iron (Rev. 12:5; cf. 2:27; 19:15)	"The Lord hath said unto me, Thou [My Anointed] art my Son; this day have I begotten thee. . . . Thou shalt break them [the heathen] with a rod of iron; thou shalt dash them in pieces like a potter's vessel." Ps. 2:7,9
The angel Michael (Rev. 12:7,8)	"At that time shall Michael [guardian angel of Israel] stand up, the great prince which standeth for the children of thy people . . . and at that time thy people shall be delivered, every one that shall be found written in the book." Dan. 12:1; cf. 10:13,21

Satan cast out of heaven (Rev. 12:9; cf. 9:1)	"How art thou fallen from heaven, O Lucifer, son of the morning! how art thou cut down to the ground, which didst weaken the nations! . . . Yet thou shalt be brought down to hell, to the sides of the pit." Is. 14:12,15
	"He [Jesus] said unto them, I beheld Satan as lightning fall from heaven." Lu. 10:18
Accuser of our brethren (Rev. 12:10)	"He [an angel] shewed me Joshua the high priest standing before the angel of the Lord, and Satan [adversary, accuser] standing at his right hand to resist him." Zech. 3:1
Wings of a great eagle (Rev. 12:14)	"Ye have seen what I did unto the Egyptians, and how I bare you on eagles' wings, and brought you unto myself." Ex. 19:4; see Deut. 32:11; Is. 40:31
A time, and times, and half a time (Rev. 12:14)	"He shall speak great words against the most High, and shall wear out the saints of the most High, and think to change times and laws: and they shall be given into his hand until a time and times and the dividing of time." Dan. 7:25; see 12:7
The remnant of the woman's seed (Rev. 12:17)	"I [Lord God] will put enmity between thee and the woman, and between thy seed and her seed; it shall bruise thy head, and thou shalt bruise his heel." Gen. 3:15
	"There shall be an highway for the remnant of his [God's] people, which shall be left, from Assyria. . . ." Is. 11:16
	"Behold, therein [in Jerusalem] shall be left a remnant that shall be brought forth, both sons and daughters . . . and ye shall see their way and their doings. . . ." Ezek. 14:22
	"Even so then at this present time also there is a remnant according to the election of grace." Rom. 11:5
Beast out of the sea (with seven heads and ten horns; like unto a leopard, a bear, a lion) blasphemes against God and wars with the saints (Rev. 13:1-7)	"Four great beasts came up from the sea. . . . The first was like a lion . . . a second, like to a bear . . . another, like a leopard . . . the beast had also four heads. . . . After this I saw . . . a fourth beast, dreadful and terrible, and strong exceedingly; and it had great iron teeth: it devoured and brake in pieces, and stamped the residue with the feet of it: and it was diverse from all the beasts that were before it; and it had ten horns. I considered the horns, and . . . there came up among them another little horn . . . in this horn were eyes like the eyes of man, and a mouth speaking great things.
	". . . the same horn made war with the saints, and prevailed against them; Until the Ancient of days came, and judgment was given to the saints of the most High; and the time came that the saints possessed the kingdom." Dan. 7:3-8,21,22
Image of the beast (Rev. 13:14)	(First of ten allusions to the *image* [see Rev. 13:15; 14:9,11; 15:2; 16:2; 19:20; 20:4].)
	"Thou shalt not make unto thee any graven image. . . . Thou shalt not bow down thyself to them, nor serve them. . . ." Ex. 20:4,5

"Nebuchadnezzar ... made an image of gold.... To you it is commanded, O people, nations, and languages, That ... ye fall down and worship the golden image...." Dan. 3:1,4,5

Mark of the beast
(Rev. 13:16)

(Symbol of allegiance to Satan; first of eight allusions to the *mark* [see Rev. 13:17; 14:9,11; 15:2; 16:2; 19:20; 20:4].)

Mount Sion
(Rev. 14:1)

"Beautiful for situation, the joy of the whole earth, is mount Zion, on the sides of the north, the city of the great King." Ps. 48:2

"Upon mount Zion shall be deliverance, and there shall be holiness; and the house of Jacob shall possess their possessions." Ob. v. 17

"Ye are come unto mount Sion, and unto the city of the living God, the heavenly Jerusalem, and to an innumerable company of angels...." Heb. 12:22

Babylon is fallen
(Rev. 14:8)

"Thus hath the Lord said unto me, Go, set a watchman, let him declare what he seeth.... And he answered ... Babylon is fallen, is fallen; and all the graven images of her gods he hath broken unto the ground." Is. 21:6,9

Wine of her fornication
(Rev. 14:8; cf. 17:2; 18:3,9)

"Babylon hath been a golden cup in the Lord's hand, that made all the earth drunken: the nations have drunken of her wine; therefore the nations are mad." Jer. 51:7

Wine of God's wrath;
cup of His indignation
(Rev. 14:10)

"In the hand of the Lord there is a cup, and the wine is red; it is full of mixture; and he poureth out of the same: but the dregs thereof, all the wicked of the earth shall wring them out, and drink them." Ps. 75:8

"Awake, awake, stand up, O Jerusalem, which hast drunk at the hand of the Lord the cup of his fury; thou hast drunken the dregs of the cup of trembling, and wrung them out.... I have taken out of thine hand the cup of trembling, even the dregs of the cup of my fury; thou shalt no more drink it again: But I will put it into the hand of them that afflict thee...." Is. 51:17,22,23

"Thus saith the Lord God of Israel unto me; Take the wine cup of this fury at my hand, and cause all the nations, to whom I send thee, to drink it. And they shall drink, and be moved, and be mad, because of the sword that I will send among them." Jer. 25:15,16

A sharp sickle;
harvest of earth ripe
(Rev. 14:14,15)

"Let the heathen be wakened, and come up to the valley of Jehoshaphat: for there will I sit to judge all the heathen round about. Put ye in the sickle, for the harvest is ripe: come, get you down; for the press is full, the fats overflow; for their wickedness is great." Joel 3:12, 13

Vine of the earth
gathered; winepress
of God's wrath
(Rev. 14:18-20; cf. 19:15)

"My wellbeloved hath a vineyard in a very fruitful hill: And he fenced it, and gathered out the stones thereof, and planted it with the choicest vine, and built a tower in the midst of it, and also made a winepress therein: and he looked that it should bring forth grapes, and it brought forth wild grapes." Is. 5:1,2

"The Lord hath trodden under foot all my mighty men in the midst of me: he hath called an assembly against me to crush my young men: the Lord hath trodden the virgin, the daughter of Judah, as in a winepress." Lam. 1:15

Seven plagues (Rev. 15:1)	"The Lord said unto Moses . . . stand before Pharaoh, and say unto him. . . . I will at this time send all my plagues upon thine heart, and upon thy servants, and upon thy people; that thou mayest know that there is none like me in all the earth." Ex. 9:13,14
Harps of God (Rev. 15:2; cf. 5:8; 14:2)	"Praise the Lord with harp: sing unto him with the psaltery and an instrument of ten strings." Ps. 33:2 "Then will I go unto the altar of God, unto God my exceeding joy: yea, upon the harp will I praise thee, O God my God." Ps. 43:4
Seven golden vials (Rev. 15:7)	(ASV bowls, vessels of the Tabernacle and Temple.) "Thou [Moses] shalt make the dishes thereof, and spoons thereof, and covers thereof, and bowls thereof, to cover withal: of pure gold shalt thou make them." Ex. 25:29 ". . . bowls before the altar." Zech. 14:20
Smoke of God's glory (Rev. 15:8)	"Then a cloud covered the tent of the congregation, and the glory of the Lord filled the tabernacle. And Moses was not able to enter into the tent . . . because the cloud abode thereon. . . ." Ex. 40:34,35 "I saw . . . the Lord sitting upon a throne, high and lifted up, and his train filled the temple. . . . And one [seraphim] cried unto another . . . Holy, holy, holy, is the Lord of hosts: the whole earth is full of his glory. . . . and the house was filled with smoke." Is. 6:1,3,4
Pouring out of the vials of God's wrath (Rev. 16:1)	"Pour out thy fury upon the heathen that know thee not, and upon the families that call not on thy name: for they have eaten up Jacob, and devoured him. . . ." Jer. 10:25 "Wait ye upon me, saith the Lord, until the day that I rise up to the prey: for my determination is to gather the nations . . . to pour upon them mine indignation, even all my fierce anger: for all the earth shall be devoured with the fire of my jealousy." Zeph. 3:8
Euphrates dried up (Rev. 16:12)	"I am the Lord that maketh all things. . . . That saith to the deep, Be dry, and I will dry up thy rivers." Is. 44:24,27 "A drought is upon her waters; and they shall be dried up: for it is the land of graven images, and they are mad upon their idols." Jer. 50:38
Nations gather for battle of Armageddon (Rev. 16:14,16; cf. 19:11-21)	(RV Har-Magedon, "Mount of Megiddo," the scene of many of Israel's most terrible battles [Ju. 5:19,20; II Ki. 23:29; cf. Zech. 12:11] .) "Behold, the day of the Lord cometh. . . . For I will gather all nations against Jerusalem to battle; and the city shall be taken, and the houses rifled, and the women ravished; and half of the city shall go forth into captivity, and the residue of the people shall not be cut off from the city. Then shall the Lord go forth, and fight against those nations, as when he fought in the day of battle." Zech. 14:1-3

Great whore sitting on many waters (Rev. 17:1,5,15,18)	"How is the faithful city [Jerusalem] become an harlot! it was full of judgment; righteousness lodged in it; but now murderers." Is. 1:21
	"Woe to the bloody city [Nineveh]! . . . Because of the multitude of the whoredoms of the wellfavoured harlot, the mistress of witchcrafts, that selleth nations through her whoredoms, and families through her witchcrafts." Na. 3:1,4
	"O thou [Babylon] that dwellest upon many waters, abundant in treasures, thine end is come, and the measure of thy covetousness." Jer. 51:13
Babylon's sins have reached unto heaven (Rev. 18:5)	"We would have healed Babylon, but she is not healed: forsake her, and let us go every one into his own country: for her judgment reacheth unto heaven, and is lifted up even to the skies." Jer. 51:9
She sits as queen and not as widow, her plagues come in one day (Rev. 18:7,8; cf. 18:10,17)	"Thou [Babylon] saidst, I shall be a lady for ever. . . . hear now this, thou that art given to pleasures, that dwellest carelessly, that sayest in thine heart, I am, and none else beside me; I shall not sit as a widow, neither shall I know the loss of children: But these two things shall come to thee in a moment in one day, the loss of children, and widowhood: they shall come upon thee in their perfection for the multitude of thy sorceries. . . . Therefore shall evil . . . desolation . . . come upon thee suddenly, which thou shalt not know. . . ." Is. 47:7-11
	"This is the rejoicing city [Nineveh] that dwelt carelessly, that said in her heart, I am, and there is none beside me: how is she become a desolation, a place for beasts to lie down in! . . ." Zeph. 2:15
Babylon burned with fire (Rev. 18:8)	"Behold, they [the astrologers of Babylon] shall be as stubble; the fire shall burn them; they shall not deliver themselves from the power of the flame. . . ." Is. 47:14; cf. Ezek. 28:18
	"Babylon is suddenly fallen and destroyed. . . . Behold, I am against thee, O destroying mountain, saith the Lord, which destroyeth all the earth: and I will stretch out mine hand upon thee . . . and will make thee a burnt mountain." Jer. 51:8,25
Wailing and lamentation over the desolation of the rich city (Rev. 18:9-19)	"All that . . . come down from their ships . . . shall cause their voice to be heard against thee, and shall cry bitterly, and shall cast up dust upon their heads, they shall wallow themselves in the ashes: And they shall make themselves utterly bald for thee, and gird them with sackcloth, and they shall weep for thee with bitterness of heart and bitter wailing. And in their wailing they shall take up a lamentation for thee, and lament over thee, saying, What city is like Tyrus, like the destroyed in the midst of the sea? When thy wares went forth out of the seas, thou filledst many people; thou didst enrich the kings of the earth with the multitude of thy riches and of thy merchandise." Ezek. 27:29-33
Babylon is cast down as a millstone in the sea (Rev. 18:21)	"When thou hast made an end of reading this book . . . thou shalt bind a stone to it, and cast it into the midst of Euphrates: And thou shalt say, Thus shall Babylon sink, and shall not rise from the evil that I [God] will bring upon her. . . ." Jer. 51:63,64

All joys of life stilled in Babylon (Rev. 18:22,23)	"I will take from them the voice of mirth, and . . . of gladness, the voice of the bridegroom, and . . . of the bride, the sound of the millstones, and the light of the candle. And this whole land shall be a desolation, and an astonishment. . . ." Jer. 25:10,11; cf. Ezek. 26:13
Marriage supper of the Lamb (Rev. 19:9)	The marriage feast, a well-known custom of Hebrew life (Gen. 29:21,22; Ju. 14:2,10) (See Jesus' parables of the Marriage of the King's Son [Mt. 22:2-14] and of the Great Supper [Lu. 14:16-24].)
Christ, as King, judges and makes war (Rev. 19:11,15,16)	"With righteousness shall he [the Branch] judge the poor, and reprove with equity for the meek of the earth: and he shall smite the earth with the rod of his mouth, and with the breath of his lips shall he slay the wicked." Is. 11:4
Vesture dipped in blood; wine-press trodden (Rev. 19:13,15)	"Wherefore art thou red in thine apparel, and thy garments like him that treadeth in the winefat? I have trodden the winepress alone; and of the people there was none with me: for I will tread them in mine anger, and trample them in my fury; and their blood shall be sprinkled upon my garments, and I will stain all my raiment. For the day of vengeance is in mine heart, and the year of my redeemed is come." Is. 63:2-4
Birds of prey invited to eat the flesh of the slain (Rev. 19:17,18)	"Thou son of man, thus saith the Lord God; Speak unto every feathered fowl, and to every beast of the field, Assemble yourselves, and come; gather yourselves on every side to my sacrifice that I do sacrifice for you . . . that ye may eat flesh, and drink blood. Ye shall eat the flesh of the mighty, and drink the blood of the princes of the earth. . . . Thus ye shall be filled at my table with horses and chariots, with mighty men, and with all men of war. . . ." Ezek. 39:17-20
Gog and Magog (Rev. 20:8)	"Thou son of man, prophesy against Gog [Gog and Magog, nomadic Asiatic heathen hordes from the north], and say, Thus saith the Lord God; Behold, I am against thee, O Gog, the chief prince of Meshech and Tubal: And I will turn thee back, and leave but the sixth part of thee, and will cause thee to come up from the north parts. . . . Thou shalt fall upon the mountains of Israel, thou, and all thy bands, and the people that is with thee. . . . And I will send a fire on Magog, and among them that dwell carelessly in the isles: and they shall know that I am the Lord." Ezek. 39:1,2,4,6; cf. chap. 38
Books of judgment opened, including the book of life (Rev. 20:12,15; cf. 21:27)	"Let them [mine adversaries] be blotted out of the book of the living, and not be written with the righteous." Ps. 69:28 "I beheld till the thrones were cast down, and the Ancient of days did sit. . . . and ten thousand times ten thousand stood before him: the judgment was set, and the books were opened." Dan. 7:9,10; cf. Ex. 32:32 "At that time shall Michael stand up, the great prince which standeth for the children of thy people: and there shall be a time of trouble, such as never was since there was a nation even to that same time: and at that time thy people shall be delivered, every one that shall be found written in the book." Dan. 12:1

New heaven,
new earth
(Rev. 21:1)

"Behold, I create new heavens and a new earth: and the former shall not be remembered, nor come into mind." Is. 65:17

"For as the new heavens and the new earth, which I will make, shall remain before me, saith the Lord, so shall your seed and your name remain." Is. 66:22

The bride, the
Lamb's wife
(Rev. 21:2,9)

"I will greatly rejoice in the Lord . . . for he hath clothed me with the garments of salvation, he hath covered me with the robe of righteousness, as a bridegroom decketh himself with ornaments, and as a bride adorneth herself with her jewels." Is. 61:10

God's tabernacle
is with men
(Rev. 21:3)

"I will set my tabernacle among you: and my soul shall not abhor you. And I will walk among you, and will be your God, and ye shall be my people." Lev. 26:11,12

God shall wipe
away all tears
(Rev. 21:4; cf. 7:17)

"He will swallow up death in victory; and the Lord God will wipe away tears from off all faces. . . ." Is. 25:8

"I will rejoice in Jerusalem, and joy in my people: and the voice of weeping shall be no more heard in her, nor the voice of crying." Is. 65:19; cf. 51:11

A great and
high mountain
(Rev. 21:10)

"In the visions of God brought he me into the land of Israel, and set me upon a very high mountain, by which was as the frame of a city on the south." Ezek. 40:2

Twelve gates of the
city inscribed with
names of the twelve
tribes of Israel
(Rev. 21:12)

"The gates of the city shall be after the names of the tribes of Israel: three gates northward; one gate of Reuben, one gate of Judah, one gate of Levi. And at the east side . . . three gates; and one gate of Joseph, one gate of Benjamin, one gate of Dan. And at the south side . . . three gates; one gate of Simeon, one gate of Issachar, one gate of Zebulun. At the west side . . . three gates; one gate of Gad, one gate of Asher, one gate of Naphtali." Ezek. 48:13-34

The city foursquare
(Rev. 21:16)

(Foreshadowed in the Holy of Holies of the Tabernacle, 10 x 10 x 10 cubits [see p. 160]; of Solomon's Temple, 20 x 20 x 20 [I Ki. 6:20]; and of Ezekiel's ideal temple, 20 x 20 x 20 [Ezek. 41:4].)

"These shall be the measures thereof [of the city]; the north side four thousand and five hundred, and the south side four thousand and five hundred, and on the east side four thousand and five hundred, and the west side four thousand and five hundred. . . . It was round about eighteen thousand measures: and the name of the city from that day shall be, The Lord is there." Ezek. 48:16,35

The light of the city
(Rev. 21:23; cf. 22:5)

"The sun shall be no more thy light by day; neither for brightness shall the moon give light unto thee: but the Lord shall be unto thee an everlasting light, and thy God thy glory." Is. 60:19

"I [Christ] am the light of the world: he that followeth me shall not walk in darkness, but shall have the light of life." Jn 8:12

Gates shall not be shut (Rev. 21:25,26)	"Thy gates shall be open continually; they shall not be shut day nor night; that men may bring unto thee the forces of the Gentiles, and that their kings may be brought." Is. 60:11
Nothing that defileth shall enter (Rev. 21:27)	"Awake, awake; put on thy strength, O Zion; put on thy beautiful garments, O Jerusalem, the holy city: for henceforth there shall no more come into thee the uncircumcised and the unclean." Is. 52:1; cf. Joel 3:17
River of water of life (Rev. 22:1)	"A river went out of Eden to water the garden; and from thence it was parted, and became into four heads [Pison, Gihon, Hiddekel, Euphrates]." Gen. 2:10
	"Afterward he brought me again unto the door of the house [the sanctuary]; and, behold, waters issued out from under the threshold of the house eastward. . . . And it shall come to pass, that every thing that liveth, which moveth, whithersoever the rivers shall come, shall live: and there shall be a very great multitude of fish, because these waters shall come thither: for they shall be healed. . . ." Ezek. 47:1,9; cf. Zech. 14:8
Fruit and leaves of tree of life (Rev. 22:2)	"By the river upon the bank thereof, on this side and on that side, shall grow all trees for meat, whose leaf shall not fade, neither shall the fruit thereof be consumed: it shall bring forth new fruit according to his months, because their waters they issued out of the sanctuary: and the fruit thereof shall be for meat, and the leaf thereof for medicine." Ezek. 47:12
No more curse (Rev. 22:3)	"Thou art cursed above . . . every beast of the field. . . ." (To the serpent) Gen. 3:14
	"Cursed is the ground for thy sake. . . ." (To Adam) Gen. 3:17
	"If thou wilt not hearken unto the voice of the Lord thy God, to observe to do all his commandments and his statutes . . . that all these curses shall come upon thee, and overtake thee." Deut. 28:15; see vv. 16-68
No night there (Rev. 22:5; cf. 21:25)	"Thy sun shall no more go down; neither shall thy moon withdraw itself: for the Lord shall be thine everlasting light, and the days of thy mourning shall be ended." Is. 60:20
	"It shall come to pass in that day, that the light shall not be clear, nor dark: But it shall be one day which shall be known to the Lord, not day, nor night: but it shall come to pass, that at evening time it shall be light." Zech. 14:6,7
His saints reign forever (Rev. 22:5; cf. 20:4,6)	"The saints of the most High shall take the kingdom, and possess the kingdom for ever. . . . The kingdom and dominion, and the greatness of the kingdom under the whole heaven, shall be given to the people of the saints of the most High, whose kingdom is an everlasting kingdom. . . " Dan. 7:18,27

PARADISE OF GOD IN CONTRAST TO EDEN

"To him that overcometh will I give to eat of the tree of life, which is in the midst of the paradise of God." Rev. 2:7

Note the marked contrasts between the Eden of Genesis (chapters 2 and 3) and the Paradise of Revelation; as well as the contrasts between the fruits of disobedience and the fruits of obedience.

Eden	Paradise of God
"The tree of life also in the midst of the garden, and the tree of knowledge of good and evil." Gen. 2:9	"On either side of the river, was there the tree of life...." Rev. 22:2
"A river went out of Eden to water the garden; and from thence it was parted, and became into four heads." Gen. 2:10	"... a pure river of water of life, clear as crystal, proceeding out of the throne of God and of the Lamb." Rev. 22:1
"Of the tree of the knowledge of good and evil, thou [Adam] shalt not eat of it: for in the day that thou eatest thereof thou shalt surely die." Gen. 2:17	"In the midst of the street of it [the city foursquare] ... was there the tree of life, which bare twelve manner of fruits, and yielded her fruit every month: and the leaves of the tree were for the healing of the nations." Rev. 22:2
The beguiling serpent "more subtil than any beast of the field" Gen. 3:1	"There shall in no wise enter into it any thing that ... maketh a lie...." Rev. 21:27
The forbidden fruit—"Ye shall not eat of it [tree of knowledge of good and evil], neither shall ye touch it, lest ye die." Gen. 3:3	"To him that overcometh will I give to eat of the hidden manna...." Rev. 2:17
"The eyes of them both [Adam and Eve] were opened, and they knew that they were naked...." Gen. 3:7	"He that overcometh, the same shall be clothed in white raiment...." Rev. 3:5

Eden	Paradise of God
"Adam and his wife hid themselves from the presence of the Lord God. . . ." Gen. 3:8	"His [God's] servants shall serve him: And they shall see his face; and his name shall be in their foreheads." Rev. 22:3,4
To the serpent: "Thou art cursed. . . ." Gen. 3:14 To Adam: "Cursed is the ground for thy sake. . . ." Gen. 3:17	"There shall be no more curse: but the throne of God and of the Lamb shall be in it. . . ." Rev. 22:3
To the woman: "I will greatly multiply thy sorrow and thy conception. . . ." Gen. 3:16 To the man: "In sorrow shalt thou eat of it [fruit of ground] all the days of thy life. . . . In the sweat of thy face shalt thou eat bread, till thou return unto the ground. . . ." Gen. 3:17,19	"God shall wipe away all tears from their eyes; and there shall be no more death, neither sorrow, nor crying, neither shall there be any more pain; for the former things are passed away." Rev. 21:4
The right to the tree of life is lost—"Lest he [Adam] put forth his hand, and take also of the tree of life, and eat, and live for ever: Therefore the Lord God sent him forth. . . ." Gen. 3:22,23	"Blessed are they that do his commandments, that they may have right to the tree of life, and may enter in through the gates into the city." Rev. 22:14
"The Lord God sent him forth from the garden of Eden, to till the ground from whence he was taken." Gen. 3:23	"They [God's servants] shall reign for ever and ever." Rev. 22:5
"So he drove out the man. . . ." Gen. 3:24	"I [Christ] will not blot out his name out of the book of life, but I will confess his name before my Father. . . ." Rev. 3:5 "He shall go no more out. . . ." Rev. 3:12 "To him that overcometh will I [Christ] grant to sit with me in my throne. . . ." Rev. 3:21
"He placed at the east of the garden of Eden Cherubims, and a flaming sword which turned every way, to keep the way of the tree of life." Gen. 3:24	"The gates of it shall not be shut at all by day: for there shall be no night there." Rev. 21:25 "There shall in no wise enter into it [the city foursquare] any thing that defileth, neither whatsoever worketh abomination, or maketh a lie: but they which are written in the Lamb's book of life." Rev. 21:27

GLIMPSES OF THE FOURTH DIMENSION

When there shall be "time no longer"

The Revelation of Jesus Christ to John starts from the triumphant standpoint of ascension "I am alive for evermore." By a study of correlated passages from the Gospels and The Apocalypse one sees Jesus' teachings and the events of his life lifted into universal application and truth—beyond time, beyond space, heavenly.

Read chart upward line by line

(Of Ascension)
- Revelation / "They [God's two witnesses] ascended up to heaven in a cloud. . . ." Rev. 11:12
- Jesus / "I ascend unto my Father, and your Father; and to my God, and your God." Jn. 20:17 (See Mk. 16:19)

(At Crucifixion)
- Revelation / After the seventh vial "there came a great voice . . . from the throne, saying, It is done." Rev. 16:17
- Jesus / On the cross Jesus said, "It is finished." Jn. 19:30

- Revelation / "To him that overcometh will I grant to sit with me in my throne, even as I also overcame. . . ." Rev. 3:21
- Jesus / "Be of good cheer, I have overcome the world." Jn. 16:33

(In Olivet Discourse)
- Revelation / "He cometh with clouds . . . and all kindreds of the earth shall wail because of him." Rev. 1:7
- Jesus / "Then shall appear the sign of the Son of man in heaven . . . then shall all . . . tribes of the earth mourn. . . ." Mt. 24:30

(In Olivet Discourse)
- Revelation / "He that overcometh, and keepeth my works unto the end, to him will I give power over the nations." Rev. 2:26
- Jesus / "He that shall endure unto the end, the same shall be saved." Mt. 24:13

- Revelation / "The great day of his wrath is come; and who shall be able to stand?" Rev. 6:17
- Jesus / "Watch . . . and pray always, that ye may be accounted worthy . . . to stand before the Son of man." Lu. 21:36

- Revelation / "Fear God, and give glory to him; for the hour of his judgment is come. . . ." Rev. 14:7
- Jesus / "Now is the judgment of this world: now shall the prince of this world be cast out." Jn. 12:31

(In parable)
- Revelation / "The marriage of the Lamb is come. . . . Blessed are they which are called unto the marriage supper of the Lamb." Rev. 19:7,9
- Jesus / "A certain king . . . made a marriage for his son. . . ." "Those bidden "would not come . . . they made light of it. . . ." Mt. 22:2,3,5

- Revelation / "And there shall in no wise enter into it [the city foursquare] any thing that defileth . . . or maketh a lie. . . ." Rev. 21:27
- Jesus / "Is it not written, My house shall be called of all nations the house of prayer? but ye have made it a den of thieves." Mk. 11:17

(Cleansing of Temple)
- Revelation / "I [John] fell down to worship before the feet of the angel. . . Then saith he unto me, See thou do it not . . . worship God." Rev. 22:8,9
- Jesus / "Why callest thou me good? none is good, save one, that is, God." Lu. 18:19 (a rebuke to personal worship)

- Revelation / "Behold, I have set before thee an open door, and no man can shut it. . . ." Rev. 3:8
- Jesus / "I am the door: by me if any man enter in, he shall be saved. . . ." Jn. 10:9

- Revelation / "There shall in no wise enter into it any thing that defileth . . . but they which are written in the Lamb's book of life." Rev. 21:27
- Jesus / "Rejoice not, that the spirits are subject unto you; but rather rejoice, because your names are written in heaven." Lu. 10:20

(To the Seventy)

—Revelation / "The great dragon . . . was cast into the earth, and his angels were cast out with him." Rev. 12:9

—Jesus / At the report of the Seventy Jesus said, "I beheld Satan as lightning fall from heaven." Lu. 10:18

(In Discourse)

—Revelation / "The city had no need of the sun . . . for . . . the Lamb is the light thereof." Rev. 21:23

—Jesus / "I am the light of the world: he that followeth me . . . shall have the light of life." Jn. 8:12

At Feast)

—Revelation / "The Spirit and the bride say, Come . . . let him that is athirst . . . take the water of life freely." Rev. 22:17

—Jesus / "If any man thirst, let him come unto me, and drink." Jn. 7:37

(At Transfiguration)

—Revelation / ". . . one like unto the Son of man . . . his countenance was as the sun shineth in his strength." Rev. 1:13,16

—Jesus / He "was transfigured . . . and his face did shine as the sun, and his raiment was white as the light." Mt. 17:2

—Revelation / "I heard the number of them . . . sealed: and there were sealed an hundred and forty and four thousand . . . of Israel." Rev. 7:4

—Of Jesus / ". . . him [the Son of man] hath God the Father sealed." Jn. 6:27

(In Parable)

—Revelation / "Out of his mouth goeth a sharp sword, that with it he should smite the nations. . . ." Rev. 19:15

—Jesus / "I came not to send peace [on earth], but a sword." Mt. 10:34

—Revelation / "Whosoever was not found written in the book of life was cast into the lake of fire." Rev. 20:15

—Jesus / ". . . his angels . . . shall gather out of his kingdom all things that offend. . . . And shall cast them into a furnace of fire. . . ." Mt. 13:41,42

(Lord's Prayer)

—Revelation / ". . . much people in heaven, saying, Alleluia; Salvation . . . glory . . . honour . . . power, unto . . . our God." Rev. 19:1

—Jesus / "After this manner . . . pray ye . . . thine is the kingdom, and the power, and the glory, for ever." Mt. 6:9,13

(At Sychar)

—Revelation / "The Lamb which is in the midst of the throne . . . shall lead them unto living fountains of waters. . . ." Rev. 7:17; cf. 22:1

—Jesus / "The water that I shall give him shall be in him a well of water springing up into everlasting life." Jn. 4:14

(Ministry)

—Revelation / When the Lamb opened the first four seals, each of the four beasts said, "Come and see." Rev. 6:1-7

—Jesus / When John's two disciples questioned Jesus "Rabbi . . . where dwellest thou?" Jesus answered, "Come and see." Jn. 1:38,39

—Revelation / "Thou [the Lamb] art worthy to take the book, and to open the seals . . . for thou . . . hast redeemed us to God by thy blood. . . ." Rev. 5:9

—Of Jesus / John the Baptist said, "Behold the Lamb of God, which taketh away the sin of the world." Jn. 1:29

—Revelation / "The dragon stood before the woman which was ready to be delivered, for to devour her child as soon as it was born." Rev. 12:4

—Of Jesus / "Herod . . . slew all the children that were in Bethlehem, and in all the coasts thereof, from two years old and under. . . ." Mt. 2:16

THE THRONE OF GOD AND OF THE LAMB

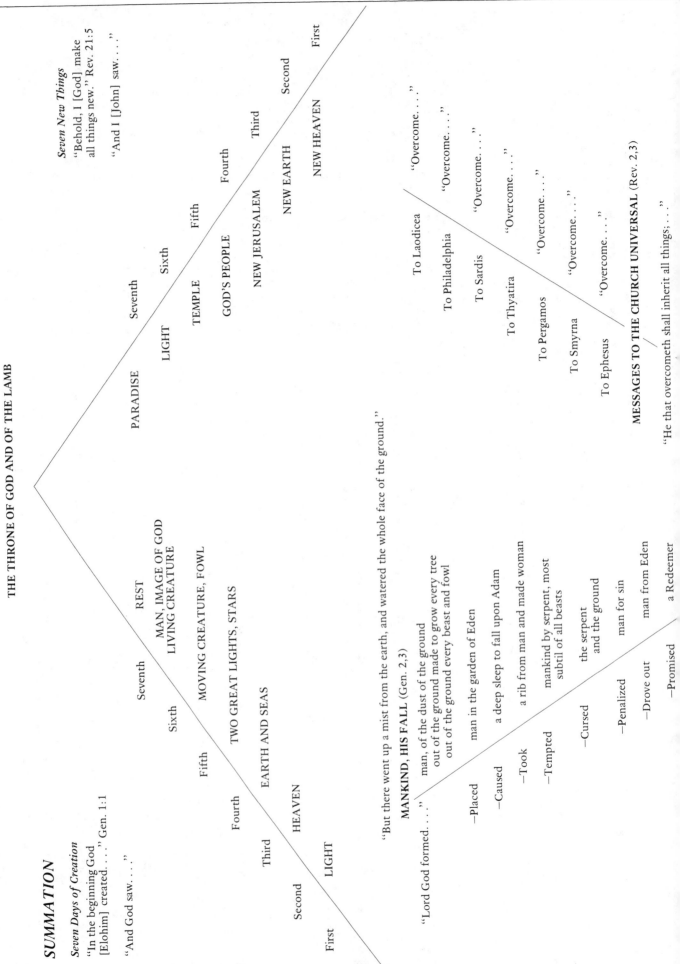

SUMMATION

Seven Days of Creation

"In the beginning God [Elohim] created. . . ." Gen. 1:1

"And God saw. . . ."

First — LIGHT
Second — HEAVEN
Third — EARTH AND SEAS
Fourth — TWO GREAT LIGHTS, STARS
Fifth — MOVING CREATURE, FOWL
Sixth — MAN, IMAGE OF GOD / LIVING CREATURE
Seventh — REST

Seven New Things

"Behold, I [God] make all things new." Rev. 21:5

"And I [John] saw. . . ."

First — NEW HEAVEN
Second — NEW EARTH
Third — NEW JERUSALEM
Fourth — GOD'S PEOPLE
Fifth — TEMPLE
Sixth — LIGHT
Seventh — PARADISE

MANKIND, HIS FALL (Gen. 2,3)

"But there went up a mist from the earth, and watered the whole face of the ground."

"Lord God formed. . . ." — man, of the dust of the ground

—Placed — man in the garden of Eden
out of the ground made to grow every tree
out of the ground every beast and fowl

—Caused — a deep sleep to fall upon Adam

—Took — a rib from man and made woman

—Tempted — mankind by serpent, most subtil of all beasts

—Cursed — the serpent and the ground

—Penalized — man for sin

—Drove out — man from Eden

—Promised — a Redeemer

MESSAGES TO THE CHURCH UNIVERSAL (Rev. 2,3)

"He that overcometh shall inherit all things; . . ."

To Ephesus "Overcome. . . ."
To Smyrna "Overcome. . . ."
To Pergamos "Overcome. . . ."
To Thyatira "Overcome. . . ."
To Sardis "Overcome. . . ."
To Philadelphia "Overcome. . . ."
To Laodicea "Overcome. . . ."

Part IV

APPROPRIATION

17

Appropriation of Scriptural Lessons

The Bible can be the possession of every one of us—with its inspiration, its revelation; its promise, its fulfillment; its first Adam, its last Adam; its old covenant, its new covenant; its law, its grace; its Son of man, its Son of God; its time, its timelessness; its individual salvation, its universal salvation. As we become increasingly familiar with our Bible, listening for its messages and the Word behind the words, and understanding its historical order and spiritual progression, we find our Bible speaking to us. It is therefore important that we train our thought to listen, our eyes to see, and our hearts to appropriate—to make use of—the great storehouse of divine revelation which has been bequeathed to us.

This section suggests to the eye and to the mind a few of the ways the truths of Scripture may be appropriated by the individual. Exploring the Bible is instructive and enlightening, but the one essential to Christian growth is that we let the Bible mold and transfigure our lives.

This quotation is part of a fragment of a papyrus found at Oxyrhynchus in Egypt in 1903 (words in brackets indicate a reconstruction of the original).

> Jesus saith, Let not him who seeks . . . cease until he finds, and when he finds he shall be astonished; astonished he shall reach the kingdom, and having reached the kingdom he shall rest.
>
> . . . the kingdom of Heaven is within you; and whoever shall know himself shall find it. [Strive therefore] to know yourselves, and ye shall be aware that ye are the sons of the [almighty] Father; [and] ye shall know that ye are in [the city of God], and ye are [the city].[1]

A Season
and
a Time

"To every thing there is a season,
  and a time to every purpose under the heaven:
"A time to be born, and a time to die;
  a time to plant, and a time to pluck up that which is planted;
"A time to kill, and a time to heal;
  a time to break down, and a time to build up;
"A time to weep, and a time to laugh;
  a time to mourn, and a time to dance;
"A time to cast away stones, and a time to gather stones together;
  a time to embrace, and a time to refrain from embracing;
"A time to get, and a time to lose;
  a time to keep, and a time to cast away;
"A time to rend, and a time to sew;
  a time to keep silence, and a time to speak;
"A time to love, and a time to hate;
  a time of war, and a time of peace."

Ec. 3:1-8

The Preacher in the book of Ecclesiastes looked upon the mortal experiences of men as vanity—indeed that "all is vanity" if life had not a deeper meaning. He epitomized mortal life as a repetitive cycle, a life that ends in death alike for both the righteous and the wicked.

Jesus Christ inaugurated a new spiritual order, in which he placed the emphasis upon immortal life, thus revealing the true purpose of man's existence. Man's days, under the divine impetus of the Master's teachings and example and those of the apostles, give "a reason of the hope" that is in him. Man's days cease to be a round "under the sun"; they move far beyond the obvious. They become an active and present walk toward the goal of eternal life.

The words of the Preacher may be a challenge and a practical help to the reader when considered in relation to the teachings of the New Testament. On the next two pages passages from the New Testament appear beside the phrases from Ecclesiastes to suggest analogies that can be made between the seasons and times of a man's mortal life and the seasons and times of his growth in Christian character.

A SEASON AND A TIME

"BEHOLD, NOW IS THE ACCEPTED TIME; BEHOLD, NOW IS THE DAY OF SALVATION." II Cor. 6:2

"TO EVERY THING THERE IS A SEASON, AND A TIME TO EVERY PURPOSE UNDER THE HEAVEN." Ec. 3:1

Read chart upward line by line

STONES TOGETHER .... an holy priesthood. . . ." I Pet. 2:5
"Ye also, as lively stones, are built up a spiritual house,

AND A TIME TO GATHER

AWAY STONES .... ("I will take the stony heart out of their flesh. . ." Ezek. 11:19)
lest any of you be hardened through the deceitfulness of sin." Heb. 3:13

A TIME TO CAST "Exhort one another daily, while it is called To day;

AND A TIME TO DANCE .... walking, and leaping, and praising God." Acts 3:8
The lame man, healed, "leaping up stood . . . walked . . . entered . . . into the temple,

A TIME TO MOURN .... "Blessed are they that mourn: for they shall be comforted." Mt. 5:4 (See Ja. 4:9,10)

AND A TIME TO LAUGH ...... "Rejoice ye in that day . . . for, behold your reward is great in heaven. . . ." Lu. 6:21,23
"Blessed are ye that weep now: for ye shall laugh. . . ."

A TIME TO WEEP .... behold . . . ye sorrowed after a godly sort, what carefulness it wrought in you. . . ." II Cor. 7:10,11
"Godly sorrow worketh repentance to salvation not to be repented of. . . .

AND A TIME TO BUILD UP ..... which built his house upon a rock." Mt. 7:24 — "Charity [love] edifieth." I Cor. 8:1
"Whosoever heareth these sayings of mine, and doeth them, I will liken him unto a wise man,

A TIME TO BREAK DOWN ..... Casting down imaginations, and every high thing that exalteth itself against the knowledge of God. . ." II Cor. 10:4,5
"The weapons of our warfare are not carnal, but mighty through God to the pulling down of strong holds;

A TIME TO HEAL .... "The prayer of faith shall save the sick, and the Lord shall raise him up. . ." Ja. 5:15
"Make straight paths for your feet, lest that which is lame be turned out of the way; but let it rather be healed." Heb. 12:13

A TIME TO KILL .... "Our old man is crucified with him, that the body of sin might be destroyed, that henceforth we should not serve sin." Rom. 6:6

AND A TIME TO PLUCK UP ... "Every plant, which my heavenly Father hath not planted, shall be rooted up." Mt. 15:13
"Every tree that bringeth not forth good fruit is hewn down, and cast into the fire." Mt. 7:19

A TIME TO PLANT .... "Now he that planteth and he that watereth are one: and every man shall receive his own reward according to his own labour." I Cor. 3:8 (See Jer. 4:3)
"If we have been planted together in the likeness of his death, we shall be also in the likeness of his resurrection." Rom. 6:5

AND A TIME TO DIE .... "How shall we, that are dead to sin, live any longer therein?" Rom. 6:2 — ". . . mortify the deeds of the body. . . ." Rom. 8:13

A TIME TO BE BORN ...... "Being born again, not of corruptible seed, but of incorruptible, by the word of God, which liveth and abideth for ever." I Pet. 1:23
"Except a man be born of water and of the Spirit, he cannot enter into the kingdom of God." Jn. 3:5

A SEASON AND A TIME—Continued

Read chart upward line by line

"WHAT PROFIT HATH HE THAT WORKETH IN THAT WHEREIN HE LABOURETH?" Ec. 3:9

"IT IS THE SPIRIT THAT QUICKENETH; THE FLESH PROFITETH NOTHING: THE WORDS THAT I SPEAK UNTO YOU, THEY ARE SPIRIT, AND THEY ARE LIFE." Jn. 6:63

AND A TIME OF PEACE .... "The fruit of righteousness is sown in peace of them that make peace." Ja. 3:18
"To be spiritually minded is life and peace." Rom. 8:6
A TIME OF WAR .... "Fight the good fight of faith, lay hold on eternal life. ..." I Tim. 6:12

AND A TIME TO HATE .... "Abhor that which is evil. ..." Rom. 12:9 (See Heb. 1:9)
"He that hateth his life in this world shall keep it unto life eternal." Jn. 12:25
and with all thy mind... Thou shalt love thy neighbour as thyself." Mt. 22:37,39
A TIME TO LOVE .... "Thou shalt love the Lord thy God with all thy heart, and with all thy soul,

AND A TIME TO SPEAK .... "Preach the word; be instant in season, out of season. ..." II Tim. 4:2
that ... I might teach others also, than ten thousand words in an unknown tongue." I Cor. 14:19
"In the church I had rather speak five words with my understanding,
"Speak not evil one of another, brethren." Ja. 4:11
A TIME TO KEEP SILENCE ..... "He that will love life, and see good days, let him refrain his tongue from evil. ..." I Pet. 3:10

AND A TIME TO SEW .... "... [desire] to be clothed upon with our house ... from heaven ... being clothed we shall not be found naked." II Cor. 5:2,3
A TIME TO REND .... "Wherefore lay apart all filthiness and superfluity of naughtiness [RV wickedness] ..." Ja. 1:21 (See II Ki. 2:12)

AND A TIME TO CAST AWAY .. "The night is far spent, the day is at hand: let us therefore cast off the works of darkness. ..." Rom. 13:12
A TIME TO KEEP .... "If ye love me [Jesus Christ], keep my commandments." Jn. 14:15 — "Prove all things; hold fast that which is good." I Th. 5:21

AND A TIME TO LOSE .... "I count all things but loss for the excellency of the knowledge of Christ Jesus my Lord. ..." Phil. 3:8
"Whosoever shall lose his life for my sake and the gospel's, the same shall save it." Mk. 8:35
"So run, that ye may obtain [an incorruptible crown]." I Cor. 9:24
A TIME TO GET [RV SEEK] ... "Seek ye first the kingdom of God, and his righteousness; and all these things shall be added unto you." Mt. 6:33

FROM EMBRACING ..... "Love not the world, neither the things that are in the world." I Jn. 2:15
AND A TIME TO REFRAIN ..... "Wherefore come out from among them, and be ye separate, saith the Lord, and touch not the unclean thing. ..." II Cor. 6:17
A TIME TO EMBRACE "Cleave to that which is good." Rom. 12:9 — "Greet ye one another with a kiss of charity." I Pet. 5:14 (See Heb. 11:13)

STEPS IN ISRAEL'S SPIRITUAL JOURNEY

In tracing the background and Old Testament history of the Children of Israel one finds revealed the progressive steps these people took which prepared them for the reception of the Messiah. The essence of their spiritual journey can be caught in a few meaningful words.

In some degree every man takes these same steps in his own spiritual journey.

Read each section upward line by line.

A RESTORATION   "Then will I [God] . . . restore them" Jer. 27:22
A REMNANT   "The holy seed . . . the substance thereof" Is. 6:13
A CAPTIVITY (Judah)   "He [the Lord] will plead with Israel" Mic. 6:2
A PLEADING (Prophets)   "The Lord's flock is carried away captive" Jer. 13:17
A DIVIDING (2 realms)   "So Israel [10 tribes] rebelled against the house of David" I Ki. 12:19
A TEMPLE (Solomon)   "So the king and all the people dedicated the house of God" II Chron. 7:5
A UNITING (David)   "I [the Lord] took thee . . . to be ruler over my people, over Israel" II Sam. 7:8
A HERITAGE (Joshua)   "When the children of Israel cried unto the Lord, the Lord raised them up a deliverer" Ju. 3:15
A LAW (Moses)   "Unto this people shalt thou divide for an inheritance the land" Josh. 1:6
A PRESERVATION (Joseph)   "I [God] will give thee tables of stone, and a law, and commandments" Ex. 24:12
A NEW NAME (Israel)   "God sent me before you to preserve you a posterity in the earth" Gen. 45:7
AN INCREASE (Abraham)   "Thy name . . . Israel: for as a prince hast thou power with God and with men, and hast prevailed" Gen. 32:28
A COVENANT (Noah's sons)   "I will establish my covenant between me and thee and thy seed after thee" Gen. 17:7
A CONTINUITY (Noah)   "Thy seed shall be as the dust of the earth, and thou shalt spread abroad" Gen. 28:14
A SAVING (Noah)   "Be fruitful, and multiply, and replenish the earth" Gen. 9:1
   "Come thou and all thy house into the ark; for thee have I seen righteous before me" Gen. 7:1

A TURNING   "Then began men to call upon the name of the Lord" Gen. 4:26
A PROMISE   To all mankind came the promise of the Redeemer (Gen. 3:15)

—ISRAEL'S JOURNEY—

A RESTORATION   He is restored to his heritage
A REMNANT   The essential purity of his nature emerges
A CAPTIVITY   Chastisement purges away his "dross"
A PLEADING   God's messengers plead for a moral regeneration
A DIVIDING   Wilfulness and idolatry divide his strength and loyalty
A TEMPLE   He dedicates himself anew to the service of God
A UNITING   Meditating on God's goodness, he is more firmly established in righteousness
A DISCIPLINE   Turning to other gods, he suffers discipline; turning to God, he is delivered
A HERITAGE   Learning patience and trust he presses forward to lay hold of his heritage
A LAW   Given God's law, he practices a purer worship
A PRESERVATION   Under God's provision and watchful care he is prevails with God
A NEW NAME   His name and nature are changed as he prevails with God
AN INCREASE   His seed increases under the blessing of the covenant
A COVENANT   As he is faithful and obedient, God's covenant is established with him
A CONTINUITY   In the seed of righteousness there is continuance
A SAVING   Under grace he and his house are saved and blessed

A TURNING   Each man must turn to God and call upon His name
A PROMISE   Redemption and salvation are promised to "every one of us"

—THE CHRISTIAN'S JOURNEY—

THE GODHEAD

The term *Godhead* is used by Paul to designate the distinctive threefold divine nature and essence of God as the Father, the Son, and the Holy Spirit (the Trinity or three in one of Christian theology). Throughout the Bible one may see the unfolding nature and self-revealing activity of this triune Being and the corresponding truth of the godlikeness of His creation.

"There are three that bear record in heaven, the Father, the Word, and the Holy Ghost: and these three are one." I Jn. 5:7

THE FATHER

Alpha and Omega

"In the beginning God. . ." Gen. 1:1

"Creator of the ends of the earth. . ." Is. 40:28

"Great is our Lord, and of great power: his understanding is infinite." Ps. 147:5

"I AM THAT I AM. . ." Ex. 3:14

"God is a Spirit. . ." Jn. 4:24

"God is love. . ." I Jn. 4:16

"I am the Lord, I change not. . ." Mal. 3:6

"There is none good but one, that is, God. . .," Mt. 19:17

"from everlasting to everlasting, thou art God." Ps. 90:2

"He is in one mind, and who can turn him?" Job 23:13

"As for God, his way is perfect. . ." Ps. 18:30

"God is light, and in him is no darkness at all." I Jn. 1:5

THE WORD—THE SON (LOGOS)

Alpha and Omega

"In the beginning was the Word, and the Word was with God, and the Word was God." Jn. 1:1

"The only begotten Son, which is in the bosom of the Father, he hath declared him." Jn. 1:18

"Before Abraham was, I am." Jn. 8:58

"I and my Father are one." Jn. 10:30

"Thou art the Christ, the Son of the living God." Mt. 16:16

"Who being the brightness of his [God's] glory, and the express image of his person. . ." Heb. 1:3

"For in him dwelleth all the fulness of the Godhead bodily." Col. 2:9

THE HOLY SPIRIT (HOLY GHOST)

"The Spirit of God moved upon the face of the waters." Gen. 1:2

"Thou sendest forth thy spirit, they are created. . .," Ps. 104:30

"Whither shall I go from thy spirit? or whither shall I flee from thy presence?"

"The Comforter, which is the Holy Ghost, whom the Father will send in my [Christ's] name, he shall teach you all things, and bring all things to your remembrance, whatsoever I have said unto you." Jn. 14:26

"When he, the Spirit of truth, is come, he will guide you into all truth. . ." Jn. 16:13

and man—the three acts of creation (Gen. 1)—stand in perfect alignment with the Creator.

HEAVEN AND EARTH

"For the invisible things of him from the creation of the world are clearly seen, being understood by the things that are made, even his eternal power and Godhead. . . ." Rom. 1:20

"Through faith we understand that the worlds were framed by the word of God, so that things which are seen were not made of things which do appear." Heb. 11:3

"God saw every thing that he had made, and, behold, it was very good." Gen. 1:31

"He hath made the earth by his power, he hath established the world by his wisdom, and hath stretched out the heavens by his discretion." Jer. 10:12

"All things were made by him [the Word]; and without him was not any thing made that was made." Jn. 1:3

EVERY LIVING CREATURE

"Thou openest thine hand, and satisfiest the desire of every living thing. The Lord is righteous in all his ways, and holy in all his works." Ps. 145:16,17

"Let every thing that hath breath praise the Lord." Ps. 150:6

"And God created . . . every living creature that moveth. . . ." Gen. 1:21

"In whose hand is the soul of every living thing. . . ." Job 12:10

"O Lord, how manifold are thy works! in wisdom hast thou made them all: the earth is full of thy riches." Ps. 104:24

MAN IN THE IMAGE AND LIKENESS OF GOD

"For in him we live, and move, and have our being . . . For we are also his offspring."
Acts 17:28

"Hereby know we that we dwell in him, and he in us, because he hath given us of his Spirit." I Jn. 4:13

"Be ye therefore perfect, even as your Father which is in heaven is perfect." Mt. 5:48

"So God created man in his own image, in the image of God created he him; male and female created he them." Gen. 1:27

"The Spirit of God hath made me, and the breath of the Almighty hath given me life." Job 33:4

"Know ye that the Lord he is God: it is he that hath made us, and not we ourselves. . . ." Ps. 100:3

SIGNIFICANCE OF CERTAIN NUMBERS IN SCRIPTURE

To the Hebrew mind certain numbers came by association to have special significance, for in addition to arithmetical values they conveyed symbolic and sacred meanings. The sacred numbers were three, four, seven, ten, twelve, forty, seventy, and their multiples.

ONE

One denotes "the idea of uniqueness, self-sufficiency, and indivisibility...."[2]

"In all languages it is the symbol of *unity*. As a cardinal number it denotes *unity*; as an ordinal it denotes *primacy*....

"*'One'* excludes all difference, for there is no second with which it can either harmonise or conflict."[3]

"Thou shalt have no other gods before me." Ex. 20:3

"Hear, O Israel: The Lord our God is one Lord." Deut. 6:4

"To whom then will ye liken me, or shall I be equal? saith the Holy One." Is. 40:25

"There shall be one fold, and one shepherd." Jn. 10:16

"I and my Father are one." Jn. 10:30

"To us there is but one God, the Father, of whom are all things, and we in him; and one Lord Jesus Christ, by whom are all things, and we by him." I Cor. 8:6

"There is one body, and one Spirit, even as ye are called in one hope of your calling; One Lord, one faith, one baptism, One God and Father of all, who is above all, and through all, and in you all." Eph. 4:4-6

TWO

The primary root in Hebrew of the word two means "'*to fold,* i.e. *duplicate'* (lit. or fig.) ... alter, double, (be given to) change, disguise, (be) diverse, pervert, prefer."[4]

"Two affirms that there is a difference—there is *another*.... It is the first number by which we can *divide* another, and therefore in all its uses we may trace this fundamental idea of *division* or *difference*."[5]

"God made two great lights; the greater light to rule the day, and the lesser light to rule the night...." Gen. 1:16

"And he gave unto Moses ... two tables of testimony, tables of stone, written with the finger of God." Ex. 31:18

"God hath spoken once; twice have I heard this; that power belongeth unto God." Ps. 62:11

"No man can serve two masters.... Ye cannot serve God and mammon." Mt. 6:24

"Where two or three are gathered together in my name, there am I in the midst of them." Mt. 18:20

"On these two commandments hang all the law and the prophets." Mt. 22:40

"I will give power unto my two witnesses, and they shall prophesy...." Rev. 11:3

THREE

Three "is the number of the Deity (the Trinity)...."[6]

"All things that are specially *complete* are stamped with this number three.

"God's attributes are *three*: omniscience, omnipresence, and omnipotence....

"*Three* denotes *divine* perfection....

"Hence the number *three* points us to what is real, essential, perfect, substantial, complete, and Divine."[7]

Threefold priestly blessing Num. 6:23-26

"Holy, holy, holy, is the Lord of hosts: the whole earth is full of his glory." Is. 6:3

Daniel "kneeled upon his knees three times a day, and prayed, and gave thanks before his God...." Dan. 6:10

"I cast out devils, and I do cures to day and to morrow, and the third day I shall be perfected." Lu. 13:32

"Destroy this temple, and in three days I [Jesus] will raise it up." Jn. 2:19

"For there are three that bear record in heaven, the Father, the Word, and the Holy Ghost: and these three are one. And there are three that bear witness in earth, the Spirit, and the water, and the blood: and these three agree in one." I Jn. 5:7,8

FOUR

"The number 4 early became a symbol of completeness. It is undoubtedly based upon the four directions which stand open to one, *i.e.,* the right hand, the left hand, before and behind. From these, in the second place, arises the recognition of the four points of the compass 'four corners of the earth. . . .'"[8]

"Four symbolizes the world or humanity."[9]

"And a river went out of Eden to water the garden; and from thence it was parted, and became into four heads." Gen. 2:10

"Also out of the midst thereof came the likeness of four living creatures. . . . And every one had four faces, and every one had four wings." Ezek. 1:5,6

"Round about the throne, were four beasts full of eyes before and behind. . . . they rest not day and night, saying, Holy, holy, holy, Lord God Almighty, which was, and is, and is to come." Rev. 4:6,8

"I saw four angels standing on the four corners of the earth, holding the four winds of the earth. . . ." Rev. 7:1

"The city lieth foursquare, and the length is as large as the breadth. . . ." Rev. 21:16

FIVE

"Five, appears in the tables of requirements and punishments. . . ."[10]

"Five. Denotes Divine *grace.* It is 4 + 1. It is God adding His gifts and blessing to the works of His hands. . . . It is the leading factor in the Tabernacle measurements."[11]

"If a man shall steal an ox . . . and kill it, or sell it; he shall restore five oxen for an ox. . . ." Ex. 22:1

"And he shall make amends for the harm that he hath done in the holy thing, and shall add the fifth part thereto, and give it unto the priest. . . ." Lev. 5:16

"Then shall the kingdom of heaven be likened unto ten virgins, which took their lamps, and went forth to meet the bridegroom. And five of them were wise, and five were foolish." Mt. 25:1,2

"Yet in the church I had rather speak five words with my understanding. . . ." I Cor. 14:19

"To them [locusts] it was given that they should not kill them [those men which have not the seal of God in their foreheads], but that they should be tormented five months. . . ." Rev. 9:5

SEVEN

In Hebrew the primary root of the word seven means "'*to be complete*'"; "a primary cardinal number; *seven* (as the sacred *full* one)."[12]

"*Seven* denotes *spiritual* perfection. . . ."[13]

". . . *seven* is the sacred number implying totality and universality. . . ."[14]

"The number seven was among the Israelites a symbolic seal of the covenant between God and their nation."[15]

"And on the seventh day God ended his work which he had made. . . ." Gen. 2:2

"But the seventh day is the sabbath of the Lord thy God: in it thou shalt not do any work. . . ." Ex. 20:10

"Seven priests shall bear before the ark seven trumpets of rams' horns: and the seventh day ye shall compass the city seven times. . . ." Josh. 6:4

"Wisdom hath builded her house, she hath hewn out her seven pillars." Pr. 9:1

"John to the seven churches . . . Grace be unto you, and peace, from him which is, and which was, and which is to come; and from the seven Spirits . . . before his throne. . . ." Rev. 1:4

"I saw in the right hand of him that sat on the throne a book . . . sealed with seven seals." Rev. 5:1

EIGHT

"*Eight* (as if a *surplus* above the 'perfect' seven)."[16]

In Hebrew the number eight comes from a root word which means "'to make fat,' 'cover with fat,' 'to super-abound.' . . . As *seven* was so called because the seventh day was the day of completion and rest, so *eight*, as the eighth day, was over and above this perfect completion and was indeed the *first* of a new series, as well as being the *eighth.*"[17]

Eight by itself "is the number specially associated with *Resurrection* and *Regeneration*, and the beginning of a new era or order."[18]

"Thou shalt not delay to offer the first of thy ripe fruits . . . the firstborn of thy sons shalt thou give unto me [God] . . . on the eighth day thou shalt give it me." Ex. 22:29,30

"Now David was the son of that Ephrathite of Beth-lehem-judah, whose name was Jesse; and he had eight sons. . . ." I Sam. 17:12

Jesus' Transfiguration came "about an eight days after" his first announcement of his coming death. Lu. 9:28

Jesus rose from the dead on "the first day of the week," of necessity the eighth day.

"Eight souls were saved by water. The like figure whereunto even baptism doth also now save us. . . ." I Pet. 3:20,21

"And spared not the old world, but saved Noah the eighth person, a preacher of righteousness. . . ." II Pet. 2:5

TEN

Ten "is one of the perfect numbers, and signifies *the perfection of Divine order. . . .*"[19]

Ten "symbolizes harmony and completeness. It is the number of the fundamental commandments."[20]

"The number Ten was, we can hardly doubt, itself significant to Moses and the Israelites. The received symbol, then and at all times, of completeness, it taught the people that the Law of Jehovah was perfect (Ps. xix. 7)."[21]

"And concerning the tithe of the herd, or of the flock . . . the tenth shall be holy unto the Lord." Lev. 27:32

"And the Lord spake unto you out of the midst of the fire: ye heard the voice of the words, but saw no similitude. . . . And he declared unto you his covenant, which he commanded you to perform, even ten commandments; and he wrote them upon two tables of stone." Deut. 4:12,13

"I will sing a new song unto thee, O God: upon a psaltery and an instrument of ten strings will I sing praises unto thee." Ps. 144:9

"Yet in it shall be a tenth [a remnant], and it shall return. . . ." Is. 6:13

"Ye shall have tribulation ten days: be thou faithful unto death, and I will give thee a crown of life." Rev. 2:10

TWELVE

"Twelve is a perfect number, signifying *perfection of government,* or of *governmental perfection.* It is found as a multiple in all that has to do with *rule.*"[22]

"'*Four* is the number which is the symbol of the world, *three* that of God. *Twelve,* therefore, is the signature of the covenant people among whom God dwells.'"[23]

"Now the sons of Jacob were twelve." Gen. 35:22

"All these are the twelve tribes of Israel. . . ." Gen. 49:28

"[Elijah] found Elisha . . . who was plowing with twelve yoke of oxen before him, and he with the twelfth: and Elijah passed by him, and cast his mantle upon him." I Ki. 19:19

Jesus came to the Temple "when he was twelve years old." Lu. 2:42

"And when it was day, he called unto him his disciples: and of them he chose twelve, whom also he named apostles. . . ." Lu. 6:13

"Thinkest thou that I cannot now pray to my Father, and he shall presently give me more than twelve legions of angels?" Mt. 26:53

The city, New Jerusalem, had "twelve gates." Rev. 21:12

FORTY	SEVENTY	OTHER MULTIPLES

Forty has long been universally recognized as an important number, both on account of the frequency of its occurrence, and the uniformity of its association with a period of *probation, trial, and chastisement....*[24]

Forty is the multiple of five times eight, (or four times ten.)

"Seventy is another combination of two of the perfect numbers, *seven* and *ten....* Hence 7 x 10 signifies *perfect* spiritual order carried out with all spiritual power and significance. Both *spirit* and *order* are greatly emphasised."[25]

"*Seventy* is *ten* multiplied by *seven*, the human moulded by the Divine."[26]

Multiples made up of combinations of the foregoing numbers conveyed the same basic meanings.

These combinations designated enlargement, fullness, and intensification.

"*Twelve* is the number of the tribes, and appropriate to *the Church:* 3 by 4: 3, the *Divine* number, multiplied by 4, the number for *world-wide extension.* 12 by 12 implies *fixity and completeness,* which is taken a thousand-fold in 144,000."[27]

"And Moses was in the mount forty days and forty nights." Ex. 24:18

"The Lord thy God led thee these forty years in the wilderness to humble thee, and to prove thee...." Deut. 8:2

"The Philistine [Goliath] drew near morning and evening, and presented himself forty days." I Sam. 17:16

"He [Elijah] arose, and did eat and drink, and went in the strength of that meat forty days and forty nights unto Horeb the mount of God." I Ki. 19:8

"He [Jesus] was there in the wilderness forty days, tempted by Satan...." Mk. 1:13

"To whom also he [Jesus] shewed himself alive after his passion by many infallible proofs, being seen of them forty days...." Acts 1:3

"All the souls of the house of Jacob, which came into Egypt, were threescore and ten." Gen. 46:27

To Moses: "Gather unto me seventy men of the elders of Israel...." Num. 11:16

"After seventy years be accomplished at Babylon I [God] will ... perform my good word toward you, in causing you to return to this place." Jer. 29:10

"The Lord appointed other seventy also, and sent them two and two before his face...." Lu. 10:1

"Seventy weeks are determined upon thy people and upon thy holy city, to finish the transgression ... and to make reconciliation for iniquity, and to bring in everlasting righteousness, and to seal up the vision and prophecy, and to anoint the most Holy." Dan. 9:24

"The chariots of God are twenty thousand, even thousands of angels...." Ps. 68:17

"He hath remembered his covenant for ever, the word which he commanded to a thousand generations." Ps. 105:8

"Lord, how oft shall my brother sin against me, and I forgive him? ... Jesus saith unto him.... Until seventy times seven." Mt. 18:21,22

"I [John] heard the voice of many angels round about the throne and the beasts and the elders: and the number of them was ten thousand times ten thousand, and thousands of thousands; Saying ... Worthy is the Lamb ... to receive ... honour...." Rev. 5:11,12

"I heard the number of them which were sealed: and there were sealed an hundred and forty and four thousand of all the tribes of the children of Israel." Rev. 7:4

"OUT OF EGYPT HAVE I CALLED MY SON"

Egypt, the dominant ancient civilization of the Nile Valley, periodically played a part in Israel's history. The early Hebrew patriarchs went into Egypt for various reasons—famine drove them down or they went to seek refuge or help. But when they or their posterity remained too long it became a place of bondage, interfering with their national growth and Messianic mission. As a result of the slavery Israel eventually suffered under the Pharaohs, Egypt came to typify to the Hebrews a state of bondage and oppression.

There are a number of historical instances which show a coming out of Egypt or the hope of doing so. These Scriptural incidents, made applicable to our present day experience, illustrate that whatever holds the human spirit in bondage and retards spiritual growth, whether it be the fleshpots of Egypt or its rigors, is, figuratively speaking, an Egypt from which God calls us out that we may serve Him.

> "Woe to them that go down to Egypt for help; and stay on horses, and trust in chariots, because they are many; and in horsemen, because they are very strong; but they look not unto the Holy One of Israel, neither seek the Lord! ... Now the Egyptians are men, and not God; and their horses flesh, and not spirit." Is. 31:1,3

Scriptural Descriptions of Egypt

"The Egyptians made ... Israel to serve with rigour." Ex. 1:13

"The oppression wherewith the Egyptians oppress" Ex. 3:9

"The house of bondage" Ex. 13:3

"The flesh pots [of Egypt]" Ex. 16:3

"The Egyptians shall help in vain, and to no purpose ... Their strength is to sit still." Is. 30:7

"The land of Egypt ... the iron furnace" Jer. 11:4

"Pharaoh king of Egypt is but a noise. ..." Jer. 46:17

"Egypt is like a very fair heifer, but destruction cometh. ..." Jer. 46:20

"The great dragon that lieth in the midst of his rivers" Ezek. 29:3

"A staff of reed to the house of Israel" Ezek. 29:6

(A type of spiritual wickedness [Rev. 11:8])

ABRAHAM in Egypt

"There was a famine in the land: and Abram went down into Egypt to sojourn there. ..."

"He said unto Sarai his wife ... thou art a fair woman ... Say, I pray thee, thou art my sister: that it may be well with me for thy sake. ...

"Pharaoh called Abram ... Why saidest thou, She is my sister? so I might have taken her to me to wife ... And Pharaoh ... sent him away. ...

"And Abram went up out of Egypt, he, and his wife, and all that he had. ..." Gen. 12:10-13:1

JOSEPH in Egypt

"They [his brethren] ... sold Joseph. ... And the Midianites sold him into Egypt unto Potiphar. ..." Gen. 37:28,36

Joseph said to his brethren: "God sent me before you to preserve you a posterity. ... and he hath made me a father to Pharaoh ... and a ruler throughout all the land of Egypt." Gen. 45:7,8

"By faith Joseph, when he died, made mention of the departing of the children of Israel; and gave commandment concerning his bones [God will surely visit you, and ye shall carry up my bones from hence]." Heb. 11:22; Gen. 50:25

JACOB (ISRAEL)
in Egypt

"Thus saith thy son Joseph, God hath made me lord of all Egypt: come down unto me...." Gen. 45:9

"God spake unto Israel [Jacob] ... fear not to go down into Egypt; for I will there make of thee a great nation: I will go down with thee into Egypt; and I will also surely bring thee up again. . . ."

"And Jacob rose up from Beer-sheba. . . . and came into Egypt, Jacob, and all his seed with him." Gen. 46:2-6

To his son Joseph, Jacob said, "Bury me not, I pray thee, in Egypt: But I will lie with my fathers, and thou shalt carry me out of Egypt...." Gen. 47: 29,30

MOSES
in Egypt

"By faith Moses, when he was come to years, refused to be called the son of Pharaoh's daughter; Choosing rather to suffer affliction with the people of God, than to enjoy the pleasures of sin for a season; Esteeming the reproach of Christ greater riches than the treasures in Egypt...." Heb. 11: 24-26

"The Lord said, I have surely seen the affliction of my people which are in Egypt.... I will send thee unto Pharaoh, that thou mayest bring forth my people ... out of Eygpt." Ex. 3:7,10

"Thou shalt say unto Pharaoh, Thus saith the Lord, Israel is my son, even my firstborn.... Let my son go, that he may serve me...." Ex. 4:22,23

ISRAELITES
in Egypt

"Wherefore say unto the children of Israel, I am the Lord, and I will bring you out from under the burdens of the Egyptians, and I will rid you out of their bondage, and I will redeem you with a stretched out arm...." Ex. 6:6

"Against all the gods of Egypt I will execute judgment: I am the Lord." Ex. 12:12

"It came to pass at the end of the four hundred and thirty years ... that all the hosts of the Lord went out from the land of Egypt." Ex. 12:41

At the Red Sea Moses said, "The Egyptians whom ye have seen to day, ye shall see them again no more for ever." Ex. 14:13

"When Israel was a child, then I loved him, and called my son out of Egypt." Hos. 11:1

A REMNANT
in Egypt

Jeremiah said, "Now therefore hear the word of the Lord, ye remnant of Judah.... If ye wholly set your faces to enter into Egypt, and go to sojourn there;

"Then it shall come to pass, that the sword, which ye feared, shall overtake you there in the land of Egypt, and the famine, whereof ye were afraid, shall follow close after you there in Egypt; and there ye shall die. . . .

"The Lord hath said . . . O ye remnant of Judah; Go ye not into Egypt: know certainly that I have admonished you this day." Jer. 42:15, 16,19

"None of the remnant of Judah ... shall return but such as shall escape.

"Then all the men ... answered Jeremiah, saying, As for the word that thou hast spoken unto us in the name of the Lord, we will not hearken unto thee." Jer. 44:14-16

BABE JESUS
in Egypt

At the angel's bidding Joseph "took the young child and his mother by night, and departed into Egypt: And was there until the death of Herod: that it might be fulfilled which was spoken of the Lord by the prophet, saying, Out of Egypt have I called my son." Mt. 2:14,15

At the angel's bidding Joseph "arose, and took the young child and his mother, and came into the land of Israel." Mt. 2:21

Truly, "out of Egypt have I called my son" applies to every Christian, for with the coming of Jesus Christ and his dispensation of grace men were in a true sense set free from bondage forever.

A LESSON FROM OLD TESTAMENT HISTORY

Read chart by column

Each period of Old Testament history shows Israel's progressive awakening to God's love and providential care.

Great characters distinguished these periods and displayed spiritual insight and qualities that were essential to Israel's salvation.

Encouraging the fuller expression within ourselves of these same desirable qualities, we discover that in "every one of us," is a Jacob, a Moses, a David, a Daniel.

Let us ask ourselves, "Am I awakening to these qualities?"

THE PROMISE TO MANKIND	THE FLOOD AND THE ARK	THE ABRAHAMIC COVENANT	A NEW NAME	PRESERVATION IN EGYPT	THE EXODUS, THE LAW, THE WANDERING
At the moment when Eve awoke to the nature of the serpent, mankind was given the first promise of the Redeemer (the seed of the woman which was to bruise the serpent's head). "I will put enmity between thee and the woman, and between thy seed and her seed: it shall bruise thy head, and thou shalt bruise his heel." Gen. 3:15 "To Seth [Adam's third son] . . . there was born a son; and he called his name Enos: then began men to call upon the name of the Lord." Gen. 4:26	Above the flood of iniquity the just find grace, and protection. "Noah found grace in the eyes of the Lord. . . . Noah was a just man and perfect in his generations, and Noah walked with God. . . . "With thee will I establish my covenant; and thou shalt come into the ark. . . ." Gen. 6:8,9,18	God makes an everlasting covenant with His obedient servant whom He has called, a covenant conditioned only by loyalty and obedience. "I am the Almighty God; walk before me, and be thou [Abram] perfect. And I will make my covenant between me and thee, and will multiply thee exceedingly." Gen. 17:1,2	Following a moral and spiritual wrestling, comes the transforming power of God; comes also the increase of "the seed." "Thy name shall not be called any more Jacob, but Israel shall be thy name: . . . I am God Almighty: be fruitful and multiply; a nation and a company of nations shall be of thee. . . ." Gen. 35:10,11	Preservation is assured to the Children of Israel, even in a strange land. "God sent me [Joseph] before you to preserve you a posterity in the earth, and to save your lives by a great deliverance." Gen. 45:7	There is "a going out" from conditions of bondage and oppression through God's power and mercy, a testing and a discipline under His guiding presence and law. "By a prophet the Lord brought Israel out of Egypt, and by a prophet was he preserved." Ho. 12:13 "God led thee these forty years in the wilderness, to humble thee, and to prove thee . . . whether thou wouldest keep his commandments, or no." Deut. 8:2
Adam	**Noah**	**Abraham**	**Jacob (Israel)**	**Joseph**	**Moses**
Our true redemption begins in our awakening and in our turning to God and His Christ, "the last Adam [who] was made a quickening spirit."	The Noah in us awakes, through righteousness, to know deliverance, safety, and grace.	The Abraham in us, chosen of God, awakes, through faith and obedience, to know a full trust in God's promises.	The Jacob in us awakes, through purified desires, to know a spiritual nature and a true birthright.	The Joseph in us awakes, through love and faithful service, to know honor and prosperity and to be a blessing to our brethren.	The Moses in us, called of God, awakes, through meekness and communion, to know an omnipotent God and His everpresent law.
awakening, turning	*righteousness*	*faith, obedience*	*purified desires*	*love, service*	*meekness, communion*

542

THE PROMISED LAND	DELIVERANCE UNDER JUDGES	UNITED KINGDOM	BUILDING OF TEMPLE	DIVISION OF KINGDOM	THE EXILE (CAPTIVITY)	THE RESTORATION AND REBUILDING OF THE TEMPLE	REBUILDING OF JERUSALEM
Israel, relying on its God, courageously battles against heathen nations and takes possession of its heritage.	Serving heathen gods results in Israel's repeated servitude to heathen nations, and these harsh experiences teach Israel to turn to its God for deliverance.	A royal line and a righteous government emerge when Israel foregoes wilful lawlessness and accepts a godly rule. Thus a national unity is furthered.	With righteous government a centralized religious worship is established. Praise and gratitude build the Temple in Jerusalem.	Failure to adhere to monotheism divides the kingdom into two kingdoms, Israel and Judah. Israel becomes apostate, suffers captivity; Judah, backsliding, has periods of reformation under godly kings and prophets, which prolong for a time its national life.	Judah's continued backsliding and disobedience lead to captivity in Babylon. There in mourning and chastisement rebellious Judah is cleansed of her persistent idolatry to attain a purer monotheism. Ezekiel and Daniel exemplify the hope of the nation.	Under Zerubbabel's leadership a willing remnant is graciously restored to its own land, there to rebuild their Temple and restore their distinctive monotheistic worship. Ezra the priest, bringing a second remnant to refresh and rekindle hope, demands and enforces a strict observance of the Law and the covenant.	The restoration continues. Under Nehemiah's zealous selfless leadership Judah is encouraged to rebuild Jerusalem's walls. The written Law is given to all the people, and succeeding centuries witness to an uncompromising monotheism, all of which further prepares the way for the coming of the Messiah.
"Joshua took the whole land, according to all that the Lord said unto Moses; and Joshua gave it for an inheritance unto Israel according to their divisions by their tribes. And the land rested from war." Josh. 11:23	"They forsook the Lord God of their fathers .. and followed other gods, of the gods of the people that were round about them. ... And the anger of the Lord was hot against Israel, and he delivered them into the hands of spoilers. ... "Nevertheless the Lord raised up judges, which delivered them out of the hand of those that spoiled them." Ju. 2:12,14,16	"He [God] chose David ... his servant, and took him from the sheepfolds. ... he brought him to feed Jacob his people, and Israel his inheritance. So he [David] fed them according to the integrity of his heart; and guided them by the skilfulness of his hands." Ps 78:70-72	"I [Solomon] ... have built an house for the name of the Lord God of Israel. And I have set there a place for the ark, wherein is the covenant of the Lord, which he made with our fathers. ..." I Ki. 8:20,21	"The Lord God of their fathers sent to them by his messengers, rising up betimes. ... But they mocked the messengers of God, and despised his words, and misused his prophets, until the wrath of the Lord arose against his people, till there was no remedy." II Chron. 36:15,16	"Like as I pleaded with your fathers in the wilderness of the land of Egypt, so will I plead with you, saith the Lord God. And I will cause you to pass under the rod, and I will bring you into the bond of the covenant. ..." Ezek. 20:36,37	"Who is there among you of all his people? his God be with him, and let him go up to Jerusalem, which is in Judah, and build the house of the Lord God of Israel. ..." Ezra 1:3	"I [Nehemiah] told them of the hand of my God which was good upon me ... And they said, Let us rise up and build. So they strengthened their hands for this good work." Neh. 2:18
Joshua	Gideon and Samuel	David	Solomon	Godly Kings, Prophets	Ezekiel, Daniel	Zerubbabel, Ezra	Nehemiah
The Joshua in us awakes, through strength and unfaltering courage, to take possession of our spiritual heritage.	The Gideon and Samuel in us awake, through reliance on God and through purity of motive, to know victory and deliverance in times of crises.	The David in us, anointed of God, awakes, through humility and love of righteousness, to sing God's praises and to know dominion and joy.	The Solomon is us awakes, through right desire and consecration, to know wisdom, peace, and prosperity. (But watchfulness is needed to guard against temptations of materialism and self-indulgence.)	The moral nobility in us awakes, through love of good and reformation, to know the regenerative forces of purer worship. The prophet in us, through spiritual insight and vision, arises to rebuke, correct, enlighten, and comfort.	The Ezekiel and Daniel in us is awake, through watchfulness, unshakable trust, and wisdom, to endure trials unflinchingly, to prove immunity from evil, and to see the power of God acknowledged.	The Zerubbabel and Ezra in us awake, through consecration and single-mindedness, to implement our spiritual ideals.	The Nehemiah in us awakes, through integrity and righteous zeal, to build the walls of our spiritual Zion so strongly they cannot be breached.
strength, courage	*reliance, purity*	*humility, righteousness*	*right desire, wisdom*	*goodness, inspiration*	*watchfulness, wisdom*	*willingness and consecration*	*integrity, zeal*

TEN ASCENDING STEPS IN THE LIFE OF JESUS AND OF THE CHRISTIAN

Read chart column by column

"from glory unto glory"

ASCENSION
RESURRECTION
CRUCIFIXION
TRANSFIGURATION
MINISTRY
TEMPTATION
BAPTISM
AT TWELVE
INCARNATION
ANNUNCIATION

ANNUNCIATION

These same ascending steps must be taken in some way in our own spiritual experience if we would follow Jesus Christ in his ascending path of glory.

Note the appropriation: Ye, your, you, thyself; he, his, him, himself; man; every one; who, whom, whomsoever; we, our, us;

JESUS

The angel Gabriel said to Mary: "The Holy Ghost shall come upon thee, and the power of the Highest shall overshadow thee: therefore also that holy thing which shall be born of thee shall be called the Son of God." Lu. 1:35

For "us"

"Verily, verily, I say unto *thee*, Except a *man* be born again, *be* cannot see the kingdom of God. . . . Except a *man* be born of water and of the Spirit, *be* cannot enter into the kingdom of God. That which is born of the flesh is flesh; and that which is born of the Spirit is spirit." Jn. 3:3,5,6

INCARNATION

JESUS

"The Word was made flesh, and dwelt among us, (and we beheld his glory, the glory as of the only begotten of the Father,) full of grace and truth." Jn. 1:14

"God . . . Hath . . . spoken unto us by his Son. . . . being the brightness of his glory, and the express image of his person. . . ." Heb. 1:1-3

For "us"

"And of his fulness have all *we* received, and grace for grace." Jn. 1:16

"For in this *we* groan, earnestly desiring to be clothed upon with *our* house which is from heaven. . . that mortality might be swallowed up of life." II Cor. 5:2,4

"Therefore if *any man* be in Christ, *be* is a new creature: old things are passed away; behold, all things are become new." II Cor. 5:17

AT TWELVE

JESUS

Joseph and Mary "found him in the temple, sitting in the midst of the doctors, both hearing them, and asking them questions. And all that heard him were astonished at his understanding and answers." Lu. 2:46,47

Jesus asked, "Wist ye not that I must be about my Father's business?" Lu. 2:49

Eighteen Silent Years

"And Jesus increased in wisdom and stature, and in favour with God and man." Lu. 2:52

For "us"

"Son, go work to day in my vineyard." Mt. 21:28

Eighteen Silent Years

"Study to shew *thyself* approved unto God, a workman that needeth not to be ashamed, rightly dividing the word of truth." II Tim. 2:15

BAPTISM

JESUS

"And Jesus, when he was baptized, went up straightway out of the water: and, lo, the heavens were opened unto him, and he saw the Spirit of God descending like a dove, and lighting upon him: And lo a voice from heaven, saying, This is my beloved Son, in whom I am well pleased." Mt. 3:16,17

For "us"

"Are *ye* able . . . to be baptized with the baptism that I am baptized with?" Mt. 20:22

"He [Christ] shall baptize *you* with the Holy Ghost and with fire." Lu. 3:16

"For by one Spirit are *we* all baptized into one body. . . ." I Cor. 12:13

"For *ye* are all the children of God by faith in Christ Jesus. For as many of *you* as have been baptized into Christ have put on Christ." Gal. 3:26,27

TEMPTATION

JESUS

Jesus said, "Get thee behind me, Satan: for it is written, Thou shalt worship the Lord thy God, and him only shalt thou serve." Lu. 4:8

"For in that he himself hath suffered being tempted, he is able to succour them that are tempted." Heb. 2:18

Jesus "was in all points tempted like as we are, yet without sin." Heb. 4:15

For "us"

"There hath no temptation taken *you* but such as is common to man: but God is faithful, who will not suffer *you* to be tempted above that *ye* are able; but will with the temptation also make a way to escape, that *ye* may be able to bear it." I Cor. 10:13

"Blessed is the *man* that endureth temptation: for when *be* is tried, *be* shall receive the crown of life, which the Lord hath promised to *them* that love him." Ja. 1:12

"Resist the devil, and he will flee from *you*. Draw nigh to God, and he will draw nigh to *you*." Ja. 4:7,8

MINISTRY

JESUS

"Jesus went about all the cities and villages, teaching in their synagogues, and preaching the gospel of the kingdom, and healing every sickness and every disease among the people." Mt. 9:35

"For even the Son of man came not to be ministered unto, but to minister, and to give his life a ransom for many." Mk. 10:45

For "us"

"Heal the sick, cleanse the lepers, raise the dead, cast out devils: freely ye have received, freely give." Mt. 10:8

"He that believeth on me, the works that I do shall he do also; and greater works than these shall be do; because I go unto my Father." Jn. 14:12

"Go ye into all the world, and preach the gospel to every creature." Mk. 16:15

TRANSFIGURATION

JESUS

"Jesus taketh Peter, James, and John his brother, and bringeth them up into an high mountain apart, And was transfigured before them: and his face did shine as the sun, and his raiment was white as the light." Mt. 17:1,2

"And as he prayed, the fashion of his countenance was altered, and his raiment was white and glistering." Lu. 9:29

For "us"

"Be not conformed to this world: but be ye transformed by the renewing of your mind...." Rom. 12:2

"But we all, with open face beholding as in a glass the glory of the Lord, are changed into the same image from glory to glory, even as by the Spirit of the Lord." II Cor. 3:18

"God, who commanded the light to shine out of darkness, hath shined in our hearts, to give the light of the knowledge of the glory of God in the face of Jesus Christ." II Cor. 4:6

CRUCIFIXION

JESUS

"The Son of man shall be betrayed into the hands of men: And they shall kill him...." Mt. 17:22,23

"And they took Jesus, and led him away. And he bearing his cross went forth into a place called the place of a skull, which is called in the Hebrew Golgotha: Where they crucified him, and two other with him, on either side one, and Jesus in the midst." Jn. 19:16-18

For "us"

"If any man will come after me, let him deny himself, and take up his cross daily, and follow me. For whosoever will save his life shall lose it: but whosoever will lose his life for my sake, the same shall save it." Lu. 9:23,24

"Our old man is crucified with him, that the body of sin might be destroyed, that henceforth we should not serve sin." Rom. 6:6

"For the preaching of the cross is to them that perish foolishness; but unto us which are saved it is the power of God." I Cor. 1:18

RESURRECTION

JESUS

"The angel of the Lord descended from heaven ... and rolled back the stone from the door, and ... said unto the women.... He is risen, as he said." Mt. 28:2,5,6

"Whom God hath raised up, having loosed the pains of death: because it was not possible that he should be holden of it." Acts 2:24

"Him God raised up the third day, and shewed him openly...." Acts 10:40

For "us"

Jesus said, "I am the resurrection, and the life: be that believeth in me, though be were dead, yet shall he live: And whosoever liveth and believeth in me shall never die." Jn. 11:25,26

"If the Spirit of him that raised up Jesus from the dead dwell in you, he that raised up Christ from the dead shall also quicken your mortal bodies by his Spirit that dwelleth in you." Rom 8:11

"God hath both raised up the Lord, and will also raise up us by his own power." I Cor. 6:14

ASCENSION

JESUS

"Go to my brethren, and say unto them, I ascend unto my Father, and your Father; and to my God, and your God." Jn. 20:17

"And he led them out as far as to Bethany, and he lifted up his hands, and blessed them. And it came to pass, while he blessed them, he was parted from them, and carried up into heaven." Lu. 24:50,51

"He was received up into heaven, and sat on the right hand of God." Mk. 16:19

For "us"

"Unto every one of us is given grace according to the measure of the gift of Christ. Wherefore he saith, When he ascended up on high, he led captivity captive, and gave gifts unto men." Eph. 4:7,8

"Giving thanks unto the Father, which hath made us meet to be partakers of the inheritance of the saints in light: Who hath delivered us from the power of darkness, and hath translated us into the kingdom of his dear Son." Col. 1:12,13

"If ye then be risen with Christ, seek those things which are above, where Christ sitteth on the right hand of God.... When Christ, who is our life, shall appear, then shall ye also appear with him in glory." Col. 3:1,4

JESUS

"To him that overcometh will I grant to sit with me in my throne, even as I also overcame, and am set down with my Father in his throne." Rev. 3:21

SOME LESSONS FROM JESUS' EARLY LIFE

Often we are inclined to regard the events in the early life of Jesus as relative only to him whereas these events, including their very order, have a practical application for us today. Figuratively speaking, we too pay a tax, make a journey to our Bethlehem, declare our lineage. . . .

Read chart column by column

A TAX	BETHLEHEM	THE LINEAGE	THE BIRTH	THE MANGER	THE PRESENTATION IN THE TEMPLE	JESUS IN TEMPLE AT AGE OF TWELVE	PREPARATORY YEARS
"There went out a decree from Caesar Augustus, that all the world should be taxed. . . " "And all went to be taxed, every one into his own city." Lu. 2:1,3	Joseph went "into Judaea, unto the city of David, which is called Bethlehem. . . . To be taxed with Mary his espoused wife, being great with child." Lu. 2:4,5	"Joseph also went up . . . (because he was of the house and lineage of David)." Lu. 2:4	"And she [Mary] brought forth her firstborn son. . . ." Lu. 2:7	Mary "laid him in a manger; because there was no room for them in the inn." Lu. 2:7	"And when the days of her purification according to the law of Moses were accomplished, they brought him to Jerusalem, to present him to the Lord. . . ." Lu. 2:22 "And the child grew, and waxed strong in spirit, filled with wisdom: and the grace of God was upon him." Lu. 2:40	Mary and Joseph "found him in the temple, sitting in the midst of the doctors, both hearing them, and asking them questions." Jesus asked, "How is it that ye sought me? wist ye not that I must be about my Father's business?" Lu. 2:46,49 (At thirteen, a Jewish boy became a servant of the Law)	"And he went down with them, and came to Nazareth, and was subject unto them. . . ." "And Jesus increased in wisdom and stature, and in favour with God and man." Lu. 2:51,52 "And Jesus himself began to be about thirty years of age. . . ." Lu. 3:23 (At thirty, under Jewish law, a man was considered mature)
Figuratively speaking—	*Figuratively speaking—*	*Figuratively speaking—*	*Figuratively speaking—*	*Figuratively speaking—*	*Figuratively speaking—*	*Figuratively speaking—*	*Figuratively speaking—*
As under the government of our day we pay a price for our human rights and freedom, so every man must be willing to pay the exaction required to obtain the rights and privileges of citizenship in the kingdom of heaven.	We must make this journey to our Bethlehem, must at some time journey toward the hallowed experience wherein the Christ child is born to individual consciousness.	"Every one of us" is of the lineage of David; the Bible records: "Now to Abraham and his seed were the promises made. He saith not, And to seeds, as of many; but as of one, And to thy seed, which is Christ" (Gal. 3:16). Thus all those of "spiritual Israel" are the lawful inheritors of this promise.	The birth of the Christ child in our individual experience gives him pre-eminence in our hearts, makes him our "first-born."	For this babe we must humbly make room—a quiet, unobtrusive resting place wherein also abide the gentle, inarticulate, submissively loving service bearers, and wherein for the moment is privacy and protection from the eyes of the world.	We must present this Christ child of our beholding before the Lord. We must come to the house of God so cleansed and purified that he may be lawfully presented and openly acknowledged, sanctified, and dedicated. This Christ child in our hearts, pre-eminent, first-born, openly acknowledged and blessed, must grow, wax strong in spirit, be filled with wisdom, and have the grace of God upon	We, as servants of God's law, must intelligently and constructively question the educational systems of our day to determine what measures up to true Christianity. We must seek and choose to be about our "Father's business."	"Every one of us" must learn obedience, must grow in practical application of Christian principles, from immaturity ("babes in Christ") to maturity (full "stature"). We must learn patience and "continuance in well-doing" through silent days and years, that we may minister not only to ourselves but to others. Thus step by step there lies before every one of us the unbounded opportunity of service in our Father's kingdom.

AN EXAMPLE OF ENDURING TRUST

Paul's Voyage to Rome
(Acts 27:1-28:16)

This is more than an arduous historical journey; it is a heartening account of endurance, trust, and preservation under great physical hardship. It affords an example of patient confidence in the face of untoward conditions of nature and of victory over the deterring forces of the human mind.

Note the positives (bold face) and the negatives (italics).

Read chart upward line by line

Theme (positives)	Scripture (Progress)	Negatives
Progress	"And so we went toward Rome."	
Succor, service	Here all were received with kindness. Paul's life preserved from viper's bite. He healed Publius and others.	
A haven	"And so it came to pass, that they [276 souls] escaped all safe to land [Melita]."	
Individual effort	The centurion commanded "they which could swim . . . get to land: And the rest . . . on broken pieces of the ship."	
Protection	"The soldiers' counsel was to kill the prisoners. . . . But the centurion . . . kept them from their purpose. . . ."	Break up
	"The forepart stuck fast . . . remained unmoveable . . . the hinder part was broken with the violence of the waves."	
	"And falling into a place where two seas met, they ran the ship aground. . . ."	
Courage	"When they had taken up the anchors, they committed themselves unto the sea . . . and made toward shore."	
Hope	"When it was day . . . they discovered a certain creek . . . into . . . which they were minded . . . to thrust in the ship."	
An unburdening	"When they had eaten enough, they lightened the ship, and cast out the wheat into the sea."	
Gratitude, cheer	"He took bread, and gave thanks to God . . . Then were they all of good cheer, and they also took some meat."	
A strengthening	"Paul besought them all to take meat . . . This day is the fourteenth day that ye have . . . taken nothing."	
A sacrificing	"Then the soldiers cut off the ropes of the [small] boat, and let her fall off."	
Justice	Paul said to the centurion and the soldiers, "Except these abide in the ship, ye cannot be saved."	
	"The shipmen were about to flee [in small boat] . . . under colour as though they would have cast anchors. . . ."	Deceit, self-interest
Wisdom, patience	"Fearing lest we should have fallen upon rocks, they cast four anchors . . . and wished for the day."	
Vigilance	They "sounded . . . twenty fathoms . . . they sounded again and found it fifteen fathoms."	
Crisis	"When the fourteenth night was come . . . about midnight the shipmen deemed that they drew near to some country. . . ."	
Grace, expectancy of safety	"God hath given thee all them that sail with thee. . . . Howbeit we must be cast upon a certain island."	
Divine promise	"For there stood by me this night the angel of God. . . . Saying, Fear not, Paul; thou must be brought before Caesar. . . ."	
Comfort	"Now I exhort you to be of good cheer: for there shall be no loss of any man's life among you, but of the ship."	
	Paul said, "Sirs, ye should have hearkened unto me, and not to have gained this harm and loss."	
	When neither sun nor stars in many days appeared . . . all hope that we should be saved was then taken away."	Discouragement, despair
	"The next day they lightened the ship; And the third day we cast out with our own hands the tackling. . . ."	Toil, depletion
	"Fearing . . . the quicksands, [they] strake sail, and so were driven . . . exceedingly tossed with a tempest. . . ."	Fear, peril, confusion
	"Running under a certain island . . . they used helps, undergirding the ship. . . ."	Fatiguing toil
	"There arose . . . a tempestuous wind . . . when the ship . . . could not bear up into the wind, we let her drive."	Violent tumult, loss of control
	"When the south wind blew softly, supposing that they had obtained their purpose . . . they sailed close by Crete."	Deceptive appearances, foolish confidence
	"Because the haven was not commodious to winter in, the more part advised to depart . . . to Phenice. . . ."	Human will, longing for ease
	"Nevertheless the centurion believed the master . . . of the ship, more than those things . . . spoken by Paul."	Heedlessness, dull ears
Foresight	Paul admonished, "This voyage will be with hurt . . . not only of the lading and ship, but also of our lives."	Procrastination, self-will
	We "came unto . . . The fair havens. . . . when much time was spent, and . . . sailing . . . now dangerous" they would leave	
	"When we had sailed slowly many days . . . the wind not suffering us, we sailed under Crete . . . hardly passing it. . . ."	Hindrance
Launching	"We sailed under Cyprus . . . winds were contrary." At Myra . . . they changed ships for Italy.	
	"We launched [from Caesarea] . . . touched at Sidon. . . . Julius . . . gave [Paul] liberty to go unto his friends. . . ."	*(Deterring forces of the human mind)*

547

Place and Time
As Dimensions of Thought

The Biblical narratives in many instances include geographic localities as part of the record. Because of the character of the events which took place in these environs, the place names themselves suggest dimensions of thought beyond the literal—a breadth of vision, a depth of insight, a spiritual altitude of understanding.

BETH-EL ("house of God"). Here Jacob saw the vision of a ladder whose top reached to heaven, and "the angels of God ascending and descending on it" (Gen. 28:12,19).

PENIEL ("face of God"). Here Jacob's name was changed to Israel (Gen. 32:24-30).

HOREB ("desert"). On this mount Moses saw the burning bush, heard God's voice, and received His law (Ex. 3; 19:20-20:17). Here Elijah heard the still small voice (I Ki. 19:8-12).

GETHSEMANE ("oil press"). In the garden of Gethsemane Jesus yielded completely to the Father's will (Mt. 26:36-44).

Conversely, certain names have become negative representations of moral darkness, bondage, or sin.

BABEL ("confusion"). Here occurred the confounding of tongues (Gen. 11:1-9).

SODOM ("to scorn") and GOMORRAH ("to be nigh"). Destroyed by brimstone and fire; proverbial symbols of great wickedness (Gen. 19; Rev. 11:8).

Frequently included in the narratives are the times of events. These time relationships also often suggest dimensions beyond the literal meaning of hours or days and imply periods of readiness, comprehension, endurance, fullness.

DAY—"And the evening and the morning were the first *day*" (Gen. 1:5). Jesus continued "all night in prayer to God. And when it was *day* . . . he chose twelve [apostles]" (Lu. 6:12,13). "The third *day* I shall be perfected" (Lu. 13:32).

MORNING—Moses was commanded, "Be ready in the *morning,* and come up in the *morning* unto mount Sinai" (Ex. 34:2). "When the *morning* was now come, Jesus stood on the shore. . . ." (Jn. 21:4).

EVEN—"At *even,* when the sun did set, they brought unto [Jesus] all that were diseased, and them that were possesed with devils" (Mk. 1:32).

HOUR—Jesus prayed, "Father save me from this *hour*: but for this cause came I unto this *hour*" (Jn. 12:27). At the Last Supper Jesus said, "Father, the *hour* is come; glorify thy Son, that thy Son also may glorify thee" (Jn. 17:1).

Conversely, certain time designations have a negative shade of meaning.

NIGHT—"By *night*" Nicodemus came to Jesus (Jn. 3:2). "It was *night*" when Judas left the Passover meal to betray Jesus (Jn. 13:30). The apostles turned to their old vocation of fishing: "That *night* they caught nothing" (Jn. 21:3).

WINTER—"It was *winter*" when the rulers resisted Jesus' claim to Messiahship (Jn. 10:22). "Pray ye that your flight be not in the *winter*. . . ." (Mt. 24:20).

548

THE SPIRITUAL GROWTH OF THE CHRISTIAN

From his rebirth at conversion to the finishing of his course, Paul strove to be a perfect follower of Christ Jesus—to reach the full "stature" of Christ. His life and teachings press the Christian to outgrow spiritual immaturity and to come "of full age."

Of himself Paul said, "When I was a child, I spake as a child, I understood as a child, I thought as a child: but when I became a man, I put away childish things" (I Cor. 13:11).

Of the Christian he said, "The Spirit itself beareth witness with our spirit, that we are the children of God: And if children, then heirs; heirs of God, and joint-heirs with Christ; if so be that we suffer with him, that we may be also glorified together" (Rom. 8:16,17).

Read chart upward line by line

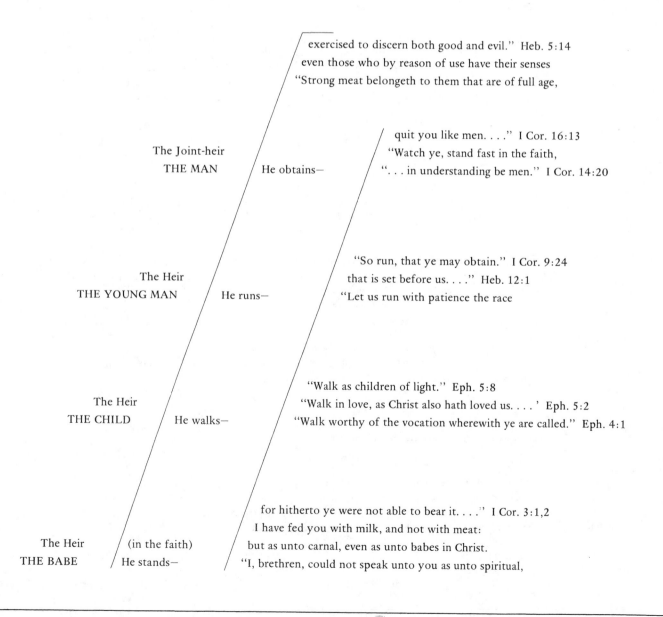

The Joint-heir
THE MAN   He obtains—

exercised to discern both good and evil." Heb. 5:14
even those who by reason of use have their senses
"Strong meat belongeth to them that are of full age,

quit you like men. . . ." I Cor. 16:13
"Watch ye, stand fast in the faith,
". . . in understanding be men." I Cor. 14:20

The Heir
THE YOUNG MAN   He runs—

"So run, that ye may obtain." I Cor. 9:24
that is set before us. . . ." Heb. 12:1
"Let us run with patience the race

The Heir
THE CHILD   He walks—

"Walk as children of light." Eph. 5:8
"Walk in love, as Christ also hath loved us. . . .' Eph. 5:2
"Walk worthy of the vocation wherewith ye are called." Eph. 4:1

The Heir
THE BABE   (in the faith)
            He stands—

for hitherto ye were not able to bear it. . . ." I Cor. 3:1,2
I have fed you with milk, and not with meat:
but as unto carnal, even as unto babes in Christ.
"I, brethren, could not speak unto you as unto spiritual,

AN EXAMPLE OF DELIVERANCE THROUGH PRAYER

Acts 12 records the imprisonment of the Apostle Peter, brought about by the enmity of Herod Agrippa toward the young church. "Prayer was made without ceasing of the church unto God for him," and Peter's liberation was so sudden, so quick, so effectual, that while it was transpiring, he thought it was a vision. His deliverance can be inspirational to anyone who at some time or other faces imprisonment, literally or figuratively, by forces from within or from without.

Read chart upward line by line

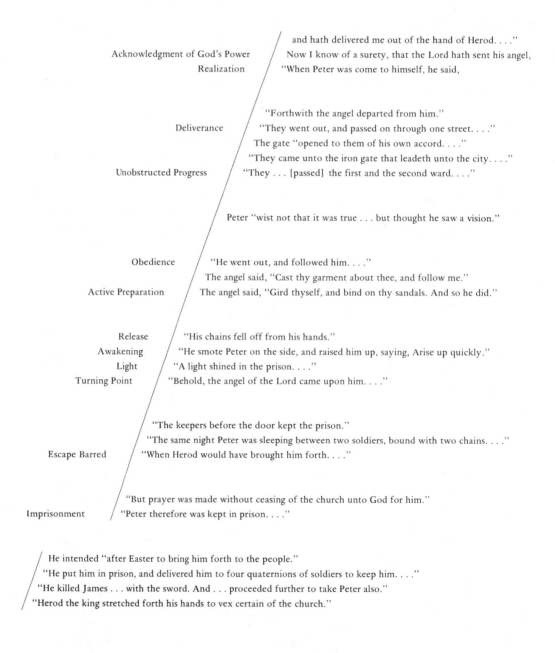

Acknowledgment of God's Power
Realization

   and hath delivered me out of the hand of Herod. . . ."
   Now I know of a surety, that the Lord hath sent his angel,
   "When Peter was come to himself, he said,

Deliverance

   "Forthwith the angel departed from him."
   "They went out, and passed on through one street. . . ."
   The gate "opened to them of his own accord. . . ."

Unobstructed Progress

   "They came unto the iron gate that leadeth unto the city. . . ."
   "They . . . [passed] the first and the second ward. . . ."

Peter "wist not that it was true . . . but thought he saw a vision."

Obedience

   "He went out, and followed him. . . ."
   The angel said, "Cast thy garment about thee, and follow me."

Active Preparation

   The angel said, "Gird thyself, and bind on thy sandals. And so he did."

Release
Awakening
Light
Turning Point

   "His chains fell off from his hands."
   "He smote Peter on the side, and raised him up, saying, Arise up quickly."
   "A light shined in the prison. . . ."
   "Behold, the angel of the Lord came upon him. . . ."

Escape Barred

   "The keepers before the door kept the prison."
   "The same night Peter was sleeping between two soldiers, bound with two chains. . . ."
   "When Herod would have brought him forth. . . ."

Imprisonment

   "But prayer was made without ceasing of the church unto God for him."
   "Peter therefore was kept in prison. . . ."

Evil Intent

   He intended "after Easter to bring him forth to the people."
   "He put him in prison, and delivered him to four quaternions of soldiers to keep him. . . ."
   "He killed James . . . with the sword. And . . . proceeded further to take Peter also."
   "Herod the king stretched forth his hands to vex certain of the church."

THE SPAN FROM GENESIS TO REVELATION

The slow but steady evolving of the divine plan and purpose for mankind's redemption may be clearly traced in the centuries of development of Scriptural history and revelation.

"We give thee thanks, O Lord God Almighty, which art, and wast, and art to come; because thou hast taken to thee thy great power, and hast reigned." Rev. 11:17

Read chart upward line by line

FINAL TRIUMPH OF KINGDOM OF GOD

With the Revelation of Jesus Christ
With Christianity and the Church
With Jesus Christ and his Grace
With Wisdom and Prophecy
With Covenant and Law

THE REVELATION OF JESUS CHRIST GIVEN

With Christianity and the Church
With Jesus Christ and his Grace
With Wisdom and Prophecy
With Covenant and Law

CHRISTIANITY AND THE CHURCH ESTABLISHED

With Jesus Christ and his Grace
With Wisdom and Prophecy
With Covenant and Law

GRACE GIVEN THROUGH JESUS CHRIST

With Prophecy
With Wisdom
With Covenant and Law

PROPHECY DEVELOPED

With Wisdom
With Law
With Covenant

WISDOM EVIDENCED

With Law
With Covenant

THE LAW ADDED

With Covenant

THE ABRAHAMIC COVENANT INSTITUTED

With Israel's beginnings

Notes

Acknowledgment is made of permission to quote from the following translations.

From *THE BIBLE: A New Translation by James Moffatt*. Copyright © 1954 by James Moffatt. By permission of Harper & Row Publishers, Inc.

The New English Bible (Oxford University Press, Cambridge University Press), 1970.

Reprinted with permission of Macmillan Publishing Co., Inc. from *The New Testament in Modern English*, Rev. Edn. by J. B. Phillips. © J. B. Phillips 1958, 1960, 1972.

Richard F. Weymouth, *The New Testament in Modern Speech*, 3rd ed. (Boston: The Pilgrim Press, 1902).

CHAPTER 1. THE BIBLE AND ITS PRESERVATION

[1] E. W. Bullinger, *Number in Scripture*, 5th rev. ed. (London: Eyre and Spottiswoode Limited, 1928), p. 159.

CHAPTER 2. LIFE AND CUSTOMS OF BIBLE TIMES

[1] M. W. Jacobus, E. C. Lane, A. C. Zenos (eds.), *Funk and Wagnalls New Standard Bible Dictionary*, 3rd rev. ed. (Philadelphia: The Blakiston Company, 1936), p. 156.

[2] *Ibid*, p. 304.

[3] *The New Analytical Bible and Dictionary of the Bible*, rev. ed. (Chicago: John A. Dickson Publishing Company, 1950), p. 166. By permission.

[4] Reprinted with permission of Macmillan Publishing Co., Inc. from *Commentary on the Holy Bible* by J. R. Dummelow, Editor, p. 51. Copyright 1908, 1909 by Macmillan Publishing Co., Inc., renewed 1936, 1937 by John R. Dummelow.

[5] William Smith (ed.), *A Dictionary of the Bible* (New York: Fleming H. Revell Company, n.d.), p. 232.

[6] From *Abingdon Bible Commentary*, p. 100. Copyright renewal © 1956 by Abingdon Press. Used by permission.

CHAPTER 3. OLD TESTAMENT HISTORY

[1] W. W. Tarn, *Alexander the Great* (Cambridge: University Press, 1948), p. 147.

CHAPTER 4. GREAT OLD TESTAMENT CHARACTERS

[1] Charles Marston, *The Bible Comes Alive* (London: Eyre and Spottiswoode, 1940), p. 84.

[2] James Hastings (ed.), *Dictionary of the Bible* (New York: Charles Scribner's Sons, 1942), p. 11.

[3] Reprinted with permission of Macmillan Publishing Co., Inc. from *Commentary on the Holy Bible* by J. R. Dummelow, Editor, p. 10. Copyright 1908, 1909 by Macmillan Publishing Co., Inc., renewed 1936, 1937 by John R. Dummelow.

[4] *The New Analytical Bible and Dictionary of the Bible*, rev. ed. (Chicago: John A. Dickson Publishing Company, 1950), p. 61. By permission. (Cited hereafter as *New Analytical Bible*)

[5] Hastings, p. 936.

[6] *Ibid*, p. 185.

[7] Leonard Woolley, *Ur of the Chaldees*, rev. ed. (Harmondsworth, Middlesex: Penguin Books Ltd., 1954), pp. 20-23.

[8] From *Abingdon Bible Commentary*, p. 259. Copyright renewal © 1956 by Abingdon Press. Used by permission.

[9] Dummelow, p. 37.

[10] R. Jamieson, A. R. Fausset, D. Brown (eds.), *A Commentary Critical and Explanatory on the Old and New Testaments*, 2nd ed. (Grand Rapids: Zondervan Publishing House, n.d.), I, 49.

[11] Samuel Fallows (ed.), *The Popular and Critical Bible Encyclopaedia and Scriptural Dictionary* (Chicago: The Howard-Severance Company, 1913), II, 1003.

[12] *New Analytical Bible*, p. 493.

[13] *Ibid*, p. 1063.

[14] Hastings, p. 253.

CHAPTER 5. CORRELATION— OLD TESTAMENT SUBJECTS

[1] *The New Analytical Bible and Dictionary of the Bible*, rev. ed. (Chicago: John A. Dickson Publishing Company, 1950). (Genesis Front Matter). By permission.

[2] *Ibid*, p. 59.

[3] Reprinted with permission of Macmillan Publishing Co., Inc. from *Commentary on the Holy Bible* by J. R. Dummelow, Editor, p. 6. Copyright 1908, 1909 by Macmillan Publishing Co., Inc., renewed 1936, 1937 by John R. Dummelow.

[4] *Ibid*, p. 10.

[5] *Ibid*, p. 739.

[6] Alfred Edersheim, *The Life and Times of Jesus the Messiah*, 8th rev. ed. (New York: Longmans, Green, and Co., 1897), I, 299.

CHAPTER 6. A STUDY OF JOB

[1] R. Jamieson, A. R. Fausset, D. Brown (eds.), *A Commentary Critical and Explanatory on the Old and New Testaments*, 2nd ed. (Grand Rapids: Zondervan Publishing House, n.d.), I, 336.

CHAPTER 7. A CONDENSATION OF THE PSALMS

[1] From *Abingdon Bible Commentary*, p. 509. Copyright renewal © 1956 by Abingdon Press. Used by permission.

[2] Reprinted with permission of Macmillan Publishing Co., Inc. from *Commentary on the Holy Bible* by J. R. Dummelow, Editor, p. 324. Copyright 1908, 1909 by Macmillan Publishing Co., Inc., renewed 1936, 1937 by John R. Dummelow.

CHAPTER 8. LIFE AND MINISTRY OF JESUS

[1] M. W. Jacobus, E. C. Lane, A. C. Zenos (eds.), *Funk and Wagnalls New Standard Bible Dictionary*, 3rd rev. ed. (Philadelphia: The Blakiston Company, 1936), p. 955. (Cited hereafter as *New Standard Bible Dictionary*)

[2] From *The Interpreter's Bible*, VII, 111. Copyright renewal © 1979 by Abingdon. Used by permission.

[3] From *Abingdon Bible Commentary*, p. Copyright renewal © 1956 by Abingdon Press. Used by permission.

[4] *The Works of Flavius Josephus with Three Dissertations* (trans. William Whiston) (Cincinnati: H. and J. Applegate, 1950), *Antiquities of the Jews*, xv. 1.3. (Cited hereafter as Josephus)

[5] James Hastings (ed.), *Dictionary of the Bible* (New York: Charles Scribner's Sons, 1942), p. 720.

[6] R. H. Charles, *Apocrypha and Pseudepigrapha of the Old Testament in English* (Oxford: Clarendon Press, 1913), Vol. II.

[7] *Ibid*.

[8] *New Standard Bible Dictionary*, p. 452.

[9] *Abingdon Bible Commentary*, p. 1067.

[10] R. A. Torrey, *Difficulties in the Bible* (Chicago: Fleming H. Revell Company, 1907), pp. 98-100. permission.

[11] Cunningham Geikie, *Life and Words of Christ* rev. ed. (New York: D. Appleton and Company, 1906), I, pp. 98-99.

[12] *New Standard Bible Dictionary*, p. 453.

[13] Geikie, II, 103.

[14] Hastings, p. 446.

[15] Frederick W. Farrar, *The Life of Christ* (New York: Funk & Wagnalls Company [published in the United States for Cassel & Company, Limited, London] n.d.), pp. 70-71.

[16] *Ibid*, p. 72.

[17] R. Jamieson, A. R. Fausset, D. Brown (eds.), *Commentary Critical and Explanatory on the Old and New Testaments*, 2nd ed. (Grand Rapids: Zondervan Publishing House, n.d.), II, 13. (Cited hereafter Jamieson *et al*.)

[18] William Smith (ed.), *A Dictionary of the Bible* (New York: Fleming H. Revell Company, n.d.), 292.

[19] Hastings, p. 447.

[20] *Abingdon Bible Commentary*, p. 893.

[21] Alfred Edersheim, *The Life and Times of Jesus the Messiah*, 8th rev. ed. (New York: Longmans, Green, and Co., 1897), I, 294.

[22] *Ibid*, II, 356-57.

[23] Samuel Fallows (ed.), *The Popular and Critical Bible Encyclopaedia and Scriptural Dictionary* (Chicago: The Howard-Severance Company, 1913), II, 948-49. (Cited hereafter as Fallows)

[24] *Ibid*, II, 946.

[25] Jamieson *et al*., II, 130-31.

[26] Geikie, I, 498.

[27] *Ibid,* I, 501.

[28] Josephus, *Antiquities of the Jews,* iv. 3.2.

[29] Geikie, II, 8-9.

[30] Farrar, p. 207.

[31] Geikie, I, 72.

[32] *Ibid,* II, 47.

[33] *Ibid,* II, 51.

[34] Jamieson *et al.,* II, 42-43.

[35] Geikie, II, 90-92.

[36] From *The Interpreter's Bible,* VII, 355-56. Copyright renewal © 1979 by Abingdon. Used by permission.

[37] Geikie, II, 191-92.

[38] Reprinted with permission of Macmillan Publishing Co., Inc. from *Commentary on the Holy Bible* by J. R. Dummelow, Editor, p. 681. Copyright 1908, 1909 by Macmillan Publishing Co., Inc., renewed 1936, 1937 by John R. Dummelow.

[39] Jamieson *et al.,* II, 107.

[40] *Abingdon Bible Commentary,* p. 898.

[41] Geikie, II, 236-37.

[42] Fallows, III, 1676.

[43] Hastings, p. 947.

[44] *Columbian Family and Pulpit Bible* (Boston: Joseph Teal, 1822), footnote on Mt. 17:24. (Cited hereafter as *Columbian Bible*)

[45] Jamieson *et al.,* II, 80.

[46] *Abingdon Bible Commentary,* p. 983.

[47] *Columbian Bible,* footnote on Jn. 8:58.

[48] Dummelow, p. 751.

[49] Geikie, II, 266-67.

[50] Jamieson *et al.,* II, 110.

[51] Richard C. Trench, *Notes on the Parables of Our Lord,* 2nd ed. (Grand Rapids: Baker Book House, 1950), p. 110. By permission.

[52] George A. Buttrick, *The Parables of Jesus* (New York: Harper & Brothers, 1928), p. 83.

[53] Dummelow, p. 758.

[54] Trench, p. 134.

[55] *Abingdon Bible Commentary,* p. 1049.

[56] *Columbian Bible,* footnote on Lu. 16:8.

[57] Trench, p. 162.

[58] From *The Interpreter's Bible,* VIII, 296. Copyright renewal © 1980 by Abingdon. Used by permission.

[59] Farrar, p. 504.

[60] Geikie, II, 357.

[61] Hastings, p. 538.

[62] *Ibid.*

[63] Jamieson *et al.,* II, 118.

[64] *Abingdon Bible Commentary,* p. 899.

[65] Geikie, II, 374.

[66] Jamieson *et al.,* II, 83.

[67] *Columbian Bible,* footnote on Mt. 22:11.

[68] Madeleine S. and J. Lane Miller, *Harper's Bible Dictionary,* 7th ed. (New York: Harper & Row, Publishers, 1961), p. 526. By permission.

[69] Farrar, p. 584.

[70] Jamieson *et al.,* II, 58.

[71] Hastings, p. 461.

[72] *Abingdon Bible Commentary,* p. 993.

[73] Dummelow, p. 802.

[74] From *The Interpreter's Bible,* VIII, 731-32. Copyright renewal © 1980 by Abingdon. Used by permission.

[75] Geikie, II, 530-31.

[76] Dummelow, p. cxxix.

[77] Fallows, II, 951.

[78] Jamieson *et al.,* II, 61.

[79] Hastings, p. 458.

[80] Jamieson *et al.,* II, 63.

[81] Hastings, p. 457.

[82] Edersheim, II, 642.

[83] James Strong, *The Exhaustive Concordance of the Bible* (New York: The Methodist Book Concern, 1936).

CHAPTER 9. CORRELATION—JESUS

[1] Harold E. Monser (ed.), *The Cross Reference Bible* (New York: The Cross Reference Bible Company, 1910), p. 1970.

[2] From *Abingdon Bible Commentary,* p. 893. Copyright renewal © 1956 by Abingdon Press. Used by permission.

[3] Cunningham Geikie, *Life and Words of Christ,* rev. ed. (New York: D. Appleton and Company, 1906), I. 157-58.

[4] By permission. From *Webster's Third New International Dictionary* © 1966 by G. & C. Merriam Co., Publishers of the Merriam-Webster Dictionaries.

[5] *Ibid.*

CHAPTER 10. THE WORK OF THE TWELVE APOSTLES

[1] Reprinted with permission of Macmillan Publishing Co., Inc. from *Commentary on the Holy Bible* by J. R. Dummelow, Editor, p. 821. Copyright 1908, 1909 by Macmillan Publishing Co., Inc., renewed 1936, 1937 by John R. Dummelow.

[2] From *The Interpreter's Bible,* IX, 90. Copyright renewal © 1982 by Abingdon. Used by permission.

[3] R. Jamieson, A. R. Fausset, D. Brown (eds.), *A Commentary Critical and Explanatory on the Old and New Testaments,* 2nd ed. (Grand Rapids: Zondervan Publishing House, n.d.), II, 180.

CHAPTER 11. LIFE AND MINISTRY OF PAUL

[1] W. J. Conybeare and J. S. Howson, *The Life and Epistles of St. Paul* (New York: Charles Scribner's Sons, 1894), I, 75. (Cited hereafter as Conybeare)

[2] *Ibid,* I, 93.

[3] F. W. Farrar, *The Life and Work of St. Paul* (New York: E. P. Dutton and Company, 1889), p. 117.

[4] Samuel Fallows (ed.), *The Popular and Critical Bible Encyclopaedia and Scriptural Dictionary* (Chicago: The Howard-Severance Company, 1913), II, 1298.

[5] Conybeare, I, 149.

[6] Farrar, pp. 247-48.

[7] William Smith (ed.), *A Dictionary of the Bible* (New York: Fleming H. Revell Company, n.d.), p. 505.

[8] *The New Analytical Bible and Dictionary of the Bible,* rev. ed. (Chicago: John A. Dickson Publishing Company, 1950), p. 1356. By permission.

[9] *The International Standard Bible Encyclopaedia* (Grand Rapids: Wm. B. Eerdmans Publishing Co., 1960), V, 2855. By permission.

[10] *The Interpreter's Bible* (New York: Abingdon Press, 1951), XI, 327. By permission.

[11] M. W. Jacobus, E. C. Lane, A. C. Zenos (eds.), *Funk and Wagnalls New Standard Bible Dictionary,* 3rd rev. ed. (Philadelphia: The Blakiston Company, 1936), p. 180.

[12] *The Companion Bible* (London: The Lamp Press Ltd., n.d.), p. 1629.

[13] From *The Interpreter's Bible,* IX, 257. Copyright renewal © 1982 by Abingdon. Used by permission.

[14] Reprinted with permission of Macmillan Publishing Co., Inc. from *Commentary on the Holy Bible* by J. R. Dummelow, Editor, p. 913. Copyright 1908, 1909 by Macmillan Publishing Co., Inc., renewed 1936, 1937 by John R. Dummelow.

[15] *Ibid,* p. 942.

[16] *Ibid,* p. 862.

[17] R. Jamieson, A. R. Fausset, D. Brown, (eds.), *A Commentary Critical and Explanatory on the Old and New Testaments,* 2nd ed. (Grand Rapids: Zondervan Publishing House, n.d.), II, 218.

[18] Madeleine S. and J. Lane Miller, *Harper's Bible Dictionary,* 7th ed. (New York: Harper & Row, Publishers, 1961), p. 548. By permission.

[19] Harold E. Monser (ed.), *The Cross Reference Bible* (New York: The Cross Reference Bible Company, 1910), p. 2229.

CHAPTER 12. PAUL'S DOCTRINAL TEACHINGS

[1] James Hastings (ed.), *Dictionary of the Bible* (New York: Charles Scribner's Sons, 1942), p. 313.

[2] From *The American College Dictionary,* copyright, 1947, 1948, 1949, 1950, 1951, 1952, 1953, 1954, 1955, 1956, 1957, 1958, 1959, 1960, 1961, 1962, 1963, 1964, 1965, 1966, 1967, 1968, 1969, by Random House, Inc. Reprinted by permission.

[3] Reprinted with permission of Macmillan Publishing Co., Inc. from *Commentary on the Holy Bible* by J. R. Dummelow, Editor, p. 869. Copyright 1908, 1909 by Macmillan Publishing Co., Inc., renewed 1936, 1937 by John R. Dummelow.

[4] Alexander Cruden, *Cruden's Complete Concordance* (Philadelphia: The John C. Winston Company, 1930), p. 199.

[5] Dummelow, p. 869.

[6] Hastings, p. 693.

CHAPTER 13. CORRELATION—CHRISTIAN AND CHURCH

[1] James Hastings (ed.), *Dictionary of the Bible* (New York: Charles Scribner's Sons, 1942), p. 140.

[2] From *Abingdon Bible Commentary,* p. 1381. Copyright renewal © 1956 by Abingdon Press. Used by permission.

[3] R. Jamieson, A. R. Fausset, D. Brown, (eds.), *A Commentary Critical and Explanatory on the Old and New Testaments,* 2nd ed. (Grand Rapids: Zondervan Publishing House, n.d.), II, 43.

CHAPTER 14. THE EPISTLE TO THE HEBREWS

[1] Harold E. Monser (ed.), *The Cross Reference Bible* (New York: The Cross Reference Bible Company, 1910), p. 2268.

[2] Reprinted with permission of Macmillan Publishing Co., Inc. from *Commentary on the Holy Bible* by J. R. Dummelow, Editor, p. 821. Copyright 1908, 1909 by Macmillan Publishing Co., Inc., renewed 1936, 1937 by John R. Dummelow.

CHAPTER 16. THE REVELATION OF ST. JOHN THE DIVINE

[1] From *Abingdon Bible Commentary,* p. 1366-67.

Copyright renewal © 1956 by Abingdon Press. Used by permission.

[2] James Hastings (ed.), *Dictionary of the Bible* (New York: Charles Scribner's Sons, 1942), p. 797.

[3] *Ibid,* p. 949.

CHAPTER 17. APPROPRIATION OF SCRIPTURAL LESSONS

[1] Bernard P. Grenfell and Arthur S. Hunt (eds.), *New Sayings of Jesus and Fragment of a Lost Gospel* (New York: Oxford University Press, 1904), pp. 13, 16.

[2] James Hastings (ed.), *Dictionary of the Bible* (New York: Charles Scribner's Sons, 1942), p. 659.

[3] E. W. Bullinger, *Number in Scripture,* 5th rev. ed. (London: Eyre and Spottiswoode Limited, 1928), p. 50.

[4] James Strong, *The Exhaustive Concordance of the Bible* (New York: The Methodist Book Concern, 1936). (Cited hereafter as *Strong's Concordance)*

[5] Bullinger, p. 92.

[6] Samuel Fallows (ed.), *The Popular and Critical Bible Encyclopaedia and Scriptural Dictionary* (Chicago: The Howard-Severance Company, 1913), II, 1245.

[7] Bullinger, pp. 107-8.

[8] M. W. Jacobus, E. C. Lane, A. C. Zenos (eds.), *Funk and Wagnalls New Standard Bible Dictionary,* 3rd rev. ed. (Philadelphia: The Blakiston Company, 1936), p. 628.

[9] Fallows, II, 1245.

[10] *Ibid,* II, 1245.

[11] *The Companion Bible* (London: The Lamp Press Ltd., n.d.), p. 14a Appendix.

[12] *Strong's Concordance.*

[13] Bullinger, p. 107.

[14] R. Jamieson, A. R. Fausset, D. Brown (eds.), *A Commentary Critical and Explanatory on the Old and New Testaments,* 2nd ed. (Grand Rapids: Zondervan Publishing House, n.d.), II, 549. (Cited hereafter as Jamieson *et al.)*

[15] *Ibid,* I, 146.

[16] *Strong's Concordance.*

[17] Bullinger, p. 196.

[18] *Ibid,* p. 200.

[19] *Ibid,* p. 243.

[20] Fallows, II, 1245.

[21] William Smith (ed.), *A Dictionary of the Bible* (New York: Fleming H. Revell Company, n.d.) p. 692.

[22] Bullinger, p. 253.

[23] Reprinted with permission of Macmillan Publishing Co., Inc. from *Commentary on the Holy Bible* by J. R. Dummelow, Editor, p. 1091. Copyright 1908, 1909 by Macmillan Publishing Co., Inc., renewed 1936, 1937 by John R. Dummelow.

[24] Bullinger, p. 266.

[25] *Ibid,* p. 270.

[26] Jamieson *et al.,* I, 641.

[27] *Ibid,* II, 570.

Index

Italic numbers indicate illustrations; *a* = left column, *b* = right column. O.T. = Old Testament, N.T. = New Testament.

Aaron, 53, 56a, 75, 77, 107, 161a, 167-68, 474
Abaddon, 166
Abba, 142b
Abed-nego, 132, 171b
Abel, 55a, 73, 97, 114-15, 479, 481
Abiathar, 53a
Abigail, 39a, 112, 357a
Abihu, 56a, 169b
Abijam (Abijah), 84
Abimelech, 46b, 100
Abiram, 77, 170a
Abner, 81
"Abomination of desolation," 93, 214a, 307b
Abram, Abraham, 13, 29, 44b, 64a, 66b, 93, 100-1, 114-15, 223-25, 292a, 540, 542; covenant with, 10b, 47a, 73, 148; Paul on, 418-20, 450-51, 464, 479-80; seed of, 150, 464
Absalom, 43a, 45b, 83, 112
Accho (Ptolemais), 229b, 422b
Accusations: against apostles, 375-77; against Jesus, 246a, 250b, 267-70, 279a, 286a, 321-23, 352-53; against Paul, 400a, 405b, 413a, 423b, 425b, 427a, 443-44; against Stephen, 378-79. *See also* Blasphemy
Accuser, 499, 515; *see also* Satan
Achaia, 401b, 403a, 407a, 412b, 417-18, 437a
Achaicus, 409b
Acropolis, 401, *401*
Acts of the Apostles, 12, 20-21, 374, 387
Adam, 13, 65-66, 73, 96-97, 114-15, 145-47, 224-25, 420a, 449-50, 522-23, 526, 542; covenant with, 47a, 148
Adam and Eve, 221b
Adonai, 142b
Adonijah, 40b, 53a, 83, 112
Adultery, 38-40, 259, 410b; woman healed of, 280a, 335, 369
Advent of Jesus, 10b, 19, 125, 147-48, 223b, 228a, 493b; *see also* Hope, Incarnation
Adversary, 165-66, 181; *see also* Satan
Advocate, 313-14, 483
Aeneas, 380a, 384
Agabus, 392b, 422b
Agriculture, 34-36; festivals, 59-61. *See also* Firstfruits, Harvest
Agrippa I, II: *see* Herod
Ahab 69, 85, 118-19, 123
Ahaz, 50a, 87, 124-25
Ahaziah: of Israel, 85, 118, 123; of Judah, 86
Ahijah, 83
Alexander the Great, 63b, 92, 213, 274a, 490
Alpha and Omega: Christ as, 492-95, 505-6, 509, 534; God as, 495, 509, 534
Altar(s), 46a, 48-50, *49-51,* 55-56, 62b, 119, 126-27, 134, 160, 162-63, *163,*

214a, 226a, 498, 506, 512
Amalek, Amalekites, 75, 81, 108, 112, 114-15
Amaziah, 86
Ammon, Ammonites, 29a, 79, 114-15, 123, 130, 138
Amorites, 63, 77, 109
Amos, 18, 87, 491b; book of, 5a, 12, 18
Amram, 75, 106
Ananias: of Damascus, 389b; high priest, 424b; husband of Sapphira, 377a
Andrew, 235a, 249b, 252-53, 306a
Angelology, 165, 217b, 222a, 433-34, 490b
Angels, 101, 103, 118-19; Jesus and, 228a, 234a, 330, 334, 471; of Revelation, 497-500, 502, 504, 506-7, 514
Anger: of God, 167b; Jesus on, 259. *See also* Judgment, Wrath of God
Animals: camels, 30-31; clean, 30b, 44a, 269a, 381a; donkeys, 30, 300a; goats, 30, 62; horses, 31-33; oxen, 30, 36a, 181; sacrificial, 55-57, 62; sheep, 30; swine, 44a, 214a, 262, 362; as symbol, 30b, 33a, 300a; unclean, 31b, 44a, 269a, 381a
Anna, 228-29
Annas, 231a, 320
Annunciation to Mary, 226b, 544
Anointed One, 10b, 220b, 222b, 471
Anthropomorphism, 48b, 145, 167b; *see also* Worship
Antichrist, 165-66, 307b, 464, 483, 485
Antigonus II, 215a
Antinomianism, 482
Antioch: Pisidia, 393-94, 398a, 406b, 440a; Syria, 392-94, 396-97, 405-6
Antiochus IV (Epiphanes), 50a, 93, 214a, 220b, 307b
Antipas: *see* Herod
Antipater, 93, 214-15
Antonia, Tower of, 322a, 424a
Antony, Mark, 250a
Apocalypse, 10b, 125, 158b, 488-94, 506, 508; *see also* Language, apocalyptic; Revelation
Apocalyptic literature, 131, 133, 135, 220-22, 490-91; *see also* Writing, apocalyptic
Apocrypha, 5-6, 216b
Apollos, 407, 410b
Apostasy, 14-16, 18, 71b, 118-20, 122, 126, 130, 307, 405a, 440a, 478-79; *see also* Doctrines, heretical; High places, Idolatry
Apostles, the Twelve: character of, 252-56; choosing of, 252; commissioned, 270b, 372; given keys of the kingdom, 275b, 376a; healings by, 271a, 384-86; persecution of, 376-77, 381b, 392, 468; training of, 252, 256b, 270-71 274-75, 328, 350b, 372-73; work of, 374-82

Apostolic Church, 383, 468; *see also* Church
Appropriation, Scriptural lessons, 529-51
Aqabah, Gulf of, 106, 116
Aquila, 403b, 405b, 407a, 414a
Arabia, 29a, 30b, 72a, 116, 390, 417b
Arabs, 29a, 63, 138
Aram: *see* Syria
Aramaic, 3, 6b, 63b, 132, 230a, 387
Ararat, Mount, 73, 99
Araunah, 36a, 83, 174a
Archelaus, 229b, 231a
Archeology, 6b, 32, 37b, 49-50, *66-69, 98, 140,* 218, *219, 221, 251*
Areopagus (Mars Hill), 402-3, *403*
Aristarchus, 413-14, 421b, 429b, 433a
Aristeas, Letter of, 221a
Aristobulus II, 93, 214b
Ark: of the Covenant, 51a, 62a, 75, 108-10, 113, 160-63, *161,* 326b, 498, 543; Noah's, 98-99, 479, 542
Armageddon, 502, 507, 517
Armenian Version, 6b
Arphaxad, 100, 114-15
Artaxerxes, 90-91, 136, 138
Asa, 51a, 84-85, 122-23, 224
Ascension of Jesus, 225b, 328, 333-34, 347, 545
Asceticism, 218a, 433b, 434a, 438a, 482; *see also* Celibacy, Fasting
Asenath, 105
Asher: son of Jacob, 74, 114-15, 151, 153; tribe of, 155, 520
Asherah, 51a, 122, 127
Ashdod, 170a, 389a
Ashtoreth, 50, 51, 117
Ass: *see* Donkey
Assos, 422a
Assumption of Moses, 221a
Assyria, 15, 17, 19, 29a, 71b, 87, 98, 125-26
Astarte: *see* Ashtoreth
Athaliah, 85-86, 123, 356
Athena, 401
Athens, 401-3
Atonement: Church and, 463; Day of, 53b, 62a; of Jesus, 53b, 57b, 62b, 326b, 434, 447; by vicarious sacrifice, 55-57, 157a. *See also* Reconciliation
Attalia, 393-94
Augustine, 6a, 257, 389a
Augustus Caesar, 93, 215a, 228a, 231a
Auranitis, 215b, 231a
Authorized Version: *see* King James Bible
Azariah: *see* Uzziah
Azotus, 380a

Baal-worship, 48a, 50-51, 117-19, 121, 123, 127
Baasha, 84, 123
Babel, Tower of, 50, 73, 550
Babylon, Babylonia, 17, 29a, 48a, 50-51, 55, 63, 72a, 98, 125, 128-29, 134; of

Revelation, 501, 507, 516, 518-19
Balaam, 77, 168b, 220a
Balak, 77
Baptism, 99, 148, 375b, 463; of Cornelius, 380-81; of Ethiopian eunuch, 379-80; by Holy Ghost, 56a, 235a; of jailor, 400a; of Jesus, 232, 234-35, 375a, 544; by John the Baptist, 231-32, 302a; of Lydia, 399b; Paul on, 395a, 411, 418a, 420a, 434-35
Barabbas, 323a
Barak, 79, 480
Barnabas, 377a, 384, 391-92, 397b
Barrenness, 37a, 41a, 150-51, 173a
Bartholomew: see Nathanael
Bartimaeus, 298a, 335, 367
Baruch, books of, 5b, 221a
Baruch, Jeremiah's scribe, 129
Baskets, 271b, 274b, 391a
Batanaea, 215b, 231a
Bath-sheba, 14, 83, 113, 116
Beatitudes, 258-59
Bedouins, 29a, *32*, 33a, 43a
Beelzebub, 165-66, 267b, 270a, 285; *see also* Satan
Beer-sheba, 67a, 100, 111
Bel and the Dragon, 5b
Belial, 166
Belshazzar, 90, 133, 171a
Belteshazzar: see Daniel
Benhadad: I, 84, 123; II, 85-86, 120-21, 171b
Benjamin: son of Jacob, 67a, 74, 105, 114-115, 150-51, 153; tribe of, 84, 117-18, 122, 388a, 504, 520
Berea, 400-1, 403a, 414b
Bethabara, 234b
Bethany, 285b, 294b, 297-98, 300-1, 311a, 333b
Beth-el, 50b, 66b, 74, 84, 100, 102, 111, 118, 120, 550
Bethesda, pool of, 250b, *251*, 360
Bethlehem, 81, 112, 134, 220b, *222*, 228-29
Bethphage, 300a
Bethsaida, 249a, 254b, 263b, 271a, 275a
Beth-shemesh, *36*, 170b
Betrothal, 38b, 226-27, 416b
Bezer, 45b
Bible: canonization, 4-6, 216; design and scope, 10-12, 551; divisions and books of, 12-24; as literature, 3, 12; preservation of, 3-10; span of, 551; versions, 6-10. *See also* Scripture
Bildad, 180, 182, 185-86, 189-90, 193-95
Bilhah, 41a, 74, 102-3, 150-51
Birth: of Jesus, 223, 225b, 228a, 546; new, 241-42, 389b, 452b
Birthright, 40b, 102-3, 105
Bishop's Bible, 9
Blasphemy, 219b, 246a, 250b, 267a, 281a, 283, 321, 378-79, 507, 515
Blemish, 54-55, 60b
Blessing(s): to Abraham's seed, 47a, 100, 450b; Beatitudes, 258-59; God's, to His creation, 144; Jacob's, 105, 152-53; Jesus', 264a, 271b, 275a, 312a, 333b; of the Law, 157; Moses', 77, 154-55; Simeon's, 228b; to Virgin Mary, 226-27
Blindness: healings of, 263a, 268, 270b,

275a, 281, 335, 361-62, 364-65, 367; smitings with, 171b, 389b, 393b; spiritual, 264a, 273b, 281b, 305a, 365, 420-21, 466
Blood: covenant, 46; efficacy of Christ's, 53b, 57b, 312a, 420a, 447a, 451b, 477-78, 497, 499; healing of issue of, 270b, 335, 362; plague of, 149, 498, 500; revenge, 44-46, 260; in sacrifice, 49a, 55-57, 59a, 62, 396a
Boaz, 14, 36a, 38a, 114-15, 224
Body: of Christ, 312a, 412a, 434-36, 448b, 459, 478; natural and spiritual, 241a, 415b, 436a, 448-49; resurrection, 329b, 412, 448a; of sin, 455; as temple, 241a, 411a, 416a, 457
Bohairic Version, 6b
Boils, 149, 173b, 182
"Book of the law," 4b, 127
Books: of N.T., 3, 12, 21-24; of O.T., 3, 12-19
Brazen altar, 49-50, *50*, 160, 162b, *163*
Brazen serpent, 77, 170a, 242a
Bread, 43b, 60, 172-73, 271b, 274-75, 376a, 404, 430b; as body of Christ, 312a, 411b (*see also* Eucharist); covenant, 46b; Feast of Unleavened, 59-60; Jesus on, 232b, 261, 272; of life, discourse on, 272, 336; wave offerings, 56b, 60b. *See also* Leaven, Shewbread
Breastplate, *52*, *53*
Bride, 38-39, 174b, 242b, 505, 519-20; *see also* Marriage
Bridegroom, 38b, 519-20; Christ as, 39a, 242b, 269b, 309; *see also* Marriage
Brotherhood, 42a, 45a, 239, 262, 278a, 288a, 376-77, 411a, 418b, 421a, 433, 435a, 452b, 483, 485
Brothers of Jesus, 229b, 270b
Burnt offering, altar of, 49-50, *50*, 55-56, 160, *163*, 279a
Bush, burning, 75, 106, 168b

Caesar: Augustus, 93, 215a, 228a, 231a, 304a; Julius, 93, 214-15
Caesarea, 215b, 389a, 422b, *426*
Caesarea Philippi, 274a, 276a
Caiaphas, 231a, 295b, 310b, 320b, 377b
Cain, 73, 97, 114-15, 479
Caleb, 68, 77, 79, 108
Calendar, Hebrew, 59a
Calf: golden, 52b, 75, 106; worship, 48a, 84, 118, 122
Calvary: see Golgotha
Cambyses, 135
Camels, 30-31, *32*, 44a, 181
Cana, 236, 246a, 254b
Canaan: Ham's son, 73, 99, 114-15; land of, 13-14, 29-30, 48, 50-51, 54b, 64b, 66b, 68, 77, 79, 100-1, 103, 105-10, 117, 154 (*see also* Palestine)
Canaanites, 29a, 38a, 50-51, 63, 77, 79, 99, 109-10
Candlestick(s): golden, 53, *53*, 135, 160, 162b, 491, 495-96, 509; the two, 498, 513
Canon of Scripture, 4-6, 12-24, 216
Canticles (Song of Solomon), 16
Capernaum, 245-46, 249, 252b, 263b, 271-72, 274a, 277-78
Captivity: of Israel, 71b, 124-27, 130; of

Judah (Exile), 15, 17, 72a, 89-90, 125, 128-30, 132, 134, 136, 543
Carmel, Mount, 119-20, 168a, 173b
Celibacy, 38a, 218a, 297a, 411a; *see also* Asceticism
Cenchrea, 403b, 405b, 421b
Centurion's servant, healing of, 263, 361
Cephas: see Peter
Chaldea, 19, 66b, 73, 100; *see also* Babylon
Charity, 260, 289a, 378a, 407a, 434a, 456, 496; *see also* Love
Chebar (river), 130
Chemosh, 50, 117
Cherith (brook), 118
Child sacrifice, 48a, 55b, 101
Children, 40-41, 434a; of God, 40b, 259-60, 304a, 418a, 420b; of Israel, 13-14, 64a, 66a, 75, 77, 103-4, 150, 418a, 464, 497; Jesus and, 40b, 278a
Children, Song of Three Holy, 5b
Chinnereth, Lake of, 245; *see also* Sea of Galilee
Chorazin, 249a, 263b
Christ: as Alpha and Omega, 493-95, 505-6, 509, 534; body of, 312a, 411-12, 434-36, 448b, 459; as bread of life, 272; as bridegroom, 39a, 242b, 269b, 309; Church and, 275b, 348, 411-12, 434-35, 459-60, 466b; Day of, 405a, 465b, 491-93; as good shepherd, 281-82; as high priest, 53b, 62b, 240, 470-78; humanity and divinity of, 220b, 222-23, 225-26, 275a, 283, 297, 305a, 330-31, 344, 471, 482-83; incarnation, 223-25, 391a, 438a, 446b, 467a, 472, 483, 544; indwelling, 296a, 434a, 466b; kingdom of, 87, 90, 125, 132-33, 289b, 307a, 467a, 498 (*see also* Kingdom of God); life in, 20a, 262, 273a, 282a, 295a, 310a, 435a, 446a, 452-53, 483-84, 490; as light of world, 223b, 280, 306a, 483, 504, 507, 520; majesty of, 220b, 493-94; ministry of (*see under* Jesus); Peter's confession of, 275a, 375-77; pre-eminence, 242a, 348, 433-34, 471; pre-existence, 281a, 305a, 344, 348, 452a, 471-72; prophecies of, 337; reconciliation through, 62b, 415b, 420a, 433a, 435a, 447, 449b, 463, 472; risen, 328, 331a, 448; as rock, 275b; Second Coming of, 56a, 125, 148, 287, 293-94, 296a, 299, 308-10, 314-15, 321b, 334a, 348, 404-5, 440a, 491-93, 494-95, 497, 502, 506-7; titles of, 220, 228a, 272, 280-81, 345, 390, 472, 448, 492-93, 495, 497, 502; as vine, 314; as water of life, 242-43, 279-80; as the way, 313a, 446, 449b, 462-63, 478; witnesses for, 228b, 234b, 250b, 275a, 331b; as the Word, 223b, 377b, 483, 534. *See also* Messiah, Son
Christian, the, 392b, 418a, 464; Jesus on life of, 257-63 (*see also* Discipleship); Paul on life of, 404, 410-11, 418b, 421a, 434-36, 438-40, 451-52; perse-

cution of, 379, 381-82, 389, 439a, 468-69, 490; ten ascending steps in life of, 544-45; walk of, 22-23, 533, 547

Christianity: and Diana worship, 412b; and emperor worship, 490a; and Epistle to the Hebrews, 470; nature of, 387, 452b, 490b; spread of, 45a, 374, 387, 445, 452b; as the Way, 262, 375b, 407a, 446b

Chronicles, books of, 5a, 12, 15

Chronology: of Apostolic Church, 383, 468; O.T. history, 73-91; Ussher's, 65, 73

Church: body of Christ, 411-12, 434-35, 459; as bride, 38-39, 466b, 502, 504; brotherhood in, 418b, 421a; comforted, in Revelation, 490b, 495, 497-500, 505; communal life, 376-77; dates of apostolic, 383, 468; doctrine for, 445-52; edification of, 435, 460-61; factions and disorders in, 405b, 409-12; of the first-born, 459, 481; healing work in, 333a, 376, 379b, 384-86, 432a; Jesus on, 275b, 278b, 348; Paul's ministry in, 387-440; persecution of, 379b, 381b, 389b, 469b, 490, 499, 503, 507; qualifications of officers, 438-40; redemptive mission of, 10-11, 333a, 462-63; seven, of Revelation, 408a, 467a; 495-96, 506; as true Israel, 459, 464; women in, 357b, 378a, 411b, 438a; work of the Twelve and, 374-82

Cilicia, 177, 388a, 391-93, 398a, 417b

Circumcision, 40-41, 48b, 101, 109, 148, 395a, 417-19, 434a, 436a, 450-51

Cisterns, 33, 34

Cities: discourse against impenitent, 263b, 336; Levitical, 54b, 77, 109; of refuge, 45b, 54-55, 77, 109

Claudius: emperor, 403b, 419a; Lysias, 424-25

Cleanness: of animals, 30b, 44a, 269a, 381a; "without blemish," 54-55. See also Purification, Sanctification

Cleansing of Temple, 241a, 299, 301b

Clement: of Alexandria, 6a, 489a; bishop of Rome, 437a

Cleopas, 330-31

Cloth, new on old garment, parable of, 269b, 336

Clothing, 42-44; of priests, 53-54; wedding garments, 39a, 303b

Coat, 42b, 104

Code: Deuteronomic, 4b, 51-52, 127; of Hammurabi, 29a, 37b, 51b, 140; Holiness, 4b, 52a; Priestly, 4b, 52a, 96, 216a

Cohort, 424a, 429

Colossae, 408a, 433, 435a

Colossians, Epistle to, 6a, 12, 23, 433-34

Comforter, 299, 311a, 313-15, 347, 375, 491; see also Holy Ghost, Second Coming of Christ

Commandments, 13, 40b, 48, 51b, 55b, 57b, 75, 107, 148, 157a, 161a; Jesus on, 273a, 304b, 312b; Paul on, 414a

Concubine, 36-37, 40-42, 51b, 357a

Conversion: of Cornelius, 380-81; of Ethiopian eunuch, 379-80; of Paul, 380a, 388-89; of Sergius Paulus, 393b

Corban, oath of, 273b

Corinth, 403b, 409-10, 412b, 417a, 437a

Corinthians, Epistles to, 6a, 12, 22, 410-12, 414-16

Cornelius, 380-81, 395b

Corner-stone, 135, 200, 303a, 376b, 461

Correlation: O.T. subjects, 141-78; Jesus, 344-73; Christian and Church, 453-69

Council: of Carthage, 6a, 470; of Jamnia, 5a; of Jerusalem, 394-96, 417-18; Sanhedrin, 217, 219a, 245, 295b, 320-21, 327, 329a, 376b, 378b, 388-89, 425, 427; of Trent, 5b

Courses, priestly, 55a, 112, 116, 226a

Court of the Gentiles, 163b, 215b, 241a, 498, 513

Covenant, 3, 46-47, 66, 148; Abrahamic, 13, 47, 73-74, 100-1, 148, 464, 542; Adamic, 47, 148; blood, 46; bread, 46b; Davidic, 47, 81, 113, 148; God's, 10b, 47, 66a, 148, 420b; Jesus, fulfillment of, 47b, 148, 475-76; Law and, 157, 418a, 450b; Mosaic, 47, 51b, 75, 107, 148; New, 47, 89, 129, 148, 312, 470-71, 476; Noahic, 47, 73, 99, 101, 148; O.T. and N.T., contrasted, 470-81; Paul on, 418a, 420-21; renewals of, 47, 74, 77, 79, 83-84, 88, 91, 102, 117, 127; salt, 46b

Coverdale's Bible, 5b, 9

Creation: first account, 13, 143-44, 526, 534; second account, 13, 96, 145-46, 526

Crete, 430a, 437-38

Crispus, 405a

Cross: Jesus' teaching of, 253a, 275-76, 290a; Paul's teaching of, 410a, 418b, 434-35, 447, 480

Crucifixion: of Jesus, 324-27, 355, 545; Paul on, 403-4, 410a, 415b, 418b, 420a, 447

Cubit, 159-60, 162b

Cuneiform, 29a, 37, 71-72, 98

Customs of Bible times, 27-64

Cyprus, 392-93, 398a

Cyrus, 72, 72, 90, 132, 134-35, 163a, 213

Dagon, 170a

Damascus, 389, 390, 391a, 417-18, 452b

Dan: son of Jacob, 74, 114-15, 150-51, 153; town of, 111, 118; tribe of, 155, 464, 520

Daniel, 17, 72a, 90, 129, 132-33, 172a, 543; book of, 5a, 12, 17, 132

Darius: I, 134-35; the Mede, 90, 132-33

Darkness, plague of, 149

Dathan, 77, 170a

David, 11b, 14-15, 43-44, 47a, 55a, 68, 80 (map), 81, 83, 111-18, 122, 174, 224, 279, 480, 510, 543; covenant with, 10b, 47a, 148; genealogy of, 114-15; psalms of, 204; seed of Messiah, 47b, 220a, 224, 305a, 446b

Day: of Atonement, 53b, 62; of Christ, 405a, 465b, 491-93; as dimension of thought, 550; of Firstfruits, 60-61, 375a; of Judgment, 16, 18-19, 222a, 405a, 491, 493

Daysman, 185, 197

Dead Sea, 29b, 46b, 174a, 243, 284

Dead Sea Scrolls, 6b, 7, 218b, 218

Deafness, healing of, 274b, 335, 363

Death: destruction of, 412b, 417a, 420a, 449a, 503-4; Jesus abolished, 248b, 326, 472; plague of, 156; raisings from, 173, 263a, 270b, 294-95, 335, 370-71, 386

Deborah, 39a, 79, 356-57

Debtors, parable of two, 264b, 336

Decalogue: see Commandments

Decapolis, 250a, 274

Dedication, Feast of, 61b, 93, 214a, 282b

Defilement, 132, 269, 273b, 322a, 521, 523; see also Uncleanness

Delilah, 79, 350

Deliverance, O.T. miracles of, 171-72

Deluge: see Flood

Demetrius, 412-13

Demoniac: healing of dumb, 270b, 335, 363; healing of Gadarene, 270a, 335, 362

Demonology, 165, 222a, 408b

Derbe, 394b, 398a, 406b

Deuteronomic Code, 4b, 51-52, 127

Deuteronomy, 4b, 12-13, 127

Devil, 267b, 270, 280b, 405a, 472; see also Demonology, Satan

Diana, Ephesian, 407b, 407, 409, 412-13, 413

Diaspora: see Dispersion

Didrachme, 277b

Dimensions, spiritual, 524-25, 550

Dinah, 45b, 74, 102

Disciples, 235a, 249a, 252-56, 315b, 349-50; see also Apostles

Discipleship, 241b, 252b, 271a, 275-76, 280b, 292b, 314, 452b; parable of cost of, 289-90, 336

Discourses (list, 336): Christ, bread of life, 272; coming of kingdom and of the Son of man, 296; denunciation of Pharisees and scribes, 285-86, 305; destruction of Jerusalem, signs of Christ's coming, Last Judgment, 306-10; going and returning, 314-15; good shepherd, 281-82; humility and forgiveness, 278; invitation to the weary, 263b; light of world, 280; new birth, 241-42; prayer, 285b; Sermon on the Mount, 257-63; Son and the Father, 250; spiritual freedom, 280-81; against traditions of elders, 273; trust in God's care, 286-87; vine and branches, 314; watchfulness for Christ's coming, 286-87; water of life, 242-43, 279-80; Way, Truth, Life, 313a; woes on impenitent cities, 263b

Dispersion, 15, 92, 213, 215-16, 221a, 229a, 388a, 393a; see also Captivity

Dives and Lazarus, parable of, 292, 336

Divided Kingdom, 15, 82 (map), 84-85, 117

Divination, maid with spirit of, 385

Divorce, 38-40, 260, 296b, 411a

Docetism, 482

Doctrines: heretical, 433b, 469, 482-83; of Paul, 395b, 417b, 419-20, 445-52

Domitian, 254b, 469, 490a

Donkey, 30b, 32, 181, 300a

Dooms of Revelation, 492, 501-3, 507

Dorcas, 357, 380a, 386

Dothan, 34b, 104
Dove, 55-56, 73, 98, 228b
Dowry, 38b
Draft of fishes, 248-49, 332a, 335
Dragnet, parable of the, 266-67, 336
Dragon, 165-66, 499, 507, 514; see also Satan, Serpent
Dreams: of Joseph, Jacob's son, 104; of Joseph of Nazareth, 229a; of Nebuchadnezzar, 132-33; of Pharaoh, 104. See also Visions
Dropsy, healing of, 294a, 335, 366
Dumbness, healings of, 263a, 270b, 285b, 335, 361, 363

Ecclesiastes, 5a, 12, 16, 117, 179
Ecclesiasticus, 5b
Eden, 96, 146-47, 522-23
Edom, Edomites, 18, 29a, 64a, 77, 86, 114-15, 130; see also Idumaea
Education, religious, 37a, 40a, 51b, 54, 216-17, 230, 246
Egypt, 540-41; gods of, 48a, 55a; Israel in, 13, 68, 74-75, 540-42; Jesus in, 229, 541; Joseph in, 104-5; Moses in, 106-7; and Ptolemies, 92, 214a
Eight, significance of, 538
El: see Elohim
Eleazar, 53a, 77
El Elyon, 142b
Eli, 53a, 79, 110-11
Elias: see Elijah
Eliezer, 85, 123
Elihu, 180, 196-99
Elijah, 55-56, 71a, 85, 118-20, 124, 168a, 171-75, 226a, 234b, 276b, 447b
Elimelech, 38a
Eliphaz, 180, 182-84, 188-89, 191-93
Elisabeth, 225-27, 356, 375a
Elisha, 55b, 71a, 85-86, 119-21, 124, 168a, 170-73, 176
Elkanah, 39a, 41a, 110
Elohim, 4b, 96, 142-45
Elohistic Document, 4b, 143, 145
Elon, 79
El Shaddai, 142b
Elymas, 393b
Emmaus, 330b
Emperor worship, 468-69, 490a
English Bible, 7-10
Enoch, 73, 114-15, 119, 174a, 224, 447b, 479
Enoch, books of, 221
Enos, 97, 114-15
Epaphras, 408a, 433
Epaphroditus, 433a, 435b, 436a
Ephesians, Epistle to, 6a, 12, 22, 433-35
Ephesus, 393b, 405b, 407a, 409a, 412-14, 414, 434b, 437a, 496
Ephraim: city of, 295b; son of Joseph, 40b, 74, 105, 114-15, 153; tribe of, 109, 153-54
Epicurus, Epicureans, 402
Epileptic, healing of, 277a, 335, 364
Epistles, general, 12, 20, 24; canon of, 6a, 468; James, 12, 20, 24; John, 12, 20, 24, 254b, 482-87; Jude, 12, 20, 24; Peter, 12, 20, 24, 253
Epistles, Pauline, 12, 20, 22-23, 437, 445; canon of, 6a, 468; Colossians, 23, 433-34; Corinthians, I, 22, 410-12; Corin-

thians, II, 22, 414-16; Ephesians, 22, 434-35; Galatians, 22, 417-18; Hebrews, 23, 470-81; Philemon, 23, 433a; Philippians, 22, 435-36; Romans, 22, 419-21; Thessalonians, I, 23, 404b; Thessalonians, II, 23, 405a; Timothy, I, 23, 438a; Timothy, II, 23, 439-40; Titus, 23, 439
Erasmus, 223a
Erastus, 409b
Error, spirit of, 486-87; see also Evil
Esau, 18, 40b, 67a, 74, 102-3, 114-15, 173a
Eschatology, 222, 307a, 310a, 447b, 491b
Esdraelon, Plain of, 29b, 34b, 229b, 245
Esdras, books of, 5b
Essenes, 218, 219
Esther: book of, 5a, 12, 15; queen, 15, 61a, 357a; Esther, 5b
Eucharist, 312a, 376a, 409a, 411b, 422a
Eunuch, 297a, 379-80
Euphrates, 29a, 64a, 66a, 116, 146, 500, 517
Eusebius, 6a, 437a, 490a
Eutychus, 386, 422a
Eve, 73, 96, 146-47, 356, 522-23; see also Seed of the woman
Evil, 165, 405a, 433b, 435b, 482, 485-86; see also Demonology, Satan, Sin
Exile: see Captivity
Exodus: book of, 4b, 12-13; from Egypt, 68, 75, 76 (map), 106-7, 542
Exorcism, 393b, 408-9
Ezekiel, 17, 50a, 89-90, 129-31, 163a, 543; book of, 5a, 12, 17
Ezion-geber, 116
Ezra, 15, 38a, 72b, 91, 136-39, 158b, 216a, 543; book of, 5a, 12, 15
Ezra IV, 221b

Fair Havens, 430a
Faith: healings by, 358, 360-62, 365-68; Jesus on, 242, 250b, 262, 272b, 279-80, 283b, 286-87, 290a, 292b, 295a, 302a, 306a, 313a, 333a; justification by, 418-21; of O.T. patriarchs and saints, 95, 100-1, 246b, 479-80; salvation by grace through, 395b, 417b, 419-20, 434a, 449-52, 473, 479-81, 485
Fall of man, 96-97, 147, 526
Family: see Society
Fan, winnowing, 36, 232a
Farming, 34-36, 59b; see also Festivals
Fasts, fasting, 61-63, 232b, 234b, 269-70; Day of Atonement, 62; of months, 62
Feast(s), 44a, 58-61, 204; of Dedication, 61b, 93, 214a, 282b; New Moon, 59; of Passover, 59-60, 75, 156, 300, 311; of Purim, 15, 61a; Sabbath, 58-59; of Tabernacles, 59, 61, 279; of Trumpets, 59a; of Unleavened Bread, 59-60; of Weeks, 59-61; of Wood Offering, 61
Feeding: of apostles at Lord's Supper, 311; of apostles at Sea of Galilee, 332a; of Elijah, 118, 172b; of Israel with manna, 75, 107, 172a, 272b; of multitudes by Jesus, 271b, 274a; of a hundred men by Elisha, 121, 173a
Felix, 425-27

Festivals: see Feasts
Festus, 427-28
Fig tree, 301-2; parables of, 288-89, 308b, 336
Fire, 55-56, 232a, 268a, 375a, 481, 491a, 512; see also Altar, Sacrifice
First-born, 40-41, 52b, 102, 105, 153, 149, 228b, 434, 481; see also Birthright, Children
Firstfruits, 35b, 54-55, 57-58, 244b, 448b; Day of, 60-61, 375
Fishing, 245, 245, 249, 332
Five, significance of, 537
Flies, plague of, 149
Flood, the, 66, 66-67, 73, 98, 145, 169b, 542
Food: see Meals
Fool, parable of the rich, 288b, 336
Foreknowledge of Jesus, 345-48
Forgiveness: 261, 302a, 324b, 414a, 433-34; of sin, 231b, 264b, 267b, 278b, 312a, 331b, 368, 375b, 381, 394a, 419b, 434a, 438a, 447a; see also Atonement, Justification, Reconciliation, Sacrifice
Fortunatus, 409b
Forty, significance of, 539
Four, significance of, 537
Fourth dimension, glimpses of, 524-25
Frogs, plague of, 149
Freedom: discourse on spiritual, 280-81; from Mosaic legalism, 395-96, 417-18; from sin, 42a, 420a, 449-51
Friend, parable of importunate, 285b, 336
Furnace, fiery, 132, 171b

Gabbatha, 323a
Gabriel, 133, 226
Gad: son of Jacob, 74, 114-115, 150-51, 153; tribe of, 153, 155
Gadarene demoniac, 270a, 335, 362
Gaius: of Corinth, 405a; of Derbe, 421b; of Macedonia, 413-14
Galatia, 398b, 407a, 417a
Galatians, Epistle to, 6a, 12, 22, 417-18
Galilee, 34b, 63b, 214a, 231a, 245-46, 250, 274a, 284-85, 332; Jesus' ministry in, 245-83; Sea of, 237, 245, 249, 271-72, 284
Gall and vinegar, 324a
Gallio, 405b
Gamaliel, 377b, 388a, 424b
Gaulanitis, 215b, 231a
Gedaliah, 89
Gehazi, 85, 121, 170b
Gemara, 217a
Genealogy: of Jesus, 134, 223-25; Messianic line to David, 114-15
Genesis: book of, 4b, 12-13
Geneva Bible, 9
Gennesaret: see Sea of Galilee
Gentile(s), 16, 64b, 99, 163b, 229a, 245, 284, 297b, 307-8, 412b; court of, 163b, 215b, 241a, 498, 513; Jews' relation to, 380-81, 392, 396b; Law and, 394-96; salvation for, 125, 274, 285, 305b, 379b, 387, 390-92, 418-21, 435a, 466
Gergasa, 249a
Gerizim, Mount, 242b

ershon (Gershom), 54b
eshem, 138
ethsemane, 299, 315-20, 436b, 452b, 550
ibeon, 50b, 83, 116
ideon, 36a, 56a, 79, 169a, 480, 543
ifts, spiritual, 411b, 421a, 461
ilgal, 77, 79, 111, 118, 120
irdle, 42b, 53-54, 231b, 422b, 495
nosticism, 433b, 482-83
oats, 30b, 56b, 62, 160; parable of sheep and, 310a
od: as Alpha and Omega, 495, 509, 534-35; covenant of, 10b, 47, 66, 148, 420b; Creator, 10b, 143-44, 180, 199-202, 534-35; developing concept of, 16-19, 48a, 107, 142a, 167, 179-80, 536; kingdom of, 10-11, 239, 257-62, 491; names of, 30b, 107, 142, 205; power of shown in miracles, 167-74, 246-48, 358-71, 384-86
odhead, 143, 402b, 419b, 433-34, 467a, 484, 493b, 534-35
og and Magog, 131, 503, 519
olan, 45b
olden altar (altar of incense), 49-50, 160, 226a, 498, 506, 512
olden Rule, 262
olgotha (Calvary), 324a
oliath, 81, 112
omorrah, 56a, 73, 169b, 550
oodman of the house, parable of, 287a, 309a, 336
oshen, 68, 74, 105
ospel, the, 246a, 287b, 307b, 333, 381a, 419b, 453, 463a
ospels, Four, 6a, 12, 20-21, 223a, 445, 468; harmony of, 338-43
race, salvation by, 389b, 395b, 417b, 419-20, 434b, 436a, 449-52, 463, 470, 480-81, 537
reat Bible, 9
reece: see Achaia
reek: language, 3, 5-6, 20, 63b, 92, 213, 230a, 387-88; philosophy, 402, 409a
roves, 50b, 127
uidance, O.T. signs of God's, 168-69
uilt offering, 57a
utenberg: Johannes, 5b; Bible, 9

abakkuk, 19, 89, 493b; book, 5a, 12, 19
agar, 40-41, 73, 101, 172a, 418a
aggai, 19, 91, 135, 163a; book of, 5a, 12, 19
agiographa, 5a
ail, 498, 500, 512; plague of, 149
allel, 142b, 204, 311b
am, 66b, 73, 98-99, 114-15
aman, 15, 61a
ammurabi, Code of, 29a, 37b, 51b, 140
anani: kinsman of Nehemiah, 138-39; seer, 84, 122
ananiah, 139
and: healing of withered, 268b, 335; Jeroboam's, 170b, 173b; leprous, 107, 167a
annah, 39a, 41a, 110, 356-57
anukkah; see Feast of Dedication
aran, 66b, 73, 100
armony of the Gospels, 223a, 338-43

Harvest, 35b, 59-60, 244b, 265-66, 418b, 449a, 500, 516; see also Feasts
Hasmoneans: see Maccabees
Hatred against Jesus, 352-55
Hattin, Horns of, 257, 258
Hazael, 86, 119, 121
Healings: see Miracles
Heaven, 143-44; kingdom of (see Kingdom of God); new, 125, 504, 507, 520
Hebrew(s), 29-31, 33, 64, 100, 106; Epistle to, 6a, 12, 23, 468, 470-81; language, 63; society, 27-28, 36-42. See also Israelites, Semites
Hebron, 14, 45b, 66b, 71a, 73, 81, 100, 113
Heli, 224-25
Hellenization of Palestine, 63b, 92-93, 213-15, 217
Heresy, 219b, 433b, 440a, 469, 482-83
Herod: Agrippa I, 381, 382, 392b; Agrippa II, 390, 427b; Antipas, tetrarch, 231a, 242b, 271b, 296b, 322b; the Great, 93, 220, 228-29, 242b, 284; Philip, Herodias' husband, 242b; Philip, tetrarch, 231a; Temple of, 50a, 163-64, 164, 215, 306b, 326b
Herodians, 303b
Herodias, 242b, 296b, 356
Hexateuch, 5a
Hezekiah, 51a, 58a, 71, 87-88, 124-26, 173b
High places, 50-51, 123, 126-27
High priest, 53, 56b, 61-62, 127, 134, 160, 231a, 295b, 310b, 320b, 377b; Christ as, 53b, 62b, 240, 470-78
Hilkiah, 127
Hillel, school of, 40a, 250a, 296b
Hiram, 83, 116, 162b
History: of Apostolic Church, 374-83, 387-440, 468; books of, 12, 14-15, 21; intertestamental, 92-93, 213-22; of Jesus, 213-334; lesson from O.T., 542-43; resume of O.T., 65-72; outline of O.T., 73-91
Hittites, 32, 109
Holiness Code, 4b, 52a
Holy Ghost, 226-28, 232, 235a, 314b, 379a; blasphemy against, 267b, 270a; as Comforter, 313-14, 347, 375; Gentiles and, 381a, 407b; at Pentecost, 56a, 375; promise of, 313b, 333b. See also Holy Spirit
Holy of Holies, 53b, 62a, 159, 159-60, 163
Holy Place, 49a, 53b, 62a, 138, 159, 159-60, 163, 307b
Holy Spirit, 314b, 374-75, 483; as Advocate, 313a, 483; as Comforter, 313-15, 347, 491b; in Godhead, 534; as Spirit of God, 143, 375a. See also Holy Ghost
Hope, Messianic, 220-22
Horeb: see Sinai
Horses, 31-33, 491, 506, 511
Hosanna, 300b
Hosea, 18, 87; book of, 5a, 12, 18
Hoshea, 87
Hospitality, 44-45, 270b, 289a
House on rock, parable of, 262-63, 336

Huldah, 39a, 127
Humility, 30b, 278a, 289a, 293b
Husbandmen, parable of wicked, 302-3
Hypocrisy, 217b, 260-61, 286, 305
Hyrcanus, John, 93, 214b

Iconium, 394, 398a, 406b, 440a
Idolatry, 15, 47b, 50-51, 68, 71-72, 84-89, 117, 122-23, 127-28, 242b; forbidden, 48, 75, 77, 110, 485; Paul on, 402-3, 410-11, 416a, 454. See also Calf
Idumaea, 214, 231a, 252a
Illyricum, 415a, 417a
Imagery, apocalyptic, 133, 490-91, 508-21
Immanuel, 125, 148, 220b, 226b, 239, 493a, 504; see also Messiah
Immortality: Greek concept of, 404a; Jesus and, 242, 250b, 281-82, 304a, 326b, 328, 530; Jewish concept of, 217-18, 222a, 304; Paul on, 415b, 446-49. See also Life, Resurrection
Importunate friend, parable of, 285b
Importunate widow: see Widow
Incarnation, 223-25, 391a, 438a, 446b, 467a, 472, 483, 544; see also Advent
Incense, 46b, 53-56, 62a, 498, 512; altar of, 49b, 51, 160
Infirm man, healing of, 250b, 267-68, 335, 360
Ingathering, Feast of: see Feast of Tabernacles
Inheritance, 38b, 40b, 59b, 287a; see also Birthright
Irenaeus, 6a, 489a
Isaac, 13, 29b, 34a, 40b, 43a, 46b, 48a, 67a, 73, 101-2, 106, 114-15, 150, 224, 418a, 480
Isaiah, 17, 87-88, 124-26, 128, 158b, 220a; book of, 5a, 12, 17, 125
Ish-bosheth, 81
Ishmael, Ishmaelites, 29a, 40b, 73-74, 101, 114-15, 418a
Israel: history, resume and outline of, 66-72, 73-91; Kingdom of, 15, 71, 82 (map), 84-87, 118, 120, 122, 125-26, 130; nation of, 10b, 12-15, 40b, 47a, 66-68, 103, 106, 148, 150, 154, 420-21, 466a, 480; spiritual, 252a, 464, 471b, 497
Israelites, 29a, 64a, 74-75, 106, 114-15, 170a, 540-41; see also Hebrews
Issachar, 74, 114-15, 151, 153, 155
Ituraea, 231a

Jacob, 13, 29b, 46b, 64a, 67a, 74, 102-3, 106, 114-15, 150-53, 173a, 224, 464, 480, 541-42
Jah, Jahweh, 142b
Jair, 79
Jairus, daughter of, 270b, 294b, 335, 357, 370
James: brother of Jesus, 333a, 382a, 391b, 395b; Epistle of, 6a, 12, 24, 468; the Less, 252b, 255b; son of Zebedee, 249b, 252-53, 297b, 306b, 316, 332a, 392b
Jamnia, Council of, 5a
Japheth, 64b, 66b, 73, 99, 114-15

Jason, 400b

Jebusites, 109

Jeconias, 223-25

Jedidiah, 116, 149

Jehoahaz: of Israel, 86; of Judah, 88, 120, 128-29

Jehoash, 86, 88, 120

Jehoiachin, 89, 128-30

Jehoiada, 86

Jehoiakim, 89, 128-29

Jehoram: of Israel, 85-86, 118, 120-21; of Judah, 85-86, 123

Jehoshaphat, 51a, 85, 120-23, 171b, 219a, 224

Jehosheba, 86

Jehovah, 4b, 68, 96-97; name and character, 48a, 75, 107, 142b, 145-46; worship of, 50b, 52a, 71a, 117, 122

Jehovah-jireh, 101

Jehovistic Document, 4b, 96, 145

Jehu: king of Israel, 85-86, 119, 121; seer, 123

Jephthah, 48a, 79, 480

Jeremiah, 17, 88-89, 127-30, 158b; book of, 5a, 12, 17

Jericho, 34b, 68, 68, 77, 109, 118, 120, 168a, 297a

Jeroboam: I, 51a, 83-84, 116, 118, 170b, 173b; II, 87

Jerome, 6, 437a

Jerusalem, 15, 71-72, 91, 113, 171b, 174, 230, 325 (map), 543; center of worship, 117, 122; Council of, 394-96, 417-18; David conquers, 72a, 113; early Church in, 375; fall of, 17, 72a, 89, 128-29, 218b, 300b, 307b, 468-69; Jesus in (see Jesus); new, 19, 125, 174b, 459, 504, 507, 520; Paul in (see Paul); prophecies on doom of, 128-31, 306-8; restoration of, 133-34, 136-39

Jeshurun, 155

Jesse, 112, 114-15, 220a, 224

Jesus: accusations against, 267-70, 279a, 286a, 321-23, 352-53; and Adam, 97, 147; Advent of, 10b, 19, 125, 147-48, 223b, 228a, 493b; and angels, 228a, 234a, 287a, 330, 334, 471; "Anointed One," 10b, 220b, 222b, 471; anointing by Mary of Bethany, 298b; appearances after Resurrection, 329-33; arrest, 319; ascension, 225b, 328, 333-34, 347, 545; atonement of, 53b, 57b, 326b, 434b, 447; authority questioned, 241a, 302; baptism, 232, 234-35, 375a, 544; betrayal, 310b, 319, 345; blood, efficacy of, 53b, 57b, 312a, 420a, 447a, 451b, 477-78, 497, 499; born in Bethlehem, 134, 220b, 228a; brethren of, 229b, 270b; calls the Four, 249a; childhood, 229-30; chooses apostles, 252-56; Church and, 275b, 278b; cleanses Temple, 241a, 299, 301b; on Commandments, 273a, 304b, 312b; commissions apostles, 270b; conspiracy against, 310b; and covenant, 47b, 148, 475-76; and the cross, 253a, 275-76, 290; crucifix-

ion of, 324-27, 355, 545; death abolished by, 248b, 326, 472; death and resurrection foretold, 275b, 277a, 297a; on discipleship, 241-42, 252b, 271a, 275-76, 280b, 289-90, 292b, 314; discourses, list of, 336 (see also Discourses); on divorce, 40a, 260, 296b; draft of fishes, 248-49, 332; on faith, 262, 272b, 280b, 286-87, 290a, 292, 302a, 306a, 313a, 333a; fast of, 63a, 234b; on fasting, 61-62, 261, 269-70; at Feast of Dedication, 282b; at Feast of Tabernacles, 279-82; feeds multitudes, 271b, 274a; first disciples, 235a; flight to Egypt, 229a, 541; foreknowledge of events, 345-48; on forgiveness, 261, 264b, 267b, 278b, 302a, 312a, 324b, 331b; and fourth dimension, 524-25; Galilean ministry, 245-83; genealogy of, 223-25; Gentiles seek, 305b; in Gethsemane, 299, 315-19; hatred of, 352-55; as high priest, 53b, 62b, 240, 470-78; on humility, 278a, 289a, 293b; as Immanuel, 148, 226b, 239; immortality and, 250b, 281-82, 304a, 326b, 328, 530; infancy, 225-29; intercessory prayer of, 315; irrefutable question, 304b; in Jerusalem, 228a, 230a, 240-42, 250, 274a, 279a, 282b, 299-301, 333a; John Baptist and, 231, 234-35, 242, 263, 302; Judaean ministry, 240-44; as king, 222-23, 225, 240, 299-300, 323-24, 493, 507, 519; and kingdom of God, 239 (see also Kingdom); as Lamb of God, 51b, 55b, 57b, 60b, 158a, 234-35, 311b, 467b, 497, 502, 504-7, 510, 512; on Last Judgment, 310, 491-92; Last Supper, 46b, 311-15; Law and, 52b, 157-58, 259, 304b; lessons from early life of, 223-31, 546; on life, 241-44, 272-73, 313a; on life of Christian, 257-67, 269b, 287-94; ministry of, 239-334, 338-43, 545; as Lion of Judah, 152, 506; on love, 45b, 57b, 223a, 259-60, 264b, 288a, 290a, 304b, 312-15, 332b; Magi and, 228b; on marriage, 38a, 296-97, 304a; as mediator, 47, 66a, 148, 438a, 471, 475-78; miracles of, 236, 241b, 246-48, 270b, 274b, 335, 358-71; mission, universality of, 223a, 228b, 333, 348, 441, 462; on new birth, 241b; parables, list of, 336 (see also Parables); and Passion Week, 299-334; at Passover, 230a, 311; Peraean ministry, 284-98; persecution of, 240, 249-50, 252a, 264a, 270a, 281, 283, 295b, 319-27, 352-55; Peter's confession of, 275a; and Pharisees, 241-42, 273-75, 280-81, 285-86, 289-93, 295-96, 300-3, 305, 351-55; on prayer, 260-62, 278b, 285b, 293, 301b; presentation in Temple, 228a; as prophet, 220a,

240, 246b, 271b, 280-81, 310b, 365, 471; propitiatory sacrifice of, 57b, 62b, 311b, 447, 451a, 477-78, 484; questions asked by, 349-51; rabbis and, 250a; raisings from the dead, 173, 263a, 270b, 294-95, 370-71; redemption through, 10b, 60b, 223b, 225a, 309a, 389a, 419b, 434b, 447b, 463-64, 493a, 551; rejection by Jews, 248-49, 270b, 273a, 284, 302-3, 306b, 321b, 323b, 346, 420b; resurrection, 275b, 277a, 297, 328-30, 355; teaching on, 241a, 289a, 295a, 304, 345, 545; on retaliation, 45b, 260; righteousness of, 232, 276, 314b, 326a, 436a, 451; and Sabbath, 59a, 250b, 268-69, 281a; and Sadducees, 217-18, 295b, 304, 351; salvation through, 227-28, 234b, 242a, 449-51, 472, 474-75; Sanhedrin's plot against, 295b; and Satan, 165, 232-34, 270a, 275b, 280b, 285-86, 313b, 326a; as Savior, 226b, 228a, 232a, 244b, 280a, 436a, 450; and scribes, 268a, 285-86, 304-5, 310b, 351; on Second Coming, 56a, 125, 148, 293-94, 296a, 299, 308-10, 314-15, 321b, 334a, 348, 491-93; as seed of David, 47b, 113, 220a, 226b, 446b; as seed of the woman, 10b, 47b, 97, 147, 223b; Sermon on the Mount, 252a, 257-63; on servants, 261, 273a, 280b, 292b, 309, 311; the Seventy, 285; silent years of, 176-77, 231, 544; on sin and sinners, 232a, 264b, 267, 269b, 280b, 290-91, 314b, 368-69; and Solomon, 117; as Son of God, 223b, 225b, 232b, 234a, 240, 242a, 250, 275a, 283, 305a, 344, 472, 530; as Son of man, 133, 222b, 225, 242a, 308a, 344-48, 471; on spiritual freedom, 280-81; on stewardship, 275b, 287a, 291b, 309; and Temple, 234a, 241a, 279b, 282b, 299, 301-2, 304-5; temptation of, 232-34, 544; ten ascending steps in life of, 544-45; tomb, 327; training of apostles, 255-56, 256b, 270-71, 274-75, 328, 372-73; transfiguration, 276-77, 545; trials of, 320-23; and tribute, 277-78, 303b; triumphal entry, 300-1; at twelve, 230-31, 544; walks on sea, 248a, 272a; washes disciples' feet, 311-12; on watchfulness, 286-87, 309, 318, 336; and withered fig tree, 301-2; "without sin," 232a, 475, 483; on worship, 48b, 244a, 262; young manhood, 231; and Zacchaeus, 298

Jethro, 75, 106

Jews, 64; of the Dispersion, 15, 92-93, 213, 215-16, 221, 229a, 375b, 388, 393a; Gentiles and, 380-81, 396b; Judaism and, 64, 137, 216; Maccabees and, 93, 214-15; Paul on, 419-21, 435a, 464, 466a; restoration

Judah, 134, 136; and Roman rule, 93, 214-15; Samaritans and, 134-35, 242-43. *See also* Hebrews, Israel, Israelites, Judaism

Jezebel, 45a, 85, 118-21, 356, 496, 509

Joab, 45b, 81, 83, 112

Joash, 86, 356

Job, book of, 5a, 12, 16, 179-203

Jochebed, 75, 106

Joel, 18, 91, 491b; book of, 5a, 12, 18

John: apostle, 44a, 119, 165, 178, 235a, 249b, 252b, 254a, 297b, 306b, 311a, 316, 320b, 324b, 329, 332b, 376b, 379b, 482-83, 488-89, 490a; the Baptist, 119, 226-27, 231-32, 234-35, 242, 263, 271b; 302; Epistles of, 6a, 12, 24, 254b, 468; Gospel of, 6a, 12, 20-21, 223a, 254b, 468; Hyrcanus I, 93, 214a

Jonah, 18, 87, 274b, 286a; book of, 5a, 12, 18

Jonathan: Maccabaeus, 214a; son of Saul, 81, 112

Joppa, 380b, 386

Jordan, 29b, 34, 76, 108, 118, 120, 168a, 231-33, *233*, 240, 245, *247*, 284

Joseph: of Arimathaea, 327; husband of Mary, 223-26, 228-30; son of Jacob, 13, 67a, 74, 104-5, 113-15, 132, 150-51, 153-54, 480, 540, 542

Josephus, 50a, 217b, 219a, 242b, 245, 300, 307a, 323b

Joshua: book of, 5a, 12, 14; high priest (Jeshua), 134-35; son of Nun, 14, 34b, 68, 77, 79, 108-9, 175, 543

Josiah, 51a, 88, 127-28, 224

Jotham, 87, 124

Jubilee, year of, 42a, 59b

Jubilees, 221a

Judaea, 213-15, 231-32, 240; Jesus' ministry in, 240-44, 250

Judah: Kingdom of, 15, 71a, *82* (map), 84-89, 103, 112-13, 117-18, 122-23, 126-27, 130, 134; son of Jacob, 74, 103, 114-15, 150, 152; tribe of, 112, 118, 122, 152, 154, 220a

Judaism, 40a, 52a, 59a, 72b, 91, 137-39, 214, 216-17, 258, 395a, 414a, 416-17, 433b, 470, 482

Judas: apostle (Thaddaeus), 252b, 255b, 313a; Iscariot, 252b, 255b, 298b, 310, 312a, 320-22, 375a; Maccabaeus, 50a, 61a, 93, 214a; zealot of Galilee, 218b, 307a

Jude, Epistle of, 6a, 12, 24, 468

Judge, parable of unjust, 292-93, 336

Judges, 14, 68, 79, 110, 543; book of, 5a, 12, 14

Judgment(s): Day of, 16, 18-19, 222a, 405a, 491-93; Last, 310, 464, 491, 503, 507; in Revelation, 497-503, 519; signs of divine, O.T., 18-19, 56a, 125, 167, 169-71. *See also* Righteousness

Judiciary, Hebrew, development of, 55a, 76, 107, 110, 123, 137, 219a; *see also* Judges, Sanhedrin

Judith, 5b

Julius, centurion, 429-30, 432b

Justification by faith, 395b, 417-20, 451, 463

Justin Martyr, 6a, 329a, 489a

Kadesh-barnea, 13, 68, 77, 106, 108

Kedesh, 45b

Khirbet Qumran, 218, *219*

Kidron Valley, 174a, 301a, 306b, 315b

King(s): books of, 5a, 12, 15; godly, 84-85, 88, 122-23, 126-27, 543; of Israel, 84-87; of Judah, 84-89; Messianic, 113, 125, 220a, 222-25, 228b, 240, 299-300, 323-24, 493, 507, 419; Ptolemies, 92, 214a, 216b; Syrian (Seleucid), 93, 214a

King James Bible, 5b, *9*, 10a

Kingdom: of God (of heaven), 10-11, 16, 133, 222-23, 232b, 234, 239, 248a, 275b, 326a, 465, 467a, 491, 498, 504, 506, 514; nature of, 257-63, 296a; parables of, 265-67, 278b, 293-94, 303, 309, 336; time of, 246a, 292-93, 296, 333b, 504; of Israel (*see* Israel); of Judah (*see* Judah); Messianic (Christ's), 87, 90, 125, 131-33, 226b, 289b, 307a, 467a, 498; United, *80* (map), 81, 112-13, 116, 543

Kirjath-jearim, 110

Kohath, 54b

Korah, 77, 170a

Laban, 46b, 48a, 67a, 74, 102-3, 150

Lamb of God: Jesus as, 51b, 55b, 57b, 158a, 234-35, 311b, 467b, 497, 504-7, 510, 512; marriage of, 502, 519; wife of, 174b, 356, 504, 507

Lamech, 37b, 73, 98, 114-15, 224

Lameness, healings of, 376, 394b

Lamentations, book of, 5a, 12, 17

Lamp, miracle of burning, 168b, 309a

Language: apocalyptic, 131, 133, 220-22, 307a, 490b; Aramaic, 3, 6b, 63, 230, 387; Greek, 3, 5-6, 63b, 92, 213, 230a, 387; Hebrew, 3-6, 63, 230, 387-88; of inspiration, 375b, 412a; Semitic, 63

Laodicea, 408a, 434b

Last Judgment: *see* Judgment

Last Supper: *see* Supper

Laver, brazen, 160, *161*, 162

Law: books of, 4b, 12-13; Jesus on, 52b, 157-58, 259, 304b; Mosaic, 10b, 13, 29b, 51-52, 54-55, 59, 157-58, 216, 450a, 538; oral, 4a, 52a, 216-17; Paul on, 158a, 418-19, 421a, 436a, 450-51; and scribes and Pharisees, 216-17, 286b, 305; "servant of," 40a, 230a, 546. *See also* Blood revenge, Commandments

Laying on of hands, 378a, 438b

Lazarus: of Bethany, 285b, 294-95, 298b, 300a, 335, 370; rich man and, parable of, 292a, 336

Leah, 39a, 67a, 74, 103, 150-51

Leaven, 56a, 60, 275a; parable of, 266b

Lebbaeus: *see* Thaddaeus

Legion, Roman, 320a

Leprosy, 57a; healings of, 107, 121, 167a, 173b, 249, 269b, 296, 335, 359, 366

Letter of Aristeas, 221a

Levi: apostle (Matthew), 252b, 255a; son

of Jacob, 74, 114-15, 150, 152; tribe of, 14, 41a, 52b, 54b, 75, 106, 109, 154

Levites, 13, 15, 52, 54-55, 57-58, 85, 123, 136, 139, 159þ, 219a, 288a, 474-75; *see also* Priesthood

Levitical cities, 54b, 77, 109, 155

Leviticus, book of, 4b, 12-13, 75

Lice, plague of, 149

Life and customs of Bible times, 27-64; agricultural, 34-36; blood revenge, 45-46; covenants, 46-47; dress, 42-43; fasts, 61-63; festivals, 58-61; Hebrew society, 36-42, 242-43, 380b, 395a; hospitality, 44-45, meals, 43-44; nomadic, 29-34; worship, 47-58

Life: book of, 503-4, 519; in Christ, 20a, 223b, 262, 273a, 282a, 295a, 310a, 435a, 446a, 452-53, 483-84, 490b; Jesus' discourses on, 241-44, 272-73, 313a; river of, 505, 521. *See also* Immortality, Resurrection

Light: Christ as, 223b, 306a, 483, 504, 507, 520; of world, discourse on, 280

Lion of Judah, 152, 506

Literature: apocalyptic, 131, 133, 135, 220-22, 490-91; apocryphal, 5a; Bible as, 3, 12; intertestamental, 216a, 220-22; N.T., 12, 20-24, 445; O.T., 4-5, 12-19, 179, 216; pseudepigraphal, 220-22; rabbinical, 216-17; Wisdom, 5a, 179. *See also* Canon, Preservation of text, Versions

Locusts, plague of, 18, 149, 498, 513

Logos, 534; *see* Word

Lord God: *see* Jehovah

Lord's Prayer, 261, 285b

Lord's Supper, 312a, 376a, 411b

Lot, 29, 44b, 66b, 73, 100, 169a; wife of, 169b

Love: God's, 10b, 16, 47, 167, 172a, 204, 260, 483-85; Jesus on, 45b, 57b, 223a, 259-60, 264b, 288a, 290a, 304b, 312-15, 332b; John the apostle on, 483-86; Paul on, 412a, 415a, 420-21, 435a, 446a, 452b. *See also* Forgiveness, Grace

Lucifer, 165-66, 493a

Luke, 374, 387, 399a, 421b, 429b, 433a, 439b; Gospel of, 6a, 12, 20-21, 223a, 468

Luther, Martin, 9

LXX: *see* Septuagint

Lycaonia, 394a, 398b

Lycias, Claudius, 424-25

Lydda, 380a

Lydia, 357, 399b

Lystra, 394b, 398a, 406b, 440a

Maccabees, 53a, 93, 214-20, 284

Maccabees, books of, 5b, 221a

Macedonia, 399-401, 414-15, 421b, 437

Machaerus, 242b

Magdala, 249a

Magi, 228b

Magnificat, 227a

Malachi, 19, 91-92, 139; book of, 5a, 12, 19

Malchus, 320a, 335, 367

Mammon, 261, 291b

Man: creation of, 143-46, 535; nature of, Paul on, 435a, 453-58; son of, Jesus as, 133, 222b, 225, 242a, 305a, 308a, 344-48

Manasseh: king of Judah, 51a, 88, 127; son of Joseph, 40b, 74, 105, 114-15, 153; tribe of, 109, 154, 464

Manasses, Prayer of, 5b

Mandrakes, 151

Manna, 75, 77, 107, 109, 161a, 172a, 272b, 496, 522

Manoah, 169a

Marah, 75, 172a

Marcion, 6a

Mariamne, 215a

Mark: Gospel of, 6a, 12, 20-21, 223a, 468; John, 21, 223a, 392-93, 397-98, 440b

Marriage, 37-38, 40b, 51-53, 137, 139, 150, 236a, 250a, 357; feast, 39a, 236, 289b; Jesus on, 38a, 296-97, 304a; of king's son, parable of, 44b, 303a, 336; of the Lamb, 39a, 289b, 502, 519; Levirate, 38a; Paul on, 38a, 411a, 434-35, 438a

Mars' Hill (Areopagus), 402a, *403*

Marston, Charles, 98

Martha, 285b, 294-95, 298b, 357

Martyrdom: of James, 253b, 381b; of Paul, 440b, 468; of Peter, 468; of Stephen, 379

Martyrdom of Isaiah, 221a

Mary: of Bethany, 285b, 294-95, 298b, 357, 595; Magdalene, 270b, 324b, 327b, 329-30, 357; mother of James, 329a; mother of John Mark, 357, 381b, 392b; Virgin, 147, 224-31, 236, 270b, 324b, 349, 356-57, 375a; wife of Cleophas, 270b

Masada, 218b, *221*

Massora, 6b

Matthew, 223, 249b, 252b, 255a; Gospel of, 6a, 12, 20-21, 255a, 468

Matthew's Bible, 9

Matthias, 375a

Meal offering, 56

Meals, 43-44; *see also* Fasts, Feasts, Manna, Sacrifice

Meat(s), 30-31, 44a, 244b, 269a, 272b, 381a, 410-11, 547

Mediator, Jesus as, 47, 66a, 148, 438a, 471, 475-78

Megiddo, 32, 49a

Melchizedek, 53b, 73, 100, 474-75

Melita, 431, *431*

Menahem, 87

Mephibosheth, 81

Mercy seat, 62a, 161

Meribah, 154, 172b

Meshach, 132, 171b

Mesopotamia, 29-30, 63b, 66b, 79, 100, 102

Messiah: hope of, 113, 135, 217b, 220-22, 235-36, 244b; incarnation of, 223-25; line of, 10-11, 15, 74, 98-99, 103, 113-15, 134, 150, 152, 224; office of, 240; O.T. prophecies of, 11b, 74, 77, 83, 97, 107, 125, 129, 133, 139, 220, 337; psalms, Messianic, 204;

seed of David, 47b, 220a, 224, 305a, 446b; suffering servant, 125, 220b, 275-76, 330-31, 393-94

Micah, 18, 87-88, 126, 134, 229a; book of, 5a, 12, 18

Michael, 133, 499, 514, 519

Michal, 81, 112

Midian, Midianites, 29a, 77, 79, 106, 114-15

Midrashim, 217a

Miletus, 422a, *423*, 437a

Millennium, 502-3, 507

Miracles: of apostles, 271a, 374, 376-77, 379b, 384-86, 411b; of Jesus, 236, 241b, 246-48, 270b, 274b, 335, 358-71; O.T., 167-74; of Paul, 384-86, 394b, 399b, 408, 422a, 431-32; of Peter, 376-77, 380, 384; of the Seventy, 285a

Miriam, 77, 173a, 357

Mishnah, 217a

Mitre, 43a, 53

Mitylene, 422a

Mizpah (Mizpeh), 81, 111

Moab, 68, 77, 79, 107, 130

Moabites, 29a, 50b, 64a, 85, 114-15, 117, 123

Molech, 50, 117

Monogamy, 37-38, 357

Monotheism, 11a, 13, 29b, 48, 91, 110, 113, 118, 137, 139, 142a, 216a

Moriah, Mount, 50b, 101, 162b, 174a

Mosaic system, 51-58, 107

Moses, 13, 43a, 46-47, 51-52, 68, 75, 77, 106-7, 119, 154, 167-68, 175, 234b, 276b, 471-72, 480, 541-42

Mount: of Olives, *284*, 300, 306b, 315-16, 336b; Sermon on the, 257-63

Murrain, plague of, 149

Mustard seed, parable of, 266a, 336

Myra, 429a

"Mysteries," N.T., 465-67

Naaman, 121, 173b, 249a

Nabal, 112

Naboth, 85, 118

Nadab: king of Israel, 84; son of Aaron, 56a, 169b

Nahum, 19, 88; book of, 5a, 12, 19

Nain, 263a, 269b, 294b, 335, 370

Names: of God, 142; new, *156*, 509, 542; of Satan, 166

Naomi, 14, 36a, 38a

Naphtali: son of Jacob, 74, 114-15, 151, 153; tribe of, 155

Nathan: prophet, 83, 113; son of David, 224-25

Nathanael, 236a, 252b, 254b, 332a

Nazarenes, 388b, 425b

Nazareth, 226b, 229b, 231a, 248b, 270b, 352

Nazarite, 227b, 231b, 424a

Neapolis, 399b

Nebo, Mount, 77, 107

Nebuchadnezzar, 72a, 89-90, 129-30, 132-34, 171a, 174b

Necho (Pharaoh), 88, 127

Negeb, 30a, 68

Nehemiah, 15, 19, 45a, 58a, 72b, 91-92,

138-39, 216a, 543; book of, 5a, 12, 1█

Nero, 437a, 439-40, 468-69

New birth, discourse on, 241-42

New Testament: books of, 3, 12, 21-2█ canonization of, 5b; language of, 63█ literature, 20, 445; summation of, 52█

New Year Festival, 59

Nicodemus, 241b, 327a, 550

Nicopolis, 437a

Nineveh, Ninevites, 18-19, 87, 89, 12█ 286a

Noah, 47a, 49a, 55a, 64b, 66, 73, 98-9█ 114-15, 148, 169b, 224, 542; cov█ nant with, 47, 73, 99, 101, 148; de█ cendants of, *114* (map)

Nobleman's son, healing of, 246a, 33█ 358

Nomadism, 29-34, 48a

Numbers: book of, 4b, 12-13; signif█ cance of sacred, 536-39

Obadiah, 18, 90; book of, 5a, 12, 18

Obed, 14, 114-15

Octavianus: see Augustus

Offerings: oblations, 55-56; sacrificia█ 55-57; *see also* Altars

Oil, 44b, 53-54, 239, 309a, 316, 471

Old Testament: canonization of, 4-5; c█ related subjects in, 141-78; divisio█ and books of, 3, 12-19; history, 65-9█ 542-43; Messianic prophecies in, 33█ miracles of, 167-74; principal chara█ ters of, 95-139; summation of, 526

Olive tree, 316, *316-19*; symbolism o█ 135, 421a, 498, 513

Omega: see Alpha

Omer, 172a

Omri, 84-85

On (Heliopolis), 104, 229a

One, significance of, 536

Onesimus, 433-34

Onesiphorus, 439b

Oral law, 4a, 52a, 216-17

Ordination, 258, 378a, 398a, 438b

Origen, 6a, 440b, 489a

Othniel, 79

Oxen, 30b, 36a, 181

Oxgoad, 389a

Padan-aram, 67a, 74, 102, 150-51

Palestine, *78*, *238* (maps); climate, 34-3█ divided among the tribes, 68, 79, 10█ 154; in intertestamental period, 21█ 222, 231a; language of, 63; under R█ man rule, 93, 214b, 218b, 220b, 222█ 231a, 284, 295b, 322, 425a, 427█ 468-69, 490; topography, 29-30, 34█ 229b, 240, 245, 284. See also Canaa█

Pamphylia, 393-94

Pantheism, 47-48, 402b; *see also* Poly█ theism

Paphos, 393b

Papyrus, 3, 5-6

Parable(s), 264 (list, 336); barren fig tre█ 288-89; cost of discipleship, 289-9█ dragnet, 266-67; faithful and faithle█ stewards, 287, 309a; fig tree an█ young leaves, 308b; of Galilean perio█ 262-78; good Samaritan, 287b; goo█

man of the house, 287a, 309a; great supper, 44b, 289b; hidden treasure, 266b; house built on rock, 262-63; importunate friend, 285b; importunate widow (unjust judge), 292-93, 296b; of the kingdom, 264-67; laborers in the vineyard, 293b, 306; leaven, 266b; lost piece of silver, 290b; lost sheep, 290; marriage of king's son, 44b, 303a; mustard seed, 266a; natural growth of the seed, 265b; new cloth on old garment, 269b; new wine in old bottles, 269b; pearl of great price, 266b; of Peraean ministry, 287-94; Pharisee and publican, 293; prodigal son, 290-91; rich fool, 288b; rich man and Lazarus, 292; sheep and goats, 310a; sower and seed, 265; talents, 309b; tares and wheat, 265-66, 491b; ten pounds, 294a; ten virgins, 309; two debtors, 264b; two sons, 302b; unjust steward, 291b; unmerciful servant, 278b; unprofitable servant, 292b; the vineyard, or wicked husbandmen, 302-3; watchful porter, 309a; watchful servants, 287a; wedding guest, 289a

_raclete, 313a

_radise, 324b, 416b, 505, 507, 522-23

_rallels, Jesus and Paul, 441-44

_ralytic, healing of, 249, 335, 360

_ran, Wilderness of, 77

_rousia, 307-8

_schal lamb, 57b, 60, 311a; see also Passover

_ssion Week, 299-327

_ssover, Feast of, 59-60, 75, 126, 149, 204, 230a, 300, 311

_tmos, 119, 468, 489, 490, 493

_triarch(s), 29b, 37a, 98, 100, 102, 104, 540; world of, 28 (map)

_ul: on Abraham, 418-20, 450-51, 464, 479-80; accusations against, 400a, 405b, 413a, 423b, 425b, 427a, 443-44; on Adam, 97, 449-50; apostleship of, 390, 395-97, 410, 412b, 415-18, 428a, 452b; in Arabia, 390, 417b; and authorship of Hebrews, 23, 470; on baptism, 395a, 411, 418a, 420a, 434-35; on Christian life, 404, 410-11, 418b, 421, 434-36, 438-40, 451-52; on Church, 38b, 411-12, 434-35, 459, 466b (see also Church); conversion, 380a, 388-89; and Council of Jerusalem, 394-96, 417; on covenant, 418a, 420-21, 470-81; on cross and crucifixion, 403-4; 410a, 415b, 418b, 420a, 434-35, 447, 480; in Damascus, 389, 428a, 448a, 452b; on divorce, 40a, 411a; doctrinal teachings, 445-52; early life and education, 388, 424b; epistles (see Epistles, Pauline); founding of churches, 445, 452b; on Godhead, 402b, 419b, 434a, 467a; on idolatry, 402-3, 410-11, 416a, 454; on immortality, 415b, 418b, 440b, 446-49; imprisonments, 400, 424-28, 432-37,

439a; on incarnation, 391a, 438a, 446b, 467a, 472; in Jerusalem, 388-89, 391-92, 395a, 405b, 423a; on Jews' unbelief, 418-21, 435a, 464, 466a; on justification by faith, 395b, 417-20, 451, 463; Law and, 158a, 418-19, 421a, 436a, 450-51; life and ministry of, 387-440; on love, 412a, 415a, 420-21, 435a, 446a, 452b; on nature of man, 435a, 453-58; on marriage, 38a, 411a, 434-35, 438a; martyrdom, 440b, 468; miracles of, 384-86, 394b, 399b, 408, 422a, 431-32; missionary journeys, 392 (map), 393-94, 397 (map), 397-425, 406 (map), 429 (map), 429-32, 437a; on "mysteries," 465-67; parallels in lives of Jesus and, 441-44; persecution of, 391-92, 394, 400-1, 405b, 412-15, 421b, 424-27, 431-32, 439-40; as Pharisee, 388, 425a, 428; on prayer, 435-36, 438a; on resurrection, 404b, 412, 415b, 420a, 434a, 436a, 447-50, 466a; Roman citizenship, 388a, 398a, 400, 405b, 424-25, 427b; on salvation by grace, 395b, 417b, 419-20, 434a, 436a, 449-52, 463, 480-81; on sanctification, 404, 411a, 420a, 451-52; and Sanhedrin, 389, 425-27; on servants, 415b, 434-35, 439; silences in life of, 177-78, 391-92, 427a; on slavery, 42a, 411a, 433, 438b; as tentmaker, 34a, 388a, 403-4; trials of, 424-28, 437, 440b; and viper, 385, 431; visions of Christ, 308a, 391b, 399a, 416b

Peace offering, 56b

Pearl, parable of, 266b, 336

Pekah, 87, 124

Pekahiah, 87

Pella, 308a, 468b

Peniel, 67a, 74, 103, 152, 550

Penitence: see Atonement, Fasting, Repentance

Penitent sinner, healing of, 264b, 335, 357b, 368

Pentateuch, 4b, 13, 52a, 137, 143, 145, 157a, 216-18, 242b

Pentecost, 61, 375-76, 419a, 438b

Peraea, 214-15, 231a, 250a, 252a, 284, 308a; Jesus' ministry in, 284-98

Perga, 393-94

Pergamos, 408, 408, 496

Persecution: of apostles, 376-77, 381b, 392, 468; of church, 378-82, 388-89, 392, 490, 495, 498-500, 503, 507; of Christians, 258-60, 271a, 307b, 314b, 439a, 468-69, 490; of Jeremiah, 128-29; of Jesus, 240, 249-50, 252a, 264a, 270a, 281, 283, 295b, 319-27, 352-55; of Paul, 391-92, 394, 400-1, 405b, 412-15, 421b, 424-27, 431-32, 439-40

Persia, 15, 92, 134, 138-39

Peter, Simon (Cephas), 252-53, 256b; Church and, 275b, 375-77, 380-81, 391b, 395-96, 418a, 468, 548; Epistles of, 6a, 12, 24, 468; healing of mother-

in-law, 249b, 335; healings by, 376-77, 380, 384; Jesus and, 236a, 249b, 272-73, 275-78, 287a, 302a, 306b, 311-12, 316, 318, 320-21, 329a, 331-32, 375-77, 410b

Pharaoh: Abraham and, 73, 100; Joseph and, 67b, 74, 104-5; Josiah and, 88, 127; Moses and, 68, 75, 106-7, 149, 169b, 229a

Pharisee(s), 93, 214b, 216-17; Jesus and, 217b, 241-42, 245-46, 250a, 259, 264, 267-70, 272-75, 280-82, 285-86, 289-93, 295-96, 300-3, 305, 351-55; Paul and, 388, 425a; and resurrection, 217b, 304a, 448a. See also Rabbinism

Phebe, 357, 421b

Philadelphia, 408a, 496

Philemon, 408a, 433a; Epistle to, 6a, 12, 23, 433a

Philip: apostle, 236a, 252b, 254b, 271b, 305-6, 313a; Evangelist, 378-79, 384, 422b; Herod, husband of Herodias, 242b; Herod, tetrarch, 231a

Philippi, 399, 399, 414a, 421b, 435b

Philippians, Epistle to, 12, 22, 433a, 435b

Philistines, 79, 81-83, 111-12, 161b, 170a

Phineas, 53a, 77, 136

Phoenicia, Phoenicians, 29a, 63, 109, 274, 422b

Phrygia, 398b, 407a

Phylacteries, 52a, 293a

Pilate, Pontius, 93, 322-23

Pisgah, Mount, 107

Pisidia, 393-94, 398

Place as dimension of thought, 550

Plagues: in Egypt, 75, 107, 149, 171a; of locusts, 18, 149, 498, 513; seven last, of Revelation, 492, 500, 507

Plumbline, 94, 332b

Poetry: books of, 5a, 12, 16; Job, 16, 179-203; Proverbs, 16; Psalms, 16, 204-9

Polycarp, 6a

Polygamy, 37, 41a, 150, 357

Polytheism, 48, 110, 142a, 145, 401-2, 407; see also Baal worship

Pompey, 93, 214b

Pools: see Bethesda, Siloam, Solomon

Porter, watching, parable of, 309a, 336

Potiphar, 67b, 74, 104; wife of, 74, 104, 356

Poti-pherah, 104

Pounds, parable of, 294, 336

Praetorium, 322a

Prayer: Jesus on, 260-62, 278b, 285b, 293, 301-2; Paul on, 435-36, 438a

Pre-eminence of Christ, 242a, 348, 433-34, 471

Pre-existence of Christ, 281a, 305a, 344, 348, 452a, 471-72

Preservation of Bible text, 4-6

Priesthood, Aaronic, 51-54, 107, 122, 217b, 473-78; see also High priest, Priests, Sadducees

Priestly Code, 4b, 52a, 143, 145, 216a

Priests, 13, 37-38, 52-57, 511; see also Levites, Priesthood, Sacrifice

Priscilla, 357, 403b, 405b, 407a, 414

Prodigal son, parable of, 290-91, 336

Promised Land, 14, 66b, 100, 107-8, 543; see also Canaan, Palestine

Prophecy: Jacob's, 152-53; Messianic, 204, 220-22, 337; rise of, 11b, 16, 71b, 111, 118, 120, 124-25, 128-33 (see also Apocalyptic literature)

Prophet(s), 16-19, 40b, 47b, 51a, 53a, 57, 71b, 124, 134, 471, 480, 543; books of major and minor, 4-5, 12, 17-19, 216a; Jesus as, 220a, 240, 246b, 271b, 280-81, 310b, 365, 471; Law and, 52b, 157-58; schools of, 111, 120

Protection, miracles of, 171-72

Proverbs, book of, 5a, 12, 16, 117, 179

Psalms, 5a , 12, 16, 113, 204-9

Psalms of Solomon, 221a

Pseudepigrapha, 220-22

Ptolemais (Accho), 229b, 422b

Ptolemies, 92, 214a, 216b

Publican(s), 255a, 260, 269b, 298a, 302b; parable of Pharisee and, 293, 336

Publius, 432a; father of, 386, 432a

Punishment, future, 217b, 222a, 304a, 310a

Purification, 119, 231b, 242a, 311b, 437a; see also Baptism, Circumcision, Sacrifice, Sanctification

Purim, Feast of, 15, 61a

Puteoli, 432a

Pythagoras, 433b

Quails, 170a, 172a

Questions asked by Jesus, 349-51

Quirinius, 218b

Rabbinism, 240, 246a, 250a, 296b; see also Pharisees, Scribes

Rabboni, 330a

Rachel, 39a, 41a, 48a, 67a, 74, 103, 150-51, 356

Rahab, 77, 480

Rainbow, 99, 148, 498, 510

Ramah, 50b, 79, 111

Ramoth-gilead, 45b, 123

Rebekah, 39-40, 43a, 67a, 74, 100, 102, 150

Reconciliation through Christ, 62b, 415b, 420a, 433a, 435a, 447, 449b, 463, 472; see also Atonement, Justification by faith, Sacrifice

Red Sea, 68, 75, 107, 167b

Redeemer, promise of, 10b, 97, 125, 134, 147-48, 152, 220a, 337, 526, 542

Redemption: of the body, 412, 420b, 436a; covenant and, 13, 47, 100-1, 148; through Jesus Christ, 10b, 60b, 223b, 225a, 309a, 389b, 419b, 434b, 447b, 463-64, 477, 493a, 551; Law and, 157-58, 450-51

Reformation, periods of, 15, 72a, 84-85, 88, 122-23, 126-27, 137, 139

Refuge, cities of, 45b, 54-55, 77, 109

Rehoboam, 84, 116-18

Rejection of Jesus, 248, 270b, 284, 294, 303, 306b, 321b, 323b, 346, 420b

Remnant, 15-16, 89-91, 130, 134, 136, 139, 158a, 220b, 420b, 499, 507, 515

Repentance, 129, 157b, 167, 191, 231-32, 242b, 246a, 288-89, 416a, 447a, 496; parables of, 290-91

Rephidim, 75, 106, 171-72

Restoration of Judah, 72b, 90-91, 129, 131, 134, 136, 138, 543

Resurrection: general, 331b, 503, 507; of Jesus, 275b, 277a, 297, 328-30, 355, 545; Jesus' teaching on, 241a, 289a, 295a, 304; Jewish concept of, 217b, 222a; Paul on, 404, 412, 415b, 420a, 434a, 436a, 447-50, 466a. See also Immortality

Retaliation, Jesus on, 45b, 260

Reuben: son of Jacob, 74, 104, 114-15, 150, 152; tribe of, 154

Revelation: book of, 6a, 12, 20, 24, 254b, 468, 488-94; glimpses of fourth dimension in, 524-25; introduction and outline, 488-507. See also Apocalypse

Revenge: see Blood

Rezin, 87, 124

Rhegium, 432a

Rheims and Douai Bible, 10a

Rich fool, parable of, 288b, 336

Rich man (Dives) and Lazarus, parable of, 292, 336

Righteousness: of Abraham, 418a, 420a, 451b; of the Christian, 416a, 418b, 420, 435b, 451-52, 457; of God, 16, 124, 167, 179-80, 197-99, 419b, 451; of Jesus Christ, 232a, 276, 314b, 326a, 436a, 451; of the kingdom, 258-62; of Law vs. grace, 157, 436a, 450-51; of the prophets, 16, 94, 124, 480. See also Justification by faith

Ritualism, 52b, 56-57, 216, 268-69, 273, 286, 423-24; see also Judaism, Worship

Rivers in Eden, 146, 521

Rock: of Christ, 275b; parable of house built on, 262-63, 336

Rod: Aaron's, 77, 161a; of iron, 205, 499, 502, 514; Moses', 107, 167-68; shepherd's, 30b, 282

Roman rule: emperor worship and, 439a, 469, 490; Jewish religious freedom and, 214-15; Palestine and, 93, 214b, 218b, 220-22, 231a, 284, 295b, 322, 425a, 427a, 468-69, 490

Romans, Epistle to, 6a, 12, 23, 419-21

Rome: church at, 419a, 435b, 452b; Paul in, 432b, 439-40, 445

Rosh Hashana, 59a

Ruler, parable of rich young, 293b, 336

Ruth, 14, 36a, 38a, 43a, 356-57; book of, 5a, 12, 14

Sabbath, 54a, 58-59, 75, 139, 148, 219b, 326b, 537; feasts, 59; Jesus and, 219b, 246a, 250b, 268-69, 281a, 359-60, 365-66; Sabbatical year, 35b, 59b, 61a

Sackcloth, 61b, 269b, 498

Sacrifice, 49-50, 55-58, 62, 157b, 450a, 473, 476-78; child, 48a, 55b, 101; Christian's, 421; Jesus' propitiatory, 62b, 158a, 311b, 447, 451a, 477-78. See also Atonement, Blood covenant, Lamb

Sadducees, 214b, 217-19, 268a, 448; apostles and, 376-78; Jesus and, 267a, 270a, 274-75, 280a, 282-83, 295b, 304, 351. See also Sanhedrin

Salamis, 393, 393

Salathiel: see Shealtiel

Salome, 253b, 270b, 329a

Salt, 46b, 56a, 259, 290a

Salvation: by grace, 389b, 395b, 417b, 419-20, 434b, 436a, 449-52, 463, 470, 480-81, 537; through Jesus, 227-28, 234b, 242a, 449-51; justification by faith and, 395-96, 417-20, 451; Law and, 157, 450; from sin, 227b, 234b, 239, 291a; universality of, 227-28, 246b, 376b, 405b, 432b, 446, 451, 472. See also Redemption

Samaria: city, 85, 215b, 379; Jesus in, 242-44, 285a, 296a; province, 18, 214a, 231a

Samaritan(s): Jews and, 135, 242-44; parable of good, 287-88, 336

Samson, 79, 172b, 227b, 480

Samuel, 14, 68, 79, 81, 110-11, 169, 480, 543; books of, 5a, 12, 14

Sanballat, 138

Sanctification of the Christian, 404, 411a, 420a, 451b, 463, 466b; see also Baptism

Sandals, 43a

Sanhedrin, 217, 219a, 241b, 245, 277, 279a, 281, 295b, 301b, 310b, 320-21, 321, 323a, 327, 329a, 376b, 378, 388-89, 425, 427

Sapphira, 356, 377a

Sarah (Sarai), 39a, 41a, 66b, 73, 100, 356-57, 418a, 479

Sardis, 408a, 409, 496

Sarepta: see Zarephath

Sargon, 124, 126

Satan, 165-66, 493, 499, 502-3, 50, 515; Jesus and, 165, 232-34, 270, 275b, 280b, 285-86, 313b, 326a (see also Beelzebub); Job and, 179-82, 20. See also Demonology, Devil

Saul: king, 15, 68, 81, 111-12; of Tarsus (see Paul)

Savior, Jesus as, 226b, 228a, 232a, 244, 280a, 436a, 450

Scapegoat, 62

Sceva, 408b

Schools, 40a, 230a, 246; of Hillel a Shammai, 40a, 250a, 296b; of t prophets, 79, 111, 120. See a Education

Scourging, 323b, 391b, 400, 400, 42

Scribes, 54b, 93, 136, 216-17, 21, 230b; Jesus and, 245-46, 250a, 26 267-70, 272-73, 285-86, 289a, 30 304-5, 310b, 351

Scripture: Christian, 3-6, 12-24; Hebre 4-5, 12-19, 136, 216-17. See also ble, Literature

Scythopolis, 285a, 296a

Sea of Galilee, 237, 245, 249, 271-284

Seal of the living God, 272b, 497, 512

Seals, vision of seven, 492, 497, 506, 5

Season and a time, 530-32

Second Coming of Christ, 56a, 125, 1

287, 293-94, 296a, 299, 308-10, 314-15, 321b, 334a, 348, 404-5, 440a, 491-93; *see also* Comforter
Secundus, 421b
Seed, 35b; of Abraham, 47a, 100-1, 148, 150, 450b, 464; of David, 47b, 113, 220a, 226b, 446b; parables of, 265-66, 336; of the woman, 10b, 47b, 97, 147, 223b, 492, 507, 515
Seleucia, 392-93
Seleucids, 93, 214a
Semite(s), 29a, 55a, 63-64, 114-15
Sennacherib, 71, 88, 125-26, 171
Septuagint, 5-6, 92, 216b, 388b
Sergius Paulus, 393b
Sermon on the Mount, 252a, 257-63, 349
Serpent: brazen, 77, 170a, 242a; Moses' rod into, 107; Tempter, the, 10b, 96-97, 147, 165-66, 514, 522-23 (*see also* Dragon)
Servant(s), 42a; Christ as suffering, 125, 220b, 223b, 275-76, 330-31, 393-94; Jesus on, 261, 278, 280b, 292b, 309, 311b; "of the law," 230a, 546; parables of, 278b, 287a, 292b, 336; Paul on, 415b, 434-35, 439a. *See also* Slavery
Seth, 10b, 65-66, 73, 97-98, 114-15, 224
Seven, significance of, 58b, 537
Seventy: significance of, 539; the, 285a
Shadrach, 132, 171b
Shallum, 87
Shalmaneser V, 126
Shamgar, 79
Shammai, school of, 40a, 250a, 296b
Sharon, Plain of, 34b
Shealtiel (Salathiel), 134, 224
Sheba, queen of, 83, 117, 286a
Shechem, 45b, 67b, 79, 100, 104
Sheep, 30b, 240; parables of, 290, 310a, 336. *See also* Sacrifice, Shepherd
Shekel, 41, 104, 228b, 310b; half-, 277
Shekinah, 108, 131, 159b, 162b, 276b
Shem, 29a, 63-64, 66b, 73, 98-100, 114-15
Sheol, 292a
Shepherd, 30, *30*, 112, 130, 228a, 281-82, 512
Shewbread, 49-50, 54a, 58b, 160, 162
Shiloh, 50b, 53a, 79, 108, 110, 113, 161
Shishak, 84, 163a
Shunammite woman, 45a, 121, 173b
Shushan, 138, *140*
Sibylline Oracles, 221a
Sidon, 109, 130, 252a, 257, 274a, 429b
Silas, 396a, 398a, 400, 403-4
Silences of Biblical history, 175-78
Siloam, Pool of, 61a, 281a
Silver, parable of lost, 290b, 336
Simeon: of Jerusalem, 228-29, 375a; son of Jacob, 74, 114-15, 150, 152; tribe of, 154
Simon: of Cyrene, 324a; the leper, 298b; Maccabaeus, 93, 214a; Magus, 379b; Peter (*see* Peter); the Pharisee, 264b; Zelotes, 252, 255b
Sin: abolished by Jesus' sacrifice, 62b, 158a, 234b, 311-12, 326a, 420a, 447, 451a, 471-72, 475, 477-78; animal sacrifices for, 55-57, 62, 157b, 476-78; of

disbelief, 280-81, 314b; Ezekiel on, 131; forgiveness (remission) of, 231b, 264b, 267b, 278b, 291a, 312a, 331b, 368, 375b, 381a, 394a, 419b, 434a, 438a, 447a; Gnostic concept of, 482-83; and God's saving grace, 419-20, 434b, 449-51, 480-81; healings of, 264b, 280a, 298, 368-69; of Israel's idolatry, 47-48, 51-52, 68, 71-72, 84-89, 110, 122-23, 127-28; Jesus on, 264b, 267, 280b, 290-91, 314b, 368-69; Jesus without, 232a, 475, 483; John on, 483-86; Law and, 157b, 420a, 449-50; moon-god, 48a; nature of man of, 405a, 412b, 420a, 434-35, 454-55, 465b; offering, 56-57; original, 96-97, 147, 179-80, 420a; salvation from, 47a, 227b, 234b, 239, 291a, 450; unpardonable, 267b, 270a
Sinai (Horeb), Mount, 13, 50-51, 68, 74, 106-7, 119, 481, 550
Sinners, Jesus' attitude to, 269b, 290-91
Sion: *see* Zion
Slavery, 37a, 41-42, 59b, 310-11, 411a, 433b, 438b
Smyrna, 408a, 496
Society, Hebrew: *see* Life and Customs
Sodom, 56a, 73, 100, 169b, 550
Sodomites, 122, 171a
Solomon, 15, 32, *32*, 40b, 44-45, 47b, 56a, 71, *80* (map), 83, 113, 116-18, 169a, 224, 286a, 530, 543; Pools of, *70-71*; Song of, 5a, 12, 16, 117; Temple of, 15, 83, 113, 116-17, 129, 162, *162*
Solomon, Wisdom of, 5b
Son(s): and the Father, discourse, 250, 336; of God, Jesus as, 223b, 225b, 232b, 234a, 240, 242a, 250, 275a, 283, 305a, 344, 472, 534; "of the law," 40a, 230a; of man, Jesus as, 133, 222b, 225, 242a, 305a, 308a, 344-48; parable of two, 302b, 336
Song of Solomon, 5a, 12, 16, 117
Song of the Three Holy Children, 5b
Sopater, 421b
Sopherim: see Scribes
Sosthenes, 405b
Sower, parable of, 265, 336
Spies sent to Canaan, 77, 106, 108, 170a
Spirit: of error, 486-87; of evil, 165; of God, 48b, 143, 244a, 375a, 420a, 465-66; parable of unclean, 286a, 336; of truth, 313-14, 486-87; healing of man with unclean, 249, 335, 359. *See also* Comforter, Godhead, Holy Ghost, Holy Spirit
Springs, 34a
Stephanas, 405a, 409b
Stephen, 378-79, 384, 388-89, 417a
Stewardship, 275b, 410b, 439; parables of, 287a, 291b, 336; *see also* Discipleship, Servants
Stoics, 402b
Stooped woman, healing of, 268b, 294a, 335, 357, 366
Stuttering, healing of, 274b, 335, 363
Sukkoth, 61a
Sumer, Sumerians, 29a, 48a
Sun and moon stayed, 108, 168a

Supper, 43b; Last, 46b, 311-15; marriage, of the Lamb, 39a, 289b, 502, 519; parable of great, 44b, 289b, 336. *See also* Lord's supper
Susanna, 270b
Susanna, Book of, 5b
Swine, 44a, 214a, 262, 362
Sychar, 243
Symbolism: *see* Apocalyptic writing
Synagogue, 40a, 52b, 59a, 216-17, 230a, 246
Syracuse, 432a
Syria (Aram), 29, 63b, 93, 177, 388a, 391-93, 397a, 406, 417b
Syrians, 63-64, 86, 93, 121, 171b
Syrophenician's daughter, healing of, 274a, 335, 357, 363

Tabernacle, 51b, 75, 79, 107-8, 159-61, *159-60*, 476-77, 504, 520; Levites and, 54b, 159b. *See also* Altars, Ark of the Covenant, Candlestick
Tabernacles, Feast of, 34a, 61, 204, 279
Tabitha, 380a
Taboos, 142a; *see also* Worship
Talents, 278b; parable of, 309b, 336
Talmud, 217a
Tamar, 83
Tares, parable of, 265-66, 336, 491b
Targums, 6b
Tarshish, 116, 122
Tarsus, 388, 391-92, 406b
Tatnai, 135
Taurus Mountains, 388a, 398, *398*
Tax: redemption of first-born, 41a, 228b; Roman, 214b, 218b, 303-4; temple, 277b, 335
Tempest, stilling of, 248a, 270a, 335
Temple: body as, 164b, 241a, 411a; Christian as, 164b, 410a, 416a, 435a; Ezekiel's ideal, 131; Herod's, 163-64, *164*, 215b, 306b, 326b, 469; Jesus and, 230, 241a, 279b, 282b, 299, 301-2, 304-7; in Revelation, 498, 504, 507, 513, 543; Solomon's, 15, 55a, 71a, 83, 116-17, 126-27, 129, 162, *162*; Zerubbabel's, 4b, 15, 19, 53a, 55a, 91, 134-35, 163a, 214a. *See also* Tabernacle
Temptation: of Adam and Eve, 73, 96-97, 147, 526; of Jesus, 232-34, 544
Tempter, the, 96, 166
Ten, significance of, 538
Tents, tentmaking, 30a, 33a, *35*, 388a, 403b
Terah, 66b, 73, 100, 114-15
Tertullian, 6a, 440b, 489-90
Tertullus, 425b
Testament, defined, 3
Testaments of the Twelve Patriarchs, 221a
Thaddaeus, 252a, 255b
Thessalonians, Epistles to, 6a, 12, 23, 404-5
Thessalonica, 400b, 403-4, 414b
Theudas, 307a
Thomas, 252b, 255a, 313a, 331-32
Thorn(s): crown of, 323b; in the flesh, 417a
Three, significance of, 536
Three Holy Children, Song of the, 5b

Threshing floor, 36, *36,* 162a, 174a
Thummim, 53b, 154
Thyatira, 408a, 496
Tiberias: emperor, 93, 231b, 322-23; Sea of, 245 (*see also* Sea of Galilee)
Tiglath-pileser (III), 87, 124, 126
Tigris, 29a, 66
Time: as dimension of thought, 550; season and a, 530-32
Timothy, 398a, 403-4, 406b, 409b, 436-37; Epistles to, 6a, 12, 23, 438-39, 468
Tirzah, 84
Tithing, 54-55, 57, 126, 139, 286b
Titus: Epistle to, 6a, 12, 23, 439a, 468; Paul's companion, 395, 406b, 410a, 414-15, 438-39; emperor, 468-69
Tobiah, 138
Tobit, 5b
Torah, 4, 52, 217a, 250a; *see also* Law
Trachonitis, 215b, 231a
Traditions, Jesus' discourse on, 273
Trajan, 489
Transfiguration, Jesus', 107, 119, 276a, 324b, 545
Translation: of Elijah, 119-20, 174; of Enoch, 73, 119, 174, 479; of Scripture, 6-10
Treasure, parable of hidden, 266b, 336
Tree: fig, 288-89, 301-2, 308b; of good and evil, 96-97, 146, 522; of life, 96, 146, 505, 521-22; olive, 135, 316, *316-19,* 421a, 498, 513; sycamine, 292b
Trent, Council of, 5b
Trespass offering, 57a
Trial: of Jesus, 320-22, 355; of Job, 179-203; of Paul, 424-28, 437, 440b; of Peter and apostles, 376-77; of Stephen, 378b. *See also* Sanhedrin
Tribes, Twelve, 14, 35a, 37a, *78* (map), 103, 108, 114-15, 153-55, 159, 464, 497, 504, 520; *see also* Children of Israel, Israel
Tribulation, great, 307b, 491a
Tribute, Jesus on, 277-78, 303b
Trinity, the, 143, 404a, 534, 536; *see also* Godhead, Holy Ghost
Troas, 399a, 414a, 422a, 437a
Trogyllium, 422a
Trophimus, 421b, 437a
Trumpets, 54b, *54,* 109; Feast of, 59a; of Revelation, 492, 498, 506, 512
Truth, spirit of, 313-14, 375a, 486-87; *see also* Comforter
Twelve: apostles, 252-56, 270-71, 274a, 328, 372-86; significance of, 538; tribes (*see* Tribes)
Two, significance of, 536
Tychicus, 421, 433-34, 439b
Tyndale's Bible, 7b, *8*
Tyrannus, 408a, 412b
Tyre, 116, 118, 130, 162b, 252a, 257, 274a, 322b

Unclean spirit: healing of man with, 249, 335, 359; parable of man with, 286a
Uncleanness: animal, 31b, 44a, 214a; ceremonial, 39b, 54a, 57a, 60a, 228b, 269a (*see also* Defilement)
United Kingdom: 71a, *80* (map), 81, 83-84, 112-13, 116, 118, 122, 543; division of, 14, 184, 117-18, 122, 543
Unleavened bread, 60; Feast of, 59-60
Ur, 66b, 98, 100
Uriah, 113
Urim, 53b, 154; *see also* Thummin
Ussher, Bishop, 65, 73
Uzzah, 81, 170b
Uzziah (Azariah), 87, 124, 170b

Veil: as clothing, 43, 411b, 415b; of the flesh, 478; of Tabernacle and Temple, 159b, 163-64, 326b, 512
Versions of the Bible, 6-10
Vespasian, 468
Vials, of Revelation, 500, 517
Vine and branches, discourse on, 314, 336
Vineyard: laborers in, parable of, 293b, 306, 336; parable of, 302-3, 336
Viper, Paul bitten by, 385, 431a
Virgins, parable of ten, 309, 336
Vision(s): Ananias', 389b; Cornelius', 380b; Daniel's, 17, 90, 133; Ezekiel's, 17, 130-31; Isaiah's, 124; Paul's 308a, 391b, 399a, 416b; Peter's, 380b; of Revelation, 490b, 492-95, 497-507; Zechariah's, 19, 135. *See also* Dreams
Vow, 110, 227b, 405b, 424a
Vulgate, 6-7

Watchfulness, 318, 404b, 496, 500; discourse on, 286-87, 336; parables of, 287a, 309, 336
Watchman, Ezekiel as, 19, 130-31
Water: living, 34b, 242-43, 279-80, 336, 521; turned into wine, 236a. *See also* Baptism, Cisterns, Wells
Waterpots, 34a, *34, 43,* 236b
Way, the: Christ as, 313a, 449b, 462-63, 478; Christianity as, 262, 375b, 407a, 446b
Wedding, 39a, 236a, 250a; garment, 303b; guest, parable of, 289a, 336. *See also* Bride, Bridegroom, Marriage
Week(s): Feast of, 59-61, 204; Passion, 299-327; seventy, in Daniel, 133
Wells, 34a, 243
Whore, great, 356, 467b, 501, 507, 518
Wicked One, 166, 405b, 465b, 493a
Widow(s), 38a, 41b, 173a, 191, 194-95, 293a, 378a, 438b, 501, 518; of Nain, 263a, 294b, 335; parable of importunate, 292-93, 296b, 336; of Zarephath, 118, 249a
Wife, 39a, 41-42, 150, 357a, 411, 434-35 (*see also* Marriage, Womanhood); Lamb's, 356, 504, 507
Wilderness (desert), 30a, 106, 119, 231-32, *235,* 391a; Wandering in, 33b, 54b, 68, *76* (map), 77, 106-8, 542
Wine: parable of new in old bottles, 269b, 336; water turned into, 236a, 335
Wisdom literature, 5a, 179
Withered hand: healing of man with, 250b, 335, 360; of Jeroboam, 84, 170b, 173b
Witnesses: cloud of, 480; two of Mosaic Law, 280a, 321a; two of Revelation, 135, 479, 498, 506, 513
Woes: on impenitent cities, discourse on, 263b, 336; three of Revelation, 498-99
Woman, women: Christian status of, 378a; creation of, 146-47; of faith, 480; with issue of blood, 270b, 335, 357, 362; healing of adulterous, 335, 369; healing of penitent, 264b; Samaritan, 243-44, 357; Shunammite, 45a, 121, 173b; slavery and, 42a; in travail of Revelation, 499, 507, 514. *See also* Concubine, Wife, Womanhood
Womanhood, 39a, 356-57
Wood Offering, Feast of, 61a
Woolley, Leonard, 98
Word, the, 3, 410a, 436a, 453, 529; Christ as, 223b, 337b, 483, 534
Worship, 47-57; Aaronic priesthood, 52-54; altars of, 48-50; centralization in Jerusalem, 14, 113, 117, 162b, 174; Christian, 258, 376a, 411-12, 422a, 436; emperor, 468-69, 490a; high places, 50-51; intertestamental period, 215-22; Jesus on, 48b, 244a, 262; Levites, 54-55; Mosaic system, 51-52; sacrificial, 51b, 55-57; synagogue, 216a, 246; tithing, 57-58. *See also* Monotheism, Prayer, Sabbath, Tabernacle, Temple
Wrath of God, 491, 511, 516-17; *see also* Anger, Judgment
Writing, apocalyptic and pseudepigrapha, 220-22, 490-91, 508
Writings, The, 5a, 216-17
Wycliffe's Bible, 5b, 7a, *8*

Yah, Yahweh: *see* Jehovah
Yahwistic Document, 4b, 145
Year: civil and religious, 59a; of Jubilee, 42a, 59; post-Flood length, 98; Sabbatical, 59
Yom Kippur, 62a

Zacchaeus, 298a, 335, 369
Zachariah, 87
Zacharias, 225-27, 375a
Zadok, 53a
Zadokite Fragments, 221a
Zarephath, *69,* 118, 173, 249a
Zealots, 218b, *221,* 255b, 307b
Zebedee, 252-54
Zebulun: son of Jacob, 74, 114-15, 150-51; tribe of, 152, 155
Zechariah: book of, 5a, 12, 19; prophet, 19, 91, 135, 163a, 300a; son of Jehoiada, 86
Zedekiah, 89, 129
Zelophehad, daughters of, 40b
Zelotes: *see* Simon
Zephaniah, 19, 88, 130; book of, 5a, 12, 19
Zerubbabel, 15, 19, 72b, 90, 134-35, 163a, 224, 543
Zidon: *see* Sidon
Zilpah, 74, 102-3, 150-51
Zimri, 84
Zion, Mount, 14, 19, 51, 113, 139, 174, 481, 500, 516; *see also* Jerusalem, new
Zipporah, 75, 106
Zophar, 180, 182, 186-87, 190-91
Zoroastrianism, 228b